EDITION 8

Quantitative Methods for Business

David R. Anderson
University of Cincinnati

Dennis J. Sweeney
University of Cincinnati

Thomas A. Williams
Rochester Institute of Technology

South-Western College Publishing
Thomson Learning™

Australia • Canada • Denmark • Japan • Mexico • New Zealand • Philippines
Puerto Rico • Singapore • South Africa • Spain • United Kingdom • United States

Quantitative Methods for Business, 8th edition by Anderson, Sweeney, and Williams
Sr. Acquisitions Editor: Charles E. McCormick, Jr.
Sr. Developmental Editor: Alice C. Denny
Sr. Marketing Manager: Joseph A. Sabatino
Production Editor: Deanna R. Quinn
Manufacturing Coordinator: Sandee Milewski
Internal Design: Michael H. Stratton
Cover Design: Paul Neff Design
Cover Photo: EyeWire, Inc.
Production House and Compositor: BookMasters, Inc.
Printer: Quebecor World

Printed in the United States of America
3   4   5   03   02

For more information contact South-Western College Publishing, 5191 Natorp Boulevard, Mason, Ohio, 45040 or find us on the Internet at http://www.swcollege.com

For permission to use material from this text or product, contact us by
• **telephone: 1-800-730-2214**
• **fax: 1-800-730-2215**
• **web: http://www.thomsonrights.com**

Library of Congress Cataloging-in-Publication Data

Anderson, David Ray
    Quantitative methods for business / David R. Anderson, Dennis J. Sweeney, Thomas A. Williams.—8th ed.
        p.   cm.
    Includes bibliographical references (p.   ) and index.
    ISBN 0-324-04499-2 (package)
    ISBN 0-324-02133-X (book)
    1. Management science.   I. Sweeney, Dennis J.   II. Williams, Thomas Arthur III. Title.
T56.A63 2000
658.4′033—dc21

                                                                                99-462384

This book is printed on acid-free paper.

Dedicated to
Krista, Justin, Mark, and Colleen
Mark, Linda, Brad, Tim, Scott, and Lisa
Cathy, David, and Kristin

Brief Contents

Contents

Chapter 5
Utility and Decision Making 148

Chapter 6
Forecasting 165

Chapter 7
Introduction to Linear Programming 216

Chapter 12
Project Scheduling: PERT/CPM 478

Chapter 13
Inventory Management: Independent Demand 514

Chapter 14
Inventory Management: Dependent Demand 565

Chapter 15
Waiting Line Models 591

Chapter 16
Simulation 633

Chapter 17
Markov Processes 690

Chapter 18
Multicriteria Decision Problems 714

Preface

The purpose of this eighth edition, as with previous editions, is to provide undergraduate and graduate students with a conceptual understanding of the role that quantitative methods play in the decision-making process. The text describes the many quantitative methods that have been developed over the years, explains how they work, and shows how the decision maker can apply and interpret them.

This book is written with the nonmathematician in mind. It is applications oriented and uses a problem scenario approach. In each chapter a problem is described in conjunction with the quantitative procedure being introduced. Development of the quantitative technique or model includes applying it to the problem to generate a solution or recommendation. We have found that this approach helps to motivate the student by demonstrating not only how the procedure works, but also how it can contribute to the decision-making process.

The mathematical prerequisite for this text is a course in algebra. The two chapters on probability and probability distributions will provide the necessary background for the use of probability in subsequent chapters.

Throughout the text we use generally accepted notation for the topic being covered. As a result, students who pursue study beyond the level of this text will have little difficulty reading more advanced material. To also assist in further study, a bibliography is included at the end of this book.

CHANGES IN THE EIGHTH EDITION

In preparing the eighth edition we were careful to maintain the overall format and approach of previous editions. However, based on our own classroom experience, changes in the field, and suggestions from users of previous editions, we made several significant changes to enhance the content, organization, and readability of the text.

Decision Analysis

Influence diagrams, risk analysis, risk profiles, and sensitivity analysis of payoffs have been added to Chapter 4. A revised approach to decision analysis provides greater emphasis on problem formulation and the decision-making process, while involving fewer technical details such as computing revised probabilities. Use of Bayes' Theorem and the detailed calculations of revised probabilities are now included in an optional section.

Linear Programming

Chapters 7 and 8 have undergone major revision. Chapter 7 now includes a step-by-step discussion of problem formulation and modeling. We emphasize the need for understanding the problem thoroughly, writing a verbal description of the objective and each constraint, defining the decision variables, writing the objective in terms of the decision variables, and writing the constraints in terms of the decision variables. We think this approach will ease the student's transition to modeling more complex problems in Chapter 8 and 9. To enhance understanding and interpretation, we have changed from the x_1 and x_2 notation for the decision variables to more descriptive notation. For example, in the RMC problem, we now use F to denote the fuel additive product and S to denote the solvent base product.

Computer solution using *The Management Scientist* has been moved to Chapter 7 to enable the student to use and interpret computer solutions of linear programs earlier in the text. Step-by-step instructions for using the software are provided in the appendix to Chapter 7. A chapter appendix is also included on LINDO for those who wish to use this software to solve linear programs. A student version of LINDO® 6.1 is available in a bundle package with the textbook.

Chapter 8 now focuses on sensitivity analysis and the interpretation of the solution to linear programs. The detailed calculations required to do a complete graphical sensitivity analysis by hand have been deleted. Sensitivity analysis concepts are still introduced and illustrated graphically. However, the focus is now on using computer software for sensitivity analysis and interpretation.

Multicriteria Decision Problem

A new section on scoring models has been added to Chapter 18. A scoring model provides a relatively easy way to identify a recommended decision alternative for a multicriteria problem. An appendix showing how to implement a scoring model with spreadsheets has been added. In addition, the section on AHP has been restructured to better match the flow of the decision process. The AHP car selection problem now involves three alternative automobiles: Accord, Saturn, and Cavalier.

New Problems and Case Problems

More than 10 percent of the problems are new, as well as new case problems in probability, decision analysis, linear programming, linear programming applications, integer linear programming, and waiting line models. The text now contains 25 case problems.

New *The Management Scientist version 5.0* Software

The new version 5.0 of *The Management Scientist* software is now available for Microsoft® Windows 95, Windows 98, and Windows NT operating systems. We have made a number of improvements in entering and editing data in several modules. For instance, in the forecasting module the user may now add and delete time series observations. The integer programming module has been reworked to provide a more stable and robust solution procedure, and the user interface has been enhanced to improve ease of use.

New and Revised Spreadsheet Appendixes

Spreadsheet appendixes to show how Microsoft® Excel can be used to implement many of the methods presented in the text were first introduced in the previous edition. Based on our teaching experience using Excel, we have added two new spreadsheet appendixes and have enhanced the existing spreadsheet appendixes. The new edition offers Excel appendixes in 13 chapters.

Crystal Ball® Spreadsheet Appendix

A new spreadsheet appendix using the Crystal Ball add-in software to perform risk analysis is presented in Chapter 16. Crystal Ball is demonstrated by solving the PortaCom simulation problem presented in the chapter. A student version of Crystal Ball is packaged inside each copy of the eighth edition textbook.

FEATURES AND PEDAGOGY

We have continued many of the features that appeared in previous editions. Some of the important ones are noted here.

- **Annotations** Annotations that highlight key points and provide additional insights for the student are a continuing feature of this edition. These annotations, which appear in the margins, are designed to provide emphasis and enhance understanding of the terms and concepts being presented in the text.
- **Notes & Comments** At the end of many sections, we provide Notes & Comments designed to give the student additional insights about the quantitative methodology and its application. Notes & Comments include warnings about or limitations of the methodology, recommendations for application, brief descriptions of additional technical considerations, and other matters.
- **Self-Test Exercises** Certain exercises are identified as self-test exercises. Completely worked-out solutions for these exercises are provided in Appendix G at the end of the text. Students can attempt the self-test exercises and immediately check the solution to evaluate their understanding of the concepts presented in the chapter.
- **Quantitative Methods in Action** Quantitative Methods in Action articles are presented throughout the text. Each Q. M. in Action presents a summary of an application of quantitative methods found in practice. Adaptations of materials from *Interfaces* and *OR/MS Today* articles provide the basis for the applications in this feature.
- **Quantitative Methods in Practice** Quantitative Methods in Practice articles are presented at the end of eleven chapters. The articles, supplied by practitioners, describe how companies have successfully used quantitative methods in practice. We believe that this feature helps motivate students by placing the chapter material in a real-world context. Companies providing these applications include Procter & Gamble, Eastman Kodak, Mead, Citibank, Pharmacia & Upjohn, CVS Corporation, and others.

COURSE OUTLINE FLEXIBILITY

The text provides instructors substantial flexibility in selecting topics to meet specific course needs. Although many variations are possible, the single-quarter and single-semester outlines that follow are illustrative of the options available.

- Suggested One-Quarter Course Outline
    Introduction (Chapter 1)
    Decision Analysis (Chapters 4 and 5)
    Linear Programming (Chapters 7, 8 and 9)
    Transportation, Assignment, and Transshipment Problems (Chapter 10)
    PERT/CPM (Chapter 12)
    Waiting-Line Models (Chapter 15)
    Simulation (Chapter 16)
- Suggested One-Semester Course Outline
    Introduction (Chapter 1)
    Probability Concepts (Chapters 2 and 3)
    Decision Analysis (Chapters 4 and 5)

Forecasting (Chapter 6)
Linear Programming (Chapters 7, 8, and 9)
Transportation, Assignment, and Transshipment Problems (Chapter 10)
Integer Linear Program (Chapter 11)
PERT/CPM (Chapter 12)
Waiting-Line Models (Chapter 15)
Simulation (Chapter 16)

Many other possibilities exist for one-term courses, depending on time available, course objectives, and backgrounds of the students.

ANCILLARY TEACHING AND LEARNING MATERIALS

As has always been the case, this new edition of *Quantitative Methods for Business* has ancillaries that will increase the value of the text to both students and instructors.

- **Study Guide** (ISBN: 0-324-02136-4) Prepared by John Loucks of St. Edward's University, the *Study Guide* will provide the student with significant supplementary study materials. Each chapter contains key concepts, a review section, sample problems with step-by-step solutions, problems with answers, and a series of self-testing questions with answers. The *Study Guide* may be purchased at a special price when bundled with the textbook.
- **Solutions Manual** - The *Solutions Manual,* prepared by the authors, includes solutions for all problems in the text. At the request of the instructor, the *Solutions Manual* can be packaged with the text for student purchase.
- **The Management Scientist, version 5.0** (ISBN: 0-324-00890-2) provides 12 computer modules for working through the problems in the course. The software is class tested to run with little or no instructor supervision. Thorough documentation including examples of how to use the software on actual problems accompanies the CD-Rom. The Management Scientist software may also be purchased at a value price when bundled with the textbook.
- **LINDO version 6.1** - An educational version of LINDO 6.10 software is sold at a discounted price when it is packaged with the text

All instructor ancillaries are now provided on a single CD-ROM. The Instructor's Resource CD (ISBN: 0-324-02134-8) is available to adopters from their Thomson Learning™ publisher's representative, the ITP Academic Resource Center at 800-423-0563, or through the online catalog at www.swcollege.com. Included in this convenient format are:

- **Solutions Manual** - The *Solutions Manual,* prepared by the authors, includes solutions for all problems in the text.
- **Instructor's Manual** - The *Instructor's Manual* also prepared by the authors, contains solutions to all case problems presented in the text.
- **PowerPoint™ Presentation Slides** - Prepared by John Loucks of St. Edward's University, the presentation slides contain a teaching outline that incorporates graphics to help instructors create even more stimulating lectures. The slides may be adapted using PowerPoint 97 software to facilitate classroom use.
- **Test Bank** and Computerized Testing Software - Prepared also by John Loucks, the *Test Bank* in Microsoft Word files includes multiple choice, true/false, short answer questions, and problems for each chapter. A separate version of the test bank in computerized testing software allows instructors to create, edit, store and print exams.

ACKNOWLEDGMENTS

We were fortunate in having the expertise of a number of reviewers as we began our work on this eighth edition of *Quantitative Methods for Business*. Our appreciation and thanks go to:

Melanie Hatch, Miami University

Christine Irujo, Westfield State College

William C. Keller, Webb Institute of the University of Phoenix

Christos Koulamas, Florida International University

Mohammad Meybodi, Indiana University–Kokomo

John Miller, Jr., Mercer University

Donald A. Ostasiewski, Thomas More College

Emre Veral, CUNY–Baruch

Writing and revising a textbook is a continuing process. We owe a debt to many of our colleagues and friends for their helpful comments and suggestions during the development of earlier editions. Among these are:

Robert L. Armacost, University of Central Florida

Uttarayan Bagchi, University of Texas at Austin

Edward Baker, University of Miami

Norman Baker, University of Cincinnati

Oded Berman, University of Toronto

Jeffrey Camm, University of Cincinnati

Rodger D. Carlson, Morehead State University

Ying Chien, University of Scranton

John Eatman, University of North Carolina–Greensboro

Ronald Ebert, University of Missouri–Columbia

Don Edwards, University of South Carolina

Ronald Ehresman, Baldwin-Wallace College

Peter Ellis, Utah State University

Lawrence Ettkin, Chattanooga

Jim Evans, University of Cincinnati

Michael Ford, Rochester Institute of Technology

Terri Friel, Eastern Kentucky University

Phil Fry, Boise State University

Robert Garfinkel, University of Connecticut

Nicholas G. Hall, Ohio State University

Michael E. Hanna, University of Houston–Clear Lake

Daniel G. Hotard, Southeastern Louisiana University

David Hott, Florida Institute of Technology

Barry Kadets, Bryant College

Birsen Karpak, Youngstown State University

John Lawrence, Jr., California State University–Fullerton

Constantine Loucopoulos, Emporia State University

Ka-sing Man, Georgetown University

William G. Marchal, University of Toledo

Kamlesh Mathur, Case Western Reserve University

Joseph Mazzola, Duke University

Patrick McKeown, University of Georgia

Constance McLaren, Indiana State University

Mario Miranda, The Ohio State University

Alan Neebe, University of North Carolina

David Pentico, Duquesne University

B. Madhusudan Rao, Bowling Green State University

Handanhal V. Ravinder, University of New Mexico

Donna Retzlaff-Roberts, University of Memphis

Don R. Robinson, Illinois State University

Richard Rosenthal, Naval Postgraduate School

Antoinette Somers, Wayne State University

Christopher S. Tang, University of California–Los Angeles

Giri Kumar Tayi, State University of New York–Albany

Willban Terpening, Gonzaga University

Edward P. Winkofsky, Mead Corporation

Neba L'Abbe Wu, Eastern Michigan University

Our associates from organizations who supplied the Quantitative Methods in Practice applications made a major contribution to the text. These individuals are cited in a credit line on the first page of each application.

We are also indebted to our senior acquisitions editor, Charles McCormick, Jr., our senior developmental editor, Alice Denny, our production editor Deanna Quinn, our designer Mike Stratton, our senior marketing manager Joe Sabatino, and others at South-Western College Publishing for their counsel and support during the preparation of this text.

David R. Anderson
Dennis J. Sweeney
Thomas A. Williams

About the Authors

David R. Anderson. David R. Anderson is Professor of Quantitative Analysis in the College of Business Administration at the University of Cincinnati. Born in Grand Forks, North Dakota, he earned his B.S., M.S., and Ph.D. degrees from Purdue University. Professor Anderson has served as Head of the Department of Quantitative Analysis and Operations Management and as Associate Dean of the College of Business Administration. In addition, he was the coordinator of the College's first Executive Program.

At the University of Cincinnati, Professor Anderson has taught introductory statistics for business students as well as graduate-level courses in regression analysis, multivariate analysis, and management science. He has also taught statistical courses at the Department of Labor in Washington, D.C. He has been honored with nominations and awards for excellence in teaching and excellence in service to student organizations.

Professor Anderson has coauthored eight textbooks in the areas of statistics, management science, linear programming, and production and operations management. He is an active consultant in the field of sampling and statistical methods.

Dennis J. Sweeney. Dennis J. Sweeney is Professor of Quantitative Analysis and Director of the Center for Productivity Improvement at the University of Cincinnati. Born in Des Moines, Iowa, he earned a B.S.B.A. degree from Drake University and his M.B.A. and D.B.A. degrees from Indiana University where he was an NDEA Fellow. During 1978–79, Professor Sweeney worked in the management science group at Procter & Gamble; during 1981–82, he was a visiting professor at Duke University. Professor Sweeney served as Head of the Department of Quantitative Analysis and as Associate Dean of the College of Business Administration at the University of Cincinnati.

Professor Sweeney has published more than 30 articles and monographs in the area of management science and statistics. The National Science Foundation, IBM, Procter & Gamble, Federated Department Stories, Kroger, and Cincinnati Gas & Electric have funded his research, which has been published in *Management Science, Operations Research, Mathematical Programming, Decision Sciences,* and other journals.

Professor Sweeney has coauthored eight textbooks in the areas of statistics, management science, linear programming, and production and operations management.

Thomas A. Williams. Thomas A. Williams is Professor of Management Science in the College of Business at Rochester Institute of Technology. Born in Elmira, New York, he earned his B.S. degree at Clarkson University. He did his graduate work at Rensselaer Polytechnic Institute, where he received his M.S. and Ph.D. degrees.

Before joining the College of Business at RIT, Professor Williams served for seven years as a faculty member in the College of Business Administration at the University of Cincinnati, where he developed the undergraduate program in Information Systems and then served as its coordinator. At RIT he was the first chairman of the Decision Sciences Department. He teaches courses in management science and statistics, as well as graduate courses in regression and decision analysis.

Professor Williams is the coauthor of nine textbooks in the areas of management science, statistics, production and operations management, and mathematics. He has been a consultant for numerous *Fortune* 500 companies and has worked on projects ranging from the use of data analysis to the development of large-scale regression models.

INTRODUCTION

CONTENTS

This book is concerned with the use of quantitative methods to assist in decision making. The emphasis is not on the methods themselves, but rather on how they can contribute to better decisions. Our approach is to describe situations in which quantitative methods have been applied successfully and then show how a manager can use the methods to make better decisions. Brief descriptions of successful applications of quantitative methods are scattered throughout the book; these are entitled Q. M. in Action. Also at the end of most chapters is a write-up describing Quantitative Methods in Practice in some organizations.

Various names have been given to the body of knowledge involving quantitative approaches to decision making. The ones most commonly used are *management science* (MS), *operations research* (OR), and *decision science*. All are concerned with rational approaches to decision making based on the scientific method. The material described in this book is the core body of knowledge in these fields.

The scientific management revolution of the early 1900s, initiated by Frederic W. Taylor, provided the foundation for the use of quantitative methods in management. But modern management science research is generally considered to have originated during the World War II period, when teams were formed to deal with strategic and tactical problems faced by the military. These teams, which often consisted of people with diverse specialties (e.g., mathematicians, engineers, and behavioral scientists), were joined together to solve a common problem using the scientific method. After the war, many of these team members continued their research into quantitative approaches to decision making.

Two developments that occurred during the post–World War II period led to the growth and use of quantitative methods in nonmilitary applications.

First, continued research resulted in numerous methodological developments. Probably the most significant development was the discovery by George Dantzig, in 1947, of the simplex method for solving linear programming problems. Many more methodological developments followed, and in 1957 the first book on operations research was published by Churchman, Ackoff, and Arnoff.[1]

Concurrent with these methodological developments was a virtual explosion in computing power made available through digital computers. Computers enabled practitioners to use the methodological advances to solve a large variety of problems. The computer technology explosion continues; personal computers are now more powerful than earlier mainframe computers. Today, variants of the post–World War II methodological developments are being used on personal computers to solve problems larger than those solved on mainframe computers just a few years ago.

1.1   PROBLEM SOLVING AND DECISION MAKING

Problem solving can be defined as the process of identifying a difference between the actual and the desired state of affairs and then taking action to resolve the difference. For problems important enough to justify the time and effort of careful analysis, the problem-solving process involves the following seven steps:

1. Identify and define the problem.
2. Determine the set of alternative solutions.
3. Determine the criterion or criteria that will be used to evaluate the alternatives.
4. Evaluate the alternatives.
5. Choose an alternative.
6. Implement the selected alternative.
7. Evaluate the results to determine whether a satisfactory solution has been obtained.

Decision making is the term generally associated with the first five steps of the problem-solving process. Thus, the first step of decision making is to identify and define the problem. Decision making ends with the choosing of an alternative, which is the act of making the decision.

Let us consider the following example of the decision-making process. For the moment assume that you are currently unemployed and that you would like a position that will lead to a satisfying career. Suppose that your job search has resulted in offers from companies in Rochester, New York; Dallas, Texas; Greensboro, North Carolina; and Pittsburgh, Pennsylvania. Thus, the alternatives for your decision problem can be stated as follows:

1. Accept the position in Rochester.
2. Accept the position in Dallas.
3. Accept the position in Greensboro.
4. Accept the position in Pittsburgh.

The next step of the problem-solving process involves determining the criteria that will be used to evaluate the four alternatives. Obviously, the starting salary is a factor of some importance. If salary were the only criterion important to you, the alternative selected as "best" would be the one with the highest starting salary. Problems in which the objective is to find the best solution with respect to one criterion are referred to as **single-criterion decision problems.**

---

1. C. W. Churchman, R. L. Ackoff, and E. L. Arnoff, *Introduction to Operations Research* (New York: Wiley, 1957).

Suppose that you have also concluded that the potential for advancement and the location of the job are two other criteria of major importance. Thus, the three criteria in your decision problem are starting salary, potential for advancement, and location. Problems that involve more than one criterion are referred to as **multicriteria decision problems.**

The next step of the decision-making process is to evaluate each of the alternatives with respect to each criterion. For example, evaluating each alternative relative to the starting salary criterion is done simply by recording the starting salary for each job alternative. Evaluating each alternative with respect to the potential for advancement and the location of the job is more difficult to do, however, because these evaluations are based primarily on subjective factors that are often difficult to quantify. Suppose for now that you decide to measure potential for advancement and job location by rating each of these criteria as poor, fair, average, good, or excellent. The data you compile are shown in Table 1.1.

You are now ready to make a choice from the available alternatives. What makes this choice phase so difficult is that the criteria are probably not all equally important, and no one alternative is "best" with regard to all criteria. Although we will present a method for dealing with situations like this one later in the text, for now let us suppose that after a careful evaluation of the data in Table 1.1, you have decided to select alternative 3; alternative 3 is thus referred to as the **decision.**

At this point in time, the decision-making process is complete. In summary, we see that this process involves five steps:

1. Define the problem.
2. Identify the alternatives.
3. Determine the criteria.
4. Evaluate the alternatives.
5. Choose an alternative.

Note that missing from this list are the last two steps in the problem-solving process: implementing the selected alternative and evaluating the results to determine whether a satisfactory solution has been obtained. This omission is not meant to diminish the importance of each of these activities, but to emphasize the more limited scope of the term *decision making* as compared to the term *problem solving.* Figure 1.1 summarizes the relationship between these two concepts.

1.2   QUANTITATIVE ANALYSIS AND DECISION MAKING

Consider the flowchart presented in Figure 1.2. Note that we have combined the first three steps of the decision-making process under the heading of "Structuring the Problem" and the latter two steps under the heading "Analyzing the Problem." Let us now consider in greater detail how to carry out the activities that make up the decision-making process.

TABLE 1.1   DATA FOR THE JOB EVALUATION DECISION-MAKING PROBLEM

Alternative	Starting Salary	Potential for Advancement	Job Location
1. Rochester	$38,500	Average	Average
2. Dallas	$36,000	Excellent	Good
3. Greensboro	$36,000	Good	Excellent
4. Pittsburgh	$37,000	Average	Good

FIGURE 1.1   THE RELATIONSHIP BETWEEN PROBLEM SOLVING AND DECISION MAKING

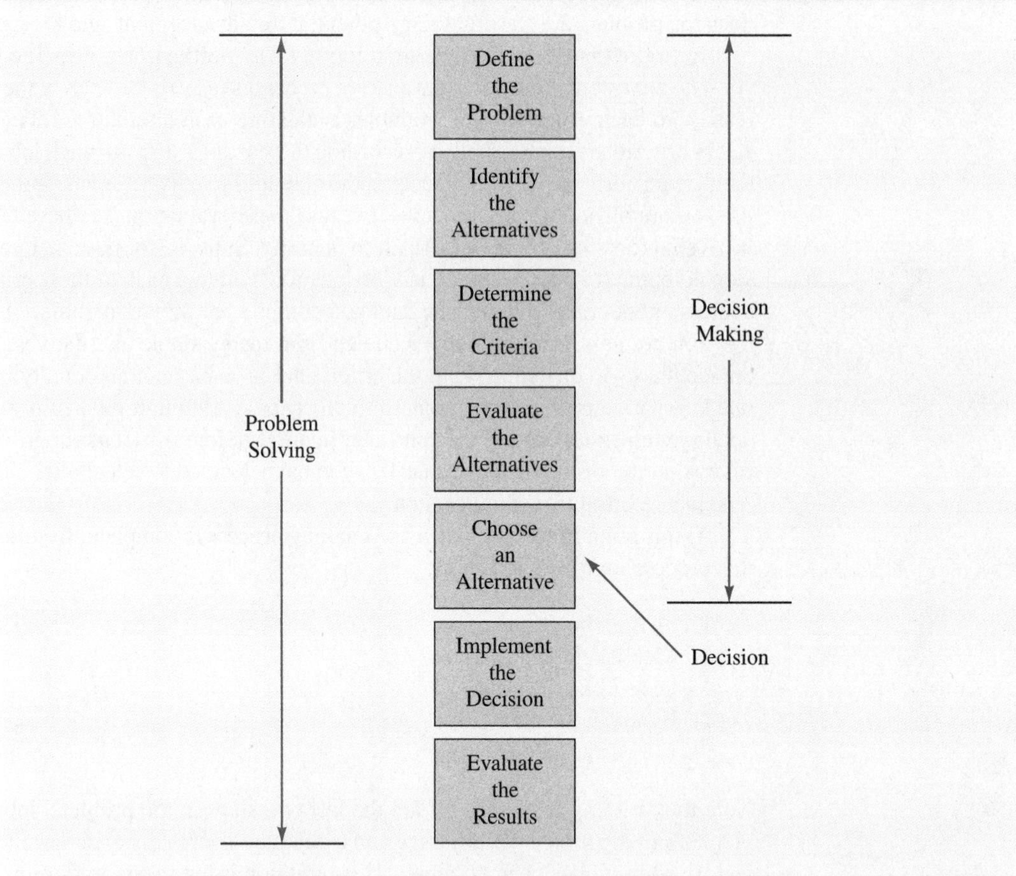

Figure 1.3 shows that the analysis phase of the decision-making process may take two basic forms: qualitative and quantitative. Qualitative analysis is based primarily on the manager's judgment and experience; it includes the manager's intuitive "feel" for the problem and is more an art than a science. If the manager has had experience with similar problems, or if the problem is relatively simple, heavy emphasis may be placed upon a qualitative analysis. However, if the manager has had little experience with similar problems, or if the problem is sufficiently complex, then a quantitative analysis of the problem can be an especially important consideration in the manager's final decision.

When using the quantitative approach, an analyst will concentrate on the quantitative facts or data associated with the problem and develop mathematical expressions that describe the objectives, constraints, and other relationships that exist in the problem. Then, by using one or more quantitative methods, the analyst will make a recommendation based on the quantitative aspects of the problem.

Quantitative methods are especially helpful with large, complex problems. For example, in the coordination of the thousands of tasks associated with landing the Apollo 11 safely on the moon, quantitative techniques helped to ensure that more than 300,000 pieces of work performed by more than 400,000 people were integrated smoothly.

Although skills in the qualitative approach are inherent in the manager and usually increase with experience, the skills of the quantitative approach can be learned only by studying the assumptions and methods of management science. A manager can increase decision-making effectiveness by learning more about quantitative methodology and by better understanding its contribution to the decision-making process. A manager who is knowledgeable in quantitative decision-making procedures is in a much better position to compare and evaluate the qualitative and quantitative sources of recommendations and ultimately to combine the two sources in order to make the best possible decision.

FIGURE 1.2   AN ALTERNATE CLASSIFICATION OF THE DECISION-MAKING PROCESS

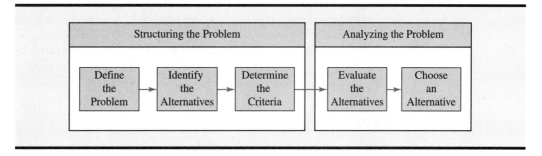

FIGURE 1.3   THE ROLE OF QUALITATIVE AND QUANTITATIVE ANALYSIS

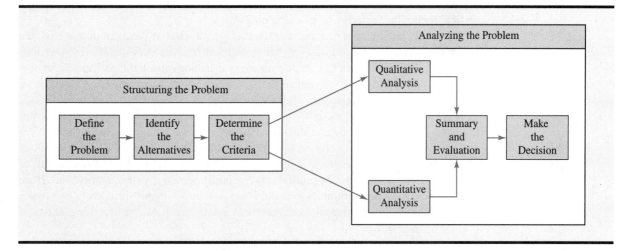

The box in Figure 1.3 entitled "Quantitative Analysis" encompasses most of the subject matter of this text. We will consider a managerial problem, introduce the appropriate quantitative methodology, and then develop the recommended decision.

In closing this section, let us briefly state some of the reasons why a quantitative approach might be used in the decision-making process:

Try Problem 4 to test your understanding of why quantitative approaches might be needed in a particular problem.

1. The problem is complex, and the manager cannot develop a good solution without the aid of quantitative analysis.
2. The problem is especially important (e.g., a great deal of money is involved), and the manager desires a thorough analysis before attempting to make a decision.
3. The problem is new, and the manager has no previous experience from which to draw.
4. The problem is repetitive, and the manager saves time and effort by relying on quantitative procedures to make routine decision recommendations.

1.3   QUANTITATIVE ANALYSIS

From Figure 1.3 we see that quantitative analysis begins once the problem has been structured. It usually takes imagination, teamwork, and considerable effort to transform a rather general problem description into a well-defined problem that can be approached via quantitative analysis. The more the analyst is involved in the process of structuring the problem, the more likely it is that the ensuing quantitative analysis will make an important contribution to the decision-making process.

To successfully apply quantitative analysis to decision making, the analyst must work closely with the manager or user of the results. When both the quantitative analyst and the manager agree that the problem has been adequately structured, work can begin on developing a model to represent the problem mathematically. Solution procedures can then be employed to find the best solution for the model. This best solution for the model then becomes a recommendation to the decision maker. The process of developing and solving models is the essence of the quantitative analysis process.

Model Development

Models are representations of real objects or situations and can be presented in various forms. For example, a scale model of an airplane is a representation of a real airplane. Similarly, a child's toy truck is a model of a real truck. The model airplane and toy truck are examples of models that are physical replicas of real objects. In modeling terminology, physical replicas are referred to as **iconic models.**

A second classification includes models that are physical in form but do not have the same physical appearance as the object being modeled. Such models are referred to as **analog models.** The speedometer of an automobile is an analog model; the position of the needle on the dial represents the speed of the automobile. A thermometer is another analog model representing temperature.

A third classification of models—the type we will primarily be studying—includes representations of a problem by a system of symbols and mathematical relationships or expressions. Such models are referred to as **mathematical models** and are a critical part of any quantitative approach to decision making. For example, the total profit from the sale of a product can be determined by multiplying the profit per unit by the quantity sold. If we let x represent the number of units sold and P the total profit, then, with a profit of $10 per unit, the following mathematical model defines the total profit earned by selling x units:

$$P = 10x \qquad (1.1)$$

The purpose, or value, of any model is that it enables us to make inferences about the real situation by studying and analyzing the model. For example, an airplane designer might test an iconic model of a new airplane in a wind tunnel to learn about the potential flying characteristics of the full-size airplane. Similarly, a mathematical model may be used to make inferences about how much profit will be earned if a specified quantity of a particular product is sold. According to the mathematical model of equation (1.1), we would expect selling three units of the product ($x = 3$) would provide a profit of $P = 10(3) = \$30$.

In general, experimenting with models requires less time and is less expensive than experimenting with the real object or situation. A model airplane is certainly quicker and less expensive to build and study than the full-size airplane. Similarly, the mathematical model in equation (1.1) allows a quick identification of profit expectations without actually requiring the manager to produce and sell x units. Models also have the advantage of reducing the risk associated with experimenting with the real situation. In particular, bad designs or bad decisions that cause the model airplane to crash or a mathematical model to project a $10,000 loss can be avoided in the real situation.

The value of model-based conclusions and decisions is dependent on how well the model represents the real situation. The more closely the model airplane represents the real airplane, the more accurate the conclusions and predictions will be. Similarly, the more closely the mathematical model represents the company's true profit-volume relationship, the more accurate the profit projections will be.

Because this text deals with quantitative analysis based on mathematical models, let us look more closely at the mathematical modeling process. When initially considering a man-

Herbert A. Simon, a Nobel prize winner in economics and an expert in decision making, said that a mathematical model does not have to be exact; it just has to be close enough to provide better results than can be obtained by common sense.

agerial problem, we usually find that the problem definition phase leads to a specific objective, such as maximization of profit or minimization of cost, and possibly a set of restrictions or **constraints,** such as production capacities. The success of the mathematical model and quantitative approach will depend heavily on how accurately the objective and constraints can be expressed in mathematical equations or relationships.

A mathematical expression that describes the problem's objective is referred to as the **objective function.** For example, the profit equation $P = 10x$ would be an objective function for a firm attempting to maximize profit. A production capacity constraint would be necessary if, for instance, 5 hours are required to produce each unit and only 40 hours are available per week. Let x indicate the number of units produced each week. The production time constraint is given by

$$5x \leq 40 \tag{1.2}$$

The value of $5x$ is the total time required to produce x units; the symbol $\leq$ indicates that the production time required must be less than or equal to the 40 hours available.

The decision problem or question is the following: How many units of the product should be scheduled each week to maximize profit? A complete mathematical model for this simple production problem is

$$\text{Maximize} \qquad P = 10x \quad \text{objective function}$$
$$\text{subject to (s.t.)}$$
$$\left.\begin{array}{c} 5x \leq 40 \\ x \geq 0 \end{array}\right\} \text{constraints}$$

The $x \geq 0$ constraint requires the production quantity x to be greater than or equal to zero, which simply recognizes the fact that it is not possible to manufacture a negative number of units. The optimal solution to this model can be easily calculated and is given by $x = 8$, with an associated profit of \$80. This model is an example of a linear programming model. In subsequent chapters we will discuss more complicated mathematical models and learn how to solve them in situations where the answers are not nearly so obvious.

In the preceding mathematical model, the profit per unit (\$10), the production time per unit (5 hours), and the production capacity (40 hours) are environmental factors not under the control of the manager or decision maker. Such environmental factors, which can affect both the objective function and the constraints, are referred to as **uncontrollable inputs** to the model. Inputs that are controlled or determined by the decision maker are referred to as **controllable inputs** to the model. In the example given, the production quantity x is the controllable input to the model. Controllable inputs are the decision alternatives specified by the manager and thus are also referred to as the **decision variables** of the model.

Once all controllable and uncontrollable inputs are specified, the objective function and constraints can be evaluated and the output of the model determined. In this sense, the output of the model is simply the projection of what would happen if those particular environmental factors and decisions occurred in the real situation. A flowchart of how controllable and uncontrollable inputs are transformed by the mathematical model into output is shown in Figure 1.4. A similar flowchart showing the specific details of the production model is shown in Figure 1.5.

As stated earlier, the uncontrollable inputs are those the decision maker cannot influence. The specific controllable and uncontrollable inputs of a model depend on the particular problem or decision-making situation. In the production problem, the production time available (40), is an uncontrollable input. However, if it were possible to hire more employees or use overtime, the number of hours of production time would become a controllable input and therefore a decision variable in the model.

FIGURE 1.4   FLOWCHART OF THE PROCESS OF TRANSFORMING MODEL INPUTS INTO OUTPUT

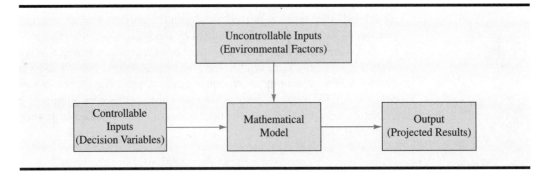

FIGURE 1.5   FLOWCHART FOR THE PRODUCTION MODEL

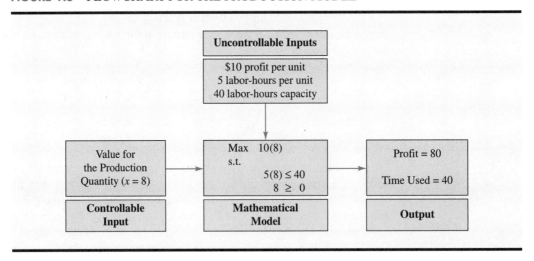

Uncontrollable inputs can either be known exactly or be uncertain and subject to variation. If all uncontrollable inputs to a model are known and cannot vary, the model is referred to as a **deterministic model.** Corporate income tax rates are not under the influence of the manager and thus constitute an uncontrollable input in many decision models. Because these rates are known and fixed (at least in the short run), a mathematical model with corporate income tax rates as the only uncontrollable input would be a deterministic model. The distinguishing feature of a deterministic model is that the uncontrollable input values are known in advance.

If any of the uncontrollable inputs are uncertain and subject to variation, the model is referred to as a **stochastic** or **probabilistic model.** An uncontrollable input to many production planning models is demand for the product. Because future demand may be any of a range of values, a mathematical model that treats demand with uncertainty would be called a stochastic model. In the production model, the number of hours of production time required per unit, the total hours available, and the unit profit were all uncontrollable inputs. Because the uncontrollable inputs were all known to take on fixed values, the model was deterministic. If, however, the number of hours of production time per unit could vary from 3 to 6 hours depending on the quality of the raw material, the model would be stochastic. The distinguishing feature of a stochastic model is that the value of the output cannot be determined even if the value of the controllable input is known because the specific values of the uncontrollable inputs are unknown. In this respect, stochastic models are often more difficult to analyze.

Data Preparation

Another step in the quantitative analysis of a problem is the preparation of the data required by the model. Data in this sense refer to the values of the uncontrollable inputs to the model. All uncontrollable inputs or data must be specified before we can analyze the model and recommend a decision or solution for the problem.

In the production model, the values of the uncontrollable inputs or data were $10 per unit for profit, 5 hours per unit for production time, and 40 hours for production capacity. In the development of the model, these data values were known and incorporated into the model as it was being developed. If the model is relatively small and the uncontrollable in-put values or data required are few, the quantitative analyst will probably combine model development and data preparation into one step. That is, in these situations the data values are inserted as the equations of the mathematical model are developed.

However, in many mathematical modeling situations, the data or uncontrollable input values are not readily available. In these situations the analyst may know that the model will need profit per unit, production time, and production capacity data, but the values will not be known until the accounting, production, and engineering departments can be consulted. Rather than attempting to collect the required data as the model is being developed, the analyst will usually adopt a general notation for the model development step and then a separate data preparation step will be performed to obtain the uncontrollable input values required by the model.

Using the general notation

$$c = \text{profit per unit}$$
$$a = \text{production time in hours per unit}$$
$$b = \text{production capacity in hours}$$

the model development step of the production problem would result in the following general model:

$$\text{Max} \quad cx$$
$$\text{s.t.}$$
$$ax \leq b$$
$$x \geq 0$$

A separate data preparation step to identify the values for c, a, and b would then be necessary to complete the model.

Many inexperienced quantitative analysts assume that once the problem has been defined and a general model developed, the problem is essentially solved. These individuals tend to be-lieve that data preparation is a trivial step in the process and can be easily handled by clerical staff. Actually, this assumption could not be further from the truth, especially with large-scale models that have numerous data input values. For example, a moderate-size linear programming model with 50 decision variables and 25 constraints could have more than 1300 data elements that must be identified in the data preparation step. The time required to prepare these data and the possibility of data collection errors will make the data preparation step a critical part of the quantitative analysis process. Often, a fairly large database is needed to support a mathematical model, and information systems specialists also become involved in the data preparation step.

Model Solution

Once the model development and data preparation steps have been completed, we can pro-ceed to the model solution step. In this step, the analyst will attempt to identify the values of the decision variables that provide the "best" output for the model. The specific decision-variable value or values providing the "best" output will be referred to as the **optimal solution** for the model. For the production problem, the model solution step involves finding the value of the production quantity decision variable x that maximizes profit while not causing a violation of the production capacity constraint.

One procedure that might be used in the model solution step involves a trial-and-error approach in which the model is used to test and evaluate various decision alternatives. In the production model, this procedure would mean testing and evaluating the model using various production quantities or values of x. Referring to Figure 1.5, note that we could input trial values for x and check the corresponding output for projected profit and satisfaction of the production capacity constraint. If a particular decision alternative does not satisfy one or more of the model constraints, the decision alternative is rejected as being **infeasible,** regardless of the objective function value. If all constraints are satisfied, the decision alternative is **feasible** and a candidate for the "best" solution or recommended decision. Through this trial-and-error process of evaluating selected decision alternatives, a decision maker can identify a good—and possibly the best—feasible solution to the problem. This solution would then be the recommended decision for the problem.

Table 1.2 shows the results of a trial-and-error approach to solving the production model of Figure 1.5. The recommended decision is a production quantity of 8 because the feasible solution with the highest projected profit occurs at $x = 8$.

Although the trial-and-error solution process is often acceptable and can provide valuable information for the manager, it has the drawbacks of not necessarily providing the best solution and of being inefficient in terms of requiring numerous calculations if many decision alternatives are tried. Thus, quantitative analysts have developed special solution procedures for many models that are much more efficient than the trial-and-error approach. Throughout this text, you will be introduced to solution procedures that are applicable to the specific mathematical models that will be formulated. Some relatively small models or problems can be solved by hand computations, but most practical applications require the use of a computer.

The model development and model solution steps are not completely separable. An analyst will want both to develop an accurate model or representation of the actual problem situation and to be able to find a solution to the model. If we approach the model development step by attempting to find the most accurate and realistic mathematical model, we may find the model so large and complex that it is impossible to obtain a solu-

TABLE 1.2 TRIAL-AND-ERROR SOLUTION FOR THE PRODUCTION MODEL OF FIGURE 1.5

Decision Alternative (Production Quantity) x	Projected Profit	Total Hours of Production	Feasible Solution? (Hours Used ≤ 40)
0	0	0	Yes
2	20	10	Yes
4	40	20	Yes
6	60	30	Yes
8	80	40	Yes
10	100	50	No
12	120	60	No

tion. In this case, a simpler and perhaps more easily understood model with a readily available solution procedure is preferred even if the recommended solution is only a rough approximation of the best decision. As you learn more about quantitative solution procedures, you will have a better idea of the types of mathematical models that can be developed and solved.

Try Problem 8 to test your understanding of the concept of a mathematical model and what is referred to as the optimal solution to the model.

After a model solution has been obtained, both the quantitative analyst and the manager will be interested in determining how good the solution really is. Even though the analyst has undoubtedly taken many precautions to develop a realistic model, often the goodness or accuracy of the model cannot be assessed until model solutions are generated. Model testing and validation are frequently conducted with relatively small "test" problems that have known or at least expected solutions. If the model generates the expected solutions, and if other output information appears correct, the go-ahead may be given to use the model on the full-scale problem. However, if the model test and validation identify potential problems or inaccuracies inherent in the model, corrective action, such as model modification and/or collection of more accurate input data, may be taken. Whatever the corrective action, the model solution will not be used in practice until the model has satisfactorily passed testing and validation.

Report Generation

An important part of the quantitative analysis process is the preparation of managerial reports based on the model's solution. Referring to Figure 1.3, we see that the solution based on the quantitative analysis of a problem is one of the inputs the manager considers before making a final decision. Thus, the results of the model must appear in a managerial report that can be easily understood by the decision maker. The report includes the recommended decision and other pertinent information about the results that may be helpful to the decision maker.

A Note Regarding Implementation

As discussed in Section 1.2, the manager is responsible for integrating the quantitative solution with qualitative considerations in order to make the best possible decision. After completing the decision-making process, the manager must oversee the implementation and follow-up evaluation of the decision. During the implementation and follow-up, the manager should continue to monitor the contribution of the model. At times, this process may lead to requests for model expansion or refinement that will cause the quantitative analyst to return to an earlier step of the process.

Successful implementation of results is of critical importance to the quantitative analyst as well as the manager. If the results of the quantitative analysis process are not correctly implemented, the entire effort may be of no value. It doesn't take many unsuccessful implementations before the quantitative analyst is out of work. Because implementation often requires people to do things differently, it often meets with resistance. People want to know, "What's wrong with the way we've been doing it?" and so on. One of the most effective ways to ensure successful implementation is to include users throughout the modeling process. A user who feels a part of identifying the problem and developing the solution is much more likely to enthusiastically implement the results. The success rate for implementing the results of a quantitative analysis project is much greater for those projects in which there has been extensive user involvement. The Q.M. in Action, Quantitative Analysis at Merrill Lynch, discusses some of the reasons for the success of quantitative analysis at Merrill Lynch.

Q. M. IN ACTION

QUANTITATIVE ANALYSIS AT MERRILL LYNCH*

Merrill Lynch, a brokerage and financial services firm with more than 56,000 employees in 45 countries, serves its client base through two business units. The Merrill Lynch Corporate and Institutional Client Group serves more than 7,000 corporations, institutions, and governments. The Merrill Lynch Private Client Group (MLPC) serves approximately four million households, as well as 225,000 small to mid-sized businesses and regional financial institutions, through more than 14,000 financial consultants in 600-plus branch offices. The management science group, established in 1986, has been part of MLPC since 1991. The mission of this group is to provide high-end quantitative analysis to support strategic management decisions and to enhance the financial consultant-client relationship.

The management science group has successfully implemented models and developed systems for asset allocation, financial planning, marketing information technology, database marketing, and portfolio performance measurement. Although technical expertise and objectivity are clearly important factors in any analytical group, the management science group attributes much of its success to communications skills, teamwork, and consulting skills.

Each project begins with face-to-face meetings with the client. A proposal is then prepared to outline the background of the problem, the objectives of the project, the approach, the required resources, the time schedule, and the implementation issues. At this stage, analysts focus on developing solutions that provide significant value and are easily implemented.

As the work progresses, frequent meetings keep the clients up to date. Because people with different skills, perspectives, and motivations must work together for a common goal, teamwork is essential. The group's members take classes in team approaches, facilitation, and conflict resolution. They possess a broad range of multifunctional and multidisciplinary capabilities, and are motivated to provide solutions that focus on the goals of the firm. This approach to problem solving and the implementation of quantitative analysis has been a hallmark of the management science group. The impact and success of the group translates into hard dollars and repeat business. The group recently received the annual Edelman award given by the Institute for Operations Research and the Management Sciences for effective use of management science for organizational success.

*Based on Russ Labe, Raj Nigam, and Steve Spence, "Management Science at Merrill Lynch Private Client Group," *Interfaces* 29, no. 2 (March–April 1999), pp. 1–14.

NOTES AND COMMENTS

1. Developments in computer technology have increased the availability of quantitative methods to decision makers. A variety of software packages are now available for personal computers. Versions of The Management Scientist, Microsoft Excel, and LINDO are widely used in quantitative methods courses.

2. The Management Scientist is a software package developed by the authors of this text. Version 5.0 is now available for Windows 95, Windows 98, and Windows NT operating systems. This software can be used to solve problems in the text as well as small-scale problems encountered in practice. Appendix 1.2 provides an overview of the features and use of The Management Scientist.

3. Various chapter appendixes provide step-by-step instructions for using The Management Scientist and Excel to solve problems in the text.

1.4   MODELS OF COST, REVENUE, AND PROFIT

Some of the most basic quantitative models arising in business and economic applications are those involving the relationship between a volume variable—such as production volume or sales volume—and cost, revenue, and profit. Through the use of these models, a manager can determine the projected cost, revenue, and/or profit associated with an established production quantity or a forecasted sales volume. Financial planning, production planning, sales quotas, and other areas of decision making can benefit from such cost, revenue, and profit models.

Cost and Volume Models

The cost of manufacturing or producing a product is a function of the volume produced. This cost can usually be defined as a sum of two costs: fixed cost and variable cost. **Fixed cost** is the portion of the total cost that does not depend on the production volume; this cost remains the same no matter how much is produced. **Variable cost,** on the other hand, is the portion of the total cost that is dependent on and varies with the production volume. To illustrate how cost and volume models can be developed, we will consider a manufacturing problem faced by Nowlin Plastics.

Nowlin Plastics produces a variety of compact disc (CD) storage cases. Nowlin's best selling product is the CD-50, a slim, plastic CD holder with a specially designed lining that protects the optical surface of the disk. Several products are produced on the same manufacturing line, and a setup cost is incurred each time a changeover is made for a new product. Suppose that the setup cost for the CD-50 is $3000. This setup cost is a fixed cost that is incurred regardless of the number of units eventually produced. In addition, suppose that variable labor and material costs are $2 for each unit produced. The cost-volume model for producing x units of the CD-50 can be written as

$$C(x) = 3000 + 2x \tag{1.3}$$

where

$$x = \text{production volume in units}$$
$$C(x) = \text{total cost of producing } x \text{ units}$$

Once a production volume is established, the model in equation (1.3) can be used to compute the total production cost. For example, the decision to produce $x = 1200$ units would result in a total cost of $C(1200) = 3000 + 2(1200) = \$5400$.

Marginal cost is defined as the rate of change of the total cost with respect to production volume. That is, it is the cost increase associated with a one-unit increase in the production volume. In the cost model of equation (1.3), we see that the total cost $C(x)$ will increase by $2 for each unit increase in the production volume. Thus, the marginal cost is $2. With more complex total cost models, marginal cost may depend on the production volume. In such cases, we could have marginal cost increasing or decreasing with the production volume x.

Revenue and Volume Models

Management of Nowlin Plastics will also want information on the projected revenue associated with selling a specified number of units. Thus, a model of the relationship between revenue and volume is also needed. Suppose that each CD-50 storage unit sells for $5. The model for total revenue can be written as

$$R(x) = 5x \tag{1.4}$$

where

$$x = \text{sales volume in units}$$
$$R(x) = \text{total revenue associated with selling } x \text{ units}$$

Marginal revenue is defined as the rate of change of total revenue with respect to sales volume. That is, it is the increase in total revenue resulting from a one-unit increase in sales volume. In the model of equation (1.4), we see that the marginal revenue is \$5. In this case, marginal revenue is constant and does not vary with the sales volume. With more complex models, we may find that marginal revenue increases or decreases as the sales volume x increases.

Profit and Volume Models

One of the most important criteria for management decision making is profit. Managers need to be able to know the profit implications of their decisions. If we assume that we will only produce what can be sold, the production volume and sales volume will be equal. We can combine equations (1.3) and (1.4) to develop a profit-volume model that will determine profit associated with a specified production-sales volume. Since total profit is total revenue minus total cost, the following model provides the profit associated with producing and selling x units:

$$P(x) = R(x) - C(x) \qquad (1.5)$$
$$= 5x - (3000 + 2x) = -3000 + 3x$$

Thus, the model for profit $P(x)$ can be derived from the models of the revenue-volume and cost-volume relationships.

Breakeven Analysis

Using equation (1.5), we can now determine the profit associated with any production volume x. For example, suppose that a demand forecast indicates that 500 units of the product can be sold. The decision to produce and sell the 500 units results in a projected profit of

$$P(500) = -3000 + 3(500) = -1500$$

In other words, a loss of \$1500 is predicted. If sales are expected to be 500 units, the manager may decide against producing the product. However, a demand forecast of 1800 units would show a projected profit of

$$P(1800) = -3000 + 3(1800) = 2400$$

This profit may be enough to justify proceeding with the production and sale of the product.

We see that a volume of 500 units will yield a loss, whereas a volume of 1800 provides a profit. The volume that results in total revenue equaling total cost (providing \$0 profit) is called the **breakeven point.** If the breakeven point is known, a manager can quickly infer that a volume above the breakeven point will result in a profit, while a volume below the breakeven point will result in a loss. Thus, the breakeven point for a product provides valuable information for a manager who must make a yes/no decision concerning production of the product.

Let us now return to the Nowlin Plastics example and show how the profit model in equation (1.5) can be used to compute the breakeven point. The breakeven point can be

FIGURE 1.6   GRAPH OF THE BREAKEVEN ANALYSIS FOR NOWLIN PLASTICS

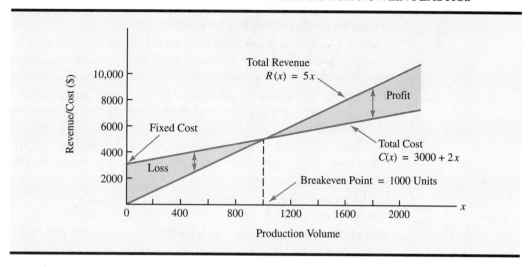

found by setting the profit expression equal to zero and solving for the production volume. Using equation (1.5), we have

$$P(x) = -3000 + 3x = 0$$
$$3x = 3000$$
$$x = 1000$$

Try Problem 15 to test your ability to determine the breakeven point for a quantitative model.

With this information, we know that production and sales of the product must be at least 1000 units before a profit can be expected. The graphs of the total cost model, the total revenue model, and the location of the breakeven point are shown in Figure 1.6. In Appendix 1.1 we also show how Excel can be used to perform a breakeven analysis for the Nowlin Plastics production example.

1.5   QUANTITATIVE METHODS IN PRACTICE

In this section we present a brief overview of the quantitative methods covered in this text. Over the years, practitioners have found numerous applications for the following:

Linear Programming.   Linear programming is a problem-solving approach that has been developed for situations involving maximizing or minimizing a linear function subject to linear constraints that limit the degree to which the objective can be pursued. The production model developed in Section 1.3 (see Figure 1.5) is an example of a simple linear programming model.

Integer Linear Programming.   Integer linear programming is an approach used for problems that can be set up as linear programs with the additional requirement that some or all of the decision recommendations be integer values.

Project Scheduling: PERT/CPM.   In many situations, managers are responsible for planning, scheduling, and controlling projects that consist of numerous separate jobs or tasks performed by a variety of departments, individuals, and so forth. The PERT (Program Evaluation and Review Technique) and CPM (Critical Path Method) techniques help managers carry out their project scheduling responsibilities.

Inventory Models. Inventory models are used by managers faced with the dual problems of maintaining sufficient inventories to meet demand for goods and, at the same time, incurring the lowest possible inventory holding costs.

Waiting-Line or Queueing Models. Waiting-line or queueing models have been developed to help managers understand and make better decisions concerning the operation of systems involving waiting lines.

Simulation. Simulation is a technique used to model the operation of a system. This technique employs a computer program to model the operation and perform simulation computations.

Decision Analysis. Decision analysis can be used to determine optimal strategies in situations involving several decision alternatives and an uncertain or risk-filled pattern of future events.

Goal Programming. Goal programming is a technique for solving multicriteria decision problems, usually within the framework of linear programming.

Analytic Hierarchy Process. This multicriteria decision-making technique permits the inclusion of subjective factors in arriving at a recommended decision.

Forecasting. Forecasting methods are techniques that can be used to predict future aspects of a business operation.

Markov-Process Models. Markov-process models are useful in studying the evolution of certain systems over repeated trials. For example, Markov processes have been used to describe the probability that a machine, functioning in one period, will function or break down in another period.

Methods Used Most Frequently

Our experience as both practitioners and educators has been that the most frequently used quantitative methods are linear programming, integer programming, network models such as transportation and transshipment models, and simulation. Depending upon the industry, the other methods in the preceding list are used more or less frequently.

Helping to bridge the gap between the manager and the quantitative analyst is a major focus of the text. We believe that the barriers to the use of quantitative methods can best be removed by increasing the manager's understanding of how quantitative analysis can be applied. The text will help you develop an understanding of which quantitative methods are most useful, how they are used, and, most importantly, how they can assist managers in making better decisions.

Q. M. in Action: Taco Bell's SMART Labor Management System shows how Taco Bell uses quantitative analysis to ensure that the maximum time customers wait in line is between three and five minutes. The SMART system consists of three models: a forecasting model, a simulation model, and an integer programming model. This system provides Taco Bell with a major competitive advantage, and is typical of the widespread role of quantitative analysis in service industries. Throughout the text we will illustrate the applications of quantitative analysis with Q. M. in Action vignettes.

NOTES AND COMMENTS

1. Operations research analyst is listed by the Bureau of Labor Statistics as one of the fastest growing occupations for careers requiring a bachelor's degree. The predicted growth is from 57,000 jobs in 1990 to 100,000 jobs in 2005, an increase of 73%.

2. The Institute for Operations Research and the Management Sciences (INFORMS) and the Decision Sciences Institute (DSI) are two professional societies that publish journals and newsletters dealing with current research and applications of operations research and management science techniques.

Q. M. IN ACTION

TACO BELL'S SMART LABOR MANAGEMENT SYSTEM*

Taco Bell turned to quantitative analysis in order to develop methods for better handling customer demand while keeping labor costs down. The company created the SMART (Scheduling Management and Restaurant Tool) Labor Management System (LMS) in order to provide a method of scheduling employees that will ensure that the maximum time customers wait in line is three to five minutes. The SMART LMS consists of three integrated models: a forecasting model, a simulation model, and an integer programming model.

The forecasting model determines how many dollars worth of business each store will generate each day. Unlike a manufacturing plant, which makes forecasts in terms of years, months, or weeks, Taco Bell needs to develop predictions of customer arrivals based on 15-minute intervals. Then, using the predictions of how much business a store will generate the following day, a simulation model determines how many employees will be needed and how they should be positioned throughout the facility. To determine the labor table for the next day, the simulation model must take into account the differences in Taco Bell fa-

cilities, the build-to-order food preparation approach used by Taco Bell, and the randomness associated with customer demand. Using the labor table generated by the simulation model, the integer programming model determines how many people are needed on the schedule for a particular day and what their shifts should be so that payroll costs are minimized. The integer programming model also takes into account all of the customer-service responsibilities and provides Taco Bell managers with the ability to schedule other tasks such as cleaning and maintenance.

The system is used in all company-owned stores, and by 1996 had been adopted by 70 percent of franchisees. From 1993–1996, the new system resulted in labor cost savings of $40.34 million. Employee feedback is positive, and other fast food companies have indicated that the new system has provided Taco Bell with a major competitive advantage.

*Based on Nancy Bistritz, "Taco Bell Finds Recipe For Success," *OR/MS Today,* (October 1997): 20–21.

SUMMARY

This text is about how quantitative methods may be used to help managers make better decisions. The focus of this text is on the decision-making process and on the role of quantitative analysis in that process. We have discussed the problem orientation of this process and in an overview have shown how mathematical models can be used in this type of analysis.

The difference between the model and the situation or managerial problem it represents is an important point. Mathematical models are abstractions of real-world situations and, as such, cannot capture all the aspects of the real situation. However, if a model can capture the major relevant aspects of the problem and can then provide a solution recommendation, it can be a valuable aid to decision making.

One of the characteristics of quantitative analysis that will become increasingly apparent as we proceed through the text is the search for a best solution to the problem. In carrying out the quantitative analysis, we shall be attempting to develop procedures for finding the "best" or optimal solution.

GLOSSARY

Problem solving   The process of identifying a difference between the actual and the desired state of affairs and then taking action to resolve the difference.

Decision making   The process of defining the problem, identifying the alternatives, determining the criteria, evaluating the alternatives, and choosing an alternative.

Single-criterion decision problem   A problem in which the objective is to find the "best" solution with respect to just one criterion.

Multicriteria decision problem   A problem that involves more than one criterion; the objective is to find the "best" solution, taking into account all the criteria.

Decision   The alternative selected.

Model   A representation of a real object or situation.

Iconic model   A physical replica, or representation, of a real object.

Analog model   While physical in form, an analog model does not have a physical appearance similar to the real object or situation it represents.

Mathematical model   Mathematical symbols and expressions used to represent a real situation.

Constraints   Restrictions or limitations imposed on a problem.

Objective function   A mathematical expression that describes the problem's objective.

Controllable input   The decision alternatives or inputs that can be specified by the decision maker.

Decision variable   Another term for controllable input.

Uncontrollable input   The environmental factors or inputs that cannot be controlled by the decision maker.

Deterministic model   A model in which all uncontrollable inputs are known and cannot vary.

Stochastic model   A model in which at least one uncontrollable input is uncertain and subject to variation; stochastic models are also referred to as probabilistic models.

Optimal solution   The specific decision variable value or values that provide the "best" output for the model.

Feasible solution   A decision alternative or solution that satisfies all constraints.

Infeasible solution   A decision alternative or solution that violates one or more constraints.

Fixed cost   The portion of the total cost that does not depend on the volume; this cost remains the same no matter how much is produced.

Variable cost   The portion of the total cost that is dependent on and varies with the volume.

Marginal cost   The rate of change of the total cost with respect to volume.

Marginal revenue   The rate of change of total revenue with respect to volume.

Breakeven point   The volume at which total revenue equals total cost.

PROBLEMS

1. Define the terms *management science* and *operations research*.

2. Describe the major reasons for the growth in the use of quantitative analysis since World War II.

3. Discuss the different roles played by the qualitative and quantitative approaches to managerial decision making. Why is it important for a manager or decision maker to have a good understanding of both of these approaches to decision making?

SELFtest   4. A firm has just completed a new plant that will produce more than 500 different products, using more than 50 different production lines and machines. The production scheduling decisions are critical in that sales will be lost if customer demand is not met on time. If no individual in the firm has had experience with this production operation, and if new production schedules must be generated each week, why should the firm consider a quantitative approach to the production scheduling problem?

5. List and discuss the steps of the decision-making process.

6. Give an example of each of the three types of models discussed in this chapter: iconic, analog, and mathematical.

7. What are the advantages of analyzing and experimenting with a model as opposed to a real object or situation?

SELFtest   8. Recall the production model from Section 1.3:

$$\text{Max} \quad 10x$$
$$\text{s.t.}$$
$$5x \leq 40$$
$$x \geq 0$$

Suppose the firm in this example considers a second product that has a unit profit of $5 and requires 2 hours for each unit produced. Use y as the number of units of product 2 produced.
  a. Show the mathematical model when both products are considered simultaneously.
  b. Identify the controllable and uncontrollable inputs for this model.
  c. Draw the flowchart of the input-output process for this model (see Figure 1.5).
  d. What are the optimal solution values of x and y?

9. Is the model developed in Problem 8 a deterministic or a stochastic model? Explain.

10. Suppose we modify the model in Problem 8 to obtain the following mathematical model:

$$\text{Max} \quad 10x$$
$$\text{s.t.}$$
$$ax \leq 40$$
$$x \geq 0$$

where a is the number of hours required for each unit produced. With $a = 5$, the optimal solution is $x = 8$. If we have a stochastic model with $a = 3$, $a = 4$, $a = 5$, or $a = 6$ as the possible values for the number of hours required per unit, what is the optimal value for x? What problems does this stochastic model cause?

11. A retail store in Des Moines, Iowa, receives shipments of a particular product from Kansas City and Minneapolis. Let

$$x = \text{units of product received from Kansas City}$$
$$y = \text{units of product received from Minneapolis}$$

  a. Write an expression for the total units of product received by the retail store in Des Moines.
  b. Shipments from Kansas City cost $0.20 per unit, and shipments from Minneapolis cost $0.25 per unit. Develop an objective function representing the total cost of shipments to Des Moines.
  c. Assuming the monthly demand at the retail store is 5000 units, develop a constraint that requires 5000 units to be shipped to Des Moines.
  d. No more than 4000 units can be shipped from Kansas City, and no more than 3000 units can be shipped from Minneapolis in a month. Develop constraints to model this situation.

e. Of course, negative amounts cannot be shipped. Combine the objective function and constraints developed to state a mathematical model for satisfying the demand at the Des Moines retail store at minimum cost.

12. Suppose you are going on a weekend trip to a city that is d miles away. Develop a model that determines your round-trip gasoline costs. What assumptions or approximations are necessary to treat this model as a deterministic model? Are these assumptions or approximations acceptable to you?

13. For most products, higher prices result in a decreased demand, whereas lower prices result in an increased demand. Let

$$d = \text{annual demand for a product in units}$$
$$p = \text{price per unit}$$

Assume that a firm accepts the following price-demand relationship as being realistic:

$$d = 800 - 10p$$

where p must be between $20 and $70.

a. How many units can the firm sell at the $20 per-unit price? At the $70 per-unit price?
b. Show the mathematical model for the total revenue (TR), which is the annual demand multiplied by the unit price.
c. Based on other considerations, the firm's management will only consider price alternatives of $30, $40, and $50. Use your model from part (b) to determine the price alternative that will maximize the total revenue.
d. What are the expected annual demand and the total revenue according to your recommended price?

14. Suppose that a manager has a choice between the following two mathematical models of a given situation: (a) a relatively simple model that is a reasonable approximation of the real situation and (b) a thorough and complex model that is the most accurate mathematical representation of the real situation possible. Why might the model described in part (a) be preferred by the manager?

SELFtest 15. The O'Neill Shoe Manufacturing Company will produce a special-style shoe if the order size is large enough to provide a reasonable profit. For each special-style order, the company incurs a fixed cost of $1000 for the production setup. The variable cost is $30 per pair, and each pair sells for $40.

a. Let x indicate the number of pairs of shoes produced. Develop a mathematical model for the total cost of producing x pairs of shoes.
b. Let P indicate the total profit. Develop a mathematical model for the total profit realized from an order for x pairs of shoes.
c. How large must the shoe order be before O'Neill will break even?

16. Eastman Publishing Company is considering publishing a paperback textbook on spreadsheet applications for business. The fixed cost of manuscript preparation, textbook design, and production setup is estimated to be $80,000. Variable production and material costs are estimated to be $3 per book. Demand over the life of the book is estimated to be 4000 copies. The publisher plans to sell the text to college and university bookstores for $20 each.

a. What is the breakeven point?
b. What profit or loss can be anticipated with a demand of 4000 copies?
c. With a demand of 4000 copies, what is the minimum price per copy that the publisher must charge to break even?
d. If the publisher believes that the price per copy could be increased to $25.95 and not affect the anticipated demand of 4000 copies, what action would you recommend? What profit or loss can be anticipated?

17. Preliminary plans are underway for the construction of a new stadium for a major league baseball team. City officials have questioned the number and profitability of the luxury corporate boxes planned for the upper deck of the stadium. Corporations and selected individuals may buy the boxes for $100,000 each. The fixed construction cost for the upper-deck area is estimated to be $1,500,000, with a variable cost of $50,000 for each box constructed.

a. What is the breakeven point for the number of luxury boxes in the new stadium?

b. Preliminary drawings for the stadium show that space is available for the construction of up to 50 luxury boxes. Promoters indicate that buyers are available and that all 50 could be sold if constructed. What is your recommendation concerning the construction of luxury boxes? What profit is anticipated?

18. Financial Analysts, Inc., is an investment firm that manages stock portfolios for a number of clients. A new client has just requested that the firm handle an $80,000 portfolio. As an initial investment strategy, the client would like to restrict the portfolio to a mix of the following two stocks:

Stock	Price/ Share	Estimated Annual Return/Share	Maximum Possible Investment
Oil Alaska	$50	$6	$50,000
Southwest Petroleum	$30	$4	$45,000

Let

$$x = \text{number of shares of Oil Alaska}$$

$$y = \text{number of shares of Southwest Petroleum}$$

a. Develop the objective function, assuming that the client desires to maximize the total annual return.

b. Show the mathematical expression for each of the following three constraints:
(1) Total investment funds available are $80,000.
(2) Maximum Oil Alaska investment is $50,000.
(3) Maximum Southwest Petroleum investment is $45,000.

Note: Adding the $x \geq 0$ and $y \geq 0$ constraints provides a linear programming model for the investment problem. A solution procedure for this model will be discussed in Chapter 2.

19. Models of inventory systems frequently consider the relationships among a beginning inventory, a production quantity, a demand or sales, and an ending inventory. For a given production period j, let

s_{j-1} = ending inventory from the previous period (beginning inventory for period j)

x_j = production quantity in period j

d_j = demand in period j

s_j = ending inventory for period j

a. Write the mathematical relationship or model that shows ending inventory as a function of beginning inventory, production, and demand.

b. What constraint should be added if production capacity for period j is given by C_j?

c. What constraint should be added if inventory requirements for period j mandate an ending inventory of at least I_j?

Appendix 1.1   THE MANAGEMENT SCIENTIST SOFTWARE

Developments in computer technology have been a major factor in making quantitative methods available to decision makers. A software package called The Management Scientist has been prepared by the authors to accompany this text. Version 5.0 is now available for Windows 95, Windows 98, and Windows NT operating systems. This software can be used to solve problems in the text as well as small-scale problems encountered in practice. Using The Management Scientist will give you an understanding and appreciation of the role of the computer in applying quantitative methods to decision problems.

The Management Scientist contains twelve modules, or programs, that will enable you to solve problems in many areas including the following:

- Chapter 4   Decision analysis
- Chapter 6   Forecasting
- Chapters 7–9   Linear programming
- Chapter 10   Transportation and assignment
- Chapter 11   Integer linear programming
- Chapter 12   PERT/CPM
- Chapter 13   Inventory models
- Chapter 15   Waiting line models
- Chapter 17   Markov processes

Use of The Management Scientist with the text is optional. Occasionally, we insert a figure in the text that shows the output The Management Scientist provides for a problem. However, familiarity with the use of the software is not necessary to understand the figure and the text material. The remainder of this appendix provides an overview of the features and the use of the software.

Selecting a Module

After starting The Management Scientist, you will encounter the module selection screen as shown in Figure 1.7. The choices provide access to the 12 modules. Simply click the desired module and select OK to load the requested module into the computer's memory.

The File Menu

After a module is loaded, you will need to click the File menu to begin working with a problem. The File menu provides the following options.

New   Select this option to begin a new problem. Dialog boxes and input templates will guide you through the data input process.

Open   Select this option to retrieve a problem that has been previously saved. When the problem is selected it will be displayed on the screen so that you can verify the problem is the one you want to solve.

Save   Once a new problem has been entered, you may want to save it for future use or modification. The Save option will guide you through the naming and saving process. If you create a folder named Problems, the Open and Save options will take you automatically to the Problems folder.

FIGURE 1.7   MODULE SELECTION SCREEN FOR THE MANAGEMENT SCIENTIST

Select A Module

○ 1. Linear Programming   ○   7. PERT/CPM
○ 2. Transportation   ○   8. Inventory
○ 3. Assignment   ○   9. Waiting Lines
○ 4. Integer Linear Programming   ○ 10. Decision Analysis
○ 5. Shortest Route   ○ 11. Forecasting
○ 6. Minimal Spanning Tree   ○ 12. Markov Processes

OK

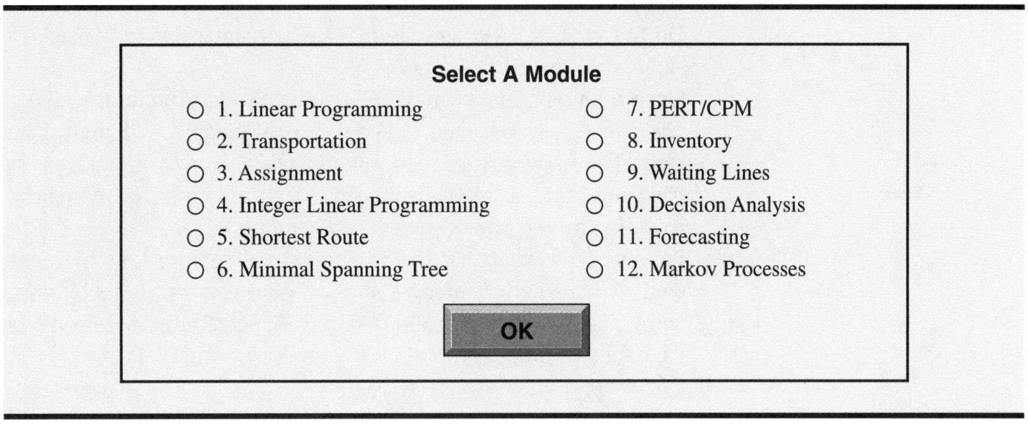

Change Modules   This option returns the user to the screen in Figure 1.7 and another module may be selected.

Exit   This option will exit The Management Scientist.

The Edit Menu

After a new problem has been solved, you may want to make one or more modifications to the problem before resolving. The Edit menu provides the option to display the problem and then make revisions in the problem before solving or saving. In the linear and integer programming modules, the Edit menu also has options to change the problem size by adding or deleting variables and adding or deleting constraints. Similar options to change the problem size are provided in the Edit menu of the transportation and assignment modules.

The Solution Menu

The Solution menu provides two options.

Solve   This option solves the current problem and displays the solution on the screen.

Print Solution   Once the solution is on the screen, the Solution menu has the Print Solution option, which sends the solution to a printer or to a text file. If the text file option is used, the file can be accessed later by a word processor so that the solution output may be displayed as part of a solution report.

Advice about Data Input

Any time a new problem is selected, the appropriate module will provide dialog boxes and forms for describing the features of the problem and for entering data. When using The Management Scientist, you may find the following data input suggestions helpful.

1. Do not enter commas (,) with your input data. For example, the value 104,000 should be entered with the six digits: 104000.

2. Do not enter the dollar sign ($) for profit or cost data. For example, a cost of $20.00 should be entered as 20.

3. Do not enter the percent sign (%) if percentage is requested. For example, 25% should be entered as 25, not 25% or .25.

4. Occasionally, a model may be formulated with fractional values such as 1/4, 2/3, 5/6, and so on. The data input for The Management Scientist must be in decimal form. The fraction 1/4 can be entered as .25. However, fractions such as 2/3 and 5/6 have repeating decimal forms. In these cases, we recommend the convention of rounding to five places such as .66667 and .83333.

5. Finally, we recommend that in general you attempt to scale extremely large input data so that smaller numbers may be input and processed by the computer. For example, costs such as $2,500,000 may be scaled to 2.5 with the understanding that the data used in the problem reflect millions of dollars.

Appendix 1.2   USING SPREADSHEETS FOR BREAKEVEN ANALYSIS

In Section 1.4 we introduced the Nowlin Plastics production example to illustrate how quantitative models can be used to help a manager determine the projected cost, revenue, and/or profit associated with an established production quantity or a forecasted sales volume. In this appendix we introduce spreadsheet applications by showing how to use Excel to perform a quantitative analysis of the Nowlin Plastics example.

Refer to the spreadsheet shown in Figure 1.8. We begin by entering the problem data into the top portion of the spreadsheet. The value of 3000 in cell B3 is the setup cost, the value of 2 in cell B5 is the variable labor and material costs per unit, and the value of 5 in

FIGURE 1.8   FORMULA SPREADSHEET FOR THE NOWLIN PLASTICS PRODUCTION EXAMPLE

	A	B
1	**Nowlin Plastics**	
2		
3	**Fixed Cost**	3000
4		
5	**Variable Cost per Unit**	2
6		
7	**Selling Price per Unit**	5
8		
9		
10	**Models**	
11		
12	**Production Volume**	800
13		
14	**Total Cost**	=B3+B5*B12
15		
16	**Total Revenue**	=B7*B12
17		
18	**Total Profit (Loss)**	=B16-B14

cell B7 is the selling price per unit. In general, whenever we perform a quantitative analysis using a spreadsheet, we will enter the problem data in the top portion of the spreadsheet and reserve the bottom portion for model development. The label "Models" in cell B10 helps to provide a visual reminder of this convention.

Cell B12 in the models portion of the spreadsheet contains the proposed production volume in units. Because the values for total cost, total revenue, and total profit depend upon the value of this decision variable, we have placed a border around cell B12 and screened the cell for emphasis. Based upon the value in cell B12, the cell formulas in cells B14, B16, and B18 are used to compute values for total cost, total revenue, and total profit (loss), respectively. First, recall that the value of total cost is the sum of the fixed cost (cell B3) and the total variable cost. Because the total variable cost is the product of the variable cost per unit (cell B5) and the production volume (cell B12), it is given by B5*B12. Thus, to compute total cost we entered the formula =B3 + B5*B12 into cell B14. Next, total revenue is the product of the selling price per unit (cell B7) and the number of units produced (cell B12), therefore in cell B16 we have entered the formula =B7*B12. Finally, the total profit (or loss) is the difference between the total revenue (cell B16) and the total cost (cell B14). Thus, in cell B18 we have entered the formula =B16 − B14. The spreadsheet shown in Figure 1.8 shows the formulas used to make these computations; we refer to it as a formula spreadsheet.

To examine the effect of selecting a particular value for the production volume, we have entered a value of 800 in cell B12. The spreadsheet shown in Figure 1.9 shows the values obtained by the formulas; a production volume of 800 units results in a total cost of $4600, a total revenue of $4000, and a loss of $600. To examine the effect of other production volumes, we only need to enter the other values into cell B12. To examine

FIGURE 1.9   SPREADSHEET SOLUTION USING A PRODUCTION VOLUME OF 800 UNITS FOR THE NOWLIN PLASTICS PRODUCTION EXAMPLE

	A	B
1	**Nowlin Plastics**	
2		
3	**Fixed Cost**	$3,000
4		
5	**Variable Cost per Unit**	$2
6		
7	**Selling Price per Unit**	$5
8		
9		
10	**Models**	
11		
12	**Production Volume**	800
13		
14	**Total Cost**	$4,600
15		
16	**Total Revenue**	$4,000
17		
18	**Total Profit (Loss)**	-$600

the effect of different costs and selling prices, we simply enter the appropriate values in the data portion of the spreadsheet; the results will be displayed in the model section of the spreadsheet.

In Section 1.4 we illustrated breakeven analysis. Let us now see how a spreadsheet can be used to compute the breakeven point for the Nowlin Plastics production example. We begin by considering a trial-and-error approach using Excel's Table command.

Determining the Breakeven Point Using Excel's Table Command

The breakeven point is the production volume that results in total revenue equal to total cost and hence a profit of $0. One way to determine the breakeven point is to use a trial-and-error approach. For example, in Figure 1.9 we saw that a trial production volume of 800 units resulted in a loss of $600. Because this trial solution resulted in a loss, a production volume of 800 units cannot be the breakeven point. We could continue to experiment with other production volumes by simply entering different values into cell B12 and observing the resulting profit or loss in cell B18. A better approach is to use Excel's Table command for doing this type of what-if analysis.

Suppose that we wanted to compute the profit or loss associated with production quantities ranging in value from 200 units to 2000 units, in increments of 200. We begin by entering these trial production values into a row or column of the spreadsheet. Note that we have entered these values into cells D13:D22 of the spreadsheet shown in Figure 1.10. Next,

FIGURE 1.10   USING EXCEL'S TABLE COMMAND TO COMPUTE THE BREAKEVEN POINT FOR THE NOWLIN PLASTICS PRODUCTION EXAMPLE

	A	B	C	D	E
1	**Nowlin Plastics**				
2					
3	**Fixed Cost**	$3,000			
4					
5	**Variable Cost per Unit**	$2			
6					
7	**Selling Price per Unit**	$5			
8					
9					
10	**Models**				
11					
12	**Production Volume**	800			-$600
13				200	-$2,400
14	**Total Cost**	$4,600		400	-$1,800
15				600	-$1,200
16	**Total Revenue**	$4,000		800	-$600
17				1000	$0
18	**Total Profit (Loss)**	-$600		1200	$600
19				1400	$1,200
20				1600	$1,800
21				1800	$2,400
22				2000	$3,000

we enter the formula for profit into cell E12. Since the formula for profit has already been entered into cell B18, we entered the formula =B18 into cell E12. The following steps used Excel's Table command to compute profit and loss projections for each trial production value.

Step 1. Select cells D12:E22
Step 2. Select the **Data** pull-down menu
Step 3. Choose the **Table** option
Step 4. When the **Table** dialog box appears
        Enter B12 in the **Column Input Cell**
        Select **OK**

The profit and loss values corresponding to each of the trial production values are displayed in cells E13:E22. Thus, we see that a production quantity of 200 units results in a loss of $2,400, a production quantity of 400 results in a loss of $1,800, and so on. Because a production quantity of 1000 results in a profit of $0, it is the breakeven point for Nowlin Plastics.

Determining the Breakeven Point Using Goal Seek

Another way to find a breakeven point using a spreadsheet is to use the Goal Seek tool. The Goal Seek tool in Microsoft Excel allows the user to determine the value for an input cell that will cause the value of a related output cell to equal some specified value (called the *goal*). In the case of breakeven analysis, the "goal" is to set Total Profit to zero by "seeking" an appropriate value for Production Volume. Goal Seek will allow us to find the value of production volume that will set Nowlin Plastics' total profit to zero. The following steps describe how to use Goal Seek to find the breakeven point for Nowlin Plastics:

Step 1. Select the **Tools** pull-down menu
Step 2. Choose the **Goal Seek** option
Step 3. When the **Goal Seek** dialog box appears:
        Enter B18 in the **Set cell** box
        Enter 0 in the **To value** box
        Enter B12 in the **By changing cell** box
        Select **OK**

The completed Goal Seek dialog box is shown in Figure 1.11, and the spreadsheet obtained after selecting OK is shown in Figure 1.12. The Total Profit in cell B18 is zero, and the Production Volume in cell B12 has been set to the breakeven point of 1000.

FIGURE 1.11   GOAL SEEK DIALOG BOX FOR THE NOWLIN PLASTICS
                PRODUCTION EXAMPLE

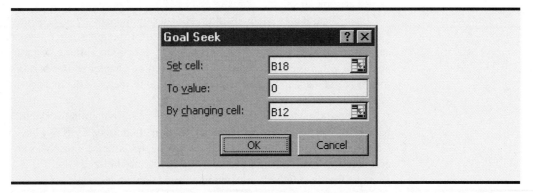

FIGURE 1.12 BREAKEVEN POINT FOUND USING GOAL SEEK FOR THE NOWLIN
PLASTICS PRODUCTION EXAMPLE

	A	B
1	**Nowlin Plastics**	
2		
3	**Fixed Cost**	$3,000
4		
5	**Variable Cost per Unit**	$2
6		
7	**Selling Price per Unit**	$5
8		
9		
10	**Models**	
11		
12	**Production Volume**	1000
13		
14	**Total Cost**	5000
15		
16	**Total Revenue**	5000
17		
18	**Total Profit (Loss)**	0

QUANTITATIVE METHODS IN PRACTICE FEATURE

Quantitative Methods in Practice write-ups prepared by practitioners are presented at the end of 14 chapters. We feel these provide a meaningful extension to the text material. The purpose of these application write-ups is to provide the reader with a better appreciation for the types of companies that use quantitative analysis and the types of problems these companies are able to solve.

Each Quantitative Methods in Practice write-up begins with a description of the company involved and continues with a discussion of the areas where the company has successfully applied quantitative analysis. The remainder of the write-up deals with an application that is closely related to the preceding chapter and/or part of the book. An effort has been made to avoid technical detail and to focus on the managerial aspects and the value of the results to the company.

Because Chapter 1 is designed to provide an introduction to quantitative analysis, we have not emphasized any particular solution methodology. Thus, we have placed the Mead Corporation write-up at the end of this first chapter because it provides an overview of several areas in which quantitative analysis can be used effectively. It is evidence of the impact quantitative methods are having at some companies.

MEAD CORPORATION*

DAYTON, OHIO

Mead is a major producer of papers for premium periodicals, books, commercial printing, and business forms, with special expertise in coating technologies. The company and its affiliates also produce pulp and lumber, a variety of specialty papers, and converted wood and paper products. Mead is a leader in the design and manufacture of packaging systems for beverage and other consumables markets. The company is a world leader in the production of coated board, and manufactures shipping containers and corrugating medium. Mead is a major manufacturer of paper-based school and office products, and operates a nationwide network of distribution centers for paper, packaging, and supplies.

Quantitative Methods at Mead Corporation

Quantitative analyses at Mead are developed and implemented by the company's Decision Analysis (DA) Department. The DA Department provides timely, efficient internal consulting services to the operating groups and corporate staff in the functional areas of operations, finance, marketing, and human resources. The department assists decision makers by providing them with analytical tools of quantitative methods as well as personal analysis and recommendations. Through conversations and observations, the department recognizes where quantitative methods are applicable, and it then recommends appropriate projects. In addition, the department provides a resource reservoir for information and assistance on quantitative methodology and assumes responsibility for keeping current in quantitative methods that could produce efficiencies at Mead. This charter results in a variety of projects and applications that span the corporation. Four examples of quantitative methods at Mead are described here.

*The authors are indebted to Dr. Edward P. Winkofsky of Mead Corporation, Dayton, Ohio, for providing this application.

A Corporate Planning System

The DA Department built and maintains a corporate planning system. This system allows business units to create and evaluate their five-year plans in an interactive computer environment.

Once the individual business units have finished their planning, the system consolidates the information at a group level. The assumptions of the units and the group are evaluated and reconciled. The use of this computer model facilitates the process by ensuring uniformity of calculations and reporting by all the planning units. Ultimately, the information is consolidated and evaluated at a corporate level.

A Timberland Financing Model

Another example of quantitative methods involves the development of a timberland financing model. Working directly with financial management, analysts assisted in the creation of a deterministic model that considered the major factors in a timberland financing arrangement. The model was used to examine the liability and profitability of timberland acquisition under various assumptions concerning forest growth rates, the inflation rate, and other financial considerations. By using the model, management was able to examine fully the acquisition and modify the financial arrangement as operating conditions warranted. The model is currently operated and modified by financial management and is considered a major tool in the examination of timberland financing.

Inventory Analysis

Inventory analysis is an area in which more sophisticated tools of quantitative analysis have been used. Simulation models have been used to describe the major factors (e.g., demand or usage rates, lead times, and production rates) in an inventory system. Typically, an inventory model includes purchase, storage, ordering, stockout, and degradation costs. The simulation model is used to evaluate reorder points, safety stocks, customer service levels, review periods, and the response time of the inventory system to extraordinary events.

Once developed and in place, the model can be updated as economic and operating conditions change. Thus, the model can be used by management to evaluate its inventory system on an ongoing basis and to ensure that it is operating in a cost-effective manner. These inventory simulation models are user friendly and can be operated and maintained by management with little formal computer training.

A Timber Harvesting Model

Mead also uses models to assist with the long-range management of the company's timberland. Through the use of large-scale linear programs, timber harvesting plans have been developed to cover a substantial time horizon. These models consider wood market conditions, mill pulpwood requirements, harvesting capacities, and general forest management principles. Within these constraints, the model develops an optimal harvesting and purchasing schedule based on discounted cash flow. Alternative schedules are developed to reflect various assumptions concerning forest growth, wood availability, and general economic conditions.

Quantitative methods are also used in the development of the inputs for the linear programming models already described. Timber prices and supplies as well as mill requirements must be forecast over the time horizon. Advanced sampling techniques are used to evaluate land holdings and to project forest growth. The harvest schedule is developed through the use of a number of quantitative methods.

Summary

The applications briefly described here—although only a few of the many quantitative analyses at Mead—convey the breadth of the activities currently in use within the company. The quantitative analyst at Mead must be able to work in a number of different environments and be proficient in a wide range of quantitative methods. In addition, the analyst must possess exceptional oral and written communication skills. Only with this background will the analyst be able to achieve the major objective of quantitative analysis at Mead—the development and implementation of user-friendly quantitative models that will support and enhance management decision making throughout the organization.

Questions

1. Which techniques listed in Section 1.5 are being used in the four applications described at the Mead Corporation?
2. Which of the Mead applications use a deterministic model, and which use a stochastic model? What conditions in the applications indicate a stochastic model is necessary?
3. Discuss how quantitative analysis described in Section 1.3 occurs in Mead's inventory analysis application.
4. Discuss the benefits associated with the quantitative applications at Mead.

INTRODUCTION TO PROBABILITY

CONTENTS

Business decisions are often based on an analysis of uncertainties such as the following:

1. What are the "chances" that sales will decrease if we increase prices?
2. What is the "likelihood" that a new assembly method will increase productivity?
3. How "likely" is it that the project will be completed on time?
4. What are the "odds" in favor of a new investment being profitable?

Probability provides a better description of uncertainty than verbal expressions such as chances are "pretty good," chances are "fair," and so on.

Probability is a numerical measure of the likelihood that an event will occur. Thus, probabilities could be used as measures of the degree of uncertainty associated with the four events previously listed. If probabilities were available, we could determine the likelihood of each event occurring.

Probability values are always assigned on a scale from 0 to 1. A probability near 0 indicates that an event is unlikely to occur; a probability near 1 indicates that an event is almost certain to occur. Other probabilities between 0 and 1 represent varying degrees of likelihood that an event will occur. Figure 2.1 depicts this view of probability.

Probability is important in decision making because it provides a way to measure, express, and analyze the uncertainties associated with future events. The Q. M. in Action: Airline Overbooking describes the role that probability plays in airline overbooking decisions.

2.1 EXPERIMENTS AND THE SAMPLE SPACE

In discussing probability, we define an **experiment** to be any process that generates well-defined outcomes. On any single repetition of an

FIGURE 2.1   PROBABILITY AS A NUMERICAL MEASURE OF THE LIKELIHOOD
OF OCCURRENCE

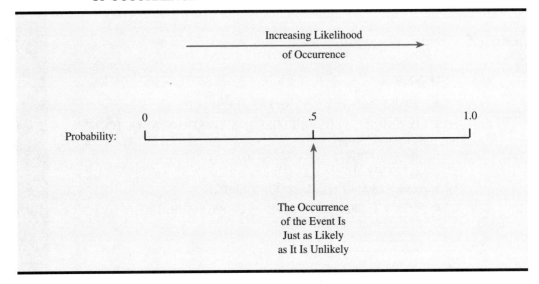

experiment *one and only one* of the possible experimental outcomes will occur. Several examples of experiments and their associated outcomes are as follows:

Experiment	Experimental Outcomes
Toss a coin	Head, tail
Select a part for inspection	Defective, nondefective
Conduct a sales call	Purchase, no purchase
Roll a die	1, 2, 3, 4, 5, 6
Play a football game	Win, lose, tie

The first step in analyzing a particular experiment is to define carefully the experimental outcomes. When we have defined *all* possible experimental outcomes, we have identified the **sample space** for the experiment. That is, the sample space is the set of all possible experimental outcomes. Any one particular experimental outcome is referred to as a **sample point** and is an element of the sample space.

Consider the experiment of tossing a coin. The experimental outcomes are defined by the upward face of the coin—a head or a tail. If we let S denote the sample space, we can use the following notation to describe the sample space and sample points for the coin-tossing experiment:

$$S = \{\text{Head, Tail}\}$$

Using this notation for the second experiment in the preceding table, selecting a part for inspection, provides a sample space with sample points as follows:

$$S = \{\text{Defective, Nondefective}\}$$

Finally, suppose that we consider the fourth experiment in the table, rolling a die. The experimental outcomes are defined as the number of dots appearing on the upward face of the

Try Problem 1 for practice in listing the experimental outcomes (sample points) for an experiment. die. In this experiment, the numerical values 1, 2, 3, 4, 5, and 6 represent the possible experimental outcomes or sample points. Thus the sample space is denoted

$$S = \{1, 2, 3, 4, 5, 6\}$$

Q.M. IN ACTION

AIRLINE OVERBOOKING*

Overbooking in the airline industry is the practice of selling more seats for a flight than the airplane's capacity. American Airlines estimates that, without overbooking, about 15% of seats would be unused at departure. As part of its yield management program, American uses quantitative decision tools to determine the optimal level of overbooking. Management attempts to maximize overbooking profitability by explicitly taking into account various probabilities and the revenue and cost implications of the decision.

Perhaps the primary consideration in determining the optimal level of overbooking is in assessing the relevant probabilities. Three probabilities are needed:

1. The probability that a passenger will cancel
2. The probability that a passenger with an active reservation will not show up on the departure day

3. The probability that a passenger who is turned away will choose another American flight (recapture probability).

These probabilities together with the costs of overbooking and underbooking are the key determinants of American Airlines' overbooking policy. Thus, considerable effort is spent in obtaining good estimates of the probabilities. American Airlines expects an annual revenue contribution of more than $500 million from this and other aspects of its yield management program.

*Based on B. C. Smith, J. F. Leimkuhler, and R. M. Darrow, "Yield Management at American Airlines." *Interfaces* 22, no. 3 (1992): 8–31.

NOTES AND COMMENTS

In probability, the notion of an experiment is somewhat different from the laboratory sciences. In the laboratory sciences, the researcher assumes that each time an experiment is repeated in exactly the same way, the same outcome will occur. For the type of experiment we study in probability, the outcome is determined by chance. Even though the experiment might be repeated in exactly the same way, a different outcome may occur. Because of this difference, the experiments we study in probability are sometimes called random experiments.

2.2   ASSIGNING PROBABILITIES TO EXPERIMENTAL OUTCOMES

With an understanding of an experiment and the sample space, let us now see how probabilities for the experimental outcomes can be determined. The probability of an experimental outcome is a numerical measure of the likelihood that the experimental outcome will occur. In assigning probabilities to experimental outcomes, two **basic requirements of probability** must be satisfied.

1. The probability values assigned to each experimental outcome (sample point) must be between 0 and 1. That is, if we let E_i indicate the ith experimental outcome and $P(E_i)$ indicate the probability of this experimental outcome, we must have

$$0 \leq P(E_i) \leq 1 \qquad \text{for all } i \qquad (2.1)$$

2. The sum of *all* of the experimental outcome probabilities must be 1. For example, if a sample space has k experimental outcomes, we must have

$$P(E_1) + P(E_2) + \cdots + P(E_k) = 1 \qquad (2.2)$$

Any method of assigning probability values to the experimental outcomes that satisfies these two requirements and results in reasonable numerical measures of the likelihood of the outcomes is acceptable. In practice, the classical method, the relative frequency method, or the subjective method are often used.

Classical Method

To illustrate the classical method of assigning probabilities, let us again consider the experiment of flipping a coin. On any one flip, we will observe one of two experimental outcomes: head or tail. A reasonable assumption is that the two possible outcomes are equally likely. Therefore, as one of the two equally likely outcomes is a head, we logically should conclude that the probability of observing a head is $\frac{1}{2}$, or 0.50. Similarly, the probability of observing a tail is 0.50. When the assumption of equally likely outcomes is used as a basis for assigning probabilities, the approach is referred to as the **classical method.** If an experiment has n possible outcomes, the classical method would assign a probability of $1/n$ to each experimental outcome.

As another illustration of the classical method, consider again the experiment of rolling a die. In Section 2.1 we described the sample space and sample points for this experiment with the notation

$$S = \{1, 2, 3, 4, 5, 6\}$$

A reasonable conclusion is that the six experimental outcomes are equally likely, and hence each outcome is assigned a probability of $\frac{1}{6}$. Thus, if $P(1)$ denotes the probability that one dot appears on the upward face of the die, then $P(1) = \frac{1}{6}$. Similarly, $P(2) = \frac{1}{6}$, $P(3) = \frac{1}{6}$, $P(4) = \frac{1}{6}$, $P(5) = \frac{1}{6}$, and $P(6) = \frac{1}{6}$. Note that this probability assignment satisfies the two basic requirements for assigning probabilities. In fact, requirements (2.1) and (2.2) are automatically satisfied when the classical method is used, because each of the n sample points is assigned a probability of $1/n$.

The classical method was developed originally to analyze gambling probabilities, where the assumption of equally likely outcomes often is reasonable. In many business problems, however, this assumption is not valid. Hence, alternative methods of assigning probabilities are required.

Relative Frequency Method

Consider a firm that is preparing to market a new product. In order to estimate the probability that a customer will purchase the product, a test market evaluation has been set up wherein salespeople call on potential customers. Each sales call conducted has two possible outcomes: The customer purchases the product, or the customer does not purchase the product. With no reason to assume that the two experimental outcomes are equally likely, the classical method of assigning probabilities is inappropriate.

Suppose that, in the test market evaluation of the product, 400 potential customers were contacted; 100 actually purchased the product, but 300 did not. In effect, then, we have repeated the experiment of contacting a customer 400 times and have found that the product was purchased 100 times. Thus, we might decide to use the relative frequency of the number of customers that purchased the product as an estimate of the probability of a customer making a purchase. We could assign a probability of $100/400 = 0.25$ to the experimental outcome of purchasing the product. Similarly, $300/400 = 0.75$ could be assigned to the ex-

Try Problems 2 and 4 for practice in assigning probabilities to experimental outcomes using the relative frequency approach.

perimental outcome of not purchasing the product. This approach to assigning probabilities is referred to as the **relative frequency method.**

Subjective Method

The classical and relative frequency methods cannot be applied to all situations where probability assignments are desired. In some situations the experimental outcomes are not equally likely and relative frequency data are not available. For example, what is the probability that the Pittsburgh Steelers will win their next football game? The experimental outcomes of a win, a loss, or a tie are not necessarily equally likely. Also, the teams involved have not played several times previously this year, so no relative frequency data relevant to this upcoming game are available. Thus, if we want an estimate of the probability that the Steelers will win, we must use a subjective opinion of its value.

The classical and relative frequency methods of assigning probabilities are objective. For the same experiment and data, we should agree on the probability assignments. However, the subjective method involves a personal "degree of belief." Different individuals looking at the same experiment can provide equally good but different subjective probabilities.

With the subjective method of assigning probabilities to the experimental outcomes, we may use any data available along with our experience and intuition. However, after we consider all available information, we must specify a probability value that expresses our *degree of belief* that the experimental outcome will occur. This method of assigning probability is referred to as the **subjective method.** Because subjective probability expresses a person's "degree of belief," it is personal. Different people can be expected to assign different probabilities to the same event. Care must be taken when using the subjective method to ensure that requirements (2.1) and (2.2) are satisfied. That is, regardless of a person's "degree of belief," the probability value assigned to each experimental outcome must be between 0 and 1, and the sum of all the experimental outcome probabilities must equal 1.

Even in situations where either the classical or relative frequency approach can be applied, management may want to provide subjective probability estimates. In such cases, the best probability estimates often are obtained by combining estimates from the classical or relative frequency approaches with subjective probability estimates.

2.3 EVENTS AND THEIR PROBABILITIES

An **event** is a collection of sample points (experimental outcomes). For example, in the experiment of rolling a die, the sample space has six sample points and is denoted $S = \{1, 2, 3, 4, 5, 6\}$. Now consider the event that the number of dots shown on the upward face of the die is an even number. The three sample points in this event are 2, 4, and 6. Using the letter A to denote this event, we write A as a collection of sample points:

$$A = \{2, 4, 6\}$$

Thus, if the experimental outcome or sample point were 2, 4, or 6, we would say that the event A has occurred.

Much of the focus of probability analysis is involved with computing probabilities for various events that are of interest to a decision maker. If the probabilities of the sample points are defined, the *probability of an event* is equal to the sum of the probabilities of the sample points in the event.

Returning to the experiment of rolling a die, we used the classical method to conclude that the probability associated with each sample point is $\frac{1}{6}$. Thus, the probability of rolling a 2 is $\frac{1}{6}$, the probability of rolling a 4 is $\frac{1}{6}$, and the probability of rolling a 6 is $\frac{1}{6}$. The probability of event A—an even number of dots on the upward face of the die—is

$$P(A) = P(2) + P(4) + P(6)$$
$$= \frac{1}{6} + \frac{1}{6} + \frac{1}{6} = \frac{3}{6} = \frac{1}{2}$$

Try Problem 6 for practice in assigning probabilities to events.

Any time that we can identify all the sample points of an experiment and assign the corresponding sample point probabilities, we can use the preceding approach to compute the probability of an event. However, in many experiments the number of sample points is large and the identification of the sample points, as well as determining their associated probabilities, becomes extremely cumbersome if not impossible. In the remainder of this chapter we present some basic probability relationships that can be used to compute the probability of an event without knowing sample point probabilities. These probability relationships require a knowledge of the probabilities for some events in the experiment. Probabilities of other events are then computed from these known probabilities using one or more of the probability relationships.

NOTES AND COMMENTS

1. The sample space, S, is itself an event. It contains all the experimental outcomes, so it has a probability of 1; that is, $P(S) = 1$.
2. When the classical method is used to assign probabilities, the assumption is that the experimental outcomes are equally likely. In such cases, the probability of an event can be computed by counting the number of experimental outcomes in the event and dividing the result by the total number of experimental outcomes.

2.4   SOME BASIC RELATIONSHIPS OF PROBABILITY

In this section we present several relationships that will be helpful in computing probabilities. The relationships are the complement of an event, the addition law, conditional probability, and the multiplication law.

Complement of an Event

For an event A, the **complement of event** A is the event consisting of all sample points that are *not* in A. The complement of A is denoted by A^c. Figure 2.2 provides a diagram, known as a **Venn diagram,** that illustrates the concept of a complement. The rectangular area represents the sample space for the experiment and as such contains all possible sample points. The circle represents event A and contains only the sample points that belong to A. The remainder of the rectangle contains all sample points not in event A, which by definition is the complement of A.

FIGURE 2.2   COMPLEMENT OF EVENT A

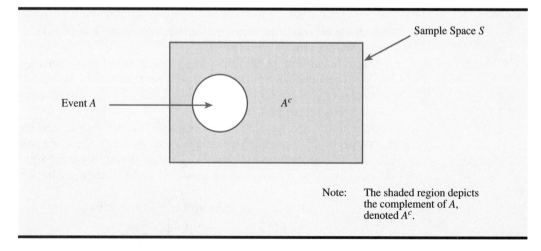

Note: The shaded region depicts the complement of A, denoted A^c.

In any probability application, event A and its complement A^c must satisfy the condition

$$P(A) + P(A^c) = 1$$

Solving for $P(A)$, we have

$$P(A) = 1 - P(A^c) \tag{2.3}$$

Equation (2.3) shows that the probability of an event A can be computed easily if the probability of its complement, $P(A^c)$, is known.

Consider the case of a sales manager who, after reviewing sales reports, states that 80% of new customer contacts result in no sale. By letting A denote the event of a sale and A^c denote the event of no sale, the manager is stating that $P(A^c) = 0.80$. Using equation (2.3), we see that

$$P(A) = 1 - P(A^c) = 1 - 0.80 = 0.20$$

which shows that there is a 0.20 probability that a sale will be made on a new customer contact.

In another case, a purchasing agent states a 0.90 probability that a supplier will send a shipment that is free of defective parts. Using the complement, we can conclude a $1 - 0.90 = 0.10$ probability that the shipment will contain some defective parts.

Addition Law

The addition law is a useful relationship when we have two events and are interested in knowing the probability that at least one of the events occurs. That is, with events A and B, we are interested in knowing the probability that event A or event B or both will occur. Before we present the addition law, we need to discuss two concepts concerning the combination of events: the *union* of events and the *intersection* of events.

Key words for the union of events (A ∪ B) *are "either A or B occurs" or "at least one of the two events occurs."*

For two events A and B, the **union of events A and B** is the event containing all sample points belonging to A or B or both. The union is denoted $A \cup B$. The Venn diagram shown in Figure 2.3 depicts the union of events A and B; the shaded region contains all the sample points in event A, as well as all the sample points in event B. The fact that the circles overlap indicates that some sample points are contained in both A and B.

FIGURE 2.3   UNION OF EVENTS A AND B

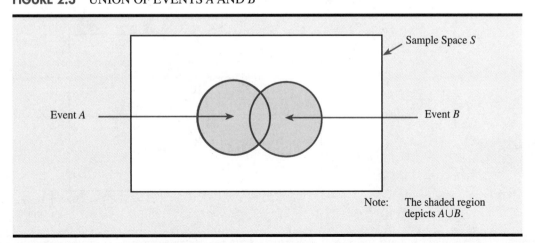

Sample Space S

Event A

Event B

Note: The shaded region depicts $A \cup B$.

For two events A and B, the **intersection of events A and B** is the event containing the sample points belonging to *both A and B*. The intersection is denoted by $A \cap B$. The Venn diagram depicting the intersection of the two events is shown in Figure 2.4. The area where the two circles overlap is the intersection; it contains the sample points that are in both A and B.

The addition law provides a way to compute the probability of event A or B or both occurring. In other words, the addition law is used to compute the probability of the union of two events, $A \cup B$. The **addition law** is formally stated as follows:

$$P(A \cup B) = P(A) + P(B) - P(A \cap B) \tag{2.4}$$

To obtain an intuitive understanding of the addition law, note that the first two terms in the addition law, $P(A) + P(B)$, account for all the sample points in $A \cup B$. However, as the sample points in the intersection $A \cap B$ are in both A and B, when we compute $P(A) + P(B)$ we in effect are counting each of the sample points in $A \cap B$ twice. We correct for this double counting by subtracting $P(A \cap B)$.

To apply the addition law, let us consider the following situations in a college course in quantitative methods for decision making. Of 200 students taking the course, 160 passed the mid-term examination and 140 passed the final examination; 124 students passed both exams. Let

$$A = \text{event of passing the mid-term exam}$$
$$B = \text{event of passing the final exam}$$

This relative frequency information leads to the following probabilities:

$$P(A) = \frac{160}{200} = 0.80$$

$$P(B) = \frac{140}{200} = 0.70$$

$$P(A \cap B) = \frac{124}{200} = 0.62$$

After reviewing the grades, the instructor decided to give a passing grade to any student who passed at least one of the two exams. That is, any student who passed the midterm, any

FIGURE 2.4   INTERSECTION OF EVENTS A AND B

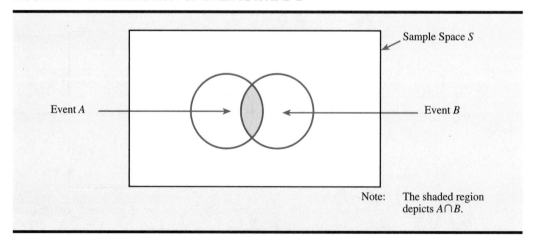

Note: The shaded region depicts $A \cap B$.

student who passed the final, and any student who passed both exams would receive a passing grade. What is the probability of a student receiving a passing grade in this course?

Your first reaction may be to try to count how many of the 200 students passed at least one exam, but note that the probability question is about the union of the events A and B. That is, we want to know the probability that a student passed the mid-term (A), passed the final (B), or passed both. Thus we want to know $P(A \cup B)$. Using the addition law (2.4) for the events A and B, we have

$$P(A \cup B) = P(A) + P(B) - P(A \cap B)$$

Knowing the three probabilities on the right-hand side of this expression, we obtain

$$P(A \cup B) = 0.80 + 0.70 - 0.62 = 0.88$$

This result indicates an 88% chance of a student passing the course because of the 0.88 probability of passing at least one of the exams.

Now consider a study involving the television viewing habits of married couples. It was reported that 30% of the husbands and 20% of the wives were regular viewers of a particular Friday evening program. For 12% of the couples in the study, both husband and wife were regular viewers of the program. What is the probability that at least one member of a married couple is a regular viewer of the program?

Let

$$H = \text{husband is a regular viewer}$$
$$W = \text{wife is a regular viewer}$$

We have $P(H) = 0.30$, $P(W) = 0.20$, and $P(H \cap W) = 0.12$; thus, the addition law yields

$$P(H \cup W) = P(H) + P(W) - P(H \cap W) = 0.30 + 0.20 - 0.12 = 0.38$$

This result shows a 0.38 probability that at least one member of a married couple is a regular viewer of the program.

Before going on, let us see how the addition law is applied to **mutually exclusive events.** Two or more events are said to be mutually exclusive if the events do not have any sample points in common—that is, there are no sample points in the intersection of the events. For two events A and B to be mutually exclusive, $P(A \cap B) = 0$. Figure 2.5 provides a Venn diagram depicting two mutually exclusive events. Because $P(A \cap B) = 0$ for the *special case of mutually exclusive events,* the addition law becomes

An event and its complement are mutually exclusive and their union is the entire sample space.

$$P(A \cup B) = P(A) + P(B) \tag{2.5}$$

For practice, try solving Problem 7.

To compute the probability of the union of two mutually exclusive events, we simply add the corresponding probabilities.

Conditional Probability

In many probability situations, being able to determine the probability of one event when another event is known to have occurred is important. Suppose that we have an event A with probability $P(A)$ and that we obtain new information or learn that another event, denoted B, has occurred. If A is related to B, we will want to take advantage of this information in computing a new or revised probability for event A.

FIGURE 2.5 MUTUALLY EXCLUSIVE EVENTS

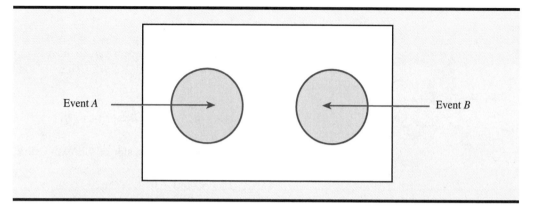

This new probability of event A is written P(A | B). The "|" denotes the fact that we are considering the probability of event A *given the condition that event B has occurred*. Thus, the notation P(A | B) is read "the probability of A given B."

With two events A and B, the general definitions of **conditional probability** for A given B and for B given A are as follows:

In conditional probability such as P(A | B) = 0.25, the probability value of 0.25 refers only to the probability of event A. The conditional probability provides the probability of event A assuming that event B has occurred. No information is provided about the probability of event B.

$$P(A \mid B) = \frac{P(A \cap B)}{P(B)} \tag{2.6}$$

$$P(B \mid A) = \frac{P(A \cap B)}{P(A)} \tag{2.7}$$

Note that for these expressions to have meaning, P(B) cannot equal 0 in equation (2.6) and P(A) cannot equal 0 in equation (2.7).

To obtain an intuitive understanding of the use of equation (2.6), consider the Venn diagram in Figure 2.6. The shaded region (both blue and gray) denotes that event B has occurred; the gray shaded region denotes the event (A ∩ B). We know that once B has occurred, the only way that we can also observe event A is for event (A ∩ B) to occur. Thus, the ratio P(A ∩ B)/P(B) provides the probability that we will observe event A when event B has already occurred.

Try Problem 12 for practice computing conditional probabilities.

We can apply conditional probability to the promotional status of male and female officers of a major metropolitan police force. It consists of 1200 officers: 960 men and 240 women. Over the past 2 years, 324 officers have been promoted. Table 2.1 shows the specific breakdown of promotions for male and female officers. Such a table is often called a *contingency table* or a *cross tabulation*.

After reviewing the promotional record, a committee of female officers filed a discrimination case on the basis that only 36 female officers had received promotions during the past 2 years. The police administration argued that the relatively low number of promotions for female officers is due not to discrimination but to the fact that few female officers are on the force. We use conditional probability to evaluate the discrimination charge.

Let

$$M = \text{event an officer is a man}$$
$$W = \text{event an officer is a woman}$$
$$B = \text{event an officer is promoted}$$

FIGURE 2.6   CONDITIONAL PROBABILITY

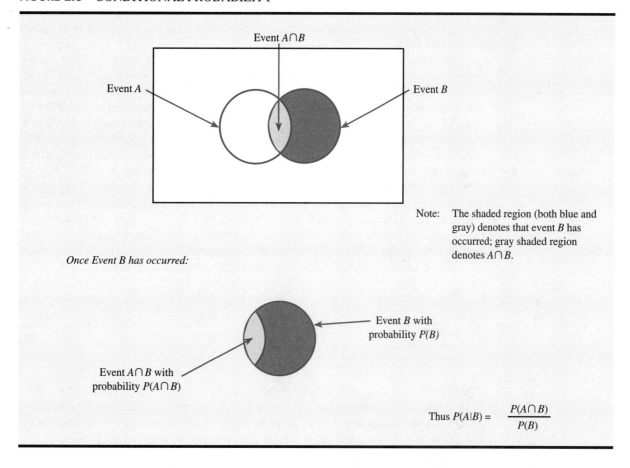

Event $A \cap B$

Event A

Event B

Note: The shaded region (both blue and gray) denotes that event B has occurred; gray shaded region denotes $A \cap B$.

Once Event B has occurred:

Event B with probability $P(B)$

Event $A \cap B$ with probability $P(A \cap B)$

Thus $P(A|B) = \dfrac{P(A \cap B)}{P(B)}$

TABLE 2.1   CONTINGENCY TABLE FOR PROMOTIONAL STATUS OF POLICE OFFICERS DURING THE PAST 2 YEARS

	Promoted	**Not Promoted**	**Total**
Men	288	672	960
Women	36	204	240
Total	324	876	1200

Dividing the data values in Table 2.1 by the total of 1200 officers permits us to summarize the available information as follows:

$$P(M \cap B) = \frac{288}{1200} = 0.24$$ probability that an officer is a man *and* is promoted

$$P(M \cap B^c) = \frac{672}{1200} = 0.56$$ probability that an officer is a man *and* is not promoted

$$P(W \cap B) = \frac{36}{1200} = 0.03$$ probability that an officer is a woman *and* is promoted

$$P(W \cap B^c) = \frac{204}{1200} = 0.17$$ probability that an officer is a woman *and* is not promoted

Because each of these values gives the probability of the intersection of two events, these probabilities are called **joint probabilities.** Table 2.2, which provides a summary of the probability information for the police officer promotion situation, is referred to as a **joint probability table.**

The values in the margins of the joint probability table provide the probabilities of each event separately. That is, $P(M) = 0.80$, $P(W) = 0.20$, $P(B) = 0.27$, and $P(B^c) = 0.73$. That is, 80% of the force is male, 20% of the force is female, 27% of all officers received promotions, and 73% were not promoted. These probabilities are referred to as **marginal probabilities** because of their location in the margins of the joint probability table. Returning to the issue of discrimination against the female officers, we see that the probability of promotion of an officer is $P(B) = 0.27$ (regardless of whether that officer is male or female). However, the critical issue in the discrimination case involves the two conditional probabilities $P(B \mid M)$ and $P(B \mid W)$. That is, what is the probability of a promotion *given* that the officer is a man and what is the probability of a promotion *given* that the officer is a woman? If these two probabilities are equal, the discrimination case has no basis because the chances of a promotion are the same for male and female officers. However, different conditional probabilities will support the position that male and female officers are treated differently in terms of promotion.

Using equation (2.7), the conditional probability relationship, we obtain

$$P(B \mid M) = \frac{P(M \cap B)}{P(M)} = \frac{0.24}{0.80} = 0.30$$

$$P(B \mid W) = \frac{P(W \cap B)}{P(W)} = \frac{0.03}{0.20} = 0.15$$

What conclusions do you draw? The probability of a promotion for a male officer is 0.30. That is twice the 0.15 probability of a promotion for a female officer. Although the use of conditional probability does not in itself prove that discrimination exists in this case, the conditional probability values strongly support the argument presented by the female officers.

In this illustration $P(B) = 0.27$, $P(B \mid M) = 0.30$, and $P(B \mid W) = 0.15$. These probabilities show clearly that promotion (event B) is influenced by whether the officer is male or female. In particular, as $P(B \mid M) \neq P(B)$, events B and M are **dependent events.** That is, the probability of event B (promotion) is altered or affected by knowing whether M (the officer is male) occurs. Similarly, with $P(B \mid W) \neq P(B)$, events B and W are dependent events. But, if the probability of event B was not changed by the existence of event M, that is, $P(B \mid M) = P(B)$, events B and M would be **independent events.** That is, two events A and B are *independent* if

$$P(B \mid A) = P(B)$$

TABLE 2.2   JOINT PROBABILITY TABLE FOR POLICE OFFICER PROMOTIONS

	Promoted	Not Promoted	Total
Men	0.24	0.56	0.80
Women	0.03	0.17	0.20
Total	0.27	0.73	1.00

Joint probabilities appear in the body of the table.

Marginal probabilities appear in the margins of the table.

or

$$P(A \mid B) = P(A)$$

For practice, try solving Problem 13.

Otherwise, the events are *dependent.*

Multiplication Law

The **multiplication law** can be used to find the probability of an intersection of two events. The multiplication law is derived from the definition of conditional probability. Using equations (2.6) and (2.7) and solving for $P(A \cap B)$, we obtain the multiplication law:

$$P(A \cap B) = P(A \mid B)P(B) \tag{2.8}$$

$$P(A \cap B) = P(B \mid A)P(A) \tag{2.9}$$

The multiplication law is useful in situations where probabilities such as $P(A)$, $P(B)$, $P(A \mid B)$, and/or $P(B \mid A)$ are known but where $P(A \cap B)$ is not. For example, suppose that a newspaper circulation department knows that 84% of its customers subscribe to the daily edition of the paper. Let D denote the event that a customer subscribes to the daily edition; hence, $P(D) = 0.84$. In addition, the department knows that the conditional probability that a customer who already holds a daily subscription also subscribes to the Sunday edition (event S) is 0.75; that is, $P(S \mid D) = 0.75$. What is the probability that a customer subscribes to both the daily and Sunday editions of the newspaper? Using equation (2.9), we compute $P(D \cap S)$:

$$P(D \cap S) = P(S \mid D)P(D) = 0.75(0.84) = 0.63$$

This result tells us that 63% of the newspaper's customers take both the daily and Sunday editions.

Before concluding this section, let us consider the special case of the multiplication law when the events involved are independent. Recall that independent events exist whenever $P(B \mid A) = P(B)$ or $P(A \mid B) = P(A)$. Returning to the multiplication law, equations (2.8) and (2.9), we can substitute $P(A)$ for $P(A \mid B)$ and $P(B)$ for $P(B \mid A)$. Hence, for the *special case of independent events,* the multiplication law becomes

$$P(A \cap B) = P(A)P(B) \tag{2.10}$$

Thus, to compute the probability of the intersection of two independent events, we simply multiply the corresponding probabilities. For example, a service station manager knows from past experience that 40% of her customers use a credit card when purchasing gasoline. What is the probability that the next two customers purchasing gasoline will both use a credit card? If we let

A = event that the first customer uses a credit card

B = event that the second customer uses a credit card

the event of interest is $A \cap B$. With no other information, a reasonable assumption is that A and B are independent events. Thus

$$P(A \cap B) = P(A)P(B) = (0.40)(0.40) = 0.16$$

NOTES AND COMMENTS

Do not confuse mutually exclusive events with independent events. Two events with nonzero probabilities cannot be both mutually exclusive and independent. If one mutually exclusive event is known to occur, the probability of the other occurring is reduced to zero. Thus, they cannot be independent.

2.5   BAYES' THEOREM

In the discussion of conditional probability, we indicated that revising probabilities when new information is obtained is an important phase of probability analysis. Often, we begin an analysis with initial or **prior probability** estimates for specific events of interest. Then, from sources such as a sample, a special report, or a product test, we obtain some additional information about the events. With this new information, we update the prior probability values by calculating revised probabilities, referred to as **posterior probabilities. Bayes' theorem** provides a means for making these probability calculations. The steps in this probability revision process are shown in Figure 2.7.

We can apply Bayes' theorem to a manufacturing firm that receives shipments of parts from two different suppliers. Let A_1 denote the event that a part is from supplier 1 and A_2 denote the event that a part is from supplier 2. Currently, 65% of the parts purchased by the company are from supplier 1, and the remaining 35% are from supplier 2. Thus, if a part is selected at random, we would assign the prior probabilities $P(A_1) = 0.65$ and $P(A_2) = 0.35$.

The quality of the purchased parts varies with the source of supply. Based on historical data, the conditional probabilities of receiving good and bad parts from the two suppliers are shown in Table 2.3. Thus, if we let G denote the event that a part is good and B denote the event that a part is bad, the information in Table 2.3 provides the following conditional probability values:

$$P(G \mid A_1) = 0.98 \qquad P(B \mid A_1) = 0.02$$
$$P(G \mid A_2) = 0.95 \qquad P(B \mid A_2) = 0.05$$

The tree diagram shown in Figure 2.8 depicts the process of the firm receiving a part from one of the two suppliers and then discovering that the part is good or bad as a two-

FIGURE 2.7   PROBABILITY REVISION USING BAYES' THEOREM

Prior Probabilities	→	New Information	→	Application of Bayes' Theorem	→	Posterior Probabilities

TABLE 2.3   CONDITIONAL PROBABILITIES OF RECEIVING GOOD AND BAD PARTS FROM TWO SUPPLIERS

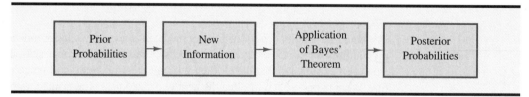

	Good Parts	**Bad Parts**	
Supplier 1	0.98	0.02	⟵ $P(B \mid A_1)$
Supplier 2	0.95	0.05	

FIGURE 2.8   TWO-STEP TREE DIAGRAM

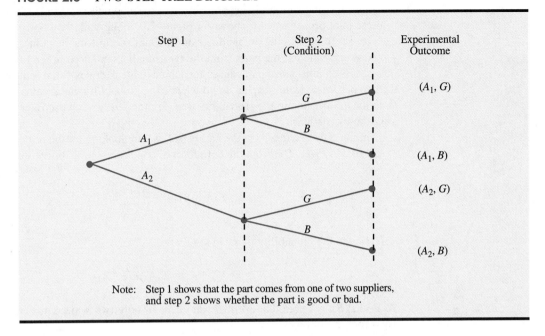

Note: Step 1 shows that the part comes from one of two suppliers,
and step 2 shows whether the part is good or bad.

step experiment. Of the four possible experimental outcomes, two correspond to the part being good, and two correspond to the part being bad.

Each of the experimental outcomes is the intersection of two events, so we can use the multiplication rule to compute the probabilities. For instance,

$$P(A_1 \cap G) = P(A_1)P(G \mid A_1)$$

The process of computing these joint probabilities can be depicted in what is sometimes called a *probability tree,* as shown in Figure 2.9. From left to right in the tree, the probabilities for each of the branches at step 1 are the prior probabilities, and the probabilities for each

FIGURE 2.9   PROBABILITY TREE FOR TWO-SUPPLIER EXAMPLE

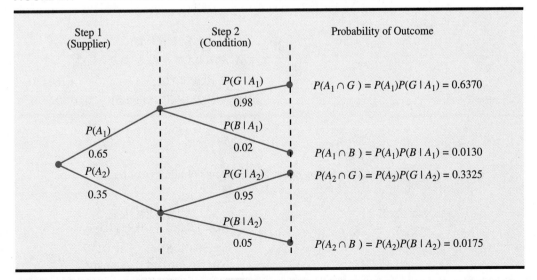

branch at step 2 are conditional probabilities. To find the probabilities of each experimental outcome, we simply multiply the probabilities on the branches leading to the outcome. Each of these joint probabilities is shown in Figure 2.9, along with the known probabilities for each branch. Note that the probabilities of the four experimental outcomes sum to 1.

Now suppose that the parts from the two suppliers are used in the firm's manufacturing process and that a bad part causes a machine to break down. What is the probability that the bad part came from supplier 1 and what is the probability that it came from supplier 2? With the information in the probability tree (Figure 2.9), we can use Bayes' theorem to answer these questions.

Letting B denote the event the part is bad, we are looking for the posterior probabilities $P(A_1 \mid B)$ and $P(A_2 \mid B)$. From the definition of conditional probability, we know that

$$P(A_1 \mid B) = \frac{P(A_1 \cap B)}{P(B)} \tag{2.11}$$

Referring to the probability tree, we see that

$$P(A_1 \cap B) = P(A_1)P(B \mid A_1) \tag{2.12}$$

To find $P(B)$, we note that event B can occur in only two ways: $(A_1 \cap B)$ and $(A_2 \cap B)$. Therefore, we have

$$P(B) = P(A_1 \cap B) + P(A_2 \cap B)$$
$$= P(A_1)P(B \mid A_1) + P(A_2)P(B \mid A_2) \tag{2.13}$$

Substituting from equations (2.12) and (2.13) into equation (2.11) and writing a similar result for $P(A_2 \mid B)$, we obtain Bayes' theorem for the case of two events.

The Reverend Thomas Bayes (1702–1761), a Presbyterian minister, is credited with the original work leading to the version of Bayes' theorem in use today.

$$P(A_1 \mid B) = \frac{P(A_1)P(B \mid A_1)}{P(A_1)P(B \mid A_1) + P(A_2)P(B \mid A_2)} \tag{2.14}$$

$$P(A_2 \mid B) = \frac{P(A_2)P(B \mid A_2)}{P(A_1)P(B \mid A_1) + P(A_2)P(B \mid A_2)} \tag{2.15}$$

Using equation (2.14) and the probability values provided in our example, we have

$$P(A_1 \mid B) = \frac{P(A_1)P(B \mid A_1)}{P(A_1)P(B \mid A_1) + P(A_2)P(B \mid A_2)}$$
$$= \frac{(0.65)(0.02)}{(0.65)(0.02) + (0.35)(0.05)} = \frac{0.0130}{0.0130 + 0.0175}$$
$$= \frac{0.0130}{0.0305} = 0.4262$$

In addition, using equation (2.15), we obtain $P(A_2 \mid B)$:

$$P(A_2 \mid B) = \frac{(0.35)(0.05)}{(0.65)(0.02) + (0.35)(0.05)}$$
$$= \frac{0.0175}{0.0130 + 0.0175} = \frac{0.0175}{0.0305} = 0.5738$$

Note that in this application we initially started with a probability of 0.65 that a part selected at random was from supplier 1. However, given information that the part is bad, we determine the probability that the part is from supplier 1 drops to 0.4262. In fact, if the part is bad, there is a better than 50-50 chance that the part came from supplier 2; that is, $P(A_2 \mid B) = 0.5738$.

Bayes' theorem is applicable when the events for which we want to compute posterior probabilities are mutually exclusive and their union is the entire sample space.[1] Bayes' theorem can be extended to the case of n mutually exclusive events $A_1, A_2, \ldots, A_n$, whose union is the entire sample space. In such a case Bayes' theorem for the computation of any posterior probability $P(A_i \mid B)$ becomes

$$P(A_i \mid B) = \frac{P(A_i)P(B \mid A_i)}{P(A_1)P(B \mid A_1) + P(A_2)P(B \mid A_2) + \cdots + P(A_n)P(B \mid A_n)} \quad (2.16)$$

Try Problem 20 for practice using Bayes' theorem to compute posterior probabilities.

With prior probabilities $P(A_1)$, $P(A_2)$, $\ldots$, $P(A_n)$ and the appropriate conditional probabilities $P(B \mid A_1)$, $P(B \mid A_2)$, $\ldots$, $P(B \mid A_n)$, equation (2.16) can be used to compute the posterior probability of the events $A_1, A_2, \ldots, A_n$.

The Tabular Approach

The tabular approach is helpful in conducting the Bayes' theorem calculations simultaneously for all events A_i. Such an approach is shown in Table 2.4. The computations shown there involve the following steps.

Step 1.   Prepare three columns:
Column 1—The mutually exclusive events for which posterior probabilities are desired
Column 2—The prior probabilities for the events
Column 3—The conditional probabilities of the new information given each event
Step 2.   In column 4, compute the joint probabilities for each event and the new information B by using the multiplication law. To get these joint probabilities, multiply the prior probabilities in column 2 by the corresponding conditional probabilities in column 3—that is, $P(A_i \cap B) = P(A_i)P(B \mid A_i)$.
Step 3.   Sum the joint probabilities in column 4 to obtain the probability of the new information, $P(B)$. In the example there is a 0.0130 probability that a part is from supplier 1 and is bad and a 0.0175 probability that a part is from supplier 2 and is bad. These are the only two ways by which a bad part can be obtained, so the sum $0.0130 + 0.0175$ shows an overall probability of 0.0305 of finding a bad part from the combined shipments of both suppliers.
Step 4.   In column 5, compute the posterior probabilities by using the basic relationship of conditional probability

$$P(A_i \mid B) = \frac{P(A_i \cap B)}{P(B)}$$

Try Problem 25 for an application of Bayes' theorem involving the tabular approach.

Note that the joint probabilities $P(A_i \cap B)$ appear in column 4, whereas $P(B)$ is the sum of the column 4 values.

---

1. If the union of events is the entire sample space, the events are often called *collectively exhaustive.*

TABLE 2.4   SUMMARY OF BAYES' THEOREM CALCULATIONS FOR THE
TWO-SUPPLIER PROBLEM

(1) Events A_i	(2) Prior Probabilities $P(A_i)$	(3) Conditional Probabilities $P(B \mid A_i)$	(4) Joint Probabilities $P(A_i \cap B)$	(5) Posterior Probabilities $P(A_i \mid B)$
A_1	0.65	0.02	0.0130	0.0130/0.0305 = 0.4262
A_2	0.35	0.05	0.0175	0.0175/0.0305 = 0.5738
	1.00		$P(B) = 0.0305$	1.0000

NOTES AND COMMENTS

1. Bayes' theorem is used in decision analysis (see Chapter 4). The prior probabilities often are subjective estimates provided by a decision maker. Sample information is obtained and posterior probabilities are computed for use in developing a decision strategy.

2. An event and its complement are mutually exclusive, and their union is the entire sample space. Thus, Bayes' theorem is always applicable for computing posterior probabilities of an event and its complement.

SUMMARY

In this chapter we introduced basic probability concepts and illustrated how probability analysis can provide helpful decision-making information. We described how probability can be interpreted as a numerical measure of the likelihood that an event will occur. In addition, we showed that the probability of an event can be computed either by summing the probabilities of the experimental outcomes (sample points) comprising the event or by using the basic relationships of probability. When additional information becomes available, we showed how conditional probability and Bayes' theorem can be used to obtain revised or posterior probabilities.

The probability concepts covered will be helpful in future chapters when we describe quantitative methods based on the use of probability information. Specific chapters and quantitative methods that make use of probability are

- Chapter 3   Probability distributions
- Chapter 4   Decision analysis
- Chapter 5   Utility and decision making
- Chapter 12   Project scheduling: PERT/CPM
- Chapter 14   Inventory management: Independent demand
- Chapter 15   Waiting line models
- Chapter 16   Simulation

GLOSSARY

Probability   A numerical measure of the likelihood that an event will occur.

Experiment   Any process that generates well-defined outcomes.

Sample space   The set of all possible sample points (experimental outcomes).

Sample point   The individual outcome of an experiment.

Basic requirements of probability   Two requirements that restrict the manner in which probability assignments can be made:

1. For each experimental outcome E_i, $0 \leq P(E_i) \leq 1$.
2. $P(E_1) + P(E_2) + \cdots + P(E_k) = 1$.

Classical method   A method of assigning probabilities that is based on the assumption that the experimental outcomes are equally likely.

Relative frequency method   A method of assigning probabilities based on experimentation or historical data.

Subjective method   A method of assigning probabilities based on judgment.

Event   A collection of sample points or experimental outcomes.

Complement of event A   The event containing all sample points that are not in A.

Venn diagram   A graphical device for representing the sample space and operations involving events.

Union of events A and B   The event containing all sample points that are in A, in B, or in both.

Intersection of events A and B   The event containing all sample points that are in both A and B.

Addition law   A probability law used to compute the probability of a union: $P(A \cup B) = P(A) + P(B) - P(A \cap B)$. For mutually exclusive events, $P(A \cap B) = 0$, and it reduces to $P(A \cup B) = P(A) + P(B)$.

Mutually exclusive events   Events that have no sample points in common; that is, $A \cap B$ is empty and $P(A \cap B) = 0$.

Conditional probability   The probability of an event given another event has occurred. The conditional probability of A given B is $P(A \mid B) = P(A \cap B)/P(B)$.

Joint probability   The probability of the intersection of two events.

Joint probability table   A table used to display joint and marginal probabilities.

Marginal probabilities   The values in the margins of the joint probability table, which provide the probability of each event separately.

Dependent events   Two events A and B, where $P(A \mid B) \neq P(A)$ or $P(B \mid A) \neq P(B)$; that is, the probability of one event is altered or affected by knowing whether the other event occurs.

Independent events   Two events A and B, where $P(A \mid B) = P(A)$ and $P(B \mid A) = P(B)$; that is, the events have no influence on each other.

Multiplication law   A probability law used to compute the probability of an intersection: $P(A \cap B) = P(A \mid B)P(B)$ or $P(A \cap B) = P(B \mid A)P(A)$. For independent events, it reduces to $P(A \cap B) = P(A)P(B)$.

Prior probabilities   Initial probabilities of events.

Posterior probabilities   Revised probabilities of events based on additional information.

Bayes' theorem   A method used to compute posterior probabilities.

PROBLEMS

SELFtest   1. In a quality control process an inspector selects a completed part for inspection. The inspector then determines whether the part has a major defect, a minor defect, or no defect. Consider the selection and classification of the part as an experiment. List the sample points for the experiment.

SELFtest   **2.** An experiment with three outcomes has been repeated 50 times, and E_1 occurred 20 times, E_2 occurred 13 times, and E_3 occurred 17 times. Assign probabilities to the outcomes. What method did you use? Why?

3. The manager of a large apartment complex provides the following subjective probability estimate about the number of vacancies that will exist next month.

Vacancies	Probability
0	0.05
1	0.15
2	0.35
3	0.25
4	0.10
5	0.10

List the sample points in each of the following events and provide the probability of
a. no vacancies.
b. at least four vacancies.
c. two or fewer vacancies.

SELFtest   **4.** Many school systems now provide Internet access for their students. As of 1996, Internet access was provided at 21,733 elementary schools, 7286 junior high schools, and 10,682 high schools (*Statistical Abstract of the United States, 1997*). The total number of schools includes 51,745 elementary schools, 14,012 junior high schools, and 17,229 high schools.
a. If you randomly choose an elementary school to visit, what is the probability it will have Internet access?
b. If you randomly choose a junior high school to visit, what is the probability it will have Internet access?
c. If you randomly choose a school to visit, what is the probability it will be an elementary school?
d. If you randomly choose a school to visit, what is the probability it will have Internet access?

5. Strom Construction has made a bid on two contracts. The owner has identified the possible outcomes and subjectively assigned the following probabilities.

Experimental Outcome	Obtain Contract 1	Obtain Contract 2	Probability
1	Yes	Yes	0.15
2	Yes	No	0.15
3	No	Yes	0.30
4	No	No	0.25

a. Are these valid probability assignments? Why or why not?
b. What would have to be done to make the probability assignments valid?

SELFtest   **6.** A sample of 100 customers of Montana Gas and Electric resulted in the following frequency distribution of monthly charges.

Amount ($)	Number
0–49	13
50–99	22
100–149	34
150–199	26
200–249	5

    a.   Let A be the event that monthly charges are $150 or more. Find $P(A)$.

    b.   Let B be the event that monthly charges are less than $150. Find $P(B)$.

SELFtest   **7.** Suppose that a sample space has five equally likely experimental outcomes: E_1, E_2, E_3, E_4, E_5. Let

$$A = \{E_1, E_2\}$$
$$B = \{E_3, E_4\}$$
$$C = \{E_2, E_3, E_5\}$$

    a.   Find $P(A)$, $P(B)$, and $P(C)$.

    b.   Find $P(A \cup B)$. Are A and B mutually exclusive?

    c.   Find A^c, C^c, $P(A^c)$, and $P(C^c)$.

    d.   Find $A \cup B^c$ and $P(A \cup B^c)$.

    e.   Find $P(B \cup C)$.

    8. According to the Census Bureau, deaths in the United States occur at a rate of 2,425,000 per year. The National Center for Health Statistics reported that the three leading causes of death during 1997 were heart disease (725,790), cancer (537,390), and stroke (159,877). Let H, C, and S represent the events that a person dies of heart disease, cancer, and stroke, respectively.

    a.   Use the data to estimate $P(H)$, $P(C)$, and $P(S)$.

    b.   Are events H and C mutually exclusive? Find $P(H \cap C)$.

    c.   What is the probability that a person dies from heart disease or cancer?

    d.   What is the probability that a person dies from cancer or stroke?

    e.   Find the probability that someone dies from a cause other than one of these three.

    9. A pharmaceutical company conducted a study to evaluate the effect of an allergy relief medicine; 250 patients with symptoms that included itchy eyes and a skin rash received the new drug. The results of the study are as follows: 90 of the patients treated experienced eye relief, 135 had their skin rash clear up, and 45 experienced relief of both itchy eyes and the skin rash. What is the probability that a patient who takes the drug will experience relief of at least one of the two symptoms?

    10. A study of 100 students who had been awarded university scholarships showed that 40 had part-time jobs, 25 had made the dean's list the previous semester, and 15 had both a part-time job and made the dean's list. What was the probability that a student had a part-time job or was on the dean's list?

    11. Let A be an event that a person's primary method of transportation to and from work is an automobile and B be an event that a person's primary method of transportation to and from work is a bus. Suppose that in a large city $P(A) = 0.45$ and $P(B) = 0.35$.

    a.   Are events A and B mutually exclusive? What is the probability that a person uses an automobile or a bus in going to and from work?

    b.   Find the probability that a person's primary method of transportation is some means other than a bus.

SELFtest **12.** For two events A and B, $P(A) = 0.5$, $P(B) = 0.60$ and $P(A \cap B) = 0.40$.
    a. Find $P(A \mid B)$.
    b. Find $P(B \mid A)$.
    c. Are A and B independent? Why or why not?

SELFtest **13.** In a survey of MBA students, the following data were obtained on "Students' first reason for application to the school in which they matriculated."

| | | **Reason for Application** | | | |
		School Quality	School Cost or Convenience	Other	**Totals**
Enrollment	Full time	421	393	76	890
Status	Part time	400	593	46	1039
	Totals	821	986	122	1929

    a. Develop a joint probability table using these data.
    b. Use the marginal probabilities of school quality, school cost or convenience, and other to comment on the most important reason for choosing a school.
    c. If a student goes full time, what is the probability that school quality will be the first reason for choosing a school?
    d. If a student goes part time, what is the probability that school quality will be the first reason for choosing a school?
    e. Let A be the event that a student is full time and let B be the event that the student lists school quality as the first reason for applying. Are events A and B independent? Justify your answer.

14. The following table shows the distribution of blood types in the general population (Hoxworth Blood Center, Cincinnati, Ohio).

	A	**B**	**AB**	**O**
Rh+	34%	9%	4%	38%
Rh−	6%	2%	1%	6%

    a. What is the probability a person will have type O blood?
    b. What is the probability a person will be Rh−?
    c. What is the probability a married couple will both be Rh−?
    d. What is the probability a married couple will both have type AB blood?
    e. What is the probability a person will be Rh− given she or he has type O blood?
    f. What is the probability a person will have type B blood given he or she is Rh+?

15. The Texas Oil Company provides a limited partnership arrangement whereby small investors can pool resources to invest in large-scale oil exploration programs. In the exploratory drilling phase, the selection of locations for new wells is based on the geologic structure of the proposed drilling sites. Experience shows that the probability of a type A structure at the site of a productive well is 0.40. The company also knows that 50% of all wells are drilled in locations with type A structure. Finally, 30% of all wells drilled are productive.

a. What is the probability of a well being drilled in a type A structure *and* being productive?
b. If the drilling process begins in a location with a type A structure, what is the proba-bility of having a productive well at that location?
c. Is finding a productive well independent of the type A geologic structure? Explain.

16. A purchasing agent has placed a rush order for a particular raw material with two differ-ent suppliers, A and B. If neither order arrives in 4 days the production process must be shut down until at least one of the orders arrives. The probability that supplier A can de-liver the material in 4 days is 0.55. The probability that supplier B can deliver the mater-ial in 4 days is 0.35.
a. What is the probability that both suppliers deliver the material in 4 days? Because two separate suppliers are involved, assume independence.
b. What is the probability that at least one supplier delivers the material in 4 days?
c. What is the probability the production process is shut down in 4 days because of a shortage in raw material (that is, both orders are late)?

17. The 1995 *Wall Street Journal* Subscriber Study provided the following data on ownership of direct broadcast satellite television. The data are broken down by the four sections of the country in which a separate edition is published.

		Geographic Region			
		East	Midwest	Southwest	West
Satellite Television	Currently own	17	8	7	13
	Likely to purchase	107	95	30	93
	Neither	488	403	98	275

a. Construct a joint probability table.
b. What is the probability of a subscriber owning satellite television?
c. What is the probability one of the subscribers surveyed is from the Southwest?
d. What is the probability of a subscriber from the Southwest owning satellite television?
e. Which region of the country is most likely to own satellite television?
f. Which region of the country is most likely to own satellite television a year from now?

18. In the evaluation of a sales training program, a firm discovered that of 50 salespeople re-ceiving a bonus last year, 20 had attended a special sales training program. The firm has 200 salespeople. Let B = the event that a salesperson makes a bonus and S = the event that a salesperson attends the sales training program.
a. Find $P(B)$, $P(S \mid B)$, and $P(S \cap B)$.
b. Assume that 40% of the salespeople have attended the training program. What is the probability that a salesperson makes a bonus given that the salesperson attended the sales training program, $P(B \mid S)$?
c. If the firm evaluates the training program in terms of its effect on the probability of a salesperson's receiving a bonus, what is your evaluation of the training program? Comment on whether B and S are dependent or independent events.

19. A company has studied the number of lost-time accidents occurring at its Brownsville, Texas, plant. Historical records show that 6% of the employees had lost-time accidents last year. Management believes that a special safety program will reduce the accidents to 5% during the current year. In addition, it estimates that 15% of those employees having had lost-time accidents last year will have a lost-time accident during the current year.
a. What percentage of the employees will have lost-time accidents in both years?
b. What percentage of the employees will have at least one lost-time accident over the 2-year period?

SELFtest 20. The prior probabilities for events A_1, A_2, and A_3 are $P(A_1) = 0.20$, $P(A_2) = 0.50$, and $P(A_3) = 0.30$. The conditional probabilities of event B given A_1, A_2, and A_3 are $P(B \mid A_1) = 0.50$, $P(B \mid A_2) = 0.40$, and $P(B \mid A_3) = 0.30$.

a. Compute $P(B \cap A_1)$, $P(B \cap A_2)$, and $P(B \cap A_3)$.

b. Apply Bayes' theorem, equation (2.16), to compute the posterior probability $P(A_2 \mid B)$.

c. Use the tabular approach to applying Bayes' theorem to compute $P(A_1 \mid B)$, $P(A_2 \mid B)$, and $P(A_3 \mid B)$.

21. A consulting firm has submitted a bid for a large research project. The firm's management initially felt there was a 50-50 chance of getting the bid. However, the agency to which the bid was submitted has subsequently requested additional information on the bid. Experience indicates that on 75% of the successful bids and 40% of the unsuccessful bids the agency requested additional information.

a. What is the prior probability the bid will be successful (i.e., prior to receiving the request for additional information)?

b. What is the conditional probability of a request for additional information given that the bid will ultimately be successful?

c. Compute a posterior probability that the bid will be successful given that a request for additional information has been received.

22. A local bank is reviewing its credit card policy with a view toward recalling some of its credit cards. In the past approximately 5% of cardholders have defaulted, and the bank has been unable to collect the outstanding balance. Thus, management has established a prior probability of 0.05 that any particular cardholder will default. The bank has further found that the probability of missing one or more monthly payments for those customers who do not default is 0.20. Of course, the probability of missing one or more payments for those who default is 1.

a. For a customer who has missed a monthly payment, compute the posterior probability that the customer will default.

b. The bank would like to recall its card if the probability that a customer will default is greater than 0.20. Should the bank recall its card if the customer misses a monthly payment? Why or why not?

23. An oil company has purchased an option on land in Alaska. Preliminary geologic studies have assigned the following prior probabilities.

$$P(\text{high-quality oil}) = 0.50$$
$$P(\text{medium-quality oil}) = 0.20$$
$$P(\text{no oil}) = 0.30$$

a. What is the probability of finding oil?

b. After 200 feet of drilling on the first well, a soil test is made. The probabilities of finding the particular type of soil identified by the test are

$$P(\text{soil} \mid \text{high-quality oil}) = 0.20$$
$$P(\text{soil} \mid \text{medium-quality oil}) = 0.80$$
$$P(\text{soil} \mid \text{no oil}) = 0.20$$

How should the firm interpret the soil test? What are the revised probabilities, and what is the new probability of finding oil?

24. A Bayesian approach can be used to revise probabilities that a prospect field will produce oil (*Oil & Gas Journal,* January 11, 1988). In one case, geological assessment indicates a 25% chance that the field will produce oil. Further, there is an 80% chance that a particular well will strike oil given that oil is present in the prospect field.

a. Suppose that one well is drilled on the field and it comes up dry. What is the probability that the prospect field will produce oil?

b. If two wells come up dry, what is the probability that the field will produce oil?

c. The oil company would like to keep looking as long as the chances of finding oil are greater than 1%. How many dry wells must be drilled before the field will be abandoned?

SELFtest   25. The Wayne Manufacturing Company purchases a certain part from suppliers A, B, and C. Supplier A supplies 60% of the parts, B 30%, and C 10%. The quality of parts varies among the suppliers, with A, B, and C parts having 0.25%, 1%, and 2% defective rates, respectively. The parts are used in one of the company's major products.

a. What is the probability that the company's major product is assembled with a defective part? Use the tabular approach to Bayes' theorem to solve.

b. When a defective part is found, which supplier is the likely source?

26. *M. D. Computing* (vol. 8, no. 5, 1991) describes the use of Bayes' theorem and conditional probability in medical diagnosis. Prior probabilities of diseases are based on the physician's assessment of factors such as geographic location, seasonal influence, and occurrence of epidemics. Assume that a patient is believed to have one of two diseases, denoted D_1 and D_2, with $P(D_1) = 0.60$ and $P(D_2) = 0.40$ and that medical research has shown a probability associated with each symptom that may accompany the diseases. Suppose that, given diseases D_1 and D_2, the probabilities a patient will have symptoms S_1, S_2, or S_3 are as follows:

		Symptoms		
		S_1	S_2	S_3
Disease	D_1	0.15	0.10	0.15 ← $P(S_3 \mid D_1)$
	D_2	0.80	0.15	0.03

After finding that a certain symptom is present, the medical diagnosis may be aided by finding the revised probabilities the patient has each particular disease. Compute the posterior probabilities of each disease for the following medical findings.

a. The patient has symptom S_1.

b. The patient has symptom S_2.

c. The patient has symptom S_3.

d. For the patient with symptom S_1 in part (a), suppose that symptom S_2 also is present? What are the revised probabilities of D_1 and D_2?

Case Problem   HAMILTON COUNTY JUDGES

Hamilton County judges try thousands of cases per year. In an overwhelming majority of the cases disposed, the verdict stands as rendered. However, some cases are appealed, and of those appealed, some of the cases are reversed. Kristen DelGuzzi of *The Cincinnati Enquirer* conducted a study of cases handled by Hamilton County judges over the years 1994 through 1996 (*The Cincinnati Enquirer,* January 11, 1998). Shown in Table 2.5 on page 57 are the results for 182,908 cases handled (disposed) by 38 judges in Common Pleas Court, Domestic Relations Court, and Municipal Court. Two of the judges (Dinkelacker and Hogan) did not serve in the same court for the entire three-year period.

The purpose of the newspaper's study was to evaluate the performance of the judges. Appeals are often the result of mistakes made by judges, and the newspaper wanted to know which judges were doing a good job and which were making too many mistakes. You have been called in to assist in the data analysis. Use your knowledge of probability and conditional probability to help with the ranking of the judges. You also may be able to analyze the likelihood of cases handled by the different courts being appealed and reversed.

Managerial Report

Prepare a report with your rankings of the judges. Also, include an analysis of the likelihood of appeal and case reversal in the three courts. At a minimum, your report should include the following:

1. The probability of cases being appealed and reversed in the three different courts.
2. The probability of a case being appealed for each judge.
3. The probability of a case being reversed for each judge.
4. The probability of reversal given an appeal for each judge.
5. Rank the judges within each court. State the criteria you used and provide a rationale for your choice.

TABLE 2.5 TOTAL CASES DISPOSED, APPEALED, AND REVERSED IN HAMILTON COUNTY COURTS DURING 1994 THROUGH 1996

Common Pleas Court

Judge	Total Cases Disposed	Appealed Cases	Reversed Cases
Fred Cartolano	3037	137	12
Thomas Crush	3372	119	10
Patrick Dinkelacker	1258	44	8
Timothy Hogan	1954	60	7
Robert Kraft	3138	127	7
William Mathews	2264	91	18
William Morrissey	3032	121	22
Norbert Nadel	2959	131	20
Arthur Ney, Jr.	3219	125	14
Richard Niehaus	3353	137	16
Thomas Nurre	3000	121	6
John O'Connor	2969	129	12
Robert Ruehlman	3205	145	18
J. Howard Sundermann	955	60	10
Ann Marie Tracey	3141	127	13
Ralph Winkler	3089	88	6
Total	43,945	1762	199

Domestic Relations Court

Judge	Total Cases Disposed	Appealed Cases	Reversed Cases
Penelope Cunningham	2729	7	1
Patrick Dinkelacker	6001	19	4
Deborah Gaines	8799	48	9
Ronald Panioto	12,970	32	3
Total	30,499	106	17

Municipal Court

Judge	Total Cases Disposed	Appealed Cases	Reversed Cases
Mike Allen	6149	43	4
Nadine Allen	7812	34	6
Timothy Black	7954	41	6
David Davis	7736	43	5
Leslie Isaiah Gaines	5282	35	13
Karla Grady	5253	6	0
Deidra Hair	2532	5	0
Dennis Helmick	7900	29	5
Timothy Hogan	2308	13	2
James Patrick Kenney	2798	6	1
Joseph Luebbers	4698	25	8
William Mallory	8277	38	9
Melba Marsh	8219	34	7
Beth Mattingly	2971	13	1
Albert Mestemaker	4975	28	9
Mark Painter	2239	7	3
Jack Rosen	7790	41	13
Mark Schweikert	5403	33	6
David Stockdale	5371	22	4
John A. West	2797	4	2
Total	108,464	500	104

MORTON INTERNATIONAL*

CHICAGO, ILLINOIS

Morton International is a company with strong businesses in salt and household products, rocket motors, and specialty chemicals. Carstab Corporation, a subsidiary of Morton, produces a variety of specialty chemical products designed to meet the unique specifications of its customers. One such product, an expensive catalyst used in chemical processing, met the customer's exact specifications in only some, but not all, of the lots produced by Carstab.

Carstab's customer agreed to test each lot as it was received to determine whether the catalyst would perform the desired function. If the catalyst did not pass the test, the lot would be returned to Carstab. The problem was that only 60% of the lots sent to the customer were passing the test. This problem meant that, although the product was still good and usable by other customers, an unacceptably high percentage (40%) of the shipments to this particular customer were being returned.

Carstab explored the possibility of duplicating the customer's test, but equipment cost made this infeasible. Therefore, to improve customer service, Carstab's chemists designed a new test that was believed to indicate whether the lot would eventually pass the customer's test. The question was, "Would the Carstab test increase the probability that a lot shipped to the customer would then pass the customer's test?"

A sample of lots was tested under both the customer's procedure and Carstab's proposed procedure. Results were that 55% of the lots passed Carstab's test, and 50% of the lots passed both the customer's and Carstab's test. In probability notation, we have

A = the event the lot passes the customer's test

B = the event the lot passes Carstab's test

where

*The authors are indebted to Michael Haskell of Morton International for providing this application.

$$P(B) = 0.55 \quad \text{and} \quad P(A \cap B) = 0.50$$

The probability information sought was the conditional probability $P(A \mid B)$ given by

$$P(A \mid B) = \frac{P(A \cap B)}{P(B)} = \frac{0.50}{0.55} = 0.909$$

Prior to Carstab's new test the probability a lot would pass the customer's test was 0.60. However, the new results showed that given a lot passed Carstab's new test it had a 0.909 probability of passing the customer's test. This result was good supporting evidence for the use of the test prior to shipment. Based on this probability analysis, the preshipment testing procedure was implemented at the company. Immediate results showed an improved level of customer service. A few lots were still being returned; however, the percentage was greatly reduced. The customer was more satisfied and return shipping costs were reduced.

Probability did not make the decision for the manager. However, some basic probability considerations provided important decision-making information and were a significant factor in the decision to implement the new testing procedure which resulted in improved service to the customer.

Questions

1. Why didn't Carstab produce a product that would meet customer specifications 100% of the time?
2. What probability information was helpful to Carstab in identifying its ability to produce a product that would meet the customer's specifications?
3. For the testing procedure described in this application, how would the results have changed if $P(B) = 0.40$ and $P(A \cap B) = 0.30$? Explain.

PROBABILITY DISTRIBUTIONS

Chapter 3

CONTENTS

In this chapter we continue the study of probability by introducing the concepts of random variables and probability distributions. We consider the probability distributions of both discrete and continuous random variables. Of particular interest are five special probability distributions: the binomial, the Poisson, the uniform, the normal, and the exponential. These probability distributions are important because they are used extensively in practice. The Q. M. in Action: Probability Distributions and a Treasure Hunt describes how the development and use of a probability distribution helped find a sunken ship.

3.1 RANDOM VARIABLES

Recall that in Chapter 2 we defined an experiment as any process that generates well-defined outcomes. We now want to concentrate on the process of assigning *numerical values* to outcomes. To do so we introduce the notion of a random variable.

For any particular experiment a random variable can be defined so that each possible experimental outcome generates exactly one numerical value for the random variable. For example, if we consider the experiment of selling automobiles for one day at a particular dealership, we could

PROBABILITY DISTRIBUTIONS AND A TREASURE HUNT*

The use of probability distributions played a key role in the location of a sunken ship. In 1857, while carrying passengers and gold from California to New York, the *SS Central America* sank in a hurricane, taking gold bars and coins worth an estimated $400 million to the ocean bottom. Central to the creation of the search plan was the development of a probability distribution for the position of the sunken ship.

Work began on developing the probability distribution in the summer of 1985. It involved combining information from various sources: Captain Herndon's last reported position, sightings by other ships, the drift of survivors, estimates of wind speed and ocean currents, and the like. Based on the information available, three separate probability distributions were developed and then merged into one, with subjective weights being assigned by the analysts. A search plan was based on these probabilities, and the actual search began during the summer of 1986.

Not until the summer of 1988 was the wreck finally discovered. In the summer of 1989, one ton of gold bars and gold coins was recovered from the wreck. The search team concluded that the sunken ship probably would not have been found without the use of the probability distribution for its location.

*Based on Lawrence D. Stone, "Search for the *SS Central America:* Mathematical Treasure Hunting," *Interfaces* 22, no. 3 (1992): 32–54.

describe the experimental outcomes in terms of the *number* of cars sold. In this case, if x = number of cars sold, x is called a random variable. The particular numerical value that the random variable takes on depends on the outcome of the experiment. That is, we will not know the specific value of the random variable until we have observed the experimental outcome. For example, if on a given day three cars are sold, the value of the random variable is 3; if on another day (a repeat of the experiment) four cars are sold, the value is 4. We define a random variable as follows:

Random variables must assume numerical values.

A **random variable** is a numerical description of the outcome of an experiment.

Some additional examples of experiments and their associated random variables are given in Table 3.1. Although many experiments have experimental outcomes that lend themselves quite naturally to numerical values, others do not. For example, for the experiment of tossing a coin one time, the experimental outcome will be either a head or a tail, neither of which has a natural numerical value. However, we still may want to express the outcomes in terms of a random variable. Thus, we need a rule that can be used to assign a numerical value to each of the experimental outcomes. One possibility is to let the random variable $x = 1$ if the experimental outcome is a head and $x = 0$ if the experimental outcome

TABLE 3.1 EXAMPLES OF RANDOM VARIABLES

Experiment	Random Variable (x)	Possible Values for the Random Variable
Make 100 sales calls	Total number of sales	0, 1, 2, . . . , 100
Inspect a shipment of 70 radios	Number of defective radios	0, 1, 2, . . . , 70
Build a new library	Percentage of project completed after 6 months	$0 \leq x \leq 100$
Operate a restaurant	Number of customers entering in one day	0, 1, 2, . . .

is a tail. Although the numerical values for *x* are arbitrary, *x* is a random variable because it describes the experimental outcomes numerically.

A random variable may be classified as either discrete or continuous, depending on the numerical values it can have. A random variable that may take on only a finite or an infinite sequence (e.g., 1, 2, 3, . . .) of values is a **discrete random variable.** The number of units sold, the number of defects observed, the number of customers that enter a bank during one day of operation, and so on, are examples of discrete random variables. The first two and the last random variables in Table 3.1 are discrete. Random variables such as weight, time, and temperature that may take on any value in a certain interval or collection of intervals are **continuous random variables.** For instance, the third random variable in Table 3.1 is a continuous random variable because it may take on any value in the interval from 0 to 100 (for example, 56.33, or 64.22).

Try Problem 1 for practice in identifying discrete and continuous random variables.

NOTES AND COMMENTS

One way to determine whether a random variable is discrete or continuous is to think of the values of the random variable as points on a line. Choose two points representing values of the random variable. If the entire line segment between the two points also represents possible values for the random variable, the random variable is continuous.

3.2   DISCRETE RANDOM VARIABLES

We can demonstrate the use of a discrete random variable by considering the sales of automobiles at DiCarlo Motors, Inc., in Saratoga, New York. The owner of DiCarlo Motors is interested in the daily sales volume for automobiles. Suppose that we let *x* be a random variable denoting the number of cars sold on a given day. Sales records show that 5 is the maximum number of cars that DiCarlo has ever sold during one day. The owner believes that the previous history of sales adequately represents what will occur in the future, so we would expect the random variable *x* to take on one of the numerical values 0, 1, 2, 3, 4, or 5. The possible values of the random variable are finite; thus we would classify *x* as a discrete random variable.

Probability Distribution of a Discrete Random Variable

Suppose that in checking DiCarlo's sales records we find that over the past year the firm has been open for business 300 days. The sales volumes generated and the frequency of their occurrence are summarized in Table 3.2. With these historical data available, the owner of DiCarlo Motors believes that the relative frequency method will provide a reasonable means

TABLE 3.2   CARS SOLD PER DAY AT DICARLO MOTORS

Sales Volume	Number of Days
No sales	54
One car	117
Two cars	72
Three cars	42
Four cars	12
Five cars	3
Total	300

of assessing the probabilities for the random variable x. The **probability function,** denoted $f(x)$, provides the probability that the random variable x takes on a specific value. Because on 54 of the 300 days of historical data DiCarlo Motors did not sell any cars and because no sales corresponds to $x = 0$, we assign to $f(0)$ the value $^{54}/_{300} = 0.18$. Similarly, $f(1)$ denotes the probability that x takes on the value 1, so we assign to $f(1)$ the value $^{117}/_{300} = 0.39$. After computing the relative frequencies for the other possible values of x, we can develop a table of x and $f(x)$ values. Table 3.3 shows one way of representing the probability distribution of the random variable x.

We can also represent the probability distribution of x graphically. In Figure 3.1 the values of the random variable x are shown on the horizontal axis. The probability that x takes on these values is shown on the vertical axis. For many discrete random variables the probability distribution also can be represented as a formula that provides $f(x)$ for every possible value of x. We illustrate this approach in the next section.

In Section 2.2 we defined the two basic requirements of all probability assignments as $0 \leq P(E_i) \leq 1$ and $\Sigma P(E_i) = 1$. Equations (3.1) and (3.2) are the analogs of these basic requirements.

In the development of a **discrete probability distribution,** two conditions must always be satisfied:

$$f(x) \geq 0 \qquad (3.1)$$
$$\Sigma f(x) = 1 \qquad (3.2)$$

TABLE 3.3   PROBABILITY DISTRIBUTION FOR THE NUMBER OF CARS SOLD PER DAY

x	$f(x)$
0	0.18
1	0.39
2	0.24
3	0.14
4	0.04
5	0.01
Total	1.00

FIGURE 3.1   PROBABILITY DISTRIBUTION FOR THE NUMBER OF CARS SOLD PER DAY

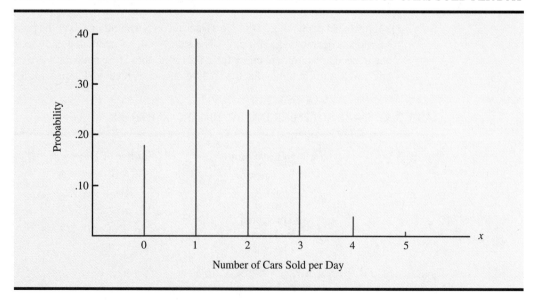

Condition (3.1) is the requirement that the probabilities associated with each value of x must be greater than or equal to zero, whereas condition (3.2) indicates that the sum of the probabilities for all values of the random variable x must be equal to 1. Table 3.3 shows that conditions (3.1) and (3.2) are satisfied. Thus, the probability distribution developed for DiCarlo Motors is a valid discrete probability distribution.

After establishing a random variable and its probability distribution, we can develop a variety of additional probability information, depending on the needs and interests of the decision maker. For example, in the DiCarlo Motors problem the probability distribution shown in Table 3.3 can be used to provide the following information.

1. There is a 0.18 probability that no cars will be sold during a day.
2. The most probable sales volume is 1, with $f(1) = 0.39$.
3. There is a 0.05 probability of an outstanding sales day with four or five cars being sold.

Try Problem 3 for practice in constructing a discrete probability distribution.

Using probability information such as that just given, DiCarlo's management can understand better the uncertainties associated with the car sales operation. Perhaps this improved understanding can serve as the basis for a new policy or decision that will increase the effectiveness of the firm.

Expected Value

After constructing the probability distribution for a random variable, we often want to compute the mean or expected value of the random variable. The **expected value** of a discrete random variable is a weighted average of all possible values of the random variable, where the weights are the probabilities associated with the values. The mathematical formula for computing the expected value of a discrete random variable x is

$$E(x) = \mu = \Sigma x f(x) \tag{3.3}$$

As equation (3.3) shows, both the notations $E(x)$ and μ are used to refer to the expected value of a random variable.

To compute the expected value of a discrete random variable, we must multiply each value of the random variable by its corresponding probability and then add the resulting terms. Calculation of the expected value of the random variable (number of daily sales) for DiCarlo Motors is shown in Table 3.4. The first column contains the values of the random variable x, and the second column contains their associated probabilities $f(x)$. Multiplying each value of x by its probability $f(x)$ provides the $xf(x)$ values in the third column. Following equation (3.3), we sum this column, $\Sigma xf(x)$, to find the expected value of 1.50 cars sold per day.

The expected value of a random variable is the mean, or average, value. That is, for experiments that can be repeated numerous times, the expected value can be interpreted as the "long-run" average value for the random variable. However, the expected value is not necessarily the number that we think the random variable will assume the next time the experiment is conducted. In fact, it is impossible for DiCarlo to sell exactly 1.50 cars on any day. However, if we envision selling cars at DiCarlo Motors for many days into the future, the expected value of 1.50 cars provides the mean, or average, daily sales volume.

The expected value can be important to the manager from both the planning and decision-making points of view. For example, suppose that DiCarlo Motors will be open 60 days during the next 3 months. How many cars will be sold during this time? Although we can't specify the exact sales for any given day, the expected value of 1.50 cars per day provides an expected or average sales estimate of $60(1.50) = 90$ cars for the next 3-month period. In terms of setting sales quotas and/or planning orders, the expected value may provide helpful decision-making information.

TABLE 3.4   EXPECTED VALUE CALCULATION

x	$f(x)$	$xf(x)$
0	0.18	$0(0.18) = 0.00$
1	0.39	$1(0.39) = 0.39$
2	0.24	$2(0.24) = 0.48$
3	0.14	$3(0.14) = 0.42$
4	0.04	$4(0.04) = 0.16$
5	0.01	$5(0.01) = \underline{0.05}$
		$E(x) = 1.50$

These calculations can be made easily in a spreadsheet See Appendix 3.1.

Variance

The expected value gives us an idea of the average or central value for the random variable, but we often want a measure of the dispersion, or variability, of the possible values of the random variable. For example, if the values of the random variable range from quite large to quite small, we would expect a large value for the measure of variability. If the values of the random variable show only modest variation, we would expect a relatively small value. The variance is a measure commonly used to summarize the variability in the values of a random variable. The mathematical expression for the *variance* of a discrete random variable is

An alternative formula for the variance of a discrete random variable is $Var(x) = \Sigma x^2 f(x) - \mu^2$.

$$\text{Var}(x) = \sigma^2 = \Sigma(x - \mu)^2 f(x) \qquad (3.4)$$

As equation (3.4) shows, an essential part of the variance formula is a *deviation*, $x - \mu$, which measures how far a particular value of the random variable is from the expected value or mean, μ. In computing the variance of a discrete random variable, we square the deviations and then weight them by the corresponding probability. The sum of these weighted squared deviations for all values of the random variable is the **variance.** In other words, the variance is a weighted average of the squared deviations.

The calculation of the variance for the number of daily sales in the DiCarlo Motors problem is summarized in Table 3.5. We see that the variance for the number of cars sold per day is 1.25. A related measure of variability is the **standard deviation,** σ, which is defined as the positive square root of the variance. For DiCarlo Motors, the standard deviation of the number of cars sold per day is

$$\sigma = \sqrt{1.25} = 1.118$$

TABLE 3.5   VARIANCE CALCULATION

x	$x - \mu$	$(x - \mu)^2$	$f(x)$	$(x - \mu)^2 f(x)$
0	$0 - 1.50 = -1.50$	2.25	0.18	$2.25(0.18) = 0.4050$
1	$1 - 1.50 = -0.50$	0.25	0.39	$0.25(0.39) = 0.0975$
2	$2 - 1.50 = 0.50$	0.25	0.24	$0.25(0.24) = 0.0600$
3	$3 - 1.50 = 1.50$	2.25	0.14	$2.25(0.14) = 0.3150$
4	$4 - 1.50 = 2.50$	6.25	0.04	$6.25(0.04) = 0.2500$
5	$5 - 1.50 = 3.50$	12.25	0.01	$12.25(0.01) = \underline{0.1225}$
				$\sigma^2 = 1.2500$

These calculations can be made easily in a spreadsheet. See Appendix 3.1.

For the purpose of easier managerial interpretation, the standard deviation may be preferred over the variance because it is measured in the same units as the random variable ($\sigma = 1.118$ cars sold per day). The variance (σ^2) is measured in squared units and is thus more difficult for a manager to interpret.

Try Problem 4 to be sure you can compute the expected value, variance, and standard deviation.

At this point our interpretation of the variance and the standard deviation is limited to comparisons of the variability of different random variables. For example, if the daily sales data from a second DiCarlo dealership in Albany, New York, provided $\sigma^2 = 2.56$ and $\sigma = 1.6$, we can conclude that the number of cars sold per day at this dealership exhibits more variability than at the first DiCarlo dealership, where $\sigma^2 = 1.25$ and $\sigma = 1.118$. Later in this chapter we discuss the normal distribution. For that probability distribution, we show that the variance and the standard deviation of the random variable are essential for making probability calculations.

3.3   BINOMIAL PROBABILITY DISTRIBUTION

In this section we consider a class of experiments that meet the following conditions.

1. The overall experiment can be described in terms of a sequence of n identical experiments called *trials.*
2. Two outcomes are possible on each trial. We refer to one outcome as a *success* and the other as a *failure.*
3. The probabilities of the two outcomes do not change from one trial to the next.
4. The trials are independent (i.e., the outcome of one trial does not affect the outcome of any other trial).

Experiments that satisfy conditions 2, 3, and 4 are said to be generated by a *Bernoulli process.* In addition, if condition 1 is satisfied (there are n identical trials), we have a *binomial experiment.* An important discrete random variable associated with the binomial experiment is the number of successful outcomes in the n trials. If we let x denote the value of this random variable, then x can have a value of 0, 1, 2, 3, . . . , n, depending on the number of successes observed in the n trials. The probability distribution associated with this random variable is called the **binomial probability distribution.**

In cases where the binomial distribution is applicable, the mathematical formula for computing the probability of any value for the random variable is the binomial probability function

Try Problem 9 (parts a–d) for practice computing binomial probabilities.

$$f(x) = \frac{n!}{x!(n - x)!} p^x (1 - p)^{n-x} \qquad x = 0, 1, \ldots, n \qquad (3.5)$$

where

$$n = \text{number of trials}$$
$$p = \text{probability of success on one trial}$$
$$x = \text{number of successes in } n \text{ trials}$$
$$f(x) = \text{probability of } x \text{ successes in } n \text{ trials}$$

The term $n!$ in the preceding expression is referred to as *n factorial* and is defined as

$$n! = n(n - 1)(n - 2) \cdots (2)(1)$$

For example, $4! = (4)(3)(2)(1) = 24$. Also, by definition, the special case of zero factorial is $0! = 1$.

Nastke Clothing Store Problem

To illustrate the binomial probability distribution, let us consider the experiment of customers entering the Nastke Clothing Store. To keep the problem relatively small, we restrict the experiment to the next three customers. If, based on experience, the store manager estimates that the probability of one customer making a purchase is 0.30, what is the probability that exactly two of the next three customers make a purchase?

We first want to demonstrate that three customers entering the clothing store and deciding whether to make a purchase can be viewed as a binomial experiment. Checking the four requirements for a binomial experiment, we note the following.

1. The experiment can be described as a sequence of three identical trials, one trial for each of the three customers who will enter the store.
2. Two outcomes—the customer makes a purchase (success) or the customer does not make a purchase (failure)—are possible for each trial.
3. The probabilities of the purchase (0.30) and no purchase (0.70) outcomes are assumed to be the same for all customers.
4. The purchase decision of each customer is independent of the purchase decision of the other customers.

Thus, if we define the random variable x as the number of customers making a purchase (i.e., the number of successes in the three trials), we satisfy the requirements of the binomial probability distribution.

With $n = 3$ trials and the probability of a purchase $p = 0.30$ for each customer, we use equation (3.5) to compute the probability of two customers making a purchase. This probability, denoted $f(2)$, is

$$f(2) = \frac{3!}{2!1!} (0.30)^2 (0.70)^1$$

$$= \frac{3 \times 2 \times 1}{2 \times 1 \times 1} (0.30)^2 (0.70)^1 = 0.189$$

Try Problem 12 for an application of the binomial distribution.

Similarly, the probability of no customers making a purchase, denoted $f(0)$, is

$$f(0) = \frac{3!}{0!3!} (0.30)^0 (0.70)^3$$

$$= \frac{3 \times 2 \times 1}{1 \times 3 \times 2 \times 1} (0.30)^0 (0.70)^3 = 0.343$$

Similarly, equation (3.5) can be used to show that the probabilities of one and three purchases are $f(1) = 0.441$ and $f(3) = 0.027$. Table 3.6 and Figure 3.2 summarize the binomial probability distribution for the Nastke Clothing Store problem.

If we consider any variation of the Nastke problem, such as 10 customers rather than 3 customers entering the store, the binomial probability function given by equation (3.5) still applies. For example, the probability that 4 of the 10 customers make a purchase is

$$f(4) = \frac{10!}{4!6!} (0.30)^4 (0.70)^6 = 0.2001$$

In this binomial experiment, $n = 10$, $x = 4$, and $p = 0.30$.

With the use of equation (3.5), tables have been developed that provide the probability of x successes in n trials for a binomial experiment. Such a table of binomial probability values is provided in Appendix A. We have included a portion of this table in Table 3.7. In

TABLE 3.6   PROBABILITY DISTRIBUTION FOR THE NUMBER OF CUSTOMERS MAKING A PURCHASE

x	$f(x)$
0	0.343
1	0.441
2	0.189
3	0.027
Total	1.000

FIGURE 3.2   PROBABILITY DISTRIBUTION FOR THE NASTKE CLOTHING STORE PROBLEM

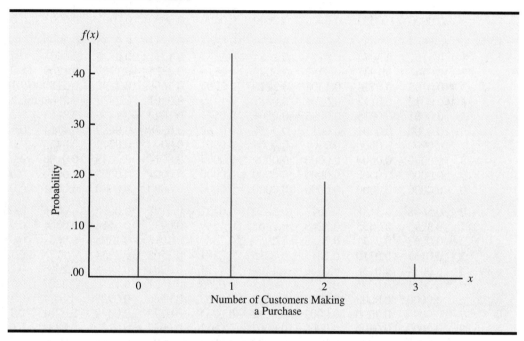

order to use this table, specify the values of n, p, and x for the binomial experiment of interest. Check the use of this table by employing it to verify the probability of four successes in ten trials for the Nastke Clothing Store problem. Note that the value of $f(4) = 0.2001$ can be read directly from the table of binomial probabilities, making it unnecessary to perform the calculations required by equation (3.5).

Expected Value and Variance for the Binomial Distribution

From the probability distribution in Table 3.6, we can use equation (3.3) to compute the expected value or expected number of customers making a purchase:

$$\mu = \Sigma x f(x) = 0(0.343) + 1(0.441) + 2(0.189) + 3(0.027) = 0.9$$

Note that we could have obtained this same expected value simply by multiplying n (the number of trials) by p (the probability of success on any one trial):

$$np = 3(0.30) = 0.9$$

TABLE 3.7   SELECTED VALUES FROM THE BINOMIAL PROBABILITY TABLES EXAMPLE: $n = 10$, $x = 4$, $p = 0.30$; $f(4) = 0.2001$

n	x					p					
		0.05	0.10	0.15	0.20	0.25	0.30	0.35	0.40	0.45	0.50
9	0	0.6302	0.3874	0.2316	0.1342	0.0751	0.0404	0.0207	0.0101	0.0046	0.0020
	1	0.2985	0.3874	0.3679	0.3020	0.2253	0.1556	0.1004	0.0605	0.0339	0.0176
	2	0.0629	0.1722	0.2597	0.3020	0.3003	0.2668	0.2162	0.1612	0.1110	0.0703
	3	0.0077	0.0446	0.1069	0.1762	0.2336	0.2668	0.2716	0.2508	0.2119	0.1641
	4	0.0006	0.0074	0.0283	0.0661	0.1168	0.1715	0.2194	0.2508	0.2600	0.2461
	5	0.0000	0.0008	0.0050	0.0165	0.0389	0.0735	0.1181	0.1672	0.2128	0.2461
	6	0.0000	0.0001	0.0006	0.0028	0.0087	0.0210	0.0424	0.0743	0.1160	0.1641
	7	0.0000	0.0000	0.0000	0.0003	0.0012	0.0039	0.0098	0.0212	0.0407	0.0703
	8	0.0000	0.0000	0.0000	0.0000	0.0001	0.0004	0.0013	0.0035	0.0083	0.0176
	9	0.0000	0.0000	0.0000	0.0000	0.0000	0.0000	0.0001	0.0003	0.0008	0.0020
10	0	0.5987	0.3487	0.1969	0.1074	0.0563	0.0282	0.0135	0.0060	0.0025	0.0010
	1	0.3151	0.3874	0.3474	0.2684	0.1877	0.1211	0.0725	0.0403	0.0207	0.0098
	2	0.0746	0.1937	0.2759	0.3020	0.2816	0.2335	0.1757	0.1209	0.0763	0.0439
	3	0.0105	0.0574	0.1298	0.2013	0.2503	0.2668	0.2522	0.2150	0.1665	0.1172
	4	0.0010	0.0112	0.0401	0.0881	0.1460	**0.2001**	0.2377	0.2508	0.2384	0.2051
	5	0.0001	0.0015	0.0085	0.0264	0.0584	0.1029	0.1536	0.2007	0.2340	0.2461
	6	0.0000	0.0001	0.0012	0.0055	0.0162	0.0368	0.0689	0.1115	0.1596	0.2051
	7	0.0000	0.0000	0.0001	0.0008	0.0031	0.0090	0.0212	0.0425	0.0746	0.1172
	8	0.0000	0.0000	0.0000	0.0001	0.0004	0.0014	0.0043	0.0106	0.0229	0.0439
	9	0.0000	0.0000	0.0000	0.0000	0.0000	0.0001	0.0005	0.0016	0.0042	0.0098
	10	0.0000	0.0000	0.0000	0.0000	0.0000	0.0000	0.0000	0.0001	0.0003	0.0010
11	0	0.5688	0.3138	0.1673	0.0859	0.0422	0.0198	0.0088	0.0036	0.0014	0.0005
	1	0.3293	0.3835	0.3248	0.2362	0.1549	0.0932	0.0518	0.0266	0.0125	0.0054
	2	0.0867	0.2131	0.2866	0.2953	0.2581	0.1998	0.1395	0.0887	0.0531	0.0269
	3	0.0137	0.0710	0.1517	0.2215	0.2581	0.2568	0.2254	0.1774	0.1259	0.0806
	4	0.0014	0.0158	0.0536	0.1107	0.1721	0.2201	0.2428	0.2365	0.2060	0.1611
	5	0.0001	0.0025	0.0132	0.0388	0.0803	0.1321	0.1830	0.2207	0.2360	0.2256
	6	0.0000	0.0003	0.0023	0.0097	0.0268	0.0566	0.0985	0.1471	0.1931	0.2256
	7	0.0000	0.0000	0.0003	0.0017	0.0064	0.0173	0.0379	0.0701	0.1128	0.1611
	8	0.0000	0.0000	0.0000	0.0002	0.0011	0.0037	0.0102	0.0234	0.0462	0.0806
	9	0.0000	0.0000	0.0000	0.0000	0.0001	0.0005	0.0018	0.0052	0.0126	0.0269
	10	0.0000	0.0000	0.0000	0.0000	0.0000	0.0000	0.0002	0.0007	0.0021	0.0054
	11	0.0000	0.0000	0.0000	0.0000	0.0000	0.0000	0.0000	0.0000	0.0002	0.0005

For the special case of a binomial probability distribution, the expected value of the random variable is given by

$$\mu = np \tag{3.6}$$

Thus, if you know that the probability distribution is binomial, you do not have to make the detailed calculations required by equation (3.3) to compute the expected value.

Suppose that during the next month Nastke's Clothing Store expects 1000 customers to enter the store. What is the expected number of customers who will make a purchase? Using equation (3.6) the answer is $\mu = np = (1000)(0.3) = 300$. To increase the expected number of sales, Nastke's must induce more customers to enter the store and/or somehow increase the probability that any individual customer will make a purchase after entering.

For the special case of a binomial distribution the variance of the random variable is

$$\sigma^2 = np(1 - p) \tag{3.7}$$

Try Problem 9 part e for practice computing the expected value, variance, and standard deviation.

For the Nastke Clothing Store problem with three customers, the variance and standard deviation for the number of customers making a purchase are

$$\sigma^2 = np(1 - p) = 3(0.3)(0.7) = 0.63$$
$$\sigma = \sqrt{0.63} = 0.79$$

3.4   POISSON PROBABILITY DISTRIBUTION

In this section we will consider a discrete random variable that often is useful when we are dealing with the number of occurrences of an event over a specified interval of time or space. For example, the random variable of interest might be the number of arrivals at a car wash in 1 hour, the number of repairs needed in 10 miles of highway, or the number of leaks in 100 miles of pipeline. If the following two assumptions are satisfied, the **Poisson probability distribution** is applicable.

1. The probability of an occurrence of the event is the same for any two intervals of equal length.
2. The occurrence or nonoccurrence of the event in any interval is independent of the occurrence or nonoccurrence in any other interval. The probability function of the Poisson random variable is given by equation (3.8):

$$f(x) = \frac{\lambda^x e^{-\lambda}}{x!} \qquad \text{for } x = 0, 1, 2, \ldots \tag{3.8}$$

where

$$\lambda = \text{mean or average number of occurrences in an interval}$$
$$e = 2.71828$$
$$x = \text{number of occurrences in the interval}$$
$$f(x) = \text{probability of } x \text{ occurrences in the interval}$$

Note that equation (3.8) shows no upper limit to the number of possible values that a Poisson random variable can take on. That is, although x is still a discrete random variable with an infinite sequence of values ($x = 0, 1, 2, \ldots$), the Poisson random variable has no specific upper limit.

An Example Involving Time Invervals

Suppose that we are interested in the number of arrivals at the drive-in teller window of a bank during a 15-minute period on weekday mornings. If we assume that the probability of a car arriving is the same for any two time periods of equal length and that the arrival or nonarrival of a car in any time period is independent of the arrival or nonarrival in any other time period, the Poisson probability function is applicable. Then if we assume that an analysis of historical data shows that the average number of cars arriving during a 15-minute interval of time is 10, the Poisson probability function with $\lambda = 10$ applies,

$$f(x) = \frac{\lambda^x e^{-\lambda}}{x!} = \frac{10^x e^{-10}}{x!} \qquad \text{for } x = 0, 1, 2, \ldots$$

Bell Labs uses the Poisson distribution in modeling the arrival of phone calls.

If we wanted to know the probability of five arrivals in 15 minutes, we would set $x = 5$ and obtain[1]

$$f(5) = \frac{10^5 e^{-10}}{5!} = 0.0378$$

Although we determined this probability by evaluating the probability function with $\lambda = 10$ and $x = 5$, the use of Poisson probability distribution tables often is easier. These tables provide probabilities for specific values of x and λ. We included such a table as Appendix B. For convenience we reproduced a portion of it as Table 3.8. To use the table of Poisson probabilities, you need know only the values of x and λ. Thus, from Table 3.8, the probability of five arrivals in a 15-minute period is the value in the row corresponding to $x = 5$ and the column corresponding to $\lambda = 10$. Hence, $f(5) = 0.0378$.

Try Problem 14 for practice computing Poisson probabilities.

An Example Involving Length or Distance Intervals

Suppose that we are concerned with the occurrence of major defects in a section of highway one month after resurfacing. We assume that the probability of a defect is the same for

TABLE 3.8   SELECTED VALUES FROM THE POISSON PROBABILITY TABLES EXAMPLE: $\lambda = 10, x = 5$; $f(5) = 0.0378$

	λ									
x	9.1	9.2	9.3	9.4	9.5	9.6	9.7	9.8	9.9	10
0	0.0001	0.0001	0.0001	0.0001	0.0001	0.0001	0.0001	0.0001	0.0001	0.0000
1	0.0010	0.0009	0.0009	0.0008	0.0007	0.0007	0.0006	0.0005	0.0005	0.0005
2	0.0046	0.0043	0.0040	0.0037	0.0034	0.0031	0.0029	0.0027	0.0025	0.0023
3	0.0140	0.0131	0.0123	0.0115	0.0107	0.0100	0.0093	0.0087	0.0081	0.0076
4	0.0319	0.0302	0.0285	0.0269	0.0254	0.0240	0.0226	0.0213	0.0201	0.0189
5	0.0581	0.0555	0.0530	0.0506	0.0483	0.0460	0.0439	0.0418	0.0398	**0.0378**
6	0.0881	0.0851	0.0822	0.0793	0.0764	0.0736	0.0709	0.0682	0.0656	0.0631
7	0.1145	0.1118	0.1091	0.1064	0.1037	0.1010	0.0982	0.0955	0.0928	0.0901
8	0.1302	0.1286	0.1269	0.1251	0.1232	0.1212	0.1191	0.1170	0.1148	0.1126
9	0.1317	0.1315	0.1311	0.1306	0.1300	0.1293	0.1284	0.1274	0.1263	0.1251
10	0.1198	0.1210	0.1219	0.1228	0.1235	0.1241	0.1245	0.1249	0.1250	0.1251
11	0.0991	0.1012	0.1031	0.1049	0.1067	0.1083	0.1098	0.1112	0.1125	0.1137
12	0.0752	0.0776	0.0799	0.0822	0.0844	0.0866	0.0888	0.0908	0.0928	0.0948
13	0.0526	0.0549	0.0572	0.0594	0.0617	0.0640	0.0662	0.0685	0.0707	0.0729
14	0.0342	0.0361	0.0380	0.0399	0.0419	0.0439	0.0459	0.0479	0.0500	0.0521
15	0.0208	0.0221	0.0235	0.0250	0.0265	0.0281	0.0297	0.0313	0.0330	0.0347
16	0.0118	0.0127	0.0137	0.0147	0.0157	0.0168	0.0180	0.0192	0.0204	0.0217
17	0.0063	0.0069	0.0075	0.0081	0.0088	0.0095	0.0103	0.0111	0.0119	0.0128
18	0.0032	0.0035	0.0039	0.0042	0.0046	0.0051	0.0055	0.0060	0.0065	0.0071
19	0.0015	0.0017	0.0019	0.0021	0.0023	0.0026	0.0028	0.0031	0.0034	0.0037
20	0.0007	0.0008	0.0009	0.0010	0.0011	0.0012	0.0014	0.0015	0.0017	0.0019
21	0.0003	0.0003	0.0004	0.0004	0.0005	0.0006	0.0006	0.0007	0.0008	0.0009
22	0.0001	0.0001	0.0002	0.0002	0.0002	0.0002	0.0003	0.0003	0.0004	0.0004
23	0.0000	0.0001	0.0001	0.0001	0.0001	0.0001	0.0001	0.0001	0.0002	0.0002
24	0.0000	0.0000	0.0000	0.0000	0.0000	0.0000	0.0000	0.0001	0.0001	0.0001

---

1. Values of $e^{-\lambda}$ are available in Appendix D and can be easily computed with most modern calculators.

any two intervals of equal length, and that the occurrence or nonoccurrence of a defect in any one interval is independent of the occurrence or nonoccurrence in any other interval. Thus, the Poisson probability distribution applies.

Suppose that major defects occur at the average rate of two per mile. We want to find the probability that no major defects will occur in a particular 3-mile section of the highway. The interval length is 3 miles, so λ = (2 defects/mile)(3 miles) = 6 represents the expected number of major defects over the 3-mile section of highway. Thus, by using equation (3.8) or Appendix B with λ = 6 and x = 0, we obtain the probability of no major defects of 0.0025. Thus, finding no major defects in the 3-mile section is very unlikely. In fact, there is a 1 − 0.0025 = 0.9975 probability of at least one major defect in that section of highway.

NOTES AND COMMENTS

When working with the Poisson probability distribution, you need to be sure that λ is the mean number of occurrences for the desired interval. For instance, suppose that you know that 30 calls come into a switchboard every 15 minutes. To compute Poisson probabilities for the number of calls coming in over a 5-minute period, you would use λ = 10; to compute probabilities for the number of calls coming in over a 1-minute period, you would use λ = 2.

3.5   CONTINUOUS RANDOM VARIABLES

In this section we introduce probability distributions for continuous random variables. Recall from Section 3.1 that random variables that can take on any value in a certain interval or collection of intervals are said to be *continuous*. Examples of continuous random variables are

1. The *number of ounces* of soup placed in a can labeled "8 ounces"
2. The *flight time* of an airplane traveling from Chicago to New York
3. The *lifetime* of the picture tube in a new television set
4. The *drilling depth* required to reach oil in an offshore drilling operation.

To understand the nature of continuous random variables more fully, suppose that, in the first example, one can of soup has 8.2 ounces and another 8.3 ounces. Other cans could weigh 8.25 ounces, 8.225 ounces, and so on. In fact, the actual weight can be any numerical value from 0 ounces for an empty can to, say, 8.5 ounces for a can filled to capacity. Because this interval contains infinitely many values, we can no longer list each value of the random variable and then identify its associated probability. In fact, for continuous random variables we need a new method for computing the probabilities associated with the values of the random variable.

Applying the Uniform Distribution

Let x denote the flight time of an airplane traveling from Chicago to New York. Assume that the minimum time is 2 hours and that the maximum time is 2 hours 20 minutes. Thus, in terms of minutes, the flight time can be any value in the interval from 120 minutes to 140 minutes (e.g., 124 minutes, 125.48 minutes, etc.). As the random variable x can take on any value from 120 to 140 minutes, x is a continuous rather than a discrete random variable. Assume that sufficient actual flight data are available to conclude that the probability of a flight time between 120 and 121 minutes is the same as the probability of a flight time within any other 1-minute interval up to and including 140 minutes. With every 1-minute interval being equally likely, the random variable x has a **uniform probability distribution.** The following **probability density function** describes the uniform probability distribution for the flight time random variable:

$$f(x) = \begin{cases} \dfrac{1}{20} & \text{for } 120 \le x \le 140 \\ 0 & \text{elsewhere} \end{cases} \tag{3.9}$$

Figure 3.3 shows a graph of this probability density function. In general, the uniform probability density function for a random variable x is

$$f(x) = \begin{cases} \dfrac{1}{b-a} & \text{for } a \le x \le b \\ 0 & \text{elsewhere} \end{cases} \tag{3.10}$$

In the flight time example, $a = 120$ and $b = 140$.

In the graph of a probability density function, $f(x)$ shows the height or value of the function at any particular value of x. Because the probability density function for flight time is *uniform,* the height or value of the function is the same for each value of x between 120 and 140. That is, $f(x) = \frac{1}{20}$ for all values of x between 120 and 140. The probability density function $f(x)$, unlike the probability function for a discrete random variable, represents the height of the function at any particular value of x and *not* probability. Recall that, for each value of a discrete random variable (say, $x = 2$), the probability function yielded the probability of x having *exactly* that value [for example, $f(2)$]. However, a continuous random variable has infinitely many values, so we can no longer identify the probability for each specific value of x. Rather, we must consider probability in terms of the likelihood that a random variable takes on a value within a *specified interval.* For example, in the flight time example an acceptable probability question is: What is the probability that the flight time is between 120 and 130 minutes? That is, what is $P(120 \le x \le 130)$? As the flight time must be between 120 and 140 minutes and as the probability is uniformly distributed over this interval, we feel comfortable saying that $P(120 \le x \le 130) = 0.50$. Indeed, as we will show, this assumption is correct.

FIGURE 3.3   UNIFORM PROBABILITY DENSITY FUNCTION FOR FLIGHT TIME

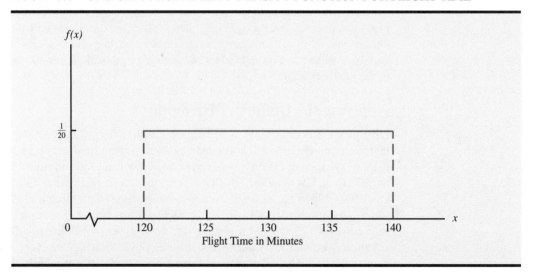

Area as a Measure of Probability

Refer to Figure 3.4 and consider the *area under the graph of f(x)* over the interval from 120 to 130. Note that the region is rectangular in shape and that the area of a rectangle is simply the width times the height. With the width of the interval equal to $130 - 120 = 10$ and the height of the graph $f(x) = \frac{1}{20}$, the area = width × height = $10(\frac{1}{20}) = \frac{10}{20} = 0.50$.

What observation can you make about the area under the graph of $f(x)$ and probability? They are identical! Indeed, that is true for all continuous random variables. In other words, once you have identified a probability density function $f(x)$ for a continuous random variable, you can obtain the probability that x takes on a value between some lower value a and some higher value b by computing the *area* under the graph of $f(x)$ over the interval a to b.

Whenever the probability is proportional to the length of the interval, the random variable is uniformly distributed.

With the appropriate probability distribution and the interpretation of area as probability, we can answer any number of probability questions. For example, what is the probability of a flight time between 128 and 136 minutes? The width of the interval is $136 - 128 = 8$. With the uniform height of $\frac{1}{20}$, $P(128 \leq x \leq 136) = \frac{8}{20} = 0.40$.

Note that $P(120 \leq x \leq 140) = 20(\frac{1}{20}) = 1$. That is, the total area under the $f(x)$ graph is equal to 1. This property holds for all continuous probability distributions and is the analog of the condition that the sum of the probabilities has to equal 1 for a discrete probability distribution. A continuous probability distribution also requires that $f(x) \geq 0$ for all values of x. It is the analog of the requirement that $f(x) \geq 0$ for discrete probability distributions.

Two principal differences between continuous random variables and probability distributions and their discrete counterparts stand out.

1. We no longer talk about the probability of the random variable taking on a particular value. Instead we talk about the probability of the random variable taking on a value within some given interval.

Try Problem 18 to practice computing probabilities using the uniform probability distribution.

2. The probability of the random variable taking on a value within some given interval is defined to be the area under the graph of the probability density function over the interval. This definition implies that the probability that a continuous random variable takes on any particular value is zero because the area under the graph of $f(x)$ at a single point is zero.

FIGURE 3.4 AREA PROVIDES PROBABILITY OF FLIGHT TIME

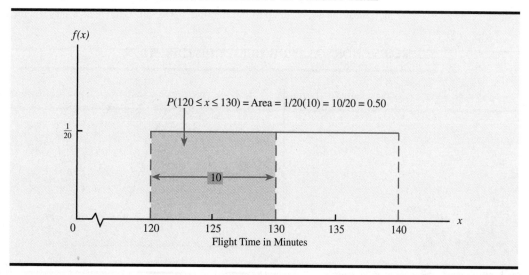

1. For any continuous random variable the probability of any particular value is zero, so $P(a \leq x \leq b) = P(a < x < b)$. Thus, the probability of a random variable assuming a value in any interval is the same whether the endpoints are included or not.

2. To see more clearly why the height of a probability density function is not a probability, think about a random variable with a uniform probability distribution of

$$f(x) = \begin{cases} 2 & \text{for } 0 \leq x \leq 0.5 \\ 0 & \text{elsewhere} \end{cases}$$

The height of the probability density function is 2 for values of x between 0 and 0.5. But, we know that probabilities can never be greater than 1.

3.6   NORMAL PROBABILITY DISTRIBUTION

Perhaps the most important probability distribution used to describe a continuous random variable is the **normal probability distribution.** It is applicable in a great many practical problem situations, and its probability density function has the form of the bell-shaped curve shown in Figure 3.5.

The normal distribution was first observed by Abraham deMoivre, a French mathematician, in the early 1700s. deMoivre's work was motivated by the study of probability associated with gambling and games of chance.

The mathematical form of the probability density function for the uniform distribution was fairly simple: $f(x) = 1/(b - a)$ for $a \leq x \leq b$. The mathematical function that provides the bell-shaped curve of the normal probability density function is more complex:

$$f(x) = \frac{1}{\sigma \sqrt{2\pi}} e^{-(x-\mu)^2/2\sigma^2} \qquad \text{for } -\infty < x < \infty \qquad (3.11)$$

where

μ = mean or expected value of the random variable x

σ^2 = variance of the random variable x

σ = standard deviation of the random variable x

π = 3.14159

e = 2.71828

Recall from the previous discussion of continuous random variables that $f(x)$ is the height of the curve at a particular value of x. Thus, once we specify the mean (μ) and either

FIGURE 3.5   NORMAL PROBABILITY DISTRIBUTION

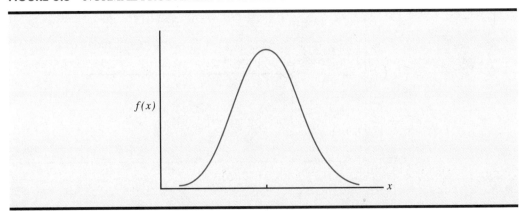

the standard deviation (σ) or variance (σ^2), we can use equation (3.11) to determine the graph for the corresponding normal distribution. Figure 3.6 shows two normal distributions, one with $\mu = 50$ and $\sigma = 15$ and another with $\mu = 50$ and $\sigma = 7.5$. Note in particular the effect that the standard deviation σ has on the general shape of the normal curve. A larger standard deviation tends to flatten and broaden the curve because larger values of σ indicate greater variability in the values of the random variable.

Fortunately, whenever we use the normal distribution to answer probability questions, we do not have to use the probability density function of equation (3.11). In fact, when we use the normal distribution, we will have tables of probability values [areas under the $f(x)$ curve] that can provide the desired probability information. To show how to use the tables of areas or probabilities for the normal distribution, we must first introduce the standard normal distribution.

Standard Normal Distribution

A random variable that has a normal distribution with a mean of 0 and a standard deviation of 1 is said to have a **standard normal distribution.** We use the letter z to designate this particular normal random variable. Figure 3.7 shows the graph of the standard normal distribution. Note that it has the same general appearance as other normal distributions, but with the special properties of $\mu = 0$ and $\sigma = 1$. The units on the horizontal axis (z) measure the number of standard deviations from the mean.

Recall the procedure for finding probabilities associated with a continuous random variable. We want to determine the probability of the random variable having a value in a specified interval from a to b. Thus we have to find the area under the curve in the interval from a to b. In the preceding section we showed that finding probabilities, or areas under the curve, for a uniform distribution was relatively easy. All we had to do was multiply the width of the interval by the height of the graph. However, finding areas under the normal distribution curve appears at first glance to be much more difficult because the height of the curve varies. The mathematical technique for obtaining these areas is beyond the scope of the text, but fortunately tables are available that provide the areas or probability values for the standard normal distribution. Table 3.9 is such a table of areas. This table is also available as Appendix C.

To use Table 3.9 to find probabilities, first note that values of z appear in the left-hand column, with the second decimal value of z appearing in the top row. For example, for a z value of 1.00 we find the 1.0 in the left-hand column and 0.00 in the top row. Then by looking in the body of the table, we find that 0.3413 corresponds to the 1.00 value for z. The

FIGURE 3.6   TWO NORMAL DISTRIBUTIONS WITH $\mu = 50$

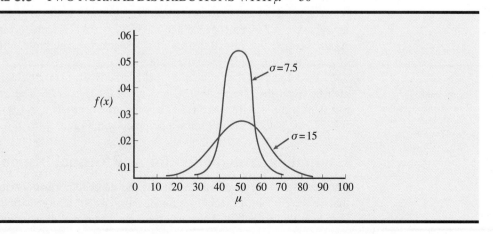

FIGURE 3.7　STANDARD NORMAL DISTRIBUTION

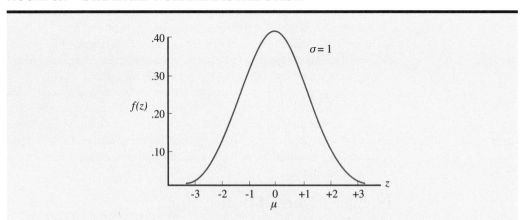

value of 0.3413 is the area under the curve between the mean ($z = 0.00$) and $z = 1.00$, shown graphically in Figure 3.8.

Thus, the values in Table 3.9 provide *the area under the curve between the mean ($z = 0.00$) and any specified positive value of z.* For another example, we can use the table to find that the area or probability of a z value in the interval $z = 0.00$ to $z = 1.25$ is 0.3944.

Suppose that we want the probability of obtaining a z value between $z = -1.00$ and $z = 1.00$. We already have used Table 3.9 to find that the probability of a z value between $z = 0.00$ and $z = 1.00$ is 0.3413. Note now that the normal distribution is symmetric. That is, the shape of the curve to the left of the mean is the mirror image of the shape of the curve to the right of the mean. Thus, the probability of a z value between $z = 0.00$ and $z = -1.00$ is the same as the probability of a z value between $z = 0.00$ and $z = 1.00$, or 0.3413. Hence, the probability of a z value between $z = -1.00$ and $z = 1.00$ is $0.3413 + 0.3413 = 0.6826$, shown graphically in Figure 3.9.

Similarly, we can find that the probability of a z value between -2.00 and $+2.00$ is $0.4772 + 0.4772 = 0.9544$ and that the probability of a z value between -3.00 and $+3.00$ is $0.4986 + 0.4986 = 0.9972$. We know that the total probability or total area under the curve for any continuous random variable must be 1.0000, so the probability of 0.9972 tells us the value of z almost always will fall between -3.00 and $+3.00$. Note that the figures depicting the standard normal distribution show this condition graphically.

We now consider two final examples of computing areas for the standard normal distribution. First let us find the probability that z is greater than 2.00. From Table 3.9 the area between $z = 0.00$ and $z = 2.00$ is 0.4772. As 0.5000 is the total area above the mean, the area above $z = 2.00$ must be $0.5000 - 0.4772 = 0.0228$, shown graphically in Figure 3.10. Again, because the normal distribution is symmetric, the probability of obtaining a value of z less than $z = -2.00$ is also 0.0228.

Try Problem 21 for practice computing probabilities with the standard normal probability distribution.

Now let us find the probability that z is between 1.00 and 2.00. We first note that the area between the mean $z = 0.00$ and $z = 2.00$ is 0.4772. The area between the mean $z = 0.00$ and $z = 1.00$ is 0.3413. Thus the area between $z = 1.00$ and $z = 2.00$ must be $0.4772 - 0.3413 = 0.1359$, shown graphically in Figure 3.11.

Computing Probabilities for Any Normal Distribution

The reason that we have been discussing the standard normal distribution so extensively is that we can compute probabilities for any normal distribution by first converting to the standard normal distribution. Thus, when we have a normal distribution with any mean μ and

TABLE 3.9   AREAS OR PROBABILITIES FOR THE STANDARD NORMAL DISTRIBUTION

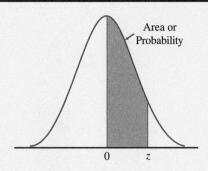

Entries in the table give the area under the curve between the mean and z standard deviations above the mean. For example, for $z = 1.25$, the area under the curve between the mean and z is 0.3944.

z	0.00	0.01	0.02	0.03	0.04	0.05	0.06	0.07	0.08	0.09
0.0	0.0000	0.0040	0.0080	0.0120	0.0160	0.0199	0.0239	0.0279	0.0319	0.0359
0.1	0.0398	0.0438	0.0478	0.0517	0.0557	0.0596	0.0636	0.0675	0.0714	0.0753
0.2	0.0793	0.0832	0.0871	0.0910	0.0948	0.0987	0.1026	0.1064	0.1103	0.1141
0.3	0.1179	0.1217	0.1255	0.1293	0.1331	0.1368	0.1406	0.1443	0.1480	0.1517
0.4	0.1554	0.1591	0.1628	0.1664	0.1700	0.1736	0.1772	0.1808	0.1844	0.1879
0.5	0.1915	0.1950	0.1985	0.2019	0.2054	0.2088	0.2123	0.2157	0.2190	0.2224
0.6	0.2257	0.2291	0.2324	0.2357	0.2389	0.2422	0.2454	0.2486	0.2518	0.2549
0.7	0.2580	0.2612	0.2642	0.2673	0.2704	0.2734	0.2764	0.2794	0.2823	0.2852
0.8	0.2881	0.2910	0.2939	0.2967	0.2995	0.3023	0.3051	0.3078	0.3106	0.3133
0.9	0.3159	0.3186	0.3212	0.3238	0.3264	0.3289	0.3315	0.3340	0.3365	0.3389
1.0	0.3413	0.3438	0.3461	0.3485	0.3508	0.3531	0.3554	0.3577	0.3599	0.3621
1.1	0.3643	0.3665	0.3686	0.3708	0.3729	0.3749	0.3770	0.3790	0.3810	0.3830
1.2	0.3849	0.3869	0.3888	0.3907	0.3925	**0.3944**	0.3962	0.3980	0.3997	0.4015
1.3	0.4032	0.4049	0.4066	0.4082	0.4099	0.4115	0.4131	0.4147	0.4162	0.4177
1.4	0.4192	0.4207	0.4222	0.4236	0.4251	0.4265	0.4279	0.4292	0.4306	0.4319
1.5	0.4332	0.4345	0.4357	0.4370	0.4382	0.4394	0.4406	0.4418	0.4429	0.4441
1.6	0.4452	0.4463	0.4474	0.4484	0.4495	0.4505	0.4515	0.4525	0.4535	0.4545
1.7	0.4554	0.4564	0.4573	0.4582	0.4591	0.4599	0.4608	0.4616	0.4625	0.4633
1.8	0.4641	0.4649	0.4656	0.4664	0.4671	0.4678	0.4686	0.4693	0.4699	0.4706
1.9	0.4713	0.4719	0.4726	0.4732	0.4738	0.4744	0.4750	0.4756	0.4761	0.4767
2.0	0.4772	0.4778	0.4783	0.4788	0.4793	0.4798	0.4803	0.4808	0.4812	0.4817
2.1	0.4821	0.4826	0.4830	0.4834	0.4838	0.4842	0.4846	0.4850	0.4854	0.4857
2.2	0.4861	0.4864	0.4868	0.4871	0.4875	0.4878	0.4881	0.4884	0.4887	0.4890
2.3	0.4893	0.4896	0.4898	0.4901	0.4904	0.4906	0.4909	0.4911	0.4913	0.4916
2.4	0.4918	0.4920	0.4922	0.4925	0.4927	0.4929	0.4931	0.4932	0.4934	0.4936
2.5	0.4938	0.4940	0.4941	0.4943	0.4945	0.4946	0.4948	0.4949	0.4951	0.4952
2.6	0.4953	0.4955	0.4956	0.4957	0.4959	0.4960	0.4961	0.4962	0.4963	0.4964
2.7	0.4965	0.4966	0.4967	0.4968	0.4969	0.4970	0.4971	0.4972	0.4973	0.4974
2.8	0.4974	0.4975	0.4976	0.4977	0.4977	0.4978	0.4979	0.4979	0.4980	0.4981
2.9	0.4981	0.4982	0.4982	0.4983	0.4984	0.4984	0.4985	0.4985	0.4986	0.4986
3.0	0.4986	0.4987	0.4987	0.4988	0.4988	0.4989	0.4989	0.4989	0.4990	0.4990

FIGURE 3.8   PROBABILITY OF z BETWEEN 0.00 AND +1.00

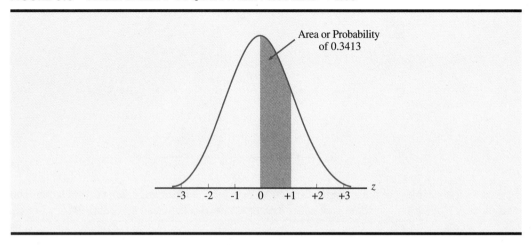

FIGURE 3.9   PROBABILITY OF z BETWEEN −1.00 AND +1.00

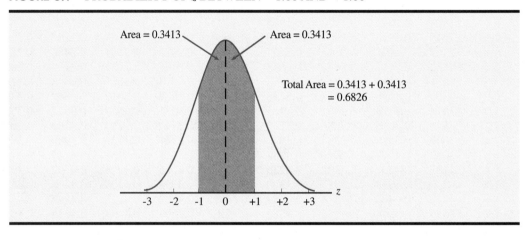

FIGURE 3.10   PROBABILITY OF z GREATER THAN 2.00

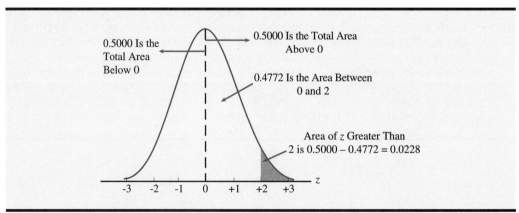

FIGURE 3.11   PROBABILITY OF z BETWEEN 1.00 AND 2.00

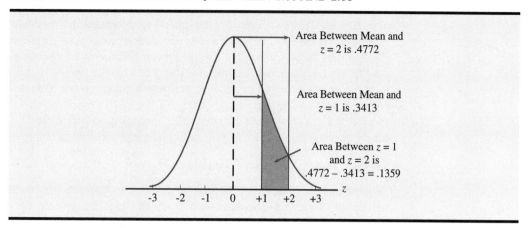

any standard deviation σ, we can answer probability questions about this distribution by converting to the standard normal distribution. We then use Table 3.9 and the appropriate z values to find the probability. The formula used to convert any normal random variable x with mean μ and standard deviation σ to the standard normal distribution is

$$z = \frac{x - \mu}{\sigma} \qquad (3.12)$$

When used in this way, z is a measure of the number of standard deviations that x is from μ.

We can most easily show how the conversion to the z value allows us to use the standard normal distribution to compute probabilities for any normal distribution with an example. Suppose that we have a normal distribution with $\mu = 10$ and $\sigma = 2$, as shown graphically in Figure 3.12. Note that, in addition to the values of the random variable shown on the x axis, we have included a second axis (the z axis) to show that for each value of x there is a corresponding value of z. For example, when $x = 10$ the corresponding z value (the number of standard deviations away from the mean) is $z = (x - \mu)/\sigma = (10 - 10)/2 = 0$. Similarly, for $x = 14$ we have $z = (x - \mu)/\sigma = (14 - 10)/2 = 2$.

FIGURE 3.12   NORMAL DISTRIBUTION WITH $\mu = 10$ AND $\sigma = 2$

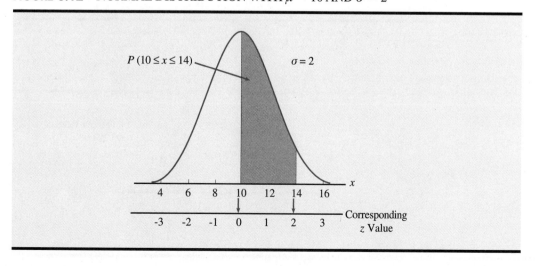

Now suppose that we want to know the probability that the random variable x is between 10 and 14—that is, $P(10 \le x \le 14)$. We do not have tables that provide this probability directly. However, note that in Figure 3.12 the area under the curve (probability) for x between 10 and 14 is the same as the area under the curve for z between 0 and 2. Using $z = 2.00$ and Table 3.9, we find that the area or probability of z being between 0 and 2 is 0.4772. Thus, we conclude that the probability of x being between 10 and 14 also is 0.4772.

This procedure applies to any normal distribution problem. That is, for any x value a corresponding z value is given by equation (3.12). To find the probability that x is in a specified interval, simply convert the x interval to its corresponding z interval. Then use the table for the standard normal distribution to answer the probability question.

Grear Tire Company Problem

Suppose that the Grear Tire Company has just developed a new steel-belted radial tire that will be sold through a national chain of discount stores. Because the tire is a new product, Grear's management believes that the mileage guarantee offered with the tire will be an important factor in the consumer acceptance of the product. Before finalizing the tire mileage guarantee policy, Grear's management wants some probability information concerning the number of miles the tires will last.

From actual road tests with the tires, Grear's engineering group estimates the mean tire mileage at $\mu = 36{,}500$ miles and the standard deviation at $\sigma = 5000$ miles. In addition, the data collected indicate that a normal distribution is a reasonable assumption.

What percentage of the tires, then, can be expected to last more than 40,000 miles? In other words, what is the probability that the tire mileage will exceed 40,000? To compute this probability, we need to find the area of the shaded region in Figure 3.13.

At $x = 40{,}000$ we have

$$z = \frac{x - \mu}{\sigma} = \frac{40{,}000 - 36{,}500}{5{,}000} = \frac{3{,}500}{5{,}000} = 0.70$$

Thus the probability that the normal distribution for tire mileage will have an x value greater than 40,000 is the same as the probability that the standard normal distribution will have a z value greater than 0.70. Using Table 3.9, we find that the area corresponding to $z = 0.70$ is 0.2580. However, remember that the table always provides the area between the mean and the z value. Thus, we know that there is a 0.2580 area between the mean and $z = 0.70$.

FIGURE 3.13   GREAR TIRE COMPANY TIRE MILEAGE

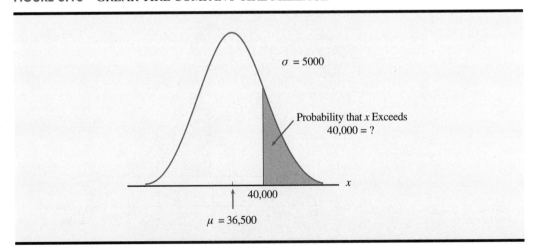

As the total area above the mean is 0.5000, we must have $0.5000 - 0.2580 = 0.2420$ as the area above $z = 0.70$. In terms of the tire mileage x, we can conclude that there is a 0.2420 probability that x will be above 40,000. Thus, about 24.2% of the tires manufactured by Grear can be expected to last more than 40,000 miles.

Let us now assume that Grear is considering a guarantee that will provide a discount on a new set of tires if the mileage on the original tires doesn't exceed the mileage stated on the guarantee. What should the guarantee mileage be if Grear wants no more than 10% of the tires to be eligible for the discount? This question is interpreted graphically in Figure 3.14. Note that 10% of the area is below the unknown guarantee mileage, so we know that 40% of the area must be between the mean and the unknown guarantee mileage. The question is, how many standard deviations (z value) do we have to be *below* the mean to find 40% of the area? If we look up 0.4000 in the *body* of Table 3.9, we see that a 0.4000 area occurs at approximately $z = 1.28$. The area is below the mean, so we know that the z value of interest must be -1.28. Hence, we must be 1.28 standard deviations less than the mean to find the desired guarantee mileage. This mileage then is

$$\text{Guarantee mileage} = \mu - 1.28\sigma$$
$$= 36,500 - 1.28(5,000) = 30,100$$

Therefore a guarantee of 30,100 miles will meet the requirement that approximately 10% of the tires will be eligible for the discount. With this information the firm might confidently set its tire mileage guarantee at 30,000 miles.

Try Problem 23 for practice finding a z value that cuts off a particular probability.

Again we see the important role that probability distributions play in providing decision-making information. Once a probability distribution is established for a particular problem, it can be used rather quickly and easily to provide probability information about the problem. Although this information does not make a decision recommendation directly, it does provide information that helps the decision maker understand the problem better. Ultimately, this information may assist the decision maker in reaching a good decision.

3.7   EXPONENTIAL PROBABILITY DISTRIBUTION

A continuous probability distribution that is often useful in describing the time needed to complete a task is the **exponential probability distribution.** The exponential random variable can be used to describe the time between arrivals at a car wash, the time required

FIGURE 3.14   GREAR'S DISCOUNT GUARANTEE

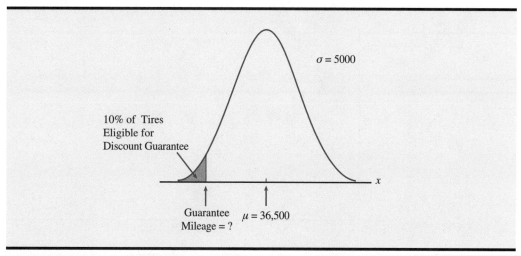

to load a truck, the distance between major defects in a highway, and so on. The exponential probability density function is

$$f(x) = \frac{1}{\mu} e^{-x/\mu} \qquad \text{for } x \geq 0, \mu > 0 \tag{3.13}$$

To provide an example of the exponential probability distribution, suppose that the time required to load a truck at the Schips loading dock follows an exponential probability distribution. If the mean, or average, time to load a truck is 15 minutes ($\mu = 15$), the appropriate probability density function is

$$f(x) = \frac{1}{15} e^{-x/15}$$

Figure 3.15 shows the graph of this density function.

Computing Probabilities for the Exponential Distribution

As with any continuous probability distribution, the area under the curve corresponding to some interval provides the probability that the random variable takes on a value in that interval. For example, for the Schips loading dock example the probability that 6 *minutes or less* ($x \leq 6$) are needed to load a truck is defined to be the area under the curve from $x = 0$ to $x = 6$. Similarly, the probability that a truck is loaded in 18 *minutes or less* ($x \leq 18$) is the area under the curve from $x = 0$ to $x = 18$. Note also that the probability of loading a truck in between 6 and 18 minutes ($6 \leq x \leq 18$) is the area under the curve from $x = 6$ to $x = 18$.

FIGURE 3.15   EXPONENTIAL DISTRIBUTION FOR THE SCHIPS LOADING
DOCK EXAMPLE

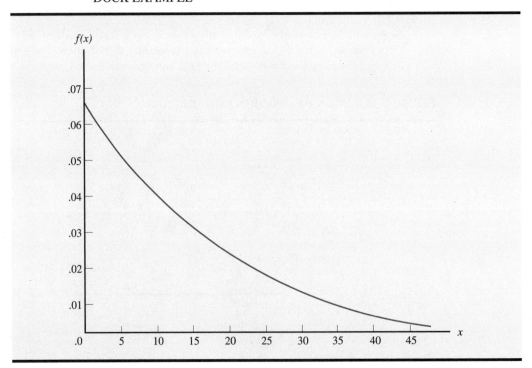

To compute exponential probabilities such as those previously described, the following formula provides the probability of obtaining a value for the exponential random variable of less than or equal to some specific value of x, denoted by x_0:

$$P(x \leq x_0) = 1 - e^{-x_0/\mu} \qquad (3.14)$$

Thus, for the Schips loading dock example, equation (3.14) becomes

$$P(\text{loading time} \leq x_0) = 1 - e^{-x_0/15}$$

Hence, the probability that 6 minutes or less ($x \leq 6$) are needed to load a truck is

$$P(\text{loading time} \leq 6) = 1 - e^{-6/15} = 0.3297$$

Note also the probability that 18 minutes or less ($x \leq 18$) are needed to load a truck is

$$P(\text{loading time} \leq 18) = 1 - e^{-18/15} = 0.6988$$

Try Problem 29 for practice finding probabilities with the exponential probability distribution.

Thus, the probability that 6 to 18 minutes are required to load a truck is $0.6988 - 0.3297 = 0.3691$. Probabilities for any other interval can be computed in a similar manner.

Relationship between the Poisson and Exponential Distributions

In Section 3.4 we introduced the Poisson distribution as a discrete probability distribution that often is useful when we are dealing with the number of occurrences over a specified interval of time or space. Recall that the Poisson probability function is

The Poisson and exponential probability distributions are used in the chapter on waiting line models (Chapter 15). In these models the Poisson distribution is used as the probability distribution for the number of arrivals while the exponential probability distribution is used as the probability distribution for the service time.

$$f(x) = \frac{\lambda^x e^{-\lambda}}{x!}$$

where

$$\lambda = \text{expected value or mean number of occurrences in an interval}$$

The continuous exponential probability distribution is related to the discrete Poisson distribution: The Poisson distribution provides an appropriate description of the number of occurrences per interval, the exponential distribution provides a description of the length of the interval between occurrences.

To illustrate this relationship, let us suppose that the number of cars that arrive at a car wash during 1 hour is described by a Poisson probability distribution with a mean of 10 cars per hour. Thus the Poisson probability function that provides the probability of x arrivals per hour is

$$f(x) = \frac{10^x e^{-10}}{x!}$$

The average number of arrivals is 10 cars per hour, so the average time between cars arriving is

$$\frac{1 \text{ hour}}{10 \text{ cars}} = 0.1 \text{ hour/car}$$

Try Problem 30 for an application of the exponential probability distribution.

Thus, the corresponding exponential distribution that describes the time between the arrival of cars has a mean of $\mu = 0.1$ hours per car. The appropriate exponential probability density function is

$$f(x) = \frac{1}{0.1} e^{-x/0.1} = 10e^{-10x}$$

SUMMARY

In this chapter we continued the discussion of probability by introducing the important concepts of random variables and probability distributions. Random variables provide numerical descriptions of the outcomes of experiments. When random variables are used, computations of the expected value, variance, and standard deviation can help the decision maker understand characteristics of the problem under study. We discussed the probability distributions for both discrete and continuous random variables.

Of particular interest are special probability distributions such as the binomial, Poisson, uniform, normal, and exponential distributions. These distributions are important because they have wide applicability and because special formulas and/or tables make the probability information easily available.

Through a variety of problems and applications we illustrated the role that probability distributions play in providing decision-making information. Although the probability values generated by the techniques and methods of this chapter do not by themselves make decision recommendations, they do provide assistance to the decision maker in terms of understanding the uncertainties inherent in the problem. Ultimately, this better understanding may lead to new and better decisions.

GLOSSARY

Random variable   A numerical description of the outcome of an experiment.

Discrete random variable   A random variable that can take on only a finite or infinite sequence of values.

Continuous random variable   A random variable that may take on any value in an interval or collection of intervals.

Probability function   A function, denoted $f(x)$, that provides the probability that a discrete random variable x takes on some specific value.

Discrete probability distribution   A table, graph, or equation describing the values of the random variable and the associated probabilities.

Expected value   A weighted average of the values of the random variable, for which the probability function provides the weights. If an experiment can be repeated a large number of times, the expected value can be interpreted as the "long-run average."

Variance   A measure of the dispersion or variability in the random variable. It is a weighted average of the squared deviations from the mean, μ.

Standard deviation   The positive square root of the variance.

Binomial probability distribution   The probability distribution for a discrete random variable. It is used to compute the probability of x successes in n trials.

Poisson probability distribution   The probability distribution for a discrete random variable. It is used to compute the probability of x occurrences over a specified interval.

Uniform probability distribution   A continuous probability distribution in which the probability that the random variable will assume a value in any interval of equal length is the same for each interval.

Probability density function   The function that describes the probability distribution of a continuous random variable.

Normal probability distribution   A continuous probability distribution. Its probability density function is bell-shaped and determined by the mean, μ, and standard deviation, σ.

Standard normal distribution   A normal distribution with a mean of 0 and a standard deviation of 1.

Exponential probability distribution   A continuous probability distribution that is useful in describing the time to complete a task or the time between occurrences of an event.

PROBLEMS

SELFtest   1.   The following examples are experiments and their associated random variables. In each case identify the values the random variable can take on and state whether the random variable is discrete or continuous.

Experiment	Random Variable (x)
a. Take a 20-question examination	Number of questions answered correctly
b. Observe cars arriving at a tollbooth for 1 hour	Number of cars arriving at the tollbooth
c. Audit 50 tax returns	Number of returns containing errors
d. Observe an employee's work for 8 hours	Number of nonproductive hours
e. Weigh a shipment of goods	Number of pounds

2.   The following table shows a partial probability distribution for the MRA Company's projected profits (in thousands of dollars) for the first year of operation (the negative value denotes a loss).

x	$f(x)$
−100	0.10
0	0.20
50	0.30
100	0.25
150	0.10
200	

a.   Find the missing value of $f(200)$. What is your interpretation of this value?
b.   What is the probability that MRA will be profitable?
c.   What is the probability that MRA will make at least $100,000?

SELFtest   3.   Data were collected on the number of operating rooms in use at Tampa General Hospital over a 20-day period. On 3 of the days only 1 operating room was used; on 5 days, 2 were used; on 8 days, 3 were used; and on 4 days all 4 rooms were used.
a.   Use the relative frequency approach to construct a probability distribution for the number of operating rooms in use on any given day.

  b. Draw a graph of the probability distribution.
  c. Show that your probability distribution satisfies the required conditions for a valid discrete probability distribution.

SELFtest   4. Shown is a probability distribution for the random variable x.

x	$f(x)$
3	0.25
6	0.50
9	0.25
Total	1.00

  a. Compute $E(x)$, the expected value of x.
  b. Compute σ^2, the variance of x.
  c. Compute σ, the standard deviation of x.

  5. Shown are the percent frequency distributions of job satisfaction scores for a sample of information systems (IS) senior executives and IS middle managers (*Computerworld*, May 26, 1997). The scores range from a low of 1 (very dissatisfied) to a high of 5 (very satisfied).

Job Satisfaction Score	IS Senior Executives (%)	IS Middle Managers (%)
1	5	4
2	9	10
3	3	12
4	42	46
5	41	28
Total	100	100

  a. Develop a probability distribution for the job satisfaction score of a senior executive.
  b. Develop a probability distribution for the job satisfaction score of a middle manager.
  c. What is the probability a senior executive will report a job satisfaction score of 4 or 5?
  d. What is the probability a middle manager is very satisfied?
  e. Compare the overall job satisfaction of senior executives and middle managers.

  6. An opinion survey of 1009 adults was conducted by Louis Harris & Associates, Inc. (*Business Week,* December 29, 1997). Shown is the probability distribution of responses to a question concerning the stock market's valuation.

Market Valuation	Random Variable (x)	Probability $f(x)$
Very undervalued	1	0.02
Somewhat undervalued	2	0.06
Fairly valued	3	0.28
Somewhat overvalued	4	0.54
Very overvalued	5	0.10

a. Show that the probability distribution satisfies the properties of all probability distributions.

b. What are the expected value and variance of the probability distribution of opinions?

c. Comment on whether people think the stock market is overvalued.

7. The demand for a product of Carolina Industries varies greatly from month to month. Based on the past 2 years of data, the following probability distribution shows the company's monthly demand.

Unit Demand	Probability
300	0.20
400	0.30
500	0.35
600	0.15

a. If the company places monthly orders equal to the expected value of the monthly demand, what should Carolina's monthly order quantity be for this product?

b. Assume that each unit demanded generates $70 in revenue and that each unit ordered costs $50. How much will the company gain or lose in a month if it places an order based on your answer to part (a) and the actual demand for the item is 300 units?

c. What are the variance and the standard deviation for the number of units demanded?

8. The J. R. Ryland Computer Company is considering a plant expansion that will enable the company to begin production of a new computer product. The company's president must determine whether to make the expansion a medium- or large-scale project. An uncertainty involves the demand for the new product, which for planning purposes may be low demand, medium demand, or high demand. The probability estimates for the demands are 0.20, 0.50 and 0.30, respectively. Letting x indicate the annual profit in $1000s, the firm's planners have developed profit forecasts for the medium- and large-scale expansion projects.

		Medium-Scale Expansion Profits		Large-Scale Expansion Profits	
		x	$f(x)$	y	$f(y)$
	Low	50	0.20	0	0.20
Demand	Medium	150	0.50	100	0.50
	High	200	0.30	300	0.30

a. Compute the expected value for the profit associated with the two expansion alternatives. Which decision is preferred for the objective of maximizing the expected profit?

b. Compute the variance for the profit associated with the two expansion alternatives. Which decision is preferred for the objective of minimizing the risk or uncertainty?

SELFtest

9. Consider a binomial experiment with 2 trials and $p = 0.4$.

a. Compute the probability of 1 success, $f(1)$.

b. Compute $f(0)$.

c. Compute $f(2)$.

d. Find the probability of at least 1 success.

e. Find the expected value, variance, and standard deviation.

10. Consider a binomial experiment with $n = 10$ and $p = 0.10$. Use the binomial tables (Appendix A) to answer parts (a) through (d).
    a. Find $f(0)$.
    b. Find $f(2)$.
    c. Find $P(x \leq 2)$.
    d. Find $P(x \geq 1)$.
    e. Find $E(x)$.
    f. Find $Var(x)$ and σ.

11. The greatest number of complaints by owners of two-year-old automobiles is in the area of electrical system performance (*Consumer Reports 1992 Buyers Guide*). In an annual questionnaire of owners of more than 300 makes and models of automobiles, *Consumer Reports* found that 10% of the owners of two-year-old automobiles experienced trouble with the electrical system that included the starter, alternator, battery, switch controls, instruments, wiring, lights, and radio.
    a. What is the probability that a sample of 12 owners of two-year-old automobiles will reveal 2 owners with electrical system problems?
    b. What is the probability that a sample of 12 owners of two-year-old automobiles will reveal at least 2 owners with electrical system problems?
    c. What is the probability that a sample of 20 owners of two-year-old automobiles will reveal at least one electrical system problem?

SELFtest 12. When a new machine is functioning properly, only 3% of the items produced are defective. Assume that we will randomly select two parts produced on the machine and that we are interested in the number of defective parts found.
    a. Describe the conditions under which this situation would be a binomial experiment.
    b. How many experimental outcomes yield 1 defect?
    c. Compute the probabilities associated with finding no defects, 1 defect, and 2 defects.

13. Military radar and missile detection systems are designed to warn a country of enemy attacks. A reliability question deals with the ability of the detection system to identify an attack and issue the warning. Assume that a particular detection system has a 0.90 probability of detecting a missile attack. Answer the following questions using the binomial probability distribution.
    a. What is the probability that 1 detection system will detect an attack?
    b. If 2 detection systems are installed in the same area and operate independently, what is the probability that at least 1 of the systems will detect the attack?
    c. If 3 systems are installed, what is the probability that at least one of the systems will detect the attack?
    d. Would you recommend that multiple detection systems be operated? Explain.

SELFtest 14. Consider a Poisson probability distribution with 2 as the average number of occurrences per time period.
    a. Write the appropriate Poisson probability function.
    b. What is the average number of occurrences in 3 time periods?
    c. Write the appropriate Poisson probability function to determine the probability of x occurrences in 3 time periods.
    d. Find the probability of 2 occurrences in 1 time period.
    e. Find the probability of 6 occurrences in 3 time periods.
    f. Find the probability of 5 occurrences in 2 time periods.

15. Telephone calls arrive at the rate of 48 per hour at the reservation desk for Regional Airways.
    a. Find the probability of receiving 3 calls in a 5-minute interval.
    b. Find the probability of receiving 10 calls in 15 minutes.
    c. Suppose that no calls are currently on hold. If the agent takes 5 minutes to complete processing the current call, how many callers do you expect to be waiting by that time? What is the probability that no one will be waiting?
    d. If no calls are currently being processed, what is the probability the agent can take 3 minutes for personal time without being interrupted?

16. The mean number of times per year that *Barron's* subscribers take domestic flights for personal reasons is four (*Barron's* 1995 Primary Reader Survey).
    a. What is the probability a subscriber takes two domestic flights for personal reasons in a year?
    b. What is the mean number of domestic flights for personal reasons in a 3-month period?
    c. What is the probability a subscriber takes one or more domestic flights for personal reasons in a 6-month period?

17. Airline passengers arrive randomly and independently at the passenger screening facility at a major international airport. The mean arrival rate is 10 passengers per minute.
    a. What is the probability of no arrivals in a 1-minute period?
    b. What is the probability of 3 or fewer arrivals in a 1-minute period?
    c. What is the probability of no arrivals in a 15-second period?
    d. What is the probability of at least 1 arrival in a 15-second period?

SELFtest   18. A random variable x is uniformly distributed between 1.0 and 1.5.
    a. Show the graph of the probability density function.
    b. Find $P(x = 1.25)$.
    c. Find $P(1.0 \leq x \leq 1.25)$.
    d. Find $P(1.20 < x < 1.5)$.

19. Delta Airlines quotes a flight time of 2 hours, 5 minutes for its flights from Cincinnati to Tampa. Suppose we believe that actual flight times are uniformly distributed between 2 hours and 2 hours, 20 minutes.
    a. Show the graph of the probability density function for flight times.
    b. What is the probability that the flight will be no more than five minutes late?
    c. What is the probability that the flight will be more than 10 minutes late?
    d. What is the expected flight time?

20. Most computer languages have a function that can be used to generate random numbers. In Microsoft's Excel, the RAND function can be used to generate random numbers between 0 and 1. If we let x denote the random number generated, then x is a continuous random variable with the probability density function:

$$f(x) = \begin{cases} 1 & \text{for } 0 \leq x \leq 1 \\ 0 & \text{elsewhere} \end{cases}$$

    a. Graph the probability density function.
    b. What is the probability of generating a random number between 0.25 and 0.75?
    c. What is the probability of generating a random number with a value less than or equal to 0.30?
    d. What is the probability of generating a random number with a value greater than 0.60?

SELFtest   21. For the standard normal random variable z, compute the following probabilities.
    a. $P(0 \leq z \leq 0.83)$
    b. $P(-1.57 \leq z \leq 0)$
    c. $P(z > 0.44)$
    d. $P(z \geq -0.23)$
    e. $P(z < 1.20)$
    f. $P(z \leq -0.71)$

22. For the standard normal random variable z, find z for each situation.
    a. The area between 0 and z is 0.4750.
    b. The area between 0 and z is 0.2291.
    c. The area to the right of z is 0.1314.
    d. The area to the left of z is 0.6700.

SELFtest   23. For the standard normal random variable z, find z for each situation.
                    a. The area to the left of z is 0.2119.
                    b. The area between $-z$ and z is 0.9030.
                    c. The area between $-z$ and z is 0.2052.
                    d. The area to the left of z is 0.9948.
                    e. The area to the right of z is 0.6915.

24. The demand for a new product is estimated to be normally distributed with $\mu = 200$ and $\sigma = 40$. Let x be the number of units demanded and find the following probabilities.
     a. $P(180 \leq x \leq 220)$
     b. $P(x \geq 250)$
     c. $P(x \leq 100)$
     d. $P(225 \leq x \leq 250)$

25. Trading volume on the New York Stock Exchange has been growing in recent years. For the first two weeks of January 1998, the average daily volume was 646 million shares (*Barron's* January 1998). The probability distribution of daily volume is approximately normal with a standard deviation of about 100 million shares.
     a. What is the probability trading volume will be less than 400 million shares?
     b. What percentage of the time does the trading volume exceed 800 million shares?
     c. If the exchange wants to issue a press release on the top 5% of trading days, what volume will trigger a release?

26. General Hospital's patient account division has compiled data on the age of accounts receivables. The data collected indicate that the age of the accounts follows a normal distribution with $\mu = 28$ days and $\sigma = 8$ days.
     a. What portion of the accounts are between 20 and 40 days old—that is, $P(20 \leq x \leq 40)$?
     b. The hospital administrator is interested in sending reminder letters to the oldest 15% of accounts. How many days old should an account be before a reminder letter is sent?
     c. The hospital administrator wants to give a discount to those accounts that pay their balance by the 21st day. What percentage of the accounts will receive the discount?

27. The Webster National Bank is reviewing its service charges and interest-paying policies on checking accounts. The average daily balance on personal checking accounts is $550, with a standard deviation of $150. In addition, the average daily balances are normally distributed.
     a. What percentage of personal checking account customers carry average daily balances in excess of $800?
     b. What percentage carry average daily balances below $200?
     c. What percentage carry average daily balances between $300 and $700?
     d. The bank is considering paying interest to customers carrying average daily balances in excess of a certain amount. If the bank does not want to pay interest to more than 5% of its customers, what is the minimum average daily balance it should be willing to pay interest on?

28. A machine fills containers with a particular product. The standard deviation of filling weights computed from past data is 0.6 ounces. If only 2% of the containers hold less than 18 ounces, what is the mean filling weight for the machine? That is, what must μ equal? Assume that the filling weights have a normal distribution.

SELFtest   29. Consider the exponential probability density function:

$$f(x) = \frac{1}{3} e^{-x/3} \qquad \text{for } x \geq 0$$

a. Write the formula for $P(x \leq x_0)$.
b. Find $P(x \leq 2)$.
c. Find $P(x \geq 3)$.

    d.   Find $P(x \leq 5)$.

    e.   Find $P(2 \leq x \leq 5)$.

SELFtest   30. There were 34 traffic fatalities in Clermont County, Ohio, during 1987 (The *Cincinnati Enquirer,* December 8, 1988). Assume that, for an average of 34 fatalities per year, an exponential distribution accurately describes the time between fatalities.

    a.   What is the probability the time between fatalities is 1 month or less?

    b.   What is the probability the time between fatalities is 1 week or more?

    31. The time between arrivals of vehicles at a particular intersection follows an exponential probability distribution with a mean of 12 seconds.

    a.   Sketch this exponential probability distribution.

    b.   What is the probability the time between vehicle arrivals is 12 seconds or less?

    c.   What is the probability the time between vehicle arrivals is 6 seconds or less?

    d.   What is the probability there will be 30 or more seconds between arriving vehicles?

    32. The lifetime (hours) of an electronic device is a random variable with the exponential probability density function:

$$f(x) = \frac{1}{50} e^{-x/50} \qquad \text{for } x \geq 0$$

    a.   What is the mean lifetime of the device?

    b.   What is the probability the device fails in the first 25 hours of operation?

    c.   What is the probability the device operates 100 or more hours before failure?

    33. The time (in minutes) between telephone calls at an insurance claims office has the exponential probability distribution:

$$f(x) = 0.50e^{-0.50x} \qquad \text{for } x \geq 0$$

    a.   What is the mean time between telephone calls?

    b.   What is the probability of 30 seconds or less between telephone calls?

    c.   What is the probability of 1 minute or less between telephone calls?

    d.   What is the probability of 5 or more minutes without a telephone call?

    34. How much do people use computers at home? According to a survey, *Barron's* subscribers who have personal computers at home use the computer an average of 7.4 hours per week (*Barron's* 1995 Primary Reader Survey). The number of hours of usage is approximately exponentially distributed.

    a.   What is the probability that a *Barron's* subscriber who has a personal computer at home spends 3 hours or less on the computer during a week?

    b.   What is the probability that a *Barron's* subscriber who has a personal computer at home uses the computer more than 10 hours during a week?

    c.   What is the probability that a *Barron's* subscriber who has a personal computer at home uses the computer between 3 and 10 hours per week?

Appendix 3.1   SPREADSHEETS FOR EXPECTED VALUE AND VARIANCE

Spreadsheets can be helpful in relieving the computational burden of computing probabilities, expected values, and variances. In this appendix we show how to use an Excel spreadsheet to compute the expected value and variance for a discrete probability distribution.

    Refer to Tables 3.4 and 3.5, which show the computations involved in computing the expected value and variance for the number of cars sold per day at DiCarlo Motors. Figure 3.16 shows the spreadsheet used to make these same calculations. The DiCarlo Motors

FIGURE 3.16   SPREADSHEET FOR COMPUTING EXPECTED VALUE AND VARIANCE

	A	B	C	D
1	x	f(x)	xf(x)	$(x-mu)^2f(x)$
2	0	0.18	0.00	0.4050
3	1	0.39	0.39	0.0975
4	2	0.24	0.48	0.0600
5	3	0.14	0.42	0.3150
6	4	0.04	0.16	0.2500
7	5	0.01	0.05	0.1225
8			1.50	1.2500

probability distribution has been entered in columns A and B of the spreadsheet. The number of cars sold x appears in cells A2:A7 and the corresponding probabilities $f(x)$ appear in cells B2:B7. The following cell formulas are used to make the expected value and variance calculations.

Calculate the expected value.

Cell C2   =A2*B2

(Copy cell C2 to cells C3:C7)

Cell C8   =SUM(C2:C7)

Calculate the variance.

Cell D2   =(A2-C$8)^2*B2

(Copy cell D2 to cells D3:D7)

Cell D8   =SUM(D2:D7)

The expected value appears in cell C8 and the variance appears in cell D8. The standard deviation for the number of cars sold can be obtained by entering the formula =SQRT(D8) in any unused cell in the spreadsheet.

Appendix 3.2   COMPUTING DISCRETE PROBABILITIES WITH SPREADSHEETS

Excel has the capability of computing probabilities for several discrete probability distributions including the binomial and Poisson. In this appendix, we describe how Excel can be used to compute the probabilities for any binomial probability distribution. The procedures for the Poisson probability distributions are similar to the one we describe for the binomial probability distribution.

Let us return to the Nastke Clothing Store problem, where the binomial probabilities of interest are based on a binomial experiment with $n = 10$ and $p = .30$. We assume that the user is interested in the probability of $x = 4$ successes in the 10 trials. The following steps describe how to use Excel to produce the desired binomial probability.

Step 1. Select a cell in the worksheet where you want the binomial probability to appear
Step 2. Select the **Insert** pull-down menu
Step 3. Choose the **Function** option

Step 4. When the **Paste Function** dialog box appears:
Choose **Statistical** from the **Function Category** box
Choose **BINOMDIST** from the **Function Name** box
Select **OK**

Step 5. When the **BINOMDIST** dialog box appears:
Enter 4 in the **Number_s** box (the value of x)
Enter 10 in the **Trials** box (the value of n)
Enter .30 in the **Probability_s** box (the value of p)
Enter false in the **Cumulative** box*

Note: At this point the desired binomial probability of .2001 is automatically computed and appears in the right center of the dialog box.

Select **OK** and the binomial probability will appear in the worksheet cell requested in Step 1.

If the user wants other binomial probabilities, there are ways of obtaining the information without repeating the steps for each probability desired. Perhaps the easiest alternative is to stay in step 5. After the four entries have been made and the first probability appears, simply return to the **Number_s** box and insert a new value of x. The new probability will appear. Repeated changes can be made in the dialog box, including changes to the trials, probability, and/or cumulative boxes. For each change, the desired probability will appear. When **OK** is selected, only the last binomial probability will be placed in the worksheet.

If the user wants to insert multiple binomial probabilities into the worksheet, the desired values of x shouuld be entered into the worksheet first. Then, in step 5, the user must enter the cell location of one of the values of x in the numbers box. After completing the steps for one binomial probability, individuals experienced with Excel can use Excel's Copy command to copy the binomial function into the cells where the other binomial probabilities are to appear.

The Excel procedure for generating Poisson probabilities is similar to the procedure we have just described. Step 4 can be used to select the POISSON function name. The dialog box in step 5 will guide the user through the input values required to compute the desired probabilities.

Appendix 3.3   COMPUTING PROBABILITIES FOR CONTINUOUS DISTRIBUTIONS WITH SPREADSHEETS

Excel has the capability of computing probabilities for several continuous probability distributions, including the normal and exponential probability distributions. In this appendix, we describe how Excel can be used to compute probabilities for any normal probability distribution. The procedures for the exponential and other continuous probability distributions are similar to the one we describe for the normal probability distribution.

Let us return to the Grear Tire Company problem where the tire mileage was described by a normal probability distribution with $\mu = 36,500$ and $\sigma = 5000$. Assume we are interested in the probability that tire mileage will exceed 40,000 miles. The following steps describe how to use Excel to produce the desired normal probability.

Step 1. Select a cell in the worksheet where you want the normal probability to appear
Step 2. Select the **Insert** pull-down menu
Step 3. Choose the **Function** option

---

*Placing false in the cumulative box provides the probability of exactly four successes. Placing true in this box provides the cumulative probability of four *or fewer* successes.

Step 4. When the **Paste Function** dialog box appears:
Choose **Statistical** from the **Function Category** box
Choose **NORMDIST** from the **Function Name** box
Select **OK**

Step 5. When the **NORMDIST** dialog box appears:
Enter 40000 in the **x** box
Enter 36500 in the **mean** box
Enter 5000 in the **standard deviation** box
Enter true in the **cumulative** box
Select **OK**

At this point, .7580 will appear in the cell selected in step 1, indicating that the probability of tire mileage being less than or equal to 40,000 miles is .7580. Therefore, the probability that tire mileage will exceed 40,000 miles is $1 - .7580 = .2420$.

Excel uses an inverse computation to convert a given cumulative normal probability into a value for the random variable. For example, what mileage guarantee should Grear offer if the company wants no more than 10% of the tires to be eligible for the guarantee? To compute the mileage guarantee by using Excel, follow the procedure just described. However, two changes are necessary: in step 4, choose **NORMINV** from the **Function Name** box; in step 5, enter the cumulative probability of .10 in the **probability** box and then enter the mean and the standard deviation. When **OK** is selected in step 5, the tire mileage guarantee of 30,092 or approximately 30,100 miles appears in the worksheet.

The Excel procedure for generating exponential probabilities is similar to the procedure just described. Step 4 can be used to choose the **EXPONDIST** function name. The dialog box in step 5 will guide the user through the input values required to compute the desired probability. Note that the value entered in the lambda box is $1/\mu$. When **OK** is selected in step 5, the cumulative exponential probability appears in the worksheet.

XEROX CORPORATION*

STAMFORD, CONNECTICUT

Xerox Corporation is in the information products and systems business worldwide. Everyone is familiar with the Xerox copy machines, but the company is involved in many other businesses as well. Xerox's Multinational Documentation & Training Services (MD&TS) provides customers with timely, cost-effective, and high-quality communication services. The four basic services of MD&TS are documentation, training, translation, and publishing.

The professional writers and translators working for MD&TS use an online computerized publication system. For this system, management was interested in determining the effect of different system configurations on performance. Specifically, for a given system configuration, management was interested in determining the following:

1. The probability of a user being refused access by the system because of an excess number of users.
2. The probability of any specific number of users being on the system simultaneously.

A computer simulation model was developed for the purpose of determining these probabilities. In order to build the simulation model, it was necessary to identify the probability distribution for two key random variables:

1. The On Time per session (the length of time a user is on the system).
2. The Idle Time per session (the length of time between sessions).

Based on a survey of users, the probability distribution of on time per session was approximated as shown in the following table. Another probability distribution was developed for the random variable indicating idle time per session. These two probability distributions

were key inputs to the simulation model. The results from the simulation study helped MD&TS determine a system configuration that ensured a near-zero probability that a user would be refused access to the system.

x	$f(x)$
10	0.05
20	0.06
30	0.08
40	0.20
50	0.25
60	0.20
70	0.08
80	0.06
90	0.02

The actual probability distribution used in the simulation study has been modified to protect proprietary information and to simplify the discussion.

Questions

1. What is the expected value of the on time per session based on the probability distribution shown in the table? What is your interpretation of this expected value?
2. What is the variance of the on time per session based on the probability distribution shown in the table?
3. What is the probability the on time per session would be between 35 and 65 minutes?
4. Another simulation model might choose to represent the on time per session with a normal probability distribution. Use a normal probability distribution with the expected value of question 1 and the variance of question 2 to answer question 3.

---

*The authors are indebted to Soterios M. Flouris for providing this application.

Chapter 4

DECISION ANALYSIS

CONTENTS

Decision analysis can be used to determine an optimal strategy when a decision maker is faced with several decision alternatives and an uncertain or risk-filled pattern of future events. For example, a global manufacturer might be interested in determining the best location for a new plant. Suppose that the manufacturer has identified five decision alternatives corresponding to five plant locations in different countries. Making the plant location decision is complicated by factors such as the world economy, demand in various regions of the world, labor availability, raw material costs, transportation costs, and so on. In such a problem, several scenarios could be developed to describe how the various factors combine to form the possible uncertain future events. Then probabilities can be assigned to the events. Using profit or cost as a measure of the consequence for each decision alternative and each future event combination, the best plant location can be selected.

Even when a careful decision analysis has been conducted, the uncertain future events make the final consequence uncertain. In some cases, the selected decision alternative may provide good or excellent results. In other cases, a relatively unlikely future event may occur causing the selected decision alternative to provide only fair or even poor results. The risk associated with any decision alternative is a direct result of the uncertainty associated with the final consequence. A good decision analysis includes risk analysis. Through risk analysis the decision maker is provided with probability information about the favorable as well as the unfavorable consequences that may occur.

We begin the study of decision analysis by considering problems having reasonably few decision alternatives and reasonably few possible future events. Influence diagrams and payoff tables are introduced to provide a structure for the decision problem and to illustrate the fundamentals of decision analysis. We then introduce decision trees to show the sequential nature of decision problems. Decision trees are used to analyze more complex problems and to identify an optimal sequence of decisions, referred to as an optimal decision strategy. Sensitivity analysis shows how changes in various aspects of the problem affect the recommended decision alternative.

4.1   PROBLEM FORMULATION

The first step in the decision analysis process is problem formulation. We begin with a verbal statement of the problem. We then identify the decision alternatives, the uncertain future events, referred to as **chance events,** and the **consequences** associated with each decision alternative and each chance event outcome. Let us begin by considering a construction project of the Pittsburgh Development Corporation.

Pittsburgh Development Corporation (PDC) has purchased land, which will be the site of a new luxury condominium complex. The location provides a spectacular view of downtown Pittsburgh and the Golden Triangle where the Allegheny and Monongahela rivers meet to form the Ohio River. PDC plans to price the individual condominium units between $300,000 and $1,400,000.

PDC has preliminary architectural drawings for three different-sized projects: one with 30 condominiums, one with 60 condominiums, and one with 90 condominiums. The financial success of the project depends upon the size of the condominium complex and the chance event concerning the demand for the condominiums. The statement of the PDC decision problem is to select the size of the new luxury condominium project that will lead to the largest profit given the uncertainty concerning the demand for the condominiums.

Given the statement of the problem, it is clear that the decision is to select the best size for the condominium complex. PDC has the following three decision alternatives:

$$d_1 = \text{a small complex with 30 condominiums}$$
$$d_2 = \text{a medium complex with 60 condominiums}$$
$$d_3 = \text{a large complex with 90 condominiums}$$

A factor in selecting the best decision alternative is the uncertainty associated with the chance event concerning the demand for the condominiums. When asked about the possible demand for the condominiums, PDC's president acknowledged a wide range of possibilities, but decided that it would be adequate to consider two possible chance event outcomes: a strong demand and a weak demand.

In decision analysis, the possible outcomes for a chance event are referred to as the **states of nature.** The states of nature are defined so that one and only one of the possible states of nature will occur. For the PDC problem, the chance event concerning the demand for the condominiums has two states of nature:

$$s_1 = \text{strong demand for the condominiums}$$
$$s_2 = \text{weak demand for the condominiums}$$

Thus, management must first select a decision alternative (complex size), then a state of nature follows (demand for the condominiums), and finally a consequence will occur. In this case, the consequence is the PDC's profit.

Influence Diagrams

An **influence diagram** is a graphical device that shows the relationships among the decisions, the chance events, and the consequences for a decision problem. The **nodes** in an influence diagram are used to represent the decisions, chance events, and consequences. Rectangles or squares are used to depict **decision nodes,** circles or ovals are used to depict **chance nodes,** and diamonds are used to depict consequence nodes. The lines connecting the nodes, referred to as *arcs,* show the direction of influence that the nodes have on one another. Figure 4.1 shows the influence diagram for the PDC problem. The complex size is the decision node, demand is the chance node, and profit is the consequence node. The arcs connecting the nodes show that both the complex size and the demand influence PDC's profit.

Payoff Tables

Given the three decision alternatives and the two states of nature, which complex size should PDC choose? To answer this question, PDC will need to know the consequence associated with each decision alternative and each state of nature. In decision analysis, we refer to the consequence resulting from a specific combination of a decision alternative and a state of nature as a **payoff.** A table showing payoffs for all combinations of decision alternatives and states of nature is a **payoff table.**

Payoffs can be expressed in terms of profit, cost, time, distance, or any other measure appropriate for the decision problem being analyzed.

Because PDC wants to select the complex size that provides the largest profit, profit is used as the consequence. The payoff table with profits expressed in millions of dollars is shown in Table 4.1. Note, for example, that if a medium complex is built and demand turns out to be strong, a profit of $14 million will be realized. We will use the notation V_{ij} to denote the payoff associated with decision alternative i and state of nature j. Using Table 4.1, $V_{31} = 20$ indicates a payoff of $20 million occurs if the decision is to build a large complex (d_3) and the strong demand state of nature (s_1) occurs. Similarly, $V_{32} = -9$ indicates a loss of $9 million if the decision is to build a large complex (d_3) and the weak demand state of nature (s_2) occurs.

Decision Trees

A **decision tree** provides a graphical representation of the decision-making process. Figure 4.2 presents a decision tree for the PDC problem. Note that the decision tree shows the natu-

FIGURE 4.1   INFLUENCE DIAGRAM FOR THE PDC PROBLEM

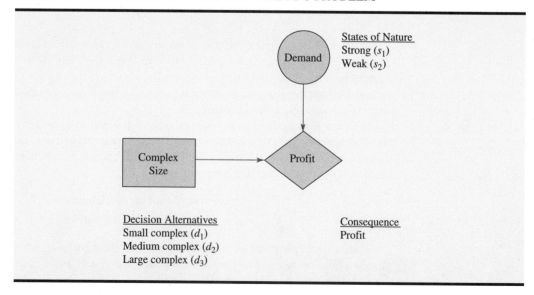

TABLE 4.1   PAYOFF TABLE FOR THE PDC CONDOMINIUM PROJECT
(PAYOFFS IN $ MILLION)

	State of Nature	
Decision Alternative	**Strong Demand s_1**	**Weak Demand s_2**
Small complex, d_1	8	7
Medium complex, d_2	14	5
Large complex, d_3	20	−9

ral or logical progression that will occur over time. First, PDC must make a decision regarding the size of the condominium complex (d_1, d_2, or d_3). Then, after the decision is implemented, either state of nature s_1 or s_2 will occur. The number at each end point of the tree indicates the payoff associated with a particular sequence. For example the topmost payoff of 8 indicates that an $8 million profit is anticipated if PDC constructs a small condominium complex (d_1) and demand turns out to be strong (s_1). The next payoff of 7 indicates an anticipated profit of $7 million if PDC constructs a small condominium complex (d_1) and demand turns out to be weak (s_2). Thus, the decision tree shows graphically the sequences of decision alternatives and states of nature that provide the six possible payoffs for PDC.

If you have a payoff table, you can develop a decision tree. Try Problem 1(a).

The decision tree in Figure 4.2 has four nodes, numbered 1–4. Squares are used to depict decision nodes and circles are used to depict chance nodes. Thus, node 1 is a decision node, and nodes 2, 3, and 4 are chance nodes. The branches, which connect the nodes, leaving the decision node correspond to the decision alternatives. The branches leaving each chance node correspond to the states of nature. The payoffs are shown at the end of the states-of-nature branches. We now turn to the question: How can the decision maker use the information in the payoff table or the decision tree to select the best decision alternative? Several approaches may be used.

FIGURE 4.2   DECISION TREE FOR THE PDC CONDOMINIUM PROJECT
(PAYOFFS IN $ MILLION)

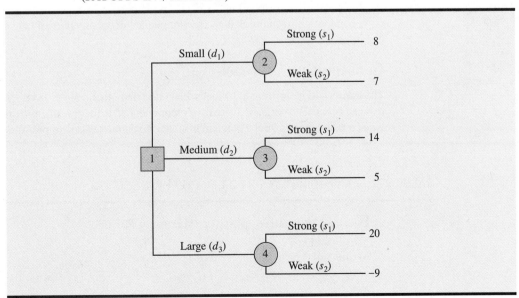

NOTES AND COMMENTS

1. Experts in problem solving agree that the first step in solving a complex problem is to decompose it into a series of smaller subproblems. Decision trees provide a useful way to show how a problem can be decomposed and the sequential nature of the decision process.

2. People often view the same problem from different perspectives. Thus, the discussion regarding the development of a decision tree may provide additional insight about the problem.

4.2   DECISION MAKING WITHOUT PROBABILITIES

Many people think of a good decision as one in which the consequence is good. However, in some instances, a good, well-thought-out decision may still lead to a bad or undesirable consequence.

In this section we consider approaches to decision making that do not require knowledge of the probabilities of the states of nature. These approaches are appropriate in situations in which the decision maker has little confidence in his or her ability to assess the probabilities, or in which a simple best-case and worst-case analysis is desirable. Because different approaches sometimes lead to different decision recommendations, the decision maker needs to understand the approaches available and then select the specific approach that, according to the decision maker's judgment, is the most appropriate.

Optimistic Approach

The **optimistic approach** evaluates each decision alternative in terms of the *best* payoff that can occur. The decision alternative that is recommended is the one that provides the best possible payoff. For a problem in which maximum profit is desired, as in the PDC problem, the optimistic approach would lead the decision maker to choose the alternative corresponding to the largest profit. For problems involving minimization, this approach leads to choosing the alternative with the smallest payoff.

For a maximization problem, the optimistic approach often is referred to as the maximax *approach; for a minimization problem, the corresponding terminology is* minimin.

To illustrate the optimistic approach, we use it to develop a recommendation for the PDC problem. First, we determine the maximum payoff for each decision alternative; then we select the decision alternative that provides the overall maximum payoff. These steps systematically identify the decision alternative that provides the largest possible profit. Table 4.2 illustrates these steps.

Because 20, corresponding to d_3, is the largest payoff, the decision to construct the large condominium complex is the recommended decision alternative using the optimistic approach.

Conservative Approach

The **conservative approach** evaluates each decision alternative in terms of the *worst* payoff that can occur. The decision alternative recommended is the one that provides the best of the worst possible payoffs. For a problem in which the output measure is profit, as in the PDC prob-

---

TABLE 4.2   MAXIMUM PAYOFF FOR EACH PDC DECISION ALTERNATIVE

Decision Alternative	Maximum Payoff	
Small complex, d_1	8	
Medium complex, d_2	14	Maximum of the
Large complex, d_3	20 ←	maximum payoff values

For a maximization problem, the conservative approach is often referred to as the maximin *approach; for a minimization problem, the corresponding terminology is* minimax.

lem, the conservative approach would lead the decision maker to choose the alternative that maximizes the minimum possible profit that could be obtained. For problems involving minimization, this approach identifies the alternative that will minimize the maximum payoff.

To illustrate the conservative approach, we use it to develop a recommendation for the PDC problem. First, we identify the minimum payoff for each of the decision alternatives; then we select the decision alternative that maximizes the minimum payoff. Table 4.3 illustrates these steps for the PDC problem.

Because 7, corresponding to d_1, yields the maximum of the minimum payoffs, the decision alternative of a small condominium complex is recommended. This decision approach is considered conservative because it identifies the worst possible payoffs and then recommends the decision alternative that avoids the possibility of extremely "bad" payoffs. In the conservative approach, PDC is guaranteed a profit of at least $7 million. Although PDC may make more, it *cannot* make less than $7 million.

Minimax Regret Approach

Minimax regret is an approach to decision making that is neither purely optimistic nor purely conservative. Let us illustrate the minimax regret approach by showing how it can be used to select a decision alternative for the PDC problem.

Suppose that the PDC constructs a small condominium complex (d_1) and demand turns out to be strong (s_1). Table 4.1 shows that the resulting profit for PDC would be $8 million. However, given that the strong demand state of nature (s_1) has occurred, we realize that the decision to construct a large condominium complex (d_3), yielding a profit of $20 million, would have been the best decision. The difference between the payoff for the best decision alternative ($20 million) and the payoff for the decision to construct a small condominium complex ($8 million) is the **opportunity loss,** or **regret,** associated with decision alternative d_1 when state of nature s_1 occurs; thus, for this case, the opportunity loss or regret is $20 million $-$ $8 million $=$ $12 million. Similarly, if PDC makes the decision to construct a medium condominium complex (d_2) and the strong demand state of nature (s_1) occurs, the opportunity loss, or regret, associated with d_2 would be $20 million $-$ $14 million $=$ $6 million.

In general the following expression represents the opportunity loss, or regret.

$$R_{ij} = \left| V_j^* - V_{ij} \right| \qquad (4.1)$$

where

R_{ij} = the regret associated with decision alternative d_i and state of nature s_j

V_j^* = the payoff value[1] corresponding to the best decision for the state of nature s_j

V_{ij} = the payoff corresponding to decision alternative d_i and state of nature s_j

TABLE 4.3   MINIMUM PAYOFF FOR EACH PDC DECISION ALTERNATIVE

Decision Alternative	Minimum Payoff	
Small complex, d_1	7 ←	Maximum of the minimum payoff values
Medium complex, d_2	5	
Large complex, d_3	−9	

---

[1]In maximization problems, V_j^* will be the largest entry in column j of the payoff table. In minimization problems, V_j^* will be the smallest entry in column j of the payoff table.

TABLE 4.4   OPPORTUNITY LOSS, OR REGRET, TABLE FOR THE PDC CONDOMINIUM PROJECT ($ MILLION)

Decision Alternative	State of Nature	
	Strong Demand s_1	Weak Demand s_2
Small complex, d_1	12	0
Medium complex, d_2	6	2
Large complex, d_3	0	16

TABLE 4.5   MAXIMUM REGRET FOR EACH PDC DECISION ALTERNATIVE

Decision Alternative	Maximum Regret	
Small complex, d_1	12	
Medium complex, d_2	6	← Minimum of the maximum regret
Large complex, d_3	16	

Note the role of the absolute value in equation (4.1). That is, for minimization problems, the best payoff, V_j^*, is the smallest entry in column j. Because this value always is less than or equal to V_{ij}, the absolute value of the difference between V_j^* and V_{ij} ensures that the regret is always the magnitude of the difference.

Using equation (4.1) and the payoffs in Table 4.1, we can compute the regret associated with each combination of decision alternative d_i and state of nature s_j. Because the PDC problem is a maximization problem, V_j^* will be the largest entry in column j of the payoff table. Thus, to compute the regret, we simply subtract each entry in a column from the largest entry in the column. Table 4.4 shows the opportunity loss, or regret, table for the PDC problem.

The next step in applying the minimax regret approach is to list the maximum regret for each decision alternative; Table 4.5 shows the results for the PDC problem. Selecting the decision alternative with the *minimum* of the *maximum* regret values—hence, the name *minimax regret*—yields the minimax regret decision. For the PDC problem, the alternative to construct the medium condominium complex, with a corresponding maximum regret of $6 million, is the recommended minimax regret decision.

For practice in developing a decision recommendation using the optimistic, conservative, and minimax regret approaches, try Problem 1(b).

Note that the three approaches discussed in this section provide different recommendations, which in itself isn't bad. It simply reflects the difference in decision-making philosophies that underlie the various approaches. Ultimately, the decision maker will have to choose the most appropriate approach and then make the final decision accordingly. The main criticism of the approaches discussed in this section is that they do not consider any information about the probabilities of the various states of nature. In the next section we discuss an approach that utilizes probability information in selecting a decision alternative.

4.3   DECISION MAKING WITH PROBABILITIES

In many decision-making situations, we can obtain probability assessments for the states of nature. When such probabilities are available, we can use the **expected value approach** to identify the best decision alternative. Let us first define the expected value of a decision alternative and then apply it to the PDC problem.

Let

$$N = \text{the number of states of nature}$$
$$P(s_j) = \text{the probability of state of nature } s_j$$

Because one and only one of the N states of nature can occur, the probabilities must satisfy two conditions:

$$P(s_j) \geq 0 \qquad \text{for all states of nature} \tag{4.2}$$

$$\sum_{j=1}^{N} P(s_j) = P(s_1) + P(s_2) + \cdots + P(s_N) = 1 \tag{4.3}$$

The **expected value (EV)** of decision alternative d_i is defined as follows.

$$\text{EV}(d_i) = \sum_{j=1}^{N} P(s_j)V_{ij} \tag{4.4}$$

In words, the expected value of a decision alternative is the sum of weighted payoffs for the decision alternative. The weight for a payoff is the probability of the associated state of nature and therefore the probability that the payoff will occur. Let us return to the PDC problem to see how the expected value approach can be applied.

PDC is optimistic about the potential for the luxury high-rise condominium complex. Suppose that this optimism leads to an initial subjective probability assessment of 0.8 that demand will be strong (s_1) and a corresponding probability of 0.2 that demand will be weak (s_2). Thus, $P(s_1) = 0.8$ and $P(s_2) = 0.2$. Using the payoff values in Table 4.1 and equation (4.4), we compute the expected value for each of the three decision alternatives as follows:

$$\text{EV}(d_1) = 0.8(8) \ + 0.2(7) \quad = 7.8$$
$$\text{EV}(d_2) = 0.8(14) + 0.2(5) \quad = 12.2$$
$$\text{EV}(d_3) = 0.8(20) + 0.2(-9) = 14.2$$

Thus, using the expected value approach, we find that the large condominium complex, with an expected value of $14.2 million, is the recommended decision.

Can you now use the expected value approach to develop a decision recommendation? Try Problem 5.

The calculations required to identify the decision alternative with the best expected value can be conveniently carried out on a decision tree. Figure 4.3 shows the decision tree for the PDC problem with state-of-nature branch probabilities. Working backward through the decision tree, we first compute the expected value at each chance node. That is, at each chance node, we weight each possible payoff by its probability of occurrence. By doing so, we obtain the expected values for nodes 2, 3, and 4, as shown in Figure 4.4.

Because the decision maker controls the branch leaving decision node 1 and because we are trying to maximize the expected profit, the best decision alternative at node 1 is d_3. Thus, the decision tree analysis leads to a recommendation of d_3 with an expected value of $14.2 million. Note that this recommendation is also obtained with the expected value approach in conjunction with the payoff table.

Computer software packages are available to help in constructing more complex decision trees.

Other decision problems may be substantially more complex than the PDC problem, but if a reasonable number of decision alternatives and states of nature are present, you can use the decision tree approach outlined here. First, draw a decision tree consisting of decision nodes, chance nodes, and branches that describe the sequential nature of the problem. If you use the expected value approach, the next step is to determine the probabilities for

FIGURE 4.3   PDC DECISION TREE WITH STATE-OF-NATURE BRANCH PROBABILITIES

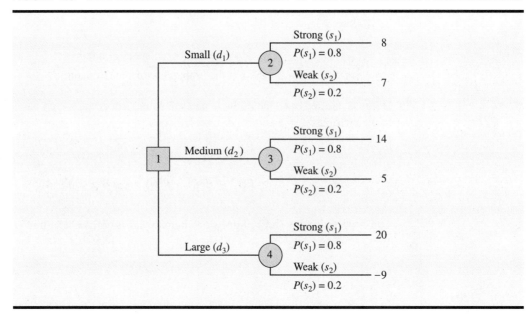

FIGURE 4.4   APPLYING THE EXPECTED VALUE APPROACH USING DECISION TREES

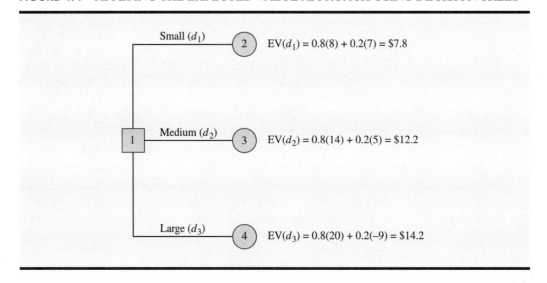

each of the states of nature and compute the expected value at each chance node. Then select the decision branch leading to the chance node with the best expected value. The decision alternative associated with this branch is the recommended decision.

Expected Value of Perfect Information

Suppose that PDC has the opportunity to conduct a market research study that would help evaluate buyer interest in the condominium project and provide information that management could use to improve the probability assessments for the states of nature. To determine the potential value of this information, we begin by supposing that the study could provide *perfect information* regarding the states of nature; that is, we assume for the moment that PDC could determine with certainty, prior to making a decision, which state of nature is going to occur. To make use of this perfect information, we will develop a decision strategy that PDC should follow once it knows which state of nature will occur. A decision strategy is simply a decision rule that specifies the decision alternative to be selected after new information becomes available.

To help determine the decision strategy for PDC, we have reproduced PDC's payoff table as Table 4.6. Note that, if PDC knew for sure that state of nature s_1 would occur, the best decision alternative would be d_3, with a payoff of $20 million. Similarly, if PDC knew for sure that state of nature s_2 would occur, the best decision alternative would be d_1, with a payoff of $7 million. Thus, we can state PDC's optimal decision strategy when the perfect information becomes available as follows:

If s_1, select d_3 and receive a payoff of $20 million.

If s_2, select d_1 and receive a payoff of $7 million.

What is the expected value for this decision strategy? To compute the expected value with perfect information, we return to the original probabilities for the states of nature: $P(s_1) = 0.8$, and $P(s_2) = 0.2$. Thus, there is a 0.8 probability that the perfect information will indicate state of nature s_1 and the resulting decision alternative d_3 will provide a $20 million profit. Similarly, with a 0.2 probability for state of nature s_2, the optimal decision alternative d_1 will provide a $7 million profit. Thus, from equation (4.4), the expected value of the decision strategy that uses perfect information is

$$0.8(20) + 0.2(7) = 17.4$$

We refer to the expected value of $17.4 million as the *expected value with perfect information* (EVwPI).

Earlier in this section we showed that the recommended decision using the expected value approach is decision alternative d_3, with an expected value of $14.2 million. Because this decision recommendation and expected value computation were made without the benefit of perfect information, $14.2 million is referred to as the *expected value without perfect information* (EVwoPI).

It would be worth $3.2 million for PDC to learn the level of market acceptance before selecting a decision alternative.

The expected value with perfect information is $17.4 million, and the expected value without perfect information is $14.2; therefore, the expected value of the perfect information (EVPI) is $17.4 − $14.2 = $3.2 million. In other words, $3.2 million represents the additional expected value that can be obtained if perfect information were available about the states of nature.

Generally speaking, a market research study will not provide "perfect" information; however, if the market research study is a good one, the information gathered might be worth a sizable portion of the $3.2 million. Given the EVPI of $3.2 million, PDC should seriously consider the market survey as a way to obtain more information about the states of nature.

TABLE 4.6   PAYOFF TABLE FOR THE PDC CONDOMINIUM PROJECT ($ MILLION)

	State of Nature	
Decision Alternative	**Strong Demand s_1**	**Weak Demand s_2**
Small complex, d_1	8	7
Medium complex, d_2	14	5
Large complex, d_3	20	−9

In general, the **expected value of perfect information** is computed as follows:

$$\text{EVPI} = |\text{EVwPI} - \text{EVwoPI}| \qquad (4.5)$$

where

> EVPI = expected value of perfect information
>
> EVwPI = expected value *with* perfect information about the states of nature
>
> EVwoPI = expected value *without* perfect information about the states of nature

For practice in determining the expected value of perfect information, try Problem 14.

Note the role of the absolute value in equation (4.5). For minimization problems the expected value with perfect information is always less than or equal to the expected value without perfect information. In this case, EVPI is the magnitude of the difference between EVwPI and EVwoPI, or the absolute value of the difference as shown in equation (4.5).

NOTES AND COMMENTS

We restate the *opportunity loss,* or *regret,* table for the PDC problem (see Table 4.4) as follows.

	State of Nature	
	Strong Demand	Weak Demand
Decision Alternative	s_1	s_2
Small complex, d_1	12	0
Medium complex, d_2	6	2
Large complex, d_3	0	16

Using $P(s_1)$, $P(s_2)$, and the opportunity loss values, we can compute the *expected opportunity loss* (EOL) for each decision alternative. With $P(s_1) = $ 0.8 and $P(s_2) = 0.2$, the expected opportunity loss for each of the three decision alternatives is

$$\text{EOL}(d_1) = 0.8(12) + 0.2(0) = 9.6$$
$$\text{EOL}(d_2) = 0.8(6) + 0.2(2) = 5.2$$
$$\text{EOL}(d_3) = 0.8(0) + 0.2(16) = 3.2$$

Regardless of whether the decision analysis involves maximization or minimization, the *minimum* expected opportunity loss always provides the best decision alternative. Thus, with $\text{EOL}(d_3) = $ 3.2, d_3 is the recommended decision. In addition, the minimum expected opportunity loss always is *equal to the expected value of perfect information.* That is, EOL(best decision) = EVPI; for the PDC problem, this value is $3.2 million.

4.4   RISK ANALYSIS AND SENSITIVITY ANALYSIS

In this section, we introduce risk analysis and sensitivity analysis. **Risk analysis** can be used to provide probabilities for the payoffs associated with a decision alternative. As a result, risk analysis helps the decision maker recognize the difference between the expected value of a decision alternative and the payoff that may actually occur. **Sensitivity analysis** also helps the decision maker by describing how changes in the state-of-nature probabilities and/or changes in the payoffs affect the recommended decision alternative.

Risk Analysis

A decision alternative and a state of nature combine to generate the payoff associated with a decision. The **risk profile** for a decision alternative shows the possible payoffs along with their associated probabilities.

Let us demonstrate risk analysis and the construction of a risk profile by returning to the PDC condominium construction project. Using the expected value approach, we identified the large condominium complex (d_3) as the best decision alternative. The expected value of $14.2 million for d_3 is based on a 0.8 probability of obtaining a $20 million profit and a 0.2 probability of obtaining a $9 million loss. The 0.8 probability for the $20 million payoff and the 0.2 probability for the $-$9 million payoff provide the risk profile for the large complex decision alternative. This risk profile is shown graphically in Figure 4.5.

Sometimes a review of the risk profile associated with an optimal decision alternative may cause the decision maker to choose another decision alternative even though the expected value of the other decision alternative is not as good. For example, the risk profile for the medium complex decision alternative (d_2) shows a 0.8 probability for a $14 million payoff and 0.2 probability for a $5 million payoff. Because no probability of a loss is associated with decision alternative d_2, the medium complex decision alternative would be judged less risky than the large complex decision alternative. As a result, a decision maker might prefer the less-risky medium complex decision alternative even though it has an expected value of $2 million less than the large complex decision alternative.

Sensitivity Analysis

Sensitivity analysis can be used to determine how changes in the probabilities for the states of nature and/or changes in the payoffs affect the recommended decision alternative. In many cases, the probabilities for the states of nature and the payoffs are based on subjective assessments. Sensitivity analysis helps the decision maker understand which of these inputs are critical to the choice of the best decision alternative. If a small change in the value of one of the inputs causes a change in the recommended decision alternative, the solution to the decision analysis problem is sensitive to that particular input. Extra effort and care should be taken to make sure the input value is as accurate as possible. On the other hand, if a modest to large change in the value of one of the inputs does not cause a change in the recommended decision alternative, the solution to the decision analysis problem is not sensitive to that particular input. No extra time or effort would be needed to refine the estimated input value.

One approach to sensitivity analysis is to select different values for the probabilities of the states of nature and/or the payoffs and then resolve the decision analysis problem. If the recommended decision alternative changes, we know that the solution is sensitive to the changes made. For example, suppose that in the PDC problem the probability for a strong demand is revised to 0.2 and the probability for a weak demand is revised to 0.8. Would the

FIGURE 4.5   RISK PROFILE FOR THE LARGE COMPLEX DECISION ALTERNATIVE FOR THE PDC CONDOMINIUM PROJECT

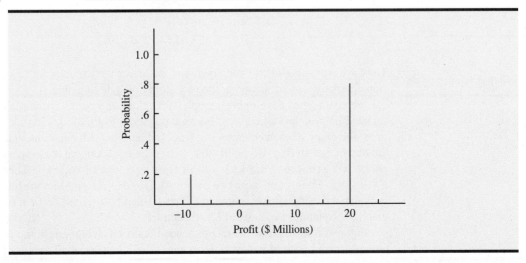

recommended decision alternative change? Using $P(s_1) = 0.2$, $P(s_2) = 0.8$, and equation (4.4), the revised expected values for the three decision alternatives are

$$
\begin{aligned}
EV(d_1) &= 0.2(8) \ \ + 0.8(7) \ \ = 7.2 \\
EV(d_2) &= 0.2(14) + 0.8(5) \ \ = 6.8 \\
EV(d_3) &= 0.2(20) + 0.8(-9) = -3.2
\end{aligned}
$$

With these probability assessments the recommended decision alternative is to construct a small condominium complex (d_1), with an expected value of $7.2 million. The probability of strong demand is only 0.2, so constructing the large condominium complex (d_3) is the least preferred alternative, with an expected value of $-$3.2 million (a loss).

Computer software packages for decision analysis, such as Precision Tree, make it easy to calculate these revised scenarios.

Thus, when the probability of strong demand is large, PDC should build the large complex; when the probability of strong demand is small, PDC should build the small complex. Obviously, we could continue to modify the probabilities of the states of nature and learn even more about how changes in the probabilities affect the recommended decision alternative. The drawback to this approach is the numerous calculations required to evaluate the effect of several possible changes in the state-of-nature probabilities.

For the special case of two states of nature, a graphical procedure can be used to determine how changes for the probabilities of the states of nature affect the recommended decision alternative. To demonstrate this procedure, we let p denote the probability of state of nature s_1; that is, $P(s_1) = p$. With only two states of nature in the PDC problem, the probability of state of nature s_2 is

$$
P(s_2) = 1 - P(s_1) = 1 - p
$$

Using equation (4.4) and the payoff values in Table 4.1, we determine the expected value for decision alternative d_1 as follows:

$$
\begin{aligned}
EV(d_1) &= P(s_1)(8) + P(s_2)(7) \\
&= p(8) + (1 - p)(7) \\
&= 8p + 7 - 7p = p + 7
\end{aligned} \tag{4.6}
$$

Repeating the expected value computations for decision alternatives d_2 and d_3, we obtain expressions for the expected value of each decision alternative as a function of p:

$$
EV(d_2) = 9p + 5 \tag{4.7}
$$

$$
EV(d_3) = 29p - 9 \tag{4.8}
$$

Thus, we have developed three equations that show the expected value of the three decision alternatives as a function of the probability of state of nature s_1.

We continue by developing a graph with values of p on the horizontal axis and the associated EVs on the vertical axis. Because equations (4.6), (4.7), and (4.8) are linear equations, the graph of each equation is a straight line. For each equation, then, we can obtain the line by identifying two points that satisfy the equation and drawing a line through the points. For instance, if we let $p = 0$ in equation (4.6), $EV(d_1) = 7$. Then, letting $p = 1$, $EV(d_1) = 8$. Connecting these two points, $(0, 7)$ and $(1, 8)$, provides the line labeled $EV(d_1)$ in Figure 4.6. Similarly, we obtain the lines labeled $EV(d_2)$ and $EV(d_3)$; these lines are the graphs of equations (4.7) and (4.8), respectively.

Figure 4.6 shows how the recommended decision changes as p, the probability of the strong demand state of nature (s_1), changes. Note that for small values of p, decision al-

FIGURE 4.6   EXPECTED VALUE FOR THE PDC DECISION ALTERNATIVES AS A
FUNCTION OF p

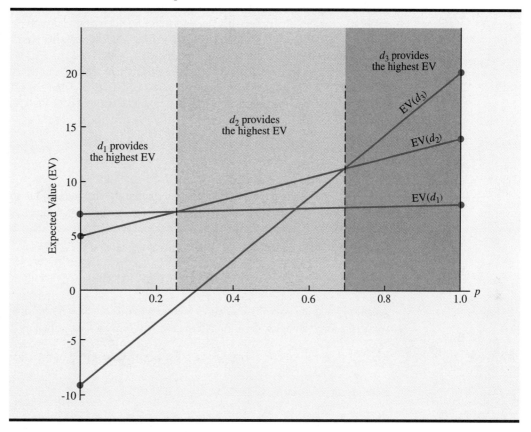

ternative d_1 (small complex) provides the largest expected value and is thus the recommended decision. When the value of p increases to a certain point, decision alternative d_2 (medium complex) provides the largest expected value and is the recommended decision. Finally, for large values of p, decision alternative d_3 (large complex) becomes the recommended decision.

The value of p for which the expected values of d_1 and d_2 are equal is the value of p corresponding to the intersection of the $EV(d_1)$ and the $EV(d_2)$ lines. To determine this value, we set $EV(d_1) = EV(d_2)$ and solve for the value of p:

$$p + 7 = 9p + 5$$
$$8p = 2$$
$$p = \frac{2}{8} = 0.25$$

Hence, when $p = 0.25$, decision alternatives d_1 and d_2 provide the same expected value. Repeating this calculation for the value of p corresponding to the intersection of the $EV(d_2)$ and $EV(d_3)$ lines we obtain $p = 0.70$.

Using Figure 4.6, we can conclude that decision alternative d_1 provides the largest expected value for $p \leq 0.25$, decision alternative d_2 provides the largest expected value for $0.25 \leq p \leq 0.70$, and decision alternative d_3 provides the largest expected value for $p \geq 0.70$. Because p is the probability of state of nature s_1 and $(1 - p)$ is the probability of state

Graphical sensitivity analysis shows how changes in the probabilities for the states of nature affect the recommended decision alternative. Try Problem 8.

of nature s_2, we now have the sensitivity analysis information that tells us how changes in the state-of-nature probabilities affect the recommended decision alternative.

Sensitivity analysis calculations can also be made for the values of the payoffs. In the original PDC problem, the expected values for the three decision alternatives were as follows: $EV(d_1) = 7.8$, $EV(d_2) = 12.2$, and $EV(d_3) = 14.2$. Decision alternative d_3 (large complex) was recommended. Note that decision alternative d_2 with $EV(d_2) = 12.2$ was the second best decision alternative. Decision alternative d_3 will remain the optimal decision alternative as long as $EV(d_3)$ is greater than or equal to the expected value of the second best decision alternative. Thus, decision alternative d_3 will remain the optimal decision alternative as long as

$$EV(d_3) \geq 12.2 \tag{4.9}$$

Let

$$S = \text{the payoff of decision alternative } d_3 \text{ when demand is strong}$$
$$W = \text{the payoff of decision alternative } d_3 \text{ when demand is weak}$$

Using $P(s_1) = 0.8$ and $P(s_2) = 0.2$, the general expression for $EV(d_3)$ is

$$EV(d_3) = 0.8S + 0.2W \tag{4.10}$$

Assuming that the payoff for d_3 stays at its original value of $-\$9$ million when demand is weak, the large complex decision alternative will remain the optimal as long as

$$EV(d_3) = 0.8S + 0.2(-9) \geq 12.2 \tag{4.11}$$

Solving for S, we have

$$0.8S - 1.8 \geq 12.2$$
$$0.8S \geq 14$$
$$S \geq 17.5$$

Recall that when demand is strong, decision alternative d_3 has an estimated payoff of $20 million. The preceding calculation shows that decision alternative d_3 will remain optimal as long as the payoff for d_3 when demand is strong is at least $17.5 million.

Assuming that the payoff for d_3 stays at its original value of $20 million, we can make a similar calculation to learn how sensitive the optimal solution is with regard to the payoff for d_3 when demand is weak. Returning to the expected value calculation of equation (4.10), we know that the large complex decision alternative will remain optimal as long as

$$EV(d_3) = 0.8(20) + 0.2W \geq 12.2 \tag{4.12}$$

Solving for W, we have

$$16 + 0.2W \geq 12.2$$
$$0.2W \geq -3.8$$
$$W \geq -19$$

Recall that when demand is weak, decision alternative d_3 has an estimated payoff of $-\$9$ million. The preceding calculation shows that decision alternative d_3 will remain optimal as long as the payoff for d_3 when demand is weak is at least $-\$19$ million.

Based on this sensitivity analysis, we conclude that the payoffs for the large complex decision alternative (d_3) could vary considerably and d_3 would remain the recommended decision alternative. Thus, we conclude that the optimal solution for the PDC decision problem is not particularly sensitive to the payoffs for the large complex decision alternative. We note, however, that this sensitivity analysis has been conducted based on only one change at a time. That is, only one payoff was changed and the probabilities for the states of nature remained $P(s_1) = 0.8$ and $P(s_2) = 0.2$. Note that similar sensitivity analysis calculations can be made for the payoffs associated with the small complex decision alternative d_1 and the medium complex decision alternative d_2. However, in these cases, decision alternative d_3 remains optimal only if the changes in the payoffs for decision alternatives d_1 and d_2 meet the requirements that $EV(d_1) \leq 14.2$ and $EV(d_2) \leq 14.2$.

Sensitivity analysis can assist management in deciding whether more time and effort should be spent obtaining better estimates of payoffs and/or probabilities.

NOTES AND COMMENTS

1. Some decision analysis software automatically provide the risk profiles for the optimal decision alternative. These packages also allow the user to obtain the risk profiles for other decision alternatives. After comparing the risk profiles, a decision maker may decide to select a decision alternative with a good risk profile even though the expected value of the decision alternative is not as good as the optimal decision alternative.

2. A *tornado diagram,* a graphical display, is particularly helpful when several inputs combine to determine the value of the optimal solution. By varying each input over its range of values, we obtain information about how each input affects the value of the optimal solution. To display this information, a bar is constructed for the input with the width of the bar showing how the input affects the value of the optimal solution. The widest bar corresponds to the input that is most sensitive. The bars are arranged in a graph with the widest bar at the top, resulting in a graph that has the appearance of a tornado.

4.5   DECISION ANALYSIS WITH SAMPLE INFORMATION

In applying the expected value approach, we have shown how probability information about the states of nature affects the expected value calculations and thus the decision recommendation. Frequently, decision makers have preliminary or **prior probability** assessments for the states of nature that are the best probability values available at that time. However, to make the best possible decision, the decision maker may want to seek additional information about the states of nature. This new information can be used to revise or update the prior probabilities so that the final decision is based on more accurate probabilities for the states of nature. Most often, additional information is obtained through experiments designed to provide **sample information** about the states of nature. Raw material sampling, product testing, and market research studies are examples of experiments (or studies) that may enable management to revise or update the state-of-nature probabilities. These revised probabilities are called **posterior probabilities.**

Let us return to the PDC problem and assume that management is considering a six-month market research study designed to learn more about potential market acceptance of the PDC condominium project. Management anticipates that the market research study will provide one of the following two results:

1. Favorable report: A significant number of the individuals contacted express interest in purchasing a PDC condominium.
2. Unfavorable report: Very few of the individuals contacted express interest in purchasing a PDC condominium.

An Influence Diagram

By introducing the possibility of conducting a market research study, the PDC problem becomes more complex. The influence diagram for the expanded PDC problem is shown in Figure 4.7. Note that the two decision nodes correspond to the research study and the complex-size decisions. The two chance nodes correspond to the research study results and demand for the condominiums. Finally, the consequence node is the profit. From the arcs of the influence diagram, we see that demand influences both the research study results and profit. Although demand is currently unknown to PDC, some level of demand for the condominiums already exists in the Pittsburgh area. If existing demand is strong, the research study is likely to find a significant number of individuals who express an interest in purchasing a condominium. However, if the existing demand is weak, the research study is more likely to find a significant number of individuals who express little interest in purchasing a condominium. In this sense, existing demand for the condominiums will influence the research study results. And clearly, demand will have an influence upon PDC's profit.

The arc from the research study decision node to the complex-size decision node indicates that the research study decision precedes the complex-size decision. No arc spans from the research study decision node to the research study results node, because the decision to conduct the research study does not actually influence the research study results. The decision to conduct the research study makes the research study results available, but it does not influence the results of the research study. Finally, the complex-size node and the demand node both influence profit. Note that if there were a stated cost to conduct the research study, the decision to conduct the research study would also influence profit. In such a case, we would need to add an arc from the research study decision node to the profit node to show the influence that the research study cost would have on profit.

A Decision Tree

The decision tree for the PDC problem with sample information shows the logical sequence for the decisions and the chance events.

First, PDC's management must decide whether the market research should be conducted. If it is conducted, PDC's management must be prepared to make a decision about the size of the condominium project if the market research report is favorable and, possibly, a different decision about the size of the condominium project if the market research report is unfavorable. The decision tree in Figure 4.8 shows this PDC decision problem. The squares are de-

FIGURE 4.7   INFLUENCE DIAGRAM FOR THE PDC PROBLEM WITH SAMPLE INFORMATION

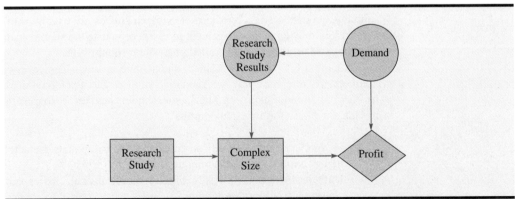

FIGURE 4.8   THE PDC DECISION TREE INCLUDING THE MARKET RESEARCH STUDY

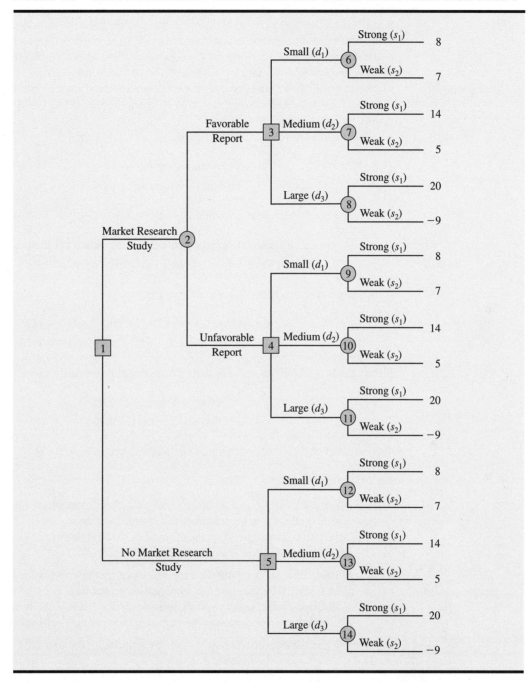

cision nodes and the circles are chance nodes. At each decision node, the branch of the tree that is taken is based on the decision made. At each chance node, the branch of the tree that is taken is based on probability or chance. For example, decision node 1 shows that PDC must first make the decision of whether to conduct the market research study. If the market research study is undertaken, chance node 2 indicates that both the favorable report branch and the unfavorable report branch are not under PDC's control and will be determined by chance. Node 3 is a decision node, indicating that PDC must make the decision to construct the small, medium, or large complex if the market research report is favorable. Node 4 is a decision node showing that PDC must make the decision to construct the small, medium, or large complex if the market research report is unfavorable. Node 5 is a decision node indicating that PDC must make the decision to construct the small, medium, or large complex if the market research is not undertaken. Nodes 6 to 14 are chance nodes indicating that the strong demand or weak demand state-of-nature branches will be determined by chance.

We explain in Section 4.6 how these probabilities can be developed.

Analysis of the decision tree and the choice of an optimal strategy requires that we know the branch probabilities corresponding to all chance nodes. PDC has developed the following branch probabilities.

If the market research study is undertaken

$$P(\text{Favorable report}) = 0.77$$
$$P(\text{Unfavorable report}) = 0.23$$

If the market research report is favorable

$$P(\text{Strong demand given a Favorable report}) = 0.94$$
$$P(\text{Weak demand given a Favorable report}) = 0.06$$

If the market research report is unfavorable

$$P(\text{Strong demand given an Unfavorable report}) = 0.35$$
$$P(\text{Weak demand given an Unfavorable report}) = 0.65$$

If the market research report is not undertaken the prior probabilities are applicable.

$$P(\text{Strong demand}) = 0.80$$
$$P(\text{Weak demand}) = 0.20$$

The branch probabilities are shown on the decision tree in Figure 4.9.

Decision Strategy

A **decision strategy** is a sequence of decisions and chance outcomes where the decisions chosen depend on the yet to be determined outcomes of chance events.

The approach used to determine the optimal **decision strategy** is based on a backward pass through the decision tree using the following steps:

1. At chance nodes, compute the expected value by multiplying the payoff at the end of each branch by the corresponding branch probabilities.
2. At decision nodes, select the decision branch that leads to the best expected value. This expected value becomes the expected value at the decision node.

Starting the backward pass calculations by computing the expected values at chance nodes 6 to 14 provides the following results.

$$
\begin{aligned}
\text{EV(Node 6)} &= 0.94(8) + 0.06(7) &&= 7.94 \\
\text{EV(Node 7)} &= 0.94(14) + 0.06(5) &&= 13.46 \\
\text{EV(Node 8)} &= 0.94(20) + 0.06(-9) &&= 18.26 \\
\text{EV(Node 9)} &= 0.35(8) + 0.65(7) &&= 7.35 \\
\text{EV(Node 10)} &= 0.35(14) + 0.65(5) &&= 8.15 \\
\text{EV(Node 11)} &= 0.35(20) + 0.65(-9) &&= 1.15 \\
\text{EV(Node 12)} &= 0.80(8) + 0.20(7) &&= 7.80
\end{aligned}
$$

$$\text{EV(Node 13)} = 0.80(14) + 0.20(5) \quad = 12.20$$
$$\text{EV(Node 14)} = 0.80(20) + 0.20(-9) = 14.20$$

Figure 4.10 shows the reduced decision tree after computing expected values at these chance nodes.

Next move to decision nodes 3, 4, and 5. For each of these nodes, we select the decision alternative branch that leads to the best expected value. For example, at node 3 we have the

FIGURE 4.9   THE PDC DECISION TREE WITH BRANCH PROBABILITIES

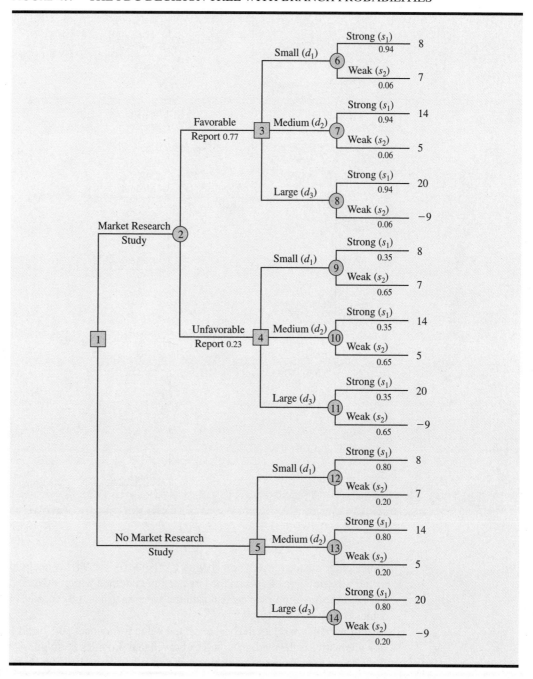

FIGURE 4.10   PDC DECISION TREE AFTER COMPUTING EXPECTED VALUES
AT CHANCE NODES 6 TO 14

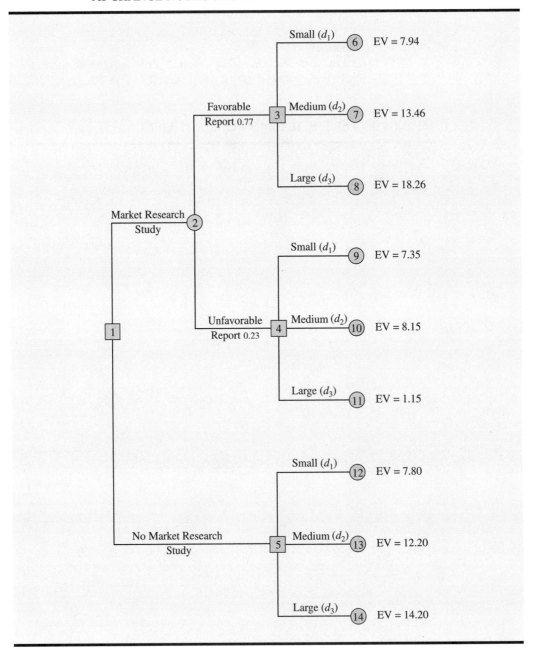

choice of the small complex branch with EV(Node 6) = 7.94, the medium complex branch
with EV(Node 7) = 13.46, and the large complex branch with EV(Node 8) = 18.26. Thus,
we select the large complex decision alternative branch and the expected value at node 3 becomes EV(Node 3) = 18.26.

For node 4, we select the best expected value from nodes 9, 10, and 11. The best decision alternative is the medium complex branch that provides EV(Node 4) = 8.15. For node
5, we select the best expected value from nodes 12, 13, and 14. The best decision alterna-

FIGURE 4.11   PDC DECISION TREE AFTER CHOOSING BEST DECISIONS AT
NODES 3, 4, AND 5

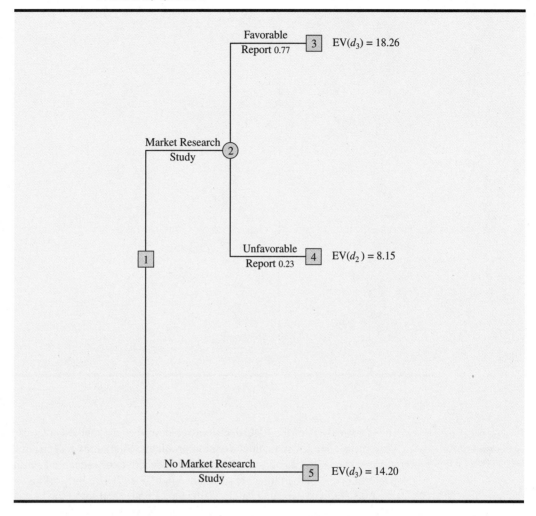

tive is the large complex branch which provides EV(Node 5) = 14.20. Figure 4.11 shows
the reduced decision tree after choosing the best decisions at nodes 3, 4, and 5.

The expected value at chance node 2 can now be computed as follows:

$$\text{EV(Node 2)} = 0.77\text{EV(Node 3)} + 0.23\text{EV(Node 4)}$$
$$= 0.77(18.26) + 0.23(8.15) = 15.93$$

This reduces the decision tree to one involving only the 2 decision branches from node 1
(see Figure 4.12).

Finally, the decision can be made at decision node 1 by selecting the best expected values from nodes 2 and 5. This action leads to the decision alternative to conduct the market
research study, which provides an overall expected value of 15.93.

The optimal decision for PDC is to conduct the market research study and then carry
out the following decision strategy:

If the market research is favorable, construct the large condominium complex.

If the market research is unfavorable, construct the medium condominium complex.

FIGURE 4.12   PDC DECISION TREE REDUCED TO 2 DECISION BRANCHES

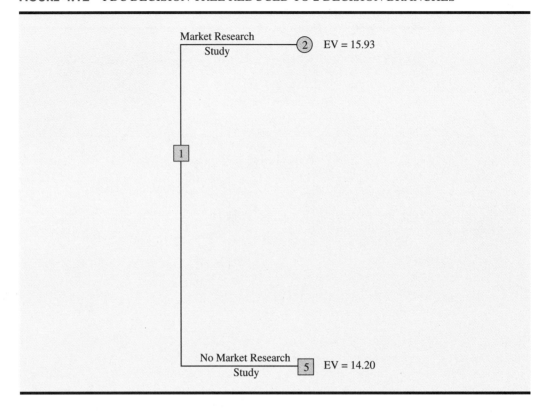

Problem 16 will test your ability to develop an optimal decision strategy.

The analysis of the PDC decision tree describes the methods that can be used to analyze more complex sequential decision problems. First, draw a decision tree consisting of decision and chance nodes and branches that describe the sequential nature of the problem. Determine the probabilities for all chance outcomes. Then, by working backward through the tree, compute expected values at all chance nodes and select the best decision branch at all decision nodes. The sequence of optimal decision branches determines the optimal decision strategy for the problem. The Q. M. in Action article on drug testing for student athletes describes how Santa Clara University used decision analysis to make a decision regarding whether to implement a drug testing program for student athletes.

Risk Profile

Figure 4.13 provides a reduced decision tree showing only the sequence of decision alternatives and chance events for the PDC optimal decision strategy. By implementing the optimal decision strategy, PDC will obtain one of the four payoffs shown at the terminal branches of the decision tree. Recall that a risk profile shows the possible payoffs with their associated probabilities. Thus, in order to construct a risk profile for the optimal decision strategy we will need to compute the probability for each of the four payoffs.

Note that each payoff results from a sequence of branches leading from node 1 to the payoff. For instance, the payoff of $20 million is obtained by following the upper branch from node 1, the upper branch from node 2, the lower branch from node 3 and the upper branch from node 8. The probability of following that sequence of branches can be found by multiplying the probabilities for the branches from the chance nodes in the sequence.

Q.M. IN ACTION

DECISION ANALYSIS AND DRUG TESTING FOR STUDENT ATHLETES*

The athletic governing board of Santa Clara University considered whether to implement a drug-testing program for the university's intercollegiate athletes. The decision analysis framework contains two decision alternatives: implement a drug-testing program and do not implement a drug-testing program. Each student athlete is either a drug user or not a drug user, so these two possibilities are considered to be the states of nature for the problem.

If the drug-testing program is implemented, student athletes will be required to take a drug-screening test. Results of the test will be either positive (test indicates a possible drug user) or negative (test does not indicate a possible drug user). The test outcomes are considered to be the sample information in the decision problem. If the test result is negative, no follow-up action will be taken.

However, if the test result is positive, follow-up action will be taken to determine whether the student athlete actually is a drug user. The payoffs include the cost of not identifying a drug user and the cost of falsely identifying a nonuser.

Decision analysis showed that if the test result is positive, a reasonably high probability still exists that the student athlete is not a drug user. The cost and other problems associated with this type of misleading test result were considered significant. Consequently, the athletic governing board decided not to implement the drug-testing program.

*Charles D. Feinstein, "Deciding Whether to Test Student Athletes for Drug Use," *Interfaces* 20, no. 3 (May–June 1990): 80–87.

Thus the probability the $20 million payoff is $(0.77)(0.94) = 0.72$. Similarly, the probabilities for each of the other payoffs are obtained by multiplying the probabilities for the branches from the chance nodes leading to the payoffs. Doing so, we find the probability of the $-\$9$ million payoff is $(0.77)(0.06) = 0.05$; the probability of the $14 million payoff is $(0.23)(0.35) = 0.08$; and the probability of the $5 million payoff is $(0.23)(0.65) = 0.15$. The following table showing the probability distribution for the payoffs for the PDC

FIGURE 4.13   PDC DECISION TREE SHOWING ONLY BRANCHES ASSOCIATED WITH OPTIMAL DECISION STRATEGY

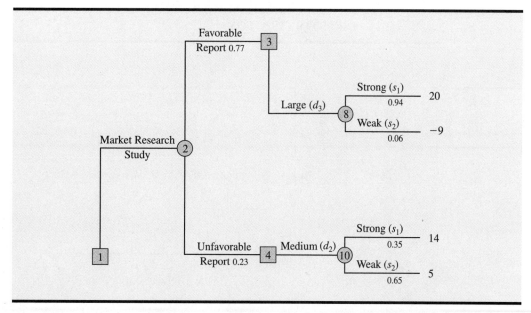

optimal decision strategy is the tabular representation of the risk profile for the optimal decision strategy.

Payoff ($ Million)	Probability
−9	0.05
5	0.15
14	0.08
20	0.72
	1.00

Figure 4.14 provides a graphical representation of the risk profile. Comparing Figures 4.5 and 4.14, we see that the PDC risk profile is changed by the strategy to conduct the market research study. In fact, the use of the market research study has lowered the probability of the $9 million loss from 0.20 to 0.05. PDC's management would most likely view that change as a significant reduction in the risk associated with the condominium project.

Expected Value of Sample Information

In the PDC problem, the market research study is the sample information used to determine the optimal decision strategy. The expected value associated with the market research study is $15.93. In Section 4.3 we showed that the best expected value if the market research study is *not* undertaken is $14.20. Thus, we can conclude that the difference, $15.93 − $14.20 = $1.73, is the **expected value of sample information.** In other words, conducting the market research study adds $1.73 million to the PDC expected value. In general, the expected value of sample information is as follows:

The EVSI = $1.73 million suggests PDC should be willing to pay up to $1.73 million to conduct the market research study.

$$\text{EVSI} = |\text{EVwSI} - \text{EVwoSI}| \qquad (4.13)$$

FIGURE 4.14   RISK PROFILE FOR PDC CONDOMINIUM PROJECT WITH SAMPLE INFORMATION SHOWING PAYOFFS ASSOCIATED WITH OPTIMAL DECISION STRATEGY

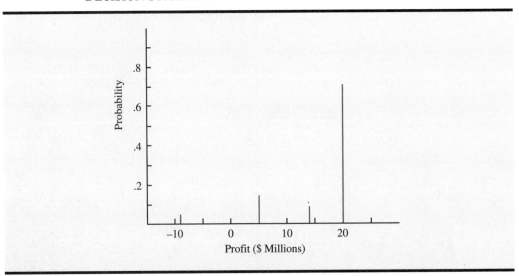

where

$\qquad$ EVSI = expected value of sample information

$\qquad$ EVwSI = expected value *with* sample information about the states of nature

$\qquad$ EVwoSI = expected value *without* sample information about the states of nature

Note the role of the absolute value in equation (4.13). For minimization problems the expected value with sample information is always less than or equal to the expected value without sample information. In this case, EVSI is the magnitude of the difference between EVwSI and EVwoSI; thus, by taking the absolute value of the difference as shown in equation (4.13), we can handle both the maximization and minimization cases with one equation.

Efficiency of Sample Information

In Section 4.3 we showed that the expected value of perfect information (EVPI) for the PDC problem is $3.2 million. We never anticipated that the market research report would obtain perfect information, but we can use an **efficiency** measure to express the value of the market research information. With perfect information having an efficiency rating of 100%, the efficiency rating E for sample information is computed as follows.

$$E = \frac{EVSI}{EVPI} \times 100 \qquad (4.14)$$

For the PDC problem,

$$E = \frac{1.73}{3.2} \times 100 = 54.1\%$$

In other words, the information from the market research study is 54.1% as efficient as perfect information.

Low efficiency ratings for sample information might lead the decision maker to look for other types of information. However, high efficiency ratings indicate that the sample information is almost as good as perfect information and that additional sources of information would not yield significantly better results.

4.6   COMPUTING BRANCH PROBABILITIES

In Section 4.5 the branch probabilities for the PDC decision tree chance nodes were specified in the problem description. No computations were required to determine these probabilities. In this section we show how **Bayes Theorem,** a topic covered in Chapter 2, can be used to compute branch probabilities for decision trees.

The PDC decision tree is shown again in Figure 4.15. Let

$\qquad F$ = Favorable market research report

$\qquad U$ = Unfavorable market research report

$\qquad s_1$ = Strong demand (state of nature 1)

$\qquad s_2$ = Weak demand (state of nature 2)

At chance node 2, we need to know the branch probabilities $P(F)$ and $P(U)$. At chance nodes 6, 7, and 8, we need to know the branch probabilities $P(s_1 \mid F)$, the probability of state of nature 1 given a favorable market research report, and $P(s_2 \mid F)$, the probability of state

FIGURE 4.15   THE PDC DECISION TREE

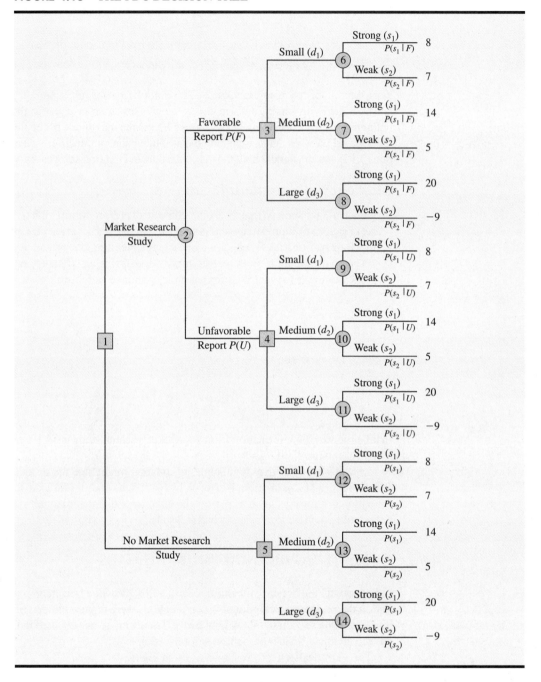

of nature 2 given a favorable market research report. $P(s_1 \mid F)$ and $P(s_2 \mid F)$ are referred to as **posterior probabilities** because they are conditional probabilities based on the outcome of the sample information. At chance nodes 9, 10, and 11, we need to know the branch probabilities $P(s_1 \mid U)$ and $P(s_2 \mid U)$; note that these are also posterior probabilities, denoting the probabilities of the two states of nature *given* that the market research report is unfavorable. Finally at chance nodes 12, 13, and 14, we need the probabilities for the states of nature, $P(s_1)$ and $P(s_2)$, if the market research study is not undertaken.

In making the probability computations, we need to know PDC's assessment of the probabilities for the two states of nature, $P(s_1)$ and $P(s_2)$; these are the prior probabilities as discussed earlier. In addition, we must know the **conditional probability** of the market research outcomes (the sample information) *given* each state of nature. For example, we need to know the conditional probability of a favorable market research report given that the state of nature is strong demand for the PDC project; note that this conditional probability of F given state of nature s_1 is written $P(F \mid s_1)$. To carry out the probability calculations, we will need conditional probabilities for all sample outcomes given all states of nature, that is, $P(F \mid s_1)$, $P(F \mid s_2)$, $P(U \mid s_1)$ and $P(U \mid s_2)$. In the PDC problem, we assume that the following assessments are available for these conditional probabilities.

	Market Research	
State of Nature	**Favorable, F**	**Unfavorable, U**
Strong demand, s_1	$P(F \mid s_1) = 0.90$	$P(U \mid s_1) = 0.10$
Weak demand, s_2	$P(F \mid s_2) = 0.25$	$P(U \mid s_2) = 0.75$

Note that the preceding probability assessments provide a reasonable degree of confidence in the market research study. If the true state of nature is s_1, the probability of a favorable market research report is 0.90, and the probability of an unfavorable market research report is 0.10. If the true state of nature is s_2, the probability of a favorable market research report is 0.25, and the probability of an unfavorable market research report is 0.75. The reason for a 0.25 probability of a potentially misleading favorable market research report for state of nature s_2 is that when some potential buyers first hear about the new condominium project, their enthusiasm may lead them to overstate their real interest in it. A potential buyer's initial favorable response can change quickly to a "no thank you" when later faced with the reality of signing a purchase contract and making a down payment.

In the following discussion, we present a tabular approach as a convenient method for carrying out the probability computations. The computations for the PDC problem based on a favorable market research report (F) are summarized in Table 4.7. The steps used to develop this table are as follows.

Step 1.   In column 1 enter the states of nature. In column 2 enter the *prior probabilities* for the states of nature. In column 3 enter the *conditional probabilities* of a favorable market research report (F) given each state of nature.

Step 2.   In column 4 compute the **joint probabilities** by multiplying the prior probability values in column 2 by the corresponding conditional probability values in column 3.

Step 3.   Sum the joint probabilities in column 4 to obtain the probability of a favorable market research report, $P(F)$.

Step 4.   Divide each joint probability in column 4 by $P(F) = 0.77$ to obtain the revised or *posterior probabilities, $P(s_1 \mid F)$ and $P(s_2 \mid F)$*.

Table 4.7 shows that the probability of obtaining a favorable market research report is $P(F) = 0.77$. In addition, $P(s_1 \mid F) = 0.94$ and $P(s_2 \mid F) = 0.06$. In particular, note that a favorable market research report will prompt a revised or posterior probability of 0.94 that the market demand of the condominium will be strong, s_1.

The tabular probability computation procedure must be repeated for each possible sample information outcome. Thus, Table 4.8 shows the computations of the branch probabilities of the PDC problem based on an unfavorable market research report. Note that the probability of obtaining an unfavorable market research report is $P(U) = 0.23$. If an

TABLE 4.7 BRANCH PROBABILITIES FOR THE PDC CONDOMINIUM PROJECT BASED ON A FAVORABLE MARKET RESEARCH REPORT

States of Nature s_j	Prior Probabilities $P(s_j)$	Conditional Probabilities $P(F \mid s_j)$	Joint Probabilities $P(F \cap s_j)$	Posterior Probabilities $P(s_j \mid F)$
s_1	0.8	0.90	0.72	0.94
s_2	0.2	0.25	0.05	0.06
	1.0		$P(F) = 0.77$	1.00

TABLE 4.8 BRANCH PROBABILITIES FOR THE PDC CONDOMINIUM PROJECT BASED ON AN UNFAVORABLE MARKET RESEARCH REPORT

States of Nature s_j	Prior Probabilities $P(s_j)$	Conditional Probabilities $P(U \mid s_j)$	Joint Probabilities $P(U \cap s_j)$	Posterior Probabilities $P(s_j \mid U)$
s_1	0.8	0.10	0.08	0.35
s_2	0.2	0.75	0.15	0.65
	1.0		$P(U) = 0.23$	1.00

unfavorable report is obtained, the posterior probability of a strong market demand, s_1, is 0.35 and of a weak market demand, s_2, is 0.65. The branch probabilities from Tables 4.7 and 4.8 were shown on the PDC decision tree in Figure 4.9.

Problem 22 asks you to compute the posterior probabilities.

The discussion in this section shows an underlying relationship between the probabilities on the various branches in a decision tree. To assume different prior probabilities, $P(s_1)$ and $P(s_2)$, without determining how these changes would alter $P(F)$ and $P(U)$, as well as the posterior probabilities $P(s_1 \mid F)$, $P(s_2 \mid F)$, $P(s_1 \mid U)$ and $P(s_2 \mid U)$ would be inappropriate.

SUMMARY

Decision analysis can be used to determine a recommended decision alternative or an optimal decision strategy when a decision maker is faced with an uncertain and risk-filled pattern of future events. The goal of decision analysis is to identify the best decision alternative or the optimal decision strategy given information about the uncertain events and the possible consequences or payoffs. The uncertain future events are called chance events and the outcomes of the chance events are called states of nature.

We showed how influence diagrams, payoff tables, and decision trees could be used to structure a decision problem and describe the relationships among the decisions, the chance events, and the consequences. We presented three approaches to decision making without probabilities: the optimistic approach, the conservative approach, and the minimax regret approach. When probability assessments are provided for the states of nature, the expected value approach can be used to identify the recommended decision alternative or decision strategy.

In cases where sample information about the chance events is available, a sequence of decisions has to be made. First we must decide whether to obtain the sample information.

If the answer to this decision is yes, an optimal decision strategy based on the specific sample information must be developed. In this situation, decision trees and the expected value approach can be used to determine the optimal decision strategy.

Even though the expected value approach can be used to obtain a recommended decision alternative or optimal decision strategy, the payoff that actually occurs will usually have a value different from the expected value. A risk profile provides a probability distribution for the possible payoffs and can assist the decision maker in assessing the risks associated with different decision alternatives. Finally, sensitivity analysis can be conducted to determine the effect changes in the probabilities for the states of nature and changes in the values of the payoffs have on the recommended decision alternative.

Decision analysis has been widely used in practice. The Q. M. in Action: Investing in a Power Transmission System describes how Oglethorpe Power Corporation used decision analysis to decide whether to invest in a major transmission system between Georgia and Florida. The Quantitative Methods in Practice at the end of the chapter describes how Ohio Edison used decision analysis to select equipment that helped the company meet emission standards.

Q. M. IN ACTION

INVESTING IN A TRANSMISSION SYSTEM

Oglethorpe Power Corporation (OPC) provides wholesale electrical power to consumer-owned cooperatives in the state of Georgia. Florida Power Corporation proposed that OPC join in the building of a major transmission line from Georgia to Florida. Deciding whether to become involved in the building of the transmission line was a major decision for OPC because it would involve the commitment of substantial OPC resources. OPC worked with Applied Decision Analysis, Inc., to conduct a comprehensive decision analysis of the problem.

In the problem formulation step, three decisions were identified: (1) deciding whether to build a transmission line from Georgia to Florida; (2) deciding whether to upgrade existing transmission facilities; and (3) deciding who would control the new facilities. Oglethorpe was faced with five chance events: (1) construction costs, (2) competition, (3) demand in Florida, (4) OPC's share of the operation, and (5) pricing. The consequence or payoff was measured in terms of dollars saved. The influence diagram for the problem had three decision nodes, five chance nodes, a consequence node,

and several intermediate nodes that described intermediate calculations. The decision tree for the problem had more than 8000 paths from the starting node to the terminal branches.

An expected value analysis of the decision tree provided an optimal decision strategy for OPC. However, the risk profile for the optimal decision strategy showed that the recommended strategy was very risky and had a significant probability of increasing OPC's cost rather than providing a savings. The risk analysis led to the conclusion that more information about the competition was needed in order to reduce OPC's risk. Sensitivity analysis involving various probabilities and payoffs showed that the value of the optimal decision strategy was stable over a reasonable range of input values. The final recommendation from the decision analysis was that OPC should begin negotiations with Florida Power Corporation concerning the building of the new transmission line.

Based on Borison, Adam, "Oglethorpe Power Corporation Decides about Investing in a Major Transmission System" *Interfaces,* March–April, 1995, pp. 25–36.

GLOSSARY

Chance event   An uncertain future event affecting the consequence, or payoff, associated with a decision.

States of nature   The possible outcomes for chance events that affect the payoff associated with a decision alternative.

Influence diagram   A graphical device that shows the relationship among decisions, chance events, and consequences for a decision problem.

Consequence   The result obtained when a decision alternative is chosen and a chance event occurs. A measure of the consequence is often called a payoff.

Payoff   A measure of the consequence of a decision such as profit, cost, or time. Each combination of a decision alternative and a state of nature has an associated payoff, (consequence).

Payoff table   A tabular representation of the payoffs for a decision problem.

Decision tree   A graphical representation of the decision problem that shows the sequential nature of the decision-making process.

Node   An intersection or junction point of an influence diagram or a decision tree.

Decision nodes   Nodes indicating points where a decision is made.

Chance nodes   Nodes indicating points where an uncertain event will occur.

Branch   Lines showing the alternatives from decision nodes and the outcomes from chance nodes.

Optimistic approach   An approach to choosing a decision alternative without using probabilities. For a maximization problem, it leads to choosing the decision alternative corresponding to the largest payoff; for a minimization problem, it leads to choosing the decision alternative corresponding to the smallest payoff.

Conservative approach   An approach to choosing a decision alternative without using probabilities. For a maximization problem, it leads to choosing the decision alternative that maximizes the minimum payoff; for a minimization problem, it leads to choosing the decision alternative that minimizes the maximum payoff.

Minimax regret approach   An approach to choosing a decision alternative without using probabilities. For each alternative, the maximum regret is computed, which leads to choosing the decision alternative that minimizes the maximum regret.

Opportunity loss, or regret   The amount of loss (lower profit or higher cost) from not making the best decision for each state of nature.

Expected value approach   An approach to choosing a decision alternative that is based on the expected value of each decision alternative. The recommended decision alternative is the one that provides the best expected value.

Expected value (EV)   For a chance node, it is the weighted average of the payoffs. The weights are the state-of-nature probabilities.

Expected value of perfect information (EVPI)   The expected value of information that would tell the decision maker exactly which state of nature is going to occur (i.e., perfect information).

Decision strategy   A strategy involving a sequence of decisions and chance outcomes to provide the optimal solution to a decision problem.

Risk analysis   The study of the possible payoffs and probabilities associated with a decision alternative or a decision strategy.

Risk profile   The probability distribution of the possible payoffs associated with a decision alternative or decision strategy.

Sensitivity analysis   The study of how changes in the probability assessments for the states of nature and/or changes in the payoffs affect the recommended decision alternative.

Prior probabilities   The probabilities of the states of nature prior to obtaining sample information.

Sample information   New information obtained through research or experimentation that enables an updating or revision of the state-of-nature probabilities.

Posterior (revised) probabilities   The probabilities of the states of nature after revising the prior probabilities based on sample information.

Expected value of sample information (EVSI)   The difference between the expected value of an optimal strategy based on sample information and the "best" expected value without any sample information.

Efficiency   The ratio of EVSI to EVPI as a percent; perfect information is 100% efficient.

Bayes theorem   A probability expression that enables the use of sample information to revise prior probabilities.

Conditional probabilities   The probability of one event given the known outcome of a (possibly) related event.

Joint probabilities   The probabilities of both sample information and a particular state of nature occurring simultaneously.

PROBLEMS

SELFtest

1. The following payoff table shows profit for a decision analysis problem with two decision alternatives and three states of nature.

	State of Nature		
Decision Alternative	s_1	s_2	s_3
d_1	250	100	25
d_2	100	100	75

    a.   Construct a decision tree for this problem.
    b.   If the decision maker knows nothing about the probabilities of the three states of nature, what is the recommended decision using the optimistic, conservative, and minimax regret approaches?

2. Suppose that a decision maker faced with four decision alternatives and four states of nature develops the following profit payoff table.

	State of Nature			
Decision Alternative	s_1	s_2	s_3	s_4
d_1	14	9	10	5
d_2	11	10	8	7
d_3	9	10	10	11
d_4	8	10	11	13

    a.   If the decision maker knows nothing about the probabilities of the four states of nature, what is the recommended decision using the optimistic, conservative, and minimax regret approaches?
    b.   Which approach do you prefer? Explain. Is establishing the most appropriate approach before analyzing the problem important for the decision maker? Explain.
    c.   Assume that the payoff table provides *cost* rather than profit payoffs. What is the recommended decision using the optimistic, conservative, and minimax regret approaches?

SELFtest

3. Southland Corporation's decision to produce a new line of recreational products has resulted in the need to construct either a small plant or a large plant. The best selection of plant size depends on how the marketplace reacts to the new product line. To conduct an analysis, marketing management has decided to view the possible long-run demand as either low, medium, or high. The following payoff table shows the projected profit in millions of dollars:

	Long-Run Demand		
Plant Size	**Low**	**Medium**	**High**
Small	150	200	200
Large	50	200	500

a. What is the decision to be made, and what is the chance event for Southland's problem?
b. Construct an influence diagram.
c. Construct a decision tree.
d. Recommend a decision based on the use of the optimistic, conservative, and minimax regret approaches.

4. Amy Lloyd is interested in leasing a new Saab and has contacted three automobile dealers for pricing information. Each dealer has offered Amy a closed-end 36-month lease with no down payment due at the time of signing. Each lease includes a monthly charge and a mileage allowance. Additional miles receive a surcharge on a per-mile basis. The monthly lease cost, the mileage allowance, and the cost for additional miles follow:

Dealer	Monthly Cost	Mileage Allowance	Cost per Additional Mile
Forno Saab	$299	36,000	$0.15
Midtown Motors	$310	45,000	$0.20
Hopkins Automotive	$325	54,000	$0.15

Amy has decided to choose the lease option that will minimize her total 36-month cost. The difficulty is that Amy is not sure how many miles she will drive over the next three years. For purposes of this decision she believes it is reasonable to assume that she will drive 12,000 miles per year, 15,000 miles per year, or 18,000 miles per year. With this assumption Amy has estimated her total costs for the three lease options. For example, she figures that the Forno Saab lease will cost her $10,764 if she drives 12,000 miles per year, $12,114 if she drives 15,000 miles per year, or $13,464 if she drives 18,000 miles per year.

a. What is the decision, and what is the chance event?
b. Construct a payoff table for Amy's problem.
c. If Amy has no idea which of the three mileage assumptions is most appropriate, what is the recommended decision (leasing option) using the optimistic, conservative, and minimax regret approaches?
d. Suppose that the probabilities that Amy drives 12,000, 15,000, and 18,000 miles per year are 0.5, 0.4, and 0.1, respectively. What option should Amy choose using the expected value approach?
e. Develop a risk profile for the decision selected in Part (d). What is the most likely cost, and what is its probability?

f. Suppose that after further consideration, Amy concludes that the probabilities that she will drive 12,000, 15,000, and 18,000 miles per year are 0.3, 0.4, and 0.3, respectively. What decision should Amy make using the expected value approach?

SELFtest   5. The following profit payoff table was presented in Problem 1. Suppose that the decision maker has obtained the probability assessments: $P(s_1) = 0.65$, $P(s_2) = 0.15$, and $P(s_3) = 0.20$. Use the expected value approach to determine the optimal decision.

	State of Nature		
Decision Alternative	s_1	s_2	s_3
d_1	250	100	25
d_2	100	100	75

6. The profit payoff table presented in Problem 2 is repeated here.

	State of Nature			
Decision Alternative	s_1	s_2	s_3	s_4
d_1	14	9	10	5
d_2	11	10	8	7
d_3	9	10	10	11
d_4	8	10	11	13

Suppose that the decision maker obtains information that enables the following probability assessments to be made: $P(s_1) = 0.5$, $P(s_2) = 0.2$, $P(s_3) = 0.2$, and $P(s_4) = 0.1$.
   a. Use the expected value approach to determine the optimal decision.
   b. Now assume that the entries in the payoff table are costs; use the expected value approach to determine the optimal decision.

SELFtest   7. Hudson Corporation is considering three options for managing its data processing operation: continuing with its own staff, hiring an outside vendor to do the managing (referred to as *outsourcing*), or using a combination of its own staff and an outside vendor. The cost of the operation depends on future demand. The annual cost of each option (in $000s) depends on demand as follows.

Staffing Options	Demand		
	High	Medium	Low
Own Staff	650	650	600
Outside Vendor	900	600	300
Combination	800	650	500

   a. If the demand probabilities are 0.2, 0.5, and 0.3, which decision alternative will minimize the expected cost of the data processing operation? What is the expected annual cost associated with that recommendation?
   b. Construct a risk profile for the optimal decision in part (a). What is the probability of the cost exceeding $700,000?

SELFtest   8.   The following payoff table shows the profit for a decision problem with two states of nature and two decision alternatives.

		State of Nature	
Decision Alternative		s_1	s_2
d_1		10	1
d_2		4	3

    a.   Use graphical sensitivity analysis to determine the range of probabilities of state of nature s_1 for which each of the decision alternatives has the largest expected value.

    b.   Suppose $P(s_1) = 0.2$ and $P(s_2) = 0.8$. What is the best decision using the expected value approach?

    c.   Perform sensitivity analysis on the payoffs for decision alternative d_1. Assume the probabilities are as given in part (b) and find the range of payoffs under states of nature s_1 and s_2 that will keep the solution found in part (b) optimal. Is the solution more sensitive to the payoff under state of nature s_1 or s_2?

9.   Myrtle Air Express has decided to offer direct service from Cleveland to Myrtle Beach. Management must decide between a full price service using the company's new fleet of jet aircraft and a discount service using smaller capacity commuter planes. It is clear that the best choice depends on the market reaction to the service Myrtle Air offers. Management has developed estimates of the contribution to profit for each type of service based upon two possible levels of demand for service to Myrtle Beach: strong and weak. The following table shows the estimated quarterly profits in thousands of dollars.

	Demand for Service	
Service	**Strong**	**Weak**
Full Price	$960	−$490
Discount	$670	$320

    a.   What is the decision to be made, what is the chance event, and what is the consequence for this problem? How many decision alternatives are there? How many outcomes are there for the chance event?

    b.   If nothing is known about the probabilities of the chance outcomes, what is the recommended decision using the optimistic, conservative, and minimax regret approaches?

    c.   Suppose that management of Myrtle Air Express believes that the probability of strong demand is 0.7 and the probability of weak demand is 0.3. Use the expected value approach to determine an optimal decision.

    d.   Suppose that the probability of strong demand is 0.8 and the probability of weak demand is 0.2. What is the optimal decision using the expected value approach?

    e.   Use graphical sensitivity analysis to determine the range of demand probabilities for which each of the decision alternatives has the largest expected value.

10.   Political Systems, Inc., is a new firm specializing in information services such as surveys and data analysis for individuals running for political office. The firm is opening its headquarters in Chicago and is considering three office locations, which differ in cost due to square footage and office equipment requirements. The profit projections shown (in thousands of dollars) for each location were based on both strong demand and weak demand states of nature.

	Demand	
Office Location	Strong	Weak
A	200	−20
B	120	10
C	100	60

    a.   Initially, management is uncomfortable stating probabilities for the states of nature. Let p denote the probability of the strong demand state of nature. What does graphical sensitivity analysis tell management about location preferences? Can any location be dropped from consideration? Why or why not?

    b.   After further review, management estimated the probability of a strong demand at 0.65. Based on the results in part (a), which location should be selected? What is the expected value associated with that decision?

11. For the Pittsburgh Development Corporation problem in Section 4.3, the decision alternative to build the large condominium complex was found to be optimal using the expected value approach. In Section 4.4 we conducted a sensitivity analysis for the payoffs associated with this decision alternative. We found that the large complex remained optimal as long as the payoff for the strong demand was greater than or equal to $17.5 million and as long as the payoff for the weak demand was greater than or equal to −$19 million.

    a.   Consider the medium complex decision. How much could the payoff under strong demand increase and still keep decision alternative d_3 the optimal solution?

    b.   Consider the small complex decision. How much could the payoff under strong demand increase and still keep decision alternative d_3 the optimal solution?

12. The distance from Potsdam to larger markets and limited air service have hindered the town in attracting new industry. Air Express, a major overnight delivery service is considering establishing a regional distribution center in Potsdam. But Air Express will not establish the center unless the length of the runway at the local airport is increased. Another candidate for new development is Diagnostic Research, Inc. (DRI), a leading producer of medical testing equipment. DRI is considering building a new manufacturing plant. Increasing the length of the runway is not a requirement for DRI, but the planning commission feels that doing so will help convince DRI to locate their new plant in Potsdam. Assuming that the town lengthens the runway, the Potsdam planning commission believes that the probabilities shown in the following table are applicable.

	New DRI Plant	No DRI Plant
New Air Express Center	.30	.10
No Air Express Center	.40	.20

For instance, the probability that Air Express will establish a new distribution center and DRI will build a new plant is .30.

The estimated annual revenue to the town, after deducting the cost of lengthening the runway, is as follows:

	New DRI Plant	No New Plant
New Air Express Center	$600,000	$150,000
No Air Express Center	$250,000	−$200,000

If the runway expansion project is not conducted, the planning commission assesses the probability DRI will locate their new plant in Potsdam at 0.6; in this case, the estimated annual revenue to the town will be $450,000. If the runway expansion project is not conducted and DRI does not locate in Potsdam, the annual revenue will be $0 since no cost will have been incurred and no revenues will be forthcoming.

a. What is the decision to be made, what is the chance event, and what is the consequence?
b. Compute the expected annual revenue associated with the decision alternative to lengthen the runway.
c. Compute the expected annual revenue associated with the decision alternative to not lengthen the runway.
d. Should the town elect to lengthen the runway? Explain.
e. Suppose that the probabilities associated with lengthening the runway were as follows:

	New DRI Plant	No DRI Plant
New Air Express Center	.40	.10
No Air Express Center	.30	.20

What effect, if any, would this change in the probabilities have on the recommended decision?

13. Seneca Hill Winery has recently purchased land for the purpose of establishing a new vineyard. Management is considering two varieties of white grapes for the new vineyard: Chardonnay and Riesling. The Chardonnay grapes would be used to produce a dry Chardonnay wine, and the Riesling grapes would be used to produce a semi-dry Riesling wine. It takes approximately four years from the time of planting before new grapes can be harvested. This length of time creates a great deal of uncertainty concerning future demand and makes the decision concerning the type of grapes to plant difficult. Three possibilities are being considered: Chardonnay grapes only; Riesling grapes only; and both Chardonnay and Riesling grapes. Seneca management decided that for planning purposes it would be adequate to consider only two demand possibilities for each type of wine: strong or weak. With two possibilities for each type of wine it was necessary to assess four probabilities. With the help of some forecasts in industry publications management made the following probability assessments.

	Riesling Demand	
Chardonnay Demand	Weak	Strong
Weak	0.05	0.50
Strong	0.25	0.20

Revenue projections show an annual contribution to profit of $20,000 if Seneca Hill only plants Chardonnay grapes and demand is weak for Chardonnay wine, and $70,000 if they only plant Chardonnay grapes and demand is strong for Chardonnay wine. If they only plant Riesling grapes, the annual profit projection is $25,000 if demand is weak for Riesling grapes and $45,000 if demand is strong for Riesling grapes. If Seneca plants both types of grapes, the annual profit projections are shown in the following table.

	Riesling Demand	
Chardonnay Demand	**Weak**	**Strong**
Weak	$22,000	$40,000
Strong	$26,000	$60,000

a. What is the decision to be made, what is the chance event, and what is the consequence? Identify the alternatives for the decisions and the possible outcomes for the chance events.

b. Develop a decision tree.

c. Use the expected value approach to recommend which alternative Seneca Hill Winery should follow in order to maximize expected annual profit.

d. Suppose management is concerned about the probability assessments when demand for Chardonnay wine is strong. Some believe it is likely for Riesling demand to also be strong in this case. Suppose the probability of strong demand for Chardonnay and weak demand for Riesling is 0.05 and that the probability of strong demand for Chardonnay and strong demand for Riesling is 0.40. How does this change the recommended decision? Assume that the probabilities when Chardonnay demand is weak are still 0.05 and 0.50.

e. Other members of the management team expect the Chardonnay market to become saturated at some point in the future causing a fall in prices. Suppose that the annual profit projections fall to $50,000 when demand for Chardonnay is strong and Chardonnay grapes only are planted. Using the original probability assessments, determine how this change would affect the optimal decision.

SELFtest   14. The following profit payoff table was presented in Problems 1 and 5.

	State of Nature		
Decision Alternative	s_1	s_2	s_3
d_1	250	100	25
d_2	100	100	75

The probabilities for the states of nature are: $P(s_1) = 0.65$, $P(s_2) = 0.15$, and $P(s_3) = 0.20$.

a. What is the optimal decision strategy if perfect information were available?

b. What is the expected value for the decision strategy developed in part (a)?

c. Using the expected value approach, what is the recommended decision without perfect information? What is its expected value?

d. What is the expected value of perfect information?

15. The Lake Placid Town Council has decided to build a new community center to be used for conventions, concerts, and other public events. But, considerable controversy surrounds the appropriate size. Many influential citizens want a large center that would be a showcase for the area. But the mayor feels that if demand does not support such a center, the community will lose a large amount of money. To provide structure for the decision process, the council narrowed the building alternatives to three sizes: small, medium, and large. Everybody agreed that the critical factor in choosing the best size is the number of people who will want to use the new facility. A regional planning consultant provided demand estimates under three scenarios: worst case, base case, and best case. The worst-case scenario corresponds to a situation in which tourism drops significantly; the base-case

scenario corresponds to a situation in which Lake Placid continues to attract visitors at current levels; and the best-case scenario corresponds to a significant increase in tourism. The consultant has provided probability assessments of 0.10, 0.60, and 0.30 for the worst-case, base-case, and best-case scenarios, respectively.

The town council suggested using net cash flow over a five-year planning horizon as the criterion for deciding on the best size. The following projections of net cash flow, in thousands of dollars, for a five-year planning horizon have been developed. All costs, including the consultant's fee, have been included.

	Demand Scenario		
Center Size	Worst Case	Base Case	Best Case
Small	400	500	660
Medium	−250	650	800
Large	−400	580	990

a. What decision should Lake Placid make using the expected value approach?

b. Construct risk profiles for the medium and large alternatives. Given the mayor's concern over the possibility of losing money and the result of part (a), which alternative would you recommend?

c. Compute the expected value of perfect information. Do you think it would be worth trying to obtain additional information concerning which scenario is likely to occur?

d. Suppose the probability of the worst-case scenario increases to 0.2, the probability of the base-case scenario decreases to 0.5, and the probability of the best-case scenario remains at 0.3. What effect, if any, would these changes have on the decision recommendation?

e. The consultant has suggested that an expenditure of $150,000 on a promotional campaign over the planning horizon will effectively reduce the probability of the worst-case scenario to zero. If the campaign can be expected to also increase the probability of the best-case scenario to 0.4, is it a good investment?

SELFtest **16.** Consider a variation of the PDC decision tree shown in Figure 4.9. The company must first decide whether to undertake the market research study. If the market research study is conducted, the outcome will either be favorable (F) or unfavorable (U). Assume there are only two decision alternatives d_1 and d_2 and two states of nature s_1 and s_2. The payoff table showing profit is as follows:

	State of Nature	
Decision Alternative	s_1	s_2
d_1	100	300
d_2	400	200

a. Show the decision tree.

b. Using the following probabilities, what is the optimal decision strategy?

$$P(F) = 0.56 \quad P(s_1 \mid F) = 0.57 \quad P(s_1 \mid U) = 0.18 \quad P(s_1) = 0.40$$
$$P(U) = 0.44 \quad P(s_2 \mid F) = 0.43 \quad P(s_2 \mid U) = 0.82 \quad P(s_2) = 0.60$$

17. A real estate investor has the opportunity to purchase land currently zoned residential. If the county board approves a request to rezone the property as commercial within the next year, the investor will be able to lease the land to a large discount firm that wants to open a new store on the property. However, if the zoning change is not approved, the investor will have to sell the property at a loss. Profits (in $000s) are shown in the following payoff table.

	State of Nature	
Decision Alternative	**Rezoning Approved** s_1	**Rezoning Not Approved** s_2
Purchase, d_1	600	−200
Do not purchase, d_2	0	0

    a. If the probability that the rezoning will be approved is 0.5, what decision is recommended? What is the expected profit?

    b. The investor can purchase an option to buy the land. Under the option, the investor maintains the rights to purchase the land anytime during the next 3 months while learning more about possible resistance to the rezoning proposal from area residents. Probabilities are as follows.

$$\text{Let}\quad H = \text{High resistance to rezoning}$$
$$L = \text{Low resistance to rezoning}$$

$$P(H) = 0.55 \quad P(s_1 \mid H) = 0.18 \quad P(s_2 \mid H) = 0.82$$
$$P(L) = 0.45 \quad P(s_1 \mid L) = 0.89 \quad P(s_2 \mid L) = 0.11$$

    What is the optimal decision strategy if the investor uses the option period to learn more about the resistance from area residents before making the purchase decision?

    c. If the option will cost the investor an additional $10,000, should the investor purchase the option? Why or why not? What is the maximum that the investor should be willing to pay for the option?

18. McHuffter Condominiums, Inc., of Pensacola, Florida, recently purchased land near the Gulf of Mexico and is attempting to determine the size of the condominium development it should build. It is considering three sizes of developments: small, d_1; medium, d_2; and large, d_3. At the same time, an uncertain economy makes ascertaining the demand for the new condominiums difficult. McHuffter's management realizes that a large development followed by low demand could be very costly to the company. However, if McHuffter makes a conservative small-development decision and then finds a high demand, the firm's profits will be lower than they might have been. With the three levels of demand—low, medium, and high—McHuffter's management has prepared the following profit (in $000s) payoff table.

	State of Nature		
Decision Alternatives	**Low, s_1**	**Medium, s_2**	**High, s_3**
Small Condo, d_1	400	400	400
Medium Condo, d_2	100	600	600
Large Condo, d_3	−300	300	900

The probabilities for the states of nature are $P(s_1) = 0.20$, $P(s_2) = 0.35$, and $P(s_3) = 0.45$. Suppose that before making a final decision, McHuffter is considering conducting a survey to help evaluate the demand for the new condominium development. The survey report is anticipated to indicate one of three levels of demand: weak (W), average (A), or strong (S). The relevant probabilities are as follows:

$P(W) = 0.30$	$P(s_1 \mid W) = 0.39$	$P(s_1 \mid A) = 0.16$	$P(s_1 \mid S) = 0.06$
$P(A) = 0.38$	$P(s_2 \mid W) = 0.46$	$P(s_2 \mid A) = 0.37$	$P(s_2 \mid S) = 0.22$
$P(S) = 0.32$	$P(s_3 \mid W) = 0.15$	$P(s_3 \mid A) = 0.47$	$P(s_3 \mid S) = 0.72$

a. Construct a decision tree for this problem.
b. What is the recommended decision if the survey is not undertaken? What is the expected value?
c. What is the expected value of perfect information?
d. What is McHuffter's optimal decision strategy?
e. What is the expected value of the survey information?
f. What is the efficiency of the survey information?

19. Hale's TV Productions is considering producing a pilot for a comedy series in the hope of selling it to a major television network. The network may decide to reject the series, but it may also decide to purchase the rights to the series for either one or two years. At this point in time, Hale may either produce the pilot and wait for the network's decision or transfer the rights for the pilot and series to a competitor for $100,000. Hale's decision alternatives and profits (in thousands of dollars) are as follows:

	State of Nature		
Decision Alternative	Reject, s_1	1 Year, s_2	2 Years, s_3
Produce Pilot, d_1	-100	50	150
Sell to Competitor, d_2	100	100	100

The probabilities for the states of nature are $P(s_1) = 0.20$, $P(s_2) = 0.30$, and $P(s_3) = 0.50$. For a consulting fee of $5,000, an agency will review the plans for the comedy series and indicate the overall chances of a favorable network reaction to the series. Assume that the agency review will result in a favorable (F) or an unfavorable (U) review and that the following probabilities are relevant.

$P(F) = 0.69$	$P(s_1 \mid F) = 0.09$	$P(s_1 \mid U) = 0.45$
$P(U) = 0.31$	$P(s_2 \mid F) = 0.26$	$P(s_2 \mid U) = 0.39$
	$P(s_3 \mid F) = 0.65$	$P(s_3 \mid U) = 0.16$

a. Construct a decision tree for this problem.
b. What is the recommended decision if the agency opinion is not used? What is the expected value?
c. What is the expected value of perfect information?
d. What is Hale's optimal decision strategy assuming the agency's information is used?
e. What is the expected value of the agency's information?
f. Is the agency's information worth the $5,000 fee? What is the maximum that Hale should be willing to pay for the information?
g. What is the recommended decision?

20. Martin's Service Station is considering entering the snowplowing business for the coming winter season. Martin can purchase either a snowplow blade attachment for the station's pick-up truck or a new heavy-duty snowplow truck. Martin has analyzed the situation and believes that either alternative would be a profitable investment if the snowfall is heavy. Smaller profits would result if the snowfall is moderate, and losses would result if the snowfall is light. The following profits have been determined.

| | State of Nature | | |
Decision Alternatives	Heavy, s_1	Moderate, s_2	Light, s_3
Blade Attachment, d_1	3500	1000	−1500
New Snowplow, d_2	7000	2000	−9000

The probabilities for the states of nature are $P(s_1) = 0.4$, $P(s_2) = 0.3$, and $P(s_3) = 0.3$. Suppose that Martin decides to wait until September before making a final decision. Assessments of the probabilities associated with a normal (N) or unseasonably cold (U) September are as follows:

$$P(N) = 0.80 \quad P(s_1 \mid N) = 0.35 \quad P(s_1 \mid U) = 0.62$$
$$P(U) = 0.20 \quad P(s_2 \mid N) = 0.30 \quad P(s_2 \mid U) = 0.31$$
$$P(s_3 \mid N) = 0.35 \quad P(s_3 \mid U) = 0.07$$

a. Construct a decision tree for this problem.
b. What is the recommended decision if Martin does not wait until September? What is the expected value?
c. What is the expected value of perfect information?
d. What is Martin's optimal decision strategy if the decision is not made until the September weather is determined? What is the expected value of this decision strategy?

21. Lawson's Department Store faces a buying decision for a seasonal product for which demand can be high, medium, and low. The purchaser for Lawson's can order 1, 2, or 3 lots of the product before the season begins but cannot reorder later. Profit projections (in $000s) are shown.

| | State of Nature | | |
| | High Demand | Medium Demand | Low Demand |
Decision Alternative	s_1	s_2	s_3
Order 1 lot, d_1	60	60	50
Order 2 lots, d_2	80	80	30
Order 3 lots, d_3	100	70	10

a. If the prior probabilities for the three states of nature are 0.3, 0.3, and 0.4, respectively, what is the recommended order quantity?
b. At each preseason sales meeting, the vice-president of sales provides a personal opinion regarding potential demand for this product. Because of the vice-president's enthusiasm and optimistic nature, the predictions of market conditions have always been either "excellent" (E) or "very good" (V). Probabilities are as follows. What is the optimal decision strategy?

$$P(E) = 0.70 \qquad P(s_1 \mid E) = 0.34 \qquad P(s_1 \mid V) = 0.20$$
$$P(V) = 0.30 \qquad P(s_2 \mid E) = 0.32 \qquad P(s_2 \mid V) = 0.26$$
$$P(s_3 \mid E) = 0.34 \qquad P(s_3 \mid V) = 0.54$$

c. Use the efficiency of sample information and discuss whether the firm should consider a consulting expert who could provide independent forecasts of market conditions for the product.

22. Suppose that you are given a decision situation with three possible states of nature: s_1, s_2, and s_3. The prior probabilities are $P(s_1) = 0.2$, $P(s_2) = 0.5$, and $P(s_3) = 0.3$. With sample information I, $P(I \mid s_1) = 0.1$, $P(I \mid s_2) = 0.05$, and $P(I \mid s_3) = 0.2$. Compute the revised or posterior probabilities: $P(s_1 \mid I)$, $P(s_2 \mid I)$, and $P(s_3 \mid I)$.

23. In the following profit payoff table for a decision problem with two states of nature and three decision alternatives, the prior probabilities, for s_1 and s_2 are $P(s_1) = 0.8$ and $P(s_2) = 0.2$.

	State of Nature	
Decision Alternative	s_1	s_2
d_1	15	10
d_2	10	12
d_3	8	20

a. What is the optimal decision?
b. Find the EVPI.
c. Suppose that sample information I is obtained, with $P(I \mid s_1) = 0.2$ and $P(I \mid s_2) = 0.75$. Find the posterior probabilities $P(s_1 \mid I)$ and $P(s_2 \mid I)$. Recommend a decision alternative based on these probabilities.

24. To save on expenses, Rona and Jerry agreed to form a carpool for traveling to and from work. Rona preferred to use the somewhat longer but more consistent Queen City Avenue. Although Jerry preferred the quicker expressway, he agreed with Rona that they should take Queen City Avenue if the expressway had a traffic jam. The following payoff table provides the one-way time estimate in minutes for traveling to or from work.

	State of Nature	
	Expressway Open	Expressway Jammed
Decision Alternative	s_1	s_2
Queen City Avenue, d_1	30	30
Expressway, d_2	25	45

Based on their experience with traffic problems, Rona and Jerry agreed on a 0.15 probability that the expressway would be jammed.

In addition, they agreed that weather seemed to affect the traffic conditions on the expressway. Let

$$C = \text{clear}$$
$$O = \text{overcast}$$
$$R = \text{rain}$$

The following conditional probabilities apply.

$$P(C \mid s_1) = 0.8 \qquad P(O \mid s_1) = 0.2 \qquad P(R \mid s_1) = 0.0$$
$$P(C \mid s_2) = 0.1 \qquad P(O \mid s_2) = 0.3 \qquad P(R \mid s_2) = 0.6$$

a. Use the Bayes' probability revision procedure to compute the probability of each weather condition and the conditional probability of the expressway open s_1 or jammed s_2 given each weather condition.
b. Show the decision tree for this problem.
c. What is the optimal decision strategy, and what is the expected travel time?

25. The Gorman Manufacturing Company must decide whether to manufacture a component part at its Milan, Michigan, plant or purchase the component part from a supplier. The resulting profit is dependent upon the demand for the product. The following payoff table shows the projected profit (in $000s).

	State of Nature		
	Low Demand	Medium Demand	High Demand
Decision Alternative	s_1	s_2	s_3
Manufacture, d_1	−20	40	100
Purchase, d_2	10	45	70

The state-of-nature probabilities are $P(s_1) = 0.35$, $P(s_2) = 0.35$, and $P(s_3) = 0.30$.
a. Use a decision tree to recommend a decision.
b. Use EVPI to determine whether Gorman should attempt to obtain a better estimate of demand.
c. A test market study of the potential demand for the product is expected to report either a favorable (F) or unfavorable (U) condition. The relevant conditional probabilities are as follows:

$$P(F \mid s_1) = 0.10 \qquad P(U \mid s_1) = 0.90$$
$$P(F \mid s_2) = 0.40 \qquad P(U \mid s_2) = 0.60$$
$$P(F \mid s_3) = 0.60 \qquad P(U \mid s_3) = 0.40$$

What is the probability that the market research report will be favorable?
d. What is Gorman's optimal decision strategy?
e. What is the expected value of the market research information?
f. What is the efficiency of the information?

Case Problem   PROPERTY PURCHASE STRATEGY

Glenn Foreman, president of Oceanview Development Corporation, is considering submitting a bid to purchase property that will be sold by sealed bid at a county tax foreclosure. Glenn's initial judgment is to submit a bid of $5 million. Based on his experience, Glenn estimates that a bid of $5 million will have a 0.2 probability of being the highest bid and securing the property for Oceanview. The current date is June 1. Sealed bids for the property must be submitted by August 15. The winning bid will be announced on September 1.

If Oceanview submits the highest bid and obtains the property, the firm plans to build and sell a complex of luxury condominiums. However, a complicating factor is that the property is currently zoned for single-family residences only. Glenn believes that a referendum could be placed on the voting ballot in time for the November election. Passage of the referendum would change the zoning of the property and permit construction of the condominiums.

The sealed-bid procedure requires the bid to be submitted with a certified check for 10% of the amount bid. If the bid is rejected, the deposit is refunded. If the bid is accepted, the deposit is the down payment for the property. However, if the bid is accepted and the bidder does not follow through with the purchase and meet the remainder of the financial obligation within six months, the deposit will be forfeited. In this case, the county will offer the property to the next highest bidder.

To determine whether Oceanview should submit the $5 million bid, Glenn has done some preliminary analysis. This preliminary work provided an assessment of 0.3 for the probability that the referendum for a zoning change will be approved and resulted in the following estimates of the costs and revenues that will be incurred if the condominiums are built.

Cost and Revenue Estimates

Revenue from condominium sales	$15,000,000
Cost	
Property	$5,000,000
Construction expenses	$8,000,000

If Oceanview obtains the property and the zoning change is rejected in November, Glenn believes that the best option would be for the firm not to complete the purchase of the property. In this case, Oceanview would forfeit the 10% deposit that accompanied the bid.

Because the likelihood that the zoning referendum will be approved is such an important factor in the decision process, Glenn has suggested that the firm hire a market research service to conduct a survey of voters. The survey would provide a better estimate of the likelihood that the referendum for a zoning change would be approved. The market research firm that Oceanview Development has worked with in the past has agreed to do the study for $15,000. The results of the study will be available August 1, so that Oceanview will have this information before the August 15 bid deadline. The results of the survey will be either a prediction that the zoning change will be approved or a prediction that the zoning change will be rejected. After considering the record of the market research service in previous studies conducted for Oceanview, Glenn has developed the following probability estimates concerning the accuracy of the market research information.

$$P(A \mid s_1) = 0.9 \qquad P(N \mid s_1) = 0.1$$
$$P(A \mid s_2) = 0.2 \qquad P(N \mid s_2) = 0.8$$

where

A = prediction of zoning change approval
N = prediction that zoning change will not be approved
s_1 = the zoning change is approved by the voters
s_2 = the zoning change is rejected by the voters

Managerial Report

Perform an analysis of the problem facing the Oceanview Development Corporation, and prepare a report that summarizes your findings and recommendations. Include the following items in your report:

1. A decision tree that shows the logical sequence of the decision problem
2. A recommendation regarding what Oceanview should do if the market research information is not available
3. A decision strategy that Oceanview should follow if the market research is conducted
4. A recommendation as to whether Oceanview should employ the market research firm, along with the value of the information provided by the market research firm. Include the details of your analysis as an appendix to your report.

Case Problem   LAWSUIT DEFENSE STRATEGY

John Campbell, an employee of Manhattan Construction Company, claims to have injured his back as a result of a fall while repairing the roof at one of the Eastview apartment buildings. He has filed a lawsuit against Doug Reynolds, the owner of Eastview Apartments, asking for damages of $1,500,000. John claims that the roof had rotten sections and that his fall could have been prevented if Mr. Reynolds had told Manhattan Construction about the problem. Mr. Reynolds has notified his insurance company, Allied Insurance, of the lawsuit. Allied must defend Mr. Reynolds and decide what action to take regarding the lawsuit.

Some depositions have been taken, and a series of discussions have taken place between both sides. As a result, John Campbell has offered to accept a settlement of $750,000. Thus, one option is for Allied to pay John $750,000 to settle the claim. Allied is also considering making John a counteroffer of $400,000 in the hope that he will accept a lesser amount to avoid the time and cost of going to trial. But, Allied's preliminary investigation has shown that John has a strong case; Allied is concerned that John may reject their counteroffer and request a jury trial. Allied's lawyers have spent some time exploring John's likely reaction if they make a counteroffer of $400,000.

The lawyers have concluded that it is adequate to consider three possible outcomes to represent John's possible reaction to a counteroffer of $400,000: (1) John will accept the counteroffer and the case will be closed; (2) John will reject the counteroffer and elect to have a jury decide the settlement amount; or (3) John will make a counteroffer to Allied of $600,000. If John does make a counteroffer, Allied has decided that they will not make additional counteroffers. They will either accept John's counteroffer of $600,000 or go to trial.

If the case goes to a jury trial, Allied has decided that it should be adequate to consider three possible outcomes: (1) the jury may reject John's claim and Allied will not be required to pay any damages; (2) the jury will find in favor of John and award him $750,000 in damages; or (3) the jury will conclude that John has a strong case and award him the full amount that he sued for, $1,500,000.

Key considerations as Allied develops its strategy for disposing of the case are the probabilities associated with John's response to an Allied counteroffer of $400,000, and the probabilities associated with the three possible trial outcomes. Allied's lawyers believe the probability that John will accept a counteroffer of $400,000 is 0.10, the probability that John will reject a counteroffer of $400,000 is 0.40, and the probability that John will, himself, make a counteroffer to Allied of $600,000 is 0.50. If the case goes to court, they believe that the probability the jury will award John damages of $1,500,000 is 0.30, the probability that the jury will award John damages of $750,000 is 0.50, and the probability that the jury will award John nothing is 0.20.

Managerial Report

Perform an analysis of the problem facing Allied Insurance and prepare a report that summarizes your findings and recommendations. Be sure to include the following items:

1. A decision tree
2. A recommendation regarding whether Allied should accept John's initial offer to settle the claim for $750,000
3. A decision strategy that Allied should follow if they decide to make John a counteroffer of $400,000
4. A risk profile for your recommended strategy

Appendix 4.1 DECISION ANALYSIS WITH SPREADSHEETS

A spreadsheet provides a convenient way to perform the basic decision analysis computations. A spreadsheet may be designed for any of the decision analysis approaches described in this chapter. We will demonstrate use of the spreadsheet in decision analysis by solving the PDC condominium problem using the expected value approach.

The Expected Value Approach

This spreadsheet solution is shown in Figure 4.16. The payoff table with appropriate headings is placed into cell A3 through cell C8. In addition, the probabilities for the two states of nature are placed in cells B9 and C9. The Excel formulas that provide the calculations and optimal solution recommendation are as follows:

Cells D6:D8	Compute the expected value for each decision alternative
	Cell D6 =B9*B6+C9*C6
	Cell D7 =B9*B7+C9*C7
	Cell D8 =B9*B8+C9*C8
Cell D11	Compute the maximum expected value
	=MAX(D6:D8)
Cell E6:E8	Determine which decision alternative is recommended
	Cell E6 =IF(D6=D11,A6," ")
	Cell E7 =IF(D7=D11,A7," ")
	Cell E8 =IF(D8=D11,A8," ")

As Figure 4.16 shows, the expected value approach recommends the large complex decision alternative with a maximum expected value of 14.2.

The only change required to convert the spreadsheet in Figure 4.16 into a minimization analysis is to change the formula in cell D11 to =MIN(D6:D8). With this change, the decision alternative with the minimum expected value will be shown in column E.

Computation of Branch Probabilities

Spreadsheets can be used to compute the branch probabilities for a decision tree as discussed in Section 4.6. A spreadsheet used to compute the branch probabilities for the PDC problem is shown in Figure 4.17. The prior probabilities are entered into cells B5 and B6.

FIGURE 4.16 SPREADSHEET SOLUTION FOR THE PDC PROBLEM USING THE EXPECTED VALUE APPROACH

	A	B	C	D	E
1	**PDC Problem - Expected Value Approach**				
2					
3	**Payoff Table**				
4		**State of Nature**		**Expected**	**Recommended**
5	**Decision Alternative**	High acceptance	Low acceptance	**Value**	**Decision**
6	Small complex	8	7	7.8	
7	Medium complex	14	5	12.2	
8	Large complex	20	-9	14.2	Large complex
9	**Probability**	0.8	0.2		
10					
11	**Maximum Expected Value**			14.2	

FIGURE 4.17 SPREADSHEET SOLUTION FOR THE PDC PROBLEM PROBABILITY CALCULATIONS

	A	B	C	D	E
1	**PDC Problem - Bayes' Probability Calculations**				
2					
3		Prior			
4	**States of Nature**	Probabilities			
5	High Acceptance	0.8			
6	Low Acceptance	0.2			
7					
8	**Conditional Probabilities**				
9		Market Research			
10	If State of Nature Is	Favorable	Unfavorable		
11	High Acceptance	0.90	0.10		
12	Low Acceptance	0.25	0.75		
13					
14					
15	**Market Research Favorable (F)**				
16		Prior	Conditional	Joint	Posterior
17	State of Nature	Probabilities	Probabilities	Probabilities	Probabilities
18	High Acceptance	0.8	0.90	0.72	0.94
19	Low Acceptance	0.2	0.25	0.05	0.06
20				P(F) =	0.77
21					
22					
23	**Market Research Unfavorable (U)**				
24		Prior	Conditional	Joint	Posterior
25	State of Nature	Probabilities	Probabilities	Probabilities	Probabilities
26	High Acceptance	0.8	0.10	0.08	0.35
27	Low Acceptance	0.2	0.75	0.15	0.65
28				P(U) =	0.23

The four conditional probabilities are entered into cells B11, B12, C11, and C12. The following cell formulas perform the probability calculations for the PDC problem based on a favorable market research report, shown previously in Table 4.7.

Cells B18 and B19	Enter the prior probabilities =B5 =B6
Cells C18 and C19	Enter the conditional probabilities for a favorable market research report =B11 =B12
Cells D18 and D19	Compute the joint probabilities =B18*C18 =B19*C19
Cell D20	Compute the probability of a favorable market research report =SUM(D18:D19)
Cells E18 and E19	Compute the posterior probabilities for each state of nature =D18/D20 =D19/D20

The same logic was used to perform the probability calculations based on an unfavorable market research report shown in cells B23:E28.

OHIO EDISON COMPANY*

AKRON, OHIO

Ohio Edison Company is an operating company of FirstEnergy Corporation. Ohio Edison and its subsidiary, Pennsylvania Power Company, provide electrical service to more than one million customers in central and northeastern Ohio and western Pennsylvania. Most of this electricity is generated by coal-fired power plants. To meet evolving air-quality standards, Ohio Edison replaced existing particulate control equipment at most of its generating plants with more efficient equipment. The combination of this program to upgrade air-quality control equipment with the continuing need to construct new generating plants to meet future power requirements resulted in a large capital investment program.

Quantitative methods at Ohio Edison are distributed throughout the company rather than centralized in a specific department, and are more or less evenly divided among the following areas: fossil and nuclear fuel planning, environmental studies, capacity planning, large equipment evaluation, and corporate planning. Applications include decision analysis, optimal ordering strategies, computer modeling, and simulation.

A Decision Analysis Application

The flue gas emitted by coal-fired power plants contains small ash particles and sulfur dioxide (SO_2). Federal and state regulatory agencies have established emission limits for both particulates and sulfur dioxide. In the late 1970s, Ohio Edison developed a plan to comply with new air-quality standards at one of its largest power plants. This plant, which consists of seven coal-fired units (most of which were constructed in the 1960s), constitutes about one-third of the generating capacity of Ohio Edison and its subsidiary company. Although all units were initially constructed with

particulate emission control equipment, that equipment was no longer capable of meeting new particulate emission requirements.

A decision had already been made to burn low-sulfur coal in four of the smaller units (units 1–4) at the plant in order to meet SO_2 emission standards. Fabric filters were to be installed on these units to control particulate emissions. Fabric filters, also known as baghouses, use thousands of fabric bags to filter out the particulates; they function in much the same way as a household vacuum cleaner.

It was considered likely, although not certain, that the three larger units (units 5–7) at this plant would burn medium- to high-sulfur coal. A method of controlling particulate emissions at these units had not yet been selected. Preliminary studies narrowed the particulate control equipment choice to a decision between fabric filters and electrostatic precipitators (which remove particulates suspended in the flue gas by passing the flue gas through a strong electric field). This decision was affected by a number of uncertainties, including the following:

- Uncertainty in the way some air-quality laws and regulations might be interpreted
- Potential requirements that either low-sulfur coal or high-sulfur Ohio coal (or neither) be burned in units 5–7
- Potential future changes to air-quality laws and regulations
- An overall plant reliability improvement program already under way at this plant
- The outcome of this program itself, which would affect the operating costs of whichever pollution control technology was installed in these units
- Uncertain construction costs of the equipment, particularly because limited space at the plant site made it necessary to install the equipment on

*The authors are indebted to Thomas J. Madden and M. S. Hyrnick of Ohio Edison Company, Akron, Ohio, for providing this application.

a massive bridge deck over a four-lane highway immediately adjacent to the power plant

- Uncertain costs associated with replacing the electrical power required to operate the particulate control equipment
- Various other factors, including potential accidents and chronic operating problems that could increase the costs of operating the generating units (the degree to which each of these factors could affect operating costs varied with the choice of technology and with the sulfur content of the coal)

Particulate Control Decision

The air-quality program involved a choice between two types of particulate control equipment (fabric filters and electrostatic precipitators) for units 5–7. Because of the complexity of the problem, the high degree of uncertainty associated with factors affecting the decision, and the importance (because of potential reliability and cost impact on Ohio Edison) of the choice, decision analysis was used in the selection process.

The decision measure used to evaluate the outcomes of the particulate technology decision analysis was the annual revenue requirements for the three large units over their remaining lifetime. Revenue requirements are the monies that would have to be collected from the utility customers to recover costs resulting from the decision. They include not only direct costs but also the cost of capital and return on investment.

A decision tree was constructed to represent the particulate control decision and its uncertainties and costs. A simplified version of this decision tree is shown in Figure 4.18. The decision and chance nodes are indicated. Note that to conserve space, a type of shorthand notation is used. The coal sulfur content chance node should actually be located at the end of each branch of the capital cost chance node, as the dashed lines indicate. Each chance node actually represents several probabilistic cost models or submodels. The total revenue requirements are the sum of the revenue requirements for capital and operating costs. Costs associated with these models were obtained from engineering calculations or estimates. Probabilities were obtained from existing data or the subjective assessments of knowledgeable persons.

Results

A decision tree similar to that shown in Figure 4.18 was used to generate cumulative probability distributions for the annual revenue requirements outcomes calculated for each of the two particulate control alternatives. Careful study of these results led to the following conclusions:

- The expected value of annual revenue requirements for the electrostatic precipitator technology was approximately $1 million lower than that for the fabric filters.
- The fabric filter alternative had a higher upside risk—that is, a higher probability of high revenue requirements—than did the precipitator alternative.
- The precipitator technology had nearly an 80% probability of lower annual revenue requirements than the fabric filters.
- Although the capital cost of the fabric filter equipment (the cost of installing the equipment) was lower than for the precipitator, this cost was more than offset by the higher operating costs associated with the fabric filter.

These results led Ohio Edison to select the electrostatic precipitator technology for the generating units in question. Had the decision analysis not been performed, the particulate control decision might have been based chiefly on capital cost, a decision measure that would have favored the fabric filter equipment. Decision analysis offers a means for effectively analyzing the uncertainties involved in a decision. Because of this analysis, the use of decision analysis methodology in this application resulted in a decision that yielded both lower expected revenue requirements and lower risk.

Questions

1. Why was decision analysis used in the selection of particulate control equipment for units 5, 6, and 7?
2. List the decision alternatives for the decision analysis problem developed by Ohio Edison.
3. What were the benefits of using decision analysis in this application?

FIGURE 4.18   SIMPLIFIED PARTICULATE CONTROL EQUIPMENT DECISION TREE

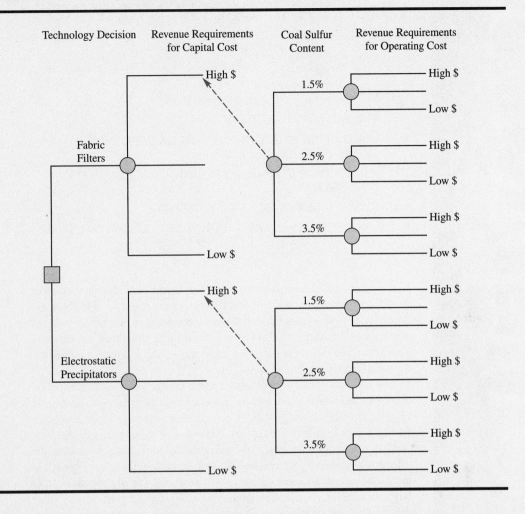

Chapter 5

UTILITY AND DECISION MAKING

CONTENTS

In the preceding chapter we frequently expressed consequences in terms of monetary values. When probability information was available about the chance events, we recommended selecting the decision alternative with the best expected monetary value. However, in some situations, the decision alternative with the best expected monetary value is not necessarily the most desirable decision.

By the most desirable decision we mean the one that is preferred by the decision maker, taking into account not only monetary value but also many other factors such as the possibility of making a very large profit and/or incurring a very large loss. Examples of situations in which selecting the decision alternative with the best expected monetary value may not lead to the selection of the most preferred decision are numerous. One such example is the decision made by most people to buy insurance. Clearly, the decision to buy insurance for a house does not provide a higher expected monetary value than not buying such insurance. Otherwise insurance companies could not pay expenses and make a profit. Similarly, many people buy tickets for state lotteries even though the expected monetary value of such a decision is negative.

Should we conclude that people or businesses that buy insurance or participate in lotteries do so because they are unable to determine which decision alternative leads to the best expected monetary value? On the contrary, we take the view that in these cases monetary value is not the sole measure of the true worth of the consequence to the decision maker. When the expected monetary value approach does not lead to the most preferred decision alternative, expressing the value (or worth) of a consequence in terms of its *utility* will permit the use of *expected utility* to identify the most desirable decision.

5.1 THE MEANING OF UTILITY

Utility is a measure of the total worth of a particular outcome; it reflects the decision maker's attitude toward a collection of factors such as profit, loss, and risk. Researchers have found that as long as the monetary value of payoffs stays within a range that the decision maker considers reasonable, selecting the decision alternative with the best expected monetary

Until 1944, when Von Neumann and Morgenstern published the book Theory of Games and Economic Behavior, *the literature on decisions involving risk consisted primarily of applications involving the use of probability in gambling.*

value usually leads to selection of the most preferred decision. However, when the payoffs become extreme, most decision makers are not satisfied with the decision that simply provides the best expected monetary value.

As an example of a situation in which utility can help in selecting the best decision alternative, let us consider the problem faced by Swofford, Inc., a relatively small real estate investment firm located in Atlanta, Georgia. Swofford currently has two investment opportunities that require approximately the same cash outlay. The cash requirements necessary prohibit Swofford from making more than one investment at this time. Consequently, three possible decision alternatives may be considered.

The three decision alternatives, denoted d_1, d_2, and d_3, are

$$d_1 = \text{make investment } A$$
$$d_2 = \text{make investment } B$$
$$d_3 = \text{do not invest}$$

The monetary payoffs associated with the investment opportunities depend on the investment decision and on the direction of the real estate market during the next 6 months (the chance event). Real estate prices will go up, remain stable, or go down. Thus the Swofford states of nature, denoted by s_1, s_2, and s_3, are

$$s_1 = \text{real estate prices go up}$$
$$s_2 = \text{real estate prices remain stable}$$
$$s_3 = \text{real estate prices go down}$$

Using the best information available, Swofford has estimated the profits, or payoffs, associated with each decision alternative and state-of-nature combination. The resulting payoff table is shown in Table 5.1.

The best estimate of the probability that real estate prices will go up is 0.30; the best estimate of the probability that prices will remain stable is 0.50; and the best estimate of the probability that prices will go down is 0.20. Thus the expected values for the three decision alternatives are

$$\text{EV}(d_1) = 0.3(30,000) + 0.5(20,000) \quad + 0.2(-50,000) = 9,000$$
$$\text{EV}(d_2) = 0.3(50,000) + 0.5(-20,000) + 0.2(-30,000) = -1,000$$
$$\text{EV}(d_3) = 0.3(0) \qquad\quad + 0.5(0) \qquad\quad + 0.2(0) \qquad\quad = 0$$

Using the expected value approach, the optimal decision is to select investment A with an expected monetary value of $9000. Is this really the best decision alternative? Let us consider some other relevant factors that relate to Swofford's capability for absorbing the loss of $50,000 if investment A is made and prices actually go down.

TABLE 5.1   PAYOFF TABLE FOR SWOFFORD, INC.

Decision Alternative	State of Nature		
	Prices Up s_1	Prices Stable s_2	Prices Down s_3
Investment A, d_1	$30,000	$20,000	−$50,000
Investment B, d_2	$50,000	−$20,000	−$30,000
Do not invest, d_3	0	0	0

Actually, Swofford's current financial position is weak. This condition is partly reflected in Swofford's ability to make only one investment currently. More important, however, the firm's president believes that, if the next investment results in a substantial loss, Swofford's future will be in jeopardy. Although the expected value approach leads to a recommendation for d_1, do you think the firm's president would prefer this decision? We suspect that the president would select d_2 or d_3 to avoid the possibility of incurring a $50,000 loss. In fact, a reasonable conclusion is that, if a loss of even $30,000 could drive Swofford out of business, the president would select d_3, believing that both investments A and B are too risky for Swofford's current financial position.

The way we resolve Swofford's dilemma is first to determine Swofford's utility for the various monetary outcomes. Recall that the utility of any outcome is the total worth of that outcome, taking into account all risks and consequences involved. If the utilities for the various consequences are assessed correctly, the decision alternative with the highest expected utility is the most preferred, or best, alternative. In the next section we show how to determine the utility of the monetary outcomes so that the alternative with the highest expected utility is most preferred.

5.2   DEVELOPING UTILITIES FOR MONETARY PAYOFFS

Utility values of 0 and 1 could have been selected here; we selected 0 and 10 in order to avoid any possible confusion between the utility value for a payoff and the probability p.

The procedure we use to establish utility values for the payoffs in Swofford's situation requires that we first assign a utility value to the best and worst possible payoffs. Any values will work as long as the utility assigned to the best payoff is greater than the utility assigned to the worst payoff. In this case, $50,000 is the best payoff and $-$50,000 is the worst. Suppose, then, that we arbitrarily make assignments to these two payoffs as follows:

$$\text{Utility of } -\$50{,}000 = U(-50{,}000) = \ 0$$
$$\text{Utility of } \ \ \$50{,}000 = U(50{,}000) \ \ = 10$$

Let us now determine the utility associated with every other payoff.

Consider the process of establishing the utility of a payoff of $30,000. First we ask Swofford's president to state a preference between a guaranteed $30,000 payoff and an opportunity to engage in the following **lottery,** or bet:

Lottery: Swofford's obtains a payoff of $50,000 with probability p
and a payoff of $-$50,000 with probability $(1 - p)$

p is often referred to as the indifference probability.

Obviously, if p is very close to 1, Swofford's president would prefer the lottery to the guaranteed payoff of $30,000 because the firm would virtually ensure itself a payoff of $50,000. But if p is very close to 0, Swofford's president would clearly prefer the guarantee of $30,000. In any event, as p changes continuously from 0 to 1, the preference for the guaranteed payoff of $30,000 will change at some point into a preference for the lottery. At this value of p, Swofford's president would have no greater preference for the guaranteed payoff of $30,000 than for the lottery. For example, let us assume that when $p = 0.95$, Swofford's president is indifferent between the guaranteed payoff of $30,000 and the lottery. For this value of p, we can compute the utility of a $30,000 payoff as follows:

$$U(30{,}000) = pU(50{,}000) + (1 - p)U(-50{,}000)$$
$$= 0.95(10) + (0.05)(0)$$
$$= 9.5$$

Obviously, if we had started with a different assignment of utilities for a payoff of $50,000 and $-$50,000, the result would have been a different utility for $30,000. For example, if we had started with an assignment of 100 for $50,000 and 10 for $-$50,000$, the utility of a $30,000 payoff would be

$$U(30,000) = 0.95(100) + 0.05(10)$$
$$= 95 + 0.5$$
$$= 95.5$$

Hence, we must conclude that the utility assigned to each payoff is not unique but merely depends on the initial choice of utilities for the best and worst payoffs. We will discuss this further at the end of this section. For now, however, we will continue to use a value of 10 for the utility of $50,000 and a value of 0 for the utility of $-$50,000$.

Before computing the utility for the other payoffs, let us consider the significance of Swofford's president assigning a utility of 9.5 to a payoff of $30,000. Clearly, when $p = 0.95$, the expected value of the lottery is

$$EV(lottery) = 0.95(\$50,000) + 0.05(-\$50,000)$$
$$= \$47,500 - \$2,500$$
$$= \$45,000$$

The difference between the expected value of the lottery and the guaranteed payoff can be viewed as the risk premium the decision maker is willing to pay.

Although the expected value of the lottery when $p = 0.95$ is $45,000, Swofford's president would just as soon take a guaranteed payoff of $30,000. Thus, Swofford's president is taking a conservative, or risk-avoiding, viewpoint. The president would rather have $30,000 for certain than risk anything greater than a 5% chance of incurring a loss of $50,000. In other words the difference between the EV of $45,000 and the guaranteed payoff of $30,000 is the risk premium that Swofford's president would be willing to pay to avoid the 5% chance of losing $50,000.

To compute the utility associated with a payoff of $-$20,000$, we must ask Swofford's president to state a preference between a guaranteed $-$20,000$ payoff and an opportunity to engage again in the following lottery:

Lottery: Swofford's obtains a payoff of $50,000 with probability p
and a payoff of $-$50,000$ with probability $(1 - p)$

Note that this lottery is exactly the same as the one we used to establish the utility of a payoff of $30,000. In fact, we use this lottery to establish the utility for any monetary value in the Swofford payoff table. We need to determine the value of p that would make the president indifferent between a guaranteed payoff of $-$20,000$ and the lottery. For example, we might begin by asking the president to choose between a certain loss of $20,000 and the lottery with a payoff of $50,000 with probability $p = 0.90$ and a payoff of $-$50,000$ with probability $(1 - p) = 0.10$. What answer do you think we would get? Surely, with this high probability of obtaining a payoff of $50,000, the president would elect the lottery. Next, we might ask whether $p = 0.85$ would result in indifference between the loss of $20,000 for certain and the lottery. Again the president might prefer the lottery. Suppose that we continue until we get to $p = 0.55$, at which point the president is indifferent between the payoff of $-$20,000$ and the lottery. That is, for any value of p less than 0.55, the president would rather take a loss of $20,000 for certain rather than risk the potential loss of $50,000 with the lottery; and for any value of p above 0.55, the president would choose the lottery. Thus, the utility assigned to a payoff of $-$20,000$ is

$$U(-\$20,000) = pU(50,000) + (1 - p)U(-\$50,000)$$
$$= 0.55(10) + 0.45(0)$$
$$= 5.5$$

Again let us compare the significance of this assignment to the expected value approach. When $p = 0.55$, the expected value of the lottery is

$$\text{EV(lottery)} = 0.55(\$50,000) + 0.45(-\$50,000)$$
$$= \$27,500 - \$22,500$$
$$= \$5,000$$

Thus, Swofford's president would just as soon absorb a loss of $20,000 for certain as take the lottery, even though the expected value of the lottery is $5000. Once again this preference demonstrates the conservative, or risk-avoiding, point of view of Swofford's president.

In these two examples we computed the utility for the monetary payoffs of $30,000 and −$20,000. We can determine the utility for any monetary payoff M in a similar fashion. First, we must find the probability p for which the decision maker is indifferent between a guaranteed payoff of M and a lottery with a payoff of $50,000 with probability p and −$50,000 with probability $(1 - p)$. The utility of M is then computed as follows:

$$U(M) = pU(\$50,000) + (1 - p)U(-\$50,000)$$
$$= p(10) + (1 - p)0$$
$$= 10p$$

Using this procedure we developed utility values for the rest of the payoffs in Swofford's problem. The results are presented in Table 5.2.

Now that we have determined the utility value of each of the possible monetary values, we can write the original payoff table in terms of utility values. Table 5.3 shows the utility for the various outcomes in the Swofford problem. The notation we use for the entries in the utility table is U_{ij}, which denotes the utility associated with decision alternative d_i and state of nature s_j. Using this notation, we see that $U_{23} = 4.0$.

TABLE 5.2   UTILITY OF MONETARY PAYOFFS FOR THE SWOFFORD, INC., PROBLEM

Monetary Value	Indifference Value of p	Utility Value
$ 50,000	Does not apply	10.0
30,000	0.95	9.5
20,000	0.90	9.0
0	0.75	7.5
−20,000	0.55	5.5
−30,000	0.40	4.0
−50,000	Does not apply	0

TABLE 5.3   UTILITY TABLE FOR SWOFFORD, INC.

Decision Alternative	State of Nature		
	Prices Up s_1	Prices Stable s_2	Prices Down s_3
Investment A, d_1	9.5	9.0	0
Investment B, d_2	10.0	5.5	4.0
Do not invest, d_3	7.5	7.5	7.5

The Expected Utility Approach

We can now apply the expected value computations introduced in Chapter 4 to the utilities in Table 5.3 in order to select an optimal decision alternative for Swofford, Inc. However, because utility values represent such a special case of expected value, we will refer to the expected value when applied to utility values as the **expected utility** (EU). Thus, the expected utility approach requires the analyst to compute the expected utility for each decision alternative and then select the alternative yielding the highest expected utility. With N possible states of nature, the expected utility of a decision alternative d_i is given by

$$EU(d_i) = \sum_{j=1}^{N} P(s_j)U_{ij} \qquad (5.1)$$

The expected utility for each of the decision alternatives in the Swofford problem is

$$EU(d_1) = 0.3(9.5) + 0.5(9.0) + 0.2(0) \quad = 7.35$$
$$EU(d_2) = 0.3(10) \ + 0.5(5.5) + 0.2(4.0) = 6.55$$
$$EU(d_3) = 0.3(7.5) + 0.5(7.5) + 0.2(7.5) = 7.50$$

Can you use the expected utility approach to determine the optimal decision? Try Problem 1.

Note that the optimal decision using the expected utility approach is d_3, do not invest. The ranking of alternatives according to the president's utility assignments and the associated monetary values are as follows.

Ranking of Decision Alternatives	Expected Utility	Expected Monetary Value
Do not invest	7.50	0
Investment A	7.35	9000
Investment B	6.55	−1000

Note that although investment A had the highest expected monetary value of $9000, the analysis indicates that Swofford should decline this investment. The rationale behind not selecting investment A is that the 0.20 probability of a $50,000 loss was considered to involve a serious risk by Swofford's president. The seriousness of this risk and its associated impact on the company were not adequately reflected by the expected monetary value of investment A. We assessed the utility for each payoff to assess this risk adequately.

NOTES AND COMMENTS

In the Swofford problem we have been using a utility of 10 for the best payoff and 0 for the worst. The choice of values could have been anything, and we might have chosen 1 for the utility of the best payoff and 0 for the utility of the worst. Had we made this choice, the utility for any monetary value M would have been the value of p at which the decision maker was indifferent between a guaranteed payoff of M and a lottery in which the best payoff is obtained with probability p and the worst payoff is obtained with probability $(1 - p)$. Thus, the utility for any monetary value would have been equal to the probability of earning the best payoff. Often this choice is made because of the ease in computation. We chose not to do so to emphasize the distinction between the utility values and the indifference probabilities for the lottery.

5.3 SUMMARY OF STEPS FOR DETERMINING THE UTILITY OF MONEY

Before considering other aspects of utility, let us summarize the steps involved in determining the utility for a monetary value and using it within the decision analysis framework. The following steps state in general terms the procedure used to solve the Swofford, Inc., investment problem.

Step 1. Develop a payoff table using monetary values.

Step 2. Identify the best and worst payoff values in the table and assign each a utility value, with U(best payoff) $> U$(worst payoff).

Step 3. For every other monetary value M in the original payoff table, do the following to determine its utility value.

    a. Define the lottery: The best payoff is obtained with probability p and the worst payoff is obtained with probability $(1 - p)$.

    b. Determine the value of p such that the decision maker is indifferent between a guaranteed payoff of M and the lottery defined in step 3a.

    c. Calculate the utility of M as follows:

$$U(M) = pU(\text{best payoff}) + (1 - p)U(\text{worst payoff})$$

Step 4. Convert the payoff table from monetary values to utility values.

Step 5. Apply the expected utility approach to the utility table developed in step 4 and select the decision alternative with the highest expected utility.

NOTES AND COMMENTS

The procedure we have described for determining the utility of monetary consequences can also be used to develop a utility measure for nonmonetary consequences. Assign the best consequence a utility of 10 and the worst a utility of 0. Then create a lottery with a probability of p for the best consequence and $(1 - p)$ for the worst consequence. For each of the other consequences, find the value of p that makes the decision maker indifferent between the lottery and the consequence. Then calculate the utility of the consequence in question as follows:

$$U(\text{consequence}) = pU(\text{best consequence}) + (1 - p)U(\text{worst consequence})$$

5.4 RISK AVOIDERS VERSUS RISK TAKERS

The financial position of Swofford, Inc., was such that the firm's president evaluated investment opportunities from a conservative, or risk-avoiding, point of view. However, if the firm had a surplus of cash and a stable future, Swofford's president might have been looking for investment alternatives that, although perhaps risky, contained a potential for substantial profit. That type of behavior would have made the president a **risk taker.** In this section we analyze the decision problem faced by Swofford from the point of view of a decision maker who would be classified as a risk taker. We then compare the conservative, or risk-avoiding, point of view of Swofford's president with the behavior of a decision maker who is a risk taker.

For the decision problem facing Swofford, Inc., and using the general procedure for developing utilities as discussed in Section 5.3, a risk taker might express the utility for the various payoffs shown in Table 5.4. As before, $U(50,000) = 10$ and $U(-50,000) = 0$. Note the difference in behavior reflected in Table 5.4 and Table 5.2. That is, in determining the

TABLE 5.4   REVISED UTILITY VALUES FOR THE SWOFFORD, INC., PROBLEM
ASSUMING A RISK TAKER

Monetary Value	Indifference Value of p	Utility Value
$ 50,000	Does not apply	10.0
30,000	0.50	5.0
20,000	0.40	4.0
0	0.25	2.5
−20,000	0.15	1.5
−30,000	0.10	1.0
−50,000	Does not apply	0

value of p at which the decision maker is indifferent between a guaranteed payoff of M and
a lottery in which $50,000 is obtained with probability p and −$50,000 with probability
$(1 - p)$, the risk taker is willing to accept a greater risk of incurring a loss of $50,000 in or-
der to gain the opportunity to realize a profit of $50,000.

To help develop the utility table for the risk taker, we have reproduced the Swofford,
Inc., payoff table in Table 5.5. Using these payoffs and the risk taker's utility values given
in Table 5.4, we can write the risk taker's utility table as shown in Table 5.6. Using the state-
of-nature probabilities $P(s_1) = 0.3$, $P(s_2) = 0.5$, and $P(s_3) = 0.2$, the expected utility for
each decision alternative is

$$EU(d_1) = 0.3(5.0) + 0.5(4.0) + 0.2(0) \quad = 3.50$$
$$EU(d_2) = 0.3(10) \; + 0.5(1.5) + 0.2(1.0) = 3.95$$
$$EU(d_3) = 0.3(2.5) + 0.5(2.5) + 0.2(2.5) = 2.50$$

What is the recommended decision? Perhaps somewhat to your surprise, the analysis recommends investment B, with the highest expected utility of 3.95. Recall that this

TABLE 5.5   PAYOFF TABLE FOR SWOFFORD, INC.

Decision Alternative	State of Nature		
	Prices Up s_1	Prices Stable s_2	Prices Down s_3
Investment A, d_1	$30,000	$20,000	−$50,000
Investment B, d_2	$50,000	−$20,000	−$30,000
Do not invest, d_3	0	0	0

TABLE 5.6   UTILITY TABLE OF A RISK TAKER FOR THE SWOFFORD, INC., PROBLEM

Decision Alternative	State of Nature		
	Prices Up s_1	Prices Stable s_2	Prices Down s_3
Investment A, d_1	5.0	4.0	0
Investment B, d_2	10.0	1.5	1.0
Do not invest, d_3	2.5	2.5	2.5

investment has a $-\$1000$ expected monetary value. Why is it now the recommended decision? Remember that the decision maker in this revised problem is a risk taker. Thus, although the expected value of investment B is negative, utility analysis has shown that this decision maker is enough of a risk taker to prefer investment B and its potential for the $50,000 profit.

The expected utility values give the following order of preference of the decision alternatives for the risk taker and the associated expected monetary values.

Ranking of Decision Alternatives	Expected Utility	Expected Monetary Value
Investment B	3.95	$-\$1000$
Investment A	3.50	$9000
Do not invest	2.50	0

Comparing the utility analysis for a risk taker with the more conservative preferences of the president of Swofford, Inc., who is a **risk avoider** we see that, even with the same decision problem, different attitudes toward risk can lead to different recommended decisions. The utility values established by Swofford's president indicated that the firm should not invest at this time, whereas the utilities established by the risk taker showed a preference for investment B. Note that both of these decisions differ from the best expected monetary value decision, which was investment A.

We can obtain another perspective of the difference between behaviors of a risk avoider and a risk taker by developing a graph that depicts the relationship between monetary value and utility. We use the horizontal axis of the graph to represent monetary values and the vertical axis to represent the utility associated with each monetary value. Now, consider the data in Table 5.2, with a utility value corresponding to each monetary value for the original Swofford, Inc., problem. These values can be plotted on a graph such as that in Figure 5.1, and a curve can be drawn through the observed points. The resulting curve is the **utility function for money** for Swofford's president. Recall that these points reflected the conservative, or risk-avoiding, nature of Swofford's president. Hence, we refer to the curve in Figure 5.1 as a utility function for a risk avoider. Using the data in Table 5.4, developed for a risk taker, we can plot these points on a graph such as that in Figure 5.2. The resulting curve depicts the utility function for a risk taker.

By looking at the utility functions of Figures 5.1 and 5.2, we can begin to generalize about the utility functions for risk avoiders and risk takers. Although the exact shape of the utility function will vary from one decision maker to another, we can see the general shape of these two types of utility functions. The utility function for a risk avoider shows a diminishing marginal return for money. For example, the increase in utility going from a monetary value of $-\$30,000$ to $0 is $7.5 - 4.0 = 3.5$, whereas the increase in utility in going from $0 to $30,000 is only $9.5 - 7.5 = 2.0$. However, the utility function for a risk taker shows an increasing marginal return for money. For example, in Figure 5.2, the increase in utility in going from $-\$30,000$ to $0 is $2.5 - 1.0 = 1.5$, whereas the increase in utility in going from $0 to $30,000 is $5.0 - 2.5 = 2.5$. Note also that in either case the utility function is always increasing. That is, more money leads to more utility. All utility functions possess this property.

We concluded that the utility function for a risk avoider shows a diminishing marginal return for money and that the utility function for a risk taker shows an increasing marginal return. When the marginal return for money is neither decreasing nor increasing but remains constant, the corresponding utility function describes the behavior of a decision

FIGURE 5.1   UTILITY FUNCTION FOR MONEY FOR THE RISK AVOIDER

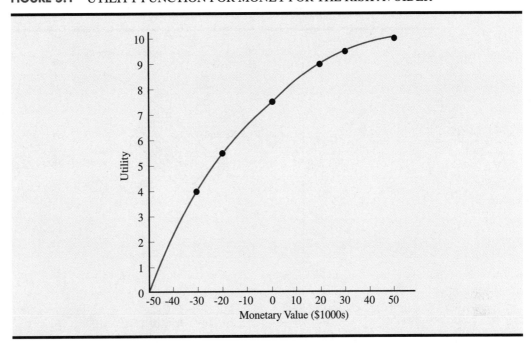

FIGURE 5.2   UTILITY FUNCTION FOR MONEY FOR THE RISK TAKER

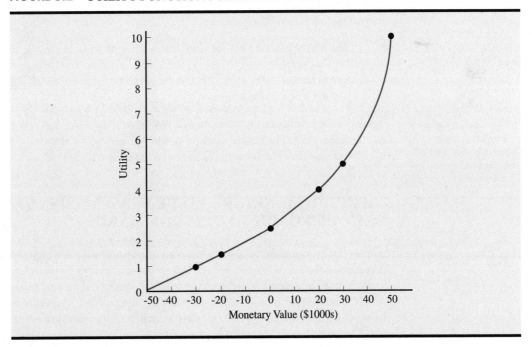

FIGURE 5.3   UTILITY FUNCTIONS FOR RISK-AVOIDER, RISK-TAKER, AND
RISK-NEUTRAL DECISION MAKERS

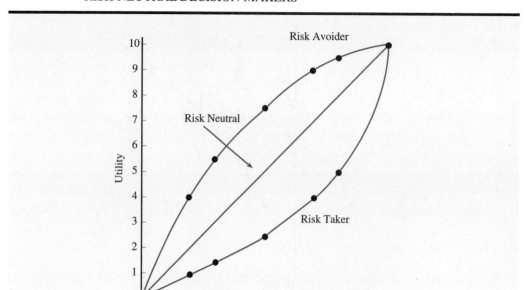

maker who is neutral to risk. The following characteristics are associated with a **risk-neutral decision maker.**

1. The utility function can be drawn as a straight line connecting the "best" and the "worst" points.
2. The expected utility approach and the expected value approach applied to monetary payoffs result in the same action.

Try Problem 5 for practice in plotting the utility function for risk-avoider, risk-taker, and risk-neutral decision makers.

Figure 5.3 depicts the utility function of a risk-neutral decision maker using the Swofford, Inc., problem data. For comparison purposes, we also show the utility functions for the cases where the decision maker is either a risk taker or a risk avoider.

5.5   EXPECTED MONETARY VALUE VERSUS EXPECTED UTILITY AS AN APPROACH TO DECISION MAKING

In many decision-making problems, expected monetary value and expected utility will lead to identical recommendations. In fact, this result will always be true if the decision maker is risk neutral. In general, if the decision maker is almost risk neutral over the range of payoffs (from lowest to highest) for a particular decision problem, the decision alternative with the best expected monetary value leads to selection of the most preferred decision alternative. The trick lies in recognizing the range of monetary values over which a decision maker's utility function is risk neutral.

Generally, when the payoffs for a particular decision-making problem fall into a reasonable range—the best is not too good and the worst is not too bad—decision makers tend to express preferences in agreement with the expected monetary value approach. Thus, we suggest asking the decision maker to consider the best and worst possible payoffs for a problem and assess their reasonableness. If the decision maker believes that they are in the reasonable range, the decision alternative with the best expected monetary value can be used. However, if the payoffs appear unreasonably large or unreasonably small (for example, a huge loss) and if the decision maker believes that monetary values do not adequately reflect her or his true preferences for the payoffs, a utility analysis of the problem should be considered.

Unfortunately, determination of the appropriate utilities is not a trivial task. As we have shown, measuring utility requires a degree of subjectivity on the part of the decision maker, and different decision makers will have different utility functions. This aspect of utility often causes decision makers to feel uncomfortable about using the expected utility approach. However, if you encounter a decision situation in which you are convinced that monetary value is not the sole measure of performance, and if you agree that a quantitative analysis of the decision problem is desirable, you should recommend that utility analysis be considered.

SUMMARY

In this chapter we suggested that expected utility be used in decision situations in which an analysis based on expected monetary value would not lead to the best decision. Unlike monetary value, utility is a measure of the total worth of a consequence resulting from the choice of a decision alternative and the occurrence of a chance event. As such, utility takes into account the decision maker's attitude toward the profit, loss, and risk associated with a consequence. The examples showed how the use of utility analysis can lead to decision recommendations that differ from those based on expected monetary value.

Admittedly, a decision maker's utility can be difficult to measure. However, we presented a step-by-step procedure that can be used to determine a decision maker's utility for any payoff value. Using the decision maker's evaluation of a lottery involving only the best and worst payoffs, the procedure provides a method whereby each entry in the payoff table can be converted to a utility value. Then expected utility can be used to select the best decision alternative.

Even with utility as a measure of worth, we demonstrated how the analysis for a conservative, or risk-avoiding, decision maker could lead to decision recommendations different from those of a risk taker. When the decision maker is risk neutral, we showed that the recommendations using expected utility are identical to the recommendations using expected monetary value.

GLOSSARY

Utility   A measure of the total worth of a consequence reflecting a decision maker's attitude toward considerations such as profit, loss, and risk.

Lottery   A hypothetical investment alternative with a probability p of obtaining the best payoff and a probability of $(1 - p)$ of obtaining the worst payoff.

Expected utility (EU)   The weighted average of the utilities associated with a decision alternative. The weights are the state-of-nature probabilities.

Risk taker   A decision maker who tends to prefer decisions that, although risky, have a possibility for an extremely good payoff.

Risk avoider   A decision maker who tends to avoid decisions that have the risk of an extremely bad payoff.

Utility function for money   A curve that depicts the relationship between monetary value and utility.

Risk-neutral decision maker   A decision maker who is neutral to risk. For this decision maker the decision alternative with the best expected monetary value is identical to the alternative with the highest expected utility.

PROBLEMS

SELFtest

1. A firm has three investment alternatives. Payoffs are in $000s.

	Economic Conditions		
Decision Alternative	Up s_1	Stable s_2	Down s_3
Investment A, d_1	100	25	0
Investment B, d_2	75	50	25
Investment C, d_3	50	50	50
Probabilities	0.40	0.30	0.30

a. Using the expected value approach, which decision is preferred?

b. For the lottery having a payoff of $100,000 with probability p and $0 with probability $(1 - p)$, two decision makers expressed the following indifference probabilities. Find the most preferred decision for each decision maker using the expected utility approach.

	Indifference Probability (p)	
Profit	Decision Maker A	Decision Maker B
$75,000	0.80	0.60
$50,000	0.60	0.30
$25,000	0.30	0.15

c. Why don't decision makers A and B select the same decision alternative?

2. Alexander Industries is considering purchasing an insurance policy for its new office building in St. Louis, Missouri. The policy has an annual cost of $10,000. If Alexander Industries doesn't purchase the insurance and minor fire damage occurs, a cost of $100,000 is anticipated; the cost if major or total destruction occurs is $200,000. The costs, including the state-of-nature probabilities, are as follows.

	Damage		
Decision Alternative	None s_1	Minor s_2	Major s_3
Purchase insurance, d_1	10,000	10,000	10,000
Do not purchase insurance, d_2	0	100,000	200,000
Probabilities	0.96	0.03	0.01

a. Using the expected value approach, what decision do you recommend?

b. What lottery would you use to assess utilities? (Note that, as the data are costs, the best payoff is $0.)

c. Assume that you found the following indifference probabilities for the lottery defined in part (b). What decision would you recommend?

Cost	Indifference Probability
10,000	$p = 0.99$
100,000	$p = 0.60$

d. Do you favor using expected value or expected utility for this decision problem? Why?

3. In a certain state lottery, a lottery ticket costs $2. In terms of the decision to purchase or not to purchase a lottery ticket, suppose that the following payoff table applies.

	State of Nature	
Decision Alternatives	**Win s_1**	**Lose s_2**
Purchase lottery ticket, d_1	300,000	−2
Do not purchase lottery ticket, d_2	0	0

a. A realistic estimate of the chances of winning are 1 in 250,000. Use the expected value approach to recommend a decision.
b. If a particular decision maker assigns an indifference probability of 0.000001 to the $0 payoff, would this individual purchase a lottery ticket? Use expected utility to justify your answer.

4. Two different routes accommodate travel between two cities. Route A normally takes 60 minutes, and route B normally takes 45 minutes. If traffic problems are encountered on route A, the travel time increases to 70 minutes; traffic problems on route B increase travel time to 90 minutes. The probability of a delay is 0.20 for route A and 0.30 for route B.
a. Using the expected value approach, what is the recommended route?
b. If utilities are to be assigned to the travel times, what is the appropriate lottery? Note that the smaller times should reflect higher utilities.
c. Use the lottery of part (b) and assume that the decision maker expresses indifference probabilities of

$$p = 0.80 \qquad \text{for 60 minutes}$$
$$p = 0.60 \qquad \text{for 70 minutes}$$

What route should this decision maker select? Is the decision maker a risk taker or a risk avoider?

SELFtest

5. Three decision makers have assessed utilities for the following decision problem (payoff in dollars).

	State of Nature		
Decision Alternative	s_1	s_2	s_3
d_1	20	50	−20
d_2	80	100	−100

The indifference probabilities are as follows.

	Indifference Probability (p)		
Payoff	Decision Maker A	Decision Maker B	Decision Maker C
100	1.00	1.00	1.00
80	0.95	0.70	0.90
50	0.90	0.60	0.75
20	0.70	0.45	0.60
−20	0.50	0.25	0.40
−100	0.00	0.00	0.00

    a. Plot the utility function for money for each decision maker.
    b. Classify each decision maker as a risk avoider, a risk taker, or risk neutral.
    c. For the payoff of 20, what is the premium that the risk avoider will pay to avoid risk? What is the premium that the risk taker will pay to have the opportunity of the high payoff?

6. In Problem 5, if $P(s_1) = 0.25$, $P(s_2) = 0.50$, and $P(s_3) = 0.25$, find a recommended decision for each of the three decision makers. Note that for the same decision problem, different utilities can lead to different decisions.

7. Suppose that the point spread for a particular sporting event is 10 points and that with this spread you are convinced you would have a 0.60 probability of winning a bet on your team. However, the local bookie will accept only a $1000 bet. Assuming that such bets are legal, would you bet on your team? (Disregard any commission charged by the bookie.) Remember that *you* must pay losses out of your own pocket. Your payoff table is as follows.

	State of Nature	
Decision Alternatives	You Win s_1	You Lose s_2
Bet, d_1	1000	−1000
Don't bet, d_2	0	0

    a. What decision does the expected value approach recommend?
    b. What is *your* indifference probability for the $0 payoff? (Although this choice isn't easy, be as realistic as possible. It is required for an analysis that reflects your attitude toward risk.)
    c. What decision would you make based on the expected utility approach? In this case are you a risk taker or risk avoider?
    d. Would other individuals assess the same utility values you do? Explain.
    e. If your decision in part (c) was to place the bet, repeat the analysis assuming a minimum bet of $10,000.

8. A Las Vegas roulette wheel has 38 different numerical values. If an individual bets on one number and wins, the payoff is 35 to 1.
    a. Show a payoff table for a $10 bet on one number for decision alternatives of bet and do not bet.
    b. What is the recommended decision using the expected value approach?

    c. Do the Las Vegas casinos want risk-taking or risk-avoiding customers? Explain.

    d. What range of utility values would a decision maker have to assign to the $0 payoff in order to have expected utility justify a decision to place the $10 bet?

9. A new product has the following profit projections and associated probabilities.

Profit	Probability
$150,000	0.10
$100,000	0.25
$ 50,000	0.20
0	0.15
−$ 50,000	0.20
−$100,000	0.10

    a. Use the expected value approach to decide whether to market the new product.

    b. Because of the high dollar values involved, especially the possibility of a $100,000 loss, the marketing vice-president has expressed some concern about the use of the expected value approach. As a consequence, if a utility analysis is performed, what is the appropriate lottery?

    c. Assume that the following indifference probabilities are assigned. Do the utilities reflect the behavior of a risk taker or a risk avoider?

Profit	Indifference Probability (p)
$100,000	0.95
$ 50,000	0.70
0	0.50
−$ 50,000	0.25

    d. Use expected utility to make a recommended decision.

    e. Should the decision maker feel comfortable with the final decision recommended by the analysis?

10. A television network has been receiving low ratings for its programs. Currently, management is considering two alternatives for the Monday night 8:00 P.M.–9:00 P.M. time slot: a western with a well-known star, or a musical variety with a relatively unknown husband-and-wife team. The percentages of viewing audience estimates depend on the degree of program acceptance. The relevant data are as follows.

Program Acceptance	Percentage of Viewing Audience	
	Western	Musical Variety
High	30%	40%
Moderate	25%	20%
Poor	20%	15%

The probabilities associated with program acceptance levels are as follows.

| Program Acceptance | Probability | |
	Western	Musical Variety
High	0.30	0.30
Moderate	0.60	0.40
Poor	0.10	0.30

a. Using the expected value approach, which program should the network choose?
b. For a utility analysis, what is the appropriate lottery?
c. Based on the lottery in part (b), assume that the network's program manager has assigned the following indifference probabilities. Based on the use of utility measures, which program would you recommend? Is the manager a risk taker or a risk avoider?

Percentage of Audience	Indifference Probability (p)
30%	0.40
25%	0.30
20%	0.10

FORECASTING

Chapter 6

CONTENTS

An essential aspect of managing any organization is planning for the future. Indeed, the long-run success of an organization is closely related to how well management is able to anticipate the future and develop appropriate strategies. Good judgment, intuition, and an awareness of the state of the economy may give a manager a rough idea or "feeling" of what is likely to happen in the future. However, converting this feeling into a number that can be used as next quarter's sales volume or next year's raw material cost per unit often is difficult. The purpose of this chapter is to introduce several forecasting methods.

Suppose that we have been asked to provide quarterly forecasts of the sales volume for a particular product during the coming year. Production schedules, raw material purchasing plans, inventory policies, and sales quotas will be affected by the quarterly forecasts that we provide. Consequently, poor forecasts may result in increased costs for the firm. How should we go about providing the quarterly sales volume forecasts?

Most companies can forecast total demand for all products, as a group, with errors of less than 5%. However, forecasting demand for individual products may result in significantly higher errors.

We will certainly want to review the actual sales data for the product in previous periods. Using these historical data, we can identify the general level of sales and any trend such as an increase or decrease in sales volume over time. A further review of the data might reveal a seasonal pattern such as peak sales occurring in the third quarter of each year and sales volume bottoming out during the first quarter. By reviewing historical data, we can often develop a better understanding of the pattern of past sales, leading to better predictions of future sales for the product.

The historical sales data form a time series. A **time series** is a set of observations of a variable measured at successive points in time or over successive periods of time. In this chapter we introduce several procedures for analyzing time series. The objective of such analyses is to provide good **forecasts** or predictions of future values of the time series.

Forecasting methods can be classified as quantitative or qualitative. Quantitative forecasting methods can be used when (1) past information about the variable being forecast is available, (2) the information can be quantified, and (3) a reasonable assumption is that the pattern of the past will continue into the future. In such cases, a forecast can be developed using a time series method or a causal method.

A forecast is simply a prediction of what will happen in the future. Managers must learn to accept the fact that, regardless of the technique used, they will not be able to develop perfect forecasts.

If the historical data are restricted to past values of the variable that we are trying to forecast, the forecasting procedure is called a *time series method.* The objective of time series methods is to discover a pattern in the historical data and then extrapolate this pattern into the future; the forecast is based solely on past values of the variable that we are trying to forecast and/or on past forecast errors. In this chapter we discuss three time series methods: smoothing (moving averages, weighted moving averages, and exponential smoothing), trend projection, and trend projection adjusted for seasonal influence.

Causal forecasting methods are based on the assumption that the variable we are trying to forecast exhibits a cause-effect relationship with one or more other variables. In this chapter we discuss the use of regression analysis as a causal forecasting method. For instance, the sales volume for many products is influenced by advertising expenditures, so regression analysis may be used to develop an equation showing how these two variables are related. Then, once the advertising budget has been set for the next period, we could substitute this value into the equation to develop a prediction or forecast of the sales volume for that period. Note that if a time series method had been used to develop the forecast, advertising expenditures would not even have been considered; that is, a time series method would have based the forecast solely on past sales.

Qualitative methods generally involve the use of expert judgment to develop forecasts. For instance, a panel of experts might develop a consensus forecast of the prime rate for a year from now. An advantage of qualitative procedures is that they can be applied when the information on the variable being forecast cannot be quantified and when historical data either are not applicable or available. Figure 6.1 provides an overview of the types of forecasting methods.

6.1   THE COMPONENTS OF A TIME SERIES

The pattern or behavior of the data in a time series has several components. The usual assumption is that four separate components—trend, cyclical, seasonal, and irregular—combine to provide specific values for the time series.

Trend Component

In time series analysis, the measurements may be taken every hour, day, week, month, or year, or at any other regular interval. Although time series data generally exhibit random fluctuations, the time series may still show gradual shifts or movements to relatively higher or lower values over a longer period of time. The gradual shifting of the time series is referred to as the **trend** in the time series; this shifting or trend is usually the result of long-

FIGURE 6.1   AN OVERVIEW OF FORECASTING METHODS

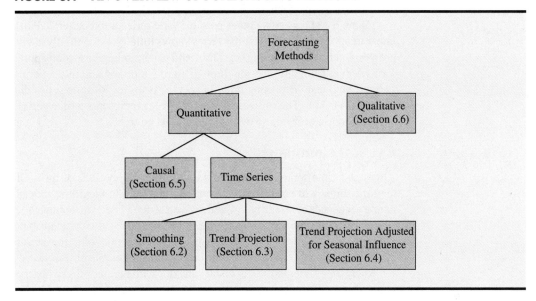

term factors such as changes in the population, demographic characteristics of the population, technology, and consumer preferences.

For example, a manufacturer of photographic equipment may observe substantial month-to-month variability in the number of cameras sold. However, in reviewing sales over the past 10 to 15 years, this manufacturer may note a gradual increase in the annual sales volume. Suppose that the sales volume was approximately 1700 cameras per month in 1990, 2300 cameras per month in 1995, and 2500 cameras per month in 2000. Although actual month-to-month sales volumes may vary substantially, this gradual growth in sales shows an upward trend for the time series. Figure 6.2 shows a straight line that may be a good approximation of the trend in camera sales. Although the trend for camera sales

FIGURE 6.2   LINEAR TREND OF CAMERA SALES

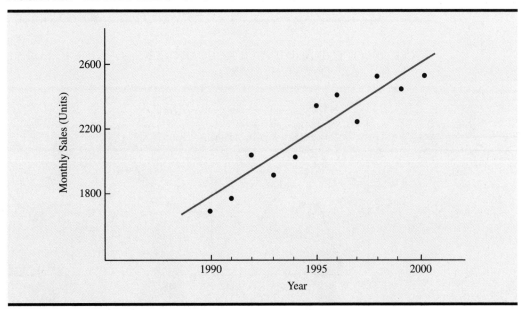

appears to be linear and increasing over time, sometimes the trend in a time series can be described better by some other pattern.

Figure 6.3 shows some other possible time series trend patterns. Part (a) shows a non-linear trend; in this case, the time series shows little growth initially, then a period of rapid growth, and finally a leveling off. This trend pattern might be a good approximation of sales for a product from introduction through a growth period and into a period of market saturation. The linear decreasing trend in part (b) is useful for time series displaying a steady decline over time. The horizontal line in part (c) represents a time series that has no consistent increase or decrease over time and thus no trend.

Cyclical Component

Although a time series may exhibit a trend over long periods of time, all future values of the time series will not fall exactly on the trend line. In fact, time series often show alternating sequences of points below and above the trend line. Any recurring sequence of points above and below the trend line lasting more than one year can be attributed to the **cyclical component** of the time series. Figure 6.4 shows the graph of a time series with an obvious cyclical component. The observations are taken at intervals of one year.

Many time series exhibit cyclical behavior with regular runs of observations below and above the trend line. Generally, this component of the time series is due to multiyear cycli-

FIGURE 6.3 EXAMPLES OF SOME POSSIBLE TIME SERIES TREND PATTERNS

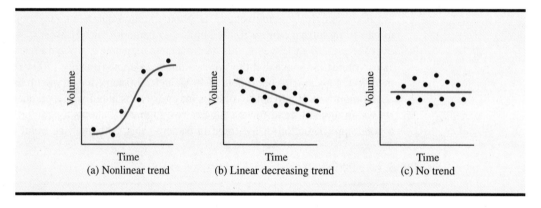

FIGURE 6.4 TREND AND CYCLICAL COMPONENTS OF A TIME SERIES (DATA POINTS ARE ONE YEAR APART)

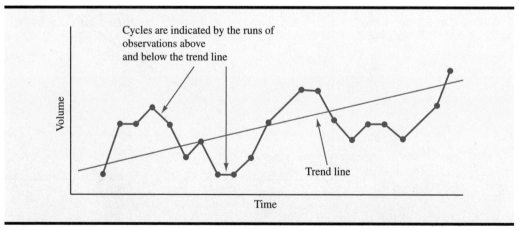

cal movements in the economy. For example, periods of modest inflation followed by periods of rapid inflation can lead to many time series that alternate below and above a generally increasing trend line (e.g., a time series for housing costs).

Seasonal Component

Whereas the trend and cyclical components of a time series are identified by analyzing multiyear movements in historical data, many time series show a regular pattern over one-year periods. For example, a manufacturer of swimming pools expects low sales activity in the fall and winter months, with peak sales occurring in the spring and summer months. Manufacturers of snow removal equipment and heavy clothing, however, expect just the opposite yearly pattern. Not surprisingly, the component of the time series that represents the variability in the data due to seasonal influences is called the **seasonal component.** Although we generally think of seasonal movement in a time series as occurring within one year, the seasonal component also may be used to represent any regularly repeating pattern that is less than one year in duration. For example, daily traffic volume data show within-the-day "seasonal" behavior, with peak levels during rush hours, moderate flow during the rest of the day, and light flow from midnight to early morning.

Irregular Component

The **irregular component** of the time series is the residual or "catchall" factor that includes deviations of actual time series values from those expected given the effects of the trend, cyclical, and seasonal components. It accounts for the random variability in the time series. The irregular component is caused by the short-term, unanticipated, and nonrecurring factors that affect the time series. Because this component accounts for the random variability in the time series, it is unpredictable. We cannot attempt to predict its impact on the time series.

6.2   USING SMOOTHING METHODS IN FORECASTING

Many manufacturing environments require forecasts for thousands of items weekly or monthly. Thus, in choosing a forecasting technique, simplicity and ease of use are important criteria. The data requirements for the techniques in this section are minimal, and the techniques are easy to use and understand.

In this section we discuss three forecasting methods: moving averages, weighted moving averages, and exponential smoothing. The objective of each of these methods is to "smooth out" the random fluctuations caused by the irregular component of the time series. Therefore, they are referred to as *smoothing methods*. Smoothing methods are appropriate for a stable time series—that is, one that exhibits no significant trend, cyclical, or seasonal effects—because they adapt well to changes in the level of the time series. However, without modification, they do not work as well when a significant trend and/or seasonal variation are present.

Smoothing methods are easy to use and generally provide a high level of accuracy for short-range forecasts such as a forecast for the next time period. One of the methods, exponential smoothing, has minimal data requirements and thus is a good method to use when forecasts are required for large numbers of items.

Moving Averages

The **moving averages** method uses the average of the *most recent n* data values in the time series as the forecast for the next period. Mathematically,

$$\text{Moving average} = \frac{\sum(\text{most recent } n \text{ data values})}{n} \qquad (6.1)$$

The term *moving* indicates that, as a new observation becomes available for the time series, it replaces the oldest observation in equation (6.1), and a new average is computed. As a result, the average will change, or move, as new observations become available.

To illustrate the moving averages method, consider the 12 weeks of data presented in Table 6.1 and Figure 6.5. These data show the number of gallons of gasoline sold by a gasoline distributor in Bennington, Vermont, over the past 12 weeks. Figure 6.5 indicates that, although random variability is present, the time series appears to be stable over time. Thus, the smoothing methods of this section are applicable.

To use moving averages to forecast gasoline sales, we must first select the number of data values to be included in the moving average. For example, let us compute forecasts

TABLE 6.1   GASOLINE SALES TIMES SERIES

Week	Sales (000s of gallons)
1	17
2	21
3	19
4	23
5	18
6	16
7	20
8	18
9	22
10	20
11	15
12	22

FIGURE 6.5   GRAPH OF GASOLINE SALES TIME SERIES

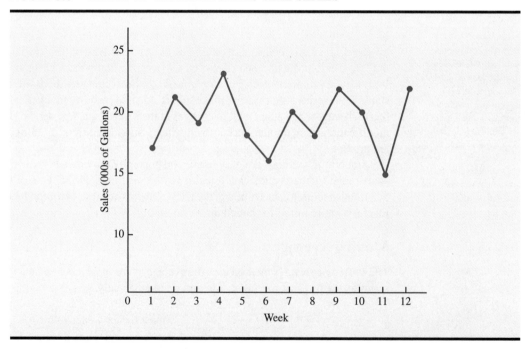

using a 3-week moving average. The moving average calculation for the first 3 weeks of the gasoline sales time series is

$$\text{Moving average (weeks 1–3)} = \frac{17 + 21 + 19}{3} = 19$$

We then use this moving average value as the forecast for week 4. The actual value observed in week 4 is 23, so the forecast error in week 4 is $23 - 19 = 4$. In general, the error associated with a forecast is the difference between the observed value of the time series and the forecast.

The calculation for the second 3-week moving average is

$$\text{Moving average (weeks 2–4)} = \frac{21 + 19 + 23}{3} = 21$$

Try Problem 1 for practice in using moving averages to compute a forecast.

Hence, the forecast for week 5 is 21, and the error associated with this forecast is $18 - 21 = -3$. Thus, the forecast error may be positive or negative, depending on whether the forecast is too low or too high. A complete summary of the 3-week moving average calculations for the gasoline sales time series is shown in Table 6.2.

To forecast gasoline sales for week 13 using a 3-month moving average, we need to compute the average of sales for weeks 10, 11, and 12. The calculation for this moving average is

$$\text{Moving average (weeks 10–12)} = \frac{20 + 15 + 22}{3} = 19$$

Hence, the forecast for week 13 is 19, or 19,000 gallons of gasoline. Figure 6.6 shows a graph of the original time series and the 3-week moving average forecasts.

Forecast Accuracy   An important consideration in selecting a forecasting method is the accuracy of the forecast. Clearly, we want forecast errors to be small. The last two columns of Table 6.2, which contain the forecast errors and the forecast errors squared, can be used to develop measures of forecast accuracy.

TABLE 6.2   SUMMARY OF 3-WEEK MOVING AVERAGE CALCULATIONS

Week	Time Series Value	Moving Average Forecast	Forecast Error	Squared Forecast Error
1	17			
2	21			
3	19			
4	23	19	4	16
5	18	21	−3	9
6	16	20	−4	16
7	20	19	1	1
8	18	18	0	0
9	22	18	4	16
10	20	20	0	0
11	15	20	−5	25
12	22	19	3	9
			Totals 0	92

FIGURE 6.6   GRAPH OF GASOLINE SALES TIME SERIES AND 3-WEEK MOVING AVERAGE FORECASTS

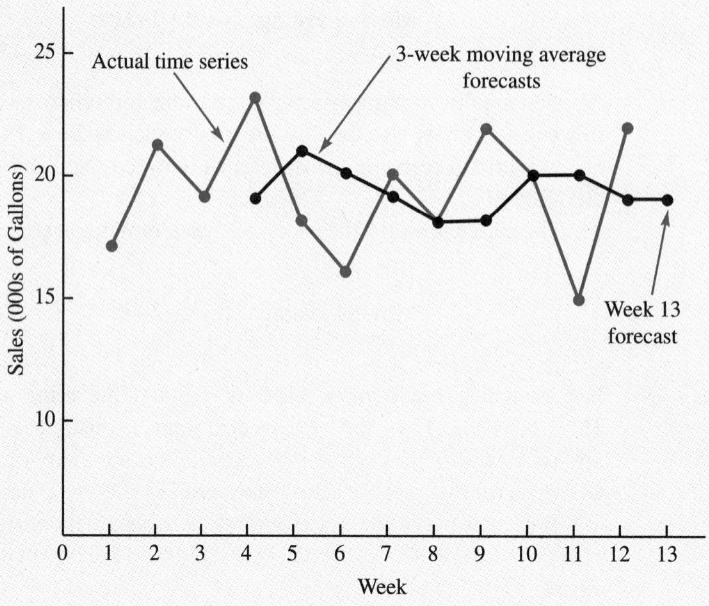

For the gasoline sales time series, we can use the last column of Table 6.2 to compute the average of the sum of the squared errors. Doing so, we obtain

$$\text{Average of the sum of squared errors} = \frac{92}{9} = 10.22$$

This average of the sum of squared errors is commonly referred to as the **mean squared error (MSE).** The MSE is an often-used measure of the accuracy of a forecasting method and is the one we use in this chapter.

As we indicated previously, to use the moving averages method, we must first select the number of data values to be included in the moving average. Not surprisingly, for a particular time series, different lengths of moving averages will affect the accuracy of the forecast. One possible approach to choosing the number of values to be included is to use trial and error to identify the length that minimizes the MSE. Then, if we assume that the length that is best for the past will also be best for the future, we would forecast the next value in the time series using the number of data values that minimized the MSE for the historical time series.

Problem 2 will test your ability to use MSE as a measure of forecast accuracy.

Weighted Moving Averages

In the moving averages method, each observation in the calculation receives the same weight. One variation, known as **weighted moving averages,** involves selecting different weights for each data value and then computing a weighted average of the most recent n data values as the forecast. In most cases, the most recent observation receives the most weight, and the weight decreases for older data values. For example, we can use the gasoline sales time series to illustrate the computation of a weighted 3-week moving average, with the most recent observation receiving a weight three times as great as that given the oldest observation, and the next oldest observation receiving a weight twice as great as the oldest. For week 4 the computation is

$$\text{Weighted moving averages forecast for week 4} = \frac{3}{6}(19) + \frac{2}{6}(21) + \frac{1}{6}(17) = 19.33$$

Note that for the weighted moving average the sum of the weights is equal to 1. Actually, this condition was also true for the simple moving average: Each weight was ⅓. However, recall that the simple or unweighted moving average provided a forecast of 19.

Forecast Accuracy   To use the weighted moving averages method, we must first select the number of data values to be included in the weighted moving average and then choose weights for each of the data values. In general, if we believe that the recent past is a better predictor of the future than the distant past, larger weights should be given to the more recent observations. However, when the time series is highly variable, selecting approximately equal weights for each data value may be best. Note that the only requirement in selecting the weights is that their sum must equal 1. To determine whether one particular combination of data values and weights provides a more accurate forecast than another combination, we will continue to use the MSE criterion as the measure of forecast accuracy. That is, if we assume that the combination that is best for the past will also be best for the future, we would use the combination of data values and weights that minimized MSE for the historical time series to forecast the next value in the time series.

Exponential Smoothing

Exponential smoothing is simple and has few data requirements. Thus, it is an inexpensive, useful approach for firms that make many forecasts each period.

Exponential smoothing uses a weighted average of past time series values as the forecast; it is a special case of the weighted moving averages method in which we select only one weight—the weight for the most recent observation. The weights for the other data values are automatically computed and get smaller and smaller as the observations move farther into the past. The basic exponential smoothing model is:

$$F_{t+1} = \alpha Y_t + (1 - \alpha)F_t \qquad (6.2)$$

where

$$F_{t+1} = \text{forecast of the time series for period } t + 1$$
$$Y_t = \text{actual value of the time series in period } t$$
$$F_t = \text{forecast of the time series for period } t$$
$$\alpha = \text{smoothing constant } (0 \leq \alpha \leq 1)$$

Equation (6.2) shows that the forecast for period $t + 1$ is a weighted average of the actual value in period t and the forecast for period t; note in particular that the weight given to the actual value in period t is α and that the weight given to the forecast in period t is $1 - \alpha$. We can demonstrate that the exponential smoothing forecast for any period also is a weighted average of *all the previous actual values* for the time series with a time series consisting of three periods of data: Y_1, Y_2, and Y_3. To start the calculations, we let F_1 equal the actual value of the time series in period 1; that is, $F_1 = Y_1$. Hence, the forecast for period 2

$$F_2 = \alpha Y_1 + (1 - \alpha)F_1$$
$$= \alpha Y_1 + (1 - \alpha)Y_1$$
$$= Y_1$$

Thus, the exponential smoothing forecast for period 2 is equal to the actual value of the time series in period 1.

The forecast for period 3 is

$$F_3 = \alpha Y_2 + (1 - \alpha)F_2 = \alpha Y_2 + (1 - \alpha)Y_1$$

Finally, substituting this expression for F_3 in the expression for F_4, we obtain

$$
\begin{aligned}
F_4 &= \alpha Y_3 + (1 - \alpha)F_3 \\
&= \alpha Y_3 + (1 - \alpha)[\alpha Y_2 + (1 - \alpha)Y_1] \\
&= \alpha Y_3 + \alpha(1 - \alpha)Y_2 + (1 - \alpha)^2 Y_1
\end{aligned}
$$

Hence, F_4 is a weighted average of the first three time series values. The sum of the coefficients, or weights, for Y_1, Y_2, and Y_3 equals 1. A similar argument can be made to show that, in general, any forecast F_{t+1} is a weighted average of all the previous time series values.

Despite the fact that exponential smoothing provides a forecast that is a weighted average of all past observations, all the past data do not need to be saved in order to compute the forecast for the next period. In fact, once the **smoothing constant** α has been selected, only two pieces of information are required to compute the forecast. Equation (6.2) shows that with a given α we can compute the forecast for period $t + 1$ simply by knowing the actual and forecast time series values for period t—that is, Y_t and F_t.

To illustrate the exponential smoothing approach to forecasting, consider the gasoline sales time series presented previously in Table 6.1 and Figure 6.5. As indicated, the exponential smoothing forecast for period 2 is equal to the actual value of the time series in period 1. Thus, with $Y_1 = 17$, we set $F_2 = 17$ to get the exponential smoothing computations started. From the time series data in Table 6.1, we find an actual time series value in period 2 of $Y_2 = 21$. Thus, period 2 has a forecast error of $21 - 17 = 4$.

Continuing with the exponential smoothing computations, using a smoothing constant of $\alpha = 0.2$, provides the forecast for period 3:

$$F_3 = 0.2Y_2 + 0.8F_2 = 0.2(21) + 0.8(17) = 17.8$$

Once the actual time series value in period 3, $Y_3 = 19$, is known, we can generate a forecast for period 4:

$$F_4 = 0.2Y_3 + 0.8F_3 = 0.2(19) + 0.8(17.8) = 18.04$$

By continuing the exponential smoothing calculations, we can determine the weekly forecast values and the corresponding weekly forecast errors, as shown in Table 6.3. Note that we have not shown an exponential smoothing forecast or the forecast error for period 1 because no forecast was made. For week 12, we have $Y_{12} = 22$ and $F_{12} = 18.48$. Can we use this information to generate a forecast for week 13 before the actual value of week 13 becomes known? Using the exponential smoothing model, we have

$$F_{13} = 0.2Y_{12} + 0.8F_{12} = 0.2(22) + 0.8(18.48) = 19.18$$

Can you now use exponential smoothing to develop forecasts? Try Problem 4.

Thus, the exponential smoothing forecast of the amount sold in week 13 is 19.18, or 19,180 gallons of gasoline. With this forecast, the firm can make plans and decisions accordingly. The accuracy of the forecast will not be known until the end of week 13.

TABLE 6.3   SUMMARY OF THE EXPONENTIAL SMOOTHING FORECASTS AND
FORECAST ERRORS FOR GASOLINE SALES WITH SMOOTHING
CONSTANT $\alpha = 0.2$

Week (t)	Time Series Value (Y_t)	Exponential Smoothing Forecast (F_t)	Forecast Error ($Y_t - F_t$)
1	17		
2	21	17.00	4.00
3	19	17.80	1.20
4	23	18.04	4.96
5	18	19.03	−1.03
6	16	18.83	−2.83
7	20	18.26	1.74
8	18	18.61	−0.61
9	22	18.49	3.51
10	20	19.19	0.81
11	15	19.35	−4.35
12	22	18.48	3.52

Figure 6.7 shows the plot of the actual and the forecast values from Table 6.3. Note in particular how the forecasts "smooth out" the irregular fluctuations in the time series.

Forecast Accuracy   In the preceding exponential smoothing calculations, we used a smoothing constant of $\alpha = 0.2$. Although any value of α between 0 and 1 is acceptable, some values will yield better forecasts than others. Insight into choosing a good value for α can be obtained by rewriting the basic exponential smoothing model as follows:

$$F_{t+1} = \alpha Y_t + (1 - \alpha)F_t \tag{6.3}$$
$$= \alpha Y_t + F_t - \alpha F_t$$
$$= F_t + \alpha(Y_t - F_t)$$

Forecast
in period t

Forecast error
in period t

Thus, the new forecast F_{t+1} is equal to the previous forecast F_t plus an adjustment, which is α times the most recent forecast error, $Y_t - F_t$. That is, the forecast in period $t + 1$ is obtained by adjusting the forecast in period t by a fraction of the forecast error. If the time series contains substantial random variability, a small value of the smoothing constant is preferred. The reason for this choice is that, because much of the forecast error is due to random variability, we do not want to overreact and adjust the forecasts too quickly. For a time series with relatively little random variability, larger values of the smoothing constant have the advantage of quickly adjusting the forecasts when forecasting errors occur and therefore allowing the forecast to react faster to changing conditions.

The criterion we use to determine a desirable value for the smoothing constant α is the same as the criterion we proposed earlier for determining the number of periods of data to include in the moving averages calculation. That is, we choose the value of α that minimizes the mean squared error. A summary of the MSE calculations for the exponential smoothing forecast of gasoline sales with $\alpha = 0.2$ is shown in Table 6.4. Note that

FIGURE 6.7 GRAPH OF ACTUAL AND FORECAST GASOLINE SALES TIME SERIES
WITH SMOOTHING CONSTANT $\alpha = 0.2$

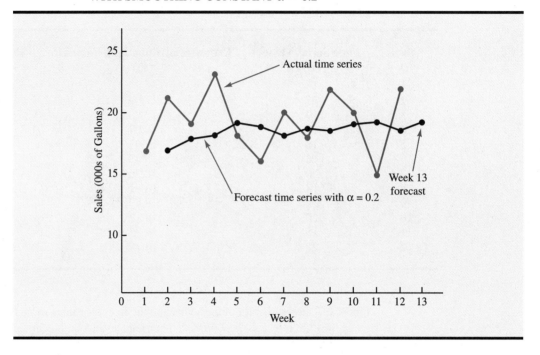

TABLE 6.4 MEAN SQUARED ERROR COMPUTATIONS FOR FORECASTING GASOLINE
SALES WITH $\alpha = 0.2$

Week (t)	Time Series Value (Y_t)	Forecast (F_t)	Forecast Error ($Y_t - F_t$)	Squared Forecast Error ($Y_t - F_t)^2$
1	17			
2	21	17.00	4.00	16.00
3	19	17.80	1.20	1.44
4	23	18.04	4.96	24.60
5	18	19.03	−1.03	1.06
6	16	18.83	−2.83	8.01
7	20	18.26	1.74	3.03
8	18	18.61	−0.61	0.37
9	22	18.49	3.51	12.32
10	20	19.19	0.81	0.66
11	15	19.35	−4.35	18.92
12	22	18.48	3.52	12.39
			Total	98.80

$$\text{MSE} = 98.80/11 = 8.98$$

Problem 5 asks you to determine whether moving averages or exponential smoothing provides the best forecasts for a given set of data.

there is one less squared error term than the number of periods of data because we had no past values with which to make a forecast for period 1. Would a different value of α have provided better results in terms of a lower MSE value? Perhaps the most straightforward way to answer this question is simply to try another value for α. We then compare its mean squared error with the MSE value of 8.98, obtained using a smoothing constant of $\alpha = 0.2$.

TABLE 6.5   MEAN SQUARED ERROR COMPUTATIONS FOR FORECASTING GASOLINE
SALES WITH $\alpha = 0.3$

Week (t)	Time Series Value (Y_t)	Forecast (F_t)	Forecast Error $(Y_t - F_t)$	Squared Forecast Error $(Y_t - F_t)^2$
1	17			
2	21	17.00	4.00	16.00
3	19	18.20	0.80	0.64
4	23	18.44	4.56	20.79
5	18	19.81	−1.81	3.28
6	16	19.27	−3.27	10.69
7	20	18.29	1.71	2.92
8	18	18.80	−0.80	0.64
9	22	18.56	3.44	11.83
10	20	19.59	0.41	0.17
11	15	19.71	−4.71	22.18
12	22	18.30	3.70	13.69
			Total	102.83

$$\text{MSE} = 102.83/11 = 9.35$$

The exponential smoothing results with $\alpha = 0.3$ are shown in Table 6.5. With MSE = 9.35, a smoothing constant of $\alpha = 0.3$ results in less forecast accuracy than a smoothing constant of $\alpha = 0.2$. Thus, we would be inclined to use the original smoothing constant of 0.2. Using a trial-and-error calculation with other values of α, we can find a "good" value for the smoothing constant. This value can be used in the exponential smoothing model to provide forecasts for the future. At a later date, after new time series observations have been obtained, we analyze the newly collected time series data to determine whether the smoothing constant should be revised to provide better forecasting results.

NOTES AND COMMENTS

1. Another commonly used measure of forecast accuracy is the **mean absolute deviation (MAD).** This measure is simply the average of the absolute values of all the forecast errors. Using the errors given in Table 6.2, we obtain

$$\text{MAD} = \frac{4 + 3 + 4 + 1 + 0 + 4 + 0 + 5 + 3}{9}$$

$$= 2.67$$

One major difference between the MSE and the MAD is that the MSE measure is influenced much more by large forecast errors than by small errors (for the MSE measure the errors are squared). The selection of the best measure of forecasting accuracy is not a simple matter. Indeed, forecasting experts often disagree as to which measure should be used. We use the MSE measure in this chapter.

2. Spreadsheet packages are an effective aid in choosing a good value of α for exponential smoothing and selecting weights for the weighted moving averages method. With the time series data and the forecasting formulas in the spreadsheets, you can experiment with different values of α (or moving average weights) and choose the value(s) providing the smallest MSE or MAD. In the chapter appendix, we show how this can be done.

6.3   USING TREND PROJECTION IN FORECASTING

In this section we show how to forecast the values of a time series that exhibits a long-term linear trend. The type of time series for which the trend projection method is applicable shows a consistent increase or decrease over time; it is not stable so the smoothing methods described in the preceding section are not applicable.

Consider the time series for bicycle sales of a particular manufacturer over the past 10 years, as shown in Table 6.6 and Figure 6.8. Note that 21,600 bicycles were sold in year 1; 22,900 were sold in year 2; and so on. In year 10, the most recent year, 31,400 bicycles were sold. Although Figure 6.8 shows some up-and-down movement over the past 10

TABLE 6.6   BICYCLE SALES TIME SERIES

Year (t)	Sales (000s) (Y_t)
1	21.6
2	22.9
3	25.5
4	21.9
5	23.9
6	27.5
7	31.5
8	29.7
9	28.6
10	31.4

FIGURE 6.8   GRAPH OF BICYCLE SALES TIME SERIES

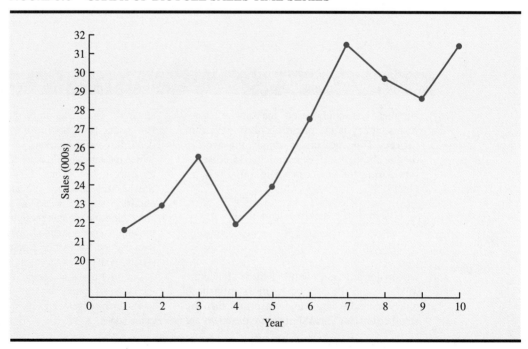

FIGURE 6.9   TREND REPRESENTED BY A LINEAR FUNCTION FOR BICYCLE SALES

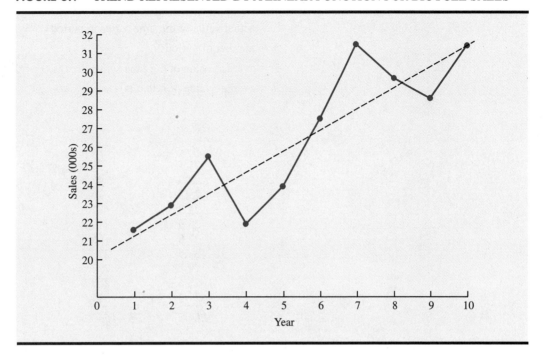

years, the time series for the number of bicycles sold seems to have an overall increasing or upward trend.

We do not want the trend component of a time series to follow each and every "up" and "down" movement. Rather, the trend component should reflect the gradual shifting—in this case, growth—of the time series values. After we view the time series data in Table 6.6 and the graph in Figure 6.8, we might agree that a linear trend as shown in Figure 6.9 provides a reasonable description of the long-run movement in the series.

We use the bicycle sales data to illustrate the calculations involved in applying regression analysis to identify a linear trend. For a linear trend, the estimated sales volume expressed as a function of time is

$$T_t = b_0 + b_1 t \qquad (6.4)$$

where

$$T_t = \text{trend value for bicycle sales in period } t$$
$$b_0 = \text{intercept of the trend line}$$
$$b_1 = \text{slope of the trend line}$$

Note that, for the time series on bicycle sales, $t = 1$ corresponds to the oldest time series value and $t = 10$ corresponds to the most recent time series value. Formulas for computing b_1 and b_0 are:

$$b_1 = \frac{\sum t Y_t - \left(\sum t \sum Y_t\right)/n}{\sum t^2 - \left(\sum t\right)^2/n} \qquad (6.5)$$
$$b_0 = \bar{Y} - b_1 \bar{t} \qquad (6.6)$$

where

$$Y_t = \text{actual value of the time series in period } t$$
$$n = \text{number of periods}$$
$$\overline{Y} = \text{average value of the time series; that is, } \overline{Y} = \Sigma Y_t/n$$
$$\overline{t} = \text{average value of } t; \text{ that is, } \overline{t} = \Sigma t/n$$

t	Y_t	tY_t	t^2
1	21.6	21.6	1
2	22.9	45.8	4
3	25.5	76.5	9
4	21.9	87.6	16
5	23.9	119.5	25
6	27.5	165.0	36
7	31.5	220.5	49
8	29.7	237.6	64
9	28.6	257.4	81
10	31.4	314.0	100
Totals 55	264.5	1545.5	385

Using these relationships for b_0 and b_1 and the bicycle sales data of Table 6.6, we obtain the following calculations.

$$\overline{t} = \frac{55}{10} = 5.5$$

$$\overline{Y} = \frac{264.5}{10} = 26.45$$

$$b_1 = \frac{1545.5 - (55)(264.5)/10}{385 - (55)^2/10} = 1.10$$

$$b_0 = 26.45 - 1.10(5.5) = 20.4$$

Therefore,

$$T_t = 20.4 + 1.1t \tag{6.7}$$

is the equation for the linear trend component for the bicycle sales time series.

Try Problem 14 for practice in developing the equation for the linear trend component of a time series.

The slope of 1.1 in the trend equation indicates that over the past 10 years the firm has experienced an average growth in sales of about 1100 units per year. If we assume that the past 10-year trend in sales is a good indicator for the future, we can use equation (6.7) to project the trend component of the time series. For example, substituting $t = 11$ into equation (6.7) yields next year's trend projection, T_{11}:

$$T_{11} = 20.4 + 1.1(11) = 32.5$$

Thus the trend component yields a sales forecast of 32,500 bicycles for next year.

FIGURE 6.10   SOME POSSIBLE FORMS OF NONLINEAR TREND PATTERNS

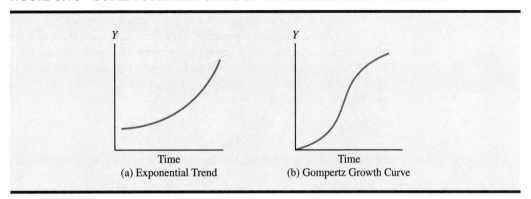

We can also use the trend line to forecast sales farther into the future. For instance, using equation (6.7), we develop forecasts for an additional 2 and 3 years into the future as follows:

$$T_{12} = 20.4 + 1.1(12) = 33.6$$
$$T_{13} = 20.4 + 1.1(13) = 34.7$$

The use of a linear function to model the trend is common. However, as we discussed earlier, sometimes time series exhibit a curvilinear (nonlinear) trend similar to those shown in Figure 6.10. More advanced texts discuss how to develop models for these more complex relationships.

6.4   USING TREND AND SEASONAL COMPONENTS IN FORECASTING

We have shown how to forecast the values of a time series that has a trend component. In this section we extend the discussion by showing how to forecast the values of a time series that has both trend and seasonal components.

Many situations in business and economics involve period-to-period comparisons. For instance, we might be interested to learn that unemployment is up 2% compared to last month, steel production is up 5% over last month, or that the production of electric power is down 3% from the previous month. Care must be exercised in using such information, however, because whenever a seasonal influence is present, such comparisons usually are not especially meaningful. For instance, the fact that electric power consumption is down by 3% from August to September might be only the seasonal effect associated with a decrease in the use of air conditioning and not because of a long-term decline in the use of electric power. Indeed, after adjusting for the seasonal effect, we might even find that the use of electric power has increased.

Removing the seasonal effect from a time series is known as *deseasonalizing the time series*. After we do so, period-to-period comparisons are more meaningful and can help identify whether a trend exists. The approach we take in this section is appropriate in situations when only seasonal effects are present or in situations when both seasonal and trend components are present. The first step is to compute seasonal indexes and use them to deseasonalize the data. Then, if a trend is apparent in the deseasonalized data, we use regression analysis on the deseasonalized data to estimate the trend.

The Multiplicative Model

In addition to a trend component T and a seasonal component S, we assume that the time series also has an irregular component I. The irregular component accounts for the random effects in the time series that cannot be explained by the trend and seasonal components. Using T_t, S_t, and I_t to identify the trend, seasonal, and irregular components at time t, we assume that the actual time series value, denoted by Y_t, can be described by the **multiplicative time series model**

$$Y_t = T_t \times S_t \times I_t \qquad (6.8)$$

In this model, T_t is the trend measured in units of the item being forecast. However, the S_t and I_t components are measured in relative terms, with values above 1.00 indicating effects above the trend, and values below 1.00 indicating effects below the trend.

We illustrate the use of the multiplicative model with trend, seasonal, and irregular components by working with the quarterly data presented in Table 6.7 and Figure 6.11. These data show television set sales (in thousands of units) for a particular manufacturer over the past 4 years. We begin by showing how to identify the seasonal component of the time series.

Calculating the Seasonal Indexes

Figure 6.11 indicates that sales are lowest in the second quarter of each year, followed by higher sales levels in quarters 3 and 4. Thus, we conclude that a seasonal pattern exists for television set sales. We begin the computational procedure used to identify each quarter's seasonal influence by computing a moving average to isolate the combined seasonal and irregular components, S_t and I_t.

To do so, we use 1 year of data in each calculation. Because we are working with a quarterly series, we use four data values in each moving average. The moving average calculation for the first 4 quarters of the television set sales data is

$$\text{First moving average} = \frac{4.8 + 4.1 + 6.0 + 6.5}{4} = \frac{21.4}{4} = 5.35$$

TABLE 6.7   QUARTERLY DATA FOR TELEVISION SET SALES

Year	Quarter	Sales (000s)
1	1	4.8
	2	4.1
	3	6.0
	4	6.5
2	1	5.8
	2	5.2
	3	6.8
	4	7.4
3	1	6.0
	2	5.6
	3	7.5
	4	7.8
4	1	6.3
	2	5.9
	3	8.0
	4	8.4

FIGURE 6.11   GRAPH OF QUARTERLY TELEVISION SET SALES TIME SERIES

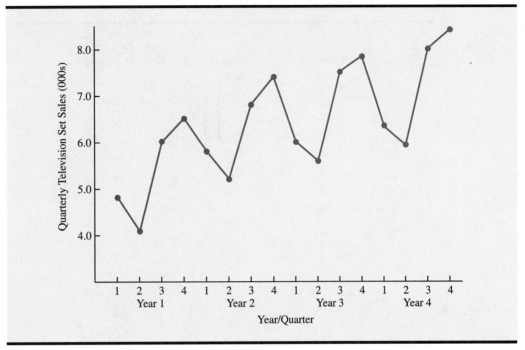

Note that the moving average calculation for the first 4 quarters yields the average quarterly sales over year 1 of the time series. Continuing the moving average calculation, we next add the 5.8 value for the first quarter of year 2 and drop the 4.8 for the first quarter of year 1. Thus, the second moving average is

$$\text{Second moving average} = \frac{4.1 + 6.0 + 6.5 + 5.8}{4} = \frac{22.4}{4} = 5.6$$

Similarly, the third moving average calculation is $(6.0 + 6.5 + 5.8 + 5.2)/4 = 5.875$.

Before we proceed with the moving average calculations for the entire time series, we return to the first moving average calculation, which resulted in a value of 5.35. The 5.35 value represents an average quarterly sales volume (across all seasons) for year 1. As we look back at the calculation of the 5.35 value, associating 5.35 with the "middle" quarter of the moving average group makes sense. Note, however, that we encounter some difficulty in identifying the middle quarter; 4 quarters in the moving average allow for no middle quarter. The 5.35 value corresponds to the last half of quarter 2 and the first half of quarter 3. Similarly, if we go to the next moving average value of 5.60, the middle corresponds to the last half of quarter 3 and the first half of quarter 4.

Recall that the reason for computing moving averages is to isolate the combined seasonal and irregular components. However, the moving average values we have computed do not correspond directly to the original quarters of the time series. We can resolve this difficulty by using the midpoints between successive moving average values. For example, because 5.35 corresponds to the first half of quarter 3 and 5.60 corresponds to the last half of quarter 3, we can use $(5.35 + 5.60)/2 = 5.475$ as the moving average value for quarter 3. Similarly, we associate a moving average value of $(5.60 + 5.875)/2 = 5.738$ with quarter 4. The result is a *centered moving average*. Table 6.8 shows a complete summary of the moving average and centered moving average calculations for the television set sales data.

TABLE 6.8   CENTERED MOVING AVERAGE CALCULATIONS FOR THE TELEVISION
              SET SALES TIME SERIES

Year	Quarter	Sales (000s)	4-Quarter Moving Average	Centered Moving Average
1	1	4.8		
	2	4.1		
	3	6.0	5.350	5.475
	4	6.5	5.600	5.738
2	1	5.8	5.875	5.975
	2	5.2	6.075	6.188
	3	6.8	6.300	6.325
	4	7.4	6.350	6.400
3	1	6.0	6.450	6.538
	2	5.6	6.625	6.675
	3	7.5	6.725	6.763
	4	7.8	6.800	6.838
4	1	6.3	6.875	6.938
	2	5.9	7.000	7.075
	3	8.0	7.150	
	4	8.4		

If the number of data points in a moving average calculation is an odd number, the middle point will correspond to one of the periods in the time series. In such cases, we would not have to center the moving average values to correspond to a particular time period, as we did in the calculations in Table 6.8.

What do the centered moving averages in Table 6.8 tell us about this time series? Figure 6.12 shows plots of the actual time series values and the corresponding centered moving average. Note particularly how the centered moving average values tend to "smooth out" both the seasonal and irregular fluctuations in the time series. The moving average values computed for 4 quarters of data do not include the fluctuations due to seasonal influences because the seasonal effect has been averaged out. Each point in the centered moving average represents what the value of the time series would be without seasonal or irregular influences.

By dividing each time series observation by the corresponding centered moving average value, we can identify the seasonal-irregular effect in the time series. For example, the third quarter of year 1 shows 6.0/5.475 = 1.096 as the combined seasonal-irregular component. Table 6.9 summarizes the resulting seasonal-irregular values for the entire time series.

Consider the third quarter. The results from years 1, 2, and 3 show third-quarter values of 1.096, 1.075, and 1.109, respectively. Thus, in all cases the seasonal-irregular component appears to have an above average influence in the third quarter. The fluctuations over the 3 years can be attributed to the irregular component, so we can average the computed values to eliminate the irregular influence and obtain an estimate of the third-quarter seasonal influence:

$$\text{Seasonal effect of third quarter} = \frac{1.096 + 1.075 + 1.109}{3} = 1.09$$

FIGURE 6.12   GRAPH OF QUARTERLY TELEVISION SET SALES TIME SERIES AND
CENTERED MOVING AVERAGE

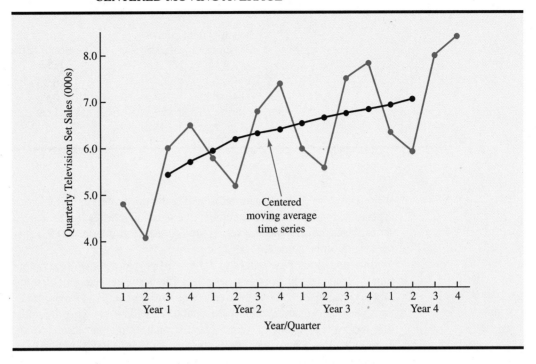

TABLE 6.9   SEASONAL-IRREGULAR VALUES FOR THE TELEVISION SET SALES
TIME SERIES

Year	Quarter	Sales (000s)	Centered Moving Average	Seasonal-Irregular Value
1	1	4.8		
	2	4.1		
	3	6.0	5.475	1.096
	4	6.5	5.738	1.133
2	1	5.8	5.975	0.971
	2	5.2	6.188	0.840
	3	6.8	6.325	1.075
	4	7.4	6.400	1.156
3	1	6.0	6.538	0.918
	2	5.6	6.675	0.839
	3	7.5	6.763	1.109
	4	7.8	6.838	1.141
4	1	6.3	6.938	0.908
	2	5.9	7.075	0.834
	3	8.0		
	4	8.4		

TABLE 6.10   SEASONAL INDEX CALCULATIONS FOR THE TELEVISION SET SALES
TIME SERIES

Quarter	Seasonal-Irregular Component Values $(S_t I_t)$	Seasonal Index (S_t)
1	0.971, 0.918, 0.908	0.93
2	0.840, 0.839, 0.834	0.84
3	1.096, 1.075, 1.109	1.09
4	1.133, 1.156, 1.141	1.14

We refer to 1.09 as the **seasonal index** for the third quarter. In Table 6.10 we summarize
the calculations involved in computing the seasonal indexes for the television set sales time
series. Thus, the seasonal indexes for all 4 quarters are: quarter 1, 0.93; quarter 2, 0.84; quarter 3, 1.09; and quarter 4, 1.14.

Interpretation of the values in Table 6.10 provides some observations about the "seasonal" component in television set sales. The best sales quarter is the fourth quarter, with
sales averaging 14% above the average quarterly value. The worst, or slowest, sales quarter is the second quarter, with its seasonal index at 0.84, showing the sales average 16% below the average quarterly sales. The seasonal component corresponds to the intuitive
expectation that television viewing interest and thus television purchase patterns tend to
peak in the fourth quarter, with its coming winter season and fewer outdoor activities. The
low second-quarter sales reflect the reduced television interest resulting from the spring and
presummer activities of the potential customers.

*Can you now compute and
interpret seasonal indexes
for a time series? Try
Problem 25.*

One final adjustment may be necessary in obtaining the seasonal indexes. The multiplicative model requires that the average seasonal index equal 1.00, so the sum of the four
seasonal indexes in Table 6.10 must equal 4.00. In other words, the seasonal effects must
even out over the year. The average of the seasonal indexes in our example is equal to 1.00,
and hence, this type of adjustment is not necessary. In other cases, a slight adjustment may
be necessary. To make the adjustment, multiply each seasonal index by the number of seasons divided by the sum of the unadjusted seasonal indexes. For instance, for quarterly data,
multiply each seasonal index by 4/(sum of the unadjusted seasonal indexes). Some of the
problems at the end of the chapter require this adjustment.

Deseasonalizing the Time Series

*With deseasonalized data,
comparing sales in
successive periods makes
sense. With data that have
not been deseasonalized,
relevant comparisons can
often be made between
sales in the current period
and sales in the same
period one year ago.*

The purpose of finding seasonal indexes is to remove the seasonal effects from a time series. This process is referred to as *deseasonalizing* the time series. Economic time series adjusted for seasonal variations (**deseasonalized time series**) are reported in the *Survey of
Current Business, The Wall Street Journal,* and *Business Week.* Using the notation of the
multiplicative model, we have

$$Y_t = T_t \times S_t \times I_t$$

By dividing each time series observation by the corresponding seasonal index, we remove
the effect of season from the time series. The deseasonalized time series for television set
sales is summarized in Table 6.11. A graph of the deseasonalized television set sales time
series is shown in Figure 6.13.

TABLE 6.11   DESEASONALIZED VALUES FOR THE TELEVISION SET SALES
TIMES SERIES

Year	Quarter	Sales (000s) (Y_t)	Seasonal Index (S_t)	Deseasonalized Sales $(Y_t/S_t = T_t I_t)$
1	1	4.8	0.93	5.16
	2	4.1	0.84	4.88
	3	6.0	1.09	5.50
	4	6.5	1.14	5.70
2	1	5.8	0.93	6.24
	2	5.2	0.84	6.19
	3	6.8	1.09	6.24
	4	7.4	1.14	6.49
3	1	6.0	0.93	6.45
	2	5.6	0.84	6.67
	3	7.5	1.09	6.88
	4	7.8	1.14	6.84
4	1	6.3	0.93	6.77
	2	5.9	0.84	7.02
	3	8.0	1.09	7.34
	4	8.4	1.14	7.37

FIGURE 6.13   DESEASONALIZED TELEVISION SET SALES TIME SERIES

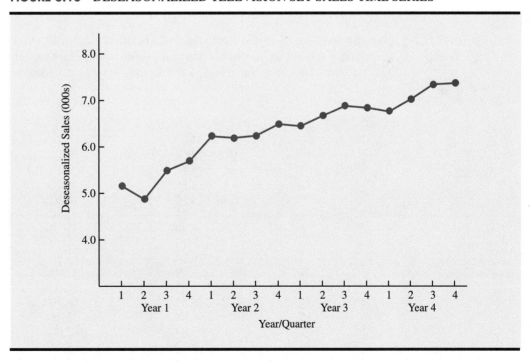

Using the Deseasonalized Time Series to Identify Trend

Although the graph in Figure 6.13 shows some up-and-down movement over the past 16 quarters, the time series seems to have an upward linear trend. To identify this trend, we use the same procedure as in the preceding section; in this case, the data used are quarterly deseasonalized sales values. Thus, for a linear trend, the estimated sales volume expressed as a function of time is

$$T_t = b_0 + b_1 t$$

where

T_t = trend value for television set sales in period t

b_0 = intercept of the trend line

b_0 = slope of the trend line

As before, $t = 1$ corresponds to the time of the first observation for the time series, $t = 2$ corresponds to the time of the second observation, and so on. Thus, for the deseasonalized television set sales time series, $t = 1$ corresponds to the first deseasonalized quarterly sales value and $t = 16$ corresponds to the most recent deseasonalized quarterly sales value. The formulas for computing the values of b_0 and b_1 again are

$$b_1 = \frac{\sum t Y_t - (\sum t \sum Y_t)/n}{\sum t^2 - (\sum t)^2/n} \quad \text{and} \quad b_0 = \bar{Y} - b_1 \bar{t}$$

Note, however, that Y_t now refers to the deseasonalized time series value at time t and not to the actual value of the time series. Using the given relationships for b_0 and b_1 and the deseasonalized sales data of Table 6.11, we make the following calculations.

t	Y_t (deseasonalized)	tY_t	t^2
1	5.16	5.16	1
2	4.88	9.76	4
3	5.50	16.50	9
4	5.70	22.80	16
5	6.24	31.20	25
6	6.19	37.14	36
7	6.24	43.68	49
8	6.49	51.92	64
9	6.45	58.05	81
10	6.67	66.70	100
11	6.88	75.68	121
12	6.84	82.08	144
13	6.77	88.01	169
14	7.02	98.28	196
15	7.34	110.10	225
16	7.37	117.92	256
Totals 136	101.74	914.98	1496

$$\bar{t} = \frac{136}{16} = 8.5$$

$$\bar{Y} = \frac{101.74}{16} = 6.359$$

$$b_1 = \frac{914.98 - (136)(101.74)/16}{1496 - (136)^2/16} = 0.148$$

$$b_0 = 6.359 - 0.148(8.5) = 5.101$$

Therefore,

$$T_t = 5.101 + 0.148t$$

is the equation for the linear trend component of the time series.

The slope of 0.148 indicates that over the past 16 quarters the firm has experienced an average deseasonalized growth in sales of about 148 sets per quarter. If we assume that the past 16-quarter trend in sales data is a reasonably good indicator of the future, we can use this equation to project the trend component of the time series for future quarters. For example, substituting $t = 17$ into the equation yields next quarter's trend projection, T_{17}:

$$T_{17} = 5.101 + 0.148(17) = 7.617$$

Thus, the trend component yields a sales forecast of 7617 television sets for the next quarter. Similarly, the trend component produces sales forecasts of 7765, 7913, and 8061 television sets in quarters 18, 19, and 20, respectively.

Seasonal Adjustments

The final step in developing the forecast when both trend and seasonal components are present is to use the seasonal index to adjust the trend projection. Returning to the television set sales example, we have a trend projection for the next 4 quarters. Now we must adjust the forecast for the seasonal effect. The seasonal index for the first quarter of year 5 ($t = 17$) is 0.93, so we obtain the quarterly forecast by multiplying the forecast based on trend ($T_{17} = 7617$) times the seasonal index (0.93). Thus, the forecast for the next quarter is $7617(0.93) = 7084$. Table 6.12 shows the quarterly forecast for quarters 17–20. The forecasts show the high-volume fourth quarter with a 9190-unit forecast and the low-volume second quarter with a 6523-unit forecast.

Models Based on Monthly Data

In the preceding television set sales example we used quarterly data to illustrate the computation of seasonal indexes. However, many businesses use monthly rather than quarterly

TABLE 6.12   QUARTERLY FORECASTS FOR THE TELEVISION SET SALES TIME SERIES

Year	Quarter	Trend Forecast	Seasonal Index (see Table 6.10)	Quarterly Forecast
5	1	7617	0.93	(7617)(0.93) = 7084
	2	7765	0.84	(7765)(0.84) = 6523
	3	7913	1.09	(7913)(1.09) = 8625
	4	8061	1.14	(8061)(1.14) = 9190

forecasts. In such cases, the procedures introduced in this section can be applied with minor modifications. First, a 12-month moving average replaces the 4-quarter moving average; second, 12 monthly seasonal indexes, rather than the 4 quarterly indexes, must be computed. Other than these changes, the computational and forecasting procedures are identical.

Cyclical Component

Mathematically, the multiplicative model of equation (6.8) can be expanded to include a cyclical component as follows:

$$Y_t = T_t \times C_t \times S_t \times I_t \tag{6.9}$$

The cyclical component is attributable to multiyear cycles in the time series. It is analogous to the seasonal component but over a longer period of time. However, because of the length of time involved, obtaining enough relevant data to estimate the cyclical component often is difficult. Another difficulty is that the length of cycles usually varies. We leave further discussion of the cyclical component to texts on forecasting methods.

6.5   USING REGRESSION ANALYSIS IN FORECASTING

Regression analysis is a statistical technique that can be used to develop a mathematical equation showing how variables are related. In regression terminology, the variable that is being predicted is called the *dependent* or *response* variable. The variable or variables being used to predict the value of the dependent variable are called the *independent* or *predictor* variables. Regression analysis involving one independent variable and one dependent variable for which the relationship between the variables is approximated by a straight line is called *simple linear regression*. Regression analysis involving two or more independent variables is called *multiple regression analysis*. In Section 6.3 we utilized simple linear regression to fit a linear trend to the bicycle sales time series. Recall that we developed a linear equation relating bicycle sales to the time period. The number of bicycles sold isn't actually causally related to time; instead, time is a surrogate for variables to which the number of bicycles sold is actually related but which are either unknown or too difficult or costly to measure. Thus, the use of regression analysis for trend projection is not a causal forecasting method because only past values of sales, the variable being forecast, were used.

When we use regression analysis to relate the variable that we want to forecast to other variables that are supposed to influence or explain that variable, it becomes a causal forecasting method. The Q. M. in Action: Spare Parts Forecasting at American Airlines explains why that company uses regression analysis as a causal forecasting method to estimate the demand for spare parts.

Using Regression Analysis as a Causal Forecasting Method

To illustrate how regression analysis is used as a causal forecasting method, we consider the sales forecasting problem faced by Armand's Pizza Parlors, a chain of Italian restaurants doing business in a five-state area. The most successful locations have been near college campuses. The managers believe that quarterly sales for these restaurants (denoted by *y*) are related positively to the size of the student population (denoted by *x*); that is, restaurants near campuses with a large population tend to generate more sales than those located near campuses with a small population. Using regression analysis we can develop an equation showing how the dependent variable *y* is related the independent variable *x*.

Q. M. IN ACTION

SPARE PARTS FORECASTING AT AMERICAN AIRLINES*

American Airlines developed the Rotables Allocation and Planning System (RAPS) to provide demand forecasts for spare parts, assist in allocating spare parts to airports, and calculate the availability level of each spare part. The demand forecasting module of RAPS provides monthly demand forecasts for more than 5000 parts, ranging from coffee makers to landing gears. The average price for parts covered by RAPS is approximately $5000.

Prior to RAPS, American Airlines used time series methodology to forecast spare parts demand. The time series methodology was slow to respond to external factors such as changes in aircraft utilization and major fleet expansions. To correct for these deficiencies, the forecasting component of

RAPS involves the use of regression analysis "to establish a relationship between monthly part removals and various functions of monthly flying hours." The RAPS system generates the monthly demand forecasts in less than an hour.

Nearly all the parts covered by the RAPS system are essential to the operation of an aircraft. A part shortage can even result in cancellation of a flight, so the cost can be substantial. The materials management group at American Airlines estimated "that using RAPS has provided a one-time savings of $7 million and recurring annual savings of nearly $1 million."

*Mark J. Tedone, "Repairable Part Management," *Interfaces* 19, no. 4 (July–August 1989): 61–68.

This equation can then be used to forecast quarterly sales for restaurants located near college campuses given the size of the student population.

In situations where time series data are not available, regression analysis can still be used to develop a forecast. For instance, suppose that management wanted to forecast sales for a new restaurant they were considering opening near a college campus. Because no historical data are available on sales for a new restaurant, Armand cannot use time series data to develop the forecast. But, as we will now illustrate, regression analysis can still be used to forecast quarterly sales.

To develop the equation relating quarterly sales and the size of the student population, Armand's collected data from a sample of 10 of its restaurants located near college campuses. These data are summarized in Table 6.13. For example, restaurant 1, with $y = 58$ and $x = 2$, had $58,000 in quarterly sales and is located near a campus with 2000 students. Figure 6.14 shows graphically the data presented in Table 6.13. The size of the student

TABLE 6.13   DATA ON QUARTERLY SALES AND STUDENT POPULATION FOR 10 RESTAURANTS

Restaurant	y = Quarterly Sales ($000s)	x = Student Population (000s)
1	58	2
2	105	6
3	88	8
4	118	8
5	117	12
6	137	16
7	157	20
8	169	20
9	149	22
10	202	26

FIGURE 6.14   SCATTER DIAGRAM OF QUARTERLY SALES VERSUS
STUDENT POPULATION

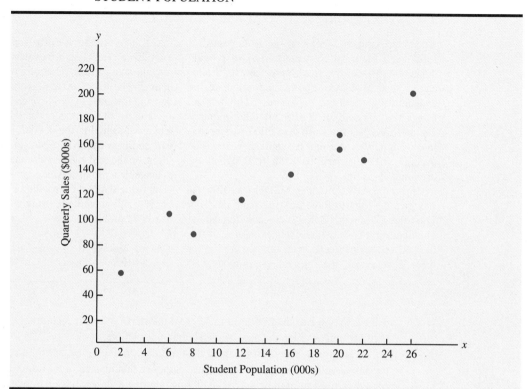

population is shown on the horizontal axis, with quarterly sales shown on the vertical axis. This type of graph is called a *scatter diagram*. Usually the independent variable is plotted on the horizontal axis, and the dependent variable is plotted on the vertical axis. The advantage of a scatter diagram is that it provides an overview of the data and enables us to draw preliminary conclusions about a possible relationship between the variables.

What preliminary conclusions can we draw from Figure 6.14? Sales appear to be higher at campuses with larger student populations. Also, it appears that the relationship between the two variables can be approximated by a straight line; indeed, there appears to be a positive relationship between x and y. In Figure 6.15 we have drawn a straight line through the data that appears to provide a good linear approximation of the relationship between the variables. Observe that the relationship isn't perfect. Indeed, few, if any, of the data fall exactly on the line. However, if we can develop the mathematical expression for this line, we may be able to use it to forecast the value of y corresponding to each possible value of x. The resulting equation of the line is called the *estimated regression equation*.

Using the least-squares method of estimation, we develop the estimated regression equation

$$\hat{y} = b_0 + b_1 x \qquad (6.10)$$

where

$\hat{y}$ = estimated value of the dependent variable (quarterly sales)

b_0 = intercept of the estimated regression equation

b_1 = slope of the estimated regression equation

x = value of the independent variable (student population)

We use the sample data and the following expression to compute the intercept b_0 and slope b_1:

$$b_1 = \frac{\sum x_i y_i - \left(\sum x_i \sum y_i\right)/n}{\sum x_i^2 - \left(\sum x_i\right)^2/n} \tag{6.11}$$

$$b_0 = \bar{y} - b_1 \bar{x} \tag{6.12}$$

where

x_i = value of the independent variable for the ith observation

y_i = value of the dependent variable for the ith observation

$\bar{x}$ = mean value for the independent variable

$\bar{y}$ = mean value for the dependent variable

n = total number of observations

Some of the calculations necessary to develop the least-squares estimated regression equation for the data on student population and quarterly sales are shown in Table 6.14. Our example contains 10 restaurants or observations; hence $n = 10$. Using equations (6.11) and

FIGURE 6.15   STRAIGHT-LINE APPROXIMATION FOR DATA ON QUARTERLY SALES AND STUDENT POPULATION

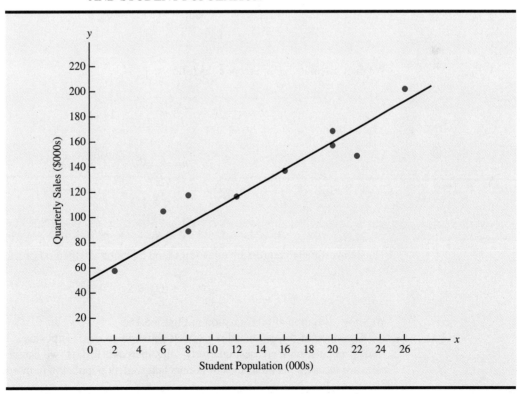

TABLE 6.14   CALCULATIONS FOR THE LEAST-SQUARES ESTIMATED REGRESSION EQUATION FOR ARMAND'S PIZZA PARLORS

Restaurant (i)	y_i	x_i	$x_i y_i$	x_i^2
1	58	2	116	4
2	105	6	630	36
3	88	8	704	64
4	118	8	944	64
5	117	12	1,404	144
6	137	16	2,192	256
7	157	20	3,140	400
8	169	20	3,380	400
9	149	22	3,278	484
10	202	26	5,252	676
Totals	1300	140	21,040	2528

(6.12), we can now compute the slope and intercept of the estimated regression equation. We calculate the slope b_1 as follows:

$$b_1 = \frac{\sum x_i y_i - (\sum x_i \sum y_i)/n}{\sum x_i^2 - (\sum x_i)^2/n}$$

$$= \frac{21,040 - (140)(1300)/10}{2528 - (140)^2/10}$$

$$= \frac{2840}{568}$$

$$= 5$$

We then calculate the intercept b_0 as follows:

$$\bar{x} = \frac{\sum x_i}{n} = \frac{140}{10} = 14$$

$$\bar{y} = \frac{\sum y_i}{n} = \frac{1300}{10} = 130$$

$$b_0 = \bar{y} - b_1 \bar{x}$$

$$= 130 - 5(14)$$

$$= 60$$

Thus, the estimated regression equation found by using the method of least squares is

$$\hat{y} = 60 + 5x$$

We show the graph of this equation in Figure 6.16.

The slope of the estimated regression equation ($b_1 = 5$) is positive, implying that, as student population increases, quarterly sales increase. In fact, we can conclude (because sales are measured in thousands of dollars and student population in thousands) that an in-

FIGURE 6.16   THE ESTIMATED REGRESSION EQUATION FOR ARMAND'S
PIZZA PARLORS

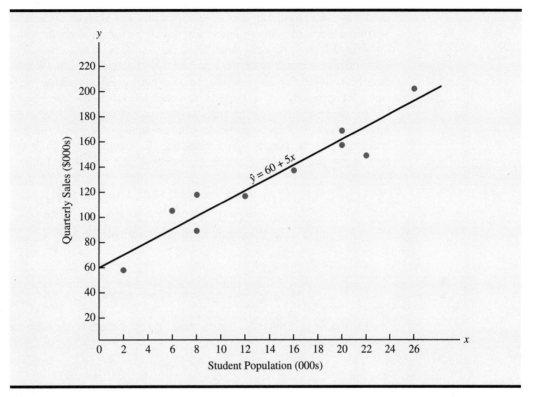

crease in the student population of 1000 is associated with an increase of $5000 in expected
quarterly sales; that is, quarterly sales are expected to increase by $5 per student.

If we believe that the least-squares estimated regression equation adequately describes
the relationship between x and y, using the estimated regression equation to forecast the
value of y for a given value of x seems reasonable. For example, if we wanted to forecast
quarterly sales for a new restaurant to be located near a campus with 16,000 students, we
would compute

*Practice using regression
analysis to develop a
forecast by working
Problem 33.*

$$\hat{y} = 60 + 5(16)$$
$$= 140$$

Hence, we would forecast quarterly sales of $140,000 per year.

The sales forecasting problem facing Armand's Pizza Parlors illustrates how simple linear regression analysis can be used to develop forecasts when time series data are not available. Multiple regression analysis also can be applied in these situations if additional data
for other independent variables are available. For example, suppose that the management
of Armand's Pizza Parlors also believes that the number of competitors near the college
campus is related to quarterly sales. Intuitively, management believes that restaurants located near campuses with fewer competitors generate more sales revenue than those located
near campuses with more competitors. With additional data, multiple regression analysis
could be used to develop an equation relating quarterly sales to the size of the student population and the number of competitors.

Using Regression Analysis with Time Series Data

In Section 6.3 we fit a linear trend to the bicycle sales time series to show how simple linear regression analysis can be used to forecast future values of a time series when past values of the time series are available. Recall that for this problem the annual sales in year t was treated as the dependent variable and the year t was treated as the independent variable. The inherent complexity of most real-world problems necessitates the consideration of more than one independent variable to predict the dependent variable. We now consider how multiple regression analysis is used to develop forecasts when time series data are available.

To use multiple regression analysis, we need a sample of observations for the dependent variable and all the independent variables. In time series analysis, the n periods of time series data provide a sample of n observations for each variable. To describe the wide variety of regression-based models that can be developed, we use the following notation:

$$Y_t = \text{actual value of the time series in period } t$$
$$x_{1t} = \text{value of independent variable 1 in period } t$$
$$x_{2t} = \text{value of independent variable 2 in period } t$$
$$\cdot$$
$$\cdot$$
$$\cdot$$
$$x_{kt} = \text{value of independent variable } k \text{ in period } t$$

The n periods of data necessary to develop the estimated regression equation would appear as follows.

Period	Time Series (Y_t)	Value of Independent Variables x_{1t}	x_{2t}	x_{3t}	· · ·	x_{kt}
1	Y_1	x_{11}	x_{21}	x_{31}	· · ·	x_{k1}
2	Y_2	x_{12}	x_{22}	x_{32}	· · ·	x_{k2}
·	·	·	·	·	· · · · ·	·
·	·	·	·	·	· · · · ·	·
·	·	·	·	·	· · · · ·	·
n	Y_n	x_{1n}	x_{2n}	x_{3n}	· · ·	x_{kn}

As you might imagine, a number of choices can be made when selecting the independent variables in a forecasting model. One possible choice is simply time. We made this choice in Section 6.3 when we estimated the trend of the time series using a linear function of the independent variable time. Letting

$$x_{1t} = t$$

we obtain an estimated regression equation of the form

$$\hat{Y}_t = b_0 + b_1 t$$

where $\hat{Y}_t$ is the estimate of the time series value Y_t and where b_0 and b_1 are the estimated regression coefficients. In a more complex model, additional terms could be added corresponding to time raised to other powers. For example, if

$$x_{2t} = t^2 \quad \text{and} \quad x_{3t} = t^3$$

the estimated regression equation would become

$$\hat{Y}_t = b_0 + b_1 x_{1t} + b_2 x_{2t} + b_3 x_{3t}$$
$$= b_0 + b_1 t + b_2 t^2 + b_3 t^3$$

Note that this model provides a forecast of a time series with curvilinear characteristics over time.

Other regression-based forecasting models involve the use of a mixture of economic and demographic independent variables. For example, in forecasting the sale of refrigerators, we might select independent variables such as

x_{1t} = price in period t

x_{2t} = total industry sales in period $t - 1$

x_{3t} = number of building permits for new houses in period $t - 1$

x_{4t} = population forecast for period t

x_{5t} = advertising budget for period t

According to the usual multiple regression procedure, an estimated regression equation with five independent variables would be used to develop forecasts in this case.

Spyros Makridakis, a noted forecasting expert, has conducted research showing that simple techniques usually outperform more complex procedures for short-term forecasting. Using a more sophisticated and expensive procedure will not guarantee better forecasts.

Whether a regression approach provides a good forecast depends largely on how well we are able to identify and obtain data for independent variables that are closely related to the time series. Generally, during the development of an estimated regression equation, we will want to consider many possible sets of independent variables. Thus, part of the regression analysis procedure should focus on the selection of the set of independent variables that provides the best forecasting model.

In the chapter introduction we stated that **causal forecasting methods** utilized time series related to the one being forecast in an effort to explain better the cause of a time series' behavior. Regression analysis is the tool most often used in developing causal models. The related time series become the independent variables, and the time series being forecast is the dependent variable.

Another type of regression-based forecasting model occurs whenever all the independent variables are previous values of the same time series. For example, if the time series values are denoted $Y_1, Y_2, \ldots, Y_n$, we might try to find an estimated regression equation relating Y_t to the most recent time series values, Y_{t-1}, Y_{t-2}, and so on. For instance, if we use the actual values of the time series for the three most recent periods as independent variables, the estimated regression equation would be

$$\hat{Y}_t = b_0 + b_1 Y_{t-1} + b_2 Y_{t-2} + b_3 Y_{t-3}$$

Regression models such as this one in which the independent variables are previous values of the time series are referred to as **autoregressive models.**

Finally, another regression-based forecasting approach is one that incorporates a mixture of the independent variables previously discussed. For example, we might select a combination of time variables, some economic/demographic variables, and some previous values of the time series variable itself.

6.6   QUALITATIVE APPROACHES TO FORECASTING

In the preceding sections we discussed several types of quantitative forecasting methods. Most of these techniques require historical data on the variable of interest, so they cannot be applied when no historical data are available. Furthermore, even when such data are available, a significant change in environmental conditions affecting the time series may make the use of past data questionable in predicting future values of the time series. For example, a government-imposed gasoline rationing program would raise questions about the validity of a gasoline sales forecast based on historical data. Qualitative forecasting techniques offer an alternative in these and other cases.

Delphi Method

If historical data are not available, managers may use a qualitative technique to develop forecasts. But the cost of using qualitative techniques can be high because of the time commitment required from the people involved.

One of the most commonly used qualitative forecasting techniques is the **Delphi method.** This technique, originally developed by a research group at the Rand Corporation, attempts to develop forecasts through "group consensus." In its usual application, the members of a panel of experts—all of whom are physically separated from and unknown to each other—are asked to respond to a series of questionnaires. The responses from the first questionnaire are tabulated and used to prepare a second questionnaire that contains information and opinions of the entire group. Each respondent is then asked to reconsider and possibly revise his or her previous response in light of the group information provided. This process continues until the coordinator feels that some degree of consensus has been reached. The goal of the Delphi method is not to produce a single answer as output, but instead to produce a relatively narrow spread of opinions within which the majority of experts concur.

Expert Judgment

Empirical evidence and theoretical arguments suggest that between 5 and 20 experts should be used in judgmental forecasting.

Qualitative forecasts often are based on the judgment of a single expert or represent the consensus of a group of experts. For example, each year a group of experts at Merrill Lynch gather to forecast the level of the Dow Jones Industrial Average and the prime rate for the next year. In doing so, the experts individually consider information that they believe will influence the stock market and interest rates; then they combine their conclusions into a forecast. No formal model is used, and no two experts are likely to consider the same information in the same way.

Expert judgment is a forecasting method that is often recommended when conditions in the past are not likely to hold in the future. Even though no formal quantitative model is used, expert judgment has provided good forecasts in many situations.

Scenario Writing

The qualitative procedure referred to as **scenario writing** consists of developing a conceptual scenario of the future based on a well-defined set of assumptions. Different sets of assumptions lead to different scenarios. The job of the decision maker is to decide how likely each scenario is and then to make decisions accordingly.

Intuitive Approaches

Subjective, or *intuitive qualitative approaches,* are based on the ability of the human mind to process information that, in most cases, is difficult to quantify. These techniques are often used in group work, wherein a committee or panel seeks to develop new ideas or solve complex problems through a series of "brainstorming sessions." In such sessions, individuals are freed from the usual group restrictions of peer pressure and criticism because they can present any idea or opinion without regard to its relevancy and, even more importantly, without fear of criticism.

SUMMARY

In this chapter we discussed how forecasts can be developed to help management develop appropriate strategies for the future. We began by defining a time series as a set of observations on a variable measured at successive points in time or over successive periods of time. A time series may involve four separate components: trend, seasonal, irregular, and cyclical. By isolating these components and measuring their apparent effects, future values of the time series can be forecast.

Quantitative forecasting methods include time series methods and causal methods. A time series method is appropriate when the historical data are restricted to past values of the variable being forecast. The three time series methods discussed in the chapter are smoothing (moving averages, weighted moving averages, and exponential smoothing), trend projection, and trend projection adjusted for seasonal influence.

Smoothing methods are appropriate for a stable time series, that is, one that exhibits no significant trend, cyclical, or seasonal effects. The moving averages approach consists of computing an average of past values and then using this average as the forecast for the next period. The weighted moving averages method allows for the possibility of unequal weights for the data; thus, the moving averages method is a special case of the weighted moving averages method in which all the weights are equal. Exponential smoothing also is a special case of the weighted moving averages method involving only one parameter: the weight for the most recent observation.

When a time series consists of random fluctuations around a long-term trend line, a linear equation may be used to estimate the trend. When seasonal effects are present, seasonal indexes can be computed and used to deseasonalize the data and to develop forecasts. When both seasonal and long-term trend effects are present, a trend line is fitted to the deseasonalized data; the seasonal indexes are then used to adjust the trend projections.

Causal forecasting methods are based on the assumption that the variable being forecast exhibits a cause-effect relationship with one or more other variables. A causal forecasting method is one that relates the variable being forecast to other variables that are thought to influence or explain it. Regression analysis is a causal forecasting method that can be used to develop forecasts when time series data are not available.

Qualitative forecasting methods may be used when little or no historical data are available. Qualitative forecasting methods also are considered most appropriate when the historical pattern of the time series is not expected to continue into the future.

GLOSSARY

Time series   A set of observations measured at successive points in time or over successive periods of time.

Forecast   A projection or prediction of future values of a time series.

Trend   The long-run shift or movement in the time series observable over several periods of data.

Cyclical component   The component of the time series model that results in periodic above-trend and below-trend behavior of the time series lasting more than one year.

Seasonal component   The component of the time series model that shows a periodic pattern over one year or less.

Irregular component   The component of the time series model that reflects the random variation of the actual time series values beyond what can be explained by the trend, cyclical, and seasonal components.

Moving averages   A method of forecasting or smoothing a time series by averaging each successive group of data points.

Mean squared error (MSE)   An approach to measuring the accuracy of a forecasting model. This measure is the average of the sum of the squared differences between the actual time series values and the forecasted values.

Weighted moving averages   A method of forecasting or smoothing a time series by computing a weighted average of past time series values. The sum of the weights must equal 1.

Exponential smoothing   A forecasting technique that uses a weighted average of past time series values to arrive at smoothed time series values that can be used as forecasts.

Smoothing constant   A parameter of the exponential smoothing model that provides the weight given to the most recent time series value in the calculation of the forecast.

Mean absolute deviation (MAD)   A measure of forecast accuracy. The average of the absolute values of the forecast errors.

Multiplicative time series model   A model that assumes that the separate components of the time series can be multiplied together to identify the actual time series value. When the four components of trend, cyclical, seasonal, and irregular are assumed present, we obtain $Y_t = T_t \times C_t \times S_t \times I_t$. When cyclical effects are not modeled, we obtain $Y_t = T_t \times S_t \times I_t$.

Seasonal index   A measure of the seasonal effect on a time series. A seasonal index above 1 indicates a positive effect, a seasonal index of 1 indicates no seasonal effect, and a seasonal index less than 1 indicates a negative effect.

Deseasonalized time series   A time series that has had the effect of season removed by dividing each original time series observation by the corresponding seasonal index.

Regression analysis   A statistical technique that can be used to develop a mathematical equation showing how variables are related.

Causal forecasting methods   Forecasting methods that relate a time series to other variables that are believed to explain or cause its behavior.

Autoregressive model   A time series model that uses a regression relationship based on historical time series values to predict the future time series values.

Delphi method   A qualitative forecasting method that obtains forecasts through group consensus.

Scenario writing   A qualitative forecasting method that consists of developing a conceptual scenario of the future based on a well-defined set of assumptions.

PROBLEMS

SELFtest

1. Corporate Triple A Bond interest rates for 12 consecutive months are 9.5, 9.3, 9.4, 9.6, 9.8, 9.7, 9.8, 10.5, 9.9, 9.7, 9.6, and 9.6.
    a. Develop 3- and 4-month moving averages for this time series. Which moving average provides the better forecasts? Explain.
    b. What is the moving average forecast for the next month?

SELFtest

2. Refer to the gasoline sales time series data in Table 6.1.
    a. Compute 4- and 5-week moving averages for the time series.
    b. Compute the MSE for the 4- and 5-week moving average forecasts.
    c. What appears to be the best number of weeks of past data to use in the moving average computation? Remember that the MSE for the 3-week moving average is 10.22.

3. Refer again to the gasoline sales time series data in Table 6.1.
    a. Use a weight of $\frac{1}{2}$ for the most recent observation, $\frac{1}{3}$ for the second most recent, and $\frac{1}{6}$ for the third most recent to compute a 3-week weighted moving average for the time series.
    b. Compute the MSE for the weighted moving average in part (a). Do you prefer this weighted moving average to the unweighted moving average? Remember that the MSE for the unweighted moving average is 10.22.
    c. Suppose that you are allowed to choose any weights as long as they sum to 1. Could you always find a set of weights that would make the MSE smaller for a weighted moving average than for an unweighted moving average? Why or why not?

SELFtest   4. Use the gasoline sales time series data from Table 6.1 to show the exponential smoothing forecasts using $\alpha = 0.1$. Using the mean squared error criterion, would you prefer a smoothing constant of $\alpha = 0.1$ or $\alpha = 0.2$?

SELFtest   5. For the Hawkins Company, the monthly percentages of all shipments that were received on time over the past 12 months are 80, 82, 84, 83, 83, 84, 85, 84, 82, 83, 84, and 83.

      a. Compare a 3-month moving average forecast with an exponential smoothing forecast for $\alpha = 0.2$. Which provides the better forecasts?

      b. What is the forecast for next month?

    6. With a smoothing constant of $\alpha = 0.2$, equation (6.2) shows that the forecast for the 13th week of the gasoline sales data from Table 6.1 is given by $F_{13} = 0.2Y_{12} + 0.8F_{12}$. However, the forecast for week 12 is given by $F_{12} = 0.2Y_{11} + 0.8F_{11}$. Thus, we could combine these two results to write the forecast for the 13th week as

$$F_{13} = 0.2Y_{12} + 0.8(0.2Y_{11} + 0.8F_{11}) = 0.2Y_{12} + 0.16Y_{11} + 0.64F_{11}$$

      a. Make use of the fact that $F_{11} = 0.2Y_{10} + 0.8F_{10}$ (and similarly for F_{10} and F_9) and continue to expand the expression for F_{13} until you have written it in terms of the past data values Y_{12}, Y_{11}, Y_{10}, Y_9, and Y_8, and the forecast for period 8.

      b. Refer to the coefficients or weights for the past data values Y_{12}, Y_{11}, Y_{10}, Y_9, and Y_8; what observation can you make about how exponential smoothing weights past data values in arriving at new forecasts? Compare this weighting pattern with the weighting pattern of the moving averages method.

    7. Alabama building contracts for a 12-month period (in millions of dollars) are 240, 350, 230, 260, 280, 320, 220, 310, 240, 310, 240, and 230.

      a. Compare a 3-month moving average forecast with an exponential smoothing forecast using $\alpha = 0.2$. Which provides the better forecasts?

      b. What is the forecast for the next month?

    8. Moving averages often are used to identify movements in stock prices. Weekly closing prices (in dollars per share) for Toys'R'Us for September 22, 1997, through December 8, 1997, follow (Prudential Securities, Inc.).

Week	Price ($)	Week	Price ($)
September 22	$34\frac{7}{8}$	November 3	$33\frac{5}{8}$
September 29	$35\frac{5}{8}$	November 10	$35\frac{1}{16}$
October 6	$34\frac{11}{16}$	November 17	$34\frac{1}{16}$
October 13	$33\frac{9}{16}$	November 24	$34\frac{1}{8}$
October 20	$32\frac{5}{8}$	December 1	$33\frac{1}{4}$
October 27	34	December 8	$32\frac{1}{16}$

      a. Use a 3-month moving average to smooth the time series. Forecast the closing price for December 15, 1997.

      b. Use a 3-month weighted moving average to smooth the time series. Use a weight of .4 for the most recent period, .4 for the next period back, and .2 for the third period back. Forecast the closing price for December 15, 1997.

      c. Use exponential smoothing with a smoothing constant of $\alpha = .35$ to smooth the time series. Forecast the closing price for December 15, 1997.

      d. Which of the three methods do you prefer? Why?

9. The following data represent 15 quarters of manufacturing capacity utilization (in percentages).

Quarter/Year	Utilization	Quarter/Year	Utilization
1/1996	82.5	1/1998	78.8
2/1996	81.3	2/1998	78.7
3/1996	81.3	3/1998	78.4
4/1996	79.0	4/1998	80.0
1/1997	76.6	1/1999	80.7
2/1997	78.0	2/1999	80.7
3/1997	78.4	3/1999	80.8
4/1997	78.0		

a. Compute 3- and 4-quarter moving averages for this time series. Which moving average provides the better forecast for the fourth quarter of 1999?
b. Use smoothing constants of $\alpha = 0.4$ and $\alpha = 0.5$ to develop forecasts for the fourth quarter of 1999. Which smoothing constant provides the better forecast?
c. Based on the analyses in parts (a) and (b), which method—moving averages or exponential smoothing—provides the better forecast? Explain.

10. The Federal Election Commission maintains data showing the voting age population, the number of registered voters, and the turnout for federal elections. The following table shows the national voter turnout as a percentage of the voting age population from 1972 to 1996. (*The Wall Street Journal Almanac*, 1998)

Year	% Turnout	Year	% Turnout
1972	55	1986	36
1974	38	1988	50
1976	54	1990	37
1978	37	1992	55
1980	53	1994	39
1982	40	1996	49
1984	53		

a. Use exponential smoothing to forecast this time series. Consider smoothing constants of $\alpha = .1$ and .2. What value of the smoothing constant provides the best forecast?
b. What is the forecast of the percentage turnout in 1998?

11. The percentage of individual investors' portfolios committed to stock depends on the state of the economy. As of April 1997, a typical portfolio consisted of cash (19%), stocks (30%), stock funds (37%), bonds (8%), and bond funds (6%) (*AAII Journal,* June 1997). The following table reports the percentage of stocks in a typical portfolio in nine quarters from 1995 to 1997.

Quarter	Stock %	Quarter	Stock %
1st—1995	29.8	2nd—1996	31.5
2nd—1995	31.0	3rd—1996	32.0
3rd—1995	29.9	4th—1996	31.9
4th—1995	30.1	1st—1997	30.0
1st—1996	32.2		

a. Use exponential smoothing to forecast this time series. Consider smoothing constants of $\alpha = .2, .3,$ and $.4$. What value of the smoothing constant provides the best forecast?

b. What is the forecast of the percentage of assets committed to stocks for the second quarter of 1997?

12. United Dairies, Inc., supplies milk to several independent grocers throughout Dade County, Florida. Management wants to develop a forecast of the number of half-gallons of milk sold per week. Sales data (in units) for the past 12 weeks are as follows.

Week	Sales	Week	Sales
1	2750	7	3300
2	3100	8	3100
3	3250	9	2950
4	2800	10	3000
5	2900	11	3200
6	3050	12	3150

Use exponential smoothing, with $\alpha = 0.4$, to develop a forecast of demand for week 13.

13. Ten weeks of data on the Commodity Futures Index are 7.35, 7.40, 7.55, 7.56, 7.60, 7.52, 7.52, 7.70, 7.62, and 7.55.

a. Compute the exponential smoothing values for $\alpha = 0.2$.

b. Compute the exponential smoothing values for $\alpha = 0.3$.

c. Which exponential smoothing model provides the better forecasts? Forecast week 11.

SELFtest 14. The enrollment data (000s) for a state college for the past 6 years are shown.

Year	1	2	3	4	5	6
Enrollment	20.5	20.2	19.5	19.0	19.1	18.8

Develop the equation for the linear trend component for this time series. Comment on what is happening to enrollment at this institution.

15. Automobile sales at B. J. Scott Motors, Inc., provided the following 10-year time series.

Year	Sales	Year	Sales
1	400	6	260
2	390	7	300
3	320	8	320
4	340	9	340
5	270	10	370

Plot the time series, and comment on the appropriateness of a linear trend. What type of functional form would be best for the trend pattern of this time series?

16. The president of a small manufacturing firm has been concerned about the continual growth in manufacturing costs over the past several years. The following is a time series of the cost per unit (in dollars) for the firm's leading product over the past 8 years.

Year	Cost Per Unit	Year	Cost Per Unit
1	20.00	5	26.60
2	24.50	6	30.00
3	28.20	7	31.00
4	27.50	8	36.00

a. Graph this time series. Does a linear trend appear?

b. Develop the equation for the linear trend component for the time series. What is the average cost increase per year?

17. In the late 1990s many firms began downsizing in order to reduce their costs. One of the results of these cost-cutting measures has been a decline in the percentage of private-industry jobs that are managerial. The following data show the percentage of females who were managers from 1990 to 1995 (*The Wall Street Journal Almanac*, 1998).

Year	1990	1991	1992	1993	1994	1995
Percentage	7.45	7.53	7.52	7.65	7.62	7.73

a. Develop a linear trend equation for this time series.

b. Use the trend equation to estimate the percentage of females who were managers for 1996 and 1997.

18. ACT Networks, Inc., develops, manufactures, and sells integrated wide-area network access products. The following are annual sales data from 1992 to 1997 (*Stock Investor Pro, American Association of Individual Investors*, August 31, 1997).

Year	Sales ($millions)
1992	5.4
1993	6.2
1994	12.7
1995	20.6
1996	28.4
1997	44.9

a. Develop a linear trend equation for this time series.

b. What is the firm's average increase in sales per year?

c. Use the trend equation to forecast sales for 1998.

19. The following data show the time series of the most recent quarterly capital expenditures (in billions of dollars) for the 1000 largest manufacturing firms: 24, 25, 23, 24, 22, 26, 28, 31, 29, 32, 37, and 42.

a. Develop a linear trend equation for the time series.

b. Graph the time series and the linear trend equation.

c. What appears to be happening to capital expenditures? What is the forecast 1 year, or 4 quarters, into the future?

20. The Costello Music Company has been in business for 5 years. During that time, the sale of electric organs has grown from 12 units in the first year to 76 units in the most recent year. Fred Costello, the firm's owner, wants to develop a forecast of organ sales for the coming year based on the historical data shown.

Year	1	2	3	4	5
Sales	12	28	34	50	76

a. Graph this time series. Does a linear trend appear?
b. Develop the equation for the linear trend component for the time series. What is the average increase in sales per year for the firm?

21. Hudson Marine has been an authorized dealer for C&D marine radios for the past 7 years. The number of radios sold each year is shown.

Year	1	2	3	4	5	6	7
Number Sold	35	50	75	90	105	110	130

a. Graph this time series. Does a linear trend appear?
b. Develop the equation for the linear trend component for the time series.
c. Use the linear trend developed in part (b) to prepare a forecast for sales in year 8.

22. The Motion Picture Association of America (MPAA) collects data that show the cost of making movies for MPAA members, including Disney, Paramount, Universal, Warner Brothers, MGM, Fox, Sony, and Turner. The following data show the average production costs (in $000s) from 1985 to 1996 for MPAA members (*The Wall Street Journal Almanac*, 1998).

Year	Average Production Costs ($000s)	Year	Average Production Costs ($000s)
1985	$16,779	1991	$26,136
1986	$17,455	1992	$28,858
1987	$20,051	1993	$29,910
1988	$18,061	1994	$34,288
1989	$23,454	1995	$36,370
1990	$26,783	1996	$39,836

a. Plot the time series and comment on the appropriateness of a linear trend.
b. Develop the equation for the linear trend component for this time series.
c. What is the average increase in production costs that MPAA members have been experiencing per year?
d. Use the trend equation to forecast the average production costs in 1997 and 1998.

23. The Garden Avenue Seven sells tapes of its musical performances. The following data show sales for the past 18 months. The group's manager wants an accurate method for forecasting future sales.

Month	Sales	Month	Sales	Month	Sales
1	293	7	381	13	549
2	283	8	431	14	544
3	322	9	424	15	601
4	355	10	433	16	587
5	346	11	470	17	644
6	379	12	481	18	660

a. Use exponential smoothing, with $\alpha = 0.3, 0.4$, and 0.5. Which value of α provides the best forecasts?
b. Use trend projection to provide a forecast. What is the value of MSE?
c. Which method of forecasting would you recommend to the manager? Why?

24. The Mayfair Department Store in Davenport, Iowa, is trying to determine the amount of sales lost while it was shut down because of summer floods. Sales data for January–June are shown.

Month	Sales ($000s)
January	185.72
February	167.84
March	205.11
April	210.36
May	255.57
June	261.19

a. Use exponential smoothing, with $\alpha = 0.4$, to develop a forecast for July and August. (Hint: Use the forecast for July as the actual sales in July in developing the August forecast.) Comment on the use of exponential smoothing for forecasts more than one period into the future.

b. Use trend projection to forecast sales for July and August.

c. Mayfair's insurance company has proposed a settlement based on lost sales of $240,000 in July and August. Is this amount fair? If not, what amount would you counter with?

SELFtest **25.** The quarterly sales data (number of copies sold) for a college textbook over the past 3 years are as follows.

Quarter	Year 1	Year 2	Year 3
1	1690	1800	1850
2	940	900	1100
3	2625	2900	2930
4	2500	2360	2615

a. Show the 4-quarter moving average values for this time series. Plot both the original time series and the moving averages on the same graph.

b. Compute seasonal indexes for the four quarters.

c. When does the textbook publisher experience the largest seasonal index? Does this result appear to be reasonable? Explain.

26. Identify the monthly seasonal indexes for the following three years of expenses for a 6-unit apartment house in southern Florida. Use a 12-month moving average calculation.

Month	Year 1	Year 2	Year 3
January	170	180	195
February	180	205	210
March	205	215	230
April	230	245	280
May	240	265	290
June	315	330	390
July	360	400	420
August	290	335	330
September	240	260	290
October	240	270	295
November	230	255	280
December	195	220	250

27. Air pollution control specialists in southern California monitor the amount of ozone, carbon dioxide, and nitrogen dioxide in the air on an hourly basis. The hourly time series data exhibit seasonality, with the levels of pollutants showing similar patterns over the hours in the day. On July 15, 16, and 17, the observed levels of nitrogen dioxide in a city's downtown area for the 12 hours from 6:00 A.M. to 6:00 P.M. were as follows.

July 15	25	28	35	50	60	60	40	35	30	25	25	20
July 16	28	30	35	48	60	65	50	40	35	25	20	20
July 17	35	42	45	70	72	75	60	45	40	25	25	25

  a. Identify the hourly seasonal indexes for the 12-hourly daily readings.
  b. Based on the seasonal indexes in part (a), the trend equation developed for the deseasonalized data is $T_t = 32.983 + 0.3922t$. Use the trend component only to develop forecasts for the 12 hours for July 18.
  c. Use the seasonal indexes from part (a) to adjust the trend forecasts in part (b).

28. Refer to Problem 21. Suppose that the following are the quarterly sales data for the past 7 years.

Year	Quarter 1	Quarter 2	Quarter 3	Quarter 4	Total Sales
1	6	15	10	4	35
2	10	18	15	7	50
3	14	26	23	12	75
4	19	28	25	18	90
5	22	34	28	21	105
6	24	36	30	20	110
7	28	40	35	27	130

  a. Show the 4-quarter moving average values for this time series. Plot both the original time series and the moving averages on the same graph.
  b. Compute the seasonal indexes for the four quarters.
  c. When does Hudson Marine experience the largest seasonal effect? Does this result seem reasonable? Explain.

29. Consider the Costello Music Company scenario presented in Problem 20 and the following quarterly sales data.

Year	Quarter 1	Quarter 2	Quarter 3	Quarter 4	Total Yearly Sales
1	4	2	1	5	12
2	6	4	4	14	28
3	10	3	5	16	34
4	12	9	7	22	50
5	18	10	13	35	76

  a. Compute the seasonal indexes for the four quarters.
  b. When does Costello Music experience the largest seasonal effect? Does this result appear to be reasonable? Explain.

30. Refer to the Hudson Marine data in Problem 28.
    a. Deseasonalize the data, and use the deseasonalized time series to identify the trend.
    b. Use the results of part (a) to develop a quarterly forecast for next year based on trend.
    c. Use the seasonal indexes developed in Problem 28 to adjust the forecasts developed in part (b) to account for the effect of season.

31. Consider the Costello Music Company time series in Problem 29.
    a. Deseasonalize the data, and use the deseasonalized time series to identify the trend.
    b. Use the results of part (a) to develop a quarterly forecast for next year based on trend.
    c. Use the seasonal indexes developed in Problem 29 to adjust the forecasts developed in part (b) to account for seasonal effects.

32. Electric power consumption is measured in kilowatt-hours (kWh). The local utility company has an interrupt program, whereby commercial customers who participate receive favorable rates but must agree to cut back consumption if the utility requests them to do so. Timko Products cut back consumption at 12:00 noon Thursday. To assess the savings, the utility must estimate Timko's usage without the interrupt. The period of interrupted service was from noon to 8:00 P.M. Data on electric consumption for the past 72 hours is available.

Time Period	Monday	Tuesday	Wednesday	Thursday
12–4 A.M.	—	19,281	31,209	27,330
4–8 A.M.	—	33,195	37,014	32,715
8–12 noon	—	99,516	119,968	152,465
12–4 P.M.	124,299	123,666	156,033	
4–8 P.M.	113,545	111,717	128,889	
8–12 midnight	41,300	48,112	73,923	

    a. Is there a seasonal effect over the 24-hour period? Compute seasonal indexes for the six 4-hour periods.
    b. Use trend adjusted for seasonal factors to estimate Timko's normal usage over the period of interrupted service.

SELFtest 33. Eddie's Restaurants collected the following data on the relationship between advertising and sales at a sample of five restaurants.

Advertising Expenditures ($000s)	1.0	4.0	6.0	10.0	14.0
Sales ($000s)	19.0	44.0	40.0	52.0	53.0

    a. Let x represent advertising expenditures and y represent sales. Use the method of least squares to develop a straight-line approximation of the relationship between the two variables.
    b. Use the equation developed in part (a) to forecast sales for an advertising expenditure of $8000.

34. The management of a chain of fast-food restaurants wants to investigate the relationship between the daily sales volume (in dollars) of a company restaurant and the number of competitor restaurants within a 1-mile radius. The following data have been collected.

Number of Competitors Within 1 Mile	Sales
1	3600
1	3300
2	3100
3	2900
3	2700
4	2500
5	2300
5	2000

    a. Develop the least-squares estimated regression equation that relates daily sales volume to the number of competitor restaurants within a 1-mile radius.

    b. Use the estimated regression equation developed in part (a) to forecast the daily sales volume for a particular company restaurant that has four competitors within a 1-mile radius.

35. The supervisor of a manufacturing process believed that assembly-line speed (in feet/ minute) affected the number of defective parts found during on-line inspection. To test this theory, management had the same batch of parts inspected visually at a variety of line speeds. The following data were collected.

Line Speed	Number of Defective Parts Found
20	21
20	19
40	15
30	16
60	14
40	17

    a. Develop the estimated regression equation that relates line speed to the number of defective parts found.

    b. Use the equation developed in part (a) to forecast the number of defective parts found for a line speed of 50 feet per minute.

Case Problem   FORECASTING SALES

The Vintage Restaurant is located on Captiva Island, a resort community near Fort Meyers, Florida. The restaurant, which is owned and operated by Karen Payne, has just completed its third year of operation. During this time, Karen has sought to establish a reputation for the restaurant as a high-quality dining establishment that specializes in fresh seafood. The efforts made by Karen and her staff have proven successful, and her restaurant has become one of the best and fastest-growing restaurants on the island.

Karen has concluded that, to plan better for the growth of the restaurant in the future, she needs to develop a system that will enable her to forecast food and beverage sales by month for up to 1 year in advance. Karen has the following data on total food and beverage sales for the 3 years of operation.

Food and Beverage Sales for the Vintage Restaurant ($000s)

Month	First Year	Second Year	Third Year
January	242	263	282
February	235	238	255
March	232	247	265
April	178	193	205
May	184	193	210
June	140	149	160
July	145	157	166
August	152	161	174
September	110	122	126
October	130	130	148
November	152	167	173
December	206	230	235

Managerial Report

Perform an analysis of the sales data for the Vintage Restaurant. Prepare a report for Karen that summarizes your findings, forecasts, and recommendations. Include the following:

1. A graph of the time series.
2. An analysis of the seasonality of the data. Indicate the seasonal indexes for each month, and comment on the high seasonal and low seasonal sales months. Do the seasonal indexes make intuitive sense? Discuss.
3. Forecast sales for January through December of the fourth year.
4. Assume that January sales for the fourth year turned out to be $295,000. What was your forecast error? If this error is large, Karen may be puzzled about the difference between your forecast and the actual sales value. What can you do to resolve her uncertainty in the forecasting procedure?
5. Recommendations as to when the system that you have developed should be updated to account for new sales data that will occur.
6. Include detailed calculations of your analysis in the appendix of your report.

Case Problem   FORECASTING LOST SALES

The Carlson Department Store suffered heavy damage when a hurricane struck on August 31, 1996. The store was closed for four months (September 1996 through December 1996), and Carlson is now involved in a dispute with its insurance company concerning the amount of lost sales during the time the store was closed. Two key issues must be resolved: (1) the amount of sales Carlson would have made if the hurricane had not struck; and (2) whether Carlson is entitled to any compensation for excess sales from increased business activity after the storm. More than $8 billion in federal disaster relief and insurance money came into the county, resulting in increased sales at department stores and numerous other businesses.

Table 6.15 shows the sales data for the 48 months preceding the storm. The U.S. Department of Commerce also has published total sales for the 48 months preceding the storm for all department stores in the county, as well as the total sales in the county for the 4 months the Carlson Department Store was closed. Table 6.16 shows these data. Management has asked you to analyze these data and develop estimates of the lost sales at the Carlson Department Store for the months of September through December 1996. Management also has asked you to determine whether a case can be made for excess storm-related sales

TABLE 6.15   SALES FOR CARLSON DEPARTMENT STORE, SEPTEMBER 1992
THROUGH AUGUST 1996

Month	1992	1993	1994	1995	1996
Jan.		1.45	2.31	2.31	2.56
Feb.		1.80	1.89	1.99	2.28
Mar.		2.03	2.02	2.42	2.69
Apr.		1.99	2.23	2.45	2.48
May		2.32	2.39	2.57	2.73
June		2.20	2.14	2.42	2.37
July		2.13	2.27	2.40	2.31
Aug.		2.43	2.21	2.50	2.23
Sept.	1.71	1.90	1.89	2.09	
Oct.	1.90	2.13	2.29	2.54	
Nov.	2.74	2.56	2.83	2.97	
Dec.	4.20	4.16	4.04	4.35	

TABLE 6.16   DEPARTMENT STORE SALES FOR THE COUNTY, SEPTEMBER 1992
THROUGH DECEMBER 1996

Month	1992	1993	1994	1995	1996
Jan.		46.8	46.8	43.8	48.0
Feb.		48.0	48.6	45.6	51.6
Mar.		60.0	59.4	57.6	57.6
Apr.		57.6	58.2	53.4	58.2
May		61.8	60.6	56.4	60.0
June		58.2	55.2	52.8	57.0
July		56.4	51.0	54.0	57.6
Aug.		63.0	58.8	60.6	61.8
Sept.	55.8	57.6	49.8	47.4	69.0
Oct.	56.4	53.4	54.6	54.6	75.0
Nov.	71.4	71.4	65.4	67.8	85.2
Dec.	117.6	114.0	102.0	100.2	121.8

during the same period. If such a case can be made, Carlson is entitled to compensation for
excess sales it would have earned in addition to ordinary sales.

Managerial Report

Prepare a report for the management of the Carlson Department store that summarizes your
findings, forecasts, and recommendations. Include the following.

1. An estimate of sales had there been no hurricane.
2. An estimate of countywide department store sales had there been no hurricane.
3. Use the countywide actual department stores sales for September through December 1996 and the estimate in part (2) to make a case for or against excess storm-related sales.
4. An estimate of lost sales for the Carlson Department Store for September through December 1996.

Appendix 6.1   SPREADSHEETS FOR FORECASTING

In this appendix we show how Excel can be used to develop forecasts using three forecasting methods: moving averages, exponential smoothing, and trend projection.

Moving Averages

To show how Excel can be used to develop forecasts using the moving averages method, we will develop a forecast for the gasoline sales time series in Table 6.1 and Figure 6.5. We assume that the user has entered the sales data for the 12 weeks into worksheet rows 1 through 12 of column A. The following steps can be used to produce a three-week moving average.

Step 1. Select the **Tools** pull-down menu
Step 2. Select the **Data Analysis** option
Step 3. When the **Data Analysis Tools** dialog box appears, choose **Moving Average**
Step 4. When the **Moving Average** dialog box appears:
Enter A1:A12 in the **Input Range** box
Enter 3 in the **Interval** box
Enter B2 in the **Output Range** box
Select **OK**

The three-week moving average forecasts will appear in column B of the worksheet. Note that forecasts for periods of other length can be computed easily by entering a different value in the Interval box.

Exponential Smoothing

To show how Excel can be used for exponential smoothing, we again develop a forecast for the gasoline sales time series in Table 6.1 and Figure 6.5. We assume that the user has entered the sales data for the 12 weeks into worksheet rows 1 through 12 of column A and that the smoothing constant is $\alpha = 0.2$. The following steps can be used to produce a forecast.

Step 1. Select the **Tools** pull-down menu
Step 2. Select the **Data Analysis** option
Step 3. When the **Data Analysis Tools** dialog box appears, choose **Exponential Smoothing**
Step 4. When the **Exponential Smoothing** dialog box appears:
Enter A1:A12 in the **Input Range** box
Enter 0.8 in the **Damping factor** box
Enter B1 in the **Output Range** box
Select **OK**

The exponential smoothing forecasts will appear in column B of the worksheet. Note that the value we entered in the Damping factor box is $1 - \alpha$; forecasts for other smoothing constants can be computed easily by entering a different value for $1 - \alpha$ in the Damping factor box.

Trend Projection

To show how Excel can be used for trend projection, we develop a forecast for the bicycle sales time series in Table 6.6 and Figure 6.8. We assume that the user has entered the year (1–10) for each observation into worksheet rows 1 through 10 of column A and the sales values into worksheet rows 1 through 10 of column B. The following steps can be used to produce a forecast for year 11 by trend projection.

Step 1. Select an empty cell in the worksheet

Step 2. Select the **Insert** pull-down menu

Step 3. Choose the **Function** option

Step 4. When the **Paste Function** dialog box appears:
Choose **Statistical** in the Function Category box
Choose **Forecast** in the Function Name box
Select **OK**

Step 5. When the **Forecast dialog** box appears:
Enter 11 in the **x** box
Enter B1:B10 in the **Known y's** box
Enter A1:A10 in the **Known x's** box
Select **OK**

The forecast for year 11, in this case 32.5, will appear in the cell selected in Step 1.

THE CINCINNATI GAS & ELECTRIC COMPANY*
CINCINNATI, OHIO

The Cincinnati Gas Light and Coke Company was chartered by the state of Ohio on April 3, 1837. Under this charter, the company manufactured gas by distillation of coal and sold it for lighting purposes. During the last quarter of the nineteenth century, the company successfully marketed gas for lighting, heating, and cooking and as fuel for gas engines.

In 1901 the Cincinnati Gas Light and Coke Company and the Cincinnati Electric Light Company merged to form The Cincinnati Gas & Electric Company (CG&E). This new company was able to shift from manufactured gas to natural gas and adopt the rapidly emerging technologies in generating and distributing electricity. CG&E operated as a subsidiary of the Columbia Gas Electric Company from 1909 until 1944.

In 1994, CG&E merged with Public Service of Indiana to form Cinergy Corporation. Today, CG&E is a subsidiary of Cinergy serving approximately 440,000 gas customers and 720,000 electric customers. The company's service area covers approximately 3000 square miles in and around the Greater Cincinnati area.

Forecasting at CG&E

As in any modern company, forecasting at CG&E is an integral part of operating and managing the business. Depending on the decision to be made, the forecasting techniques used range from judgment and graphical trend projections to sophisticated multiple regression models.

Forecasting in the utility industry offers some unique perspectives. Because electricity cannot take the form of finished-goods or in-process inventories, this product must be generated to meet the instantaneous requirements of the customers. Electrical shortages are not just lost sales, but "brownouts" or "blackouts." This

situation places an unusual burden on the utility forecaster. On the positive side, the demand for energy and the sale of energy are more predictable than for many other products. Also, unlike the situation in a multi-product firm, a great amount of forecasting effort and expertise can be concentrated on the two products: gas and electricity.

Forecasting Electric Energy and Peak Loads

The two types of forecasts discussed in this section are the long-range forecasts of electric peak load and electric energy. The largest observed electric demand for any given period, such as an hour, a day, a month, or a year, is defined as the peak load. The cumulative amount of energy generated and used over the period of an hour is referred to as electric energy.

Until the mid-1970s the seasonal patterns of both electric energy and electric peak load were very regular; the time series for both of these exhibited a fairly steady exponential growth. Business cycles had little noticeable effect on either. Perhaps the most serious shift in the behavior of these time series came from the increasing installation of air conditioning units in the Greater Cincinnati area, which caused an accelerated growth in the trend component and also in the relative magnitude of the summer peaks. Nevertheless, the two time series remained regular and generally quite predictable.

Trend projection was the most popular method used to forecast electric energy and electric peak load. The forecast accuracy was quite acceptable and even enviable when compared to forecast errors experienced in other industries.

A New Era in Forecasting

In the mid-1970s a variety of actions by the government, the off-and-on energy shortages, and price sig-

*The authors are indebted to Dr. Richard Evans of The Cincinnati Gas & Electric Company, Cincinnati, Ohio, for providing this application.

nals to the consumer began to affect the consumption of electric energy. The behavior of the peak load and electric energy time series became less predictable, and a simple trend projection forecasting model was no longer adequate. As a result, a special forecasting model—referred to as an econometric model—was developed by CG&E to better account for the behavior of these time series.

The purpose of the econometric model is to forecast the annual energy consumption by residential, commercial, and industrial classes of service. These forecasts are then used to develop forecasts of summer and winter peak loads. First, energy consumption in the industrial and commercial classes is forecast. For an assumed level of economic activity, the projection of electric energy is made along with a forecast of employment in the area. The employment forecast is converted to a forecast of adult population through the use of unemployment rates and labor force participation rates. Household forecasts are then developed through the use of demographic statistics on the average number of persons per household. The resulting forecast of households is used as an indicator of residential customers.

At this point, a comparison is made with the demographic projections for the area population. The differences between the residential customers forecast and the population forecast are reconciled to produce the final forecast of residential customers. This forecast becomes the principal independent variable in forecasting residential electric energy.

Summer and winter peak loads are then forecast by applying class peak contribution factors to the energy forecasts. The contributions that each class makes toward the peak are summed to establish the peak forecast.

A number of economic and demographic time series are used in the construction of this econometric model. Simply speaking, the entire forecasting system is a compilation of several statistically verified multiple regression equations.

Impact and Value of the Forecasts

The forecast of the annual electric peak load guides the timing decisions for constructing future generating units, and the financial impact of these decisions is great. For example, a large generating unit built by the company cost nearly $600 million, and the interest rate on a recent first mortgage bond was 16%. At this rate, annual interest costs would be nearly $100 million. Obviously, a timing decision that leads to having the unit available no sooner than necessary is crucial.

The energy forecasts are important in other ways also. For example, purchases of coal as fuel for the generating units are based on the forecast levels of energy needed. The revenue from the electric operations of the company is determined from forecasted sales, which in turn enters into the planning of rate changes and external financing. These planning and decision-making processes are among the most important management activities in the company. It is imperative that the decision makers have the best forecast information available to assist them in arriving at these decisions.

Questions

1. Describe some of the unique perspectives associated with forecasting in the utility industry as compared with other industries.
2. What type of forecasting procedure was used by CG&E into the mid-1970s? What necessitated a change?
3. Briefly describe CG&E's current approach to forecasting.
4. What are the benefits of accurate forecasts for CG&E?

Chapter 7

INTRODUCTION TO LINEAR PROGRAMMING

CONTENTS

Linear programming is a problem-solving approach developed to help managers make decisions. The following situations describe some typical applications of linear programming:

1. A manufacturer wants to develop a production schedule and an inventory policy that will satisfy sales demand in future periods. Ideally, the schedule and policy will enable the company to satisfy demand and at the same time *minimize* the total production and inventory costs.

2. A financial analyst must select an investment portfolio from a variety of stock and bond investment alternatives. The analyst would like to establish the portfolio that *maximizes* the return on investment.

3. A marketing manager wants to determine how best to allocate a fixed advertising budget among alternative advertising media such as radio, television, newspaper, and magazine. The manager would like to determine the media mix that *maximizes* advertising effectiveness.

4. A company has warehouses in a number of locations. Given specific customer demands, the company would like to determine how much each warehouse should ship to each customer so that total transportation costs are *minimized.*

Linear programming was initially referred to as "programming in a linear structure." In 1948 Tjalling Koopmans suggested to George Dantzig that the name was much too long; Koopman's suggestion was to shorten it to linear programming. George Dantzig agreed and the field we now know as linear programming was named.

These examples are only a few of the situations in which linear programming has been used successfully, but they illustrate the diversity of linear programming applications. A close scrutiny reveals one basic property they all have in common. In each example, we were concerned with *maximizing* or *minimizing* some quantity. In example 1, the manufacturer wanted to minimize costs; in example 2, the financial analyst wanted to maximize return on investment; in example 3, the marketing manager wanted to maximize advertising effectiveness; and in example 4, the company wanted to minimize total transportation costs. *In all linear programming problems, the maximization or minimization of some quantity is the objective.*

All linear programming problems also have a second property: restrictions or **constraints** that limit the degree to which the objective can be pursued. In example 1, the manufacturer is restricted by constraints requiring product demand to be satisfied and by the constraints limiting production capacity. The financial analyst's portfolio problem is constrained by the total amount of investment funds available and the maximum amounts that can be invested in each stock or bond. The marketing manager's media selection decision is constrained by a fixed advertising budget and the availability of the various media. In the transportation problem, the minimum-cost shipping schedule is constrained by the supply of product available at each warehouse. *Thus, constraints are another general feature of every linear programming problem.*

7.1   A SIMPLE MAXIMIZATION PROBLEM

RMC, Inc., is a small firm that produces a variety of chemical-based products. In a particular production process, three raw materials are used to produce two products: a fuel additive and a solvent base. The fuel additive is sold to oil companies and is used in the production of gasoline and related fuels. The solvent base is sold to a variety of chemical firms and is used in both home and industrial cleaning products. The three raw materials are blended to form the fuel additive and solvent base as indicated in Table 7.1. It shows that a ton of fuel additive is a mixture of 0.4 ton of material 1 and 0.6 ton of material 3. A ton of solvent base is a mixture of 0.5 ton of material 1, 0.2 ton of material 2, and 0.3 ton of material 3.

RMC's production is constrained by a limited availability of the three raw materials. For the current production period, RMC has available the following quantities of each raw material.

Material	Amount Available for Production
Material 1	20 tons
Material 2	5 tons
Material 3	21 tons

Because of spoilage and the nature of the production process, any materials not used for current production are useless and must be discarded.

It is important to understand that we are maximizing profit contribution, not profit. Overhead and other shared costs must be deducted before arriving at a profit figure.

The accounting department has analyzed the production figures, assigned all relevant costs, and arrived at prices for both products that will result in a profit contribution[1] of $40 for every ton of fuel additive produced and $30 for every ton of solvent base produced. Let us now use linear programming to determine the number of tons of fuel additive and the number of tons of solvent base to produce in order to maximize total profit contribution.

---

1. From an accounting perspective, profit contribution is more correctly described as the contribution margin per ton; overhead and other shared costs have not been allocated to the fuel additive and solvent base costs.

TABLE 7.1   MATERIAL REQUIREMENTS PER TON FOR THE RMC PROBLEM

	Product	
	Fuel Additive	**Solvent Base**
Material 1	0.4	0.5
Material 2		0.2
Material 3	0.6	0.3

0.6 ton of material 3 is used in
each ton of fuel additive

Problem Formulation

Problem formulation is the process of translating a verbal statement of a problem into a mathematical statement. The mathematical statement of the problem is referred to as a **mathematical model.** Developing an appropriate mathematical model is an art that can only be mastered with practice and experience. Even though every problem has at least some unique features, most problems also have many common or similar features. As a result, some general guidelines for developing a mathematical model can be helpful. We will illustrate these guidelines by developing a mathematical model for the RMC problem.

Understand the Problem Thoroughly   The RMC problem is relatively easy to understand. RMC wants to determine how much of each product to produce in order to maximize the total contribution to profit. The number of tons available for the three materials that are required to produce the two products will limit the number of tons of each product that can be produced. More complex problems will require more work in order to understand the problem. However, understanding the problem thoroughly is the first step in developing any mathematical model.

Describe the Objective   RMC's objective is to maximize the total contribution to profit.

Describe Each Constraint   Three constraints limit the number of tons of fuel additive and the number of tons of solvent base that can be produced.

Constraint 1:   The number of tons of material 1 used must be less than or equal to the 20 tons available.

Constraint 2:   The number of tons of material 2 used must be less than or equal to the 5 tons available.

Constraint 3:   The number of tons of material 3 used must be less than or equal to the 21 tons available.

Define the Decision Variables   The **decision variables** are the controllable inputs in the problem. For the RMC problem the two decision variables are (1) the number of tons of fuel additive produced, and (2) the number of tons of solvent base produced. In developing the mathematical model for the RMC problem, we will use the following notation for the decision variables.

$$F = \text{number of tons of fuel additive}$$
$$S = \text{number of tons of solvent base}$$

Write the Objective in Terms of the Decision Variables   RMC's profit contribution comes from the production of F tons of fuel additive and S tons of solvent base. Because RMC makes $40 for every ton of fuel additive produced and $30 for every ton of solvent base produced, the company will make $40F from the production of the fuel additive and $30S from the production of the solvent base. Thus,

$$\text{Total profit contribution} = 40F + 30S$$

Because the objective—maximize total profit contribution—is a function of the decision variables F and S, we refer to $40F + 30S$ as the **objective function.** Using "Max" as an abbreviation for maximize, we can write RMC's objective as follows:

$$\text{Max}\quad 40F + 30S \tag{7.1}$$

Write the Constraints in Terms of the Decision Variables

Constraint 1:

$$\text{Tons of material 1 used} \leq \text{Tons of material 1 available}$$

Every ton of fuel additive that RMC produces will use 0.4 tons of material 1. Thus, $0.4F$ tons of material 1 is used to produce F tons of fuel additive. Similarly, every ton of solvent base that RMC produces will use 0.5 tons of material 1. Thus, $0.5S$ tons of material 1 is used to produce S tons of solvent base. Therefore, the number of tons of material 1 used to produce F tons of fuel additive and S tons of solvent base is

$$\text{Tons of material 1 used} = 0.4F + 0.5S$$

Because 20 tons of material 1 are available for use in production, the mathematical statement of constraint 1 is

$$0.4F + 0.5S \leq 20 \tag{7.2}$$

Constraint 2:

$$\text{Tons of material 2 used} \leq \text{Tons of material 2 available}$$

Fuel additive does not use material 2. However, every ton of solvent base that RMC produces will use 0.2 tons of material 2. Thus, $0.2S$ tons of material 2 is used to produce S tons of solvent base. Therefore, the number of tons of material 2 used to produce F tons of fuel additive and S tons of solvent base is

$$\text{Tons of material 2 used} = 0.2S$$

Because 5 tons of material 2 are available for production, the mathematical statement of constraint 2 is

$$0.2S \leq 5 \tag{7.3}$$

Constraint 3:

$$\text{Tons of material 3 used} \leq \text{Tons of material 3 available}$$

Every ton of fuel additive RMC produces will use 0.6 tons of material 3. Thus, $0.6F$ tons of material 1 is used to produce F tons of fuel additive. Similarly, every ton of solvent base RMC produces will use 0.3 tons of material 3. Thus, $0.3S$ tons of material 1 is used to produce S tons of solvent base. Therefore, the number of tons of material 3 used to produce F tons of fuel additive and S tons of solvent base is

$$\text{Tons of material 3 used} = 0.6F + 0.3S$$

Because 21 tons of material 3 are available for production, the mathematical statement of constraint 3 is

$$0.6F + 0.3S \leq 21 \tag{7.4}$$

Add the Nonnegativity Constraints   RMC cannot produce a negative number of tons of fuel additive or a negative number of tons of solvent base. Therefore, **nonnegativity constraints** must be added to prevent the decision variables F and S from having negative values. These nonnegativity constraints are

$$F \geq 0 \quad \text{and} \quad S \geq 0$$

Nonnegativity constraints are a general feature of all linear programming problems and may be written in the abbreviated form:

$$F, S \geq 0 \tag{7.5}$$

Mathematical Model for the RMC Problem

Problem formulation is now complete. We have succeeded in translating the verbal statement of the RMC problem into the following mathematical model.

$$\text{Max} \quad 40F + 30S$$

Subject to (s.t.)

$$
\begin{aligned}
0.4F + 0.5S &\leq 20 \quad \text{Material 1} \\
0.2S &\leq 5 \quad \text{Material 2} \\
0.6F + 0.3S &\leq 21 \quad \text{Material 3} \\
F, S &\geq 0
\end{aligned}
$$

Our job now is to find the product mix (i.e., the combination of F and S) that satisfies all the constraints and, at the same time, yields a maximum value for the objective function. Once these values of F and S are calculated, we will have found the optimal solution to the problem.

This mathematical model of the RMC problem is a **linear program.** The problem has the objective and constraints that, as we said earlier, are common properties of all *linear* programs. But what is the special feature of this mathematical model that makes it a linear program? The special feature that makes it a linear program is that the objective function and all constraint functions (the left-hand sides of the constraint inequalities) are linear functions of the decision variables.

Mathematical functions in which each variable appears in a separate term and is raised to the first power are called **linear functions.** The objective function ($40F + 30S$) is linear because each decision variable appears in a separate term and has an exponent of 1. The amount of material 1 used ($0.4F + 0.5S$) is also a linear function of the decision variables for the same reason. Similarly, the functions on the left-hand side of the material 2 and material 3 constraint inequalities (the constraint functions) are also linear functions. Thus, the mathematical formulation is referred to as a linear program.

Try Problem 1 to test your ability to recognize the types of mathematical relationships that can be found in a linear program.

Linear *programming* has nothing to do with computer programming. The use of the word *programming* here means "choosing a course of action." Linear programming involves choosing a course of action when the mathematical model of the problem contains only linear functions.

NOTES AND COMMENTS

1. The three assumptions necessary for a linear programming model to be appropriate are proportionality, additivity, and divisibility. *Proportionality* means that the contribution to the objective function and the amount of resources used in each constraint are proportional to the value of each decision variable. *Additivity* means that the value of the objective function and the total resources used can be found by summing the objective function contribution and the resources used for all decision variables. *Divisibility* means that the decision variables are continuous. The divisibility assumption plus the nonnegativity constraints mean that decision variables can take on any value greater than or equal to zero.

2. Quantitative analysts formulate and solve a variety of mathematical models that contain an objective function and a set of constraints. Models of this type are referred to as *mathematical programming models.* Linear programming models are a special type of mathematical programming model in that the objective function and all constraint functions are linear.

7.2   GRAPHICAL SOLUTION PROCEDURE

A linear programming problem involving only two decision variables can be solved using a graphical solution procedure. Let us begin the graphical solution procedure by developing a graph that displays the possible solutions (F and S values) for the RMC problem. The graph in Figure 7.1 has values of F on the horizontal axis and values of S on the vertical axis. Any point on the graph can be identified by its F and S values, which indicate the position of the point along the horizontal and vertical axes, respectively. Thus, every point on the graph corresponds to a possible solution. The solution of $F = 0$ and $S = 0$ is referred to as the origin. Because both F and S must be nonnegative, the graph in Figure 7.1 only displays solutions where $F \geq 0$ and $S \geq 0$.

Earlier we determined that the inequality representing the material 1 constraint was

$$0.4F + 0.5S \leq 20$$

To show all solutions that satisfy this relationship, we start by graphing the line corresponding to the equation

$$0.4F + 0.5S = 20$$

We graph this equation by identifying two points that satisfy this equation and then drawing a line through the points. Setting $F = 0$ and solving for S gives $0.5S = 20$ or $S = 40$; hence the solution ($F = 0$, $S = 40$) satisfies the preceding equation. To find a second solution satisfying this equation, we set $S = 0$ and solve for F. Doing so, we obtain $0.4F = 20$, or $F = 50$. Thus a second solution satisfying the equation is ($F = 50$, $S = 0$). With these two points, we can now graph the line. This line, called the *material 1 constraint line,* is shown in Figure 7.2.

Recall that the inequality representing the material 1 constraint is

$$0.4F + 0.5S \leq 20$$

Can you identify all the solutions that satisfy this constraint? First, note that any point on the line $0.4F + 0.5S = 20$ must satisfy the constraint. But where are the solutions satisfying $0.4F + 0.5S < 20$? Consider two solutions ($F = 10$, $S = 10$) and ($F = 40$, $S = 30$). Figure 7.2 shows that the first solution is below the constraint line and the second solution is above the constraint line. Which of these solutions satisfies the material 1 constraint? For ($F = 10$, $S = 10$) we have

$$0.4F + 0.5S = 0.4(10) + 0.5(10) = 9$$

FIGURE 7.1   GRAPH SHOWING TWO SOLUTIONS FOR THE TWO-VARIABLE
RMC PROBLEM

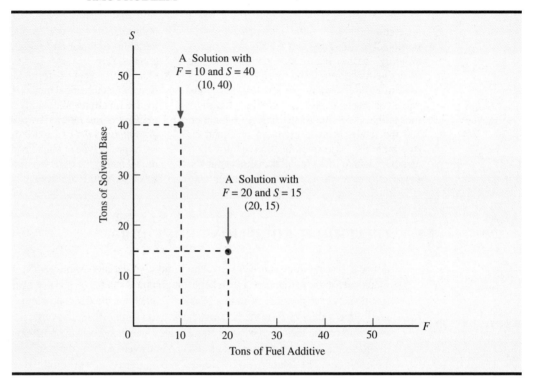

FIGURE 7.2   THE MATERIAL 1 CONSTRAINT LINE

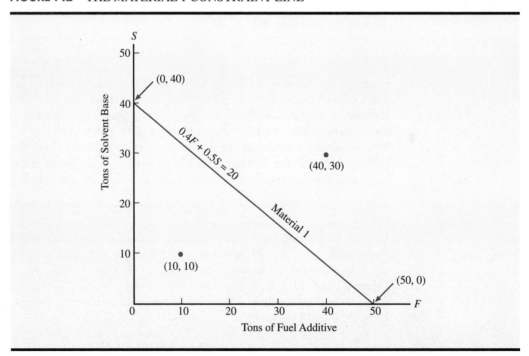

Because 9 tons is less than the 20 tons of material 1 available, the $F = 10$, $S = 10$ solution satisfies the constraint. For $F = 40$ and $S = 30$ we have

$$0.4F + 0.5S = 0.4(40) + 0.5(30) = 31$$

The 31 tons is greater than the 20 tons available, so the $F = 40$, $S = 30$ solution does not satisfy the constraint.

You should now be able to graph a constraint line and find the solution points that satisfy the constraint. Try Problem 2.

If a particular solution satisfies the constraint, all other solutions on the same side of the constraint line will also satisfy the constraint. If a particular solution does not satisfy the constraint, all other solutions on the same side of the constraint line will not satisfy the constraint. Thus, you need to evaluate only one solution to determine which side of a constraint line provides solutions that will satisfy the constraint. The shaded area in Figure 7.3 shows all the solutions that satisfy the material 1 constraint.

Next let us identify all solutions that satisfy the material 2 constraint:

$$0.2S \leq 5$$

We start by drawing the constraint line corresponding to the equation $0.2S = 5$. Because this equation is equivalent to the equation $S = 25$, we simply draw a line whose S value is 25 for every value of F; this line is parallel to and 25 units above the horizontal axis. In Figure 7.4 we have drawn the line corresponding to the material 2 constraint. Following the approach we used for the material 1 constraint, we realize that only solutions on or below the line will satisfy the material 2 constraint. Thus, in Figure 7.4 the shaded area corresponds to the solutions that satisfy the material 2 constraint.

Similarly, we can determine the solutions that satisfy the material 3 constraint. Figure 7.5 shows the result. For practice, try to graph the feasible solutions that satisfy the material 3 constraint and determine whether your result agrees with that shown in Figure 7.5.

FIGURE 7.3   SOLUTIONS THAT SATISFY THE MATERIAL 1 CONSTRAINT

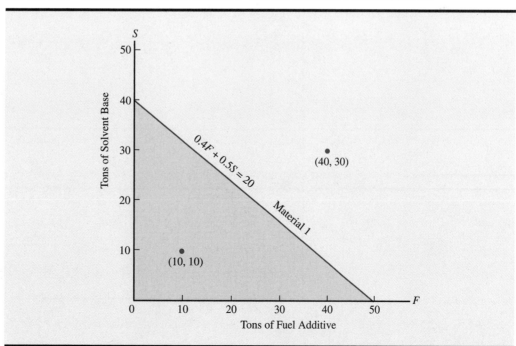

FIGURE 7.4   SOLUTIONS THAT SATISFY THE MATERIAL 2 CONSTRAINT

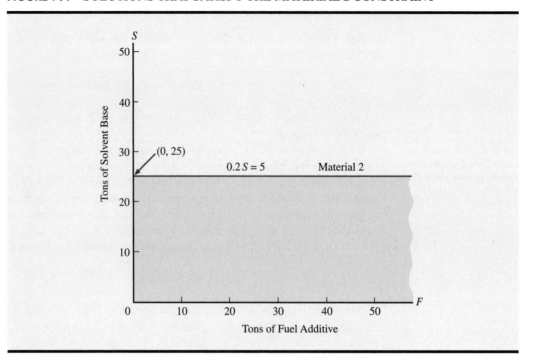

FIGURE 7.5   SOLUTIONS THAT SATISFY THE MATERIAL 3 CONSTRAINT

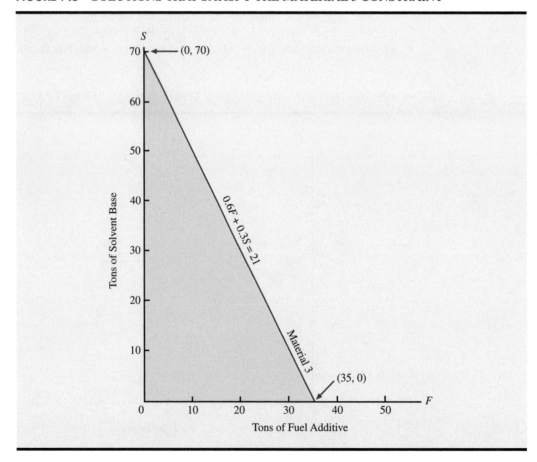

We now have three separate graphs showing the solutions that satisfy each of the three constraints. In a linear programming problem, we need to identify the solutions that satisfy *all* the constraints *simultaneously*. To find these solutions we can draw the three constraints on one graph and observe the region containing the points that do in fact satisfy all the constraints simultaneously.

The graphs in Figures 7.3–7.5 can be superimposed to obtain one graph with all three constraints. Figure 7.6 shows this combined constraint graph. The shaded region in this figure includes every solution point that satisfies all the constraints simultaneously. Because solutions that satisfy all the constraints simultaneously are termed **feasible solutions,** the shaded region is called the *feasible solution region,* or simply the **feasible region.** Any point on the boundary of the feasible region, or within the feasible region, is a *feasible solution point* for the linear programming problem.

Can you now find the feasible region given several constraints? Try Problem 7.

Now that we have identified the feasible region, we are ready to proceed with the graphical solution method and find the optimal solution to the RMC problem. Recall that the optimal solution for a linear programming problem is the feasible solution that provides the best possible value of the objective function. Let us start the optimizing step of the graphical solution procedure by redrawing the feasible region on a separate graph. Figure 7.7 shows the graph.

One approach to finding the optimal solution would be to evaluate the objective function for each feasible solution; the optimal solution would then be the one yielding the largest value. The difficulty with this approach is that there are too many feasible solutions

FIGURE 7.6   FEASIBLE REGION FOR THE RMC PROBLEM

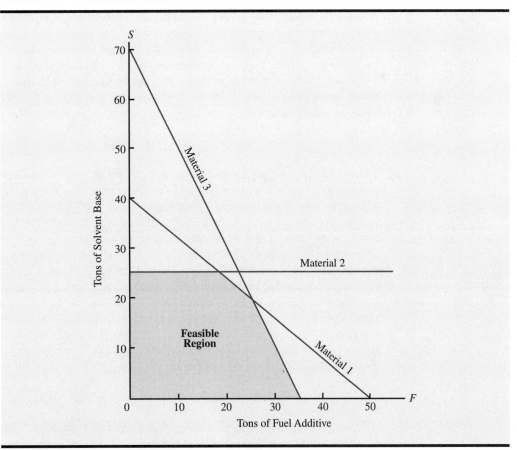

FIGURE 7.7   FEASIBLE REGION FOR THE RMC PROBLEM

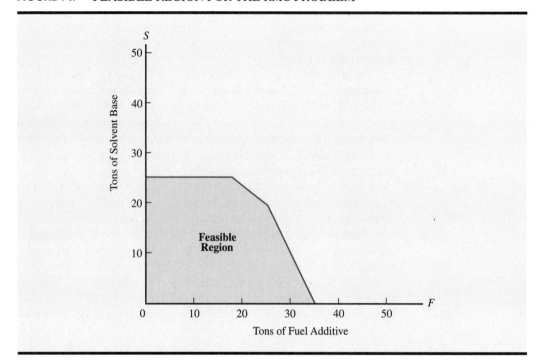

(actually infinitely many); thus, evaluating all feasible solutions would not be possible. Hence, this trial-and-error procedure cannot be used to identify the optimal solution.

Rather than trying to compute the profit contribution for each feasible solution, we select an arbitrary value for profit contribution and identify all the feasible solutions that yield the selected value. For example, what feasible solutions provide a profit contribution of $240? These solutions are given by the values of F and S in the feasible region that will make the objective function

$$40F + 30S = 240$$

This expression is simply the equation of a line. Thus all feasible solutions (F, S) yielding a profit contribution of $240 must be on the line. We learned earlier in this section how to graph a constraint line. The procedure for graphing the profit or objective function line is the same. Letting $F = 0$, we see that S must be 8; thus the solution point $(F = 0, S = 8)$ is on the line. Similarly, by letting $S = 0$ we see that the solution point $(F = 6, S = 0)$ is also on the line. Drawing the line through these two points identifies all the solutions that have a profit contribution of $240. A graph of this profit line is presented in Figure 7.8. It shows that an infinite number of feasible production combinations will provide a $240 profit contribution.

The objective is to find the feasible solution yielding the highest profit contribution, so we proceed by selecting higher profit contributions and finding the solutions that yield the stated values. For example, what solutions provide a profit contribution of $720? What solutions provide a profit contribution of $1200? To answer these questions we must find the F and S values that are on the profit lines

$$40F + 30S = 720 \quad \text{and} \quad 40F + 30S = 1200$$

Using the previous procedure for graphing profit and constraint lines, we graphed the $720 and $1200 profit lines presented in Figure 7.9. Not all solution points on the $1200

FIGURE 7.8 $240 PROFIT LINE FOR THE RMC PROBLEM

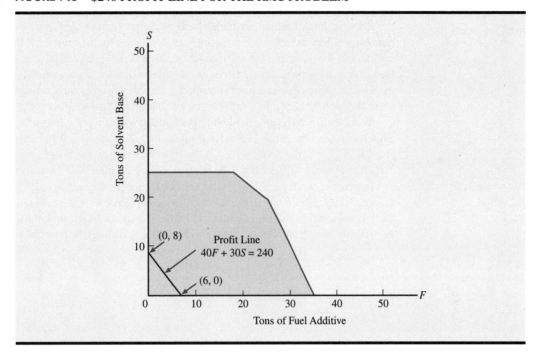

FIGURE 7.9   SELECTED PROFIT LINES FOR THE RMC PROBLEM

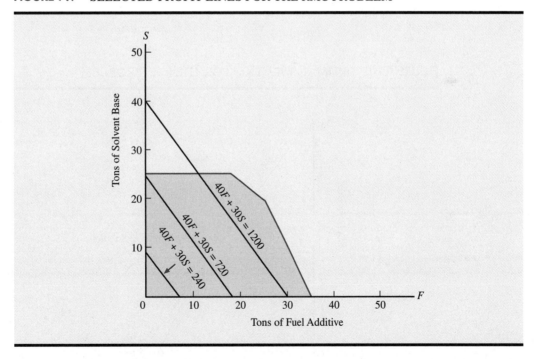

profit line are in the feasible region, but at least some points on the line are; thus, we can obtain a feasible solution that provides a $1200 profit contribution.

Can we find a feasible solution yielding an even higher profit contribution? Look at Figure 7.9 and make some general observations about the profit lines. You should be able to identify the following properties: (1) the profit lines are *parallel* to each other; and (2) profit lines with higher profit contributions are farther from the origin.

Because the profit lines are parallel and higher profit lines are farther from the origin, we can obtain solutions that yield increasingly higher values for the objective function by continuing to move the profit line farther from the origin but keeping it parallel to the other profit lines. However, at some point any further outward movement will place the profit line entirely outside the feasible region. Because points outside the feasible region are unacceptable, the point in the feasible region that lies on the highest profit line is an optimal solution to the linear program.

You should now be able to identify the optimal solution point for the RMC problem. Use a ruler and move the profit line as far from the origin as you can. What is the last point in the feasible region? This point, which is the optimal solution, is shown graphically in Figure 7.10. The optimal values for the decision variables are the F and S values at this point.

Depending on the accuracy of your graph, you may or may not be able to determine the exact optimal values of F and S directly from the graph. However, refer to Figure 7.6 and note that the optimal solution point for the RMC example is at the *intersection* of the material 1 and material 3 constraint lines. That is, the optimal solution is on both the material 1 constraint line,

$$0.4F + 0.5S = 20 \qquad (7.6)$$

and the material 3 constraint line,

$$0.6F + 0.3S = 21 \qquad (7.7)$$

Thus, the values of the decision variables F and S must satisfy both equations (7.6) and (7.7) simultaneously. Using (7.6) and solving for F gives

$$0.4F = 20 - 0.5S$$

FIGURE 7.10   OPTIMAL SOLUTION FOR THE RMC PROBLEM

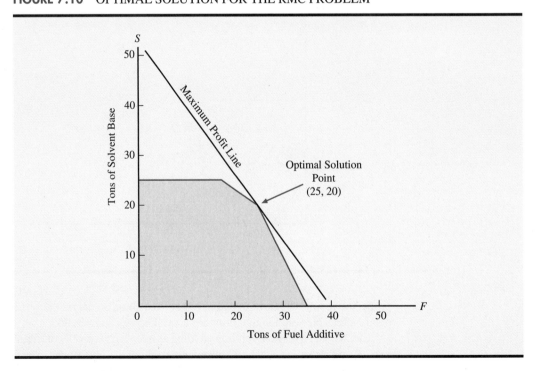

or

$$F = 50 - 1.25S \qquad (7.8)$$

Substituting this expression for F into equation (7.7) and solving for S yields

$$0.6(50 - 1.25S) + 0.3S = 21$$
$$30 - 0.75S + 0.3S = 21$$
$$-0.45S = -9$$
$$S = 20$$

Although the optimal solution to the RMC problem consists of integer values for the decision variables, this result will not always be the case.

Substituting $S = 20$ in equation (7.8) and solving for F provides

$$F = 50 - 1.25(20)$$
$$= 50 - 25 = 25$$

Thus, the exact location of the optimal solution point is $F = 25$ and $S = 20$. This solution point provides the optimal production quantities for RMC at 25 tons of fuel additive and 20 tons of solvent base and yields a profit contribution of $40(25) + 30(20) = \$1600$.

For practice in using the graphical solution procedure to identify the optimal solution and find the exact values of the decision variables at the optimal solution, try Problem 11.

For a linear programming problem with two decision variables, you can determine the exact values of the decision variables at the optimal solution by first using the graphical procedure to identify the optimal solution point and then solving the two simultaneous equations associated with this point.

A Note on Graphing Lines

An important aspect of the graphical method is the ability to graph lines showing the constraints and the objective function of the linear program. The procedure we have used for graphing the equation of a line is to find any two points satisfying the equation and then draw the line through the two points. For the RMC constraints, the two points were easily found by the setting $F = 0$ and solving the constraint equation for S. Then we set $S = 0$ and solved for F. For the material 1 constraint line

$$0.4F + 0.5S = 20$$

This procedure identified the two points $(F = 0, S = 40)$ and $(F = 50, S = 0)$. The material 1 constraint line was then graphed by drawing a line through these two points.

All constraints and objective function lines in two-variable linear programs can be graphed if two points on the line can be identified. However, finding the two points on the line is not always as easy as shown in the RMC problem. For example, suppose a company manufactures two models of a small hand-held computer: the Professional (P) and the Assistant (A). Management needs 50 units of the Professional model for its own salesforce, and expects sales of the remaining Professionals to be less than or equal to 50% of the sales of the Assistant. A constraint enforcing this requirement is

$$P - 50 \leq 0.5A$$

or

$$P - 0.5A \leq 50$$

Using the equality form of the constraint and setting $P = 0$, we find the point ($P = 0$, $A = -100$) is on the constraint line. Setting $A = 0$, we find a second point ($P = 50, A = 0$) on the constraint line. If we have drawn only the nonnegative ($P \geq 0, A \geq 0$) portion of the graph, the first point ($P = 0, A = -100$) cannot be plotted because $A = -100$ is not on the graph. Whenever we have two points on the line, but one or both of the points cannot be plotted in the nonnegative portion of the graph, the simplest approach is to enlarge the graph. In this example, the point ($P = 0, A = -100$) can be plotted by extending the graph to include the negative A axis. Once both points satisfying the constraint equation have been located, the line can be drawn. The constraint line and the solutions that satisfy the constraint $P - 0.5A \leq 50$ are shown in Figure 7.11.

As another example, consider a problem involving two decision variables, R and T. Suppose that the number of units of R produced has to be at least equal to the number of units of T produced. A constraint enforcing this requirement is

$$R \geq T$$

or

$$R - T \geq 0$$

Can you graph a constraint line when the origin is on the constraint line? Try Problem 5.

To find all solutions satisfying the constraint as an equality, we first set $R = 0$ and solve for T. This result shows that the origin ($T = 0, R = 0$) is on the constraint line. Setting $T = 0$ and solving for R provides the same point. However, we can obtain a second point on the line by setting T equal to any value other than zero and then solving for R. For instance, setting $T = 100$ and solving for R, we find that the point ($T = 100, R = 100$) is on the line. With the two points ($R = 0, T = 0$) and ($R = 100, T = 100$), the constraint line $R - T = 0$ and the solutions that satisfy the constraint $R - T \geq 0$ can be plotted as shown in Figure 7.12.

FIGURE 7.11   SOLUTIONS THAT SATISFY THE CONSTRAINT $P - 0.5A \leq 50$

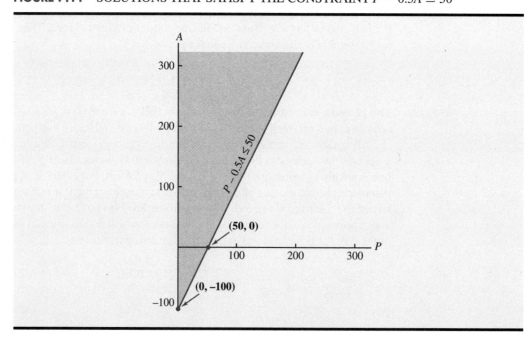

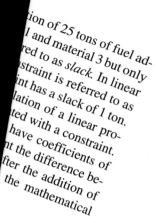

HE CONSTRAINT $R - T \geq 0$

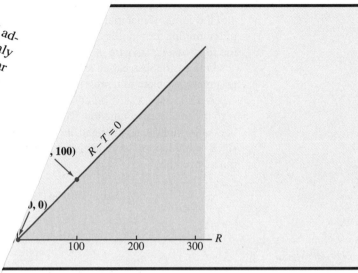

tion of 25 tons of fuel ad-
and material 3 but only
red to as *slack*. In linear
straint is referred to as
int has a slack of 1 ton.
ation of a linear pro-
ted with a constraint.
have coefficients of
t the difference be-
fter the addition of
the mathematical

is said to be

al solution

f the Graphical Solution Procedure
ization Problems

een, the graphical solution procedure is a method for solving two-variable lin-
ming problems such as the RMC problem. The steps of the graphical solution
for a maximization problem are summarized here:

Prepare a graph for each constraint that shows the solutions that satisfy the constraint.
Determine the feasible region by identifying the solutions that satisfy all the constraints simultaneously.
3. Draw an objective function line showing the values of the decision variables that
yield a specified value of the objective function.
4. Move parallel objective function lines toward larger objective function values until
further movement would take the line completely outside the feasible region.
5. Any feasible solution on the objective function line with the largest value is an optimal solution.

Slack Variables

In addition to the optimal solution and its associated profit contribution, the management
of RMC will want information about the production requirements for the three materials.
We can determine this information by substituting the optimal solution values ($F = 25$,
$S = 20$) into the constraints of the linear program.

Constraint	Tons Required for $F = 25$, $S = 20$ Tons	Tons Available	Unused Tons
Material 1	$0.4(25) + 0.5(20) = 20$	20	0
Material 2	$0.2(20) = 4$	5	1
Material 3	$0.6(25) + 0.3(20) = 21$	21	0

on?
l 1
nt.
e
,

Can you identify the slack associated with a constraint? Try Problem 22(e).

Thus, the complete solution tells management that the produc[...] ditive and 20 tons of solvent base will require all available material[...] 4 of the 5 tons of material 2. The 1 ton of unused material 2 is refer[...] programming terminology, any unused or idle capacity for a $\leq$ co[...] the *slack associated with the constraint.* Thus, the material 2 constra[...]

Often variables, called **slack variables,** are added to the formu[...] gramming problem to represent the slack, or unused capacity, associa[...] Unused capacity makes no contribution to profit, so slack variables[...] zero in the objective function. More generally, slack variables represe[...] tween the right-hand side and the left-hand side of a $\leq$ constraint. A[...] slack variables to the mathematical statement of the RMC problem[...] model becomes

Can you write a linear program in standard form? Try Problem 18.

$$\text{Max} \quad 40F + 30S + 0S_1 + 0S_2 + 0S_3$$
$$\text{s.t.}$$
$$0.4F + 0.5S + 1S_1 \qquad\qquad = 20$$
$$0.2S \quad + 1S_2 \qquad = 5$$
$$0.6F + 0.3S \qquad\qquad + 1S_3 = 21$$
$$F, S, S_1, S_2, S_3$$

Whenever all the constraints in a linear program are expressed as equalities, it[...] written in **standard form.**

Referring to the standard form of the RMC problem, we see that at the optim[...] ($F = 25$, $S = 20$) the values for the slack variables are

Constraint	Value of Slack Variable
Material 1	$S_1 = 0$
Material 2	$S_2 = 1$
Material 3	$S_3 = 0$

Could we have used the graphical analysis to provide some of the previous informat[...] The answer is yes. By finding the optimal solution in Figure 7.6, we see that the materi[...] constraint and the material 3 constraint restrict, or *bind,* the feasible region at this poi[...] Thus, the optimal solution requires the use of all of these two resources. In other words, t[...] graph shows that at the optimal solution material 1 and material 3 will have zero slack. Bu[...] because the material 2 constraint is not binding the feasible region at the optimal solution[...] we can expect some slack for this resource.

Recognizing redundant constraints is easy with the graphical solution method. In problems with more than two decision variables, however, redundant constraints usually will not be apparent.

Finally, some linear programs may have one or more constraints that do not affect[...] the feasible region. That is, the feasible region remains the same whether or not the con- straint is included in the problem. Because such a constraint does not affect the feasible re- gion and thus cannot affect the optimal solution, it is called a **redundant constraint.** Redundant constraints can be dropped from the problem without having any effect on the optimal solution. However, in most linear programming problems redundant con- straints are not discarded because they are not immediately recognizable as being redun- dant. The RMC problem had no redundant constraints because each constraint had an effect on the feasible region.

FIGURE 7.12   FEASIBLE SOLUTIONS FOR THE CONSTRAINT $R - T \geq 0$

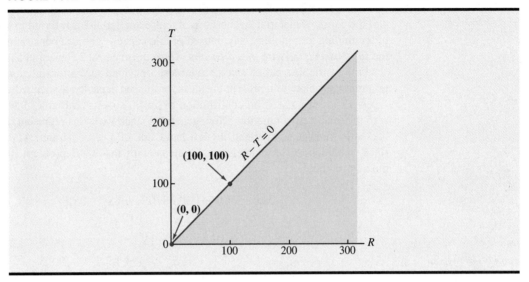

Summary of the Graphical Solution Procedure for Maximization Problems

For additional practice in using the graphical solution procedure, try Problem 22(b), 22(c), and 22(d).

As we have seen, the graphical solution procedure is a method for solving two-variable linear programming problems such as the RMC problem. The steps of the graphical solution procedure for a maximization problem are summarized here:

1. Prepare a graph for each constraint that shows the solutions that satisfy the constraint.
2. Determine the feasible region by identifying the solutions that satisfy all the constraints simultaneously.
3. Draw an objective function line showing the values of the decision variables that yield a specified value of the objective function.
4. Move parallel objective function lines toward larger objective function values until further movement would take the line completely outside the feasible region.
5. Any feasible solution on the objective function line with the largest value is an optimal solution.

Slack Variables

In addition to the optimal solution and its associated profit contribution, the management of RMC will want information about the production requirements for the three materials. We can determine this information by substituting the optimal solution values ($F = 25$, $S = 20$) into the constraints of the linear program.

Constraint	Tons Required for $F = 25, S = 20$ Tons	Tons Available	Unused Tons
Material 1	$0.4(25) + 0.5(20) = 20$	20	0
Material 2	$0.2(20) = 4$	5	1
Material 3	$0.6(25) + 0.3(20) = 21$	21	0

*Can you identify the
slack associated with
a constraint? Try
Problem 22(e).*

Thus, the complete solution tells management that the production of 25 tons of fuel additive and 20 tons of solvent base will require all available material 1 and material 3 but only 4 of the 5 tons of material 2. The 1 ton of unused material 2 is referred to as *slack*. In linear programming terminology, any unused or idle capacity for a $\leq$ constraint is referred to as the *slack associated with the constraint*. Thus, the material 2 constraint has a slack of 1 ton.

Often variables, called **slack variables,** are added to the formulation of a linear programming problem to represent the slack, or unused capacity, associated with a constraint. Unused capacity makes no contribution to profit, so slack variables have coefficients of zero in the objective function. More generally, slack variables represent the difference between the right-hand side and the left-hand side of a $\leq$ constraint. After the addition of slack variables to the mathematical statement of the RMC problem, the mathematical model becomes

*Can you write a linear
program in standard form?
Try Problem 18.*

$$\text{Max} \quad 40F + 30S + 0S_1 + 0S_2 + 0S_3$$

$$\text{s.t.}$$

$$0.4F + 0.5S + 1S_1 \qquad\qquad = 20$$
$$0.2S \qquad + 1S_2 \qquad = 5$$
$$0.6F + 0.3S \qquad\qquad + 1S_3 = 21$$
$$F, S, S_1, S_2, S_3$$

Whenever all the constraints in a linear program are expressed as equalities, it is said to be written in **standard form.**

Referring to the standard form of the RMC problem, we see that at the optimal solution $(F = 25, S = 20)$ the values for the slack variables are

Constraint	Value of Slack Variable
Material 1	$S_1 = 0$
Material 2	$S_2 = 1$
Material 3	$S_3 = 0$

Could we have used the graphical analysis to provide some of the previous information? The answer is yes. By finding the optimal solution in Figure 7.6, we see that the material 1 constraint and the material 3 constraint restrict, or *bind,* the feasible region at this point. Thus, the optimal solution requires the use of all of these two resources. In other words, the graph shows that at the optimal solution material 1 and material 3 will have zero slack. But, because the material 2 constraint is not binding the feasible region at the optimal solution, we can expect some slack for this resource.

*Recognizing redundant
constraints is easy with the
graphical solution method.
In problems with more than
two decision variables,
however, redundant
constraints usually will not
be apparent.*

Finally, some linear programs may have one or more constraints that do not affect the feasible region. That is, the feasible region remains the same whether or not the constraint is included in the problem. Because such a constraint does not affect the feasible region and thus cannot affect the optimal solution, it is called a **redundant constraint.** Redundant constraints can be dropped from the problem without having any effect on the optimal solution. However, in most linear programming problems redundant constraints are not discarded because they are not immediately recognizable as being redundant. The RMC problem had no redundant constraints because each constraint had an effect on the feasible region.

NOTES AND COMMENTS

1. In the standard form representation of a linear program, the objective function coefficients for slack variables are zero. This condition implies that slack variables, which represent unused resources, do not affect the value of the objective function. However, in some applications, some or all of the unused resources can be sold and contribute to profit. In such cases the corresponding slack variables become decision variables representing the amount of resources to be sold. For each of these variables, a nonzero coefficient in the objective function would reflect the profit associated with selling a unit of the corresponding resource.

2. Redundant constraints do not affect the feasible region; as a result they can be removed from a linear programming model without affecting the optimal solution. However, if the linear programming model is to be resolved later, changes in some of the data might change a previously redundant constraint into a binding constraint. Thus, we recommend keeping all constraints in the linear programming model even though one or more of the constraints may be redundant.

7.3   EXTREME POINTS AND THE OPTIMAL SOLUTION

Suppose that the profit contribution for 1 ton of solvent base increases from $30 to $60 while the profit contribution for 1 ton of fuel additive and all the constraints remain unchanged. The complete linear programming model of this new problem is identical to the mathematical model in Section 7.2, except for the revised objective function:

$$\text{Max} \quad 40F + 60S$$

How does this change in the objective function affect the optimal solution to the RMC problem? Figure 7.13 shows the graphical solution of the RMC problem with the revised objective function. Note that since the constraints have not changed, the feasible region has not changed. However, the profit lines have been altered to reflect the new objective function.

By moving the profit line in a parallel manner away from the origin, we find the optimal solution as shown in Figure 7.13. The values of the decision variables at this point are $F = 18.75$ and $S = 25$. The increased profit for the solvent base has caused a change in the optimal solution. In fact, as you may have suspected, we are cutting back the production of the lower profit fuel additive and increasing the production of the higher profit solvent base.

What have you noticed about the location of the optimal solutions in the linear programming problems that we have solved thus far? Look closely at the graphical solutions in Figures 7.10 and 7.13. An important observation that you should be able to make is that the optimal solutions occur at one of the vertices or "corners" of the feasible region. In linear programming terminology these vertices are referred to as the **extreme points** of the feasible region. Thus, the RMC has five vertices or five extreme points (Figure 7.14). We can now state our observation about the location of optimal solutions[2]:

> The optimal solution to a linear programming problem can be found at an extreme point of the feasible region for the problem.

---

2. In Section 7.6 we show that two special cases (infeasibility and unboundedness) in linear programming have no optimal solution. The observation stated does not apply to these cases.

FIGURE 7.13   OPTIMAL SOLUTION FOR THE RMC PROBLEM WITH AN OBJECTIVE FUNCTION OF $40F + 60S$

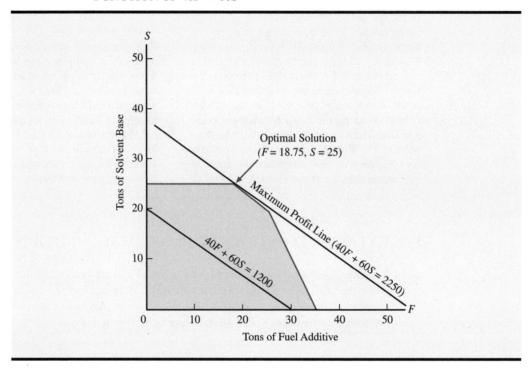

FIGURE 7.14   THE FIVE EXTREME POINTS OF THE FEASIBLE REGION FOR THE RMC PROBLEM

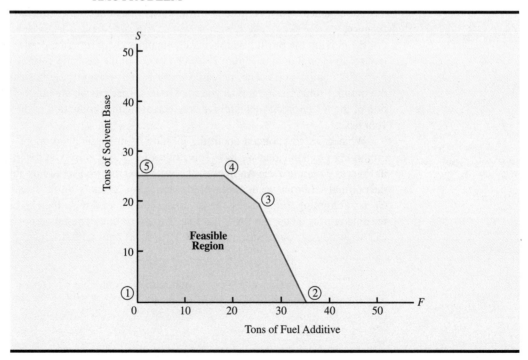

For additional practice in identifying the extreme points of the feasible region and determining the optimal solution by computing and comparing the objective function value at each extreme point, try Problem 13.

This property means that, if you are looking for the optimal solution to a linear programming problem, you do not have to evaluate all feasible solution points. In fact, you have to consider *only* the feasible solutions that occur at the extreme points of the feasible region. Thus, for the RMC problem, instead of computing and comparing the profit for all feasible solutions, we can find the optimal solution by evaluating the five extreme-point solutions and selecting the one that provides the highest profit. Actually, the graphical solution procedure is nothing more than a convenient way of identifying an optimal extreme point for two-variable problems.

7.4 COMPUTER SOLUTION OF THE RMC PROBLEM

In January 1952 the first successful computer solution of a linear programming problem was performed on the SEAC (Standards Eastern Automatic Computer). The SEAC, the first digital computer built by the National Bureau of Standards under U.S. Air Force sponsorship, had a 512-word memory and magnetic tape for external storage.

Instructions on how to solve linear programs using The Management Scientist, LINDO, and Excel are provided in appendixes at the end of the chapter.

Computer programs designed to solve linear programming problems are now widely available. Most companies and universities have access to these computer programs. After a short period of familiarization with the specific features of the program, most users can solve linear programming problems with few difficulties. Problems involving thousands of variables and thousands of constraints are now routinely solved with computer packages. Most large linear programs can be solved with just a few minutes of computer time; small linear programs usually require only a few seconds.

As a result of the recent explosion of software for personal computers, a large number of user-friendly computer programs that can solve linear programs are now available. These programs, developed by academicians and small software companies, are almost all easy to use. Most of these programs are designed to solve smaller linear programs (a few hundred variables). But some can be used to solve problems involving thousands of variables and constraints. Linear programming solvers are now part of many spreadsheet packages. In Appendix 7.3, we show how to use the solver available with Excel.

The Management Scientist, a software package developed by the authors of this text, contains a linear programming module. Let us demonstrate its use by solving the RMC problem. The linear program is as follows.

$$\text{Max} \quad 40F + 30S$$

s.t.

$$0.4F + 0.5S \le 20 \quad \text{Material 1}$$
$$0.2S \le 5 \quad \text{Material 2}$$
$$0.6F + 0.3S \le 21 \quad \text{Material 3}$$
$$F, S \ge 0$$

The solution[3] generated by The Management Scientist is shown in Figure 7.15.

Interpretation of Computer Output

Let us look more closely at The Management Scientist output in Figure 7.15 and interpret the computer solution provided for the RMC problem. First, note that the number 1600.000, which appears to the right of objective function value, indicates that the optimal solution to this problem will provide a profit of $1600. Directly below the objective function value are the values of the decision variables at the optimal solution. Thus, we have $F = 25$ tons of fuel additive and $S = 20$ tons of solvent base as the optimal production quantities.

3. The steps required to generate this solution are described in Appendix 7.1.

FIGURE 7.15   THE MANAGEMENT SCIENTIST SOLUTION FOR THE RMC PROBLEM

```
Objective Function Value =                    1600.000

          Variable              Value              Reduced Costs
       --------------       --------------        -----------------

             F                  25.000                  0.000
             S                  20.000                  0.000


         Constraint          Slack/Surplus           Dual Prices
       --------------       --------------        -----------------

             1                   0.000                 33.333
             2                   1.000                  0.000
             3                   0.000                 44.444


OBJECTIVE COEFFICIENT RANGES

       Variable          Lower Limit         Current Value        Upper Limit
     ------------       --------------       --------------      --------------

          F                24.000               40.000              60.000
          S                20.000               30.000              50.000


RIGHT HAND SIDE RANGES

       Constraint        Lower Limit         Current Value        Upper Limit
     ------------       --------------       --------------      --------------

           1               14.000               20.000              21.500
           2                4.000                5.000         No Upper Limit
           3               18.750               21.000              30.000
```

The information in the Reduced Costs column indicates how much the objective function coefficient of each decision variable would have to improve[4] before it would be possible for that variable to assume a positive value in the optimal solution. If a decision variable is already positive in the optimal solution, its reduced cost is zero. For the RMC problem, the optimal solution is $F = 25$ and $S = 20$. Both variables already have positive values, so their corresponding reduced costs are zero. In Chapter 8 we interpret the reduced cost for a decision variable that does not have a positive value in the optimal solution.

Immediately following the optimal F and S values and the reduced cost information, the computer output provides information about the status of the constraints. Recall that the RMC problem had three less-than-or-equal-to constraints corresponding to the tons available for each of the three raw materials. The information shown in the Slack/Surplus column provides the value of the slack variable for each of the three materials. This information is summarized as follows:

---

4. For a maximization problem, *improve* means get bigger; for a minimization problem, *improve* means get smaller.

Constraint Number	Constraint Name	Slack
1	Material 1	0
2	Material 2	1
3	Material 3	0

Thus, we see that the binding constraints (the material 1 and material 3 constraints) have zero slack at the optimal solution. The material 2 constraint has 1 ton of slack, or unused capacity.

The rest of the output in Figure 7.15 can be used to determine how a change in a coefficient of the objective function or a change in the right-hand-side value of a constraint will affect the optimal solution. We will discuss the use of this information in Chapter 8 when we study the topic of sensitivity analysis.

NOTES AND COMMENTS

Linear programming solvers are now a standard feature of most spreadsheet packages. Excel, Lotus 1-2-3, and Quattro Pro all come with built-in solvers capable of solving optimization problems, including linear programs. The solver in each of these spreadsheet packages was developed by Frontline Systems and provides a similar user interface. In Appendix 7.3 we show how spreadsheets can be used to solve linear programs by using Excel to solve the RMC problem.

7.5　A SIMPLE MINIMIZATION PROBLEM

M&D Chemicals produces two products that are sold as raw materials to companies manufacturing bath soaps and laundry detergents. Based on an analysis of current inventory levels and potential demand for the coming month, M&D's management has specified that the combined production for products A and B must total at least 350 gallons. Separately, a major customer's order for 125 gallons of product A must also be satisfied. Product A requires 2 hours of processing time per gallon while product B requires 1 hour of processing time per gallon, and for the coming month, 600 hours of processing time are available. M&D's objective is to satisfy these requirements at a minimum total production cost. Production costs are $2 per gallon for product A and $3 per gallon for product B.

To find the minimum-cost production schedule, we will formulate the M&D Chemicals problem as a linear program. Following a procedure similar to the one used for the RMC problem we first define the decision variables and the objective function for the problem. Let

$$A = \text{number of gallons of product A}$$
$$B = \text{number of gallons of product B}$$

Because the production costs are $2 per gallon for product A and $3 per gallon for product B, the objective function that corresponds to the minimization of the total production cost can be written as

$$\text{Min}\quad 2A + 3B$$

Next consider the constraints placed on the M&D Chemicals problem. To satisfy the major customer's demand for 125 gallons of product A, we know A must be at least 125. Thus, we write the constraint

$$1A \geq 125$$

Because the combined production for both products must total at least 350 gallons, we can write the constraint

$$1A + 1B \geq 350$$

Finally, the limitation on available processing time of 600 hours means that we need to add the constraint

$$2A + 1B \leq 600$$

After adding the nonnegativity constraints ($A, B \geq 0$), we have the following linear program for the M&D Chemicals problem:

$$\text{Min} \quad 2A + 3B$$

s.t.

$1A$		≥ 125	Demand for product A
$1A$	$+ 1B$	≥ 350	Total production
$2A$	$+ 1B$	≤ 600	Processing time
	A, B	≥ 0	

Because the linear programming model has only two decision variables, the graphical solution procedure can be used to find the optimal production quantities. The graphical method for this problem, just as in the RMC problem, requires us to first graph the constraint lines to find the feasible region. By graphing each constraint line separately and then checking points on either side of the constraint line, the solutions that satisfy each constraint can be identified. By combining the solutions that satisfy each constraint on the same graph, we obtain the feasible region shown in Figure 7.16.

To find the minimum-cost solution, we now draw the objective function line corresponding to a particular total cost value. For example, we might start by drawing the line $2A + 3B = 1200$. This line is shown in Figure 7.17. Clearly some points in the feasible region would provide a total cost of $1200. To find the values of A and B that provide smaller total cost values, we move the objective function line in a lower left direction until, if we moved it any farther, it would be entirely outside the feasible region. Note that the objective function line $2A + 3B = 800$ intersects the feasible region at the extreme point $A = 250$ and $B = 100$. This extreme point provides the minimum-cost solution with an objective function value of 800. From Figures 7.16 and 7.17, we can see that the total production constraint and the processing time constraint are binding. Just as in every linear programming problem, the optimal solution occurs at an extreme point of the feasible region.

Summary of the Graphical Solution Procedure for Minimization Problems

Can you use the graphical solution procedure to determine the optimal solution for a minimization problem? Try Problem 29.

The steps of the graphical solution procedure for a minimization problem are summarized here:

1. Prepare a graph for each constraint that shows the solutions that satisfy the constraint.
2. Determine the feasible region by identifying the solutions that satisfy all the constraints simultaneously.
3. Draw an objective function line showing the values of the decision variables that yield a specified value of the objective function.

FIGURE 7.16   THE FEASIBLE REGION FOR THE M&D CHEMICALS PROBLEM

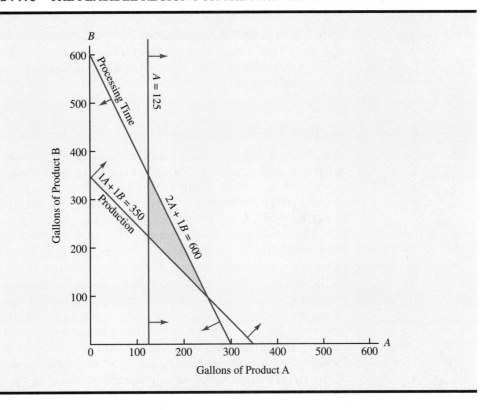

FIGURE 7.17   GRAPHICAL SOLUTION FOR THE M&D CHEMICALS PROBLEM

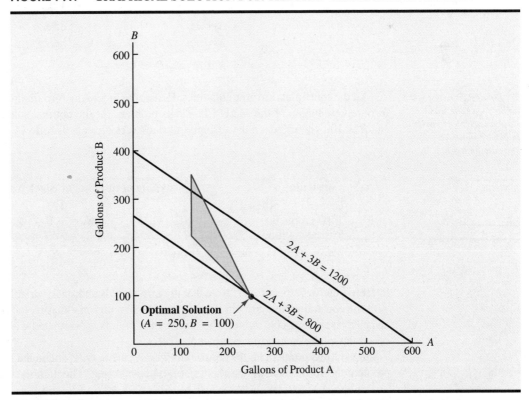

4. Move parallel objective function lines toward smaller objective function values until further movement would take the line completely outside the feasible region.
5. Any feasible solution on the objective function line with the smallest value is an optimal solution.

Surplus Variables

The optimal solution to the M&D Chemicals problem shows that the desired total production of $A + B = 350$ gallons has been achieved by using all available processing time of $2A + 1B = 2(250) + 1(100) = 600$ hours. In addition, note that the constraint requiring that product A demand be met has been satisfied with $A = 250$ gallons. In fact, the production of product A exceeds its minimum level by $250 - 125 = 125$ gallons. This excess production for product A is referred to as *surplus*. In linear programming terminology, any excess quantity corresponding to a $\geq$ constraint is referred to as surplus.

Recall that with a $\leq$ constraint, a slack variable can be added to the left-hand side of the inequality to convert the constraint to equality form. With a $\geq$ constraint, a **surplus variable** can be subtracted from the left-hand side of the inequality to convert the constraint to equality form. Just as with slack variables, surplus variables are given a coefficient of zero in the objective function because they have no effect on its value. After including two surplus variables, S_1 and S_2, for the $\geq$ constraints and one slack variable, S_3, for the $\leq$ constraint, the linear programming model of the M&D Chemicals problem becomes

$$
\begin{aligned}
\text{Min} \quad & 2A + 3B + 0S_1 + 0S_2 + 0S_3 \\
\text{s.t.} \quad & \\
& 1A \quad\quad\; - 1S_1 \quad\quad\quad\quad = 125 \\
& 1A + 1B \quad\quad - 1S_2 \quad\quad = 350 \\
& 2A + 1B \quad\quad\quad\quad + 1S_3 = 600 \\
& A, B, S_1, S_2, S_3 \geq 0
\end{aligned}
$$

Try Problem 33 to test your ability to use slack and surplus variables to write a linear program in standard form.

All the constraints are now equalities. Hence, the preceding formulation is the standard-form representation of the M&D Chemicals problem. At the optimal solution of $A = 250$ and $B = 100$, the values of the surplus and slack variables are as follows:

Constraint	Value of Surplus or Slack Variables
Demand for product A	$S_1 = 125$
Total production	$S_2 = 0$
Processing time	$S_3 = 0$

Refer to Figures 7.16 and 7.17. Note that the zero surplus and slack variables are associated with the constraints that are binding at the optimal solution—that is, the total production and processing time constraints. The surplus of 125 units is associated with the nonbinding constraint on the demand for product A.

In the RMC problem all the constraints were of the $\leq$ type, and in the M&D Chemicals problem the constraints were a mixture of $\geq$ and $\leq$ types. The number and types of constraints encountered in a particular linear programming problem depend on the specific conditions existing in the problem. Linear programming problems may have some $\leq$ constraints, some $\geq$ constraints, and some $=$ constraints. For an equality constraint, feasible solutions must lie directly on the constraint line.

Try Problem 32 to practice solving a linear program with all three constraint forms.

An example of a linear program with two decision variables, G and H, and all three constraint forms is given here:

$$\text{Min} \quad 2G + 2H$$
$$\text{s.t.}$$
$$1G + 3H \leq 12$$
$$3G + 1H \geq 13$$
$$1G - 1H = 3$$
$$G, H \geq 0$$

The standard-form representation of this problem is

$$\text{Min} \quad 2G + 2H + 0S_1 + 0S_2$$
$$\text{s.t.}$$
$$1G + 3H + 1S_1 \qquad\quad = 12$$
$$3G + 1H \qquad - 1S_2 = 13$$
$$1G - 1H \qquad\qquad = 3$$
$$G, H, S_1, S_2 \geq 0$$

The standard form requires a slack variable for the $\leq$ constraint and a surplus variable for the $\geq$ constraint. However, neither a slack nor a surplus variable is required for the third constraint because it is already in equality form.

When solving linear programs graphically, it is not necessary to write the problem in its standard form. Nevertheless, it is helpful to be able to compute the values of the slack and surplus variables and understand what they mean. A final point: The standard form of the linear programming problem is equivalent to the original formulation of the problem. That is, the optimal solution to any linear programming problem is the same as the optimal solution to the standard form of the problem. The standard form has not changed the basic problem; it has only changed how we write the constraints for the problem.

Computer Solution of the M&D Chemicals Problem

The solution obtained using The Management Scientist is presented in Figure 7.18. The computer output shows that the minimum-cost solution yields an objective function value of $800. The values of the decision variables show that 250 gallons of product A and 100 gallons of product B provide the minimum-cost solution.

The Slack/Surplus column shows that the $\geq$ constraint corresponding to the demand for product A (see constraint 1) has a surplus of 125 units. This column tells us that production of product A in the optimal solution exceeds demand by 125 gallons. The Slack/Surplus values are zero for the total production requirement (constraint 2) and the processing time limitation (constraint 3), which indicates that these constraints are binding at the optimal solution. We will discuss the rest of the computer output in Figure 7.18 in Chapter 8 when we study the topic of sensitivity analysis.

FIGURE 7.18   THE MANAGEMENT SCIENTIST SOLUTION FOR THE M&D CHEMICALS PROBLEM

```
Objective Function Value =            800.000

        Variable             Value             Reduced Costs
    -------------     ---------------     -------------------
          A               250.000                   0.000
          B               100.000                   0.000

        Constraint       Slack/Surplus           Dual Prices
    -------------     ---------------     -------------------
          1               125.000                   0.000
          2                 0.000                  -4.000
          3                 0.000                   1.000

OBJECTIVE COEFFICIENT RANGES

      Variable       Lower Limit     Current Value     Upper Limit
    ------------   ---------------   ---------------   ---------------
          A        No Lower Limit           2.000             3.000
          B                 2.000           3.000      No Upper Limit

RIGHT HAND SIDE RANGES

      Constraint     Lower Limit     Current Value     Upper Limit
    ------------   ---------------   ---------------   ---------------
          1        No Lower Limit         125.000           250.000
          2               300.000         350.000           475.000
          3               475.000         600.000           700.000
```

7.6   SPECIAL CASES

In this section we discuss three special situations that can arise when we attempt to solve linear programming problems.

Alternative Optimal Solutions

From our discussion of the graphical solution procedure, we know that optimal solutions can be found at the extreme points of the feasible region. Now let us consider the special case where the optimal objective function line coincides with one of the binding constraint lines. It can lead to **alternative optimal solutions,** whereby more than one solution provides the optimal value for the objective function.

To illustrate the case of alternative optimal solutions, we return to the RMC problem. However, let us assume that the profit contribution for the solvent base (S) has increased to $50. The revised objective function is $40F + 50S$. Figure 7.19 shows the graphical solution to this problem. Note that the optimal solution still occurs at an extreme point. In fact, it occurs at two extreme points: extreme point ③ ($F = 25$, $S = 20$) and extreme point ④ ($F = 18.75$, $S = 25$).

FIGURE 7.19   OPTIMAL SOLUTIONS FOR THE RMC PROBLEM WITH AN OBJECTIVE
FUNCTION OF $40x_1 + 50x_2$

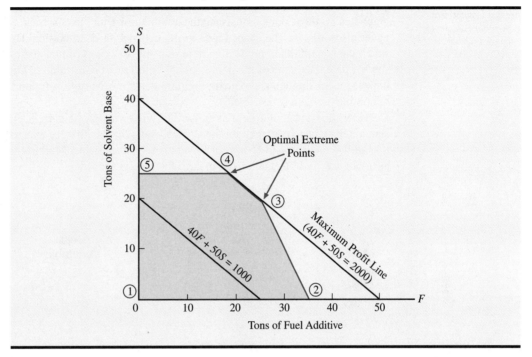

The objective function values at these two extreme points are identical; that is,

$$40F + 50S = 40(25) + 50(20) = 2000$$

and

$$40F + 50S = 40(18.75) + 50(25) = 2000$$

Furthermore, any point on the line connecting the two optimal extreme points also provides an optimal solution. For example, the solution point ($F = 21.875$, $S = 22.5$), which is half-way between the two extreme points, also provides the optimal objective function value of

$$40F + 50S = 40(21.875) + 50(22.5) = 2000$$

A linear programming problem with alternative optimal solutions is generally a good situation for the manager or decision maker. It means that several combinations of the decision variables are optimal and that the manager can select the most desirable optimal solution. Unfortunately, determining whether a problem has alternative optimal solutions is not a simple matter.

Infeasibility

Infeasibility means that no solution to the linear programming problem satisfies all constraints, including the nonnegativity constraints. Graphically, infeasibility means that a feasible region does not exist; that is, no points satisfy all constraint equations and non-negativity conditions simultaneously. To illustrate this situation, let us return to the problem facing RMC.

Problems with no feasible solution do arise in practice, most often because management's expectations are too high or because too many restrictions have been placed on the problem.

Suppose that management had specified that at least 30 tons of fuel additive and at least 15 tons of solvent base must be produced. Figure 7.20 shows the graph of the solution region that reflects these requirements. The shaded area in the lower left-hand portion of the graph depicts those points satisfying the less-than-or-equal-to constraints on the amount of materials available. The shaded area in the upper right-hand portion depicts those points satisfying the minimum production requirements of 30 tons of fuel additive and 15 tons of solvent base. But none of the points satisfy both sets of constraints. Thus, if management imposes these minimum production requirements, no feasible solution to the linear programming problem is possible.

How should we interpret this infeasibility in terms of the current problem? First, we should tell management that, for the available amounts of the three materials, producing 30 tons of fuel additive and 15 tons of solvent base isn't possible. Moreover, we can tell management exactly how much more of each material is needed.

Material	Minimum Tons Required for $F = 30, S = 15$	Tons Available	Additional Tons Required
Material 1	$0.4(30) + 0.5(15) = 19.5$	20	—
Material 2	$0.2(15) = 3$	5	—
Material 3	$0.6(30) + 0.3(15) = 22.5$	21	1.5

Thus, RMC has a sufficient supply of materials 1 and 2 but will need 1.5 additional tons of material 3 to meet management's production requirements of 30 tons of fuel additive and

FIGURE 7.20 NO FEASIBLE REGION FOR THE RMC PROBLEM WITH MINIMUM PRODUCTION REQUIREMENTS

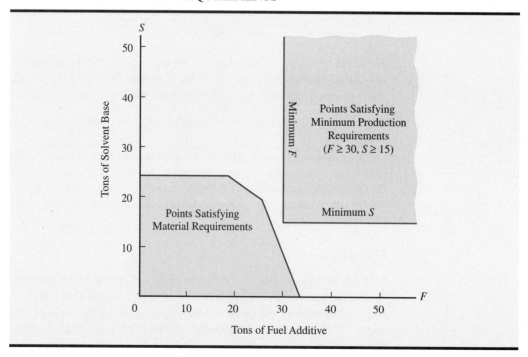

15 tons of solvent base. If, after reviewing the preceding analysis, management still wants this level of production for the two products, RMC will have to obtain the additional 1.5 tons of material 3.

Often, many possibilities are available for corrective management action, once we discover the lack of a feasible solution. The important thing to realize is that linear programming analysis can help determine whether management's plans are feasible. By analyzing the problem using linear programming, we are often able to point out infeasible conditions and initiate corrective action.

Whenever you attempt to solve a problem that is infeasible using The Management Scientist, you will obtain a message that says "No Feasible Solution." In this case you know that no solution to the linear programming problem will satisfy all constraints. Careful inspection of your formulation is necessary to identify why the problem is infeasible. In some situations, the only reasonable approach is to drop one or more constraints and resolve the problem. If you are able to find an optimal solution for this revised problem, you will know that the constraint(s) that were omitted are causing the problem to be infeasible.

Unbounded

The solution to a maximization linear programming problem is **unbounded** if the value of the solution may be made infinitely large without violating any of the constraints; for a minimization problem, the solution is unbounded if the value may be made infinitely small. This condition might be termed *managerial utopia;* for example, if this condition were to occur in a profit maximization problem, the manager could achieve an unlimited profit.

However, in linear programming models of real problems, the occurrence of an unbounded solution means that the problem has been improperly formulated. We know it is not possible to increase profits indefinitely. Therefore, we must conclude that if a profit maximization problem results in an unbounded solution, the mathematical model doesn't represent the real-world problem sufficiently. Usually, what has happened is that a constraint has been inadvertently omitted during problem formulation.

As an illustration, consider the following linear program with two decision variables, X and Y.

$$\text{Max} \quad 20X + 10Y$$
$$\text{s.t.}$$
$$1X \qquad \geq 2$$
$$1Y \leq 5$$
$$X, Y \geq 0$$

In Figure 7.21 we have graphed the feasible region associated with this problem. Note that we can only indicate part of the feasible region since the feasible region extends indefinitely in the direction of the X axis. Looking at the objective function lines in Figure 7.21, we see that the solution to this problem may be made as large as we desire. That is, no matter what solution we pick, we will always be able to reach some feasible solution with a larger value. Thus, we say that the solution to this linear program is *unbounded.*

Can you recognize whether a linear program involves alternative optimal solutions, infeasibility, or is unbounded? Try Problems 40 and 41.

Whenever you attempt to solve a problem that is unbounded using The Management Scientist, you will obtain a message that says, "Problem is Unbounded." Because unbounded solutions cannot occur in real problems, the first thing you should do is to review your model to determine whether you have incorrectly formulated the problem. In many cases, this error is the result of inadvertently omitting a constraint during problem formulation.

FIGURE 7.21   EXAMPLE OF AN UNBOUNDED PROBLEM

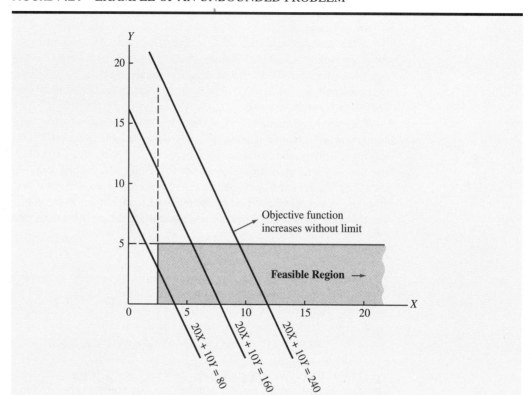

NOTES AND COMMENTS

1. Infeasibility is independent of the objective function. It exists because the constraints are so restrictive that they allow no feasible region for the linear programming model. Thus, when you encounter infeasibility, making changes in the coefficients of the objective function will not help; the problem will remain infeasible.

2. The occurrence of an unbounded solution is often the result of a missing constraint. However, a change in the objective function may cause a previously unbounded problem to become bounded with an optimal solution. For example, the graph in Figure 7.21 shows an unbounded solution for the objective function Max $20X + 10Y$. However, changing the objective function to Max $-20X - 10Y$ will provide the optimal solution $X = 2$ and $Y = 0$ even though no changes have been made in the constraints.

7.7   GENERAL LINEAR PROGRAMMING NOTATION

In this chapter we showed how to formulate mathematical models for the RMC and M&D Chemicals linear programming problems. To formulate a mathematical model of the RMC problem we began by defining two decision variables: F = number of tons of fuel additive, and S = number of tons of solvent base. In the M&D Chemicals problem, the two decision variables were defined as A = number of gallons of product A, and B = number of gallons of product B. We selected decision variable names of F and S in the RMC problem and A and B in the M&D Chemicals problem to make it easier to recall what these decision variables represented in the problem. Although this approach works well for linear programs involving a small number of decision variables, it can become difficult when dealing with problems involving a large number of decision variables.

A more general notation that is often used for linear programs uses the letter x with a subscript. For instance, in the RMC problem, we could have defined the decision variables as follows:

$$x_1 = \text{number of tons of fuel additive}$$
$$x_2 = \text{number of tons of solvent base}$$

In the M&D Chemicals problem, the same variable names would be used, but their definitions would change:

$$x_1 = \text{number of gallons of product A}$$
$$x_2 = \text{number of gallons of product B}$$

A disadvantage of using general notation for decision variable is that we are no longer able to easily identify what the decision variables actually represent in the mathematical model. However, the advantage of general notation is that formulating a mathematical model for a problem that involves a large number of decision variables is much easier. For instance, for a linear programming problem with three decision variables, we would use variable names of x_1, x_2, and x_3; for a problem with four decision variables, we would use variable names of x_1, x_2, x_3, and x_4, and so on. Clearly, if a problem involved 1000 decision variables, trying to identify 1000 unique names would be difficult. However, using the general linear programming notation, the decision variables would be defined as $x_1, x_2, x_3, \ldots, x_{1000}$.

To illustrate the graphical solution procedure for a linear program written using general linear programming notation, consider the following mathematical model for a maximization problem involving two decision variables:

$$\text{Max} \quad 3x_1 + 2x_2$$

s.t.

$$2x_1 + 2x_2 \le 8$$
$$1x_1 + 0.5x_2 \le 3$$
$$x_1, x_2 \ge 0$$

We must first develop a graph that displays the possible solutions (x_1 and x_2 values) for the problem. The usual convention is to plot values of x_1 along the horizontal axis and values of x_2 along the vertical axis. Figure 7.22 shows the graphical solution for this two-variable problem. Note that for this problem the optimal solution is $x_1 = 2$ and $x_2 = 2$, with an objective function value of 10.

Using general linear programming notation we can write the standard form of the preceding problem as follows:

$$\text{Max} \quad 3x_1 + 2x_2 + 0s_1 + 0s_2$$

s.t.

$$2x_1 + 2x_2 + 1s_1 \qquad = 8$$
$$1x_1 + 0.5x_2 + \qquad 1s_2 = 3$$
$$x_1, x_2, s_1, s_2 \ge 0$$

Thus, at the optimal solution $x_1 = 2$ and $x_2 = 2$; the values of the slack variables are $s_1 = s_2 = 0$.

FIGURE 7.22 GRAPHICAL SOLUTION OF A TWO-VARIABLE LINEAR PROGRAM WITH GENERAL NOTATION

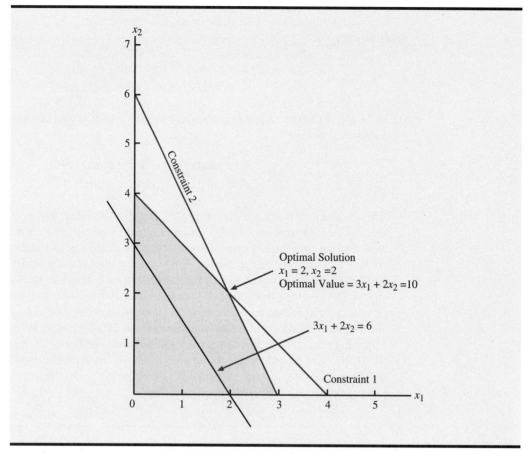

SUMMARY

We formulated linear programming models for the RMC maximization problem and the M&D Chemicals minimization problem. For both problems we showed how a graphical solution procedure and The Management Scientist software package can be used to identify an optimal solution. In formulating a linear programming model of these problems, we developed a general definition of a linear program.

A linear program is a mathematical model that has

1. a linear objective function that is to be maximized or minimized,
2. a set of linear constraints, and
3. variables that are all restricted to nonnegative values.

Slack variables may be used to write less-than-or-equal-to constraints in equality form and surplus variables may be used to write greater-than-or-equal-to constraints in equality form. The value of a slack variable can usually be interpreted as the amount of unused resource, while the value of a surplus variable indicates the amount over and above some stated minimum requirement. When all constraints have been written as equalities, the linear program has been written in its standard form.

If the solution to a linear program is infeasible or unbounded, no optimal solution to the problem can be found. In the case of infeasibility, no feasible solutions are possible;

whereas, in the case of an unbounded solution, the objective function can be made infinitely large for a maximization problem and infinitely small for a minimization problem. In the case of alternative optimal solutions, two or more optimal extreme points exist, and all the points on the line segment connecting them are also optimal.

The chapter concluded with a section showing how to write a mathematical model using general linear programming notation. The Q. M. in Action: Using Linear Programming for Traffic Control provides just one of many examples of the widespread use of linear programming. In the next two chapters we will see many more applications of linear programming.

Q. M. IN ACTION

USING LINEAR PROGRAMMING FOR TRAFFIC CONTROL*

The Hanshin Expressway was the first urban toll expressway in Osaka, Japan. Although in 1964 its length was only 2.3 kilometers, today it is a large-scale urban expressway network of 200 kilometers. The Hanshin Expressway provides service for the Hanshin (Osaka-Kobe) area, the second-most populated area in Japan. An average of 828,000 vehicles use the expressway each day, with daily traffic sometimes exceeding 1,000,000 vehicles. In 1990, the Hanshin Expressway Public Corporation started using an automated traffic control system in order to maximize the number of vehicles flowing into the expressway network.

The automated traffic control system relies on two control methods: (1) limiting the number of cars that enter the expressway at each entrance ramp; and (2) providing drivers with up-to-date and accurate traffic information, including expected travel times and information about accidents. The approach used to limit the number of vehicles depends upon whether the expressway is in a normal or steady state of operation, or whether some type of unusual event, such as an accident or a breakdown, has occurred.

In the first phase of the steady-state case, the Hanshin system uses a linear programming model to maximize the total number of vehicles entering the system, while preventing traffic congestion and adverse effects on surrounding road networks. The data that drive the linear programming model are collected from detectors installed every 500 meters along the expressway and at all entrance and exit ramps. Every five minutes the real-time data collected from the detectors are used to update the model coefficients, and a new linear program computes the maximum number of vehicles the expressway can accommodate.

The automated traffic control system has been successful. According to surveys, traffic control has decreased the length of congested portions of the expressway by 30 percent and the duration by 20 percent. It has proved to be extremely cost effective, and drivers consider it an indispensable service.

*Based on T. Yoshino, T. Sasaki, and T. Hasegawa, "The Traffic-Control System on the Hanshin Expressway," *Interfaces* (January–February 1995): 94–108.

GLOSSARY

Constraint   An equation or inequality that rules out certain combinations of decision variables as feasible solutions.

Problem formulation   The process of translating the verbal statement of a problem into a mathematical statement called the *mathematical model*.

Mathematical model   A representation of a problem where the objective and all constraint conditions are described by mathematical expressions.

Decision variable   A controllable input for a linear programming model.

Objective function   The expression that defines the quantity to be maximized or minimized in a linear programming model.

Nonnegativity constraints A set of constraints that requires all variables to be nonnegative.

Linear program A mathematical model with a linear objective function, a set of linear constraints, and nonnegative variables.

Linear functions Mathematical expressions in which the variables appear in separate terms and are raised to the first power.

Feasible solution A solution that satisfies all the constraints.

Feasible region The set of all feasible solutions.

Slack variable A variable added to the left-hand side of a less-than-or-equal-to constraint to convert the constraint into an equality. The value of this variable can usually be interpreted as the amount of unused resource.

Standard form A linear program in which all the constraints are written as equalities. The optimal solution of the standard form of a linear program is the same as the optimal solution of the original formulation of the linear program.

Redundant constraint A constraint that does not affect the feasible region. If a constraint is redundant, it can be removed from the problem without affecting the feasible region.

Extreme point Graphically speaking, extreme points are the feasible solution points occurring at the vertices or "corners" of the feasible region. With two-variable problems, extreme points are determined by the intersection of the constraint lines.

Surplus variable A variable subtracted from the left-hand side of a greater-than-or-equal-to constraint to convert the constraint into an equality. The value of this variable can usually be interpreted as the amount over and above some required minimum level.

Alternative optimal solutions The case in which more than one solution provides the optimal value for the objective function.

Infeasibility The situation in which no solution to the linear programming problem satisfies all the constraints.

Unbounded If the value of the solution may be made infinitely large in a maximization linear programming problem or infinitely small in a minimization problem without violating any of the constraints the problem is said to be unbounded.

PROBLEMS

SELFtest

1. Which of the following mathematical relationships could be found in a linear programming model, and which could not? For the relationships that are unacceptable for linear programs, state why.
   a. $-1x_1 + 2x_2 - 1x_3 \leq 70$
   b. $2x_1 - 2x_3 = 50$
   c. $1x_1 - 2x_2^2 + 4x_3 \leq 10$
   d. $3\sqrt{x_1} + 2x_2 - 1x_3 \geq 15$
   e. $1x_1 + 1x_2 + 1x_3 = 6$
   f. $2x_1 + 5x_2 + 1x_1x_2 \leq 25$

SELFtest

2. Find the solutions that satisfy the following constraints:
   a. $4x_1 + 2x_2 \leq 16$
   b. $4x_1 + 2x_2 \geq 16$
   c. $4x_1 + 2x_2 = 16$

3. Show a separate graph of the constraint lines and the solutions that satisfy each of the following constraints:
   a. $3x_1 + 2x_2 \leq 18$
   b. $12x_1 + 8x_2 \geq 480$
   c. $5x_1 + 10x_2 = 200$

4. Show a separate graph of the constraint lines and the solutions that satisfy each of the following constraints:
   a. $3x_1 - 4x_2 \geq 60$
   b. $-6x_1 + 5x_2 \leq 60$
   c. $5x_1 - 2x_2 \leq 0$

5. Show a separate graph of the constraint lines and the solutions that satisfy each of the following constraints:
   a. $x_1 \geq 0.25 (x_1 + x_2)$
   b. $x_2 \leq 0.10 (x_1 + x_2)$
   c. $x_1 \leq 0.50 (x_1 + x_2)$

SELFtest 6. Three objective functions for linear programming problems are $7x_1 + 10x_2$, $6x_1 + 4x_2$, and $-4x_1 + 7x_2$. Show the graph of each for objective function values equal to 420.

SELFtest 7. Identify the feasible region for the following set of constraints:

$$0.5x_1 + 0.25x_2 \geq 30$$
$$1x_1 + 5x_2 \geq 250$$
$$0.25x_1 + 0.5x_2 \leq 50$$
$$x_1, x_2 \geq 0$$

8. Identify the feasible region for the following set of constraints:

$$2x_1 - 1x_2 \leq 0$$
$$-1x_1 + 1.5x_2 \leq 200$$
$$x_1, x_2 \geq 0$$

9. Identify the feasible region for the following set of constraints:

$$3x_1 - 2x_2 \geq 0$$
$$2x_1 - 1x_2 \leq 200$$
$$1x_1 \leq 150$$
$$x_1, x_2 \geq 0$$

SELFtest 10. For the linear program

$$\text{Max} \quad 2x_1 + 3x_2$$
s.t.
$$1x_1 + 2x_2 \leq 6$$
$$5x_1 + 3x_2 \leq 15$$
$$x_1, x_2 \geq 0$$

find the optimal solution using the graphical solution procedure. What is the value of the objective function at the optimal solution?

11. Solve the following linear program using the graphical solution procedure.

$$\text{Max} \quad 5x_1 + 5x_2$$
s.t.
$$1x_1 \leq 100$$
$$1x_2 \leq 80$$
$$2x_1 + 4x_2 \leq 400$$
$$x_1, x_2 \geq 0$$

12. Consider the following linear programming problem:

$$\text{Max} \quad 3x_1 + 3x_2$$

s.t.

$$2x_1 + 4x_2 \leq 12$$
$$6x_1 + 4x_2 \leq 24$$
$$x_1, x_2 \geq 0$$

a. Find the optimal solution using the graphical solution procedure.
b. If the objective function is changed to $2x_1 + 6x_2$, what will the optimal solution be?
c. How many extreme points are there? What are the values of x_1 and x_2 at each extreme point?

SELFtest   13. Consider the following linear program:

$$\text{Max} \quad 1x_1 + 2x_2$$

s.t.

$$1x_1 \qquad \leq 5$$
$$1x_2 \leq 4$$
$$2x_1 + 2x_2 = 12$$
$$x_1, x_2 \geq 0$$

a. Show the feasible region.
b. What are the extreme points of the feasible region?
c. Find the optimal solution using the graphical procedure.

14. Embassy Motorcycles (EM) manufacturers two lightweight motorcycles designed for easy handling and safety. The EZ-Rider model has a new engine and a low profile that make it easy to balance. The Lady-Sport model is slightly larger, uses a more traditional engine, and is specifically designed to appeal to women riders. Embassy produces the engines for both models at its Des Moines, Iowa, plant. Each EZ-Rider engine requires 6 hours of manufacturing time and each Lady-Sport engine requires 3 hours of manufacturing time. The Des Moines plant has 2100 hours of engine manufacturing time available for the next production period. Embassy's motorcycle frame supplier can supply as many EZ-Rider frames as needed. However, the Lady-Sport frame is more complex and the supplier can only provide up to 280 Lady-Sport frames for the next production period. Final assembly and testing requires 2 hours for each EZ-Rider model and 2.5 hours for each Lady-Sport model. A maximum of 1000 hours of assembly and testing time are available for the next production period. The company's accounting department projects a profit contribution of $2400 for each EZ-Rider produced and $1800 for each Lady-Sport produced.
a. Formulate a linear programming model that can be used to determine the number of units of each model that should be produced in order to maximize the total contribution to profit.
b. Solve the problem graphically. What is the optimal solution?
c. Which constraints are binding?

15. Par, Inc., is a small manufacturer of golf equipment and supplies. Par has been convinced by its distributor that there is an existing market for both a medium-priced golf bag, referred to as a standard model, and a high-priced golf bag, referred to as a deluxe model. The distributor is so confident of the market that, if Par can make the bags at a competitive price, the distributor has agreed to purchase all the bags that Par can manufacture over the next three months. A careful analysis of the manufacturing requirements resulted in the following table, which shows the production time requirements for the four required manufacturing operations and the accounting department's estimate of the profit contribution per bag.

	Production Time (hours)				
Product	**Cutting and Dyeing**	**Sewing**	**Finishing**	**Inspection and Packaging**	**Profit per Bag**
Standard	7/10	1/2	1	1/10	$10
Deluxe	1	5/6	2/3	1/4	$ 9

The director of manufacturing estimates that 630 hours of cutting and dyeing time, 600 hours of sewing time, 708 hours of finishing time, and 135 hours of inspection and packaging time will be available for the production of golf bags during the next 3 months.
  a. If the company wants to maximize total profit contribution, how many bags of each model should it manufacture?
  b. What profit contribution can Par earn on those production quantities?
  c. How many hours of production time will be scheduled for each operation?
  d. What is the slack time in each operation?

16. Suppose that Par's management (Problem 15) encounters the following situations.
  a. The accounting department revises its estimate of the profit contribution for the deluxe bag to $18 per bag.
  b. A new low-cost material is available for the standard bag, and the profit contribution per standard bag can be increased to $20 per bag. (Assume that the profit contribution of the deluxe bag is the original $9 value.)
  c. New sewing equipment is available that would increase the sewing operation capacity to 750 hours. (Assume that $10x_1 + 9x_2$ is the appropriate objective function.)
If each of these situations is encountered separately, what is the optimal solution and the total profit contribution?

17. Refer to the feasible region for Par, Inc., in Problem 15.
  a. Develop an objective function that will make extreme point (0,540) the optimal extreme point.
  b. What is the optimal solution for the objective function you selected in part (a)?
  c. What are the values of the slack variables associated with this solution?

SELFtest   18. Write the following linear program in standard form:

$$\text{Max} \quad 5x_1 + 2x_2 + 8x_3$$
$$\text{s.t.}$$
$$1x_1 - 2x_2 + 0.5x_3 \leq 420$$
$$2x_1 + 3x_2 - 1x_3 \leq 610$$
$$6x_1 - 1x_2 + 3x_3 \leq 125$$
$$x_1, x_2, x_3 \geq 0$$

19. For the linear program

$$\text{Max} \quad 4x_1 + 1x_2$$
$$\text{s.t.}$$
$$10x_1 + 2x_2 \leq 30$$
$$3x_1 + 2x_2 \leq 12$$
$$2x_1 + 2x_2 \leq 10$$
$$x_1, x_2 \geq 0$$

a. Write this problem in standard form.
b. Solve the problem using the graphical solution procedure.
c. What are the values of the three slack variables at the optimal solution?

20. Given the linear program

$$\text{Max} \quad 3x_1 + 4x_2$$

s.t.

$$-1x_1 + 2x_2 \le 8$$
$$1x_1 + 2x_2 \le 12$$
$$2x_1 + 1x_2 \le 16$$
$$x_1, x_2 \ge 0$$

a. Write the problem in standard form.
b. Solve the problem using the graphical solution procedure.
c. What are the values of the three slack variables at the optimal solution?

21. For the linear program

$$\text{Max} \quad 3x_1 + 2x_2$$

s.t.

$$x_1 + x_2 \ge 4$$
$$3x_1 + 4x_2 \le 24$$
$$x_1 \ge 2$$
$$x_1 - x_2 \le 0$$
$$x_1, x_2 \ge 0$$

a. Write the problem in standard form.
b. Solve the problem.
c. What are the values of the slack and surplus variables at the optimal solution?

SELFtest

22. Kelson Sporting Equipment, Inc., makes two different types of baseball gloves: a regular model and a catcher's model. The firm has 900 hours of production time available in its cutting and sewing department, 300 hours available in its finishing department, and 100 hours available in its packaging and shipping department. The production time requirements and the profit contribution per glove are given in the following table.

Model	Production Time (hours)			Profit/Glove
	Cutting and Sewing	Finishing	Packaging and Shipping	
Regular model	1	$\frac{1}{2}$	$\frac{1}{8}$	$5
Catcher's model	$\frac{3}{2}$	$\frac{1}{3}$	$\frac{1}{4}$	$8

Assuming that the company is interested in maximizing the total profit contribution, answer the following:
a. What is the linear programming model for this problem?
b. Find the optimal solution using the graphical solution procedure. How many gloves of each model should Kelson manufacture?
c. What is the total profit contribution Kelson can earn with the given production quantities?

d. How many hours of production time will be scheduled in each department?

e. What is the slack time in each department?

23. George Johnson recently inherited a large sum of money; he wants to use a portion of this money to set up a trust fund for his two children. The trust fund has two investment options: (1) a bond fund and (2) a stock fund. The projected returns over the life of the investments are 6% for the bond fund and 10% for the stock fund. Whatever portion of the inheritance he finally decides to commit to the trust fund, he wants to invest at least 30% of that amount in the bond fund. In addition, he wants to select a mix that will enable him to obtain a total return of at least 7.5%.

    a. Formulate a linear programming model that can be used to determine the percentage that should be allocated to each of the possible investment alternatives.

    b. Solve the problem using the graphical solution procedure.

24. The Sea Wharf Restaurant would like to determine the best way to allocate a monthly advertising budget of $1000 between newspaper advertising and radio advertising. Management has decided that at least 25% of the budget must be spent on each type of media, and that the amount of money spent on local newspaper advertising must be at least twice the amount spent on radio advertising. A marketing consultant has developed an index that measures audience exposure per dollar of advertising on a scale from 0 to 100, with higher values implying greater audience exposure. If the value of the index for local newspaper advertising is 50 and the value of the index for spot radio advertising is 80, how should the restaurant allocate its advertising budget in order to maximize the value of total audience exposure?

    a. Formulate a linear programming model that can be used to determine how the restaurant should allocate its advertising budget in order to maximize the value of total audience exposure.

    b. Solve the problem using the graphical solution procedure.

25. Blair & Rosen, Inc. (B&R), is a brokerage firm that specializes in investment portfolios designed to meet the specific risk tolerances of its clients. A client who contacted B&R this past week has a maximum of $50,000 to invest. B&R's investment advisor has decided to recommend a portfolio consisting of two investment funds: an Internet fund and a Blue Chip fund. The Internet fund has a projected annual return of 12%, while the Blue Chip fund has a projected annual return of 9%. The investment advisor requires that at most $35,000 of the client's funds should be invested in the Internet fund. B&R services include a risk rating for each investment alternative. The Internet fund, which is the more risky of the two investment alternatives, has a risk rating of 6 per thousand dollars invested. The Blue Chip fund has a risk rating of 4 per thousand dollars invested. For example, if $10,000 is invested in each of the two investment funds, B&R's risk rating for the portfolio would by $6(10) + 4(10) = 100$. Finally, B&R has developed a questionnaire to measure each client's risk tolerance. Based on the responses, each client is classified as a conservative, moderate, or aggressive investor. Suppose that the questionnaire results have classified the current client as a moderate investor. B&R recommends that a client who is a moderate investor limit his or her portfolio to a maximum risk rating of 240.

    a. What is the recommended investment portfolio for this client? What is the annual return for the portfolio?

    b. Suppose that a second client with $50,000 to invest has been classified as an aggressive investor. B&R recommends that the maximum portfolio risk rating for an aggressive investor is 320. What is the recommended investment portfolio for this aggressive investor? Discuss what happens to the portfolio under the aggressive investor strategy.

    c. Suppose that a third client with $50,000 to invest has been classified as a conservative investor. B&R recommends that the maximum portfolio risk rating for a conservative investor is 160. Develop the recommended investment portfolio for the conservative investor. Discuss the interpretation of the slack variable for the total investment fund constraint.

26. Tom's, Inc., produces various Mexican food products and sells them to Western Foods, a chain of grocery stores located in Texas and New Mexico. Tom's, Inc., makes two salsa products: Western Foods Salsa and Mexico City Salsa. Essentially, the two products have different blends of whole tomatoes, tomato sauce, and tomato paste. The Western Foods Salsa is a blend of 50% whole tomatoes, 30% tomato sauce, and 20% tomato paste. The Mexico City Salsa, which has a thicker and chunkier consistency, consists of 70% whole tomatoes, 10% tomato sauce, and 20% tomato paste. Each jar of salsa produced weighs 10 ounces. For the current production period Tom's, Inc., can purchase up to 280 pounds of whole tomatoes, 130 pounds of tomato sauce, and 100 pounds of tomato paste; the price per pound for these ingredients is $0.96, $0.64, and $0.56, respectively. The cost of the spices and the other ingredients is approximately $0.10 per jar. Tom's, Inc., buys empty glass jars for $0.02 each, and labeling and filling costs are estimated to be $0.03 for each jar of salsa produced. Tom's contract with Western Foods results in sales revenue of $1.64 for each jar of Western Foods Salsa and $1.93 for each jar of Mexico City Salsa.

    a. Develop a linear programming model that will enable Tom's to determine the mix of salsa products that will maximize the total profit contribution.

    b. Find the optimal solution.

27. The production editor for Rayburn Publishing Company has 1800 pages of manuscript that must be copyedited. Because of the short time frame involved, only two copyeditors are available: Erhan Mergen and Sue Smith. Erhan has 10 days available and Sue has 12 days available. Erhan can process 100 pages of manuscript per day and Sue can process 150 pages of manuscript per day. Rayburn Publishing has developed an index used to measure the overall quality of a copyeditor on a scale from 1 (worst) to 10 (best). Erhan's quality rating is 9 and Sue's quality rating is 6. In addition, Erhan charges $3 per page of copyedited manuscript and Sue charges $2 per page. If a budget of $4800 has been allocated for copyediting, how many pages should be assigned to each copyeditor in order to complete the project with the highest possible quality?

28. A financial advisor at Diehl Investments has identified two companies that are likely candidates for a takeover in the near future. Eastern Cable is a leading manufacturer of flexible cable systems used in the construction industry, and ComSwitch is a new firm specializing in digital switching systems. Eastern Cable is currently trading for $40 per share, and ComSwitch is currently trading for $25 per share. If the takeovers occur, the financial advisor estimates that the price of Eastern Cable will go to $55 per share and ComSwitch will go to $43 per share. At this point in time, the financial advisor has identified ComSwitch as the higher risk alternative. Assume that a client has indicated a willingness to invest a maximum of $50,000 in the two companies. The client wants to invest at least $15,000 in Eastern Cable and at least $10,000 in ComSwitch. Because of the higher risk associated with ComSwitch, the financial advisor has recommended that at most $25,000 should be invested in ComSwitch.

    a. Formulate a linear programming model that can be used to determine the number of shares of Eastern Cable and the number of shares of ComSwitch that will meet the investment constraints and maximize the total return for the investment.

    b. Graph the feasible region.

    c. Determine the coordinates of each extreme point.

    d. Find the optimal solution.

SELFtest   **29.** Consider the following linear program:

$$\text{Min} \quad 3x_1 + 4x_2$$

s.t.

$$1x_1 + 3x_2 \geq 6$$
$$1x_1 + 1x_2 \geq 4$$
$$x_1, x_2 \geq 0$$

Identify the feasible region and find the optimal solution using the graphical solution procedure. What is the value of the objective function?

30. Identify the three extreme-point solutions for the M&D Chemicals problem (see Section 7.5). Identify the value of the objective function and the values of the slack and surplus variables at each extreme point.

31. Consider the following linear programming problem:

$$\text{Min} \quad x_1 + 2x_2$$

s.t.

$$x_1 + 4x_2 \le 21$$
$$2x_1 + x_2 \ge 7$$
$$3x_1 + 1.5x_2 \le 21$$
$$-2x_1 + 6x_2 \ge 0$$
$$x_1, x_2 \ge 0$$

a. Find the optimal solution using the graphical solution procedure and the value of the objective function.
b. Determine the amount of slack or surplus for each constraint.
c. Suppose the objective function is changed to max $5x_1 + 2x_2$. Find the optimal solution and the value of the objective function.

SELFtest   32. Consider the following linear program:

$$\text{Min} \quad 2x_1 + 2x_2$$

s.t.

$$1x_1 + 3x_2 \le 12$$
$$3x_1 + 1x_2 \ge 13$$
$$1x_1 - 1x_2 = 3$$
$$x_1, x_2 \ge 0$$

a. Show the feasible region.
b. What are the extreme points of the feasible region?
c. Find the optimal solution using the graphical solution procedure.

SELFtest   33. For the linear program

$$\text{Min} \quad 6x_1 + 4x_2$$

s.t.

$$2x_1 + 1x_2 \ge 12$$
$$1x_1 + 1x_2 \ge 10$$
$$1x_2 \le 4$$
$$x_1, x_2 \ge 0$$

a. Write the problem in standard form.
b. Solve the problem using the graphical solution procedure.
c. What are the values of the slack and surplus variables?

34. As part of a quality improvement initiative, Consolidated Electronics employees complete a three-day training program on teaming and a two-day training program on problem solving. The manager of quality improvement has requested that at least 8 training programs

on teaming and at least 10 training programs on problem solving be offered during the next six months. In addition, senior-level management has specified that at least 25 training programs must be offered during this period. Consolidated Electronics uses a consultant to teach the training programs. During the next quarter, the consultant has 84 days of training time available. Each training program on teaming costs $10,000 and each training program on problem solving costs $8,000.

a. Formulate a linear programming model that can be used to determine the number of training programs on teaming and the number of training programs on problem solving that should be offered in order to minimize total cost.

b. Graph the feasible region.

c. Determine the coordinates of each extreme point.

d. Solve for the minimum cost solution.

35. The New England Cheese Company produces two cheese spreads by blending mild cheddar cheese with extra sharp cheddar cheese. The cheese spreads are packaged in 12-ounce containers, which are then sold to distributors throughout the Northeast. The Regular blend contains 80% mild cheddar and 20% extra sharp, and the Zesty blend contains 60% mild cheddar and 40% extra sharp. This year, a local dairy cooperative has offered to provide up to 8100 pounds of mild cheddar cheese for $1.20 per pound and up to 3000 pounds of extra sharp cheddar cheese for $1.40 per pound. The cost to blend and package the cheese spreads, excluding the cost of the cheese, is $0.20 per container. If each container of Regular is sold for $1.95 and each container of Zesty is sold for $2.20, how many containers of Regular and Zesty should New England Cheese produce?

36. Healthtech Food Products is considering developing a new low-fat snack food. It is to be a blend of two types of cereals, each of which has different fiber, fat, and protein characteristics. The following table shows these nutrition characteristics for one ounce of each type of cereal.

Cereal	Dietary Fiber (grams)	Fat (grams)	Protein (grams)
A	2	2	4
B	1.5	3	3

Note that each ounce of cereal A provides 2 grams of dietary fiber and that each ounce of cereal B provides 1.5 grams of dietary fiber. Thus, if Healthtech were to develop the new product using a mix consisting of 50% of cereal A and 50% cereal B, 1 ounce of the snack food would contain 1.75 grams of dietary fiber. Healthtech's nutrition requirements call for each ounce of the new food to have at least 1.7 grams of dietary fiber, no more than 2.8 grams of fat, and no more than 3.6 grams of protein. The cost of cereal A is $0.02 per ounce and the cost of cereal B is $0.025 per ounce. Healthtech wants to determine how much of each cereal is needed to produce 1 ounce of the new food product at the lowest possible cost.

a. Formulate a linear programming model for this situation.

b. Solve the problem using the graphical solution procedure.

c. What are the values of the slack and surplus variables?

d. If Healthtech markets the new snack food in an 8-ounce package, what is the cost per package?

37. Innis Investments manages funds for a number of companies and wealthy clients. The investment strategy is tailored to each client's needs. For a new client, Innis has been authorized to invest up to $1.2 million in two investment funds: a stock fund and a money market fund. Each unit of the stock fund costs $50 and provides an annual rate of return

of 10%; each unit of the money market fund costs $100 and provides an annual rate of return of 4%.

The client wants to minimize risk subject to the requirement that the annual income from the investment be at least $60,000. According to Innis's risk measurement system, each unit invested in the stock fund has a risk index of 8, and each unit invested in the money market fund has a risk index of 3; the higher risk index associated with the stock fund simply indicates that it is the riskier investment. Innis's client has also specified that at least $300,000 be invested in the money market fund.

a. Determine how many units of each fund Innis should purchase for the client to minimize the total risk index for the portfolio.

b. How much annual income will this investment strategy generate?

c. Suppose the client desires to maximize annual return. How should the funds be invested?

38. Photo Chemicals produces two types of photographic developing fluids. Both products cost Photo Chemicals $1 per gallon to produce. Based on an analysis of current inventory levels and outstanding orders for the next month, Photo Chemicals' management has specified that at least 30 gallons of product 1 and at least 20 gallons of product 2 must be produced during the next 2 weeks. Management has also stated that an existing inventory of highly perishable raw material required in the production of both fluids must be used within the next 2 weeks. The current inventory of the perishable raw material is 80 pounds. While more of this raw material can be ordered if necessary, any of the current inventory that is not used within the next 2 weeks will spoil—hence, the management requirement that at least 80 pounds be used in the next 2 weeks. Furthermore, it is known that product 1 requires 1 pound of this perishable raw material per gallon and product 2 requires 2 pounds of the raw material per gallon. Because Photo Chemicals' objective is to keep its production costs at the minimum possible level, the firm's management is looking for a minimum cost production plan that uses all the 80 pounds of perishable raw material and provides at least 30 gallons of product 1 and at least 20 gallons of product 2. What is the minimum cost solution?

39. Southern Oil Company produces two grades of gasoline: regular and premium. The profit contributions are $0.30 per gallon for regular gasoline and $0.50 per gallon for premium gasoline. Each gallon of regular gasoline contains 0.3 gallons of grade A crude oil and each gallon of premium gasoline contains 0.6 gallons of grade A crude oil. For the next production period, Southern has 18,000 gallons of grade A crude oil available. The refinery used to produce the gasolines has a production capacity of 50,000 gallons for the next production period. Southern Oil's distributors have indicated that demand for the premium gasoline for the next production period will be at most 20,000 gallons.

a. Formulate a linear programming model that can be used to determine the number of gallons of regular gasoline and the number of gallons of premium gasoline that should be produced in order to maximize total profit contribution.

b. What is the optimal solution?

c. What are the values and interpretations of the slack variables?

d. What are the binding constraints?

SELFtest **40.** Does the following linear program involve infeasibility, unbounded, and/or alternative optimal solutions? Explain.

$$\text{Max} \quad 4x_1 + 8x_2$$
$$\text{s.t.}$$
$$2x_1 + 2x_2 \leq 10$$
$$-1x_1 + 1x_2 \geq 8$$
$$x_1, x_2 \geq 0$$

SELFtest   **41.** Does the following linear program involve infeasibility, unbounded, and/or alternative optimal solutions? Explain.

$$\text{Max}\quad 1x_1 + 1x_2$$

s.t.

$$8x_1 + 6x_2 \geq 24$$
$$2x_2 \geq 4$$
$$x_1, x_2 \geq 0$$

42. Consider the following linear program:

$$\text{Max}\quad 1x_1 + 1x_2$$

s.t.

$$5x_1 + 3x_2 \leq 15$$
$$3x_1 + 5x_2 \leq 15$$
$$x_1, x_2 \geq 0$$

    a. What is the optimal solution for this problem?
    b. Suppose that the objective function is changed to $1x_1 + 2x_2$. Find the new optimal solution.

43. Consider the following linear program:

$$\text{Max}\quad 1x_1 - 2x_2$$

s.t.

$$-4x_1 + 3x_2 \leq 3$$
$$1x_1 - 1x_2 \leq 3$$
$$x_1, x_2 \geq 0$$

    a. Graph the feasible region for the problem.
    b. Is the feasible region unbounded? Explain.
    c. Find the optimal solution.
    d. Does an unbounded feasible region imply that the optimal solution to the linear program will be unbounded?

44. The manager of a small independent grocery store is trying to determine the best use of her shelf space for soft drinks. The store carries national and generic brands and currently has 200 square feet of shelf space available. The manager wants to allocate at least 60% of the space to the national brands and, regardless of the profitability, allocate at least 10% of the space to the generic brands. How many square feet of space should the manager allocate to the national brands and the generic brands if
    a. The national brands are more profitable than the generic brands?
    b. Both brands are equally profitable?
    c. The generic brand is more profitable than the national brand?

45. Discuss what happens to the M&D Chemicals problem (see Section 7.5) if the cost per gallon for product A is increased to $3.00 per gallon. What would you recommend? Explain.

46. For the M&D Chemicals problem in Section 7.5, discuss the effect of management's requiring total production of 500 gallons for the two products. List two or three actions M&D should consider to correct the situation you encounter.

47. Reconsider the Kelson Sporting Equipment, Inc., production example in Problem 22. Discuss the concepts of infeasibility, unbounded solutions, and alternative optimal solutions as they occur in each of the following situations:

a. Management has requested that the production of baseball gloves (regular model plus catcher's model) be such that the total number of gloves produced is at least 750.

b. The original problem has to be solved again because the profit contribution for the regular model is adjusted downward to $4 per glove.

c. What would have to happen for this problem to be unbounded?

48. Expedition Outfitters manufactures a variety of specialty clothing for hiking, skiing, and mountain climbing. They have decided to begin production on two new parkas designed for use in extremely cold weather: the Mount Everest Parka and the Rocky Mountain Parka. Their manufacturing plant has 120 hours of cutting time and 120 hours of sewing time available for producing these two parkas. Each Mount Everest Parka requires 30 minutes of cutting time and 45 minutes of sewing time, and each Rocky Mountain Parka requires 20 minutes of cutting time and 15 minutes of sewing time. The labor and material cost is $150 for each Mount Everest Parka and $50 for each Rocky Mountain Parka, and the retail prices through the firm's mail order catalog are $250 for the Mount Everest Parka and $200 for the Rocky Mountain Parka. Because management believes that the Mount Everest Parka is a unique coat that will enhance the image of the firm, they have specified that at least 20% of the total production must consist of this model. Assuming that Expedition Outfitters can sell as many coats of each type as they can produce, how many units of each model should they manufacture to maximize the total profit contribution?

49. English Motors, Ltd. (EML), has developed a new all-wheel-drive sports utility vehicle. As part of the marketing campaign, EML has developed a video tape sales presentation to send to both owners of current EML four-wheel-drive vehicles as well as to owners of four-wheel-drive sports utility vehicles offered by competitors; EML refers to these two target markets as the current customer market and the new customer market. Individuals who receive the new promotion video will also receive a coupon for a test drive of the new EML model for one weekend. A key factor in the success of the new promotion is the response rate, the percentage of individuals that receives the new promotion and test drives the new model. EML estimates that the response rate for the current customer market is 25% and the response rate for the new customer market is 20%. For the customers who test drive the new model the sales rate is the percentage of individuals that makes a purchase. Marketing research studies indicate that the sales rate is 12% for the current customer market and 20% for the new customer market. The cost for each promotion, excluding the test drive costs, are $4 for each promotion sent to the current customer market and $6 for each promotion sent to the new customer market. Management has also specified that a minimum of 30,000 current customers should test drive the new model and a minimum of 10,000 new customers should test drive the new model. In addition, the number of current customers that test drives the new vehicle must be at least twice the number of new customers that test drives the new vehicle. If the marketing budget, excluding test drive costs, is $1,200,000, how many promotions should be sent to each group of customers in order to maximize total sales?

50. Creative Sports Design (CSD) manufactures a standard-size racket and an oversize racket. The firm's rackets are extremely light due to the use of a magnesium-graphite alloy that was invented by the firm's founder. Each standard-size racket uses 0.125 kilograms of the alloy and each oversize racket uses 0.4 kilograms; over the next two-week production period only 80 kilograms of the alloy are available. Each standard-size racket uses 10 minutes of manufacturing time and each oversize racket uses 12 minutes. The profit contributions are $10 for each standard-size racket and $15 for each oversize racket, and 40 hours of manufacturing time are available each week. Management has specified that at least 20% of the total production must be the standard-size racket. How many rackets of each type should CSD manufacture over the next two weeks to maximize the total profit contribution? Assume that because of the unique nature of their products, CSD can sell as many rackets as they can produce.

51. Management of High Tech Services (HTS) would like to develop a model that will help allocate their technicians' time between service calls to regular contract customers and new

customers. A maximum of 80 hours of technician time is available over the two-week planning period. To satisfy cash flow requirements, at least $800 in revenue (per technician) must be generated during the two-week period. Technician time for regular customers generates $25 per hour. However, technician time for new customers only generates an average of $8 per hour because in many cases a new customer contact does not provide billable services. To ensure that new customer contacts are being maintained, the technician time spent on new customer contacts must be at least 60% of the time spent on regular customer contacts. Given these revenue and policy requirements, HTS would like to determine how to allocate technician time between regular customers and new customers so that the total number of customers contacted during the two-week period will be maximized. Technicians require an average of 50 minutes for each regular customer contact and 1 hour for each new customer contact.

    a. Develop a linear programming model that will enable HTS to allocate technician time between regular customers and new customers.

    b. Find the optimal solution.

52. Jackson Hole Manufacturing is a small manufacturer of plastic products used in the automotive and computer industries. One of its major contracts is with a large computer company and involves the production of plastic printer cases for the computer company's portable printers. The printer cases are produced on two injection molding machines. The M-100 machine has a production capacity of 25 printer cases per hour, and the M-200 machine has a production capacity of 40 cases per hour. Both machines use the same chemical material to produce the printer cases; the M-100 uses 40 pounds of the raw material per hour and the M-200 uses 50 pounds per hour. The computer company has asked Jackson Hole to produce as many of the cases during the upcoming week as possible and has said that it will pay $18 for each case Jackson Hole can deliver. However, next week is a regularly scheduled vacation period for most of Jackson Hole's production employees; during this time, annual maintenance is performed for all equipment in the plant. Because of the downtime for maintenance, the M-100 will be available for no more than 15 hours, and the M-200 will be available for no more than 10 hours. However, because of the high setup cost involved with both machines, management has a requirement that, if production is scheduled on either machine, the machine must be operated for at least 5 hours. The supplier of the chemical material used in the production process has informed Jackson Hole that a maximum of 1000 pounds of the chemical material will be available for next week's production; the cost for this raw material is $6 per pound. In addition to the raw material cost, Jackson Hole estimates that the hourly cost of operating the M-100 and the M-200 are $50 and $75, respectively.

    a. Formulate a linear programming model that can be used to maximize the contribution to profit.

    b. Find the optimal solution.

Case Problem   ADVERTISING STRATEGY

Midtown Motors, Inc., has hired a marketing services firm to develop an advertising strategy for promoting Midtown's used car sales. The marketing firm has recommended that Midtown use spot announcements on both television and radio as the advertising media for the proposed promotional campaign. Advertising strategy guidelines are expressed as follows:

1. Use at least 30 announcements for combined television and radio coverage.
2. Do not use more than 25 radio announcements.
3. The number of radio announcements cannot be less than the number of television announcements.

The television station has quoted a cost of $1200 per spot announcement, and the radio station has quoted a cost of $300 per spot announcement. Midtown's advertising budget has been set at $25,500. The marketing services firm has rated the various advertising media in terms of audience coverage and recall power of the advertisement. For Midtown's media alternatives, the television announcement is rated at 600, and the radio announcement is rated at 200. Midtown's president would like to know how many television and how many radio spot announcements should be used to maximize the overall rating of the advertising campaign.

Midtown's president believes the television station will consider running the Midtown spot announcement on its highly rated evening news program (at the same cost) if Midtown will consider using additional television announcements.

Managerial Report

Perform an analysis of advertising strategy for Midtown Motors, and prepare a report to Midtown's president presenting your findings and recommendations. Include (but do not limit your discussion to) a consideration of the following:

1. The recommended number of television and radio spot announcements
2. The relative merits of each advertising medium
3. The news program rating that would be necessary before it would make sense to increase the number of television spots
4. The number of television spots that should be purchased if the news program is rated highly enough to make increasing the number of television spots advisable
5. The restrictions placed on the advertising strategy that Midtown might want to consider relaxing or altering
6. The best use of any possible increase in the advertising budget
7. Any other information that may help Midtown's president make the advertising strategy decision

Include a copy of your linear programming model and graphical solution in the appendix to your report.

Case Problem   PRODUCTION STRATEGY

Better Fitness, Inc. (BFI), manufactures exercise equipment at its plant in Freeport, Long Island. It recently designed two universal weight machines for the home exercise market. Both machines use BFI-patented technology that provides the user with an extremely wide range of motion capability for each type of exercise performed. Until now, such capabilities have been available only on expensive weight machines used primarily by physical therapists.

At a recent trade show, demonstrations of the machines resulted in significant dealer interest. In fact, the number of orders that BFI received at the trade show far exceeded its manufacturing capabilities for the current production period. As a result, management decided to begin production of the two machines. The two machines, which BFI has named the BodyPlus 100 and the BodyPlus 200, require different amounts of resources to produce.

The BodyPlus 100 consists of a frame unit, a press station, and a pec-dec station. Each frame produced uses 4 hours of machining and welding time and 2 hours of painting and finishing time. Each press station requires 2 hours of machining and welding time and 1 hour of painting and finishing time, and each pec-dec station uses 2 hours of machining and welding time and 2 hours of painting and finishing time. In addition, 2 hours are spent assembling, testing, and packaging each BodyPlus 100. The raw material costs are $450 for each frame, $300 for each press station, and $250 for each pec-dec station; packaging costs are estimated to be $50 per unit.

The BodyPlus 200 consists of a frame unit, a press station, a pec-dec station, and a leg-press station. Each frame produced uses 5 hours of machining and welding time and 4 hours of painting and finishing time. Each press station requires 3 hours machining and welding time and 2 hours of painting and finishing time, each pec-dec station uses 2 hours of machining and welding time and 2 hours of painting and finishing time, and each leg-press station requires 2 hours of machining and welding time and 2 hours of painting and finishing time. In addition, 2 hours are spent assembling, testing, and packaging each Body-Plus 200. The raw material costs are $650 for each frame, $400 for each press station, $250 for each pec-dec station, and $200 for each leg-press station; packaging costs are estimated to be $75 per unit.

For the next production period, management estimates that 600 hours of machining and welding time, 450 hours of painting and finishing time, and 140 hours of assembly, testing, and packaging time will be available. Current labor costs are $20 per hour for machining and welding time, $15 per hour for painting and finishing time, and $12 per hour for assembly, testing, and packaging time. The market in which the two machines must compete suggests a retail price of $2400 for the BodyPlus 100 and $3500 for the BodyPlus 200, although some flexibility may be available to BFI because of the unique capabilities of the new machines. Authorized BFI dealers can purchase machines for 70% of the suggested retail price.

BFI's president believes that the unique capabilities of the BodyPlus 200 can help position BFI as one of the leaders in high-end exercise equipment. Consequently, he has stated that the number of units of the BodyPlus 200 produced must be at least 25% of the total production.

Managerial Report

Analyze the production problem at Better Fitness, Inc., and prepare a report for BFI's president presenting your findings and recommendations. Include (but do not limit your discussion to) a consideration of the following items:

1. The recommended number of BodyPlus 100 and BodyPlus 200 machines to produce
2. The effect on profits of the requirement that the number of units of the BodyPlus 200 produced must be at least 25% of the total production
3. Where efforts should be expended in order to increase contribution to profits

Include a copy of your linear programming model and graphical solution in an appendix to your report.

Case Problem   HART VENTURE CAPITAL

Hart Venture Capital (HVC) specializes in providing venture capital for software development and Internet applications. Currently HVC has two investment opportunities: (1) Security Systems, a firm that needs additional capital to develop an Internet security software package; and (2) Market Analysis, a market research company that needs additional capital to develop a software package for conducting customer satisfaction surveys. In exchange for Security Systems stock, the firm has asked HVC to provide $600,000 in year 1, $600,000 in year 2, and $250,000 in year 3 over the coming three-year period. In exchange for their stock, Market Analysis has asked HVC to provide $500,000 in year 1, $350,000 in year 2, and $400,000 in year 3 over the same three-year period. HVC believes that both investment opportunities are worth pursuing. However, because of other investments, they are willing to commit at most $800,000 for both projects in the first year, at most $700,000 in the second year, and $500,000 in the third year.

HVC's financial analysis team has reviewed both projects and has recommended that the company's objective should be to maximize the net present value of the total investment in Security Systems and Market Analysis. The net present value takes into account the estimated value of the stock at the end of the three-year period as well as the capital outflows that are necessary during each of the three years. Using an 8% rate of return, HVC's financial analysis team estimates that 100% funding of the Security Systems project has a net present value of $1,800,000 and 100% funding of the Market Analysis project has a net present value of $1,600,000.

HVC has the option to fund any percentage of the Security Systems and Market Analysis projects. For example, if HVC decides to fund 40% of the Security Systems project, investments of 0.40($600,000) = $240,000 would be required in year 1, 0.40($600,000) = $240,000 would be required in year 2, and 0.40($250,000) = $100,000 would be required in year 3. In this case, the net present value of the Security Systems project would be 0.40($1,800,000) = $720,000. The investment amounts and the net present value for partial funding of the Market Analysis project would be computed in the same manner.

Managerial Report

Perform an analysis of HVC's investment problem and prepare a report that presents your findings and recommendations. Be sure to include information on the following:

1. The recommended percentage of each project that HVC should fund and the net present value of the total investment
2. A capital allocation plan for Security Systems and Market Analysis for the coming three-year period and the total HVC investment each year
3. The effect, if any, on the recommended percentage of each project that HVC should fund if HVC is willing to commit an additional $100,000 during the first year
4. A capital allocation plan if an additional $100,000 is made available
5. Your recommendation as to whether HVC should commit the additional $100,000 in the first year

Provide model details and relevant computer output in a report appendix.

Appendix 7.1   SOLVING LINEAR PROGRAMS WITH THE MANAGEMENT SCIENTIST

In this appendix we describe how The Management Scientist software package can be used to solve the RMC linear programming problem. After starting The Management Scientist, execute the following steps.

Step 1. Select the **Linear Programming** module
Step 2. Select the **File** pull-down menu
     Select **New**
Step 3. When the **Problem Features** dialog box appears:
     Enter 2 in the **Number of Decision Variables** box
     Enter 3 in the **Number of Constraints** box
     Select **Maximize** in the **Optimization Type** box
     Select **OK**
Step 4. When the data input worksheet appears (see Figure 7.23):
     Change **Variable Names** from X1 and X2 to F and S respectively.
     Enter the **Objective Function Coefficients**
     For each constraint:
       Enter the **Coefficients**
       Enter the **Relation** (<, =, >)
       Enter the **Right-Hand-Side** value
Step 5. Select the **Solution** pull-down menu
     Select **Solve**

FIGURE 7.23   DATA INPUT WORKSHEET FOR THE RMC PROBLEM USING THE MANAGEMENT
SCIENTIST

Optimization Type: Maximize				
Variable Names: [Change if Desired]	F	S		
Objective Function Coefficients	40	30		

	Coefficients			
Subject To:	F	S	Relation (<, =, >)	Right-Hand-Side
Constraint 1	0.4	0.5	<	20
Constraint 2		0.2	<	5
Constraint 3	0.6	0.3	<	21

The user entries for the data input sheet are shown in color in Figure 7.23. The output from
The Management Scientist is shown in Figure 7.15. The original problem can be edited or
changed by selecting the **Edit** pull-down menu. Finally, printed output can be obtained by
selecting the **Solution** pull-down menu and then selecting the **Print Solution** option.

Appendix 7.2   SOLVING LINEAR PROGRAMS WITH LINDO®

LINDO (Linear, INteractive, and Discrete Optimizer) was developed by Linus E. Schrage at the
University of Chicago; it is available in Command-line and Windows versions. In this appendix we describe how to use the Windows version by entering and solving the RMC problem.

When you start LINDO, two windows are immediately displayed. The outer window labeled
"LINDO" contains all the command menus and the command toolbar. The smaller window labeled "<untitled>" is the model window. This window is used to enter and edit the linear programming model that you want to solve. The first item you must enter into the model window is
the objective function. Thus, for the RMC problem, enter MAX $40F + 30S$. To indicate that
the objective function has been completely entered and that the model constraints will follow,
press the return key and type the words SUBJECT TO (or just the letters ST). Next, after
pressing the return key to move to a new line, enter the first RMC constraint $0.4F + 0.5S < 20$.
Note that LINDO interprets the $<$ symbol as $\leq$. Then, after pressing the return key, enter the
second constraint $0.2S < 5$. Press the return key again and enter the third and final constraint,
$0.6F + 0.3S < 21$. Finally, after pressing the return key, type END to signal LINDO that the
model input is complete. The model window will now contain the following model:

$$\text{Max } 40F + 30S$$
$$\text{ST}$$
$$0.4F + 0.5S < 20$$
$$0.2S < 5$$
$$0.6F + 0.3S < 21$$
$$\text{END}$$

If you make an error entering the model, you can correct it at any time by simply position-
ing the cursor where you made the error and entering the necessary corrections.

To solve the model, you must select the Solve command from the Solve menu, or press
the Solve button on the LINDO toolbar. If LINDO does not find any errors in the model
input, it will begin to solve the model. As part of the solution process, LINDO displays a

FIGURE 7.24   SOLUTION TO THE RMC PROBLEM USING LINDO

```
         OBJECTIVE FUNCTION VALUE

    1)       1600.000


VARIABLE        VALUE            REDUCED COST
     F        25.000000            0.000000
     S        20.000000            0.000000


    ROW    SLACK OR SURPLUS     DUAL PRICES
    2)        0.000000          33.333332
    3)        1.000000           0.000000
    4)        0.000000          44.444443


NO. ITERATIONS=       2


RANGES IN WHICH THE BASIS IS UNCHANGED:

                               OBJ COEFFICIENT RANGES
VARIABLE         CURRENT          ALLOWABLE          ALLOWABLE
                 COEF             INCREASE           DECREASE
     F        40.000000          20.000000          16.000000
     S        30.000000          19.999998          10.000000


                               RIGHTHAND SIDE RANGES
    ROW          CURRENT          ALLOWABLE          ALLOWABLE
                 RHS              INCREASE           DECREASE
    2         20.000000           1.500000           6.000000
    3          5.000000           INFINITY           1.000000
    4         21.000000           9.000000           2.250000
```

Status Window that can be used to monitor the progress of the solver. When the solver is finished, LINDO will ask whether you want to do range (sensitivity) analysis. If you select the "YES" button and close the Status Window, LINDO displays the complete solution to the RMC problem on a new window titled "Reports Window." The output that appears in the Reports Window is shown in Figure 7.24.

The first section of the output shown in Figure 7.24 is self-explanatory. For example, we see that the optimal solution is $F = 25$ and $S = 20$, the value of the optimal solution is 1600, and the slack variables for the three constraints are 0, 1, and 0. The rest of the output in Figure 7.24 can be used to determine how a change in a coefficient of the objective function or a change in the right-hand-side value of a constraint will affect the optimal solution. We will discuss the use of this information in Chapter 8 when we study the topic of sensitivity analysis.

Appendix 7.3   SOLVING LINEAR PROGRAMS WITH SPREADSHEETS

In this appendix, we will use an Excel spreadsheet to solve the RMC linear programming problem. We will enter the problem data for the RMC problem in the top part of the spreadsheet and develop the linear programming model in the bottom part of the spreadsheet.

Spreadsheet Formulation

Whenever we formulate a spreadsheet model of a linear program, we perform the following steps:

Step 1. Enter the problem data in the top part of the spreadsheet
Step 2. Specify cell locations for the decision variables
Step 3. Select a cell and enter a formula for computing the value of the objective function
Step 4. Select a cell and enter a formula for computing the left-hand side of each constraint
Step 5. Select a cell and enter a formula for computing the right-hand side of each constraint

The formula spreadsheet that we developed for the RMC problem using these five steps is shown in Figure 7.25. Let us review each of the preceding steps as they apply to the RMC problem.

Step 1. Enter the problem data in the top part of the spreadsheet.
Cells B5 to C7 show the material requirements per ton of each product.
Cells B8 and C8 show the profit contribution per ton for the two products.
Cells D5 to D7 show the maximum amounts available for each of the three materials.

FIGURE 7.25   FORMULA SPREADSHEET FOR THE RMC PROBLEM

	A	B	C	D
1	**RMC Problem**			
2				
3		**Material Requierments**		
4	**Material**	**Fuel Additive**	**Solvent Base**	**Amount Available**
5	Material 1	0.4	0.5	20
6	Material 2		0.2	5
7	Material 3	0.6	0.3	21
8	**Profit Per Ton**	40	30	
9				
10				
11	**Model**			
12				
13		**Decision Variables**		
14		**Fuel Additive**	**Solvent Base**	
15	**Tons Produced**			
16				
17	**Maximize Total Profit**	=B8*B15+C8*C15		
18				
19	**Constraints**	**Amount Used (LHS)**		**Amount Available (RHS)**
20	Material 1	=B5*B15+C5*C15	<=	=D5
21	Material 2	=C6*C15	<=	=D6
22	Material 3	=B7*B15+C7*C15	<=	=D7

Step 2. Specify cell locations for the decision variables.

Cell B15 will contain the number of tons of fuel additive produced, and cell C15 will contain the number of tons of solvent base produced.

Step 3. Select a cell and enter a formula for computing the value of the objective function.

Cell B17:   =B8*B15+C8*C15

Step 4. Select a cell and enter a formula for computing the left-hand side of each constraint.

With three constraints, we have

Cell B20:   =B5*B15+C5*C15
Cell B21:   =C6*C15
Cell B22:   =B7*B15+C7*C15

Step 5. Select a cell and enter a formula for computing the right-hand side of each constraint.

With three constraints, we have

Cell D20:   =D5
Cell D21:   =D6
Cell D22:   =D7

Note descriptive labels make the model section of the spreadsheet easier to read and understand. For example, we have added "Fuel Additive," "Solvent Base," and "Tons Produced" in rows 14 and 15 so that the values of the decision variables appearing in Cells B15 and C15 can be easily interpreted. In addition, we have entered "Maximum Profit" in cell A17 to indicate that the value of the objective function appearing in cell B17 is the maximum profit contribution. In the constraint section of the spreadsheet we have added the constraint names as well as the "<=" symbols to show the relationship that exists between the left-hand side and the right-hand side of each constraint. Although these descriptive labels are not necessary to use Excel Solver to find a solution to the RMC problem, the labels make it easier for the user to understand and interpret the optimal solution.

Spreadsheet Solution

The following steps describe how Excel Solver can be used to obtain the optimal solution to the RMC problem.

Step 1. Select the **Tools** pull-down menu

Step 2. Select the **Solver** option

Step 3. When the **Solver Parameters** dialog box appears:

Enter B17 into the **Set Target Cell** box
Select the **Equal To: Max** option
Enter B15:C15 into the **By Changing Cells** box
Select **Add**

Step 4. When the **Add Constraint** dialog box appears:

Enter B20:B22 in the **Cell Reference** box
Select <=
Enter D20:D22 in the **Constraint** box
Select **OK**

Step 5. When the **Solver Parameters** dialog box appears:

Choose **Options**

Step 6. When the **Solver Options** dialog box appears:

Select **Assume Linear Model**
Select **Assume Non-Negative**
Select **OK**

Step 7. When the **Solver Parameters** dialog box appears:
Choose **Solve**
Step 8. When the **Solver Results** dialog box appears:
Select **Keep Solver Solution**
Select **OK**

Figure 7.26 shows the optimal solution to the RMC problem as previously discussed.

FIGURE 7.26 SOLUTION TO THE RMC PROBLEM USING EXCEL

	A	B	C	D
1	**RMC Problem**			
2				
3		**Material Requirements**		
4	**Material**	**Fuel Additive**	**Solvent Base**	**Amount Available**
5	Material 1	0.4	0.5	20
6	Material 2		0.2	5
7	Material 3	0.6	0.3	21
8	**Profit Per Ton**	40	30	
9				
10				
11	**Model**			
12				
13		**Decision Variables**		
14		**Fuel Additive**	**Solvent Base**	
15	**Tons Produced**	25	20	
16				
17	**Maximum Profit**	1600		
18				
19	**Constraints**	**Amount Used (LHS)**		**Amount Available (RHS)**
20	Material 1	20	<=	20
21	Material 2	4	<=	5
22	Material 3	21	<=	21

LINEAR PROGRAMMING: SENSITIVITY ANALYSIS AND INTERPRETATION OF SOLUTION

CONTENTS

Sensitivity analysis is the study of how changes in the coefficients of a linear programming problem affect the optimal solution. Using sensitivity analysis, we can answer questions such as the following:

1. How will a change in an *objective function coefficient* affect the optimal solution?
2. How will a change in a *right-hand-side value* for a constraint affect the optimal solution?

Because sensitivity analysis is concerned with how these changes affect the optimal solution, sensitivity analysis does not begin until the optimal solution to the original linear programming problem has been obtained. For this reason, sensitivity analysis is often referred to as *postoptimality analysis.*

Our approach to sensitivity analysis parallels the approach used to introduce linear programming in Chapter 7. We introduce sensitivity analysis by using the graphical method for a linear programming problem with two decision variables. Then, we show how The Management Scientist software package can be used to provide more complete sensitivity analysis information.

Finally, we extend the discussion of problem formulation started in Chapter 7 by formulating and solving three larger linear programming problems. In discussing the solution for each of these problems, we focus on managerial interpretation of the optimal solution and sensitivity analysis information.

8.1   INTRODUCTION TO SENSITIVITY ANALYSIS

Sensitivity analysis is important to decision makers because real-world problems exist in a changing environment. Prices of raw materials change, product demands change, production capacities change, stock prices change, and so on. If a linear programming model has been used in such an environment, we can expect some of the coefficients in the model to change over time. As a result, we will want to determine how these changes affect the optimal solution. Sensitivity analysis provides information needed to respond to such changes without requiring a complete solution of a revised linear program.

Recall the RMC problem introduced in Chapter 7. RMC wanted to determine the number of tons of fuel additive (F) and the number of tons of solvent base (S) to produce in order to maximize the total profit contribution for the two products. Three raw material constraints limit the amounts of the two products that can be produced. The RMC linear programming model is restated here:

$$\text{Max} \quad 40F + 30S$$

$$\text{s.t.}$$

$$0.4F + 0.5S \leq 20 \quad \text{Material 1}$$
$$0.2S \leq 5 \quad \text{Material 2}$$
$$0.6F + 0.3S \leq 21 \quad \text{Material 3}$$
$$F, S \geq 0$$

The optimal solution, $F = 25$ tons and $S = 20$ tons, provided a maximum profit contribution of $1600.

The optimal solution was based on profit contributions of $40 per ton for the fuel additive and $30 per ton for the solvent base. However, suppose that we later learn that a price reduction causes the profit contribution for the fuel additive to fall from $40 to $30 per ton. Sensitivity analysis can be used to determine whether producing 25 tons of fuel additive and 20 tons of solvent base is still best. If it is, solving a modified linear programming problem with $30F + 30S$ as the new objective function is not necessary.

Sensitivity analysis can also be used to determine which coefficients in a linear programming model are crucial. For example, suppose that management believes that the $30 per ton profit contribution for the solvent base is only a rough estimate of the profit contribution that will actually be obtained. If sensitivity analysis shows that 25 tons of fuel additive and 20 tons of solvent base will be the optimal solution as long as the profit contribution for the solvent base is between $20 and $50, management should feel comfortable with the $30 per ton estimate and the recommended production quantities. However, if sensitivity analysis shows that 25 tons of fuel additive and 20 tons solvent base will be the optimal solution only if the profit contribution for the solvent base is between $29.90 and $30.20 per ton, management may want to review the accuracy of the $30 per ton estimate.

Another aspect of sensitivity analysis concerns changes in the right-hand-side values of the constraints. Recall that in the RMC problem the optimal solution used all available material 1 and material 3. What would happen to the optimal solution and total profit contribution if RMC could obtain additional quantities of either of these resources? Sensitivity analysis can help determine how much each added ton of material is worth and how many tons can be added before diminishing returns set in.

8.2   OBJECTIVE FUNCTION COEFFICIENTS

Let us begin sensitivity analysis by using the graphical solution procedure to demonstrate how a change in an objective function coefficient can affect the optimal solution to a linear programming problem. We begin with the graphical solution to the original RMC problem shown in Figure 8.1. The feasible region is shaded. The objective function $40F + 30S$ takes on its maximum value at the extreme point $F = 25$ and $S = 20$. Thus, $F = 25$ and $S = 20$ is the optimal solution and $40(25) + 30(20) = 1600$ is the value of the optimal solution.

Now suppose RMC learns that a price reduction in the fuel additive has reduced its profit contribution to \$30 per ton. With this reduction, RMC's management may question the desirability of maintaining the original optimal solution of $F = 25$ tons and $S = 20$ tons. Perhaps a different solution is now optimal. The RMC linear program with the revised objective function is as follows:

$$\text{Max} \quad 30F + 30S$$

s.t.

$$
\begin{array}{lll}
0.4F + 0.5S \leq 20 & \text{Material 1} \\
0.2S \leq 5 & \text{Material 2} \\
0.6F + 0.3S \leq 21 & \text{Material 3} \\
F, S \geq 0 &
\end{array}
$$

Note that only the objective function has changed. Because the constraints have not changed, the feasible region for the revised RMC problem remains the same as the original problem. The graphical solution to the RMC problem with the objective function $30F + 30S$ is shown in Figure 8.2. Note that the extreme point providing the optimal solution is still $F = 25$ and $S = 20$. Thus, although the total profit contribution has decreased to $30(25) + 30(20) = 1350$, the decrease in the profit contribution for the fuel additive from \$40 per ton to \$30 per ton has not changed the optimal solution $F = 25$ and $S = 20$.

Now let us suppose that a further price reduction causes the profit contribution for the fuel additive to be reduced to \$20 per ton. Is $F = 25$ and $S = 20$ still the optimal solution?

FIGURE 8.1   OPTIMAL SOLUTION TO THE ORIGINAL RMC PROBLEM

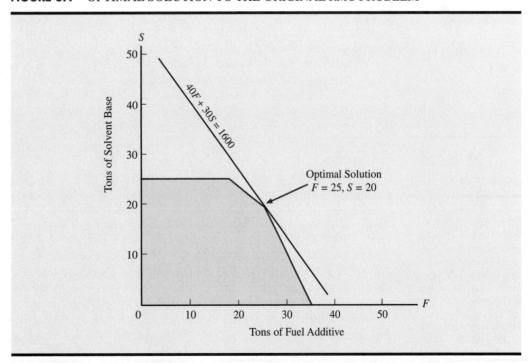

FIGURE 8.2 REVISED OPTIMAL SOLUTION WITH THE RMC OBJECTIVE FUNCTION
$30F + 30S$

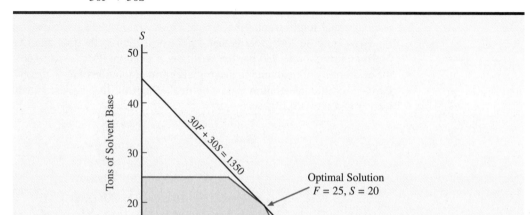

Figure 8.3 shows the graphical solution to the RMC problem with the objective function re-vised to $20F + 30S$. The extreme point providing the optimal solution is now $F = 18.75$ and $S = 25$. The total profit contribution has decreased to $20(18.75) + 30(25) = 1125$. However, in this case, we see that decreasing the profit contribution for the fuel additive to $20 per ton has changed the optimal solution. That is, the solution $F = 25$ tons and $S = 20$ is no longer optimal. The solution $F = 18.75$ and $S = 25$ now provides the optimal pro-duction quantities for RMC.

What have we learned from the graphical solutions in Figures 8.1, 8.2, and 8.3? First of all, changing one objective function coefficient changes the slope of the objective function line but leaves the feasible region unchanged. If the change in the objective func-tion coefficient is small, the extreme point that provided the optimal solution to the origi-nal problem may still provide the optimal solution. However, if the change in the objective function coefficient is large enough, a different extreme point will provide a new opti-mal solution.

Fortunately, the linear programming computer solution to the original RMC linear programming problem provides the sensitivity analysis information about the objective function coefficients. *You do not have to reformulate and resolve the linear program-ming problem to obtain the sensitivity analysis information.* The computer solution to the original RMC linear programming problem is shown in Figure 8.4. Refer to the shaded section labeled OBJECTIVE COEFFICIENT RANGES. Consider the row for the fuel ad-ditive F. The Lower Limit is $24, the Current Value is $40, and the Upper Limit is $60. The range $24 to $60 provides the objective coefficient range for the fuel additive. Thus, assuming that all other aspects of the original RMC problem do not change, the profit contribution for the fuel additive can be from $24 per ton to $60 per ton and the solution $F = 25$ tons and $S = 20$ tons will remain the optimal solution. Indeed, this result is what we observed with the graphical solution in Figures 8.2 and 8.3. When the profit contribu-

FIGURE 8.3   REVISED OPTIMAL SOLUTION WITH THE RMC OBJECTIVE FUNCTION
$20F + 30S$

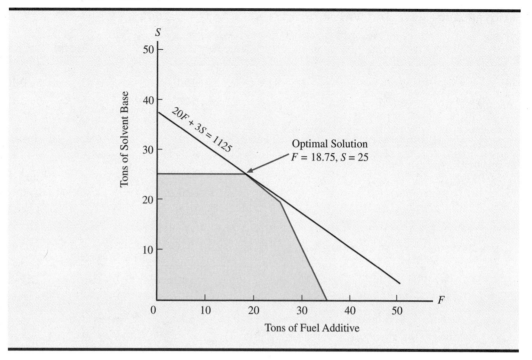

tion of the fuel additive was reduced to $30 per ton (within the $24 to $60 objective co-efficient range), the solution $F = 25$ and tons and $S = 20$ tons remained optimal. However, when the profit contribution of the fuel additive was reduced to $20 per ton (outside the $24 to $60 objective coefficient range), the solution $F = 25$ tons and $S = 20$ tons was no longer optimal. In summary, if the objective function coefficient for the fuel additive is within its objective coefficient range, $24 to $60, and all other aspects of the original RMC problem remain unchanged, the optimal solution to the RMC problem will still be $F = 25$ tons and $S = 20$ tons.

Now let us use the sensitivity analysis information in Figure 8.4 to interpret what it tells us about changes in the objective function coefficient for the solvent base. Assuming that the profit contribution for the fuel additive is $40 per ton and that all other aspects of the original RMC problem remain unchanged, the objective coefficient range for the solvent base is $20 to $50. Thus, we conclude that as long as the profit contribution for the solvent base is within the $20 to $50 range, the solution $F = 25$ and $S = 20$ will remain optimal. If the profit contribution for the solvent base is outside this range, a different extreme point and a different solution will become optimal.

NOTES AND COMMENTS

If two objective function coefficients change simultaneously, both may move outside their respective objective coefficient ranges and not affect the optimal solution. For instance, in a two-variable linear program, the slope of the objective function will not change at all if both coefficients are changed by the same percentage.

FIGURE 8.4 THE MANAGEMENT SCIENTIST SOLUTION FOR THE RMC PROBLEM

```
Objective Function Value =                    1600.000

          Variable              Value            Reduced Costs
       -------------        ---------------     ------------------
            F                   25.000               0.000
            S                   20.000               0.000


          Constraint          Slack/Surplus         Dual Prices
       -------------        ---------------     ------------------
            1                    0.000               33.333
            2                    1.000               0.000
            3                    0.000               44.444


  OBJECTIVE COEFFICIENT RANGES

      Variable         Lower Limit      Current Value      Upper Limit
   -----------      ---------------   ---------------   ---------------
        F                 24.000           40.000            60.000
        S                 20.000           30.000            50.000


  RIGHT HAND SIDE RANGES

      Constraint       Lower Limit      Current Value      Upper Limit
   -----------      ---------------   ---------------   ---------------
        1                 14.000           20.000            21.500
        2                  4.000            5.000       No Upper Limit
        3                 18.750           21.000            30.000
```

Simultaneous Changes

The sensitivity analysis information provided for the objective function coefficients is based on the assumption that only one objective function coefficient changes at a time and that all other aspects of the original problem remain unchanged. Thus, an objective coefficient range is only applicable for changes to a single objective coefficient. However, in some cases, we may be interested in what happens if two or more objective function coefficients change simultaneously. As we will demonstrate, some analysis of simultaneous changes is possible with the help of the **100 percent rule.**

Referring to the computer solution in Figure 8.4, we restate the objective coefficient ranges for the RMC problem in Table 8.1. The Allowable Decrease and Allowable Increase columns indicate how much the current value of the objective function coefficient can decrease or increase without changing the optimal solution. The Allowable Decrease and Allowable Increase values are computed as follows:

Sensitivity analysis information assumes that only one objective function coefficient changes at a time. Other coefficients in the problem are assumed to be as stated in the original problem.

$$\text{Allowable Decrease} = \text{Current Value} - \text{Lower Limit}$$
$$\text{Allowable Increase} = \text{Upper Limit} - \text{Current Value}$$

TABLE 8.1 OBJECTIVE COEFFICIENT RANGES, ALLOWABLE DECREASES, AND
ALLOWABLE INCREASES FOR THE RMC PROBLEM

Decision Variable	Objective Coefficient Range			Allowable Decrease	Allowable Increase
	Lower Limit	Current Value	Upper Limit		
F	24	40	60	16	20
S	20	30	50	10	20

Suppose RMC's accounting department reviews both the price and cost data for the two products. As a result, the profit contribution for the fuel additive is increased to $48 per ton and the profit contribution for the solvent base is decreased to $27 per ton. Thus, the fuel additive has a $48 − $40 = $8 per ton increase. From Table 8.1 we see that the allowable increase for the fuel additive coefficient is $20. Thus, the increase in the fuel additive objective function coefficient is 8/20 = 0.40, or 40%, of its allowable increase. Similarly, the solvent base has a $30 − $27 = $3 per ton decrease. With an allowable decrease of $10, the solvent base objective function decrease is 3/10 = 0.30, or 30%, of its allowable decrease. The sum of the percentage increase for the fuel additive and the percentage decrease for the solvent base is 40% + 30% = 70%.

Let us now state the 100 percent rule as it applies to simultaneous changes in the objective function coefficients.

100 Percent Rule for Objective Function Coefficients

For all objective function coefficients that are changed, sum the percentages of the allowable increases and the allowable decreases. If the sum of the percentages is less than or equal to 100%, the optimal solution does not change.

Applying the 100 percent rule to the RMC problem, we see that the sum of the percentages of the allowable increases and the allowable decreases is 70%. Thus, the 100% rule indicates that if the profit contribution for the fuel additive increases to $48 per ton and the profit contribution for the solvent base decreases to $27 per ton, the solution of $F = 25$ tons and $S = 20$ tons will remain optimal. Thus, with the revised objective function coefficients and the same optimal solution, the total profit contribution becomes $48(25) + 27(20) = \$1740$.

Finally, note that the 100 percent rule *does not* say that the optimal solution will change if the sum of the percentages of the allowable increases and the allowable decreases is greater than 100%. All we can say is that if the sum of the percentages is greater than 100%, a different optimal solution *may exist*. Thus, whenever the sum of the percentage changes is greater than 100%, the revised problem must be solved in order to determine the new optimal solution.

8.3 RIGHT-HAND SIDES

Let us expand the discussion of sensitivity analysis by considering how a change in the right-hand side of a constraint affects the feasible region and the optimal solution to a linear programming problem. As with sensitivity analysis for the objective function coefficients, we consider what happens when we make *one change at a time*. For example, suppose that in the RMC problem an additional 4.5 tons of material 3 becomes available.

Sensitivity analysis for right-hand sides is based on the assumption that only one right-hand side changes at a time. All other aspects of the problem are assumed to be as stated in the original problem.

In this case, the right-hand side of the third constraint increases from 21 tons to 25.5 tons. The revised RMC linear programming model is as follows:

$$\text{Max} \quad 40F + 30S$$

s.t.

$$0.4F + 0.5S \leq 20 \qquad \text{Material 1}$$
$$0.2S \leq 5 \qquad \text{Material 2}$$
$$0.6F + 0.3S \leq 25.5 \quad \text{Material 3}$$
$$F, S \geq 0$$

The graphical solution to this problem is shown in Figure 8.5. Note how the feasible region has expanded because of the additional 4.5 tons of material 3. Application of the graphical solution procedure shows that the extreme point $F = 37.5$ tons and $S = 10$ tons is the new optimal solution. The value of the optimal solution is $40(37.5) + 30(10) = \$1800$. Recall that the optimal solution to the original RMC problem was $F = 25$ tons and $S = 20$ tons and the value of the optimal solution was \$1600. Thus, the additional 4.5 tons of material 3 in the revised problem has provided a new optimal solution and has increased the value of the optimal solution by $\$1800 - \$1600 = \$200$. On a per ton basis, the additional 4.5 tons of material 3 has increased the value of the optimal solution at the rate of $\$200/4.5 = \$44.44$ per ton.

Dual prices often provide the economic information that helps make decisions about acquiring additional resources.

The **dual price** is the *improvement* in the value of the optimal solution per unit increase in the right-hand side of a constraint. Hence, the dual price for material 3 is \$44.44 per ton. In other words, if we increase the right-hand side of the material 3 constraint by 1 ton, the value of the optimal solution will improve \$44.44. Conversely, if we decrease the right-hand side of the material 3 constraint by 1 ton, the value of the optimal solution will worsen by \$44.44. In general, the dual price tells us what will happen to the value of the optimal solution if we make a one-unit change in the right-hand side of a constraint.

FIGURE 8.5   GRAPHICAL SOLUTION TO THE RMC PROBLEM WITH CONSTRAINT 3
$0.6F + 0.5S \leq 24.5$

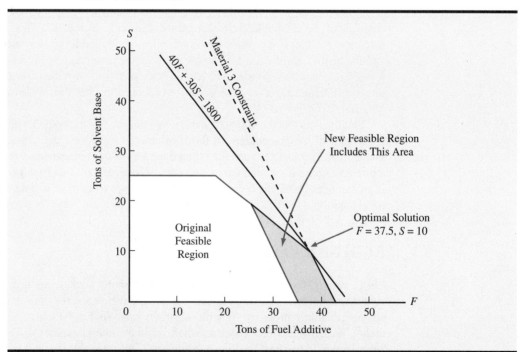

Computer solutions typically provide the dual price and right-hand-side range information for each constraint.

Fortunately, the linear programming computer solution to the original linear programming problem provides the dual prices for all the constraints. *You do not have to reformulate and resolve the linear programming problem to obtain the dual price information.* The computer solution to the original RMC linear programming problem is shown in Figure 8.6. The column labeled Dual Prices provides the following information:

Constraint	Dual Price
Material 1	$33.33
Material 2	$ 0.00
Material 3	$44.44

Note that the dual price for material 3, $44.44 per ton, agrees with the calculations we made using the graphical solution procedure. We also observe that the dual price for material 1 indicates that the value of the optimal solution will improve at the rate of $33.33 per ton of

FIGURE 8.6 THE MANAGEMENT SCIENTIST SOLUTION FOR THE RMC PROBLEM

```
Objective Function Value =                      1600.000

         Variable              Value              Reduced Costs
      -------------        -------------        -----------------

            F                 25.000                  0.000
            S                 20.000                  0.000


        Constraint         Slack/Surplus          Dual Prices
      -------------        -------------        -----------------

            1                  0.000                 33.333
            2                  1.000                  0.000
            3                  0.000                 44.444


OBJECTIVE COEFFICIENT RANGES

     Variable         Lower Limit         Current Value        Upper Limit
   ------------     -------------        -------------        -------------

        F               24.000              40.000               60.000
        S               20.000              30.000               50.000


RIGHT HAND SIDE RANGES

    Constraint        Lower Limit         Current Value        Upper Limit
   ------------     -------------        -------------        -------------

        1               14.000              20.000               21.500
        2                4.000               5.000           No Upper Limit
        3               18.750              21.000               30.000
```

material 1. Finally, note that the dual price for material 2 is $0.00. Referring to Figure 8.6, we see that optimal solution to the RMC problem shows that material 2 has a slack of one ton. Thus, at the optimal solution, one ton of material 2 is unused. The dual price of $0.00 tells us that additional tons of material 2 will simply add to the amount of slack for constraint 2 and will not change the value of the optimal solution.

The right-hand-side range is often referred to as the range of feasibility.

We caution here that the value of a dual price may be applicable only for small increases in the right-hand side. As more and more resources are obtained and as the right-hand side continues to increase, other constraints will become binding and limit the change in the value of the optimal solution. At some point, the dual price can no longer be used to determine the improvement in the value of the optimal solution. To determine the range where the dual price is applicable, refer to Figure 8.6 and the section labeled RIGHT HAND SIDE RANGES. As long as the right-hand side for a constraint stays within its corresponding right-hand-side range, the dual price is applicable. For example, referring to constraint 3, we see that the dual price of $44.44 per ton for material 3 applies as long as the right-hand side of constraint 3 is between 18.75 tons and 30 tons. This range tells us that for each additional ton of material 3 that RMC could obtain, up to a total of 30 tons, the value of the optimal solution would improve by $44.44 for each ton added. However, if more than 30 tons were made available, RMC cannot expect the dual price of $44.44 per ton to be applicable. Similarly, the dual price for constraint 1 is $33.33 per ton as long as the amount of material 1 available is between 14 and 21.5 tons. Note also that the dual price of $0.00 for constraint 2 is applicable as long as the amount of material 2 available is at least 4 tons.

NOTES AND COMMENTS

Some texts associate the term *shadow price* with each constraint. The concept of a shadow price is closely related to the concept of a dual price. The shadow price associated with a constraint is the *change* in the value of the optimal solution per-unit increase in the right-hand side of the constraint. In general, the dual price and the shadow price are the *same* for all *maximization* linear programs. In *minimization* linear programs, the shadow price is the *negative* of the corresponding dual price.

Simultaneous Changes

Keep in mind that the right-hand-side sensitivity analysis information is based on the assumption that only one right-hand side changes at a time. However, in some cases, we may be interested in what happens if two or more right-hand sides change simultaneously. Some analysis of simultaneous changes is possible with the help of the 100 percent rule.

Referring to the computer solution in Figure 8.6, we restate the right-hand-side range information for the RMC problem in Table 8.2. The Allowable Decrease and Allowable Increase columns indicate how much the current value of the right-hand side can decrease or increase without changing the dual price. The Allowable Decrease and Allowable Increase values are computed as follows:

Allowable Decrease = Current Value − Lower Limit

Allowable Increase = Upper LImit − Current Value

Now suppose that RMC's management decides to purchase an additional 0.5 tons of material 1 and an additional 4.5 tons of material 3. As Table 8.2 shows, material 1 has an allowable increase of 1.5 tons; therefore, the material 1 right-hand-side increase is 0.5/1.5 = 0.333, or 33.3%, of its allowable increase. Similarly, because material 3 has an allowable increase of 9 tons, the material 3 right-hand-side increase is 4.5/9 = 0.50, or

TABLE 8.2 RIGHT-HAND-SIDE RANGES, ALLOWABLE DECREASES, AND
ALLOWABLE INCREASES FOR THE RMC PROBLEM

| | Right-Hand-Side Ranges | | | | |
Constraint	Lower Limit	Current Value	Upper Limit	Allowable Decrease	Allowable Increase
Material 1	14	20	21.5	6	1.5
Material 2	4	5	No Upper Limit	1	No Upper Limit
Material 3	18.75	21	30	2.25	9

50%, of its allowable increase. The sum of the percentages for the two right-hand sides is
33.3% + 50% = 83.3%.

Let us now state the 100 percent rule as it applies to simultaneous changes in the right-
hand sides of a linear programming problem.

100 Percent Rule for Right-Hand Sides

For all right-hand sides that are changed, sum the percentages of the allowable increases
and the allowable decreases. If the sum of the percentages is less than or equal to 100%, the
dual prices do not change.

Applying the 100 percent rule to the RMC problem, we see that the sum of the percentages of the allowable increases and the allowable decreases is 83.3%. Thus, the 100
percent rule indicates that the dual price for material 1 remains $33.33 per ton, and the dual
price for material 3 remains $44.44 per ton. Thus, the 0.5 additional tons of material 1 and
4.5 additional tons of material 3 will improve the value of the objective function
0.5(33.33) + 4.5(44.44) = $216.67. Note, however, that the revised linear program will
have to be solved to determine the production quantities, F and S, that provide the new optimal solution.

The 100 percent rule *does not* say that the dual prices will change if the sum of the percentages of the allowable increases and the allowable decreases is greater than 100%. All
we can say is that if the sum of the percentages is greater than 100%, different dual prices
may exist. Thus, whenever the sum of the percentage changes is greater than 100%, a revised problem must be solved in order to determine the new optimal solution and the new
dual prices.

A Second Example

As another example, let us consider the M&D Chemicals minimization problem introduced
in Section 7.5. The decision variables are A = number of gallons of product A and B =
number of gallons of product B. The linear programming model is as follows:

$$\text{Min} \quad 2A + 3B$$

s.t.

$$1A \qquad \geq 125 \quad \text{Demand for product } A$$
$$1A + 1B \geq 350 \quad \text{Total production}$$
$$2A + 1B \leq 600 \quad \text{Processing time}$$
$$A, B \geq 0$$

The solution obtained using The Management Scientist is presented in Figure 8.7. The computer output shows that the value of the optimal solution is $800. The values of the decision variables show that 250 gallons of product A and 100 gallons of product B provide the minimum cost solution.

The Slack/Surplus column shows that the $\geq$ constraint corresponding to the demand for product A (constraint 1) has a surplus of 125 units. In other words, the production of product A in the optimal solution exceeds demand by 125 gallons. The Slack/Surplus values are zero for the constraints corresponding to the total production (constraint 2) and the processing time (constraint 3); thus, these constraints are binding at the optimal solution.

The dual price shows the *improvement* in the value of the optimal solution per unit increase in the right-hand side of the constraint. Focusing first on the dual price of 1.00 for the processing time constraint (constraint 3), we see that if we can increase the processing time from 600 to 601 hours, the value of the optimal solution will *improve* by $1. Because the objective is to minimize costs, improvement in this case means a lowering of costs. Thus, if 601 hours of processing time are available, the value of the optimal solution will improve to $800 − $1 = $799. The RIGHT HAND SIDE RANGES section of the output shows that the upper limit for processing time (constraint 3) is 700 hours. Thus, the dual price of $1 per unit would be applicable for every additional hour of processing time up to a total of 700 hours.

Let us again return to the Dual Prices section of the output and consider the dual price for total production (constraint 2). The *negative dual price* tells us that the value of the optimal

FIGURE 8.7 THE MANAGEMENT SCIENTIST SOLUTION FOR THE M&D CHEMICALS PROBLEM

```
Objective Function Value =            800.000

      Variable               Value              Reduced Costs
   --------------        --------------        ------------------

         A                  250.000                  0.000
         B                  100.000                  0.000


     Constraint          Slack/Surplus            Dual Prices
   --------------        --------------        ------------------

         1                  125.000                  0.000
         2                    0.000                 -4.000
         3                    0.000                  1.000


OBJECTIVE COEFFICIENT RANGES

    Variable        Lower Limit        Current Value        Upper Limit
  ------------    ---------------    ---------------    ---------------

       A          No Lower Limit             2.000                3.000
       B                  2.000             3.000        No Upper Limit


RIGHT HAND SIDE RANGES

   Constraint       Lower Limit        Current Value        Upper Limit
  ------------    ---------------    ---------------    ---------------

        1         No Lower Limit           125.000              250.000
        2                300.000           350.000              475.000
        3                475.000           600.000              700.000
```

solution *will not improve* if the right-hand side is increased by one unit. In fact, the dual price of −4.00 tells us that if the right-hand side of the total production constraint is increased from 350 to 351 units, the value of the optimal solution will worsen by the amount of $4. Because worsening means an increase in cost, the value of the optimal solution will become $800 + $4 = $804 if the one-unit increase in the total production requirement is made.

Because the dual price refers to improvement in the value of the optimal solution per unit increase in the right-hand side, a constraint with a negative dual price should not have its right-hand side increased. In fact, if the dual price is negative, efforts should be made to reduce the right-hand side of the constraint. If the right-hand side of the total production constraint were decreased from 350 to 349 units, the dual price indicates that the total cost could be lowered by $4 to $800 − $4 = $796.

Even though the dual price is the improvement in the value of the optimal solution per unit increase in the right-hand side of a constraint, the interpretation of an *improvement* in the value of an objective function depends on whether we are solving a maximization or a minimization problem. The dual price for a ≤ constraint will always be greater than or equal to zero because increasing the right-hand side cannot make the value of the objective function worse. Similarly, the dual price for a ≥ constraint will always be less than or equal to zero because increasing the right-hand side cannot improve the value of the optimal solution.

Finally, consider the right-hand-side ranges provided in Figure 8.7. The ranges for the M&D Chemicals problem are summarized here:

Constraint	Min RHS	Max RHS
Product A demand	No lower limit	250
Total production	300	475
Processing time	475	700

Try Problem 10 to test your ability to interpret the computer output for a minimization problem.

As long as the right-hand sides are within these ranges, the dual prices shown on the computer printout are applicable.

Cautionary Note on the Interpretation of Dual Prices

As stated previously, the dual price is the improvement in the value of the optimal solution per unit increase in the right-hand side of a constraint. When the right-hand side of the constraint represents the amount of a resource available, the associated dual price is often interpreted as the maximum amount one should be willing to pay for one additional unit of the resource. However, such an interpretation is not always correct. To see why, we need to understand the difference between sunk and relevant costs. A **sunk cost** is one that is not affected by the decision made. It will be incurred no matter what values the decision variables assume. A **relevant cost** is one that depends on the decision made. The amount of a relevant cost will vary depending on the values of the decision variables.

Let us reconsider the RMC problem. The amount of material 1 available is 20 tons. The cost of material 1 is a sunk cost if it must be paid regardless of the number of tons of fuel additive and solvent base produced. It would be a relevant cost if RMC only had to pay for the number of tons of material 1 actually used to produce fuel additive and solvent base. All relevant costs should be included in the objective function of a linear program. Sunk costs should not be included in the objective function. For RMC we have been assuming that the company has already paid for materials 1, 2, and 3. Therefore, the cost of the raw materials for RMC is a sunk cost and has not been included in the objective function.

When the cost of a resource is *sunk,* the dual price can be interpreted as the maximum amount the company should be willing to pay for one additional unit of the resource. When

Only relevant costs should be included in the objective function.

the cost of a resource used is relevant, the dual price can be interpreted as the amount by which the value of the resource exceeds its cost. Thus, when the resource cost is relevant, the dual price can be interpreted as the maximum premium over the normal cost that the company should be willing to pay for one unit of the resource.

NOTES AND COMMENTS

1. Computer software packages for solving linear programs are readily available. Most of these provide the optimal solution, dual or shadow price information, the objective coefficient ranges, and the right-hand-side ranges. The labels used for these ranges may vary, but the meaning is the same as what we have described here.

2. Whenever one of the right-hand sides is at an end point of its range, the dual and shadow prices only provide one-sided information. In this case, they only predict the change in the optimal value of the objective function for changes toward the interior of the range.

3. A condition called *degeneracy* can cause a subtle difference in how we interpret changes in the objective function coefficients beyond the end points of the objective coefficient range. Degeneracy occurs when the dual price equals zero for one of the binding constraints. Degeneracy does not affect the interpretation of changes toward the interior of the objective coefficient range. However, when degeneracy is present, changes beyond the end points of the range do not necessarily mean a different solution will be optimal. From a practical point of view, changes beyond the end points of the range necessitate resolving the problem.

4. The 100 percent rule permits an analysis of multiple changes in the right-hand sides or multiple changes in the objective function coefficients. But the 100 percent rule cannot be applied to changes in both objective function coefficients *and* right-hand sides at the same time. In order to consider simultaneous changes for *both* right-hand-side values and objective function coefficients, the problem must be resolved.

5. Managers are frequently called on to provide an economic justification for new technology. Often the new technology is developed, or purchased, in order to conserve resources. The dual price can be helpful in such cases because it can be used to determine the savings attributable to the new technology by showing the savings per unit of resource conserved.

8.4 MORE THAN TWO DECISION VARIABLES

The graphical solution procedure is useful only for linear programs involving two decision variables. Computer software packages are designed to handle linear programs involving large numbers of variables and constraints. In this section we discuss the formulation and computer solution for two linear programs with three decision variables. In doing so, we will show how to interpret the reduced-cost portion of the computer output and will also illustrate the interpretation of dual prices for constraints that involve percentages.

Modified RMC Problem

The RMC linear programming problem was introduced in Section 7.1. The original problem formulation is restated here:

$$\text{Max} \quad 40F + 30S$$

s.t.

$$0.4F + 0.5S \leq 20 \quad \text{Material 1}$$
$$0.2S \leq 5 \quad \text{Material 2}$$
$$0.6F + 0.3S \leq 21 \quad \text{Material 3}$$
$$F, S \geq 0$$

Recall that F is the number of tons of fuel additive produced and that S is the number of tons of solvent base produced. Suppose that management also is considering producing a carpet cleaning fluid. Estimates are that each ton of carpet cleaning fluid will require 0.6 tons of material 1, 0.1 tons of material 2, and 0.3 tons of material 3. Because of the unique capabilities of the new product, RMC's management believes that the company will realize a profit contribution of $50 for each ton of carpet cleaning fluid produced during the current production period.

Let us consider the modifications in the original linear programming model that are needed to incorporate the effect of this additional decision variable. We let C denote the number of tons of carpet cleaning fluid produced. After adding C to the objective function and to each of the three constraints, we obtain the linear program for the modified problem:

$$\text{Max} \quad 40F + 30S + 50C$$

$$\text{s.t.}$$

$$0.4F + 0.5S + 0.6C \leq 20 \quad \text{Material 1}$$
$$0.2S + 0.1C \leq 5 \quad \text{Material 2}$$
$$0.6F + 0.3S + 0.3C \leq 21 \quad \text{Material 3}$$
$$F, S, C \geq 0$$

Figure 8.8 shows The Management Scientist solution to the modified RMC problem. The optimal solution calls for the production of 27.5 tons of fuel additive, 0 tons of solvent base, and 15 tons of carpet cleaning fluid. The value of the optimal solution is $1850.

Note the information contained in the reduced costs column. The **reduced cost** indicates how much the objective function coefficient for a particular variable would have to improve before that decision variable could assume a positive value in the optimal solution. As the computer output shows, the reduced costs for decision variables F and C are zero because these decision variables already have positive values in the optimal solution. The reduced cost of 12.50 for decision variable S tells us that the profit contribution for the solvent base would have to increase to at least $30 + $12.50 = $42.50 before S *could* assume a positive value in the optimal solution.[1] In other words, unless the profit contribution for S increases by at least $12.50 the value of S will remain at zero in the optimal solution.

Suppose that we increase the coefficient of S by $12.501 and then resolve the problem using The Management Scientist. Figure 8.9 shows the new solution. Although S assumes a positive value in the new solution ($S = 20.000$), the value of the optimal solution ($1850.020) has only increased by two cents. Note that the difference of two cents is just 20, the number of units of S produced in the new solution, times 0.001, the amount we increased the coefficient of S beyond 12.50. In some computer software packages, increasing the objective function coefficient of S by *exactly* $12.50 will result in a solution in which S assumes a positive value and the value of the objective function remains at 1850. In other words, increasing the profit contribution of S by exactly the amount of the reduced cost will result in alternative optimal solutions. However, whenever the profit contribution of S is increased by *more than* $12.50, S will not remain at zero in the optimal solution.

Figure 8.8 also shows that the dual prices for constraints 1 and 3 are 75.000 and 16.667, respectively, indicating that these two constraints are binding in the optimal solution. Thus, each additional ton of material 1 would increase the value of the optimal solution by $75 and each additional ton of material 3 would increase the value of the optimal solution by $16.667.

---

1. In the case of degeneracy, a decision variable may not assume a positive value in the optimal solution even when the improvement in the profit contribution exceeds the value of the reduced costs. Our definition of reduced costs, stated as "... *could* assume a positive value ...," provides for such special cases. More advanced texts on mathematical programming discuss these special types of situations.

FIGURE 8.8   THE MANAGEMENT SCIENTIST SOLUTION FOR THE MODIFIED RMC PROBLEM

```
Objective Function Value =                    1850.000

        Variable              Value              Reduced Costs
      -------------       ---------------      -------------------
           F                 27.500                 0.000
           S                  0.000                12.500
           C                 15.000                 0.000


        Constraint         Slack/Surplus            Dual Prices
      -------------       ---------------      -------------------
           1                  0.000                75.000
           2                  3.500                 0.000
           3                  0.000                16.667

OBJECTIVE COEFFICIENT RANGES

     Variable        Lower Limit      Current Value      Upper Limit
   ------------    ---------------    ---------------    ---------------
        F                33.333           40.000            100.000
        S          No Lower Limit         30.000             42.500
        C                33.333           50.000             60.000

RIGHT HAND SIDE RANGES

    Constraint       Lower Limit      Current Value      Upper Limit
   ------------    ---------------    ---------------    ---------------
        1               14.000           20.000             34.000
        2                1.500            5.000      No Upper Limit
        3               10.000           21.000             30.000
```

Suppose that after reviewing the solution shown in Figure 8.8, management decides to add the requirement that the number of tons of solvent base produced must be at least 25% of the number of tons of fuel additive produced. Writing this requirement using the decision variables F and S, we obtain

$$S \geq 0.25F \quad \text{or} \quad -0.25F + S \geq 0$$

Adding this new constraint to the modified RMC linear program and resolving the problem using The Management Scientist, we obtain the optimal solution shown in Figure 8.10.

Let us interpret the dual price for constraint 4, the requirement that the number of tons of solvent base produced must be at least 25% of the number of tons of fuel additive produced. The dual price of −12.121 indicates that a 1-unit increase in the right side of the con-

FIGURE 8.9   THE MANAGEMENT SCIENTIST SOLUTION FOR THE MODIFIED RMC PROBLEM WITH
THE COEFFICIENT OF *S* INCREASED BY $12.50

Objective Function Value =   1850.020

Variable	Value	Reduced Costs
F	25.000	0.000
S	20.000	0.000
C	0.000	0.001

Constraint	Slack/Surplus	Dual Prices
1	0.000	75.003
2	1.000	0.000
3	0.000	16.664

OBJECTIVE COEFFICIENT RANGES

Variable	Lower Limit	Current Value	Upper Limit
F	34.001	40.000	40.008
S	42.500	42.501	50.000
C	No Lower Limit	50.000	50.001

RIGHT HAND SIDE RANGES

Constraint	Lower Limit	Current Value	Upper Limit
1	14.000	20.000	21.500
2	4.000	5.000	No Upper Limit
3	18.750	21.000	30.000

straint will lower profits by $12.121. Thus, what the dual price of −12.121 is actually telling us is what will happen to the value of the optimal solution if the constraint is changed to

$$S \geq 0.25F + 1$$

The correct interpretation of the dual price of −12.121 can now be stated as follows: If we are forced to produce 1 ton of solvent base over and above the minimum 25% requirement, total profit will decrease by $12.121. Conversely, if we relax the minimum 25% requirement by 1 ton ($S \geq 0.25F - 1$), total profit will increase by $12.121.

The dual price for a percentage (or ratio) constraint such as this will not directly provide answers to questions concerning a percentage increase or decrease in the right-hand side of the constraint. For example, what would happen to the value of the optimal solution

FIGURE 8.10 THE MANAGEMENT SCIENTIST SOLUTION FOR THE MODIFIED RMC PROBLEM WITH THE 25% SOLVENT BASE REQUIREMENT

```
Objective Function Value =                    1766.667

      Variable                Value              Reduced Costs
   --------------         --------------        ------------------

        F                    26.667                  0.000
        S                     6.667                  0.000
        C                    10.000                  0.000


      Constraint           Slack/Surplus           Dual Prices
   --------------         --------------        ------------------

        1                     0.000                 78.788
        2                     2.667                  0.000
        3                     0.000                  9.091
        4                     0.000                -12.121


OBJECTIVE COEFFICIENT RANGES

    Variable          Lower Limit          Current Value        Upper Limit
  ------------       --------------       --------------       --------------

       F                36.250               40.000              105.000
       S                15.000               30.000               42.500
       C                33.333               50.000               54.286


RIGHT HAND SIDE RANGES

   Constraint         Lower Limit          Current Value        Upper Limit
  ------------       --------------       --------------       --------------

       1                16.333               20.000               32.571
       2                 2.333                5.000          No Upper Limit
       3                10.000               21.000               25.714
       4                -6.875                0.000               13.750
```

if the number of tons of solvent base produced has to be at least 26% of the number of standard bags? To answer such a question, we would resolve the problem using the constraint $-0.26F + S \geq 0$.

Because percentage (or ratio) constraints frequently occur in linear programming models, we need to consider another example. For instance, suppose that RMC's management states that the number of tons of carpet cleaning fluid produced may not exceed 20% of total production. Because total production is $F + S + C$, we can write this constraint as

$$C \leq 0.2(F + S + C)$$
$$C \leq 0.2F + 0.2S + 0.2C$$
$$-0.2F - 0.2S + 0.8C \leq 0$$

The solution obtained using The Management Scientist for the model that incorporates both the effects of this new percentage requirement and the previous requirement $(-0.25F + S \geq 0)$ is shown in Figure 8.11. After rounding, the dual price corresponding to the new constraint (constraint 5) is 16.13. Thus, every additional ton of carpet cleaning fluid that we are allowed to produce over the current 20% limit will increase the value of the objective function by $16.13; moreover, the right-hand-side range for this constraint shows that this interpretation is valid for increases of up to 1.333 tons.

FIGURE 8.11   THE MANAGEMENT SCIENTIST SOLUTION FOR THE MODIFIED RMC PROBLEM WITH 25% SOLVENT BASE AND 20% CARPET CLEANING FLUID REQUIREMENTS

```
Objective Function Value =                      1745.161

        Variable              Value           Reduced Costs
        --------              -----           -------------

           F                 26.452               0.000
           S                  8.387               0.000
           C                  8.710               0.000


      Constraint          Slack/Surplus          Dual Prices
      ----------          -------------          -----------

           1                  0.000               38.710
           2                  2.452                0.000
           3                  0.000               46.237
           4                  1.774                0.000
           5                  0.000               16.129


OBJECTIVE COEFFICIENT RANGES

     Variable        Lower Limit      Current Value      Upper Limit
     --------        -----------      -------------      -----------

        F              23.462            40.000             64.000
        S              16.667            30.000             42.500
        C              33.333            50.000          No Upper Limit


RIGHT HAND SIDE RANGES

    Constraint        Lower Limit      Current Value      Upper Limit
    ----------        -----------      -------------      -----------

        1               19.463            20.000             24.000
        2                2.548             5.000          No Upper Limit
        3               15.698            21.000             21.579
        4          No Lower Limit          0.000              1.774
        5               -9.000             0.000              1.333
```

Bluegrass Farms Problem

To provide additional practice in formulating and interpreting the computer solution for linear programs involving more than two decision variables, we consider a minimization problem involving three decision variables. Bluegrass Farms, located in Lexington, Kentucky, has been experimenting with a special diet for its racehorses. The feed components available for the diet are a standard horse feed product, an enriched oat product, and a new vitamin and mineral feed additive. The nutritional values in units per pound and the costs for the three feed components are summarized in Table 8.3; for example, each pound of the standard feed component contains 0.8 unit of ingredient A, 1 unit of ingredient B, and 0.1 unit of ingredient C. The minimum daily diet requirements for each horse are three units of ingredient A, six units of ingredient B, and four units of ingredient C. In addition, to control the weight of the horses, the total daily feed for a horse should not exceed 6 pounds. Bluegrass Farms would like to determine the minimum-cost mix that will satisfy the daily diet requirements.

To formulate a linear programming model for the Bluegrass Farms problem, we introduce three decision variables:

$$S = \text{number of pounds of the standard horse feed product}$$
$$E = \text{number of pounds of the enriched oat product}$$
$$A = \text{number of pounds of the vitamin and mineral feed additive}$$

Using the data in Table 8.3, the objective function that will minimize the total cost associated with the daily feed can be written as follows:

$$\text{Min} \quad 0.25S + 0.50E + 3A$$

Because the minimum daily requirement for ingredient A is three units, we obtain the constraint

$$0.8S + 0.2E \geq 3$$

The constraint for ingredient B is

$$1.0S + 1.5E + 3.0A \geq 6$$

and the constraint for ingredient C is

$$0.1S + 0.6E + 2.0A \geq 4$$

Finally, the constraint that restricts the mix to at most 6 pounds is

$$S + E + A \leq 6$$

TABLE 8.3   NUTRITIONAL VALUE AND COST DATA FOR THE BLUEGRASS FARMS PROBLEM

Feed Component	Standard	Enriched Oat	Additive
Ingredient A	0.8	0.2	0.0
Ingredient B	1.0	1.5	3.0
Ingredient C	0.1	0.6	2.0
Cost per pound	$0.25	$0.50	$3.00

Combining all the constraints with the nonnegativity requirements enables us to write the complete linear programming model for the Bluegrass Farms problem as follows:

$$\text{Min} \quad 0.25S + 0.50E + 3A$$

s.t.

$$
\begin{array}{llll}
0.8S + & 0.2E & & \geq 3 \quad \text{Ingredient A} \\
1.0S + & 1.5E + & 3.0A & \geq 6 \quad \text{Ingredient B} \\
0.1S + & 0.6E + & 2.0A & \geq 4 \quad \text{Ingredient C} \\
S + & E + & A & \leq 6 \quad \text{Weight} \\
\end{array}
$$

$$S, E, A \geq 0$$

The output obtained using The Management Scientist to solve the Bluegrass Farms problem is shown in Figure 8.12. After rounding, we see that the optimal solution calls for a daily diet consisting of 3.514 pounds of the standard horse feed product, 0.956 pound of the enriched oat product, and 1.541 pounds of the vitamin and mineral feed additive. Thus, with feed component costs of $0.25, $0.50, and $3.00, the total cost of the optimal diet is

$$
\begin{array}{rl}
3.514 \text{ pounds @ } \$0.25 \text{ per pound} = & \$0.879 \\
0.956 \text{ pound } \text{ @ } \$0.50 \text{ per pound} = & 0.478 \\
1.541 \text{ pounds @ } \$3.00 \text{ per pound} = & \underline{4.623} \\
\text{Total cost} = & \$5.980 \\
\end{array}
$$

Looking at the Slack/Surplus section of the computer output, we find a value of 3.554 for constraint 2. Because constraint 2 is a greater-than-or-equal-to constraint, 3.554 is the surplus; the optimal solution exceeds the minimum daily diet requirement for ingredient B (6 units) by 3.554 units. Because the surplus values for constraints 1 and 3 are both zero, we see that the optimal diet just meets the minimum requirements for ingredients A and C; moreover, a slack value of zero for constraint 4 shows that the optimal solution provides a total daily feed weight of 6 pounds.

The dual price (after rounding) for ingredient A is −1.22. To interpret this value properly, we first look at the sign; it is negative. Thus increasing the right-hand side of constraint 1 will cause the solution value to worsen. In this minimization problem, "worsen" means that the total daily cost will increase. Thus a one-unit increase in the right-hand side of constraint 1 will increase the total cost of the daily diet by $1.22. Conversely, it is also correct to conclude that a decrease of one unit in the right-hand side will decrease the total cost by $1.22. Looking at the RIGHT HAND SIDE RANGES section of the computer output, we see that these interpretations are correct as long as the right-hand side of constraint 1 is between 1.143 and 3.368.

Suppose that the Bluegrass management is willing to reconsider their position regarding the maximum weight of the daily diet. The dual price of 0.92 (after rounding) for constraint 4 shows that a one-unit increase in the right-hand side of constraint 4 will reduce total cost by $0.92. The RIGHT HAND SIDE RANGES section of the output shows that this interpretation is correct for increases in the right-hand side up to a maximum of 8.478 pounds. Thus, the effect of increasing the right-hand side of constraint 4 from 6 to 8 pounds is a decrease in the total daily cost of 2 × $0.92 or $1.84. Keep in mind that if this change were made, the feasible region would change, and we would obtain a new optimal solution.

The OBJECTIVE COEFFICIENT RANGES section of the computer output shows a lower limit of −0.393 for S. Clearly, in a real problem, the objective function coefficient of S (the cost of the standard horse feed product) cannot take on a negative value. So, from a practical point of view, we can think of the lower limit for the objective function coefficient

FIGURE 8.12 THE MANAGEMENT SCIENTIST SOLUTION FOR THE BLUEGRASS FARMS PROBLEM

```
Objective Function Value =              5.973

        Variable              Value              Reduced Costs
      --------------     ----------------      ------------------
            S                 3.514                  0.000
            E                 0.946                  0.000
            A                 1.541                  0.000

        Constraint          Slack/Surplus          Dual Prices
      --------------     ----------------      ------------------
            1                 0.000                 -1.216
            2                 3.554                  0.000
            3                 0.000                 -1.959
            4                 0.000                  0.919

OBJECTIVE COEFFICIENT RANGES

    Variable       Lower Limit       Current Value       Upper Limit
  ------------   ---------------    ---------------    ---------------
        S            -0.393              0.250         No Upper Limit
        E         No Lower Limit         0.500              0.925
        A             1.522              3.000         No Upper Limit

RIGHT HAND SIDE RANGES

    Constraint     Lower Limit       Current Value       Upper Limit
  ------------   ---------------    ---------------    ---------------
        1             1.143              3.000              3.368
        2         No Lower Limit         6.000              9.554
        3             2.100              4.000              4.875
        4             5.562              6.000              8.478
```

of S as being zero. We can thus conclude that no matter how much the cost of the standard mix were to decrease, the optimal solution would not change. Even if Bluegrass Farms could obtain the standard horse feed product for free, the optimal solution would still specify a daily diet of 3.51 pounds of the standard horse feed product, 0.95 pound of the enriched oat product, and 1.54 pounds of the vitamin and mineral feed additive. However, any decrease in the per-unit cost of the standard feed would result in a decrease in the total cost for the optimal daily diet.

Note that the objective coefficient ranges for S and A have no upper limit. Even if the cost of A were to increase, for example, from $3.00 to $13.00 per pound, the optimal solution would not change; the total cost of the solution, however, would increase by $10 (the amount of the increase) times 1.541 or $15.41. You must always keep in mind that the interpretations we have made using the sensitivity analysis information in the computer output are only appropriate if all other coefficients in the problem do not change. To consider simultaneous changes we must use the 100 percent rule or resolve the problem after making the changes.

Linear programming has been successfully applied to a variety of applications involving food products and nutrition. The Q. M. in Action: Estimation of Food Nutrient Values discusses how the Nutrition Coordinating Center of the University of Minnesota uses linear programming to help estimate the nutrient amounts in new food products.

Q. M. IN ACTION

ESTIMATION OF FOOD NUTRIENT VALUES

The Nutrition Coordinating Center (NCC) of the University of Minnesota maintains a food-composition database that is used by nutritionists and researchers throughout the world. Nutrient information provided by NCC is used to estimate the nutrient intake of individuals, to plan menus, to research links between diet and disease, and to meet regulatory requirements.

Nutrient intake calculations require data on an enormous number of food nutrient values. NCC's food composition database contains information on 93 different nutrients for each food product. With many new brand-name products introduced each year, NCC has the significant task of maintaining an accurate and timely database. The task is made more difficult by the fact that new brand-name products only provide data on a relatively small number of nutrients. Because of the high cost of chemically analyzing the new products, NCC uses a linear programming model to help estimate thousands of nutrient values per year.

The decision variables in the linear programming model are the amounts of each ingredient in a food product. The objective is to minimize the difference between the estimated nutrient values and the known nutrient values for the food product. Constraints are that ingredients must be in descending order by weight, ingredients must be within nutritionist-specified bounds, and the differences between the calculated nutrient values and the known nutrient values must be within specified tolerances.

In practice, a NCC nutritionist employs the linear programming model to derive estimates of the amounts of each ingredient in a new food product. Given these estimates, the nutritionist refines the estimates based on his or her knowledge of the product formulation and the food composition. Once the amounts of each ingredient are obtained, the amounts of each nutrient in the food product can be calculated. With approximately 1000 products evaluated each year, the time and cost savings provided by using linear programming to help estimate the nutrient values are significant.

*Based on Brian J. Westrich, Michael A. Altmann, and Sandra J. Potthoff, "Minnesota's Nutrition Coordinating Center Uses Mathematical Optimization to Estimate Food Nutrient Values," *Interfaces* (September–October 1998): 86–99.

8.5   ELECTRONIC COMMUNICATIONS PROBLEM

The Electronic Communications problem is a maximization problem involving four decision variables, two less-than-or-equal-to constraints, one equality constraint, and one greater-than-or-equal-to constraint. We will use this problem to provide a summary of the process of formulating a mathematical model, using The Management Scientist to obtain an optimal solution, and interpreting the solution and sensitivity report information. In the next chapter we will continue to illustrate how linear programming can be applied by showing additional examples from the areas of marketing, finance, and production management.

Electronic Communications manufactures portable radio systems that can be used for two-way communications. The company's new product, which has a range of up to 25 miles, is suitable for use in a variety of business and personal applications. The distribution channels for the new radio are as follows:

1. Marine equipment distributors
2. Business equipment distributors
3. National chain of retail stores
4. Direct mail

Because of differing distribution and promotional costs, the profitability of the product will vary with the distribution channel. In addition, the advertising cost and the personal sales

TABLE 8.4 PROFIT, ADVERTISING COST, AND PERSONAL SALES TIME DATA FOR THE ELECTRONIC COMMUNICATIONS PROBLEM

Distribution Channel	Profit per Unit Sold	Advertising Cost per Unit Sold	Personal Sales Effort per Unit Sold
Marine distributors	$90	$10	2 hours
Business distributors	$84	$ 8	3 hours
National retail stores	$70	$ 9	3 hours
Direct mail	$60	$15	None

effort required will vary with the distribution channels. Table 8.4 summarizes the contribution to profit, advertising cost, and personal sales effort data for the Electronic Communications problem. The firm has set the advertising budget at $5000, and a maximum of 1800 hours of salesforce time is available for allocation to the sales effort. Management has also decided to produce exactly 600 units for the current production period. Finally, an ongoing contract with a national chain of retail stores requires that at least 150 units be distributed through this distribution channel.

Electronic Communications is now faced with the problem of determining the number of units that should be produced for each of the distribution channels in order to maximize the total contribution to profit. In addition to determining how many units should be allocated to each of the four distribution channels, Electronic Communications must also determine how to allocate the advertising budget and salesforce effort to each of the four distribution channels.

Problem Formulation

We will now write the objective function and the constraints for the Electronic Communications problem. We begin with the objective function.

Objective function: Maximize profit

Four constraints are needed to account for the following restrictions: (1) a limited advertising budget; (2) limited salesforce availability; (3) a production requirement; and (4) a retail stores distribution requirement.

Constraint 1 Advertising expenditure ≤ Budget

Constraint 2 Sales time used ≤ Time available

Constraint 3 Radios produced = Management requirement

Constraint 4 Retail distribution ≥ Contract requirement

These expressions provide descriptions of the objective function and the constraints. We are now ready to define the decision variables that will represent the decisions the manager must make. For the Electronic Communications problem, we introduce the following four decision variables:

M = the number of units produced for the marine equipment distribution channel

B = the number of units produced for the business equipment distribution channel

R = the number of units produced for the national retail chain distribution channel

D = the number of units produced for the direct mail distribution channel

Using the data in Table 8.4, we can write the objective function for maximizing the total contribution to profit associated with the radios as follows:

$$\text{Max } 90M + 84B + 70R + 60D$$

Let us now develop a mathematical statement of the constraints for the problem. Because the advertising budget has been set at \$5000, the constraint that limits the amount of advertising expenditure can be written as follows:

$$10M + 8B + 9R + 15D \leq 5000$$

Similarly, with sales time limited to 1800 hours, we obtain the constraint

$$2M + 3B + 3R \leq 1800$$

Management's decision to produce exactly 600 units during the current production period is expressed as

$$M + B + R + D = 600$$

Finally, to account for the fact that the number of units distributed by the national chain of retail stores must be at least 150, we add the constraint

$$R \geq 150$$

Combining all of the constraints with the nonnegativity requirements enables us to write the complete linear programming model for the Electronic Communications problem as follows:

$$
\begin{aligned}
\text{Max } \quad & 90M + 84B + 70R + 60D \\
\text{s.t.} \quad & \\
& 10M + 8B + 9R + 15D \leq 5000 \quad \text{Advertising budget} \\
& 2M + 3B + 3R \leq 1800 \quad \text{Salesforce availability} \\
& M + B + R + D = 600 \quad \text{Production level} \\
& R \geq 150 \quad \text{Retail stores requirement} \\
& M, B, R, D \geq 0
\end{aligned}
$$

Computer Solution and Interpretation

A portion of the output obtained using The Management Scientist to solve the Electronic Communications problem is shown in Figure 8.13. The Objective Function Value section shows that the optimal solution to the problem will provide a maximum profit of \$48,450. The optimal values of the decision variables are $M = 25$, $B = 425$, $R = 150$, and $D = 0$. Thus, the optimal strategy for Electronic Communications is to concentrate on the business equipment distribution channel with $B = 425$ units. In addition, the firm should allocate 25 units to the marine distribution channel ($M = 25$) and meet its 150-unit commitment to the national retail chain store distribution channel ($R = 150$). With $D = 0$, the optimal solution indicates that the firm should not use the direct mail distribution channel.

Now consider the information contained in the Reduced Costs column. Recall that the reduced costs indicate how much each objective function coefficient would have to improve before the corresponding decision variable could assume a positive value in the optimal solution. As the computer output shows, the first three reduced costs are zero because the corresponding decision variables already have positive values in the optimal solution. However,

FIGURE 8.13   A PORTION OF THE MANAGEMENT SCIENTIST SOLUTION FOR THE
ELECTRONIC COMMUNICATIONS PROBLEM

```
Objective Function Value =          48450.000

     Variable              Value            Reduced Costs
  --------------      --------------       ----------------

        M                 25.000                0.000
        B                425.000                0.000
        R                150.000                0.000
        D                  0.000               45.000


   Constraint        Slack/Surplus            Dual Prices
  --------------      --------------       ----------------

        1                  0.000                3.000
        2                 25.000                0.000
        3                  0.000               60.000
        4                  0.000              -17.000
```

the reduced cost of 45 for decision variable *D* tells us that the profit for the new radios distributed via the direct mail channel would have to increase from its current value of $60 per
unit to at least $60 + $45 = $105 per unit before it would be profitable to use the direct
mail distribution channel.

The computer output information for the slack/surplus variables and the dual prices is
restated here:

Constraint Number	Constraint Name	Type of Constraint	Slack or Surplus	Dual Price
1	Advertising budget	$\leq$	0	3
2	Salesforce availability	$\leq$	25	0
3	Production level	$=$	0	60
4	Retail stores requirement	$\geq$	0	-17

The advertising budget constraint has a slack of zero, indicating that the entire budget
of $5000 has been used. The corresponding dual price of 3 tells us that an additional dollar
added to the advertising budget will improve the objective function (increase the profit) by
$3. Thus, the possibility of increasing the advertising budget should be seriously consid-
ered by the firm. The slack of 25 hours for the salesforce availability constraint shows that
the allocated 1800 hours of sales time are adequate to distribute the radios produced and
that 25 hours of sales time will remain unused. Because the production level constraint is
an equality constraint, the zero slack/surplus shown on the output is expected. However,
the dual price of 60 associated with this constraint shows that if the firm were to consider
increasing the production level for the radios, the value of the objective function, or profit,
would improve at the rate of $60 per radio produced. Finally, the surplus of zero associ-
ated with the retail store distribution channel commitment is a result of this constraint being binding. The negative dual price indicates that increasing the commitment from 150 to
151 units will actually decrease the profit by $17. Thus, Electronic Communications may

want to consider reducing its commitment to the retail store distribution channel. A *decrease* in the commitment will actually improve profit at the rate of $17 per unit.

We now consider the additional sensitivity analysis information provided by the computer output shown in Figure 8.14. The objective coefficient ranges are

$$84 \leq C_M < \text{No upper limit}$$
$$50 \leq C_B \leq 90$$
$$\text{No lower limit} < C_R \leq 87$$
$$\text{No lower limit} < C_D \leq 105$$

The current solution, or strategy, remains optimal, provided that the objective function coefficients remain in the given ranges. Note in particular the range associated with the direct mail distribution channel coefficient, C_D. This information is consistent with the earlier observation for the Reduced Costs portion of the output. In both instances, we see that the per-unit profit would have to increase to $105 before the direct mail distribution channel could be in the optimal solution with a positive value.

Finally, the sensitivity analysis information on RIGHT HAND SIDE RANGES, as shown in Figure 8.14, provides the following ranges:

Constraint	Min RHS	Current Value	Max RHS
Advertising budget	4950	5000	5850
Salesforce	1775	1800	No upper limit
Production level	515	600	603.57
Retail stores requirement	0	150	200

Several interpretations of these right-hand-side ranges are possible. In particular, recall that the dual price for the advertising budget enabled us to conclude that each $1 increase in the budget would improve the profit by $3. The range for the advertising budget shows that this statement about the value of increasing the budget is appropriate up to an advertising budget of $5850. Increases above this level would not necessarily be beneficial. Also note that the dual price of -17 for the retail stores requirement suggested the desirability of reducing this commitment. The right-hand-side range for this constraint shows that the commitment could be reduced to zero and the value of the reduction would be at the rate of $17 per unit.

Again, the *sensitivity analysis* or *postoptimality analysis* provided by computer software packages for linear programming problems considers only *one change at a time*, with all other coefficients of the problem remaining as originally specified. As mentioned earlier, simultaneous changes can sometimes be analyzed without resolving the problem, provided that the cumulative changes are not large enough to violate the 100 percent rule.

Finally, recall that the complete solution to the Electronic Communications problem requested information not only on the number of units to be distributed over each channel, but also on the allocation of the advertising budget and the salesforce effort to each distribution channel. Because the optimal solution is $M = 25, B = 425, R = 150,$ and $D = 0$, we can simply evaluate each term in a given constraint to determine how much of the constraint resource is allocated to each distribution channel. For example, the advertising budget constraint of

$$10M + 8B + 9R + 15D \leq 5000$$

shows that $10M = 10(25) = \$250$, $8B = 8(425) = \$3400$, $9R = 9(150) = \$1350$, and $15D = 15(0) = \$0$. Thus, the advertising budget allocations are, respectively, $250, $3400,

FIGURE 8.14 OBJECTIVE COEFFICIENT AND RIGHT-HAND-SIDE RANGES PROVIDED BY THE MANAGEMENT SCIENTIST FOR THE ELECTRONIC COMMUNICATIONS PROBLEM

```
OBJECTIVE COEFFICIENT RANGES

    Variable        Lower Limit      Current Value     Upper Limit
  ------------    ---------------   ---------------   ---------------
       M                 84.000           90.000      No Upper Limit
       B                 50.000           84.000             90.000
       R          No Lower Limit          70.000             87.000
       D          No Lower Limit          60.000            105.000


RIGHT HAND SIDE RANGES

    Constraint      Lower Limit      Current Value     Upper Limit
  ------------    ---------------   ---------------   ---------------
       1               4950.000         5000.000           5850.000
       2               1775.000         1800.000      No Upper Limit
       3                515.000          600.000            603.571
       4                  0.000          150.000            200.000
```

$1350, and $0 for each of the four distribution channels. Making similar calculations for the salesforce constraint results in the managerial summary of the Electronic Communications optimal solution as shown in Table 8.5.

TABLE 8.5 PROFIT-MAXIMIZING STRATEGY FOR THE ELECTRONIC COMMUNICATIONS PROBLEM

Distribution Channel	Volume	Advertising Allocation	Salesforce Allocation (hours)
Marine distributors	25	$ 250	50
Business distributors	425	3400	1275
National retail stores	150	1350	450
Direct mail	0	0	0
Totals	600	$5000	1775

Projected total profit = $48,450

SUMMARY

We began the chapter with a discussion of sensitivity analysis, the study of how changes in the coefficients of a linear program affect the optimal solution. Specifically, we showed how a change in one of the objective function coefficients or a change in the right-hand-side value for a constraint will affect the optimal solution to the problem.

We continued our discussion of problem formulation, sensitivity analysis, and the interpretation of the solution by introducing modifications of the RMC problem. These modifications involved an additional decision variable and percentage, or ratio, constraints. Then, in order to provide additional practice in formulating and interpreting the solution for linear programs involving more than two decision variables, we introduced the Bluegrass Farms problem, a minimization problem involving three decision variables. In the last section we summarized all the work to date using the Electronic Communications problem, a maximization problem with four decision variables, two less-than-or-equal-to constraints, one equality constraint, and one greater-than-or-equal-to constraint.

The Q. M. in Action: An Optimal Wood Procurement Policy illustrates the diversity of problem situations to which linear programming can be applied. In this application, Wellborn Cabinet, Inc., was able to reduce annual raw material costs for one of its production systems by $412,000 as a result of formulating and solving a linear programming model. Your ability to formulate, solve, and interpret the solution to problems like the Electronic Communications problem is critical to understanding how more complex problems, such as the one encountered by Wellborn Cabinet, Inc., can be modeled using linear programming.

Q. M. IN ACTION

AN OPTIMAL WOOD PROCUREMENT POLICY*

Wellborn Cabinet, Inc., operates an integrated sawmill and cabinet manufacturing system in Alabama. Its manufacturing facility consists of a sawmill, four dry kilns, and a wood cabinet assembly plant; the assembly plant includes a rough mill for producing cabinet components that are referred to as blanks. Because of the pressure to market quality products at competitive prices, a major concern for Wellborn Cabinet is to maintain consistency in product quality. A key factor in maintaining this quality depends on controlling the quality and costs of raw materials.

To produce blanks, Wellborn Cabinet purchases #1 and #2 grade hardwood logs, as well as #1 and #2 dry or green common grade lumber. During a typical five-day week of operation, the sawmill can process up to 1550 logs with a small-end diameter from 9 to 22 inches. Usually, the lumber is purchased in bundles containing random sizes. Both the logs processed by the sawmill and the green lumber purchased from outside suppliers are dried at the kilns to an average moisture content

of 7%; the dried material is then planed and converted into about 130 different sizes of blanks at the rough mill.

Wellborn developed a linear programming model of the blank production system. The objective was to determine a procurement plan that would minimize the total cost of producing blanks for a five-day work week. Constraints included capacities of the sawmill and dry kilns, the demand for blanks at the manufacturing plant, and the available supply of raw materials. The initial results indicate that the company can minimize the total cost of producing blanks by purchasing only #2 grade logs and #2 common green lumber; approximately 88% of the rough mill dry lumber requirements should come from #2 grade logs and the rest from purchased #2 common green lumber. The projected annual savings in raw material costs were $412,000.

*Based on H. F. Carino and C. H. LeNoir, Jr., "Optimizing Wood Procurement in Cabinet Manufacturing," *Interfaces* (March–April 1988): 10–19.

GLOSSARY

Sensitivity analysis   The study of how changes in the coefficients of a linear programming problem affect the optimal solution.

100 percent rule   A rule indicating when simultaneous changes in two or more objective function coefficients will not cause a change in the optimal values for the decision variables. It can also be applied to indicate when two or more right-hand-side changes will not cause a change in any of the dual prices.

Dual price The improvement in the value of the optimal solution per unit increase in the right-hand side of a constraint.

Sunk cost A cost that is not affected by the decision made. It will be incurred no matter what values the decision variables assume.

Relevant cost A cost that depends upon the decision made. The amount of a relevant cost will vary depending on the values of the decision variables.

Reduced cost The amount by which an objective function coefficient would have to improve (increase for a maximization problem, decrease for a minimization problem) before it would be possible for the corresponding variable to assume a positive value in the optimal solution.

PROBLEMS

SELFtest   1. Consider the following linear program:

$$\text{Max} \quad 3A + 2B$$

s.t.

$$1A + 1B \leq 10$$
$$3A + 1B \leq 24$$
$$1A + 2B \leq 16$$
$$A, B \geq 0$$

a. Use the graphical solution procedure to find the optimal solution.
b. Assume that the objective function coefficient for A changes from 3 to 5. Does the optimal solution change? Use the graphical solution procedure to find the new optimal solution.
c. Assume that the objective function coefficient for A remains 3, but the objective function coefficient for B changes from 2 to 4. Does the optimal solution change? Use the graphical solution procedure to find the new optimal solution.
d. The Management Scientist computer solution for the linear program in part (a) provides the following objective coefficient range information:

Variable	Lower Limit	Current Value	Upper Limit
A	2	3	6
B	1	2	3

Use this objective coefficient range information to answer parts (b) and (c).

SELFtest   2. Consider the linear program in Problem 1. The value of the optimal solution is 27. Suppose that the right-hand side for constraint 1 is increased from 10 to 11.
a. Use the graphical solution procedure to find the new optimal solution.
b. Use the solution to part (a) to determine the dual price for constraint 1.
c. The Management Scientist computer solution for the linear program in Problem 1 provides the following right-hand-side range information:

Constraint	Lower Limit	Current Value	Upper Limit
1	8	10	11.2
2	18	24	30
3	13	16	No Upper Limit

What does the right-hand side range information for constraint 1 tell you about the dual price for constraint 1?

   d. The dual price for constraint 2 is 0.5. Using this dual price and the right-hand-side range information in part (c), what conclusion can be drawn about the effect of changes to the right-hand side of constraint 2?

3. Consider the following linear program:

$$\text{Min} \quad 8X + 12Y$$

$$\text{s.t.}$$

$$1X + 3Y \geq 9$$
$$2X + 2Y \geq 10$$
$$6X + 2Y \geq 18$$
$$X, Y \geq 0$$

   a. Use the graphical solution procedure to find the optimal solution.

   b. Assume that the objective function coefficient for X changes from 8 to 6. Does the optimal solution change? Use the graphical solution procedure to find the new optimal solution.

   c. Assume that the objective function coefficient for X remains 8, but the objective function coefficient for Y changes from 12 to 6. Does the optimal solution change? Use the graphical solution procedure to find the new optimal solution.

   d. The Management Scientist computer solution for the linear program in part (a) provides the following objective coefficient range information:

Variable	Lower Limit	Current Value	Upper Limit
X	4	8	12
Y	8	12	24

How would this objective coefficient range information help you answer parts (b) and (c) prior to resolving the problem?

4. Consider the linear program in Problem 3. The value of the optimal solution is 48. Suppose that the right-hand side for constraint 1 is increased from 9 to 10.

   a. Use the graphical solution procedure to find the new optimal solution.

   b. Use the solution to part (a) to determine the dual price for constraint 1.

   c. The Management Scientist computer solution for the linear program in Problem 1 provides the following right-hand-side range information:

Constraint	Lower Limit	Current Value	Upper Limit
1	5	9	11
2	9	10	18
3	No Lower Limit	18	22

What does the right-hand-side range information for constraint 1 tell you about the dual price for constraint 1?

   d. The dual price for constraint 2 is -3. Using this dual price and the right-hand-side range information in part (c), what conclusion can be drawn about the effect of changes to the right-hand side of constraint 2?

SELFtest   5.   Refer to the Kelson Sporting Equipment problem (Chapter 7, Problem 22). Letting

$$R = \text{number of regular gloves}$$
$$C = \text{number of catcher's mitts}$$

leads to the following formulation:

$$\text{Max} \quad 5R + 8C$$

s.t.

$$R + \tfrac{3}{2}C \leq 900 \quad \text{Cutting and sewing}$$
$$\tfrac{1}{2}R + \tfrac{1}{3}C \leq 300 \quad \text{Finishing}$$
$$\tfrac{1}{8}R + \tfrac{1}{4}C \leq 100 \quad \text{Packaging and shipping}$$
$$R, C \geq 0$$

The computer solution obtained using The Management Scientist is shown in Figure 8.15.
   a. What is the optimal solution, and what is the value of the total profit contribution?
   b. Which constraints are binding?
   c. What are the dual prices for the resources? Interpret each.
   d. If overtime can be scheduled in one of the departments, where would you recommend doing so?

SELFtest   6.   Refer to the computer solution of the Kelson Sporting Equipment problem in Figure 8.15 (see Problem 5).
   a. Determine the objective coefficient ranges.
   b. Interpret the ranges in part (a).
   c. Interpret the right-hand-side ranges.
   d. How much will the value of the optimal solution improve if 20 extra hours of packaging and shipping time are made available?

7.   Investment Advisors, Inc., is a brokerage firm that manages stock portfolios for a number of clients. A particular portfolio consists of U shares of U.S. Oil and H shares of Huber Steel. The annual return for U.S. Oil is $3 per share and the annual return for Huber Steel is $5 per share. U.S. Oil sells for $25 per share and Huber Steel sells for $50 per share. The portfolio has $80,000 to be invested. The portfolio risk index (0.50 per share of U.S. Oil and 0.25 per share for Huber Steel) has a maximum of 700. In addition, the portfolio is limited to a maximum of 1000 shares of U.S. Oil. The linear programming formation that will maximum the total annual return of the portfolio is as follows:

$$\text{Max} \quad 3U + 5H \qquad\qquad \text{Maximize total annual return}$$

s.t.

$$25U + 50H \leq 80{,}000 \quad \text{Funds available}$$
$$0.50U + 0.25H \leq 700 \quad \text{Risk maximum}$$
$$1U \qquad\quad \leq 1000 \quad \text{U.S. Oil maximum}$$
$$U, H \geq 0$$

The computer solution of this problem is shown in Figure 8.16.
   a. What is the optimal solution, and what is the value of the total annual return?
   b. Which constraints are binding? What is your interpretation of these constraints in terms of the problem?
   c. What are the dual prices for the constraints? Interpret each.
   d. Would it be beneficial to increase the maximum amount invested in U.S. Oil? Why or why not?

FIGURE 8.15   THE MANAGEMENT SCIENTIST SOLUTION FOR THE KELSON SPORTING
EQUIPMENT PROBLEM

```
Objective Function Value =        3700.00146

        Variable              Value              Reduced Costs
     -------------       ---------------      -------------------
          R                500.00153               0.00000
          C                149.99924               0.00000

       Constraint         Slack/Surplus            Dual Prices
     -------------       ---------------      -------------------
           1               174.99962               0.00000
           2                 0.00000               2.99999
           3                 0.00000              28.00006

OBJECTIVE COEFFICIENT RANGES

     Variable        Lower Limit        Current Value       Upper Limit
   ------------     ---------------     ---------------     ------------
        R               4.00000            5.00000           12.00012
        C               3.33330            8.00000           10.00000

RIGHT HAND SIDE RANGES

    Constraint       Lower Limit        Current Value       Upper Limit
   ------------     ---------------     ---------------     ------------
        1              725.00037          900.00000        No Upper Limit
        2              133.33199          300.00000          400.00000
        3               75.00000          100.00000          134.99982
```

8. Refer to Figure 8.16, which shows the computer solution of Problem 7.
   a. How much would the return for U.S. Oil have to increase before it would be beneficial to increase the investment in this stock?
   b. How much would the return for Huber Steel have to decrease before it would be beneficial to reduce the investment in this stock?
   c. How much would the total annual return be reduced if the U.S. Oil maximum were reduced to 900 shares?

9. Recall the Tom's, Inc., problem (Chapter 7, Problem 26). Letting

$$W = \text{jars of Western Foods Salsa}$$
$$M = \text{jars of Mexico City Salsa}$$

leads to the formulation:

$$\text{Max} \quad 1W + 1.25M$$

s.t.

$$5W + 7M \leq 4480 \quad \text{Whole tomatoes}$$
$$3W + 1M \leq 2080 \quad \text{Tomato sauce}$$
$$2W + 2M \leq 1600 \quad \text{Tomato paste}$$
$$W, M \geq 0$$

The Management Scientist solution is shown in Figure 8.17.

FIGURE 8.16   THE MANAGEMENT SCIENTIST SOLUTION FOR THE INVESTMENT
ADVISORS PROBLEM

```
Objective Function Value =              8400.000

        Variable              Value           Reduced Costs
    --------------      ---------------     ------------------
           U                 800.000                 0.000
           H                1200.000                 0.000

       Constraint         Slack/Surplus          Dual Prices
    --------------      ---------------     ------------------
           1                   0.000                 0.093
           2                   0.000                 1.333
           3                 200.000                 0.000

OBJECTIVE COEFFICIENT RANGES

      Variable        Lower Limit      Current Value      Upper Limit
    ------------     ------------     ---------------     ------------
          U              2.500             3.000             10.000
          H              1.500             5.000              6.000

RIGHT HAND SIDE RANGES

     Constraint       Lower Limit      Current Value      Upper Limit
    ------------     ------------     ---------------     ------------
          1           65000.000         80000.000         140000.000
          2             400.000           700.000            775.000
          3             800.000          1000.000         No Upper Limit
```

a. What is the optimal solution, and what are the optimal production quantities?
b. Specify the objective function ranges.
c. What are the dual prices for each constraint? Interpret each.
d. Identify each of the right-hand-side ranges.

SELFtest   10. Recall the Innis Investments problem (Chapter 7, Problem 37). Letting

$$S = \text{units purchased in the stock fund}$$

$$M = \text{units purchased in the money market fund}$$

leads to the following formulation:

$$\text{Min} \quad 8S + 3M$$

s.t.

$$50S + 100M \leq 1{,}200{,}000 \quad \text{Funds available}$$
$$5S + 4M \geq 60{,}000 \quad \text{Annual income}$$

FIGURE 8.17   THE MANAGEMENT SCIENTIST SOLUTION FOR THE TOM'S, INC., PROBLEM

OPTIMAL SOLUTION

Objective Function Value =   860.000

Variable	Value	Reduced Costs
W	560.000	0.000
M	240.000	0.000

Constraint	Slack/Surplus	Dual Prices
1	0.000	0.125
2	160.000	0.000
3	0.000	0.187

OBJECTIVE COEFFICIENT RANGES

Variable	Lower Limit	Current Value	Upper Limit
W	0.893	1.000	1.250
M	1.000	1.250	1.400

RIGHT HAND SIDE RANGES

Constraint	Lower Limit	Current Value	Upper Limit
1	4320.000	4480.000	5600.000
2	1920.000	2080.000	No Upper Limit
3	1280.000	1600.000	1640.000

$$M \geq \quad 3{,}000 \quad \text{Units in money market}$$
$$S, M \geq 0$$

The computer solution is shown in Figure 8.18.
a. What is the optimal solution, and what is the minimum total risk?
b. Specify the objective coefficient ranges.
c. How much annual income will be earned by the portfolio?
d. What is the rate of return for the portfolio?
e. What is the dual price for the funds available constraint?
f. What is the marginal rate of return on extra funds added to the portfolio?

11. Refer to Problem 10 and the computer solution shown in Figure 8.18.
   a. Suppose the risk index for the stock fund (the value of C_S) increases from its current value of 8 to 12. How does the optimal solution change, if at all?
   b. Suppose the risk index for the money market fund (the value of C_M) increases from its current value of 3 to 3.5. How does the optimal solution change, if at all?
   c. Suppose C_S increases to 12 and C_M increases to 3.5. How does the optimal solution change, if at all?

FIGURE 8.18   THE MANAGEMENT SCIENTIST SOLUTION FOR THE INNIS INVESTMENTS PROBLEM

```
Objective Function Value =          62000.000

        Variable              Value              Reduced Costs
    ---------------      ---------------      -------------------
           S               4000.000                  0.000
           M              10000.000                  0.000


       Constraint         Slack/Surplus          Dual Prices
    ---------------      ---------------      -------------------
           1                  0.000                  0.057
           2                  0.000                 -2.167
           3               7000.000                  0.000


OBJECTIVE COEFFICIENT RANGES

      Variable        Lower Limit      Current Value       Upper Limit
    ------------      ------------      -------------      ------------
           S             3.750             8.000          No Upper Limit
           M         No Lower Limit        3.000              6.400


RIGHT HAND SIDE RANGES

     Constraint       Lower Limit      Current Value       Upper Limit
    ------------      ------------      -------------      ------------
           1          780000.000        1200000.000        1500000.000
           2           48000.000          60000.000         102000.000
           3         No Lower Limit        3000.000          10000.000
```

SELFtest   **12.** Suppose that in a product-mix problem x_1, x_2, x_3, and x_4 indicate the units of products 1, 2, 3, and 4, respectively, and the linear program is

$$\text{Max} \quad 4x_1 + 6x_2 + 3x_3 + 1x_4$$
$$\text{s.t.}$$
$$1.5x_1 + 2x_2 + 4x_3 + 3x_4 \le 550 \quad \text{Machine A hours}$$
$$4x_1 + 1x_2 + 2x_3 + 1x_4 \le 700 \quad \text{Machine B hours}$$
$$2x_1 + 3x_2 + 1x_3 + 2x_4 \le 200 \quad \text{Machine C hours}$$
$$x_1, x_2, x_3, x_4 \ge 0$$

The computer solution developed using The Management Scientist is shown in Figure 8.19.
a. What is the optimal solution, and what is the value of the objective function?
b. Which constraints are binding?
c. Which machines have excess capacity available? How much?
d. If the objective function coefficient of x_1 is increased by 0.50, will the optimal solution change?

SELFtest   **13.** Refer to the computer solution of Problem 12 in Figure 8.19.
a. Identify the objective coefficient ranges.
b. Suppose the objective function coefficient for x_1 is decreased by 3, the objective function coefficient of x_2 is increased by 1.5, and the objective function coefficient for x_4 is increased by 1. What will the new optimal solution be?

FIGURE 8.19   THE MANAGEMENT SCIENTIST SOLUTION FOR PROBLEM 18

```
Objective Function Value =          525.000

        Variable              Value              Reduced Costs
        --------              -----              -------------
           X1                 0.000                  0.050
           X2                25.000                  0.000
           X3               125.000                  0.000
           X4                 0.000                  3.500

       Constraint         Slack/Surplus            Dual Prices
       ----------         -------------            -----------
           1                  0.000                  0.300
           2                425.000                  0.000
           3                  0.000                  1.800
```

OBJECTIVE COEFFICIENT RANGES

Variable	Lower Limit	Current Value	Upper Limit
X1	No Lower Limit	4.000	4.050
X2	5.923	6.000	9.000
X3	2.000	3.000	12.000
X4	No Lower Limit	1.000	4.500

RIGHT HAND SIDE RANGES

Constraint	Lower Limit	Current Value	Upper Limit
1	133.333	550.000	800.000
2	275.000	700.000	No Upper Limit
3	137.500	200.000	825.000

    c. Identify the right-hand-side ranges.

    d. If the number of hours available on machine A is increased by 300, will the dual price for that constraint change?

14. Consider the following linear program and computer solution shown in Figure 8.20.

$$\text{Min}\quad 15x_1 + 15x_2 + 16x_3$$

s.t.

$$1x_1 + \qquad\quad 1x_3 \le 30$$
$$0.5x_1 - 1x_2 + 6x_3 \ge 15$$
$$3x_1 + 4x_2 - 1x_3 \ge 20$$
$$x_1, x_2, x_3 \ge 0$$

    a. What is the optimal solution, and what is the value for the objective function?

    b. Which constraints are binding?

    c. What are the dual prices? Interpret each.

    d. If you could change the right-hand side of one constraint by one unit, which one would you choose? What would be the new value of the right-hand side?

FIGURE 8.20   THE MANAGEMENT SCIENTIST SOLUTION FOR PROBLEM 14

```
Objective Function Value =           139.730

      Variable              Value              Reduced Costs
    -------------       --------------       -----------------
         X1                 7.297                 0.000
         X2                 0.000                 0.676
         X3                 1.892                 0.000

      Constraint         Slack/Surplus           Dual Prices
    -------------       --------------       -----------------
          1                20.811                 0.000
          2                 0.000                -3.405
          3                 0.000                -4.432

OBJECTIVE COEFFICIENT RANGES

     Variable        Lower Limit      Current Value      Upper Limit
   ------------     -------------    ---------------    ---------------
         X1              1.333            15.000             15.543
         X2             14.324            15.000        No Upper Limit
         X3             13.500            16.000            180.000

RIGHT HAND SIDE RANGES

    Constraint       Lower Limit      Current Value      Upper Limit
   ------------     -------------    ---------------    ---------------
         1              9.189            30.000        No Upper Limit
         2              3.333            15.000            111.250
         3             -2.500            20.000             90.000
```

15. Refer to the computer solution of Problem 14 in Figure 8.20.
    a. Interpret the objective coefficient ranges.
    b. Suppose the objective function coefficient of x_1 is increased by 0.25. What is the new optimal solution?
    c. Suppose the objective function coefficient of x_1 is increased by 0.25 and the objective function coefficient of x_2 is decreased by 0.25. What is the new optimal solution?

16. Supersport Footballs, Inc., has to determine the best number of All-Pro (A), College (C), and High School (H) models of footballs to produce in order to maximize profits. Constraints include production capacity limitations (time available in minutes) in each of three departments (cutting and dyeing, sewing, and inspection and packaging) as well as a constraint that requires the production of at least 1000 All-Pro footballs. The linear programming model of Supersport's problem is shown here:

$$\text{Max} \quad 3A + 5C + 4H$$

s.t.

$$12A + 10C + 8H \leq 18{,}000 \quad \text{Cutting and dyeing}$$
$$15A + 15C + 12H \leq 18{,}000 \quad \text{Sewing}$$

$$3A + 4C + 2H \le 9,000 \quad \text{Inspection and packaging}$$
$$1A \qquad\qquad \ge 1,000 \quad \text{All-Pro model}$$
$$A, C, H \ge 0$$

The computer solution to the Supersport problem is shown in Figure 8.21.

a. How many footballs of each type should Supersport produce to maximize the total profit contribution?

b. Which constraints are binding?

c. Interpret the slack and/or surplus in each constraint.

d. Interpret the objective coefficient ranges.

17. Refer to the computer solution of Problem 16 (see Figure 8.21).

a. Overtime rates in the sewing department are $12 per hour. Would you recommend that the company consider using overtime in that department? Explain.

b. What is the dual price for the fourth constraint? Interpret its value for management.

FIGURE 8.21   THE MANAGEMENT SCIENTIST SOLUTION FOR THE SUPERSPORT
FOOTBALLS PROBLEM

```
Objective Function Value =          4000.000

        Variable              Value            Reduced Costs
        --------              -----            -------------
           A                1000.000               0.000
           C                 200.000               0.000
           H                   0.000               0.000


        Constraint        Slack/Surplus          Dual Prices
        ----------        -------------          -----------
            1               4000.000               0.000
            2                  0.000               0.333
            3               5200.000               0.000
            4                  0.000              -2.000


OBJECTIVE COEFFICIENT RANGES

      Variable     Lower Limit      Current Value       Upper Limit
      --------     -----------      -------------       -----------
         A        No Lower Limit        3.000              5.000
         C            5.000             5.000         No Upper Limit
         H        No Lower Limit        4.000              4.000


RIGHT HAND SIDE RANGES

     Constraint     Lower Limit      Current Value       Upper Limit
     ----------     -----------      -------------       -----------
         1         14000.000          18000.000       No Upper Limit
         2         15000.000          18000.000          24000.000
         3          3800.000           9000.000       No Upper Limit
         4             0.000           1000.000           1200.000
```

  c. Note that the reduced cost for H, the High-School football, is zero, but H is not in the solution at a positive value. What is your interpretation of this value?

  d. Suppose that the profit contribution of the College ball is increased by $1. How do you expect the solution to change?

18. Adirondack Savings Bank (ASB) has $1,000,000 in new funds that must be allocated to home loans, personal loans, and automobile loans. The annual rates of return for the three types of loans are 7% for home loans, 12% for personal loans, and 9% for automobile loans. The bank's planning committee has decided that at least 40% of the new funds must be allocated to home loans. In addition, the planning committee has specified that the amount allocated to personal loans cannot exceed 60% of the amount allocated to automobile loans.

  a. Formulate a linear programming model that can be used to determine the amount of funds ASB should allocate to each type of loan in order to maximize the total annual return for the new funds.

  b. How much should be allocated to each type of loan? What is the total annual return? What is the annual percentage return?

  c. If the interest rate on home loans increased to 9%, would the amount allocated to each type of loan change? Explain.

  d. Suppose the total amount of new funds available was increased by $10,000. What effect would this have on the total annual return? Explain.

  e. Assume that ASB has the original $1,000,000 in new funds available and that the planning committee has agreed to relax the requirement that at least 40% of the new funds must be allocated to home loans by 1%. How much would the annual return change? How much would the annual percentage return change?

19. Better Products, Inc., manufactures three products on two machines. In a typical week, 40 hours are available on each machine. The profit contribution and production time in hours per unit are as follows:

Category	Product 1	Product 2	Product 3
Profit/unit	$30	$50	$20
Machine 1 time/unit	0.5	2.0	0.75
Machine 2 time/unit	1.0	1.0	0.5

Two operators are required for machine 1; thus, 2 hours of labor must be scheduled for each hour of machine 1 time. Only one operator is required for machine 2. A maximum of 100 labor-hours is available for assignment to the machines during the coming week. Other production requirements are that product 1 cannot account for more than 50% of the units produced and that product 3 must account for at least 20% of the units produced.

  a. How many units of each product should be produced to maximize the total profit contribution? What is the projected weekly profit associated with your solution?

  b. How many hours of production time will be scheduled on each machine?

  c. What is the value of an additional hour of labor?

  d. Assume that labor capacity can be increased to 120 hours. Would you be interested in using the additional 20 hours available for this resource? Develop the optimal product mix assuming the extra hours are made available.

20. Industrial Designs has been awarded a contract to design a label for a new wine produced by Lake View Winery. The company estimates that 150 hours will be required to complete the project. Three of the firm's graphics designers are available for assignment to this project: Lisa, a senior designer and team leader; David, a senior designer; and Sarah, a junior designer. Because Lisa has worked on several projects for Lake View Winery, management has specified that Lisa must be assigned at least 40% of the total number of hours that are assigned to the two senior designers. To provide label-designing experience for Sarah, Sarah must be assigned at least 15% of the total project time. However, the number of hours assigned to Sarah must not exceed 25% of the total number of hours that are assigned to the two senior designers. Due to other project commitments, Lisa has a maximum of 50 hours available to work on this project. Hourly wage rates are $30 for Lisa, $25 for David, and $18 for Sarah.

a. Formulate a linear program that can be used to determine the number of hours each graphic designer should be assigned to the project in order to minimize total cost.

b. How many hours should each graphic designer be assigned to the project? What is the total cost?

c. Suppose Lisa could be assigned more than 50 hours. What effect would this have on the optimal solution? Explain.

d. If Sarah were not required to work a minimum number of hours on this project, would the optimal solution change? Explain.

21. Vollmer Manufacturing makes three components for sale to refrigeration companies. The components are processed on two machines: a shaper and a grinder. The times (in minutes) required on each machine are as follows:

	Machine	
Component	Shaper	Grinder
1	6	4
2	4	5
3	4	2

The shaper is available for 120 hours, and the grinder is available for 110 hours. No more than 200 units of component 3 can be sold, but up to 1000 units of each of the other components can be sold. In fact, the company already has orders for 600 units of component 1 that must be satisfied. The profit contributions for components 1, 2, and 3 are $8, $6, and $9, respectively.

a. Formulate and solve for the recommended production quantities.

b. What are the objective coefficient ranges for the three components? Interpret these ranges for company management.

c. What are the right-hand-side ranges? Interpret these ranges for company management.

d. If more time could be made available on the grinder, how much would it be worth?

e. If more units of component 3 can be sold by reducing the sales price by $4, should the company reduce the price?

22. National Insurance Associates carries an investment portfolio of stocks, bonds, and other investment alternatives. Currently $200,000 of funds are available and must be considered for new investment opportunities. The four stock options National is considering and the relevant financial data are as follows:

	Stock			
	A	B	C	D
Price per share	$100	$50	$80	$40
Annual rate of return	0.12	0.08	0.06	0.10
Risk measure per dollar invested	0.10	0.07	0.05	0.08

The risk measure indicates the relative uncertainty associated with the stock in terms of its realizing the projected annual return; higher values indicate greater risk. The risk measures are provided by the firm's top financial advisor.

National's top management has stipulated the following investment guidelines: the annual rate of return for the portfolio must be at least 9% and no one stock can account for more than 50% of the total dollar investment.

a. Use linear programming to develop an investment portfolio that minimizes risk.
b. If the firm ignores risk and uses a maximum return-on-investment strategy, what is the investment portfolio?
c. What is the dollar difference between the portfolios in parts (a) and (b)? Why might the company prefer the solution developed in part (a)?

23. Georgia Cabinets manufactures kitchen cabinets that are sold to local dealers throughout the Southeast. The company has a large backlog of orders for oak and cherry cabinets and has decided to contract with three smaller cabinetmakers to do the final finishing operation. For the three cabinetmakers, the number of hours required to complete all the oak cabinets, the number of hours required to complete all the cherry cabinets, the number of hours available for the final finishing operation, and the cost per hour to perform the work are shown here.

	Cabinetmaker 1	Cabinetmaker 2	Cabinetmaker 3
Hours required to complete all the oak cabinets	50	42	30
Hours required to complete all the cherry cabinets	60	48	35
Hours available	40	30	35
Cost per hour	$36	$42	$55

For example, Cabinetmaker 1 estimates it will take 50 hours to complete all the oak cabinets and 60 hours to complete all the cherry cabinets. However, Cabinetmaker 1 only has 40 hours available for the final finishing operation. Thus, Cabinetmaker 1 can only complete $40/50 = 0.80$ or 80% of the oak cabinets if it worked only on oak cabinets. Similarly, Cabinetmaker 1 can only complete $40/60 = 0.67$ or 67% of the cherry cabinets if it worked only on cherry cabinets.

a. Formulate a linear programming model that can be used to determine the percentage of the oak cabinets and the percentage of the cherry cabinets that should be given to each of the three cabinetmakers in order to minimize the total cost of completing both projects.
b. Solve the model formulated in part (a). What percentage of the oak cabinets and what percentage of the cherry cabinets should be assigned to each cabinetmaker? What is the total cost of completing both projects?
c. If Cabinetmaker 1 has additional hours available, would the optimal solution change? Explain.
d. If Cabinetmaker 2 has additional hours available, would the optimal solution change? Explain.
e. Suppose Cabinetmaker 2 reduced its cost to $38 per hour. What effect would this change have on the optimal solution? Explain.

24. Benson Electronics manufactures three components used to produce cell telephones and other communication devices. In a given production period, demand for the three components may exceed Benson's manufacturing capacity. In this case, the company meets de-

mand by purchasing the components from another manufacturer at an increased cost per unit. Benson's manufacturing cost per unit and purchasing cost per unit for the three components are as follows:

Source	Component 1	Component 2	Component 3
Manufacture	$4.50	$5.00	$2.75
Purchase	$6.50	$8.80	$7.00

Manufacturing times in minutes per unit for Benson's three departments are as follows:

Department	Component 1	Component 2	Component 3
Production	2	3	4
Assembly	1	1.5	3
Testing & Packaging	1.5	2	5

For instance, each unit of component 1 that Benson manufactures requires 2 minutes of production time, 1 minute of assembly time, and 1.5 minutes of testing and packaging time. For the next production period, Benson has capacities of 360 hours in the production department, 250 hours in the assembly department, and 300 hours in the testing and packaging department.

a. Formulate a linear programming model that can be used to determine how many units of each component to manufacture and how many units of each component to purchase. Assume that component demands that must be satisfied are 6000 units for component 1, 4000 units for component 2, and 3500 units for component 3. The objective is to minimize the total manufacturing and purchasing costs.

b. What is the optimal solution? How many units of each component should be manufactured and how many units of each component should be purchased?

c. Which departments are limiting Benson's manufacturing quantities? Use the dual price to determine the value of an *extra hour* in each of these departments.

d. Suppose that Benson had to obtain one additional unit of component 2. Discuss what the dual price for the component 2 constraint tells us about the cost to obtain the additional unit.

25. Golf Shafts, Inc. (GSI), produces graphite shafts for several manufacturers of golf clubs. Two GSI manufacturing facilities, one located in San Diego and the other in Tampa, have the capability to produce shafts in varying degrees of stiffness, ranging from regular models used primarily by average golfers to extra stiff models used primarily by low-handicap and professional golfers. GSI has just received a contract for the production of 200,000 regular shafts and 75,000 stiff shafts. Because both plants are currently producing shafts for previous orders, neither plant has sufficient capacity by itself to fill the new order. The San Diego plant can produce up to a total of 120,000 shafts and the Tampa plant can produce up to a total of 180,000 shafts. Because of equipment differences at each of the plants and differing labor costs, the per-unit production costs vary as shown here:

	San Diego Cost	Tampa Cost
Regular Shaft	$5.25	$4.95
Stiff Shaft	$5.45	$5.70

    a. Formulate a linear programming model to determine how GSI should schedule production for the new order in order to minimize the total production cost.

    b. Solve the model that you developed in part (a).

    c. Suppose that some of the previous orders at the Tampa plant could be rescheduled in order to free up additional capacity for the new order. Would this option be worthwhile? Explain.

    d. Suppose that the cost to produce a stiff shaft in Tampa had been incorrectly computed, and that the correct cost is $5.30 per shaft. What effect, if any, would this have on the optimal solution developed in part (b)? What effect would this have on total production cost?

26. The Pfeiffer Company manages approximately $15 million for clients. For each client, Pfeiffer chooses a mix of three investment vehicles: a growth stock fund, an income fund, and a money market fund. Each client has different investment objectives and different tolerances for risk. To accommodate these differences, Pfeiffer places limits on the percentage of each portfolio that may be invested in the three funds and assigns a portfolio risk index to each client.

Here's how the system works for Dennis Hartmann, one of Pfeiffer's clients. Based on an evaluation of Hartmann's risk tolerance, Pfeiffer has assigned Hartmann's portfolio a risk index of 0.05. Furthermore, to maintain diversity, the fraction of Hartmann's portfolio invested in the growth and income funds must be at least 10% for each, and at least 20% must be in the money market fund.

The risk ratings for the growth, income, and money market funds are 0.10, 0.05, and 0.01, respectively. A portfolio risk index is computed as a weighted average of the risk ratings for the three funds where the weights are the fraction of the portfolio invested in each of the funds. Hartmann has given Pfeiffer $300,000 to manage. Pfeiffer is currently forecasting a yield of 20% on the growth fund, 10% on the income fund, and 6% on the money market fund.

    a. Develop a linear programming model to select the best mix of investments for Hartmann's portfolio.

    b. Solve the model you developed in part (a).

    c. How much may the yields on the three funds vary before it will be necessary for Pfeiffer to modify Hartmann's portfolio?

    d. If Hartmann were more risk tolerant, how much of a yield increase could he expect? For instance, what if his portfolio risk index is increased to 0.06?

    e. If Pfeiffer revised the yield estimate for the growth fund downward to 0.10, how would you recommend modifying Hartmann's portfolio?

    f. What information must Pfeiffer maintain on each client in order to use this system to manage client portfolios?

    g. On a weekly basis Pfeiffer revises the yield estimates for the three funds. Suppose Pfeiffer has 50 clients. Describe how you would envision Pfeiffer making weekly modifications in each client's portfolio and allocating the total funds managed among the three investment funds.

27. La Jolla Beverage Products is considering producing a wine cooler that would be a blend of a white wine, a rosé wine, and fruit juice. To meet taste specifications, the wine cooler must consist of at least 50% white wine, at least 20% and no more than 30% rosé, and exactly 20% fruit juice. La Jolla purchases the wine from local wineries and the fruit juice from a processing plant in San Francisco. For the current production period, 10,000 gallons of white wine and 8000 gallons of rosé wine can be purchased; an unlimited amount of fruit juice can be ordered. The costs for the wine are $1.00 per gallon for the white and $1.50 per gallon for the rosé; the fruit juice can be purchased for $0.50 per gallon. La Jolla Beverage Products can sell all of the wine cooler they can produce for·$2.50 per gallon.

    a. Is the cost of the wine and fruit juice a sunk cost or a relevant cost in this situation? Explain.

    b. Formulate a linear program to determine the blend of the three ingredients that will maximize the total profit contribution. Solve the linear program to determine the number of gallons of each ingredient La Jolla should purchase and the total profit contribution they will realize from this blend.

c. If La Jolla could obtain additional amounts of the white wine, should they do so? If so, how much should they be willing to pay for each additional gallon, and how many additional gallons would they want to purchase?

d. If La Jolla Beverage Products could obtain additional amounts of the rosé wine, should they do so? If so, how much should they be willing to pay for each additional gallon, and how many additional gallons would they want to purchase?

e. Interpret the dual price for the constraint corresponding to the requirement that the wine cooler must contain at least 50% white wine. What is your advice to management given this dual price?

f. Interpret the dual price for the constraint corresponding to the requirement that the wine cooler must contain exactly 20% fruit juice. What is your advice to management given this dual price?

28. The program manager for Channel 10 would like to determine the best way to allocate the time for the 11:00–11:30 evening news broadcast. Specifically, she would like to determine the number of minutes of broadcast time to devote to local news, national news, weather, and sports. Over the 30-minute broadcast, 10 minutes are set aside for advertising. The station's broadcast policy states that at least 15% of the time available should be devoted to local news coverage; the time devoted to local news or national news must be at least 50% of the total broadcast time; the time devoted to the weather segment must be less than or equal to the time devoted to the sports segment; the time devoted to the sports segment should be no longer than the total time spent on the local and national news; and at least 20% of the time should be devoted to the weather segment. The production costs per minute are $300 for local news, $200 for national news, $100 for weather, and $100 for sports.

a. Formulate and solve a linear program that can determine how the 20 available minutes should be used to minimize the total cost of producing the program.

b. Interpret the dual price for the constraint corresponding to the available time. What advice would you give the station manager given this dual price?

c. Interpret the dual price for the constraint corresponding to the requirement that at least 15% of the available time should be devoted to local coverage. What advice would you give the station manager given this dual price?

d. Interpret the dual price for the constraint corresponding to the requirement that the time devoted to the local and the national news must be at least 50% of the total broadcast time. What advice would you give the station manager given this dual price?

e. Interpret the dual price for the constraint corresponding to the requirement that the time devoted to the weather segment must be less than or equal to the time devoted to the sports segment. What advice would you give the station manager given this dual price?

29. Gulf Coast Electronics is ready to award contracts for printing their annual report. For the past several years, the four-color annual report has been printed by Johnson Printing and Lakeside Litho. A new firm, Benson Printing, has inquired into the possibility of doing a portion of the printing. The quality and service level provided by Lakeside Litho has been extremely high; in fact, only 0.5% of their reports have had to be discarded because of quality problems. Johnson Printing has also had a high quality level historically, producing an average of only 1% unacceptable reports. Because Gulf Coast Electronics has had no experience with Benson Printing, they have estimated their defective rate to be 10%. Gulf Coast would like to determine how many reports should be printed by each firm to obtain 75,000 acceptable-quality reports. To ensure that Benson Printing will receive some of the contract, management has specified that the number of reports awarded to Benson Printing must be at least 10% of the volume given to Johnson Printing. In addition, the total volume assigned to Benson Printing, Johnson Printing, and Lakeside Litho should not exceed 30,000, 50,000, and 50,000 copies, respectively. Because of the long-term relationship that has developed with Lakeside Litho, management has also specified that at least 30,000

reports should be awarded to Lakeside Litho. The cost per copy is $2.45 for Benson Printing, $2.50 for Johnson Printing, and $2.75 for Lakeside Litho.

a. Formulate and solve a linear program for determining how many copies should be assigned to each printing firm to minimize the total cost of obtaining 75,000 acceptable-quality reports.

b. Suppose that the quality level for Benson Printing is much better than estimated. What effect, if any, would this quality level have?

c. Suppose that management is willing to reconsider their requirement that Lakeside Litho be awarded at least 30,000 reports. What effect, if any, would this consideration have?

Case Problem   PRODUCT MIX

TJ's, Inc., makes three nut mixes for sale to grocery chains located in the Southeast. The three mixes, referred to as the Regular Mix, the Deluxe Mix, and the Holiday Mix, are made by mixing different percentages of five types of nuts.

In preparation for the fall season, TJ's has just purchased the following shipments of nuts at the prices shown:

Type of Nut	Shipment Amount (pounds)	Cost per Shipment
Almond	6000	$7500
Brazil	7500	$7125
Filbert	7500	$6750
Pecan	6000	$7200
Walnut	7500	$7875

The Regular Mix consists of 15% almonds, 25% Brazil nuts, 25% filberts, 10% pecans, and 25% walnuts. The Deluxe Mix consists of 20% of each type of nut, and the Holiday Mix consists of 25% almonds, 15% Brazil nuts, 15% filberts, 25% pecans, and 20% walnuts.

TJ's accountant has analyzed the cost of packaging materials, sales price per pound, and so forth, and has determined that the profit contribution per pound is $1.65 for the Regular Mix, $2.00 for the Deluxe Mix, and $2.25 for the Holiday Mix. These figures do not include the cost of specific types of nuts in the different mixes because that cost can vary greatly in the commodity markets.

Customer orders already received are summarized here:

Type of Mix	Orders (pounds)
Regular	10,000
Deluxe	3,000
Holiday	5,000

Because demand is running high, it is expected that TJ's will receive many more orders than can be satisfied.

TJ's is committed to using the available nuts to maximize profit over the fall season; nuts not used will be given to the Free Store. But even if it is not profitable to do so, TJ's president has indicated that the orders already received must be satisfied.

Managerial Report

Perform an analysis of TJ's product mix problem, and prepare a report for TJ's president that summarizes your findings. Be sure to include information and analysis on the following:

1. The cost per pound of the nuts included in the Regular, Deluxe, and Holiday mixes
2. The optimal product mix and the total profit contribution
3. Recommendations regarding how the total profit contribution can be increased if additional quantities of nuts can be purchased
4. A recommendation as to whether TJ's should purchase an additional 1000 pounds of almonds for $1000 from a supplier who overbought
5. Recommendations on how profit contribution could be increased (if at all) if TJ's does not satisfy all existing orders

Case Problem   INVESTMENT STRATEGY

J. D. Williams, Inc., is an investment advisory firm that manages more than $120 million in funds for its numerous clients. The company uses an asset allocation model that recommends the portion of each client's portfolio to be invested in a growth stock fund, an income fund, and a money market fund. To maintain diversity in each client's portfolio, the firm places limits on the percentage of each portfolio that may be invested in each of the three funds. General guidelines indicate that the amount invested in the growth fund must be between 20% and 40% of the total portfolio value. Similar percentages for the other two funds stipulate that between 20% and 50% of the total portfolio value must be in the income fund and at least 30% of the total portfolio value must be in the money market fund.

In addition, the company attempts to assess the risk tolerance of each client and adjust the portfolio to meet the needs of the individual investor. For example, Williams has just contracted with a new client who has $800,000 to invest. Based on an evaluation of the client's risk tolerance, Williams has assigned a maximum risk index of 0.05 for the client. The firm's risk indicators show the risk of the growth fund at 0.10, the income fund at 0.07, and the money market fund at 0.01. An overall portfolio risk index is computed as a weighted average of the risk rating for the three funds where the weights are the fraction of the client's portfolio invested in each of the funds.

Additionally, Williams is currently forecasting annual yields of 18% for the growth fund, 12.5% for the income fund, and 7.5% for the money market fund. Based on the information provided, how should the new client be advised to allocate the $800,000 among the growth, income, and money market funds? Develop a linear programming model that will provide the maximum yield for the portfolio. Use your model to develop a managerial report.

Managerial Report

1. Recommend how much of the $800,000 should be invested in each of the three funds. What is the annual yield you anticipate for the investment recommendation?
2. Assume that the client's risk index could be increased to 0.055. How much would the yield increase and how would the investment recommendation change?
3. Refer again to the original situation where the client's risk index was assessed to be 0.05. How would your investment recommendation change if the annual yield for the growth fund were revised downward to 16% or even to 14%?
4. Assume that the client has expressed some concern about having too much money in the growth fund. How would the original recommendation change if the amount

invested in the growth fund is not allowed to exceed the amount invested in the income fund?
5. The asset allocation model you have developed may be useful in modifying the portfolios for all of the firm's clients whenever the anticipated yields for the three funds are periodically revised. What is your recommendation as to whether use of this model is possible?

Appendix 8.1   SENSITIVITY ANALYSIS WITH SPREADSHEETS

Previously we showed how Excel Solver could be used to solve the RMC problem (Appendix 7.3). In the following appendix we show how Excel can also be used to provide sensitivity analysis information.

Whenever Excel Solver finds the optimal solution to a linear program, the Solver Results dialog box appears on the computer screen (see Figure 8.22). If the solution to the linear program is all that is desired, select **OK.** However, if sensitivity analysis information is desired, the following steps are necessary.

Step 1. Select **Sensitivity** in the **Reports** box
Step 2. Select **OK**

The solution to the RMC problem is shown in Figure 8.23; the accompanying sensitivity report is shown in Figure 8.24.

The Adjustable Cells section of the sensitivity report provides the optimal values of the decision variables. Using the Final Value column, we see that the optimal solution to the RMC problem is 25 tons of fuel additive and 20 tons of solvent base. The Reduced Cost column indicates how much the objective function coefficient of each decision variable would have to improve before that decision variable could have a positive value in the optimal solution. The reduced costs are both zero because both RMC decision variables already have positive values.

In the last three columns we find Objective Coefficient, Allowable Increase, and Allowable Decrease information. The entries in these columns can be used to compute the objective coefficient ranges. For example, the objective function coefficient for the fuel additive is $40. The allowable decrease of $16 per ton provides a lower limit of $40 − $16 = $24, while the allowable increase of $20 provides an upper limit of $40 + $20 = $60. Thus, the objective coefficient range for the fuel additive is $24 to $60. As long as the objective function coefficient is in this range, the optimal solution of 25 tons of fuel additive and

FIGURE 8.22   EXCEL SOLVER RESULTS DIALOG BOX

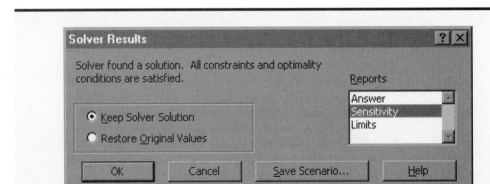

FIGURE 8.23   EXCEL SOLUTION FOR THE RMC PROBLEM

	A	B	C	D
1	**RMC Problem**			
2				
3		**Material Requirements**		
4	**Material**	**Fuel Additive**	**Solvent Base**	**Amount Available**
5	Material 1	0.4	0.5	20
6	Material 2		0.2	5
7	Material 3	0.6	0.3	21
8	**Profit Per Ton**	40	30	
9				
10				
11	**Model**			
12				
13		**Decision Variables**		
14		**Fuel Additive**	**Solvent Base**	
15	**Tons Produced**	25	20	
16				
17	**Maximum Profit**	1600		
18				
19	**Constraints**	**Amount Used (LHS)**		**Amount Available (RHS)**
20	Material 1	20	<=	20
21	Material 2	4	<=	5
22	Material 3	21	<=	21

20 tons of solvent base will not change. Similarly, the allowable decrease of $10 and allowable increase of $20 show that the objective coefficient range for the solvent base is $30 − $10 = $20 to $30 + $20 = $50.

Next, consider the information in the Constraints section of the sensitivity report. The entries in the Final Value column indicate the number of tons of each material required by the optimal solution. Thus, RMC will need 20 tons of material 1, 4 tons of material 2 and 21 tons of material 3 in order to produce the optimal solution of 25 tons of fuel additive and 20 tons of solvent base.

FIGURE 8.24   EXCEL'S SENSITIVITY REPORT FOR THE RMC PROBLEM

Adjustable Cells

Cell	Name	Final Value	Reduced Cost	Objective Coefficient	Allowable Increase	Allowable Decrease
$B$15	Tons Produced Fuel Additive	25	0	40	20	16
$C$15	Tons Produced Solvent Base	20	0	30	20	10

Constraints

Cell	Name	Final Value	Shadow Price	Constraint R.H. Side	Allowable Increase	Allowable Decrease
$B$20	Material 1 Amount Used (LHS)	20	33.33	20	1.5	6
$B$21	Material 2 Amount Used (LHS)	4	0.00	5	1E+30	1
$B$22	Material 3 Amount Used (LHS)	21	44.44	21	9	2.25

The values in the Constraint R.H. Side column are the right-hand sides of the constraints for the RMC problem. The differences between the entries in the Constraint R.H. Side column and the Final Value column provide the values of the slack variables for the RMC problem. Thus, there are $20 - 20 = 0$ tons of slack for material 1, $5 - 4 = 1$ ton of slack for material 2, and $21 - 21 = 0$ tons of slack for material 3.

The entries in the Shadow Price column provide the *change* in the value of the objective function per unit increase in the right-hand side of the constraint. For example, the shadow price for material 1 is $33.33. Thus, the value of the objective function will change from $1600 to $1600 + $33.33 = $1633.33 if one additional ton of material 1 is obtained. Similarly, the shadow price for material 3 is $44.44. Thus, the value of the objective function will change from $1600 to $1600 + $44.44 = $1644.44 if one additional ton of material 3 is obtained. The shadow price of material 2 is $0, which shows that the objective function will not change if one additional ton of material 2 is obtained. Indeed, because a slack of 1 ton of material 2 is already indicated at the optimal solution, an additional ton of material 2 will only add slack and will not change the value of the objective function.

The dual price indicates improvement in the value of the objective function while the shadow price indicates change in the value of the objective function. In minimization problems, the dual price is positive while the shadow price is negative.

Recall that The Management Scientist uses the term *dual price* to describe the *improvement* in the objective function per unit increase in the right-hand side of a constraint. The dual price and shadow price are the same for maximization problems; the *improvement* indicated by the dual price is the same as the positive *change* indicated in the shadow price. However, for minimization problems, the dual price and shadow price have opposite signs. The *improvement* (lower value of the objective function) indicated by a positive dual price differs in sign from the negative *change* indicated by a shadow price to show a decrease in the value of the objective function.

The sensitivity analysis interpretations provided in this appendix are based on the assumption that only one objective function coefficient or only one right-hand side change occurs at a time.

Finally, the last two columns of the Constraints section in Figure 8.24 provide the range information for the right-hand sides. For material 1, the allowable decrease of 6 tons and allowable increase of 1.5 tons show that the right-hand-side range for material 1 constraint is $20 - 6 = 14$ tons to $20 + 1.5 = 21.5$ tons. Thus, if 14 tons to 21.5 tons of material 1 available, the shadow price for material 1 will be $33.33. The allowable increase of $1E + 30$ for material 2 is an extremely large number used to indicate no upper limit for the increase. Thus, as long as at least $5 - 1 = 4$ tons of material 2 are available, the shadow price for material 2 will be $0. Finally, as long as $21 - 2.25 = 18.75$ tons to $21 + 9 = 30$ tons of material 3 are available, the shadow price for material 3 will be $44.44. If any change causes a right-hand side to be outside its corresponding right-hand-side range, the problem must be resolved to find the new optimal solution and the new shadow price.

EASTMAN KODAK*

ROCHESTER, NEW YORK

In 1881 entrepreneur/inventor George Eastman formed the Eastman Dry Plate Company with a vision that it would become a worldwide manufacturer and marketer of photographic goods. Today, Eastman Kodak is a $20-billion enterprise with manufacturing operations on four continents, and customers in more than 150 countries. Headquartered in Rochester, New York, Kodak's imaging products include amateur roll film, photographic paper, medical and industrial X-ray film, motion picture film, and graphic arts materials. In addition, Kodak is a manufacturer of imaging equipment and chemicals.

Quantitative Methods at Kodak

Applications involving quantitative methods at Kodak can be traced back to pioneering efforts in the 1950s. Since then, quantitative methods have been employed to solve a variety of problems involving most of the operational areas of the company. Today, the majority of the applications are conducted by the Management Services Division, while a small group called Distribution Operations Research focuses on applying quantitative analysis to worldwide logistics issues.

Assigning Products to Worldwide Facilities

The sensitizing operation is the heart of the manufacturing process for photographic paper and film. In this operation, a light-sensitive emulsion is coated on a base to produce a sensitized master roll. The sensitized master rolls are then sent to a finishing operation where they are cut into proper dimensions. The sensitizing operation, by virtue of its centrality to the overall process and the peculiarity of the manufacturing technologies required, receives a great deal of managerial attention, both at the operational and strategic levels.

One of Kodak's major planning issues involves the allocation of product to the various sensitizing facilities located throughout the world. The assignment of product to facilities is called the "world load." In determining the world load, Kodak is confronted with a number of interesting trade-offs. For instance, in terms of manufacturing costs, not all sensitizing facilities are equally efficient for all products. Some facilities tend to be more cost efficient over a broad range of products, but the margins by which they are better varies from product to product. However, many product-facility combinations are essentially impossible because of unique product specifications and machine capabilities. Nonetheless, there is a choice of facilities for practically every product.

The product-facility manufacturing costs are only part of the picture. The cheapest place to sensitize a particular product might, for example, be Australia. But, if most of the customers for that product are in Europe, then Australia becomes less favorable because of the high transportation costs involved. Transportation costs are therefore among the costs considered in determining the world load.

Another cost that must be considered involves the duties and duty drawbacks for the various countries throughout the world. Duty drawback is the "forgiving" of duty for a manufacturer who brings a semifinished product into a country, adds value to it, and then ships it out of that country. The effects of duty and duty drawback can significantly affect the allocation decision.

To assist in determining the world load, Kodak developed a linear programming model that accounts for the physical nature of the distribution problem and the various cost elements already described. More specifically, the program's objective is to minimize total cost

*The authors are indebted to Greg Sampson of Eastman Kodak for providing this application.

(manufacturing, transportation, and duties) subject to "natural" constraints such as satisfying demand and capacity constraints for each facility.

Sensitivity Analysis and Interpretation

The linear programming model is a static representation of the problem situation, and the real world is always changing. Thus, Kodak cannot simply solve the linear program and implement the optimal solution; the static linear programming model must be used in a dynamic way. For instance, when demand expectations change, the model can be used to determine the effect the change will have on the world load. Or, suppose that country A and country B tear down duty barriers between them; what effect will it have on the world load? Suppose that the currency of country A rises compared to the currency of country B; how should the world load be modified? These are but a few of the situations of how the world load must be reevaluated based on the impact of external stimuli.

In addition to using the linear programming model in a "how-to-react" mode, the model is useful in a more active mode by considering questions such as the following: Is it worthwhile for facility F to spend D dollars to lower the unit manufacturing cost of product P from X to Y? If such an investment is made, the effect may go well beyond the simple first-order impact at facility F; in fact, it is likely that the change at facility F will result in a reshuffling of the world load. The linear programming model helps evaluate the overall effect of possible changes at any facility.

Managerial Use

The world-load model gives excellent directional advice and integrates the complex interaction of many factors, but many aspects of the world-load problem do not fall neatly into specific cost categories. Although it might be possible to construct a model that would account for almost every aspect of the real-world situation, the time and cost needed to develop it would be prohibitive. Kodak has chosen to use a simpler world-load model; sensitivity analysis is then used to explore many of the questions that management may want to address. In the final analysis, managers recognize that they cannot use the model by simply turning it on, reading the results, and executing the solution. The model's recommendations combined with managerial judgment provide the final decisions and actions for world-load allocation.

Questions

1. What are some of the trade-offs associated with allocating the products to the various sensitizing facilities?
2. What costs are included in the objective function of the world-load model?
3. Briefly describe the role of sensitivity analysis in this application.
4. The world-load model does not account for all issues involved in assigning products to sensitizing facilities. What reason did Kodak have for not addressing *all* the issues, and what implications does this decision have for management?

LINEAR PROGRAMMING APPLICATIONS

CONTENTS

Linear programming has proven to be one of the most successful quantitative approaches to decision making. Applications have been reported in almost every industry. Problems studied include production scheduling, media selection, financial planning, capital budgeting, transportation, distribution system design, product mix, staffing, blending, and many others. As the variety of applications suggests, linear programming is a flexible problem-solving tool. In this chapter we present a variety of applications, including several from the traditional business areas of marketing, finance, and operations management. Modeling, computer solution, and interpretation of output are emphasized.

A mathematical model is developed for each problem studied. These models can be solved using a variety of computer packages including The Management Scientist, LINDO, and Excel Solver. In the chapter, computer solutions obtained using The Management Scientist are presented for most of the applications. The solution output for LINDO is similar; in the chapter appendix we illustrate the use of Excel Solver by solving a financial planning problem.

9.1 MARKETING APPLICATIONS

Applications of linear programming in marketing are numerous. In this section we discuss applications in media selection and marketing research.

Media Selection

In Section 7.1 we provided some general guidelines for modeling linear programming problems. You may want to review Section 7.1 before proceeding with the linear programming applications in this chapter.

Media selection applications of linear programming are designed to help marketing managers allocate a fixed advertising budget to various advertising media. Potential media include newspapers, magazines, radio, television, and direct mail. In these applications, the objective is to maximize reach, frequency, and quality of exposure. Restrictions on the allowable allocation usually arise during consideration of company policy, contract requirements, and media availability. In the application that follows, we illustrate how a media selection problem might be formulated and solved using a linear programming model.

Relax-and-Enjoy Lake Development Corporation is developing a lakeside community at a privately owned lake. The primary market for the lakeside lots and homes includes all middle- and upper-income families within approximately 100 miles of the development. Relax-and-Enjoy has employed the advertising firm of Boone, Phillips, and Jackson (BP&J) to design the promotional campaign.

After considering possible advertising media and the market to be covered, BP&J has recommended that the first month's advertising be restricted to five media. At the end of the month, BP&J will then reevaluate its strategy based on the month's results. BP&J has collected data on the number of potential customers reached, the cost per advertisement, the maximum number of times each medium is available, and the exposure quality rating for each of the five media. The quality rating is measured in terms of an exposure quality unit, a measure of the relative value of one advertisement in each of the media. This measure, based on BP&J's experience in the advertising business, takes into account factors such as audience demographics (age, income, and education of the audience reached), image presented, and quality of the advertisement. The information collected is presented in Table 9.1.

Relax-and-Enjoy provided BP&J with an advertising budget of $30,000 for the first month's campaign. In addition, Relax-and-Enjoy imposed the following restrictions on how BP&J may allocate these funds: At least 10 television commercials must be used, at least 50,000 potential customers must be reached, and no more than $18,000 may be spent on television advertisements. What advertising media selection plan should be recommended?

TABLE 9.1 ADVERTISING MEDIA ALTERNATIVES FOR THE RELAX-AND-ENJOY LAKE DEVELOPMENT CORPORATION

Advertising Media	Number of Potential Customers Reached	Cost ($) per Advertisement	Maximum Times Available per Month*	Exposure Quality Units
1. Daytime TV (1 min), station WKLA	1000	1500	15	65
2. Evening TV (30 sec), station WKLA	2000	3000	10	90
3. Daily newspaper (full page), *The Morning Journal*	1500	400	25	40
4. Sunday newspaper magazine (½ page color), *The Sunday Press*	2500	1000	4	60
5. Radio, 8:00 A.M. or 5:00 P.M. news (30 sec), station KNOP	300	100	30	20

*The maximum number of times the medium is available is either the maximum number of times the advertising medium occurs (e.g., four Sundays per month or the maximum number of times BP&J recommends that the medium be used).

The decision to be made is how many times to use each medium. We begin by defining the decision variables:

$$DTV = \text{number of times daytime TV is used}$$
$$ETV = \text{number of times evening TV is used}$$
$$DN = \text{number of times daily newspaper is used}$$
$$SN = \text{number of times Sunday newspaper is used}$$
$$R = \text{number of times radio is used}$$

The data on quality of exposure in Table 9.1 show that each daytime TV (DTV) advertisement is rated at 65 exposure quality units. Thus, an advertising plan with DTV advertisements will provide a total of $65DTV$ exposure quality units. Continuing with the data in Table 9.1, we find evening TV (ETV) rated at 90 exposure quality units, daily newspaper (DN) rated at 40 exposure quality units, Sunday newspaper (SN) rated at 60 exposure quality units, and radio (R) rated at 20 exposure quality units. With the objective of maximizing the total exposure quality units for the overall media selection plan, the objective function becomes

$$\text{Max} \quad 65DTV + 90ETV + 40DN + 60SN + 20R \qquad \text{Exposure quality}$$

We now formulate the constraints for the model from the information given:

Care must be taken to ensure the linear programming model accurately reflects the real problem. Always review your formulation thoroughly before attempting to solve the model.

$$
\begin{aligned}
DTV & \leq 15 \\
ETV & \leq 10 \\
DN & \leq 25 \\
SN & \leq 4 \\
R & \leq 30
\end{aligned}
\Bigg\} \;
\begin{aligned}
& \text{Availability} \\
& \text{of media}
\end{aligned}
$$

$$1500DTV + 3000ETV + 400DN + 1000SN + 100R \leq 30{,}000 \quad \text{Budget}$$

$$
\begin{aligned}
DTV + ETV & \geq 10 \\
1500DTV + 3000ETV & \leq 18{,}000
\end{aligned}
\Bigg\} \;
\begin{aligned}
& \text{Television} \\
& \text{restrictions}
\end{aligned}
$$

$$1000DTV + 2000ETV + 1500DN + 2500SN + 300R \geq 50{,}000 \quad \text{Customers reached}$$

$$DTV, ETV, DN, SN, R \geq 0$$

Problem 1 provides practice at formulating a similar media selection model.

The computer solution to this five-variable, nine-constraint linear programming model is shown in Figure 9.1; a summary is presented in Table 9.2.

The optimal solution calls for advertisements to be distributed among daytime TV, daily newspaper, Sunday newspaper, and radio. The maximum number of exposure quality units is 2370, and the total number of customers reached is 61,500. The reduced costs column in Figure 9.1 indicates that the number of exposure quality units for evening TV would have to increase by at least 65 before this media alternative could appear in the optimal solution. Note that the budget constraint (constraint 6) has a dual price of 0.060. That is, a $1.00 increase in the advertising budget will lead to an increase of 0.06 exposure quality units. The dual price of -25.000 for constraint 7 indicates that reducing the number of television commercials by 1 will increase the exposure quality of the advertising plan by 25 units. Thus, Relax-and-Enjoy should consider reducing the requirement of having at least 10 television commercials.

More complex media selection models may include considerations such as the reduced exposure quality value for repeat media usage, cost discounts for repeat media usage, audience overlap by different media, and/or timing recommendations for the advertisements.

A possible shortcoming of this model is that, even if the exposure quality measure were not subject to error, it offers no guarantee that maximization of total exposure quality will lead to a maximization of profit or of sales (a common surrogate for profit). However, this issue is not a shortcoming of linear programming; rather, it is a shortcoming of the use of

FIGURE 9.1   THE MANAGEMENT SCIENTIST SOLUTION FOR THE RELAX-AND-ENJOY LAKE
DEVELOPMENT CORPORATION PROBLEM

```
Objective Function Value =           2370.000

        Variable              Value              Reduced Costs
    --------------      ---------------      ------------------
          DTV              10.000                  0.000
          ETV               0.000                 65.000
          DN               25.000                  0.000
          SN                2.000                  0.000
          R                30.000                  0.000


       Constraint       Slack/Surplus           Dual Prices
    --------------      ---------------      ------------------
           1                5.000                  0.000
           2               10.000                  0.000
           3                0.000                 16.000
           4                2.000                  0.000
           5                0.000                 14.000
           6                0.000                  0.060
           7                0.000                -25.000
           8             3000.000                  0.000
           9            11500.003                  0.000
```

Media Availability

Budget

Television Restrictions

Audience Coverage

TABLE 9.2   ADVERTISING PLAN FOR THE RELAX-AND-ENJOY LAKE
DEVELOPMENT CORPORATION

Media	Frequency	Budget
Daytime TV	10	$15,000
Daily newspaper	25	10,000
Sunday newspaper	2	2,000
Radio	30	3,000
		$30,000

Exposure quality units = 2370
Total customers reached = 61,500

exposure quality as a criterion. If we could directly measure the effect of an advertisement on profit, we could use total profit as the objective to be maximized.

Marketing Research

An organization conducts marketing research to learn about consumer characteristics, attitudes, and preferences. Marketing research firms that specialize in providing such information often do the actual research for client organizations. Typical services offered by a marketing research firm include designing the study, conducting market surveys, analyzing the data collected, and providing summary reports and recommendations for the client. In

NOTES AND COMMENTS

1. The media selection model required subjective evaluations of the exposure quality for the media alternatives. Marketing managers may have substantial data concerning exposure quality, but the final coefficients used in the objective function may also include considerations based primarily on managerial judgment. Judgment is an acceptable way of obtaining input for a linear programming model.

2. The media selection model presented in this section uses exposure quality as the objective function and places a constraint on the number of customers reached. An alternative formulation of this problem would be to use the number of customers reached as the objective function and add a constraint indicating the minimum total exposure quality required for the media plan.

---

the research design phase, targets or quotas may be established for the number and types of respondents to be surveyed. The marketing research firm's objective is to conduct the survey so as to meet the client's needs at a minimum cost.

Market Survey, Inc. (MSI), specializes in evaluating consumer reaction to new products, services, and advertising campaigns. A client firm has requested MSI's assistance in ascertaining consumer reaction to a recently marketed household product. During meetings with the client, MSI agreed to conduct door-to-door personal interviews to obtain responses from households with children and households without children. In addition, MSI agreed to conduct both day and evening interviews. Specifically, the client's contract called for MSI to conduct 1000 interviews under the following quota guidelines.

1. Interview at least 400 households with children.
2. Interview at least 400 households without children.
3. The total number of households interviewed during the evening must be at least as great as the number of households interviewed during the day.
4. At least 40% of the interviews for households with children must be conducted during the evening.
5. At least 60% of the interviews for households without children must be conducted during the evening.

Because the interviews for households with children take additional interviewer time and because evening interviewers are paid more than daytime interviewers, the cost varies with the type of interview. Based on previous research studies, estimates of the interview costs are as follows:

Household	Interview Cost	
	Day	Evening
Children	$20	$25
No children	$18	$20

What is the household, time-of-day interview plan that will satisfy the contract requirements at a minimum total interviewing cost?

In formulating the linear programming model for the MSI problem, we utilize the following decision-variable notation:

DC = the number of daytime interviews of households with children

EC = the number of evening interviews of households with children

DNC = the number of daytime interviews of households without children

ENC = the number of evening interviews of households without children

We begin the linear programming model formulation by using the cost-per-interview data to develop the objective function:

$$\text{Min} \quad 20DC + 25EC + 18DNC + 20ENC$$

The constraint requiring a total of 1000 interviews is

$$DC + EC + DNC + ENC = 1000$$

The five specifications concerning the types of interviews are as follows.

- Households with children:

$$DC + EC \geq 400$$

- Households without children:

$$DNC + ENC \geq 400$$

- At least as many evening interviews as day interviews:

$$EC + ENC \geq DC + DNC$$

The usual format for linear programming model formulation and computer input places all decision variables on the left side of the inequality and a constant (possibly zero) on the right side. Thus, we rewrite this constraint as

$$-DC + EC - DNC + ENC \geq 0$$

- At least 40% of interviews of households with children during the evening:

$$EC \geq 0.4(DC + EC) \quad \text{or} \quad -0.4DC + 0.6EC \geq 0$$

- At least 60% of interviews of households without children during the evening:

$$ENC \geq 0.6(DNC + ENC) \quad \text{or} \quad 20.6DNC + 0.4ENC \geq 0$$

When we add the nonnegativity requirements, the four-variable and six-constraint linear programming model becomes

$$\text{Min} \quad 20DC + 25EC + 18DNC + 20ENC$$

s.t.

$DC +$	$EC +$	$DNC +$	ENC	$=$	1000	Total interviews
$DC +$	EC			$\geq$	400	Households with children
		$DNC +$	ENC	$\geq$	400	Households without children
$-DC +$	$EC -$	$DNC +$	ENC	$\geq$	0	Evening interviews
$-0.4DC +$	$0.6EC$			$\geq$	0	Evening interviews in households with children
		$-0.6DNC +$	$0.4ENC$	$\geq$	0	Evening interviews in households without children

$$DC, EC, DNC, ENC \geq 0$$

The computer solution for this linear program is shown in Figure 9.2. The solution reveals that the minimum cost of $20,320 occurs with the following interview schedule.

Household	Number of Interviews		
	Day	Evening	Totals
Children	240	160	400
No children	240	360	600
Totals	480	520	1000

Hence, 480 interviews will be scheduled during the day and 520 during the evening. Households with children will be covered by 400 interviews, and households without children will be covered by 600 interviews.

Selected sensitivity analysis information from Figure 9.2 shows a dual price of −19.200 for constraint 1. In other words, the value of the optimal solution will get worse (the total interviewing cost will increase) by $19.20 if the number of interviews is increased from 1000 to 1001. Thus, $19.20 is the incremental cost of obtaining additional interviews. It also is the savings that could be realized by reducing the number of interviews from 1000 to 999.

The surplus variable, with a value of 200.000, for constraint 3 shows that 200 more households without children will be interviewed than required. Similarly, the surplus variable, with a value of 40.000, for constraint 4 shows that the number of evening interviews exceeds the number of daytime interviews by 40. The zero values for the surplus variables in constraints 5 and 6 indicate that the more expensive evening interviews are being held at a minimum. Indeed, the dual price of −5.000 for constraint 5 indicates that if one more household (with children) than the minimum requirement must be interviewed during the evening, the total interviewing cost will go up by $5.00. Similarly, constraint 6 shows that

FIGURE 9.2   THE MANAGEMENT SCIENTIST SOLUTION FOR THE MARKET
SURVEY PROBLEM

```
Objective Function Value =           20320.000

       Variable              Value             Reduced Costs
    --------------      --------------      -----------------
          DC                240.000               0.000
          EC                160.000               0.000
          DNC               240.000               0.000
          ENC               360.000               0.000

     Constraint         Slack/Surplus           Dual Prices
    --------------      --------------      -----------------
          1                  0.000               -19.200
          2                  0.000                -2.800
          3                200.000                 0.000
          4                 40.000                 0.000
          5                  0.000                -5.000
          6                  0.000                -2.000
```

requiring one more household (without children) to be interviewed during the evening will increase costs by $2.00.

9.2   FINANCIAL APPLICATIONS

In finance, linear programming has been applied in problem situations involving capital budgeting, make-or-buy decisions, asset allocation, portfolio selection, financial planning, and many more. In this section, we describe a portfolio selection problem and a problem involving funding of an early retirement program.

Portfolio Selection

Portfolio selection problems involve situations in which a financial manager must select specific investments—for example, stocks and bonds—from a variety of investment alternatives. Managers of mutual funds, credit unions, insurance companies, and banks frequently encounter this type of problem. The objective function for portfolio selection problems usually is maximization of expected return or minimization of risk. The constraints usually take the form of restrictions on the type of permissible investments, state laws, company policy, maximum permissible risk, and so on. Problems of this type have been formulated and solved using a variety of mathematical programming techniques. In this section we formulate and solve a portfolio selection problem as a linear program.

Consider the case of Welte Mutual Funds, Inc., located in New York City. Welte has just obtained $100,000 by converting industrial bonds to cash and is now looking for other investment opportunities for these funds. Based on Welte's current investments, the firm's top financial analyst recommends that all new investments be made in the oil industry, steel industry, or in government bonds. Specifically, the analyst has identified five investment opportunities and projected their annual rates of return. The investments and rates of return are shown in Table 9.3.

Management of Welte has imposed the following investment guidelines.

1. Neither industry (oil or steel) should receive more than $50,000.
2. Government bonds should be at least 25% of the steel industry investments.
3. The investment in Pacific Oil, the high-return but high-risk investment, cannot be more than 60% of the total oil industry investment.

What portfolio recommendations—investments and amounts—should be made for the available $100,000? Given the objective of maximizing projected return subject to the budgetary and managerially imposed constraints, we can answer this question by formulating and solving a linear programming model of the problem. The solution will provide investment recommendations for the management of Welte Mutual Funds.

TABLE 9.3   INVESTMENT OPPORTUNITIES FOR WELTE MUTUAL FUNDS

Investment	Projected Rate of Return (%)
Atlantic Oil	7.3
Pacific Oil	10.3
Midwest Steel	6.4
Huber Steel	7.5
Government bonds	4.5

Let

$$A = \text{dollars invested in Atlantic Oil}$$
$$P = \text{dollars invested in Pacific Oil}$$
$$M = \text{dollars invested in Midwest Steel}$$
$$H = \text{dollars invested in Huber Steel}$$
$$G = \text{dollars invested in government bonds}$$

Using the projected rates of return shown in Table 9.3, we write the objective function for maximizing the total return for the portfolio as

$$\text{Max} \quad 0.073A + 0.103P + 0.064M + 0.075H + 0.045G$$

The constraint specifying investment of the available $100,000 is

$$A + P + M + H + G = 100,000$$

The requirements that neither the oil nor the steel industry should receive more than $50,000 are

$$A + P \le 50,000$$
$$M + H \le 50,000$$

The requirement that government bonds be at least 25% of the steel industry investment is expressed as

$$G \ge 0.25(M + H) \quad \text{or} \quad -0.25M - 0.25H + G \ge 0$$

Finally, the constraint that Pacific Oil cannot be more than 60% of the total oil industry investment is

$$P \le 0.60(A + P) \quad \text{or} \quad -0.60A + 0.40P \le 0$$

By adding the nonnegativity restrictions, we obtain the complete linear programming model for the Welte Mutual Fund investment problem:

Max $0.073A + 0.103P + 0.064M + 0.075H + 0.045G$

s.t.

$A +$	$P +$	$M +$	$H +$	$G =$	100,000	Available funds
$A +$	P			$\le$	50,000	Oil industry maximum
		$M +$	H	$\le$	50,000	Steel industry maximum
		$-\ 0.25M -$	$0.25H +$	$G \ge$	0	Government bonds maximum
$-\ 0.6A +$	$0.4P$			$\le$	0	Pacific Oil restriction

$$A, P, M, H, G \ge 0$$

FIGURE 9.3 THE MANAGEMENT SCIENTIST SOLUTION FOR THE WELTE MUTUAL
FUNDS PROBLEM

```
Objective Function Value =            8000.000

        Variable              Value              Reduced Costs
      -------------       ---------------      -------------------
           A               20000.000                 0.000
           P               30000.000                 0.000
           M                   0.000                 0.011
           H               40000.000                 0.000
           G               10000.000                 0.000


       Constraint         Slack/Surplus            Dual Prices
      -------------       ---------------      -------------------
           1                   0.000                 0.069
           2                   0.000                 0.022
           3               10000.000                 0.000
           4                   0.000                -0.024
           5                   0.000                 0.030
```

We solved this problem using The Management Scientist; the output is shown in Figure 9.3. Table 9.4 shows how the funds are divided among the securities. Note that the optimal solution indicates that the portfolio should be diversified among all the investment opportunities except Midwest Steel. The projected annual return for this portfolio is $8000, which is an overall return of 8%.

The computer printout shows the dual price for constraint 3 is zero. The reason is that the steel industry maximum isn't a binding constraint; increases in the steel industry limit of $50,000 will not improve the value of the optimal solution. Indeed, the slack variable for this constraint shows that the current steel industry investment is $10,000 below its limit of $50,000. The dual prices for the other constraints are nonzero, indicating that these constraints are binding.

The dual price of 0.069 for constraint 1 shows that the value of the optimal solution can be increased by 0.069 if one more dollar can be made available for the portfolio investment.

TABLE 9.4 OPTIMAL PORTFOLIO SELECTION FOR WELTE MUTUAL FUNDS

Investment	Amount	Expected Annual Return
Atlantic Oil	$ 20,000	$1,460
Pacific Oil	30,000	3,090
Huber Steel	40,000	3,000
Government bonds	10,000	450
Totals	$100,000	$8,000

Expected annual return of $8,000
Overall rate of return = 8%

The dual price for the available funds constraint provides information on the rate of return from additional investment funds.

If more funds can be obtained at a cost of less than 6.9%, management should consider obtaining them. However, if a return in excess of 6.9% can be obtained by investing funds elsewhere (other than in these five securities), management should question the wisdom of investing the entire $100,000 in this portfolio.

Similar interpretations can be given to the other dual prices. Note that the dual price for constraint 4 is negative at -0.024. This result indicates that increasing the value on the right-hand side of the constraint by one unit can be expected to worsen the value of the optimal solution by 0.024. That is, in terms of the optimal portfolio, if Welte invests one more dollar in government bonds (beyond the minimum requirement), the total return will decrease by $0.024. To see why this decrease occurs, note again from the dual price for constraint 1 that the marginal return on the funds invested in the portfolio is 6.9% (the average return is 8%). The rate of return on government bonds is 4.5%. Thus, the cost of investing one more dollar in government bonds is the difference between the marginal return on the portfolio and the marginal return on government bonds: $6.9\% - 4.5\% = 2.4\%$.

Practice formulating a variation of the Welte problem by working Problem 9.

Note that the optimal solution shows that Midwest Steel should not be included in the portfolio ($M = 0$). The associated reduced cost for M of 0.011 tells us that the objective function coefficient for Midwest Steel would have to increase by 0.011 before considering the Midwest Steel investment alternative would be advisable. With such an increase the Midwest Steel return would be $0.064 + 0.011 = 0.075$, making this investment just as desirable as the currently used Huber Steel investment alternative.

Finally, a simple modification of the Welte linear programming model permits determining the fraction of available funds invested in each security. That is, we divide each of the right-hand-side values by 100,000. Then the optimal values for the variables will give the fraction of funds that should be invested in each security for a portfolio of any size.

Financial Planning

Linear programming has been used for a variety of financial planning applications. The Q.M. in Action: Using Linear Programming for Optimal Lease Structuring describes how GE Capital used linear programming to optimize the structure of a leveraged lease.

Hewlitt Corporation has established an early retirement program as part of its corporate restructuring. At the close of the voluntary sign-up period, 68 employees had elected early retirement. As a result of these early retirements, the company has incurred the

NOTES AND COMMENTS

1. The optimal solution to the Welte Mutual Funds problem indicates that $20,000 is to be spent on the Atlantic Oil stock. If Atlantic Oil sells for $75 per share, we would have to purchase exactly $266\frac{2}{3}$ shares in order to spend exactly $20,000. The difficulty of purchasing fractional shares is usually handled by purchasing the largest possible integer number of shares with the allotted funds (e.g., 266 shares of Atlantic Oil). This approach guarantees that the budget constraint will not be violated. This approach, of course, introduces the possibility that the solution will no longer be optimal, but the danger is slight if a large number of securities are involved. In cases where the analyst believes that the decision variables *must* have integer values, the problem must be formulated as an integer linear programming model. Integer linear programming is the topic of Chapter 11.

2. Financial portfolio theory stresses obtaining a proper balance between risk and return. In the Welte problem, we explicitly considered return in the objective function. Risk is controlled by choosing constraints that ensure diversity among oil and steel stocks and a balance between government bonds and the steel industry investment.

USING LINEAR PROGRAMMING FOR OPTIMAL LEASE STRUCTURING*

GE Capital is a $70-billion subsidiary of General Electric. As one of the nation's largest and most diverse financial services companies, GE Capital arranges leases in both domestic and international markets, including leases for telecommunications; data processing; construction; and fleets of cars, trucks, and commercial aircraft. To help allocate and schedule the rental and debt payments of a leveraged lease, GE Capital analysts have developed an optimization model, which is available as an optional component of the company's lease analysis proprietary software.

Leveraged leases are designed to provide financing for assets with economic lives of at least five years, which require large capital outlays. A leveraged lease represents an agreement among the lessor (the owner of the asset), the lessee (the user of the asset), and the lender who provides a nonrecourse loan of 50% to 80% of the lessor's purchase price. In a nonrecourse loan, the lenders cannot turn to the lessor for repayment in the event of default. As the lessor in such arrangements, GE Capital is able to claim ownership and realize income tax benefits such as depreciation and interest deductions. These deductions usually produce tax losses during the early years of the lease, which reduces the total tax liability. Approximately 85% of

all financial leases in the United States are leveraged leases.

In its simplest form, the leveraged lease structuring problem can be formulated as a linear program. The linear program models the after-tax cash flow for the lessor, taking into consideration rental receipts, borrowing and repaying of the loan, and income taxes. Constraints are formulated to ensure compliance with IRS guidelines and to enable customizing of leases to meet lessee and lessor requirements. The objective function can be entered in a custom fashion or selected from a predefined list. Typically, the objective is to minimize the lessee's cost, expressed as the net present value of rental payments, or to maximize the lessor's after-tax yield.

GE Capital developed an optimization approach that could be applied to single-investor lease structuring. In a study with the department most involved with these transactions, the optimization approach yielded substantial benefits. The approach has helped GE Capital win some single-investor transactions ranging in size from $1 million to $20 million.

*Based on C. J. Litty, "Optimal Lease Structuring at GE Capital," *Interfaces* (May–June 1994): 34–45.

---

following obligations over the next 8 years. Cash requirements (in $000s) are due at the beginning of each year.

Year	1	2	3	4	5	6	7	8
Cash Requirement	430	210	222	231	240	195	225	255

The corporate treasurer must determine how much money must be set aside today to meet the eight yearly financial obligations as they come due. The financing plan for the retirement program includes investments in government bonds as well as savings. The investments in government bonds are limited to three choices:

Bond	Price	Rate	Years to Maturity
1	$1150	8.875	5
2	1000	5.500	6
3	1350	11.750	7

The government bonds have a par value of $1000, which means that even with different prices each bond pays $1000 at maturity. The rates shown are based on the par value. For purposes of planning, the treasurer has assumed that any funds not invested in bonds will be placed in savings and earn interest at an annual rate of 4%.

We define the decision variables as follows:

F = total dollars required to meet the retirement plan's 8-year obligation

B_1 = units of bond 1 purchased at the beginning of year 1

B_2 = units of bond 2 purchased at the beginning of year 1

B_3 = units of bond 3 purchased at the beginning of year 1

S_i = amount placed in savings at the beginning of the year i for $i = 1, \ldots, 8$

The objective function is to minimize the total dollars needed to meet the retirement plan's 8-year obligation, or

$$\text{Min}\quad F$$

A key feature of this type of financial planning problem is that a constraint must be formulated for each year of the planning horizon. In general, each constraint takes the form:

$$\begin{pmatrix} \text{Funds available at} \\ \text{the beginning of the year} \end{pmatrix} - \begin{pmatrix} \text{Funds invested in bonds} \\ \text{and placed in savings} \end{pmatrix} = \begin{pmatrix} \text{Cash obligation for} \\ \text{the current year} \end{pmatrix}$$

The funds available at the beginning of year 1 is given by F. With a current price of $1150 for bond 1 and investments expressed in thousands of dollars, the total investment for B_1 units of bond 1 would be $1.15B_1$. Similarly, the total investment in bonds 2 and 3 would be $1B_2$ and $1.35B_3$, respectively. The investment in savings for year 1 is S_1. Using these results and the first-year obligation of 430, we obtain the constraint for year 1:

$$F - 1.15B_1 - 1B_2 - 1.35B_3 - S_1 = 430 \quad \text{Year 1}$$

We do not consider future investments in bonds because the future price of bonds depends on interest rates and cannot be known in advance.

Investments in bonds can take place only in this first year, and the bonds will be held until maturity.

The funds available at the beginning of year 2 include the investment returns of 8.875% on the par value of bond 1, 5.5% on the par value of bond 2, 11.75% on the par value of bond 3, and 4% on savings. The new amount to be invested in savings for year 2 is S_2. With an obligation of 210, the constraint for year 2 is

$$0.08875B_1 + 0.055B_2 + 0.1175B_3 + 1.04S_1 - S_2 = 210 \quad \text{Year 2}$$

Similarly, the constraints for years 3 to 8 are

$$0.08875B_1 + 0.055B_2 + 0.1175B_3 + 1.04S_2 - S_3 = 222 \quad \text{Year 3}$$
$$0.08875B_1 + 0.055B_2 + 0.1175B_3 + 1.04S_3 - S_4 = 231 \quad \text{Year 4}$$
$$0.08875B_1 + 0.055B_2 + 0.1175B_3 + 1.04S_4 - S_5 = 240 \quad \text{Year 5}$$
$$1.08875B_1 + 0.055B_2 + 0.1175B_3 + 1.04S_5 - S_6 = 195 \quad \text{Year 6}$$
$$1.055B_2 + 0.1175B_3 + 1.04S_6 - S_7 = 225 \quad \text{Year 7}$$
$$1.1175B_3 + 1.04S_7 - S_8 = 255 \quad \text{Year 8}$$

Note that the constraint for year 6 shows that funds available from bond 1 are $1.08875B_1$. The coefficient of 1.08875 reflects the fact that bond 1 matures at the end of year 5. As a result, the par value plus the interest from bond 1 during year 5 is available at the beginning of year 6. Also, because bond 1 matures in year 5 and becomes available for use at the beginning of year 6, the variable B_1 does not appear in the constraints for years 7 and 8. Note the similar interpretation for bond 2, which matures at the end of year 6 and has the par value plus interest available at the beginning of year 7. In addition, bond 3 matures at the end of year 7 and has the par value plus interest available at the beginning of year 8.

Finally, note that a variable S_8 appears in the constraint for year 8. The retirement fund obligation will be completed at the beginning of year 8, so we anticipate that S_8 will be zero and no funds will be put into savings. However, the formulation includes S_8 in the event that the bond income plus interest from the savings in year 7 exceed the 255 cash requirement for year 8. Thus, S_8 is a surplus variable that shows any funds remaining after the 8-year cash requirements have been satisfied.

The solution to the 12 variable, 8 constraint linear program is shown in Figure 9.4. With an objective function value of 1728.79385, the total investment required to meet the retirement plan's 8-year obligation is $1,728,794. Using the current prices of $1150, $1000, and $1350 for each of the bonds respectively, we can summarize the initial investments in the three bonds as follows:

Bond	Units Purchased	Investment Amount
1	$B_1 = 144.988$	$1150(144.988) = $166,736
2	$B_2 = 187.856$	$1000(187.856) = $187,856
3	$B_3 = 228.188$	$1350(228.188) = $308,054

The solution also shows that $636,148 (see S_1) will be placed in savings at the beginning of the first year. By starting with $1,728,794, the company can make the specified bond and savings investments and have enough left over to meet the retirement program's first-year cash requirement of $430,000.

The optimal solution in Figure 9.4 shows that the decision variables S_1, S_2, S_3, and S_4 all are greater than zero, indicating investments in savings are required in each of the first four years. However, interest from the bonds plus the bond maturity incomes will be sufficient to cover the retirement program's cash requirements in years 5 through 8.

In this application, the dual price can be thought of as the negative of the present value of each dollar in the cash requirement. For example, each dollar that must be paid in year 8 has a present value of $0.67084.

The dual prices have an interesting interpretation in this application. Each right-hand-side value corresponds to the payment that must be made in that year. Note that the dual prices are negative, indicating that reducing the payment in any year would be beneficial because the total funds required for the retirement program's obligation would be less. Also note that the dual prices show that reductions are more beneficial in the early years, with decreasing benefits in subsequent years. As a result, Hewlitt would benefit by reducing cash requirements in the early years even if it had to make equivalently larger cash payments in later years.

NOTES AND COMMENTS

1. The optimal solution for the Hewlitt Corporation problem shows fractional numbers of government bonds at 144.988, 187.856, and 228.188 units, respectively. However, fractional bond units usually are not available. If we were conservative and rounded up to 145, 188, and 229 units, respectively, the total funds required for the 8-year retirement program obligation would be approximately $1254 more than the total funds indicated by the objective function. Because of the magnitude of the funds involved, rounding up probably would provide a workable solution. If an optimal integer solution were required, the methods of integer linear programming covered in Chapter 11 would have to be used.

2. We implicitly assumed that interest from the government bonds is paid annually. Investments such as treasury notes actually provide interest payments every 6 months. In such cases, the model can be reformulated with 6-month periods, with interest and/or cash payments occurring every 6 months.

FIGURE 9.4   THE MANAGEMENT SCIENTIST SOLUTION FOR THE HEWLITT
CORPORATION CASH REQUIREMENTS PROBLEM

```
Objective Function Value =            1728.79385

      Variable              Value            Reduced Costs
   --------------      ---------------     ------------------
         F               1728.79385            0.00000
         B1               144.98815            0.00000
         B2               187.85585            0.00000
         B3               228.18792            0.00000
         S1               636.14794            0.00000
         S2               501.60571            0.00000
         S3               349.68179            0.00000
         S4               182.68091            0.00000
         S5                 0.00000            0.06403
         S6                 0.00000            0.01261
         S7                 0.00000            0.02132
         S8                 0.00000            0.67084


    Constraint          Slack/Surplus          Dual Prices
   --------------      ---------------     ------------------
         1                 0.00000              -1.00000
         2                 0.00000              -0.96154
         3                 0.00000              -0.92456
         4                 0.00000              -0.88900
         5                 0.00000              -0.85480
         6                 0.00000              -0.76036
         7                 0.00000              -0.71899
         8                 0.00000              -0.67084
```

9.3   PRODUCTION MANAGEMENT APPLICATIONS

Many linear programming applications have been developed for production and operations
management, including scheduling, staffing, inventory control, and capacity planning. In
this section we describe examples with make-or-buy decisions, production scheduling, and
workforce assignments.

A Make-or-Buy Decision

We illustrate the use of a linear programming model to determine how much of each of several component parts a company should manufacture and how much it should purchase
from an outside supplier. Such a decision is referred to as a make-or-buy decision.

The Janders Company markets various business and engineering products. Currently,
Janders is preparing to introduce two new calculators: one for the business market called
the Financial Manager and one for the engineering market called the Technician. Each calculator has three components: a base, an electronic cartridge, and a face plate or top. The
same base is used for both calculators, but the cartridges and tops are different. All components can be manufactured by the company or purchased from outside suppliers. The manufacturing costs and purchase prices for the components are summarized in Table 9.5.

TABLE 9.5   MANUFACTURING COSTS AND PURCHASE PRICES FOR JANDERS CALCULATOR COMPONENTS

Component	Cost per Unit Manufacture (regular time)	Purchase
Base	$0.50	$0.60
Financial cartridge	3.75	4.00
Technician cartridge	3.30	3.90
Financial top	0.60	0.65
Technician top	0.75	0.78

Janders' forecasters indicate that 3000 Financial Manager calculators and 2000 Technician calculators will be needed. However, manufacturing capacity is limited. The company has 200 hours of regular manufacturing time and 50 hours of overtime that can be scheduled for the calculators. Overtime involves a premium at the additional cost of $9 per hour. Table 9.6 shows manufacturing times (in minutes) for the components.

The problem for Janders is to determine how many units of each component to manufacture and how many units of each component to purchase. We define the decision variables as follows:

$$BM = \text{number of bases manufactured}$$
$$BP = \text{number of bases purchased}$$
$$FCM = \text{number of Financial cartridges manufactured}$$
$$FCP = \text{number of Financial cartridges purchased}$$
$$TCM = \text{number of Technician cartridges manufactured}$$
$$TCP = \text{number of Technician cartridges purchased}$$
$$FTM = \text{number of Financial tops manufactured}$$
$$FTP = \text{number of Financial tops purchased}$$
$$TTM = \text{number of Technician tops manufactured}$$
$$TTP = \text{number of Technician tops purchased}$$

One additional decision variable is needed to determine the hours of overtime that must be scheduled:

$$OT = \text{number of hours of overtime to be scheduled}$$

TABLE 9.6   MANUFACTURING TIMES IN MINUTES PER UNIT FOR JANDERS CALCULATOR COMPONENTS

Component	Manufacturing Time
Base	1.0
Financial cartridge	3.0
Technician cartridge	2.5
Financial top	1.0
Technician top	1.5

The objective function is to minimize the total cost, including manufacturing costs, purchase costs, and overtime costs. Using the cost-per-unit data in Table 9.5 and the overtime premium cost rate of $9 per hour, we write the objective function as

$$\text{Min} \quad 0.5BM + 0.6BP + 3.75FCM + 4FCP + 3.3TCM + 3.9TCP + 0.6FTM$$
$$+ 0.65FTP + 0.75TTM + 0.78TTP + 9OT$$

The first five constraints specify the number of each component needed to satisfy the demand for 3000 Financial Manager calculators and 2000 Technician calculators. A total of 5000 base components are needed, with the number of other components depending on the demand for the particular calculator. The five demand constraints are

$$\begin{aligned}
BM + BP &= 5000 & \text{Bases} \\
FCM + FCP &= 3000 & \text{Financial cartridges} \\
TCM + TCP &= 2000 & \text{Technician cartridges} \\
FTM + FTP &= 3000 & \text{Financial tops} \\
TTM + TTP &= 2000 & \text{Technician tops}
\end{aligned}$$

Two constraints are needed to guarantee that manufacturing capacities for regular time and overtime cannot be exceeded. The first constraint limits overtime capacity to 50 hours, or

$$OT \leq 50$$

The same units of measure must be used for both the left-hand side and right-hand side of the constraint. In this case, minutes are used.

The second constraint states that the total manufacturing time required for all components must be less than or equal to the total manufacturing capacity, including regular time plus overtime. The manufacturing times for the components are expressed in minutes so we state the total manufacturing capacity constraint in minutes, with the 200 hours of regular time capacity becoming $60(200) = 12,000$ minutes. The actual overtime required is unknown at this point, so we write the overtime as $60OT$ minutes. Using the manufacturing times from Table 9.6, we have

$$BM + 3FCM + 2.5TCM + FTM + 1.5TTM \leq 12,000 + 60OT$$

Moving the decision variable for overtime to the left-hand side of the constraint provides the manufacturing capacity constraint:

$$BM + 3FCM + 2.5TCM + FTM + 1.5TTM - 60OT \leq 12,000$$

The complete formulation of Janders' make-or-buy problem with all decision variables greater than or equal to zero is

$$\text{Min} \quad 0.5BM + 0.6BP + 3.75FCM + 4FCP + 3.3TCM + 3.9TCP$$
$$+ 0.6FTM + 0.65FTP + 0.75TTM + 0.78TTP + 9OT$$

s.t.

BM				$+ BP =$	5000	Bases
	FCM			$+ FCP =$	3000	Financial cartridges
		TCM		$+ TCP =$	2000	Technician cartridges
			FTM	$+ FTP =$	3000	Financial tops
			$TTM +$	$TTP =$	2000	Technician tops
				$OT \leq$	50	Overtime hours
$BM + 3FCM + 2.5TCM + FTM + 1.5TTM - 60OT \leq 12,000$						Manufacturing capacity

The computer solution to this 11-variable, 7-constraint linear program is shown in Figure 9.5. The optimal solution indicates that all 5000 bases (BM), 667 Financial Manager cartridges (FCM), and 2000 Technician cartridges (TCM) should be manufactured. The remaining 2333 Financial Manager cartridges (FCP), all the Financial Manager tops (FTP), and all Technician tops (TTP) should be purchased. No overtime manufacturing is necessary, and the total cost associated with the optimal make-or-buy plan is $24,443.33.

Try Problem 12 for practice with a variation of the Janders make-or-buy problem.

Sensitivity analysis provides some additional information about the unused overtime capacity. The Reduced Costs column shows that the overtime (OT) premium would have to decrease by $4 per hour before overtime production should be considered. That is, if the overtime premium is $9 − $4 = $5 or less, Janders may want to replace some of the purchased components with components manufactured on overtime. Problem 12 at the end of the chapter asks you to reconsider the Janders problem with a lower overtime premium to show how the optimal make-or-buy solution changes.

The dual price for the manufacturing capacity constraint 7 is 0.083. This price indicates that an additional hour of manufacturing capacity is worth $0.083 per minute or ($0.083)(60) = $5 per hour. The right-hand-side range for constraint 7 shows that this conclusion is valid until the amount of regular time increases to 19,000 minutes, or 316.7 hours.

Sensitivity analysis also indicates that a change in prices charged by the outside suppliers can affect the optimal solution. For instance, the objective coefficient range for BP is 0.583 to no upper limit. If the purchase price for bases remains at $0.583 or more, the number of bases purchased (BP) will remain at zero. However, if the purchase price drops below $0.583, Janders should begin to purchase rather than manufacture the base component. Similar sensitivity analysis conclusions about the purchase price ranges can be drawn for the other components.

NOTES AND COMMENTS

The proper interpretation of the dual price for manufacturing capacity (constraint 7) in the Janders problem is that an additional hour of manufacturing capacity is worth ($0.083)(60) = $5 per hour. Thus, the company should be willing to pay a premium of $5 per hour over and above the current regular time cost per hour, which is already included in the manufacturing cost of the product. Thus, if the regular time cost is $18 per hour, Janders should be willing to pay up to $18 + $5 = $23 per hour to obtain additional labor capacity.

Production Scheduling

One of the most important applications of linear programming deals with multiperiod planning such as production scheduling. The solution to a production scheduling problem enables the manager to establish an efficient low-cost production schedule for one or more products over several time periods (weeks or months). Essentially, a production scheduling problem can be viewed as a product-mix problem for each of several periods in the future. The manager must determine the production levels that will allow the company to meet product demand requirements, given limitations on production capacity, labor capacity, and storage space, while minimizing total production costs.

One advantage of using linear programming for production scheduling problems is that they recur. A production schedule must be established for the current month, then again for the next month, for the month after that, and so on. When looking at the problem each month, the production manager will find that, although demand for the products has changed, production times, production capacities, storage space limitations, and so on are roughly the same. Thus, the production manager is basically resolving the same problem handled in

```
Objective Function Value =          24443.333

        Variable              Value            Reduced Costs
       ----------          ------------        -------------
          BM                5000.000               0.000
          BP                   0.000               0.017
          FCM                666.667               0.000
          FCP               2333.333               0.000
          TCM               2000.000               0.000
          TCP                  0.000               0.392
          FTM                  0.000               0.033
          FTP               3000.000               0.000
          TTM                  0.000               0.095
          TTP               2000.000               0.000
          OT                   0.000               4.000


        Constraint       Slack/Surplus          Dual Prices
       ------------      -------------        ---------------
           1                 0.000               -0.583
           2                 0.000               -4.000
           3                 0.000               -3.508
           4                 0.000               -0.650
           5                 0.000               -0.780
           6                50.000                0.000
           7                 0.000                0.083


OBJECTIVE COEFFICIENT RANGES

Variable        Lower Limit       Current Value       Upper Limit
--------       -------------      -------------      -------------
   BM          No Lower Limit         0.500               0.517
   BP               0.583             0.600          No Upper Limit
   FCM              3.700             3.750               3.850
   FCP              3.900             4.000               4.050
   TCM          No Lower Limit        3.300               3.692
   TCP              3.508             3.900          No Upper Limit
   FTM              0.567             0.600          No Upper Limit
   FTP          No Lower Limit        0.650               0.683
   TTM              0.655             0.750          No Upper Limit
   TTP          No Lower Limit        0.780               0.875
   OT               5.000             9.000          No Upper Limit


RIGHT HAND SIDE RANGES

Constraint      Lower Limit       Current Value       Upper Limit
----------     -------------      -------------      -------------
    1               0.000           5000.000            7000.000
    2             666.667           3000.000        No Upper Limit
    3               0.000           2000.000            2800.000
    4               0.000           3000.000        No Upper Limit
    5               0.000           2000.000        No Upper Limit
    6               0.000             50.000        No Upper Limit
    7           10000.000          12000.000           19000.000
```

previous months, and a general linear programming model of the production scheduling procedure may be frequently applied. Once the model has been formulated, the manager can simply supply the data—demand, capacities, and so on—for the given production period and use the linear programming model repeatedly to develop the production schedule.

Let us consider the case of the Bollinger Electronics Company, which produces two different electronic components for a major airplane engine manufacturer. The airplane engine manufacturer notifies the Bollinger sales office each quarter of its monthly requirements for components for each of the next 3 months. The monthly requirements for the components may vary considerably, depending on the type of engine the airplane engine manufacturer is producing. The order shown in Table 9.7 has just been received for the next 3-month period.

After the order is processed, a demand statement is sent to the production control department. The production control department must then develop a 3-month production plan for the components. In arriving at the desired schedule, the production manager will want to identify the following:

1. Total production cost
2. Inventory holding cost
3. Change-in-production-level costs

In the remainder of this section, we show how to formulate a linear programming model of the production and inventory process for Bollinger Electronics to minimize the total cost.

To develop the model, we let x_{im} denote the production volume in units for product i in month m. Here $i = 1, 2$, and $m = 1, 2, 3$; $i = 1$ refers to component 322A, $i = 2$ refers to component 802B, $m = 1$ refers to April, $m = 2$ refers to May, and $m = 3$ refers to June. The purpose of the double subscript is to provide a more descriptive notation. We could simply use x_6 to represent the number of units of product 2 produced in month 3, but x_{23} is more descriptive, identifying directly the product and month represented by the variable.

If component 322A costs \$20 per unit produced and component 802B costs \$10 per unit produced, the total production cost part of the objective function is

$$\text{Total production cost} = 20x_{11} + 20x_{12} + 20x_{13} + 10x_{21} + 10x_{22} + 10x_{23}$$

Because the production cost per unit is the same each month, we don't need to include the production costs in the objective function; that is, regardless of the production schedule selected, the total production cost will remain the same. In other words, production costs are not relevant costs for the production scheduling decision under consideration. In cases in which the production cost per unit is expected to change each month, the variable production costs per unit per month must be included in the objective function. The solution for the Bollinger Electronics problem will be the same whether these costs are included, therefore we included them so that the value of the linear programming objective function will include all the costs associated with the problem.

To incorporate the relevant inventory holding costs into the model, we let s_{im} denote the inventory level for product i at the end of month m. Bollinger has determined that on a

TABLE 9.7 THREE-MONTH DEMAND SCHEDULE FOR BOLLINGER
ELECTRONICS COMPANY

Component	April	May	June
322A	1000	3000	5000
802B	1000	500	3000

monthly basis inventory holding costs are 1.5% of the cost of the product; that is, $(0.015)(\$20) = \$0.30$ per unit for component 322A and $(0.015)(\$10) = \$0.15$ per unit for component 802B. A common assumption made in using the linear programming approach to production scheduling is that monthly ending inventories are an acceptable approximation to the average inventory levels throughout the month. Making this assumption, we write the inventory holding cost portion of the objective function as

$$\text{Inventory holding cost} = 0.30s_{11} + 0.30s_{12} + 0.30s_{13} + 0.15s_{21} + 0.15s_{22} + 0.15s_{23}$$

To incorporate the costs of fluctuations in production levels from month to month, we need to define two additional variables:

$$I_m = \text{increase in the total production level necessary during month } m$$
$$D_m = \text{decrease in the total production level necessary during month } m$$

After estimating the effects of employee layoffs, turnovers, reassignment training costs, and other costs associated with fluctuating production levels, Bollinger estimates that the cost associated with increasing the production level for any month is $0.50 per unit increase. A similar cost associated with decreasing the production level for any month is $0.20 per unit. Thus, we write the third portion of the objective function as

$$\text{Change-in-production-level costs} = 0.50I_1 + 0.50I_2 + 0.50I_3$$
$$+ 0.20D_1 + 0.20D_2 + 0.20D_3$$

Note that the cost associated with changes in production level is a function of the change in the total number of units produced in month m compared to the total number of units produced in month $m - 1$. In other production scheduling applications, fluctuations in production level might be measured in terms of machine hours or labor-hours required rather than in terms of the total number of units produced.

Combining all three costs, the complete objective function becomes

$$\text{Min} \quad 20x_{11} + 20x_{12} + 20x_{13} + 10x_{21} + 10x_{22} + 10x_{23} + 0.30s_{11}$$
$$+0.30s_{12} + 0.30s_{13} + 0.15s_{21} + 0.15s_{22} + 0.15s_{23} + 0.50I_1$$
$$+0.50I_2 + 0.50I_3 + 0.20D_1 + 0.20D_2 + 0.20D_3$$

We now consider the constraints. First, we must guarantee that the schedule meets customer demand. Because the units shipped can come from the current month's production or from inventory carried over from previous months, the demand requirement takes the form

$$\begin{pmatrix} \text{Ending} \\ \text{inventory} \\ \text{from previous} \\ \text{month} \end{pmatrix} + \begin{pmatrix} \text{Current} \\ \text{production} \end{pmatrix} - \begin{pmatrix} \text{Ending} \\ \text{inventory} \\ \text{for this} \\ \text{month} \end{pmatrix} = \begin{pmatrix} \text{This month's} \\ \text{demand} \end{pmatrix}$$

Suppose that the inventories at the beginning of the 3-month scheduling period were 500 units for component 322A and 200 units for component 802B. The demand for both products in the first month (April) was 1000 units, so the constraints for meeting demand in the first month become

$$500 + x_{11} - s_{11} = 1000$$
$$200 + x_{21} - s_{21} = 1000$$

Moving the constants to the right-hand side, we have

$$x_{11} - s_{11} = 500$$
$$x_{21} - s_{21} = 800$$

Similarly, we need demand constraints for both products in the second and third months. We write them as follows.

Month 2

$$s_{11} + x_{12} - s_{12} = 3000$$
$$s_{21} + x_{22} - s_{22} = 500$$

Month 3

$$s_{12} + x_{13} - s_{13} = 5000$$
$$s_{22} + x_{23} - s_{23} = 3000$$

If the company specifies a minimum inventory level at the end of the 3-month period of at least 400 units of component 322A and at least 200 units of component 802B, we can add the constraints

$$s_{13} \geq 400$$
$$s_{23} \geq 200$$

Suppose that we have the additional information on machine, labor, and storage capacity shown in Table 9.8. Machine, labor, and storage space requirements are given in Table 9.9. To reflect these limitations, the following constraints are necessary.

Machine Capacity

$$0.10x_{11} + 0.08x_{21} \leq 400 \quad \text{Month 1}$$
$$0.10x_{12} + 0.08x_{22} \leq 500 \quad \text{Month 2}$$
$$0.10x_{13} + 0.08x_{23} \leq 600 \quad \text{Month 3}$$

Labor Capacity

$$0.05x_{11} + 0.07x_{21} \leq 300 \quad \text{Month 1}$$
$$0.05x_{12} + 0.07x_{22} \leq 300 \quad \text{Month 2}$$
$$0.05x_{13} + 0.07x_{23} \leq 300 \quad \text{Month 3}$$

Storage Capacity

$$2s_{11} + 3s_{21} \leq 10,000 \quad \text{Month 1}$$
$$2s_{12} + 3s_{22} \leq 10,000 \quad \text{Month 2}$$
$$2s_{13} + 3s_{23} \leq 10,000 \quad \text{Month 3}$$

One final set of constraints must be added to guarantee that I_m and D_m will reflect the increase or decrease in the total production level for month m. Suppose that the production levels for March, the month before the start of the current production scheduling period, had been 1500 units of component 322A and 1000 units of component 802B for a total pro-

TABLE 9.8   MACHINE, LABOR, AND STORAGE CAPACITIES FOR
BOLLINGER ELECTRONICS

Month	Machine Capacity (hours)	Labor Capacity (hours)	Storage Capacity (square feet)
April	400	300	10,000
May	500	300	10,000
June	600	300	10,000

duction level of $1500 + 1000 = 2500$ units. We can find the amount of the change in production for April from the relationship

$$\text{April production} - \text{March production} = \text{Change}$$

Using the April production variables, x_{11} and x_{21}, the March production of 2500 units, we have

$$(x_{11} + x_{21}) - 2500 = \text{Change}$$

Note that the change can be positive or negative. A positive change reflects an increase in the total production level, and a negative change reflects a decrease in the total production level. We can use the increase in production for April, I_1, and the decrease in production for April, D_1, to specify the constraint for the change in total production for the month of April:

$$(x_{11} + x_{21}) - 2500 = I_1 - D_1$$

Of course, we cannot have an increase in production and a decrease in production during the same 1-month period; thus, either I_1 or D_1 will be zero. If April requires 3000 units of production, $I_1 = 500$ and $D_1 = 0$. If April requires 2200 units of production, $I_1 = 0$ and $D_1 = 300$. This approach of denoting the change in production level as the difference between two nonnegative variables, I_1 and D_1, permits both positive and negative changes in the total production level. If a single variable (say, c_m) had been used to represent the change in production level, only positive changes would be possible because of the nonnegativity requirement.

Using the same approach in May and June (always subtracting the previous month's total production from the current month's total production), we obtain the constraints for the second and third months of the production scheduling period:

$$(x_{12} + x_{22}) - (x_{11} + x_{21}) = I_2 - D_2$$
$$(x_{13} + x_{23}) - (x_{12} + x_{22}) = I_3 - D_3$$

TABLE 9.9   MACHINE, LABOR, AND STORAGE REQUIREMENTS FOR COMPONENTS
322A AND 802B

Component	Machine (hours/unit)	Labor (hours/unit)	Storage (square feet/unit)
322A	0.10	0.05	2
802B	0.08	0.07	3

Placing the variables on the left-hand side and the constants on the right-hand side yields the complete set of what are commonly referred to as production-smoothing constraints:

$$x_{11} + x_{21} \qquad\qquad -I_1 + D_1 = 2500$$
$$-x_{11} - x_{21} + x_{12} + x_{22} \qquad -I_2 + D_2 = 0$$
$$-x_{12} - x_{22} + x_{13} + x_{23} - I_3 + D_3 = 0$$

The initially rather small, 2-product, 3-month scheduling problem has now developed into an 18-variable, 20-constraint linear programming problem. Note that in this problem we were concerned only with one type of machine process, one type of labor, and one type of storage area. Actual production scheduling problems usually involve several machine types, several labor grades, and/or several storage areas, requiring large-scale linear programs. For instance, a problem involving 100 products over a 12-month period could have more than 1000 variables and constraints.

Problem 19 involves a production scheduling application with labor-smoothing constraints.

Figure 9.6 shows the computer solution to the Bollinger Electronics production scheduling problem. Table 9.10 contains a portion of the managerial report based on the computer solution.

Consider the monthly variation in the production and inventory schedule shown in Table 9.10. Recall that the inventory cost for component 802B is one-half the inventory cost for component 322A. Therefore, as might be expected, component 802B is produced heavily in the first month (April) and then held in inventory for the demand that will occur in future months. Component 322A tends to be produced when needed, and only small amounts are carried in inventory.

The costs of increasing and decreasing the total production volume tend to smooth the monthly variations. In fact, the minimum-cost schedule calls for a 500-unit increase in

TABLE 9.10   MINIMUM COST PRODUCTION SCHEDULE INFORMATION FOR THE BOLLINGER ELECTRONICS PROBLEM

Activity	April	May	June
Production			
Component 322A	500	3,200	5,200
Component 802B	2,500	2,000	0
Totals	3,000	5,200	5,200
Ending inventory			
Component 322A	0	200	400
Component 802B	1,700	3,200	200
Machine usage			
Scheduled hours	250	480	520
Slack capacity hours	150	20	80
Labor usage			
Scheduled hours	200	300	260
Slack capacity hours	100	0	40
Storage usage			
Scheduled storage	5,100	10,000	1,400
Slack capacity	4,900	0	8,600
Total production, inventory, and production-smoothing cost = $225,295			

FIGURE 9.6   THE MANAGEMENT SCIENTIST SOLUTION FOR THE BOLLINGER
ELECTRONICS PROBLEM

```
Objective Function Value =        225295.000

        Variable              Value           Reduced Costs
      --------------      --------------      ------------------
           X11              500.000               0.000
           X12             3200.000               0.000
           X13             5200.000               0.000
           X21             2500.000               0.000
           X22             2000.000               0.000
           X23                0.000               0.128
           S11                0.000               0.172
           S12              200.000               0.000
           S13              400.000               0.000
           S21             1700.000               0.000
           S22             3200.000               0.000
           S23              200.000               0.000
           I1               500.000               0.000
           I2              2200.000               0.000
           I3                 0.000               0.072
           D1                 0.000               0.700
           D2                 0.000               0.700
           D3                 0.000               0.628

        Constraint        Slack/Surplus         Dual Prices
      --------------      --------------      ------------------
            1                 0.000              -20.000
            2                 0.000              -10.000
            3                 0.000              -20.128
            4                 0.000              -10.150
            5                 0.000              -20.428
            6                 0.000              -10.300
            7                 0.000              -20.728
            8                 0.000              -10.450
            9               150.000                0.000
           10                20.000                0.000
           11                80.000                0.000
           12               100.000                0.000
           13                 0.000                1.111
           14                40.000                0.000
           15              4900.000                0.000
           16                 0.000                0.000
           17              8600.000                0.000
           18                 0.000                0.500
           19                 0.000                0.500
           20                 0.000                0.428
```

total production in April and a 2200-unit increase in total production in May. The May production level of 5200 units is then maintained during June.

The machine usage section of the report shows ample machine capacity in all 3 months. However, labor capacity is at full utilization (slack = 0 for constraint 13 in Figure 9.6) in the month of May. The dual price shows that an additional hour of labor capacity in May will improve the value of the optimal solution (lower cost) by approximately $1.11.

A linear programming model of a 2-product, 3-month production system can provide valuable information in terms of identifying a minimum-cost production schedule. In larger production systems, where the number of variables and constraints is too large to track manually, linear programming models can provide a significant advantage in developing cost-saving production schedules. The Q. M. in Action: Libbey-Owens-Ford shows just how large linear programming models can be for applications involving production scheduling.

Workforce Assignment

Workforce assignment problems frequently occur when production managers must make decisions involving staffing requirements for a given planning period. Workforce assignments often have some flexibility, and at least some personnel can be assigned to more than one department or work center. Such is the case when employees have been cross-trained on two or more jobs or, for instance, when sales personnel can be transferred between stores. In the following application, we show how linear programming can be used to determine not only an optimal product mix, but also an optimal workforce assignment.

McCormick Manufacturing Company produces two products with contributions to profit per unit of $10 and $9, respectively. The labor requirements per unit produced and the total hours of labor available from personnel assigned to each of four departments are shown in Table 9.11. Assuming that the number of hours available in each department is fixed, we can formulate McCormick's problem as a standard product-mix linear program with the following decision variables:

$$P_1 = \text{units of product 1}$$
$$P_2 = \text{units of product 2}$$

Q. M. IN ACTION

LIBBEY-OWENS-FORD*

Libbey-Owens-Ford utilizes a large-scale linear programming model to achieve integrated production, distribution, and inventory planning for its flat glass products. The linear programming model is called FLAGPOL. Schedulers and planners in the flat-glass products group must coordinate production schedules for more than 200 different glass products. The products are made in 4 colors (clear, gray, bronze, and blue-green) and 26 thicknesses. Other options include 3 quality levels, 2 cutting classifications, 4 packaging modes, and various fabrication methods, including tempered glass and/or coated glass.

To integrate production, distribution, and inventory planning, company analysts developed a linear programming model that optimizes opera-

tions for all products over a 12-month planning horizon. The model is applied monthly, and its output helps planners react to unexpected changes in the operating environment and deal with strategic issues such as adding new plants and expanding capacity. A typical linear programming model has approximately 100,000 variables and 26,000 constraints. The company estimates that the FLAGPOL model provides an annual savings of more than $2 million.

*Based on Clarence H. Martin, Denver C. Dent, and James C. Eckhart, "Integrated Production, Distribution and Inventory Planning at Libbey-Owens-Ford," *Interfaces* (May–June 1993): 68–78.

TABLE 9.11   DEPARTMENTAL LABOR-HOURS PER UNIT AND TOTAL HOURS AVAILABLE FOR THE McCORMICK MANUFACTURING COMPANY

| Department | Labor-Hours per Unit | | Total Hours Available |
	Product 1	Product 2	
1	0.65	0.95	6500
2	0.45	0.85	6000
3	1.00	0.70	7000
4	0.15	0.30	1400

The linear program is

$$\text{Max} \quad 10P_1 + 9P_2$$

s.t.

$$0.65P_1 + 0.95P_2 \leq 6500$$
$$0.45P_1 + 0.85P_2 \leq 6000$$
$$1.00P_1 + 0.70P_2 \leq 7000$$
$$0.15P_1 + 0.30P_2 \leq 1400$$
$$P_1, P_2 \geq 0$$

The optimal solution to the linear programming model is shown in Figure 9.7. After rounding, it calls for 5744 units of product 1, 1795 units of product 2, and a total profit of $73,590. With this optimal solution, departments 3 and 4 are operating at capacity, and departments 1 and 2 have a slack of approximately 1062 and 1890 hours, respectively. We would anticipate that the product mix would change and that the total profit would increase if the workforce assignment could be revised so that the slack, or unused hours, in departments 1 and 2 could be transferred to the departments currently working at capacity.

FIGURE 9.7   THE MANAGEMENT SCIENTIST SOLUTION FOR THE McCORMICK MANUFACTURING COMPANY PROBLEM WITH NO WORKFORCE TRANSFERS PERMITTED

```
Objective Function Value =          73589.744

        Variable            Value           Reduced Costs
    --------------      --------------      ------------------
          P1               5743.590              0.000
          P2               1794.872              0.000


       Constraint       Slack/Surplus          Dual Prices
    --------------      --------------      ------------------
           1               1061.538              0.000
           2               1889.744              0.000
           3                  0.000              8.462
           4                  0.000             10.256
```

However, the production manager may be uncertain as to how the workforce should be re-allocated among the four departments. Let us expand the linear programming model to include decision variables that will help determine the optimal workforce assignment in addition to the profit-maximizing product mix.

Suppose that McCormick has a cross-training program that enables some employees to be transferred between departments. By taking advantage of the cross-training skills, a limited number of employees and labor-hours may be transferred from one department to another. For example, suppose that the cross-training permits transfers as shown in Table 9.12. Row 1 of this table shows that some employees assigned to department 1 have cross-training skills that permit them to be transferred to department 2 or 3. The right-hand column shows that, for the current production planning period, a maximum of 400 hours can be transferred from department 1. Similar cross-training transfer capabilities and capacities are shown for departments 2, 3, and 4.

When workforce assignments are flexible, we do not automatically know how many hours of labor should be assigned to or be transferred from each department. We need to add decision variables to the linear programming model to account for such changes.

$$b_i = \text{the labor-hours allocated to department } i \text{ for } i = 1, 2, 3, \text{ and } 4$$

$$t_{ij} = \text{the labor-hours transferred from department } i \text{ to department } j$$

The right-hand sides are now treated as decision variables.

With the addition of decision variables b_1, b_2, b_3, and b_4, we write the capacity restrictions for the four departments as follows:

$$0.65P_1 + 0.95P_2 \leq b_1$$
$$0.45P_1 + 0.85P_2 \leq b_2$$
$$1.00P_1 + 0.70P_2 \leq b_3$$
$$0.15P_1 + 0.30P_2 \leq b_4$$

Because b_1, b_2, b_3, and b_4 are now decision variables, we follow the standard practice of placing these variables on the left side of the inequalities, and the first four constraints of the linear programming model become

$$0.65P_1 + 0.95P_2 - b_1 \qquad\qquad\qquad \leq 0$$
$$0.45P_1 + 0.85P_2 \qquad - b_2 \qquad\qquad \leq 0$$
$$1.00P_1 + 0.70P_2 \qquad\qquad - b_3 \quad \leq 0$$
$$0.15P_1 + 0.30P_2 \qquad\qquad\qquad - b_4 \leq 0$$

The labor-hours ultimately allocated to each department must be determined by a series of labor balance equations, or constraints, that include the number of hours initially

TABLE 9.12   CROSS-TRAINING ABILITY AND CAPACITY INFORMATION

From Department	Cross-Training Transfers Permitted to Department				Maximum Hours Transferable
	1	2	3	4	
1	—	yes	yes	—	400
2	—	—	yes	yes	800
3	—	—	—	yes	100
4	yes	yes	—	—	200

assigned to each department plus the number of hours transferred into the department minus the number of hours transferred out of the department. Using department 1 as an example, we determine the workforce allocation as follows:

$$b_1 = \begin{pmatrix} \text{Hours} \\ \text{initially in} \\ \text{department 1} \end{pmatrix} + \begin{pmatrix} \text{Hours} \\ \text{transferred into} \\ \text{department 1} \end{pmatrix} - \begin{pmatrix} \text{Hours} \\ \text{transferred out of} \\ \text{department 1} \end{pmatrix}$$

Table 9.11 shows 6500 hours initially assigned to department 1. We use the transfer decision variables t_{i1} to denote transfers into department 1 and t_{1j} to denote transfers from department 1. Table 9.12 shows that the cross-training capabilities involving department 1 are restricted to transfers from department 4 (variable t_{41}) and transfers to either department 2 or department 3 (variables t_{12} and t_{13}). Thus, we can express the total workforce allocation for department 1 as

$$b_1 = 6500 + t_{41} - t_{12} - t_{13}$$

Moving the decision variables for the workforce transfers to the left-hand side, we have the labor balance equation or constraint

$$b_1 - t_{41} + t_{12} + t_{13} = 6500$$

This form of constraint will be needed for each of the four departments. Thus, the following labor balance constraints for departments 2, 3, and 4 would be added to the model.

$$b_2 - t_{12} - t_{42} + t_{23} + t_{24} = 6000$$
$$b_3 - t_{13} - t_{23} + t_{34} = 7000$$
$$b_4 - t_{24} - t_{34} + t_{41} + t_{42} = 1400$$

Finally, Table 9.12 shows the number of hours that may be transferred from each department is limited, indicating that a transfer capacity constraint must be added for each of the four departments. The additional constraints are

$$t_{12} + t_{13} \leq 400$$
$$t_{23} + t_{24} \leq 800$$
$$t_{34} \leq 100$$
$$t_{41} + t_{42} \leq 200$$

The complete linear programming model has 2 product decision variables (P_1 and P_2), 4 department workforce assignment variables (b_1, b_2, b_3, and b_4), 7 transfer variables t_{12}, t_{13}, t_{23}, t_{24}, t_{34}, t_{41}, and t_{42}), and 12 constraints. Figure 9.8 shows the optimal solution to this linear program provided by The Management Scientist.

Variations in the workforce assignment model could be used in situations such as allocating raw material resources to products, allocating machine time to products, and allocating salesforce time to stores or sales territories.

McCormick's profit can be increased by $10,421 to $84,011 by taking advantage of cross-training and workforce transfers. The optimal product mix of 6825 units of product 1 and 1751 units of product 2 can be achieved if $t_{13} = 400$ hours are transferred from department 1 to department 3; $t_{23} = 651$ hours are transferred from department 2 to department 3; and $t_{24} = 149$ hours are transferred from department 2 to department 4. The resulting workforce assignments for departments 1–4 would provide 6100, 5200, 8051, and 1549 hours, respectively.

FIGURE 9.8   THE MANAGEMENT SCIENTIST SOLUTION FOR THE McCORMICK
MANUFACTURING COMPANY PROBLEM

```
Objective Function Value =          84011.299

         Variable              Value           Reduced Costs
       --------------      ---------------    -----------------
           P1                 6824.859              0.000
           P2                 1751.412              0.000
           B1                 6100.000              0.000
           B2                 5200.000              0.000
           B3                 8050.847              0.000
           B4                 1549.153              0.000
           T12                   0.000              8.249
           T13                 400.000              0.000
           T23                 650.847              0.000
           T24                 149.153              0.000
           T34                   0.000              0.000
           T41                   0.000              7.458
           T42                   0.000              8.249

        Constraint         Slack/Surplus        Dual Prices
       --------------      ---------------    -----------------
            1                   0.000              0.791
            2                 640.113              0.000
            3                   0.000              8.249
            4                   0.000              8.249
            5                   0.000              0.791
            6                   0.000              0.000
            7                   0.000              8.249
            8                   0.000              8.249
            9                   0.000              7.458
           10                   0.000              8.249
           11                 100.000              0.000
           12                 200.000              0.000
```

If a manager has the flexibility to assign personnel to different departments, reduced workforce idle time, improved workforce utilization, and improved profit should result. The linear programming model in this section automatically assigns employees and labor-hours to the departments in the most profitable manner.

9.4   BLENDING PROBLEMS

Blending problems arise whenever a manager must decide how to blend two or more re-sources to produce one or more products. In these situations, the resources contain one or more essential ingredients that must be blended into final products that will contain specific percentages of each. In most of these applications, then, management must decide how much of each resource to purchase to satisfy product specifications and product demands at minimum cost.

Blending problems occur frequently in the petroleum industry (e.g., blending crude oil to produce different octane gasolines), chemical industry (e.g., blending chemicals to produce fertilizers and weed killers), and food industry (e.g., blending ingredients to produce soft drinks and soups). In this section we illustrate how to apply linear programming to a blending problem in the petroleum industry.

The Grand Strand Oil Company produces regular and premium gasoline for independent service stations in the southeastern United States. The Grand Strand refinery manufactures the gasoline products by blending three petroleum components. The gasolines are sold at different prices, and the petroleum components have different costs. The firm wants to determine how to mix or blend the three components into the two gasoline products and maximize profits.

Data available show that regular gasoline can be sold for $1.00 per gallon and premium gasoline for $1.08 per gallon. For the current production planning period, Grand Strand can obtain the three petroleum components at the cost per gallon and in the quantities shown in Table 9.13.

Product specifications for the regular and premium gasolines restrict the amounts of each component that can be used in each gasoline product. Table 9.14 lists the product specifications. Current commitments to distributors require Grand Strand to produce at least 10,000 gallons of regular gasoline.

The Grand Strand blending problem is to determine how many gallons of each component should be used in the regular gasoline blend and how many should be used in the premium gasoline blend. The optimal blending solution should maximize the firm's profit, subject to the constraints on the available petroleum supplies shown in Table 9.13, the product specifications shown in Table 9.14, and the required 10,000 gallons of regular gasoline.

We define the decision variables as

$$x_{ij} = \text{gallons of component } i \text{ used in gasoline } j,$$
$$\text{where } i = 1, 2, \text{ or } 3 \text{ for components } 1, 2, \text{ or } 3,$$
$$\text{and } j = r \text{ if regular or } j = p \text{ if premium}$$

TABLE 9.13   PETROLEUM COST AND SUPPLY FOR THE GRAND STRAND
BLENDING PROBLEM

Petroleum Component	Cost/Gallon	Maximum Available
1	$0.50	5,000 gallons
2	$0.60	10,000 gallons
3	$0.84	10,000 gallons

TABLE 9.14   PRODUCT SPECIFICATIONS FOR THE GRAND STRAND
BLENDING PROBLEM

Product	Specifications
Regular gasoline	At most 30% component 1
	At least 40% component 2
	At most 20% component 3
Premium gasoline	At least 25% component 1
	At most 40% component 2
	At least 30% component 3

The six decision variables are

$$x_{1r} = \text{gallons of component 1 in regular gasoline}$$
$$x_{2r} = \text{gallons of component 2 in regular gasoline}$$
$$x_{3r} = \text{gallons of component 3 in regular gasoline}$$
$$x_{1p} = \text{gallons of component 1 in premium gasoline}$$
$$x_{2p} = \text{gallons of component 2 in premium gasoline}$$
$$x_{3p} = \text{gallons of component 3 in premium gasoline}$$

The total number of gallons of each type of gasoline produced is the sum of the number of gallons produced using each of the three petroleum components.

Total Gallons Produced

$$\text{Regular gasoline} = x_{1r} + x_{2r} + x_{3r}$$
$$\text{Premium gasoline} = x_{1p} + x_{2p} + x_{3p}$$

The total gallons of each petroleum component are computed in a similar fashion.

Total Petroleum Component Use

$$\text{Component 1} = x_{1r} + x_{1p}$$
$$\text{Component 2} = x_{2r} + x_{2p}$$
$$\text{Component 3} = x_{3r} + x_{3p}$$

We develop the objective function of maximizing the profit contribution by identifying the difference between the total revenue from both gasolines and the total cost of the three petroleum components. By multiplying the $1.00 per gallon price by the total gallons of regular gasoline, the $1.08 per gallon price by the total gallons of premium gasoline, and the component cost per gallon figures in Table 9.13 by the total gallons of each component used, we obtain the objective function:

$$\text{Max} \quad 1.00(x_{1r} + x_{2r} + x_{3r}) + 1.08(x_{1p} + x_{2p} + x_{3p})$$
$$- 0.50(x_{1r} + x_{1p}) - 0.60(x_{2r} + x_{2p}) - 0.84(x_{3r} + x_{3p})$$

When we combine terms, the objective function becomes

$$\text{Max} \quad 0.50x_{1r} + 0.40x_{2r} + 0.16x_{3r} + 0.58x_{1p} + 0.48x_{2p} + 0.24x_{3p}$$

The limitations on the availability of the three petroleum components are

$$x_{1r} + x_{1p} \leq 5{,}000 \quad \text{Component 1}$$
$$x_{2r} + x_{2p} \leq 10{,}000 \quad \text{Component 2}$$
$$x_{3r} + x_{3p} \leq 10{,}000 \quad \text{Component 3}$$

Six constraints are now required to meet the product specifications stated in Table 9.14. The first specification states that component 1 can account for no more than 30% of the total gallons of regular gasoline produced. That is,

$$x_{1r} \leq 0.30(x_{1r} + x_{2r} + x_{3r})$$

Rewriting this constraint with the variables on the left-hand side and a constant on the right-hand side yields

$$0.70x_{1r} - 0.30x_{2r} - 0.30x_{3r} \leq 0$$

The second product specification listed in Table 9.14 becomes

$$x_{2r} \geq 0.40(x_{1r} + x_{2r} + x_{3r})$$

and thus,

$$-0.40x_{1r} + 0.60x_{2r} - 0.40x_{3r} \geq 0$$

Similarly, we write the four remaining blending specifications listed in Table 9.14 as

$$-0.20x_{1r} - 0.20x_{2r} + 0.80x_{3r} \leq 0$$
$$+0.75x_{1p} - 0.25x_{2p} - 0.25x_{3p} \geq 0$$
$$-0.40x_{1p} + 0.60x_{2p} - 0.40x_{3p} \leq 0$$
$$-0.30x_{1p} - 0.30x_{2p} + 0.70x_{3p} \geq 0$$

The constraint for at least 10,000 gallons of regular gasoline is

$$x_{1r} + x_{2r} + x_{3r} \geq 10,000$$

The complete linear programming model with 6 decision variables and 10 constraints is

$$\text{Max} \quad 0.50x_{1r} + 0.40x_{2r} + 0.16x_{3r} + 0.58x_{1p} + 0.48x_{2p} + 0.24x_{3p}$$

s.t.

$$
\begin{array}{llll}
x_{1r} & & + \ x_{1p} & & \leq \ 5{,}000 \\
& x_{2r} & + \ x_{2p} & & \leq \ 10{,}000 \\
& x_{3r} & + \ x_{3p} & & \leq \ 10{,}000 \\
0.70x_{1r} - 0.30x_{2r} - 0.30x_{3r} & & & \leq \ 0 \\
-0.40x_{1r} + 0.60x_{2r} - 0.40x_{3r} & & & \geq \ 0 \\
-0.20x_{1r} - 0.20x_{2r} + 0.80x_{3r} & & & \leq \ 0 \\
& 0.75x_{1p} - 0.25x_{2p} - 0.25x_{3p} & & \geq \ 0 \\
& -0.40x_{1p} + 0.60x_{2p} - 0.40x_{3p} & & \leq \ 0 \\
& -0.30x_{1p} - 0.30x_{2p} + 0.70x_{3p} & & \geq \ 0 \\
x_{1r} + x_{2r} + x_{3r} & & & \geq \ 10{,}000 \\
\end{array}
$$

$$x_{1r}, x_{2r}, x_{3r}, x_{1p}, x_{2p}, x_{3p} \geq 0$$

Try Problem 15 as another example of a blending model.

The computer solution to the Grand Strand blending problem is shown in Figure 9.9. The optimal solution providing a profit of $9300 is summarized in Table 9.15. The optimal blending strategy shows that 10,000 gallons of regular gasoline should be produced. The regular gasoline will be manufactured as a blend of 8000 gallons of component 2 and 2000 gallons of component 3. The 15,000 gallons of premium gasoline will be manufactured as a blend of 5000 gallons of component 1, 2000 gallons of component 2, and 8000 gallons of component 3.

FIGURE 9.9   THE MANAGEMENT SCIENTIST SOLUTION FOR THE GRAND STRAND
BLENDING PROBLEM

```
Objective Function Value =            9300.000

         Variable             Value              Reduced Costs
      --------------     ---------------      ------------------
           X1R                0.000                  0.000
           X2R             8000.000                  0.000
           X3R             2000.000                  0.000
           X1P             5000.000                  0.000
           X2P             2000.000                  0.000
           X3P             8000.000                  0.000

         Constraint        Slack/Surplus           Dual Prices
      --------------     ---------------      ------------------
             1                 0.000                  0.580
             2                 0.000                  0.480
             3                 0.000                  0.240
             4              3000.000                  0.000
             5              4000.000                  0.000
             6                 0.000                  0.000
             7              1250.000                  0.000
             8              4000.000                  0.000
             9              3500.000                  0.000
            10                 0.000                 -0.080
```

TABLE 9.15   GRAND STRAND GASOLINE BLENDING SOLUTION

| Gasoline | Gallons of Component (percentage) | | | Total |
	Component 1	Component 2	Component 3	
Regular	0 (0%)	8000 (80%)	2000 (20%)	10,000
Premium	5000 (33⅓%)	2000 (13⅓%)	8000 (53⅓%)	15,000

The interpretation of the slack and surplus variables associated with the product specification constraints (constraints 4–9) in Figure 9.9 needs some clarification. If the constraint
is a ≤ constraint, the value of the slack variable can be interpreted as the gallons of component use below the maximum amount of the component use specified by the constraint.
For example, the slack of 3000.000 for constraint 4 shows that component 1 use is 3000
gallons below the maximum amount of component 1 that could have been used in the production of 10,000 gallons of regular gasoline. If the product specification constraint is a
≥ constraint, a surplus variable shows the gallons of component use above the minimum
amount of component use specified by the blending constraint. For example, the surplus
of 4000.000 for constraint 5 shows that component 2 use is 4000 gallons above the minimum amount of component 2 that must be used in the production of 10,000 gallons of regular gasoline.

NOTES AND COMMENTS

A convenient way to define the decision variables in a blending problem is to use a matrix in which the rows correspond to the raw materials and the columns correspond to the final products. For example, in the Grand Strand blending problem, we could define the decision variables as follows:

		Final Products	
		Regular Gasoline	Premium Gasoline
Raw Materials	Component 1	x_{1r}	x_{1p}
	Component 2	x_{2r}	x_{2p}
	Component 3	x_{3r}	x_{3p}

This approach has two advantages: (1) it provides a systematic way to define the decision variables for any blending problem; and (2) it provides a visual image of the decision variables in terms of how they are related to the raw materials, products, and each other.

9.5   DATA ENVELOPMENT ANALYSIS

Data envelopment analysis (DEA) is an application of linear programming used to measure the relative efficiency of operating units with the same goals and objectives. For example, DEA has been used within individual fast food outlets in the same chain. In this case, the goal of DEA was to identify the inefficient outlets that should be targeted for further study and, if necessary, corrective action. Other applications of DEA have measured the relative efficiencies of hospitals, banks, courts, schools, and so on. In these applications, the performance of each institution or organization was measured relative to the performance of all operating units in the same system. Q. M. in Action: Efficiency of Bank Branches describes how a large nationally known bank used DEA to determine which branches were operating inefficiently.

The operating units of most organizations have multiple inputs such as staff size, salaries, hours of operation, and advertising budget, as well as multiple outputs such as profit, market share, and growth rate. In these situations, it is often difficult for a manager to determine which operating units are inefficient in converting their multiple inputs into multiple outputs. This particular area is where data envelopment analysis has proven to be a helpful managerial tool. We illustrate the application of data envelopment analysis by evaluating the performance of a group of four hospitals.

Evaluating the Performance of Hospitals

The hospital administrators at General Hospital, University Hospital, County Hospital, and State Hospital have been meeting to discuss ways in which they can help one another improve the performance at each of their hospitals. A consultant has suggested that they consider using DEA to measure the performance of each hospital relative to the performance of all four hospitals. In discussing how this evaluation could be done, the following three input measures and four output measures were identified:

Input Measures

1. The number of full-time equivalent (FTE) nonphysician personnel
2. The amount spent on supplies
3. The number of bed-days available

EFFICIENCY OF BANK BRANCHES*

Management of a large, nationally known bank wanted to improve operations at the branch level. A total of 182 branch banks located in four major cities were selected for the study. Data envelopment analysis (DEA) was used to determine which branches were operating inefficiently.

The DEA model compared the actual operating results of each branch with those of all other branches. A less-productive branch was one that required more resources to produce the same output as the best-performing branches. The best-performing branches are identified by a DEA efficiency rating of 100 percent ($E = 1.00$). The inefficient or less-productive branches are identified by an efficiency rating less than 100 percent ($E < 1.00$).

The inputs used for each branch were the number of teller full-time equivalents, the number of nonteller personnel full-time equivalents, the number of parking spaces, the number of ATMs, and the advertising expense per customer. The outputs were the amount of loans (direct, indirect, commercial, and equity), the amount of deposits (checking, savings, and CDs), the average number of accounts per customer, and the customer satisfaction score based on a quarterly customer survey. Data were collected over six consecutive quarters to determine how the branches were operating over time.

The solution to the DEA linear programming model showed that 92 of the 182 branches were fully efficient. Only 5 branches fell below the 70 percent efficiency level, and approximately 25% of the branches had efficiency ratings between 80% to 89%. DEA identified the specific branches that were relatively inefficient and provided insights as to how these branches could improve productivity. Focusing on the less-productive branches, the bank was able to identify ways to reduce the input resources required without significantly reducing the volume and quality of service. In addition, the DEA analysis provided management with a better understanding of the factors that contribute most to the efficiency of the branch banks.

*Based on B. Golany and J. E. Storbeck, "A Data Envelopment Analysis of the Operational Efficiency of Bank Branches," *Interfaces* (May–June 1999): 14–26.

Problem 26 asks you to formulate and solve a linear program to assess the relative efficiency of General Hospital.

Output Measures

1. Patient-days of service under Medicare
2. Patient-days of service not under Medicare
3. Number of nurses trained
4. Number of interns trained

Summaries of the input and output measures for a one-year period at each of the four hospitals are shown in Tables 9.16 and 9.17. Let us show how DEA can use these data to identify relatively inefficient hospitals.

Overview of the DEA Approach

In this application of DEA, a linear programming model will be developed for each hospital whose efficiency is to be evaluated. To illustrate the modeling process, we will formulate a linear program that can be used to determine the relative efficiency of County Hospital.

TABLE 9.16   ANNUAL RESOURCES CONSUMED (INPUTS) BY THE FOUR HOSPITALS

Input Measure	Hospital			
	General	**University**	**County**	**State**
Full-time equivalent nonphysicians	285.20	162.30	275.70	210.40
Supply expense ($000s)	123.80	128.70	348.50	154.10
Bed-days available (000s)	106.72	64.21	104.10	104.04

TABLE 9.17   ANNUAL SERVICES PROVIDED (OUTPUTS) BY THE FOUR HOSPITALS

	Hospital			
Input Measure	**General**	**University**	**County**	**State**
Medicare patient-days (000s)	48.14	34.62	36.72	33.16
Non-Medicare patient-days (000s)	43.10	27.11	45.98	56.46
Nurses trained	253	148	175	160
Interns trained	41	27	23	84

First, using a linear programming model, we construct a **hypothetical composite,** in this case a composite hospital, based on the outputs and inputs for all operating units with the same goals. For each of the four hospitals' output measures, the output for the composite hospital is determined by computing a weighted average of the corresponding outputs for all four hospitals. For each of the three input measures, the input for the composite hospital is determined by using the same weights to compute a weighted average of the corresponding inputs for all four hospitals. Constraints in the linear programming model require all outputs for the composite hospital to be *greater than or equal to* the outputs of County Hospital, the hospital being evaluated. If the inputs for the composite unit can be shown to be *less than* the inputs for County Hospital, the composite hospital is shown to have the same, or more, output for *less input.* In this case, the model shows that the composite hospital is more efficient than County Hospital. In other words, the hospital being evaluated is *less efficient* than the composite hospital. Because the composite hospital is based on all four hospitals, the hospital being evaluated can be judged *relatively inefficient* when compared to the other hospitals in the group.

DEA Linear Programming Model

To determine the weight that each hospital will have in computing the outputs and inputs for the composite hospital, we use the following decision variables:

$$wg = \text{weight applied to inputs and outputs for General Hospital}$$
$$wu = \text{weight applied to inputs and outputs for University Hospital}$$
$$wc = \text{weight applied to inputs and outputs for County Hospital}$$
$$ws = \text{weight applied to inputs and outputs for State Hospital}$$

The DEA approach requires that the sum of these weights equal 1. Thus, the first constraint is

$$wg + wu + wc + ws = 1$$

In general, every DEA linear programming model will include a constraint that requires the weights for the operating units to sum to 1.

As we stated previously, for each output measure, the output for the composite hospital is determined by computing a weighted average of the corresponding outputs for all four hospitals. For instance, for output measure 1, the number of patient days of service under Medicare, the output for the composite hospital is

$$\begin{aligned}\text{Medicare patient-days} \atop \text{for Composite Hospital} &= \left(\text{Medicare patient-days} \atop \text{for General Hospital}\right)wg + \left(\text{Medicare patient-days} \atop \text{for University Hospital}\right)wu \\ &+ \left(\text{Medicare patient-days} \atop \text{for County Hospital}\right)wc + \left(\text{Medicare patient-days} \atop \text{for State Hospital}\right)ws\end{aligned}$$

Substituting the number of medicare patient-days for each hospital as shown in Table 9.17, we obtain the following expression:

$$\text{Medicare patient-days for Composite Hospital} = 48.14wg + 34.62wu + 36.72wc + 33.16ws$$

The other output measures for the composite hospital are computed in a similar fashion. Figure 9.10 provides a summary of the results.

For each of the four output measures, we need to write a constraint that requires the output for the composite hospital to be greater than or equal to the output for County Hospital. Thus, the general form of the output constraints is

$$\text{Output for the Composite Hospital} \geq \text{Output for County Hospital}$$

Because the number of Medicare patient-days for County Hospital is 36.72, the output constraint corresponding to the number of Medicare patient-days is

$$48.14wg + 34.62wu + 36.72wc + 33.16ws \geq 36.72$$

In a similar fashion, we formulated a constraint for each of the other three output measures, with the results as shown:

$$
\begin{array}{rl}
43.10wg + 27.11wu + 45.98wc + 56.46ws \geq 45.98 & \text{Non-Medicare} \\
253wg + \quad 148wu + \quad 175wc + \quad 160ws \geq \quad 175 & \text{Nurses} \\
41wg + \quad 27wu + \quad 23wc + \quad 84ws \geq \quad 23 & \text{Interns}
\end{array}
$$

The four output constraints require the linear programming solution to provide weights that will make each output measure for the composite hospital greater than or equal to the corresponding output measure for County Hospital. Thus, if a solution satisfying the output constraints can be found, the composite hospital will have produced at least as much of each output as County Hospital.

Next, we need to consider the constraints needed to model the relationship between the inputs for the composite hospital and the resources available to the composite hospital. A

FIGURE 9.10   RELATIONSHIP BETWEEN THE OUTPUT MEASURES FOR THE FOUR HOSPITALS AND THE OUTPUT MEASURES FOR THE COMPOSITE HOSPITAL

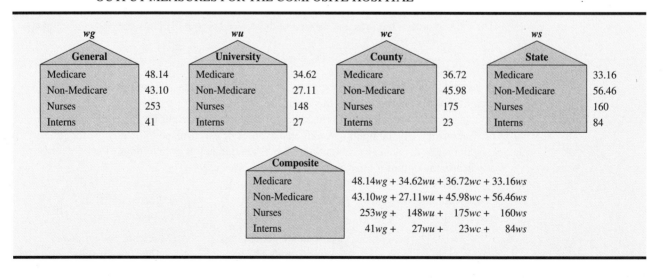

constraint is required for each of the three input measures. The general form for the input constraints is as follows:

$$\text{Input for the Composite Hospital} \leq \text{Resources available to the Composite Hospital}$$

For each input measure, the input for the composite hospital is a weighted average of the corresponding input for each of the four hospitals. Thus, for input measure 1, the number of full-time equivalent nonphysicians, the input for the composite hospital is

$$\text{FTE nonphysicians for Composite Hospital} = \left(\text{FTE nonphysicians for General Hospital}\right)wg + \left(\text{FTE nonphysicians for University Hospital}\right)wu$$
$$+ \left(\text{FTE nonphysicians for County Hospital}\right)wc + \left(\text{FTE nonphysicians for State Hospital}\right)ws$$

Substituting the values for the number of full-time equivalent nonphysicians for each hospital as shown in Table 9.16, we obtain the following expression for the number of full-time equivalent nonphysicians for the composite hospital:

$$285.20wg + 162.30wu + 275.70wc + 210.40ws$$

In a similar manner, we can write expressions for each of the other two input measures as shown in Figure 9.11.

To complete the formulation of the input constraints, we must write expressions for the right-hand-side values for each constraint. First, note that the right-hand-side values are the resources available to the composite hospital. In the DEA approach, these right-hand-side values are a percentage of the input values for County Hospital. Thus, we must introduce the following decision variables:

$$E = \text{the fraction of County Hospital's input available to the composite hospital}$$

To illustrate the important role that E plays in the DEA approach, we show how to write the expression for the number of FTE nonphysicians available to the composite hospital. Table

FIGURE 9.11   RELATIONSHIP BETWEEN THE INPUT MEASURES FOR THE FOUR HOSPITALS AND THE INPUT MEASURES FOR THE COMPOSITE HOSPITAL

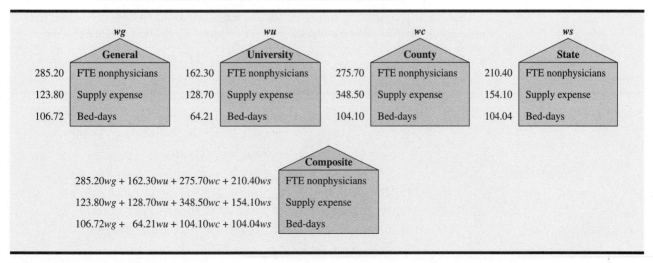

9.16 shows that the number of FTE nonphysicians used by County Hospital was 275.70; thus, 275.70E is the number of FTE nonphysicians available to the composite hospital. If $E = 1$, the number of FTE nonphysicians available to the composite hospital is 275.70, the same as the number of FTE nonphysicians used by County Hospital. However, if E is greater than 1, the composite hospital would have available proportionally more nonphysicians, while if E is less than 1, the composite hospital would have available proportionally fewer FTE nonphysicians. Because of the effect that E has in determining the resources available to the composite hospital, E is referred to as the **efficiency index.**

We can now write the input constraint corresponding to the number of FTE nonphysicians available to the composite hospital:

$$285.20wg + 162.30wu + 275.70wc + 210.40ws \leq 275.70E$$

In a similar manner, we can write the input constraints for the supplies and bed-days available to the composite hospital. First, using the data in Table 9.16, we note that for each of these resources, the amount that is available to the composite hospital is 348.50E and 104.10E, respectively. Thus, the input constraints for the supplies and bed-days are written as follows:

$$123.80wg + 128.70wu + 348.50wc + 154.10ws \leq 348.50E \quad \text{Supplies}$$
$$106.72wg + 64.21wu + 104.10wc + 104.04ws \leq 104.10E \quad \text{Bed-days}$$

If a solution with $E < 1$ can be found, the composite hospital does not need as many resources as County Hospital needs to produce the same level of output.

The objective function for the DEA model is to minimize the value of E, which is equivalent to minimizing the input resources available to the composite hospital. Thus, the objective function is written as

$$\text{Min } E$$

The DEA efficiency conclusion is based on the optimal value for E. The decision rule is as follows:

If $E = 1$, the composite hospital requires *as much input* as County Hospital does, offering no evidence that County Hospital is inefficient.

If $E < 1$, the composite hospital requires *less input* to obtain the output achieved by County Hospital, indicating that the composite hospital is more efficient, and thus, County Hospital can be judged relatively inefficient.

The DEA linear programming model for the efficiency evaluation of County Hospital has five decision variables and eight constraints. The complete model is rewritten as follows:

$$\text{Min} \quad E$$
$$\text{s.t.}$$

$$
\begin{aligned}
wg + wu + wc + ws &= 1 \\
48.14wg + 34.62wu + 36.72wc + 33.16ws &\geq 36.72 \\
43.10wg + 27.11wu + 45.98wc + 56.46ws &\geq 45.98 \\
253wg + 148wu + 175wc + 160ws &\geq 175 \\
41wg + 27wu + 23wc + 84ws &\geq 23 \\
-275.70E + 285.20wg + 162.30wu + 275.70wc + 210.40ws &\leq 0 \\
-348.50E + 123.80wg + 128.70wu + 348.50wc + 154.10ws &\leq 0 \\
-104.10E + 106.72wg + 64.21wu + 104.10wc + 104.04ws &\leq 0 \\
E, wg, wu, wc, ws &\geq 0
\end{aligned}
$$

Note that in this formulation of the model, we have moved the terms involving E to the left side of the three input constraints because E is a decision variable. This linear program was solved using The Management Scientist software package. The computer solution is shown in Figure 9.12.

We first note that the objective function shows that the efficiency score for County Hospital is 0.905. This score tells us that the composite hospital can obtain at least the level of each output that County Hospital obtains by having available no more than 90.5% of the input resources required by County Hospital. Thus, the composite hospital is more efficient, and the DEA analysis has identified County Hospital as being relatively inefficient.

From the solution in Figure 9.12, we see that the composite hospital is formed from the weighted average of General Hospital ($wg = 0.212$), University Hospital ($wu = 0.260$), and State Hospital ($ws = 0.527$). Each input and output of the composite hospital is determined by the same weighted average of the inputs and outputs of these three hospitals.

The Slack/Surplus column provides some additional information about the efficiency of County Hospital compared to the composite hospital. Specifically, the composite hospital has at least as much of each output as County Hospital has (constraints 2–5) and provides 1.6 more nurses trained (surplus for constraint 4) and 37 more interns trained (surplus for constraint 5). The slack of zero from constraint 8 shows that the composite hospital uses approximately 90.5% of the bed-days used by County Hospital. The slack values for constraints 6 and 7 show that less than 90.5% of the FTE nonphysician and the supplies expense resources used at County Hospital are used by the composite hospital.

Clearly, the composite hospital is more efficient than County Hospital, and we are justified in concluding that County Hospital is relatively inefficient compared to the other hospitals in the group. Given the results of the DEA analysis, hospital administrators should examine operations to determine how County Hospital resources can be more effectively utilized.

FIGURE 9.12   THE MANAGEMENT SCIENTIST SOLUTION FOR THE DATA
ENVELOPMENT ANALYSIS COUNTY HOSPITAL PROBLEM

```
Objective Function Value =            0.905

        Variable              Value              Reduced Costs
        --------              -----              -------------

           E                  0.905                  0.000
          WG                  0.212                  0.000
          WU                  0.260                  0.000
          WC                  0.000                  0.095
          WS                  0.527                  0.000


       Constraint         Slack/Surplus            Dual Prices
       ----------         -------------            -----------

           1                  0.000                  0.239
           2                  0.000                 -0.014
           3                  0.000                 -0.014
           4                  1.615                  0.000
           5                 37.027                  0.000
           6                 35.643                  0.000
           7                174.422                  0.000
           8                  0.000                  0.010
```

Summary of the DEA Approach

To use data envelopment analysis to measure the relative efficiency of County Hospital, we used a linear programming model to construct a hypothetical composite hospital based on the outputs and inputs for the four hospitals in the problem. The approach to solving other types of problems using DEA is similar. That is, for each operating unit that we want to measure the efficiency of, we must formulate and solve a linear programming model similar to the linear program we solved to measure the relative efficiency of County Hospital. The following step-by-step procedure should help you in formulating a linear programming model for other types of DEA applications. Note that the operating unit that we want to measure the relative efficiency of is referred to as the jth operating unit.

Step 1. Define decision variables or weights (one for each operating unit) that can be used to determine the inputs and outputs for the composite operating unit.

Step 2. Write a constraint that requires the weights to sum to 1.

Step 3. For each output measure, write a constraint that requires the output for the composite operating unit to be greater than or equal to the corresponding output for the jth operating unit.

Step 4. Define a decision variable, E, which determines the fraction of the jth operating unit's input available to the composite operating unit.

Step 5. For each input measure, write a constraint that requires the input for the composite operating unit to be less than or equal to the resources available to the composite operating unit.

Step 6. Write the objective function as Min E.

NOTES AND COMMENTS

1. Remember that the goal of data envelopment analysis is to identify operating units that are relatively inefficient. The method *does not* necessarily identify the operating units that are *relatively efficient*. Just because the efficiency index is $E = 1$, we cannot conclude that the unit being analyzed is relatively efficient. Indeed, any unit that has the largest output on any one of the output measures cannot be judged relatively inefficient.

2. It is possible for DEA to show all but one unit to be relatively inefficient. Such would be the case

if a unit producing the most of every output also consumes the least of every input. Such cases are extremely rare in practice.

3. In applying data envelopment analysis to problems involving a large group of operating units, practitioners have found that roughly 50% of the operating units can be identified as inefficient. Comparing each relatively inefficient unit to the units contributing to the composite unit may be helpful in understanding how the operation of each relatively inefficient unit can be improved.

SUMMARY

In this chapter we presented a broad range of applications that demonstrate how to use linear programming to assist in the decision-making process. We formulated and solved problems from marketing, finance, and production management, and illustrated how linear programming can be applied to blending problems and data envelopment analysis.

Many of the illustrations presented in this chapter are scaled-down versions of actual situations in which linear programming has been applied. In real-world applications, the problem may not be so concisely stated, the data for the problem may not be as readily available, and the problem most likely will involve numerous decision variables and/or constraints. However, a thorough study of the applications in this chapter is a good place to begin in applying linear programming to real problems.

GLOSSARY

Data envelopment analysis (DEA)   A linear programming application used to measure the relative efficiency of operating units with the same goals and objectives.

Hypothetical composite   A weighted average of outputs and inputs of all operating units with similar goals.

Efficiency index   Percentage of an individual operating unit's resources that are available to the composite operating unit.

PROBLEMS

Note: The following problems have been designed to give you an understanding and appreciation of the broad range of problems that can be formulated as linear programs. You should be able to formulate a linear programming model for each of the problems. However, you will need access to a linear programming computer package to develop the solutions and make the requested interpretations.

SELFtest

1. The Westchester Chamber of Commerce periodically sponsors public service seminars and programs. Currently, promotional plans are under way for this year's program. Advertising alternatives include television, radio, and newspaper. Audience estimates, costs, and maximum media usage limitations are as shown.

Constraint	Television	Radio	Newspaper
Audience per advertisement	100,000	18,000	40,000
Cost per advertisement	$2,000	$300	$600
Maximum media usage	10	20	10

To ensure a balanced use of advertising media, radio advertisements must not exceed 50% of the total number of advertisements authorized. In addition, television should account for at least 10% of the total number of advertisements authorized.

a. If the promotional budget is limited to $18,200, how many commercial messages should be run on each medium to maximize total audience contact? What is the allocation of the budget among the three media, and what is the total audience reached?

b. By how much would audience contact increase if an extra $100 were allocated to the promotional budget?

2. The management of Hartman Company is trying to determine the amount of each of two products to produce over the coming planning period. The following information concerns labor availability, labor utilization, and product profitability.

Department	Product (hours/unit)		Labor-Hours Available
	1	2	
A	1.00	0.35	100
B	0.30	0.20	36
C	0.20	0.50	50
Profit contribution/unit	$30.00	$15.00	

a. Develop a linear programming model of the Hartman Company problem. Solve the model to determine the optimal production quantities of products 1 and 2.

b. In computing the profit contribution per unit, management doesn't deduct labor costs because they are considered fixed for the upcoming planning period. However, suppose that overtime can be scheduled in some of the departments. Which departments would you recommend scheduling for overtime? How much would you be willing to pay per hour of overtime in each department?

c. Suppose that 10, 6, and 8 hours of overtime may be scheduled in departments A, B, and C, respectively. The cost per hour of overtime is $18 in department A, $22.50 in department B, and $12 in department C. Formulate a linear programming model that can be used to determine the optimal production quantities if overtime is made available. What are the optimal production quantities, and what is the revised total contribution to profit? How much overtime do you recommend using in each department? What is the increase in the total contribution to profit if overtime is used?

3. The employee credit union at State University is planning the allocation of funds for the coming year. The credit union makes four types of loans to its members. In addition, the credit union invests in risk-free securities to stabilize income. The various revenue-producing investments together with annual rates of return are as follows:

Type of Loan/Investment	Annual Rate of Return (%)
Automobile loans	8
Furniture loans	10
Other secured loans	11
Signature loans	12
Risk-free securities	9

The credit union will have $2,000,000 available for investment during the coming year. State laws and credit union policies impose the following restrictions on the composition of the loans and investments.

- Risk-free securities may not exceed 30% of the total funds available for investment.
- Signature loans may not exceed 10% of the funds invested in all loans (automobile, furniture, other secured, and signature loans).
- Furniture loans plus other secured loans may not exceed the automobile loans.
- Other secured loans plus signature loans may not exceed the funds invested in risk-free securities.

How should the $2,000,000 be allocated to each of the loan/investment alternatives to maximize total annual return? What is the projected total annual return?

4. Hilltop Coffee manufactures a coffee product by blending three types of coffee beans. The cost per pound and the available pounds of each bean are as follows:

Bean	Cost per Pound	Available Pounds
1	$0.50	500
2	$0.70	600
3	$0.45	400

Consumer tests with coffee products were used to provide ratings on a scale of 0–100, with higher ratings indicating higher quality. Product quality standards for the blended coffee require a consumer rating for aroma to be at least 75 and a consumer rating for taste to be at least 80. The individual ratings of the aroma and taste for coffee made from 100% of each bean are as follows.

Bean	Aroma Rating	Taste Rating
1	75	86
2	85	88
3	60	75

Assume that the aroma and taste attributes of the coffee blend will be a weighted average of the attributes of the beans used in the blend.
  a. What is the minimum cost blend that will meet the quality standards and provide 1000 pounds of the blended coffee product?
  b. What is the cost per pound for the coffee blend?
  c. Determine the aroma and taste ratings for the coffee blend.
  d. If additional coffee were to be produced, what would be the expected cost per pound?

5. Ajax Fuels, Inc., is developing a new additive for airplane fuels. The additive is a mixture of three ingredients: A, B, and C. For proper performance, the total amount of additive (amount of A + amount of B + amount of C) must be at least 10 ounces per gallon of fuel. However, because of safety reasons, the amount of additive must not exceed 15 ounces per gallon of fuel. The mix or blend of the three ingredients is critical. At least 1 ounce of ingredient A must be used for every ounce of ingredient B. The amount of ingredient C must be greater than one-half the amount of ingredient A. If the costs per ounce for ingredients A, B, and C are $0.10, $0.03, and $0.09, respectively, find the minimum cost mixture of A, B, and C for each gallon of airplane fuel.

6. G. Kunz and Sons, Inc., manufactures two products used in the heavy equipment industry. Both products require manufacturing operations in two departments. The following are the production time (in hours) and profit contribution figures for the two products.

		Labor-Hours	
Product	Profit per Unit	Dept. A	Dept. B
1	$25	6	12
2	$20	8	10

For the coming production period, Kunz has available a total of 900 hours of labor that can be allocated to either of the two departments. Find the production plan and labor allocation (hours assigned in each department) that will maximize the total contribution to profit.

7. As part of the settlement for a class action lawsuit, Hoxworth Corporation must provide sufficient cash to make the following annual payments (in $000s).

Year	1	2	3	4	5	6
Payment	190	215	240	285	315	460

The annual payments must be made at the beginning of each year. The judge will approve an amount that, along with earnings on its investment, will cover the annual payments. Investment of the funds will be limited to savings (at 4% annually) and government securities, at prices and rates currently quoted in *The Wall Street Journal*.

368

Hoxworth wants to develop a plan for making the annual payments by investing in the following securities (par value = $1000). Funds not invested in these securities will be placed in savings.

Security	Current Price	Rate (%)	Years to Maturity
1	$1055	6.750	3
2	$1000	5.125	4

Assume that interest is paid annually. The plan will be submitted to the judge and, if approved, Hoxworth will be required to pay a trustee the amount that will be required to fund the plan.

a. Use linear programming to find the minimum cash settlement necessary to fund the annual payments.

b. Use the dual price to determine how much more Hoxworth should be willing to pay now to reduce the payment at the beginning of year 6 to $400,000.

c. Use the dual price to determine how much more Hoxworth should be willing to pay to reduce the year 1 payment to $150,000.

d. Suppose that the annual payments are to be made at the end of each year. Reformulate the model to accommodate this change. How much would Hoxworth save if this change could be negotiated?

8. The Clark County Sheriff's Department schedules police officers for 8-hour shifts. The beginning times for the shifts are 8:00 A.M., noon, 4:00 P.M., 8:00 P.M., midnight, and 4:00 A.M. An officer beginning a shift at one of these times works for the next 8 hours. During normal weekday operations, the number of officers needed varies depending on the time of day. The department staffing guidelines require the following minimum number of officers on duty:

Time of Day	Minimum Officers on Duty
8:00 A.M.–noon	5
Noon–4:00 P.M.	6
4:00 P.M.–8:00 P.M.	10
8:00 P.M.–MIDNIGHT	7
MIDNIGHT–4:00 A.M.	4
4:00 A.M.–8:00 A.M.	6

Determine the number of police officers that should be scheduled to begin the 8-hour shifts at each of the six times (8:00 A.M., noon, 4:00 P.M., 8:00 P.M., midnight, and 4:00 A.M.) to minimize the total number of officers required. (Hint: Let x_1 = the number of officers beginning work at 8:00 A.M., x_2 = the number of officers beginning work at noon, and so on.)

SELFtest   9. Reconsider the Welte Mutual Funds problem from Section 9.2. Define your decision variables as the fraction of funds invested in each security. Also, modify the constraints limiting investments in the oil and steel industries as follows: No more than 50% of the total funds invested in stock (oil and steel) may be invested in the oil industry, and no more than 50% of the funds invested in stock (oil and steel) may be invested in the steel industry.

a. Solve the revised linear programming model. What fraction of the portfolio should be invested in each type of security?

b. How much should be invested in each type of security?

c. What are the total earnings for the portfolio?

d. What is the marginal rate of return on the portfolio? That is, how much more could be earned by investing one more dollar in the portfolio?

10. Lurix Electronics manufactures two products that can be produced on two different production lines. Both products have their lowest production costs when produced on the more modern of the two production lines. However, the modern production line does not have the capacity to handle the total production. As a result, some production will have to be routed to the older production line. The following data show total production requirements, production line capacities, and production costs.

| | Production Cost/Unit | | Minimum Production |
Product	Modern Line	Old Line	Requirements
1	$ 3.00	$ 5.00	500 units
2	$ 2.50	$ 4.00	700 units
Production line capacities	800	600	

Formulate a linear programming model that can be used to make the production routing decision. What is the recommended decision and the total cost?

11. Edwards Manufacturing Company purchases two component parts from three different suppliers. The suppliers have limited capacity, and no one supplier can meet all the company's needs. In addition, the suppliers charge different prices for the components. Component price data (in price per unit) are as follows:

| | Supplier | | |
Component	1	2	3
1	$12	$13	$14
2	$10	$11	$10

Each supplier has a limited capacity in terms of the total number of components it can supply. However, as long as Edwards provides sufficient advance orders, each supplier can devote its capacity to component 1, component 2, or any combination of the two components, if the total number of units ordered is within its capacity. Supplier capacities are as follows.

Supplier	1	2	3
Capacity	600	1000	800

If the Edwards production plan for the next period includes 1000 units of component 1 and 800 units of component 2, what purchases do you recommend? That is, how many units of each component should be ordered from each supplier? What is the total purchase cost for the components?

SELFtest 12. Refer to the Janders application in Section 9.3. Consider each of the following variations of the original problem separately.
   a. Suppose that Janders' supplier lowers the price for the bases to $0.55 per unit. What is the new optimal solution and its value?
   b. Suppose that the supplier of the tops for the Technician calculator raises the unit price to $0.82. What is the new optimal solution and its value?
   c. If Janders' employees were willing to work overtime for an overtime premium of only $2 per hour, should Janders schedule overtime? Why or why not? What is the new optimal solution and its value?

13. Reconsider the McCormick Manufacturing Company problem in Section 9.3. Each of the following parts presents a variation of the original problem. Consider each question separately.

a. Suppose that no more than 600 hours can be transferred from department 2. Based on the dual price information, how does the value of the optimal solution change?

b. Modify the linear programming model to reflect the change described in part (a). Solve the revised formulation to verify your conclusion in part (a). What transfers are recommended?

c. Suppose that the employees transferred from department 1 to department 3 are only 80% as productive in department 3 as the employees originally assigned to that department. Reformulate the original model in Section 9.3 accordingly and solve. What is the new optimal solution? (Hint: Modify the labor balance equation for department 3.)

14. The production manager for the Classic Boat Corporation must determine how many units of the Classic 21 model to produce over the next four quarters. The company has a beginning inventory of 100 Classic 21 boats, and demand for the four quarters is 2000 units in quarter 1, 4000 units in quarter 2, 3000 units in quarter 3, and 1500 units in quarter 4. The firm has limited production capacity in each quarter. That is, up to 4000 units can be produced in quarter 1, 3000 units in quarter 2, 2000 units in quarter 3, and 4000 units in quarter 4. Each boat held in inventory in quarters 1 and 2 incurs an inventory holding cost of $250 per unit; the holding cost for quarters 3 and 4 is $300 per unit. The production costs for the first quarter are $10,000 per unit; these costs are expected to increase by 10% each quarter because of increases in labor and material costs. Management has specified that the ending inventory for quarter 4 must be at least 500 boats.

a. Formulate a linear programming model that can be used to determine the production schedule that will minimize the total cost of meeting demand in each quarter subject to the production capacities in each quarter and also to the required ending inventory in quarter 4.

b. Solve the linear program formulated in part (a). Then develop a table that will show for each quarter the number of units to manufacture, the ending inventory, and the costs incurred.

c. Interpret each of the dual prices corresponding to the constraints developed to meet demand in each quarter. Based on these dual prices what advice would you give the production manager?

d. Interpret each of the dual prices corresponding to the production capacity in each quarter. Based on each of these dual prices what advice would you give the production manager?

SELFtest 15. Seastrand Oil Company produces two grades of gasoline: regular and high octane. Both gasolines are produced by blending two types of crude oil. Although both types of crude oil contain the two important ingredients required to produce both gasolines, the percentage of important ingredients in each type of crude oil differs, as does the cost per gallon. The percentage of ingredients A and B in each type of crude oil and the cost per gallon are shown.

Crude Oil	Cost	Ingredient A	Ingredient B	
1	$0.10	20%	60%	Crude oil 1 is 60% ingredient B
2	$0.15	50%	30%	

Each gallon of regular gasoline must contain at least 40% of ingredient A, whereas each gallon of high octane can contain at most 50% of ingredient B. Daily demand for regular and high-octane gasoline is 800,000 and 500,000 gallons, respectively. How many gallons of each type of crude oil should be used in the two gasolines to satisfy daily demand at a minimum cost?

16. The Ferguson Paper Company produces rolls of paper for use in adding machines, desk calculators, and cash registers. The rolls, which are 200 feet long, are produced in widths of 1½, 2½, and 3½ inches. The production process provides 200-foot rolls in 10-inch widths only. The firm must therefore cut the rolls to the desired final product sizes. The seven cutting alternatives and the amount of waste generated by each are as follows.

| Cutting | Number of Rolls | | | Waste |
Alternative	1½ in.	2½ in.	3½ in.	(inches)
1	6	0	0	1
2	0	4	0	0
3	2	0	2	0
4	0	1	2	½
5	1	3	0	1
6	1	2	1	0
7	4	0	1	½

The minimum requirements for the three products are

Roll Width (inches)	1½	2½	3½
Units	1000	2000	4000

a. If the company wants to minimize the number of 10-inch rolls that must be manufactured, how many 10-inch rolls will be processed on each cutting alternative? How many rolls are required, and what is the total waste (inches)?

b. If the company wants to minimize the waste generated, how many 10-inch units will be processed on each cutting alternative? How many rolls are required, and what is the total waste (inches)?

c. What are the differences in parts (a) and (b) to this problem? In this case, which objective do you prefer? Explain. What types of situations would make the other objective more desirable?

17. Frandec Company manufactures, assembles, and rebuilds material handling equipment used in warehouses and distribution centers. One product, called a Liftmaster, is assembled from four components: a frame, a motor, two supports, and a metal strap. Frandec's production schedule calls for 5000 Liftmasters to be made next month. Frandec purchases the motors from an outside supplier, but the frames, supports, and straps may either be manufactured by the company or purchased from an outside supplier. Manufacturing and purchase costs per unit are shown.

Component	Manufacturing Cost	Purchase Cost
Frame	$38.00	$51.00
Support	11.50	15.00
Strap	6.50	7.50

Three departments are involved in the production of these components. The time (in minutes per unit) required to process each component in each department and the available capacity (in hours) for the three departments are as follows.

Component	Department		
	Cutting	Milling	Shaping
Frame	3.5	2.2	3.1
Support	1.3	1.7	2.6
Strap	0.8	—	1.7
Capacity (hours)	350	420	680

a. Formulate and solve a linear programming model for this make-or-buy application. How many of each component should be manufactured and how many should be purchased?
b. What is the total cost of the manufacturing and purchasing plan?
c. How many hours of production time are used in each department?
d. How much should Frandec be willing to pay for an additional hour of time in the shaping department?
e. Another manufacturer has offered to sell frames to Frandec for $45 each. Could Frandec improve its position by pursuing this opportunity? Why or why not?

18. The Two-Rivers Oil Company near Pittsburgh transports gasoline to its distributors by truck. The company has recently contracted to supply gasoline distributors in southern Ohio, and it has $600,000 available to spend on the necessary expansion of its fleet of gasoline tank trucks. Three models of gasoline tank trucks are available.

Truck Model	Capacity (gallons)	Purchase Cost	Monthly Operating Cost, Including Depreciation
Super Tanker	5000	$67,000	$550
Regular Line	2500	$55,000	$425
Econo-Tanker	1000	$46,000	$350

The company estimates that the monthly demand for the region will be 550,000 gallons of gasoline. Because of the size and speed differences of the trucks, the number of deliveries or round trips possible per month for each truck model will vary. Trip capacities are estimated at 15 trips per month for the Super Tanker, 20 trips per month for the Regular Line, and 25 trips per month for the Econo-Tanker. Based on maintenance and driver availability, the firm does not want to add more than 15 new vehicles to its fleet. In addition, the company has decided to purchase at least three of the new Econo-Tankers for use on short-run, low-demand routes. As a final constraint, the company does not want more than half the new models to be Super Tankers.
a. If the company wishes to satisfy the gasoline demand with a minimum monthly operating expense, how many models of each truck should be purchased?
b. If the company did not require at least three Econo-Tankers and did not limit the number of Super Tankers to at most half the new models, how many models of each truck should be purchased?

SELFtest 19. The Silver Star Bicycle Company will be manufacturing both men's and women's models for its Easy-Pedal 10-speed bicycles during the next 2 months. Management wants to develop a production schedule indicating how many bicycles of each model should be produced in each month. Current demand forecasts call for 150 men's and 125 women's models to be shipped during the first month and 200 men's and 150 women's models to be shipped during the second month. Additional data are shown.

Model	Production Costs	Labor Requirements (hours)		Current Inventory
		Manufacturing	Assembly	
Men's	$120	2.0	1.5	20
Women's	$ 90	1.6	1.0	30

Last month the company used a total of 1000 hours of labor. The company's labor relations policy will not allow the combined total hours of labor (manufacturing plus assembly) to increase or decrease by more than 100 hours from month to month. In addition, the company charges monthly inventory at the rate of 2% of the production cost based on the inventory levels at the end of the month. The company would like to have at least 25 units of each model in inventory at the end of the 2 months.

a. Establish a production schedule that minimizes production and inventory costs and satisfies the labor-smoothing, demand, and inventory requirements. What inventories will be maintained and what are the monthly labor requirements?

b. If the company changed the constraints so that monthly labor increases and decreases could not exceed 50 hours, what would happen to the production schedule? How much will the cost increase? What would you recommend?

20. Filtron Corporation produces filtration containers used in water treatment systems. Although business has been growing, the demand each month varies considerably. As a result, the company utilizes a mix of part-time and full-time employees to meet production demands. Although this approach provides Filtron with great flexibility, it has resulted in increased costs and morale problems among employees. For instance, if Filtron needs to increase production from one month to the next, additional part-time employees have to be hired and trained, and costs go up. If Filtron has to decrease production, the workforce has to be reduced and Filtron incurs additional costs in terms of unemployment benefits and decreased morale. Best estimates are that increasing the number of units produced from one month to the next will increase production costs by $1.25 per unit, and that decreasing the number of units produced will increase production costs by $1.00 per unit. In February Filtron produced 10,000 filtration containers but only sold 7500 units; 2500 units are currently in inventory. The sales forecasts for March, April, and May are for 12,000 units, 8,000 units, and 15,000 units, respectively. In addition, Filtron has the capacity to store up to 3000 filtration containers at the end of any month. Management would like to determine the number of units to be produced in March, April, and May that will minimize the total cost of the monthly production increases and decreases.

21. Greenville Cabinets has received a contract to produce speaker cabinets for a major speaker manufacturer. The contract calls for the production of 3300 bookshelf speakers and 4100 floor speakers over the next two months, with the following delivery schedule.

Model	Month 1	Month 2
Bookshelf	2100	1200
Floor	1500	2600

Greenville estimates that the production time for each bookshelf model is 0.7 hour and the production time for each floor model is 1 hour. The raw material costs are $10 for each bookshelf model and $12 for each floor model. Labor costs are $22 per hour using regular production time and $33 using overtime. Greenville has up to 2400 hours of regular production time available each month and up to 1000 additional hours of overtime available each month. If production for either cabinet exceeds demand in month 1, the cabinets can be stored at a cost of $5 per cabinet. For each product, determine the number of units that should be manufactured each month on regular time and on overtime to minimize total production and storage costs.

22. TriCity Manufacturing (TCM) makes Styrofoam cups, plates, and sandwich and meal containers. Next week's schedule calls for the production of 80,000 small sandwich containers, 80,000 large sandwich containers, and 65,000 meal containers. To make these containers, Styrofoam sheets are melted and formed into final products using three machines: M1, M2, and M3. Machine M1 can process Styrofoam sheets with a maximum width of 12 inches. The width capacity of machine M2 is 16 inches, and the width capacity of machine M3 is 20 inches. The small sandwich containers require 10-inch wide Styrofoam sheets; thus, these containers can be produced on each of the three machines. The large sandwich containers require 12-inch wide sheets; thus, these containers can also be produced on each of the three machines. However, the meal containers require 16-inch wide Styrofoam sheets, so the meal containers cannot be produced on machine M1. Waste is incurred in the production of all three containers because Styrofoam is lost in the heating and forming process as well as in the final trimming of the product. The amount of waste generated varies depending upon the container produced and the machine used. The following table shows the waste in square inches for each machine and product combination. The waste material is recycled for future use.

Machine	Small Sandwich	Large Sandwich	Meal
M1	20	15	—
M2	24	28	18
M3	32	35	36

Production rates also depend upon the container produced and the machine used. The following table shows the production rates in units per minute for each machine and product combination. Machine capacities are limited for the next week. Time available is 35 hours for machine M1, 35 hours for machine M2, and 40 hours for machine M3.

Machine	Small Sandwich	Large Sandwich	Meal
M1	30	25	—
M2	45	40	30
M3	60	52	44

a. Costs associated with reprocessing the waste material have been increasing. Thus, TCM would like to minimize the amount of waste generated in meeting next week's production schedule. Formulate a linear programming model that can be used to determine the best production schedule.

b. Solve the linear program formulated in part (a) to determine the production schedule. How much waste is generated? Which machines, if any, have idle capacity?

23. EZ-Windows, Inc., manufactures replacement windows for the home remodeling business. In January, the company produced 15,000 windows and ended the month with 9000 windows in inventory. EZ-Windows management team would like to develop a production

schedule for the next three months. A smooth production schedule is obviously desirable as it maintains the current workforce and provides a similar month-to-month operation. However, given the sales forecasts, the production capacities, and the storage capabilities as shown, the management team does not think a smooth production schedule with the same production quantity each month possible.

	February	March	April
Sales forecast	15,000	16,500	20,000
Production capacity	14,000	14,000	18,000
Storage capacity	6,000	6,000	6,000

The company's cost accounting department estimates that increasing production by one window from one month to the next will increase total costs by $1.00 for each unit increase in the production level. In addition, decreasing production by one unit from one month to the next will increase total costs by $0.65 for each unit decrease in the production level. Ignoring production and inventory carrying costs, formulate and solve a linear programming model that will minimize the cost of changing production levels while still satisfying the monthly sales forecasts.

24. Morton Financial must decide on the percentage of available funds to commit to each of two investments, referred to as A and B, over the next four periods. The following table shows the amount of new funds available for each of the four periods, as well as the cash expenditure required for each investment (negative values) or the cash income from the investment (positive values). The data shown (in $000s) reflect the amount of expenditure or income if 100% of the funds available in any period are invested in either A or B. For example, if Morton decides to invest 100% of the funds available in any period in investment A, it will incur cash expenditures of $1000 in period 1, $800 in period 2, $200 in period 3, and income of $200 in period 4. Note, however, if Morton made the decision to invest 80% in investment A, the cash expenditures or income would be 80% of the values shown.

Period	New Investment Funds Available	Investment A	Investment B
1	1500	-1000	-800
2	400	-800	-500
3	500	-200	-300
4	100	200	300

The amount of funds available in any period is the sum of the new investment funds for the period, the new loan funds, the savings from the previous period, the cash income from investment A, and the cash income from investment B. The funds available in any period can be used to pay the loan and interest from the previous period, placed in savings, used to pay the cash expenditures for investment A, or used to pay the cash expenditures for investment B.

Assume an interest rate of 10% per period for savings and an interest rate of 18% per period on borrowed funds. Let

$$S(t) = \text{the savings for period } t$$
$$L(t) = \text{the new loan funds for period } t$$

Then, in any period t, the savings income from the previous period is $1.1S(t-1)$ and the loan and interest expenditure from the previous period is $1.18L(t-1)$.

At the end of period 4, investment A is expected to have a cash value of $3200 (assuming a 100% investment in A), and investment B is expected to have a cash value of $2500 (assuming a 100% investment in B). Additional income and expenses at the end of period 4 will be income from savings in period 4 less the repayment of the period 4 loan plus interest.

Suppose that the decision variables are defined as

$$x_1 = \text{the proportion of investment A undertaken}$$
$$x_2 = \text{the proportion of investment B undertaken}$$

For example, if $x_1 = 0.5$, $500 would be invested in investment A during the first period, and all remaining cash flows and ending investment A values would be multiplied by 0.5. The same holds for investment B. The model must include constraints $x_1 \leq 1$ and $x_2 \leq 1$ to make sure that no more than 100% of the investments can be undertaken.

If no more than $200 can be borrowed in any period, determine the proportions of investments A and B and the amount of savings and borrowing in each period that will maximize the cash value for the firm at the end of the four periods.

25. Western Family Steakhouse offers a variety of low-cost meals and quick service. Other than management, the steakhouse operates with two full-time employees who work 8 hours per day. The rest of the employees are part-time employees who are scheduled for 4-hour shifts during peak meal times. On Saturdays the steakhouse is open from 11:00 A.M. to 10:00 P.M. Management wants to develop a schedule for part-time employees that will minimize labor costs and still provide excellent customer service. The average wage rate for the part-time employees is $7.60 per hour. The total number of full-time and part-time employees needed varies with the time of day as shown.

Time	Total Number of Employees Needed
11:00 A.M.–noon	9
Noon–1:00 P.M.	9
1:00 P.M.–2:00 P.M.	9
2:00 P.M.–3:00 P.M.	3
3:00 P.M.–4:00 P.M.	3
4:00 P.M.–5:00 P.M.	3
5:00 P.M.–6:00 P.M.	6
6:00 P.M.–7:00 P.M.	12
7:00 P.M.–8:00 P.M.	12
8:00 P.M.–9:00 P.M.	7
9:00 P.M.–10:00 P.M.	7

One full-time employee comes on duty at 11:00 A.M., works 4 hours, takes an hour off, and returns for another 4 hours. The other full-time employee comes to work at 1:00 P.M. and works the same 4-hours-on, 1-hour-off, 4-hours-on pattern.

a. Develop a minimum cost schedule for part-time employees.

b. What is the total payroll for the part-time employees? How many part-time shifts are needed? Use the surplus variables to comment on the desirability of scheduling at least some of the part-time employees for 3-hour shifts.

c. Assume that part-time employees can be assigned either a 3-hour or 4-hour shift. Develop a minimum cost schedule for the part-time employees. How many part-time shifts are needed and what is the cost savings compared to the previous schedule?

26. In Section 9.5 data envelopment analysis was used to evaluate the relative efficiencies of four hospitals. Data for three input measures and four output measures were provided in Tables 9.16 and 9.17.

    a. Use these data to develop a linear programming model that could be used to evaluate the performance of General Hospital.

    b. The following computer solution was obtained using The Management Scientist. Does the solution indicate that General Hospital is relatively inefficient?

Objective Function Value = 1.000000

Variable	Value	Reduced Costs
E	1.000	0.000
WG	1.000	0.000
WU	0.000	0.000
WC	0.000	0.331
WS	0.000	0.215

    c. Explain which hospital or hospitals make up the composite unit used to evaluate General Hospital and why.

27. Data envelopment analysis has been used to measure the relative efficiency of a group of hospitals. A particular study involved seven teaching hospitals; data on three input measures and four output measures are contained in the following tables.

	Input Measures		
Hospital	Full-Time Equivalent Nonphysicians	Supply Expense ($000s)	Bed-Days Available ($000s)
A	310.0	134.60	116.00
B	278.5	114.30	106.80
C	165.6	131.30	65.52
D	250.0	316.00	94.40
E	206.4	151.20	102.10
F	384.0	217.00	153.70
G	530.1	770.80	215.00

	Output Measures			
Hospital	Patient-Days (65 or older) (000s)	Patient-Days (under 65) (000s)	Nurses Trained	Interns Trained
A	55.31	49.52	291	47
B	37.64	55.63	156	3
C	32.91	25.77	141	26
D	33.53	41.99	160	21
E	32.48	55.30	157	82
F	48.78	81.92	285	92
G	58.41	119.70	111	89

a. Formulate a linear programming model so that data envelopment analysis can be used to evaluate the performance of hospital D.
b. Solve the model.
c. Is hospital D relatively inefficient? What is the interpretation of the value of the objective function?
d. How many patient-days of each type are produced by the composite hospital?
e. Which hospitals would you recommend hospital D consider emulating to improve the efficiency of its operation?

28. Refer again to the data presented in Problem 27.
a. Formulate a linear programming model that can be used to perform data envelopment analysis for hospital E.
b. Solve the model.
c. Is hospital E relatively inefficient? What is the interpretation of the value of the objective function?
d. Which hospitals are involved in making up the composite hospital? Can you make a general statement about which hospitals will make up the composite unit associated with a unit that is not inefficient?

29. The Ranch House, Inc., operates five fast food restaurants. Input measures for the restaurants include weekly hours of operation, full-time equivalent staff, and weekly supply expenses. Output measures of performance include average weekly contribution to profit, market share, and annual growth rate. Data for the input and output measures are shown in the following tables.

| | Input Measures | | |
Restaurant	Hours of Operation	FTE Staff	Supplies ($)
Bardstown	96	16	850
Clarksville	110	22	1400
Jeffersonville	100	18	1200
New Albany	125	25	1500
St. Matthews	120	24	1600

| | Output Measures | | |
Restaurant	Weekly Profit	Market Share (%)	Growth Rate (%)
Bardstown	$3800	25	8.0
Clarksville	$4600	32	8.5
Jeffersonville	$4400	35	8.0
New Albany	$6500	30	10.0
St. Matthews	$6000	28	9.0

a. Develop a linear programming model that can be used to evaluate the performance of the Clarksville Ranch House restaurant.
b. Solve the model.
c. Is the Clarksville Ranch House restaurant relatively inefficient? Discuss.
d. Where does the composite restaurant have more output than the Clarksville restaurant? How much less of each input resource does the composite restaurant require when compared to the Clarksville restaurant?
e. What other restaurants should be studied to find suggested ways for the Clarksville restaurant to improve its efficiency?

Case Problem ENVIRONMENTAL PROTECTION

Skillings Industrial Chemicals, Inc., operates a refinery in southwestern Ohio near the Ohio River. The company's primary product is manufactured from a chemical process that requires the use of two raw materials—material A and material B. The production of 1 pound of the primary product requires the use of 1 pound of material A and 2 pounds of material B. The output of the chemical process is 1 pound of the primary product, 1 pound of liquid waste material, and 1 pound of solid waste by-product. The solid waste by-product is given to a local fertilizer plant as payment for picking it up and disposing of it. The liquid waste material has no market value, so the refinery has been dumping it directly into the Ohio River. The company's manufacturing process is shown schematically in Figure 9.13.

Government pollution guidelines established by the Environmental Protection Agency will no longer permit disposal of the liquid waste directly into the river. The refinery's research group has developed the following set of alternative uses for the liquid waste material.

1. Produce a secondary product K by adding 1 pound of raw material A to every pound of liquid waste.
2. Produce a secondary product M by adding 1 pound of raw material B to every pound of liquid waste.
3. Specially treat the liquid waste so that it meets pollution standards before dumping it into the river.

These three alternatives are depicted in Figure 9.14.

The company's management knows that the secondary products will be low in quality and may not be very profitable. However, management also recognizes that the special treatment alternative will be a relatively expensive operation. The company's problem is to determine how to satisfy the pollution regulations and still maintain the highest possible profit. How should the liquid waste material be handled? Should Skillings produce product K, produce product M, use the special treatment, or employ some combination of the three alternatives?

FIGURE 9.13 MANUFACTURING PROCESS AT SKILLINGS INDUSTRIAL
CHEMICALS, INC.

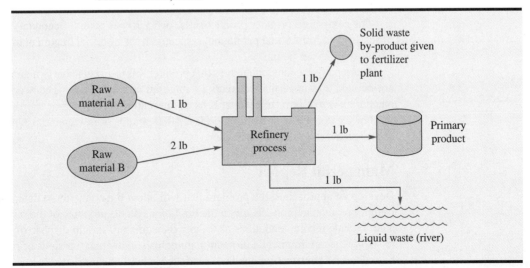

FIGURE 9.14   ALTERNATIVES FOR HANDLING THE REFINERY LIQUID WASTE

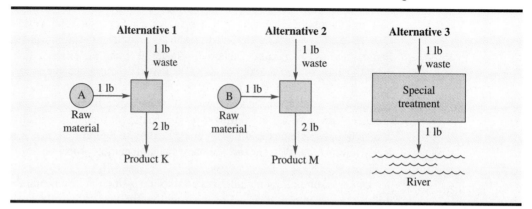

Last month 10,000 pounds of the company's primary product were produced. The accounting department has prepared a cost report showing the breakdown of fixed and variable expenses that were incurred during the month.

**Cost Analysis for 10,000 Pounds
of Primary Product**

Fixed costs	
Administrative expenses	$12,000
Refinery overhead	4,000
Variable costs	
Raw material A	15,000
Raw material B	16,000
Direct labor	5,000
Total	$52,000

In this cost analysis, the fixed-cost portion of the expenses is the same every month regardless of production level. Direct labor costs are expected to run $0.20 per pound for product K and $0.10 per pound for product M.

The company's primary product sells for $5.70 per pound. Secondary products K and M sell for $0.85 and $0.65 per pound, respectively. The special treatment of the liquid waste will cost $0.25 per pound.

A company accountant believes that product K is too expensive to manufacture and cannot be sold at a price that recovers its material and labor cost. The accountant's recommendation is to eliminate product K as an alternative.

For the upcoming production period, 5000 pounds of raw material A and 7000 pounds of raw material B will be available.

Managerial Report

Develop an approach to the problem that will allow the company to determine how much primary product to produce, given the limitations on the amounts of the raw material available. Include recommendations as to how the company should dispose of the liquid waste to satisfy the environmental protection guidelines. How many pounds of product K should be produced? How many pounds of product M should be produced? How many pounds of liquid waste should be specially treated and dumped into the river? Include a discussion and analysis of the following in your report:

1. A cost analysis showing the profit contribution per pound for the primary product, product K, and product M
2. The optimal production quantities and waste disposal plan, including the projected profit
3. A discussion of the value of additional pounds of each raw material
4. A discussion of the sensitivity analysis of the objective function coefficients
5. Comments on the accountant's recommendation to eliminate product K as an alternative: Does the recommendation appear reasonable? What is your reaction to the recommendation? How would the optimal solution change if product K were eliminated?

Case Problem   TRUCK LEASING STRATEGY

Reep Construction has recently won a contract for the excavation and site preparation of a new rest area on the Pennsylvania turnpike. In preparing his bid for the job, Bob Reep, founder and president of Reep Construction, estimated that it would take 4 months to perform the work and that 10, 12, 14, and 8 trucks would be needed in months 1 through 4, respectively.

The firm currently has 20 trucks of the type needed to perform the work on the new project. These trucks were obtained last year when Bob signed a long-term lease with PennState Leasing. Although most of these trucks are currently being used on existing jobs, Bob estimates that one truck will be available for use on the new project in month 1, two trucks will be available in month 2, three trucks will be available in month 3, and one truck will be available in month 4. Thus, to complete the project, Bob will have to lease additional trucks.

The long-term leasing contract with PennState has a monthly cost of $600 per truck. Reep Construction pays its truck drivers $20 an hour, and daily fuel costs are approximately $100 per truck. All maintenance costs are paid by PennState Leasing. For planning purposes, Bob estimates that each truck used on the new project will be operating 8 hours a day, 5 days a week for approximately 4 weeks each month.

Bob does not believe that current business conditions justify committing the firm to additional long-term leases. In discussing the short-term leasing possibilities with PennState Leasing, Bob has learned that he can obtain short-term leases of 1–4 months. Short-term leases differ from long-term leases in that the short-term leasing plans include the cost of both a truck and a driver. Maintenance costs for short-term leases also are paid by PennState Leasing. The following costs for each of the 4 months cover the lease of a truck and driver.

Length of Lease	Cost per Month
1	$4000
2	$3700
3	$3225
4	$3040

Bob Reep would like to acquire a lease that would minimize the cost of meeting the monthly trucking requirements for his new project, but he also takes great pride in the fact that his company has never laid off employees. Bob is committed to maintaining his no-layoff policy; that is, he will use his own drivers even if costs are higher.

Managerial Report

Perform an analysis of Reep Construction's leasing problem and prepare a report for Bob Reep that summarizes your findings. Be sure to include information on and analysis of the following items.

1. The optimal leasing plan
2. The costs associated with the optimal leasing plan
3. The cost for Reep Construction to maintain its current policy of no layoffs

Case Problem   PHOENIX COMPUTER

Phoenix Computer manufactures and sells personal computers directly to customers. Orders are accepted by phone and through the company's web site. Phoenix will be introducing several new laptop models over the next few months and management has recognized a need to develop technical support personnel to specialize in the new laptop systems. One option being considered is to hire new employees and put them through a 3-month training program. Another option is to put current customer service specialists through a 2-month training program on the new laptop models. Phoenix estimates that the need for laptop specialists will grow from 0 to 100 during the months of May through September as follows: May—20; June—30; July—85; August—85; and September—100. After September, Phoenix expects that maintaining a staff of 100 laptop specialists will be sufficient.

The annual salary for a new employee is estimated to be $27,000 whether the person is hired to enter the training program or to replace a current employee who is entering the training program. The annual salary for the current Phoenix employees who are being considered for the training program is approximately $36,000. The cost of the 3-month training program is $1500 per person, and the cost of the 2-month training program is $1000 per person. Note that the length of the training program means that a lag will occur between the time when a new person is hired and the time a new laptop specialist is available. The number of current employees who will be available for training is limited. Phoenix estimates that the following numbers can be made available in the coming months: March—15; April—20; May—0; June—5; and July—10. The training center has the capacity to start new 3-month and 2-month training classes each month; however, the total number of students (new and current employees) that begin training each month can not exceed 25.

Phoenix needs to determine the number of new hires that should begin the 3-month training program each month and the number of current employees that should begin the 2-month training program each month. The objective is to satisfy staffing needs during May through September at the lowest possible total cost; that is, minimize the incremental salary cost and the total training cost.

It is currently January, and Phoenix Computer would like to develop a plan for hiring new employees and determining the mix of new hires and current employees to place in the training program.

Managerial Report

Perform an analysis of the Phoenix Computer problem and prepare a report that summarizes your findings. Be sure to include information on and analysis of the following items.

1. The incremental salary and training cost associated with hiring a new employee and training him/her to be a laptop specialist
2. The incremental salary and training cost associated with putting a current employee through the training program (Don't forget that a replacement must be hired when the current employee enters the program)

3. Recommendations regarding the hiring and training plan that will minimize the salary and training costs over the February through August period as well as answers to these questions: What is the total cost of providing technical support for the new laptop models? How much higher will monthly payroll costs be in September than in January?

Case Problem   TEXTILE MILL SCHEDULING

The Scottsville Textile Mill* produces five different fabrics. Each fabric can be woven on one or more of the mill's 38 looms. The sales department has forecast demand for the next month. The demand data are shown in Table 9.18, along with data on the selling price per yard, variable cost per yard, and purchase price per yard. The mill operates 24 hours a day and is scheduled for 30 days during the coming month.

The mill has two types of looms: dobbie and regular. The dobbie looms are more versatile and can be used for all five fabrics. The regular looms can produce only three of the fabrics. The mill has a total of 38 looms: 8 are dobbie and 30 are regular. The rate of production for each fabric on each type of loom is given in Table 9.19. The time required to change over from producing one fabric to another is negligible and does not have to be considered.

The Scottsville Textile Mill satisfies all demand with either its own fabric or fabric purchased from another mill. That is, fabrics that cannot be woven at the Scottsville Mill because of limited loom capacity will be purchased from another mill. The purchase price of each fabric is also shown in Table 9.18.

TABLE 9.18   MONTHLY DEMAND, SELLING PRICE, VARIABLE COST, AND PURCHASE PRICE DATA FOR SCOTTSVILLE TEXTILE MILL FABRICS

Fabric	Demand (yards)	Selling Price ($/yard)	Variable Cost ($/yard)	Purchase Price ($/yard)
1	16,500	0.99	0.66	0.80
2	22,000	0.86	0.55	0.70
3	62,000	1.10	0.49	0.60
4	7,500	1.24	0.51	0.70
5	62,000	0.70	0.50	0.70

TABLE 9.19   LOOM PRODUCTION RATES FOR THE SCOTTSVILLE TEXTILE MILL

Fabric	Loom Rate (yards/hour) Dobbie	Loom Rate (yards/hour) Regular
1	4.63	—
2	4.63	—
3	5.23	5.23
4	5.23	5.23
5	4.17	4.17

Note: Fabrics 1 and 2 can be manufactured only on the dobbie loom.

*This case is based on the Calhoun Textile Mill Case by Jeffrey D. Camm, P. M. Dearing, and Suresh K. Tadisnia, 1987.

Managerial Report

Develop a model that can be used to schedule production for the Scottsville Textile Mill, and at the same time, determine how many yards of each fabric must be purchased from another mill. Include a discussion and analysis of the following items in your report.

1. The final production schedule and loom assignments for each fabric
2. The projected total contribution to profit
3. A discussion of the value of additional loom time (The mill is considering purchasing a ninth dobbie loom. What is your estimate of the monthly profit contribution of this additional loom?)
4. A discussion of the objective coefficients ranges
5. A discussion of how the objective of minimizing total costs would provide a different model than the objective of maximizing total profit contribution: How would the interpretation of the objective coefficients ranges differ for these two models?

Case Problem   WORKFORCE SCHEDULING

Davis Instruments has two manufacturing plants located in Atlanta, Georgia. Product demand varies considerably from month to month, causing Davis extreme difficulty in workforce scheduling. Recently Davis started hiring temporary workers supplied by WorkForce Unlimited, a company that specializes in providing temporary employees for firms in the greater Atlanta area. WorkForce Unlimited has offered to provide temporary employees under three contract options that differ in terms of the length of employment and the cost. The three options are summarized:

Option	Length of Employment	Cost
1	One month	$2000
2	Two months	$4800
3	Three months	$7500

The longer contract periods are more expensive because WorkForce Unlimited has greater difficulty finding temporary workers who are willing to commit to longer work assignments.

Over the next six months, Davis has projected the following needs for additional employees.

Month	January	February	March	April	May	June
Employees Needed	10	23	19	26	20	14

Each month, Davis can hire as many temporary employees as needed under each of the three options. For instance, if Davis hires five employees in January under Option 2, WorkForce Unlimited will supply Davis with five temporary workers who will work two months: January and February. For this, Davis will have to pay 5($4800) = $24,000. Because of some merger negotiations underway, Davis does not want to commit to any contractual obligations for temporary employees that extend beyond June.

Davis has a quality control program that requires each temporary employee to receive training at the time of hire. The training program is required even if the person has worked for Davis Instruments in the past. Davis estimates that the cost of training is $875 each time a temporary employee is hired. Thus, if a temporary employee is hired for one month, Davis will incur a training cost of $875, but will incur no additional training cost if the employee is on a two- or three-month contract.

Managerial Report

Develop a model that can be used to determine the number of temporary employees Davis should hire each month under each contract plan in order to meet the projected needs at a minimum total cost. Include the following items in your report:

1. A schedule that shows the number of temporary employees that Davis should hire each month for each contract option.
2. A summary table that shows the number of temporary employees that Davis should hire under each contract option, the associated contract cost for each option, and the associated training cost for each option. Provide summary totals showing the total number temporary employees hired, total contract costs, and total training costs.
3. If the cost to train each temporary employee could be reduced to $700 per month, what effect would this have on the hiring plan? Explain. Discuss the implications that this has for identifying methods for reducing training costs. How much of a reduction in training costs would be required to change the hiring plan based on a training cost of $875 per temporary employee?
4. Suppose that Davis was to hire 10 full-time employees at the beginning of January in order to satisfy part of the labor requirements over the next six months. If Davis can hire full-time employees for $16.50 per hour, including fringe benefits, what effect would this have on total labor and training costs over the six-month period as compared to hiring only temporary employees? Assume that full-time and temporary employees both work approximately 160 hours per month. Provide a recommendation regarding the decision to hire additional full-time employees.

Appendix 9.1   SPREADSHEET SOLUTION OF HEWLITT CORPORATION FINANCIAL PLANNING PROBLEM

In Appendix 7.3 we showed how Excel could be used to solve the RMC linear programming problem. To illustrate the use of Excel in solving a more complex linear programming problem, we show the solution to the Hewlitt Corporation financial planning problem presented in Section 9.2.

The spreadsheet formulation and solution of the Hewlitt Corporation problem are shown in Figure 9.15. As described in Appendix 7.1, our practice is to put the data required for the problem in the top part of the spreadsheet and build the model in the bottom part of the spreadsheet. The model consists of a set of cells for the decision variables, a cell for the objective function, a set of cells for the left-hand-side functions, and a set of cells for the right-hand sides of the constraints. The cells for each of these model components are screened; the cells for the decision variables are also enclosed by a boldface line. Descriptive labels are used to make the spreadsheet easy to read.

Spreadsheet Formulation

The data and descriptive labels are contained in cells A1:G12. The screened cells in the bottom portion of the spreadsheet contain the key elements of the model required by the Excel Solver.

FIGURE 9.15 SPREADSHEET SOLUTION FOR THE HEWLITT CORPORATION PROBLEM

	A	B	C	D	E	F	G	H	I	J	K	L
1	Hewlitt Corporation Cash Requirements											
2												
3		Cash										
4	Year	Rqmt.				Bond						
5	1	430			1	2	3					
6	2	210		Price ($1000)	1.15	1	1.35					
7	3	222		Rate	0.08875	0.055	0.1175					
8	4	231		Years to Maturity	5	6	7					
9	5	240										
10	6	195		Annual Savings Multiple		1.04						
11	7	225										
12	8	255										
13												
14	Model											
15												
16	F	B1	B2	B3	S1	S2	S3	S4	S5	S6	S7	S8
17	1728.79385	144.9881	187.8558	228.1879195	636.1479	501.6057	349.68179	182.6809	0	0	0	0
18												
19					Cash Flow		Net Cash		Cash			
20	Min Funds	1728.794		Constraints	In	Out	Flow		Rqmt.			
21				Year 1	1728.794	1298.794	430	=	430			
22				Year 2	711.6057	501.6057	210	=	210			
23				Year 3	571.6818	349.6818	222	=	222			
24				Year 4	413.6809	182.6809	231	=	231			
25				Year 5	240	0	240	=	240			
26				Year 6	195	0	195	=	195			
27				Year 7	225	0	225	=	225			
28				Year 8	255	0	255	=	255			

Decision Variables Cells A17:L17 are reserved for the decision variables. The optimal values (rounded to 3 places), are shown to be $F = 1728.794$, $B_1 = 144.988$, $B_2 = 187.856$, $B_3 = 228.188$, $S_1 = 636.148$, $S_2 = 501.606$, $S_3 = 349.682$, $S_4 = 182.681$, and $S_5 = S_6 = S_7 = S_8 = 0$.

Objective Function The formula $=A17$ has been placed into cell B20 to reflect the total funds required. It is simply the value of the decision variable, F. The total funds required by the optimal solution is shown to be $1,728,794.

Left-Hand Sides The left-hand sides for the 8 constraints represent the annual net cash flow. They are placed into cells G21:G28.
Cell G21 $=E21-F21$ (Copy to G22:G28)

For this problem, some of the left-hand-side cells reference other cells that contain formulas. These referenced cells provide Hewlitt's cash flow in and cash flow out for each of the eight years.* The cells and their formulas are as follows:

Cell E21 $=A17$

Cell E22 $=SUMPRODUCT(\$E\$7:\$G\$7,\$B\$17:\$D\$17)+\$F\$10*E17$

Cell E23 $=SUMPRODUCT(\$E\$7:\$G\$7,\$B\$17:\$D\$17)+\$F\$10*F17$

Cell E24 $=SUMPRODUCT(\$E\$7:\$G\$7,\$B\$17:\$D\$17)+\$F\$10*G17$

Cell E25 $=SUMPRODUCT(\$E\$7:\$G\$7,\$B\$17:\$D\$17)+\$F\$10*H17$

---

*The cash flow in is the sum of the positive terms in each constraint equation in the mathematical model, and the cash flow out is the sum of the negative terms in each constraint equation.

Cell E26 =(1+E7)*B17+F7*C17+G7*D17+F10*I17

Cell E27 =(1+F7)*C17+G7*D17+F10*J17

Cell E28 =(1+G7)*D17+F10*K17

Cell F21 =SUMPRODUCT(E6:G6,B17:D17)+E17

Cell F22 =F17

Cell F23 =G17

Cell F24 =H17

Cell F25 =I17

Cell F26 =J17

Cell F27 =K17

Cell F28 =L17

Right-Hand Sides   The right-hand sides for the 8 constraints represent the annual cash requirements. They are placed into cells I21:I28.

Cell I21 =B5 (Copy to I22:I28)

Spreadsheet Solution

We are now ready to use the information in the spreadsheet to determine the optimal solution to the Hewlitt Corporation problem. The following steps describe how to use Excel to obtain the optimal solution.

Step 1. Select the **Tools** pull-down menu
Step 2. Select the **Solver** option
Step 3. When the **Solver Parameters** dialog box appears:
    Enter B20 in the **Set Target Cell** box
    Select the **Equal to: Min** option
    Enter A17:L17 in the **By Changing Cells** box
    Choose **Add**
Step 4. When the **Add Constraint** dialog box appears:
    Enter G21:G28 in the **Cell Reference** box
    Select **=**
    Enter I21:I28 in the **Constraint** box
    Select **OK**
Step 5. When the **Solver Parameters** dialog box appears:
    Choose **Options**
Step 6. When the **Solver Options** dialog box appears:
    Select **Assume Linear Model**
    Select **Assume Non-Negative**
    Select **OK**
Step 7. When the **Solver Parameters** dialog box appears:
    Choose **Solve**
Step 8. When the **Solver Results** dialog box appears:
    Select **Keep Solver Solution**
    Select **Sensitivity** in the **Reports** box
    Select **OK**

The solver parameters dialog box is shown in Figure 9.16. The optimal solution is shown in Figure 9.15; the accompanying sensitivity report is shown in Figure 9.17.

FIGURE 9.16   SOLVER PARAMETERS DIALOG BOX FOR THE HEWLITT
CORPORATION PROBLEM

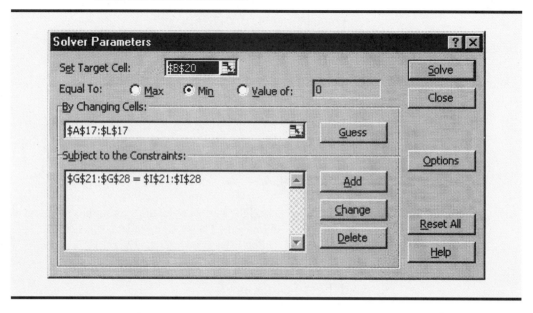

FIGURE 9.17   CONSTRAINTS SECTION OF THE SENSITIVITY REPORT FOR THE
HEWLITT CORPORATION PROBLEM

Constraints

Cell	Name	Final Value	Shadow Price	Constraint R.H. Side	Allowable Increase	Allowable Decrease
$G$21	Year 1 Flow	430	1	430	1E+30	1728.793855
$G$22	Year 2 Flow	210	0.961538462	210	1E+30	661.5938616
$G$23	Year 3 Flow	222	0.924556213	222	1E+30	521.6699405
$G$24	Year 4 Flow	231	0.888996359	231	1E+30	363.6690626
$G$25	Year 5 Flow	240	0.854804191	240	1E+30	189.9881496
$G$26	Year 6 Flow	195	0.760364454	195	2149.927647	157.8558478
$G$27	Year 7 Flow	225	0.718991202	225	3027.962172	198.1879195
$G$28	Year 8 Flow	255	0.670839393	255	1583.881915	255

Discussion

Figures 9.15 and 9.17 contain essentially the same information as that provided by The
Management Scientist solution in Figure 9.4. Recall that the Excel sensitivity report uses
the term *shadow price* to describe the *change* in value of the solution per-unit increase in
the right-hand side of a constraint. The Management Scientist and LINDO use the term *dual
price* to describe the *improvement* in value of the solution per-unit increase in the right-hand
side of a constraint. For maximization problems, the shadow price and dual price are the
same; for minimization problems, the shadow price and dual price have opposite signs. Because the Hewlitt financial planning problem involves minimization, the shadow prices in
the Excel sensitivity report (Figure 9.17) are the negative of the dual prices in The Management Scientist solution (Figure 9.4).

MARATHON OIL COMPANY*

FINDLAY, OHIO

Marathon Oil Company was founded in 1887 when 14 oilmen pooled their properties to organize an oil-producing company in the Trenton Rock oil fields of Ohio. In 1924 Marathon entered the refining and marketing phase of the petroleum industry. Today Marathon is a fully integrated oil company with significant international operations. In the United States the company markets petroleum products in 21 states, primarily in the Midwest and Southeast.

Quantitative Methods at Marathon Oil Company

Marathon Oil's Operations Research Department was formed in 1963 in order to aid problem solving and decision making in all areas of the company. Approximately 50% of the applications involve linear programming. Typical problems include refinery models, distribution models, gasoline and fuel oil blending models, and crude oil evaluation studies. Another 30% of the applications involve complex chemical engineering simulation models of process operations. The remaining applications involve solution techniques using nonlinear programming, network flow algorithms, and statistical techniques such as regression analysis.

A Marketing Planning Model

Marathon Oil Company has four refineries within the United States, operates 50 light products terminals, and has product demand at more than 95 locations. The Supply and Transportation Division is faced with the problem of determining which refinery should supply which terminal and, at the same time, determining which products should be transported via which pipeline, barge, or tanker to minimize cost. Product demand must be satisfied, and the supply capability of each refinery must not be exceeded. To help solve this difficult problem, Marathon's Operations Research Department developed a marketing planning model for the Operations Planning Department.

The marketing planning model is a large-scale linear programming model that takes into account sales not only at Marathon product terminals but also at all exchange locations. An exchange contract is an agreement with other oil product marketers that involves exchanging or trading Marathon's products for theirs at different locations. Thus, some geographic imbalance between supply and demand can be reduced. Both sides of the exchanges are represented since the results not only affect the net requirements at a demand location, but in addition have important financial implications. All pipelines, barges, and tankers within Marathon's marketing area are also represented in the linear programming model. The objective of the linear programming model is to minimize the cost of meeting a given demand structure, taking into account sales price, pipeline tariffs, exchange contract costs, product demand, terminal operating costs, refining costs, and product purchases.

The marketing planning model is used to solve a wide variety of planning problems. These vary from evaluating gasoline blending economics to analyzing the economics of a new terminal or pipeline. Although the types of problems that can be solved are almost unlimited, the model is most effective in handling the following:

1. Evaluating additional product demand locations, pipelines, and exchange contracts
2. Determining profitability of shifting sales from one product demand location to another
3. Determining the effects on supply and distribution when a pipeline increases its tariff
4. Optimizing production of the grades at the five refineries based on distribution

*The authors are indebted to Robert W. Wernert of Marathon Oil Company, Findlay, Ohio, for providing this application.

The linear programming model not only solves these problems, but also gives the financial impact of each solution.

Benefits

With daily sales of about 10 million gallons of refined light product, a savings of even one-thousandth of a cent per gallon can result in significant long-term savings. At the same time, what may appear to be a savings in one area, such as refining or transportation, may actually add to overall costs when the effects are fully realized throughout the system. The marketing planning model allows a simultaneous examination of this total effect.

Questions

1. What is the primary objective of Marathon's marketing planning model?
2. Describe the types of problems the marketing planning model is most effective in handling.
3. If daily savings using the model are one-tenth of a cent per gallon sold, what is the projected daily savings?

TRANSPORTATION, ASSIGNMENT, AND TRANSSHIPMENT PROBLEMS

CONTENTS

Transportation, assignment, and transshipment problems belong to a special class of linear programming problems called *network flow problems.* A separate chapter is devoted to these problems for two reasons. First, a wide variety of applications can be modeled as transportation, assignment, or transshipment problems. Second, these problems have a mathematical structure that has enabled management scientists to develop efficient specialized solution procedures for solving them; as a result, even large problems can be solved with just a few seconds of computer time.

We approach the network flow problems by illustrating each problem with a specific application. We first develop a graphical representation, called a **network,** of the problem and then show how each can be formulated and solved as a linear program.

10.1 THE TRANSPORTATION PROBLEM: THE NETWORK MODEL AND A LINEAR PROGRAMMING FORMULATION

The **transportation problem** arises frequently in planning for the distribution of goods and services from several supply locations to several demand locations. Typically, the quantity of goods available at each supply location (origin) is limited, and the quantity of goods needed at each of several demand locations (destinations) is known. The usual objective in a transportation problem is to minimize the cost of shipping goods from the origins to the destinations.

Let us illustrate by considering a transportation problem faced by Foster Generators. This problem involves the transportation of a product from

three plants to four distribution centers. Foster Generators has plants in Cleveland, Ohio; Bedford, Indiana; and York, Pennsylvania. Production capacities over the next 3-month planning period for one particular type of generator are as follows:

Origin	Plant	3-Month Production Capacity (units)
1	Cleveland	5,000
2	Bedford	6,000
3	York	2,500
	Total	13,500

The firm distributes its generators through four regional distribution centers located in Boston, Chicago, St. Louis, and Lexington; the 3-month forecast of demand for the distribution centers is as follows:

Destination	Distribution Center	3-Month Demand Forecast (units)
1	Boston	6,000
2	Chicago	4,000
3	St. Louis	2,000
4	Lexington	1,500
	Total	13,500

Management would like to determine how much of its production should be shipped from each plant to each distribution center. Figure 10.1 shows graphically the 12 distribution routes Foster can use. Such a graph is called a *network;* the circles are referred to as **nodes** and the lines connecting the nodes as **arcs.** Each origin and destination is represented by a node, and each possible shipping route is represented by an arc. The amount of the supply is written next to each origin node, and the amount of the demand is written next to each destination node. The goods shipped from the origins to the destinations represent the flow in the network. Note that the direction of flow (from origin to destination) is indicated by the arrows.

Try Problem 1 for practice in developing a network model of a transportation problem.

For Foster's transportation problem, the objective is to determine the routes to be used and the quantity to be shipped via each route that will provide the minimum total transportation cost. The cost for each unit shipped on each route is given in Table 10.1 and is shown on each arc in Figure 10.1.

The first subscript identifies the "from" node of the corresponding arc and the second subscript identifies the "to" node of the arc.

A linear programming model can be used to solve this transportation problem. We use double-subscripted decision variables, with x_{11} denoting the number of units shipped from origin 1 (Cleveland) to destination 1 (Boston), x_{12} denoting the number of units shipped from origin 1 (Cleveland) to destination 2 (Chicago), and so on. In general, the decision variables for a transportation problem having m origins and n destinations are written as follows:

$$x_{ij} = \text{number of units shipped from origin } i \text{ to destination } j$$
$$\text{where } i = 1, 2, \ldots, m \text{ and } j = 1, 2, \ldots, n$$

FIGURE 10.1   THE NETWORK REPRESENTATION OF THE FOSTER GENERATORS
TRANSPORTATION PROBLEM

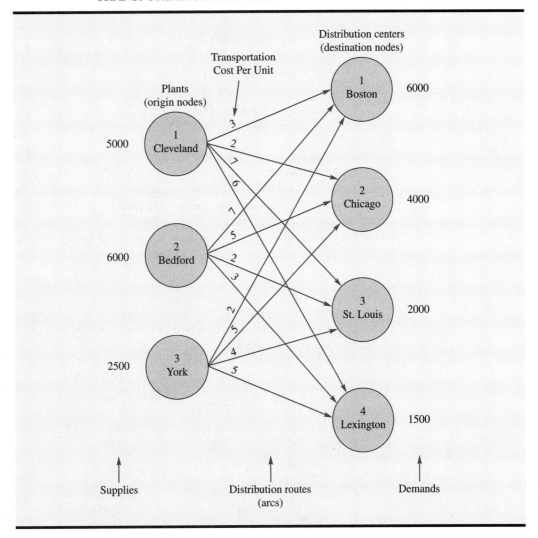

TABLE 10.1   TRANSPORTATION COST PER UNIT FOR THE FOSTER GENERATORS
TRANSPORTATION PROBLEM

Origin	Destination			
	Boston	**Chicago**	**St. Louis**	**Lexington**
Cleveland	3	2	7	6
Bedford	7	5	2	3
York	2	5	4	5

Because the objective of the transportation problem is to minimize the total transportation cost, we can use the cost data in Table 10.1 or on the arcs in Figure 10.1 to develop the following cost expressions:

Transportation costs for
units shipped from Cleveland $= 3x_{11} + 2x_{12} + 7x_{13} + 6x_{14}$

Transportation costs for
units shipped from Bedford $= 7x_{21} + 5x_{22} + 2x_{23} + 3x_{24}$

Transportation costs for
units shipped from York $= 2x_{31} + 5x_{32} + 4x_{33} + 5x_{34}$

The sum of these expressions provides the objective function showing the total transportation cost for Foster Generators.

Transportation problems need constraints because each origin has a limited supply and each destination has a demand requirement. We consider the supply constraints first. The capacity at the Cleveland plant is 5000 units. With the total number of units shipped from the Cleveland plant expressed as $x_{11} + x_{12} + x_{13} + x_{14}$, the supply constraint for the Cleveland plant is

$$x_{11} + x_{12} + x_{13} + x_{14} \leq 5000 \quad \text{Cleveland supply}$$

With three origins (plants), the Foster transportation problem has three supply constraints. Given the capacity of 6000 units at the Bedford plant and 2500 units at the York plant, the two additional supply constraints are

$$x_{21} + x_{22} + x_{23} + x_{24} \leq 6000 \quad \text{Bedford supply}$$
$$x_{31} + x_{32} + x_{33} + x_{34} \leq 2500 \quad \text{York supply}$$

With the four distribution centers as the destinations, four demand constraints are needed to ensure that destination demands will be satisfied:

$$x_{11} + x_{21} + x_{31} = 6000 \quad \text{Boston demand}$$
$$x_{12} + x_{22} + x_{32} = 4000 \quad \text{Chicago demand}$$
$$x_{13} + x_{23} + x_{33} = 2000 \quad \text{St. Louis demand}$$
$$x_{14} + x_{24} + x_{34} = 1500 \quad \text{Lexington demand}$$

Combining the objective function and constraints into one model provides a 12-variable, 7-constraint linear programming formulation of the Foster Generators transportation problem:

To obtain a feasible solution, the total supply must be greater than or equal to the total demand.

$$\text{Min} \quad 3x_{11} + 2x_{12} + 7x_{13} + 6x_{14} + 7x_{21} + 5x_{22} + 2x_{23} + 3x_{24} + 2x_{31} + 5x_{32} + 4x_{33} + 5x_{34}$$

s.t.

$$
\begin{aligned}
x_{11} + x_{12} + x_{13} + x_{14} & & & \leq 5000 \\
x_{21} + x_{22} + x_{23} + x_{24} & & & \leq 6000 \\
x_{31} + x_{32} + x_{33} + x_{34} & & & \leq 2500 \\
x_{11} \quad\quad\quad + x_{21} \quad\quad\quad + x_{31} & & & = 6000 \\
x_{12} \quad\quad\quad + x_{22} \quad\quad\quad + x_{32} & & & = 4000 \\
x_{13} \quad\quad\quad + x_{23} \quad\quad\quad + x_{33} & & & = 2000 \\
x_{14} \quad\quad\quad + x_{24} \quad\quad\quad + x_{34} & & & = 1500
\end{aligned}
$$

$$x_{ij} \geq 0 \quad \text{for } i = 1, 2, 3 \text{ and } j = 1, 2, 3, 4$$

Comparing the linear programming formulation to the network in Figure 10.1 leads to several observations. All the information needed for the linear programming formulation is on the network. Each node has one constraint, and each arc has one variable. The sum of the variables corresponding to arcs from an origin node must be less than or equal to the origin's supply, and the sum of the variables corresponding to the arcs into a destination node must be equal to the destination's demand.

Can you now use the computer to solve a linear programming model of a transportation problem? Try Problem 2.

We solved the Foster Generators problem with the linear programming module of The Management Scientist. The computer solution (see Figure 10.2) shows that the minimum total transportation cost is $39,500. The values for the decision variables show the optimal amounts to ship over each route. For example, with $x_{11} = 3500$, 3500 units should be shipped from Cleveland to Boston, and with $x_{12} = 1500$, 1500 units should be shipped from Cleveland to Chicago. Other values of the decision variables indicate the remaining shipping quantities and routes. Table 10.2 shows the minimum cost transportation schedule and Figure 10.3 summarizes the optimal solution on the network.

FIGURE 10.2   THE MANAGEMENT SCIENTIST SOLUTION FOR THE FOSTER GENERATORS TRANSPORTATION PROBLEM

```
Objective Function Value =            39500.000

        Variable              Value              Reduced Costs
     --------------       ---------------       ------------------
           X11              3500.000                 0.000
           X12              1500.000                 0.000
           X13                 0.000                 8.000
           X14                 0.000                 6.000
           X21                 0.000                 1.000
           X22              2500.000                 0.000
           X23              2000.000                 0.000
           X24              1500.000                 0.000
           X31              2500.000                 0.000
           X32                 0.000                 4.000
           X33                 0.000                 6.000
           X34                 0.000                 6.000
```

TABLE 10.2   OPTIMAL SOLUTION TO THE FOSTER GENERATORS TRANSPORTATION PROBLEM

| Route | | Units | Cost | Total |
From	To	Shipped	per Unit	Cost
Cleveland	Boston	3500	$3	$10,500
Cleveland	Chicago	1500	$2	3,000
Bedford	Chicago	2500	$5	12,500
Bedford	St. Louis	2000	$2	4,000
Bedford	Lexington	1500	$3	4,500
York	Boston	2500	$2	5,000
				$39,500

FIGURE 10.3   OPTIMAL SOLUTION TO THE FOSTER GENERATORS
TRANSPORTATION PROBLEM

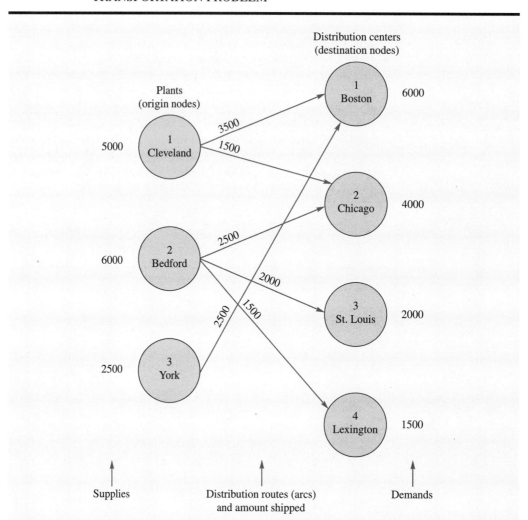

Problem Variations

The Foster Generators problem illustrates use of the basic transportation model. Variations of the basic transportation problem may involve one or more of the following situations:

1. Total supply not equal to total demand
2. Maximization objective function
3. Route capacities or route minimums
4. Unacceptable routes

With slight modifications in the linear programming model, we can easily accommodate these situations.

Total Supply Not Equal to Total Demand   Often *the total supply is not equal to the total demand*. If total supply exceeds total demand, no modification in the linear programming formulation is necessary. Excess supply will appear as slack in the linear programming solution. Slack for any particular origin can be interpreted as the unused supply or amount not shipped from the origin.

Whenever total supply is less than total demand, the model does not determine how the unsatisfied demand is handled (e.g., backorders). The manager must handle this aspect of the problem.

If total supply is less than total demand, the linear programming model of a transportation problem will not have a feasible solution. In this case, we modify the network representation by adding a **dummy origin** with a supply equal to the difference between the total demand and the total supply. With the addition of the dummy origin, and an arc from the dummy origin to each destination, the linear programming model will have a feasible solution. A zero cost per unit is assigned to each arc leaving the dummy origin so that the value of the optimal solution for the revised problem will represent the shipping cost for the units actually shipped (no shipments actually will be made from the dummy origin). When the optimal solution is implemented, the destinations showing shipments being received from the dummy origin will be the destinations experiencing a shortfall or unsatisfied demand.

Try Problem 8 to see whether you can handle a case where demand is greater than supply with a maximization objective.

Maximization Objective Function   In some transportation problems, the objective is to find a solution that maximizes profit or revenue. Using the values for profit or revenue per unit as coefficients in the objective function, we simply solve a maximization rather than a minimization linear program. This change does not affect the constraints.

Route Capacities and/or Route Minimums   The linear programming formulation of the transportation problem also can accommodate capacities and/or minimum quantities for one or more of the routes. For example, suppose that in the Foster Generators problem the York–Boston route (origin 3 to destination 1) had a capacity of 1000 units because of limited space availability on its normal mode of transportation. With x_{31} denoting the amount shipped from York to Boston, the route capacity constraint for the York–Boston route would be

$$x_{31} \leq 1000$$

Similarly, route minimums can be specified. For example,

$$x_{22} \geq 2000$$

would guarantee that a previously committed order for a Bedford–Chicago delivery of at least 2000 units would be maintained in the optimal solution.

Unacceptable Routes   Finally, establishing a route from every origin to every destination may not be possible. To handle this situation, we simply drop the corresponding arc from the network and remove the corresponding variable from the linear programming formulation. For example, if the Cleveland–St. Louis route were unacceptable or unusable, the arc from Cleveland to St. Louis could be dropped in Figure 10.1, and x_{13} could be removed from the linear programming formulation. Solving the resulting 11-variable, 7-constraint model would provide the optimal solution while guaranteeing that the Cleveland–St. Louis route is not used.

A General Linear Programming Model of the Transportation Problem

To show the general linear programming model of the transportation problem, we use the notation:

$$i = \text{index for origins, } i = 1, 2, \ldots, m$$

$$j = \text{index for destinations, } j = 1, 2, \ldots, n$$

$$x_{ij} = \text{number of units shipped from origin } i \text{ to destination } j$$

$$c_{ij} = \text{cost per unit of shipping from origin } i \text{ to destination } j$$

$$s_i = \text{supply or capacity in units at origin } i$$

$$d_j = \text{demand in units at destination } j$$

The general linear programming model of the m-origin, n-destination transportation problem is

$$\text{Min} \quad \sum_{i=1}^{m} \sum_{j=1}^{n} c_{ij} x_{ij}$$

s.t.

$$\sum_{j=1}^{n} x_{ij} \le s_i \qquad i = 1, 2, \ldots, m \quad \text{Supply}$$

$$\sum_{i=1}^{m} x_{ij} = d_j \qquad j = 1, 2, \ldots, n \quad \text{Demand}$$

$$x_{ij} \ge 0 \qquad \text{for all } i \text{ and } j$$

As mentioned previously, we can add constraints of the form $x_{ij} \le L_{ij}$ if the route from origin i to destination j has capacity L_{ij}. A transportation problem that includes constraints of this type is called a **capacitated transportation problem.** Similarly, we can add route minimum constraints of the form $x_{ij} \ge M_{ij}$ if the route from origin i to destination j must handle at least M_{ij} units.

NOTES AND COMMENTS

1. Transportation problems encountered in practice usually lead to large linear programs. Transportation problems with 100 origins and 100 destinations are not unusual. Such a problem would involve $(100)(100) = 10,000$ variables. For such a problem, special-purpose solution procedures are more efficient than general-purpose linear programming codes. But if speed is not an issue, a general-purpose linear programming code that has the capability to solve large problems will solve most transportation problems.

2. To handle a situation in which some routes may be unacceptable, we stated that you could drop the corresponding arc from the network and remove the corresponding variable from the linear programming formulation. Another approach often used is to assign an extremely large objective function cost coefficient to any unacceptable arc. If the problem has already been formulated, another option is to add a constraint to the formulation that sets the variable you want to remove equal to zero.

3. The optimal solution to a transportation model will consist of integer values for the decision variables as long as all supply and demand values are integers. The reason is the special mathematical structure of the linear programming model. Each variable appears in exactly one supply and one demand constraint, and all coefficients in the constraint equations are 1 or 0.

4. Although many transportation problems involve minimizing the cost of transporting goods between locations, many other applications of the transportation model exist. The Q. M. in Action: Marine Corps Mobilization illustrates the use of a transportation model to send Marine Corps officers to billets.

10.2   THE ASSIGNMENT PROBLEM: THE NETWORK MODEL AND A LINEAR PROGRAMMING FORMULATION

The **assignment problem** arises in a variety of decision-making situations; typical assignment problems involve assigning jobs to machines, agents to tasks, sales personnel to sales territories, contracts to bidders, and so on. A distinguishing feature of the assignment problem is that *one* agent is assigned to *one and only one* task. Specifically, we look for the set of assignments that will optimize a stated objective, such as minimize cost, minimize time, or maximize profits.

To illustrate the assignment problem, let us consider the case of Fowle Marketing Research, which has just received requests for market research studies from three new clients. The company faces the task of assigning a project leader (agent) to each client (task). Currently, three individuals have no other commitments and are available for the project leader assignments. Fowle's management realizes, however, that the time required to complete each study will depend on the experience and ability of the project leader assigned. The three projects have approximately the same priority, and management wants to assign project leaders to minimize the total number of days required to complete all three projects. If a project leader is to be assigned to one client only, what assignments should be made?

To answer the assignment question, Fowle's management must first consider all possible project leader-client assignments and then estimate the corresponding project completion times. With three project leaders and three clients, nine assignment alternatives are possible. The alternatives and the estimated project completion times in days are summarized in Table 10.3.

Try part (a) of Problem 12 to see whether you can develop a network model for an assignment problem.

Figure 10.4 shows the network representation of Fowle's assignment problem. The nodes correspond to the project leaders and clients, and the arcs represent the possible assignments of project leaders to clients. The supply at each origin node and the demand at each destination node are 1; the cost of assigning a project leader to a client is the time it takes that project leader to complete the client's task. Note the similarity between the

TABLE 10.3   ESTIMATED PROJECT COMPLETION TIMES (DAYS) FOR THE FOWLE
MARKETING RESEARCH ASSIGNMENT PROBLEM

	Client		
Project Leader	**1**	**2**	**3**
1. Terry	10	15	9
2. Carle	9	18	5
3. McClymonds	6	14	3

network models of the assignment problem (Figure 10.4) and the transportation problem
(Figure 10.1). The assignment problem is a special case of the transportation problem in
which all supply and demand values equal 1, and the amount shipped over each arc is either 0 or 1.

Because the assignment problem is a special case of the transportation problem, a linear programming formulation can be developed. Again, we need a constraint for each node
and a variable for each arc. As in the transportation problem, we use double-subscripted decision variables, with x_{11} denoting the assignment of project leader 1 (Terry) to client 1, x_{12}

FIGURE 10.4   A NETWORK MODEL OF THE FOWLE MARKETING RESEARCH
ASSIGNMENT PROBLEM

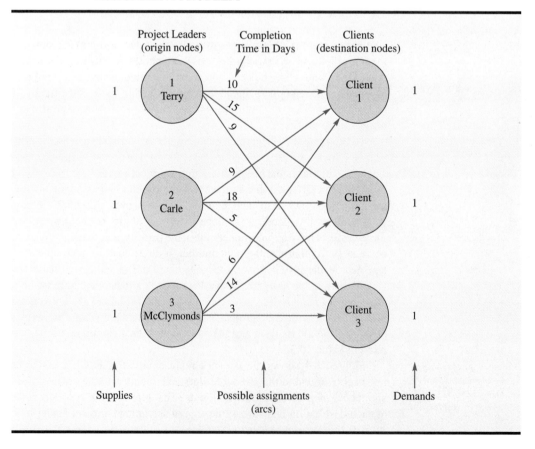

denoting the assignment of project leader 1 (Terry) to client 2, and so on. Thus, we define the decision variables for Fowle's assignment problem as

$$x_{ij} = \begin{cases} 1 \text{ if project leader } i \text{ is assigned to client } j \\ 0 \text{ otherwise} \end{cases}$$

where $i = 1, 2, 3$, and $j = 1, 2, 3$

Using this notation and the completion time data in Table 10.3, we develop completion time expressions:

$$\text{Days required for Terry's assignment} = 10x_{11} + 15x_{12} + 9x_{13}$$
$$\text{Days required for Carle's assignment} = 9x_{21} + 18x_{22} + 5x_{23}$$
$$\text{Days required for McClymonds's assignment} = 6x_{31} + 14x_{32} + 3x_{33}$$

The sum of the completion times for the three project leaders will provide the total days required to complete the three assignments. Thus, the objective function is

$$\text{Min} \quad 10x_{11} + 15x_{12} + 9x_{13} + 9x_{21} + 18x_{22} + 5x_{23} + 6x_{31} + 14x_{32} + 3x_{33}$$

Because the number of project leaders equals the number of clients, all the constraints could be written as equalites. But when the number of project leaders exceeds the number of clients, less-than-or-equal-to constraints must be used for the project leader constraints.

The constraints for the assignment problem reflect the conditions that each project leader can be assigned to at most one client and that each client must have one assigned project leader. These constraints are written as follows:

$$x_{11} + x_{12} + x_{13} \leq 1 \quad \text{Terry's assignment}$$
$$x_{21} + x_{22} + x_{23} \leq 1 \quad \text{Carle's assignment}$$
$$x_{31} + x_{32} + x_{33} \leq 1 \quad \text{McClymonds's assignment}$$
$$x_{11} + x_{21} + x_{31} = 1 \quad \text{Client 1}$$
$$x_{12} + x_{22} + x_{32} = 1 \quad \text{Client 2}$$
$$x_{13} + x_{23} + x_{33} = 1 \quad \text{Client 3}$$

Note that each node in Figure 10.4 has one constraint.

Combining the objective function and constraints into one model provides the following 9-variable, 6-constraint linear programming model of the Fowle Marketing Research assignment problem.

Try part (b) of Problem 12 for practice in formulating and solving a linear programming model for an assignment problem on the computer.

$$\text{Min} \quad 10x_{11} + 15x_{12} + 9x_{13} + 9x_{21} + 18x_{22} + 5x_{23} + 6x_{31} + 14x_{32} + 3x_{33}$$
s.t.
$$
\begin{aligned}
x_{11} + x_{12} + x_{13} & \qquad\qquad\qquad\qquad\qquad\qquad\qquad \leq 1 \\
x_{21} + x_{22} + x_{23} & \qquad\qquad\qquad\qquad\quad \leq 1 \\
x_{31} + x_{32} + x_{33} & \leq 1 \\
x_{11} \qquad + x_{21} \qquad\quad + x_{31} & = 1 \\
x_{12} \qquad + x_{22} \qquad\quad + x_{32} & = 1 \\
x_{13} \qquad + x_{23} \qquad\quad + x_{33} & = 1 \\
x_{ij} \geq 0 \quad \text{for } i = 1, 2, 3; j = 1, 2, 3
\end{aligned}
$$

Figure 10.5 shows the computer solution for this model. Terry is assigned to client 2 ($x_{12} = 1$), Carle is assigned to client 3 ($x_{23} = 1$), and McClymonds is assigned to client 1 ($x_{31} = 1$). The total completion time required is 26 days. This solution is summarized in Table 10.4.

FIGURE 10.5   THE MANAGEMENT SCIENTIST SOLUTION FOR THE FOWLE
MARKETING RESEARCH ASSIGNMENT PROBLEM

```
Objective Function Value =              26.000

        Variable            Value              Reduced Costs
     --------------     --------------       ------------------
          X11              0.000                  0.000
          X12              1.000                  0.000
          X13              0.000                  3.000
          X21              0.000                  0.000
          X22              0.000                  4.000
          X23              1.000                  0.000
          X31              1.000                  0.000
          X32              0.000                  3.000
          X33              0.000                  1.000
```

TABLE 10.4   OPTIMAL PROJECT LEADER ASSIGNMENTS FOR THE FOWLE
MARKETING RESEARCH ASSIGNMENT PROBLEM

Project Leader	Assigned Client	Days
Terry	2	15
Carle	3	5
McClymonds	1	6
		Total 26

Problem Variations

Because the assignment problem can be viewed as a special case of the transportation problem, the problem variations that may arise in an assignment problem parallel those for the transportation problem. Specifically, we can handle

1. Total number of agents (supply) not equal to the total number of tasks (demand)
2. A maximization objective function
3. Unacceptable assignments

In the linear programming formulation of a problem with five clients and only three project leaders, we could get by with one dummy project leader by placing a 2 on the right-hand side of the constraint for the dummy project leader.

The situation in which the number of agents does not equal the number of tasks is analogous to total supply not equaling total demand in a transportation problem. If the number of agents exceeds the number of tasks, the extra agents simply remain unassigned in the linear programming solution. If the number of tasks exceeds the number of agents, the linear programming model will not have a feasible solution. In this situation, a simple modification is to add enough dummy agents to equalize the number of agents and the number of tasks. For instance, in the Fowle problem we might have had five clients (tasks) and only three project leaders (agents). By adding two dummy project leaders, we can create a new assignment problem with the number of project leaders equal to the number of clients. The objective function coefficients for the assignment of dummy project leaders would be zero so that the value of the optimal solution would represent the total number of days required by the assignments actually made (no assignments will actually be made to the clients receiving dummy project leaders).

If the assignment alternatives are evaluated in terms of revenue or profit rather than time or cost, the linear programming formulation can be solved as a maximization rather than a minimization problem. In addition, if one or more assignments are unacceptable, the corresponding decision variable can be removed from the linear programming formulation. This situation could happen, for example, if an agent did not have the experience necessary for one or more of the tasks.

A General Linear Programming Model of the Assignment Problem

The general assignment problem involves m agents and n tasks. If we let $x_{ij} = 1$ or 0 according to whether agent i is assigned to task j or not, and if c_{ij} denotes the cost of assigning agent i to task j, we can write the general assignment model as

$$\text{Min} \quad \sum_{i=1}^{m} \sum_{j=1}^{n} c_{ij}x_{ij}$$

s.t.

$$\sum_{j=1}^{n} x_{ij} \leq 1 \quad i = 1, 2, \ldots, m \quad \text{Agents}$$

$$\sum_{i=1}^{m} x_{ij} = 1 \quad j = 1, 2, \ldots, n \quad \text{Tasks}$$

$$x_{ij} \geq 0 \quad \text{for all } i \text{ and } j$$

Multiple Assignments

At the beginning of this section, we indicated that a distinguishing feature of the assignment problem is that *one* agent is assigned to *one and only one* task. In generalizations of the assignment problem where one agent can be assigned to two or more tasks, the linear programming formulation of the problem can be easily modified. For example, let us assume that in the Fowle Marketing Research problem Terry could be assigned up to two clients; in this case, the constraint representing Terry's assignment would be $x_{11} + x_{12} + x_{13} \leq 2$. In general, if a_i denotes the upper limit for the number of tasks to which agent i can be assigned, we write the agent constraints as

If some tasks require more than one agent, the linear programming formulation can also accommodate the situation. Use the number of agents required as the right-hand side of the appropriate task constraint.

$$\sum_{j=1}^{n} x_{ij} \leq a_i \quad i = 1, 2, \ldots, m$$

Thus, we see that one advantage of formulating and solving assignment problems as linear programs is that special cases such as the situation involving multiple assignments can be easily handled.

NOTES AND COMMENTS

1. As noted, the assignment model is a special case of the transportation model. We stated in the notes and comments at the end of the preceding section that the optimal solution to the transportation problem will consist of integer values for the decision variables as long as the supplies and demands are integers. For the assignment problem, all supplies and demands equal 1; thus, the optimal solution must be integer valued and the integer values must be 0 or 1.

2. Combining the method for handling multiple assignments with the notion of a dummy agent provides another means of dealing with situations when the number of tasks exceeds the number of agents. That is, we add one dummy agent, but provide the dummy agent with the capability to handle multiple tasks. The number of tasks the dummy agent can handle is equal to the difference between the number of tasks and the number of agents.

10.3   THE TRANSSHIPMENT PROBLEM: THE NETWORK MODEL AND A LINEAR PROGRAMMING FORMULATION

The **transshipment problem** is an extension of the transportation problem in which intermediate nodes, referred to as *transshipment nodes,* are added to account for locations such as warehouses. In this more general type of distribution problem, shipments may be made between any pair of the three general types of nodes: origin nodes, transshipment nodes, and destination nodes. For example, the transshipment problem permits shipments of goods from origins to intermediate nodes and on to destinations, from one origin to another origin, from one intermediate location to another, from one destination location to another, and directly from origins to destinations.

As was true for the transportation problem, the supply available at each origin is limited, and the demand at each destination is specified. The objective in the transshipment problem is to determine how many units should be shipped over each arc in the network so that all destination demands are satisfied with the minimum possible transportation cost.

Try part (a) of Problem 23 for practice in developing a network representation of a transshipment problem.

Let us consider the transshipment problem faced by Ryan Electronics. Ryan is an electronics company with production facilities in Denver and Atlanta. Components produced at either facility may be shipped to either of the firm's regional warehouses, which are located in Kansas City and Louisville. From the regional warehouses, the firm supplies retail outlets in Detroit, Miami, Dallas, and New Orleans. The key features of the problem are shown in the network model depicted in Figure 10.6. Note that the supply at each origin and demand at each destination are shown in the left and right margins, respectively. Nodes 1 and 2 are the origin nodes; nodes 3 and 4 are the transshipment nodes; and nodes 5, 6, 7, and 8 are the destination nodes. The transportation cost per unit for each distribution route is shown in Table 10.5 and on the arcs of the network model in Figure 10.6.

As with the transportation and assignment problems, we can formulate a linear programming model of the transshipment problem from a network representation. Again, we need a constraint for each node and a variable for each arc. Let x_{ij} denote the number of units shipped from node i to node j. For example, x_{13} denotes the number of units shipped from the Denver plant to the Kansas City warehouse, x_{14} denotes the number of units shipped from the Denver plant to the Louisville warehouse, and so on. Because the supply at the Denver plant is 600 units, the amount shipped from the Denver plant must be less than or equal to 600. Mathematically, we write this supply constraint as

$$x_{13} + x_{14} \leq 600$$

Similarly, for the Atlanta plant we have

$$x_{23} + x_{24} \leq 400$$

We now consider how to write the constraints corresponding to the two transshipment nodes. For node 3 (the Kansas City warehouse), we must guarantee that the number of units shipped out must equal the number of units shipped into the warehouse. If

Number of units
shipped out of node $3 = x_{35} + x_{36} + x_{37} + x_{38}$

and

Number of units
shipped into node $3 = x_{13} + x_{23}$

FIGURE 10.6   NETWORK REPRESENTATION OF THE RYAN ELECTRONICS
TRANSSHIPMENT PROBLEM

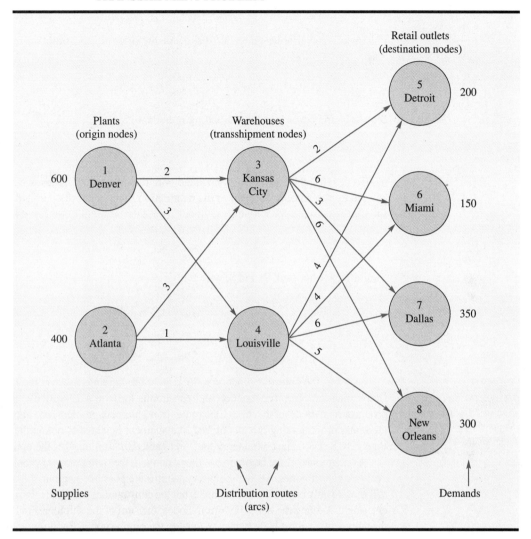

TABLE 10.5   TRANSPORTATION COSTS PER UNIT FOR THE RYAN ELECTRONICS
TRANSSHIPMENT PROBLEM

	Warehouse	
Plant	**Kansas City**	**Louisville**
Denver	2	3
Atlanta	3	1

	Retail Outlet			
Warehouse	**Detroit**	**Miami**	**Dallas**	**New Orleans**
Kansas City	2	6	3	6
Louisville	4	4	6	5

we obtain

$$x_{35} + x_{36} + x_{37} + x_{38} = x_{13} + x_{23}$$

Placing all the variables on the left-hand side provides the constraint corresponding to node 3 as

$$-x_{13} - x_{23} + x_{35} + x_{36} + x_{37} + x_{38} = 0$$

Similarly, the constraint corresponding to node 4 is

$$-x_{14} - x_{24} + x_{45} + x_{46} + x_{47} + x_{48} = 0$$

To develop the constraints associated with the destination nodes, we recognize that for each node the amount shipped to the destination must equal the demand. For example, to satisfy the demand for 200 units at node 5 (the Detroit retail outlet), we write

$$x_{35} + x_{45} = 200$$

Similarly, for nodes 6, 7, and 8, we have

$$x_{36} + x_{46} = 150$$
$$x_{37} + x_{47} = 350$$
$$x_{38} + x_{48} = 300$$

Try parts (b) and (c) of Problem 23 for practice in developing the linear programming model and in solving a transshipment problem on the computer.

As usual, the objective function reflects the total shipping cost over the 12 shipping routes. Combining the objective function and constraints leads to a 12-variable, 8-constraint linear programming model of the Ryan Electronics transshipment problem (see Figure 10.7). We used the linear programming module of The Management Scientist to obtain the optimal solution. Figure 10.8 shows the computer output, and Table 10.6 summarizes the optimal solution.

As mentioned at the beginning of this section, in the transshipment problem arcs may connect any pair of nodes. All such shipping patterns are possible in a transshipment problem. We still require only one constraint per node, but the constraint must include a variable for every arc entering or leaving the node. For origin nodes, the sum of the shipments out minus the sum of the shipments in must be less than or equal to the origin supply. For destination nodes, the sum

FIGURE 10.7   LINEAR PROGRAMMING FORMULATION OF THE RYAN ELECTRONICS
TRANSSHIPMENT PROBLEM

Min $2x_{13} + 3x_{14} + 3x_{23} + 1x_{24} + 2x_{35} + 6x_{36} + 3x_{37} + 6x_{38} + 4x_{45} + 4x_{46} + 6x_{47} + 5x_{48}$
s.t.

$$
\begin{array}{llll}
x_{13} + x_{14} & & \leq 600 & \left.\begin{array}{l} \\ \\ \end{array}\right\} \text{Origin node constraints} \\
\quad\quad x_{23} + x_{24} & & \leq 400 & \\
-x_{13} \quad\quad - x_{23} \quad + x_{35} + x_{36} + x_{37} + x_{38} & & = 0 & \left.\begin{array}{l} \\ \\ \end{array}\right\} \text{Transshipment node} \\
\quad - x_{14} \quad\quad - x_{24} \quad\quad\quad\quad + x_{45} + x_{46} + x_{47} + x_{48} & = 0 & & \text{constraints} \\
\quad\quad\quad\quad\quad\quad x_{35} & + x_{45} & = 200 & \left.\begin{array}{l} \\ \\ \\ \end{array}\right\} \text{Destination node constraints} \\
\quad\quad\quad\quad\quad\quad\quad x_{36} & + x_{46} & = 150 & \\
\quad\quad\quad\quad\quad\quad\quad\quad x_{37} & + x_{47} & = 350 & \\
\quad\quad\quad\quad\quad\quad\quad\quad\quad x_{38} & + x_{48} & = 300 &
\end{array}
$$

$x_{ij} \geq 0$ for all i and j

FIGURE 10.8   THE MANAGEMENT SCIENTIST SOLUTION FOR THE RYAN
ELECTRONICS TRANSSHIPMENT PROBLEM

```
Objective Function Value =          5200.000

        Variable              Value            Reduced Costs
     -------------        -------------      -----------------
            X13             550.000               0.000
            X14              50.000               0.000
            X23               0.000               3.000
            X24             400.000               0.000
            X35             200.000               0.000
            X36               0.000               1.000
            X37             350.000               0.000
            X38               0.000               0.000
            X45               0.000               3.000
            X46             150.000               0.000
            X47               0.000               4.000
            X48             300.000               0.000
```

TABLE 10.6   OPTIMAL SOLUTION TO THE RYAN ELECTRONICS
TRANSSHIPMENT PROBLEM

Route				
From	**To**	**Units Shipped**	**Cost per Unit**	**Total Cost**
Denver	Kansas City	550	$2	$1100
Denver	Louisville	50	$3	150
Atlanta	Louisville	400	$1	400
Kansas City	Detroit	200	$2	400
Kansas City	Dallas	350	$3	1050
Louisville	Miami	150	$4	600
Louisville	New Orleans	300	$5	1500
				$5200

of the shipments in minus the sum of the shipments out must equal demand. For transshipment
nodes, the sum of the shipments out must equal the sum of the shipments in, as before.

For an illustration of this more general type of transshipment problem, let us modify the Ryan
Electronics problem. Suppose that it is possible to ship directly from Atlanta to New Orleans at
$4 per unit and from Dallas to New Orleans at $1 per unit. The network model corresponding to
this modified Ryan Electronics problem is shown in Figure 10.9, the linear programming formulation is shown in Figure 10.10, and the computer solution is shown in Figure 10.11.

*Try Problem 24 for practice
working with transshipment
problems with this more
general structure.*

In Figure 10.9 we added two new arcs to the network model. Thus, two new variables
are necessary in the linear programming formulation. Figure 10.10 shows that the new variables x_{28} and x_{78} appear in the objective function and in the constraints corresponding to
the nodes to which the new arcs are connected. Figure 10.11 shows that the value of the
optimal solution has been reduced $600 by adding the two new shipping routes; $x_{28} = 250$
units are being shipped directly from Atlanta to New Orleans, and $x_{78} = 50$ units are being
shipped from Dallas to New Orleans.

FIGURE 10.9 NETWORK REPRESENTATION OF THE MODIFIED RYAN ELECTRONICS TRANSSHIPMENT PROBLEM

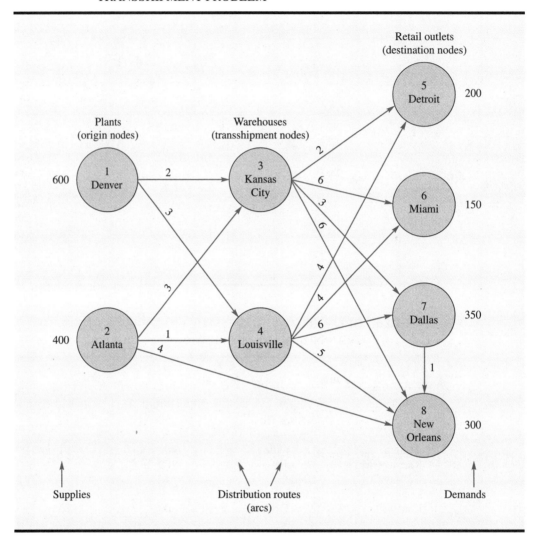

FIGURE 10.10 LINEAR PROGRAMMING FORMULATION OF THE MODIFIED RYAN ELECTRONICS TRANSSHIPMENT PROBLEM

Min $2x_{13} + 3x_{14} + 3x_{23} + 1x_{24} + 2x_{35} + 6x_{36} + 3x_{37} + 6x_{38} + 4x_{45} + 4x_{46} + 6x_{47} + 5x_{48} + 4x_{28} + 1x_{78}$

s.t.

$$
\begin{array}{llll}
x_{13} + x_{14} & & \leq 600 \quad\left.\right\} \text{Origin node constraints} \\
\quad x_{23} + x_{24} & + x_{28} & \leq 400 \\
-x_{13} \quad - x_{23} \quad + x_{35} + x_{36} + x_{37} + x_{38} & & = 0 \quad\left.\right\} \text{Transshipment node} \\
\quad - x_{14} \quad - x_{24} & + x_{45} + x_{46} + x_{47} + x_{48} & = 0 \quad\left.\right\} \text{constraints} \\
\quad\quad x_{35} & + x_{45} & = 200 \\
\quad\quad\quad x_{36} & + x_{46} & = 150 \quad\left.\right\} \text{Destination node} \\
\quad\quad\quad\quad x_{37} & + x_{47} \quad - x_{78} & = 350 \quad\left.\right\} \text{constraints} \\
\quad\quad\quad\quad\quad x_{38} & + x_{48} + x_{28} + x_{78} & = 300 \\
\end{array}
$$

$x_{ij} \geq 0$ for all i and j

FIGURE 10.11   THE MANAGEMENT SCIENTIST SOLUTION FOR THE MODIFIED RYAN ELECTRONICS TRANSSHIPMENT PROBLEM

```
Objective Function Value =          4600.000

        Variable              Value           Reduced Costs
    --------------       ---------------      ------------------
          X13               600.000                0.000
          X14                 0.000                0.000
          X23                 0.000                3.000
          X24               150.000                0.000
          X35               200.000                0.000
          X36                 0.000                1.000
          X37               400.000                0.000
          X38                 0.000                2.000
          X45                 0.000                3.000
          X46               150.000                0.000
          X47                 0.000                4.000
          X48                 0.000                2.000
          X28               250.000                0.000
          X78                50.000                0.000
```

Problem Variations

As with transportation and assignment problems, transshipment problems may be formulated with several variations, including

1. Total supply not equal to total demand
2. Maximization objective function
3. Route capacities or route minimums
4. Unacceptable routes

The linear programming model modifications required to accommodate these variations are identical to the modifications required for the transportation problem described in Section 10.1. When we add one or more constraints of the form $x_{ij} \leq L_{ij}$ to show that the route from node i to node j has capacity L_{ij}, we refer to the transshipment problem as a **capacitated transshipment problem.**

A General Linear Programming Model of the Transshipment Problem

The general linear programming model of the transshipment problem is

$$\text{Min} \quad \sum_{\text{all arcs}} c_{ij} x_{ij}$$

s.t.

$$\sum_{\text{arcs out}} x_{ij} - \sum_{\text{arcs in}} x_{ij} \leq s_i \quad \text{Origin nodes } i$$

$$\sum_{\text{arcs out}} x_{ij} - \sum_{\text{arcs in}} x_{ij} = 0 \quad \text{Transshipment nodes}$$

$$\sum_{\text{arcs in}} x_{ij} - \sum_{\text{arcs out}} x_{ij} = d_j \quad \text{Destination nodes } j$$

$$x_{ij} \geq 0 \text{ for all } i \text{ and } j$$

where

$$x_{ij} = \text{number of units shipped from node } i \text{ to node } j$$
$$c_{ij} = \text{cost per unit of shipping from node } i \text{ to node } j$$
$$s_i = \text{supply at origin node } i$$
$$d_j = \text{demand at destination node } j$$

NOTES AND COMMENTS

1. In more advanced treatments of linear programming and network flow problems, the capacitated transshipment problem is called the *pure network flow problem*. Efficient special-purpose solution procedures are available for network flow problems and their special cases.
2. In the general linear programming formulation of the transshipment problem, the constraints for the destination nodes are often written as

$$\sum_{\text{arcs out}} x_{ij} - \sum_{\text{arcs in}} x_{ij} = -d_j$$

The advantage of writing the constraints this way is that the left-hand side of each constraint then represents the flow out of the node minus the flow in. But such constraints would then have to be multiplied by -1 to obtain nonnegative right-hand sides before solving the problem by many linear programming codes.

10.4   A PRODUCTION AND INVENTORY APPLICATION

The introduction to the transportation and transshipment problems in Sections 10.1 and 10.3 involved applications for the shipment of goods from several supply locations or origins to several demand sites or destinations. Although the shipment of goods is the subject of many transportation and transshipment problems, transportation and/or transshipment models can be developed for applications that have nothing to do with the physical shipment of goods from origins to destinations. In this section we show how to use a transshipment model to solve a production scheduling and inventory problem.

Contois Carpets is a small manufacturer of carpeting for home and office installations. Production capacity, demand, production cost per square yard, and inventory holding cost per square yard for the next four quarters are shown in Table 10.7. Note that production capacity, demand, and production costs vary by quarter, whereas the cost of carrying inventory from one quarter to the next is constant at $0.25 per yard. Contois wants to determine how many yards of carpeting to manufacture each quarter to minimize the total production and inventory cost for the four-quarter period.

The network flows into and out of demand nodes are what makes the model a transshipment model.

We begin by developing a network representation of the problem. First, we create four nodes corresponding to the production in each quarter and four nodes corresponding to the demand in each quarter. Each production node is connected by an outgoing arc to the demand node for the same period. The flow on the arc represents the number of square yards of carpet manufactured for the period. For each demand node, an outgoing arc represents the amount of inventory (square yards of carpet) carried over to the demand node for the next period. Figure 10.12 shows the network model. Note that nodes 1–4 represent the production for each quarter and that nodes 5–8 represent the demand for each quarter. The quarterly production capacities are shown in the left margin, and the quarterly demands are shown in the right margin.

The objective is to determine a production scheduling and inventory policy that will minimize the total production and inventory cost for the four quarters. Constraints involve production capacity and demand in each quarter. As usual, a linear programming model can

TABLE 10.7   PRODUCTION, DEMAND, AND COST ESTIMATES FOR CONTOIS CARPETS

Quarter	Production Capacity (square yards)	Demand (square yards)	Production Cost ($/square yard)	Inventory Cost ($/square yard)
1	600	400	2	0.25
2	300	500	5	0.25
3	500	400	3	0.25
4	400	400	3	0.25

FIGURE 10.12   NETWORK REPRESENTATION OF THE CONTOIS CARPETS PROBLEM

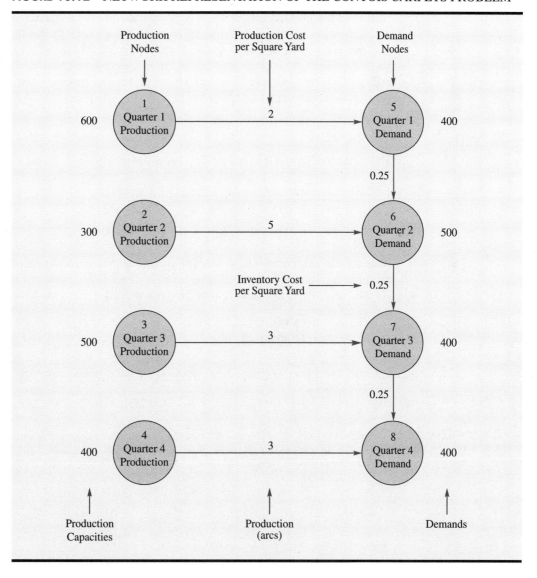

be developed from the network by establishing a constraint for each node and a variable for each arc.

Let x_{15} denote the number of square yards of carpet manufactured in quarter 1. The capacity of the facility is 600 square yards in quarter 1, so the production capacity constraint is

$$x_{15} \leq 600$$

Using similar decision variables, we obtain the production capacities for quarters 2–4:

$$x_{26} \leq 300$$
$$x_{37} \leq 500$$
$$x_{48} \leq 400$$

We now consider the development of the constraints for each of the demand nodes. For node 5, one arc enters the node, which represents the number of square yards of carpet produced in quarter 1, and one arc leaves the node, which represents the number of square yards of carpet that will not be sold in quarter 1 and will be carried over for possible sale in quarter 2. In general, for each quarter the beginning inventory plus the production minus the ending inventory must equal demand. However, because quarter 1 has no beginning inventory, the constraint for node 5 is

$$x_{15} - x_{56} = 400$$

The constraints associated with the demand nodes in quarters 2, 3, and 4 are

$$x_{56} + x_{26} - x_{67} = 500$$
$$x_{67} + x_{37} - x_{78} = 400$$
$$x_{78} + x_{48} = 400$$

Note that the constraint for node 8 (fourth-quarter demand) involves only two variables because no provision is made for holding inventory for a fifth quarter.

The objective is to minimize total production and inventory cost, so we write the objective function as

$$\text{Min} \quad 2x_{15} + 5x_{26} + 3x_{37} + 3x_{48} + 0.25x_{56} + 0.25x_{67} + 0.25x_{78}$$

The complete linear programming formulation of the Contois Carpets problem is

$$\text{Min} \quad 2x_{15} + 5x_{26} + 3x_{37} + 3x_{48} + 0.25x_{56} + 0.25x_{67} + 0.25x_{78}$$

s.t.

$$
\begin{aligned}
x_{15} & & & & & & & & & \leq 600 \\
& x_{26} & & & & & & & & \leq 300 \\
& & x_{37} & & & & & & & \leq 500 \\
& & & x_{48} & & & & & & \leq 400 \\
x_{15} & & & & - & x_{56} & & & & = 400 \\
& x_{26} & & & + & x_{56} & - & x_{67} & & = 500 \\
& & x_{37} & & & & + & x_{67} & - & x_{78} = 400 \\
& & & x_{48} & & & & & + & x_{78} = 400
\end{aligned}
$$

$$x_{ij} \geq 0 \quad \text{for all } i \text{ and } j$$

We used the linear programming module of The Management Scientist to solve the Contois Carpets problem. Figure 10.13 shows the results: Contois Carpets should manufacture 600 square yards of carpet in quarter 1, 300 square yards in quarter 2, 400 square yards in quarter 3, and 400 square yards in quarter 4. Note also that 200 square yards will be carried over from quarter 1 to quarter 2. The total production and inventory cost is $5150.

FIGURE 10.13   THE MANAGEMENT SCIENTIST SOLUTION FOR THE CONTOIS CARPETS PROBLEM

```
Objective Function Value =            5150.000

        Variable              Value              Reduced Costs
        --------------     ---------------     -------------------
            X15              600.000                 0.000
            X26              300.000                 0.000
            X37              400.000                 0.000
            X48              400.000                 0.000
            X56              200.000                 0.000
            X67                0.000                 2.250
            X78                0.000                 0.000
```

NOTES AND COMMENTS

1. Often the same problem can be modeled in different ways. In this section we modeled the Contois Carpets problem as a transshipment problem. It also can be modeled as a transportation problem.
2. In the network model we developed for the transshipment problem, the amount leaving the starting node for an arc is always equal to the amount entering the ending node for that arc. An extension of such a network model is the case where a gain or a loss occurs as an arc is traversed. The amount entering the destination node may be greater or smaller than the amount leaving the origin node. For instance, if cash is the commodity flowing across an arc, the cash earns interest from one period to the next. Thus, the amount of cash entering the next period is greater than the amount leaving the previous period by the amount of interest earned. Networks with gains or losses are treated in more advanced texts on network flow programming.

SUMMARY

In this chapter we introduced transportation, assignment, and transshipment problems. All three types of problems belong to the special category of linear programs called *network flow problems*. The network model of a transportation problem consists of nodes representing a set of origins and a set of destinations. In the basic model, an arc is used to represent the route from each origin to each destination. Each origin has a supply, and each destination has a demand. The problem is to determine the optimal amount to ship from each origin to each destination.

The assignment model is a special case of the transportation model in which all supply and all demand values are equal to 1. We represent each agent as an origin node and each task as a destination node. The transshipment model is an extension of the transportation model to distribution problems involving transfer points referred to as transshipment nodes.

In this more general model, we allow arcs between any pair of nodes. A variation of the transshipment problem allows for placing capacities on the arcs. This variation, called the *capacitated transshipment problem,* is also known in the network flow literature as the *pure network problem.*

We showed how each of these network flow problems could be modeled as a linear program, and we solved each using a general-purpose linear programming computer package. In network flow problems, the optimal solution will be integral as long as all supplies and demands are integral. Therefore, when solving any transportation, assignment, or transshipment problem in which the supplies and demands are integral, we can expect to obtain an integer-valued solution.

In Appendix 10.1, we show how to formulate and solve transportation and assignment problems using an Excel spreadsheet.

GLOSSARY

Network   A graphical representation of a problem consisting of numbered circles (nodes) interconnected by a series of lines (arcs); arrowheads on the arcs show the direction of flow. Transportation, assignment, and transshipment problems are network flow problems.

Transportation problem   A network flow problem that often involves minimizing the cost of shipping goods from a set of origins to a set of destinations; it can be formulated and solved as a linear program by including a variable for each arc and a constraint for each node.

Nodes   The intersection or junction points of a network.

Arcs   The lines connecting the nodes in a network.

Dummy origin   An origin added to a transportation problem to make the total supply equal to the total demand. The supply assigned to the dummy origin is the difference between the total demand and the total supply.

Capacitated transportation problem   A variation of the basic transportation problem in which some or all of the arcs are subject to capacity restrictions.

Assignment problem   A network flow problem that often involves the assignment of agents to tasks; it can be formulated as a linear program and is a special case of the transportation problem.

Transshipment problem   An extension of the transportation problem to distribution problems involving transfer points and possible shipments between any pair of nodes.

Capacitated transshipment problem   A variation of the transshipment problem in which some or all of the arcs are subject to capacity restrictions.

PROBLEMS

Note: In many cases, we ask you to formulate and solve the problem as a linear program. Where the solution method is not specified, you may also use the transportation or assignment modules of The Management Scientist or some other software package.

SELFtest   1.   A company imports goods at two ports: Philadelphia and New Orleans. Shipments of one product are made to customers in Atlanta, Dallas, Columbus, and Boston. For the next planning period, the supplies at each port, customer demands, and shipping costs per case from each port to each customer are as follows:

| | Customers | | | | Port |
Port	Atlanta	Dallas	Columbus	Boston	Supply
Philadelphia	2	6	6	2	5000
New Orleans	1	2	5	7	3000
Demand	1400	3200	2000	1400	

Develop a network representation of the distribution system (transportation problem).

SELFtest   **2.** Consider the following network representation of a transportation problem:

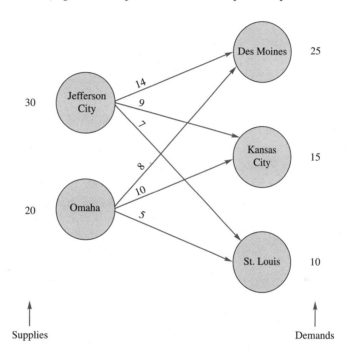

The supplies, demands, and transportation costs per unit are shown on the network.
- **a.** Develop a linear programming model for this problem; be sure to define the variables in your model.
- **b.** Solve the linear program to determine the optimal solution.

3. Reconsider the distribution system described in Problem 1.
- **a.** Develop a linear programming model that can be solved to minimize transportation cost.
- **b.** Solve the linear program to determine the minimum cost shipping schedule.

4. A product is produced at three plants and shipped to three warehouses (the transportation costs per unit are shown in the following table).

| | Warehouse | | | Plant |
Plant	W_1	W_2	W_3	Capacity
P_1	20	16	24	300
P_2	10	10	8	500
P_3	12	18	10	100
Warehouse demand	200	400	300	

a. Show a network representation of the problem.
b. Develop a linear programming model for minimizing transportation costs; solve this model to determine the minimum cost solution.
c. Suppose that the entries in the table represent profit per unit produced at plant i and sold to warehouse j. How does the model formulation change from that in part (b)?

5. Tri-County Utilities, Inc., supplies natural gas to customers in a three-county area. The company purchases natural gas from two companies: Southern Gas and Northwest Gas. Demand forecasts for the coming winter season are Hamilton County, 400 units; Butler County, 200 units; and Clermont County, 300 units. Contracts to provide the following quantities have been written: Southern Gas, 500 units; and Northwest Gas, 400 units. Distribution costs for the counties vary, depending upon the location of the suppliers. The distribution costs per unit (in thousands of dollars) are as follows:

	To		
From	**Hamilton**	**Butler**	**Clermont**
Southern Gas	10	20	15
Northwest Gas	12	15	18

a. Develop a network representation of this problem.
b. Develop a linear programming model that can be used to determine the plan that will minimize total distribution costs.
c. Describe the distribution plan and show the total distribution cost.
d. Recent residential and industrial growth in Butler County has the potential for increasing demand by as much as 100 units. Which supplier should Tri-County contract with to supply the additional capacity?

6. Arnoff Enterprises manufactures the central processing unit (CPU) for a line of personal computers. The CPUs are manufactured in Seattle, Columbus, and New York and shipped to warehouses in Pittsburgh, Mobile, Denver, Los Angeles, and Washington, D.C., for further distribution. The following table shows the number of CPUs available at each plant, the number of CPUs required by each warehouse, and the shipping costs (dollars per unit).

	Warehouse					
Plant	**Pittsburgh**	**Mobile**	**Denver**	**Los Angeles**	**Washington**	**CPUs Available**
Seattle	10	20	5	9	10	9000
Columbus	2	10	8	30	6	4000
New York	1	20	7	10	4	8000
CPUs Required	3000	5000	4000	6000	3000	21,000

a. Develop a network representation of this problem.
b. Determine the amount that should be shipped from each plant to each warehouse to minimize the total shipping cost.
c. The Pittsburgh warehouse has just increased its order by 1000 units, and Arnoff has authorized the Columbus plant to increase its production by 1000 units. Will this production increase lead to an increase or decrease in total shipping costs? Solve for the new optimal solution.

7. Premier Consulting has two consultants, Avery and Baker, who can be scheduled to work for clients up to a maximum of 160 hours each over the next four weeks. A third consultant, Campbell, has some administrative assignments already planned and is available for clients up to a maximum of 140 hours over the next four weeks. The company has four clients with projects in process. The estimated hourly requirements for each of the clients over the four-week period are

Client	Hours
A	180
B	75
C	100
D	85

Hourly rates vary for the consultant-client combination and are based on several factors, including project type and the consultant's experience. The rates (dollars per hour) for each consultant-client combination are

Consultant	Client A	Client B	Client C	Client D
Avery	100	125	115	100
Baker	120	135	115	120
Campbell	155	150	140	130

a. Develop a network representation of the problem.
b. Formulate the problem as a linear program, with the optimal solution providing the hours each consultant should be scheduled for each client to maximize the consulting firm's billings. What is the schedule and what is the total billing?
c. New information shows that Avery doesn't have the experience to be scheduled for client B. If this consulting assignment is not permitted, what impact does it have on total billings? What is the revised schedule?

SELFtest   8. Klein Chemicals, Inc., produces a special oil-base material that is currently in short supply. Four of Klein's customers have already placed orders that together exceed the combined capacity of Klein's two plants. Klein's management faces the problem of deciding how many units it should supply to each customer. Because the four customers are in different industries, different prices can be charged because of the various industry pricing structures. However, slightly different production costs at the two plants and varying transportation costs between the plants and customers make a "sell to the highest bidder" strategy unacceptable. After considering price, production costs, and transportation costs, Klein has established the following profit per unit for each plant-customer alternative.

	Customer			
Plant	D_1	D_2	D_3	D_4
Clifton Springs	$32	$34	$32	$40
Danville	$34	$30	$28	$38

The plant capacities and customer orders are as follows:

Plant Capacity (units)		Distributor Orders (units)	
Clifton Springs	5000	D_1	2000
		D_2	5000
Danville	3000	D_3	3000
		D_4	2000

How many units should each plant produce for each customer to maximize profits? Which customer demands will not be met? Show your network model and linear programming formulation.

9. Sound Electronics, Inc., produces a battery-operated tape recorder at plants located in Martinsville, North Carolina; Plymouth, New York; and Franklin, Missouri. The unit transportation cost for shipments from the three plants to distribution centers in Chicago, Dallas, and New York are as follows:

	To		
From	Chicago	Dallas	New York
Martinsville	$1.45	$1.60	$1.40
Plymouth	$1.10	$2.25	$0.60
Franklin	$1.20	$1.20	$1.80

After considering transportation costs, management has decided that under no circumstances will it use the Plymouth–Dallas route. The plant capacities and distributor orders for the next month are as follows:

Plant	Capacity (units)		Distributor	Orders (units)
Martinsville	400		Chicago	400
Plymouth	600		Dallas	400
Franklin	300		New York	400

Because of different wage scales at the three plants, the unit production cost varies from plant to plant. Assuming the costs are $29.50 per unit at Martinsville, $31.20 per unit at Plymouth, and $30.35 per unit at Franklin, find the production and distribution plan that minimizes production and transportation costs.

10. The Ace Manufacturing Company has orders for three similar products:

Product	Orders (units)
A	2000
B	500
C	1200

Three machines are available for the manufacturing operations. All three machines can produce all the products at the same production rate. However, due to varying defect percentages of each product on each machine, the unit costs of the products vary depending on the machine used. Machine capacities for the next week, and the unit costs, are as follows:

Machine	Capacity (units)
1	1500
2	1500
3	1000

Machine	Product A	B	C
1	$1.00	$1.20	$0.90
2	$1.30	$1.40	$1.20
3	$1.10	$1.00	$1.20

Use the transportation model to develop the minimum cost production schedule for the products and machines. Show the linear programming formulation.

11. Forbelt Corporation has a one-year contract to supply motors for all refrigerators produced by the Ice Age Corporation. Ice Age manufactures the refrigerators at four locations around the country: Boston, Dallas, Los Angeles, and St. Paul. Plans call for the following number (in 1000s) of refrigerators to be produced at each location.

Boston	50
Dallas	70
Los Angeles	60
St. Paul	80

Forbelt has three plants that are capable of producing the motors. The plants and production capacities (in 1000s) are

Denver	100
Atlanta	100
Chicago	150

Because of varying production and transportation costs, the profit that Forbelt earns on each lot of 1000 units depends on which plant produced the lot and which destination it was shipped to. The following table gives the accounting department estimates of the profit per unit (shipments will be made in lots of 1000 units).

	Shipped To			
Produced At	**Boston**	**Dallas**	**Los Angeles**	**St. Paul**
Denver	7	11	8	13
Atlanta	20	17	12	10
Chicago	8	18	13	16

With profit maximization as a criterion, Forbelt's management wants to determine how many motors should be produced at each plant and how many motors should be shipped from each plant to each destination.

a. Develop a network representation of this problem.
b. Find the optimal solution.

SELFtest 12. Scott and Associates, Inc., is an accounting firm that has three new clients. Project leaders will be assigned to the three clients. Based on the different backgrounds and experiences of the leaders, the various leader-client assignments differ in terms of projected completion times. The possible assignments and the estimated completion times in days are

Project Leader	Client		
	1	**2**	**3**
Jackson	10	16	32
Ellis	14	22	40
Smith	22	24	34

a. Develop a network representation of this problem.
b. Formulate the problem as a linear program, and solve. What is the total time required?

13. Assume that in Problem 12 an additional employee is available for possible assignment. The following table shows the assignment alternatives and the estimated completion times.

Project Leader	Client		
	1	**2**	**3**
Jackson	10	16	32
Ellis	14	22	40
Smith	22	24	34
Burton	14	18	36

a. What is the optimal assignment?
b. How did the assignment change compared to the best assignment possible in Problem 12? Was any savings associated with considering Burton as a possible project leader?
c. Which project leader remains unassigned?

14. Wilson Distributors, Inc., is opening two new sales territories in the western states. Three individuals currently selling in the Midwest and the East are being considered for promotion to regional sales manager positions in the new sales territories. Management has esti-

mated total annual sales (in thousands of dollars) for the assignment of each individual to each sales territory. The management sales projections are as follows:

	Sales Region	
Regional Managers	Northwest	Southwest
Bostock	$100	$95
McMahon	$85	$80
Miller	$90	$75

a. Develop a network representation of the problem.
b. Formulate and solve a linear programming model to obtain the optimal solution to this problem.

15. Fowle Marketing Research has four project leaders available for assignment to three clients. Find the assignment of project leaders to clients that will minimize the total time to complete all projects. The estimated project completion times in days are as follows:

	Client		
Project Leader	1	2	3
Terry	10	15	9
Carle	9	18	5
McClymonds	6	14	3
Higley	8	16	6

16. Salisbury Discounts has just leased a new store and is attempting to determine where various departments should be located within the store. The store manager has four locations that have not yet been assigned a department and is considering five departments that might occupy the four locations. The departments under consideration are shoe, toy, auto parts, housewares, and video. After a careful study of the layout of the remainder of the store, the store manager has made estimates of the expected profit ($1000s) for each department in each location. These estimates are presented in Table 10.8.
a. Develop a network representation of the Salisbury Discount department location assignment problem using the estimated annual profit data.
b. Formulate a linear programming model, and solve for the department location assignment that maximizes profit.

TABLE 10.8 ESTIMATED ANNUAL PROFIT ($000s) FOR EACH DEPARTMENT-LOCATION COMBINATION

	Location			
Department	1	2	3	4
Shoe	10	6	12	8
Toy	15	18	5	11
Auto parts	17	10	13	16
Housewares	14	12	13	10
Video	14	16	6	12

17. Consider again the Salisbury Discounts problem (see Problem 16). Suppose that the store manager believed that the toy department should not be considered for location 2 and that the auto parts department should not be considered for location 4. Essentially the store manager is saying that, based on other considerations, such as size of the area, adjacent departments, and so on, these two assignments are unacceptable alternatives.
    a. Develop a network representation of the problem.
    b. Formulate and solve a linear programming model.

18. The U.S. Cable Company uses a distribution system with five distribution centers and eight customer zones. Each customer zone is assigned a sole source supplier and receives all of its cable products from the same distribution center. In an effort to balance demand and workload at the distribution centers, the company's vice-president of logistics has specified that distribution centers may not be assigned more than three customer zones. The following table shows the five distribution centers and cost of supplying each customer zone ($000s).
    a. Determine the assignment of customer zones to distribution centers that will minimize cost.
    b. Which distribution centers, if any, are not used?
    c. Suppose that each distribution center is limited to a maximum of two customer zones. How does this constraint change the assignment and the cost of supplying customer zones?

| | Customer Zones | | | | | | | |
Distribution Centers	Los Angeles	Chicago	Columbus	Atlanta	Newark	Kansas City	Denver	Dallas
Plano	70	47	22	53	98	21	27	13
Nashville	75	38	19	58	90	34	40	26
Flagstaff	15	78	37	82	111	40	29	32
Springfield	60	23	8	39	82	36	32	45
Boulder	45	40	29	75	86	25	11	37

19. Mayfax Distributors, Inc., has four sales territories, each of which must be assigned a sales representative. From experience the firm's sales manager estimated the annual sales volume (in $000s) for each sales representative in each sales territory. Find the sales representative territory assignments that will maximize sales.

| | Sales Territory | | | |
Sales Representative	A	B	C	D
Washington	44	80	52	60
Benson	60	56	40	72
Fredricks	36	60	48	48
Hodson	52	76	36	40

20. The department head of a quantitative methods department at a major midwestern university will be scheduling faculty to teach courses during the coming autumn term. Four core courses need to be covered. The four courses are at the UG, MBA, MS, and Ph.D. levels. Four professors will be assigned to the courses, with each professor receiving one of the courses. Student evaluations of professors are available from previous terms. Based on a rating scale of 4 (excellent), 3 (very good), 2 (average), 1 (fair), and 0 (poor), the average

student evaluations for each professor are shown. Professor D does not have a Ph.D. and cannot be assigned to teach the Ph.D. level course. If the department head makes teaching assignments based on maximizing the student evaluation ratings over all four courses, what staffing assignments should be made?

Professor	Course			
	UG	MBA	MS	Ph.D.
A	2.8	2.2	3.3	3.0
B	3.2	3.0	3.6	3.6
C	3.3	3.2	3.5	3.5
D	3.2	2.8	2.5	—

21. A market research firm has three clients who have each requested that the firm conduct a sample survey. Four available statisticians can be assigned to these three projects; however, all four statisticians are busy, and therefore each can handle only one client. The following data show the number of hours required for each statistician to complete each job; the differences in time are based on experience and ability of the statisticians.

Statistician	Client		
	A	B	C
1	150	210	270
2	170	230	220
3	180	230	225
4	160	240	230

a. Formulate and solve a linear programming model for this problem.
b. Suppose that the time statistician 4 needs to complete the job for client A is increased from 160 to 165 hours. What effect will this change have on the solution?
c. Suppose that the time statistician 4 needs to complete the job for client A is decreased to 140 hours. What effect will this change have on the solution?
d. Suppose that the time statistician 3 needs to complete the job for client B increases to 250 hours. What effect will this change have on the solution?

22. Hatcher Enterprises uses a chemical called Rbase in production operations at five divisions. Only six suppliers of Rbase meet Hatcher's quality control standards. All six suppliers can produce Rbase in sufficient quantities to accommodate the needs of each division. The quantity of Rbase needed by each Hatcher division and the price per gallon charged by each supplier are as follows:

Division	Demand (000s of gallons)	Supplier	Price per Gallon ($)
1	40	1	12.60
2	45	2	14.00
3	50	3	10.20
4	35	4	14.20
5	45	5	12.00
		6	13.00

The cost per gallon ($) for shipping from each supplier to each division is provided in the following table.

Division	Supplier					
	1	2	3	4	5	6
1	2.75	2.50	3.15	2.80	2.75	2.75
2	0.80	0.20	5.40	1.20	3.40	1.00
3	4.70	2.60	5.30	2.80	6.00	5.60
4	2.60	1.80	4.40	2.40	5.00	2.80
5	3.40	0.40	5.00	1.20	2.60	3.60

Hatcher believes in spreading its business among suppliers so that the company will be less affected by supplier problems (e.g., labor strikes or resource availability). Company policy requires that each division have a separate supplier.

    a. For each supplier-division combination, compute the total cost of supplying the division's demand.

    b. Determine the optimal assignment of suppliers to divisions.

SELFtest   **23.** The distribution system for the Herman Company consists of three plants, two warehouses, and four customers. Plant capacities and shipping costs (in $) from each plant to each warehouse are

Plant	Warehouse		Capacity
	1	2	
1	4	7	450
2	8	5	600
3	5	6	380

Customer demand and shipping costs per unit (in $) from each warehouse to each customer are

Warehouse	Customer			
	1	2	3	4
1	6	4	8	4
2	3	6	7	7
Demand	300	300	300	400

    a. Develop a network representation of this problem.

    b. Formulate a linear programming model of the problem.

    c. Solve the linear program to determine the optimal shipping plan.

    24. Refer to Problem 23. Suppose that shipments between the two warehouses are permitted at $2 per unit and that direct shipments can be made from plant 3 to customer 4 at a cost of $7 per unit.

    a. Develop a network representation of this problem.

    b. Formulate a linear programming model of this problem.

    c. Solve the linear program to determine the optimal shipping plan.

25. CARD, Cleveland Area Rapid Delivery, operates a delivery service in the Cleveland metropolitan area. Most of CARD's business involves rapid delivery of documents and parcels between offices during the business day. CARD promotes its ability to make fast and on-time deliveries anywhere in the metropolitan area. When a customer calls with a delivery request, CARD quotes a guaranteed delivery time. The following network shows the street routes of seven pickup and delivery locations. The numbers above each arc indicate the travel time in minutes between the two locations.

   a. Develop a linear programming model of a transshipment problem that can be used to find the minimum time required to make a delivery from location 1 to location 7.

   b. How long does it take to make a delivery from location 1 to location 7?

   c. Assume that it is now 1:00 P.M. CARD has just received a request for a pickup at location 1, and the closest CARD courier is 8 minutes away from location 1. If CARD provides a 20% safety margin in guaranteeing a delivery time, what is the guaranteed delivery time if the package picked up at location 1 is to be delivered to location 7?

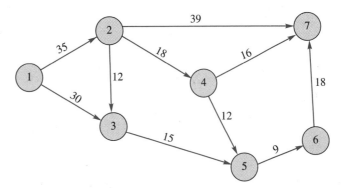

26. Adirondack Paper Mills, Inc., has paper plants in Augusta, Maine, and Tupper Lake, New York. Warehouse facilities are located in Albany, New York, and Portsmouth, New Hampshire. Distributors are located in Boston, New York, and Philadelphia. The plant capacities and distributor demands for the next month are as follows:

Plant	Capacity (units)	Distributor	Demand (units)
Augusta	300	Boston	150
Tupper Lake	100	New York	100
		Philadelphia	150

The unit transportation costs ($) for shipments from the two plants to the two warehouses and from the two warehouses to the three distributors are as follows:

	Warehouse	
Plant	Albany	Portsmouth
Augusta	7	5
Tupper Lake	3	4

	Distributor		
Warehouse	**Boston**	**New York**	**Philadelphia**
Albany	8	5	7
Portsmouth	5	6	10

    a. Draw the network representation of the Adirondack Paper Mills problem.

    b. Formulate the Adirondack Paper Mills problem as a linear programming problem.

    c. Solve the linear program to determine the minimum cost shipping schedule for the problem.

27. Consider a transshipment problem consisting of three origin nodes, two transshipment nodes, and four destination nodes. The supplies at the origin nodes and the demands at the destination nodes are as follows:

Origin	**Supply**		**Destination**	**Demand**
1	400		1	200
2	450		2	500
3	350		3	300
			4	200

The shipping costs per unit ($) are provided in the following table.

			To					
From			**Transshipment**		**Destination**			
			1	2	1	2	3	4
Origin	1		6	8	—	—	—	—
	2		8	12	—	—	—	—
	3		10	5	—	—	—	—
Transshipment	1		—	—	9	7	6	10
	2		—	—	7	9	6	8

    a. Draw the network representation of this problem.

    b. Formulate it as a linear programming problem.

    c. Solve for the optimal solution.

28. The Moore & Harman Company is in the business of buying and selling grain. An important aspect of the company's business is arranging for the purchased grain to be shipped to customers. If the company can keep freight costs low, profitability will improve.

    Currently, the company has purchased three rail cars of grain at Muncie, Indiana; six rail cars at Brazil, Indiana; and five rail cars at Xenia, Ohio. Twelve carloads of grain have been sold. The locations and the amount sold at each location are as follows:

Location	Number of Rail Car Loads
Macon, Ga.	2
Greenwood, S.C.	4
Concord, S.C.	3
Chatham, N.C.	3

All shipments must be routed through either Louisville or Cincinnati. Shown are the shipping costs per bushel (in cents) from the origins to Louisville and Cincinnati and the costs per bushel to ship from Louisville and Cincinnati to the destinations.

	To	
From	**Louisville**	**Cincinnati**
Muncie	8	6
Brazil	3	8
Xenia	9	3

← Cost per bushel from Muncie to Cincinnati is 6¢

	To			
From	**Macon**	**Greenwood**	**Concord**	**Chatham**
Louisville	44	34	34	32
Cincinnati	57	35	28	24

Cost per bushel from Cincinnati to Greenwood is 35¢

Determine a shipping schedule that will minimize the freight costs necessary to satisfy demand. Which (if any) rail cars of grain must be held at the origin until buyers can be found?

29. A rental car company has an imbalance of cars at seven of its locations. The following network shows the locations of concern (the nodes) and the cost to move a car between locations. A positive number by a node indicates an excess supply at the node, and a negative number indicates an excess demand.

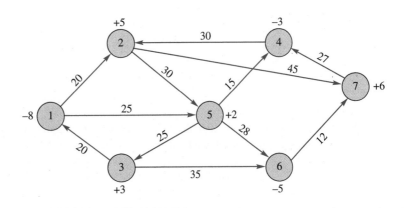

a. Develop a linear programming model of this problem.
b. Solve the model formulated in part (a) to determine how the cars should be redistributed among the locations.

30. The following linear programming formulation is for a transshipment problem.

$$\text{Min} \quad 11x_{13} + 12x_{14} + 10x_{21} + 8x_{34} + 10x_{35} + 11x_{42} + 9x_{45} + 12x_{52}$$

s.t.

$$
\begin{aligned}
x_{13} + x_{14} - x_{21} & & & & \leq 5 \\
x_{21} & & - x_{42} & - x_{52} & \leq 3 \\
x_{13} & - x_{34} - x_{35} & & & = 6 \\
- x_{14} & - x_{34} & + x_{42} + x_{45} & & \leq 2 \\
& x_{35} & + x_{45} - & x_{52} & = 4
\end{aligned}
$$

$$x_{ij} \geq 0 \quad \text{for all } i, j$$

Show the network representation of this problem.

31. Refer to the Contois Carpets problem for which the network representation is shown in Figure 10.12. Suppose that Contois has a beginning inventory of 50 yards of carpet and requires an inventory of 100 yards at the end of quarter 4.
a. Develop a network representation of this modified problem.
b. Develop a linear programming model and solve for the optimal solution.

32. Sanders Fishing Supply of Naples, Florida, manufactures a variety of fishing equipment that it sells throughout the United States. For the next three months, Sanders estimates demand for a particular product at 150, 250, and 300 units, respectively. Sanders can supply this demand by producing on regular time or overtime. Because of other commitments and anticipated cost increases in month 3, the production capacities in units and the production costs per unit are as follows:

Production	Capacity (units)	Cost per Unit
Month 1—Regular	275	$50
Month 1—Overtime	100	80
Month 2—Regular	200	50
Month 2—Overtime	50	80
Month 3—Regular	100	60
Month 3—Overtime	50	100

Inventory may be carried from one month to the next, but the cost is $20 per unit per month. For example, regular production from month 1 used to meet demand in month 2 would cost Sanders $50 + $20 = $70 per unit. This same month 1 production used to meet demand in month 3 would cost Sanders $50 + 2($20) = $90 per unit.
a. Develop a network representation of this production scheduling problem as a transportation problem. (Hint: Use six origin nodes; the supply for origin node 1 is the maximum that can be produced in month 1 on regular time, and so on.)
b. Develop a linear programming model that can be used to schedule regular and overtime production for each of the three months.
c. What is the production schedule, how many units are carried in inventory each month, and what is the total cost?
d. Is there any unused production capacity? If so, where?

Case Problem   DISTRIBUTION SYSTEM DESIGN

The Darby Company manufactures and distributes meters used to measure electric power consumption. The company started with a small production plant in El Paso and gradually built a customer base throughout Texas. A distribution center was established in Ft. Worth, Texas, and later, as business expanded, a second distribution center was established in Santa Fe, New Mexico.

The El Paso plant was expanded when the company began marketing its meters in Arizona, California, Nevada, and Utah. With the growth of the West Coast business, the Darby Company opened a third distribution center in Las Vegas and just two years ago opened a second production plant in San Bernardino, California.

Manufacturing costs differ between the company's production plants. The cost of each meter produced at the El Paso plant is $10.50. The San Bernardino plant utilizes newer and more efficient equipment; as a result, manufacturing costs are $0.50 per meter less than at the El Paso plant.

Due to the company's rapid growth, not much attention had been paid to the efficiency of the distribution system, but Darby's management has decided that it is time to address this issue. The cost of shipping a meter from each of the two plants to each of the three distribution centers is shown in Table 10.9.

The quarterly production capacity is 30,000 meters at the older El Paso plant and 20,000 meters at the San Bernardino plant. Note that no shipments are allowed from the San Bernardino plant to the Ft. Worth distribution center.

The company serves nine customer zones from the three distribution centers. The forecast of the number of meters needed in each customer zone for the next quarter is shown in Table 10.10.

TABLE 10.9   SHIPPING COST PER UNIT FROM PRODUCTION PLANTS TO
              DISTRIBUTION CENTERS (IN $)

	Distribution Center		
Plant	**Ft. Worth**	**Santa Fe**	**Las Vegas**
El Paso	3.20	2.20	4.20
San Bernardino	—	3.90	1.20

TABLE 10.10   QUARTERLY DEMAND FORECAST

Customer Zone	**Demand (meters)**
Dallas	6300
San Antonio	4880
Wichita	2130
Kansas City	1210
Denver	6120
Salt Lake City	4830
Phoenix	2750
Los Angeles	8580
San Diego	4460

TABLE 10.11   SHIPPING COST FROM THE DISTRIBUTION CENTERS TO THE CUSTOMER ZONES

Distribution Center	Customer Zone								
	Dallas	San Antonio	Wichita	Kansas City	Denver	Salt Lake City	Phoenix	Los Angeles	San Diego
Ft. Worth	0.3	2.1	3.1	4.4	6.0	—	—	—	—
Santa Fe	5.2	5.4	4.5	6.0	2.7	4.7	3.4	3.3	2.7
Las Vegas	—	—	—	—	5.4	3.3	2.4	2.1	2.5

The cost per unit of shipping from each distribution center to each customer zone is given in Table 10.11; note that some distribution centers cannot serve certain customer zones.

In the current distribution system, demand at the Dallas, San Antonio, Wichita, and Kansas City customer zones is satisfied by shipments from the Ft. Worth distribution center. In a similar manner, the Denver, Salt Lake City, and Phoenix customer zones are served by the Santa Fe distribution center, and the Los Angeles and San Diego customer zones are served by the Las Vegas distribution center. To determine how many units to ship from each plant, the quarterly customer demand forecasts are aggregated at the distribution centers, and a transportation model is used to minimize the cost of shipping from the production plants to the distribution centers.

Managerial Report

You have been called in to make recommendations for improving the distribution system. Your report should address, but not be limited to, the following issues.

1. If the company does not change its current distribution strategy, what will its distribution costs be for the following quarter?
2. Suppose that the company is willing to consider dropping the distribution center limitations; that is, customers could be served by any of the distribution centers for which costs are available. Can costs be reduced? By how much?
3. The company wants to explore the possibility of satisfying some of the customer demand directly from the production plants. In particular, the shipping cost is $0.30 per unit from San Bernardino to Los Angeles and $0.70 from San Bernardino to San Diego. The cost for direct shipments from El Paso to San Antonio is $3.50 per unit. Can distribution costs be further reduced by considering these direct plant to customer shipments?
4. Over the next five years, Darby is anticipating moderate growth (5000 meters) to the North and West. Would you recommend that they consider plant expansion at this time?

Appendix   SPREADSHEET SOLUTION OF TRANSPORTATION AND ASSIGNMENT PROBLEMS

In this appendix we show how Excel Solver can be used to solve transportation and assignment problems. We start with the Foster Generators transportation problem (see Section 10.1).

Transportation Problem

The first step is to enter the data for the transportation costs, the origin supplies, and the destination demands in the top part of the spreadsheet. Then the linear programming model is developed in the bottom part of the spreadsheet. As with all linear programs the model has four key elements: the decision variables, the objective function, the constraint left-hand sides, and the constraint right-hand sides. For a transportation problem, the decision variables are the amounts shipped from each origin to each destination; the objective function is the total transportation cost; the left-hand sides are the number of units shipped from each origin and the number of units shipped into each destination; and the right-hand sides are the origin supplies and the destination demands.

The spreadsheet formulation and solution of the Foster Generators problem are shown in Figure 10.14. The data are in the top portion of the spreadsheet. The model appears in the bottom portion of the spreadsheet; the key elements are screened.

Spreadsheet Formulation

The data and descriptive labels are contained in cells A1:F8. The transportation costs are in cells B5:E7. The origin supplies are in cells F5:F7, and the destination demands are in cells B8:E8. The key elements of the model required by the Excel Solver are the decision variables, the objective function, the constraint left-hand sides, and the constraint right-hand sides. These cells are screened in the bottom portion of the spreadsheet.

FIGURE 10.14   SPREADSHEET SOLUTION OF THE FOSTER GENERATORS PROBLEM

	A	B	C	D	E	F	G	H
1	**Foster Generators**							
2								
3			**Destination**					
4	**Origin**	Boston	Chicago	St. Louis	Lexington	**Supply**		
5	Cleveland	3	2	7	6	5000		
6	Bedford	7	5	2	3	6000		
7	York	2	5	4	5	2500		
8	**Demand**	6000	4000	2000	1500			
9								
10								
11	**Model**							
12								
13		**Min Cost**	39500					
14								
15			**Destination**					
16	**Origin**	Boston	Chicago	St. Louis	Lexington	**Total**		
17	Cleveland	3500	1500	0	0	5000	<=	5000
18	Bedford	0	2500	2000	1500	6000	<=	6000
19	York	2500	0	0	0	2500	<=	2500
20	**Total**	6000	4000	2000	1500			
21		=	=	=	=			
22		6000	4000	2000	1500			

Decision Variables   Cells B17:E19 are reserved for the decision variables. The optimal values are shown to be $x_{11} = 3500$, $x_{12} = 1500$, $x_{22} = 2500$, $x_{23} = 2000$, $x_{24} = 1500$, and $x_{41} = 2500$. All other decision variables equal zero indicating nothing will be shipped over the corresponding routes.

Objective Function   The formula =SUMPRODUCT(B5:E7,B17:E19) has been placed into cell C13 to compute the cost of the solution. The minimum cost solution is shown to have a value of $39,500.

Left-Hand Sides   Cells F17:F19 contain the left-hand sides for the supply constraints, and cells B20:E20 contain the left-hand sides for the demand constraints.

      Cell F17   =SUM(B17:E17)   (Copy to F18:F19)
      Cell B20   =SUM(B17:B19)   (Copy to C20:E20)

Right-Hand Sides   Cells H17:H19 contain the right-hand sides for the supply constraints and Cells B22:E22 contain the right-hand sides for the demand constraints.

      Cell H17   =F5   (Copy to H18:H19)
      Cell B22   =B8   (Copy to C22:E22)

Spreadsheet Solution

With the formulation complete we are now ready to use Excel's solver to find the optimal solution. The following steps are necessary.

Step 1. Select the **Tools** pull-down menu
Step 2. Select the **Solver** option
Step 3. When the **Solver Parameters** dialog box appears:
    Enter C13 in the **Set Target Cell** box
    Select the **Equal to: Min** option
    Enter B17:E19 in the **By Changing Cells** box
    Choose **Add**
Step 4. When the **Add Constraint** dialog box appears:
    Enter F17:F19 in the **Cell Reference** box
    Select **<=**
    Enter H17:H19 in the **Constraint** box
    Choose **Add**
    Enter B20:E20 in the **Cell Reference** box
    Select **=**
    Enter B22:E22 in the **Constraint** box
    Select **OK**
Step 5. When the **Solver Parameters** dialog box appears:
    Choose **Options**
Step 6. When the **Solver Options** dialog box appears:
    Select **Assume Linear Model**
    Select **Assume Non-Negative**
    Select **OK**
Step 7. When the **Solver Parameters** dialog box appears:
    Choose **Solve**
Step 8. When the **Solver Results** dialog box appears:
    Select **Keep Solver Solution**
    Select **OK**

FIGURE 10.15   SOLVER PARAMETERS DIALOG BOX FOR FOSTER
GENERATORS PROBLEM

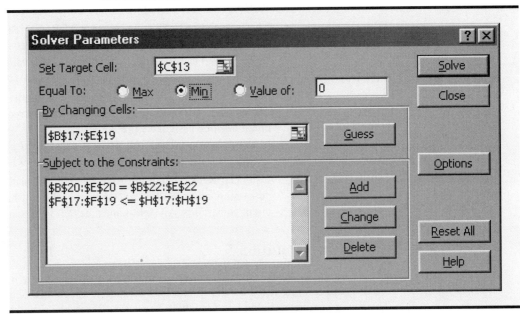

The completed solver parameters dialog box is shown in Figure 10.15. The optimal solution is shown in Figure 10.14.

The Assignment Problem

The first step is to enter the data for the assignment costs in the top part of the spreadsheet. Even though the assignment model is a special case of the transportation model, it is not necessary to enter values for origin supplies and destination demands because they are always equal to one.

The linear programming model is developed in the bottom part of the spreadsheet. As with all linear programs the model has four key elements: the decision variables, the objective function, the constraint left-hand sides, and the constraint right-hand sides. For an assignment problem the decision variables indicate whether an agent is assigned to a task (with a 1 for yes or 0 for no); the objective function is the total cost of all assignments; the constraint left-hand sides are the number of tasks that are assigned to each agent and the number of agents that are assigned to each task; and the right-hand sides are the number of tasks each agent can handle (1) and the number of agents each task requires (1).

The spreadsheet formulation and solution for the Fowle Marketing Research Assignment problem (see section 10.2) are shown in Figure 10.16.

Spreadsheet Formulation

The data and descriptive labels are contained in cells A1:D7. Note that we have not inserted supply and demand values because they are always equal to 1 in an assignment problem. The model appears in the bottom portion of the spreadsheet with the key elements screened.

Decision Variables	Cells B16:D18 are reserved for the decision variables. The optimal values are shown to be $x_{12} = 1$, $x_{23} = 1$, and $x_{31} = 1$ with all other variables $= 0$.
Objective Function	The formula =SUMPRODUCT(B5:D7,B16:D18) has been placed into cell C12 to compute the number of days required to complete all the jobs. The minimum time solution has a value of 26 days.
Left-Hand Sides	Cells E16:E18 contain the left-hand sides of the constraints for the number of clients each project leader can handle. Cells B19:D19 contain the left-hand sides of the constraints requiring that each client must be assigned a project leader.

> Cell E16   =SUM(B16:D16)   (Copy to E17:E18)
> Cell B19   =SUM(B16:B18)   (Copy to C19:D19)

Right-Hand Sides	Cells G16:G18 contain the right-hand sides for the project leader constraints and cells B21:D21 contain the right-hand sides for the client constraints. All right-hand side cell values are 1.

Spreadsheet Solution

The steps used to develop the optimal solution to the Fowle Marketing Research problem are the same as those listed for the spreadsheet solution to the Foster Generators problem. The solver parameter dialog box for Fowle Marketing Research is shown in Figure 10.17 and the optimal solution is shown in Figure 10.16

FIGURE 10.16   SPREADSHEET SOLUTION OF THE FOWLE MARKETING RESEARCH PROBLEM

	A	B	C	D	E	F	G	H
1	**Fowle Marketing Research**							
2								
3			**Client**					
4	**Project Leader**	1	2	3				
5	Terry	10	15	9				
6	Carle	9	18	5				
7	McClymonds	6	14	3				
8								
9								
10	**Model**							
11								
12		**Min Time**	26					
13								
14			**Client**					
15	**Project Leader**	1	2	3	**Total**			
16	Terry	0	1	0	1	<=	1	
17	Carle	0	0	1	1	<=	1	
18	McClymonds	1	0	0	1	<=	1	
19	**Total**	1	1	1				
20		=	=	=				
21		1	1	1				

FIGURE 10.17   SOLVER PARAMETERS DIALOG BOX FOR FOWLE MARKETING
RESEARCH PROBLEM

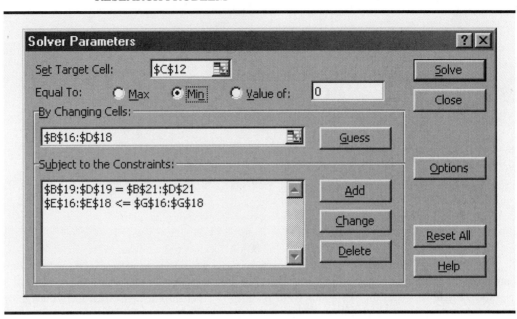

PROCTER & GAMBLE*

CINCINNATI, OHIO

Procter & Gamble (P&G) is in the consumer-products business worldwide. P&G produces and markets such products as detergents, disposable diapers, coffee, over-the-counter pharmaceuticals, dentifrices, bar soaps, mouthwashes, and paper towels. It has the leading brand in more categories than any other consumer-products company in the United States.

To maintain its leadership position in its many markets, P&G makes extensive use of quantitative methods. Some of the methodologies employed include probability and risk analysis, linear and integer programming, network flow analysis, and simulation. The individuals employing these methodologies are scattered throughout P&G's numerous divisions with perhaps the largest concentration being in the management systems division. P&G employs engineers, operations researchers, computer scientists, and businesspeople who are skilled in employing quantitative methodologies.

When P&G embarked on a major strategic planning initiative, the North American Product Sourcing Study, it was interested in consolidating its product sources and optimizing its distribution system design throughout North America. One of the decision support systems that proved to be a great aid in this project was called the Product Sourcing Heuristic (PSH). This heuristic was based on a transshipment model much like the ones described in this chapter.

In a preprocessing phase, all P&G products were aggregated into groups that shared the same technology and could be made at the same plant. The PSH was used by product strategy teams that had responsibility for developing product sourcing options for the separate product groups. The various plants that could produce the product group were source nodes, the company's regional distribution centers were the transshipment nodes, and P&G's customer zones were the destinations. Direct shipments to customer zones as well as shipments through distribution centers were employed.

The product strategy teams used the heuristic interactively to explore a variety of questions concerning product sourcing and distribution. For instance, the team might be interested in the impact of closing two plants and consolidating production in three remaining plants. The product sourcing heuristic would then delete the source nodes corresponding to the two closed plants, make any capacity modifications recommended to the sources corresponding to the remaining three plants, and resolve the transshipment problem. The product strategy team could then examine the new solution, make some more modifications, solve again, and so on.

The Product Sourcing Heuristic was viewed as a valuable decision support system by all who used it. Probably the most valuable feature was that the model permitted a rapid evaluation of a variety of strategic options. A feature that was viewed as a big plus by all who used it was that solutions provided by the PSH were displayed on a map of North America using a geographic information system. This map enabled strategic planners to review immediately the impact of their sourcing decisions across North America. The PSH has proven so successful that P&G is using it in other markets around the world.

*The authors are indebted to Mr. Franz Dill and Mr. Tom Chorman of Procter & Gamble for providing this application.

INTEGER LINEAR PROGRAMMING

CONTENTS

In this chapter we discuss a class of problems that are modeled as linear programs with the additional requirement that one or more variables must be integer. Such problems are called **integer linear programs.** If all variables must be integer, we have an all-integer linear program. If some, but not all, variables must be integer, we have a mixed-integer linear program. In many applications of integer linear programming, one or more integer variables are required to equal either 0 or 1. Such variables are called *0–1* or *binary variables.* If all variables are 0–1 variables, we have a 0–1 integer linear program.

Integer variables—especially 0–1 variables—provide substantial modeling flexibility. As a result, the number of applications that can be addressed with linear programming methodology is expanded. The cost of the added modeling flexibility is that problems involving integer variables are often much more difficult to solve. A linear programming problem with several thousand continuous variables can be solved with any of several commercial linear programming solvers. However, an all-integer linear programming problem with less than 100 variables can sometimes be extremely difficult to solve. Experienced quantitative analysts can help identify the types of integer linear programs that are easy, or at least reasonable, to solve. Commercial computer software packages, such as MPSX-MIP®, OSL®, CPLEX®, and LINDO®, have extensive integer programming capability. The Management Scientist and spreadsheet packages, such as Excel, have the capability for solving smaller integer linear programs.

The objective of this chapter is to provide an applications-oriented introduction to integer linear programming. First, we discuss the different types of integer linear programming models. Then we show the formulation,

graphical solution, and computer solution of an all-integer linear program. In Section 11.3, we discuss four applications of integer linear programming that make use of 0–1 variables: capital budgeting, fixed cost, distribution system design, and bank location problems. In Section 11.4, we provide additional illustrations of the modeling flexibility provided by 0–1 variables. A chapter appendix illustrates the use of Excel for solving integer programs.

NOTES AND COMMENTS

1. Because integer linear programs are harder to solve than linear programs, one should not try to solve a problem as an integer program if simply rounding the linear programming solution is adequate. In many linear programming problems, such as those in previous chapters, rounding has little economic consequences on the objective function, and feasibility is not an issue. But, in problems such as determining how many jet engines to manufacture, the consequences of rounding can be substantial and integer programming methodology should be employed.
2. Some linear programming problems have a special structure, which guarantees that the variables will have integer values. The assignment, transportation, and transshipment problems of Chapter 10 have such structures. If the supply and the demand for transportation and transshipment problems are integer, the optimal linear programming solution will provide integer amounts shipped. For the assignment problem, the optimal linear programming solution will consist of 0s and 1s. So, for these specially structured problems, linear programming methodology can be used to find optimal integer solutions. Integer linear programming algorithms are not necessary.

11.1   TYPES OF INTEGER LINEAR PROGRAMMING MODELS

The only difference between the problems studied in this chapter and the ones studied in earlier chapters on linear programming is that one, or more, variables are required to be integer. If all variables are required to be integer, we have an **all-integer linear program.** The following is a two-variable, all-integer linear programming model.

$$\text{Max} \quad 2x_1 + 3x_2$$
$$\text{s.t.}$$
$$3x_1 + 3x_2 \le 12$$
$$\tfrac{2}{3}x_1 + 1x_2 \le 4$$
$$1x_1 + 2x_2 \le 6$$
$$x_1, x_2 \ge 0 \text{ and integer}$$

Note that if we drop the phrase "and integer" from this model, we have the familiar two-variable linear program. The linear program that results from dropping the integer requirements is called the **LP Relaxation** of the integer linear program.

If some, but not all, variables are required to be integer, we have a **mixed-integer linear program.** The following is a two-variable, mixed-integer linear program.

$$\text{Max} \quad 3x_1 + 4x_2$$
$$\text{s.t.}$$
$$-1x_1 + 2x_2 \le 8$$
$$1x_1 + 2x_2 \le 12$$
$$2x_1 + 1x_2 \le 16$$
$$x_1, x_2 \ge 0 \text{ and } x_2 \text{ integer}$$

We obtain the LP Relaxation of this mixed-integer linear program by dropping the requirement that x_2 be integer.

In some applications, the integer variables may only take on the values 0 or 1. Then we have a **0–1 linear integer program.** As we see later in the chapter, 0–1 variables provide additional modeling capability. The Q. M. in Action: Planning the Size of KLM's Aircraft Maintenance Teams describes how integer and 0–1 integer variables are used to determine the size of the engineering teams that perform maintenance on KLM's aircraft.

PLANNING THE SIZE OF KLM'S AIRCRAFT MAINTENANCE TEAMS*

KLM Royal Dutch Airlines has been the major Dutch carrier since 1919. Currently, KLM owns 90 aircraft of 8 different types and operates flights to 150 cities in 79 countries. To guarantee safety, KLM has a high-quality aircraft maintenance program with a workforce that includes 250 engineers and 150 nontechnical employees.

Preventive maintenance on an aircraft consists of both major and minor inspections. Major inspections require several hours to several months to complete. Minor inspections are conducted during the ground time between aircraft arrival and departure at an airport. Engineers from KLM's aircraft maintenance group are organized into teams that carry out the maintenance tasks.

The engineers are highly skilled and well trained. A governmental rule specifies that maintenance engineers are allowed to carry out inspections on a specific aircraft type only if licensed for that aircraft type. KLM's internal safety rules further limit engineers to licenses on at most two aircraft types. When licensed for a particular aircraft, an individual engineer's skills are certified as being mechanical, electrical, or radio.

KLM's management strives to develop a good match between workload requirements and the abilities of the assigned workforce. Given a set of maintenance jobs, management attempts to minimize the number of engineers with appropriate license and skill combinations necessary to complete the jobs. An integer linear programming model helps with this task. The objective function is to minimize the number of engineers required per maintenance team. Integer decision variables are required because the number of engineers with each license and skill combination cannot be fractional. In addition, 0–1 integer variables are included in the model to guarantee that each maintenance job is carried out exactly once. Another integer programming model is used to determine the maximum number of maintenance jobs that can be scheduled given the size and composition of the maintenance workforce. KLM has found integer linear programming to be a valuable tool for solving problems dealing with personnel planning for aircraft maintenance.

* Based on M. C. Dijkstra, L. G. Kroon, M. Slomon, J. A. E. E. Van Nunen, and L. N. Van Wassenhove, "Planning the Size and Organization of KLM's Aircraft Maintenance Personnel," *Interfaces* (November–December 1994): 47–58.

11.2   GRAPHICAL AND COMPUTER SOLUTIONS FOR AN ALL-INTEGER LINEAR PROGRAM

Eastborne Realty has $2,000,000 available for the purchase of new rental property. After an initial screening. Eastborne has reduced the investment alternatives to townhouses and apartment buildings. Each townhouse can be purchased for $282,000, and five are available. Each apartment building can be purchased for $400,000, and the developer will construct as many buildings as Eastborne wants to purchase.

Eastborne's property manager can devote up to 140 hours per month to these new properties; each townhouse is expected to require 4 hours per month, and each apartment building is expected to require 40 hours per month. The annual cash flow, after deducting mortgage payments and operating expenses, is estimated to be $10,000 per townhouse and $15,000 per apartment building. Eastborne's owner would like to determine the number of townhouses and the number of apartment buildings to purchase to maximize annual cash flow.

We begin by defining the decision variables as follows:

$$T = \text{number of townhouses}$$
$$A = \text{number of apartment buildings}$$

The objective function for cash flow ($000s) is

$$\text{Max} \quad 10T + 15A$$

Three constraints must be satisfied:

$$282T + 400A \leq 2000 \quad \text{Funds available}$$
$$4T + 40A \leq 140 \quad \text{Manager's time}$$
$$T \leq 5 \quad \text{Townhouses available}$$

The variables T and A must be nonnegative. In addition, the purchase of a fractional number of townhouses and/or a fractional number of apartment buildings is unacceptable. Thus, T and A must be integer. The model for the Eastborne Realty problem is the following all-integer linear program.

$$\text{Max} \quad 10T + 15A$$
$$\text{s.t.}$$
$$282T + 400A \leq 2000$$
$$4T + 40A \leq 140$$
$$T \leq 5$$
$$T, A \geq 0 \text{ and integer}$$

Graphical Solution of the LP Relaxation

Suppose that we drop the integer requirements for T and A and solve the LP Relaxation of the Eastborne Realty Problem. Using the graphical solution procedure, as presented in Chapter 7, the optimal linear programming solution is shown in Figure 11.1. It is $T = 2.479$ townhouses and $A = 3.252$ apartment buildings. The optimal value of the objective function is 73.574, which indicates an annual cash flow of $73,574. Unfortunately, Eastborne cannot purchase fractional numbers of townhouses and apartment buildings; further analysis is necessary.

Rounding to Obtain an Integer Solution

In many cases, a noninteger solution can be rounded to obtain an acceptable integer solution. For instance, a linear programming solution to a production scheduling problem might call for the production of 15,132.4 cases of breakfast cereal. The rounded integer solution of 15,132 cases would probably have minimal impact on the value of the objective function and the feasibility of the solution. Rounding would be a sensible approach. Indeed, whenever rounding has a minimal impact on the objective function and constraints, most managers find it acceptable. A near-optimal solution is fine.

However, rounding may not always be a good strategy. When the decision variables take on small values that have a major impact on the value of the objective function and/or feasibility, an optimal integer solution is needed. Let us return to the Eastborne Realty problem and examine the impact of rounding. The optimal solution to the LP Relaxation for Eastborne Realty resulted in $T = 2.479$ townhouses and $A = 3.252$ apartment buildings. Because each

FIGURE 11.1   GRAPHICAL SOLUTION TO THE LP RELAXATION OF THE EASTBORNE
REALTY PROBLEM

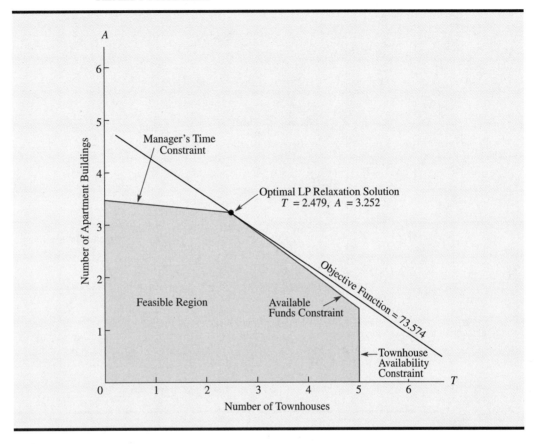

townhouse costs $282,000 and each apartment building costs $400,000, rounding to an integer solution can be expected to have a significant economic impact on the problem.

If a problem has only less-than-or-equal-to constraints with positive coefficients for the variables, rounding down will always provide a feasible integer solution.

Suppose that we round the solution to the LP Relaxation to obtain the integer solution $T = 2$ and $A = 3$, with an objective function value of $10(2) + 15(3) = 65$. The annual cash flow of $65,000 is substantially less than the annual cash flow of $73,574 provided by the solution to the LP Relaxation. Do other rounding possibilities exist? Exploring other rounding alternatives shows that the integer solution $T = 3$ and $A = 3$ is infeasible because it requires more funds than the $2,000,000 Eastborne has available. The rounded solution of $T = 2$ and $A = 4$ is also infeasible for the same reason. At this point, rounding has led to two townhouses and three apartment buildings with an annual cash flow of $65,000 as the best feasible integer solution to the problem. Unfortunately, we don't know whether this solution is the best integer solution to the problem.

Rounding to an integer solution is a trial-and-error approach. Each rounded solution must be evaluated for feasibility as well as for its impact on the value of the objective function. Even in cases where a rounded solution its feasible, we do not have a guarantee that we have found the optimal integer solution. We will see shortly that the rounded solution ($T = 2$ and $A = 3$) is not optimal for Eastborne Realty.

Graphical Solution of the All-Integer Problem

Figure 11.2 shows the changes in the linear programming graphical solution procedure required to solve the Eastborne Realty integer linear programming problem. First, the graph

FIGURE 11.2   GRAPHICAL SOLUTION OF THE EASTBORNE REALTY INTEGER PROBLEM

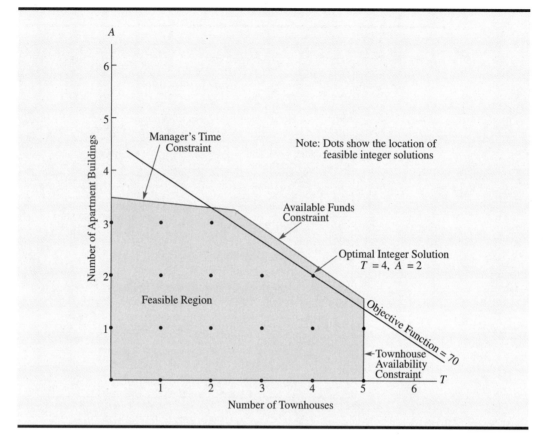

of the feasible region is drawn exactly as in the LP Relaxation of the problem. Then, because the optimal solution must have integer values, we identify the feasible integer solutions with the dots shown in Figure 11.2. Finally, instead of moving the objective function line to the best extreme point in the feasible region, we move it in an improving direction as far as possible until reaching the dot (feasible integer point) providing the best value for the objective function. Viewing Figure 11.2, we see that the optimal integer solution occurs at $T = 4$ townhouses and $A = 2$ apartment buildings. The objective function value is $10(4) + 15(2) = 70$ providing an annual cash flow of $70,000. This solution is significantly better than the best solution found by rounding: $T = 2$, $A = 3$ with an annual cash flow of $65,000. Thus, we see that rounding would not have been the best strategy for Eastborne Realty.

Try Problem 2 for practice with the graphical solution of an integer program.

Using the LP Relaxation to Establish Bounds

An important observation can be made from the analysis of the Eastborne Realty problem. It has to do with the relationship between the value of the optimal integer solution and the value of the optimal solution to the LP Relaxation.

> For integer linear programs involving maximization, the value of the optimal solution to the LP Relaxation provides an upper bound on the value of the optimal integer solution. For integer linear programs involving minimization, the value of the optimal solution to the LP Relaxation provides a lower bound on the value of the optimal integer solution.

This observation is valid for the Eastborne Realty problem. The value of the optimal integer solution is $70,000, and the value of the optimal solution to the LP Relaxation is $73,574. Thus, we know from the LP Relaxation solution that the upper bound for the value of the objective function is $73,574.

The bounding property of the LP Relaxation allows us to conclude that if, by chance, the solution to an LP Relaxation turns out to be an integer solution, it is also optimal for the integer linear program. This bounding property can also be helpful in determining whether a rounded solution is "good enough." If a rounded LP Relaxation solution is feasible and provides a value of the objective function that is "almost as good as" the value of the objective function for the LP Relaxation, we know the rounded solution is a near-optimal integer solution. In such a case, we can avoid having to solve the problem as an integer linear program.

Try Problem 5 for the graphical solution of a mixed integer program.

Computer Solution

As mentioned earlier, commercial software packages that can solve integer linear programs are widely available. Generally, these packages are reliable for problems having up to approximately 100 integer variables and may be used to solve specially structured problems with several thousand integer variables.

The Management Scientist can be used to solve the integer linear programs in this chapter. To use The Management Scientist to solve the Eastborne Realty problem, the data input worksheet is completed in the same way as for any linear program (see Appendix 7.1). Then after instructing the computer to solve the problem, the user will be asked to indicate which of the variables are integer. Specifying both T and A as integers provides the optimal integer solution shown in Figure 11.3. The solution of $T = 4$ townhouses and $A = 2$ apartment buildings has a maximum annual cash flow of $70,000. The values of the slack variables tell us that the optimal solution has $72,000 of available funds unused, 44 hours of the manager's time still available, and 1 of the available townhouses not purchased.

FIGURE 11.3   THE MANAGEMENT SCIENTIST SOLUTION FOR THE EASTBORNE REALTY PROBLEM

```
Objective Function Value =                         70.000

          Variable                        Value
             T                            4.000
             A                            2.000

          Constraint                   Slack/Surplus
             1                            72.000
             2                            44.000
             3                            1.000
```

NOTES AND COMMENTS

In Appendix 11.1 we show the use of spreadsheets to solve integer programs by using Excel to solve the Eastborne Realty problem.

11.3 APPLICATIONS INVOLVING 0–1 VARIABLES

Much of the modeling flexibility provided by integer linear programming is due to the use of 0–1 variables. In many applications, 0–1 variables provide selections or choices with the value of the variable equal to 1 if a corresponding activity is undertaken and equal to 0 if the corresponding activity is not undertaken. The capital budgeting, fixed cost, distribution system design, and bank location applications presented in this section make use of 0–1 variables.

Capital Budgeting

The Ice-Cold Refrigerator Company is considering investing in several projects that have varying capital requirements over the next four years. Faced with limited capital each year, management would like to select the most profitable projects. The estimated net present value for each project,[1] the capital requirements, and the available capital over the four-year period are shown in Table 11.1.

The four 0–1 decision variables are as follows:

$P = 1$ if the plant expansion project is accepted; 0 if rejected

$W = 1$ if the warehouse expansion project is accepted; 0 if rejected

$M = 1$ if the new machinery project is accepted; 0 if rejected

$R = 1$ if the new product research project is accepted; 0 if rejected

The company's objective function is to maximize the net present value of the capital budgeting projects. The problem has four constraints: one for the funds available in each of the next four years.

A 0–1 integer linear programming model with dollars in thousands is as follows:

$$\text{Max} \quad 90P + 40W + 10M + 37R$$

s.t.

$$15P + 10W + 10M + 15R \le 40 \quad \text{(Year 1 capital available)}$$
$$20P + 15W \quad\quad\quad + 10R \le 50 \quad \text{(Year 2 capital available)}$$
$$20P + 20W \quad\quad\quad + 10R \le 40 \quad \text{(Year 3 capital available)}$$
$$15P + 5W + 4M + 10R \le 35 \quad \text{(Year 4 capital available)}$$
$$P, W, M, R = 0, 1$$

The integer programming solution from The Management Scientist is shown in Figure 11.4. The optimal solution is $P = 1$, $W = 1$, $M = 1$, $R = 0$, with a total estimated net present value of $140,000. Thus, the company should fund the plant expansion, the warehouse expansion, and the new machinery projects. The new product research project should be put on hold unless additional capital funds become available. The values of the slack variables (see Figure 11.4) show that the company will have $5000 remaining in year 1, $15,000 remaining in year 2, and $11,000 remaining in year 4. Checking the capital requirements for the new product research project, we see that enough funds are available for this project in year 2 and year 4. However, the company would have to find additional capital funds of $10,000 in year 1 and $10,000 in year 3 to fund the new product research project.

---

1. The estimated net present value is the net cash flow discounted back to the beginning of year 1.

TABLE11.1 PROJECT NET PRESENT VALUE, CAPITAL REQUIREMENTS, AND AVAILABLE CAPITAL
FOR THE ICE-COLD REFRIGERATOR COMPANY

	Project				
	Plant Expansion	**Warehouse Expansion**	**New Machinery**	**New Product Research**	**Total Capital Available**
Present Value	$90,000	$40,000	$10,000	$37,000	
Year 1 Capital	$15,000	$10,000	$10,000	$15,000	$40,000
Year 2 Capital	$20,000	$15,000		$10,000	$50,000
Year 3 Capital	$20,000	$20,000		$10,000	$40,000
Year 4 Capital	$15,000	$ 5,000	$ 4,000	$10,000	$35,000

Fixed Cost

In many applications, the cost of production has two components: a setup cost, which is a
fixed cost, and a variable cost, which is directly related to the production quantity. The use of
0–1 variables makes including the setup cost possible in a model for a production application.

Consider the RMC problem. Three raw materials are used to produce 3 products: a fuel
additive, a solvent base, and a carpet cleaning fluid. The following decision variables are used.

$$F = \text{tons of fuel additive produced}$$
$$S = \text{tons of solvent base produced}$$
$$C = \text{tons of carpet cleaning fluid produced}$$

The profit contributions are $40 per ton for the fuel additive, $30 per ton for the solvent
base, and $50 per ton for the carpet cleaning fluid. Each ton of fuel additive is a blend of

FIGURE 11.4 THE MANAGEMENT SCIENTIST SOLUTION FOR THE ICE-COLD
REFRIGERATOR COMPANY PROBLEM

```
     Objective Function Value =              140.000

          Variable                            Value
     _ _ _ _ _ _ _ _ _ _                   _ _ _ _ _ _ _ _
               P                              1.000

               W                              1.000

               M                              1.000

               R                              0.000


        Constraint                        Slack/Surplus
     _ _ _ _ _ _ _ _ _                    _ _ _ _ _ _ _ _ _
               1                              5.000

               2                             15.000

               3                              0.000

               4                             11.000
```

0.4 tons of material 1 and 0.6 tons of material 3. Each ton of solvent base requires 0.5 tons of material 1, 0.2 tons of material 2, and 0.3 tons of material 3. Each ton of carpet cleaning fluid is a blend of 0.6 tons of material 1, 0.1 tons of material 2, and 0.3 tons of material 3. RMC has 20 tons of material 1, 5 tons of material 2, and 21 tons of material 3, and is interested in determining the optimal production quantities for the upcoming planning period.

A linear programming model of the RMC problem is shown.

$$\text{Max} \quad 40F + 30S + 50C$$

$$\text{s.t.}$$

$$
\begin{array}{rll}
0.4F + 0.5S + 0.6C \leq 20 & \text{Material 1} \\
0.2S + 0.1C \leq 5 & \text{Material 2} \\
0.6F + 0.3S + 0.3C \leq 21 & \text{Material 3} \\
F, S, C \geq 0 &
\end{array}
$$

Using the linear programming module of The Management Scientist, we obtained an optimal solution consisting of 27.5 tons of fuel additive, 0 tons of solvent base, and 15 tons of carpet cleaning fluid, with a value of $1850. See Figure 11.5.

This linear programming formulation of the RMC problem does not include a fixed cost for production setup of the products. Suppose that the following data are available concerning the setup cost and the maximum production quantity for each of the 3 products.

Product	Setup Cost	Maximum Production
Fuel additive	$200	50 tons
Solvent base	$ 50	25 tons
Carpet cleaning fluid	$400	40 tons

The modeling flexibility provided by 0–1 variables can now be used to incorporate the fixed setup costs into the production model. The 0–1 variables are defined as follows:

$$SF = 1 \text{ if the fuel additive is produced; 0 if not}$$

$$SS = 1 \text{ if the solvent base is produced; 0 if not}$$

$$SC = 1 \text{ if the carpet cleaning fluid is produced; 0 if not}$$

Using these setup variables, the total setup cost is

$$200SF + 50SS + 400SC$$

FIGURE 11.5   THE MANAGEMENT SCIENTIST SOLUTION TO THE RMC PROBLEM

```
Objective Function Value =   1850.000

     Variable              Value              Reduced Costs
   ------------          ----------          ----------------
        F                 27.500                  0.000
        S                  0.000                 12.500
        C                 15.000                  0.000
```

We can now rewrite the objective function to include the setup cost. Thus, the net profit objective function becomes

$$\text{Max} \quad 40F + 30S + 50C - 200SF - 50SS - 400SC$$

Next, we must write production capacity constraints so that if a setup variable equals 0, production of the corresponding product is not permitted and, if a setup variable equals 1, production is permitted up to the maximum quantity. For the fuel additive, we do so by adding the following constraint:

$$F \leq 50SF$$

Note that, with this constraint present, production of the fuel additive is not permitted when $SF = 0$. When $SF = 1$, production of up to 50 tons of fuel additive is permitted. We can think of the setup variable as a switch. When it is off ($SF = 0$), production is not permitted; when it is on ($SF = 1$), production is permitted.

Similar production capacity constraints, using 0–1 variables, are added for the solvent base and carpet cleaning products

$$S \leq 25SS$$
$$C \leq 40SC$$

Moving all the variables to the left-hand side of the constraints provides the following fixed cost model for the RMC problem.

$$\text{Max} \quad 40F + 30S + 50C - 200SF - 50SS - 400SC$$

s.t.

$$
\begin{array}{llll}
0.4F + 0.5S + 0.6C & & \leq 20 & \text{Material 1} \\
0.2S + 0.1C & & \leq 5 & \text{Material 2} \\
0.6F + 0.3S + 0.3C & & \leq 21 & \text{Material 3} \\
F \hspace{3.5cm} - 50SF & & \leq 0 & \text{Maximum } F \\
S \hspace{3cm} - 25SS & & \leq 0 & \text{Maximum } S \\
C \hspace{1.2cm} - 40SC & \leq 0 & & \text{Maximum } C
\end{array}
$$

$$F, S, C \geq 0; \; SF, SS, SC = 0, 1$$

We solved the RMC problem with setup costs using The Management Scientist. As shown in Figure 11.6, the optimal solution shows 25 tons of fuel additive and 20 tons of solvent base. The value of the objective function after deducting the setup cost is $1350. The setup cost for the fuel additive and the solvent base is $200 + $50 = $250. The optimal solution shows $SC = 0$, which indicates that the more expensive $400 setup cost for the carpet cleaning fluid should be avoided. Thus the carpet cleaning fluid is not produced.

The key to developing a fixed-cost model is the introduction of a 0–1 variable for each fixed cost and the specification of an upper bound for the corresponding production variable. For a production quantity x, a constraint of the form $x \leq My$ can then be used to allow production when the setup variable $y = 1$ and not to allow production when the setup variable $y = 0$. The value of the maximum production quantity M should be large enough to allow for all reasonable levels of production. But, research has shown that choosing values of M too large will slow the solution procedure.

FIGURE 11.6   THE MANAGEMENT SCIENTIST SOLUTION TO THE RMC PROBLEM
WITH SETUP COSTS

```
           Objective Function Value = 1350.000

           Variable                      Value
           --------                      -----
              F                         25.000
              S                         20.000
              C                          0.000
             SF                          1.000
             SS                          1.000
             SC                          0.000
```

Distribution System Design

The Martin-Beck Company operates a plant in St. Louis with an annual capacity of 30,000 units. Product is shipped to regional distribution centers located in Boston, Atlanta, and Houston. Because of an anticipated increase in demand, Martin-Beck plans to increase capacity by constructing a new plant in one or more of the following cities: Detroit, Toledo, Denver, or Kansas City. The estimated annual fixed cost and the annual capacity for the four proposed plants are as follows:

Proposed Plant	Annual Fixed Cost	Annual Capacity
Detroit	$175,000	10,000
Toledo	$300,000	20,000
Denver	$375,000	30,000
Kansas City	$500,000	40,000

The company's long-range planning group has developed forecasts of the anticipated annual demand at the distribution centers as follows:

Distribution Center	Annual Demand
Boston	30,000
Atlanta	20,000
Houston	20,000

The shipping cost per unit from each plant to each distribution center is shown in Table 11.2. A network representation of the potential Martin-Beck distribution system is shown in Figure 11.7. Each potential plant location is shown; capacities and demands are shown in thousands of units. This network representation is for a transportation problem with a plant at St. Louis and at all four proposed sites. However, the decision has not yet been made as to which new plant or plants will be constructed.

Let us now show how 0–1 variables can be used to develop a model for choosing the best plant locations and for determining how much to ship from each plant to each

TABLE 11.2   SHIPPING COST PER UNIT FOR THE MARTIN-BECK DISTRIBUTION
SYSTEM

Plant Site	Distribution Centers		
	Boston	**Atlanta**	**Houston**
Detroit	5	2	3
Toledo	4	3	4
Denver	9	7	5
Kansas City	10	4	2
St. Louis	8	4	3

FIGURE 11.7   THE NETWORK REPRESENTATION OF THE MARTIN-BECK COMPANY
DISTRIBUTION SYSTEM PROBLEM

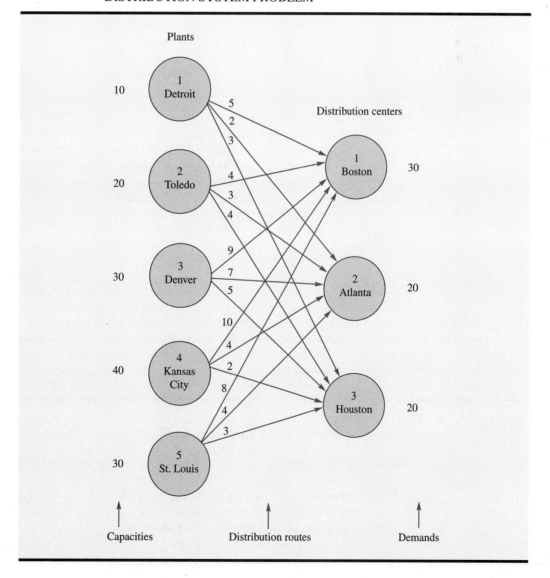

distribution center. We can use the following 0–1 variables to represent the plant construction decision.

$$y_1 = 1 \text{ if a plant is constructed in Detroit; 0 if not}$$
$$y_2 = 1 \text{ if a plant is constructed in Toledo; 0 if not}$$
$$y_3 = 1 \text{ if a plant is constructed in Denver; 0 if not}$$
$$y_4 = 1 \text{ if a plant is constructed in Kansas City; 0 if not}$$

The variables representing the amount shipped from each plant site to each distribution center are defined just as for a transportation problem.

$$x_{ij} = \text{the units shipped in thousands from plant } i \text{ to distribution center } j$$
$$i = 1, 2, 3, 4, 5 \quad \text{and} \quad j = 1, 2, 3$$

Using the shipping cost data in Table 11.2, the annual transportation cost in thousand of dollars is written

$$5x_{11} + 2x_{12} + 3x_{13} + 4x_{21} + 3x_{22} + 4x_{23} + 9x_{31} + 7x_{32} + 5x_{33}$$
$$+ 10x_{41} + 4x_{42} + 2x_{43} + 8x_{51} + 4x_{52} + 3x_{53}$$

The annual fixed cost of operating the new plant or plants in thousand of dollars is written as

$$175y_1 + 300y_2 + 375y_3 + 500y_4$$

Note that the 0–1 variables are defined so that the annual fixed cost of operating the new plants is only calculated for the plant or plants that are actually constructed (i.e., $y_i = 1$). If a plant is not constructed, $y_i = 0$ and the corresponding annual fixed cost is $0.

The Martin-Beck objective function is the sum of the annual transportation cost plus the annual fixed cost of operating the newly constructed plants.

Now let us consider the capacity constraints at the four proposed plants. Using Detroit as an example, we write the following constraint:

$$x_{11} + x_{12} + x_{13} \leq 10y_1$$

If the Detroit plant is constructed, $y_1 = 1$ and the total amount shipped from Detroit to the three distribution centers must be less than or equal to Detroit's 10,000-unit capacity. If the Detroit plant is not constructed, $y_1 = 0$ will result in a 0 capacity at Detroit. In this case, the variables corresponding to the shipments from Detroit must all equal zero: $x_{11} = 0$, $x_{12} = 0$, and $x_{13} = 0$. By placing all variables on the left-hand side of the constraints, we have the following Detroit capacity constraint:

$$x_{11} + x_{12} + x_{13} - 10y_1 \leq 0 \quad \text{Detroit capacity}$$

In a similar fashion, the capacity constraint for the proposed plant in Toledo can be written

$$x_{21} + x_{22} + x_{23} - 20y_2 \leq 0 \quad \text{Toledo capacity}$$

Similar constraints can be written for the proposed plants in Denver and Kansas City. Note that because a plant already exists in St. Louis, we do not define a 0–1 variable for this plant. Its capacity constraint can be written as follows:

$$x_{51} + x_{52} + x_{53} \leq 30 \quad \text{St. Louis capacity}$$

Three demand constraints will be needed, one for each of the three distribution centers. The demand constraint for the Boston distribution center with units in thousands is written as

$$x_{11} + x_{21} + x_{31} + x_{41} + x_{51} = 30 \quad \text{Boston demand}$$

Similar constraints appear for the Atlanta and Houston distribution centers.

The complete model for the Martin-Beck distribution system design problem is as follows:

$$\text{Min} \quad 5x_{11} + 2x_{12} + 3x_{13} + 4x_{21} + 3x_{22} + 4x_{23} + 9x_{31} + 7x_{32} + 5x_{33} + 10x_{41} + 4x_{42}$$
$$+ 2x_{43} + 8x_{51} + 4x_{52} + 3x_{53} + 175y_1 + 300y_2 + 375y_3 + 500y_4$$

s.t.

$x_{11} + x_{12} + x_{13} \qquad\qquad - 10y_1 \qquad\qquad\qquad\qquad \leq 0$	Detroit capacity
$x_{21} + x_{22} + x_{23} \qquad\qquad\qquad - 20y_2 \qquad\qquad\qquad \leq 0$	Toledo capacity
$x_{31} + x_{32} + x_{33} \qquad\qquad\qquad\qquad - 30y_3 \qquad\qquad \leq 0$	Denver capacity
$x_{41} + x_{42} + x_{43} \qquad\qquad\qquad\qquad\qquad - 40y_4 \leq 0$	Kansas City capacity
$x_{51} + x_{52} + x_{53} \qquad\qquad\qquad\qquad\qquad\qquad\quad \leq 30$	St. Louis capacity
$x_{11} + x_{21} + x_{31} + x_{41} + x_{51} \qquad\qquad\qquad\qquad = 30$	Boston demand
$x_{12} + x_{22} + x_{32} + x_{42} + x_{52} \qquad\qquad\qquad\qquad = 20$	Atlanta demand
$x_{13} + x_{23} + x_{33} + x_{43} + x_{53} \qquad\qquad\qquad\qquad = 20$	Houston demand

$$x_{ij} \geq \text{ for all } i \text{ and } j; \; y_1, y_2, y_3, y_4 = 0, 1$$

Using the integer linear programming module of The Management Scientist, we obtained the solution shown in Figure 11.8. The optimal solution calls for the construction of a plant in Kansas City ($y_4 = 1$); 20,000 units will be shipped from Kansas City to Atlanta ($x_{42} = 20$), 20,000 units will be shipped from Kansas City to Houston ($x_{43} = 20$), and 30,000 units will be shipped from St. Louis to Boston ($x_{51} = 30$). Note that the total cost of this solution including the fixed cost of $500,000 for the plant in Kansas City is $860,000.

This basic model can be expanded to accommodate distribution systems involving direct shipments from plants to warehouses, from plants to retail outlets, and of multiple products.[2] Using the special properties of 0–1 variables, the model can also be expanded to accommodate a variety of configuration constraints on the plant locations. For example, suppose in another problem, site 1 was in Dallas and site 2 was in Fort Worth. A company might not want to locate plants in both Dallas and Fort Worth because the cities are so close together. To prevent it from happening, the following constraint can be added to the model:

Problem 13, which is based on the Martin-Beck distribution system problem, provides additional practice involving 0–1 variables.

$$y_1 + y_2 \leq 1$$

This constraint allows either y_1 or y_2 to equal 1, but not both. If we had written the constraints as an equality, it would require that a plant be located in either Dallas or Fort Worth.

Bank Location

The long-range planning department for the Ohio Trust Company is considering expanding its operation into a 20-county region in northeastern Ohio (see Figure 11.9). Currently, Ohio

---

2. For computational reasons, it is usually preferable to replace the m plant capacity constraints with mn shipping route capacity constraints of the form $x_{ij} \leq \text{Min } \{s_i, d_j\} \, y_i$ for $i = 1, \ldots, m$, and $j = 1, \ldots, n$. The coefficient for y_i in each of these constraints is the smaller of the origin capacity (s_i) or the destination demand (d_j). These additional constraints often have the desirable feature of causing the solution of the LP Relaxation to be integer.

FIGURE 11.8 THE MANAGEMENT SCIENTIST SOLUTION FOR THE MARTIN-BECK
COMPANY DISTRIBUTION SYSTEM PROBLEM

```
OPTIMAL SOLUTION

Objective Function Value =                    860.000

        Variable                              Value
          X11                                 0.000
          X12                                 0.000
          X13                                 0.000
          X21                                 0.000
          X22                                 0.000
          X23                                 0.000
          X31                                 0.000
          X32                                 0.000
          X33                                 0.000
          X41                                 0.000
          X42                                20.000
          X43                                20.000
          X51                                30.000
          X52                                 0.000
          X53                                 0.000
          Y1                                  0.000
          Y2                                  0.000
          Y3                                  0.000
          Y4                                  1.000


        Constraint                         Slack/Surplus
            1                                 0.000
            2                                 0.000
            3                                 0.000
            4                                 0.000
            5                                 0.000
            6                                 0.000
            7                                 0.000
            8                                 0.000
```

Trust does not have a principal place of business in any of the 20 counties. According to the
banking laws in Ohio, if a bank establishes a principal place of business (PPB) in any
county, branch banks can be established in that county and in any adjacent county. However, to establish a new principal place of business, Ohio Trust must either obtain approval
for a new bank from the state's superintendent of banks or purchase an existing bank.

Table 11.3 lists the 20 counties in the region and adjacent counties. For example,
Ashtabula County is adjacent to Lake, Geauga, and Trumbull counties; Lake County is adjacent to Ashtabula, Cuyahoga, and Geauga counties; and so on.

As an initial step in its planning, Ohio Trust would like to determine the minimum number of PPBs necessary to do business throughout the 20-county region. A 0–1 integer programming model can be used to solve this problem for Ohio Trust. We define the variables as

$$x_i = 1 \text{ if a PPB is established in county } i; 0 \text{ otherwise}$$

To minimize the number of PPBs needed, we write the objective function as

$$\text{Min} \quad x_1 + x_2 + \cdots + x_{20}$$

FIGURE 11.9 THE 20-COUNTY AREA IN NORTHEASTERN OHIO

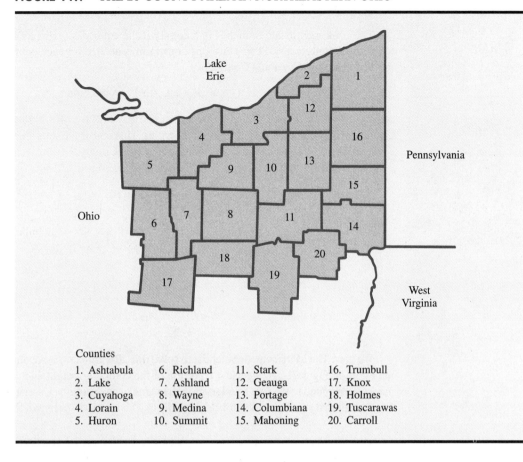

Counties

1. Ashtabula	6. Richland	11. Stark	16. Trumbull
2. Lake	7. Ashland	12. Geauga	17. Knox
3. Cuyahoga	8. Wayne	13. Portage	18. Holmes
4. Lorain	9. Medina	14. Columbiana	19. Tuscarawas
5. Huron	10. Summit	15. Mahoning	20. Carroll

TABLE 11.3 COUNTIES IN THE OHIO TRUST EXPANSION REGION

Counties Under Consideration	Adjacent Counties (by Number)
1. Ashtabula	2, 12, 16
2. Lake	1, 3, 12
3. Cuyahoga	2, 4, 9, 10, 12, 13
4. Lorain	3, 5, 7, 9
5. Huron	4, 6, 7
6. Richland	5, 7, 17
7. Ashland	4, 5, 6, 8, 9, 17, 18
8. Wayne	7, 9, 10, 11, 18
9. Medina	3, 4, 7, 8, 10
10. Summit	3, 8, 9, 11, 12, 13
11. Stark	8, 10, 13, 14, 15, 18, 19, 20
12. Geauga	1, 2, 3, 10, 13, 16
13. Portage	3, 10, 11, 12, 15, 16
14. Columbiana	11, 15, 20
15. Mahoning	11, 13, 14, 16
16. Trumbull	1, 12, 13, 15
17. Knox	6, 7, 18
18. Holmes	7, 8, 11, 17, 19
19. Tuscarawas	11, 18, 20
20. Carroll	11, 14, 19

The bank may locate branches in a county if the county contains a PPB or is adjacent to another county with a PPB. Thus, one constraint is needed for each county. For example, the constraint for Ashtabula County is

$$x_1 + x_2 + x_{12} + x_{16} \geq 1 \quad \text{Ashtabula}$$

Note that satisfaction of this constraint ensures that a PPB will be placed in Ashtabula County *or* in one or more of the adjacent counties. This constraint thus guarantees that Ohio Trust will be able to place branch banks in Ashtabula County.

The complete statement of the bank location problem is

$$\text{Min} \quad x_1 + x_2 + \quad \cdots \quad + x_{20}$$

s.t.

$$
\begin{aligned}
x_1 + x_2 \quad\quad + x_{12} + x_{16} \quad\quad &\geq 1 \quad \text{Ashtabula} \\
x_1 + x_2 + x_3 + x_{12} \quad\quad\quad &\geq 1 \quad \text{Lake} \\
\vdots \quad\quad\quad\quad\quad &\quad\quad \vdots \\
x_{11} + x_{14} + x_{19} + x_{20} &\geq 1 \quad \text{Carroll} \\
x_i = 0, 1 \quad i = 1, 2, \ldots, 20
\end{aligned}
$$

We used The Management Scientist to solve this 20-variable, 20-constraint problem formulation. In Figure 11.10 we show a portion of the computer output. Note that the variable names correspond to the first four letters in the name of each county. Using the output, we see that the optimal solution calls for principal places of business in Ashland, Stark, and Geauga

FIGURE 11.10 THE MANAGEMENT SCIENTIST SOLUTION FOR THE OHIO TRUST PPB LOCATION PROBLEM

```
OPTIMAL SOLUTION

Objective Function Value = 3.000

        Variable              Value
        --------              -----
          ASHT                0.000
          LAKE                0.000
          CUYA                0.000
          LORA                0.000
          HURO                0.000
          RICH                0.000
          ASHL                1.000
          WAYN                0.000
          MEDI                0.000
          SUMM                0.000
          STAR                1.000
          GEAU                1.000
          PORT                0.000
          COLU                0.000
          MAHO                0.000
          TRUM                0.000
          KNOX                0.000
          HOLM                0.000
          TUSC                0.000
          CARR                0.000
```

counties. With PPBs in these three counties, Ohio Trust can place branch banks in all 20 counties (see Figure 11.11). All other decision variables have an optimal value of zero, indicating that a PPB should not be placed in these counties. Clearly the integer programming model could be enlarged to allow for expansion into a larger area or throughout the entire state.

FIGURE 11.11   PRINCIPAL PLACE OF BUSINESS COUNTIES FOR OHIO TRUST

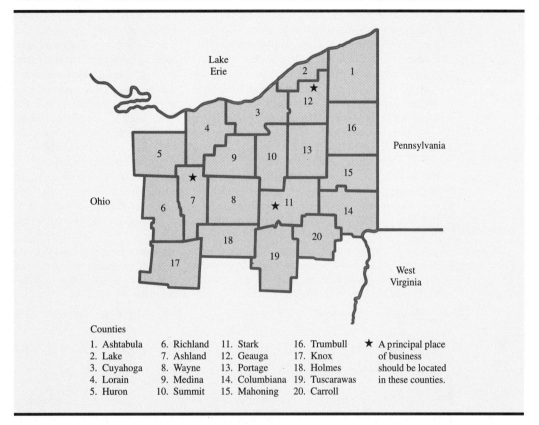

Counties

1. Ashtabula	6. Richland	11. Stark	16. Trumbull	★ A principal place
2. Lake	7. Ashland	12. Geauga	17. Knox	of business
3. Cuyahoga	8. Wayne	13. Portage	18. Holmes	should be located
4. Lorain	9. Medina	14. Columbiana	19. Tuscarawas	in these counties.
5. Huron	10. Summit	15. Mahoning	20. Carroll	

NOTES AND COMMENTS

1. Most practical applications of integer linear programming involve only 0–1 integer variables. Indeed, some mixed-integer computer codes are designed to handle only integer variables with binary values. However, if a clever mathematical trick is employed, these codes can still be used for problems involving general integer variables. The trick is called *binary expansion* and requires that an upper bound be established for each integer variable. More advanced texts on integer programming show how this can be done.

2. The Q. M. in Action: Analyzing Price Quotations Under Business Volume Discounts describes how 0–1 variables can be used in a model designed to take advantage of business volume discounts. Bellcore clients have saved millions of dollars by using a mixed-integer programming model.

3. General-purpose mixed-integer linear programming codes and some spreadsheet packages can be used for linear programming problems, all-integer problems, and problems involving some continuous and some integer variables. General-purpose codes are seldom the fastest for solving problems with special structure (such as the transportation, assignment, and transshipment problems); however, unless the problems are very large, speed is usually not a critical issue. Thus, most practitioners prefer to use one general-purpose computer package that can be used on a variety of problems rather than to maintain a variety of computer programs designed for special problems.

ANALYZING PRICE QUOTATIONS UNDER BUSINE*SS* VOLUME DISCOUNTS*

Bellcore was formed in 1984 to provide various support services for the regional Bell operating telephone companies. To reduce the cost of buying goods and services, Bellcore client companies are increasingly requesting business volume discounts from suppliers in place of traditional quantity discounts. With traditional quantity discounts, the price of each item purchased is discounted on the basis of the amount of the item purchased. Business volume discounts differ from single-item quantity discounts in that the supplier discounts the price of each item by a percentage that is based on the total dollar volume of business over all items awarded to the supplier; whatever this percentage, it remains the same for each item. In general, a firm can realize lower overall purchasing costs with business volume discounts and a supplier can increase total revenues by obtaining a large volume of that firm's business. However, business volume discounts greatly increase the complexity of the procurement process because the discount obtained depends on the purchase quantities and prices of all products purchased.

To assist Bellcore client companies in using business volume discounts, Bellcore developed the procurement decision support system (PDSS), a PC-based decision support program that uses a mixed-integer programming model to minimize the total cost of purchases. The model uses 0–1 integer variables to model the discount categories applicable to the problem and includes a variety of constraints involving factors such as supplier capacity and limits on the dollar amount awarded to a supplier. Since 1990, one Bellcore client company has reported two savings, one of $4.5 million and another of $15 million; these figures represent approximately 10% on the cost of purchases. Another client company has realized a reduction of approximately 80% in the cost of analyzing quotations, and users generally believe that PDSS is a useful tool in identifying opportunities in negotiations with suppliers.

*Based on P. Katz, A. Sadrian, and P. Tendick, "Telephone Companies Analyze Price Quotations with Bellcore's PDSS Software," *Interfaces* (January–February 1994): 50–63.

11.4   MODELING FLEXIBILITY PROVIDED BY 0–1 INTEGER VARIABLES

In Section 11.3 we presented four applications involving 0–1 integer variables. In this section we continue the discussion of the use of 0–1 integer variables in modeling. First, we show how 0–1 integer variables can be used to model multiple-choice and mutually exclusive constraints. Then, we show how 0–1 integer variables can be used to model situations in which k projects out of a set of n projects must be selected, as well as situations in which the acceptance of one project is conditional on the acceptance of another. We close the section with a cautionary note on the role of sensitivity analysis in integer linear programming.

Multiple-Choice and Mutually Exclusive Constraints

Recall the Ice-Cold Refrigerator capital budgeting problem introduced in Section 11.3. The decision variables were defined as

$P = 1$ if the plant expansion project is accepted; 0 if rejected

$W = 1$ if the warehouse expansion project is accepted; 0 if rejected

$M = 1$ if the new machinery project is accepted; 0 if rejected

$R = 1$ if the new product research project is accepted; 0 if rejected

Suppose that, instead of one warehouse expansion project, the Ice-Cold Refrigerator Company actually has three warehouse expansion projects under consideration. One of the warehouses *must* be expanded because of increasing product demand, but new demand isn't sufficient to make expansion of more than one warehouse necessary. The following variable definitions and **multiple-choice constraint** could be incorporated into the previous 0–1 integer linear programming model to reflect this situation. Let

$W_1 = 1$ if the original warehouse expansion project is accepted; 0 if rejected

$W_2 = 1$ if the second warehouse expansion project is accepted; 0 if rejected

$W_3 = 1$ if the third warehouse expansion project is accepted; 0 if rejected

The multiple-choice constraint reflecting the requirement that exactly one of these projects must be selected is

$$W_1 + W_2 + W_3 = 1$$

Because W_1, W_2, and W_3 are allowed to assume only the values 0 or 1, one and only one of these projects must be selected from among the three choices.

If the requirement that one warehouse must be expanded did not exist, the multiple-choice constraint could be modified as follows:

$$W_1 + W_2 + W_3 \leq 1$$

This modification allows for the case of no warehouse expansion ($W_1 = W_2 = W_3 = 0$) but does not permit more than one warehouse to be expanded. This type of constraint is often called a **mutually exclusive constraint.**

k out of n Alternatives Constraint

An extension of the notion of a multiple-choice constraint can be used to model situations in which k out of a set of n projects must be selected—a **k out of n alternatives constraint.** Suppose that W_1, W_2, W_3, W_4, and W_5 represent five potential warehouse expansion projects and that two of the five projects must be accepted. The constraint that satisfies this new requirement is

$$W_1 + W_2 + W_3 + W_4 + W_5 = 2$$

If no more than two of the projects are to be selected, we would use the following less-than-or-equal-to constraint:

$$W_1 + W_2 + W_3 + W_4 + W_5 \leq 2$$

Again, each of these variables must be restricted to 0–1 values.

Conditional and Corequisite Constraints

Sometimes the acceptance of one project is conditional on the acceptance of another. For example, suppose for the Ice-Cold Refrigerator Company that the warehouse expansion project was conditional on the plant expansion project. That is, management will not consider expanding the warehouse unless the plant is expanded. With P representing plant expansion and W representing warehouse expansion, a **conditional constraint** could be introduced to enforce this requirement:

$$W \leq P$$

As both P and W must be 0 or 1, whenever P is 0, W will be forced to 0. When P is 1, W is also allowed to be 1; thus, both the plant and the warehouse can be expanded. However, we note that the preceding constraint does not force the warehouse expansion project (W) to be accepted if the plant expansion project (P) is accepted.

If the warehouse expansion project had to be accepted whenever the plant expansion project was, and vice versa, we would say that P and W represented **corequisite constraint** projects. To model such a situation, we simply write the preceding constraint as an equality:

$$W = P$$

Try Problem 7 for practice with the modeling flexibility provided by 0–1 variables.

The constraint forces P and W to take on the same value.

A Cautionary Note about Sensitivity Analysis

Sensitivity analysis often is more crucial for integer linear programming problems than for linear programming problems. A small change in one of the coefficients in the constraints can cause a relatively large change in the value of the optimal solution. To understand why, consider the following integer programming model of a simple capital budgeting problem involving four projects and a budgetary constraint for a single time period:

$$\text{Max} \quad 40x_1 + 60x_2 + 70x_3 + 160x_4$$
$$\text{s.t.}$$
$$16x_1 + 35x_2 + 45x_3 + 85x_4 \leq 100$$
$$x_1, x_2, x_3, x_4 = 0, 1$$

Dual prices cannot be used for integer programming sensitivity analysis because they are designed for linear programs. Multiple computer runs usually are necessary for sensitivity analysis of integer linear programs.

We obtain the optimal solution to this problem by enumerating the alternatives. It is $x_1 = 1$, $x_2 = 1$, $x_3 = 1$, and $x_4 = 0$, with an objective function value of $170. However, note that if the budget available is increased by $1 (from $100 to $101), the optimal solution changes to $x_1 = 1$, $x_2 = 0$, $x_3 = 0$, and $x_4 = 1$, with an objective function value of $200. That is, one additional dollar in the budget would lead to a $30 increase in the return. Surely management, when faced with such a situation, would increase the budget by $1. Because of the extreme sensitivity of the value of the optimal solution to the constraint coefficients, practitioners usually recommend resolving the integer linear program several times with slight variations in the coefficients before attempting to choose the best solution for implementation.

SUMMARY

In this chapter, we introduced the important extension of linear programming referred to as *integer linear programming*. The only difference between the integer linear programming problems discussed in this chapter and the linear programming problems studied in previous chapters is that one or more of the variables must be integer. If all variables must be integer, we have an all-integer linear program. If some, but not all, variables must be integer, we have a mixed-integer linear program. If all variables are 0–1 or binary variables, we have a 0–1 integer linear program.

Studying integer linear programming is important for two major reasons. First, integer linear programming may be helpful when fractional values for the variables are not permitted. Because rounding a linear programming solution may not provide an optimal integer solution, methods for finding optimal integer solutions are needed when the economic consequences of rounding are significant. A second reason for studying integer linear programming is the increased modeling flexibility provided through the use of 0–1 variables.

We showed how 0–1 variables could be used to model important managerial considerations in capital budgeting, fixed cost, distribution system design, and bank location applications.

The number of applications of integer linear programming has been growing in recent years. This growth is due in part to the availability of commercial integer linear programming software packages. As researchers develop solution procedures capable of solving larger integer linear programs and as computer speed increases, a continuation of this growth of integer programming applications is expected.

GLOSSARY

Integer linear program   A linear program with the additional requirement that at least one of the variables must be integer.

All-integer linear program   An integer linear program in which all variables are required to be integer.

LP Relaxation   The linear program that results from dropping the integer requirements for the variables in an integer linear program.

Mixed-integer linear program   An integer linear program in which some, but not all, variables are required to be integer.

0–1 integer linear program   An all-integer or mixed-integer linear program in which the integer variables are only permitted to assume the values 0 or 1. Also called *binary integer program*.

Multiple-choice constraint   A constraint requiring that the sum of two or more 0–1 variables equal 1. Thus, any feasible solution makes a choice of which variable to set equal to 1.

Mutually exclusive constraint   A constraint requiring that the sum of two or more 0–1 variables be less than or equal to 1. Thus, if one of the variables equals 1, the others must equal 0. However, all variables could equal 0.

k out of n alternatives constraint   An extension of the multiple-choice constraint. This constraint requires that the sum of n 0–1 variables equal k.

Conditional constraint   A constraint involving 0–1 variables that does not allow certain variables to equal 1 unless certain other variables are equal to 1.

Corequisite constraint   A constraint requiring that two 0–1 variables be equal. Thus, they are both in or out of solution together.

PROBLEMS

1. Indicate which of the following is an all-integer linear program and which is a mixed-integer linear program. Write the LP Relaxation for the problem but do not attempt to solve.

   a. Max $30x_1 + 25x_2$

   s.t.

   $$3x_1 + 1.5x_2 \leq 400$$
   $$1.5x_1 + 2x_2 \leq 250$$
   $$1x_1 + 1x_2 \leq 150$$
   $$x_1, x_2 \geq 0 \text{ and } x_2 \text{ integer}$$

   b. Min $3x_1 + 4x_2$

   s.t.

   $$2x_1 + 4x_2 \geq 8$$
   $$2x_1 + 6x_2 \geq 12$$
   $$x_1, x_2 \geq 0 \text{ and integer}$$

SELFtest **2.** Consider the following all-integer linear program.

$$\text{Max} \quad 5x_1 + 8x_2$$

s.t.

$$6x_1 + 5x_2 \leq 30$$
$$9x_1 + 4x_2 \leq 36$$
$$1x_1 + 2x_2 \leq 10$$
$$x_1, x_2 \geq 0 \text{ and integer}$$

     a. Graph the constraints for this problem. Use dots to indicate all feasible integer solutions.
     b. Find the optimal solution to the LP Relaxation. Round down to find a feasible integer solution.
     c. Find the optimal integer solution. Is it the same as the solution obtained in part (b) by rounding down?

3. Consider the following all-integer linear program.

$$\text{Max} \quad 1x_1 + 1x_2$$

s.t.

$$4x_1 + 6x_2 \leq 22$$
$$1x_1 + 5x_2 \leq 15$$
$$2x_1 + 1x_2 \leq 9$$
$$x_1, x_2 \geq 0 \text{ and integer}$$

     a. Graph the constraints for this problem. Use dots to indicate all feasible integer solutions.
     b. Solve the LP Relaxation of this problem.
     c. Find the optimal integer solution.

4. Consider the following all-integer linear program.

$$\text{Max} \quad 10x_1 + 3x_2$$

s.t.

$$6x_1 + 7x_2 \leq 40$$
$$3x_1 + 1x_2 \leq 11$$
$$x_1, x_2 \geq 0 \text{ and integer}$$

     a. Formulate and solve the LP Relaxation of the problem. Solve it graphically, and round down to find a feasible solution. Specify an upper bound on the value of the optimal solution.
     b. Solve the integer linear program graphically. Compare the value of this solution with the solution obtained in part (a).
     c. Suppose the objective function changes to Max $3x_1 + 6x_2$. Repeat parts (a) and (b).

SELFtest **5.** Consider the following mixed-integer linear program.

$$\text{Max} \quad 2x_1 + 3x_2$$

s.t.

$$4x_1 + 9x_2 \leq 36$$
$$7x_1 + 5x_2 \leq 35$$
$$x_1, x_2 \geq 0 \text{ and } x_1 \text{ integer}$$

a. Graph the constraints for this problem. Indicate on your graph all feasible mixed-integer solutions.
b. Find the optimal solution to the LP Relaxation. Round the value of x_1 down to find a feasible mixed-integer solution. Is this solution optimal? Why or why not?
c. Find the optimal solution for the mixed-integer linear program.

6. Consider the following mixed-integer linear program.

$$\text{Max}\quad 1x_1 + 1x_2$$

s.t.

$$7x_1 + 9x_2 \le 63$$
$$9x_1 + 5x_2 \le 45$$
$$3x_1 + 1x_2 \le 12$$
$$x_1, x_2 \ge 0 \text{ and } x_2 \text{ integer}$$

a. Graph the constraints for this problem. Indicate on your graph all feasible mixed-integer solutions.
b. Find the optimal solution to the LP Relaxation. Round the value of x_2 down to find a feasible mixed-integer solution. Specify upper and lower bounds on the value of the optimal solution to the mixed-integer linear program.
c. Find the optimal solution to the mixed-integer linear program.

SELFtest
7. The following questions refer to a capital budgeting problem with six projects represented by 0–1 variables $x_1, x_2, x_3, x_4, x_5,$ and x_6.
a. Write a constraint modeling a situation in which two of the projects 1, 3, 5, and 6 must be undertaken.
b. Write a constraint modeling a situation in which, if projects 3 and 5 must be undertaken, they must be undertaken simultaneously.
c. Write a constraint modeling a situation in which project 1 or 4 must be undertaken, but not both.
d. Write constraints modeling a situation where project 4 cannot be undertaken unless projects 1 and 3 also are undertaken.
e. Revise the requirement in part (d) to accommodate the case in which, when projects 1 and 3 are undertaken, project 4 also must be undertaken.

8. Spencer Enterprises is attempting to choose among a series of new investment alternatives. The potential investment alternatives, the net present value of the future stream of returns, the capital requirements, and the available capital funds over the next 3 years are summarized as follows:

Alternative	Net Present Value ($)	Capital Requirements ($)		
		Year 1	Year 2	Year 3
Limited warehouse expansion	4,000	3,000	1,000	4,000
Extensive warehouse expansion	6,000	2,500	3,500	3,500
Test market new product	10,500	6,000	4,000	5,000
Advertising campaign	4,000	2,000	1,500	1,800
Basic research	8,000	5,000	1,000	4,000
Purchase new equipment	3,000	1,000	500	900
Capital funds available		10,500	7,000	8,750

a. Develop and solve an integer linear programming model for maximizing the net present value.

b. Assume that only one of the warehouse expansion projects can be implemented. Modify your model of part (a).

c. Suppose that, if test marketing of the new product is carried out, the advertising campaign also must be conducted. Modify your formulation of part (b) to reflect this new situation.

9. Hawkins Manufacturing Company produces connecting rods for 4- and 6-cylinder automobile engines using the same production line. The cost required to set up the production line to produce the 4-cylinder connecting rods is $2000, and the cost required to set up the production line for the 6-cylinder connecting rods is $3500. Manufacturing costs are $15 for each 4-cylinder connecting rod and $18 for each 6-cylinder connecting rod. Hawkins makes a decision at the end of each week as to which product will be manufactured the following week. If a production changeover is needed from one week to the next, the weekend is used to reconfigure the production line. Once the line has been set up, the weekly production capacities are 6,000 6-cylinder connecting rods and 8000 4-cylinder connecting rods. Let

x_4 = the number of 4-cylinder connecting rods produced next week

x_6 = the number of 6-cylinder connecting rods produced next week

s_4 = 1 if the production line is set up to produce the 4-cylinder connecting rods; 0 otherwise

s_6 = 1 if the production line is set up to produce the 6-cylinder connecting rods; 0 otherwise

a. Using the decision variables x_4 and s_4, write a constraint that limits next week's production of the 4-cylinder connecting rods to either 0 or 8000 units.

b. Using the decision variables x_6 and s_6, write a constraint that limits next week's production of the 6-cylinder connecting rods to either 0 or 6000 units.

c. Write 3 constraints that, taken together, limit the production of connecting rods for next week.

d. Write an objective function for minimizing the cost of production for next week.

10. Grave City is considering the relocation of several police substations to obtain better enforcement in high-crime areas. The locations under consideration together with the areas that can be covered from these locations are given in the following table.

Potential Locations for Substations	Areas Covered
A	1, 5, 7
B	1, 2, 5, 7
C	1, 3, 5
D	2, 4, 5
E	3, 4, 6
F	4, 5, 6
G	1, 5, 6, 7

a. Formulate an integer linear programming model that could be used to find the minimum number of locations necessary to provide coverage to all areas.

b. Solve the problem in part (a).

11. Hart Manufacturing makes three products. Each product requires manufacturing operations in three departments: A, B, and C. The labor-hour requirements, by department, are

Department	Product 1	Product 2	Product 3
A	1.50	3.00	2.00
B	2.00	1.00	2.50
C	0.25	0.25	0.25

During the next production period, the labor-hours available are 450 in department A, 350 in department B, and 50 in department C. The profit contributions per unit are $25 for product 1, $28 for product 2, and $30 for product 3.

a. Formulate a linear programming model for maximizing total profit contribution.

b. Solve the linear program formulated in part (a). How much of each product should be produced and what is the projected total profit contribution?

c. After evaluating the solution obtained in part (b), one of the production supervisors noted that production setup costs had not been taken into account. She noted that setup costs are $400 for product 1, $550 for product 2, and $600 for product 3. If the solution developed in part (b) is to be used, what is the total profit contribution after taking into account the setup costs?

d. Management realized that the optimal product mix, taking setup costs into account, might be different from the one recommended in part (b). Formulate a mixed-integer linear program that takes setup costs into account. Management has also stated that we should not consider making more than 175 units of product 1, 150 units of product 2, or 140 units of product 3.

e. Solve the mixed-integer linear program formulated in part (d). How much of each product should be produced and what is the projected total profit contribution? Compare this profit contribution to that obtained in part (c).

12. Yates Company supplies road salt to county highway departments. The company has three trucks, and the dispatcher is trying to schedule tomorrow's deliveries to Polk, Dallas, and Jasper counties. Two trucks have 15-ton capacities, and the third truck has a 30-ton capacity. Based on these truck capacities, two counties will receive 15 tons and the third will receive 30 tons of road salt. The dispatcher wants to determine how much to ship to each county. Let

$$x_1 = \text{amount shipped to Polk County}$$
$$x_2 = \text{amount shipped to Dallas County}$$
$$x_3 = \text{amount shipped to Jasper County}$$

and

$$y_i = \begin{cases} 1 \text{ if the 30-ton truck is assigned to county } i \\ 0 \text{ otherwise} \end{cases}$$

a. Use these variable definitions and write constraints that appropriately restrict the amount shipped to each county.

b. The cost of assigning the 30-ton truck to the three counties is $100 to Polk, $85 to Dallas, and $50 to Jasper. Formulate and solve a mixed-integer linear program to determine how much to ship to each county.

SELFtest   13. Recall the Martin-Beck Company distribution system problem in Section 11.3.

a. Modify the formulation shown in Section 11.3 to account for the policy restriction that one plant, but not two, must be located either in Detroit or in Toledo.

b. Modify the formulation shown in Section 11.3 to account for the policy restriction that no more than two plants can be located in Denver, Kansas City, and St. Louis.

14. An automobile manufacturer has five outdated plants: one each in Michigan, Ohio, and California, and two in New York. Management is considering modernizing these plants to manufacture engine blocks and transmissions for a new model car. The cost to modernize each plant and the manufacturing capacity after modernization are as follows:

Plant	Cost ($ millions)	Engine Blocks (000s)	Transmissions (000s)
Michigan	25	500	300
New York	35	800	400
New York	35	400	800
Ohio	40	900	600
California	20	200	300

The projected needs are for total capacities of 900,000 engine blocks and 900,000 transmissions. Management wants to determine which plants to modernize to meet projected manufacturing needs and, at the same time, minimize the total cost of modernization.

a. Develop a table that lists every possible option available to management. As part of your table, indicate the total engine block capacity and transmission capacity for each possible option, whether the option is feasible based on the projected needs, and the total modernization cost for each option.

b. Based on your analysis in part (a), what recommendation would you provide management?

c. Formulate a 0–1 integer programming model that could be used to determine the optimal solution to the modernization question facing management.

d. Solve the model formulated in part (c) to provide a recommendation for management.

15. CHB, Inc., is a bank holding company that is evaluating the potential for expanding into a 13-county region in the southwestern part of the state. State law permits establishing branches in any county that is adjacent to a county in which a PPB (principal place of business) is located. The following map shows the 13-county region with the population of each county indicated.

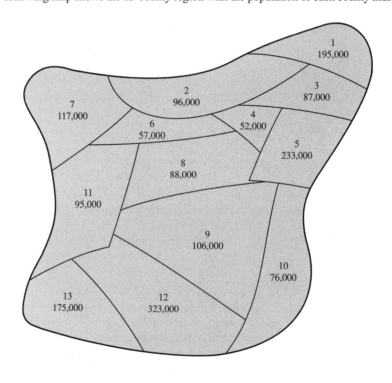

a. Assume that only one PPB can be established in the region. Where should it be located to maximize the population served? (Hint: Review the Ohio Trust formulation in Section 11.3. Consider minimizing the population not served, and introduce variable $y_i = 1$ if it is not possible to establish a branch in county i, and $y_i = 0$ otherwise).

b. Suppose that two PPBs can be established in the region. Where should they be located to maximize the population served?

c. Management has learned that a bank located in county 5 is considering selling. If CHB purchases this bank, the requisite PPB will be established in county 5, and a base for beginning expansion in the region will also be established. What advice would you give the management of CHB?

16. The Northshore Bank is working to develop an efficient work schedule for full-time and part-time tellers. The schedule must provide for efficient operation of the bank including adequate customer service, employee breaks, and so on. On Fridays the bank is open from 9:00 A.M. to 7:00 P.M. The number of tellers necessary to provide adequate customer service during each hour of operation is summarized here.

Time	Number of Tellers	Time	Number of Tellers
9:00 A.M.–10:00 A.M.	6	2:00 P.M.–3:00 P.M.	6
10:00 A.M.–11:00 A.M.	4	3:00 P.M.–4:00 P.M.	4
11:00 A.M.–Noon	8	4:00 P.M.–5:00 P.M.	7
Noon–1:00 P.M.	10	5:00 P.M.–6:00 P.M.	6
1:00 P.M.–2:00 P.M.	9	6:00 P.M.–7:00 P.M.	6

Each full-time employee starts on the hour and works a four-hour shift, followed by one hour for lunch and then a three-hour shift. Part-time employees work one four-hour shift beginning on the hour. Considering salary and fringe benefits, full-time employees cost the bank $15 per hour ($105 a day), and part-time employees cost the bank $8 per hour ($32 per day).

a. Formulate an integer linear programming model that can be used to develop a schedule that will satisfy customer service needs at a minimum employee cost. (Hint: Let x_i = number of full-time employees coming on duty at the beginning of hour i and y_i = number of part-time employees coming on duty at the beginning of hour i.)

b. Solve the LP Relaxation of your model in part (a).

c. Solve for the optimal schedule of tellers. Comment on the solution.

d. After reviewing the solution to part (c), the bank manager has realized that some additional requirements must be specified. Specifically, she wants to ensure that one full-time employee is on duty at all times from a staff of at least five full-time employees. Revise your model to incorporate these additional requirements and solve for the optimal solution.

17. Refer to the Ohio Trust bank location problem introduced in Section 11.3. Table 11.3 shows the counties under consideration and the adjacent counties.

a. Write the complete integer programming model for expansion into the following counties only: Loraine, Huron, Richland, Ashland, Wayne, Medina, and Knox.

b. Use trial and error to solve the problem in part (a).

c. Solve the problem with a computer code.

18. Refer to Problem 14. Suppose that management determined that its cost estimates to modernize the New York plants were too low. Specifically, suppose that the actual cost is $40 million to modernize each plant.

a. What changes in your previous 0–1 integer linear programming model are needed to incorporate these changes in costs?

    b. For these cost changes, what recommendations would you now provide management regarding the modernization plan?

    c. Reconsider the solution obtained using the revised cost figures. Suppose that management decides that closing two plants in the same state is not acceptable. How could this policy restriction be added to your 0–1 integer programming model?

    d. Based on the cost revision and the policy restriction presented in part (c), what recommendations would you now provide management regarding the modernization plan?

19. The Bayside Art Gallery is considering installing a video camera security system to reduce its insurance premiums. A diagram of the eight display rooms that Bayside uses for exhibitions is shown in Figure 11.12; the openings between the rooms are numbered 1–13. A security firm has proposed that two-way cameras be installed at some room openings. Each camera has the ability to monitor the two rooms between which the camera is located. For example, if a camera were located at opening number 4, rooms 1 and 4 would be covered; if a camera were located at opening 11, rooms 7 and 8 would be covered; and so on. Management has decided not to locate a camera system at the entrance to the display rooms. The objective is to provide security coverage for all eight rooms using the minimum number of two-way cameras.

    a. Formulate a 0–1 integer linear programming model that will enable Bayside's management to determine the locations for the camera systems.

    b. Solve the model formulated in part (a) to determine how many two-way cameras to purchase and where they should be located.

    c. Suppose that management wants to provide additional security coverage for room 7. Specifically, management wants room 7 to be covered by two cameras. How would your model formulated in part (a) have to change to accommodate this policy restriction?

    d. With the policy restriction specified in part (c), determine how many two-way camera systems will need to be purchased and where they will be located.

20. The Delta Group is a management consulting firm specializing in the health care industry. A team is being formed to study possible new markets, and a linear programming model has been developed for selecting team members. However, one constraint the president has imposed is a team size of three, five, or seven members. The staff can't figure out how to incorporate this requirement in the model. The current model requires that team members be selected from three departments and uses the following variable definitions.

$$x_1 = \text{the number of employees selected from department 1}$$

$$x_2 = \text{the number of employees selected from department 2}$$

$$x_3 = \text{the number of employees selected from department 3}$$

Show the staff how to write constraints that will ensure that the team will consist of three, five, or seven employees. The following integer variables should be helpful.

$$y_1 = \begin{cases} 1 & \text{if team size is 3} \\ 0 & \text{otherwise} \end{cases}$$

$$y_2 = \begin{cases} 1 & \text{if team size is 5} \\ 0 & \text{otherwise} \end{cases}$$

$$y_3 = \begin{cases} 1 & \text{if team size is 7} \\ 0 & \text{otherwise} \end{cases}$$

FIGURE 11.12   DIAGRAM OF DISPLAY ROOMS FOR BAYSIDE ART GALLERY

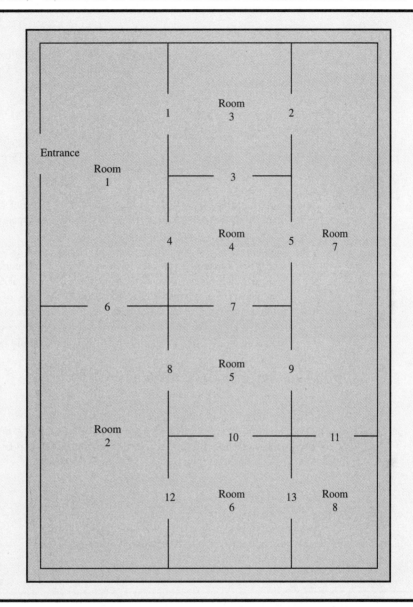

21. Roedel Electronics produces a variety of electrical components, including a remote controller for televisions and a remote controller for VCRs. Each controller consists of three subassemblies that are manufactured by Roedel: a base; a cartridge, and a keypad. Both controllers use the same base subassembly, but different cartridge and keypad subassemblies.

   Roedel's sales forecast indicates that 7000 TV controllers and 5000 VCR controllers will be needed to satisfy demand during the upcoming Christmas season. Because only 500 hours of in-house manufacturing time are available, Roedel is considering purchasing some, or all, of the subassemblies from outside suppliers. If Roedel manufactures a subassembly in-house, it incurs a fixed setup cost as well as a variable manufacturing cost. The following table shows the setup cost, the manufacturing time per subassembly, the

QUANTITATIVE METHODS FOR BUSINESS

manufacturing cost per subassembly, and the cost to purchase each of the subassemblies from an outside supplier.

Subassembly	Setup Cost ($)	Manufacturing Time per Unit (min.)	Manufacturing Cost per Unit ($)	Purchase Cost per Unit ($)
Base	1000	0.9	0.40	0.65
TV cartridge	1200	2.2	2.90	3.45
VCR cartridge	1900	3.0	3.15	3.70
TV keypad	1500	0.8	0.30	0.50
VCR keypad	1500	1.0	0.55	0.70

a. Determine how many units of each subassembly Roedel should manufacture and how many units Roedel should purchase. What is the total manufacturing and purchase cost associated with your recommendation?

b. Suppose Roedel is considering purchasing new machinery to produce VCR cartridges. For the new machinery, the setup cost is $3000; the manufacturing time is 2.5 minutes per cartridge, and the manufacturing cost is $2.60 per cartridge. Assuming that the new machinery is purchased, determine how many units of each subassembly Roedel should manufacture and how many units of each subassembly Roedel should purchase. What is the total manufacturing and purchase cost associated with your recommendation? Do you think the new machinery should be purchased? Explain.

Case Problem   TEXTBOOK PUBLISHING

ASW Publishing, Inc., a small publisher of college textbooks, must make a decision regarding which books to publish next year. The books under consideration are listed in the following table, along with the projected three-year sales expected from each book.

Book Subject	Type of Book	Projected Sales (000s)
Business calculus	New	20
Finite mathematics	Revision	30
General statistics	New	15
Mathematical statistics	New	10
Business statistics	Revision	25
Finance	New	18
Financial accounting	New	25
Managerial accounting	Revision	50
English literature	New	20
German	New	30

The books that are listed as revisions are texts that ASW already has under contract; these texts are being considered for publication as new editions. The books that are listed as new have been reviewed by the company, but contracts have not yet been signed.

The company has three individuals who can be assigned to these projects, all of whom have varying amounts of time available; John has 60 days available, and Susan and Monica both have 40 days available. The days required by each person to complete each project are shown in the following table. For instance, if the business calculus book is published, it will require 30 days of John's time and 40 days of Susan's time. An "X" indicates that the person will not be used on the project. Note that at least two staff members will be assigned to each project except the finance book.

Book Subject	John	Susan	Monica
Business calculus	30	40	X
Finite mathematics	16	24	X
General statistics	24	X	30
Mathematical statistics	20	X	24
Business statistics	10	X	16
Finance	X	X	14
Financial accounting	X	24	26
Managerial accounting	X	28	30
English literature	40	34	30
German	X	50	36

ASW will not publish more than two statistics books or more than one accounting text in a single year. In addition, management has decided that one of the mathematics books (business calculus or finite math) must be published, but not both.

Managerial Report

Prepare a report for the editorial director of ASW that describes your findings and recommendations regarding the best publication strategy for next year. In carrying out your analysis, assume that the fixed costs and the sales revenues per unit are approximately equal for all books; management is interested primarily in maximizing the total unit sales volume.

The editorial director has also asked that you include recommendations regarding the following possible changes.

1. If it would be advantageous to do so, Susan can be moved off another project to allow her to work 12 more days.
2. If it would be advantageous to do so, Monica can also be made available for another 10 days.
3. If one or more of the revisions could be postponed for another year, should they be? Clearly the company will risk losing market share by postponing a revision.

Include details of your analysis in an appendix to your report.

Case Problem   YEAGER NATIONAL BANK

Using aggressive mail promotion and low introductory interest rates, Yeager National Bank (YNB) has built a large base of credit card customers throughout the continental United States. Currently, all customers send their regular payments to the bank's corporate office located in Charlotte, North Carolina. Daily collections from customers making their regular payments are substantial, with an average of approximately $600,000. YNB estimates that it makes about 15% on its funds, and would like to ensure that customer payments are credited to the bank's account as soon as possible. For instance, if it takes 5 days for a customer's payment to be sent through the mail, processed, and credited to the bank's account, YNB has potentially lost 5 days worth of interest income. Although the time needed for this collection process cannot be completely eliminated, reducing it can be beneficial given the large amounts of money involved.

Instead of having all its credit card customers send their payments to Charlotte, YNB is considering having customers send their payments to one or more regional collection centers, referred to in the banking industry as lockboxes. Four lockbox locations have been proposed: Phoenix, Salt Lake City, Atlanta, and Boston. To determine which lockboxes to open and where lockbox customers should send their payments, YNB has divided its customer base into 5 geographical regions: Northwest, Southwest, Central, Northeast, and Southeast. Every customer in the same region will be instructed to send his or her payment to the same lockbox. The following table shows the average number of days it takes before a customer's payment is credited to the bank's account when the payment is sent from each of the regions to each of the potential lockboxes.

Customer	Location of Lockbox				Daily Collection
Zone	Phoenix	Salt Lake City	Atlanta	Boston	($000s)
Northwest	4	2	4	4	80
Southwest	2	3	4	6	90
Central	5	3	3	4	150
Northeast	5	4	3	2	180
Southeast	4	6	2	3	100

Managerial Report

Dave Wolff, the vice-president for cash management, has asked you to prepare a report containing your recommendations for the number of lockboxes and the best lockbox locations. Mr. Wolff is primarily concerned with minimizing lost interest income, but he wants you to also consider the effect of an annual fee charged for maintaining a lockbox at any location. Although the amount of the fee is unknown at this time, we can assume that the fees will be in the range of $20,000 to $30,000 per location. Once good potential locations have been selected, Mr. Wolff will seek more information on the annual fees.

Case Problem **PRODUCTION SCHEDULING WITH CHANGEOVER COSTS**

Buckeye Manufacturing produces heads for engines used in the manufacture of trucks. The production line is highly complex, and it measures 900 feet in length. Two types of engine heads are produced on this line: the P-Head and the H-Head. The P-Head is used in heavy-duty trucks and the H-Head is used in smaller trucks. Because only one type of head can be produced at a time, the line is either set up to manufacture the P-Head or the H-Head, but not both. Changeovers are made over a weekend; costs are $500 in going from a setup for the P-Head to a setup for the H-Head, and vice versa. When set up for the P-Head, the maximum production rate is 100 units per week and when set up for the H-Head, the maximum production rate is 80 units per week.

Buckeye has just shut down for the week; the line has been producing the P-Head. The manager wants to plan production and changeovers for the next eight weeks. Currently, Buckeye has an inventory of 125 P-Heads and 143 H-Heads. Inventory carrying costs are charged at an annual rate of 19.5% of the value of inventory. The production cost for the P-Head is $225, and the production cost for the H-Head is $310. The objective in developing a production schedule is to minimize the sum of production cost, plus inventory carrying cost, plus changeover cost.

Buckeye has received the following requirements schedule from its customer (an engine assembly plant) for the next nine weeks.

	Product Demand	
Week	P-Head	H-Head
1	55	38
2	55	38
3	44	30
4	0	0
5	45	48
6	45	48
7	36	58
8	35	57
9	35	58

Safety stock requirements are such that week-ending inventory must provide for at least 80% of the next week's demand.

Managerial Report

Prepare a report for Buckeye's management with a production and changeover schedule for the next eight weeks. Be sure to note how much of the total cost is due to production, how much is due to inventory, and how much is due to changeover.

Appendix 11.1   SPREADSHEET SOLUTION OF INTEGER LINEAR PROGRAMS

Spreadsheet formulation and solution for integer linear programs is similar to that for linear programming problems. Let us demonstrate the spreadsheet solution of an integer linear program by showing how Excel can be used to solve the Eastborne Realty problem. The spreadsheet with the optimal solution is shown in Figure 11.13. We will describe the key elements of the spreadsheet, and then describe how to obtain the optimal solution.

Spreadsheet Formulation

The data and descriptive labels appear in cells A1:G7 of the spreadsheet in Figure 11.13. The screened cells in the lower portion of the spreadsheet contain the information required by the Excel Solver (decision variables, objective function, constraint left-hand sides, and constraint right-hand sides).

Decision Variables   Cells B17:C17 are reserved for the decision variables. The optimal solution is to purchase 4 townhouses and 2 apartment buildings.

Objective Function   The formula =SUMPRODUCT(B7:C7,B17:C17) has been placed into cell B13 to reflect the annual cash flow associated with the solution. The optimal solution provides an annual cash flow of $70,000.

Left-Hand Sides   The left-hand sides for the 3 constraints are placed into cells F15:F17.
      Cell F15   =SUMPRODUCT (B4:C4, $B$17:$C$17)
               (Copy to sell F16)
      Cell F17   =B17

Right-Hand Sides   The right-hand sides for the 3 constraints are placed into cells H15:H17.
      Cell H15   =G4 (Copy to cells H16:H17)

FIGURE 11.13 SPREADSHEET SOLUTION FOR THE EASTBORNE REALTY PROBLEM

	A	B	C	D	E	F	G	H
1	**Eastborne Realty Problem**							
2								
3		**Townhouse**	**Apt. Bldg.**					
4	**Price($000s)**	282	400		**Funds Avl.($000s)**		2000	
5	**Mgr. Time**	4	40		**Mgr. Time Avl.**		140	
6					**Townhouses Avl.**		5	
7	**Ann. Cash Flow ($1000s)**	10	15					
8								
9								
10	**Model**							
11								
12								
13	**Max Cash Flow**	70						
14					**Constraints**	**LHS**		**RHS**
15		**Number of**			Funds	1928	<=	2000
16		**Townhouses**	**Apt. Bldgs.**		Time	96	<=	140
17	**Purchase Plan**	4	2		Twnhses	4	<=	5

Spreadsheet Solution

We are now ready to use Excel's solver to find the optimal solution. The following steps are necessary.

Step 1. Select the **Tools** pull-down menu

Step 2. Select the **Solver** option

Step 3. When the **Solver Parameters** dialog box appears:
Enter B13 in the **Set Target Cell** box
Select the **Equal to: Max** option
Enter B17:C17 in the **By Changing Cells** box
Choose **Add**

Step 4. When the **Add Constraint** dialog box appears:
Enter F15:F17 in the **Cell Reference** box
Select **<=**
Enter H15:H17 in the **Constraint** box
Choose **Add**
Enter B17:C17 in the **Cell Reference** box
Select **int**
Select **OK**

Step 5. When the **Solver Parameters** dialog box appears:
Choose **Options**

Step 6. When the **Solver Options** dialog box appears:
Set **Tolerance** at 0%
Select **Assume Linear Model**
Select **Assume Non-Negative**
Select **OK**

Step 7. When the **Solver Parameters** dialog box appears:
Choose **Solve**

Step 8. When the **Solver Results** dialog box appears:
Select **Keep Solver Solution**
Select **OK**

The solvers parameters dialog box is shown in Figure 11.14, and the solver options dialog box is shown in Figure 11.15. The optimal solution for the Eastborne Realty problem appears in Figure 11.13.

FIGURE 11.14   SOLVER PARAMETERS DIALOG BOX FOR THE EASTBORNE
REALTY PROBLEM

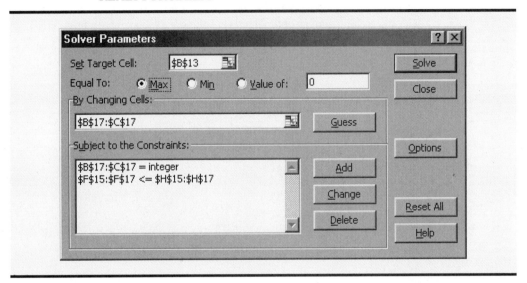

FIGURE 11.15   SOLVER OPTIONS DIALOG BOX FOR EASTBORNE REALTY PROBLEM

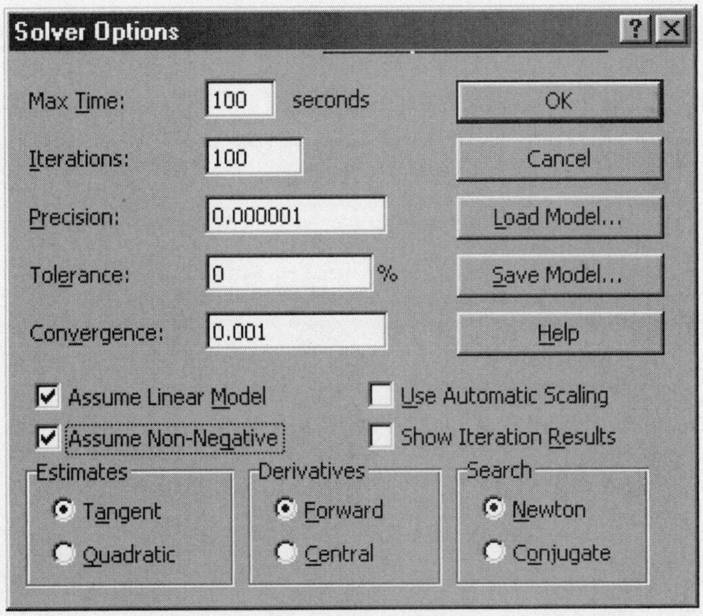

The last part of Step 4 in the spreadsheet solution procedure requires the user to Select **int** in the Add Constraints dialog box. This selection makes the decision variables in cells B17 and C17 integer variables and makes sure the optimal solution will be an integer solution. If an integer linear programming problem contains 0–1 (binary) integer variables, you must select **bin** rather than **int** for these variables in the Add Constraints dialog box. The selection of **bin** restricts the decision variables to values of 0 or 1.

Step 6 of the spreadsheet solution procedure sets the solver options dialog box **Tolerance** at 0%. This tolerance replaces Excel's default tolerance of 5%. The tolerance of 5% means that Solver will stop the search for the optimal integer solution whenever it finds an integer solution that is within 5% of the value of the optimal solution (e.g., within 5% of the value of the optimal solution to the LP Relaxation). To guarantee that Solver will keep searching until an optimal integer solution is found, 0 must be entered in the Tolerance box.

KETRON*

ARLINGTON, VIRGINIA

Ketron Division of The Bionetics Corporation is an operations research organization with offices throughout the United States. An important part of Ketron's business involves work for local, state, and national governmental agencies.

The Ketron Management Science group is responsible for the development, enhancement, marketing, and support of MPSIII, a proprietary mathematical programming system that runs on a wide range of computers—from PCs to mainframes. Ketron Management Science provides consulting services for the design and implementation of mathematical programming applications. One such mixed-integer programming (MIP) application developed for a major sporting equipment company is outlined in the following sections.

A Customer Order Allocation Model

A major sporting equipment company satisfies demand for its products by making shipments from its factories and other locations around the country where inventories are maintained. The company markets approximately 300 products and has about 30 sources of supply (factory and warehouse locations). The problem of interest is to determine how best to allocate customer orders to the various sources of supply such that the total manufacturing cost is minimized. Although transportation cost is not directly considered, it can be accounted for indirectly by not including variables corresponding to shipments from distant locations. Figure 11.16 provides a graphical representation of this problem. Note in the figure that each customer can receive shipments from only a few of the various sources of supply. For example,

we see that customer 1 may be supplied by source A or B, customer 2 may be supplied only by source A, and so on.

The customer order allocation problem is solved periodically. In a typical period, between 30 and 40 customers are to be supplied. Because most customers require several products, usually between 600 and 800 orders must be assigned to the sources of supply.

The sporting equipment company classifies each customer order as either a "guaranteed" or a "secondary" order. Guaranteed orders are single-source

FIGURE 11.16 GRAPHICAL REPRESENTATION OF THE CUSTOMER ORDER ALLOCATION PROBLEM

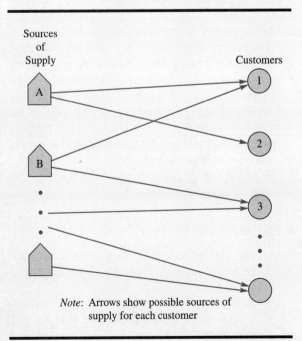

Note: Arrows show possible sources of supply for each customer

---

*The authors are indebted to J. A. Tomlin for providing this application.

orders in that they must be filled by a single supplier to ensure that the complete order will be delivered to the customer at one time. This single-source requirement necessitates the use of integer variables in the model. Approximately 80% of the company's orders are guaranteed orders.

Secondary orders can be split among the various sources of supply. These orders are made by customers restocking inventory, and receiving partial shipments from different sources at different times is not a problem. The total of all secondary orders for a given product is treated as a goal or target in the model formulation. Deviations below the goal are permitted, but a penalty cost is associated with these deviations in the objective function. When deviations occur in the optimal solution, the secondary orders will not be completely satisfied; the shortfall is spread among customers in specified proportions.

Manufacturing considerations are such that raw material availability and the type of process used constrain the amount of production. In addition, groups of items that are similar may belong to a "model group" that must be jointly constrained at some factories. Several restrictions are also placed on international shipping. For various policy reasons, shipments between sources and customers in certain countries may not be made. This restriction reduces the number of variables in the model, but it necessitates extensive data checking to ensure that all guaranteed orders have a permissible source. If they do not, some means must be found to make the problem feasible before beginning to solve the mixed-integer programming model.

The primary objective of the model is to minimize the total manufacturing costs subject to the requirement that the guaranteed orders be met. As indicated previously, the deviations below the secondary demand goals are dealt with by defining variables that indicate the amount of any shortage. The cost associated with these variables represents a penalty for not having the item in inventory when it is required.

A description of the constraints and the objective function for the model follows.

Constraints

- *Guaranteed orders:* Each customer's order for each product is assigned to a single supplier (a multiple-choice constraint).
- *Secondary orders:* For each product, the total amount of secondary demand assigned plus the shortfall must equal the total demand goal (target).

- *Raw material capacities:* The amount of each type of raw material used at a supply source cannot exceed the amount available.
- *Manufacturing capacities:* At each supply source, the capacity for each type of production process cannot be exceeded.
- *Individual product capacities:* The amount of product produced at a site cannot exceed that site's capacity for the product.
- *Group capacities:* The total production for a group of similar products at a site cannot exceed that site's capacity for the group of products.

Objective Function

The objective is to minimize the sum of (1) the manufacturing cost for guaranteed orders, (2) the manufacturing cost for secondary orders, and (3) the penalty cost for unsatisfied secondary demand.

Model Solution

Expecting to obtain an optimal solution for a problem of this complexity is unreasonable. Furthermore, the goal programming methodology for handling the secondary demand means that an "optimum" is of questionable interpretation. A "good" feasible mixed-integer solution is needed. If an integer solution is found whose value is within a few percent of the value of the LP Relaxation solution, the room for improvement is obviously small.

A fairly typical problem has about 800 constraints, 2000 0–1 assignment variables for the guaranteed orders, and 500 continuous variables associated with the secondary orders. This model is solved using Ketron's MPSIII system.

Implementation Notes

In large-scale applications such as this one, considerable systems work is involved in generating the data for the model and the managerial reports. Special data processing languages are often available to ease the programming burden of these phases. The DATAFORM language facility of MPSIII is used to generate the data for this model and to prepare the reports.

In this application, making a completely separate preprocessing run is necessary to check for internal consistency and errors in the data. Only when the data appear logically error-free is the model generated and solved. Although tedious, this kind of preprocessing effort is critical for mixed-integer models because the cost of solving the wrong model can be significant. Furthermore, in some cases the data preprocessing step permits the size of the model to be reduced. Such a reduction is possible in this application when a demand for a product has only one legitimate source. The computational benefits of such reductions can be substantial.

Questions

1. Discuss the relationship between the method for handling secondary orders and feasibility.
2. Discuss what is meant by the statement, an "optimum" is of questionable interpretation. Does it mean that any feasible solution is acceptable?

Chapter 12

PROJECT SCHEDULING: PERT/CPM

CONTENTS

In many situations, managers are responsible for planning, scheduling, and controlling projects that consist of numerous separate jobs or tasks performed by a variety of departments and individuals. Often these projects are so large and/or complex that the manager cannot possibly remember all the information pertaining to the plan, schedule, and progress of the project. In these situations the **program evaluation and review technique (PERT)** and the **critical path method (CPM)** have proven to be extremely valuable.

PERT and CPM have been used to plan, schedule, and control a wide variety of projects:

Henry L. Gantt developed the Gantt Chart as a graphical aid to scheduling jobs on machines in 1918. This application was the first of what has become known as project scheduling techniques.

1. Research and development of new products and processes
2. Construction of plants, buildings, and highways
3. Maintenance of large and complex equipment
4. Design and installation of new systems

In these types of projects, project managers must schedule and coordinate the various jobs or **activities** so that the entire project is completed on time. A complicating factor in carrying out this task is the interdependence of the activities; for example, some activities depend on the completion of other activities before they can be started. Because projects may have as many as several thousand activities, project managers look for procedures that will help them answer questions such as the following.

1. What is the total time to complete the project?
2. What are the scheduled start and finish dates for each specific activity?
3. Which activities are "critical" and must be completed *exactly* as scheduled to keep the project on schedule?
4. How long can "noncritical" activities be delayed before they cause an increase in the total project completion time?

PERT and CPM can help answer these questions.

PERT (Navy) and CPM (Du Pont and Remington Rand) differ because they were developed by different people working on different projects. Today, the best aspects of each have been combined to provide a valuable project scheduling technique.

Although PERT and CPM have the same general purpose and utilize much of the same terminology, the techniques were developed independently. PERT was developed in the late 1950s specifically for the Polaris missile project. Many activities associated with this project had never been attempted previously, so PERT was developed to handle uncertain activity times. CPM was developed primarily for industrial projects for which activity times generally were known. CPM offered the option of reducing activity times by adding more workers and/or resources, usually at an increased cost. Thus, a distinguishing feature of CPM was that it identified trade-offs between time and cost for various project activities.

Today's computerized versions of PERT and CPM have combined the best features of both approaches. Thus, the distinction between the two techniques is no longer necessary. As a result, we refer to the project scheduling procedures covered in this chapter as PERT/CPM. We begin the discussion of PERT/CPM by considering a project for the expansion of the Western Hills Shopping Center.

12.1   PROJECT SCHEDULING WITH KNOWN ACTIVITY TIMES

The effort that goes into identifying activities, determining interrelationships among activities, and estimating activity times is crucial to the success of PERT/CPM. A significant amount of time may be needed to complete this initial phase of the project scheduling process.

The owner of the Western Hills Shopping Center is planning to modernize and expand the current 32-business shopping center complex. The project is expected to provide room for 8 to 10 new businesses. Financing has been arranged through a private investor. All that remains is for the owner of the shopping center to plan, schedule, and complete the expansion project. Let us show how PERT/CPM can help.

The first step in the PERT/CPM scheduling process is to develop a list of the activities that make up the project. Table 12.1 shows the list of activities for the Western Hills Shopping Center expansion project. Nine activities are described and denoted A through I for later reference. Table 12.1 also shows the immediate predecessor(s) and the activity time (in weeks) for each activity. For a given activity, the **immediate predecessor** column identifies the activities that must be completed *immediately prior* to the start of that activity. Activities A and B do not have immediate predecessors and can be started as soon as the project begins; thus, a dash is written in the immediate predecessor column for these activities. The other entries in the immediate predecessor column show that activities C, D, and E cannot be started until activity A has been completed; activity F cannot be started until activity E has been completed; activity G cannot be started until both activities D and F have been completed; activity H cannot be started until both activities B and C have been completed;

TABLE 12.1   LIST OF ACTIVITIES FOR THE WESTERN HILLS SHOPPING CENTER PROJECT

Activity	Activity Description	Immediate Predecessor	Activity Time
A	Prepare architectural drawings	—	5
B	Identify potential new tenants	—	6
C	Develop prospectus for tenants	A	4
D	Select contractor	A	3
E	Prepare building permits	A	1
F	Obtain approval for building permits	E	4
G	Perform construction	D, F	14
H	Finalize contracts with tenants	B, C	12
I	Tenants move in	G, H	2
		Total	51

Immediate predecessor information determines whether activities can be completed in parallel (worked on simultaneously) or in series (one completed before another begins). Generally, the more series relationships present in a project, the more time will be required to complete the project.

A project network is extremely helpful in visualizing the interrelationships among the activities. No rules guide the conversion of a list of activities and immediate predecessor information into a project network. The process of constructing a project network generally improves with practice and experience.

Try Problem 3. This problem provides the immediate predecessor information for a project with seven activities and asks you to develop the project network.

and, finally, activity I cannot be started until both activities G and H have been completed. The project is finished when activity I is completed.

The last column in Table 12.1 shows the number of weeks required to complete each activity. For example, activity A takes 5 weeks, activity B takes 6 weeks, and so on. The sum of activity times is 51. As a result, you may think that the total time required to complete the project is 51 weeks. However, as we show, two or more activities often may be scheduled concurrently, thus shortening the completion time for the project. Ultimately, PERT/CPM will provide a detailed activity schedule for completing the project in the shortest time possible.

Using the immediate predecessor information in Table 12.1, we can construct a graphical representation of the project, or the **project network.** Figure 12.1 depicts the project network for Western Hills Shopping Center. The activities correspond to the *nodes* of the network (drawn as rectangles) and the *arcs* (the lines with arrows) show the precedence relationships among the activities. In addition, nodes have been added to the network to denote the start and the finish of the project. A project network will help a manager visualize the activity relationships and provide a basis for carrying out the PERT/CPM computations.

The Concept of a Critical Path

To facilitate the PERT/CPM computations, we modified the project network as shown in Figure 12.2. Note that the upper left-hand corner of each node contains the corresponding activity letter. The activity time appears immediately below the letter.

To determine the project completion time, we have to analyze the network and identify what is called the **critical path** for the network. However, before doing so, we need to define the concept of a path through the network. A **path** is a sequence of connected nodes that leads from the Start node to the Finish node. For instance, one path for the network in Figure 12.2 is defined by the sequence of nodes A-E-F-G-I. By inspection, we see that other paths are possible, such as A-D-G-I, A-C-H-I, and B-H-I. All paths in the network must be traversed in order to complete the project, so we will look for the path that requires the most time. Because all other paths are shorter in duration, this *longest* path determines the total time required to complete the project. If activities on the longest path are delayed,

FIGURE 12.1   PROJECT NETWORK FOR THE WESTERN HILLS SHOPPING CENTER

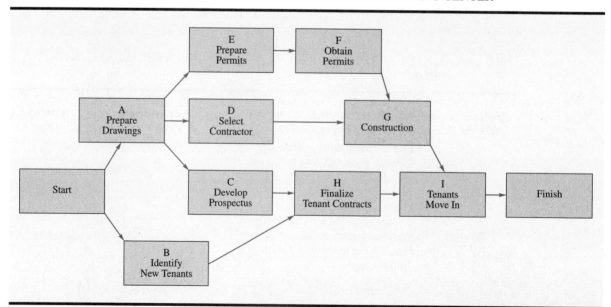

FIGURE 12.2   WESTERN HILLS SHOPPING CENTER PROJECT NETWORK WITH ACTIVITY TIMES

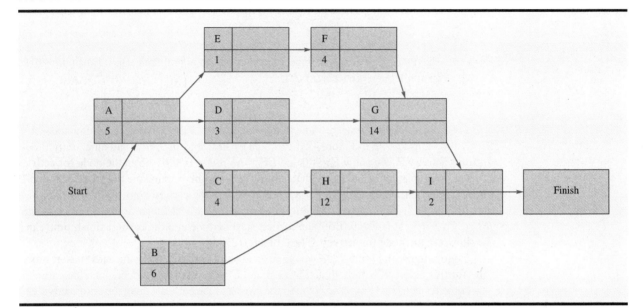

For convenience, we use the convention of referencing activities with letters. Generally, we assign the letters in approximate order as we move from left to right through the project network.

the entire project will be delayed. Thus, the longest path is the *critical path*. Activities on the critical path are referred to as the **critical activities** for the project. The following discussion presents a step-by-step algorithm for finding the critical path in a project network.

Determining the Critical Path

We begin by finding the **earliest start time** and a **latest start time** for all activities in the network. Let

$$ES = \text{earliest start time for an activity}$$
$$EF = \text{earliest finish time for an activity}$$
$$t = \text{activity time}$$

The **earliest finish time** for any activity is

$$EF = ES + t \tag{12.1}$$

Activity A can start as soon as the project starts, so we set the earliest start time for activity A equal to 0. With an activity time of 5 weeks, the earliest finish time for activity A is $EF = ES + t = 0 + 5 = 5$.

We will write the earliest start and earliest finish times in the node to the right of the activity letter. Using activity A as an example, we have

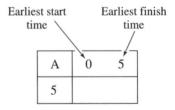

Because an activity cannot be started until *all* immediately preceding activities have been finished, the following rule can be used to determine the earliest start time for each activity.

> The earliest start time for an activity is equal to the *largest* of the earliest finish times for all its immediate predecessors.

Let us apply the earliest start time rule to the portion of the network involving nodes A, B, C, and H, as shown in Figure 12.3. With an earliest start time of 0 and an activity time of 6 for activity B, we show $ES = 0$ and $EF = ES + t = 0 + 6 = 6$ in the node for activity B. Looking at node C, we note that activity A is the only immediate predecessor for activity C. The earliest finish time for activity A is 5, so the earliest start time for activity C must be $ES = 5$. Thus, with an activity time of 4, the earliest finish time for activity C is $EF = ES + t = 5 + 4 = 9$. Both the earliest starting time and the earliest finish time can be shown in the node for activity C (see Figure 12.4).

Continuing with Figure 12.4, we move on to activity H and apply the earliest start time rule for this activity. With both activities B and C as immediate predecessors, the earliest start time for activity H must be equal to the largest of the earliest finish times for activities B and C. Thus, with $EF = 6$ for activity B and $EF = 9$ for activity C, we select the largest value, 9, as the earliest start time for activity H ($ES = 9$). With an activity time of 12 as shown in the node for activity H, the earliest finish time is $EF = ES + t = 9 + 12 = 21$. The $ES = 9$ and $EF = 21$ values can now be entered in the node for activity H in Figure 12.4.

Continuing with this **forward pass** through the network, we can establish the earliest start times and the earliest finish times for all activities in the network. Figure 12.5 shows the Western Hills Shopping Center project network with the ES and EF values for each activity. Note that the earliest finish time for activity I, the last activity in the project, is 26 weeks. Therefore, we now know that the total completion time for the project is 26 weeks.

FIGURE 12.3 A PORTION OF THE WESTERN HILLS SHOPPING CENTER PROJECT NETWORK, SHOWING ACTIVITIES A, B, C, AND H

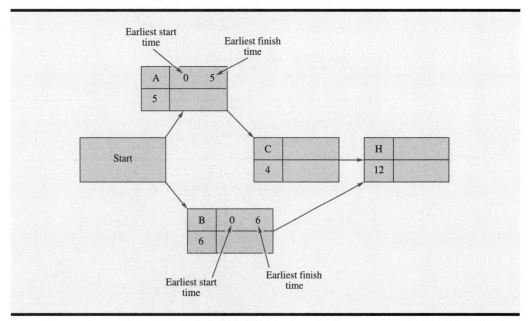

FIGURE 12.4   DETERMINING THE EARLIEST START TIME FOR ACTIVITY H

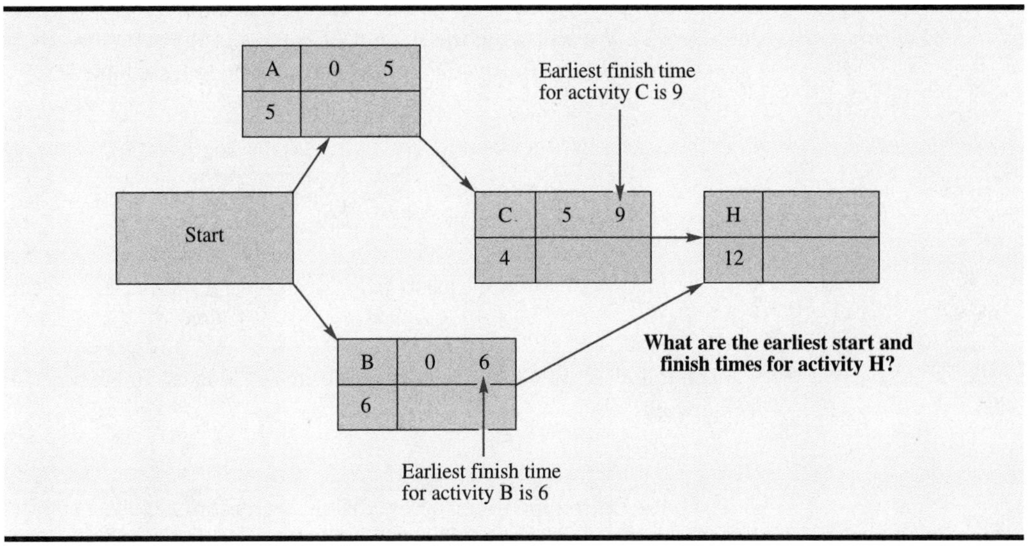

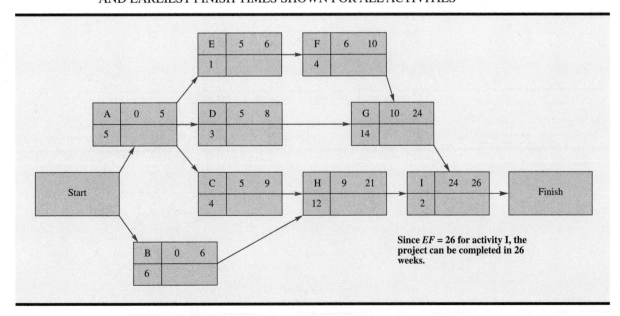

We now continue the algorithm for finding the critical path by making a **backward pass** through the network. Since the project can be completed in 26 weeks, we begin the backward pass with a **latest finish time** of 26 for activity I. Once the latest finish time for an activity is known, the *latest start time* for an activity can be computed as follows. Let

$$LS = \text{latest start time for an activity}$$

$$LF = \text{latest finish time for an activity}$$

then

$$LS = LF - t \tag{12.2}$$

FIGURE 12.5   WESTERN HILLS SHOPPING CENTER PROJECT NETWORK WITH EARLIEST START
AND EARLIEST FINISH TIMES SHOWN FOR ALL ACTIVITIES

Beginning the backward pass with activity I, we know that the latest finish time is $LF = 26$ and that the activity time is $t = 2$. Thus, the latest start time for activity I is $LS = LF - t = 26 - 2 = 24$. We will write the LS and LF values in the node directly below the earliest start (ES) and earliest finish (EF) times. Thus, for node I, we have

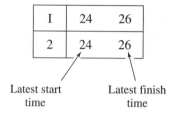

Latest start   Latest finish
time   time

The following rule can be used to determine the latest finish time for each activity in the network.

> The latest finish time for an activity is the *smallest* of the latest start times for all activities that immediately follow the activity.

Logically, this rule states that the latest time an activity can be finished equals the earliest (smallest) value for the latest start time of following activities. Figure 12.6 shows the complete project network with the LS and LF backward pass results. We can use the latest finish time rule to verify the LS and LF values shown for activity H. The latest finish time for activity H must be the latest start time for activity I. Thus, we set $LF = 24$ for activity H. Using equation (12.2), we find that $LS = LF - t = 24 - 12 = 12$ as the latest start time for activity H. These values are shown in the node for activity H in Figure 12.6.

Activity A requires a more involved application of the latest start time rule. First, note that three activities (C, D, and E) immediately follow activity A. Figure 12.6 shows that the

FIGURE 12.6   WESTERN HILLS SHOPPING CENTER PROJECT NETWORK WITH LATEST START AND LATEST FINISH TIMES SHOWN IN EACH NODE

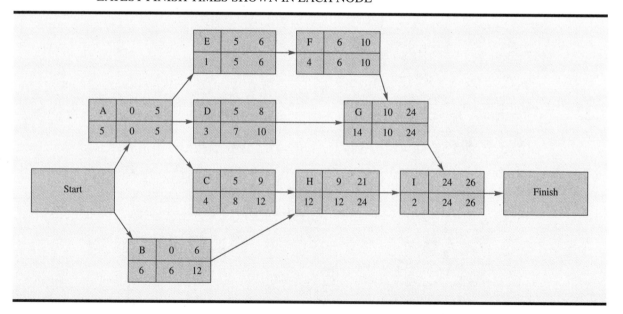

latest start times for activities C, D, and E are $LS = 8$, $LS = 7$, and $LS = 5$, respectively. The latest finish time rule for activity A states that the LF for activity A is the smallest of the latest start times for activities C, D, and E. With the smallest value being 5 for activity E, we set the latest finish time for activity A to $LF = 5$. Verify this result and the other latest start times and latest finish times shown in the nodes in Figure 12.6.

The slack for each activity indicates the length of time the activity can be delayed without increasing the project completion time.

After we have completed the forward and backward passes, we can determine the amount of slack associated with each activity. **Slack** is the length of time an activity can be delayed without increasing the project completion time. The amount of slack for an activity is computed as follows:

$$\text{Slack} = LS - ES = LF - EF \tag{12.3}$$

For example, the slack associated with activity C is $LS - ES = 8 - 5 = 3$ weeks. Hence, activity C can be delayed up to 3 weeks, and the entire project can still be completed in 26 weeks. In this sense, activity C is not critical to the completion of the entire project in 26 weeks. Next, we consider activity E. Using the information in Figure 12.6, we find that the slack is $LS - ES = 5 - 5 = 0$. Thus, activity E has zero, or no, slack. Thus, this activity cannot be delayed without increasing the completion time for the entire project. In other words, completing activity E exactly as scheduled is critical in terms of keeping the project on schedule. Thus, activity E is a critical activity. In general, the *critical activities* are the activities with zero slack.

One of the primary contributions of PERT/CPM is the identification of the critical activities. The project manager will want to monitor critical activities closely because a delay in any one of these activities will lengthen the project completion time.

The start and finish times shown in Figure 12.6 can be used to develop a detailed start time and finish time schedule for all activities. Putting this information in tabular form provides the activity schedule shown in Table 12.2. Note that the slack column shows that activities A, E, F, G, and I have zero slack. Hence, these activities are the critical activities for the project. The path formed by nodes A-E-F-G-I is the *critical path* in the Western Hills Shopping Center project network. The detailed schedule shown in Table 12.2 indicates the slack or delay that can be tolerated for the noncritical activities before these activities will increase project completion time.

The critical path algorithm is essentially a longest path algorithm. From the start node to the finish node, the critical path identifies the path that requires the most time.

Contributions of PERT/CPM

Previously, we stated that project managers look for procedures that will help answer important questions regarding the planning, scheduling, and controlling of projects. Let us reconsider these questions in light of the information that the critical path calculations have given us.

TABLE 12.2　ACTIVITY SCHEDULE FOR THE WESTERN HILLS SHOPPING CENTER PROJECT

Activity	Earliest Start (ES)	Latest Start (LS)	Earliest Finish (EF)	Latest Finish (LF)	Slack (LS − ES)	Critical Path?
A	0	0	5	5	0	Yes
B	0	6	6	12	6	
C	5	8	9	12	3	
D	5	7	8	10	2	
E	5	5	6	6	0	Yes
F	6	6	10	10	0	Yes
G	10	10	24	24	0	Yes
H	9	12	21	24	3	
I	24	24	26	26	0	Yes

If the total time required to complete the project is too long, judgment about where and how to shorten the time of critical activities must be exercised. If any activity times are altered, the critical path calculations should be repeated to determine the impact on the activity schedule and the impact on total project completion time. In Section 12.3 we show how to use linear programming to find the least-cost way to shorten the project completion time.

Software packages such as The Management Scientist perform the critical path calculations quickly and efficiently. The project manager can modify any aspect of the project and quickly determine how the modification affects the activity schedule and the total time required to complete the project.

1. How long will the project take to complete?
   Answer: The project can be completed in 26 weeks if each activity is completed on schedule.
2. What are the scheduled start and completion times for each activity?
   Answer: The activity schedule (see Table 12.2) shows the earliest start, latest start, earliest finish, and latest finish times for each activity.
3. Which activities are critical and must be completed *exactly* as scheduled to keep the project on schedule?
   Answer: A, E, F, G, and I are the critical activities.
4. How long can noncritical activities be delayed before they cause an increase in the completion time for the project?
   Answer: The activity schedule (see Table 12.2) shows the slack associated with each activity.

Such information is valuable in managing any project. Although larger projects may increase substantially the time required to make the necessary calculations, the procedure and contributions of PERT/CPM to larger projects are identical to those for the shopping center expansion project. Furthermore, computer packages may be used to carry out the steps of the PERT/CPM procedure. Figure 12.7 shows the activity schedule for the shopping center expansion project developed by The Management Scientist software package. Input to the program included the activities, their immediate predecessors, and the expected activity times. Only a few minutes were required to input the information and generate the critical path and activity schedule.

Summary of the PERT/CPM Critical Path Procedure

Before leaving this section, let us summarize the PERT/CPM critical path procedure.

Step 1. Develop a list of the activities that make up the project.
Step 2. Determine the immediate predecessor(s) for each activity in the project.

FIGURE 12.7   THE MANAGEMENT SCIENTIST ACTIVITY SCHEDULE FOR THE WESTERN HILLS SHOPPING CENTER PROJECT

```
                  ***    ACTIVITY SCHEDULE    ***

              EARLIEST  LATEST   EARLIEST  LATEST          CRITICAL
   ACTIVITY    START    START     FINISH   FINISH  SLACK   ACTIVITY
   ---------------------------------------------------------------

      A          0        0         5        5       0      YES
      B          0        6         6       12       6
      C          5        8         9       12       3
      D          5        7         8       10       2
      E          5        5         6        6       0      YES
      F          6        6        10       10       0      YES
      G         10       10        24       24       0      YES
      H          9       12        21       24       3
      I         24       24        26       26       0      YES

   ---------------------------------------------------------------

        CRITICAL PATH:    A-E-F-G-I

        PROJECT COMPLETION TIME = 26
```

Step 3. Estimate the completion time for each activity.

Step 4. Draw a project network depicting the activities and immediate predecessors listed in steps 1 and 2.

Step 5. Use the project network and the activity time estimates to determine the earliest start and the earliest finish time for each activity by making a forward pass through the network. The earliest finish time for the last activity in the project identifies the total time required to complete the project.

Step 6. Use the project completion time identified in step 5 as the latest finish time for the last activity and make a backward pass through the network to identify the latest start and latest finish time for each activity.

Step 7. Use the difference between the latest start time and the earliest start time for each activity to determine the slack for each activity.

Step 8. Find the activities with zero slack; these are the critical activities.

Step 9. Use the information from steps 5 and 6 to develop the activity schedule for the project.

NOTES AND COMMENTS

Suppose that if after analyzing a PERT/CPM network the project manager finds that the project completion time is unacceptable (i.e., the project is going to take too long). In this case, the manager must take one or both of the following steps. First, review the original PERT/CPM network to see whether any immediate predecessor relationships can be modified so that at least some of the critical path activities can be done simultaneously. Second, consider adding resources to critical path activities in an attempt to shorten the critical path; we discuss this alternative, referred to as *crashing,* in Section 12.3.

12.2   PROJECT SCHEDULING WITH UNCERTAIN ACTIVITY TIMES

In this section we consider the details of project scheduling for a problem involving new-product research and development. Because many of the activities in this project have never been attempted, the project manager wants to account for uncertainties in the activity times. Let us show how project scheduling can be conducted with uncertain activity times.

The Daugherty Porta-Vac Project

The H. S. Daugherty Company has manufactured industrial vacuum cleaning systems for many years. Recently, a member of the company's new-product research team submitted a report suggesting that the company consider manufacturing a cordless vacuum cleaner. The new product, referred to as Porta-Vac, could contribute to Daugherty's expansion into the household market. Management hopes that it can be manufactured at a reasonable cost and that its portability and no-cord convenience will make it extremely attractive.

Daugherty's management wants to study the feasibility of manufacturing the Porta-Vac product. The feasibility study will recommend the action to be taken. To complete this study, information must be obtained from the firm's research and development (R&D), product testing, manufacturing, cost estimating, and market research groups. How long will this feasibility study take? In the following discussion, we show how to answer this question and provide an activity schedule for the project.

Again, the first step in the project scheduling process is to identify all activities that make up the project and then determine the immediate predecessor(s) for each activity. Table 12.3 shows these data for the Porta-Vac project.

The Porta-Vac project network is shown in Figure 12.8. Verify that the network does in fact maintain the immediate predecessor relationships shown in Table 12.3.

TABLE 12.3   ACTIVITY LIST FOR THE PORTA-VAC PROJECT

Activity	Description	Immediate Predecessor
A	Develop product design	—
B	Plan market research	—
C	Prepare routing (manufacturing engineering)	A
D	Build prototype model	A
E	Prepare marketing brochure	A
F	Prepare cost estimates (industrial engineering)	C
G	Do preliminary product testing	D
H	Complete market survey	B, E
I	Prepare pricing and forecast report	H
J	Prepare final report	F, G, I

FIGURE 12.8   PORTA-VAC CORDLESS VACUUM CLEANER PROJECT NETWORK

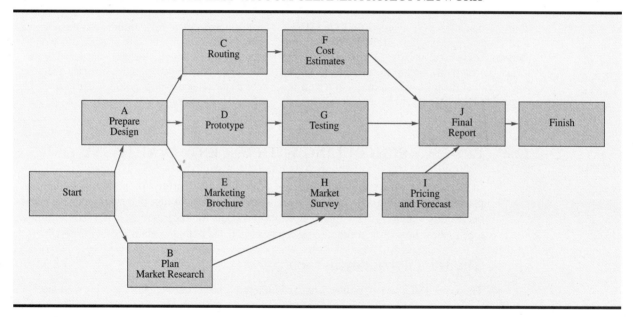

Uncertain Activity Times

Accurate activity time estimates are important in the development of an activity schedule. When activity times are uncertain, the three time estimates—optimistic, most probable, and pessimistic—allow the project manager to take uncertainty into consideration in determining the critical path and the activity schedule. This approach was developed by the designers of PERT.

Once we have developed the project network, we will need information on the time required to complete each activity. This information is used in the calculation of the total time required to complete the project and in the scheduling of specific activities. For repeat projects, such as construction and maintenance projects, managers may have the experience and historical data necessary to provide accurate activity time estimates. However, for new or unique projects, estimating the time for each activity may be quite difficult. In fact, in many cases, activity times are uncertain and are best described by a range of possible values rather than by one specific time estimate. In these instances, the uncertain activity times are treated as random variables with associated probability distributions. As a result, probability statements will be provided about the ability to meet a specific project completion date.

To incorporate uncertain activity times into the analysis, we need to obtain three time estimates for each activity:

Optimistic time a = the minimum activity time if everything progresses ideally

Most probable time m = the most probable activity time under normal conditions

Pessimistic time b = the maximum activity time if significant delays are encountered

To illustrate the PERT/CPM procedure with uncertain activity times, let us consider the optimistic, most probable, and pessimistic time estimates for the Porta-Vac activities as presented in Table 12.4 Using activity A as an example, we see that the most probable time is 5 weeks with a range from 4 weeks (optimistic) to 12 weeks (pessimistic). If the activity could be repeated a large number of times, what is the average time for the activity? This average or **expected time** (t) is as follows:

$$t = \frac{a + 4m + b}{6} \tag{12.4}$$

For activity A we have an average or expected time of

$$t_A = \frac{4 + 4(5) + 12}{6} = \frac{36}{6} = 6 \text{ weeks}$$

With uncertain activity times, we can use the *variance* to describe the dispersion or variation in the activity time values. The variance of the activity time is given by the formula[1]

$$\sigma^2 = \left(\frac{b - a}{6}\right)^2 \tag{12.5}$$

The difference between the pessimistic (b) and optimistic (a) time estimates greatly affects the value of the variance. Large differences in these two values reflect a high degree of uncertainty in the activity time. Using equation (12.5), we obtain the measure of uncertainty—that is, the variance—of activity A, denoted σ_A^2:

$$\sigma_A^2 = \left(\frac{12 - 4}{6}\right)^2 = \left(\frac{8}{6}\right)^2 = 1.78$$

TABLE 12.4   OPTIMISTIC, MOST PROBABLE, AND PESSIMISTIC ACTIVITY TIME
ESTIMATES (IN WEEKS) FOR THE PORTA-VAC PROJECT

Activity	Optimistic (a)	Most Probable (m)	Pessimistic (b)
A	4	5	12
B	1	1.5	5
C	2	3	4
D	3	4	11
E	2	3	4
F	1.5	2	2.5
G	1.5	3	4.5
H	2.5	3.5	7.5
I	1.5	2	2.5
J	1	2	3

---

1. The variance equation is based on the notion that a standard deviation is approximately $\frac{1}{6}$ of the difference between the extreme values of the distribution: $(b - a)/6$. The variance is the square of the standard deviation.

Equations (12.4) and (12.5) are based on the assumption that the activity time distribution can be described by a **beta probability distribution.**[2] With this assumption, the probability distribution for the time to complete activity A is as shown in Figure 12.9. Using equations (12.4) and (12.5) and the data in Table 12.4, we calculated the expected times and variances for all Porta-Vac activities; the results are summarized in Table 12.5. The Porta-Vac project network with expected activity times is shown in Figure 12.10.

The Critical Path

When uncertain activity times are used, the critical path calculations will determine only the expected or average time to complete the project. The actual time required to complete the project may differ. However, for planning purposes, the expected time should be valuable information for the project manager.

When we have the project network and the expected activity times, we are ready to proceed with the critical path calculations necessary to determine the expected time required to complete the project and determine the activity schedule. In these calculations, we treat the expected activity times (Table 12.5) as the fixed length or known duration of each activity. As a result, we can use the PERT/CPM critical path procedure introduced in Section 12.1 to find the critical path for the Porta-Vac project. After the critical activities and the expected time to complete the project have been determined, we analyze the effect of the activity time variability.

Proceeding with a forward pass through the network shown in Figure 12.10, we can establish the earliest start (*ES*) and earliest finish (*EF*) times for each activity. Figure 12.11 shows the project network with the *ES* and *EF* values. Note that the earliest finish time for activity J, the last activity, is 17 weeks. Thus, the expected completion time for the project is 17 weeks. Next, we make a backward pass through the network. The backward pass provides the latest start (*LS*) and latest finish (*LF*) times shown in Figure 12.12.

Activities that have larger variances show a greater degree of uncertainty. The project manager should monitor the progress of any activity with a large variance even if the expected times do not identify the activity as a critical activity.

The activity schedule for the Porta-Vac project is shown in Table 12.6. Note that the slack time (*LS − ES*) is also shown for each activity. The activities with zero slack (A, E, H, I, and J) form the critical path for the Porta-Vac project network.

Variability in Project Completion Time

We know that for the Porta-Vac project the critical path of A-E-H-I-J resulted in an expected total project completion time of 17 weeks. However, variation in critical activities can cause vari-

FIGURE 12.9 ACTIVITY TIME DISTRIBUTION FOR PRODUCT DESIGN (ACTIVITY A) FOR THE PORTA-VAC PROJECT

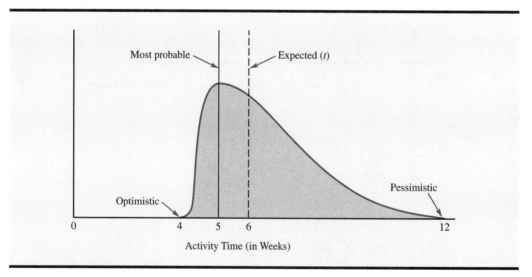

---

2. The equations for t and σ^2 require additional assumptions about the parameters of the beta probability distribution. However, even when these additional assumptions are not made, the equations still provide good approximations of t and σ^2.

TABLE 12.5 EXPECTED TIMES AND VARIANCES FOR THE PORTA-VAC PROJECT ACTIVITIES

Activity	Expected Time (weeks)	Variance
A	6	1.78
B	2	0.44
C	3	0.11
D	5	1.78
E	3	0.11
F	2	0.03
G	3	0.25
H	4	0.69
I	2	0.03
J	2	0.11
Total	32	

ation in the project completion time. Variation in noncritical activities ordinarily has no effect on the project completion time because of the slack time associated with these activities. However, if a noncritical activity is delayed long enough to expend its slack time, it becomes part of a new critical path and may affect the project completion time. Variability leading to a longer-than-expected total time for the critical activities will always extend the project completion time, and conversely, variability that results in a shorter-than-expected total time for the critical activities will reduce the project completion time, unless other activities become critical. Let us now use the variance in the critical activities to determine the variance in the project completion time.

Let T denote the total time required to complete the project. The expected value of T, which is the sum of the expected times for the critical activities is

$$E(T) = t_A + t_E + t_H + t_I + t_J$$
$$= 6 + 3 + 4 + 2 + 2 = 17 \text{ weeks}$$

FIGURE 12.10 PORTA-VAC PROJECT NETWORK WITH EXPECTED ACTIVITY TIMES

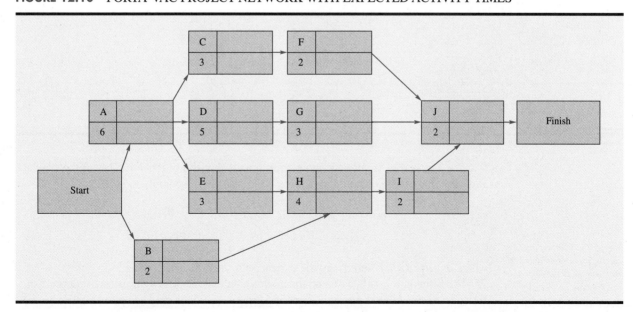

FIGURE 12.11 PORTA-VAC PROJECT NETWORK WITH EARLIEST START AND EARLIEST FINISH TIMES

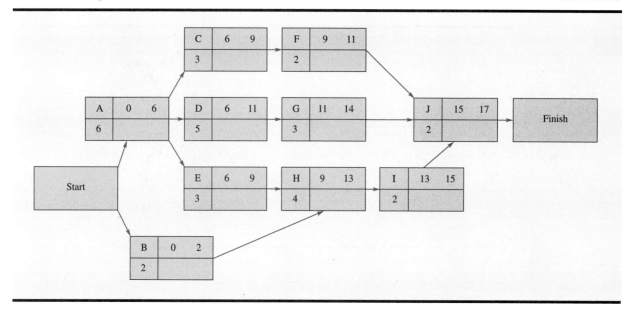

FIGURE 12.12 PORTA-VAC PROJECT NETWORK WITH LATEST START AND LATEST FINISH TIMES

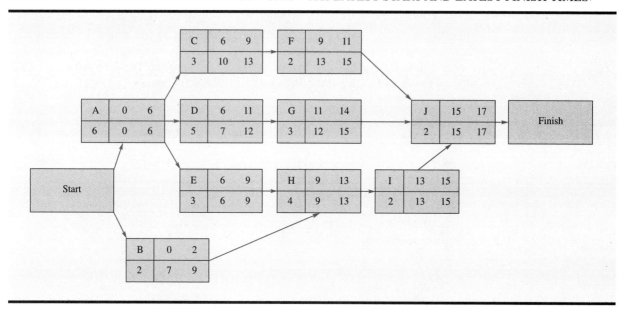

The variance in the project completion time is the sum of the variances of the critical path activities. Thus, the variance for the Porta-Vac project completion time is

$$\sigma^2 = \sigma_A^2 + \sigma_E^2 + \sigma_H^2 + \sigma_I^2 + \sigma_J^2$$
$$= 1.78 + 0.11 + 0.69 + 0.03 + 0.11 = 2.72$$

Problem 10 involves a project with uncertain activity times and asks you to compute the expected completion time and the variance for the project.

where σ_A^2, σ_E^2, σ_H^2, σ_I^2, and σ_J^2 are the variances of the critical activities.

The formula for σ^2 is based on the assumption that the activity times are independent. If two or more activities are dependent, the formula provides only an approximation to the

TABLE 12.6   ACTIVITY SCHEDULE FOR THE PORTA-VAC PROJECT

Activity	Earliest Start (ES)	Latest Start (LS)	Earliest Finish (EF)	Latest Finish (LF)	Slack (LS − ES)	Critical Path?
A	0	0	6	6	0	Yes
B	0	7	2	9	7	
C	6	10	9	13	4	
D	6	7	11	12	1	
E	6	6	9	9	0	Yes
F	9	13	11	15	4	
G	11	12	14	15	1	
H	9	9	13	13	0	Yes
I	13	13	15	15	0	Yes
J	15	15	17	17	0	Yes

variance of the project completion time. The closer the activities are to being independent, the better the approximation.

Knowing that the standard deviation is the square root of the variance, we compute the standard deviation σ for the Porta-Vac project completion time as

$$\sigma = \sqrt{\sigma^2} = \sqrt{2.72} = 1.65$$

The normal distribution tends to be a better approximation of the distribution of total time for larger projects where the critical path has many activities.

Assuming that the distribution of the project completion time T follows a normal or bell-shaped distribution[3] allows us to draw the distribution shown in Figure 12.13. With this distribution, we can compute the probability of meeting a specified project completion date. For example, suppose that management has allotted 20 weeks for the Porta-Vac project. What is the probability that we will meet the 20-week deadline? Using the normal probability distribution shown in Figure 12.14, we are asking for the probability that $T \leq 20$; this

FIGURE 12.13   NORMAL DISTRIBUTION OF THE PROJECT COMPLETION TIME FOR THE PORTA-VAC PROJECT

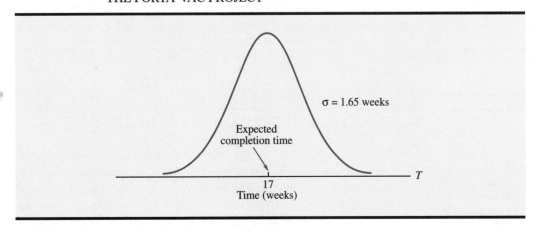

σ = 1.65 weeks

Expected completion time

17
Time (weeks)

T

---

3. Use of the normal distribution as an approximation is based on the central limit theorem, which indicates that the sum of independent random variables (activity times) follows a normal distribution as the number of random variables becomes large.

probability is shown graphically as the shaded area in the figure. The z value for the normal probability distribution at $T = 20$ is

$$z = \frac{20 - 17}{1.65} = 1.82$$

Using $z = 1.82$ and the table for the normal distribution (see Appendix C), we find that the probability of the project meeting the 20-week deadline is $0.4656 + 0.5000 = 0.9656$. Thus, even though activity time variability may cause the completion time to exceed 17 weeks, calculations indicate an excellent chance that the project will be completed before the 20-week deadline. Similar probability calculations can be made for other project deadline alternatives.

FIGURE 12.14   PROBABILITY THE PORTA-VAC PROJECT WILL MEET THE 20-WEEK DEADLINE

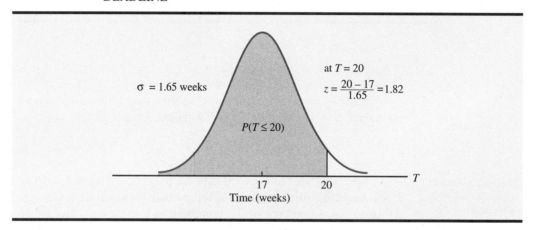

NOTES AND COMMENTS

For projects involving uncertain activity times, the probability that the project can be completed within a specified amount of time is helpful managerial information. However, remember that this probability estimate is based *only* on the critical activities. When uncertain activity times exist, longer-than-expected completion times for one or more noncritical activities may cause an original noncritical activity to become critical and hence increase the time required to complete the project. By frequently monitoring the progress of the project to make sure all activities are on schedule, the project manager will be better prepared to take corrective action if a noncritical activity begins to lengthen the duration of the project.

12.3   CONSIDERING TIME-COST TRADE-OFFS

Using more resources to reduce activity times was proposed by the developers of CPM. The shortening of activity times is referred to as crashing.

The original developers of CPM provided the project manager with the option of adding resources to selected activities to reduce project completion time. Added resources (such as more workers, overtime, and so on) generally increase project costs, so the decision to reduce activity times must take into consideration the additional cost involved. In effect, the project manager has to make a decision that involves trading reduced activity time for additional project cost.

Table 12.7 defines a two-machine maintenance project consisting of five activities. Because management has had substantial experience with similar projects, the times for main-

TABLE 12.7   ACTIVITY LIST FOR THE TWO-MACHINE MAINTENANCE PROJECT

Activity	Description	Immediate Predecessor	Expected Time (days)
A	Overhaul machine I	—	7
B	Adjust machine I	A	3
C	Overhaul machine II	—	6
D	Adjust machine II	C	3
E	Test system	B, D	2

tenance activities are considered to be known; hence, a single time estimate is given for each activity. The project network is shown in Figure 12.15.

The procedure for making critical path calculations for the maintenance project network is the same one used to find the critical path in the networks for both the Western Hills Shopping Center expansion project and the Porta-Vac project. Making the forward pass and backward pass calculations for the network in Figure 12.15, we obtained the activity schedule shown in Table 12.8. The zero slack times, and thus the critical path, are associated with activities A-B-E. The length of the critical path, and thus the total time required to complete the project, is 12 days.

FIGURE 12.15   TWO-MACHINE MAINTENANCE PROJECT NETWORK

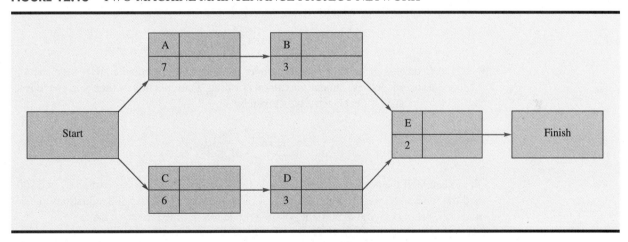

TABLE 12.8   ACTIVITY SCHEDULE FOR THE TWO-MACHINE MAINTENANCE PROJECT

Activity	Earliest Start (ES)	Latest Start (LS)	Earliest Finish (EF)	Latest Finish (LF)	Slack ($LS - ES$)	Critical Path?
A	0	0	7	7	0	Yes
B	7	7	10	10	0	Yes
C	0	1	6	7	1	
D	6	7	9	10	1	
E	10	10	12	12	0	Yes

Crashing Activity Times

Now suppose that current production levels make completing the maintenance project within 10 days imperative. By looking at the length of the critical path of the network (12 days), we realize that meeting the desired project completion time is impossible unless we can shorten selected activity times. This shortening of activity times, which usually can be achieved by adding resources, is referred to as **crashing.** However, the added resources associated with crashing activity times usually result in added project costs, so we will want to identify the activities that cost the least to crash and then crash those activities only the amount necessary to meet the desired project completion time.

To determine just where and how much to crash activity times, we need information on how much each activity can be crashed and how much the crashing process costs. Hence, we must ask for the following information:

1. Activity cost under the normal or expected activity time
2. Time to complete the activity under maximum crashing (i.e., the shortest possible activity time)
3. Activity cost under maximum crashing

Let

$$\tau_i = \text{expected time for activity } i$$

$$\tau_i' = \text{time for activity } j \text{ under maximum crashing}$$

$$M_i = \text{maximum possible reduction in time for activity } i \text{ due to crashing}$$

Given τ_i and τ_i', we can compute M_i:

$$M_i = \tau_i - \tau_i' \tag{12.6}$$

Next, let C_i denote the cost for activity i under the normal or expected activity time and C_i' denote the cost for activity i under maximum crashing. Thus, per unit of time (e.g., per day), the crashing cost K_i for each activity is given by

$$K_i = \frac{C_i' - C_i}{M_i} \tag{12.7}$$

For example, if the normal or expected time for activity A is 7 days at a cost of $C_A = \$500$ and the time under maximum crashing is 4 days at a cost of $C_A' = \$800$, equations (12.6) and (12.7) show that the maximum possible reduction in time for activity A is

$$M_A = 7 - 4 = 3 \text{ days}$$

with a crashing cost of

$$K_A = \frac{C_A' - C_A}{M_A} = \frac{800 - 500}{3} = \frac{300}{3} = \$100 \text{ per day}$$

We make the assumption that any portion or fraction of the activity crash time can be achieved for a corresponding portion of the activity crashing cost. For example, if we decided to crash activity A by only $1\frac{1}{2}$ days, the added cost would be $1\frac{1}{2}(\$100) = \$150$, which results in a total activity cost of $\$500 + \$150 = \$650$. Figure 12.16 shows the graph of the time-cost relationship for activity A. The complete normal and crash activity data for the two-machine maintenance project are given in Table 12.9.

FIGURE 12.16   TIME-COST RELATIONSHIP FOR ACTIVITY A

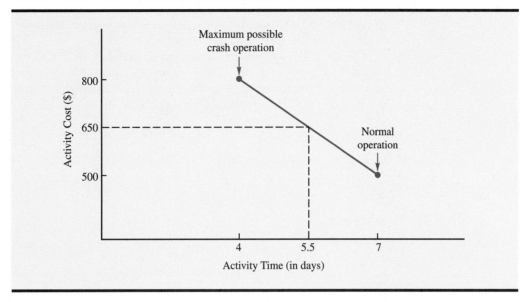

Which activities should be crashed—and by how much—to meet the 10-day project completion deadline at minimum cost? Your first reaction to this question may be to consider crashing the critical activities—A, B, or E. Activity A has the lowest crashing cost per day of the three, and crashing this activity by 2 days will reduce the A-B-E path to the desired 10 days. Keep in mind, however, that as you crash the current critical activities, other paths may become critical. Thus, you will need to check the critical path in the revised network and perhaps either identify additional activities to crash or modify your initial crashing decision. For a small network, this trial-and-error approach can be used to make crashing decisions; in larger networks, however, a mathematical procedure is required to determine the optimal crashing decisions. The following discussion shows how linear programming can be used to solve the network crashing problem.

Linear Programming Model for Crashing

In the PERT/CPM procedure, we used

$$EF = ES + t$$

TABLE 12.9   NORMAL AND CRASH ACTIVITY DATA FOR THE TWO-MACHINE MAINTENANCE PROJECT

Activity	Time (days) Normal	Time (days) Crash	Total Cost Normal (C)	Total Cost Crash (C_i')	Maximum Reduction in Time (M_i)	Crash Cost per day $\left(K_i = \dfrac{C_i' - C_i}{M_i}\right)$
A	7	4	$ 500	$ 800	3	$100
B	3	2	200	350	1	150
C	6	4	500	900	2	200
D	3	1	200	500	2	150
E	2	1	300	550	1	250
			$1700	$3100		

to determine the earliest finish time for an activity. Note that if ES, the earliest start time for an activity, is known, the effect of crashing a particular activity will be to reduce t and hence EF, the earliest finish time. In essence, we use linear programming to determine which activities to crash and how much they should be crashed.

Consider activity A, which has an expected time of 7 days. Let x_A = earliest finish time for activity A, and y_A = amount of time activity A is crashed. If we assume that the project begins at time 0, the earliest start time for activity A is 0. Because the time for activity A is reduced by the amount of time that activity A is crashed, the earliest finish time for activity A is

$$x_A \geq 0 + (7 - y_A)$$

Moving y_A to the left side,

$$x_A + y_A \geq 7$$

In general, let

$$x_i = \text{the earliest finish time for activity } i \quad i = A, B, C, D, E$$
$$y_i = \text{the amount of time activity } i \text{ is crashed} \quad i = A, B, C, D, E$$

If we follow the same approach that we used for activity A, the constraint corresponding to the earliest finish time for activity C (expected time = 6 days) is

$$x_C \geq 0 + (6 - y_C) \quad \text{or} \quad x_C + y_C \geq 6$$

Continuing with the forward pass of the PERT/CPM procedure, we see that the earliest start time for activity B is x_A, the earliest finish time for activity A. Thus, the constraint corresponding to the earliest finish time for activity B is

$$x_B \geq x_A + (3 - y_B) \quad \text{or} \quad x_B + y_B - x_A \geq 3$$

Similarly, we obtain the constraint for the earliest finish time for activity D:

$$x_D \geq x_C + (3 - y_D) \quad \text{or} \quad x_D + y_D - x_C \geq 3$$

Finally, we consider activity E. The earliest start time for activity E equals the *largest* of the earliest finish times for activities B and D. Because the earliest finish times for both activities B and D will be determined by the crashing procedure, we must write two constraints for activity E, one based on the earliest finish time for activity B and one based upon the earliest finish time for activity D:

$$x_E + y_E - x_B \geq 2 \quad \text{and} \quad x_E + y_E - x_D \geq 2$$

Recall that current production levels made completing the maintenance project within 10 days imperative. Thus, the constraint for the earliest finish time for activity E is

$$x_E \leq 10$$

In addition, we must add the following five constraints corresponding to the maximum allowable crashing time for each activity:

$$y_A \leq 3, \quad y_B \leq 1, \quad y_C \leq 2, \quad y_D \leq 2, \quad \text{and} \quad y_E \leq 1$$

As with all linear programs, we add the usual nonnegativity requirements for the decision variables.

All that remains is to develop an objective function for the model. Because the total project cost for a normal completion time is fixed at $1700 (see Table 12.9), we can minimize the total project cost (normal cost plus crashing cost) by minimizing the total crashing costs. Thus, the linear programming objective function becomes

$$\text{Min} \quad 100y_A + 150y_B + 200y_C + 150y_D + 250y_E$$

Thus, to determine the optimal crashing for each of the activities, we must solve a 10-variable, 12-constraint linear programming model. The linear programming module of The Management Scientist provides the optimal solution of crashing activity A by 1 day and activity E by 1 day, with a total crashing cost of $350. We can now develop a detailed activity schedule by using $7 - 1 = 6$ as the revised time for activity A and $2 - 1 = 1$ day as the revised time for activity E.

NOTES AND COMMENTS

Note that the two-machine maintenance project network for the crashing illustration (see Figure 12.15) has only one activity, activity E, leading directly to the Finish node. As a result, the project completion time is equal to the completion time for activity E. Thus, the linear programming constraint requiring the project completion in 10 days or less could be written $x_E \leq 10$.

If two or more activities lead directly to the Finish node of a project network, a slight modification is required in the linear programming model for crashing. Consider the portion of the project network shown below. In this case, we suggest creating an additional variable, x_{FIN}, which indicates the finish or completion time for the entire project. The fact that the project cannot be finished until both activities E and G are completed can be modeled by the two constraints

$$x_{FIN} \geq x_E \quad \text{or} \quad x_{FIN} - x_E \geq 0$$
$$x_{FIN} \geq x_G \quad \text{or} \quad x_{FIN} - x_G \geq 0$$

The constraint that the project must be finished by time T can be added as $x_{FIN} \leq T$. Problem 22 gives you practice with this type of project network.

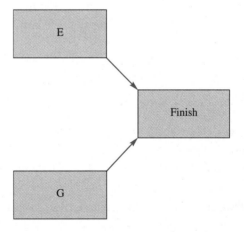

SUMMARY

In this chapter we showed how PERT/CPM can be used to plan, schedule, and control a wide variety of projects. The key to this approach to project scheduling is the development of a PERT/CPM project network that depicts the activities and their precedence relationships. From this project network and activity time estimates, the critical path for the network and the associated critical activities can be identified. In the process, an activity schedule showing the earliest start and earliest finish times, the latest start and latest finish times, and the slack for each activity can be identified.

We showed how we can include capabilities for handling variable or uncertain activity times and how to use this information to provide a probability statement about the chances the project can be completed in a specified period of time. We introduced crashing as a procedure for reducing activity times to meet project completion deadlines, and showed how a linear programming model can be used to determine the crashing decisions that will minimize the cost of reducing the project completion time.

GLOSSARY

Program evaluation and review technique (PERT)   A network-based project scheduling procedure.

Critical path method (CPM)   A network-based project scheduling procedure.

Activities   Specific jobs or tasks that are components of a project. Activities are represented by nodes in a project network.

Immediate predecessors   The activities that must be completed immediately prior to the start of a given activity.

Project network   A graphical representation of a project that depicts the activities and shows the predecessor relationships among the activities.

Critical path   The longest path in a project network.

Path   A sequence of connected nodes that leads from the Start node to the Finish node.

Critical activities   The activities on the critical path.

Earliest start time   The earliest time an activity may begin.

Latest start time   The latest time an activity may begin without increasing the project completion time.

Earliest finish time   The earliest time an activity may be completed.

Latest finish time   The latest time an activity may be completed without increasing the project completion time.

Forward pass   Part of the PERT/CPM procedure that involves moving forward through the project network to determine the earliest start and earliest finish times for each activity.

Backward pass   Part of the PERT/CPM procedure that involves moving backward through the network to determine the latest start and latest finish times for each activity.

Slack   The length of time an activity can be delayed without affecting the project completion time.

Optimistic time   The minimum activity time if everything progresses ideally.

Most probable time   The most probable activity time under normal conditions.

Pessimistic time   The maximum activity time if significant delays are encountered.

Expected time   The average activity time.

Beta probability distribution   A probability distribution used to describe activity times.

Crashing   The shortening of activity times by adding resources and hence usually increasing cost.

PROBLEMS

1. The Mohawk Discount Store is designing a management training program for individuals at its corporate headquarters. The company wants to design the program so that trainees

can complete it as quickly as possible. Important precedence relationships must be maintained between assignments or activities in the program. For example, a trainee cannot serve as an assistant to the store manager until the trainee has obtained experience in the credit department and at least one sales department. The following activities are the assignments that must be completed by each trainee in the program. Construct a project network for this problem. Do not perform any further analysis.

Activity	A	B	C	D	E	F	G	H
Immediate Predecessor	—	—	A	A, B	A, B	C	D, F	E, G

2. Bridge City Developers is coordinating the construction of an office complex. As part of the planning process, the company generated the following activity list. Draw a project network that can be used to assist in the scheduling of the project activities.

Activity	A	B	C	D	E	F	G	H	I	J
Immediate Predecessor	—	—	—	A, B	A, B	D	E	C	C	F, G, H, I

SELFtest   3. Construct a project network for the following project. The project is completed when activities F and G are both complete.

Activity	A	B	C	D	E	F	G
Immediate Predecessor	—	—	A	A	C, B	C, B	D, E

4. Assume that the project in Problem 3 has the following activity times (in months).

Activity	A	B	C	D	E	F	G
Time	4	6	2	6	3	3	5

   a. Find the critical path.
   b. The project must be completed in 1½ years. Do you anticipate difficulty in meeting the deadline? Explain.

5. Management Decision Systems (MDS) is a consulting company that specializes in the development of decision support systems. MDS has just obtained a contract to develop a computer system to assist the management of a large company in formulating its capital expenditure plan. The project leader has developed the following list of activities and immediate predecessors. Construct a project network for this problem.

Activity	A	B	C	D	E	F	G	H	I	J
Immediate Predecessor	—	—	—	B	A	B	C, D	B, E	F, G	H

SELFtest   6. Consider the following project network and activity times (in weeks).

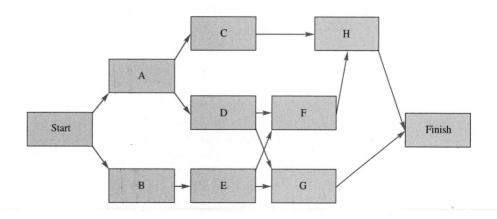

Activity	A	B	C	D	E	F	G	H
Activity Times	5	3	7	6	7	3	10	8

a. Identify the critical path.

b. How much time will be needed to complete this project?

c. Can activity D be delayed without delaying the entire project? If so, by how many weeks?

d. Can activity C be delayed without delaying the entire project? If so, by how many weeks?

e. What is the schedule for activity E?

7. A project involving the installation of a computer system comprises eight activities. The following table lists immediate predecessors and activity times (in weeks).

Activity	Immediate Predecessor	Time
A	—	3
B	—	6
C	A	2
D	B, C	5
E	D	4
F	E	3
G	B, C	9
H	F, G	3

a. Draw a project network.

b. What are the critical activities?

c. What is the expected project completion time?

8. Colonial State College is considering building a new multipurpose athletic complex on campus. The complex would provide a new gymnasium for intercollegiate basketball games, expanded office space, classrooms, and intramural facilities. The following activities would have to be undertaken before construction can begin.

Activity	Description	Immediate Predecessor	Time (weeks)
A	Survey building site	—	6
B	Develop initial design	—	8
C	Obtain board approval	A, B	12
D	Select architect	C	4
E	Establish budget	C	6
F	Finalize design	D, E	15
G	Obtain financing	E	12
H	Hire contractor	F, G	8

a. Draw a project network.

b. Identify the critical path.

c. Develop the activity schedule for the project.

d. Does it appear reasonable that construction of the athletic complex could begin one year after the decision to begin the project with the site survey and initial design plans? What is the expected completion time for the project?

9. Hamilton County Parks is planning to develop a new park and recreational area on a recently purchased 100-acre tract. Project development activities include clearing playground and picnic areas, constructing roads, constructing a shelter house, purchasing picnic equipment, and so on. The following network and activity times (in weeks) are being used in the planning, scheduling, and controlling of this project.

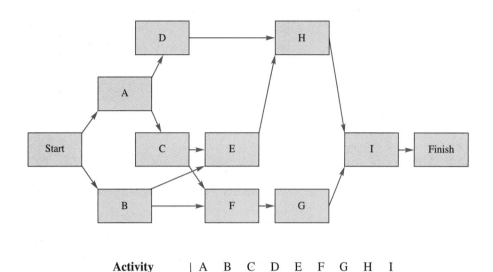

Activity	A	B	C	D	E	F	G	H	I
Activity Time	9	6	6	3	0	3	2	6	3

a. What is the critical path for this network?
b. Show the activity schedule for this project.
c. The park commissioner would like to open the park to the public within six months from the time the work on the project is started. Does this opening date appear to be feasible? Explain.

SELFtest   10. The following estimates of activity times (in days) are available for a small project.

Activity	Optimistic	Most Probable	Pessimistic
A	4	5.0	6
B	8	9.0	10
C	7	7.5	11
D	7	9.0	10
E	6	7.0	9
F	5	6.0	7

a. Compute the expected activity completion times and the variance for each activity.
b. An analyst determined that the critical path consists of activities B–D–F. Compute the expected project completion time and the variance.

11. Building a backyard swimming pool consists of nine major activities. The activities and their immediate predecessors are shown. Develop the project network.

Activity	A	B	C	D	E	F	G	H	I
Immediate Predecessor	—	—	A, B	A, B	B	C	D	D, F	E, G, H

12. Assume that the activity time estimates (in days) for the swimming pool construction project in Problem 11 are

Activity	Optimistic	Most Probable	Pessimistic
A	3	5	6
B	2	4	6
C	5	6	7
D	7	9	10
E	2	4	6
F	1	2	3
G	5	8	10
H	6	8	10
I	3	4	5

    a. What are the critical activities?
    b. What is the expected time to complete the project?
    c. What is the probability that the project can be completed in 25 or fewer days?

SELFtest **13.** Suppose that the following estimates of activity times (in weeks) were provided for the network shown in Problem 6.

Activity	Optimistic	Most Probable	Pessimistic
A	4.0	5.0	6.0
B	2.5	3.0	3.5
C	6.0	7.0	8.0
D	5.0	5.5	9.0
E	5.0	7.0	9.0
F	2.0	3.0	4.0
G	8.0	10.0	12.0
H	6.0	7.0	14.0

What is the probability that the project will be completed
    a. Within 21 weeks?
    b. Within 22 weeks?
    c. Within 25 weeks?

14. Consider the following project network.

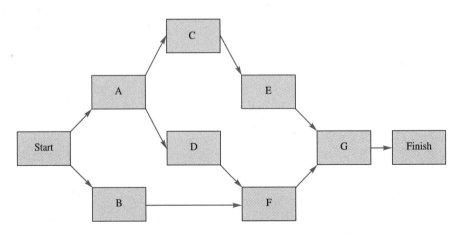

Estimates of the optimistic, most probable, and pessimistic times (in days) for the activities are

Activity	Optimistic	Most Probable	Pessimistic
A	5	6	7
B	5	12	13
C	6	8	10
D	4	10	10
E	5	6	13
F	7	7	10
G	4	7	10

a. Find the critical path.
b. How much slack time, if any, is in activity C?
c. Determine the expected project completion time and the variance.
d. Find the probability that the project will be completed in 30 or fewer days.

15. Doug Casey is in charge of planning and coordinating next spring's sales management training program for his company. Doug has listed the following activity information for this project.

Activity	Description	Immediate Predecessor	Time (weeks) Optimistic	Most Probable	Pessimistic
A	Plan topic	—	1.5	2.0	2.5
B	Obtain speakers	A	2.0	2.5	6.0
C	List meeting locations	—	1.0	2.0	3.0
D	Select location	C	1.5	2.0	2.5
E	Finalize speaker travel plans	B, D	0.5	1.0	1.5
F	Make final check with speakers	E	1.0	2.0	3.0
G	Prepare and mail brochure	B, D	3.0	3.5	7.0
H	Take reservations	G	3.0	4.0	5.0
I	Handle last-minute details	F, H	1.5	2.0	2.5

a. Draw a project network.
b. Prepare an activity schedule.
c. What are the critical activities and what is the expected project completion time?
d. If Doug wants a 0.99 probability of completing the project on time, how far ahead of the scheduled meeting date should he begin working on the project?

16. The Daugherty Porta-Vac project discussed in Section 12.2 had an expected project completion time of 17 weeks. The probability that the project could be completed in 20 weeks or less was 0.9656. The noncritical paths in the Porta-Vac project network are

A–D–G–J

A–C–F–J

B–H–I–J

a. Use the information in Table 12.5 to compute the expected time and variance for each path shown.

b. Compute the probability that each path will be completed in the desired 20-week period.

c. Why is the computation of the probability of completing a project on time based on the analysis of the critical path? In what case, if any, would making the probability computation for a noncritical path be desirable?

17. The Porsche Shop, founded in 1985 by Dale Jensen, specializes in the restoration of vintage Porsche automobiles. One of Jensen's regular customers asked him to prepare an estimate for the restoration of a 1964 model 356SC Porsche. To estimate the time and cost to perform such a restoration, Jensen broke the restoration process into four separate activities: disassembly and initial preparation work (A), body restoration (B), engine restoration (C), and final assembly (D). Once activity A has been completed, activities B and C can be performed independently of each other; however, activity D can be started only if both activities B and C have been completed. Based on his inspection of the car, Jensen believes that the following time estimates (in days) are applicable.

Activity	Optimistic	Most Probable	Pessimistic
A	3	4	8
B	5	8	11
C	2	4	6
D	4	5	12

Jensen estimates that the parts needed to restore the body will cost $3000 and that the parts needed to restore the engine will cost $5000. His current labor costs are $400 a day.

a. Develop a project network.

b. What is the expected project completion time?

c. Jensen's business philosophy is based on making decisions using a best- and worst-case scenario. Develop cost estimates for completing the restoration based on both a best- and worst-case analysis. Assume that the total restoration cost is the sum of the labor cost plus the material cost.

d. If Jensen obtains the job with a bid that is based on the costs associated with an expected completion time, what is the probability that he will lose money on the job?

e. If Jensen obtains the job based on a bid of $16,800, what is the probability that he will lose money on the job?

18. The manager of the Oak Hills Swimming Club is planning the club's swimming team program. The first team practice is scheduled for May 1. The activities, their immediate predecessors, and the activity time estimates (in weeks) are as follows.

Activity	Description	Immediate Predecessor	Time (weeks) Optimistic	Most Probable	Pessimistic
A	Meet with board	—	1	1	2
B	Hire coaches	A	4	6	8
C	Reserve pool	A	2	4	6
D	Announce program	B, C	1	2	3
E	Meet with coaches	B	2	3	4
F	Order team suits	A	1	2	3
G	Register swimmers	D	1	2	3
H	Collect fees	G	1	2	3
I	Plan first practice	E, H, F	1	1	1

    a. Draw a project network.

    b. Develop an activity schedule.

    c. What are the critical activities and what is the expected project completion time?

    d. If the club manager plans to start the project on February 1, what is the probability the swimming program will be ready by the scheduled May 1 date (13 weeks)? Should the manager begin planning the swimming program before February 1?

19. The product development group at Landon Corporation has been working on a new computer software product that has the potential to capture a large market share. Through outside sources, Landon's management has learned that a competitor is working to introduce a similar product. As a result, Landon's top management has increased its pressure on the product development group. The group's leader has turned to PERT/CPM as an aid to scheduling the activities remaining before the new product can be brought to the market. The project network is as follows.

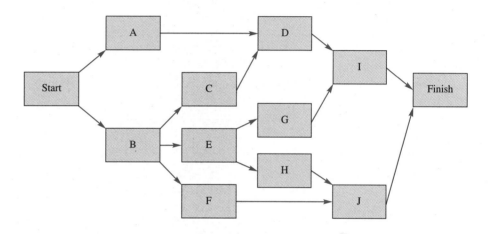

The activity time estimates (in weeks) are

Activity	Optimistic	Most Probable	Pessimistic
A	3.0	4.0	5.0
B	3.0	3.5	7.0
C	4.0	5.0	6.0
D	2.0	3.0	4.0
E	6.0	10.0	14.0
F	7.5	8.5	12.5
G	4.5	6.0	7.5
H	5.0	6.0	13.0
I	2.0	2.5	6.0
J	4.0	5.0	6.0

    a. Develop an activity schedule for this project and identify the critical path activities.

    b. What is the probability that the project will be completed so that Landon Corporation may introduce the new product within 25 weeks? Within 30 weeks?

20. Return to the computer installation project in Problem 7 and assume that the project has to be completed in 16 weeks. Crashing of the project is necessary. Use the following relevant information.

	Time (weeks)		Cost ($)	
Activity	Normal	Crash	Normal	Crash
A	3	1	900	1700
B	6	3	2000	4000
C	2	1	500	1000
D	5	3	1800	2400
E	4	3	1500	1850
F	3	1	3000	3900
G	9	4	8000	9800
H	3	2	1000	2000

a. Formulate a linear programming model that can be used to make the crashing decisions for this project.

b. Solve the linear programming model and make the minimum cost crashing decisions. What is the added cost of meeting the 16-week completion time?

c. Develop a complete activity schedule based on the crashed activity times.

SELFtest   21. Consider the following project network and activity times (in days).

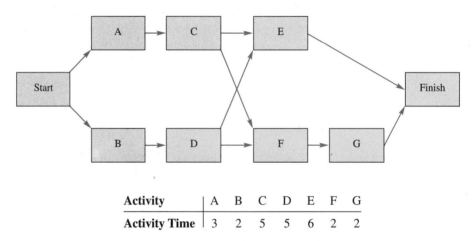

Activity	A	B	C	D	E	F	G
Activity Time	3	2	5	5	6	2	2

The crashing data for this project are as follows.

	Time (days)		Cost ($)	
Activity	Normal	Crash	Normal	Crash
A	3	2	800	1400
B	2	1	1200	1900
C	5	3	2000	2800
D	5	3	1500	2300
E	6	4	1800	2800
F	2	1	600	1000
G	2	1	500	1000

a. Find the critical path and the expected project completion time.

b. What is the total project cost using the normal times?

SELFtest   22. Refer to Problem 21. Assume that management desires a 12-day project completion time.
   a. Formulate a linear programming model that can be used to assist with the crashing
       decisions.
   b. What activities should be crashed?
   c. What is the total project cost for the 12-day completion time?

23. Consider the following project network. Note that the normal or expected activity
     times are denoted τ_i, $i = A, B, \ldots, I$. Let x_i = the earliest finish time for activity i. For-
     mulate a linear programming model that can be used to determine the length of the criti-
     cal path.

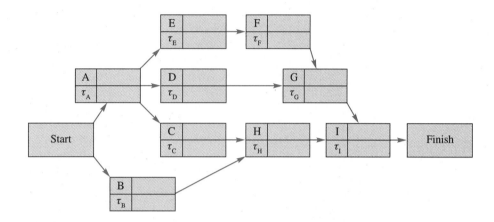

24. Office Automation, Inc., has developed a proposal for introducing a new computerized of-
     fice system that will improve word processing and interoffice communications for a par-
     ticular company. Contained in the proposal is a list of activities that must be accomplished
     to complete the new office system project. Use the following relevant information about
     the activities.

Activity	Description	Immediate Predecessor	Time (weeks)		Cost ($000s)	
			Normal	Crash	Normal	Crash
A	Plan needs	—	10	8	30	70
B	Order equipment	A	8	6	120	150
C	Install equipment	B	10	7	100	160
D	Set up training lab	A	7	6	40	50
E	Conduct training course	D	10	8	50	75
F	Test system	C, E	3	3	60	—

   a. Develop a project network.
   b. Develop an activity schedule.
   c. What are the critical activities and what is the expected project completion time?
   d. Assume that the company wants to complete the project in 6 months or 26 weeks.
       What crashing decisions do you recommend to meet the desired completion time at
       the least possible cost? Work through the network and attempt to make the crashing
       decisions by inspection.
   e. Develop an activity schedule for the crashed project.
   f. What added project cost is required to meet the 6-month completion time?

25. Because Landon Corporation (see Problem 19) is being pressured to complete the product development project at the earliest possible date, the project leader has requested that the possibility of crashing the project be evaluated.
  a. Formulate a linear programming model that could be used in making the crashing decisions.
  b. What information would have to be provided before the linear programming model could be implemented?

Case Problem   WAREHOUSE EXPANSION

R. C. Coleman distributes a variety of food products that are sold through grocery store and supermarket outlets. The company receives orders directly from the individual outlets, with a typical order requesting the delivery of several cases of anywhere from 20 to 50 different products. Under the company's current warehouse operation, warehouse clerks dispatch order-picking personnel to fill each order and have the goods moved to the warehouse shipping area. Because of the high labor costs and relatively low productivity of hand order-picking, management has decided to automate the warehouse operation by installing a computer-controlled order-picking system, along with a conveyor system for moving goods from storage to the warehouse shipping area.

R. C. Coleman's director of material management has been named the project manager in charge of the automated warehouse system. After consulting with members of the engineering staff and warehouse management personnel, the director has compiled a list of activities associated with the project. The optimistic, most probable, and pessimistic times (in weeks) have also been provided for each activity.

Activity	Description	Immediate Predecessor
A	Determine equipment needs	—
B	Obtain vendor proposals	—
C	Select vendor	A, B
D	Order system	C
E	Design new warehouse layout	C
F	Design warehouse	E
G	Design computer interface	C
H	Interface computer	D, F, G
I	Install system	D, F
J	Train system operators	H
K	Test system	I, J

	Time		
Activity	Optimistic	Most Probable	Pessimistic
A	4	6	8
B	6	8	16
C	2	4	6
D	8	10	24
E	7	10	13
F	4	6	8
G	4	6	20
H	4	6	8
I	4	6	14
J	3	4	5
K	2	4	6

Managerial Report

Develop a report that presents the activity schedule and expected project completion time for the warehouse expansion project. Include a project network in the report. In addition, take into consideration the following issues.

1. R. C. Coleman's top management has established a required 40-week completion time for the project. Can this completion time be achieved? Include probability information in your discussion. What recommendations do you have if the 40-week completion time is required?

2. Suppose that management requests that activity times be shortened to provide an 80% chance of meeting the 40-week completion time. If the variance in the project completion time is the same as you found in part (a), how much should the expected project completion time be shortened to achieve the goal of an 80% chance of completion within 40 weeks?

3. Using the expected activity times as the normal times and the following crashing information, determine the activity crashing decisions and revised activity schedule for the warehouse expansion project.

Activity	Crashed Activity Time (weeks)	Cost ($) Normal	Cost ($) Crashed
A	4	1,000	1,900
B	7	1,000	1,800
C	2	1,500	2,700
D	8	2,000	3,200
E	7	5,000	8,000
F	4	3,000	4,100
G	5	8,000	10,250
H	4	5,000	6,400
I	4	10,000	12,400
J	3	4,000	4,400
K	3	5,000	5,500

SEASONGOOD & MAYER

CINCINNATI, OHIO

Seasongood & Mayer, established in 1887, is an investment securities firm that engages in the following areas of municipal finance:

1. Underwriting new issues of municipal bonds
2. Trading—for example, acting as a market maker for the buying and selling of previously issued bonds
3. Investment banking—that is, the process of obtaining money from the capital markets at the lowest possible cost

The major applications of quantitative methods at Seasongood & Mayer are in the investment banking area. One particular application involved the use of PERT/CPM in the introduction of a $31 million hospital revenue bond issue.

Scheduling the Introduction of a Bond Issue

Any major building project involves certain common steps:

1. Defining the project
2. Determining the cost of the project
3. Financing the project

The investment banker's role in building projects is to develop the method of financing that will result in the owner's receiving the necessary funds in a timely manner. In a hospital building project, the typical method of financing is tax-free hospital revenue bonds.

The construction cost for the building project is an important factor in determining the best approach to financing. Normally, the construction cost is based on a bid submitted by a contractor or a construction manager. However, this cost is usually guaranteed only for a specified period of time, such as 60–90 days. The major function of the hospital's investment banker is to arrange the timing of the financing in such a way that the proceeds

of the bond issue can be made available within the time limit of the guaranteed-price construction bid. Since most hospitals must have the proceeds of their permanent long-term financing in hand prior to committing to major construction contracts, the investment banker's role is a significant one.

To arrange for the financing, the investment banker must coordinate the activities of hospital attorneys, the bond counsel, and so on. The cooperation of all parties and the coordination of project activities are best achieved if everyone recognizes the interdependency of the activities and the necessity of completing individual tasks in a timely manner. Seasongood & Mayer has found PERT/CPM to be useful in scheduling and coordinating such a project.

As managing underwriter for a $31,050,000 issue of Hospital Facilities Revenue Bonds for Providence Hospital in Hamilton County, Ohio, Seasongood & Mayer used the PERT/CPM critical path procedure to coordinate and schedule the project financing activities. Descriptions of the activities, times required, and immediate predecessors are given in Table 12.10. The project network is shown in Figure 12.17. The critical path activities K-L-M-N-P-Q-R-S-U-W resulted in a scheduled project completion time of 29.14 weeks. Specific schedules showing start and finish times for all activities were used to keep the entire project on track. The use of PERT/CPM was instrumental in helping Seasongood & Mayer obtain financing for this project within the time specified in the construction bid.

Questions

1. What is the role of the investment banker in building projects?
2. For the hospital project described, what is the primary objective of the investment banker?
3. Perform the critical path calculations for the project network shown in Figure 12.17. Is there more than one critical path? Discuss.

TABLE 12.10 ACTIVITIES FOR THE SEASONGOOD & MAYER PROJECT

Activity	Time Required (weeks)	Description of Activity	Immediate Predecessor
A	4	Drafting and distribution of legal documents	—
B	3	Preparation and distribution of unaudited financial statements of hospital	—
C	2	Drafting and distribution of hospital history, description of services, and existing facilities for Preliminary Official Statement (POS)	—
D	8	Drafting and distribution of demand portion of feasibility study	—
E	4	Review (additions/deletions) and approval as to form of legal documents	A
F	1	Review (additions/deletions) and approval of history, etc., for POS	C
G	4	Review (additions/deletions) and approval of demand portion of feasibility study	D
H	2	Drafting and distribution of financial portion (as to form) of feasibility study	E, G
I	2	Drafting and distribution of plan of financing and all pertinent facts relevant to the bond transaction for POS	E
J	0.5	Review and approval of unaudited financial statements	B
K	20	Receipt of firm price for project	—
L	1	Review (additions/deletions), approval, and completion of financial portion of feasibility study	H, K
M	1	Drafting of POS completed	F, I, J, L
N	0.14	Distribution of all material to bond rating services	M
O	0.28	Printing and distribution of POS to all interested parties	M
P	1	Presentation to bond rating services (Standard & Poor's, Moody's)	N
Q	1	Receipt of bond rating	P
R	2	Marketing of bonds	O, Q
S	0	Execution of Purchase Contract	R
T	0.14	Authorization and completion of Final Official Statement, completion of legal documents	S
U	3	Fulfillment of all terms and conditions of Purchase Contract	S
V	0	Bond proceeds available to hospital	T, U
W	0	Hospital able to sign construction contract	T, U

FIGURE 12.17 SEASONGOOD & MAYER PROJECT NETWORK

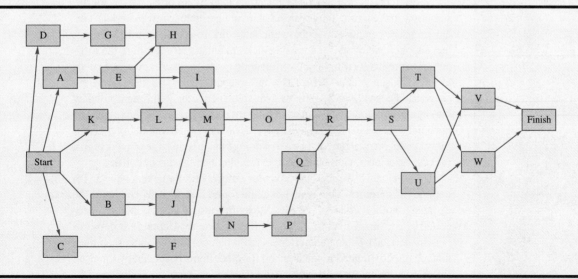

Chapter 13

INVENTORY MANAGEMENT: INDEPENDENT DEMAND

CONTENTS

Inventory refers to idle goods or materials held by an organization for use sometime in the future. Items carried in inventory include raw materials, purchased parts, components, subassemblies, work-in-process, finished goods, and supplies. Some reasons organizations maintain inventory are the difficulties in predicting sales levels, production times, demand, and usage needs exactly. Thus, inventory serves as a buffer against uncertain and fluctuating usage and keeps a supply of items available in case the items are needed by the organization or its customers. While inventory serves an important and essential role, the expense associated with financing and maintaining inventories is a substantial part of the cost of doing business. In large organizations, the cost associated with inventory can run into the millions of dollars.

In this chapter, we consider inventory models for items that have an **independent demand.** That is, the demand for an item is independent of the demand for other products or items. Most often independent demand is generated by customers placing orders for finished goods. **Dependent demand** is characterized by demand for items such as components and subassemblies that are directly related to the demand for other items produced by the firm. We discuss inventory management with dependent demand in Chapter 14.

Independent demand does not depend on demand for other items produced by the firm. The topic of inventory management with dependent demand is discussed in Chapter 14.

In applications involving inventory management with independent demand, managers must answer two important questions.

1. *How much* should be ordered when the inventory is replenished?
2. *When* should the inventory be replenished?

The purpose of this chapter is to show how quantitative models can assist in making these decisions.

We will first consider *deterministic* inventory models in which we assume that the rate of demand for the item is constant or nearly constant. Later we will consider *probabilistic* inventory models in which the demand for the item fluctuates and can be described only in probabilistic terms.

13.1   ECONOMIC ORDER QUANTITY (EOQ) MODEL

The cost associated with developing and maintaining inventory is larger than many people think. Models such as the ones presented in this chapter can be used to develop cost-effective inventory management decisions.

The **economic order quantity (EOQ)** model is applicable when the demand for an item has a constant, or nearly constant, rate and when the entire quantity ordered arrives in inventory at one point in time. The **constant demand rate** assumption means that the same number of units is taken from inventory each period of time such as 5 units every day, 25 units every week, 100 units every 4-week period, and so on.

To illustrate the EOQ model, let us consider the situation faced by the R & B Beverage Company. R & B Beverage is a distributor of beer, wine, and soft drink products. From a main warehouse located in Columbus, Ohio, R & B supplies nearly 1000 retail stores with beverage products. The beer inventory, which constitutes about 40% of the company's total inventory, averages approximately 50,000 cases. With an average cost per case of approximately $8, R & B estimates the value of its beer inventory to be $400,000.

The warehouse manager has decided to do a detailed study of the inventory costs associated with Bub Beer, the number-one-selling R & B beer. The purpose of the study is to establish the *how-much*-to-order and the *when*-to-order decisions for Bub Beer that will result in the lowest possible total cost. As the first step in the study, the warehouse manager has obtained the following demand data for the past 10 weeks:

One of the most criticized assumptions of the EOQ model is the constant demand rate. Obviously, the model would be inappropriate for items with widely fluctuating and variable demand rates. However, as this example attempts to show, the EOQ model can provide a realistic approximation of the optimal order quantity when demand is relatively stable and occurs at a nearly constant rate.

Week	Demand (cases)
1	2,000
2	2,025
3	1,950
4	2,000
5	2,100
6	2,050
7	2,000
8	1,975
9	1,900
10	2,000
Total cases	20,000
Average cases per week	2,000

Strictly speaking, these weekly demand figures do not show a constant demand rate. However, given the relatively low variability exhibited by the weekly demand, inventory planning with a constant demand rate of 2000 cases per week appears acceptable. In practice, you will find that the actual inventory situation seldom, if ever, satisfies the assumptions of the model exactly. Thus, in any particular application, the manager must determine whether the model assumptions are close enough to reality for the model to be useful. In this situation, because demand varies from a low of 1900 cases to a high of 2100 cases, the assumption of constant demand of 2000 cases per week appears to be a reasonable approximation.

The how-much-to-order decision involves selecting an order quantity that draws a compromise between (1) keeping small inventories and ordering frequently and (2) keeping large inventories and ordering infrequently. The first alternative can result in undesirably high ordering costs, while the second alternative can result in undesirably high inventory holding costs. To find an optimal compromise between these conflicting alternatives, let us consider a mathematical model that shows the total cost as the sum of the holding cost and the ordering cost.[1]

Holding costs are the costs associated with maintaining or carrying a given level of inventory; these costs depend on the size of the inventory. The first holding cost to consider is the cost of financing the inventory investment. When a firm borrows money, it incurs an interest charge. If the firm uses its own money, it experiences an opportunity cost associated with not being able to use the money for other investments. In either case, an interest cost exists for the capital tied up in inventory. This **cost of capital** is usually expressed as a percentage of the amount invested. R & B estimates its cost of capital at an annual rate of 18%.

As with other quantitative models, accurate estimates of cost parameters are critical. In the EOQ model, estimates of both the inventory holding cost and the ordering cost are needed. Also see footnote 1, which refers to relevant costs.

A number of other holding costs such as insurance, taxes, breakage, pilferage, and warehouse overhead also depend on the value of the inventory. R & B estimates these other costs at an annual rate of approximately 7% of the value of its inventory. Thus, the total holding cost for the R & B beer inventory is 25% of the value of the inventory.

Assume that the cost of one case of Bub Beer is $8. If R & B estimates its annual holding cost to be 25% of the value of its inventory, the cost of holding one case of Bub Beer in inventory for 1 year is 0.25($8) = $2.00. Note that defining the holding cost as a percentage of the value of the product is convenient because it is easily transferable to other products. For example, a case of Carle's Red Ribbon Beer, which costs $7.00 per case, would have an annual holding cost of 0.25($7.00) = $1.75 per case.

The next step in the inventory analysis is to determine the **ordering cost.** This cost, which is considered fixed regardless of the order quantity, covers the preparation of the voucher, the processing of the order including payment, postage, telephone, transportation, invoice verification, receiving, and so on. For R & B Beverage, the largest portion of the ordering cost involves the salaries of the purchasers. An analysis of the purchasing process showed that a purchaser spends approximately 45 minutes preparing and processing an order for Bub Beer. With a wage rate and fringe benefit cost for purchasers of $20 per hour, the labor portion of the ordering cost is $15. Making allowances for paper, postage, telephone, transportation, and receiving costs at $17 per order, the manager estimates that the ordering cost is $32 per order. That is, R & B is paying $32 per order regardless of the quantity requested in the order.

The holding cost, ordering cost, and demand information are the three data items that must be known prior to the use of the EOQ model. After developing these data for the R & B problem, we can look at how they are used to develop a total cost model. We begin by defining Q to be the order quantity. Thus, the how-much-to-order decision involves finding the value of Q that will minimize the sum of holding and ordering costs.

The inventory for Bub Beer will have a maximum value of Q units when an order of size Q is received from the supplier. R & B will then satisfy customer demand from inventory until the inventory is depleted, at which time another shipment of Q units will be received. Thus, assuming a constant demand, the graph of the inventory for Bub Beer is as shown in Figure 13.1. Note that the graph indicates an average inventory of $\frac{1}{2}Q$ for the period in question. This level should appear reasonable because the maximum inventory is Q, the minimum is zero, and the inventory declines at a constant rate over the period.

---

1. While quantitative analysts typically refer to "total-cost" models for inventory systems, often these models describe only the total *variable* or total *relevant* costs for the decision being considered. Costs that are not affected by the how-much-to-order decision are considered fixed or constant and are not included in the model.

FIGURE 13.1   INVENTORY FOR BUB BEER

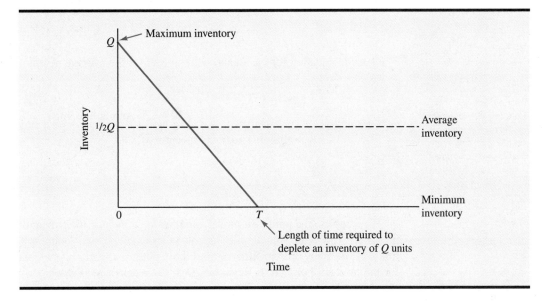

Figure 13.1 shows the inventory pattern during one order cycle of length *T*. As time goes on, this pattern will repeat. The complete inventory pattern is shown in Figure 13.2. If the average inventory during each cycle is ½*Q*, the average inventory over any number of cycles is also ½*Q*.

Most inventory cost models use an annual *cost. Thus, demand should be expressed in units per year and inventory holding cost should be based on an annual rate.*

The holding cost can be calculated using the average inventory. That is, we can calculate the holding cost by multiplying the average inventory by the cost of carrying one unit in inventory for the stated period. The period selected for the model is up to you; it could be 1 week, 1 month, 1 year, or more. However, because the holding cost for many industries and businesses is expressed as an *annual* percentage, most inventory models are developed on an *annual* cost basis.

Let

$$I = \text{annual holding cost rate}$$

$$C = \text{unit cost of the inventory item}$$

$$C_h = \text{annual cost of holding one unit in inventory}$$

FIGURE 13.2   INVENTORY PATTERN FOR THE EOQ INVENTORY MODEL

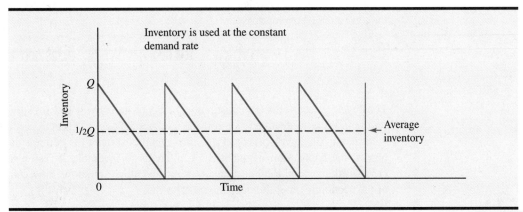

The annual cost of holding one unit in inventory is

$$C_h = IC \tag{13.1}$$

The general equation for the annual holding cost for the average inventory of $\frac{1}{2}Q$ units is as follows:

$$\begin{matrix} \text{Annual} \\ \text{holding cost} \end{matrix} = \begin{pmatrix} \text{Average} \\ \text{inventory} \end{pmatrix}\begin{pmatrix} \text{Annual holding} \\ \text{cost} \\ \text{per unit} \end{pmatrix}$$

$$= \frac{1}{2} QC_h \tag{13.2}$$

To complete the total cost model, we must now include the annual ordering cost. The goal is to express the annual ordering cost in terms of the order quantity Q. The first question is, How many orders will be placed during the year? Let D denote the annual demand for the product. For R & B Beverage, $D = (52 \text{ weeks})(2000 \text{ cases per week}) = 104,000$ cases per year. We know that by ordering Q units every time we order, we will have to place D/Q orders per year. If C_o is the cost of placing one order, the general equation for the annual ordering cost is as follows:

$$\begin{matrix} \text{Annual} \\ \text{ordering cost} \end{matrix} = \begin{pmatrix} \text{Number of} \\ \text{orders} \\ \text{per year} \end{pmatrix}\begin{pmatrix} \text{Cost} \\ \text{per} \\ \text{order} \end{pmatrix}$$

$$= \left(\frac{D}{Q}\right)C_o \tag{13.3}$$

Thus, the total annual cost, denoted TC, can be expressed as follows:

$$\begin{matrix} \text{Total} \\ \text{annual} \\ \text{cost} \end{matrix} = \begin{matrix} \text{Annual} \\ \text{holding} \\ \text{cost} \end{matrix} + \begin{matrix} \text{Annual} \\ \text{ordering} \\ \text{cost} \end{matrix}$$

$$TC = \frac{1}{2} QC_h + \frac{D}{Q} C_o \tag{13.4}$$

Using the Bub Beer data [$C_h = IC = (0.25)(\$8) = \$2$, $C_o = \$32$, and $D = 104,000$], the total annual cost model is

$$TC = \frac{1}{2} Q(\$2) + \frac{104,000}{Q} (\$32) = Q + \frac{3,328,000}{Q}$$

The development of the total cost model has gone a long way toward solving the inventory problem. We now are able to express the total annual cost as a function of *how much* should be ordered. The development of a realistic total cost model is perhaps the most important part of the application of quantitative methods to inventory decision making. Equation (13.4) is the general total cost equation for inventory situations in which the assumptions of the economic order quantity model are valid.

The How-Much-to-Order Decision

The next step is to find the order quantity Q that will minimize the total annual cost for Bub Beer. Using a trial-and-error approach, we can compute the total annual cost for several possible order quantities. As a starting point, let us consider $Q = 8000$. The total annual cost for Bub Beer is

$$TC = Q + \frac{3{,}328{,}000}{Q}$$

$$= 8000 + \frac{3{,}328{,}000}{8000} = \$8416$$

A trial order quantity of 5000 gives

$$TC = 5000 + \frac{3{,}328{,}000}{5000} = \$5666$$

The results of several other trial order quantities are shown in Table 13.1. As can be seen, the lowest cost solution is around 2000 cases. Graphs of the annual holding and ordering costs, and total annual costs are shown in Figure 13.3.

The advantage of the trial-and-error approach is that it is rather easy to do and provides the total annual cost for a number of possible order quantity decisions. In this case, the minimum cost order quantity appears to be approximately 2000 cases. The disadvantage of this approach, however, is that it does not provide the exact minimum cost order quantity.

The EOQ formula determines the optimal order quantity by balancing the annual holding cost and the annual ordering cost.

Refer to Figure 13.3. The minimum total cost order quantity is denoted by an order size of Q^*. By using differential calculus, it can be shown (see Appendix 13.2) that the value of Q^* that minimizes the total annual cost is given by the formula

In 1915 F. W. Harris derived the mathematical formula for the economic order quantity. It was the first application of quantitative methods to the area of inventory management.

$$Q^* = \sqrt{\frac{2DC_o}{C_h}} \tag{13.5}$$

This formula is referred to as the *economic order quantity (EOQ) formula.*

Using equation (13.5), the minimum total annual cost order quantity for Bub Beer is

$$Q^* = \sqrt{\frac{2(104{,}000)32}{2}} = 1824 \text{ cases}$$

TABLE 13.1   ANNUAL HOLDING, ORDERING, AND TOTAL COSTS FOR VARIOUS ORDER QUANTITIES OF BUB BEER

| | Annual Cost | | |
Order Quantity	Holding	Ordering	Total
5000	$5000	$ 666	$5666
4000	4000	832	4832
3000	3000	1109	4109
2000	2000	1664	3664
1000	1000	3328	4328

FIGURE 13.3   ANNUAL HOLDING, ORDERING, AND TOTAL COSTS FOR BUB BEER

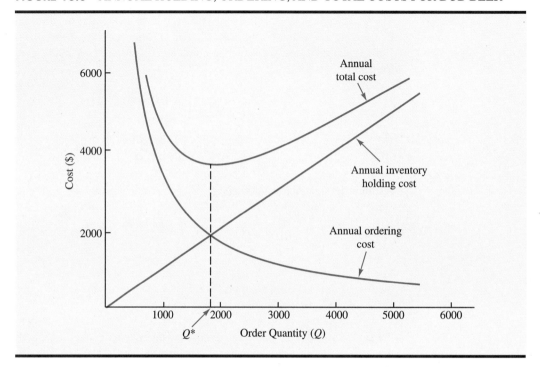

Problem 2 at the end of the chapter asks you to show that equal holding and ordering costs is a property of the EOQ model.

The use of an order quantity of 1824 in equation (13.4) shows that the minimum cost inventory policy for Bub Beer has a total annual cost of $3649. Note that $Q^* = 1824$ has balanced the holding and ordering costs. Check for yourself to see that these costs are equal.[2]

The When-to-Order Decision

Now that we know how much to order, we want to address the question of *when* to order. To answer this question, we need to introduce the concept of inventory position. The **inventory position** is defined as the amount of inventory on hand plus the amount of inventory on order. The when-to-order decision is expressed in terms of a **reorder point**—the inventory position at which a new order should be placed.

The reorder point is expressed in terms of inventory position, the amount of inventory on hand plus the amount on order. Some people think that the reorder point is expressed in terms of inventory on hand. With short lead times, inventory position is usually the same as the inventory on hand. However, with long lead times, inventory position may be larger than inventory on hand.

The manufacturer of Bub Beer guarantees a 2-day delivery on any order placed by R & B Beverage. Hence, assuming R & B Beverage operates 250 days per year, the annual demand of 104,000 cases implies a daily demand of $104,000/250 = 416$ cases. Thus, we expect (2 days)(416 cases per day) = 832 cases of Bub to be sold during the 2 days it takes a new order to reach the R & B warehouse. In inventory terminology, the 2-day delivery period is referred to as the **lead time** for a new order, and the 832-case demand anticipated during this period is referred to as the **lead-time demand.** Thus, R & B should order a new shipment of Bub Beer from the manufacturer when the inventory reaches 832 cases. For inventory systems using the constant demand rate assumption and a fixed lead time, the reorder point is the same as the lead-time demand. For these systems, the general expression for the reorder point is as follows:

$$r = dm \tag{13.6}$$

2. Actually, Q^* from equation (13.5) is 1824.28, but because we cannot order fractional cases of beer, a Q^* of 1824 is shown. This value of Q^* may cause a few cents deviation between the two costs. If Q^* is used at its exact value, the holding and ordering costs will be exactly the same.

where

$$r = \text{reorder point}$$

$$d = \text{demand per day}$$

$$m = \text{lead time for a new order in days}$$

The cycle time can be expressed in years with T = Q*/D. Because inventory managers may wish to think of cycle time in other units, T can be adjusted to months by multiplying by 12; to weeks by multiplying by 52; or as we show, to days by multiplying by the number of working days per year, which may vary from firm to firm.

The question of how frequently the order will be placed can now be answered. The period between orders is referred to as the **cycle time.** Previously in equation (13.2), we defined D/Q as the number of orders that will be placed in a year. Thus, $D/Q^* = 104,000/1824 = 57$ is the number of orders R & B Beverage will place for Bub Beer each year. If R & B places 57 orders over 250 working days, it will order approximately every $250/57 = 4.39$ working days. Thus, the cycle time is 4.39 working days. The general expression for a cycle time[3] of T days is given by

$$T = \frac{250}{D/Q^*} = \frac{250Q^*}{D} \tag{13.7}$$

Sensitivity Analysis in the EOQ Model

Even though substantial time may have been spent in arriving at the cost per order ($32) and the holding cost rate (25%), we should realize that these figures are at best good estimates. Thus, we may want to consider how much the recommended order quantity would change if the estimated ordering and holding costs had been different. To determine the effects of various cost scenarios, we can calculate the recommended order quantity under several different cost conditions. Table 13.2 shows the minimum total cost order quantity for several cost possibilities. As you can see from the table, the value of Q^* appears relatively stable, even with some variations in the cost estimates. Based on these results, the best order quantity for Bub Beer is somewhere around 1700–2000 cases. If operated properly, the total cost for the Bub Beer inventory system should be close to $3400–$3800 per year. We also note that little risk is associated with implementing the calculated order quantity of 1824. For example, if holding cost rate = 24%, C_o = $34, and the true optimal order quantity Q^* = 1919, R & B experiences only a $5 increase in the total annual cost; that is, $3690 − $3685 = $5, with Q = 1824.

From the preceding analysis, we would say that this EOQ model is insensitive to small variations or errors in the cost estimates. This insensitivity is a property of EOQ models in

TABLE 13.2   OPTIMAL ORDER QUANTITIES FOR SEVERAL COST POSSIBILITIES

Possible Inventory Holding Cost (%)	Possible Cost per Order	Optimal Order Quantity (Q^*)	Projected Total Annual Cost	
			Using Q^*	Using Q = 1824
24	$30	1803	$3461	$3462
24	34	1919	3685	3690
26	30	1732	3603	3607
26	34	1844	3835	3836

3. This general expression for cycle time is based on 250 working days per year. If the firm operated 300 working days per year and wanted to express cycle time in terms of working days, the cycle time would be given by $T = 300Q^*/D$.

general, which indicates that if we have at least reasonable estimates of ordering cost and holding cost, we can expect to obtain a good approximation of the true minimum cost order quantity.

Managers' Use of the EOQ Model

The EOQ model results in a recommended order quantity of 1824 units. Is this quantity the final decision, or should the manager's judgment enter into the establishment of the final inventory policy? Although the model has provided a good order quantity recommendation, it may not have taken into account all aspects of the inventory situation. As a result, the decision maker may want to modify the final order quantity recommendation to meet the unique circumstances of the inventory situation. In this case, the warehouse manager felt that increasing the order quantity from 1824 cases to 2000 cases to have an order quantity equal to 5 working days' demand would be desirable. By doing so, R & B Beverage can maintain a weekly order cycle.

The total cost curve in Figure 13.3 is relatively flat near the value of Q*. Consequently, the inventory manager can adjust the EOQ slightly to a more convenient level without seriously affecting the total cost.

    The warehouse manager also realized that the EOQ model was based on the constant demand rate assumption of 104,000 cases per year or 416 cases per day. While this rate is a good approximation, we must also recognize that sometimes the demand exceeds 432 cases per day. If a reorder point of 832 cases is used, we would be expecting an 832-case demand during the lead time and the new order to arrive exactly when the inventory reached zero. Such close timing would have little room for error, and the scheduling of arrivals would be critical if stockouts (shortages) were to be avoided. To protect against shortages due to higher-than-expected demands or slightly delayed incoming orders, the warehouse manager recommended a 3-day, 1248-case reorder point. Thus, under normal conditions, R & B Beverage will order 2000 cases of Bub whenever the current inventory reaches 1248 cases. During the expected 2-day lead time, 832 cases should be demanded, and 416 cases should be in inventory when an order arrives. The extra 416 cases serve as a safety precaution against a higher-than-expected demand or a delayed incoming order. In general, the amount by which the reorder point exceeds the expected lead-time demand is referred to as **safety stock.**

    The decisions to adjust the order quantity and reorder point were purely judgment decisions and were not necessarily made with a minimum cost objective in mind. However, they are examples of how managerial judgment might interface with the inventory decision model to arrive at a sound inventory policy. The final decision of $Q = 2000$ with a 416-case safety stock resulted in a total annual cost of $4528.[4]

How Has the EOQ Model Helped?

The EOQ model has objectively included holding and ordering costs and, with the aid of some management judgment, has led to a low-cost inventory policy. In addition, the general optimal order quantity model, equation (13.5), is applicable to other R & B products. For example, Red Ribbon Beer ($7 per case), which has an ordering cost of $32, a constant demand rate of 62,400 cases per year, and a 2-day lead time, has a recommended order quantity of

$$Q^* = \sqrt{\frac{2(62,400)(32)}{(0.25)(7)}} = 1511 \text{ cases}$$

Problem 1 provides practice in applying the EOQ model to another R & B product.

a cycle time of $T = [250(1511)]/62,400 = 6.05$ days, and a reorder point of $r = (62,400/250)(2) = 499.2$ cases.

---

4. A Q of 2000 units resulted in a total cost of $3664 (see Table 13.1). The additional safety stock inventory of 432 units increases the average inventory by 432 units because it is on hand all year long. Thus, the inventory carrying charge is increased by 2(432) = $864, the total cost of the revised policy is $3664 + $864 = $4528.

Summary of the EOQ Model Assumptions

You should carefully review the assumptions of the inventory model before applying it in an actual situation. Several inventory models discussed later in this chapter alter one or more of the assumptions of the EOQ model.

To use the optimal order quantity and reorder point model described here, an analyst must make assumptions about how the inventory system operates. The EOQ model with its economic order quantity formula is based on some specific assumptions about the R & B inventory system. A summary of the assumptions for this model is provided in Table 13.3. Before using the EOQ formula, carefully review these assumptions to ensure that they are applicable to the inventory system being analyzed. If the assumptions are not reasonable, seek a different inventory model.

Various types of inventory systems are used in practice, and the inventory models presented in the following sections alter one or more of the EOQ model assumptions shown in Table 13.3 to meet the needs of the different systems. When the assumptions change, a different inventory model with different optimal operating policies becomes necessary.

TABLE 13.3   SUMMARY OF THE EOQ MODEL ASSUMPTIONS

1. Demand D is deterministic and occurs at a constant rate.
2. The order quantity Q is the same for each order. The inventory level increases by Q units each time an order is received.
3. The cost per order, C_o, is constant and does not depend on the quantity ordered.
4. The purchase cost per unit, C, is constant and does not depend on the quantity ordered.
5. The inventory holding cost per unit per time period, C_h, is constant. The total inventory holding cost depends on both C_h and the size of the inventory.
6. Shortages such as stockouts or backorders are not permitted.
7. The lead time for an order is constant.
8. The inventory position is reviewed continuously. As a result, an order is placed as soon as the inventory position reaches the reorder point.

NOTES AND COMMENTS

With relatively long lead times, the lead-time demand and the resulting reorder point r, determined by equation (13.6), may exceed Q^*. If this condition occurs, at least one order will be outstanding when a new order is placed. For example, assume that Bub Beer has a lead time of $m = 6$ days. With a daily demand of $d = 432$ cases, equation (13.6) shows that the reorder point would be $r = dm = 6 \times 432 = 2592$ cases. Thus, a new order for Bub Beer should be placed whenever the inventory position (the amount of inventory on hand plus the amount of inventory on order) reaches 2592. With an order quantity of $Q = 2000$ cases, the inventory position of 2592 cases occurs when one order of 2000 cases is outstanding and $2592 - 2000 = 592$ cases are on hand.

13.2   ECONOMIC PRODUCTION LOT-SIZE MODEL

The inventory model in this section alters assumption 2 of the EOQ model (see Table 13.3). The assumption concerning the arrival of Q units each time an order is received is changed to a constant production supply rate.

The inventory model presented in this section is similar to the EOQ model in that we are attempting to determine *how much* we should order and *when* the order should be placed. We again assume a constant demand rate. However, instead of assuming that the goods arrive in a shipment of size Q^*, as in the EOQ model, we assume that units are supplied to inventory at a constant rate over several days or several weeks. The **constant supply rate** assumption implies that the same number of units is supplied to inventory each period of time (e.g., 10 units every day or 50 units every week). This model is designed for production situations in which, once an order is placed, production begins and a constant number of units is added to inventory each day until the production run has been completed.

If we have a production system that produces 50 units per day and we decide to schedule 10 days of production, we have a 50(10) = 500-unit production lot size. The **lot size** is the number of units in an order. In general, if we let Q indicate the production lot size, the approach to the inventory decisions is similar to the EOQ model; that is, we build a holding and ordering cost model that expresses the total cost as a function of the production lot size. Then we attempt to find the production lot size that minimizes the total cost.

One other condition that should be mentioned at this time is that the model only applies to situations where the production rate is greater than the demand rate; the production system must be able to satisfy demand. For instance, if the constant demand rate is 400 units per day, the production rate must be at least 400 units per day to satisfy demand.

During the production run, demand will be reducing the inventory while production will be adding to inventory. Because we have assumed that the production rate exceeds the demand rate, each day during a production run we will be producing more units than are demanded. Thus, the excess production will cause a gradual inventory buildup during the production period. When the production run is completed, the continuing demand will cause the inventory to gradually decline until a new production run is started. The inventory pattern for this system is shown in Figure 13.4.

This model differs from the EOQ model in that a setup cost replaces the ordering cost and the saw-tooth inventory pattern shown in Figure 13.4 differs from the inventory pattern shown in Figure 13.2.

As in the EOQ model, we are now dealing with two costs, the holding cost and the ordering cost. While the holding cost is identical to the definition in the EOQ model, the interpretation of the ordering cost is slightly different. In fact, in a production situation the ordering cost is more correctly referred to as the production **setup cost.** This cost, which includes labor, material, and lost production costs incurred while preparing the production system for operation, is a fixed cost that occurs for every production run regardless of the production lot size.

Total Cost Model

Let us begin building the production lot size model by writing the holding cost in terms of the production lot size Q. Again, the approach is to develop an expression for average inventory and then establish the holding costs associated with the average inventory. We use a 1-year time period and an annual cost for the model.

In the EOQ model the average inventory is one-half the maximum inventory or $\frac{1}{2}Q$. Figure 13.4 shows that for a production lot size model a constant inventory buildup rate occurs during the production run and a constant inventory depletion rate occurs during the nonproduction period; thus, the average inventory will be one-half the maximum inventory.

FIGURE 13.4   INVENTORY PATTERN FOR THE PRODUCTION LOT SIZE
INVENTORY MODEL

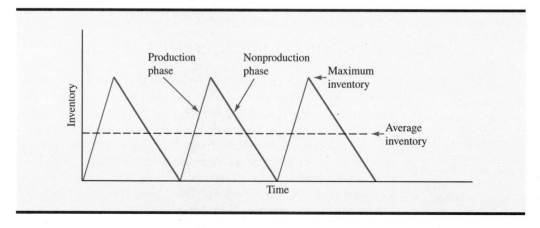

However, in this inventory system the production lot size Q does not go into inventory at one point in time, and thus the inventory never reaches a level of Q units.

To show how we can compute the maximum inventory, let

$$d = \text{daily demand rate}$$

$$p = \text{daily production rate}$$

$$t = \text{number of days for a production run}$$

At this point, the logic of the production lot size model is easier to follow using a daily demand rate d and a daily production rate p. However, when the total annual cost model is eventually developed (see equation 13.15), we recommend that inputs to the model be expressed in terms of the annual demand rate D and the annual production rate P.

Because we are assuming that p will be larger than d, the daily inventory buildup rate during the production phase is $p - d$. If we run production for t days and place $p - d$ units in inventory each day, the inventory at the end of the production run will be $(p - d)t$. From Figure 13.4 we can see that the inventory at the end of the production run is also the maximum inventory. Thus

$$\text{Maximum inventory} = (p - d)t \tag{13.8}$$

If we know we are producing a production lot size of Q units at a daily production rate of p units, then $Q = pt$, and the length of the production run t must be

$$t = \frac{Q}{P} \text{ days} \tag{13.9}$$

Thus

$$\text{Maximum inventory} = (p - d)t = (p - d)\left(\frac{Q}{p}\right)$$

$$= \left(1 - \frac{d}{p}\right)Q \tag{13.10}$$

The average inventory, which is one-half the maximum inventory, is given by

$$\text{Average inventory} = \frac{1}{2}\left(1 - \frac{d}{p}\right)Q \tag{13.11}$$

With an annual per unit holding cost of C_h, the general equation for annual holding cost is as follows:

$$\text{Annual holding cost} = \left(\begin{array}{c}\text{Average} \\ \text{inventory}\end{array}\right)\left(\begin{array}{c}\text{Annual} \\ \text{cost} \\ \text{per unit}\end{array}\right)$$

$$= \frac{1}{2}\left(1 - \frac{d}{p}\right)QC_h \tag{13.12}$$

If D is the annual demand for the product and C_o is the setup cost for a production run, then the annual setup cost, which takes the place of the annual ordering cost in the EOQ model, is as follows:

$$\text{Annual setup cost} = \left(\begin{array}{c}\text{Number of production} \\ \text{runs per year}\end{array}\right)\left(\begin{array}{c}\text{Setup cost} \\ \text{per run}\end{array}\right)$$

$$= \frac{D}{Q}C_o \tag{13.13}$$

Thus, the total annual cost (TC) model is

$$TC = \frac{1}{2}\left(1 - \frac{d}{p}\right)QC_h + \frac{D}{Q}C_o \tag{13.14}$$

Suppose that a production facility operates 250 days per year. Then we can write daily demand d in terms of annual demand D as follows:

$$d = \frac{D}{250}$$

Now let P denote the annual production for the product if the product were produced every day. Then

$$P = 250p \quad \text{and} \quad p = \frac{P}{250}$$

Thus[5]

$$\frac{d}{p} = \frac{D/250}{P/250} = \frac{D}{P}$$

Therefore, we can write the total annual cost model as follows:

$$TC = \frac{1}{2}\left(1 - \frac{D}{P}\right)QC_h + \frac{D}{Q}C_o \tag{13.15}$$

Equations (13.14) and (13.15) are equivalent. However, equation (13.15) may be used more frequently because an *annual* cost model tends to make the analyst think in terms of collecting *annual* demand data (D) and *annual* production data (P) rather than daily data.

Finding the Economic Production Lot Size

Given estimates of the holding cost (C_h), setup cost (C_o), annual demand rate (D), and annual production rate (P), we could use a trial-and-error approach to compute the total annual cost for various production lot sizes (Q). However, this trial-and-error is not necessary; we can use the minimum cost formula for Q^* that has been developed using differential calculus (see Appendix 13.3). The equation is as follows:

As the production rate P approaches infinity, D/P approaches zero. In this case, equation (13.16) is equivalent to the EOQ model in equation (13.5).

$$Q^* = \sqrt{\frac{2DC_o}{(1 - D/P)C_h}} \tag{13.16}$$

An Example. Beauty Bar Soap is produced on a production line that has an annual capacity of 60,000 cases. The annual demand is estimated at 26,000 cases, with the demand rate essentially constant throughout the year. The cleaning, preparation, and setup of the production line cost approximately $135. The manufacturing cost per case is $4.50, and the annual holding cost is figured at a 24% rate. Thus, $C_h = IC = 0.24(\$4.50) = \$1.08$. What is the recommended production lot size?

---

5. The ratio $d/p = D/P$ holds regardless of the number of days of operation; 250 days is used here merely as an illustration.

Using equation (13.16), we have

$$Q^* = \sqrt{\frac{2(26,000)(135)}{(1 - 26,000/60,000)(1.08)}} = 3387$$

The total annual cost using equation (13.15) and $Q^* = 3387$ is \$2073.

Work Problem 13 as an example of an economic production lot size model.

Other relevant data include a 5-day lead time to schedule and set up a production run and 250 working days per year. Thus, the lead-time demand of $(26,000/250)(5) = 520$ cases is the reorder point. The cycle time is the time between production runs. Using equation (13.7), the cycle time is $T = 250Q^*/D = [(250)(3387)]/26,000$, or 33 working days. Thus, we should plan a production run of 3387 units every 33 working days.

Certainly the manager will want to review the model recommendations. Adjusting the recommended $Q^* = 3387$ to a slightly different figure and/or adding safety stock may be desirable.

13.3   INVENTORY MODEL WITH PLANNED SHORTAGES

A **shortage** or **stockout** is a demand that cannot be supplied. In many situations, shortages are undesirable and should be avoided if at all possible. However, in other cases it may be desirable—from an economic point of view—to plan for and allow shortages. In practice, these types of situations are most commonly found where the value of the inventory per unit is high and hence the holding cost is high. An example of this type of situation is a new car dealer's inventory. Often a specific car that a customer wants may not be in stock. However, if the customer is willing to wait a few weeks, the dealer is usually able to order it.

The assumptions of the EOQ model in Table 13.3 apply to this inventory model with the exception that shortages, referred to as backorders, *are now permitted.*

The model developed in this section takes into account a type of shortage known as a **backorder.** In a backorder situation, we assume that when a customer places an order and discovers that the supplier is out of stock, the customer waits until the new shipment arrives, and then the order is filled. Frequently, the waiting period in backordering situations is relatively short. Thus, by promising the customer top priority and immediate delivery when the goods become available, companies may be able to convince the customer to wait until the order arrives. In these cases, the backorder assumption is valid.

The backorder model that we develop is an extension of the EOQ model presented in Section 13.1. We use the EOQ model in which all goods arrive in inventory at one time and are subject to a constant demand rate (see Table 13.3 for a summary of the EOQ model assumptions). If we let S indicate the number of backorders that are accumulated when a new shipment of size Q is received, then the inventory system for the backorder case has the following characteristics:

- If S backorders exist when a new shipment of size Q arrives, then S backorders are shipped to the appropriate customers, and the remaining $Q - S$ units are placed in inventory. Therefore, $Q - S$ is the maximum inventory.
- The inventory cycle of T days is divided into two distinct phases; t_1 days when inventory is on hand and orders are filled as they occur, and t_2 days when stockouts occur and all new orders are placed on backorder.

The inventory pattern for the inventory model with backorders, where negative inventory represents the number of backorders, is shown in Figure 13.5.

With the inventory pattern now defined, we can proceed with the basic step of all inventory models—namely, the development of a total cost model. For the inventory model with backorders, we encounter the usual holding costs and ordering costs. We also incur a backorder cost in terms of the labor and special delivery costs directly associated with the handling of the backorders. Another portion of the backorder cost accounts for the loss of

FIGURE 13.5   INVENTORY PATTERN FOR AN INVENTORY MODEL WITH BACKORDERS

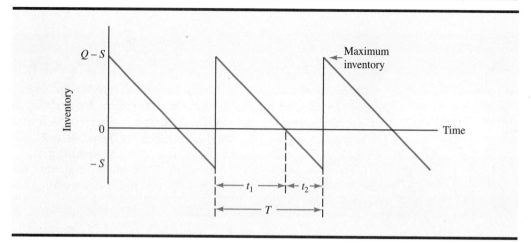

goodwill because some customers will have to wait for their orders. Because the **goodwill cost** depends on how long a customer has to wait, it is customary to adopt the convention of expressing backorder cost in terms of the cost of having a unit on backorder for a stated period of time. This method of costing backorders on a time basis is similar to the method used to compute the inventory holding cost, and we can use it to compute a total annual cost of backorders once the average backorder level and the backorder cost per unit per period are known.

Let us begin the development of a total cost model by calculating the average inventory for a hypothetical problem. If we have an average inventory of two units for 3 days and no inventory on the fourth day, what is the average inventory over the 4-day period? It is

$$\frac{2 \text{ units } (3 \text{ days}) + 0 \text{ units } (1 \text{ day})}{4 \text{ days}} = \frac{6}{4} = 1.5 \text{ units}$$

Refer to Figure 13.5. You can see that this situation is what happens in the backorder model. With a maximum inventory of $Q - S$ units, the t_1 days we have inventory on hand will have an average inventory of $(Q - S)/2$. No inventory is carried for the t_2 days in which we experience backorders. Thus, over the total cycle time of $T = t_1 + t_2$ days, we can compute the average inventory as follows:

$$\text{Average inventory} = \frac{\frac{1}{2}(Q - S)t_1 + 0t_2}{t_1 + t_2} = \frac{\frac{1}{2}(Q - S)t_1}{T} \tag{13.17}$$

Can we find other ways of expressing t_1 and T? Because we know that the maximum inventory is $Q - S$ and that d represents the constant daily demand, we have

$$t_1 = \frac{Q - S}{d} \text{ days} \tag{13.18}$$

That is, the maximum inventory of $Q - S$ units will be used up in $(Q - S)/d$ days. Because Q units are ordered each cycle, we know the length of a cycle must be

$$T = \frac{Q}{d} \text{ days} \tag{13.19}$$

Combining equations (13.18) and (13.19) with equation (13.17), we can compute the average inventory as follows:

$$\text{Average inventory} = \frac{\frac{1}{2}(Q - S)[(Q - S)/d]}{Q/d} = \frac{(Q - S)^2}{2Q} \qquad (13.20)$$

Thus, the average inventory is expressed in terms of two inventory decisions: how much we will order (Q) and the maximum number of backorders (S).

The formula for the annual number of orders placed using this model is identical to that for the EOQ model. With D representing the annual demand, we have

$$\text{Annual number of orders} = \frac{D}{Q} \qquad (13.21)$$

The next step is to develop an expression for the average backorder level. Because we know the maximum for backorders is S, we can use the same logic we used to establish average inventory in finding the average number of backorders. We have an average number of backorders during the period t_2 of $\frac{1}{2}$ the maximum number of backorders or $\frac{1}{2}S$. We do not have any backorders during the t_1 days we have inventory, therefore we can calculate the average backorders in a manner similar to equation (13.17). Using this approach, we have

$$\text{Average backorders} = \frac{0t_1 + (S/2)t_2}{T} = \frac{(S/2)t_2}{T} \qquad (13.22)$$

When we let the maximum number of backorders reach an amount S at a daily rate of d, the length of the backorder portion of the inventory cycle is

$$t_2 = \frac{S}{d} \qquad (13.23)$$

Using equations (13.23) and (13.19) in equation (13.22), we have

$$\text{Average backorders} = \frac{(S/2)(S/d)}{Q/d} = \frac{S^2}{2Q} \qquad (13.24)$$

Let

$$C_h = \text{cost to maintain one unit in inventory for 1 year}$$
$$C_o = \text{cost per order}$$
$$C_b = \text{cost to maintain one unit on backorder for 1 year}$$

The total annual cost (TC) for the inventory model with backorders becomes

$$TC = \frac{(Q - S)^2}{2Q} C_h + \frac{D}{Q} C_o + \frac{S^2}{2Q} C_b \qquad (13.25)$$

Given the cost estimates C_h, C_o, and C_b and the annual demand D, the minimum cost values for the order quantity Q^* and the planned backorders S^* are as follows (see Appendix 13.4):

$$Q^* = \sqrt{\frac{2DC_o}{C_h}\left(\frac{C_h + C_b}{C_b}\right)} \qquad (13.26)$$

$$S^* = Q^*\left(\frac{C_h}{C_h + C_b}\right) \qquad (13.27)$$

An Example.   Suppose that the Higley Radio Components Company has a product for which the assumptions of the inventory model with backorders are valid. Information obtained by the company is as follows:

$$D = 2000 \text{ units per year}$$
$$I = 0.20$$
$$C = \$50 \text{ per unit}$$
$$C_h = IC = (0.20)(\$50) = \$10 \text{ per unit per year}$$
$$C_o = \$25 \text{ per order}$$

The backorder cost C_b is one of the most difficult costs to estimate in inventory models. The reason is that it attempts to measure the cost associated with the loss of goodwill when a customer must wait for an order. Expressing this cost on an annual basis adds to the difficulty.

   The company is considering the possibility of allowing some backorders to occur for the product. The annual backorder cost has been estimated to be \$30 per unit per year. Using equations (13.26) and (13.27), we have

$$Q^* = \sqrt{\frac{2(2000)(25)}{10}\left(\frac{10 + 30}{20}\right)} = 115.47$$

and

$$S^* = 115\left(\frac{10}{10 + 30}\right) = 28.87$$

An inventory situation that incorporates backorder costs is considered in Problem 15.

If this solution is implemented, the system will operate with the following properties:

$$\text{Maximum inventory} = Q - S = 115.47 - 28.87 = 86.6$$
$$\text{Cycle time} = T = \frac{Q}{D}(250) = \frac{115.47}{2000}(250) = 14.43 \text{ working days}$$

The total annual cost is

$$\text{Holding cost} = \frac{(86.6)^2}{2(115.47)}(10) = \$325$$
$$\text{Ordering cost} = \frac{2000}{115.47}(25) = \$433$$
$$\text{Backorder cost} = \frac{(28.87)^2}{2(115.47)}(30) = \$108$$
$$\text{Total cost} = \$866$$

If backorders can be tolerated, the total cost including the backordering cost will be less than the total cost of the EOQ model. Some people think the model with backordering will have a greater cost because it includes a backordering cost in addition to the usual inventory holding and ordering costs. You can point out the fallacy in this thinking by noting that the backorder model leads to lower inventory and hence lower inventory holding costs.

If the company had chosen to prohibit backorders and had adopted the regular EOQ model, the recommended inventory decision would have been

$$Q^* = \sqrt{\frac{2(2000)(25)}{10}} = \sqrt{10,000} = 100$$

This order quantity would have resulted in a holding cost and an ordering cost of \$500 each or a total annual cost of \$1000. Thus, in this problem, allowing backorders is projecting a \$1000 − \$866 = \$134 or 13.4% savings in cost from the no-stockout EOQ model. The preceding comparison and conclusion are based on the assumption that the backorder model with an annual cost per backordered unit of \$30 is a valid model for the actual inventory situation. If the company is concerned that stockouts might lead to lost sales, then the savings might not be enough to warrant switching to an inventory policy that allowed for planned shortages.

NOTES AND COMMENTS

Equation (13.27) shows that the optimal number of planned backorders S^* is proportional to the ratio $C_h/(C_h + C_b)$, where C_h is the annual holding cost per unit and C_b is the annual backorder cost per unit. Whenever C_h increases, this ratio becomes larger, and the number of planned backorders increases. This explains why items that have a high per-unit cost and a correspondingly high annual holding cost are more economically handled on a backorder basis. On the other hand, whenever the backorder cost C_b increases, the ratio becomes smaller, and the number of planned backorders decreases. Thus, the model provides the intuitive result that items with high backordering costs will be handled with few backorders. In fact, with high backorder costs, the backorder model and the EOQ model with no backordering allowed provide similar inventory policies.

13.4 QUANTITY DISCOUNTS FOR THE EOQ MODEL

In the quantity discount model, assumption 4 of the EOQ model in Table 13.3 is altered. The cost per unit varies depending on the quantity ordered.

Quantity discounts occur in numerous situations in which suppliers provide an incentive for large order quantities by offering a lower purchase cost when items are ordered in larger quantities. In this section we show how the EOQ model can be used when quantity discounts are available.

Assume that we have a product in which the basic EOQ model (see Table 13.3) is applicable. Instead of a fixed unit cost, the supplier quotes the following discount schedule.

Discount Category	Order Size	Discount (%)	Unit Cost
1	0 to 999	0	$5.00
2	1000 to 2499	3	4.85
3	2500 and over	5	4.75

The 5% discount for the 2500-unit minimum order quantity looks tempting. However, realizing that higher order quantities result in higher inventory holding costs, we should prepare a thorough cost analysis before making a final ordering and inventory policy recommendation.

Suppose that the data and cost analyses show an annual holding cost rate of 20%, an ordering cost of $49 per order, and an annual demand of 5000 units; what order quantity should we select? The following three-step procedure shows the calculations necessary to make this decision. In the preliminary calculations, we use Q_1 to indicate the order quantity for discount category 1, Q_2 for discount category 2, and Q_3 for discount category 3.

Step 1. For each discount category, compute a Q^* using the EOQ formula based on the unit cost associated with the discount category.

Recall that the EOQ model provides $Q^* = \sqrt{2DC_o/C_h}$, where $C_h = IC = (0.20)C$. With three discount categories providing three different unit costs C, we obtain

$$Q_1^* = \sqrt{\frac{2(5000)49}{(0.20)(5.00)}} = 700$$

$$Q_2^* = \sqrt{\frac{2(5000)49}{(0.20)(4.85)}} = 711$$

$$Q_3^* = \sqrt{\frac{2(5000)49}{(0.20)(4.75)}} = 718$$

Because the only differences in the EOQ formulas are slight differences in the holding cost, the economic order quantities resulting from this step will be approximately the same. However, these order quantities will usually not all be of the size necessary to qualify for the discount price assumed. In the preceding case, both Q_2^* and Q_3^* are insufficient order quantities to obtain their assumed discounted costs of $4.85 and $4.75, respectively. For those order quantities for which the assumed price cannot be obtained, the following procedure must be used.

> Step 2. For the Q^* that is too small to qualify for the assumed discount price, adjust the order quantity upward to the nearest order quantity that will allow the product to be purchased at the assumed price.

In our example, this adjustment causes us to set

$$Q_2^* = 1000$$

and

$$Q_3^* = 2500$$

Problem 23 at the end of the chapter asks you to show that this property is true.

If a calculated Q^* for a given discount price is large enough to qualify for a bigger discount, that value of Q^* cannot lead to an optimal solution. Although the reason may not be obvious, it does turn out to be a property of the EOQ quantity discount model.

In the EOQ model with quantity discounts, the annual purchase cost must be included because purchase cost depends on the order quantity. Thus, it is a relevant cost.

In the previous inventory models considered, the annual purchase cost of the item was not included because it was constant and never affected by the inventory order policy decision. However, in the quantity discount model, the annual purchase cost depends on the order quantity and the associated unit cost. Thus, annual purchase cost (annual demand $D \times$ unit cost C) is included in the equation for total cost as shown here.

$$TC = \frac{Q}{2} C_h + \frac{D}{Q} C_o + DC \tag{13.28}$$

Using this total cost equation, we can determine the optimal order quantity for the EOQ discount model in step 3.

> Step 3. For each order quantity resulting from steps 1 and 2, compute the total annual cost using the unit price from the appropriate discount category and equation (13.28). The order quantity yielding the minimum total annual cost is the optimal order quantity.

Problem 21 will give you practice in applying the EOQ model to situations with quantity discounts.

The Step 3 calculations for the example problem are summarized in Table 13.4. As you can see, a decision to order 1000 units at the 3% discount rate yields the minimum cost solution. While the 2500-unit order quantity would result in a 5% discount, its exces-

TABLE 13.4 TOTAL ANNUAL COST CALCULATIONS FOR THE EOQ MODEL WITH QUANTITY DISCOUNTS

Discount Category	Unit Cost	Order Quantity	Annual Cost			
			Holding	Ordering	Purchase	Total
1	$5.00	700	$ 350	$350	$25,000	$25,700
2	4.85	1000	485	245	24,250	24,980
3	4.75	2500	1188	98	23,750	25,036

FIGURE 13.6   TOTAL COST CURVES FOR THE THREE DISCOUNT CATEGORIES

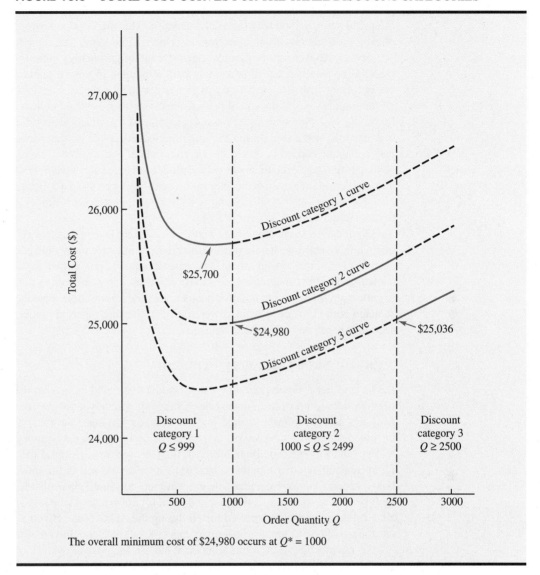

The overall minimum cost of $24,980 occurs at $Q^* = 1000$

sive holding cost makes it the second-best solution. Figure 13.6 shows the total cost curve for each of the three discount categories. Note that $Q^* = 1000$ provides the minimum cost order quantity.

13.5   SINGLE-PERIOD INVENTORY MODEL WITH PROBABILISTIC DEMAND

This inventory model is the first in the chapter that explicitly treats probabilistic demand. Unlike the EOQ model, it is for a single period with unused inventory not carried over to future periods.

The inventory models that we have discussed thus far have been based on the assumption that the demand rate is constant and **deterministic** throughout the year. We developed minimum cost order quantity and reorder point policies based on this assumption. In situations in which the demand rate is not deterministic, models have been developed that treat demand as **probabilistic** and best described by a probability distribution. In this section we consider a **single-period inventory model** with probabilistic demand.

The single-period inventory model refers to inventory situations in which *one* order is placed for the product; at the end of the period, the product has either sold out, or a surplus of unsold items will be sold for a salvage value. The single-period inventory model is applicable in situations involving seasonal or perishable items that cannot be carried in inventory and sold in future periods. Seasonal clothing (such as bathing suits and winter coats) are typically handled in a single-period manner. In these situations, a buyer places one preseason order for each item and then experiences a stockout or holds a clearance sale on the surplus stock at the end of the season. No items are carried in inventory and sold the following year. Newspapers are another example of a product that is ordered one time and is either sold or not sold during the single period. Although newspapers are ordered daily, they cannot be carried in inventory and sold in later periods. Thus, newspaper orders may be treated as a sequence of single-period models; that is, each day or period is separate, and a single-period inventory decision must be made each period (day). Because we order only once for the period, the only inventory decision we must make is *how much* of the product to order at the start of the period.

Obviously, if the demand were known for a single-period inventory situation, the solution would be easy; we would simply order the amount we knew would be demanded. However, in most single-period models, the exact demand is not known. In fact, forecasts may show that demand can have a wide variety of values. If we are going to analyze this type of inventory problem in a quantitative manner, we need information about the probabilities associated with the various demand values. Thus, the single-period model presented in this section is based on probabilistic demand.

Johnson Shoe Company Problem

Let us consider a single-period inventory model that could be used to make a how-much-to-order decision for the Johnson Shoe Company. The buyer for the Johnson Shoe Company has decided to order a shoe for men that has just been shown at a buyers' meeting in New York City. The shoe will be part of the company's spring-summer promotion and will be sold through nine retail stores in the Chicago area. Because the shoe is designed for spring and summer months, it cannot be expected to sell in the fall. Johnson plans to hold a special August clearance sale in an attempt to sell all shoes that have not been sold by July 31. The shoes cost $40 a pair and retail for $60 a pair. At the sale price of $30 a pair, all surplus shoes can be expected to sell during the August sale. If you were the buyer for the Johnson Shoe Company, how many pairs of the shoes would you order?

An obvious question at this time is, What are the possible values of demand for the shoe? We need this information to answer the question of how much to order. Let us suppose that the uniform probability distribution shown in Figure 13.7 can be used to describe the demand for the size 10D shoes. In particular, note that the range of demand is from 350 to 650 pairs of shoes, with an average, or expected, demand of 500 pairs of shoes.

Incremental analysis is a method that can be used to determine the optimal order quantity for a single-period inventory model. Incremental analysis addresses the how-much-to-order question by comparing the cost or loss of *ordering one additional unit* with the cost or loss of *not ordering one additional unit*. The costs involved are defined as follows:

c_o = cost per unit of *overestimating* demand. This cost represents the loss of ordering one additional unit and finding that it cannot be sold.

c_u = cost per unit of *underestimating* demand. This cost represents the opportunity loss of not ordering one additional unit and finding that it could have been sold.

In the Johnson Shoe Company problem, the company will incur the cost of overestimating demand whenever it orders too much and has to sell the extra shoes during the Au-

FIGURE 13.7   UNIFORM PROBABILITY DISTRIBUTION OF DEMAND FOR THE
JOHNSON SHOE COMPANY PROBLEM

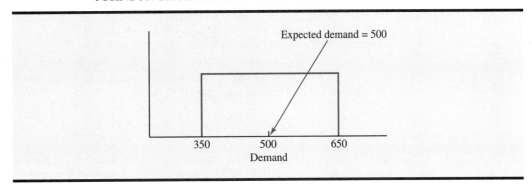

The cost of underestimating demand is usually harder to determine than the cost of overestimating demand. The reason is that the cost of underestimating demand includes a lost profit and may include a customer goodwill cost because the customer is unable to purchase the item when desired.

gust sale. Thus, the cost per unit of overestimating demand is equal to the purchase cost per unit minus the August sales price per unit; that is, $c_o = \$40 - \$30 = \$10$. Therefore, Johnson will lose $10 for each pair of shoes that it orders over the quantity demanded. The cost of underestimating demand is the lost profit because a pair of shoes that could have been sold was not available in inventory. Thus, the per-unit cost of underestimating demand is the difference between the regular selling price per unit and the purchase cost per unit; that is, $c_u = \$60 - \$40 = \$20$.

Because the exact level of demand for the size 10D shoes is unknown, we have to consider the probability of demand and thus the probability of obtaining the associated costs or losses. For example, let us assume that Johnson Shoe Company management wishes to consider an order quantity equal to the average or expected demand for 500 pairs of shoes. In incremental analysis, we consider the possible losses associated with an order quantity of 501 (ordering one additional unit) and an order quantity of 500 (not ordering one additional unit). The order quantity alternatives and the possible losses are summarized here.

Order Quantity Alternatives	Loss Occurs If	Possible Loss	Probability Loss Occurs
$Q = 501$	Demand overestimated; the additional unit *cannot* be sold	$c_o = \$10$	$P(\text{demand} \leq 500)$
$Q = 500$	Demand underestimated; an additional unit *could have* been sold	$c_u = \$20$	$P(\text{demand} > 500)$

By looking at the demand probability distribution in Figure 13.7, we see that $P(\text{demand} \leq 500) = 0.50$ and that $P(\text{demand} > 500) = 0.50$. By multiplying the possible losses, $c_o = \$10$ and $c_u = \$20$, by the probability of obtaining the loss, we can compute the expected value of the loss, or simply the *expected loss* (EL), associated with the order quantity alternatives. Thus

$$EL(Q = 501) = c_o P(\text{demand} \leq 500) = \$10(0.50) = \$5$$
$$EL(Q = 500) = c_u P(\text{demand} > 500) = \$20(0.50) = \$10$$

Based on these expected losses, do you prefer an order quantity of 501 or 500 pairs of shoes? Because the expected loss is greater for $Q = 500$, and because we want to avoid this higher cost or loss, we should make $Q = 501$ the preferred decision. We could now consider incrementing the order quantity one additional unit to $Q = 502$ and repeating the expected loss calculations.

Although we could continue this unit-by-unit analysis, it would be time-consuming and cumbersome. We would have to evaluate $Q = 502$, $Q = 503$, $Q = 504$, and so on, until we found the value of Q where the expected loss of ordering one incremental unit is equal to the expected loss of not ordering one incremental unit; that is, the optimal order quantity Q^* occurs when the incremental analysis shows that

$$EL(Q^* + 1) = EL(Q^*) \tag{13.29}$$

When this relationship holds, increasing the order quantity by one additional unit has no economic advantage. Using the logic with which we computed the expected losses for the order quantities of 501 and 500, the general expressions for $EL(Q^* + 1)$ and $EL(Q^*)$ can be written

$$EL(Q^* + 1) = c_o P(\text{demand} \leq Q^*) \tag{13.30}$$
$$EL(Q^*) = c_u P(\text{demand} > Q^*) \tag{13.31}$$

Because we know from basic probability that

$$P(\text{demand} \leq Q^*) + P(\text{demand} > Q^*) = 1 \tag{13.32}$$

we can write

$$P(\text{demand} > Q^*) = 1 - P(\text{demand} \leq Q^*) \tag{13.33}$$

Using this expression, equation (13.31) can be rewritten as

$$EL(Q^*) = c_u[1 - P(\text{demand} \leq Q^*)] \tag{13.34}$$

Equations (13.30) and (13.34) can be used to show that $EL(Q^* + 1) = EL(Q^*)$ whenever

$$c_o P(\text{demand} \leq Q^*) = c_u[1 - P(\text{demand} \leq Q^*)] \tag{13.35}$$

Solving for $P(\text{demand} \leq Q^*)$, we have

$$P(\text{demand} \leq Q^*) = \frac{c_u}{c_u + c_o} \tag{13.36}$$

This expression provides the general condition for the optimal order quantity Q^* in the single-period inventory model.

In the Johnson Shoe Company problem $c_o = \$10$ and $c_u = \$20$. Thus, equation (13.36) shows that the optimal order size for Johnson shoes must satisfy the following condition:

$$P(\text{demand} \leq Q^*) = \frac{c_u}{c_u + c_o} = \frac{20}{20 + 10} = \frac{20}{30} = \frac{2}{3}$$

We can find the optimal order quantity Q^* by referring to the probability distribution shown in Figure 13.7 and finding the value of Q that will provide $P(\text{demand} \leq Q^*) = \frac{2}{3}$.

To find this solution, we note that in the uniform distribution the probability is evenly distributed over the entire range of 350–650 pairs of shoes. Thus, we can satisfy the expression for Q^* by moving two-thirds of the way from 350 to 650. Because this range is $650 - 350 = 300$, we move 200 units from 350 toward 650. Doing so provides the optimal order quantity of 550 pairs of size 10D shoes.

In summary, the key to establishing an optimal order quantity for single-period inventory models is to identify the probability distribution that describes the demand for the item and the costs of overestimation and underestimation. Then, using the information for the costs of overestimation and underestimation, equation (13.36) can be used to find the location of Q^* in the probability distribution.

Kremer Chemical Company Problem

As another example of a single-period inventory model with probabilistic demand, consider the situation faced by the Kremer Chemical Company. Kremer has a contract with one of its customers to supply a unique liquid chemical product. Historically, the customer places orders approximately every 6 months. Because a 2-month aging condition exists for the product, Kremer will have to make its production quantity decision before the customer places an order. Kremer's inventory problem is to determine the number of pounds of the chemical to produce in anticipation of the customer's order.

Kremer's manufacturing costs for the chemical are $15 per pound, and the product sells at the fixed contract price of $20 per pound. If Kremer underproduces, it will be unable to satisfy the customer's demand. If this condition occurs, Kremer has agreed to absorb the added cost of filling the order by purchasing a higher quality substitute product from another chemical firm. The substitute product, including additional transportation expenses, will cost Kremer $19 per pound. If Kremer overproduces, it will have more product in inventory than the customer requires. Because of the spoilage potential for the product, Kremer cannot store excess production until the customer's next order. As a result, Kremer reprocesses the excess production and sells the surplus for $5 per pound.

Based on previous experience with the customer's orders, Kremer believes that the normal probability distribution shown in Figure 13.8 best describes the possible demand. Note that the normal distribution shows an average or expected demand of $\mu = 1000$ pounds with a standard deviation of $\sigma = 100$ pounds. Using Kremer's price and cost data as well as the

FIGURE 13.8   NORMAL PROBABILITY DISTRIBUTION OF DEMAND FOR THE KREMER CHEMICAL COMPANY PROBLEM

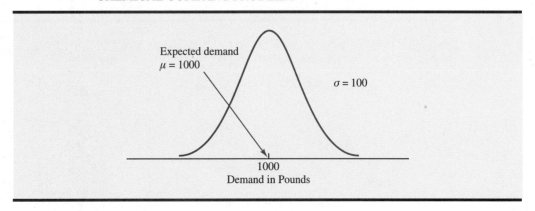

probability distribution of demand shown in Figure 13.8, how much production should Kremer plan for in anticipation of the customer's order for the liquid chemical?

Let us compute the cost of underestimation, c_u, and the cost of overestimation, c_o, as required for equation (13.36). First, if Kremer underproduces, it will have to purchase a substitute product at a higher cost per unit to satisfy the customer's demand for the product. Because the substitute product costs $19 per pound and Kremer could have manufactured the product for $15 per pound, a cost of $c_u = \$19 - \$15 = \$4$ exists for every pound of underestimated demand. If Kremer overestimates demand, the company incurs a cost of $15 per pound to manufacture the product and then sells the reprocessed excess product for $5 per pound. Thus, Kremer has a per-unit cost of $c_o = \$15 - \$5 = \$10$ for overestimating demand.

Applying equation (13.36) indicates that the optimal order quantity must satisfy the following condition:

$$P(\text{demand} \leq Q^*) = \frac{c_u}{c_u + c_o} = \frac{4}{4 + 10} = 0.2857$$

We can use the normal probability distribution for demand as shown in Figure 13.9 to find the order quantity that satisfies the condition that $P(\text{demand} \leq Q^*) = 0.2857$. From Appendix C, we see that 0.2857 of the area in the left tail of the curve of the normal probability distribution occurs approximately $z = 0.57$ standard deviations *below* the mean. Because the mean or expected demand is given by $\mu = 1000$ and the standard deviation is $\sigma = 100$, we have

An example of a single-period inventory model with probabilistic demand described by a normal probability distribution is considered in Problem 25.

$$Q^* = \mu - 0.57\sigma$$
$$= 1000 - 0.57(100) = 943$$

Thus, with the assumed normal probability distribution of demand, the Kremer Chemical Company should produce 943 pounds of the chemical in anticipation of the customer's order. Note that in this case the cost of underestimation is less than the cost of overestimation. Thus, Kremer is willing to risk a higher probability of underestimation and hence a higher probability of a stockout. In fact, Kremer's optimal order quantity has a 0.2857 probability of having a surplus and a $1 - 0.2857 = 0.7143$ probability of a stockout.

FIGURE 13.9 PROBABILITY DISTRIBUTION OF DEMAND FOR THE KREMER CHEMICAL COMPANY PROBLEM SHOWING THE LOCATION OF THE OPTIMAL ORDER QUANTITY Q^*

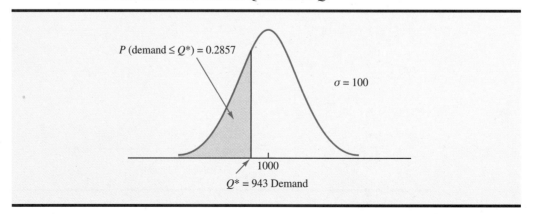

NOTES AND COMMENTS

1. In any probabilistic inventory model, the assumption about the probability distribution for demand is critical and can affect the recommended inventory decision. In the problems presented in this section, we used the uniform and the normal probability distributions to describe demand. In some situations, other probability distributions may be more appropriate. In using probabilistic inventory models, we must exercise care in selecting the probability distribution that most realistically describes demand.

2. In the single-period inventory model, the value of $c_u/(c_u + c_o)$ plays a critical role in selecting the order quantity [see equation (13.36)]. Whenever $c_u = c_o$, $c_u/(c_u + c_o)$ equals 0.50; in this case, we should select an order quantity corresponding to the median demand. With this choice, a stockout is just as likely as a surplus because the two costs are equal. However, whenever $c_u < c_o$, a smaller order quantity will be recommended. In this case, the smaller order quantity will provide a higher probability of a stockout; however, the more expensive cost of overestimating demand and having a surplus will tend to be avoided. Finally, whenever $c_u > c_o$, a larger order quantity will be recommended. In this case, the larger order quantity provides a lower probability of a stockout in an attempt to avoid the more expensive cost of underestimating demand and experiencing a stockout.

13.6   ORDER-QUANTITY, REORDER POINT MODEL WITH PROBABILISTIC DEMAND

The inventory model in this section is based on the assumptions of the EOQ model shown in Table 13.3 with the exception that demand is probabilistic rather than deterministic. With probabilistic demand, occasional shortages may occur.

In the previous section we considered a single-period inventory model with probabilistic demand. In this section we extend our discussion to a multiperiod order-quantity, reorder point inventory model with probabilistic demand. In the multiperiod model, the inventory system operates continuously with many repeating periods or cycles; inventory can be carried from one period to the next. Whenever the inventory position reaches the reorder point, an order for Q units is placed. Because demand is probabilistic, the time the reorder point will be reached, the time between orders, and the time the order of Q units will arrive in inventory cannot be determined in advance.

The inventory pattern for the order-quantity, reorder point model with probabilistic demand will have the general appearance shown in Figure 13.10. Note that the increases or jumps in the inventory occur whenever an order of Q units arrives. The inventory decreases

FIGURE 13.10   INVENTORY PATTERN FOR AN ORDER-QUANTITY, REORDER POINT MODEL WITH PROBABILISTIC DEMAND

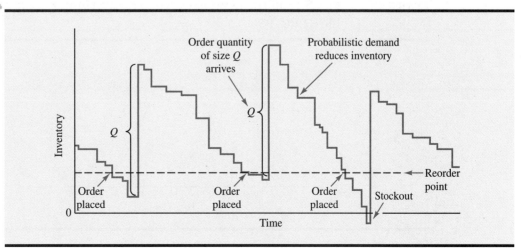

at a nonconstant rate based on the probabilistic demand. A new order is placed whenever the reorder point is reached. At times, the order quantity of Q units will arrive before inventory reaches zero. However, at other times, higher demand will cause a stockout before a new order is received. As with other order-quantity, reorder point models, the manager must determine the order quantity Q and the reorder point r for the inventory system.

The exact mathematical formulation of an order-quantity, reorder point inventory model with probabilistic demand is beyond the scope of this text. However, we present a procedure that can be used to obtain good, workable order quantity and reorder point inventory policies. The solution procedure can be expected to provide only an approximation of the optimal solution, but it can yield good solutions in many practical situations.

Let us consider the inventory problem of Dabco Industrial Lighting Distributors. Dabco purchases a special high-intensity light bulb for industrial lighting systems from a well-known light bulb manufacturer. Dabco would like a recommendation on how much to order and when to order so that a low-cost inventory policy can be maintained. Pertinent facts are that the ordering cost is $12 per order, one bulb costs $6, and Dabco uses a 20% annual holding cost rate for its inventory ($C_h = IC = 0.20 \times \$6 = \$1.20$). Dabco, which has more than 1000 customers, experiences a probabilistic demand; in fact, the number of units demanded varies considerably from day to day and from week to week. The lead time for a new order of light bulbs is 1 week. Historical sales data indicate that demand during a 1-week lead time can be described by a normal probability distribution with a mean of 154 light bulbs and a standard deviation of 25 light bulbs. The normal distribution of demand during the lead time is shown in Figure 13.11. Because the mean demand during 1-week is 154 units, Dabco can anticipate a mean or expected annual demand of 154 units per week $\times$ 52 weeks per year $=$ 8008 units per year.

The How-Much-to-Order Decision

Although we are in a probabilistic demand situation, we have an estimate of the expected annual demand of 8008 units. We can apply the EOQ model from Section 13.1 as an approximation of the best order quantity, with the expected annual demand used for D. In Dabco's case

$$Q^* = \sqrt{\frac{2DC_o}{C_h}} = \sqrt{\frac{2(8008)(12)}{(1.20)}} = 400 \text{ units}$$

When we studied the sensitivity of the EOQ model, we learned that the total cost of operating an inventory system was relatively insensitive to order quantities that were in the

FIGURE 13.11   LEAD-TIME DEMAND PROBABILITY DISTRIBUTION FOR DABCO LIGHT BULBS

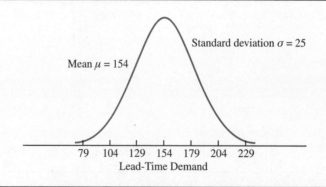

neighborhood of Q^*. Using this knowledge, we expect 400 units per order to be a good approximation of the optimal order quantity. Even if annual demand were as low as 7000 units or as high as 9000 units, an order quantity of 400 units should be a relatively good low-cost order size. Thus, given our best estimate of annual demand at 8008 units, we will use $Q^* = 400$.

We have established the 400-unit order quantity by ignoring the fact that demand is probabilistic. Using $Q^* = 400$, Dabco can anticipate placing approximately $D/Q^* = 8008/400 = 20$ orders per year with an average of approximately $250/20 = 12.5$ working days between orders.

The When-to-Order Decision

We now want to establish a when-to-order decision rule or reorder point that will trigger the ordering process. With a mean lead-time demand of 154 units, you might first suggest a 154-unit reorder point. However, considering the probability of demand now becomes extremely important. If 154 is the mean lead-time demand, and if demand is symmetrically distributed about 154, then the lead-time demand will be more than 154 units roughly 50% of the time. When the demand during the 1-week lead time exceeds 154 units, Dabco will experience a shortage or stockout. Thus, using a reorder point of 154 units, approximately 50% of the time (10 of the 20 orders a year) Dabco will be short of bulbs before the new supply arrives. This shortage rate would most likely be viewed as unacceptable.

The probability of a stockout during any one inventory cycle is easiest to estimate by first determining the number of orders that are expected during the year. The inventory manager can usually state a willingness to allow perhaps one, two, or three stockouts during the year. The allowable stockouts per year divided by the number of orders per year will provide the desired probability of a stockout.

Refer to the **lead-time demand distribution** shown in Figure 13.11. Given this distribution, we can now determine how the reorder point r affects the probability of a stockout. Because stockouts occur whenever the demand during the lead time exceeds the reorder point, we can find the probability of a stockout by using the lead-time demand distribution to compute the probability that demand will exceed r.

We could now approach the when-to-order problem by defining a cost per stockout and then attempting to include this cost in a total cost equation. Alternatively, we can ask management to specify the average number of stockouts that can be tolerated per year. If demand for a product is probabilistic, a manager who will never tolerate a stockout is being somewhat unrealistic because attempting to avoid stockouts completely will require high reorder points, high inventory, and an associated high holding cost.

Suppose in this case that Dabco management is willing to tolerate an average of one stockout per year. Because Dabco places 20 orders per year, this decision implies that management is willing to allow demand during lead time to exceed the reorder point one time in 20, or 5% of the time. The reorder point r can be found by using the lead-time demand distribution to find the value of r with a 5% chance of having a lead-time demand that will exceed it. This situation is shown graphically in Figure 13.12.

From the standard normal probability distribution table in Appendix C, we see that the r value is 1.645 standard deviations above the mean. Therefore, for the assumed normal distribution for lead-time demand with $\mu = 154$ and $\sigma = 25$, the reorder point r is

$$r = 154 + 1.645(25) = 195$$

If a normal distribution is used for lead-time demand, the general equation for r is

$$r = \mu + z\sigma \tag{13.37}$$

where z is the number of standard deviations necessary to obtain the acceptable stockout probability.

FIGURE 13.12   REORDER POINT r THAT ALLOWS A 5% CHANCE OF A STOCKOUT FOR
DABCO LIGHT BULBS

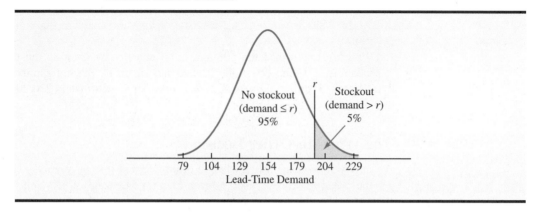

Thus, the recommended inventory decision is to order 400 units whenever the inventory reaches the reorder point of 195. Because the mean or expected demand during the lead time is 154 units, the $195 - 154 = 41$ units serve as a safety stock, which absorbs higher-than-usual demand during the lead time. Roughly 95% of the time, the 195 units will be able to satisfy demand during the lead time. The anticipated annual cost for this system is as follows:

Ordering cost $\qquad\qquad (D/Q)C_o = (8008/400)12 = \$240.24$

Holding cost, normal inventory $(Q/2)C_h = (400/2)(1.20) = \$240.00$

Holding cost, safety stock $\qquad (41)C_h = \quad 41(1.20) \quad = \underline{\$\ 49.20}$

$\qquad\qquad\qquad\qquad\qquad\qquad\qquad\qquad\qquad$ Total $\quad \$529.44$

Try Problem 29 as an example of an order quantity, reorder point model with probabilistic demand.

If Dabco could have assumed that a known, constant demand rate of 8008 units per year existed for the light bulbs, then $Q^* = 400$, $r = 154$, and a total annual cost of $\$240 + \$240 = \$480$ would have been optimal. When demand is uncertain and can only be expressed in probabilistic terms, a larger total cost can be expected. The larger cost occurs in the form of larger holding costs because more inventory must be maintained to limit the number of stockouts. For Dabco, this additional inventory or safety stock was 41 units, with an additional annual holding cost of $49.20. The Q. M. in Action: Information from a Netherlands Supplier Lowers Inventory Cost describes how a warehouser in the Netherlands has implemented an order-quantity, reorder point system with probabilistic demand.

NOTES AND COMMENTS

The Dabco reorder point was based on a 5% probability of a stockout during the lead-time period. Thus, on 95% of all order cycles Dabco will be able to satisfy customer demand without experiencing a stockout. Defining *service level* as the percentage of all order cycles that do not experience a stockout, we would say that Dabco has a 95% service level. However, other definitions of service level may include the percentage of all customer demand that can be satisfied from inventory. Thus, when an inventory manager expresses a desired service level, it is a good idea to clarify exactly what the manager means by the term *service level*.

INFORMATION FROM A NETHERLANDS SUPPLIER LOWERS INVENTORY COST*

In the Netherlands, companies such as Philips, Rank Xerox, and Fokker have followed the trend of developing closer relations between the firm and its suppliers. As teamwork, coordination, and information sharing improve, opportunities are available for better cost control in the operation of inventory systems.

One Dutch public warehouser has a contract with its supplier under which the supplier routinely provides information regarding the status and schedule of upcoming production runs. The warehouser's inventory system operates as an order-quantity, reorder point system with probabilistic demand. When the order-quantity Q has been determined, the warehouser selects the desired reorder point for the product. The distribution of the lead-time demand is essential in determining the reorder point. Usually, the lead-time demand distribution is approximated directly, taking into account both the probabilistic demand and the probabilistic length of the lead-time period.

The supplier's information concerning scheduled production runs provides the warehouser with a better understanding of the lead time involved for a product and the resulting lead-time demand distribution. With this information, the warehouse can modify the reorder point accordingly. Information sharing by the supplier thus enables the order-quantity, reorder point system to operate with a lower inventory holding cost.

*Based on F. A. van der Duyn Schouten, M. J. G. van Eijs, and R. M. J. Heuts, "The Value of Supplier Information to Improve Management of a Retailer's Inventory," *Decision Sciences,* vol. 25, no. 1 (January–February 1994): 1–14.

13.7   PERIODIC REVIEW MODEL WITH PROBABILISTIC DEMAND

The order-quantity, reorder point inventory models previously discussed require a **continuous review** inventory system. In a continuous review inventory system, the inventory position is monitored continuously so that an order can be placed whenever the reorder point is reached. Computerized inventory systems can easily provide the continuous review required by the order-quantity, reorder point models.

Up to this point, we have assumed that the inventory position is reviewed continuously so that an order can be placed as soon as the inventory position reaches the reorder point. The inventory model in this section assumes probabilistic demand and a periodic review of the inventory position.

An alternative to the continuous review system is the **periodic review inventory system.** With a periodic review system, the inventory is checked and reordering is done only at specified points in time. For example, inventory may be checked and orders placed on a weekly, biweekly, monthly, or some other periodic basis. When a firm or business handles multiple products, the periodic review system has the advantage of requiring that orders for several items be placed at the same preset periodic review time. With this type of inventory system, the shipping and receiving of orders for multiple products are easily coordinated. Under the previously discussed order-quantity, reorder point systems, the reorder points for various products can be encountered at substantially different points in time, making the coordination of orders for multiple products more difficult.

To illustrate this system, let us consider Dollar Discounts, a firm with several retail stores that carry a wide variety of products for household use. The company operates its inventory system with a two-week periodic review. Under this system, a retail store manager may order any number of units of any product from the Dollar Discounts central warehouse every two weeks. Orders for all products going to a particular store are combined into one shipment. When making the order quantity decision for each product at a given review period, the store manager knows that a reorder for the product cannot be made until the next review period.

Assuming that the lead time is less than the length of the review period, an order placed at a review period will be received prior to the next review period. In this case, the how-much-to-order decision at any review period is determined using the following:

$$Q = M - H$$

(13.38)

where

$$Q = \text{the order quantity}$$
$$M = \text{the replenishment level}$$
$$H = \text{the inventory on hand at the review period}$$

Because the demand is probabilistic, the inventory on hand at the review period, H, will vary. Thus, the order quantity that must be sufficient to bring the inventory position back to its maximum or replenishment level M can be expected to vary each period. For example, if the replenishment level for a particular product is 50 units, and the inventory on hand at the review period is $H = 12$ units, an order of $Q = M - H = 50 - 12 = 38$ units should be made. Thus, under the periodic review model, enough units are ordered each review period to bring the inventory position back up to the replenishment level.

A typical inventory pattern for a periodic review system with probabilistic demand is shown in Figure 13.13. Note that the time between periodic reviews is predetermined and fixed. The order quantity Q at each review period can vary and is shown to be the difference between the replenishment level and the inventory on hand. Finally, as with other probabilistic models, an unusually high demand can result in an occasional stockout.

The decision variable in the periodic review model is the replenishment level M. To determine M, we could begin by developing a total cost model, including holding, ordering, and stockout costs. Instead, we describe an approach that is often used in practice. In this approach, the objective is to determine a replenishment level that will meet a desired performance level, such as a reasonably low probability of stockout or a reasonably low number of stockouts per year.

In the Dollar Discounts problem, we assume that management's objective is to determine the replenishment level with only a 1% chance of a stockout. In the periodic review

FIGURE 13.13   INVENTORY PATTERN FOR PERIODIC REVIEW MODEL WITH PROBABILISTIC DEMAND

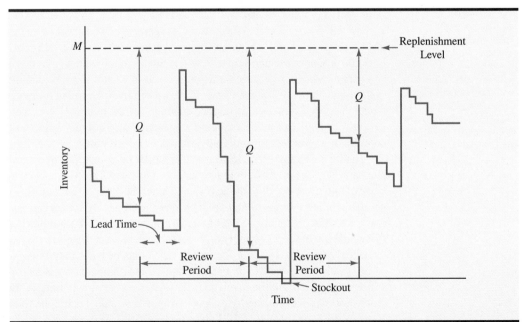

model, the order quantity at each review period must be sufficient to cover demand for the *review period plus the demand for the following lead time.* That is, the order quantity that brings the inventory position up to the replenishment level M must last until the order made at the next review period is received in inventory. The length of this time is equal to the review period plus the lead time. Figure 13.14 shows the normal probability distribution of demand during the review period plus the lead-time period for one of the Dollar Discounts products. The mean demand is 250 units, and the standard deviation of demand is 45 units. Given this situation, the logic used to establish M is similar to the logic used to establish the reorder point in Section 13.6. Figure 13.15 shows the replenishment level M with a 1% chance that demand will exceed that replenishment level. In other words, Figure 13.15 shows the replenishment level that allows a 1% chance of a stockout associated with the replenishment decision. Using the normal probability distribution table in Appendix C, we see that a value of M that is 2.33 standard deviations above the mean will allow stockouts with a 1% probability. Therefore, for the assumed normal probability distribution with $\mu = 250$ and $\sigma = 45$, the replenishment level is determined by

$$M = 250 + 2.33(45) = 355$$

FIGURE 13.14   PROBABILITY DISTRIBUTION OF DEMAND DURING THE REVIEW PERIOD AND LEAD TIME FOR THE DOLLAR DISCOUNTS PROBLEM

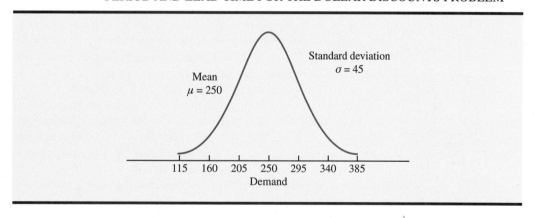

FIGURE 13.15   REPLENISHMENT LEVEL M THAT ALLOWS A 1% CHANCE OF A STOCKOUT FOR THE DOLLAR DISCOUNTS PROBLEM

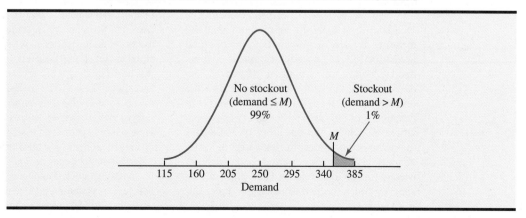

Problem 33 gives you practice in computing the replenishment level for a periodic review model with probabilistic demand.

While other probability distributions can be used to express the demand during the review period plus the lead-time period, if the normal probability distribution is used, the general expression for M is

$$M = \mu + z\sigma \tag{13.39}$$

where z is the number of standard deviations necessary to obtain the acceptable stockout probability.

Periodic review systems provide advantages of coordinated orders for multiple items. However, periodic review systems require larger safety stock levels than corresponding continuous review systems.

If demand had been deterministic rather than probabilistic, the replenishment level would have been the demand during the review period plus the demand during the lead-time period. In this case, the replenishment level would have been 250 units, and no stock-out would have occurred. However, with the probabilistic demand, we have seen that higher inventory are necessary to allow for uncertain demand and to control the probability of a stockout. In the Dollar Discounts problem, $355 - 250 = 105$ is the safety stock that is necessary to absorb any higher-than-usual demand during the review period plus the demand during the lead-time period. This safety stock limits the probability of a stockout to 1%. The Q. M. in Action: Inventory Model Helps Hewlett-Packard's Product Design for Worldwide Markets describes a periodic review inventory system at Hewlett-Packard.

More Complex Periodic Review Models

The periodic review model that we have just discussed is one approach to determining a replenishment level for the periodic review inventory system with probabilistic demand. More complex versions of the periodic review model incorporate a reorder point as another decision variable. That is, instead of ordering at every periodic review, a reorder point is established. If the inventory on hand at the periodic review is at or below the reorder point, a decision is made to order up to the replenishment level. However, if the inventory on hand at the periodic review is greater than the reorder level, such an order is not placed, and the system continues until the next periodic review. In this case, the cost of ordering is a relevant cost and can be included in a cost model along with holding and stockout costs. Optimal policies can be reached based on minimizing the expected total cost. Situations with lead times longer than the review period add to the complexity of the model. The mathematical level required to treat these more extensive periodic review models is beyond the scope of this text.

NOTES AND COMMENTS

1. The periodic review model presented in this section is based on the assumption that the lead time for an order is less than the periodic review period. Most periodic review systems operate under this condition. However, the case in which the lead time is longer than the review period can be handled by defining H in equation (13.38) as the inventory position, where H includes the inventory on hand plus the inventory on order. In this case, the order quantity at any review period is the amount needed for the inventory on hand plus *all* outstanding orders needed to reach the replenishment level.

2. In the order-quantity, reorder point model discussed in Section 13.6, a continuous review was used to initiate an order whenever the reorder point was reached. The safety stock for this model was based on the probabilistic demand during the lead time. The periodic review model presented in this section also determined a recommended safety stock. However, because the inventory review was only periodic, the safety stock was based on the probabilistic demand during the *review period plus the lead-time period.* This longer period for the safety stock computation means that periodic review systems tend to require a larger safety stock than do continuous review systems.

INVENTORY MODEL HELPS HEWLETT-PACKARD'S PRODUCT DESIGN FOR
WORLDWIDE MARKETS*

Product design always affects the efficiency of manufacturing operations. At Hewlett-Packard's Vancouver, Washington, division, managers are also learning how product design affects product customization, distribution, and delivery to worldwide markets. In most cases, different markets require different product configurations because of language, environment, and/or government regulations. Should Hewlett-Packard design variations of each product to meet the unique requirements of each market, or should it design a more general product with product customization being completed in the local market area?

An inventory model was used to study the inventory and costs associated with the product design alternatives for the Hewlett-Packard Deskjet-Plus printer. Inventory levels for the printer are maintained on a periodic review basis. Planners review the inventory position (on-hand inventory plus in-

ventory in the pipeline) weekly. Orders are placed for quantities needed to return the inventory position to the target inventory. Demand during the lead time is assumed to follow a normal probability distribution.

The inventory model projected the inventory cost associated with each product design alternative. As a result, Hewlett-Packard's Vancouver, Washington, division redesigned its products to support final customization of the product at the local distribution center level. The inventory model projected an 18% reduction in the total inventory investment, which saved millions of dollars.

*Based on H. L. Lee, C. Billington, and B. Carter, "Hewlett-Packard Gains Control of Inventory and Service through Design for Localization," *Interfaces* 23, no. 4 (July–August 1993): 1–11.

SUMMARY

In this chapter we presented some of the approaches quantitative analysts use to assist managers in establishing low-cost inventory policies. We first considered cases in which the demand rate for the product is constant. In analyzing these inventory systems, total cost models were developed, which included ordering costs, holding costs, and, in some cases, backordering costs. Then minimum cost formulas for the order quantity Q were presented. A reorder point r can be established by considering the lead-time demand.

In addition, we discussed inventory models in which a deterministic and constant rate could not be assumed, and thus, demand was described by a probability distribution. A critical issue with these probabilistic inventory models is obtaining a probability distribution that most realistically approximates the demand distribution. We first described a single-period model where only one order is placed for the product and, at the end of the period, either the product has sold out or a surplus remains of unsold products that will be sold for a salvage value. Solution procedures were then presented for multiperiod models based on either an order-quantity, reorder point, continuous review system or a replenishment-level, periodic review system.

In closing this chapter, we reemphasize that inventory and inventory systems can be an expensive phase of a firm's operation. It is very important for managers to be aware of the cost of inventory systems and to make the best possible operating policy decisions for the inventory system. Inventory models, as presented in this chapter, can help managers to develop good inventory policies.

GLOSSARY

Independent demand   Demand for an item that is independent of the demand for other products or items. Usually independent demand is generated by customers placing orders for finished goods.

Dependent demand Demand for a product, component, subassembly, or item that is dependent on the demand for another product or item.

Economic order quantity (EOQ) The order quantity that minimizes the annual holding cost plus the annual ordering cost.

Constant demand rate An assumption of many inventory models that states that the same number of units are taken from inventory each period of time.

Holding cost The cost associated with maintaining an inventory investment, including the cost of the capital investment in the inventory, insurance, taxes, warehouse overhead, and so on. This cost may be stated as a percentage of the inventory investment or as a cost per unit.

Cost of capital The cost a firm incurs to obtain capital for investment. It may be stated as an annual percentage rate, and it is part of the holding cost associated with maintaining inventory.

Ordering cost The fixed cost (salaries, paper, transportation, etc.) associated with placing an order for an item.

Inventory position The inventory on hand plus the inventory on order.

Reorder point The inventory position at which a new order should be placed.

Lead time The time between the placing of an order and its receipt in the inventory system.

Lead-time demand The number of units demanded during the lead-time period.

Cycle time The length of time between the placing of two consecutive orders.

Safety stock Inventory maintained in order to reduce the number of stockouts resulting from higher-than-expected demand.

Constant supply rate A situation in which the inventory is built up at a constant rate over a period of time.

Lot size The order quantity in the production inventory model.

Setup cost The fixed cost (labor, materials, lost production) associated with preparing for a new production run.

Shortage or Stockout Demand that cannot be supplied from inventory.

Backorder The receipt of an order for a product when no units are in inventory. These backorders become shortages, which are eventually satisfied when a new supply of the product becomes available.

Goodwill cost A cost associated with a backorder, a lost sale, or any form of stockout or unsatisfied demand. This cost may be used to reflect the loss of future profits because a customer experienced an unsatisfied demand.

Quantity discounts Discounts or lower unit costs offered by the manufacturer when a customer purchases larger quantities of the product.

Deterministic inventory model A model where demand is considered known and not subject to uncertainty.

Probabilistic inventory model A model where demand is not known exactly; probabilities must be associated with the possible values for demand.

Single-period inventory model An inventory model in which only one order is placed for the product, and at the end of the period either the item has sold out, or a surplus of unsold items will be sold for a salvage value.

Incremental analysis A method used to determine an optimal order quantity by comparing the cost of ordering an additional unit with the cost of not ordering an additional unit.

Lead-time demand distribution The distribution of demand that occurs during the lead-time period.

Continuous review inventory system   A system in which the inventory position is monitored or reviewed on a continuous basis so that a new order can be placed as soon as the reorder point is reached.

Periodic review inventory system   A system in which the inventory position is checked or reviewed at predetermined periodic points in time. Reorders are placed only at periodic review points.

PROBLEMS

SELFtest

1. Suppose that the R & B Beverage Company has a soft drink product that has a constant annual demand rate of 3600 cases. A case of the soft drink costs R & B $3. Ordering costs are $20 per order and holding costs are 25% of the value of the inventory. R & B has 250 working days per year, and the lead time is 5 days. Identify the following aspects of the inventory policy.
    a. Economic order quantity
    b. Reorder point
    c. Cycle time
    d. Total annual cost

2. A general property of the EOQ inventory model is that total inventory holding and total ordering costs are equal at the optimal solution. Use the data in Problem 1 to show that this result is true. Use equations (13.1), (13.2), and (13.3) to show that, in general, total holding costs and total ordering costs are equal whenever Q^* is used.

3. The reorder point [see equation (13.6)] is defined as the lead-time demand for an item. In cases of long lead times, the lead-time demand and thus the reorder point may exceed the economic order quantity Q^*. In such cases, the inventory position will not equal the inventory on hand when an order is placed, and the reorder point may be expressed in terms of either the inventory position or the inventory on hand. Consider the economic order quantity model with $D = 5000$, $C_o = \$32$, $C_h = \$2$, and 250 working days per year. Identify the reorder point in terms of the inventory position and in terms of the inventory on hand for each of the following lead times.
    a. 5 days
    b. 15 days
    c. 25 days
    d. 45 days

4. Westside Auto purchases a component used in the manufacture of automobile generators directly from the supplier. Westside's generator production operation, which is operated at a constant rate, will require 1000 components per month throughout the year (12,000 units annually). Assume that the ordering costs are $25 per order, the unit cost is $2.50 per component, and annual holding costs are 20% of the value of the inventory. Westside has 250 working days per year and a lead time of 5 days. Answer the following inventory policy questions.
    a. What is the EOQ for this component?
    b. What is the reorder point?
    c. What is the cycle time?
    d. What are the total annual holding and ordering costs associated with your recommended EOQ ?

5. Suppose that Westside's management in Problem 4 likes the operational efficiency of ordering once each month and in quantities of 1000 units. How much more expensive would this policy be than your EOQ recommendation? Would you recommend in favor of the 1000-unit order quantity? Explain. What would the reorder point be if the 1000-unit quantity were acceptable?

6. Tele-Reco is a new specialty store that sells television sets, videotape recorders, video games, and other television-related products. A new Japanese-manufactured videotape recorder costs Tele-Reco $600 per unit. Tele-Reco's annual holding cost rate is 22%. Ordering costs are estimated to be $70 per order.
   a. If demand for the new videotape recorder is expected to be constant with a rate of 20 units per month, what is the recommended order quantity for the videotape recorder?
   b. What are the estimated annual inventory holding and ordering costs associated with this product?
   c. How many orders will be placed per year?
   d. With 250 working days per year, what is the cycle time for this product?

7. A large distributor of oil-well drilling equipment has operated over the past 2 years with EOQ policies based on an annual holding cost rate of 22%. Under the EOQ policy, a particular product has been ordered with a $Q^* = 80$. A recent evaluation of holding costs shows that because of an increase in the interest rate associated with bank loans, the annual holding cost rate should be 27%.
   a. What is the new economic order quantity for the product?
   b. Develop a general expression showing how the economic order quantity changes when the annual holding cost rate is changed from I to I'.

8. Nation-Wide Bus Lines is proud of its 6-week bus driver training program that it conducts for all new Nation-Wide drivers. As long as the class size remains less than or equal to 35, a 6-week training program costs Nation-Wide $22,000 for instructors, equipment, and so on. The Nation-Wide training program must provide the company with approximately five new drivers per month. After completing the training program, new drivers are paid $1600 per month but do not work until a full-time driver position is open. Nation-Wide views the $1600 per month paid to each idle new driver as a holding cost necessary to maintain a supply of newly trained drivers available for immediate service. Viewing new drivers as inventory-type units, how large should the training classes be to minimize Nation-Wide's total annual training and new driver idle-time costs? How many training classes should the company hold each year? What is the total annual cost associated with your recommendation?

9. Cress Electronic Products manufactures components used in the automotive industry. Cress purchases parts for use in its manufacturing operation from a variety of different suppliers. One particular supplier provides a part where the assumptions of the EOQ model are realistic. The annual demand is 5000 units, the ordering cost is $80 per order, and the annual holding cost rate is 25%.
   a. If the cost of the part is $20 per unit, what is the economic order quantity?
   b. Assume 250 days of operation per year. If the lead time for an order is 12 days, what is the reorder point?
   c. If the lead time for the part is 7 weeks (35 days), what is the reorder point?
   d. What is the reorder point for part (c) if the reorder point is expressed in terms of the inventory on hand rather than the inventory position?

10. All-Star Bat Manufacturing, Inc., supplies baseball bats to major and minor league baseball teams. After an initial order in January, demand over the 6-month baseball season is approximately constant at 1000 bats per month. Assuming that the bat production process can handle up to 4000 bats per month, the bat production setup costs are $150 per setup, the production cost is $10 per bat, and that holding costs have a monthly rate of 2%, what production lot size would you recommend to meet the demand during the baseball season? If All-Star operates 20 days per month, how often will the production process operate, and what is the length of a production run?

11. Assume that a production line operates such that the production lot-size model of Section 13.2 is applicable. Given $D = 6400$ units per year, $C_o = \$100$, and $C_h = \$2$ per unit per year, compute the minimum cost production lot size for each of the following production rates:

a. 8000 units per year
b. 10,000 units per year
c. 32,000 units per year
d. 100,000 units per year

Compute the EOQ recommended lot size using equation (13.5). What two observations can you make about the relationship between the EOQ model and the production lot-size model?

12. Assume that you are reviewing the production lot size decision associated with a production operation where $P = 8000$ units per year, $D = 2000$ units per year, $C_o = \$300$, and $C_h = \$1.60$ per unit per year. Also assume that current practice calls for production runs of 500 units every 3 months. Would you recommend changing the current production lot size? Why or why not? How much could be saved by converting to your production lot-size recommendation?

SELFtest

13. Wilson Publishing Company produces books for the retail market. Demand for a current book is expected to occur at a constant annual rate of 7200 copies. The cost of one copy of the book is $14.50. The holding cost is based on an 18% annual rate, and production setup costs are $150 per setup. The equipment on which the book is produced has an annual production volume of 25,000 copies. Wilson has 250 working days per year, and the lead time for a production run is 15 days. Use the production lot-size model to compute the following values:
a. Minimum cost production lot size
b. Number of production runs per year
c. Cycle time
d. Length of a production run
e. Maximum inventory
f. Total annual cost
g. Reorder point

14. A well-known manufacturer of several brands of toothpaste uses the production lot-size model to determine production quantities for its various products. The product known as Extra White is currently being produced in production lot sizes of 5000 units. The length of the production run for this quantity is 10 days. Because of a recent shortage of a particular raw material, the supplier of the material has announced a cost increase that will be passed along to the manufacturer of Extra White. Current estimates are that the new raw material cost will increase the manufacturing cost of the toothpaste products by 23% per unit. What will be the effect of this price increase on the production lot sizes for Extra White?

SELFtest

15. Suppose that Westside Auto of Problem 4, with $D = 12,000$ units per year, $C_h = (2.50)(0.20) = \$0.50$, and $C_o = \$25$, decided to operate with a backorder inventory policy. Backorder costs are estimated to be $5 per unit per year. Identify the following:
a. Minimum cost order quantity
b. Maximum number of backorders
c. Maximum inventory
d. Cycle time
e. Total annual cost

16. Assuming 250 days of operation per year and a lead time of 5 days, what is the reorder point for Westside Auto in Problem 15? Show the general formula for the reorder point for the EOQ model with backorders. In general, is the reorder point when backorders are allowed greater than or less than the reorder point when backorders are not allowed? Explain.

17. A manager of an inventory system believes that inventory models are important decision-making aids. While often using an EOQ policy, the manager has never considered a back-order model because of the assumption that backorders were "bad" and should be avoided. However, with upper management's continued pressure for cost reduction, you have been asked to analyze the economics of a backordering policy for some products that can possibly be backordered. For a specific product with $D = 800$ units per year, $C_o = \$150$,

$C_h = \$3$, and $C_b = \$20$, what is the difference in total annual cost between the EOQ model and the planned shortage or backorder model? If the manager adds constraints that no more than 25% of the units can be backordered and that no customer will have to wait more than 15 days for an order, should the backorder inventory policy be adopted? Assume 250 working days per year.

18. If the lead time for new orders is 20 days for the inventory system discussed in Problem 17, find the reorder point for both the EOQ and the backorder models.

19. The A&M Hobby Shop carries a line of radio-controlled model racing cars. Demand for the cars is assumed to be constant at a rate of 40 cars per month. The cars cost $60 each, and ordering costs are approximately $15 per order, regardless of the order size. The annual holding cost rate is 20%.
    a. Determine the economic order quantity and total annual cost under the assumption that no backorders are permitted.
    b. Using a $45 per unit per year backorder cost, determine the minimum cost inventory policy and total annual cost for the model racing cars.
    c. What is the maximum number of days a customer would have to wait for a backorder under the policy in part (b)? Assume that the Hobby Shop is open for business 300 days per year.
    d. Would you recommend a no-backorder or a backorder inventory policy for this product? Explain.
    e. If the lead time is 6 days, what is the reorder point for both the no-backorder and backorder inventory policies?

20. Assume that the following quantity discount schedule is appropriate. If annual demand is 120 units, ordering costs are $20 per order, and the annual holding cost rate is 25%, what order quantity would you recommend?

Order Size	Discount (%)	Unit Cost
0 to 49	0	$30.00
50 to 99	5	28.50
100 or more	10	27.00

SELFtest 21. Apply the EOQ model to the following quantity discount situation in which $D = 500$ units per year, $C_o = \$40$, and the annual holding cost rate is 20%. What order quantity do you recommend?

Discount Category	Order Size	Discount (%)	Unit Cost
1	0 to 99	0	$10.00
2	100 or more	3	9.70

22. Keith Shoe Stores carries a basic black dress shoe for men that sells at an approximate constant rate of 500 pairs of shoes every 3 months. Keith's current buying policy is to order 500 pairs each time an order is placed. It costs Keith $30 to place an order. The annual holding cost rate is 20%. With the order quantity of 500, Keith obtains the shoes at the lowest possible unit cost of $28 per pair. Other quantity discounts offered by the manufacturer are as follows. What is the minimum cost order quantity for the shoes? What are the annual savings of your inventory policy over the policy currently being used by Keith?

Order Quantity	Price per Pair
0–99	$36
100–199	32
200–299	30
300 or more	28

23. In the EOQ model with quantity discounts, we stated that if the Q^* for a price category is larger than necessary to qualify for the category price, the category cannot be optimal. Use the two discount categories in Problem 21 to show that this statement is true. That is, plot total cost curves for the two categories and show that if the category 2 minimum cost Q is an acceptable solution, we do not have to consider category 1.

24. The J&B Card Shop sells calendars depicting a different Colonial scene each month. The once-a-year order for each year's calendar arrives in September. From past experience, the September-to-July demand for the calendars can be approximated by a normal probability distribution with $\mu = 500$ and $\sigma = 120$. The calendars cost $1.50 each, and J&B sells them for $3 each.
    a. If J&B throws out all unsold calendars at the end of July (i.e., salvage value is zero), how many calendars should be ordered?
    b. If J&B reduces the calendar price to $1 at the end of July and can sell all surplus calendars at this price, how many calendars should be ordered?

SELFtest   25. The Gilbert Air-Conditioning Company is considering the purchase of a special shipment of portable air conditioners manufactured in Japan. Each unit will cost Gilbert $80, and it will be sold for $125. Gilbert does not want to carry surplus air conditioners over until the following year. Thus, all surplus air conditioners will be sold to a wholesaler for $50 per unit. Assume that the air conditioner demand follows a normal probability distribution with $\mu = 20$ and $\sigma = 8$.
    a. What is the recommended order quantity?
    b. What is the probability that Gilbert will sell all units it orders?

26. A popular newsstand is attempting to determine how many copies of the local newspaper it should purchase each day. Demand for the newspaper can be approximated by a normal probability distribution with $\mu = 450$ and $\sigma = 100$. The newspaper costs the newsstand 35¢ a copy and sells for 50¢ a copy. The newsstand does not receive any value from surplus papers and thus absorbs a 100% loss on all unsold papers.
    a. How many copies of the newspaper should be purchased each day?
    b. What is the probability that the newsstand will have a stockout?
    c. The manager of the newsstand is concerned about the newsstand's image if the probability of stockout is high. Customers often purchase other items after coming to the newsstand. Frequent stockouts would cause customers to go to another newsstand. The manager agrees that a 50¢ goodwill cost should be assigned to any stockout. What is the new recommended order quantity and the new probability of a stockout?

27. A perishable dairy product is ordered daily at a particular supermarket. The product, which costs $1.19 per unit, sells for $1.65 per unit. If units are unsold at the end of the day, the supplier takes them back at a rebate of $1 per unit. Assume that daily demand is approximately normally distributed with $\mu = 150$ and $\sigma = 30$.
    a. What is your recommended daily order quantity for the supermarket?
    b. What is the probability that the supermarket will sell all the units it orders?
    c. In problems such as these, why would the supplier offer a rebate as high as $1? For example, why not offer a nominal rebate of, say, 25¢ per unit? What happens to the supermarket order quantity as the rebate is reduced?

28. A retail outlet sells a seasonal product for $10 per unit. The cost of the product is $8 per unit. All units not sold during the regular season are sold for half the retail price in an end-of-season clearance sale. Assume that demand for the product is uniformly distributed between 200 and 800.
   a. What is the recommended order quantity?
   b. What is the probability that at least some customers will ask to purchase the product after the outlet is sold out? That is, what is the probability of a stockout using your order quantity in part (a)?
   c. To keep customers happy and returning to the store later, the owner feels that stockouts should be avoided if at all possible. What is your recommended order quantity if the owner is willing to tolerate a 0.15 probability of a stockout?
   d. Using your answer to part (c), what is the goodwill cost you are assigning to a stockout?

SELFtest 29. Floyd Distributors, Inc., provides a variety of auto parts to small local garages. Floyd purchases parts from manufacturers according to the EOQ model and then ships the parts from a regional warehouse direct to its customers. For a particular type of muffler, Floyd's EOQ analysis recommends orders with $Q^* = 25$ to satisfy an annual demand of 200 mufflers. Floyd's has 250 working days per year, and the lead time averages 15 days.
   a. What is the reorder point if Floyd assumes a constant demand rate?
   b. Suppose that an analysis of Floyd's muffler demand shows that the lead-time demand follows a normal probability distribution with $\mu = 12$ and $\sigma = 2.5$. If Floyd's management can tolerate one stockout per year, what is the revised reorder point?
   c. What is the safety stock for part (b)? If $C_h = \$5/\text{unit/year}$, what is the extra cost due to the uncertainty of demand?

30. For Floyd Distributors in Problem 29, we were given $Q^* = 25$, $D = 200$, $C_h = \$5$, and a normal lead-time demand distribution with $\mu = 12$ and $\sigma = 2.5$.
   a. What is Floyd's reorder point if the firm is willing to tolerate two stockouts during the year?
   b. What is Floyd's reorder point if the firm wants to restrict the probability of a stockout on any one cycle to at most 1%?
   c. What are the safety stock levels and the annual safety stock costs for the reorder points found in parts (a) and (b)?

31. A product with an annual demand of 1000 units has $C_o = \$25.50$ and $C_h = \$8$. The demand exhibits some variability such that the lead-time demand follows a normal probability distribution with $\mu = 25$ and $\sigma = 5$.
   a. What is the recommended order quantity?
   b. What are the reorder point and safety stock if the firm desires at most a 2% probability of stockout on any given order cycle?
   c. If a manager sets the reorder point at 30, what is the probability of a stockout on any given order cycle? How many times would you expect to stockout during the year if this reorder point were used?

32. The B&S Novelty and Craft Shop in Bennington, Vermont, sells a variety of quality hand-made items to tourists. B&S will sell 300 hand-carved miniature replicas of a Colonial soldier each year, but the demand pattern during the year is uncertain. The replicas sell for $20 each, and B&S uses a 15% annual inventory holding cost rate. Ordering costs are $5 per order, and demand during the lead time follows a normal probability distribution with $\mu = 15$ and $\sigma = 6$.
   a. What is the recommended order quantity?
   b. If B&S is willing to accept a stockout roughly twice a year, what reorder point would you recommend? What is the probability that B&S will have a stockout in any one order-cycle?
   c. What are the safety stock and annual safety stock costs for this product?

SELFtest   33. A firm uses a 1-week periodic review inventory system. A 2-day lead time is needed for any order, and the firm is willing to tolerate an average of one stockout per year.

  a. Using the firm's service guideline, what is the probability of a stockout associated with each replenishment decision?

  b. What is the replenishment level if demand during the review period plus lead-time period is normally distributed with a mean of 60 units and a standard deviation of 12 units?

  c. What is the replenishment level if demand during the review period plus lead-time period is uniformly distributed between 35 and 85 units?

34. Foster Drugs, Inc., handles a variety of health and beauty aid products. A particular hair conditioner product costs Foster Drugs $2.95 per unit. The annual holding cost rate is 20%. An order-quantity, reorder point inventory model recommends an order quantity of 300 units per order.

  a. Lead time is one week and the lead-time demand is normally distributed with a mean of 150 units and a standard deviation of 40 units. What is the reorder point if the firm is willing to tolerate a 1% chance of stockout on any one cycle?

  b. What safety stock and annual safety stock cost are associated with your recommendation in part (a)?

  c. The order-quantity, reorder point model requires a continuous review system. Management is considering making a transition to a periodic review system in an attempt to coordinate ordering for many of its products. The demand during the proposed two-week review period and the one-week lead-time period is normally distributed with a mean of 450 units and a standard deviation of 70 units. What is the recommended replenishment level for this periodic review system if the firm is willing to tolerate the same 1% chance of stockout associated with any replenishment decision?

  d. What safety stock and annual safety stock cost are associated with your recommendation in part (c)?

  e. Compare your answers to parts (b) and (d). The company is seriously considering the periodic review system. Would you support this decision? Explain.

  f. Would you tend to favor the continuous review system for more expensive items? For example, assume that the product in the preceding example sold for $295 per unit. Explain.

35. Statewide Auto Parts uses a 4-week periodic review system to reorder parts for its inventory stock. A 1-week lead time is required to fill the order. Demand for one particular part during the 5-week replenishment period is normally distributed with a mean of 18 units and a standard deviation of 6 units.

  a. At a particular periodic review, 8 units are in inventory. The parts manager places an order for 16 units. What is the probability that this part will have a stockout before an order that is placed at the next 4-week review period arrives?

  b. Assume that the company is willing to tolerate a 2.5% chance of a stockout associated with a replenishment decision. How many parts should the manager have ordered in part (a)? What is the replenishment level for the 4-week periodic review system?

36. Rose Office Supplies, Inc., which is open 6 days a week, uses a 2-week periodic review for its store inventory. On alternating Monday mornings, the store manager fills out an order sheet requiring a shipment of various items from the company's warehouse. A particular three-ring notebook sells at an average rate of 16 notebooks per week. The standard deviation in sales is 5 notebooks per week. The lead time for a new shipment is 3 days. The mean lead-time demand is 8 notebooks with a standard deviation of 3.5.

  a. What is the mean or expected demand during the review period plus the lead-time period?

  b. Under the assumption of independent demand from week to week, the variances in demands are additive. Thus, the variance of the demand during the review period plus the lead-time period is equal to the variance of demand during the first week plus the variance of demand during the second week plus the variance of demand during the lead-time period. What is the variance of demand during the review period plus the lead-time period? What is the standard deviation of demand during the review period plus the lead-time period?

c. Assuming that demand has a normal probability distribution, what is the replenishment level that will provide an expected stockout rate of one per year?

d. On Monday, March 22, 18 notebooks remain in inventory at the store. How many notebooks should the store manager order?

Case Problem   A MAKE-OR-BUY ANALYSIS

Managers at Wagner Fabricating Company are reviewing the economic feasibility of manufacturing a part that it currently purchases from a supplier. Forecasted annual demand for the part is 3200 units. Wagner operates 250 days per year.

Wagner's financial analysts have established a cost of capital of 14% for the use of funds for investments within the company. In addition, over the past year $600,000 has been the average investment in the company's inventory. Accounting information shows that a total of $24,000 was spent on taxes and insurance related to the company's inventory. In addition, an estimated $9000 was lost due to inventory shrinkage, which included damaged goods as well as pilferage. A remaining $15,000 was spent on warehouse overhead, including utility expenses for heating and lighting.

An analysis of the purchasing operation shows that approximately 2 hours are required to process and coordinate an order for the part regardless of the quantity ordered. Purchasing salaries average $28 per hour, including employee benefits. In addition, a detailed analysis of 125 orders showed that $2375 was spent on telephone, paper, and postage directly related to the ordering process.

A 1-week lead time is required to obtain the part from the supplier. An analysis of demand during the lead time shows it approximately normally distributed with a mean of 64 units and a standard deviation of 10 units. Service level guidelines indicate that one stockout per year is acceptable.

Currently, the company has a contract to purchase the part from a supplier at a cost of $18 per unit. However, over the past few months, the company's production capacity has been expanded. As a result, excess capacity is now available in certain production departments, and the company is considering the alternative of producing the parts itself.

Forecasted utilization of equipment shows that production capacity will be available for the part being considered. The production capacity is available at the rate of 1000 units per month, with up to 5 months of production time available. Management believes that with a 2-week lead time, schedules can be arranged so that the part can be produced whenever needed. The demand during the 2-week lead time is approximately normally distributed, with a mean of 128 units and a standard deviation of 20 units. Production costs are expected to be $17 per part.

A concern of management is that setup costs will be significant. The total cost of labor and lost production time is estimated to be $50 per hour, and a full 8-hour shift will be needed to set up the equipment for producing the part.

Managerial Report

Develop a report for management of Wagner Fabricating that will address the question of whether the company should continue to purchase the part from the supplier or begin to produce the part itself. Include the following factors in your report:

1. An analysis of the holding costs, including the appropriate annual holding cost rate
2. An analysis of ordering costs, including the appropriate cost per order from the supplier

3. An analysis of setup costs for the production operation
4. A development of the inventory policy for the following two alternatives:
   a. Ordering a fixed quantity Q from the supplier
   b. Ordering a fixed quantity Q from in-plant production
5. Include the following in the policies of parts 4(a) and 4(b):
   a. Optimal quantity Q^*
   b. Number of order or production runs per year
   c. Cycle time
   d. Reorder point
   e. Amount of safety stock
   f. Expected maximum inventory
   g. Average inventory
   h. Annual holding cost
   i. Annual ordering cost
   j. Annual cost of the units purchased or manufactured
   k. Total annual cost of the purchase policy and the total annual cost of the production policy
6. Make a recommendation as to whether the company should purchase or manufacture the part. What savings are associated with your recommendation as compared with the other alternative?

Appendix 13.1   INVENTORY MODELS WITH SPREADSHEETS

In this appendix we show how a spreadsheet can be used to implement the economic order quantity (EOQ) model introduced in Section 13.1. The spreadsheet for the EOQ model can be modified to accommodate the other inventory models presented in this chapter.

Figure 13.16 shows the Excel spreadsheet for the Bub Beer economic order quantity model presented in Section 13.1. The annual demand, ordering cost, annual inventory holding rate, cost per unit, working days per year, and lead time in days are entered into cells B3:B8. The cell formulas used to compute the optimal inventory policy are as follows:

Cell B13	Economic Order Quantity	=SQRT(2*B3*B4/(B6*B5/100))
Cell B14	Total Annual Cost	=(B13/2)*(B6*B5/100)+B3*B4/B13
Cell B16	Economic Order Quantity from cell B13	=B13
Cell B18	Annual Inventory Holding Cost	=(B16/2)*(B5*B6/100)
Cell B19	Annual Ordering Cost	=(B3/B16)*B4
Cell B20	Total Annual Cost	=B18+B19
Cell B21	Maximum Inventory Level	=B16
Cell B22	Average Inventory Level	=B21/2
Cell B23	Reorder Point	=(B3/B7)*B8

Cell B24   Number of Orders per Year
=B3/B16

Cell B25   Cycle Time (Days)
=B7/B24

Cell B27   Annual Cost over EOQ
=B20−B14

Cell B28   Percentage Annual Cost over EOQ Annual Cost
=B27/B14

Using equation (13.5), the spreadsheet places the economic order quantity, Q^*, in cell B13. Cell B14 contains the total annual cost assuming the economic order quantity is implemented. The remaining spreadsheet cells provide additional information that will help the manager understand the inventory operation and determine the final order quantity to be used.

After viewing the spreadsheet solution in Figure 13.16, the manager can easily evaluate alternative order quantities. For example, assume that the manager believes that an or-

FIGURE 13.16   SPREADSHEET FOR THE BUB BEER EOQ INVENTORY MODEL

	A	B
1	**Bub Beer Economic Order Quantity**	
2		
3	Annual Demand	104,000
4	Ordering Cost	$32.00
5	Annual Inventory Holding Rate %	25
6	Cost per Unit	$8.00
7	Working Days per Year	250
8	Lead Time (Days)	2
9		
10		
11	**Optimal Inventory Policy**	
12		
13	Economic Order Quantity	1824.28
14	Total Annual Cost	$3,648.56
15		
16	**Requested Order Quantity**	1824.28
17		
18	Annual Inventory Holding Cost	$1,824.28
19	Annual Ordering Cost	$1,824.28
20	Total Annual Cost	$3,648.56
21	Maximum Inventory Level	1,824.28
22	Average Inventory Level	912.14
23	Reorder Point	832.00
24	Number of Orders per Year	57.01
25	Cycle Time (Days)	4.39
26		
27	Annual Cost over EOQ	$0.00
28	Percentage	0.00%

der quantity of 2000 cases would be easier to implement than the economic order quantity model's recommendation of $Q^* = 1824.28$. In this case, the manager simply enters 2000 as the requested order quantity in cell B16. The spreadsheet will automatically revise the inventory policy information. Figure 13.17 shows the results based on the requested order quantity of 2000 cases. In particular, note that the last two entries on the spreadsheet, cells B27 and B28, show that the added cost with $Q = 2000$ is only $15.44 per year, or only 0.42%. Other inventory order quantities can be evaluated by placing the requested economic order quantity in cell B16. In this case, the manager preferred the 2000-case order quantity with its slight cost increase over the economic order quantity model's recommendation of $Q^* = 1824.28$.

As with most other spreadsheet applications, the manager may change one or more of the models inputs and quickly learn how any change affects the optimal order quantity and the total annual cost. For example, changing the inventory holding cost rate and/or the order cost would show how sensitive the recommended economic order quantity and the total annual cost are to these input values.

FIGURE 13.17   SPREADSHEET FOR THE BUB BEER EOQ INVENTORY MODEL WITH $Q = 2000$

	A	B
1	**Bub Beer Economic Order Quantity**	
2		
3	Annual Demand	104,000
4	Ordering Cost	$32.00
5	Annual Inventory Holding Rate %	25
6	Cost per Unit	$8.00
7	Working Days per Year	250
8	Lead Time (Days)	2
9		
10		
11	**Optimal Inventory Policy**	
12		
13	Economic Order Quantity	1824.28
14	Total Annual Cost	$3,648.56
15		
16	**Requested Order Quantity**	2000.00
17		
18	Annual Inventory Holding Cost	$2,000.00
19	Annual Ordering Cost	$1,664.00
20	Total Annual Cost	$3,664.00
21	Maximum Inventory Level	2,000.00
22	Average Inventory Level	1000.00
23	Reorder Point	832.00
24	Number of Orders per Year	52.00
25	Cycle Time (Days)	4.81
26		
27	Annual Cost over EOQ	$15.44
28	Percentage	0.42%

Appendix 13.2   DEVELOPMENT OF THE OPTIMAL ORDER QUANTITY (Q) FORMULA FOR THE EOQ MODEL

Given equation (13.4) as the total annual cost for the EOQ model,

$$TC = \frac{1}{2} Q C_h + \frac{D}{Q} C_o \qquad (13.4)$$

we can find the order quantity Q that minimizes the total cost by setting the derivative, dTC/dQ, equal to zero and solving for Q^*.

$$\frac{dTC}{dQ} = \frac{1}{2} C_h - \frac{D}{Q^2} C_o = 0$$

$$\frac{1}{2} C_h = \frac{D}{Q^2} C_o$$

$$C_h Q^2 = 2DC_o$$

$$Q^2 = \frac{2DC_o}{C_h}$$

Hence,

$$Q^* = \sqrt{\frac{2DC_o}{C_h}} \qquad (13.5)$$

The second derivative is

$$\frac{d^2TC}{dQ^2} = \frac{2D}{Q^3} C_o$$

Because the value of the second derivative is greater than zero for D, C_o, and Q greater than zero, Q^* from equation (13.5) is the minimum cost solution.

Appendix 13.3   DEVELOPMENT OF THE OPTIMAL LOT-SIZE (Q^*) FORMULA FOR THE PRODUCTION LOT-SIZE MODEL

Given equation (13.15) as the total annual cost for the production lot-size model,

$$TC = \frac{1}{2}\left(1 - \frac{D}{P}\right)Q C_h + \frac{D}{Q} C_o \qquad (13.15)$$

we can find the order quantity Q that minimizes the total cost by setting the derivative, dTC/dQ, equal to zero and solving for Q^*.

$$\frac{dTC}{dQ} = \frac{1}{2}\left(1 - \frac{D}{P}\right)C_h + \frac{D}{Q^2} C_o = 0$$

Solving for Q^*, we have

$$\frac{1}{2}\left(1 - \frac{D}{P}\right)C_h = \frac{D}{Q^2}\,C_o$$

$$\left(1 - \frac{D}{P}\right)C_h Q^2 = 2DC_o$$

$$Q^2 = \frac{2DC_o}{(1 - D/P)C_h}$$

Hence,

$$Q^* = \sqrt{\frac{2DC_o}{(1 - D/P)C_h}} \tag{13.28}$$

The second derivative is

$$\frac{d^2TC}{dQ^2} = \frac{2DC_o}{Q^3}$$

Because the value of the second derivative is greater than zero for D, C_o, and Q greater than zero, Q^* from equation (13.16) is a minimum cost solution.

Appendix 13.4   DEVELOPMENT OF THE OPTIMAL ORDER QUANTITY (Q^*) AND OPTIMAL BACKORDER (S^*) FORMULAS FOR THE PLANNED SHORTAGE MODEL

Given equation (13.25) as the total annual cost for the planned shortage model,

$$TC = \frac{(Q - S^2)}{2Q}\,C_h + \frac{D}{Q}\,C_o + \frac{S^2}{2Q}\,C_b \tag{13.25}$$

we have two inventory decision variables, Q and S. To find the Q and S values that minimize equation (13.25), we must set the two partial derivatives, $\partial TC/\partial Q$ and $\partial TC/\partial S$, equal to zero. First, let us rewrite equation (13.25) as follows:

$$\begin{aligned}
TC &= \left(\frac{Q^2 - 2QS + S^2}{2Q}\right)C_h + \frac{D}{Q}\,C_o + \frac{S^2}{2Q}\,C_b \\
&= \frac{Q}{2}\,C_h - SC_h + \frac{C_h}{2Q}\,S^2 + \frac{DC_o}{Q} + \frac{C_b}{2Q}\,S^2 \\
&= \left(\frac{C_h + C_b}{2Q}\right)S^2 - SC_h + \frac{QC_h}{2} + \frac{DC_o}{Q}
\end{aligned}$$

Then setting $\partial TC/\partial S = 0$, we obtain

$$\frac{\partial TC}{\partial S} = \left(\frac{C_h + C_b}{Q}\right)S - C_h = 0$$

Solving for S^*, we have

$$\left(\frac{C_h - C_b}{Q}\right)S = C_h$$

Thus

$$S^* = Q\left(\frac{C_h}{C_h + C_b}\right) \tag{13.27}$$

Setting $\partial TC/\partial Q = 0$, we obtain

$$\frac{\partial TC}{\partial Q} = \frac{-(C_h + C_b)S^2}{2Q^2} + \frac{C_h}{2} - \frac{DC_o}{Q^2} = 0$$

Substituting S^* of equation (13.27), we have

$$\frac{\partial TC}{\partial Q} = \frac{-(C_h + C_b)Q^2(C_h)^2/(C_h + C_b)^2}{2Q^2} + \frac{C_h}{2} - \frac{DC_o}{Q^2} = 0$$

We can solve for Q^* as follows:

$$\frac{-C_h^2}{2(C_h + C_b)} + \frac{C_h}{2} = \frac{DC_o}{Q^2}$$

$$\frac{-C_h^2 + C_h(C_h + C_b)}{2(C_h + C_b)} = \frac{DC_o}{Q^2}$$

$$Q^2 = \frac{2(C_h + C_b)DC_o}{C_h C_b}$$

$$Q^2 = \frac{2C_h DC_o}{C_h C_b} + \frac{2C_b DC_o}{C_h C_b}$$

$$Q^2 = \frac{2DC_o}{C_h}\left(\frac{C_h}{C_b} + \frac{C_b}{C_b}\right)$$

Hence

$$Q^* = \sqrt{\frac{2DC_o}{C_h}\left(\frac{C_h + C_b}{C_b}\right)} \tag{13.26}$$

The second-order conditions will show that equations (13.26) and (13.27) are the minimum cost solutions.

CVS CORPORATION*

WOONSOCKET, RHODE ISLAND

The first CVS store opened in Lowell, Massachusetts, in 1963, under the name "Consumer Value Store." In the 1990s, CVS mergers and acquisition included drugstore chains formerly known as Peoples, SuperRx, Revco, and Arbor Drugs. The Revco acquisition in 1997 and the Arbor Drugs acquisition in 1998 made CVS the largest drugstore chain in the United States with 4100 stores in 25 states. In 1998, CVS dispensed approximately 12% of all retail prescriptions in the United States.

General inventory management in the drugstore business involves several product categories: basic products carried on an everyday basis, seasonal products carried only during certain times of the year (such as fruitcakes during holidays), and special items bought on an in-and-out basis throughout the year.

By far the most critical inventory issue is the replenishment of basic products. At most retail drug chains, this type of product is ordered under a periodic review inventory system, with the review period being one week. The weekly review uses electronic ordering equipment that scans an order label affixed to the shelf. Such a label is located on the shelf directly below each item. Among other information on this label is the "order-to-quantity." (*Note:* This replenishment level is referenced in the periodic review inventory model of Section 13.7.) The store employee placing the order determines the quantity to order by subtracting the number of units of product on the shelf from the order-to-quantity (OTQ). For example, if the OTQ is 6 and two units of product are on the shelf, the quantity ordered would be 4. The OTQ is the key factor in inventory control for basic products.

Several factors are considered in determining individual item OTQs. The most obvious is average weekly demand or movement. Suppose, for example, an item averages two units per week per store in warehouse deliveries. Setting the OTQ equal to 2 would not allow for sales fluctuations that exceeded the average of 2. To compensate, and to avoid stockouts, the OTQ is set equal to a 3-week demand or movement. Thus, in this example, the OTQ would become 6.

Another factor to consider is whether an item can be ordered in units or cases. In some instances, delivering in anything less than case quantities is not feasible for the warehouse. An example would be candy bars. Stores must order a minimum of one case (36 units), no matter what the movement indicates. Thus, the OTQ is 36 or a multiple of 36 to accommodate the case order restriction. Merchandising esthetics must also be considered when determining an OTQ. If an item has four facings or open positions on the shelf, but the optimum OTQ determined by movement is 3, one space would be without product. This vacancy would create an out-of-stock impression to the customer, and, thus, the OTQ would be increased to at least 4. Seasonal fluctuations in movement must be considered when OTQs are determined. For example, the OTQ for a cough and cold item would be significantly higher in January than it would be in July. Adhesive bandages would be just the opposite, with higher usage in the summer than in the winter.

Today, OTQs are based on average company warehouse movement into the stores. A computer program determines OTQs by item by individual store, based on that store's movement, rather than on the company movement.

Good inventory management does not occur in a vacuum, but must be interrelated with sales, gross margin, and expense control objectives. This inventory management system allows merchandisers to act out "what if" scenarios relating to OTQs, product costs, retail sales prices, inventory carrying costs, sales, and other factors.

*The authors are indebted to Bob Carver for providing this application. This inventory system was originally implemented in the CVS stores formerly known as SuperRx.

As an example, optimum order-to-quantities normally result in some percentage of missed sales because of individual item movement fluctuations. On the other hand, increasing the OTQs to maximize sales also increases inventory, decreases inventory turnover, and thus ties up capital that could otherwise be used for building new stores, remodeling existing locations, and so on. By using the new inventory management techniques, the company can maximize both sales and inventory turnover. Rapidly becoming a necessity rather than a luxury, the use of this technology ensures the maximization of sales, profits, and inventory turnovers that ultimately determine the success or failure of a drug chain.

Questions

1. Does the inventory system in this application use continuous review or periodic review? Why would this system be preferred for a retail business such as CVS?
2. What is the decision rule that is used to provide a safety stock and minimize stockouts?

INVENTORY MANAGEMENT: DEPENDENT DEMAND

Chapter 14

CONTENTS

The first book on material requirements planning, written by Joseph Orlicky, was published in 1975. In 1973, while preparing a study guide on material requirements planning for the American Production and Inventory Control Society (APICS), Joseph Orlicky found that the entire MRP literature consisted of only 26 items.

The inventory management techniques discussed in the previous chapter are most appropriate for managing **finished goods inventories.** In this chapter we focus on the management of **manufacturing inventories.** They consist of the raw materials, parts, and subassemblies that make up a finished good or product. Manufacturing inventories are converted into finished products, so the amount needed depends on the demand for the finished goods they will become part of. Once the demand for the finished good is known, the demand for the raw materials, parts, and subassemblies that comprise the item can be determined.

Because the demand for manufacturing inventories depends on the demand for the final product, the independent demand models of the preceding chapter should not be used to manage manufacturing inventories. Instead, techniques that apply to **dependent demand** should be used.

Material requirements planning (MRP) is a technique that can be used to translate a set of period-by-period requirements for finished products into a set of period-by-period requirements for the raw materials, parts, and subassemblies that make up the finished product. One of the goals of MRP is to minimize the investment in manufacturing inventories. Another goal is to ensure that all raw materials, parts, and subassemblies are available when needed and thereby prevent production delays from occurring.

First, we discuss the difference between managing finished goods inventories and manufacturing inventories. Then, we discuss the inputs to an MRP system: the master production schedule, the bill of materials, and inventory records. Next, we show how to use these inputs to determine the net requirements for any component over the planning horizon. Then, we illustrate lot sizing and safety stock issues and the MRP time-phasing calculations that result in a period-by-period production schedule for all

items. Finally, we present some issues involved in implementing an MRP system and provide a brief overview of just-in-time operations.

14.1   INDEPENDENT VERSUS DEPENDENT DEMAND

To illustrate the differences between managing finished goods inventories (independent demand) and managing manufacturing inventories (dependent demand), we consider an example involving the Clark Furniture Company. Clark manufactures a variety of Early American furniture at its New Bern, North Carolina, plant. To begin, we consider the factors involved in managing the finished kitchen chair inventory and the inventory of the seats used in the manufacture of these chairs. The seats are purchased from a supplier.

The top panel of Figure 14.1 shows the inventory level for the finished kitchen chairs. When the inventory level drops to the reorder point, R, a production order is issued. A lead time is needed for processing the paperwork and making the setup. Production begins at point A on the time axis. When production of the finished product is initiated, seats are withdrawn from inventory to support manufacturing needs. The inventory level for the seats is shown in the bottom panel of Figure 14.1. Note that it starts decreasing when production of the finished product begins at time A.

If we were using an independent demand inventory model to manage the seat inventory, an order for seats would be placed with the supplier whenever the inventory level falls below its reorder point. Depending on the lead time, the shipment of seats will be received at some time in the future; suppose that it is time B in Figure 14.1. However, the next production run for the chairs is not scheduled to begin until time C, so we have incurred an unnecessary holding cost for the seats that must be carried in inventory between their arrival time at B and use at time C.

FIGURE 14.1   FINISHED PRODUCT AND COMPONENT INVENTORY LEVELS USING AN INDEPENDENT DEMAND INVENTORY MODEL

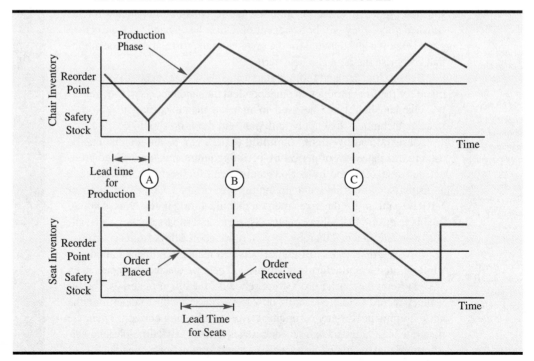

FIGURE 14.2   FINISHED PRODUCT AND COMPONENT PART INVENTORY LEVELS
WITH A TIME-PHASED ORDER POLICY

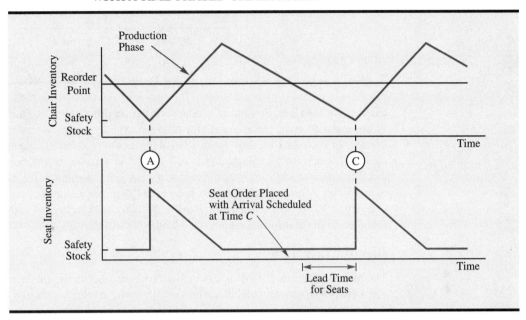

We could have eliminated this unnecessary holding cost by delaying ordering the seats so that they will not arrive prior to time *C*. That is, we could "back up" from time *C* by the amount of the lead time and place the order then. Figure 14.2 shows the reduction in the seat inventory resulting from such an ordering policy. In Figure 14.2 the order policy takes into account the fact that the demand for the seat depends on the demand for the finished product (kitchen chair).

This simple example demonstrates that, in the management of manufacturing inventories, savings in inventory holding costs can be realized by taking into account the dependent nature of demand. An approach used to manage manufacturing inventories is called *material requirements planning (MRP)*. When implemented correctly, an MRP system can reduce the investment in inventory, improve work flow, reduce shortages of raw materials, parts, and subassemblies, and help achieve more reliable delivery schedules.

14.2   INPUTS TO MATERIAL REQUIREMENTS PLANNING

An MRP system has three key inputs: the master production schedule, the bill of materials, and inventory records. The master production schedule (MPS) shows the demand for finished goods over the planning horizon, which usually is several weeks into the future. The bill of materials (BOM) is a structured parts list that shows how raw materials, parts, and subassemblies are combined to make up the finished product. Finally, an MRP inventory record is prepared for each raw material, part, or subassembly that shows the inventory level and ordering policy over the planning horizon. Each of these inputs must be available before MRP can be implemented.

Master Production Schedule

The master production schedule is meant to be a statement of what can and will be produced rather than a management wish list.

The **master production schedule (MPS)** shows the number of end items needed in each time period of the **planning horizon.** The time periods, also called *time buckets,* may be of any length that makes sense for the particular firm; however, most firms use time buckets of 1 week duration. The master production schedule is developed by taking into account sales forecasts, customer orders, economic production lot sizes, production capacity, and

TABLE 14.1   MASTER PRODUCTION SCHEDULE FOR KITCHEN CHAIRS

	Week					
	1	**2**	**3**	**4**	**5**	**6**
Production Quantity	700		600	600		700

the like. For the Clark Furniture Company the master production schedule would show the future manufacturing requirements for all products the firm produces over the planning horizon. In Table 14.1 we show the portion of the master production schedule for the kitchen chairs; note that the planning horizon is 6 weeks. The master production schedule shows that Clark must produce 700 kitchen chairs in week 1, 0 chairs in week 2, 600 chairs in week 3, and so on. After this schedule has been established, the number of components needed to produce the 700 kitchen chairs in week 1, the 600 chairs in week 3, and so on, can be determined from the information provided by the bill of materials.

Bill of Materials

The **bill of materials (BOM)** is a structured parts list that shows the hierarchical relationship between an end item and its various components; in other words, the BOM shows how the finished products are made. Figure 14.3 shows a graphical representation of the BOM for the kitchen chair produced by the Clark Furniture Company; it is called a **product structure tree.** The finished product (end item) is shown at the top (level 0). Level 1 shows that each chair is composed of 1 base assembly, 1 seat, and 1 back assembly. Level 2 shows that each base assembly is made from 4 legs and 1 brace subassembly and that each back assembly is composed of 2 outer back supports, 1 upper back support, and 5 middle back supports. Finally, level 3 shows that each brace subassembly consists of 4 braces.

The component parts or subassemblies shown at each level are said to be the *parents* of the parts or subassemblies directly below them. Each item in the BOM, except the top item, has a parent.

FIGURE 14.3   PRODUCT STRUCTURE TREE FOR THE KITCHEN CHAIR

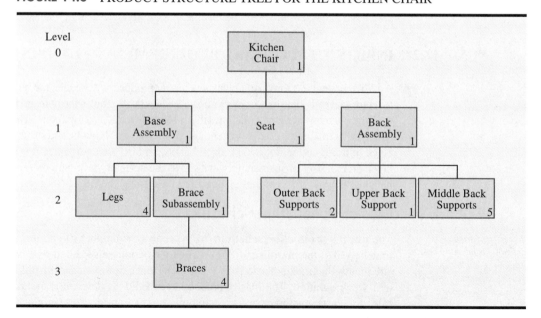

In general, the product structure tree shows how the final product is assembled from its components. Although in the Clark Furniture example we chose to show only the parts and subassemblies that make up the kitchen chair, any needed raw materials, such as wood or glue, could have been included. In practice, considerable thought must be given to the components that should be included in the BOM, and specialized reference books have been written to help manufacturers carry out this process.

The BOM clearly shows the dependent nature of demand for the components needed to produce the end item. Thus, using the BOM, we can determine exactly how many components are needed to produce the quantity of finished products stated in the master production schedule. For instance, the product structure tree shows that a demand for 700 kitchen chairs in week 1 creates a demand for 700 base assemblies, 700 seats, and 700 back assemblies. The demand for the 700 base assemblies in turn creates a demand for 2800 legs and 700 brace subassemblies. The demand for the 700 brace subassemblies in turn creates a demand for 2800 braces. Similarly, the demand for the 700 back assemblies creates a demand for 1400 outer back supports, 700 upper back supports, and 3500 middle back supports. Before showing how a production schedule is developed for these dependent demand components, we first discuss the concept of an MRP inventory record.

MRP Inventory Record

Inventory status information such as how many units are in inventory must be maintained for each item in the BOM. In general, the information contained in the **inventory record** for each component can be classified as (1) inventory transaction information or (2) planning information. The inventory transaction information includes inventory events such as the receipt of goods from a supplier, the disbursement of items from inventory to satisfy production, the generation of scrap during manufacturing, and so on. The planning information includes the lead time required to obtain the item, the safety stock (if any), the lot sizing method used for the item, and so on.

14.3   DETERMINING NET REQUIREMENTS

To illustrate how an MRP system can be used to manage inventories for dependent demand items, let us return to the example involving the kitchen chairs produced by the Clark Furniture Company, and consider the seat component. In Table 14.1 we showed the master production schedule for the next 6-week planning period, and in Figure 14.3 we showed the BOM (as a product structure tree) for the kitchen chair. Suppose that the inventory record for the seat shows a balance of 300 seats in inventory, a lead time of 1 week, a lot size of 800 seats, and a safety stock of 0 units. Suppose also that a previous order of 800 units has been scheduled to arrive at the beginning of week 1 of the current planning period. We must now determine how many seats will be needed at the beginning of each week to meet the requirements of the master production schedule. This quantity is referred to as **net requirements.**

A primary function of material requirements planning is to convert gross requirements into net requirements. Once the net requirements are established, shop orders and purchase orders can be issued to cover the net requirements.

To compute net requirements, we use a worksheet referred to as the *MRP planning worksheet.* First, recall that the master production schedule provides **gross requirements** for each week. The gross requirements are the number of kitchen chairs needed to satisfy the MPS without taking into account the number of kitchen chairs currently in inventory. The BOM shows that one seat is needed for each kitchen chair we produce, so the gross requirements for the seats are the same as the gross requirements for the finished product. Table 14.2 shows the initial MRP planning worksheet for the kitchen seats, which contains the gross requirements data and the information from the inventory record for the seats.

To determine the net requirements in week 1, we first note that 800 seats are scheduled to arrive in week 1 (**scheduled receipts**). As is customary with MRP, we assume that these

TABLE 14.2   MRP PLANNING WORKSHEET

SEAT Lot size: 800	Lead time: 1 wk Safety stock: 0		Week				
		1	2	3	4	5	6
Gross requirements		700	0	600	600	0	700
Scheduled receipts		800					
Projected balance	300						
Net requirements							
Planned order receipts							
Planned order releases							

units arrive at the beginning of week 1. Thus, because 300 seats are currently in inventory (**projected balance**) at the beginning of week 1, the number of seats available for use in this period is $800 + 300 = 1100$. If the gross requirements are 700 seats, the net requirements in period 1 are 0. We now enter 400 as the projected ending inventory balance for week 1 and 0 for the net requirements. The gross requirements are 0 in period 2, so the projected balance of 400 in week 1 is carried over to week 2. Table 14.3 shows the revised worksheet.

Looking forward to week 3, however, we see that the projected balance of 400 seats at the end of week 2 is insufficient to satisfy the gross requirements of 600 seats in week 3. Therefore, with a lead time of 1 week to obtain a seat from the supplier, we must release an order at the beginning of week 2 to provide sufficient inventory in week 3. Because this order is placed during the current planning period, we refer to its placement at the beginning of week 2 as a **planned order release,** and its arrival at the beginning of week 3 as a **planned order receipt.** Now, we are ready to determine the net requirements for week 3. With a projected balance for week 2 of 400 units and a planned order receipt of 800 units (the lot size) at the beginning of week 3, the number of seats available in week 3 is 1200. Since the gross requirements are 600, the projected balance at the end of week 3 is 600. Moreover, as we had a beginning balance of 400 seats, only 200 units of the planned order receipts are actually needed to cover the gross requirements for the period; thus, we refer to the 200 seats as the net requirements for week 3. The worksheet now appears as shown in Table 14.4.

We continue this process for week 4. With a projected balance at the end of week 3 of 600 and gross requirements in week 4 of 600, we have a projected balance of 0 at the end of week 4 and a net requirement of 0 in week 4. In week 5 the gross requirement is 0, and thus we have a projected balance, and a net requirement of 0. In week 6, however, the gross

TABLE 14.3   MRP PLANNING WORKSHEET AT WEEK 2

SEAT Lot size: 800	Lead time: 1 wk Safety stock: 0		Week				
		1	2	3	4	5	6
Gross requirements		700	0	600	600	0	700
Scheduled receipts		800					
Projected balance	300	400	400				
Net requirements		0					
Planned order receipts							
Planned order releases							

TABLE 14.4   MRP PLANNING WORKSHEET AT WEEK 3

SEAT Lot size: 800	Lead time: 1 wk Safety stock: 0	Week					
		1	**2**	**3**	**4**	**5**	**6**
Gross requirements		700	0	600	600	0	700
Scheduled receipts		800					
Projected balance	300	400	400	600			
Net requirements		0	0	200			
Planned order receipts				800			
Planned order releases			800				

requirements are 700, so an order for 800 units is released in week 5. Table 14.5 shows the resulting MRP planning worksheet.

The MRP worksheet shows that, for an initial inventory of 300 seats and an order quantity (lot size) of 800 seats, we will need to release orders for 800 seats at the beginning of weeks 2 and 5 to ensure that the required number of seats will be available each week. Before continuing our discussion of how MRP can be used to manage dependent demand inventories, let us briefly review some of the major concepts illustrated in this example.

1. The gross requirements indicate the number of components needed at the *beginning of each week* to meet the requirements stated in the MPS; the gross requirements do not take into account any beginning inventory or scheduled receipts.
2. Scheduled receipts, such as the 800 units in week 1, are items that were ordered prior to the beginning of the current planning horizon (weeks 1–6 in our example); these items are assumed to arrive at the *beginning of the week.*
3. The initial projected balance of 300 is the number of units available at the beginning of the current planning horizon. In weeks 1–6, the projected balance is the number of units that are available at the *end of the week.*

For practice in completing an MRP worksheet, try Problem 1.

4. The net requirements tell us, once any scheduled receipts and/or projected balances have been accounted for, how many units are needed at the *beginning of each week.* A positive value for net requirements initiates a planned order release.
5. Planned order releases represent orders placed during the current planning horizon. Planned order receipts represent orders received as the result of planned order releases. Planned order releases and planned order receipts are assumed to occur at the *beginning of each week.*

TABLE 14.5   FINAL MRP PLANNING WORKSHEET

SEAT Lot size: 800	Lead time: 1 wk Safety stock: 0	Week					
		1	**2**	**3**	**4**	**5**	**6**
Gross requirements		700	0	600	600	0	700
Scheduled receipts		800					
Projected balance	300	400	400	600	0	0	100
Net requirements		0	0	200	0	0	700
Planned order receipts				800			800
Planned order releases			800			800	

> **NOTES AND COMMENTS**
>
> A master production schedule usually consists of a combination of forecasts of customer orders and booked customer orders. Because forecasts are often wrong, the resulting incorrect entries in the master production schedule can lead to disastrous results. Obtaining accurate forecasts and establishing a system to deal with the inherent problems associated with forecasting (such as revising the MRP when forecasts are revised) is one of the biggest challenges facing manufacturers.

14.4   LOT SIZING AND SAFETY STOCK

To develop a production schedule using the MRP approach, we must know the lot size, the production or purchase lead time, and the amount of safety stock necessary for each component. Two commonly employed lot sizing rules are the *fixed order size* and the *lot-for-lot* rules. The **fixed order-size rule** calls for each order to be for the same number of items such as an economic order quantity. In the preceding section we used a fixed order-size rule in managing the kitchen chair seat inventory. Recall that each time a planned order release occurred, an order was placed for 800 seats; the MRP worksheet shown in Table 14.5 contains the results of using the fixed order-size rule to manage the seat inventory. Orders will be placed at the beginning of weeks 2 and 5.

The fixed order-size rule is appropriate for purchased components when such a lot size is necessary to take advantage of quantity discounts or when an economic order quantity rule (see Chapter 13) is being used. The fixed order-size rule also is appropriate for manufactured items when batches must be of a certain size because of machine or equipment capacities.

Another commonly employed method for lot sizing is called the **lot-for-lot rule.** When this rule is used, the lot size equals the net requirement in the period the lot will become available. Table 14.6 shows a completed MRP worksheet for the seats based on the lot-for-lot rule.

The lot-sizing rule doesn't affect the gross requirements, so the first row of Table 14.6 is the same as the first row of Table 14.5. In Table 14.6 we assumed that the lot-for-lot rule also had been used in the prior planning horizon and that the projected balance at the beginning of the current planning horizon is 0. Note that the scheduled receipts in week 1, 700, are just enough to cover the gross requirements in week 1; thus, the projected balance at the end of week 1 is 0. Indeed, there is no projected balance (ending inventory) at the end of any week because all lot sizes are just large enough to cover gross requirements. The planned order releases in the last row indicate that the amount of each planned order release is the same as the gross requirements in the next period. Except for week 1, the gross requirements are equal to the net requirements.

TABLE 14.6   MRP PLANNING WORKSHEET BASED ON THE LOT-FOR-LOT RULE

SEAT Lot-for-Lot	Lead time: 1 wk Safety stock: 0		Week					
			1	2	3	4	5	6
Gross requirements			700	0	600	600	0	700
Scheduled receipts			700					
Projected balance		0	0	0	0	0	0	0
Net requirements			0	0	600	600	0	700
Planned order receipts					600	600		700
Planned order releases				600	600		700	

In theory, when the lot-for-lot rule is used, the projected balance at the end of each week is 0, and the planned order release for each week equals the gross requirements in the next week. In practice, however, this situation often is not the case. For instance, suppose that, in the week prior to week 1 of the current planning horizon, the gross requirements for kitchen chairs turned out to be 100 units fewer than forecast in the master production schedule. In this case, the gross requirements for seats for that week would have been overstated by 100 units; thus, the projected balance at the beginning of the current planning horizon would be 100 and not 0. Table 14.7 shows the MRP worksheet based on the lot-for-lot rule with a projected balance of 100 seats at the beginning of the planning horizon. Note that in this case the projected balance isn't 0 each week. The planned order release for week 2 is not equal to the gross requirement for week 3; instead, the planned order release for week 2 is equal to the *net requirement* in week 3.

The lot-for-lot rule is designed to minimize inventory investment. Orders are released in the smallest amount necessary to prevent shortages. As we pointed out previously, in theory, the lot-for-lot rule leads to a projected balance of zero at the end of each week in the planning horizon. However, we also demonstrated that projected balances of greater than 0 can occur in situations where the gross requirements have been overstated in any period.

Try Problem 3 for practice in completing an MRP worksheet using the lot-for-lot rule.

A more serious situation can occur with the lot-for-lot rule if defective parts are discovered, materials are damaged, or other problems are encountered. In such cases, if there is no safety stock, the lot-for-lot rule will lead to stockouts that may result in production stoppages. Another potential difficulty with the lot-for-lot rule is that it may result in lot sizes that are too small to be economically justified. In these cases the usual procedure is to modify the lot-for-lot rule by establishing a minimum lot size.

Safety stock can buffer the production system against unexpected events such as uncertainty about gross requirements, uncertainty about lead times, defective parts produced in-house or purchased from suppliers, pilferage, and so on. As noted in the preceding chapter, safety stock increases inventory holding cost; as a result, no more safety stock than necessary should be used.

To illustrate how the use of safety stock for an item affects the development of the MRP worksheet, suppose that a safety stock of 20 units is utilized for the kitchen chair seat example in conjunction with a lot-for-lot order sizing rule. Table 14.8 shows how the safety stock affects the MRP worksheet; note that we assumed that in the prior planning horizon the lot-for-lot rule also had been used with a safety stock of 20 units. The projected balance of 20 seats, which represents the safety stock, remains at that level for the rest of the planning horizon. The safety stock of 20 units is available to buffer the production process against unexpected occurrences that would affect the inventory level. The cost of protecting the production process is the additional holding cost of the 20 units.

TABLE 14.7   MRP PLANNING WORKSHEET BASED ON THE LOT-FOR-LOT RULE WITH A BEGINNING PROJECTED BALANCE OF 100 SEATS

SEAT Lot-for-Lot	Lead time: 1 wk Safety stock: 0	Week					
		1	2	3	4	5	6
Gross requirements		700	0	600	600	0	700
Scheduled receipts		700					
Projected balance	100	100	100	0	0	0	0
Net requirements		0	0	500	600	0	700
Planned order receipts				500	600		700
Planned order releases			500	600		700	

TABLE 14.8   MRP PLANNING WORKSHEET BASED ON THE LOT-FOR-LOT RULE WITH A SAFETY STOCK OF 20 UNITS

SEAT Lot-for-Lot	Lead time: 1 wk Safety stock: 20	Week					
		1	2	3	4	5	6
Gross requirements		700	0	600	600	0	700
Scheduled receipts		700					
Projected balance	20	20	20	20	20	20	20
Net requirements		0	0	600	600	0	700
Planned order receipts				600	600		700
Planned order releases			600	600		700	

Try Problem 7 for practice in completing an MRP worksheet with safety stock.

The determination of the appropriate amount of safety stock to carry (if any) involves weighing the trade-off between inventory holding costs and production downtime. The determination of the best lot-sizing rule involves a trade-off between inventory holding cost and setup cost; larger lot sizes increase holding cost but decrease setup cost. More advanced books and research articles on manufacturing planning provide procedures for balancing these costs in determining optimal lot sizes and safety stocks.

14.5   MRP AND A TIME-PHASED PRODUCTION SCHEDULE

A schematic diagram of an MRP system is shown in Figure 14.4. As noted earlier, customer orders and forecasts are used to develop the master production schedule. The MPS, BOM, and current inventory files are the inputs needed to begin the MRP computations. The outputs from

FIGURE 14.4   AN MRP SYSTEM

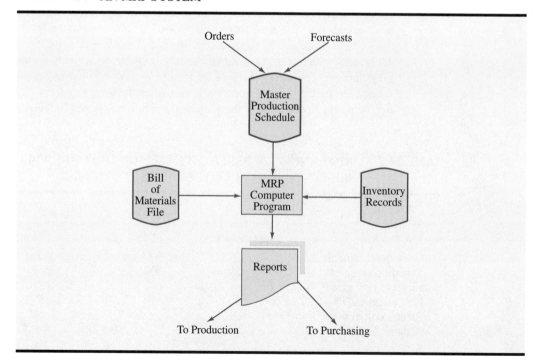

the MRP system are the net requirements for each item in the BOM, along with the dates each item is needed. This information is used to plan order releases for production and purchasing.

In this section we show how the MRP system uses the inputs in Figure 14.4 to develop a time-phased production schedule. To illustrate how MRP can result in the right component being available at exactly the right time, we develop the MRP worksheets for each item in the BOM for the kitchen chair produced by the Clark Furniture Company. To differentiate the computations in this section from those in the previous sections of this chapter, suppose that the current planning horizon corresponds to weeks 19–24. Table 14.9 shows the MPS for this planning horizon.

Suppose that the time required to assemble the three level-1 components (the base assembly, the seat, and the back assembly) into a finished chair is 1 week. Because the MPS calls for the final assembly of 400 chairs during week 19, 400 base assemblies, 400 seats, and 400 back assemblies must be available at the beginning of week 19. To determine when each of the remaining components must be available to meet the requirements of 400 chairs during week 19, we need to know the lead times associated with each of the components used to produce the kitchen chair. Table 14.10 shows this information, which would be contained in the inventory record for each item.

Using the lead times in Table 14.10, we can determine when production of each component must take place to permit the final assembly of 400 kitchen chairs during week 19. Figure 14.5 shows the result of these calculations: the time-phased requirement for each component. Figure 14.5 was developed by backscheduling from the time each item is required by the amount of its lead time.

The focus of an MRP system is on timing.

Figure 14.5 shows that to complete the final assembly of the kitchen chairs in week 19, production of the braces must start at the beginning of week 14. Thus, a 1-week lead time will ensure that the braces will be available at the beginning of week 15 so that production may begin on the brace subassembly. Note that with the 2-week lead time for the brace subassembly, the brace subassembly will be available for use in the base assembly at the beginning of week 17. The legs, which also are needed to produce the base assembly, have a

TABLE 14.9 MASTER PRODUCTION SCHEDULE FOR KITCHEN CHAIRS
FOR WEEKS 19–24

	Week					
	19	**20**	**21**	**22**	**23**	**24**
Production Quantity	400	750	600	100	850	700

TABLE 14.10 LEAD TIMES FOR COMPONENTS OF KITCHEN CHAIR

Component	Lead Time (weeks)
Base Assembly	2
Legs	1
Brace Subassembly	2
Braces	1
Seat	1
Back Assembly	3
Outer Back Supports	1
Upper Back Support	1
Middle Back Supports	1

FIGURE 14.5   TIME-PHASED PRODUCTION SCHEDULE FOR THE KITCHEN CHAIR

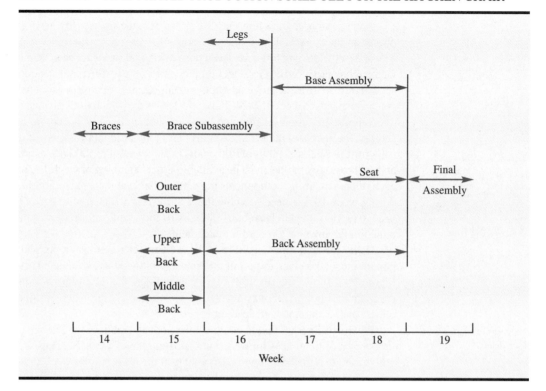

1-week lead time. Therefore, production of the legs must start at the beginning of week 16 so that they will be available at the beginning of week 17. An order is released to begin production of the base assembly at the beginning of week 17; with a 2-week lead time the base assemblies will be available for use in the final assembly during week 19.

The MPS calls for the final assembly of 400 chairs during week 19. The time-phased requirements shown in Figure 14.5 indicate that, to meet such a schedule, production of the components must begin sooner. Indeed, production of the braces must begin 5 weeks before the chairs are to be assembled. However, we still have not determined how many units of each component must be produced in each week. Thus, we now need to develop the MRP worksheets for each of the components to determine the net requirements for each item.

Table 14.11 shows the MRP planning worksheets needed to perform the time-phased calculations for each component. Note that there is one MRP worksheet for each part or subassembly shown in the bill of materials. The information shown in Table 14.11 was developed by backscheduling from the time each item is required by the amount of its lead time. In performing the calculations we assumed that the beginning inventory of each component is 0, lot sizes are determined by the lot-for-lot method, and there are no scheduled receipts.

We begin by looking at the MRP worksheets corresponding to the base assembly, the seat, and the back assembly. As we previously stated, to produce 400 chairs in week 19, we must have 400 base assemblies, 400 seats, and 400 back assemblies available at the beginning of week 19. Because each kitchen chair consists of 1 base assembly, 1 seat, and 1 back assembly, the gross requirements for these components in week 19 are also 400. With no units in inventory and no scheduled receipts, the net requirements are also 400.

Table 14.10 indicates that the lead time for the base assembly is 2 weeks. Thus, to satisfy the net requirement of 400 base assemblies at the beginning of week 19, an order for 400 base assemblies must be released at the beginning of week 17. Note that this planned

TABLE 14.11   MRP WORKSHEETS SHOWING TIME-PHASED MATERIAL REQUIREMENTS
TO SUPPORT PRODUCTION OF 400 CHAIRS IN WEEK 19

BASE ASSEMBLY
Lot-for-Lot

Lead time: 2 wks
Safety stock: 0

		Week					
		14	15	16	17	18	19
Gross requirements							400
Scheduled receipts							
Projected balance	0					0	400
Net requirements							400
Planned order receipts							400
Planned order releases					(400)		

4 legs required

LEGS
Lot-for-Lot

Lead time: 1 wk
Safety stock: 0

		Week					
		14	15	16	17	18	19
Gross requirements					(1600)		
Scheduled receipts							
Projected balance	0			0			
Net requirements					1600		
Planned order receipts					1600		
Planned order releases				1600			

BRACE SUBASSEMBLY
Lot-for-Lot

Lead time: 2 wks
Safety stock: 0

		Week					
		14	15	16	17	18	19
Gross requirements					(400)		
Scheduled receipts							
Projected balance	0			0			
Net requirements					400		
Planned order receipts					400		
Planned order releases			(400)				

4 braces required

BRACES
Lot-for-Lot

Lead time: 1 wk
Safety stock: 0

		Week					
		14	15	16	17	18	19
Gross requirements			(1600)				
Scheduled receipts							
Projected balance	0	0					
Net requirements			1600				
Planned order receipts			1600				
Planned order releases		1600					

SEAT
Lot-for-Lot

Lead time: 1 wk
Safety stock: 0

		Week					
		14	15	16	17	18	19
Gross requirements							400
Scheduled receipts							
Projected balance	0					0	
Net requirements							400
Planned order receipts							400
Planned order releases						400	

TABLE 14.11 (CONTINUED)

BACK ASSEMBLY
Lot-for-Lot

Lead time: 3 wks
Safety stock: 0

		Week					
		14	15	16	17	18	19
Gross requirements							400
Scheduled receipts							
Projected balance	0					0	
Net requirements							400
Planned order receipts							400
Planned order releases				(400)			

2 outer back supports required

OUTER BACK SUPPORT
Lot-for-Lot

Lead time: 1 wk
Safety stock: 0

		Week					
		14	15	16	17	18	19
Gross requirements				(800)			
Scheduled receipts							
Projected balance	0		0				
Net requirements				800			
Planned order receipts				800			
Planned order releases			800				

1 upper back support required

UPPER BACK SUPPORT
Lot-for-Lot

Lead time: 1 wk
Safety stock: 0

		Week					
		14	15	16	17	18	19
Gross requirements				(400)			
Scheduled receipts							
Projected balance	0		0				
Net requirements				400			
Planned order receipts				400			
Planned order releases			400				

5 middle back supports required

MIDDLE BACK
Lot-for-Lot

Lead time: 1 wk
Safety stock: 0

		Week					
		14	15	16	17	18	19
Gross requirements				(2000)			
Scheduled receipts							
Projected balance	0		0				
Net requirements				2000			
Planned order receipts				2000			
Planned order releases			2000				

order release shows up in week 19 as a planned order receipt. Recall that each base assembly consists of 4 legs and 1 brace subassembly; hence, at the beginning of week 17 we must have available 4(400) = 1600 legs and 1(400) = 400 brace subassemblies. The 1600 legs and the 400 brace subassemblies are entered as the gross requirements in week 17 for these two components. The legs have a lead time of 1 week, so we show a planned order release of 1600 legs at the beginning of week 16. Note that these 1600 legs also show up as a planned order receipt of 1600 at the beginning of week 17. The net requirements also are 1600 because no units were in inventory and no receipts are scheduled.

The lead time for the brace subassembly is 2 weeks. Thus, to have 400 brace subassemblies available at the beginning of week 17, we must release an order for 400 brace subassemblies at the beginning of week 15. This planned order release then shows up as a planned order receipt of 400 units at the beginning of week 17.

Backtracking one step further, we see that each brace subassembly consists of 4 braces; thus, we will need to have available 4(400) = 1600 braces at the beginning of week 15. The lead time for the braces is 1 week, so we will need to release an order for 1600 braces at the beginning of week 14. This planned order release shows up as planned order receipts of 1600 units in week 15.

Recall that the seat has no components below it in the product structure tree (Figure 14.3), so it doesn't generate requirements for any other items. Looking at the back assembly, the final level-1 component, we see that it has a lead time of 3 weeks and that an order for 400 back assemblies must be released at the beginning of week 16 to ensure that 400 units are available at the beginning of week 19. Each back assembly consists of 2 outer back supports, 1 upper back support, and 5 middle back supports, giving gross requirements in week 16 of 2(400) = 800 outer back supports, 1(400) = 400 upper back supports, and 5(400) = 2000 middle back supports. These gross requirements lead to planned order releases of 800, 400, and 2000 units in week 15, and show up as planned order receipts in week 16.

The process of generating net requirements for components from the MPS for an end item is called a **BOM explosion.** Note also that the use of lead times to backschedule planned order releases allows the MRP system to generate a production schedule for all the items in the BOM.

When the projected balance for an item is not 0, as we assumed in our example, the gross requirements for each item are still computed as multiples of the planned order releases for its parent item. But, in these cases the net requirements will be less than the gross requirements by the amount of the projected balance at the end of the previous period and any scheduled receipts. In this case, the planned order receipts will be the same as the net requirements for the item.

When there are safety stock requirements for some, or possibly all, items, the planned order receipts must be adjusted by the amount of the safety stock requirements. That is, planned order sizes should be just large enough to leave a projected balance equal to the amount of safety stock required after the gross requirements have been satisfied.

In Table 14.12 we show part of the BOM explosion for the kitchen chair for a projected balance of 50 units in week 18 for the base assembly and a fixed lot size of 450. Table 14.12 also shows a projected balance of 100 braces in week 14 and a safety stock requirement of 500 braces. In this revised example we show MRP worksheets only for the base assembly and its descendant items.

We look first at the MRP worksheet for the base assembly. The projected balance of 50 units at the beginning of week 18 means 50 base assemblies in inventory at the beginning of week 19. Thus, only 350 units are needed to satisfy the gross requirements of 400 base assemblies in week 19; hence, the net requirements for week 19 are 350. But, with a fixed lot size of 450 units, we must plan for an order release of 450 units at the beginning of week 17 and the receipt of those units at the beginning of week 19. Thus, the projected balance for the base assembly at the end of week 19 is 100.

As in Table 14.11, the planned order releases at one level of the BOM generates the gross requirements (the appropriate multiplier must be used) for the next level down. Thus, we have gross requirements for 1800 legs and 450 brace subassemblies in week 17. The planned order releases of 450 for the brace subassembly in week 15, in turn, generates gross requirements for 1800 braces in week 15.

Let us now look more closely at the MRP inventory record for the braces to see how the safety stock affects the situation. The gross requirements for 1800 braces could be satisfied by the projected beginning balance of 100 braces plus a lot of 1700 braces. But, such a lot size would cause the inventory level to be reduced to zero and thus the safety stock requirement of 500 would be violated. Therefore, a lot size of 2200 units must be scheduled; planned

TABLE 14.12   A PORTION OF THE MRP WORKSHEETS SHOWING TIME-PHASED
MATERIAL REQUIREMENTS TO SUPPORT PRODUCTION OF 400 CHAIRS
IN WEEK 19 (SHOWS EFFECT OF INVENTORIES, FIXED LOT SIZE, AND
SAFETY STOCK)

BASE ASSEMBLY
Lot size: 450

Lead time: 2 wks
Safety stock: 0

		Week					
		14	15	16	17	18	19
Gross requirements							400
Scheduled receipts							
Projected balance						50	100
Net requirements							350
Planned order receipts							450
Planned order releases						450	

LEGS
Lot-for-Lot

Lead time: 1 wk
Safety stock: 0

		Week					
		14	15	16	17	18	19
Gross requirements					1800		
Scheduled receipts							
Projected balance					0		
Net requirements					1800		
Planned order receipts					1800		
Planned order releases				1800			

BRACE SUBASSEMBLY
Lot-for-Lot

Lead time: 2 wks
Safety stock: 0

		Week					
		14	15	16	17	18	19
Gross requirements					450		
Scheduled receipts							
Projected balance					0		
Net requirements					450		
Planned order receipts					450		
Planned order releases				450			

BRACES
Lot-for-Lot

Lead time: 1 wk
Safety stock: 500

		Week					
		14	15	16	17	18	19
Gross requirements			1800				
Scheduled receipts							
Projected balance		100	100	500			
Net requirements			1700				
Planned order receipts			2200				
Planned order releases		2200					

*Try Problem 10 for practice
in developing a time-
phased production
schedule.*

order releases of 2200 units are shown in week 14. When this lot is received at the beginning
of week 15, the gross requirements can be satisfied with a safety stock of 500 units.

In this section we have shown how the MRP system links the production plans for all
the items in a bill of materials for an end item (final product). The value of an MRP system
should now be apparent. It ensures that materials are available when they are needed for
production but not before. Thus, inventory investment is minimized and the flow of materials is smoothed.

14.6 IMPLEMENTING AN MRP SYSTEM

Large amounts of data and records must be stored and processed during implementation of an MRP system. As a result, most MRP systems require a fairly sophisticated computer information system. Referring to Figure 14.4, we see that an MRP system must obtain information from the MPS, the BOM file, and the inventory records. The system prepares a variety of reports for production and purchasing and updates MRP inventory records. In other words, successful implementation of an MRP system depends on accurate records.

Inaccuracies in MPS, BOM, and/or inventory records will lead to inaccuracies in the output of the MRP system. Inaccuracies in these system inputs can wreak havoc with MRP because the dependent nature of component requirements can amplify any errors throughout the system. Such errors can result in the failure to order materials when needed and/or in the right amounts, can cause production shutdowns because of a lack of raw materials, parts, or subassemblies, and can lead to many other scheduling problems.

Accurate data and timely updating of records are essential to the proper functioning of an MRP system. When engineering makes a change in product design, the BOM must be updated. When changes are made in the MPS because of forecast errors or changes in customer orders, these updates must be entered in the MRP system. Finally, changes often are necessary in the inventory records because of damage to parts, the need to use some parts in quality control testing, and the like. Needless to say, any changes in MPS, BOM, or inventory records must be communicated to the MRP system as soon as possible.

Updating MRP Records

Until now, we have been concerned only with using MRP to develop period-by-period net requirements for components in response to the master production schedule needs of an end item. However, conditions change rapidly and the MRP system must be capable of responding to changes in forecasts, lead times, product design, and so on. We must be able to update MRP records in a timely fashion to adapt to such changes. Essentially, two issues must be considered: How frequently should the records be updated and which records need to be updated?

Two approaches are used to update MRP records: regeneration and net change. In the **regeneration approach** the records for all items are updated periodically. For instance, we might choose to update completely all the records in the MRP system each week with current information. Thus, we would extend the MPS 1 week into the future, update BOM and inventory records to incorporate any changes, and then completely recalculate net requirements.

In the **net change approach,** the MRP system recalculates net requirements whenever changes make it necessary; however, only the records affected by the new or revised information are updated. Both approaches to updating records are used and are effective; in practice, the regeneration approach is used more often. The key differences between the approaches involve the frequency of updating and the cost of updating. Because more records are updated each time, the regeneration approach is more costly. But, the net change approach requires more frequent processing.

Capacity Requirements Planning

MRP generates a time-phased production schedule for all items in the BOM but doesn't take into account capacity limitations. The planned order releases may call for more production at a work center than is possible with the labor and machine resources available. In such cases, the MPS may have to be modified, earlier production of an item may have to be scheduled, or overtime may have to be scheduled. But, if the MRP system calls for underutilization of a critical work center during one period, it may be necessary to modify the schedule to increase utilization of the work center.

Capacity requirements planning is the process of determining the time-phased labor and machine resources necessary to meet the MPS. The integration of capacity requirements with the MRP leads to what is often called a *closed-loop MRP system.* The MRP process has also been extended to encompass the financial plans necessary to support production and provide resources. Moreover, in some companies, MRP now has the capability to provide "what-if" analysis of company-wide operations. This company-wide view of MRP is called **manufacturing resource planning (MRP II).**

The Q. M. in Action: Integrating Process Planning with MRP describes how process planning has been integrated with an MRP system to move a company closer to complete computer-integrated manufacturing.

Q. M. IN ACTION

INTEGRATING PROCESS PLANNING WITH MRP*

Computer-aided process planning (CAPP) was integrated with an existing MRP system at one of Turkey's largest manufacturers of domestic appliances, Arcelik A.S. The company installed a computerized MRP system in 1984 and later added the CAPP system. Process planning involves determining the operations necessary to manufacture a component, their sequence, the necessary machining and tooling, setup times, and material requirements. The CAPP system obviously needed to be integrated with the company's MRP system. A benefit of implementing the CAPP system was use of the information content of the process plans to improve the accuracy of the MRP system.

Arcelik has developed several application programs to make use of the integrated CAPP/ MRP database. The integration of process planning and MRP provides the foundation for a real-time, work-in-process tracking system and is viewed by the company as a major step toward complete computer-integrated manufacturing. The computer-aided process planning system has replaced manual systems completely at two Istanbul plants. The authors believe that the manufacturing database resulting from the CAPP and MRP systems provides the information base the company needs to apply quantitative methods to production planning and control.

*Based on G. Ulusoy and R. Uzsoy, "Computer-Aided Process Planning and Material Requirements Planning: First Steps toward Computer-Integrated Manufacturing," *Interfaces* (March–April 1992): 76–86.

NOTES AND COMMENTS

1. Inventory systems can be designed to determine what can be produced with a given capacity *or* to determine what must be produced to meet a given master production schedule. An MRP system is designed to the latter requirement.
2. The first continuous net change material requirements planning system was designed and installed in 1961 for the J. I. Case Tractor Com-

pany under the direction of Joseph Orlicky. The computer system used was an IBM 305 RAMAC with 15 million characters of disk file capacity. The development of the computer software for this system took a team of programmers 10 months and expended approximately 6 person-years in the programming effort.

14.7   JUST-IN-TIME

Just-in-time (JIT) is a philosophy of operations management that focuses on eliminating waste. The JIT approach strives for zero inventory, zero employee nonproductive time, zero defects, and so on. We provide a brief overview of some of the goals and objectives of JIT in this section, emphasizing the impact of JIT on inventory.

Inventory can be viewed as expensive waste because it represents idle resources and incurs a holding cost. Ideally, inventory would not be needed in a manufacturing system. Each part should be made available at the right time and at the right place; that is, "just in time" to be used. That would mean no inventory holding cost and small production lot sizes. Recall, however, that the optimal production lot size involves a trade-off between setup cost and inventory holding cost. Larger setup costs lead to larger lot sizes and more inventory. Thus, just-in-time systems strive to reduce setup time and cost so that production lot sizes may be smaller and production runs more frequent. A goal of JIT is continuous production at just the rate the product, or part, is being used (i.e., sold or used in downstream production).

With a just-in-time system, a defective part can halt production. Because no inventory is available, workers cannot discard a defective part and use another. Thus, just-in-time systems automatically focus workers' attention on minimizing defects and, when one is found, correcting it immediately. Each worker must be acutely aware of the quality of the product being produced and know how to correct defects.

One of the consequences of a JIT system is an integrated manufacturing process. With no, or small, inventories to provide a buffer between successive workstations, a production process must be integrated. A common approach to providing this integration is the *pull system of production*. With the pull system, items are not produced at an upstream workstation until they are needed by the downstream workstation using them. No manufacturing is done just to keep workers busy. With a *push system,* a workstation would produce parts according to its own schedule and "push" them on to the next station when finished, leading to a buildup of system inventories.

The implementation of JIT systems has led to shorter cycle times and reductions in inventory cost, labor cost, space requirements, and material costs. Achieving these improvements requires a tightly integrated production system and the wholehearted involvement of both blue-collar and white-collar employees. JIT approaches also are being applied successfully in service industries. The Q. M. in Action: Ecuador's Community Health Workers use JIT describes how JIT principles have improved the health care delivery system in Ecuador.

Q. M. IN ACTION

ECUADOR'S COMMUNITY HEALTH WORKERS USE JIT*

Just-in-time approaches are as valid in service industries as they are in manufacturing industries. A key JIT issue for the Ecuadorian Ministry of Public Health (MOH) was the economical and efficient distribution of medical supplies to the country's community health workers so that sufficient supplies were available at the right place at the right time. Community health workers provide primary health care to most of the nation's population; each worker is responsible for one or several communities.

Community health workers obtain medical supplies from MOH or mission pharmacies, private pharmacies, and other outlets. Various problems (e.g., availability of supplies, cost, and travel to the supply facility) made keeping adequate supplies in the hands of the workers difficult. With the objective of providing same-day replenishment at low

cost, the MOH decided to assign workers to decentralized facilities (centers and subcenters) for supply replenishment. The MOH used quantitative methods to determine the optimal number of facilities and assign workers to them. The approach ultimately chosen involved trade-offs between supply site operational costs and transportation costs for community health workers. Interestingly, transportation costs were not always proportional to distance because the mode of transportation varied from airplanes to buses to canoes to foot travel through dense jungle.

*Based on H. L. Smith, K. R. Mangelsdorf, J. C. Luna, and R. A. Reid, "Supplying Ecuador's Health Workers Just in Time," *Interfaces* (May–June 1989): 1–12.

SUMMARY

We began this chapter with a discussion of the differences involved in managing independent and dependent demand inventory systems. Dependent demand systems are common with manufactured goods; the key is that once the demand for the end item is known, the demand for each of its components is also known. We noted that the inventory models of Chapter 13 were inappropriate for managing manufacturing inventories. Material requirements planning (MRP) is the approach used by many companies to manage manufacturing inventories.

The objective of MRP is to have the right components available at the right time in order to minimize inventory holding costs and to ensure a smooth flow of materials. The three key inputs to the MRP system are the master production schedule (MPS), the bill of materials (BOM), and inventory records. The MPS shows the production schedule for end items, the BOM shows the product structure of the end item, and the inventory records contain information such as how many units of each item are in inventory at the beginning of the planning period. The MRP system takes into account item lead times, lot sizes, and components and develops a time-phased production schedule for each item in the BOM. We noted that two approaches to updating the MRP are used in practice: regeneration and net change.

Planned order releases, an output of the MRP system, can be used to compute the labor and machine capacities required to implement the MRP. In this sense, MRP facilitates capacity requirements planning. If sufficient capacity isn't available to implement the MRP, management must find ways to either expand capacity or modify the schedule.

MRP and JIT can be thought of as two sides of the same coin. MRP addresses the need for good planning and JIT addresses the need for good execution.

With an increasing emphasis on lowering costs and improving productivity, the continued use of quantitative models for optimal inventory decisions, as well as the development of new methods of inventory management, can be expected. A development that evolved from the Japanese approach to material management and control is just-in-time (JIT). JIT is based on the goal of producing or delivering parts and materials only when and where they are needed. The JIT approach results in less inventory investment, reduces scrap, provides higher quality, and in general improves productivity. Although a full discussion of JIT is beyond the scope of this text, further information can be found in a variety of texts dealing with modern techniques of production and operations management.

GLOSSARY

Finished goods inventory   Inventory of products ready for shipment to customers.

Manufacturing inventories   Consist of the raw materials, parts, and subassemblies that make up a finished good or product.

Dependent demand   Demand for a component is dependent on demand for the finished product it is used in.

Material requirements planning (MRP)   A technique that is used to translate a set of period-by-period requirements for finished products (end items) into a set of period-by-period requirements for the raw materials, parts, and subassemblies that make up the finished products.

Master production schedule (MPS)   The schedule showing how many units of the finished product are to be produced for each period in the planning horizon.

Planning horizon   The number of periods into the future for which plans are developed.

Bill of materials (BOM)   A structured parts list that shows the hierarchical relationship between an end item and its various components; the BOM shows how the finished product is made from each of its components.

Product structure tree   A graphical representation of the bill of materials.

Inventory record   A record containing information on the availability of each item in the bill of materials.

Net requirements   The quantity that must be ordered or produced in a period; net requirements take into account any scheduled receipts and the projected balance.

Gross requirements   The total number of units of an item that are needed in a period, without taking into account any projected balance or scheduled receipts.

Scheduled receipts   Items that were ordered prior to the current planning horizon. Scheduled receipts are assumed to be available at the beginning of the period in which they arrive.

Projected balance   The amount of inventory available at the end of a period that can be used to satisfy gross requirements in future periods.

Planned order release   An order placed during the current planning horizon. Planned order releases are assumed to be placed at the beginning of the period.

Planned order receipt   An item expected to be received at some period in the future as a result of planned order releases. Planned order receipts are assumed to arrive at the beginning of the period.

Fixed order-size rule   A rule stating that the lot size must be the same each time an order is placed.

Lot-for-lot rule   A rule for computing lot sizes. The lot size varies from order to order; it is chosen just large enough to satisfy the net requirements, taking into account the lead time and any required safety stock.

BOM explosion   The process of translating the end item requirements into requirements for its components.

Regeneration approach   An approach to updating the materials requirement plan at fixed intervals of time. All records are updated at once.

Net change approach   An approach to updating the materials requirement plan whenever changes make it necessary. Only those records affected by the changes are updated.

Capacity requirements planning   The process of determining time-phased labor and machine resources necessary to meet the MPS.

Manufacturing resource planning (MRP II)   A broader view of MRP that encompasses company-wide operations.

Just-in-time (JIT)   An approach to operations management that focuses on minimizing waste. Its goals include zero inventories and zero defects.

PROBLEMS

SELFtest

1. Table 14.13 contains a partially completed MRP worksheet for a wheel subassembly.
   a. Complete the worksheet by showing the appropriate entries in the remaining cells. (It is not necessary to show zero entries.)
   b. Suppose that the beginning projected balance is 180 (instead of 80). Complete the worksheet.
   c. Suppose that the beginning projected balance is 80 and that the lot size is 500. Complete the worksheet.

2. Refer to the partially completed worksheet for a wheel subassembly in Table 14.13.
   a. Complete the worksheet for a lead time of 1 week (instead of 2 weeks).
   b. Complete the worksheet for a lead time of 3 weeks.
   c. What effect, if any, do the different lead times have on the inventory level?

TABLE 14.13   PARTIAL MRP WORKSHEET FOR WHEEL SUBASSEMBLY

WHEEL SUBASSEMBLY Lot size 400	Lead time: 2 wks Safety stock: 0	Week					
		1	2	3	4	5	6
Gross requirements			250		300		260
Scheduled receipts			400				
Projected balance	80						
Net requirements							
Planned order receipts							
Planned order releases							

SELFtest

3. Refer to the partially completed worksheet for a wheel subassembly in Table 14.13.
   a. Complete the worksheet using the lot-for-lot rule instead of a fixed lot size of 400.
   b. Suppose that the beginning projected balance is 180 (instead of 80). Complete the worksheet using the lot-for-lot rule.

4. One component used in manufacturing a dresser is a drawer subassembly. Table 14.14 contains a partially completed MRP worksheet for the drawer subassembly.
   a. Complete the worksheet by showing the appropriate entries in the remaining cells. (It is not necessary to show zero entries.)
   b. Suppose that the beginning projected balance is 120 (instead of 0). Complete the worksheet.
   c. Suppose that the beginning projected balance is 0, as in part (a). Change the lot size to 800 and complete the entries in the MRP worksheet.
   d. Would you expect the inventory holding cost to be higher using a lot size of 500 or a lot size of 800? Under what conditions would the lot size of 800 be preferable?

5. Refer to Table 14.14, which shows the partially completed MRP worksheet for a drawer subassembly. Complete the worksheet for a lead time of 2 weeks.

6. Refer to Table 14.14, which shows the partially completed MRP worksheet for a drawer subassembly.
   a. Complete the worksheet using the lot-for-lot rule for choosing a lot size.
   b. Suppose that the beginning projected balance is 120 (instead of 0). Complete the MRP worksheet using the lot-for-lot rule.
   c. What is the relationship between net requirements and planned order releases when the lot-for-lot rule is used?
   d. In Problem 4(b), a fixed lot size of 500 was used; in Problem 6(c) the lot-for-lot rule was used. In both cases the beginning projected balance, the gross requirements, and

TABLE 14.14   PARTIAL MRP WORKSHEET FOR DRAWER SUBASSEMBLY

DRAWER SUBASSEMBLY Lot size 500	Lead time: 1 wk Safety stock: 0	Week					
		1	2	3	4	5	6
Gross requirements		450		300	250		500
Scheduled receipts		500					
Projected balance	0						
Net requirements							
Planned order receipts							
Planned order releases							

the scheduled receipts were the same. Which lot-sizing rule results in the lower inventory holding cost?

SELFtest

7. Refer to Table 14.14, which shows the partially completed MRP worksheet for a drawer subassembly.
   a. Complete the worksheet for a safety stock of 30. What effect does the safety stock have on inventory holding cost?
   b. Suppose that the beginning projected balance is 120 (instead of 0). Complete the worksheet using a safety stock of 100. What effect does the safety stock have on the inventory holding cost?

8. One component of a stapler is the base subassembly. A partially completed MRP worksheet for the base subassembly is shown in Table 14.15.
   a. Complete the worksheet by showing the appropriate entries in the remaining cells. Use a fixed lot size of 400.
   b. Complete the worksheet using the lot-for-lot rule.
   c. Compare the effect of the lot-sizing rules in parts (a) and (b) on inventory holding cost. What are the conditions under which each rule would be preferable?

9. Refer to Table 14.15, which shows the partially completed MRP worksheet for the stapler base subassembly.
   a. Complete the worksheet for a safety stock of 100 and a fixed lot size of 400.
   b. Complete the worksheet for a safety stock of 100 and the lot-for-lot rule.
   c. What effect does safety stock have on inventory holding cost? Why would the company consider using safety stock?

SELFtest

10. Figure 14.6 shows the product structure tree for an end item referred to as product E. A partially completed MRP worksheet for component B is shown in Table 14.16.
    a. Complete the worksheet for component B for weeks 21–26.
    b. Part D has a projected balance of 50 at the end of week 19 and a lead time of 1 week. Show the MRP worksheet for this part for weeks 20–23 using the lot-for-lot rule and no safety stock.

11. The product structure tree for product F is shown in Figure 14.7. A partially completed worksheet for subassembly E is shown in Table 14.17.
    a. Complete the MRP worksheet for subassembly E.
    b. Prepare an MRP worksheet for part B for weeks 11–15. Use a lead time of 2 weeks and a lot size of 400. The beginning projected balance is 400 with no scheduled receipts.
    c. Prepare an MRP worksheet for part A for weeks 11–15. The beginning projected balance is 500, and the lead time is 1 week. Use the lot-for-lot rule. Note that 2 units of A are needed for each unit of E.

TABLE 14.15   PARTIALLY COMPLETED MRP WORKSHEET FOR STAPLER BASE SUBASSEMBLY

BASE SUBASSEMBLY	Lead time: 1 wk Safety stock: 0	Week					
		1	2	3	4	5	6
Gross requirements		200	250	200	200	150	200
Scheduled receipts		150					
Projected balance	150						
Net requirements							
Planned order receipts							
Planned order releases							

FIGURE 14.6   PRODUCT STRUCTURE TREE FOR PRODUCT E

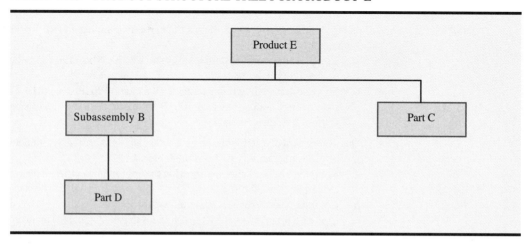

TABLE 14.16   PARTIALLY COMPLETED MRP WORKSHEET FOR PART B

PART B	**Lead time: 3 wks**					Week		
Lot size: 500	**Safety stock: 0**		**21**	**22**	**23**	**24**	**25**	**26**
Gross requirements				450		600		400
Scheduled receipts				500				
Projected balance		150						
Net requirements								
Planned order receipts								
Planned order releases								

FIGURE 14.7   PRODUCT STRUCTURE TREE FOR PRODUCT F

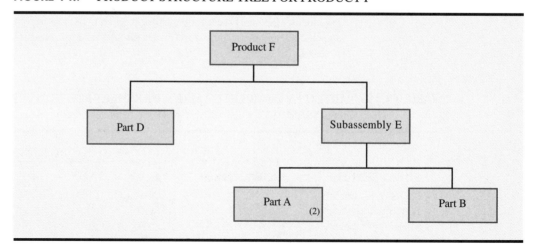

TABLE 14.17   PARTIALLY COMPLETED MRP WORKSHEET FOR SUBASSEMBLY E

SUBASSEMBLY E Lot size: 300	Lead time: 1 wk Safety stock: 0	Week					
		11	12	13	14	15	16
Gross requirements			250	200	280	250	230
Scheduled receipts		200					
Projected balance	80						
Net requirements							
Planned order receipts							
Planned order releases							

12. The Spiecker Company manufactures a 14-inch snowblower. Figure 14.8 shows the product structure tree. The master production schedule for the snowblower results in a gross requirement of 1250 for the engine assembly during week 20. Lead times (in weeks) for the engine assembly and its components are

Component	Lead time
Engine assembly	4
Air cleaner subassembly	1
Filter housing	2

The inventory on hand of the engine assembly at the beginning of week 20 is 450. Assume that no inventory is on hand for the air cleaner subassembly and the filter housing.

FIGURE 14.8   PRODUCT STRUCTURE TREE FOR THE SPIECKER 14-INCH SNOWBLOWER

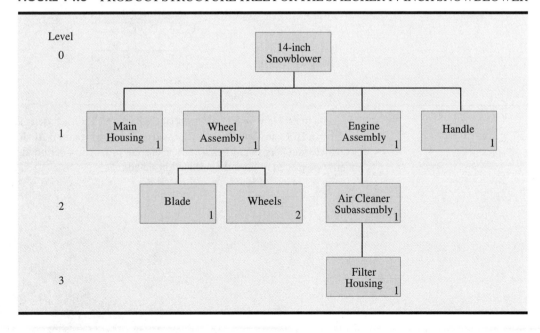

    a. Compute the net requirement for the engine assembly in week 20.

    b. When must the order be released for the air cleaner subassemblies? How many air cleaner subassemblies must be ordered using the lot-for-lot rule?

    c. When must the order be released for the filter housings? How many filter housings must be ordered using the lot-for-lot rule?

13. Refer to Figure 14.8, the product structure tree for the 14-inch snowblower. Gross requirements for the wheel assembly during week 22 are 800. The projected balance at the end of week 21 is 450. Lead times are 2 weeks for the wheel assembly, 2 weeks for the blade, and 1 week for the wheels. The lot-for-lot rule is being used for all three items.

    a. When must the order be released for the wheel assemblies needed? How many wheel assemblies must be ordered?

    b. When must the order be released for the wheels? How many wheels must be ordered? Assume that none are in inventory.

    c. When must the order be released for the blade? How many blades must be ordered? Assume a projected balance of 200 when the net requirements are computed.

14. C & D Lawn Products manufactures a rotary spreader for applying fertilizer. The following is a portion of the product structure tree. If 3000 lawn spreaders are needed to satisfy a customer's order, determine the net requirements for the base assembly, wheel subassembly, and tires (sets of 2). Assume that 1000 base assemblies, 1500 wheel subassemblies, and 800 tires are currently in inventory.

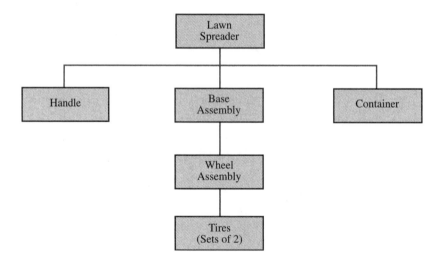

15. Refer again to Problem 14 and assume that the lead time for the base assembly, wheel subassembly, and tires are 2 weeks, 4 weeks, and 5 weeks, respectively. If all components must be completed no later than week 15 of the current production period, determine when orders must be placed to meet the production schedule.

WAITING LINE MODELS

Recall the last time that you had to wait at a supermarket checkout counter, for a teller at your local bank, or to be served at a fast food restaurant. In these and many other waiting line situations, the time spent waiting is undesirable. Adding more checkout clerks, bank tellers, or servers is not always the most economical strategy for improving service, so businesses need to determine ways to keep waiting times within tolerable limits.

Models have been developed to help managers understand and make better decisions concerning the operation of waiting lines. In quantitative analysis terminology, a waiting line is also known as a **queue,** and the body of knowledge dealing with waiting lines is known as **queuing theory.** In the

early 1900s A. K. Erlang, a Danish telephone engineer, began a study of the congestion and waiting times occurring in the completion of telephone calls. Since then, queueing theory has grown far more sophisticated and has been applied to a wide variety of waiting line situations.

Waiting line models consist of mathematical formulas and relationships that can be used to determine the **operating characteristics** (performance measures) for a waiting line. Some of the operating characteristics of interest include the following:

1. The probability that no units are in the system
2. The average number of units in the waiting line
3. The average number of units in the system (the number of units in the waiting line plus the number of units being served)
4. The average time a unit spends in the waiting line
5. The average time a unit spends in the system (the waiting time plus the service time)
6. The probability that an arriving unit has to wait for service

Managers who have such information are better able to make decisions that balance desirable service levels against the cost of providing the service.

15.1   STRUCTURE OF A WAITING LINE SYSTEM

To illustrate the basic features of a waiting line model, we consider the waiting line at the Burger Dome fast food restaurant. Burger Dome sells hamburgers, cheeseburgers, french fries, soft drinks, and milk shakes, as well as a limited number of specialty items and dessert selections. Although Burger Dome would like to serve each customer immediately, at times more customers arrive than can be handled by the Burger Dome food service staff. Thus, customers wait in line to place and receive their orders.

Burger Dome is concerned that the methods currently used to serve customers are resulting in excessive waiting times. Management has asked that a waiting line study be performed to help determine the best approach to reducing waiting times and improving service.

Single-Channel Waiting Line

In the current Burger Dome operation, a server takes a customer's order, determines the total cost of the order, takes the money from the customer, and then fills the order. Once the first customer's order is filled, the server takes the order of the next customer waiting for service. This operation is an example of a **single-channel waiting line.** Each customer entering the Burger Dome restaurant must pass through the *one* channel—one order-taking and order-filling station—to place an order, pay the bill, and receive the food. When more customers arrive than can be served immediately, they form a waiting line and wait for the order-taking and order-filling station to become available. A diagram of the Burger Dome single-channel waiting line is shown in Figure 15.1.

Distribution of Arrivals

Defining the arrival process for a waiting line involves determining the probability distribution for the number of arrivals in a given period of time. For many waiting line situations, the arrivals occur *randomly and independently* of other arrivals, and we cannot predict when an arrival will occur. In such cases, management scientists have found that the **Poisson probability distribution** provides a good description of the arrival pattern.

FIGURE 15.1   THE BURGER DOME SINGLE-CHANNEL WAITING LINE

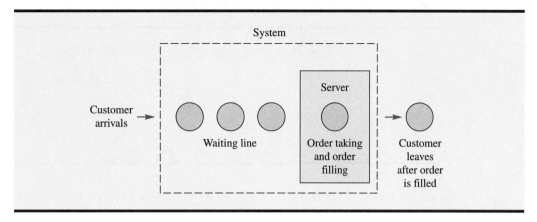

The Poisson probability function provides the probability of x arrivals in a specific time period. The probability function is as follows.[1]

$$P(x) = \frac{\lambda^x e^{-\lambda}}{x!} \quad \text{for } x = 0, 1, 2, \ldots \tag{15.1}$$

where

x = the number of arrivals in the time period

λ = the mean number of arrivals per time period

e = 2.71828

Values of $e^{-\lambda}$ can be found using a calculator or by using Appendix D.

Suppose that Burger Dome has analyzed data on customer arrivals and has concluded that the mean arrival rate is 45 customers per hour. For a 1-minute period, the mean arrival rate would be λ = 45 customers/60 minutes = 0.75 customers per minute. Thus, we can use the following Poisson probability function to compute the probability of x customer arrivals during a 1-minute period:

$$P(x) = \frac{\lambda^x e^{-\lambda}}{x!} = \frac{0.75^x e^{-0.75}}{x!} \tag{15.2}$$

Thus, the probabilities of 0, 1, and 2 customer arrivals during a 1-minute period are

$$P(0) = \frac{(0.75)^0 e^{-0.75}}{0!} = e^{-0.75} = 0.4724$$

$$P(1) = \frac{(0.75)^1 e^{-0.75}}{1!} = 0.75 e^{-0.75} = 0.75(0.4724) = 0.3543$$

$$P(2) = \frac{(0.75)^2 e^{-0.75}}{2!} = \frac{(0.75)^2 e^{-0.75}}{2!} = \frac{(0.5625)(0.4724)}{2} = 0.1329$$

The probability of no customers in a 1-minute period is 0.4724, the probability of 1 customer in a 1-minute period is 0.3543, and the probability of 2 customers in a 1-minute

---

1. The term $x!$, x *factorial*, is defined as $x! = x(x - 1)(x - 2) \ldots (2)(1)$. For example $4! = (4)(3)(2)(1) = 24$. For the special case of $x = 0$, $0! = 1$ by definition.

TABLE 15.1   POISSON PROBABILITIES FOR THE NUMBER OF CUSTOMER ARRIVALS AT A BURGER DOME RESTAURANT DURING A 1-MINUTE PERIOD ($\lambda = 0.75$)

Number of Arrivals	Probability
0	0.4724
1	0.3543
2	0.1329
3	0.0332
4	0.0062
5 or more	0.0010

period is 0.1329. Table 15.1 shows the Poisson probabilities for customer arrivals during a 1-minute period.

The waiting line models that will be presented in Sections 15.2 and 15.3 use the Poisson probability distribution to describe the customer arrivals at Burger Dome. In practice, you should record the actual number of arrivals per time period for several days or weeks and compare the frequency distribution of the observed number of arrivals to the Poisson probability distribution to determine whether the Poisson probability distribution provides a reasonable approximation of the arrival distribution.

Distribution of Service Times

The service time is the time a customer spends at the service facility once the service has started. At Burger Dome, the service time starts when a customer begins to place the order with the food server and continues until the customer has received the order. Service times are rarely constant. At Burger Dome, the number of items ordered and the mix of items ordered vary considerably from one customer to the next. Small orders can be handled in a matter of seconds, but large orders may require more than 2 minutes.

Quantitative analysts have found that if the probability distribution for the service time can be assumed to follow an **exponential probability distribution,** formulas are available for providing useful information about the operation of the waiting line. Using an exponential probability distribution, the probability that the service time will be less than or equal to a time of length t is

$$P(\text{service time} \le t) = 1 - e^{-\mu t} \qquad (15.3)$$

where

μ = the mean number of units that can be served per time period

$e = 2.71828$

Suppose that Burger Dome has studied the order-taking and order-filling process and has found that the single food server can process an average of 60 customer orders per hour. On a 1-minute basis, the mean service rate would be $\mu = 60$ customers/60 minutes = 1 customer per minute. For example, with $\mu = 1$, we can use equation (15.3) to compute probabilities such as the probability an order can be processed in $\frac{1}{2}$ minute or less, 1 minute or less, and 2 minutes or less. These computations are

$$P(\text{service time} \le 0.5 \text{ min.}) = 1 - e^{-1(0.5)} = 1 - 0.6065 = 0.3935$$
$$P(\text{service time} \le 1.0 \text{ min.}) = 1 - e^{-1(1.0)} = 1 - 0.3679 = 0.6321$$
$$P(\text{service time} \le 2.0 \text{ min.}) = 1 - e^{-1(2.0)} = 1 - 0.1353 = 0.8647$$

A property of the exponential probability distribution is that there is a 0.6321 probability that the random variable takes on a value less than its mean. In waiting line applications, the exponential probability distribution indicates that approximately 63% of the service times are less than the mean service time and approximately 37% of the service times are greater than the mean service time.

Thus, we would conclude that there is a 0.3935 probability that an order can be processed in ½ minute or less, a 0.6321 probability that it can be processed in 1 minute or less, and a 0.8647 probability that it can be processed in 2 minutes or less.

In several waiting line models presented in this chapter, we assume that the probability distribution for the service time follows an exponential probability distribution. In practice, you should collect data on actual service times to determine whether the exponential probability distribution is a reasonable approximation of the service times for your application.

Queue Discipline

In describing a waiting line system, we must define the manner in which the waiting units are arranged for service. For the Burger Dome waiting line, and in general for most customer-oriented waiting lines, the units waiting for service are arranged on a **first-come, first-served** basis; this approach is referred to as an **FCFS** queue discipline. However, some situations call for different queue disciplines. For example, when people wait for an elevator, the last one on the elevator is often the first one to complete service (i.e., the first to leave the elevator). Other types of queue disciplines assign priorities to the waiting units and then serve the unit with the highest priority first. In this chapter we consider only waiting lines based on a first-come, first-served queue discipline.

Steady-State Operation

When the Burger Dome restaurant opens in the morning, no customers are in the restaurant. Gradually, activity builds up to a normal or steady state. The beginning or start-up period is referred to as the **transient period.** The transient period ends when the system reaches the normal or **steady-state operation.** Waiting line models describe the steady-state operating characteristics of a waiting line.

15.2   SINGLE-CHANNEL WAITING LINE MODEL WITH POISSON ARRIVALS AND EXPONENTIAL SERVICE TIMES

Waiting line models are often based on assumptions such as Poisson arrivals and exponential service times. When applying any waiting line model, data should be collected on the actual system to ensure that the assumptions of the model are reasonable.

In this section we present formulas that can be used to determine the steady-state operating characteristics for a single-channel waiting line. The formulas are applicable if the arrivals follow a Poisson probability distribution and the service times follow an exponential probability distribution. As these assumptions apply to the Burger Dome waiting line problem introduced in Section 15.1, we show how formulas can be used to determine Burger Dome's operating characteristics and thus provide management with helpful decision-making information.

The mathematical methodology used to derive the formulas for the operating characteristics of waiting lines is rather complex. However, our purpose in this chapter is not to provide the theoretical development of waiting line models, but rather to show how the formulas that have been developed can provide information about operating characteristics of the waiting line. Readers interested in the mathematical development of the formulas can consult the specialized texts listed in the References and Bibliography appendix at the end of the text.

Operating Characteristics

The following formulas can be used to compute the steady-state operating characteristics for a single-channel waiting line with Poisson arrivals and exponential service times, where

λ = the mean number of arrivals per time period (the mean arrival rate)

μ = the mean number of services per time period (the mean service rate)

Equations (15.4) through (15.10) do not provide formulas for optimal conditions. Rather, these equations provide information about the steady-state operating characteristics of a waiting line.

1. The probability that no units are in the system:

$$P_0 = 1 - \frac{\lambda}{\mu} \tag{15.4}$$

2. The average number of units in the waiting line:

$$L_q = \frac{\lambda^2}{\mu(\mu - \lambda)} \tag{15.5}$$

3. The average number of units in the system:

$$L = L_q + \frac{\lambda}{\mu} \tag{15.6}$$

4. The average time a unit spends in the waiting line:

$$W_q = \frac{L_q}{\lambda} \tag{15.7}$$

5. The average time a unit spends in the system:

$$W = W_q + \frac{1}{\mu} \tag{15.8}$$

6. The probability that an arriving unit has to wait for service:

$$P_w = \frac{\lambda}{\mu} \tag{15.9}$$

7. The probability of n units in the system:

$$P_n = \left(\frac{\lambda}{\mu}\right)^n P_0 \tag{15.10}$$

The values of the **mean arrival rate** λ and the **mean service rate** μ are clearly important components in determining the operating characteristics. Equation (15.9) shows that the ratio of the mean arrival rate to the mean service rate, λ/μ, provides the probability that an arriving unit has to wait because the service facility is in use. Hence, λ/μ often is referred to as the *utilization factor* for the service facility.

The operating characteristics presented in equations (15.4) through (15.10) are applicable only when the mean service rate μ is *greater than* the mean arrival rate λ—in other words, when $\lambda/\mu < 1$. If this condition does not exist, the waiting line will continue to grow without limit because the service facility does not have sufficient capacity to handle the arriving units. Thus, in using equations (15.4) through (15.10), we must have $\mu > \lambda$.

Operating Characteristics for the Burger Dome Problem

Recall that for the Burger Dome problem we had a mean arrival rate of $\lambda = 0.75$ customers per minute and a mean service rate of $\mu = 1$ customer per minute. Thus, with $\mu > \lambda$, equations (15.4) through (15.10) can be used to provide operating characteristics for the Burger Dome single-channel waiting line:

$$P_0 = 1 - \frac{\lambda}{\mu} = 1 - \frac{0.75}{1} = 0.25$$

$$L_q = \frac{\lambda^2}{\mu(\mu - \lambda)} = \frac{0.75^2}{1(1 - 0.75)} = 2.25 \text{ customers}$$

$$L = L_q = \frac{\lambda}{\mu} + 2.25 + \frac{0.75}{1} = 3 \text{ customers}$$

$$W_q = \frac{L_q}{\lambda} = \frac{2.25}{0.75} = 3 \text{ minutes}$$

$$W = W_q + \frac{1}{\mu} = 3 + \frac{1}{1} = 4 \text{ minutes}$$

$$P_w = \frac{\lambda}{\mu} = \frac{0.75}{1} = 0.75$$

Problem 5 asks you to compute the operating characteristics for a single-channel waiting line application.

Equation (15.10) can be used to determine the probability of any number of customers in the system. Applying it provides the probability information in Table 15.2.

Managers' Use of Waiting Line Models

The results of the single-channel waiting line for Burger Dome show several important things about the operation of the waiting line. In particular, customers wait an average of 3 minutes before beginning to place an order, which appears somewhat long for a business based on fast service. In addition, the facts that the average number of customers waiting in line is 2.25 and that 75% of the arriving customers have to wait for service are indicators that something should be done to improve the waiting line operation. Table 15.2 shows a 0.1335 probability that seven or more customers are in the Burger Dome system at one time. This condition indicates a fairly high probability that Burger Dome will experience some long waiting lines if it continues to use the single-channel operation.

If the operating characteristics are unsatisfactory in terms of meeting company standards for service, Burger Dome's management should consider alternative designs or plans for improving the waiting line operation.

Improving the Waiting Line Operation

Waiting line models often indicate where improvements in operating characteristics are desirable. However, the decision of how to modify the waiting line configuration to

TABLE 15.2   THE PROBABILITY OF n CUSTOMERS IN THE SYSTEM FOR THE BURGER DOME WAITING LINE PROBLEM

Number of Customers	Probability
0	0.2500
1	0.1875
2	0.1406
3	0.1055
4	0.0791
5	0.0593
6	0.0445
7 or more	0.1335

improve the operating characteristics must be based on the insights and creativity of the analyst.

After reviewing the operating characteristics provided by the waiting line model, Burger Dome's management concluded that improvements designed to reduce waiting times are desirable. To make improvements in the waiting line operation, analysts often focus on ways to improve the service rate. Generally, service rate improvements are obtained by making either or both the following changes:

1. Increase the mean service rate μ by making a creative design change or by using new technology.
2. Add service channels so that more customers can be served simultaneously.

Assume that in considering alternative 1, Burger Dome's management decides to employ an order filler who will assist the order taker at the cash register. The customer begins the service process by placing the order with the order taker. As the order is placed, the order taker announces the order over an intercom system, and the order filler begins filling the order. When the order is completed, the order taker handles the money, while the order filler continues to fill the order. With this design, Burger Dome's management estimates the mean service rate can be increased from the current service rate of 60 customers per hour to 75 customers per hour. Thus, the mean service rate for the revised system is $\mu = 75$ customers/60 minutes $= 1.25$ customers per minute. For $\lambda = 0.75$ customers per minute and $\mu = 1.25$ customers per minute, equations (15.4) through (15.10) can be used to provide the new operating characteristics for the Burger Dome waiting line. These operating characteristics are summarized in Table 15.3.

The information in Table 15.3 indicates that all operating characteristics have improved because of the increased service rate. In particular, the average time a customer spends in the waiting line has been reduced from 3 to 1.2 minutes and the average time a customer spends in the system has been reduced from 4 to 2 minutes. Are any other alternatives available that Burger Dome can use to increase the service rate? If so, and if the mean service rate μ can be identified for each alternative, equations (15.4) through (15.10) can be used to determine the revised operating characteristics and any improvements in the waiting line system. The added cost of any proposed change can be compared to the corresponding service improvements to help the manager determine whether the proposed service improvements are worthwhile.

Problem 11 asks you to determine whether a change in the mean service rate will meet the company's service guideline for its customers.

As mentioned previously, another option often available is to provide one or more additional service channels so that more than one customer may be served at the same time. The extension of the single-channel waiting line model to the multiple-channel waiting line model is the topic of the next section.

TABLE 15.3   OPERATING CHARACTERISTICS FOR THE BURGER DOME SYSTEM WITH THE MEAN SERVICE RATE INCREASED TO $\mu = 1.25$ CUSTOMERS PER MINUTE

Probability of no customers in the system	0.400
Average number of customers in the waiting line	0.900
Average number of customers in the system	1.500
Average time in the waiting line	1.200 minutes
Average time in the system	2.000 minutes
Probability that an arriving customer has to wait	0.600
Probability that seven or more customers are in the system	0.028

NOTES AND COMMENTS

1. The assumption that arrivals follow a Poisson probability distribution is equivalent to the assumption that the time between arrivals has an exponential probability distribution. For example, if the arrivals for a waiting line follow a Poisson probability distribution with a mean of 20 arrivals per hour, the time between arrivals will follow an exponential probability distribution, with a mean time between arrivals of $\frac{1}{20}$ or 0.05 hour.

2. Many individuals believe that whenever the mean service rate μ is greater than the mean arrival rate λ, the system should be able to handle or serve all arrivals. However, as the Burger Dome example shows, the variability of arrival times and service times may result in long waiting times even when the mean service rate exceeds the mean arrival rate. A contribution of waiting line models is that they can point out undesirable waiting line operating characteristics even when the $\mu > \lambda$ condition appears satisfactory.

15.3 MULTIPLE-CHANNEL WAITING LINE MODEL WITH POISSON ARRIVALS AND EXPONENTIAL SERVICE TIMES

You may be familiar with multiple-channel systems that also have multiple waiting lines. The waiting line model in this section has multiple channels, but only a single waiting line. Operating characteristics for a multiple-channel system are better when a single waiting line, rather than multiple waiting lines, is used.

A **multiple-channel waiting line** consists of two or more service channels that are assumed to be identical in terms of service capability. In the multiple-channel system, arriving units wait in a single waiting line and then move to the first available channel to be served.

The single-channel Burger Dome operation can be expanded to a two-channel system by opening a second service channel. Figure 15.2 shows a diagram of the Burger Dome two-channel waiting line.

In this section we present formulas that can be used to determine the steady-state operating characteristics for a multiple-channel waiting line. These formulas are applicable if the following conditions exist.

1. The arrivals follow a Poisson probability distribution.
2. The service time for each channel follows an exponential probability distribution.
3. The means service rate μ is the same for each channel.
4. The arrivals wait in a single waiting line and then move to the first open channel for service.

FIGURE 15.2   THE BURGER DOME TWO-CHANNEL WAITING LINE

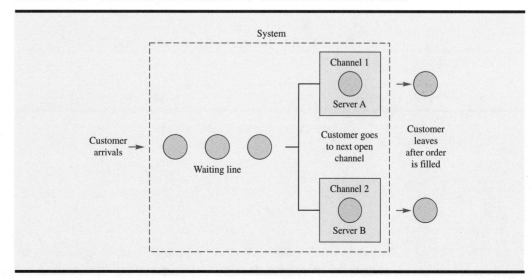

Operating Characteristics

The following formulas can be used to compute the steady-state operating characteristics for multiple-channel waiting lines, where

$$\lambda = \text{the mean arrival rate for the system}$$
$$\mu = \text{the mean service rate for } each \text{ channel}$$
$$k = \text{the number of channels}$$

1. The probability that no units are in the system:

$$P_0 = \frac{1}{\displaystyle\sum_{n=0}^{k-1} \frac{(\lambda/\mu)^n}{n!} + \frac{(\lambda/\mu)^k}{k!}\left(\frac{k\mu}{k\mu - \lambda}\right)} \qquad (15.11)$$

2. The average number of units in the waiting line:

$$L_q = \frac{(\lambda/\mu)^k \lambda\mu}{(k-1)!(k\mu - \lambda)^2} P_0 \qquad (15.12)$$

3. The average number of units in the system:

$$L = L_q + \frac{\lambda}{\mu} \qquad (15.13)$$

4. The average time a unit spends in the waiting line:

$$W_q = \frac{L_q}{\lambda} \qquad (15.14)$$

5. The average time a unit spends in the system:

$$W = W_q + \frac{1}{\mu} \qquad (15.15)$$

6. The probability that an arriving unit has to wait for service:

$$P_w = \frac{1}{k!}\left(\frac{\lambda}{\mu}\right)^k \left(\frac{k\mu}{k\mu - \lambda}\right) P_0 \qquad (15.16)$$

7. The probability of n units in the system:

$$P_n = \frac{(\lambda/\mu)^n}{n!} P_0 \quad \text{for } n \le k \qquad (15.17)$$

$$P_n = \frac{(\lambda/\mu)^n}{k! k^{(n-k)}} P_0 \quad \text{for } n > k \qquad (15.18)$$

Because μ is the mean service rate for each channel, $k\mu$ is the mean service rate for the multiple-channel system. As was true for the single-channel waiting line model, the formulas for the operating characteristics of multiple-channel waiting lines can be applied only in situations where the mean service rate for the system is greater than the mean arrival rate for the system; in other words, the formulas are applicable only if $k\mu$ is greater than λ.

Some expressions for the operating characteristics of multiple-channel waiting lines are more complex than their single-channel counterparts. However, equations (15.11) through (15.18) provide the same information as provided by the single-channel model. To help simplify the use of the multiple-channel equations, Table 15.4 contains values of P_0 for selected values of λ/μ and k. The values provided in the table correspond to cases where $k\mu > \lambda$, and hence the service rate is sufficient to process all arrivals.

TABLE 15.4   VALUES OF P_0 FOR MULTIPLE-CHANNEL WAITING LINES WITH POISSON ARRIVALS AND EXPONENTIAL SERVICE TIMES

	Number of Channels (k)			
Ratio λ/μ	2	3	4	5
0.15	0.8605	0.8607	0.8607	0.8607
0.20	0.8182	0.8187	0.8187	0.8187
0.25	0.7778	0.7788	0.7788	0.7788
0.30	0.7391	0.7407	0.7408	0.7408
0.35	0.7021	0.7046	0.7047	0.7047
0.40	0.6667	0.6701	0.6703	0.6703
0.45	0.6327	0.6373	0.6376	0.6376
0.50	0.6000	0.6061	0.6065	0.6065
0.55	0.5686	0.5763	0.5769	0.5769
0.60	0.5385	0.5479	0.5487	0.5488
0.65	0.5094	0.5209	0.5219	0.5220
0.70	0.4815	0.4952	0.4965	0.4966
0.75	0.4545	0.4706	0.4722	0.4724
0.80	0.4286	0.4472	0.4491	0.4493
0.85	0.4035	0.4248	0.4271	0.4274
0.90	0.3793	0.4035	0.4062	0.4065
0.95	0.3559	0.3831	0.3863	0.3867
1.00	0.3333	0.3636	0.3673	0.3678
1.20	0.2500	0.2941	0.3002	0.3011
1.40	0.1765	0.2360	0.2449	0.2463
1.60	0.1111	0.1872	0.1993	0.2014
1.80	0.0526	0.1460	0.1616	0.1646
2.00		0.1111	0.1304	0.1343
2.20		0.0815	0.1046	0.1094
2.40		0.0562	0.0831	0.0889
2.60		0.0345	0.0651	0.0721
2.80		0.0160	0.0521	0.0581
3.00			0.0377	0.0466
3.20			0.0273	0.0372
3.40			0.0186	0.0293
3.60			0.0113	0.0228
3.80			0.0051	0.0174
4.00				0.0130
4.20				0.0093
4.40				0.0063
4.60				0.0038
4.80				0.0017

Operating Characteristics for the Burger Dome Problem

To illustrate the multiple-channel waiting line model, we return to the Burger Dome fast food restaurant waiting line problem. Suppose that management wants to evaluate the desirability of opening a second order-processing station so that two customers can be served simultaneously. Assume a single waiting line with the first customer in line moving to the first available server. Let us evaluate the operating characteristics for this two-channel system.

We use equations (15.12) through (15.18) for the $k = 2$ channel system. For a mean arrival rate of $\lambda = 0.75$ customers per minute and mean service rate of $\mu = 1$ customer per minute for each channel, we obtain the operating characteristics:

$$P_0 = 0.4545 \quad \text{(from Table 15.4 with } \lambda/\mu = 0.75\text{)}$$

$$L_q = \frac{(0.75/1)^2(0.75)(1)}{(2 - 1)![2(1) - 0.75]^2}(0.4545) = 0.1227 \text{ customer}$$

$$L = L_q + \frac{\lambda}{\mu} = 0.1227 + \frac{0.75}{1} = 0.8727 \text{ customer}$$

$$W_q = \frac{L_q}{\lambda} = \frac{0.1227}{0.75} = 0.1636 \text{ minute}$$

$$W = W_q + \frac{1}{\mu} = 0.1636 + \frac{1}{1} = 1.1636 \text{ minutes}$$

$$P_w = \frac{1}{2!}\left(\frac{0.75}{1}\right)^2\left[\frac{2(1)}{2(1) - 0.75}\right](0.4545) = 0.2045$$

Try Problem 19, which will give you practice in determining the operating characteristics for a two-channel waiting line.

Using equations (15.17) and (15.18), we can compute the probabilities of n customers in the system. The results from these computations are summarized in Table 15.5.

We can now compare the steady-state operating characteristics of the two-channel system to the operating characteristics of the original single-channel system discussed in Section 15.2.

1. The average time a customer spends in the system (waiting time plus service time) is reduced from $W = 4$ minutes to $W = 1.1636$ minutes.
2. The average number of customers in the waiting line is reduced from $L_q = 2.25$ customers to $L_q = 0.1227$ customers.
3. The average time a customer spends in the waiting line is reduced from $W_q = 3$ minutes to $W_q = 0.1636$ minutes.
4. The probability that a customer has to wait for service is reduced from $P_w = 0.75$ to $P_w = 0.2045$.

Clearly the two-channel system will significantly improve the operating characteristics of the waiting line. However, adding an order filler at each service station would further increase

TABLE 15.5   THE PROBABILITY OF n CUSTOMERS IN THE SYSTEM FOR THE BURGER DOME TWO-CHANNEL WAITING LINE

Number of Customers	Probability
0	0.4545
1	0.3409
2	0.1278
3	0.0479
4	0.0180
5 or more	0.0109

the mean service rate and improve the operating characteristics. The final decision regarding the staffing policy at Burger Dome rests with the Burger Dome management. The waiting line study has simply provided the operating characteristics that can be anticipated under three configurations: a single-channel system with one employee, a single-channel system with two employees, and a two-channel system with an employee for each channel. After considering these results, what action would you recommend? In this case, Burger Dome adopted the following policy statement: For periods when customer arrivals are expected to average 45 customers per hour, Burger Dome will open two order-processing channels with one employee assigned to each.

By changing the mean arrival rate λ to reflect arrival rates at different times of the day, and then computing the operating characteristics, Burger Dome's management can establish guidelines and policies that tell the store managers when they should schedule service operations with a single channel, two channels, or perhaps even three or more channels. The Q. M. in Action article for Lourdes Hospital shows how a multiple-channel waiting line model has been used to help make hospital staffing decisions.

NOTES AND COMMENTS

The multiple-channel waiting line model is based on a single waiting line. You may have also encountered situations where each of the k channels has its own waiting line. Quantitative analysts have shown that the operating characteristics of multiple-channel systems are better if a single waiting line is used. People like them better also; no one who comes in after you can be served ahead of you. Thus, when possible, banks, airline reservation counters, food-service establishments, and other businesses frequently use a single waiting line for a multiple-channel system.

Q. M. IN ACTION

HOSPITAL STAFFING BASED ON A MULTIPLE-CHANNEL WAITING LINE MODEL*

Lourdes Hospital in Binghamton, New York, uses a centralized staff to schedule appointments for the hospital's outpatient, inpatient, and ambulance services. Physicians, their staffs, hospital personnel, and patients contact the centralized scheduling office by telephone to establish desired appointment times.

Efficiency of the scheduling process depends on the department's staff being able to process incoming telephone calls in a timely manner. Periodically, incoming requests for services overload the staff's ability to answer the telephone and process the appointments. As a result, users reported undesirable delays and lengthy waiting times. Management used a waiting line model to study the operation and suggest staffing changes that could improve the efficiency of the centralized scheduling process.

Data were collected on the number of telephone calls that arrived during each 15-minute period. The calls were random, not depending on the day of the week. A Poisson probability distribution was a good description of the random arrivals, with peak arrival times occurring between 9:00 A.M. and 11:30 A.M. and between 2:00 P.M. and 3:45 P.M.

each day. An investigation of service times found that, although service times were not exactly exponential, the exponential probability distribution provided a reasonable approximation.

In effect, the hospital's scheduling service was viewed as a multiple-channel waiting line with Poisson arrivals and exponential service times. The number of channels was simply the number of individuals on the scheduling staff. With the mean arrival rate adjusted for the different periods of the day, a waiting line model with k channels was used to estimate the probability that an arriving call would have to wait for service. The staff size was determined by selecting the number of channels that kept the steady state probability of waiting to no more than 10%. Staff schedules and workloads were adjusted, efficiency improved, and the number of complaints about waiting for service declined.

*Based on S. R. Agnihothri and P. F. Taylor, "Staffing a Centralized Appointment Scheduling Department in Lourdes Hospital," *Interfaces* 21, no. 5 (September–October 1991): 1–11.

15.4   SOME GENERAL RELATIONSHIPS FOR WAITING LINE MODELS

In Sections 15.2 and 15.3 we presented formulas for computing the operating characteristics for single-channel and multiple-channel waiting lines with Poisson arrivals and exponential service times. The operating characteristics of interest included

L_q = the average number of units in the waiting line

L = the average number of units in the system

W_q = the average time a unit spends in the waiting line

W = the average time a unit spends in the system

John D. C. Little showed that several relationships exist among these four characteristics and that these relationships apply to a variety of different waiting line systems. Two of the relationships, referred to as *Little's flow equations,* are

$$L = \lambda W \qquad (15.19)$$

$$L_q = \lambda W_q \qquad (15.20)$$

Equation (15.19) shows that the average number of units in the system, L, can be found by multiplying the mean arrival rate, λ, by the average time a unit spends in the system, W. Equation (15.20) shows that the same relationship holds between the average number of units in the waiting line, L_q, and the average time a unit spends in the waiting line, W_q.

Using equation (15.20) and solving for W_q, we obtain

$$W_q = \frac{L_q}{\lambda} \qquad (15.21)$$

Equation (15.21) follows directly from Little's second flow equation. We used it for the single-channel waiting line model in Section 15.2 and the multiple-channel waiting line model in Section 15.3 [see equations (15.7) and (15.14)]. Once L_q is computed for either of these models, equation (15.21) can then be used to compute W_q.

Another general expression that applies to waiting line models is that the average time in the system, W, is equal to the average time in the waiting line, W_q, plus the average service time. For a system with a mean service rate μ, the mean service time is $1/\mu$. Thus, we have the general relationship

$$W = W_q + \frac{1}{\mu} \qquad (15.22)$$

The advantage of Little's flow equations is that they show how operating characteristics L, L_q, W, and W_q are related in any waiting line system. Arrivals and service times do not have to follow specific probability distributions for the flow equations to be applicable.

Recall that we used equation (15.22) to provide the average time in the system for both the single- and multiple-channel waiting line models [see equations (15.8) and (15.15)].

The importance of Little's flow equations is that they apply to *any waiting line model* regardless of whether arrivals follow the Poisson probability distribution and regardless of whether service times follow the exponential probability distribution. For example, in a study of the grocery checkout counters at Murphy's Foodliner, an analyst concluded that arrivals follow the Poisson probability distribution with the mean arrival rate of 24 customers per hour or $\lambda = 24/60 = 0.40$ customers per minute. However, the analyst found that service times follow a normal probability distribution rather than an exponential probability distribution. The mean service rate was found to be 30 customers per hour or $\mu = 30/60 = 0.50$ customers per minute. A time study of actual customer waiting times showed that, on average, a customer spends 4.5 minutes in the system (waiting time plus checkout time); that is, $W = 4.5$. Using the waiting line relationships discussed in this section, we can now compute other operating characteristics for this waiting line.

First, using equation (15.22) and solving for W_q, we have

$$W_q = W - \frac{1}{\mu} = 4.5 - \frac{1}{0.50} = 2.5 \text{ minutes}$$

The application of Little's flow equations is demonstrated in Problem 25.

With both W and W_q known, we can use Little's flow equations, (15.19) and (15.20), to compute

$$L = \lambda W = 0.40(4.5) = 1.8 \text{ customers}$$
$$L_q = \lambda W_q = 0.40(2.5) = 1 \text{ customer}$$

The manager of Murphy's Foodliner can now review these operating characteristics to see whether action should be taken to improve the service and to reduce the waiting time and the length of the waiting line.

NOTES AND COMMENTS

In waiting line systems where the length of the waiting line is limited (e.g., a small waiting area), some arriving units will be blocked from joining the waiting line and will be lost. In this case, the blocked or lost arrivals will make the mean number of units entering the system something less than the mean arrival rate. By defining λ as the mean number of units *joining the system,* rather than the mean arrival rate, the relationships discussed in this section can be used to determine W, L, W_q, and L_q.

15.5   ECONOMIC ANALYSIS OF WAITING LINES

Frequently, decisions involving the design of waiting lines will be based on a subjective evaluation of the operating characteristics of the waiting line. For example, a manager may decide that an average waiting time of one minute or less and an average of two customers or fewer in the system are reasonable goals. The waiting line models presented in the preceding sections can be used to determine the number of channels that will meet the manager's waiting line performance goals.

On the other hand, a manager may want to identify the cost of operating the waiting line system and then base the decision regarding system design on a minimum hourly or daily operating cost. Before an economic analysis of a waiting line can be conducted, a total cost model, which includes the cost of waiting and the cost of service, must be developed.

To develop a total cost model for a waiting line, we begin by defining the notation to be used:

$$c_w = \text{the waiting cost per time period for each unit}$$
$$L = \text{the average number of units in the system}$$
$$c_s = \text{the service cost per time period for each channel}$$
$$k = \text{the number of channels}$$
$$TC = \text{the total cost per time period}$$

Waiting cost is based on average number of units in the system. It includes the time spent waiting in line plus the time spent being served.

The total cost is the sum of the waiting cost and the service cost; that is,

$$TC = c_w L + c_s k \qquad (15.23)$$

To conduct an economic analysis of a waiting line, we must obtain reasonable estimates of the waiting cost and the service cost. Of these two costs, the waiting cost is usually the more difficult to evaluate. In the Burger Dome restaurant problem, the waiting cost would be the cost per minute for a customer waiting for service. This cost is not a direct cost to Burger Dome. However, if Burger Dome ignores this cost and allows long waiting lines, customers ultimately will take their business elsewhere. Thus, Burger Dome will experience lost sales and, in effect, incur a cost.

Adding more channels always improves the operating characteristics of the waiting line and reduces the waiting cost. However, additional channels increase the service cost. An economic analysis of waiting lines attempts to find the number of channels that will minimize total cost by balancing the waiting cost and the service cost.

The service cost is generally easier to determine. This cost is the relevant cost associated with operating each service channel. In the Burger Dome problem, this cost would include the server's wages, benefits, and any other direct costs associated with operating the service channel. At Burger Dome, this cost is estimated to be $7 per hour.

To demonstrate the use of equation (15.23), we assume that Burger Dome is willing to assign a cost of $10 per hour for customer waiting time. We use the average number of units in the system, L, as computed in Sections 15.2 and 15.3 to obtain the total hourly cost for the single-channel and two-channel systems:

Single-channel system ($L = 3$ customers)

$$TC = c_w L + c_s k$$
$$= 10(3) + 7(1) = \$37.00 \text{ per hour}$$

Two-channel system ($L = 0.8727$ customer):

$$TC = c_w L + c_s k$$
$$= 10(0.8727) + 7(2) = \$22.73 \text{ per hour}$$

Problem 21 will test your ability to conduct an economic analysis of proposed single-channel and two-channel waiting line systems.

Thus, based on the cost data provided by Burger Dome, the two-channel system provides the most economical operation.

Figure 15.3 shows the general shapes of the cost curves in the economic analysis of waiting lines. The service cost increases as the number of channels is increased. However,

FIGURE 15.3   THE GENERAL SHAPE OF WAITING COST, SERVICE COST, AND TOTAL-COST CURVES IN WAITING LINE MODELS

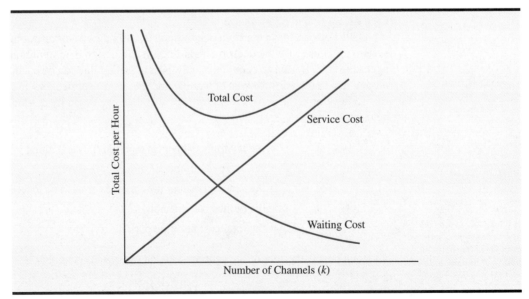

with more channels, the service is better. As a result, waiting time and cost decrease as the number of channels is increased. The number of channels that will provide a good approximation of the minimum total cost design can be found by evaluating the total cost for several design alternatives.

NOTES AND COMMENTS

1. In dealing with government agencies and utility companies, customers may not be able to take their business elsewhere. In these situations, no lost business occurs when long waiting times are encountered. This condition is one reason that service in such organizations may be poor and that customers in such situations may experience long waiting times.
2. In some instances, the organization providing the service also employs the units waiting for the service. For example, consider the case of a company that owns and operates the trucks used to deliver goods to and from its manufacturing plant. In addition to the costs associated with the trucks waiting to be loaded or unloaded, the firm also pays the wages of the truck loaders and unloaders who operate the service channel. In this case, the cost of having the trucks wait and the cost of operating the service channel are direct expenses to the firm. An economic analysis of the waiting line system is highly recommended for these types of situations.

15.6   OTHER WAITING LINE MODELS

D. G. Kendall suggested a notation that is helpful in classifying the wide variety of different waiting line models that have been developed. The three-symbol Kendall notation is as follows:

$$A/B/k$$

where

A denotes the probability distribution for the arrivals

B denotes the probability distribution for the service time

k denotes the number of channels

Depending on the letter appearing in the A or B position, a variety of waiting line systems can be described. The letters that are commonly used are as follows:

M designates a Poisson probability distribution for the arrivals or an exponential probability distribution for service time

D designates that the arrivals or the service time is deterministic or constant

G designates that the arrivals or the service time has a general probability distribution with a known mean and variance

Using the Kendall notation, the single-channel waiting line model with Poisson arrivals and exponential service times is classified as an $M/M/1$ model. The 2-channel waiting line model with Poisson arrivals and exponential service times presented in Section 15.3 would be classified as an $M/M/2$ model.

NOTES AND COMMENTS

In some cases, the Kendall notation is extended to five symbols. The fourth symbol indicates the largest number of units that can be in the system, and the fifth symbol indicates the size of the population. The fourth symbol is used in situations where the waiting line can hold a finite or maximum number of units, and the fifth sym- bol is necessary when the population of arriving units or customers is finite. When the fourth and fifth symbols of the Kendall notation are omitted, the waiting line system is assumed to have infinite capacity, and the population is assumed to be infinite.

15.7 SINGLE-CHANNEL WAITING LINE MODEL WITH POISSON ARRIVALS AND ARBITRARY SERVICE TIMES

Let us return to the single-channel waiting line model where arrivals are described by a Poisson probability distribution. However, we now assume that the probability distribution for the service times is not an exponential probability distribution. Thus, using the Kendall notation, the waiting line model that is appropriate is an $M/G/1$ model, where G denotes a general or unspecified probability distribution.

Operating Characteristics for the $M/G/1$ Model

When providing input to the M/G/1 model, be consistent in terms of the time period. For example, if λ and μ are expressed in terms of the number of units per hour, the standard deviation of the service time should be expressed in hours. The example that follows uses minutes as the time period for the arrival and service data.

The notation used to describe the operating characteristics for the $M/G/1$ model is

$$\lambda = \text{the mean arrival rate}$$
$$\mu = \text{the mean service rate}$$
$$\sigma = \text{the standard deviation of the service time}$$

Some of the steady-state operating characteristics of the $M/G/1$ waiting line model are as follows:

1. The probability that no units are in the system:

$$P_0 = 1 - \frac{\lambda}{\mu} \tag{15.24}$$

2. The average number of units in the waiting line:

$$L_q = \frac{\lambda^2 \sigma^2 + (\lambda/\mu)^2}{2(1 - \lambda/\mu)} \tag{15.25}$$

3. The average number of units in the system:

$$L = L_q + \frac{\lambda}{\mu} \tag{15.26}$$

4. The average time a unit spends in the waiting line:

$$W_q = \frac{L_q}{\lambda} \tag{15.27}$$

5. The average time a unit spends in the system:

$$W = W_q + \frac{1}{\mu} \tag{15.28}$$

6. The probability that an arriving unit has to wait for service:

$$P_w = \frac{\lambda}{\mu} \tag{15.29}$$

Note that the relationships for L, W_q, and W are the same as the relationships used for the waiting line models in Sections 15.2 and 15.3. They are given by Little's flow equations.

An Example.   Retail sales at Hartlage's Seafood Supply are handled by one clerk. Customer arrivals are random, and the average arrival rate is 21 customers per hour or $\lambda = 21/60 = 0.35$ customers per minute. A study of the service process shows that the average or mean service time is 2 minutes per customer, with a standard deviation of $\sigma = 1.2$ minutes. The mean time of 2 minutes per customer shows that the clerk has a mean service rate of $\mu = \frac{1}{2} = 0.50$ customers per minute. The operating characteristics of this *M/G/1* waiting line system are

Problem 27 provides another application of a single-channel waiting line with Poisson arrivals and arbitrary service times.

$$P_0 = 1 - \frac{\lambda}{\mu} = 1 - \frac{0.35}{0.50} = 0.30$$

$$L_q = \frac{(0.35)^2(1.2)^2 + (0.35/0.50)^2}{2(1 - 0.35/0.50)} = 1.1107 \text{ customers}$$

$$L = L_q + \frac{\lambda}{\mu} = 1.1107 + \frac{0.35}{0.50} = 1.8107 \text{ customers}$$

$$W_q = \frac{L_q}{\lambda} = \frac{1.1107}{0.35} = 3.1733 \text{ minutes}$$

$$W = W_q + \frac{1}{\mu} = 3.1733 + \frac{1}{0.50} = 5.1733 \text{ minutes}$$

$$P_w = \frac{\lambda}{\mu} = \frac{0.35}{0.50} = 0.70$$

Hartlage's manager can review these operating characteristics to determine whether scheduling a second clerk appears to be worthwhile.

Constant Service Times

We want to comment briefly on the single-channel waiting line model that assumes random arrivals but constant service times. Such a waiting line can occur in production and manufacturing environments where machine-controlled service times are constant. This waiting line is described by the *M/D/1* model, with the *D* referring to the deterministic service times. With the *M/D/1* model, the average number of units in the waiting line, L_q, can be found by using equation (15.25) with the condition that the standard deviation of the constant service time is $\sigma = 0$. Thus, the expression for the average number of units in the waiting line for the *M/D/1* waiting line becomes

$$L_q = \frac{(\lambda/\mu)^2}{2(1 - \lambda/\mu)} \tag{15.30}$$

The other expressions presented earlier in this section can be used to determine additional operating characteristics of the *M/D*/1 system.

NOTES AND COMMENTS

Whenever the operating characteristics of a waiting line are unacceptable, managers often try to improve service by increasing the mean service rate μ. This is a good idea, but equation (15.25) shows that the variation in the service times also affects the operating characteristics of the waiting line. Because the standard deviation of service times, σ, appears in the numerator of equation (15.25), a larger variation in service times results in a larger average number of units in the waiting line. Hence, another alternative for improving the service capabilities of a waiting line is to reduce the variation in the service times. Thus, even when the mean service rate of the service facility cannot be increased, a reduction in σ will reduce the average number of units in the waiting line and improve the other operating characteristics of the system.

15.8   MULTIPLE-CHANNEL MODEL WITH POISSON ARRIVALS, ARBITRARY SERVICE TIMES, AND NO WAITING LINE

An interesting variation of the waiting line models discussed so far involves a system in which no waiting is allowed. Arriving units or customers seek service from one of several service channels. If all channels are busy, arriving units are denied access to the system. In waiting line terminology, arrivals occurring when the system is full are **blocked** and are cleared from the system. Such customers may be lost or may attempt a return to the system later.

The specific model considered in this section is based on the following assumptions.

1. The system has k channels.
2. The arrivals follow a Poisson probability distribution, with mean arrival rate λ.
3. The service times for each channel may have any probability distribution.
4. The mean service rate μ is the same for each channel.
5. An arrival enters the system only if at least one channel is available. An arrival occurring when all channels are busy is blocked—that is, denied service and not allowed to enter the system.

With G denoting a general or unspecified probability distribution for service times, the appropriate model for this situation is referred to as an *M/G/k* model with "blocked customers cleared." The question addressed in this type of situation is, How many channels or servers should be used?

A primary application of this model involves the design of telephone and other communication systems where the arrivals are the calls and the channels are the number of telephone or communication lines available. In such a system, the calls are made to one telephone number, with each call automatically switched to an open channel if possible. When all channels are busy, additional calls receive a busy signal and are denied access to the system.

Operating Characteristics for the *M/G/k* Model with Blocked Customers Cleared

We approach the problem of selecting the best number of channels by computing the steady-state probabilities that j of the k channels will be busy. These probabilities are

$$P_j = \frac{(\lambda/\mu)^j/j!}{\sum_{i=0}^{k} (\lambda/\mu)^i/i!} \tag{15.31}$$

where

$$\lambda = \text{the mean arrival rate}$$
$$\mu = \text{the mean service rate for each channel}$$
$$k = \text{the number of channels}$$
$$P_j = \text{the probability that } j \text{ of the } k \text{ channels are busy}$$
$$\text{for } j = 0, 1, 2, \ldots, k$$

With no waiting allowed, operating characteristics L_q and W_q considered in previous waiting line models are automatically zero regardless of the number of service channels. In this situation, the more important design consideration involves determining how the percentage of blocked customers is affected by the number of service channels.

The most important probability value is P_k, which is the probability that all k channels are busy. On a percentage basis, P_k indicates the percentage of arrivals that are blocked and denied access to the system.

Another operating characteristic of interest is the average number of units in the system; note that this number is equivalent to the average number of channels in use. Letting L denote the average number of units in the system, we have

$$L = \frac{\lambda}{\mu}(1 - P_k) \qquad (15.32)$$

An Example. Microdata Software, Inc., uses a telephone ordering system for its computer software products. Callers place orders with Microdata by using the company's 800 telephone number. Assume that calls to this telephone number arrive at an average rate of $\lambda = 12$ calls per hour. The time required to process a telephone order varies considerably from order to order. However, each Microdata sales representative can be expected to handle an average of $\mu = 6$ calls per hour. Currently, the Microdata 800 telephone number has three internal lines or channels, each operated by a separate sales representative. Calls received on the 800 number are automatically transferred to an open line or channel if available.

Whenever all three lines are busy, callers receive a busy signal. In the past, Microdata's management has assumed that callers receiving a busy signal will call back later. However, recent research on telephone ordering has shown that a substantial number of callers who are denied access do not call back later. These lost calls represent lost revenues for the firm, so Microdata's management has requested an analysis of the telephone ordering system. Specifically, management wants to know the percentage of callers who are getting busy signals and are being blocked from the system. If management's goal is to provide sufficient capacity to handle 90% of the callers, how many telephone lines and sales representatives should Microdata use?

We can demonstrate the use of equation (15.31) by computing P_3, the probability that all three of the currently available telephone lines will be in use and additional callers will be blocked:

$$P_3 = \frac{(^{12}\!/_6)^3/3!}{(^{12}\!/_6)^0/0! + (^{12}\!/_6)^1/1! + (^{12}\!/_6)^2/2! + (^{12}\!/_6)^3/3!} = \frac{1.3333}{6.3333} = 0.2105$$

With $P_3 = 0.2105$, approximately 21% of the calls, or slightly more than one in five calls, are being blocked. Only 79% of the calls are being handled immediately by the 3-line system.

Let us assume that Microdata expands to a 4-line system. Then, the probability that all four channels will be in use and that callers will be blocked is

$$P_4 = \frac{(^{12}\!/_6)^4/4!}{(^{12}\!/_6)^0/0! + (^{12}\!/_6)^1/1! + (^{12}\!/_6)^2/2! + (^{12}\!/_6)^3/3! + (^{12}\!/_6)^4/4!} = \frac{0.6667}{7} = 0.0952$$

With only 9.52% of the callers blocked, 90.48% of the callers will reach the Microdata sales representatives. Thus, Microdata should expand its order-processing operation to 4 lines to

Problem 30 provides practice in calculating probabilities for multiple-channel systems with no waiting line.

meet management's goal of providing sufficient capacity to handle at least 90% of the callers. The average number of calls in the 4-line system and thus the average number of lines and sales representatives that will be busy is

$$L = \frac{\lambda}{\mu}(1 - P_4) = \frac{12}{6}(1 - 0.0952) = 1.8095$$

Although an average of fewer than 2 lines will be busy, the 4-line system is necessary to provide the capacity to handle at least 90% of the callers. We used equation (15.31) to calculate the probability that 0, 1, 2, 3, or 4 lines will be busy. These probabilities are summarized in Table 15.6.

As we discussed in Section 15.5, an economic analysis of waiting lines can be used to guide system design decisions. In the Microdata system, the cost of the additional line and additional sales representative should be relatively easy to establish. This cost can be balanced against the cost of the blocked calls. With 9.52% of the calls blocked and $\lambda = 12$ calls per hour, an 8-hour day will have an average of $8(12)(0.0952) = 9.1$ blocked calls. If Microdata can estimate the cost of possible lost sales, the cost of these blocked calls can be established. The economic analysis based on the service cost and the blocked-call cost can assist in determining the optimal number of lines for the system.

TABLE 15.6   PROBABILITIES OF BUSY LINES FOR THE MICRODATA 4-LINE SYSTEM

Number of Busy Lines	Probability
0	0.1429
1	0.2857
2	0.2857
3	0.1905
4	0.0952

NOTES AND COMMENTS

Many of the operating characteristics we have considered in previous sections are not relevant for the *M/G/k* model with blocked customers cleared. In particular, the average time in the waiting line, W_q, and the average number of units in the waiting line, L_q, are no longer considered because waiting is not permitted in this type of system.

15.9   WAITING LINE MODELS WITH FINITE CALLING POPULATIONS

For the waiting line models introduced so far, the population of units or customers arriving for service has been considered to be unlimited. In technical terms, when no limit is placed on how many units may seek service, the model is said to have an **infinite calling population.** Under this assumption, the mean arrival rate λ remains constant regardless of how many units are in the waiting line system. This assumption of an infinite calling population is made in most waiting line models.

In other cases, the maximum number of units or customers that may seek service is assumed to be finite. In this situation, the mean arrival rate for the system changes, depending on the number of units in the waiting line, and the waiting line model is said to have a **finite calling population.** The formulas for the operating characteristics of the previous waiting line models must be modified to account for the effect of the finite calling population.

In previous waiting line models, the arrival rate was constant and independent of the number of units in the system. With a finite calling population, the arrival rate decreases as the number of units in the system increases because, with more units in the system, fewer units are available for arrivals.

The finite calling population model discussed in this section is based on the following assumptions.

1. The arrivals for *each unit* follow a Poisson probability distribution, with mean arrival rate λ.
2. The service times follow an exponential probability distribution, with mean service rate μ.
3. The population of units that may seek service is finite.

With a single channel, the waiting line model is referred to as an *M/M/*1 model with a finite calling population.

The mean arrival rate λ is defined differently for the finite calling population model. Specifically, λ is defined in terms of the mean arrival rate for each unit.

The mean arrival rate for the *M/M/*1 model with a finite calling population is defined in terms of how often *each unit* arrives or seeks service. This situation differs from that for previous waiting line models in which λ denoted the mean arrival rate for the system. With a finite calling population, the mean arrival rate for the system varies, depending on the number of units in the system. Instead of adjusting for the changing system arrival rate, in the finite calling population model λ indicates the mean arrival rate for each unit.

Operating Characteristics for the *M/M/*1 Model with a Finite Calling Population

The following formulas are used to determine the steady-state operating characteristics for an *M/M/*1 model with a finite calling population, where

$$\lambda = \text{the mean arrival rate for each unit}$$
$$\mu = \text{the mean service rate}$$
$$N = \text{the size of the population}$$

1. The probability that no units are in the system:

$$P_0 = \frac{1}{\displaystyle\sum_{n=0}^{N} \frac{N!}{(N-n)!}\left(\frac{\lambda}{\mu}\right)^n} \tag{15.33}$$

2. The average number of units in the waiting line:

$$L_q = N - \frac{\lambda + \mu}{\lambda}(1 - P_0) \tag{15.34}$$

3. The average number of units in the system:

$$L = L_q + (1 - P_0) \tag{15.35}$$

4. The average time a unit spends in the waiting line:

$$W_q = \frac{L_q}{(N - L)\lambda} \tag{15.36}$$

5. The average time a unit spends in the system:

$$W = W_q + \frac{1}{\mu} \tag{15.37}$$

6. The probability an arriving unit has to wait for service:

$$P_w = 1 - P_0 \tag{15.38}$$

7. The probability of n units in the system:

$$P_n = \frac{N!}{(N - n)!}\left(\frac{\lambda}{\mu}\right)^n P_0 \quad \text{for } n = 0, 1, \dots, N \tag{15.39}$$

One of the primary applications of the $M/M/1$ model with a finite calling population is referred to as the *machine repair problem*. In this problem, a group of machines is considered to be the finite population of "customers" that may request repair service. Whenever a machine breaks down, an arrival occurs in the sense that a new repair request is initiated. If another machine breaks down before the repair work has been completed on the first machine, the second machine begins to form a "waiting line" for repair service. Additional breakdowns by other machines will add to the length of the waiting line. The assumption of first-come, first-served indicates that machines are repaired in the order they break down. The $M/M/1$ model shows that one person or one channel is available to perform the repair service. To return the machine to operation, each machine with a breakdown must be repaired by the single-channel operation.

An Example. The Kolkmeyer Manufacturing Company has a group of six identical machines; each machine operates an average of 20 hours between breakdowns. Thus, the mean arrival rate or request for repair service for each machine is $\lambda = \frac{1}{20} = 0.05$ per hour. With randomly occurring breakdowns, the Poisson probability distribution is used to describe the machine breakdown arrival process. One person from the maintenance department provides the single-channel repair service for the six machines. The exponentially distributed service times have a mean of 2 hours per machine or a mean service rate of $\mu = \frac{1}{2} = 0.50$ machines per hour.

With $\lambda = 0.05$ and $\mu = 0.50$, we use equations (15.33) through (15.38) to compute the operating characteristics for this system. Note that the use of equation (15.33) makes the computations involved somewhat cumbersome. Confirm for yourself that equation (15.33) provides the value of $P_0 = 0.4845$. The computations for the other operating characteristics are

$$L_q = 6 - \left(\frac{0.05 + 0.50}{0.05}\right)(1 - 0.4845) = 0.3297 \text{ machine}$$

$$L = 0.3295 + (1 - 0.4845) = 0.8451 \text{ machine}$$

$$W_q = \frac{0.3295}{(6 - 0.845)0.05} = 1.279 \text{ hours}$$

$$W = 1.279 + \frac{1}{0.50} = 3.279 \text{ hours}$$

$$P_w = 1 - P_0 = 1 - 0.4845 = 0.5155$$

Finally, equation (15.39) can be used to compute the probabilities of any number of machines being in the repair system.

FIGURE 15.4 THE MANAGEMENT SCIENTIST SOLUTION FOR THE KOLKMEYER TWO-CHANNEL
MACHINE REPAIR PROBLEM

```
WAITING LINE MODELS
* * * * * * * * * * * * * * * * * * *
    NUMBER OF CHANNELS = 2
    POISSON ARRIVALS WITH MEAN RATE = .05
    EXPONENTIAL SERVICE TIMES WITH MEAN RATE = .5 PER CHANNEL
    FINITE CALLING POPULATION OF SIZE = 6

OPERATING CHARACTERISTICS
-------------------------
THE PROBABILITY OF NO UNITS IN THE SYSTEM              0.5602
THE AVERAGE NUMBER OF UNITS IN THE WAITING LINE        0.0227
THE AVERAGE NUMBER OF UNITS IN THE SYSTEM              0.5661
THE AVERAGE TIME A UNIT SPENDS IN THE WAITING LINE     0.0834
THE AVERAGE TIME A UNIT SPENDS IN THE SYSTEM           2.0834
THE PROBABILITY THAT AN ARRIVING UNIT HAS TO WAIT      0.1036


Number of Units in the System          Probability
-----------------------------          -----------
              0                            0.5602
              1                            0.3361
              2                            0.0840
              3                            0.0168
              4                            0.0025
              5                            0.0003
              6                            0.0000
```

As with other waiting line models, the operating characteristics provide the manager with information about the waiting line operation. Whether these operating characteristics suggest that better repair service is needed depends on the cost of the idle machine waiting time compared to the cost of assigning an additional person to make the repair operation either a two-channel system or a faster one-channel system.

Operating characteristics of an M/M/1 waiting line with a finite calling population are considered in Problem 34.

Computations for the multiple-channel finite calling population model are more complex than those for the single-channel model. A computer solution is virtually mandatory in this case. The Management Scientist software package that accompanies this text has the capability of analyzing the finite calling population model. The computer output for the Kolkmeyer machine repair problem with a two-person, two-channel repair system is shown in Figure 15.4. By considering the cost of machine waiting or downtime and the cost of repair personnel, management can determine whether the two-channel system is cost effective.

SUMMARY

In this chapter we presented a variety of waiting line models that have been developed to help managers make better decisions concerning the operation of waiting lines. For each model, we presented formulas that could be used to develop operating characteristics or performance measures for the system being studied. The operating characteristics presented include the following:

1. Probability that no units are in the system
2. Average number of units in the waiting line

3. Average number of units in the system
4. Average time a unit spends in the waiting line
5. Average time a unit spends in the system
6. Probability that arriving units will have to wait for service

We also showed how an economic analysis of the waiting line could be conducted by developing a total cost model that includes the cost associated with units waiting for service and the cost required to operate the service facility.

As many of the examples in this chapter show, the most obvious applications of waiting line models are situations in which customers arrive for service such as at a grocery checkout counter, bank, or restaurant. However, with a little creativity, waiting line models can be applied to many different situations such as telephone calls waiting for connections, mail orders waiting for processing, machines waiting for repairs, manufacturing jobs waiting to be processed, and money waiting to be spent or invested. The Q. M. in Action article describes how a waiting line model provided the basis for improving productivity of a fire department in New Haven, Connecticut.

The complexity and diversity of waiting line systems found in practice often prevents an analyst from finding an existing waiting line model that fits the specific application being studied. Simulation, the topic discussed in Chapter 16, provides an approach to determining the operating characteristics of such waiting line systems.

Q. M. IN ACTION

IMPROVING FIRE DEPARTMENT PRODUCTIVITY*

The New Haven, Connecticut, Fire Department implemented a reorganization plan with cross-trained fire and medical personnel responding to both fire and medical emergencies. A waiting line model provided the basis for the reorganization by demonstrating that substantial improvements in emergency medical response time could be achieved with only a small reduction in fire protection. Annual savings were reported to be $1.4 million.

The model was based on Poisson arrivals and exponential service times for both fire and medical emergencies. It was used to estimate the average time that a person placing a call would have to wait for the appropriate emergency unit to arrive at the location. Waiting times were estimated by the model's prediction of the average travel time to reach each of the city's 28 census tracts.

The model was first applied to the original system of 16 fire units and 4 emergency medical units that operated independently. It was then applied to the proposed reorganization plan that involved cross-trained department personnel qualified to respond to both fire and medical emergencies. Results from the model demonstrated that average travel times could be reduced under the reorganization plan. Various facility location alternatives also were evaluated. When implemented, the reorganization plan reduced operating cost and improved public safety services.

*Based on A. J. Swersey, L. Goldring, and E. D. Geyer, "Improving Fire Department Productivity: Merging Fire and Emergency Medical Units in New Haven," *Interfaces* 23, no. 1 (January–February 1993): 109–129.

GLOSSARY

Queue   A waiting line.

Queuing theory   The body of knowledge dealing with waiting lines.

Operating characteristics   The performance measures for a waiting line including the probability that no units are in the system, the average number of units in the waiting line, the average waiting time, and so on.

Single-channel waiting line   A waiting line with only one service facility.

Poisson probability distribution   A probability distribution used to describe the arrival pattern for some waiting line models.

Exponential probability distribution   A probability distribution used to describe the service time for some waiting line models.

First-come, first-served (FCFS)   The queue discipline that serves waiting units on a first-come, first-served basis.

Transient period   The start-up period for a waiting line, occurring before the waiting line reaches a normal or steady-state operation.

Steady-state operation   The normal operation of the waiting line after it has gone through a start-up or transient period. The operating characteristics of waiting lines are computed for steady-state conditions.

Mean arrival rate   The average number of customers or units arriving in a given period of time.

Mean service rate   The average number of customers or units that can be served by one service facility in a given period of time.

Multiple-channel waiting line   A waiting line with two or more parallel service facilities.

Blocked   When arriving units cannot enter the waiting line because the system is full. Blocked units can occur when waiting lines are not allowed or when waiting lines have a finite capacity.

Infinite calling population   The population of customers or units who may seek service has no specified upper limit.

Finite calling population   The population of customers or units who may seek service has a fixed and finite value.

PROBLEMS

1. Willow Brook National Bank operates a drive-up teller window that allows customers to complete bank transactions without getting out of their cars. On weekday mornings, arrivals to the drive-up teller window occur at random, with a mean arrival rate of 24 customers per hour or 0.4 customers per minute.
   a. What is the mean or expected number of customers that will arrive in a 5-minute period?
   b. Assume that the Poisson probability distribution can be used to describe the arrival process. Use the mean arrival rate in part (a) and compute the probabilities that exactly 0, 1, 2, and 3 customers will arrive during a 5-minute period.
   c. Delays are expected if more than 3 customers arrive during any 5-minute period. What is the probability that delays will occur?

2. In the Willow Brook National Bank waiting line system (see Problem 1), assume that the service times for the drive-up teller follow an exponential probability distribution with a mean service rate of 36 customers per hour or 0.6 customer per minute. Use the exponential probability distribution to answer the following questions.
   a. What is the probability the service time is 1 minute or less?
   b. What is the probability the service time is 2 minutes or less?
   c. What is the probability the service time is more than 2 minutes?

3. Use the single-channel drive-up bank teller operation referred to in Problems 1 and 2 to determine the following operating characteristics for the system.
   a. The probability that no customers are in the system
   b. The average number of customers waiting

c. The average number of customers in the system
d. The average time a customer spends waiting
e. The average time a customer spends in the system
f. The probability that arriving customers will have to wait for service

4. Use the single-channel drive-up bank teller operation referred to in Problems 1–3 to determine the probabilities of 0, 1, 2, and 3 customers in the system. What is the probability that more than 3 customers will be in the drive-up teller system at the same time?

SELFtest

5. The reference desk of a university library receives requests for assistance. Assume that a Poisson probability distribution with a mean rate of 10 requests per hour can be used to describe the arrival pattern and that service times follow an exponential probability distribution with a mean service rate of 12 requests per hour.
a. What is the probability that no requests for assistance are in the system?
b. What is the average number of requests that will be waiting for service?
c. What is the average waiting time in minutes before service begins?
d. What is the average time at the reference desk in minutes (waiting time plus service time)?
e. What is the probability that a new arrival has to wait for service?

6. Trucks using a single-channel loading dock arrive according to a Poisson probability distribution. The time required to load/unload follows an exponential probability distribution. The mean arrival rate is 12 trucks per day, and the mean service rate is 18 trucks per day.
a. What is the probability that no trucks are in the system?
b. What is the average number of trucks waiting for service?
c. What is the average time a truck waits for the loading/unloading service to begin?
d. What is the probability that an arriving truck will have to wait for service?

7. Speedy Oil provides a single-channel automobile oil change and lubrication service. New arrivals occur at the rate of 2.5 cars per hour and the mean service rate is 5 cars per hour. Assume that arrivals follow a Poisson probability distribution and that service times follow an exponential probability distribution.
a. What is the average number of cars in the system?
b. What is the average time that a car waits for the oil and lubrication service to begin?
c. What is the average time a car spends in the system?
d. What is the probability that an arrival has to wait for service?

8. For the Burger Dome single-channel waiting line in Section 15.2, assume that the arrival rate is increased to 1 customer per minute and that the mean service rate is increased to 1.25 customers per minute. Compute the following operating characteristics for the new system: P_0, L_q, L, W_q, W, and P_w. Does this system provide better or poorer service compared to the original system? Discuss any differences and the reason for these differences.

9. Marty's Barber Shop has one barber. Customers arrive at the rate of 2.2 customers per hour, and haircuts are given at the average rate of 5 per hour. Use the Poisson arrivals and exponential service times model to answer the following questions.
a. What is the probability that no units are in the system?
b. What is the probability that 1 customer is receiving a haircut and no one is waiting?
c. What is the probability that 1 customer is receiving a haircut and 1 customer is waiting?
d. What is the probability that 1 customer is receiving a haircut and 2 customers are waiting?
e. What is the probability that more than 2 customers are waiting?
f. What is the average time a customer waits for service?

10. Trosper Tire Company has decided to hire a new mechanic to handle all tire changes for customers ordering a new set of tires. Two mechanics have applied for the job. One mechanic has limited experience, can be hired for $14 per hour, and can service an average of 3 customers per hour. The other mechanic has several years of experience, can service an average of 4 customers per hour, but must be paid $20 per hour. Assume that customers arrive at the Trosper garage at the rate of 2 customers per hour.

a. What are the waiting line operating characteristics using each mechanic, assuming Poisson arrivals and exponential service times?

b. If the company assigns a customer waiting cost of $30 per hour, which mechanic provides the lower operating cost?

SELFtest

11. Agan Interior Design provides home and office decorating assistance to its customers. In normal operation, an average of 2.5 customers arrive each hour. One design consultant is available to answer customer questions and make product recommendations. The consultant averages 10 minutes with each customer.

a. Compute the operating characteristics of the customer waiting line, assuming Poisson arrivals and exponential service times.

b. Service goals dictate that an arriving customer should not wait for service more than an average of 5 minutes. Is this goal being met? If not, what action do you recommend?

c. If the consultant can reduce the average time spent per customer to 8 minutes, what is the mean service rate? Will the service goal be met?

12. Pete's Market is a small local grocery store with only one checkout counter. Assume that shoppers arrive at the checkout lane according to a Poisson probability distribution, with a mean arrival rate of 15 customers per hour. The checkout service times follow an exponential probability distribution, with a mean service rate of 20 customers per hour.

a. Compute the operating characteristics for this waiting line.

b. If the manager's service goal is to limit the waiting time prior to beginning the checkout process to no more than 5 minutes, what recommendations would you provide regarding the current checkout system?

13. After reviewing the waiting line analysis of Problem 12, the manager of Pete's Market wants to consider one of the following alternatives for improving service. What alternative would you recommend? Justify your recommendation.

a. Hire a second person to bag the groceries while the cash register operator is entering the cost data and collecting money from the customer. With this improved single-channel operation, the mean service rate could be increased to 30 customers per hour.

b. Hire a second person to operate a second checkout counter. The two-channel operation would have a mean service rate of 20 customers per hour for each channel.

14. Ocala Software Systems operates a technical support center for its software customers. If customers have installation and/or use problems with Ocala software products, they may telephone the technical support center and obtain free consultation. Currently, Ocala operates its support center with one consultant. If the consultant is busy when a new customer call arrives, the customer hears a recorded message stating that all consultants are currently busy with other customers. The customer is then asked to hold and a consultant will provide assistance as soon as possible. The customer calls follow a Poisson probability distribution with a mean arrival rate of 5 calls per hour. On average, it takes 7.5 minutes for a consultant to answer a customer's questions. The service time follows an exponential probability distribution.

a. What is the mean service rate in terms of customers per hour?

b. What is the probability that no customers are in the system and the consultant is idle?

c. What is the average number of customers waiting for a consultant?

d. What is the average time a customer waits for a consultant?

e. What is the probability that a customer will have to wait for a consultant?

f. Ocala's customer service department has recently received several letters from customers complaining about the difficulty in obtaining technical support. If Ocala's customer service guidelines state that no more than 35% of all customers should have to wait for technical support and that the average waiting time should be 2 minutes or less, does your waiting line analysis indicate that Ocala is or is not meeting its customer service guidelines? What action, if any, would you recommend?

15. To improve customer service, Ocala Software Systems (see Problem 14) wants to investigate the effect of using a second consultant at its technical support center. What effect

would the additional consultant have on customer service? Would two technical consultants enable Ocala to meet its service guidelines with no more than 35% of all customers having to wait for technical support and an average customer waiting time of 2 minutes or less? Discuss.

16. The new Fore and Aft Marina is to be located on the Ohio River near Madison, Indiana. Assume that Fore and Aft has decided to build a docking facility where one boat at a time can stop for gas and servicing. Assume that arrivals follow a Poisson probability distribution, with a mean of 5 boats per hour, and that service times follow an exponential probability distribution, with a mean of 10 boats per hour. Answer the following questions.
    a. What is the probability that no boats are in the system?
    b. What is the average number of boats that will be waiting for service?
    c. What is the average time a boat will spend waiting for service?
    d. What is the average time a boat will spend at the dock?
    e. If you were the manager of Fore and Aft Marina, would you be satisfied with the service level your system will be providing? Why or why not?

17. The manager of the Fore and Aft Marina in Problem 16 wants to investigate the possibility of enlarging the docking facility so that two boats can stop for gas and servicing simultaneously. Assume that the mean arrival rate is 5 boats per hour and that the mean service rate for each channel is 10 boats per hour.
    a. What is the probability that the boat dock will be idle?
    b. What is the average number of boats that will be waiting for service?
    c. What is the average time a boat will spend waiting for service?
    d. What is the average time a boat will spend at the dock?
    e. If you were the manager of Fore and Aft Marina, would you be satisfied with the service level your system will be providing? Why or why not?

18. The City Beverage Drive-Thru is considering a two-channel service system. Cars arrive according to the Poisson probability distribution, with a mean arrival rate of 6 cars per hour. The service times have an exponential probability distribution, with a mean service rate of 10 cars per hour for each channel.
    a. What is the probability that no cars are in the system?
    b. What is the average number of cars waiting for service?
    c. What is the average time waiting for service?
    d. What is the average time in the system?
    e. What is the probability that an arriving car will have to wait for service?

SELFtest   19. Consider a two-channel waiting line with Poisson arrivals and exponential service times. The mean arrival rate is 14 units per hour, and the mean service rate is 10 units per hour for each channel.
    a. What is the probability that no units are in the system?
    b. What is the average number of units in the system?
    c. What is the average time a unit waits for service?
    d. What is the average time a unit is in the system?
    e. What is the probability of having to wait for service?

20. Refer to Problem 19. Assume that the system is expanded to a three-channel operation.
    a. Compute the operating characteristics for this waiting line system.
    b. If the service goal is to provide sufficient capacity so that no more than 25% of the customers have to wait for service, is the two- or three-channel system preferred?

SELFtest   21. Refer to the Agan Interior Design situation in Problem 11. Agan's management would like to evaluate two alternatives:
    • Use one consultant with an average service time of 8 minutes per customer.
    • Expand to two consultants, each of whom has an average service time of 10 minutes per customer.

If the consultants are paid $16 per hour and the customer waiting time is valued at $25 per hour for waiting time prior to service, should Agan expand to the two-consultant system? Explain.

22. A fast food franchise is considering operating a drive-up window food-service operation. Assume that customer arrivals follow a Poisson probability distribution, with a mean arrival rate of 24 cars per hour, and that service times follow an exponential probability distribution. Arriving customers place orders at an intercom station at the back of the parking lot and then drive to the service window to pay for and receive their orders. The following three service alternatives are being considered.
   • A single-channel operation in which one employee fills the order and takes the money from the customer. The average service time for this alternative is 2 minutes.
   • A single-channel operation in which one employee fills the order while a second employee takes the money from the customer. The average service time for this alternative is 1.25 minutes.
   • A two-channel operation with two service windows and two employees. The employee stationed at each window fills the order and takes the money for customers arriving at the window. The average service time for this alternative is 2 minutes for each channel.

Answer the following questions and recommend an alternative design for the fast food franchise.
   a. What is the probability that no cars are in the system?
   b. What is the average number of cars waiting for service?
   c. What is the average number of cars in the system?
   d. What is the average time a car waits for service?
   e. What is the average time in the system?
   f. What is the probability that an arriving car will have to wait for service?

23. The following cost information is available for the fast food franchise in Problem 22.
   • Customer waiting time is valued at $25 per hour to reflect the fact that waiting time is costly to the fast food business.
   • The cost of each employee is $6.50 per hour.
   • To account for equipment and space, an additional cost of $20 per hour is attributable to each channel.

What is the lowest-cost design for the fast food business?

24. Patients arrive at a dentist's office at a mean rate of 2.8 patients per hour. The dentist can treat patients at the mean rate of 3 patients per hour. A study of patient waiting times shows that, on average, a patient waits 30 minutes before seeing the dentist.
   a. What are the mean arrival and treatment rates in terms of patients per minute?
   b. What is the average number of patients in the waiting room?
   c. If a patient arrives at 10:10 A.M., at what time is the patient expected to leave the office?

SELFtest 25. A study of the multichannel food-service operation at the Red Birds' baseball park shows that the average time between the arrival of a customer at the food-service counter and his or her departure with a filled order is 10 minutes. During the game, customers arrive at the average rate of 4 per minute. The food-service operation requires an average of 2 minutes per customer order.
   a. What is the mean service rate per channel in terms of customers per minute?
   b. What is the average waiting time in the line prior to placing an order?
   c. On average, how many customers are in the food-service system?

26. Manning Autos operates an automotive service counter. While completing the repair work, Manning mechanics arrive at the company's parts department counter at the mean rate of 4 per hour. The parts coordinator spends an average of 6 minutes with each mechanic, discussing the parts the mechanic needs and retrieving the parts from inventory.

a. Currently, Manning has one parts coordinator. On average, each mechanic waits 4 minutes before the parts coordinator is available to answer questions and/or retrieve parts from inventory. Find L_q, W, and L for this single-channel parts operation.

b. A trial period with a second parts coordinator showed that, on average, each mechanic waited only 1 minute before a parts coordinator was available. Find L_q, W, and L for this two-channel parts operation.

c. If the cost of each mechanic is $20 per hour and the cost of each parts coordinator is $12 per hour, is the one-channel or the two-channel system more economical?

SELFtest 27. Gubser Welding, Inc., operates a welding service for construction and automotive repair jobs. Assume that the arrival of jobs at the company's office can be described by a Poisson probability distribution with a mean arrival rate of 2 jobs per 8-hour day. The time required to complete the jobs follows a normal probability distribution with a mean time of 3.2 hours and a standard deviation of 2 hours. Answer the following questions, assuming that Gubser uses one welder to complete all jobs.

a. What is the mean arrival rate in jobs per hour?

b. What is the mean service rate in jobs per hour?

c. What is the average number of jobs waiting for service?

d. What is the average time a job waits before the welder can begin working on it?

e. What is the average number of hours between when a job is received and when it is completed?

f. What percentage of the time is Gubser's welder busy?

28. Jobs arrive randomly at a particular assembly plant; assume that the mean arrival rate is 5 jobs per hour. Service times (in minutes per job) do not follow the exponential probability distribution. Two proposed designs for the plant's assembly operation are shown.

| | Service Time | |
Design	Mean	Standard Deviation
A	6.0	3.0
B	6.25	0.6

a. What is the mean service rate in jobs per hour for each design?

b. For the mean service rates in part (a), what design appears to provide the best or fastest service rate?

c. What are the standard deviations of the service times in hours?

d. Use the $M/G/1$ model in Section 15.7 to compute the operating characteristics for each design.

e. Which design provides the best operating characteristics? Why?

29. The Robotics Manufacturing Company operates an equipment repair business where emergency jobs arrive randomly at the rate of 3 jobs per 8-hour day. The company's repair facility is a single-channel system operated by a repair technician. The service time varies with a mean repair time of 2 hours and a standard deviation of 1.5 hours. The company's cost of the repair operation is $28 per hour. In the economic analysis of the waiting line system, Robotics uses $35 per hour cost for customers waiting during the repair process.

a. What are the arrival rate and service rate in jobs per hour?

b. Show the operating characteristics including the total cost per hour.

c. The company is considering purchasing a computer-based equipment repair system that would enable a constant repair time of 2 hours. For practical purposes, the standard deviation is 0. Because of the computer-based system, the company's cost of the new operation would be $32 per hour. The firm's director of operations has said no to the request for the new system because the hourly cost is $4 higher and the mean repair time is the same. Do you agree? What effect will the new system have on the waiting line characteristics of the repair service?

d. Does paying for the computer-based system to reduce the variation in service time make economic sense? How much will the new system save the company during a 40-hour work week?

SELFtest

30. A large insurance company has a central computing system that contains a variety of information about customer accounts. Insurance agents in a six-state area use telephone lines to access the customer information database. Currently, the company's central computer system allows 3 users to access the central computer simultaneously. Agents who attempt to use the system when it is full are denied access; no waiting is allowed. Management realizes that with its expanding business, more requests will be made to the central information system. Being denied access to the system is inefficient as well as annoying for agents. Access requests follow a Poisson probability distribution, with a mean of 42 calls per hour. The mean service rate per line is 20 calls per hour.

a. What is the probability that 0, 1, 2, and 3 access lines will be in use?
b. What is the probability that an agent will be denied access to the system?
c. What is the average number of access lines in use?
d. In planning for the future, management wants to be able to handle $\lambda = 50$ calls per hour; in addition, the probability that an agent will be denied access to the system should be no greater than the value computed in part (b). How many access lines should this system have?

31. Mid-West Publishing Company publishes college textbooks. The company operates an 800 telephone number whereby potential adopters can ask questions about forthcoming texts, request examination copies of texts, and place orders. Currently, two extension lines are used, with two representatives handling the telephone inquiries. Calls occurring when both extension lines are being used receive a busy signal; no waiting is allowed. Each representative can accommodate an average of 12 calls per hour. The mean arrival rate is 20 calls per hour.

a. How many extension lines should be used if the company wants to handle 90% of the calls immediately?
b. What is the average number of extension lines that will be busy if your recommendation in part (a) is used?
c. What percentage of calls receive a busy signal for the current telephone system with two extension lines?

32. City Cab, Inc., uses two dispatchers to handle requests for service and to dispatch the cabs. The telephone calls that are made to City Cab use a common telephone number. When both dispatchers are busy, the caller hears a busy signal; no waiting is allowed. Callers who receive a busy signal can call back later or call another cab service. Assume that the arrival of calls follows a Poisson probability distribution, with a mean of 40 calls per hour, and that each dispatcher can handle a mean of 30 calls per hour.

a. What percentage of time are both dispatchers idle?
b. What percentage of time are both dispatchers busy?
c. What is the probability callers will receive a busy signal if 2, 3, or 4 dispatchers are used?
d. If management wants no more than 12% of the callers to receive a busy signal, how many dispatchers should be used?

33. Kolkmeyer Manufacturing Company (see Section 15.9) is considering adding 2 machines to its manufacturing operation. This addition will bring the number of machines to 8. Mr. Andrews, president of Kolkmeyer, has asked for a study of the need to add a second employee to the repair operation. The mean arrival rate is 0.05 machine per hour for each machine, and the mean service rate for each individual assigned to the repair operation is 0.50 machine per hour.

a. Compute the operating characteristics if the company retains the single-employee repair operation.

b. Compute the operating characteristics if a second employee is added to the machine repair operation.

c. Each employee is paid $20 per hour. Machine downtime is valued at $80 per hour. From an economic point of view, should one or two employees handle the machine repair operation? Explain.

SELFtest

34. Five administrative assistants use an office copier. The average time between arrivals for each assistant is 40 minutes, which is equivalent to a mean arrival rate of $1/40 = 0.025$ arrivals per minute. The mean time each assistant spends at the copier is 5 minutes, which is equivalent to a mean service rate of $\frac{1}{5} = 0.20$ users per minute. Use the $M/M/1$ model with a finite calling population to determine the following:

a. The probability that the copier is idle
b. The average number of administrative assistants in the waiting line
c. The average number of administrative assistants at the copier
d. The average time an assistant spends waiting for the copier
e. The average time an assistant spends at the copier
f. During an 8-hour day, how many minutes does an assistant spend at the copier? How much of this time is waiting time?
g. Should management consider purchasing a second copier? Explain.

35. Schips Department Store operates a fleet of 10 trucks. The trucks arrive at random times throughout the day at the store's truck dock to be loaded with new deliveries or to have incoming shipments from the regional warehouse unloaded. Each truck returns to the truck dock for service 2 times per 8-hour day. Thus, the mean arrival rate per truck is 0.25 trucks per hour. The mean service rate is 4 trucks per hour. Using the Poisson arrivals and exponential service times model with a finite calling population of 10 trucks, determine the following operating characteristics:

a. The probability no trucks are at the truck dock
b. The average number of trucks waiting for loading/unloading
c. The average number of trucks in the truck dock area
d. The average waiting time before loading/unloading begins
e. The average waiting time in the system
f. What is the hourly cost of operation if the cost is $50 per hour for each truck and $30 per hour for the truck dock?
g. Consider a two-channel truck dock operation where the second channel could be operated for an additional $30 per hour. How much would the average number of trucks waiting for loading/unloading have to be reduced to make the two-channel truck dock economically feasible?
h. Should the company consider expanding to the two-channel truck dock? Explain.

Case Problem AIRLINE RESERVATIONS

Regional Airlines is establishing a new telephone system for handling flight reservations. During the 10:00 A.M. to 11:00 A.M. time period, calls to the reservation agent occur randomly at an average of one call every 3.75 minutes. Historical service time data show that a reservation agent spends an average of 3 minutes with each customer. The waiting line model assumptions of Poisson arrivals and exponential service times appear reasonable for the telephone reservation system.

Regional Airlines' management believes that offering an efficient telephone reservation system is an important part of establishing an image as a service-oriented airline. If the system is properly implemented, Regional Airlines will establish good customer relations, which in the long run will increase business. However, if the telephone reservation system is frequently overloaded and customers have difficulty contacting an agent, a negative customer reaction may lead to an eventual loss of business. The cost of a ticket reservation agent is $20 per hour. Thus, management wants to provide good service, but it does not want to incur the cost of overstaffing the telephone reservation operation by using more agents than necessary.

At a planning meeting, Regional's management team agreed that an acceptable customer service goal is to answer at least 85% of the incoming calls immediately. During the planning meeting, Regional's vice-president of administration pointed out that the data show that the average service rate for an agent is faster than the average arrival rate of the telephone calls. The vice-president's conclusion was that personnel costs could be minimized by using one agent and that the single agent should be able to handle the telephone reservations and still have some idle time. The vice-president of marketing restated the importance of customer service and expressed support for at least two reservation agents.

The current telephone reservation system design does not allow callers to wait. Callers who attempt to reach a reservation agent when all agents are occupied receive a busy signal and are blocked from the system. A representative from the telephone company suggested that Regional Airlines consider an expanded system that accommodates waiting. In the expanded system, when a customer calls and all agents are busy, a recorded message tells the customer that the call is being held in the order received and that an agent will be available shortly. The customer can stay on the line and listen to background music while waiting for an agent. Regional's management will need more information before switching to the expanded system.

Managerial Report

Prepare a managerial report for Regional Airlines analyzing the telephone reservation system. Evaluate both the system that does not allow waiting and the expanded system that allows waiting. Include the following information in your report.

1. A detailed analysis of the operating characteristics of the reservation system with one agent as proposed by the vice-president of administration. What is your recommendation concerning a single-agent system?
2. A detailed analysis of the operating characteristics of the reservation system based on your recommendation regarding the number of agents Regional should use.
3. What appear to be the advantages or disadvantages of the expanded system? Discuss the number of waiting callers the expanded system would need to accommodate.
4. The telephone arrival data presented are for the 10:00 A.M. to 11:00 A.M. time period; however, the arrival rate of incoming calls is expected to change from hour to hour. Describe how your waiting line analysis could be used to develop a ticket agent staffing plan that would enable the company to provide different levels of staffing for the ticket reservation system at different times during the day. Indicate the information that you would need to develop this staffing plan.

Case Problem   OFFICE EQUIPMENT, INC.

Office Equipment, Inc. (OEI), leases automatic mailing machines to business customers in Fort Wayne, Indiana. The company's success has been built on establishing a reputation of providing timely maintenance and repair service. Each OEI service contract states that a service technician will arrive at a customer's business site within an average of 3 hours from the time that the customer notifies OEI of an equipment problem.

Currently, OEI has 10 customers with service contracts. One service technician is responsible for handling all service calls. A statistical analysis of historical service records indicates that a customer requests a service call at an average rate of 1 call per 50 hours of operation. If the service technician is available when a customer calls for service, it takes the technician an average of one hour of travel time to reach the customer's office and an average of 1.5 hours to complete the repair service. However, if the service technician is busy with another customer when a new customer calls for service, the technician completes the current service call and any other waiting service calls before responding to the new service call. In such cases, once the technician is free from all existing service commitments, the technician takes an average of one hour of travel time to reach the new customer's office and an average of 1.5 hours to complete the repair service. The cost of the service technician is $80 per hour. The downtime cost (wait time and service time) for customers is $100 per hour.

OEI is planning to expand its business. Within one year, OEI projects that it will have 20 customers, and within two years, OEI projects that it will have 30 customers. Although OEI is satisfied that one service technician can handle the 10 existing customers, management is concerned about the ability of one technician to meet the average 3-hour service call guarantee when the OEI customer base expands. In a recent planning meeting, the marketing manager made a proposal to add a second service technician when OEI reaches 20 customers and to add a third service technician when OEI reaches 30 customers. Before making a final decision, management has asked for an analysis of OEI service capabilities. OEI is particularly interested in meeting the average 3-hour waiting time guarantee at the lowest possible total cost.

Managerial Report

Develop a managerial report summarizing your analysis of the OEI service capabilities. Make recommendations regarding the number of technicians to be used when OEI reaches 20 customers and when OEI reaches 30 customers. Include a discussion of the following in your report.

1. What is the mean arrival rate for each customer per hour?
2. What is the mean service rate in terms of the number of customers per hour? Note that the average travel time of one hour becomes part of the service time because the time that the service technician is busy handling a service call includes the travel time plus the time required to complete the repair.
3. Waiting line models generally assume that the arriving customers are in the same location as the service facility. Discuss the OEI situation in light of the fact that a service technician travels an average of one hour to reach each customer. How should the travel time and the waiting time predicted by the waiting line model be combined to determine the total customer waiting time?
4. OEI is satisfied that one service technician can handle the 10 existing customers. Use a waiting line model to determine the following information:
   - Probability that no customers are in the system
   - Average number of customers in the waiting line
   - Average number of customers in the system
   - Average time a customer waits until the service technician arrives
   - Average time a customer waits until the machine is back in operation
   - Probability that a customer will have to wait more than one hour for the service technician to arrive
   - The number of hours a week the technician is not making service calls
   - The total cost per hour for the service operation

   Do you agree with OEI management that one technician can meet the average 3-hour service call guarantee? Explain.
5. What is your recommendation for the number of service technicians to hire when OEI expands to 20 customers? Use the information that you developed in part 4 to justify your answer.

6. What is your recommendation for the number of service technicians to hire when OEI expands to 30 customers? Use the information that you developed in part 4 to justify your answer.

7. What are the annual savings of your recommendation in part 6 compared to the planning committee's proposal that 30 customers will require three service technicians? Assume 250 days of operation per year.

Appendix 15.1   WAITING LINE MODELS WITH SPREADSHEETS

Single-Channel Waiting Lines

Spreadsheets provide a fast and relatively easy way to compute the operating characteristics of a waiting line system. Figure 15.5 shows the Excel spreadsheet for the Burger Dome single-channel waiting line presented in Section 15.2. Note that we have listed the assumptions of Poisson arrivals and exponential service times in cells A4 and A5 as a reminder that these assumptions characterize the waiting line model being used to analyze the Burger Dome system.

Only two input values are required: the mean arrival rate, $\lambda = 0.75$ customers per minute, shown in cell B7; and the mean service rate, $\mu = 1$ customer per minute, shown in cell B8. The operating characteristics provided by equations (15.4) through (15.9) are computed using the following cell formulas:

Cell C13   Probability that no customers are in the system, P_0
=1−B7/B8

Cell C14   Average number of customers in the waiting line, L_q
=B7^2/(B8*(B8−B7))

Cell C15   Average number of customers in the system, L
=C14+B7/B8

Cell C16   Average time a customer spends in the waiting line, W_q
=C14/B7

Cell C17   Average time a customer spends in the system, W
=C16+1/B8

Cell C18   Probability an arriving customer waits for service, P_w
=B7/B8

By changing the mean arrival rate and/or mean service rate in cells B7 and B8, the spreadsheet will automatically calculate the operating characteristics for the modified single-channel waiting line.

Multiple-Channel Waiting Lines

To show how a spreadsheet can be used to compute the operating characteristics of a multiple-channel waiting line with Poisson arrivals and exponential service times, we use the same spreadsheet format that we used for the single-channel waiting line model in Figure 15.5. The only differences are that we input the number of channels and that we use equations (15.11) through (15.16) for the computations. Figure 15.6 shows the spreadsheet for the Burger Dome multiple-channel waiting line system. The assumptions of Poisson arrivals and exponential service times are shown in cells A4 and A5. The three required inputs and their cell locations are as follows: the number of channels, $k = 2$, shown in cell B7; the mean arrival rate, $\lambda = 0.75$ customers per minute, shown in cell B8; and the mean service rate, $\mu = 1$ customer per minute, shown in cell B9. The six operating characteristics in Figure 15.6 are based upon the values of k, λ and μ.

FIGURE 15.5 SPREADSHEET SOLUTION FOR THE BURGER DOME SINGLE-CHANNEL PROBLEM

	A	B	C
1	**Burger Dome Single-Channel Waiting Line**		
2			
3	**Assumptions**		
4	**Poisson Arrivals**		
5	**Exponential Service Times**		
6			
7	Mean Arrival Rate	0.75	
8	Mean Service Rate	1	
9			
10			
11	**Operating Characteristics**		
12			
13	Probability that no customers are in the system, P_o		0.2500
14	Average number of customers in the waiting line, L_q		2.2500
15	Average number of customers in the system, L		3.0000
16	Average time a customer spends in the waiting line, W_q		3.0000
17	Average time a customer spends in the system, W		4.0000
18	Probability an arriving customer has to wait, P_w		0.7500

FIGURE 15.6 SPREADSHEET SOLUTION FOR THE BURGER DOME MULTIPLE-CHANNEL PROBLEM

	A	B	C
1	**Burger Dome Multiple-Channel Waiting Line**		
2			
3	**Assumptions**		
4	**Poisson Arrivals**		
5	**Exponential Service Times**		
6			
7	Number of Channels	2	
8	Mean Arrival Rate	0.75	
9	Mean Service Rate per Channel	1	
10			
11			
12	**Operating Characteristics**		
13			
14	Probability that no customers are in the system, P_o		0.4545
15	Average number of customers in the waiting line, L_q		0.1227
16	Average number of customers in the system, L		0.8727
17	Average time a customer spends in the waiting line, W_q		0.1636
18	Average time a customer spends in the system, W		1.1636
19	Probability an arriving customer has to wait, P_w		0.2045

In some cases, the equations used to compute the operating characteristics for a multiple-channel waiting line are more complex than the equations used for a single-channel waiting line. Note in particular equation (15.11), which provides the probability that no units are in the system, P_0. This equation is substantially more complex than the equation for P_0 shown in equation (15.4). In fact, equation (15.11) is so complex that we will develop a special Excel function to evaluate it.

The equation used to compute P_0 for the multiple-channel waiting line model in Section 15.3 is

$$P_0 = \frac{1}{\displaystyle\sum_{n=0}^{k-1} \frac{(\lambda/\mu)^n}{n!} + \frac{(\lambda/\mu)^k}{k!}\left(\frac{k\mu}{k\mu - \lambda}\right)}$$

Note that the number of channels, k, the mean arrival rate λ (lambda), and the mean service rate μ (mu) must be known in order to compute P_0.

The steps required to create the P_0 function with Excel are as follows:

Step 1.　Select the **Tools** pull-down menu
Step 2.　Select the **Macro** option
Step 3.　Choose the **Visual Basic Editor**
Step 4.　When the **Visual Basic Editor** appears
　　　　　Select the **Insert** pull-down menu
　　　　　Choose the **Module** option
Step 5.　When the **Module** sheet appears enter

　　　　　　Function Your_Function_Name(Arg1, Arg2, . . .)

　　　　where **Your_Function_Name** is any name you wish to use for the function and where **Arg1, Arg2,** etc., are the arguments of the function or the inputs that you will need to evaluate the function. For the multiple-channel waiting line model, we named the function P0 and listed the three arguments or inputs as k, lamda, and mu. Thus, we entered the following:

　　　　　　　　Function P0(k,lambda,mu)

Step 6.　Next write a Visual Basic program to evaluate the function. The exact statement sequence may vary and depends upon the programming skills of the user. The Visual Basic program we entered for P_0 is shown in Figure 15.7. End Function appears as the last line of the program
Step 7.　Select the **File** pull-down menu
　　　　　Choose the **Close and Return to Microsoft Excel** option

FIGURE 15.7　THE VISUAL BASIC PROGRAM FOR P_0 IN THE MULTIPLE-CHANNEL WAITING LINE MODEL IN SECTION 15.3

```
Function P0(k, lambda, mu)
Sum = 0
For n = 0 To k − 1
Sum = Sum + (lambda/mu)^n/Application.Fact(n)
Next
P0 = 1/(Sum + ((lambda/mu)^k/Application.Fact(k))*(k*mu(k*mu − lambda)))
End Function
```

You will be returned to the spreadsheet application. You can now choose the cell where the P_0 function is to appear. Using the spreadsheet in Figure 15.6, we can enter the newly created P_0 function in the spreadsheet as follows:

Cell C14   Probability that no customers are in the system, P_0
               =P0(B7,B8,B9)

As shown in Figure 15.6, this function provides the probability of no customers in the system, $P_0 = 0.4545$.

The operating characteristics provided by equations (15.12) through (15.16) are computed using the following cell formulas:[2]

Cell C15   Average number of customers in the waiting line, L_q
               =(((B8/B9)^B7*B8*B9)/(FACT (B7−1)*(B7*B9−B8)^2))*C14

Cell C16   Average number of customers in the system, L
               =C15+B8/B9

Cell C17   Average time a customer spends in the waiting line, W_q
               =C15/B8

Cell C18   Average time a customer spends in the system, W
               =C17+1/B9

Cell C19   Probability an arriving customer has to wait for service, P_w
               =(1/FACT(B7))*(B8/B9)^B7*(B7*B9/(B7*B9−B8))*C14

The spreadsheet shown in Figure 15.6 can be used to compute the operating characteristics for both single-channel and multiple-channel waiting lines with Poisson arrivals and exponential service times. For example, entering 1 for the number of channels into cell B7 will provide the Burger Dome single-channel operating characteristics shown previously in Figure 15.5. In fact, the spreadsheet in Figure 15.6 is a general spreadsheet that can be used for any waiting line where the assumptions of Poisson arrivals and exponential service times are appropriate. Entering the number of channels, the mean arrival rate and the mean service rate is all that is necessary to compute the desired operating characteristic information. Thus, the spreadsheet provides a quick and easy way to determine how alternative designs affect the operating characteristics of the waiting line.

Other Waiting Line Models

Spreadsheets can be developed for all of the waiting line models presented in this chapter. The format of each spreadsheet will be similar to the spreadsheets shown in Figures 15.5 and 15.6. The cell formulas must be based on the equations for the operating characteristics presented for the corresponding waiting line model. The equations for the single-channel waiting line model with Poisson arrivals and arbitrary service times in Section 15.7 are relatively easily expressed with Excel cell formulas. The multiple-channel model with Poisson arrivals, arbitrary service times, and no waiting in Section 15.8 and the multiple-channel model with a finite calling population presented in Section 15.9 are more complex and require special Excel functions. For example, equation (15.31) for P_j and equation (15.33) for P_0 require the special functions. The details of developing spreadsheets for these other waiting line models are presented in *Contemporary Management Science with Spreadsheets,* by D. R. Anderson, D. J. Sweeney, and T. A. Williams, South-Western College Publishing, 1999.

---

2. Cell formulas C15 and C19 use Excel's FACT worksheet function to compute the factorial of a number. For instance, FACT (B7 − 1) in cell formula C15 is used to compute the value of $(k − 1)!$ in equation (15.12).

CITIBANK*

LONG ISLAND CITY, NEW YORK

Citibank, a division of Citigroup, makes available a wide range of financial services, including checking and savings accounts, loans and mortgages, insurance, and investment services, within the framework of a unique strategy for delivering those services called Citibanking. Citibanking entails a consistent brand identity all over the world, consistent product offerings, and high-level customer service. Citibanking lets you manage your money anytime, anywhere, anyway you choose. Whether you need to save for the future or borrow for today, you can do it all at Citibank.

Citibanking's state-of-the-art automatic teller machines (ATMs) located in Citicard Banking Centers (CBCs), let customers do all their banking in one place with the touch of a finger, 24 hours a day, 7 days a week. More than 150 different banking functions from deposits to managing investments can be performed with ease. Citibanking ATMs are so much more than just cash machines that customers today use them for 80% of their transactions.

A Waiting Line Application

The New York franchise of U.S. Citibanking operates approximately 250 CBCs. Each CBC provides customers with one or more ATMs, called customer activated terminals (or CATs), which are capable of performing a variety of banking transactions. Approximately 70% of the CBCs are located in Manhattan, the Bronx, Brooklyn, Queens, and Staten Island. The remaining 30% are suburban CBCs located in Nassau, Suffolk, Orange, Rockland, and Westchester counties. Measuring performance and service capacity at each CBC is an important part of Citibank's emphasis on providing superior access and convenience for its customers.

Each Citibank CBC operates as a waiting line system with randomly arriving customers seeking service at

a CAT. Based on the use at each site, the number of CATs ranges from 1 to 20 with each site operating with a single queue. If 1 CAT is present, the system operates as a single-channel waiting line, with arriving customers waiting whenever the CAT is being used by another customer. At most CBC sites, multiple CATs provide a multiple-channel waiting line system.

A periodic CBC capacity study is used to determine the capacity needed at each center. The hardware supply at the center is measured in terms of the transactional volume (transactions per CAT per hour) the site is capable of supporting. Customer demand is measured in terms of the peak number of arrivals per hour at the site. Comparing supply and demand enables Citibank to classify each CBC as either

- Highly endangered—average peak hour waiting time exceeds 5 minutes.
- Borderline—average peak hour waiting time is 3–5 minutes.
- Sufficient—average peak hour waiting time is 3 minutes or less.

In a recent capacity study, demand data suggested approximately 6% of the CBCs should be classified as highly endangered and approximately 8% should be classified as borderline. In total, 34 sites were listed as candidates for possible capacity expansion with incremental CATs desired.

In order to make recommendations on the number of CATs to add at the selected sites, management needed additional information concerning the customer service levels at each site. Operating characteristics information provided by a waiting line model would be helpful in determining the number of CATs each center should have. Typical information provided by the model included:

- The average number of customers in the waiting line
- The average number of customers in the system

*The authors are indebted to Stacey Karter, Citibank, for providing this application.

- The average time a customer spends in the waiting line
- The average time a customer spends in the system
- The probability that an arriving customer has to wait

In-house management information system (MIS) data on arrival rates and service times were collected to determine whether a multiple-channel waiting line model with Poisson arrivals and exponential service time could be used to model a CBC waiting line system. Customer arrivals were indeed random and adequately represented by a Poisson probability distribution. The mean arrival rate varied, depending on time of day and day of week. However, developing operating characteristic information for the peak or high demand periods was important. An average of the top 10 hourly demands was used to determine the mean arrival rate for each CBC site. Observed service times showed that the exponential probability distribution provided a reasonable approximation of the service time distribution.

For example, one midtown Manhattan branch site was classified as an endangered center operating with 5 CATs. Onsite observations were conducted to verify the MIS data and the peak arrival rate of 172 customers per hour. From the observed session times of 2 minutes per customer, the mean service rate per CAT was estimated to be 30 per hour. Five CATs were insufficient to meet this peak demand. A multiple-channel waiting line model with an expansion to 6 CATs showed that 88% of the customers would still have to wait and that the average waiting time would be 6 to 7 minutes. Expansion to 6 CATs still provided an unacceptable level of service. Expansion to 7 CATs provided acceptable service levels with an average of 2.4 customers in the waiting line. Hence, expansion to 8 CATs was not necessary at that time.

Even though peak demand periods were not always long enough to reach the steady-state conditions projected by the waiting line model, the operating characteristics indicated by the model provided general guidelines for capacity decisions. Use of the observed mean arrival and service rates unique to each site enabled the waiting line model to provide useful information for making the incremental CAT decisions at each CBC location.

Questions

1. How did Citibank's CBCs operate as a waiting line system?
2. How did Citibank ensure appropriate arrival and service time rates for the CBC waiting line operation?
3. What information did the waiting line model provide? How was this information helpful in making the incremental CAT decisions for each site?

SIMULATION

CONTENTS

Simulation is one of the most widely used quantitative approaches to decision making. It is a method for learning about a real system by experimenting with a model that represents the system. The simulation model contains the mathematical expressions and logical relationships that describe how to compute the value of the outputs given the values of the inputs. Any simulation model has two inputs: controllable inputs and probabilistic inputs. Figure 16.1 shows a conceptual diagram of a simulation model.

In conducting a **simulation experiment,** an analyst selects the value, or values, for the **controllable inputs.** Then values for the **probabilistic inputs** are randomly generated. The simulation model uses the values of the controllable inputs and the values of the probabilistic inputs to compute the value, or values, of the output. By conducting a series of experiments using a variety of values for the controllable inputs, the analyst learns how values of the controllable inputs affect or change the output of the simulation model. After reviewing the simulation results, the analyst is often able to make decision recommendations for the controllable inputs that will provide the desired output for the real system.

Simulation has been successfully applied in a variety of applications. The following examples are typical.

1. **New Product Development** The objective of this simulation is to determine the probability that a new product will be profitable. A model is developed relating profit (the output measure) to various probabilistic inputs such as demand, parts cost, and labor cost.

FIGURE 16.1   DIAGRAM OF A SIMULATION MODEL

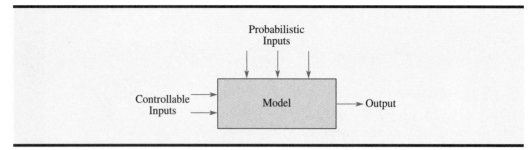

The only controllable input is whether to introduce the product. A variety of possible values will be generated for the probabilistic inputs, and the resulting profit will be computed. We develop a simulation model for this type of application in Section 16.1.

2. **Airline Overbooking**   The objective of this simulation is to determine the number of reservations an airline should accept for a particular flight. A simulation model is developed relating profit for the flight to a probabilistic input, the number of passengers with a reservation who show up and use their reservation, and a controllable input, the number of reservations accepted for the flight. For each selected value for the controllable input, a variety of possible values will be generated for the number of passengers who show up, and the resulting profit can be computed. Similar simulation models are applicable for hotel and car rental reservation systems.

3. **Inventory Policy**   The objective of this simulation is to choose an inventory policy that will provide good customer service at a reasonable cost. A model is developed relating two output measures, total inventory cost and the service level, to probabilistic inputs, such as product demand and delivery lead time from vendors, and controllable inputs, such as the order quantity and the reorder point. For each setting of the controllable inputs, a variety of possible values would be generated for the probabilistic inputs, and the resulting cost and service levels would be computed.

4. **Traffic Flow**   The objective of this simulation is to determine the effect of installing a left turn signal on the flow of traffic through a busy intersection. A model is developed relating waiting time for vehicles to get through the intersection to probabilistic inputs such as the number of vehicle arrivals and the fraction that want to make a left turn, and controllable inputs such as the length of time the left turn signal is on. For each setting of the controllable inputs, values would be generated for the probabilistic inputs, and the resulting vehicle waiting times would be computed.

5. **Waiting Lines**   The objective of this simulation is to determine the waiting times for customers at a bank's automated teller machine (ATM). A model is developed relating customer waiting times to probabilistic inputs such as customer arrivals and service times, and a controllable input, the number of ATM machines installed.

For each value of the controllable input (the number of ATM machines), a variety of values would be generated for the probabilistic inputs and the customer waiting times would be computed. We develop a simulation model for this type of application in Section 16.3.

Simulation is not an optimization technique. It is a method that can be used to describe or predict how a system will operate given certain choices for the controllable inputs and randomly generated values for the probabilistic inputs. Quantitative analysts often use simulation to determine values for the controllable inputs that are likely to lead to desirable system outputs. In this sense, simulation can be an effective tool in designing a system to provide good performance.

In this chapter we begin by showing how simulation can be used to study the financial risks associated with the development of a new product. We continue with illustrations showing how simulation can be used to establish an effective inventory policy and how simulation can be used to design waiting line systems. Other issues, such as verifying the simulation program, validating the model, and selecting a simulation software package, are discussed in Section 16.4.

16.1   RISK ANALYSIS

Risk analysis is the process of predicting the outcome of a decision in the face of uncertainty. In this section, we describe a problem that involves considerable uncertainty: the development of a new product. We first show how risk analysis can be conducted without using simulation; then, we show how a more comprehensive risk analysis can be conducted with the aid of simulation.

The PortaCom Project

PortaCom manufactures personal computers and related equipment. PortaCom's product design group has developed a prototype for a new high-quality portable printer. The new printer has an innovative design and the potential to capture a significant share of the portable printer market. Preliminary marketing and financial analyses have provided the following selling price, first-year administrative cost, and first-year advertising cost.

$$\text{Selling price} = \$249 \text{ per unit}$$
$$\text{Administrative cost} = \$400,000$$
$$\text{Advertising cost} = \$600,000$$

In the simulation model for the PortaCom problem, the preceding values are constants and are referred to as **parameters** of the model.

The cost of direct labor, the cost of parts, and the first-year demand for the printer are not known with certainty and are considered probabilistic inputs. At this stage of the planning process, PortaCom's best estimates of these inputs are $45 per unit for the direct labor cost, $90 per unit for the parts cost, and 15,000 units for the first-year demand. PortaCom would like an analysis of the first-year profit potential for the printer. Because of PortaCom's tight cash flow situation, management is particularly concerned about the potential for a loss.

What-If Analysis

One approach to risk analysis is called **what-if analysis.** A what-if analysis involves generating values for the probabilistic inputs (direct labor cost, parts cost, and first-year demand) and computing the resulting value for the output (profit). With a selling price of $249 per unit and administrative plus advertising costs equal to $400,000 + $600,000 = $1,000,000, the PortaCom profit model is

$$\text{Profit} = (\$249 - \text{Direct labor cost per unit} - \text{Parts cost per unit})(\text{Demand}) - \$1,000,000$$

Letting

$$c_1 = \text{direct labor cost per unit}$$
$$c_2 = \text{parts cost per unit}$$

and

$$x = \text{first-year demand}$$

the profit model for the first year can be written as follows:

$$\text{Profit} = (249 - c_1 - c_2)x - 1{,}000{,}000 \qquad (16.1)$$

The PortaCom profit model can be depicted as shown in Figure 16.2.

Recall that PortaCom's best estimates of the direct labor cost per unit, the parts cost per unit, and first-year demand are $45, $90, and 15,000 units, respectively. These values constitute the **base-case scenario** for PortaCom. Substituting these values into equation (16.1) yields the following profit projection.

$$\text{Profit} = (249 - 45 - 90)(15{,}000) - 1{,}000{,}000 = 710{,}000$$

Thus, the base-case scenario leads to an anticipated profit of $710,000.

In risk analysis we are concerned with both the probability of a loss and the magnitude of a loss. Although the base-case scenario looks appealing, PortaCom might be interested in what happens if the estimates of the direct labor cost per unit, parts cost per unit, and first-year demand do not turn out to be as expected under the base-case scenario. For instance, suppose that PortaCom believes that direct labor costs could range from $43 to $47 per unit, parts cost could range from $80 to $100 per unit, and first-year demand could range from 1500 to 28,500 units. Using these ranges, what-if analysis can be used to evaluate a **worst-case scenario** and a **best-case scenario.**

The worst-case value for the direct labor cost is $47 (the highest value), the worst-case value for the parts cost is $100 (the highest value), and the worst-case value for demand is 1500 units (the lowest value). Thus, in the worst-case scenario, $c_1 = 47$, $c_2 = 100$, and $x = 1500$. Substituting these values into equation (16.1) leads to the following profit projection:

$$\text{Profit} = (249 - 47 - 100)(1500) - 1{,}000{,}000 = -847{,}000$$

So, the worst-case scenario leads to a projected loss of $847,000.

The best-case value for the direct labor cost is $c_1 = 43$ (the lowest value), the best-case value for the parts cost is 80 (the lowest value), and the best-case value for demand is 28,500 units (the highest value). Substituting these values into equation (16.1) leads to the following profit projection:

Problem 2 will give you practice using what-if analysis.

$$\text{Profit} = (249 - 43 - 80)(28{,}500) - 1{,}000{,}000 = 2{,}591{,}000$$

So, the best-case scenario leads to a projected profit is $2,591,000.

FIGURE 16.2 PORTACOM PROFIT MODEL

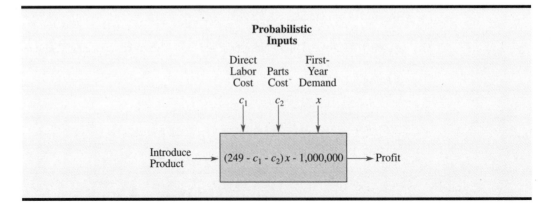

At this point the what-if analysis provides the conclusion that profits can range from a loss of $847,000 to a profit of $2,591,000 with a base-case scenario value of $710,000. Although the base-case profit of $710,000 is possible, the what-if analysis indicates that either a substantial loss or a substantial profit is possible. Other scenarios that PortaCom might want to consider can also be evaluated. However, the difficulty with what-if analysis is that it does indicate the likelihood of the various profit or loss values. In particular, we do not know anything about the *probability* of a loss.

Simulation

Using simulation to perform risk analysis for the PortaCom problem is like playing out many what-if scenarios by randomly generating values for the probabilistic inputs. The advantage of simulation is that it allows us to assess the probability of a profit and the probability of a loss.

Using the what-if approach to risk analysis, we selected values for the probabilistic inputs [direct labor cost per unit (c_1), parts cost per unit (c_2), and first-year demand (x)], and then computed the resulting profit. Applying simulation to the PortaCom problem requires generating values for the probabilistic inputs that are representative of what we might observe in practice. To generate such values, we must know the probability distribution for each probabilistic input. Further analysis by PortaCom has led to the following probability distributions for the direct labor cost per unit, the parts cost per unit, and first-year demand:

One advantage of simulation is the ability to use probability distributions that are unique to the system being studied.

Direct Labor Cost.   PortaCom believes that the direct labor cost will range from $43 to $47 per unit and is described by the discrete probability distribution shown in Table 16.1. Thus, we see a 0.1 probability that the direct labor cost will be $43 per unit, a 0.2 probability that the direct labor cost will be $44 per unit, and so on. The highest probability of 0.4 is associated with a direct labor cost of $45 per unit.

Parts Cost.   This cost depends upon the general economy, the overall demand for parts, and the pricing policy of PortaCom's parts suppliers. PortaCom believes that the parts cost will range from $80 to $100 per unit and is described by the uniform probability distribution shown in Figure 16.3. Costs per unit between $80 and $100 are equally likely.

First-Year Demand.   PortaCom believes that first-year demand is described by the normal probability distribution shown in Figure 16.4. The mean or expected value of first-year demand is 15,000 units. The standard deviation of 4500 units describes the variability in the first-year demand.

To simulate the PortaCom problem, we must generate values for the three probabilistic inputs, and compute the resulting profit. Then, we generate another set of values for the probabilistic inputs, compute a second value for profit, and so on. We continue this process until we are satisfied that enough trials have been conducted to describe the probability

TABLE 16.1   PROBABILITY DISTRIBUTION FOR DIRECT LABOR COST PER UNIT

Direct Labor Cost per Unit	Probability
$43	0.1
$44	0.2
$45	0.4
$46	0.2
$47	0.1

FIGURE 16.3   UNIFORM PROBABILITY DISTRIBUTION FOR THE PARTS COST PER UNIT

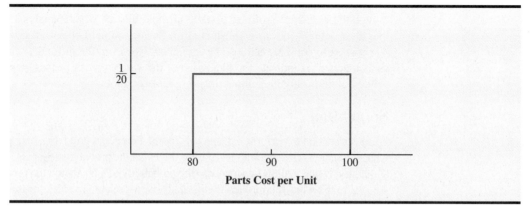

FIGURE 16.4   NORMAL PROBABILITY DISTRIBUTION OF FIRST-YEAR DEMAND

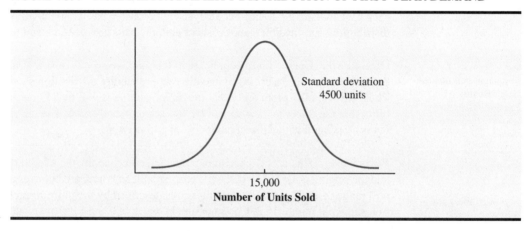

A flowchart provides a graphical representation that helps describe the logic of the simulation model.

distribution for profit. This process of generating probabilistic inputs and computing the value of the output is called *simulation*. The sequence of logical and mathematical operations required to conduct a simulation can be depicted with a flowchart. A flowchart for the PortaCom simulation is shown in Figure 16.5.

Following the logic described by the flowchart we see that the model parameters—selling price, administrative cost, and advertising cost—are $249, $400,000, and $600,000, respectively. These values will remain fixed throughout the simulation.

The next three blocks depict the generation of values for the probabilistic inputs. First, a value for the direct labor cost (c_1) is generated. Then a value for the parts cost (c_2) is generated, followed by a value for the first-year demand (x). These probabilistic input values are combined using the profit model given by equation (16.1).

$$\text{Profit} = (249 - c_1 - c_2)x - 1,000,000$$

The computation of profit completes one trial of the simulation. We then return to the block where we generated the direct labor cost and begin another trial. This process is repeated until a satisfactory number of trials has been generated.

At the end of the simulation, output measures of interest can be developed. For example, we will be interested in computing the average profit and the probability of a loss.

FIGURE 16.5   FLOWCHART FOR THE PORTACOM SIMULATION

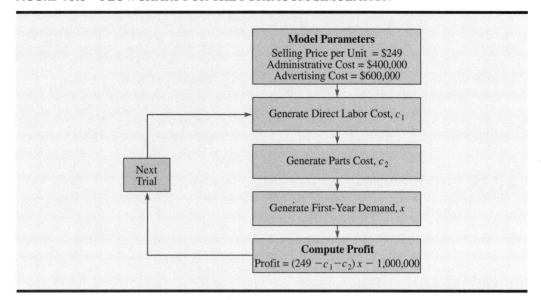

For the output measures to be meaningful, the values of the probabilistic inputs must be representative of what is likely to happen when the PortaCom printer is introduced into the market. An essential part of the simulation procedure is the ability to generate representative values for the probabilistic inputs. We now discuss how to generate these values.

Random Numbers and Generating Probabilistic Input Values.   In the PortaCom simulation, representative values must be generated for the direct labor cost per unit (c_1), the parts cost per unit (c_2), and the first-year demand (x). Random numbers and the probability distributions associated with each probabilistic input are used to generate representative values. To illustrate how to generate these values, we need to introduce the concept of *computer-generated random numbers*.

Computer-generated random numbers[1] are randomly selected decimal numbers from 0 up to, but not including, 1. The computer-generated random numbers are equally likely and are uniformly distributed over the interval from 0 to 1. Computer-generated random numbers can be obtained using built-in functions available in computer simulation packages and spreadsheets. For instance, placing = RAND() in a cell of an Excel spreadsheet will result in a random number between 0 and 1 being placed into that cell.

Table 16.2 contains 500 random numbers generated using Excel. These numbers can be viewed as a random sample of 500 values from a uniform probability distribution over the interval from 0 to 1. Let us show how random numbers can be used to generate values for the PortaCom probability distributions. We begin by showing how to generate a value for the direct labor cost per unit. The approach described is applicable for generating values from any discrete probability distribution.

An interval of random numbers is assigned to each possible value of the direct labor cost in such a fashion that the probability of generating a random number in the interval is equal to the probability of the corresponding direct labor cost. Table 16.3 shows how this process is

Because random numbers are equally likely, quantitative analysts can assign ranges of random numbers to corresponding values of probabilistic inputs so that the probability of any input value to the simulation model is identical to the probability of its occurrence in the real system.

---

1. Computer-generated random numbers are called *pseudorandom numbers*. Because they are generated through the use of mathematical formulas, they are not technically random. The difference between random numbers and pseudorandom numbers is primarily philosophical, and we use the term *random numbers* regardless of whether they are generated by a computer.

TABLE 16.2 500 COMPUTER-GENERATED RANDOM NUMBERS

0.6953	0.5247	0.1368	0.9850	0.7467	0.3813	0.5827	0.7893	0.7169	0.8166
0.0082	0.9925	0.6874	0.2122	0.6885	0.2159	0.4299	0.3467	0.2186	0.1033
0.6799	0.1241	0.3056	0.5590	0.0423	0.6515	0.2750	0.8156	0.2871	0.4680
0.8898	0.1514	0.1826	0.0004	0.5259	0.2425	0.8421	0.9248	0.9155	0.9518
0.6515	0.5027	0.9290	0.5177	0.3134	0.9177	0.2605	0.6668	0.1167	0.7870
0.3976	0.7790	0.0035	0.0064	0.0441	0.3437	0.1248	0.5442	0.9800	0.1857
0.0642	0.4086	0.6078	0.2044	0.0484	0.4691	0.7058	0.8552	0.5029	0.3288
0.0377	0.5250	0.7774	0.2390	0.9121	0.5345	0.8178	0.8443	0.4154	0.2526
0.5739	0.5181	0.0234	0.7305	0.0376	0.5169	0.5679	0.5495	0.7872	0.5321
0.5827	0.0341	0.7482	0.6351	0.9146	0.4700	0.7869	0.1337	0.0702	0.4219
0.0508	0.7905	0.2932	0.4971	0.0225	0.4466	0.5118	0.1200	0.0200	0.5445
0.4757	0.1399	0.5668	0.9569	0.7255	0.4650	0.4084	0.3701	0.9446	0.8064
0.6805	0.9931	0.4166	0.1091	0.7730	0.0691	0.9411	0.3468	0.0014	0.7379
0.2603	0.7507	0.6414	0.9907	0.2699	0.4571	0.9254	0.2371	0.8664	0.9553
0.8143	0.7625	0.1708	0.1900	0.2781	0.2830	0.6877	0.0488	0.8635	0.3155
0.5681	0.7854	0.5016	0.9403	0.1078	0.5255	0.8727	0.3815	0.5541	0.9833
0.1501	0.9363	0.3858	0.3545	0.5448	0.0643	0.3167	0.6732	0.6283	0.2631
0.8806	0.7989	0.7484	0.8083	0.2701	0.5039	0.9439	0.1027	0.9677	0.4597
0.4582	0.7590	0.4393	0.4704	0.6903	0.3732	0.6587	0.8675	0.2905	0.3058
0.0785	0.1467	0.3880	0.5274	0.8723	0.7517	0.9905	0.8904	0.8177	0.6660
0.1158	0.6635	0.4992	0.9070	0.2975	0.5686	0.8495	0.1652	0.2039	0.2553
0.2762	0.7018	0.6782	0.4013	0.2224	0.4672	0.5753	0.6219	0.6871	0.9255
0.9382	0.6411	0.7984	0.0608	0.5945	0.3977	0.4570	0.9924	0.8398	0.8361
0.5102	0.7021	0.4353	0.3398	0.8038	0.2260	0.1250	0.1884	0.3432	0.1192
0.2354	0.7410	0.7089	0.2579	0.1358	0.8446	0.1648	0.3889	0.5620	0.6555
0.9082	0.7906	0.7589	0.8870	0.1189	0.7125	0.6324	0.1096	0.5155	0.3449
0.6936	0.0702	0.9716	0.0374	0.0683	0.2397	0.7753	0.2029	0.1464	0.8000
0.4042	0.8158	0.3623	0.6614	0.7954	0.7516	0.6518	0.3638	0.3107	0.2718
0.9410	0.2201	0.6348	0.0367	0.0311	0.0688	0.2346	0.3927	0.7327	0.9994
0.0917	0.2504	0.2878	0.1735	0.3872	0.6816	0.2731	0.3846	0.6621	0.8983
0.8532	0.4869	0.2685	0.6349	0.9364	0.3451	0.4998	0.2842	0.0643	0.6656
0.8980	0.0455	0.8314	0.8189	0.6783	0.8086	0.1386	0.4442	0.9941	0.6812
0.8412	0.8792	0.2025	0.9320	0.7656	0.3815	0.5302	0.8744	0.4584	0.3585
0.5688	0.8633	0.5818	0.0692	0.2543	0.5453	0.9955	0.1237	0.7535	0.5993
0.5006	0.1215	0.8102	0.1026	0.9251	0.6851	0.1559	0.1214	0.2628	0.9374
0.5748	0.4164	0.3427	0.2809	0.8064	0.5855	0.2229	0.2805	0.9139	0.9013
0.1100	0.0873	0.9407	0.8747	0.0496	0.4380	0.5847	0.4183	0.5929	0.4863
0.5802	0.7747	0.1285	0.0074	0.6252	0.7747	0.0112	0.3958	0.3285	0.5389
0.1019	0.6628	0.8998	0.1334	0.2798	0.7351	0.7330	0.6723	0.6924	0.3963
0.9909	0.8991	0.2298	0.2603	0.6921	0.5573	0.8191	0.0384	0.2954	0.0636
0.6292	0.4923	0.0276	0.6734	0.6562	0.4231	0.1980	0.6551	0.3716	0.0507
0.9430	0.2579	0.7933	0.0945	0.3192	0.3195	0.7772	0.4672	0.7070	0.5925
0.9938	0.7098	0.7964	0.7952	0.8947	0.1214	0.8454	0.8294	0.5394	0.9413
0.4690	0.1395	0.0930	0.3189	0.6972	0.7291	0.8513	0.9256	0.7478	0.8124
0.2028	0.3774	0.0485	0.7718	0.9656	0.2444	0.0304	0.1395	0.1577	0.8625
0.6141	0.4131	0.2006	0.2329	0.6182	0.5151	0.6300	0.9311	0.3837	0.7828
0.2757	0.8479	0.7880	0.8492	0.6859	0.8947	0.6246	0.1574	0.4936	0.8077
0.0561	0.0126	0.6531	0.0378	0.4975	0.1133	0.3572	0.0071	0.4555	0.7563
0.1419	0.4308	0.8073	0.4681	0.0481	0.2918	0.2975	0.0685	0.6384	0.0812
0.3125	0.0053	0.9209	0.9768	0.3584	0.0390	0.2161	0.6333	0.4391	0.6991

TABLE 16.3   RANDOM NUMBER INTERVALS FOR GENERATING VALUES OF DIRECT
LABOR COST PER UNIT

Direct Labor Cost per Unit	Probability	Interval of Random Numbers
$43	0.1	0.0 but less than 0.1
$44	0.2	0.1 but less than 0.3
$45	0.4	0.3 but less than 0.7
$46	0.2	0.7 but less than 0.9
$47	0.1	0.9 but less than 1.0

done. The interval of random numbers 0.0 but less than 0.1 is associated with a direct labor cost of $43, the interval of random numbers 0.1 but less than 0.3 is associated with a direct labor cost of $44, and so on. With this assignment of random number intervals to the possible values of the direct labor cost, the probability of generating a random number in any interval is equal to the probability of obtaining the corresponding value for the direct labor cost. Thus, to select a value for the direct labor cost, we generate a random number between 0 and 1. If the random number is 0.0 but less than 0.1, we set the direct labor cost equal to $43. If the random number is 0.1 but less than 0.3, we set the direct labor cost equal to $44, and so on.

Problem 5 gives you the opportunity to establish intervals of random numbers and simulate demand from a discrete probability distribution.

Each trial of the simulation requires a value for the direct labor cost. Suppose that on the first trial the random number is 0.9109. From Table 16.3, the simulated value for the direct labor cost is $47 per unit. Suppose that on the second trial the random number is 0.2841. From Table 16.3, the simulated value for the direct labor cost is $44 per unit. Table 16.4 shows the results obtained for the first 10 simulation trials.

Each trial in the simulation requires a value of the direct labor cost, parts cost, and first-year demand. Let us now turn to the issue of generating values for the parts cost. The probability distribution for the parts cost per unit is the uniform distribution shown in Figure 16.3. Because this random variable has a different probability distribution than direct labor cost, we use random numbers in a slightly different way to generate values for parts cost. With a uniform probability distribution, the following relationship between the random number and the associated value of the parts cost is used.

$$\text{Parts cost} = a + r(b - a) \tag{16.2}$$

TABLE 16.4   RANDOM GENERATION OF TEN VALUES FOR THE DIRECT LABOR COST
PER UNIT

Trial	Random Number	Direct Labor Cost ($)
1	0.9109	47
2	0.2841	44
3	0.6531	45
4	0.0367	43
5	0.3451	45
6	0.2757	44
7	0.6859	45
8	0.6246	45
9	0.4936	45
10	0.8077	46

where

$$r = \text{random number between 0 and 1}$$
$$a = \text{smallest value for parts cost}$$
$$b = \text{largest value for parts cost}$$

For PortaCom, the smallest value for the parts cost is $80, and the largest value is $100. Applying equation (16.2) with $a = 80$ and $b = 100$ leads to the following formula for generating the parts cost given a random number, r.

$$\text{Parts cost} = 80 + r(100 - 80) = 80 + r20 \qquad (16.3)$$

Let us use equation (16.3) to generate a value for the parts cost. Suppose that a random number of 0.2680 is obtained. The value for the parts cost is

$$\text{Parts cost} = 80 + 0.2680(20) = 85.36 \text{ per unit}$$

Suppose that a random number of 0.5842 is generated on the next trial. The value for the parts cost is

$$\text{Parts cost} = 80 + 0.5842(20) = 91.68 \text{ per unit}$$

With appropriate choices of a and b, equation (16.2) can be used to generate values for any uniform probability distribution. Table 16.5 shows the generation of ten values for the parts cost per unit.

Finally, we need a random number procedure for generating the first-year demand. Because first-year demand is normally distributed with a mean of 15,000 units and a standard deviation of 4500 units (see Figure 16.4), we need a procedure for generating random values from a normal probability distribution. Because of the mathematical complexity, a detailed discussion of the procedure for generating random values from a normal probability distribution is omitted. However, computer simulation packages and spreadsheets include a built-in function that provides randomly generated values from a normal probability distribution. In most cases the user only needs to provide the mean and standard deviation of the normal distribution. For example, using Excel the following formula can be placed into a cell to obtain a value for a probabilistic input that is normally distributed:

Spreadsheet packages such as Excel have built-in functions that make simulations based on probability distributions such as the normal probability distribution relatively easy.

=NORMINV(RANDO(),Mean,Standard Deviation)

TABLE 16.5   RANDOM GENERATION OF TEN VALUES FOR THE PARTS COST PER UNIT

Trial	Random Number	Parts Cost ($)
1	0.2680	85.36
2	0.5842	91.68
3	0.6675	93.35
4	0.9280	98.56
5	0.4180	88.36
6	0.7342	94.68
7	0.4325	88.65
8	0.1186	82.37
9	0.6944	93.89
10	0.7869	95.74

Because the mean for the first-year demand in the PortaCom problem is 15,000 and the standard deviation is 4500, the Excel statement

$$=\text{NORMINV(RAND(),15000,4500)} \qquad (16.4)$$

will provide a normally distributed value for first-year demand. For example, if Excel's RAND() function generates the random number 0.7005, the Excel function shown in equation (16.4) will provide a first-year demand of 17,366 units. If RAND() generates the random number 0.3204, equation (16.4) will provide a first-year demand of 12,900. Table 16.6 shows the results for the first ten randomly generated values for demand. Note that random numbers less than 0.5 generate first-year demand values below the mean and that random numbers greater than 0.5 generate first-year demand values greater than the mean.

Running the Simulation Model.   Running the simulation model means implementing the sequence of logical and mathematical operations described in the flowchart in Figure 16.5. The model parameters are \$249 per unit for the selling price, \$400,000 for the administrative cost, and \$600,000 for the advertising cost. Each trial in the simulation involves randomly generating values for the probabilistic inputs (direct labor cost, parts cost, and first-year demand) and computing profit. The simulation is complete when a satisfactory number of trials have been conducted.

Let us compute the profit for the first trial assuming the following probabilistic inputs:

$$
\begin{aligned}
\text{Direct labor cost:} && c_1 &= 47 \\
\text{Parts cost:} && c_2 &= 85.36 \\
\text{First-year demand:} && x &= 17{,}366
\end{aligned}
$$

Referring to the flowchart in Figure 16.5, we see that the profit obtained is

$$
\begin{aligned}
\text{Profit} &= (249 - c_1 - c_2)x - 1{,}000{,}000 \\
&= (249 - 47 - 85.36)17{,}366 - 1{,}000{,}000 = 1{,}025{,}570
\end{aligned}
$$

The first row of Table 16.7 shows the result of this trial of the PortaCom simulation.

The simulated profit for the PortaCom printer if the direct labor cost is \$47 per unit, the parts cost is \$85.36 per unit, and first-year demand is 17,366 units is \$1,025,570. Of course, one simulation trial does not provide a complete understanding of the possible profit and

TABLE 16.6   RANDOM GENERATION OF TEN VALUES FOR FIRST-YEAR DEMAND

Trial	Random Number	Demand
1	0.7005	17,366
2	0.3204	12,900
3	0.8968	20,686
4	0.1804	10,888
5	0.4346	14,259
6	0.9605	22,904
7	0.5646	15,732
8	0.7334	17,804
9	0.0216	5,902
10	0.3218	12,918

TABLE 16.7   PORTACOM SIMULATION RESULTS FOR TEN TRIALS

Trial	Direct Labor Cost per Unit ($)	Parts Cost per Unit ($)	Units Sold	Profit ($)
1	47	85.36	17,366	1,025,570
2	44	91.68	12,900	461,828
3	45	93.35	20,686	1,288,906
4	43	98.56	10,888	169,807
5	45	88.36	14,259	648,911
6	44	94.68	22,904	1,526,769
7	45	88.65	15,732	814,686
8	45	82.37	17,804	1,165,501
9	45	93.89	5,902	−350,131
10	46	95.74	12,918	385,585
Total	449	912.64	151,359	7,137,432
Average	$44.90	$91.26	15,136	$713,743

loss. Because other values are possible for the probabilistic inputs, we can benefit from additional simulation trials.

Suppose that on a second simulation trial, random numbers of 0.2841, 0.5842, and 0.3204 are generated for the direct labor cost, the parts cost, and first-year demand, respectively. These random numbers will provide the probabilistic inputs of $44 for the direct labor cost, $91.68 for the parts cost, and 12,900 for first-year demand. These values provide a simulated profit of $461,828 on the second simulation trial (see the second row of Table 16.7).

Repetition of the simulation process with different values for the probabilistic inputs is an essential part of any simulation. Through the repeated trials, management will begin to understand what might happen when the product is introduced into the real world. We have shown the results of ten simulation trials in Table 16.7. For these 10 cases, we find a profit as high as $1,526,769 for the 6th trial and a loss of $350,131 for the 9th trial. Thus, we see both the possibility of a profit and a loss. Averages for the ten trials are presented at the bottom of the table. We see that the average profit for the ten trials is $713,743. The probability of a loss is 0.10, because one of the ten trials (the 9th) resulted in a loss. We note also that the average values for labor cost, parts cost, and first-year demand are fairly close to their means of $45, $90, and 15,000, respectively.

Simulation of the PortaCom Problem

Using an Excel spreadsheet, we simulated the PortaCom project 500 times. The spreadsheet used to carry out the simulation is shown in Figure 16.6. Note that the simulation results for trials 6 through 495 have been hidden so that the results can be shown in a reasonably sized figure. If desired, the rows for these trials can be shown and the simulation results displayed for all 500 trials. The details of the Excel spreadsheet that provided the PortaCom simulation are described in Appendix 16.1.

The simulation summary statistics in Figure 16.6 provide information about the risk associated with PortaCom's new printer. The worst result obtained in a simulation of 500 trials is a loss of $785,234, and the best result is a profit of $2,367,058. The mean profit is $698,457. Fifty-one of the trials resulted in a loss; thus, the estimated probability of a loss is 51/500 = 0.1020.

FIGURE 16.6 SPREADSHEET SIMULATION FOR THE PORTACOM PROBLEM

	A	B	C	D	E	F
1	**PortaCom Risk Analysis**					
2						
3	Selling Price per Unit		$249			
4	Administrative Cost		$400,000			
5	Advertising Cost		$600,000			
6						
7	**Direct Labor Cost**			**Parts Cost (Uniform Distribution)**		
8	Lower	Upper		Smallest Value	$80	
9	Random No.	Random No.	Cost per Unit	Largest Value	$100	
10	0.0	0.1	$43			
11	0.1	0.3	$44			
12	0.3	0.7	$45	**Demand (Normal Distribution)**		
13	0.7	0.9	$46	Mean	15000	
14	0.9	1.0	$47	Standard Dev	4500	
15						
16						
17	**Simulation Trials**					
18						
19		Direct Labor	Parts	First-Year		
20	Trial	Cost per Unit	Cost per Unit	Demand	Profit	
21	1	47	$85.36	17,366	$1,025,570	
22	2	44	$91.68	12,900	$461,828	
23	3	45	$93.35	20,686	$1,288,906	
24	4	43	$98.56	10,888	$169,807	
25	5	45	$88.36	14,259	$648,911	
516	496	44	$98.67	8,730	($71,659)	
517	497	45	$94.38	19,257	$1,110,841	
518	498	44	$90.85	14,920	$703,102	
519	499	43	$90.37	13,471	$557,662	
520	500	46	$92.50	18,614	$1,056,927	
521						
522			**Summary Statistics**			
523			Mean Profit		$698,457	
524			Standard Deviation		$520,485	
525			Minimum Profit		($785,234)	
526			Maximum Profit		$2,367,058	
527			Number of Losses		51	
528			Probability of Loss		0.1020	

Simulation studies enable an objective estimate of the probability of a loss, which is an important aspect of risk analysis.

A histogram of simulated profit values is shown in Figure 16.7. We note that the distribution of profit values is fairly symmetric with a large number of values in the range of $250,000 to $1,250,000. The probability of a large loss or a large gain is small. Only 3 trials resulted in a loss more than $500,000, and only 3 trials resulted in a profit greater than $2,000,000. However, the probability of a loss is significant. Forty-eight of the 500 trials resulted in a loss in the $0 to $500,000 range—almost 10%. The modal category, the one with the largest number of values, is the range of profits between $750,000 and $1,000,000.

In comparing the simulation approach to risk analysis to the what-if approach, we see that much more information is obtained by using simulation. With the what-if analysis, we learned that the base-case scenario projected a profit of $710,000. The worst-case scenario projected a loss of $847,000, and the best-case scenario projected a profit of $2,591,000. From the 500 trials of the simulation run, we see that the worst- and best-case scenarios, although possible, are unlikely. None of the 500 trials provided a loss as low as the worst-case or a profit as high as the best-case. Indeed, the advantage of simulation for risk analysis is the information it provides on the likely values of the output. We now know the probability of a loss, how the profit values are distributed over their range, and what profit values are most likely.

For practice working through a simulation problem, try Problems 9 and 14.

The simulation results help PortaCom's management better understand the profit/loss potential of the PortaCom portable printer. The 0.1020 probability of a loss may be acceptable to management given a probability of almost 0.80 (see Figure 16.7) that profit will exceed $250,000. On the other hand, PortaCom might want to conduct further market research before deciding whether to introduce the product. In any case, the simulation results should be helpful in reaching an appropriate decision.

FIGURE 16.7   HISTOGRAM OF SIMULATED PROFIT FOR 500 TRIALS OF THE PORTACOM SIMULATION

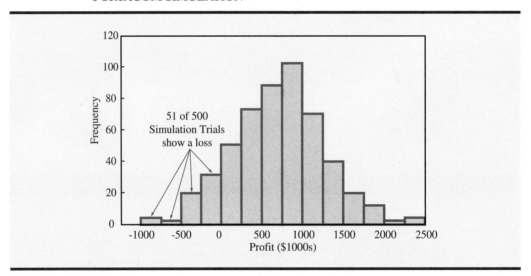

NOTES AND COMMENTS

1. The PortaCom simulation model is based on independent trials in which the results for one trial do not affect what happens in subsequent trials. Historically, simulation studies such as this were referred to as *Monte Carlo simulations*. The term *Monte Carlo simulation* was used because early practitioners of simulation saw similarities between the models they were developing and the gambling games played in the casinos of Monte Carlo. Today, many individuals interpret the term Monte Carlo simulation more broadly to mean any simulation that involves randomly generating values for the probabilistic inputs.

2. The probability distribution used to generate values for probabilistic inputs in a simulation model is often developed using historical data. For instance, suppose that an analysis of daily sales at a new car dealership for the past 50 days showed that on 2 days no cars were sold, on 5 days 1 car was sold, on 9 days 2 cars were sold, on 24 days 3 cars were sold, on 7 days 4 cars were sold, and on 3 days 5 cars were sold. We can estimate the probability distribution of daily demand using the relative frequencies for the observed data. An estimate of the probability that no cars are sold on a given day is

2/50 = 0.04, an estimate of the probability that 1 car is sold is 5/50 = 0.10 and so on. The estimated probability distribution of daily demand is as follows:

Daily Sales	0	1	2	3	4	5
Probability	0.04	0.10	0.18	0.48	0.14	0.06

3. Spreadsheet add-in packages such as @RISK® and Crystal Ball® have been developed to make spreadsheet simulation easier. For instance, using Crystal Ball we could simulate the PortaCom new product introduction by first entering the formulas showing the relationships between the probabilistic inputs and the output measure, profit. Then, a probability distribution type is selected for each probabilistic input from among a number of available choices. Crystal Ball will generate random values for each probabilistic input, compute the profit, and repeat the simulation for as many trials as specified. Graphical displays and a variety of descriptive statistics can be easily obtained. Appendix 16.2 shows how to perform a simulation of the PortaCom problem using Crystal Ball.

16.2 INVENTORY SIMULATION

In this section we describe how simulation can be used to establish an inventory policy for a product that has an uncertain demand. The product is a home ventilation fan distributed by the Butler Electrical Supply Company. Each fan costs Butler $75 and sells for $125. Thus Butler realizes a gross profit of $125 - $75 = $50 for each fan sold. Monthly demand for the fan is described by a normal probability distribution with a mean of 100 units and a standard deviation of 20 units.

Butler receives monthly deliveries from its supplier and replenishes its inventory to a level of Q at the beginning of each month. This beginning inventory level is referred to as the replenishment level. If monthly demand is less than the replenishment level, an inventory holding cost of $15 is charged for each unit that is not sold. However, if monthly demand is greater than the replenishment level, a stockout occurs and a shortage cost is incurred. Because Butler assigns a goodwill cost of $30 for each customer turned away, a shortage cost of $30 is charged for each unit of demand that cannot be satisfied. Management would like to use a simulation model to determine the average monthly net profit resulting from using a particular replenishment level. Management would also like information on the percentage of total demand that will be satisfied. This percentage is referred to as the *service level*.

The controllable input to the Butler simulation model is the replenishment level, Q. The probabilistic input is the monthly demand, D. The two output measures are the average monthly net profit and the service level. Computation of the service level requires that we keep track of the number of fans sold each month and the total demand for fans for each month. The service level will be computed at the end of the simulation run as the ratio of total units sold to total demand. A diagram showing the relationship between the inputs and the outputs is shown in Figure 16.8.

When demand is less than or equal to the replenishment level ($D \leq Q$), D units are sold, and an inventory holding cost of $15 is incurred for each of the $Q - D$ units that remain in inventory. Net profit for this case is computed as follows:

Case 1: $D \leq Q$

$$\text{Gross profit} = \$50D$$

$$\text{Holding cost} = \$15(Q - D)$$

$$\text{Net profit} = \text{Gross profit} - \text{Holding cost} = \$50D - \$15(Q - D) \quad (16.5)$$

FIGURE 16.8   BUTLER INVENTORY SIMULATION MODEL

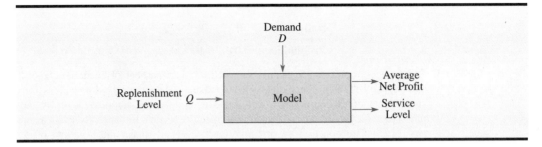

When demand is greater than the replenishment level ($D > Q$), Q fans are sold, and a shortage cost of \$30 is imposed for each of the $D - Q$ units of demand not satisfied. Net profit for this case is computed as follows:

Case 2: $D > Q$

$$\text{Gross profit} = \$50Q$$

$$\text{Shortage cost} = \$30(D - Q)$$

$$\text{Net profit} = \text{Gross profit} - \text{Shortage cost} = \$50Q - \$30(D - Q) \quad (16.6)$$

Figure 16.9 shows a flowchart that defines the sequence of logical and mathematical operations required to simulate the Butler inventory system. Each trial in the simulation represents one month of operation. The simulation is run for 300 months using a given replenishment level, Q. Then, the average profit and service level output measures are computed. Let us describe the steps involved in the simulation by illustrating the results for the first two months of a simulation run using a replenishment level of $Q = 100$.

The first block of the flowchart in Figure 16.9 sets the values of the model parameters: gross profit = \$50 per unit, holding cost = \$15 per unit, and shortage cost = \$30 per unit. The next block shows that a replenishment level of Q is selected; in our illustration, $Q = 100$. Then, a value for monthly demand is generated. Because monthly demand is normally distributed with a mean of 100 units and a standard deviation of 20 units, we can use the Excel function =NORMINV(RAND(),100,20), as described in Section 16.1, to generate a value for monthly demand. Suppose that a value of $D = 79$ is generated on the first trial. This value of demand is then compared with the replenishment level, Q. With the replenishment level set at $Q = 100$, demand is less than the replenishment level, and the left branch of the flowchart is followed. Sales are set equal to demand (79), and gross profit, holding cost, and net profit are computed as follows:

$$\text{Gross profit} = 50D = 50(79) = 3950$$

$$\text{Holding cost} = 15(Q - D) = 15(100 - 79) = 315$$

$$\text{Net profit} = \text{Gross profit} - \text{Holding cost} = 3950 - 315 = 3635$$

The values of demand, sales, gross profit, holding cost, and net profit are recorded for the first month. The first row of Table 16.8 summarizes the information for this first trial.

For the second month, suppose that a value of 111 is generated for monthly demand. Because demand is greater than the replenishment level, the right branch of the flowchart is followed. Sales are set equal to the replenishment level (100), and gross profit, shortage cost, and net profit are computed as follows:

$$\text{Gross profit} = 50Q = 50(100) = 5000$$
$$\text{Shortage cost} = 30(D - Q) = 30(111 - 100) = 330$$
$$\text{Net profit} = \text{Gross profit} - \text{Shortage cost} = 5000 - 330 = 4670$$

The values of demand, sales, gross profit, holding cost, shortage cost, and net profit are recorded for the second month. The second row of Table 16.8 summarizes the information generated in the second trial.

Results for the first 5 months of the simulation are shown in Table 16.8. The totals show that we have an accumulated total net profit of $22,310, which is an average monthly net

FIGURE 16.9   FLOWCHART FOR THE BUTLER INVENTORY SIMULATION

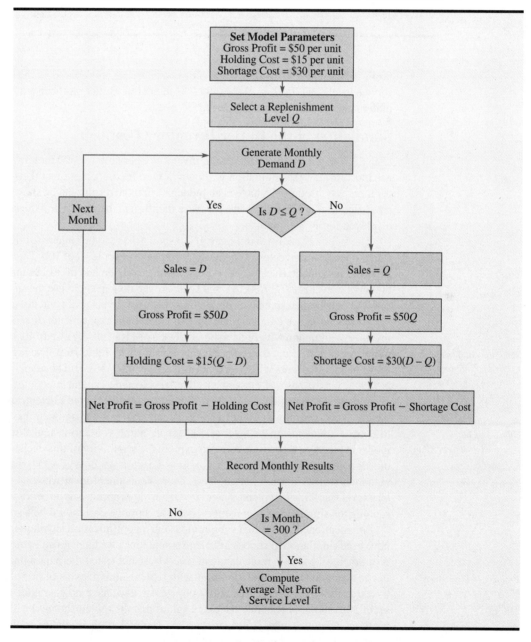

TABLE 16.8 BUTLER INVENTORY SIMULATION RESULTS FOR FIVE TRIALS WITH $Q = 100$

Month	Demand	Sales	Gross Profit ($)	Holding Cost ($)	Shortage Cost ($)	Net Profit ($)
1	79	79	3950	315	0	3635
2	111	100	5000	0	330	4670
3	93	93	4650	105	0	4545
4	100	100	5000	0	0	5000
5	118	100	5000	0	540	4460
Totals	501	472	23,600	420	870	22,310
Average	100	94	$4,720	$ 84	$174	$4,462

profit of $22,310/5 = $4,462. Total unit sales are 472, and total demand is 501. Thus, the service level is 472/501 = .942, or 94.2%, indicating Butler has been able to satisfy 94.2% of demand during the 5-month period.

Simulation of the Butler Inventory Problem

Using Excel, we simulated the Butler inventory operation for 300 months. The spreadsheet used to carry out the simulation is shown in Figure 16.10. Note that the simulation results for months 6 through 295 have been hidden so that the results can be shown in a reasonably sized figure. If desired, the rows for these months can be shown and the simulation results displayed for all 300 months.

The summary statistics in Figure 16.10 show what can be anticipated over 300 months if Butler operates its inventory system using a replenishment level of 100. The average net profit is $4,293 per month. Because 27,917 units of the total demand of 30,181 units were satisfied, the service level is 27,917/30,181 = 92.5%. We are now ready to use the simulation model to consider other replenishment levels that may improve the net profit and the service level.

At this point, we conducted a series of simulation experiments by repeating the Butler inventory simulation with replenishment levels of 110, 120, 130, and 140 units. The average monthly net profits and the service levels are shown in Table 16.9. The highest monthly net profit of $4,575 occurs with a replenishment level of $Q = 120$. The associated service level is 98.6%. On the basis of these results, Butler selected a replenishment level of $Q = 120$.

Simulation allows the user to consider different operating policies and changes to model parameters and then to observe the impact of the changes on output measures such as profit or service level.

Experimental simulation studies, such as this one for Butler's inventory policy, can help identify good operating policies and decisions. Butler's management has used simulation to choose a replenishment level of 120 for its home ventilation fan. With the simulation model in place, management can also explore the sensitivity of this decision to some of the model parameters. For instance, we assigned a shortage cost of $30 for any customer demand not met. With this shortage cost, the replenishment level was $Q = 120$ and the service level was 98.6%. If management felt a more appropriate shortage cost was $10 per unit, running the simulation again using $10 as the shortage cost would be a simple matter.

Problem 18 gives you a chance to develop a different simulation model.

We mentioned earlier that simulation is not an optimization technique. Even though we have used simulation to choose a replenishment level, we have no guarantee that this choice is optimal. All possible replenishment levels were not tested. Perhaps a manager would like to consider additional simulation runs with replenishment levels of $Q = 115$ and $Q = 125$ to search for an even better inventory policy. Also, we have no guarantee that with another set of 300 randomly generated demand values that the replenishment level with the highest profit would not change. However, with a large number of simulation trials, we should find a good and, at least, near optimal solution.

FIGURE 16.10   SPREADSHEET SIMULATION FOR THE BUTLER INVENTORY PROBLEM

	A	B	C	D	E	F	G
1	**Butler Inventory**						
2							
3	Gross Profit per Unit		$50				
4	Holding Cost per Unit		$15				
5	Shortage Cost per Unit		$30				
6							
7	**Replenishment Level**		100				
8							
9	**Demand (Normal Distribution)**						
10	Mean	100					
11	Standard Dev	20					
12							
13							
14	**Simulation**						
15							
16	Month	Demand	Sales	Gross Profit	Holding Cost	Shortage Cost	Net Profit
17	1	79	79	$3,950	$315	$0	$3,635
18	2	111	100	$5,000	$0	$330	$4,670
19	3	93	93	$4,650	$105	$0	$4,545
20	4	100	100	$5,000	$0	$0	$5,000
21	5	118	100	$5,000	$0	$540	$4,460
312	296	89	89	$4,450	$165	$0	$4,285
313	297	91	91	$4,550	$135	$0	$4,415
314	298	122	100	$5,000	$0	$660	$4,340
315	299	93	93	$4,650	$105	$0	$4,545
316	300	126	100	$5,000	$0	$780	$4,220
317							
318	**Totals**	30,181	27,917		**Summary Statistics**		
319					Mean Profit		$4,293
320					Standard Deviation		$658
321					Minimum Profit		($206)
322					Maximum Profit		$5,000
323					Service Level		92.5%

TABLE 16.9   BUTLER INVENTORY SIMULATION RESULTS FOR 300 TRIALS

Replenishment Level	Average Net Profit ($)	Service Level (%)
100	4293	92.5
110	4524	96.5
120	4575	98.6
130	4519	99.6
140	4399	99.9

SIMULATION HELPS PETROLEUM DISTRIBUTION IN THE GULF OF MEXICO*

Domestic suppliers who operate oil refineries along the Gulf Coast are helping to satisfy Florida's increasing demand for refined petroleum products. Barge fleets, operated either by independent shipping companies or by the petroleum companies themselves, are used to transport more than 20 different petroleum products to 15 Florida petroleum companies. The petroleum products are loaded at refineries in Texas, Louisiana, and Mississippi, and are discharged at tank terminals concentrated in Tampa, Port Everglades, and Jacksonville.

Barges operate under three types of contracts between the fleet operator and the client petroleum company:

- The client assumes total control of a barge and uses it for trips between its own refinery and one or more discharging ports.
- The client is guaranteed a certain volume will be moved during the contract period. Schedules vary considerably depending upon the customer's needs and the fleet operator's capabilities.
- The client hires a barge for a single trip.

A simulation model was developed to analyze the complex process of operating barge fleets in the Gulf of Mexico. An appropriate probability distribution was used to simulate requests for shipments by the petroleum companies. Additional probability distributions were used to simulate the travel times depending upon the size and type of barge. Using this information, the simulation model was used to track barge loading times, barge discharge times, barge utilization, and total cost.

Analysts used simulation runs with a variety of what-if scenarios to answer questions about the petroleum distribution system and to make recommendations for improving the efficiency of the operation. Simulation helped determine the following:

- The optimal trade-off between fleet utilization and on-time delivery
- The recommended fleet size
- The recommended barge capacities
- The best service contract structure to balance the trade-off between customer service and delivery cost

Implementation of the simulation-based recommendations demonstrated a significant improvement in the operation and a significant lowering of petroleum distribution costs.

*Based on E. D. Chajakis, "Sophisticated Crude Transportation," *OR/MS Today* (December 1997): 30–34.

16.3 WAITING LINE SIMULATION

The simulation models discussed thus far have been based on independent trials in which the results for one trial do not affect what happens in subsequent trials. In this sense, the system being modeled does not change or evolve over time. Simulation models such as these are referred to as **static simulation models.** In this section, we develop a simulation model of a waiting line system where the state of the system, including the number of customers in the waiting line and whether the service facility is busy or idle, change or evolves over time. To incorporate time into the simulation model, we use a simulation clock to record the time that each customer arrives for service as well as the time that each customer completes service. Simulation models that must take into account how the system changes or evolves over time are referred to as **dynamic simulation models.** In situations where the arrivals and departures of customers are **events** that occur at *discrete* points in time, the simulation model is also referred to as a **discrete-event simulation model.**

In Chapter 15, we presented formulas that could be used to compute the steady-state operating characteristics of a waiting line, including the average waiting time, the average number of units in the waiting line, the probability of waiting, and so on. In most cases, the waiting line formulas were based on specific assumptions about the probability distribution for arrivals, the probability distribution for service times, the queue discipline, and so on. Simulation, as an alternative for studying waiting lines, is more flexible. In applications where the assumptions required by the waiting line formulas are not reasonable, simulation may be the only feasible approach to studying the waiting line system. In this section we discuss the simulation of the waiting line for the Hammondsport Savings Bank automated teller machine (ATM).

The Hammondsport Savings Bank ATM Waiting Line

Hammondsport Savings Bank will open several new branch banks during the coming year. Each new branch is designed to have one automated teller machine (ATM). A concern is that during busy periods several customers may have to wait to use the ATM. This concern has led the bank to undertake a study of the ATM waiting line system. The bank's vice-president wants to determine whether one ATM will be sufficient. The bank has established service guidelines for its ATM system stating that the average customer waiting time for an ATM should be one minute or less. Let us show how a simulation model can be used to study the ATM waiting line at a particular branch.

Customer Arrival Times

One probabilistic input to the ATM simulation model is the arrival times of customers who use the ATM. In waiting line simulations, arrival times are determined by randomly generating the time between two successive arrivals, referred to as the *interarrival time*. For the branch bank being studied, the customer interarrival times are assumed to be uniformly distributed between 0 and 5 minutes as shown in Figure 16.11. With r denoting a random number between 0 and 1, an interarrival time for two successive customers can be simulated by using the formula for generating values from a uniform probability distribution.

$$\text{Interarrival time} = a + r(b - a) \tag{16.7}$$

where

$$r = \text{random number between 0 and 1}$$
$$a = \text{minimum interarrival time}$$
$$b = \text{maximum interarrival time}$$

FIGURE 16.11   UNIFORM PROBABILITY DISTRIBUTION OF INTERARRIVAL TIMES
FOR THE ATM WAITING LINE SYSTEM

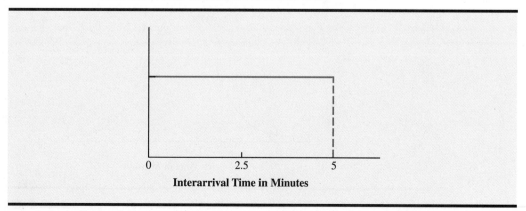

Interarrival Time in Minutes

A uniform probability distribution of interarrival times is used here to illustrate the simulation computations. Actually, any interarrival time probability distribution can be assumed, and the logic of the waiting line simulation model will not change.

For the Hammondsport ATM system, the minimum interarrival time is $a = 0$ minutes, and the maximum interarrival time is $b = 5$ minutes; therefore, the formula for generating an interarrival time is

$$\text{Interarrival time} = 0 + r(5 - 0) = 5r \qquad (16.8)$$

Assume that the simulation run begins at time $= 0$. A random number of $r = 0.2804$ generates an interarrival time of $5(0.2804) = 1.4$ minutes for customer 1. Thus, customer 1 arrives 1.4 minutes after the simulation run begins. A second random number of $r = 0.2598$ generates an interarrival time of $5(0.2598) = 1.3$ minutes, indicating that customer 2 arrives 1.3 minutes after customer 1. Thus, customer 2 arrives $1.4 + 1.3 = 2.7$ minutes after the simulation begins. Continuing, a third random number of $r = 0.9802$ indicates that customer 3 arrives 4.9 minutes after customer 2, which is 7.6 minutes after the simulation begins.

Customer Service Times

Another probabilistic input in the ATM simulation model is the service time, which is the time a customer spends using the ATM machine. Past data from similar ATMs indicates that a normal probability distribution with a mean of 2 minutes and a standard deviation of 0.5 minutes, as shown in Figure 16.12, can be used to describe service times. As discussed in Sections 16.1 and 16.2, values from a normal probability distribution with mean 2 and standard deviation 0.5 can be generated using the Excel function =NORMINV(RAND(),2,0.5). For example, the random number of 0.7257 generates a customer service time of 2.3 minutes.

Simulation Model

The probabilistic inputs to the Hammondsport Savings Bank ATM simulation model are the interarrival time and the service time. The controllable input is the number of ATMs used. The output will consist of various operating characteristics such as the probability of waiting, the average waiting time, the maximum waiting time, and so on. We show a diagram of the ATM simulation model in Figure 16.13.

FIGURE 16.12   NORMAL PROBABILITY DISTRIBUTION OF SERVICE TIMES FOR THE ATM WAITING LINE SYSTEM

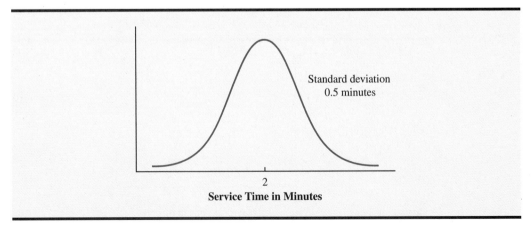

FIGURE 16.13   HAMMONDSPORT SAVINGS BANK ATM SIMULATION MODEL

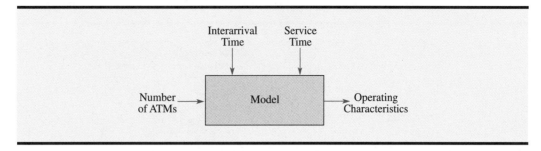

Figure 16.14 shows a flowchart that defines the sequence of logical and mathematical operations required to simulate the Hammondsport ATM system. The flowchart uses the following notation:

$$IAT = \text{Interarrival time generated}$$
$$\text{Arrival time } (i) = \text{Time at which customer } i \text{ arrives}$$
$$\text{Start time } (i) = \text{Time at which customer } i \text{ starts service}$$
$$\text{Wait time } (i) = \text{Waiting time for customer } i$$
$$ST = \text{Service time generated}$$
$$\text{Completion time } (i) = \text{Time at which customer } i \text{ completes service}$$
$$\text{System time } (i) = \text{System time for customer } i \text{ (completion time } - \text{ arrival time)}$$

Referring to Figure 16.14, we see that the simulation is initialized in the first block of the flowchart. Then a new customer is created. An interarrival time is generated to determine the time since the preceding customer arrived.[2] The arrival time for the new customer is then computed by adding the interarrival time to the arrival time of the preceding customer.

The arrival time for the new customer must be compared to the completion time of the preceding customer to determine whether the ATM is idle or busy. If the arrival time of the new customer is greater than the completion time of the preceding customer, the preceding customer will have finished service prior to the arrival of the new customer. In this case, the ATM will be idle, and the new customer can begin service immediately. The service start time for the new customer is equal to the arrival time of the new customer. However, if the arrival time for the new customer is not greater than the completion time of the preceding customer, the new customer has arrived before the preceding customer has finished service. In this case, the ATM is busy; the new customer must wait to use the ATM until the preceding customer has completed service. The service start time for the new customer is equal to the completion time of the preceding customer.

Note that the time the new customer has to wait to use the ATM is the difference between the customer's service start time and the customer's arrival time. At this point, the customer is ready to use the ATM, and the simulation run continues with the generation of the customer's service time. The time at which the customer begins service plus the service time generated determine the customer's completion time. Finally, the total time the customer spends in the system is the difference between the customer's service completion time and the customer's arrival time. At this point, the computations are complete for the

The decision rule for deciding whether the ATM is idle or busy is the most difficult aspect of the logic in a waiting line simulation model.

---

2. For the first customer, the interarrival time determines the time since the simulation started. Thus, the first interarrival time determines the time the first customer arrives.

FIGURE 16.14   FLOWCHART OF THE HAMMONDSPORT SAVINGS BANK ATM WAITING LINE
SIMULATION

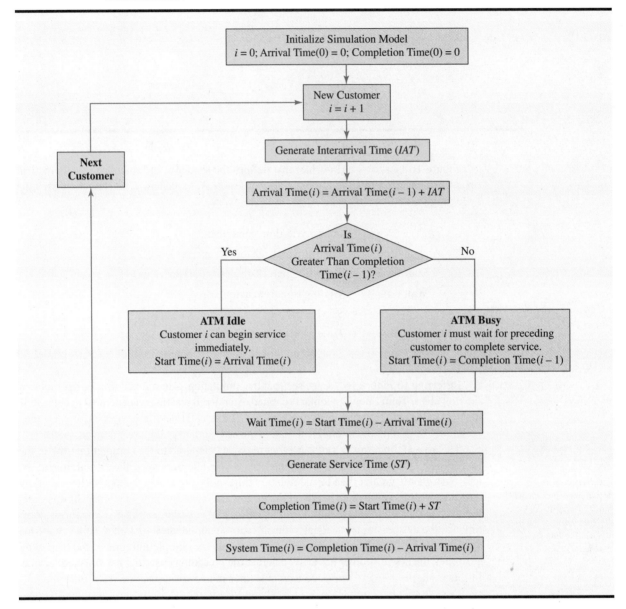

current customer, and the simulation continues with the next customer. The simulation is
continued until a specified number of customers have been served by the ATM.

Simulation results for the first ten customers are shown in Table 16.10. We discuss the
computations for the first 3 customers to illustrate the logic of the simulation model and to
show how the information in Table 16.10 was developed.

Customer 1

- An interarrival time of $IAT = 1.4$ minutes is generated.
- Because the simulation run begins at time 0, the arrival time for customer 1 is
  $0 + 1.4 = 1.4$ minutes.

- Customer 1 may begin service immediately with a start time of 1.4 minutes.
- The waiting time for customer 1 is the start time minus the arrival time: 1.4 − 1.4 = 0 minutes.
- A service time of ST = 2.3 minutes is generated for customer 1.
- The completion time for customer 1 is the start time plus the service time: 1.4 + 2.3 = 3.7 minutes.
- The time in the system for customer 1 is the completion time minus the arrival time: 3.7 − 1.4 = 2.3 minutes.

Customer 2

- An interarrival time of IAT = 1.3 minutes is generated.
- Because the arrival time of customer 1 is 1.4, the arrival time for customer 2 is 1.4 + 1.3 = 2.7 minutes.
- Because the completion time of customer 1 is 3.7 minutes, the arrival time of customer 2 is not greater than the completion time of customer 1; thus, the ATM is busy when customer 2 arrives.
- Customer 2 must wait for customer 1 to complete service before beginning service. Customer 1 completes service at 3.7 minutes, which becomes the start time for customer 2.
- The waiting time for customer 2 is the start time minus the arrival time: 3.7 − 2.7 = 1 minute.
- A service time of ST = 1.5 minutes is generated for customer 2.
- The completion time for customer 2 is the start time plus the service time: 3.7 + 1.5 = 5.2 minutes.
- The time in the system for customer 2 is the completion time minus the arrival time: 5.2 − 2.7 = 2.5 minutes.

Customer 3

- An interarrival time of IAT = 4.9 minutes is generated.
- Because the arrival time of customer 2 was 2.7 minutes, the arrival time for customer 3 is 2.7 + 4.9 = 7.6 minutes.

TABLE 16.10   SIMULATION RESULTS FOR TEN ATM CUSTOMERS

Customer	Interarrival Time	Arrival Time	Service Start Time	Wait Time	Service Time	Completion Time	Time in System
1	1.4	1.4	1.4	0.0	2.3	3.7	2.3
2	1.3	2.7	3.7	1.0	1.5	5.2	2.5
3	4.9	7.6	7.6	0.0	2.2	9.8	2.2
4	3.5	11.1	11.1	0.0	2.5	13.6	2.5
5	0.7	11.8	13.6	1.8	1.8	15.4	3.6
6	2.8	14.6	15.4	0.8	2.4	17.8	3.2
7	2.1	16.7	17.8	1.1	2.1	19.9	3.2
8	0.6	17.3	19.9	2.6	1.8	21.7	4.4
9	2.5	19.8	21.7	1.9	2.0	23.7	3.9
10	1.9	21.7	23.7	2.0	2.3	26.0	4.3
Totals	21.7			11.2	20.9		32.1
Averages	2.17			1.12	2.09		3.21

- The completion time of customer 2 is 5.2 minutes, so the arrival time for customer 3 is greater than the completion time of customer 2. Thus, the ATM is idle when customer 3 arrives.
- Customer 3 begins service immediately with a start time of 7.6 minutes.
- The waiting time for customer 3 is the start time minus the arrival time: $7.6 - 7.6 = 0$ minutes.
- A service time of $ST = 2.2$ minutes is generated for customer 3.
- The completion time for customer 3 is the start time plus the service time: $7.6 + 2.2 = 9.8$ minutes.
- The time in the system for customer 3 is the completion time minus the arrival time: $9.8 - 7.6 = 2.2$ minutes.

Using the totals in Table 16.10, we can compute an average waiting time for the 10 customers of $11.2/10 = 1.12$ minutes, and an average time in the system of $32.1/10 = 3.21$ minutes. Table 16.10 shows that seven of the ten customers had to wait. The total time for the ten-customer simulation is given by the completion time of the tenth customer: 26.0 minutes. However, at this point, we realize that a simulation for ten customers is much too short a period to draw any firm conclusions about the operation of the waiting line.

Simulation of the Hammondsport Savings Bank ATM Problem

Using an Excel spreadsheet, we simulated the operation of the Hammondsport ATM waiting line system for 1000 customers. The spreadsheet used to carry out the simulation is shown in Figure 16.15. Note that the simulation results for customers 6 through 995 have been hidden so that the results can be shown in a reasonably sized figure. If desired, the rows for these customers can be shown and the simulation results displayed for all 1000 customers.

Ultimately, summary statistics will be collected in order to describe the results of 1000 customers. Before collecting the summary statistics, let us point out that most simulation studies of dynamic systems focus on the operation of the system during its long-run or steady-state operation. To ensure that the effect of start-up conditions are not included in the steady-state calculations, a dynamic simulation model is usually run for a specified period without collecting any data about the operation of the system. The length of the startup period can vary depending on the application. For the Hammondsport Savings Bank ATM simulation, we treated the results for the first 100 customers as the start-up period. Thus, the summary statistics shown in Figure 16.15 are for the 900 customers arriving during the steady-state period.

The summary statistics show that 549 of the 900 Hammondsport customers had to wait. This result provides a $549/900 = 0.61$ probability that a customer will have to wait for service. Or, in other words, approximately 61% of the customers will have to wait because the ATM is in use. The average waiting time is 1.59 minutes per customer with at least one customer waiting the maximum time of 13.5 minutes. The utilization rate of 0.7860 indicates that the ATM is in use 78.6% of the time. Finally, 393 of the 900 customers had to wait more than 1 minute (43.67% of all customers). A histogram of waiting times for the 900 customers is shown in Figure 16.16. This figure shows that 45 customers (5%) had a waiting time greater than six minutes.

The simulation supports the conclusion that the branch will have a busy ATM system. With an average customer wait time of 1.59 minutes, the branch does not satisfy the bank's customer service guideline. This branch is a good candidate for installation of a second ATM.

FIGURE 16.15   SPREADSHEET SIMULATION OF THE HAMMONDSPORT SAVINGS BANK
WITH ONE ATM

	A	B	C	D	E	F	G	H
1	**Hammondsport Savings Bank with One ATM**							
2								
3	**Interarrival Times (Uniform Distribution)**							
4	Smallest Value	0						
5	Largest Value	5						
6								
7	**Service Times (Normal Distribution)**							
8	Mean	2						
9	Standard Dev	0.5						
10								
11								
12	**Simulation**							
13								
14		Interarrival	Arrival	Service	Wait	Service	Completion	Time
15	Customer	Time	Time	Start Time	Time	Time	Time	in System
16	1	1.4	1.4	1.4	0.0	2.3	3.7	2.3
17	2	1.3	2.7	3.7	1.0	1.5	5.2	2.5
18	3	4.9	7.6	7.6	0.0	2.2	9.8	2.2
19	4	3.5	11.1	11.1	0.0	2.5	13.6	2.5
20	5	0.7	11.8	13.6	1.8	1.8	15.4	3.6
1011	996	0.5	2496.8	2498.1	1.3	0.6	2498.7	1.9
1012	997	0.2	2497.0	2498.7	1.7	2.0	2500.7	3.7
1013	998	2.7	2499.7	2500.7	1.0	1.9	2502.5	2.8
1014	999	3.7	2503.4	2503.4	0.0	2.5	2505.8	2.5
1015	1000	4.1	2507.4	2507.4	0.0	1.9	2509.3	1.9
1016								
1017		**Summary Statistics**						
1018		Number Waiting			549			
1019		Probability of Waiting			0.6100			
1020		Average Wait Time			1.59			
1021		Maximum Wait Time			13.5			
1022		Utilization of ATM			0.7860			
1023		Number Waiting > 1 Min			393			
1024		Probability of Waiting > 1 Min			0.4367			

Simulation with Two ATMs

We extended the simulation model to the case of two ATMs. For the second ATM we
also assume that the service time is normally distributed with a mean of 2 minutes and
a standard deviation of 0.5 minutes. Table 16.11 shows the simulation results for the
first ten customers. In comparing the 2-ATM system results in Table 16.11 with the single
ATM simulation results shown in Table 16.10, we see that 2 additional columns are
needed. These two columns show when each ATM becomes available for customer
service. We assume that, when a new customer arrives, the customer will be served by

FIGURE 16.16 HISTOGRAM SHOWING THE WAITING TIME FOR 900 ATM CUSTOMERS

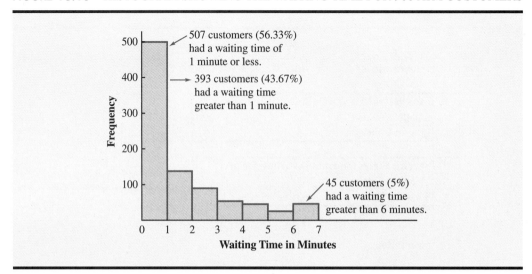

TABLE 16.11 SIMULATION RESULTS FOR TEN CUSTOMERS FOR A TWO-ATM SYSTEM

Customer	Interarrival Time	Arrival Time	Service Start Time	Wait Time	Service Time	Completion Time	Time in System	Time Available ATM 1	Time Available ATM 2
1	1.7	1.7	1.7	0.0	2.1	3.8	2.1	3.8	0.0
2	0.7	2.4	2.4	0.0	2.0	4.4	2.0	3.8	4.4
3	2.0	4.4	4.4	0.0	1.4	5.8	1.4	5.8	4.4
4	0.1	4.5	4.5	0.0	0.9	5.4	0.9	5.8	5.4
5	4.6	9.1	9.1	0.0	2.2	11.3	2.2	5.8	11.3
6	1.3	10.4	10.4	0.0	1.6	12.0	1.6	12.0	11.3
7	0.6	11.0	11.3	0.3	1.7	13.0	2.0	12.0	13.0
8	0.3	11.3	12.0	0.7	2.2	14.2	2.9	14.2	13.0
9	3.4	14.7	14.7	0.0	2.9	17.6	2.9	14.2	17.6
10	0.1	14.8	14.8	0.0	2.8	17.6	2.8	17.6	17.6
Totals	14.8			1.0	19.8		20.8		
Averages	1.48			0.1	1.98		2.08		

the ATM that frees up first. When the simulation begins, the first customer is assigned to ATM 1.

Table 16.11 shows that customer 7 is the first customer who has to wait to use an ATM. We describe how customers 6, 7, and 8 are processed to show how the logic of the simulation run for two ATMs differs from that with a single ATM.

Customer 6

- An interarrival time of 1.3 minutes is generated, and customer 6 arrives $9.1 + 1.3 = 10.4$ minutes into the simulation.
- From the customer 5 row, we see that ATM 1 frees up at 5.8 minutes, and ATM 2 will free up at 11.3 minutes into the simulation. Because ATM 1 is free, customer 6 does not wait and begins service on ATM 1 at the arrival time of 10.4 minutes.

- A service time of 1.6 minutes is generated for customer 6. So customer 6 has a completion time of $10.4 + 1.6 = 12.0$ minutes.
- The time ATM 1 will next become available is set at 12.0 minutes; the time available for ATM 2 remains 11.3 minutes.

Customer 7

- An interarrival time of 0.6 minutes is generated, and customer 7 arrives $10.4 + 0.6 = 11.0$ minutes into the simulation.
- From the previous row, we see that ATM 1 will not be available until 12.0 minutes, and ATM 2 will not be available until 11.3 minutes. So customer 7 must wait to use an ATM. Because ATM 2 will free up first, customer 7 begins service on that machine at a start time of 11.3 minutes. With an arrival time of 11.0 and a service start time of 11.3, customer 7 experiences a waiting time of $11.3 - 11.0 = 0.3$ minutes.
- A service time of 1.7 minutes is generated leading to a completion time of $11.3 + 1.7 = 13.0$ minutes.
- The time available for ATM 2 is updated to 13.0 minutes, and the time available for ATM 1 remains at 12.0 minutes.

Customer 8

- An interarrival time of 0.3 minutes is generated, and customer 8 arrives $11.0 + 0.3 = 11.3$ minutes into the simulation.
- From the previous row, we see that ATM 1 will be the first available. Thus, customer 8 starts service on ATM 1 at 12.0 minutes resulting in a waiting time of $12.0 - 11.3 = 0.7$ minutes.
- A service time of 2.2 minutes is generated resulting in a completion time of $12.0 + 2.2 = 14.2$ minutes and a system time of $0.7 + 2.2 = 2.9$ minutes.
- The time available for ATM 1 is updated to 14.2 minutes, and the time available for ATM 2 remains at 13.0 minutes.

From the totals in Table 16.11, we see that the average waiting time for these ten customers is only $1.0/10 = 0.1$ minutes. Of course, a much longer simulation will be necessary before any conclusions can be drawn.

Simulation Results with Two ATMs

The Excel spreadsheet that we used to conduct a simulation for 1000 customers is shown in Figure 16.17. Results for the first 100 customers were discarded to account for the start-up period. With 2 ATMs, the number of customers who had to wait was reduced from 549 to 78. This reduction provides a $78/900 = 0.0867$ probability that a customer will have to wait for service when 2 ATMs are used. The 2-ATM system also reduced the average wait time to 0.07 minutes (4.2 seconds) per customer. The maximum wait time was reduced from 13.5 to 2.9 minutes, and each ATM was in use 40.84% of the time. Finally, only 23 of the 900 customers had to wait more than 1 minute for an ATM to become available. Thus, only 2.56% of customers had to wait more than one minute. The simulation results provide evidence that Hammondsport Savings Bank needs to expand to the 2-ATM system.

The simulation models that we have developed can now be used to study the ATM operation at other branch banks. In each case, assumptions must be made about the appropriate interarrival time and service time probability distributions. However, once appropriate assumptions have been made, the same simulation models can be used to determine the operating characteristics of the ATM waiting line system. The IBM and Air Canada simulation model described in the Q. M. in Action possesses many of the same characteristics associated with the ATM simulation models that we developed in this section.

FIGURE 16.17 SPREADSHEET SIMULATION OF THE HAMMONDSPORT SAVINGS BANK WITH 2 ATMs

	A	B	C	D	E	F	G	H	I	J
1	**Hammondsport Savings Bank with Two ATMs**									
2										
3	**Interarrival Times (Uniform Distribution)**									
4	Smallest Value	0								
5	Largest Value	5								
6										
7	**Service Times (Normal Distribution)**									
8	Mean	2								
9	Standard Dev	0.5								
10										
11										
12	**Simulation**									
13										
14		Interarrival	Arrival	Service	Wait	Service	Completion	Time	Time Available	
15	Customer	Time	Time	Start Time	Time	Time	Time	in System	ATM 1	ATM 2
16	1	1.7	1.7	1.7	0.0	2.1	3.8	2.1	3.8	0.0
17	2	0.7	2.4	2.4	0.0	2.0	4.4	2.0	3.8	4.4
18	3	2.0	4.4	4.4	0.0	1.4	5.8	1.4	5.8	4.4
19	4	0.1	4.5	4.5	0.0	0.9	5.4	0.9	5.8	5.4
20	5	4.6	9.1	9.1	0.0	2.2	11.3	2.2	5.8	11.3
1011	996	3.3	2483.2	2483.2	0.0	2.2	2485.4	2.2	2485.4	2482.1
1012	997	4.5	2487.7	2487.7	0.0	1.9	2489.6	1.9	2485.4	2489.6
1013	998	3.7	2491.5	2491.5	0.0	3.2	2494.7	3.2	2494.7	2489.6
1014	999	0.0	2491.5	2491.5	0.0	2.4	2493.9	2.4	2494.7	2493.9
1015	1000	2.6	2494.1	2494.1	0.0	2.8	2496.9	2.8	2494.7	2496.9
1016										
1017		**Summary Statistics**								
1018		Number Waiting			78					
1019		Probability of Waiting			0.0867					
1020		Average Wait Time			0.07					
1021		Maximum Wait Time			2.9					
1022		Utilization of ATMs			0.4084					
1023		Number Waiting > 1 Min			23					
1024		Probability of Waiting > 1 Min			0.0256					

NOTES AND COMMENTS

1. The ATM waiting line model was based on uniformly distributed interarrival times and normally distributed service times. One advantage of simulation is its flexibility in accommodating a variety of different probability distributions. For instance, if we believe an exponential distribution is more appropriate for interarrival times, the ATM simulation could be repeated by simply changing the way the interarrival times are generated.

2. At the beginning of this section, we defined *discrete-event simulation* as involving a dynamic system that evolves over time. The simulation computations focus on the sequence of events as they occur at discrete points in time. In the ATM waiting line ex-

ample, customer arrivals and the customer service completions were the discrete events. Referring to the arrival times and completion times in Table 16.10, we see that the first 5 discrete events for the ATM waiting line simulation were as follows:

Event	Description	Time Event Occurred
1	Customer 1 arrives	1.4
2	Customer 2 arrives	2.7
3	Customer 1 completes service	3.7
4	Customer 2 completes service	5.2
5	Customer 3 arrives	7.6

3. We did not keep track of the number of customers in the ATM waiting line as we carried out the ATM simulation computations on a customer-by-customer basis. However, we can determine the average number of customers in the waiting line from other information in the simulation output. The following relationship is valid for any waiting line system:

$$\frac{\text{Average number}}{\text{in waiting line}} = \frac{\text{Total waiting time}}{\text{Total time of simulation}}$$

For the system with 1 ATM, the 100th customer completed service at 247.8 minutes into the simulation. Thus, the total time of the simulation for the next 900 customers was $2509.3 - 247.8 = 2261.5$ minutes. The average wait time was 1.59 minutes. During the simulation, the 900 customers had a total wait time of $900(1.59) = 1431$ minutes. Therefore, the average number of customers in the waiting line is

$$\text{Average number in waiting line} = 1431/2261.5$$
$$= 0.63 \text{ customers}$$

Q. M. IN ACTION

IBM SIMULATION MODEL HELPS IMPROVE CUSTOMER SERVICE FOR AIR CANADA*

IBM and Air Canada formed a partnership to develop a simulation model of Air Canada's domestic passenger process at the Toronto airport. Specifically, the simulation model is being used to track the flow of passengers from arrival at the airport terminal to final boarding. Simulated passengers move through activities including ticketing, coach passenger check-in, first-class passenger check-in, special assistance services (e.g., wheelchairs, unaccompanied minors, oversized baggage, pets), and the final boarding process at the gate.

The airline flight schedule is used to determine passenger arrivals at the airport. Each passenger entity is assigned an airport terminal appearance time based on the distribution of arrival times prior to the flight's scheduled departure. Based on appropriate statistical information about the percentage of passengers in each category, a passenger is identified as being business or leisure, domestic or regional, and originating or connecting. These passenger attributes vary with the time of day. Given the set of arriving passengers, the logic of the simulation model tracks flow of the passengers through the Air Canada system.

Multiple simulation runs have been used to forecast passenger service performance measures including peak and average wait times, peak and average number of passengers waiting in line, and Air Canada's resource utilization. Simulation results have identified passenger flow bottlenecks during the ticketing process and during the coach check-in process. A detailed analysis showed that excessive wait times were occurring during a one-hour period in the morning. This information gave Air Canada a better understanding of its passenger flow process and identified areas where new technology and/or additional agents could be employed to improve the efficiency of the operation.

The simulation model is flexible in that it can be used to support what-if analysis. For example, what if a passenger self-ticketing booth were added, what if a passenger seat selection booth were added, what if advanced electronic ticketing were increased, and/or what if Air Canada agent schedules were modified. These what-if simulation runs help identify the best strategies for improving the passenger flow performance measures. In addition, the simulation model can be easily modified to simulate the passenger process at other airports.

*Based on P. Bitauld, K. Burch, S. El-Taji, E. Fanucchi, M. Montevecchi, J. Ohlsson, A. Palella, R. Rushmeier, and J. Snowdon, "Journey Management," *OR/MS Today* (October 1997): 30–33.

16.4   OTHER SIMULATION ISSUES

Because simulation is one of the most widely used quantitative analysis techniques, various software tools have been developed to help analysts implement a simulation model on a computer. In this section we comment on the software available and discuss some issues involved in verifying and validating a simulation model. We close the section with a discussion of some of the advantages and disadvantages of using simulation to study a real system.

Computer Implementation

The use of spreadsheets for simulation has grown rapidly in recent years, and third-party software vendors have developed spreadsheet add-ins that make building simulation models on a spreadsheet much easier. These add-in packages provide an easy facility for generating random values from a variety of probability distributions and provide a rich array of statistics describing the simulation output. Two popular spreadsheet add-ins are Crystal Ball from Decisioneering and @RISK from Palisade Corporation. Although spreadsheets can be a valuable tool for some simulation studies, they are generally limited to smaller, less complex systems.

With the growth of simulation applications, both users of simulation and software developers began to realize that computer simulations have many common features: model development, generating values from probability distributions, maintaining a record of what happens during the simulation, and recording and summarizing the simulation output. A variety of special-purpose simulation packages are available, including GPSS®, SIMSCRIPT®, SLAM®, and Arena®. These packages have built-in simulation clocks, simplified methods for generating probabilistic inputs, and procedures for collecting and summarizing the simulation output. Special-purpose simulation packages enable management scientists to simplify the process of developing and implementing the simulation model.

Simulation models can also be developed using general-purpose computer programming languages such as BASIC, FORTRAN, PASCAL, C, and C++. The disadvantage of using these languages is that special simulation procedures are not built in. One command in a special-purpose simulation package often performs the computations and record-keeping tasks that would require several BASIC, FORTRAN, PASCAL, C, or C++ statements to duplicate. The advantage of using a general-purpose programming language is that they offer greater flexibility in terms of being able to model more complex systems.

The computational and record-keeping aspects of simulation models are assisted by special simulation software packages. The packages ease the tasks of developing a computer simulation model.

To decide which software to use, an analyst will have to consider the relative merits of a spreadsheet, a special-purpose simulation package, and a general-purpose computer programming language. The goal is to select the method that is easy to use while still providing an adequate representation of the system being studied.

Verification and Validation

An important aspect of any simulation study involves confirming that the simulation model accurately describes the real system. Inaccurate simulation models cannot be expected to provide worthwhile information. Thus, before using simulation results to draw conclusions about a real system, one must take steps to verify and validate the simulation model.

Verification is the process of determining that the computer procedure that performs the simulation calculations is logically correct. Verification is largely a debugging task to make sure that no errors are in the computer procedure that implements the simulation. In some cases, an analyst may compare computer results for a limited number of events with independent hand calculations. In other cases, tests may be performed to verify that the probabilistic inputs are being generated correctly and that the output from the simulation model seems reasonable. The verification step is not complete until the user has developed a high degree of confidence that the computer procedure is error free.

Validation is the process of ensuring that the simulation model provides an accurate representation of a real system. Validation requires an agreement among analysts and managers that the logic and the assumptions used in the design of the simulation model accurately reflect how the real system operates. The first phase of the validation process is done prior to, or in conjunction with, the development of the computer procedure for the simulation process. Validation continues after the computer program has been developed with the analyst reviewing the simulation output to see whether the simulation results closely approximate the performance of the real system. If possible, the output of the simulation model is compared to the output of an existing real system to make sure that the simulation output closely approximates the performance of the real system. If this form of validation is not possible, an analyst can experiment with the simulation model and have one or more individuals experienced with the operation of the real system review the simulation output to determine whether it is a reasonable approximation of what would be obtained with the real system under similar conditions.

Verification and validation are not tasks to be taken lightly. They are key steps in any simulation study and are necessary to ensure that decisions and conclusions based on the simulation results are appropriate for the real system.

Advantages and Disadvantages of Using Simulation

The primary advantages of simulation are that it is easy to understand and that the methodology can be used to model and learn about the behavior of complex systems that would be difficult, if not impossible, to deal with analytically. Simulation models are flexible; they can be used to describe systems without requiring the assumptions that are often required by mathematical models. In general, the larger the number of probabilistic inputs a system has, the more likely that a simulation model will provide the best approach for studying the system. Another advantage of simulation is that a simulation model provides a convenient experimental laboratory for the real system. Changing assumptions or operating policies in the simulation model and rerunning it can provide results that help predict how such changes will affect the operation of the real system. Experimenting directly with a real system is often not feasible.

Using simulation, we can ask what-if questions and project how the real system will behave. Although simulation does not guarantee optimality, it will usually provide near-optimal solutions. In addition, simulation models often warn against poor decision strategies by projecting disastrous outcomes such as system failures, large financial losses, and so on.

Simulation is not without some disadvantages. For complex systems, the process of developing, verifying, and validating a simulation model can be time-consuming and expensive. In addition, each simulation run only provides a sample of how the real system will operate. As such, the summary of the simulation data only provides estimates or approximations about the real system. Consequently, simulation does not guarantee an optimal solution. Nonetheless, the danger of obtaining poor solutions is slight if the analyst exercises good judgment in developing the simulation model and if the simulation process is run long enough under a wide variety of conditions so that the analyst has sufficient data to predict how the real system will operate.

SIMULATION AT MEXICO'S VILPAC TRUCK COMPANY*

In increasing numbers, U.S. firms are joining diverse geographical and cultural partners in Western Europe, Asia, and Mexico to capitalize on each other's advantages and remain competitive in world markets. Mexico, the United States' third largest trading partner, offers a unique opportunity for integrating manufacturing operations. For example, Mexican and U.S. firms have been working together to turn the Mexican truck company, Vilpac, into a world-class manufacturing firm.

The selection of manufacturing configurations and the design of new plants at Vilpac are being guided by a simulation model of the firm's manufacturing operations. A network simulation language, SIMNET II®, has been used to model the manufacturing system that comprises some 95 machines and 1900 parts. Various simulation runs were used to validate the model. When applied to a plant that was producing 20 trucks per day, the simulation model accurately predicted production at 19.8 trucks per day.

The three interrelated modules of the simulation model include operations, corrective maintenance, and preventive maintenance. Various components of the model include capabilities for handling changes in customer demand, manufacturing cost, capacity, and work-in-process and inventory levels. Experimentation with the model investigated capacity requirements, product-mix effects, new products, inventory policies, product flow, setup times, production planning and control strategies, plant expansion, and new plant design. Tangible benefits include an increase in production of 260%, a reduction in work-in-process of 70%, and an increase in market share.

*Based on J. P. Nuno, D. L. Shunk, J. M. Padillo, and B. Beltran, "Mexico's Vilpac Truck Company Uses a CIM Implementation to Become a World Class Manufacturer," *Interfaces* no. 1 (January–February 1993): 59–75.

SUMMARY

Simulation is a method for learning about a real system by experimenting with a model that represents the system. Some of the reasons simulation is frequently used are:

1. It can be used for a wide variety of practical problems.
2. The simulation approach is relatively easy to explain and understand. As a result, management confidence is increased, and acceptance of the results is more easily obtained.
3. Spreadsheet packages now provide another alternative for model implementation, and third-party vendors have developed add-ins that expand the capabilities of the spreadsheet packages.
4. Computer software developers have produced simulation packages that make it easier to develop and implement simulation models for more complex problems.

We first showed how simulation can be used for risk analysis by analyzing a situation involving the development of a new product: the PortaCom printer. We then showed how simulation can be used to select an inventory replenishment level that would provide both a good profit and a good customer service level. Finally, we developed a simulation model for the Hammondsport Savings Bank ATM waiting line system. This model is an example of a dynamic simulation model in which the state of the system changes or evolves over time.

Our approach was to develop a simulation model that contained both controllable inputs and probabilistic inputs. Procedures were developed for randomly generating values for the probabilistic inputs, and a flowchart was developed to show the sequence of logical and mathematical operations that describe the steps of the simulation process. Simulation results were obtained by running the simulation for a suitable number of trials or length of time. Simulation results were obtained and conclusions were drawn about the operation of the real system.

GLOSSARY

Simulation   A method for learning about a real system by experimenting with a model that represents the system.

Simulation experiment   The generation of a sample of values for the probabilistic inputs of a simulation model and computing the resulting values of the model outputs.

Controllable input   Input to a simulation model that is selected by the decision maker.

Probabilistic input   Input to a simulation model that is subject to uncertainty. A probabilistic input is described by a probability distribution.

Risk analysis   The process of predicting the outcome of a decision in the face of uncertainty.

Parameters   Numerical values that appear in the mathematical relationships of a model. Parameters are considered known and remain constant over all trials of a simulation.

What-if analysis   A trial-and-error approach to learning about the range of possible outputs for a model. Trial values are chosen for the model inputs (these are the what-ifs) and the value of the output(s) is computed.

Base-case scenario   Determining the output given the most likely values for the probabilistic inputs of a model.

Worst-case scenario   Determining the output given the worst values that can be expected for the probabilistic inputs of a model.

Best-case scenario   Determining the output given the best values that can be expected for the probabilistic inputs of a model.

Static simulation model   A simulation model used in situations where the state of the system at one point in time does not affect the state of the system at future points in time. Each trial of the simulation is independent.

Dynamic simulation model   A simulation model used in situations where the state of the system affects how the system changes or evolves over time.

Event   An instantaneous occurrence that changes the state of the system in a simulation model.

Discrete-event simulation model   A simulation model that describes how a system evolves over time by using events that occur at discrete points in time.

Verification   The process of determining that a computer program implements a simulation model as it is intended.

Validation   The process of determining that a simulation model provides an accurate representation of a real system.

PROBLEMS

Note: Problems 1–12 are designed to give you practice in setting up a simulation model and demonstrating how random numbers can be used to generate values for the probabilistic inputs. These problems, which ask you to provide a small number of simulation trials, can be done with hand calculations. This approach should give you a good understanding of the simulation process, but the simulation results will not be sufficient for you to draw final conclusions or make decisions about the situation. Problems 13–24 are more realistic in that they ask you to generate simulation output(s) for a large number of trials and use the results to draw conclusions about the behavior of the system being studied. These problems require the use of a computer to carry out the simulation computations. The ability to use Excel or some other spreadsheet package will be necessary when you attempt Problems 13–24.

1. Consider the PortaCom project discussed in Section 16.1
   a. An engineer on the product development team believes that first-year sales for the new printer will be 20,000 units. Using estimates of $45 per unit for the direct labor cost and $90 per unit for the parts cost, what is the first-year profit using the engineer's sales estimate?
   b. The financial analyst on the product development team is more conservative, indicating that parts cost may well be $100 per unit. In addition, the analyst suggests that a sales volume of 10,000 units is more realistic. Using the most likely value of $45 per unit for the direct labor cost, what is the first-year profit using the financial analyst's estimates?
   c. Why is the simulation approach to risk analysis preferable to generating a variety of what-if scenarios such as those suggested by the engineer and the financial analyst?

SELFtest

2. The management of Madeira Manufacturing Company is considering the introduction of a new product. The fixed cost to begin the production of the product is $30,000. The variable cost for the product is expected to be between $16 and $24 with a most likely value of $20 per unit. The product will sell for $50 per unit. Demand for the product is expected to range from 300 to 2100 units, with 1200 units the most likely demand.
   a. Develop the profit model for this product.
   b. Provide the base-case, worst-case, and best-case analyses.
   c. Discuss why simulation would be desirable.

3. Use the random numbers 0.3753, 0.9218, 0.0336, 0.5145, 0.7000 to generate five simulated values for the PortaCom direct labor cost per unit.

4. A retail store experiences the following probability distribution for sales of a product.

Sales (units)	0	1	2	3	4	5	6
Probability	0.08	0.12	0.28	0.24	0.14	0.10	0.04

   a. Set up intervals of random numbers that can be used to simulate sales.
   b. Random numbers generated for the first 10 days of a simulation are as follows: 0.4627, 0.8745, 0.4479, 0.6712, 0.4557, 0.8435, 0.2162, 0.1699, 0.1338, 0.2278. What is the sales value generated for each day?
   c. What are the total sales over the 10-day period?

SELFtest

5. The price of a share of a particular stock listed on the New York Stock Exchange is currently $39. The following probability distribution shows how the price per share is expected to change over a three-month period.

Stock Price Change ($)	Probability
−2	0.05
−1	0.10
0	0.25
+1	0.20
+2	0.20
+3	0.10
+4	0.10

   a. Set up intervals of random numbers that can be used to generate the change in stock price over a three-month period.

b. With the current price of $39 per share and the random numbers 0.1091, 0.9407, 0.1941, and 0.8083, simulate the price per share for the next four 3-month periods. What is the ending simulated price per share?

6. The Statewide Auto Insurance Company has developed the following probability distribution for automobile collision claims paid during the past year.

Payment($)	Probability
0	0.83
500	0.06
1,000	0.05
2,000	0.02
5,000	0.02
8,000	0.01
10,000	0.01

a. Set up intervals of random numbers that can be used to generate automobile collision claim payments.

b. Using the first 20 random numbers in column 4 of Table 16.2, simulate the payments for 20 policyholders. How many claims are paid and what is the total amount paid to the policyholders?

7. A variety of routine maintenance checks are made on commercial airplanes prior to each takeoff. A particular maintenance check of an airplane's landing gear requires between 10 and 18 minutes of a maintenance engineer's time. In fact, the exact time required is uniformly distributed over this interval. As part of a larger simulation model designed to determine total on-ground maintenance time for an airplane, we will need to simulate the actual time required to perform this maintenance check on the airplane's landing gear. Using random numbers of 0.1567, 0.9823, 0.3419, 0.5572, and 0.7758, compute the time required for each of five simulated maintenance checks of the airplane's landing gear.

8. Baseball's World Series is a maximum of 7 games, with the winner being the first team to win 4 games. Assume that the Atlanta Braves are in the World Series and that the first 2 games are to be played in Atlanta, the next 3 games at the opponent's ball park, and the last 2 games, if necessary, back in Atlanta. Taking into account the projected starting pitchers for each game and the homefield advantage, the probabilities of Atlanta winning each game are as follows:

Game	1	2	3	4	5	6	7
Probability of Win	0.60	0.55	0.48	0.45	0.48	0.55	0.50

a. Set up random number intervals that can be used to determine the winner of each game. Let the smaller random numbers indicate that Atlanta wins the game. For example, the random number interval "0.00 but less than 0.60" corresponds to Atlanta winning game 1.

b. Use the random numbers in column 6 of Table 16.2 beginning with 0.3813 to simulate the playing of the World Series. Do the Atlanta Braves win the series? How many games are played?

c. Discuss how repeated simulation trials could be used to estimate the overall probability of Atlanta winning the series as well as the most likely number of games in the series.

SELFtest 9. A project has four activities (A, B, C, and D) that must be performed sequentially. The probability distributions for the time required to complete each of the activities are as follows:

Activity	Activity Time (weeks)	Probability
A	5	0.25
	6	0.35
	7	0.25
	8	0.15
B	3	0.20
	5	0.55
	7	0.25
C	10	0.10
	12	0.25
	14	0.40
	16	0.20
	18	0.05
D	8	0.60
	10	0.40

a. Provide the base-case, worst-case, and best-case calculations for the time to complete the project.

b. Use the random numbers 0.1778, 0.9617, 0.6849, and 0.4503 to simulate the completion time of the project in weeks.

c. Discuss how simulation could be used to estimate the probability the project can be completed in 35 weeks or less.

10. Larkin Corporation conducted a test designed to evaluate the effectiveness of a new television advertisement for one of its household products. The particular television advertisement was shown in a test market for a two-week period. In a follow-up study, randomly selected individuals were contacted by telephone and asked a series of questions to determine whether they could recall the message in the television advertisement and how likely they were to purchase the product. The test market study provided the following probabilities.

Individual could recall the message   0.40

Individual could not recall the message   0.60

Response to the question of how likely they were to purchase the product provided the following probabilities.

Recall Response	Purchase Response		
	Definitely No	**Uncertain**	**Definitely Yes**
Could recall message	0.30	0.30	0.40
Could not recall message	0.50	0.40	0.10

a. Set up intervals of random numbers that can be used to determine whether a sampled individual could recall the message and then how the individual responded to the purchase question.

b. Use the following pairs of random numbers to simulate the results for three sampled individuals: individual 1 (0.5521, 0.6318), individual 2 (0.2189, 0.8432), individual 3

(0.3812, 0.1831). Which individual, if any, answered "definitely yes" to the purchase question?

c. Discuss how a large number of simulation trials could be used to estimate the overall probability of an individual answering "definitely yes" to the likelihood of purchase question.

11. A bowler has the following probability distribution for the number of pins knocked over on the first ball thrown.

Number of Pins	Probability
7	0.12
8	0.15
9	0.18
10	0.55

The probability distributions for the number of pins on the second ball are as follows:

First-Ball Pins	Second-Ball Pins			
	0	1	2	3
7	0.02	0.10	0.45	0.43
8	0.04	0.20	0.76	
9	0.06	0.94		

a. Set up intervals of random numbers that can be used to generate the number of pins knocked over on each ball.

b. The first two random numbers in column 6 of Table 16.2 are 0.3813 and 0.2159. Use these to simulate what the bowler did on the first two balls rolled.

c. Assume that the results in part (b) are for the first bowling frame. If you know how bowling scores are computed, continue to use the random numbers in Table 16.2 to compute the bowler's score for a full 10-frame game. The bowler's opponent rolled a 206 game. Did the simulated bowler beat the opponent?

12. The management of Brinkley Corporation is interested in using simulation to estimate the profit per unit for a new product. Probability distributions for the purchase cost, the labor cost, and the transportation cost are as follows:

Purchase Cost ($)	Probability	Labor Cost ($)	Probability	Transportation Cost ($)	Probability
10	0.25	20	0.10	3	0.75
11	0.45	22	0.25	5	0.25
12	0.30	24	0.35		
		25	0.30		

Assume that these are the only costs and that the selling price for the product will be $45 per unit.

a. Provide the base-case, worst-case, and best-case calculations for the profit per unit.

b. Set up intervals of random numbers that can be used to randomly generate the three cost components.

    c. Using the random numbers 0.3726, 0.5839 and 0.8275, calculate the profit per unit.

    d. Using the random numbers 0.1862, 0.7466, and 0.6171, calculate the profit per unit.

    e. Management believes the project may not be profitable if the profit per unit is less than $5. Explain how simulation can be used to estimate the probability the profit per unit will be less than $5.

13. Using the PortaCom Risk Analysis spreadsheet in Figure 16.6, develop your own spreadsheet for the PortaCom simulation model.

    a. Compute the mean profit, the minimum profit, and the maximum profit.

    b. What is your estimate of the probability of a loss?

SELFtest   14. Develop a spreadsheet simulation for the following problem. The management of Madeira Manufacturing Company is considering the introduction of a new product. The fixed cost to begin the production of the product is $30,000. The variable cost for the product is uniformly distributed between $16 and $24 per unit. The product will sell for $50 per unit. Demand for the product is best described by a normal probability distribution with a mean of 1200 units and a standard deviation of 300 units. Use a spreadsheet simulation similar to Figure 16.6. Use 500 simulation trials to answer the following questions.

    a. What is the mean profit for the simulation?

    b. What is the probability the project will result in a loss?

    c. What is your recommendation concerning the introduction of the product?

15. Use a spreadsheet to simulate the rolling of dice. Use the VLOOKUP function as described in Appendix 16.1 to select the outcome for each die. Place the number for the first die in column B and the number for the second die in column C. Show the sum in column D. Repeat the simulation for 1000 rolls of the dice. What is your simulation estimate of the probability of rolling a 7?

16. Based on experience, the time required to complete a college statistics exam is normally distributed with a mean of 42 minutes and a standard deviation of 8 minutes. A class has 70 students. Use a spreadsheet to simulate the exam completion times for 70 students. How many students are still working when the professor stops the exam at 50 minutes?

17. Grear Tire Company has produced a new tire with an estimated mean lifetime mileage of 36,500 miles. Management also believes that the standard deviation is 5000 miles and that tire mileage is normally distributed. Use a spreadsheet to simulate the miles obtained for a sample of 500 tires.

    a. Use the Excel COUNTIF function to determine the number of tires that last longer than 40,000 miles. What is your estimate of the percentage of tires that will exceed 40,000 miles?

    b. Use COUNTIF to find the number of tires that obtain mileage less than 32,000 miles. Then, find the number with less than 30,000 miles and the number with less than 28,000 miles.

    c. If management would like to advertise a tire mileage guarantee such that approximately no more than 10% of the tires would obtain mileage low enough to qualify for the guarantee, what tire mileage considered in part (b) would you recommend for the guarantee?

SELFtest   18. A building contractor is preparing a bid on a new construction project. Two other contractors will be submitting bids for the same project. Based on past bidding practices, bids from the other contractors can be described by the following probability distributions:

Contractor	Probability Distribution of Bid
A	Uniform probability distribution between $600,000 and $800,000
B	Normal probability distribution with a mean bid of $700,000 and a standard deviation of $50,000

a. If the building contractor submits a bid of $750,000, what is the probability the building contractor will obtain the bid? Use a spreadsheet to simulate 1000 trials of the contract bidding process.

b. The building contractor is also considering bids of $775,000 and $785,000. If the building contractor would like to bid such that the probability of winning the bid is about 0.80, what bid would you recommend? Repeat the simulation process with bids of $775,000 and $785,000 to justify your recommendation.

19. Develop your own spreadsheet for the Butler inventory simulation model shown in Figure 16.10. Suppose that management prefers not to charge for loss of goodwill. Run the Butler inventory simulation model with replenishment levels of 110, 115, 120, and 125. What is your recommendation?

20. In preparing for the upcoming holiday season, Mandrell Toy Company has designated a new doll called Freddy. The fixed cost to produce the doll is $100,000. The variable cost, which includes material, labor, and shipping costs, is $34 per doll. During the holiday selling season, Mandrell will sell the dolls for $42 each. If Mandrell overproduces the dolls, the excess dolls will be sold in January through a distributor who has agreed to pay Mandrell $10 per doll. Demand for new toys during the holiday selling season is extremely uncertain. Forecasts are for expected sales of 60,000 dolls with a standard deviation of 15,000. The normal probability distribution is assumed to be a good description of the demand.

a. Create a spreadsheet similar to the inventory spreadsheet in Figure 16.10. Include columns showing demand, sales, revenue from sales, amount of surplus, revenue from sales of surplus, total cost, and net profit. Use your spreadsheet to simulate the sales of the Freddy doll using a production quantity of 60,000 units. Using 500 simulation trials, what is the estimate of the mean profit associated with the production quantity of 60,000 dolls?

b. Before making a final decision on the production quantity, management has requested an analysis of a more aggressive 70,000 unit production quantity and a more conservative 50,000 unit production quantity. Run your simulation with these two production quantities. What is the mean profit associated with each? What is your recommendation on the production of the Freddy doll?

c. Assuming that Mandrell's management adopts your recommendation, what is the probability of a stockout and a shortage of the Freddy dolls during the holiday season?

21. South Central Airlines operates a commuter flight between Atlanta and Charlotte. The plane holds 30 passengers, and the airline makes a $100 profit on each passenger on the flight. When South Central takes 30 reservations for the flight, experience has shown an average of 2 passengers do not show up. As a result, with 30 reservations, South Central is averaging 28 passengers with a profit of 28(100) = $2800 per flight. The airline operations office has asked for an evaluation of an overbooking strategy where they would accept 32 reservations even though the airplane holds only 30 passengers. The probability distribution for the number of passengers showing up when 32 reservations are accepted is as follows.

Passengers Showing Up	Probability
28	0.05
29	0.25
30	0.50
31	0.15
32	0.05

The airline will receive a profit of $100 for each passenger on the flight up to the capacity of 30 passengers. The airline will incur a cost for any passenger denied seating on the flight. This cost covers added expenses of rescheduling the passenger as well as loss of goodwill, estimated to be $150 per passenger. Develop a spreadsheet model that will simulate the performance of the overbooking system. Simulate the number of passengers showing up for each of 500 flights by using the VLOOKUP function. Use the results to compute the profit for each flight.

a. Does your simulation recommend the overbooking strategy? What is the mean profit per flight if overbooking is implemented?

b. Explain how your simulation model can be used to evaluate other overbooking levels such as 31, 33, 34 and ultimately recommending a best overbooking strategy.

22. Develop your own waiting line simulation model for the Hammondsport Savings Bank problem (see Figure 16.15). Assume that a new branch is expected to open with interarrival times uniformly distributed between 0 and 4 minutes. The service times at this branch are anticipated to be normal with a mean of 2 minutes and a standard deviation of 0.5 minutes. Simulate the operation of this system for 600 customers using one ATM. What is your assessment of the ability to operate this branch with one ATM? What happens to the average wait time for customers near the end of the simulation period?

23. The Burger Dome waiting line model in Section 15.1 studies the wait time of customers at its fast food restaurant. Burger Dome's single-channel waiting line system has a mean of 0.75 arrivals per minute and a service rate of 1 customer per minute.

a. Use a spreadsheet based on Figure 16.15 to simulate the operation of this waiting line. Assuming that customer arrivals follow a Poisson probability distribution, the inter-arrival times can be simulated with the cell formula $-(1/\lambda)*LN(RAND())$, where $\lambda = 0.75$. Assuming that the service time follows an exponential probability distribution, the service times can be simulated with the cell formula $-\mu*LN(RAND())$, where $\mu = 1$. Run the Burger Dome simulation for 500 customers. The analytical model in Chapter 15 indicates an average waiting time of 3 minutes per customer. What average waiting time does your simulation model show?

b. One advantage of using simulation is that a simulation model can be altered easily to reflect other assumptions about the probabilistic inputs. Assume that the service time is more accurately described by a normal probability distribution with a mean of 1 minute and a standard deviation of 0.2 minutes. This distribution has less service time variability than the exponential probability distribution used in part (a). What is the impact of this change on the average wait time?

24. Telephone calls come into an airline reservations office randomly at the mean rate of 15 calls per hour. The time between calls follows an exponential distribution with a mean of 4 minutes. When the two reservations agents are busy, a telephone message tells the caller that the call is important and to please wait on the line until the next reservation agent becomes available. The service time for each reservation agent is normally distributed with a mean of 4 minutes and a standard deviation of 1 minute. Use a two-channel waiting line simulation model to evaluate this waiting line system. Use the spreadsheet design shown in Figure 16.17. The cell formula $=-4*LN(RAND())$ can be used to generate the inter-arrival times. Simulate the operation of the telephone reservation system for 600 customers. Discard the first 100 customers and collect data over the next 500 customers.

a. Compute the mean interval arrival time and the mean service time. If your simulation model is operating correctly, both of these should have means of approximately 4 minutes.

b. What is the mean customer wait time for this system?

c. Use the $=$COUNTIF function to determine the number of customers who have to wait for a reservation agent. What percentage of the customers have to wait?

Case Problem   COUNTY BEVERAGE DRIVE-THRU

County Beverage Drive-Thru, Inc., operates a chain of beverage supply stores in Northern Illinois. Each store has a single service lane; cars enter at one end of the store and exit at the other end. Customers pick up soft drinks, beer, snacks, and party supplies without getting out of their cars. When a new customer arrives at the store, the customer waits until the preceding customer's order is complete and then drives into the store for service.

Typically, three employees operate each store during peak periods; two clerks take and fill orders, and a third clerk serves as cashier and store supervisor. County Beverage is considering a revised store design in which computerized order-taking and payment are integrated with specialized warehousing equipment. Management hopes that the new design will permit operating each store with one clerk. To determine whether the new design is beneficial, management has decided to build a new store using the revised design.

County Beverage's new store will be located near a major shopping center. Based on experience at other locations, management believes that during the peak late afternoon and evening hours, the time between arrivals follows an exponential probability distribution with a mean of 6 minutes. These peak hours are the most critical time period for the company; most of their profit is generated during these peak hours.

An extensive study of times required to fill orders with a single clerk has led to the following probability distribution of service times.

Service Time (minutes)	Probability
2	0.24
3	0.20
4	0.15
5	0.14
6	0.12
7	0.08
8	0.05
9	0.02
Total	1.00

In case customer wait times prove too long with just a single clerk, County Beverage's management is considering two alternatives: add a second clerk to help with bagging, taking orders, etc., or enlarge the drive-thru area so that two cars can be served at once (a two-channel system). With either of these options, two clerks will be needed. With the two-channel option, service times are expected to be the same for each channel. With the second clerk helping with a single channel, service times will be reduced. The following probability distribution describes service times given that option.

Service Time (minutes)	Probability
1	0.20
2	0.35
3	0.30
4	0.10
5	0.05
Total	1.00

County Beverage's management would like you to develop a spreadsheet simulation model of the new system and use it to compare the operation of the system using the following three designs:

Design

A   One channel, one clerk
B   One channel, two clerks
C   Two channels, each with one clerk

Management is especially concerned with how long customers have to wait for service. Research has shown that 30% of the customers will wait no longer than 6 minutes and that 90% will wait no longer than 10 minutes. As a guideline, management requires the average wait time to be less than 1.5 minutes.

Managerial Report

Prepare a report that discusses the general development of the spreadsheet simulation model, and make any recommendations that you have regarding the best store design and staffing plan for County Beverage. One additional consideration is that the design allowing for a two-channel system will cost an additional $10,000 to build.

1. List the information the spreadsheet simulation model should generate so that a decision can be made on the store design and the desired number of clerks.
2. Run the simulation for 1000 customers for each alternative considered. You may want to consider making more than one run with each alternative. [*Note:* Values from an exponential probability distribution with mean μ can be generated in Excel using the following function: $=-\mu*LN(RAND())$.]
3. Be sure to note the number of customers County Beverage is likely to lose due to long customer wait times with each design alternative.

Appendix 16.1   SIMULATION WITH SPREADSHEETS

Spreadsheets enable small and moderate-sized simulation models to be implemented relatively easily and quickly. In this appendix we show the Excel spreadsheets for the three simulation models presented in the chapter.

The PortaCom Simulation Model

We simulated the PortaCom problem 500 times. The spreadsheet used to carry out the simulation is shown again in Figure 16.18. Note that the simulation results for trials 6 through 495 have been hidden so that the results can be shown in a reasonably sized figure. If desired, the rows for these trials can be shown and the simulation results displayed for all 500 trials. Let us describe the details of the Excel spreadsheet that provided the PortaCom simulation.

First, the PortaCom data are presented in the first 14 rows of the spreadsheet. The selling price per unit, administrative cost, and advertising cost parameters are entered directly into cells C3, C4, and C5. The discrete probability distribution for the direct labor cost per unit is shown in a tabular format. Note that the random number intervals are entered first followed by the corresponding cost per unit. For example, 0.0 in cell A10 and 0.1 in cell B10 show that a cost of $43 per unit will be assigned if the random number is

FIGURE 16.18   SPREADSHEET SIMULATION FOR THE PORTACOM PROBLEM

	A	B	C	D	E	F
1	**PortaCom Risk Analysis**					
2						
3	Selling Price per Unit		$249			
4	Administrative Cost		$400,000			
5	Advertising Cost		$600,000			
6						
7	**Direct Labor Cost**			**Parts Cost (Uniform Distribution)**		
8	Lower	Upper		Smallest Value	$80	
9	Random No.	Random No.	Cost per Unit	Largest Value	$100	
10	0.0	0.1	$43			
11	0.1	0.3	$44			
12	0.3	0.7	$45	**Demand (Normal Distribution)**		
13	0.7	0.9	$46	Mean	15000	
14	0.9	1.0	$47	Standard Dev	4500	
15						
16						
17	**Simulation Trials**					
18						
19		Direct Labor	Parts	First-Year		
20	Trial	Cost per Unit	Cost per Unit	Demand	Profit	
21	1	47	$85.36	17,366	$1,025,570	
22	2	44	$91.68	12,900	$461,828	
23	3	45	$93.35	20,686	$1,288,906	
24	4	43	$98.56	10,888	$169,807	
25	5	45	$88.36	14,259	$648,911	
516	496	44	$98.67	8,730	($71,659)	
517	497	45	$94.38	19,257	$1,110,841	
518	498	44	$90.85	14,920	$703,102	
519	499	43	$90.37	13,471	$557,662	
520	500	46	$92.50	18,614	$1,056,927	
521						
522			**Summary Statistics**			
523			Mean Profit		$698,457	
524			Standard Deviation		$520,485	
525			Minimum Profit		($785,234)	
526			Maximum Profit		$2,367,058	
527			Number of Losses		51	
528			Probability of Loss		0.1020	

in the interval 0.0 but less than 0.1. Thus, approximately 10% of the simulated direct labor costs will be $43 per unit. The uniform probability distribution with a smallest value of $80 in cell E8 and a largest value of $100 in cell E9 describes the parts cost per unit. Finally, a normal probability distribution with a mean of 15,000 units in cell E13 and a standard deviation of 4500 units in cell E14 describes the first-year demand distribution for the product. At this point we are ready to insert the Excel formulas that will carry out each simulation trial.

Simulation information for the first trial appears in row 21 of the spreadsheet. The cell formulas for row 21 are as follows:

Cell A21   Enter 1 for the first simulation trial

Cell B21   Simulate the direct labor cost per unit[3]
           =VLOOKUP(RAND(),$A$10:$C$14,3)

Cell C21   Simulate the parts cost per unit (uniform distribution)
           =$E$8+($E$9−$E$8)*RAND()

Cell D21   Simulate the first-year demand (normal distribution)
           =NORMINV(RAND(),$E$13,$E$14)

Cell E21   The profit obtained for the first trial
           =($C$3−B21−C21)*D21−$C$4−$C$5

Cells A21:E21 can be copied to A520:E520 in order to provide the 500 simulation trials.

Ultimately, summary statistics will be collected in order to describe the results of the 500 simulated trials. Using the standard Excel functions, the following summary statistics are computed for the 500 simulated profits appearing in cells E21 to E520.

Cell E523   The mean profit per trial =AVERAGE(E21:E520)

Cell E524   The standard deviation of profit = STDEV(E21:E520)

Cell E525   The minimum profit =MIN(E21:E520)

Cell E526   The maximum profit =MAX(E21:E520)

Cell E527   The count of the number of trials where a loss occurred
           (i.e., profit < $0) =COUNTIF(E21:E520,"<0")

Cell E528   The percentage or probability of a loss based on the 500 trials =E527/500

The F9 key can be used to perform another complete simulation of PortaCom. In this case, the entire spreadsheet will be recalculated and a set of new simulation results will be provided. Any data summaries, measures, or functions that have been built into the spreadsheet earlier will be updated automatically.

The Butler Inventory Simulation Model

We simulated the Butler inventory operation for 300 months. The spreadsheet used to carry out the simulation is shown again in Figure 16.19. Note that the simulation results for months 6 through 295 have been hidden so that the results can be shown in a reasonably sized figure. If desired, the rows for these months can be shown and the simulation results displayed for all 300 months. Let us describe the details of the Excel spreadsheet that provided the Butler inventory simulation.

First, the Butler inventory data are presented in the first 11 rows of the spreadsheet. The gross profit per unit, holding cost per unit, and shortage cost per unit data are entered directly into cells C3, C4, and C5. The replenishment level is entered into cell C7, and the mean and standard deviation of the normal probability distribution for demand are entered into cells B10 and B11. At this point we are ready to insert Excel formulas that will carry out each simulation month or trial.

Simulation information for the first month or trial appears in row 17 of the spreadsheet. The cell formulas for row 17 are as follows:

Cell A17   Enter 1 for the first simulation month

Cell B17   Simulate demand (normal distribution)
           =NORMINV(RAND(),$B$10,$B$11)

---

3. The VLOOKUP function generates a random number using the RAND() function. Then, using the table defined by the region from cells $A$10 to $C$14, the function identifies the row containing the RAND() random number and assigns the corresponding direct labor cost per unit shown in column C.

FIGURE 16.19   SPREADSHEET SIMULATION FOR THE BUTLER INVENTORY PROBLEM

	A	B	C	D	E	F	G
1	**Butler Inventory**						
2							
3	Gross Profit per Unit		$50				
4	Holding Cost per Unit		$15				
5	Shortage Cost per Unit		$30				
6							
7	**Replenishment Level**		100				
8							
9	**Demand (Normal Distribution)**						
10	Mean	100					
11	Standard Dev	20					
12							
13							
14	**Simulation**						
15							
16	Month	Demand	Sales	Gross Profit	Holding Cost	Shortage Cost	Net Profit
17	1	79	79	$3,950	$315	$0	$3,635
18	2	111	100	$5,000	$0	$330	$4,670
19	3	93	93	$4,650	$105	$0	$4,545
20	4	100	100	$5,000	$0	$0	$5,000
21	5	118	100	$5,000	$0	$540	$4,460
312	296	89	89	$4,450	$165	$0	$4,285
313	297	91	91	$4,550	$135	$0	$4,415
314	298	122	100	$5,000	$0	$660	$4,340
315	299	93	93	$4,650	$105	$0	$4,545
316	300	126	100	$5,000	$0	$780	$4,220
317							
318	**Totals**	30,181	27,917		**Summary Statistics**		
319					Mean Profit		$4,293
320					Standard Deviation		$658
321					Minimum Profit		($206)
322					Maximum Profit		$5,000
323					Service Level		92.5%

Next compute the sales, which is equal to demand (cell B17) if demand is less than or equal to the replenishment level, or is equal to the replenishment level (cell C7) if demand is greater than the replenishment level.

Cell C17   Compute sales =IF(B17<=$C$7,B17,$C$7)

Cell D17   Calculate gross profit =$C$3*C17

Cell E17   Calculate the holding cost if demand is less than or equal
to the replenishment level
=IF(B17<=$C$7,$C$4*($C$7−B17),0)

Cell F17   Calculate the shortage cost if demand is greater than the replenishment level
=IF(B17>$C$7,$C$5*(B17−$C$7),0)

Cell G17   Calculate net profit =D17−E17−F17

Cells A17:G17 can be copied to cells A316:G316 in order to provide the 300 simulation months.

Finally, summary statistics will be collected in order to describe the results of the 300 simulated trials. Using the standard Excel functions, the following totals and summary statistics are computed for the 300 months.

Cell B318   Total Demand =SUM(B17:B316)

Cell C319   Total Sales =SUM(C17:C316)

Cell G319   The mean profit per month =AVERAGE(G17:G316)

Cell G320   The standard deviation of net profit
             =STDEV(G17:G316)

Cell G321   The minimum net profit =MIN(G17:G316)

Cell G322   The maximum net profit =MAX(G17:G316)

Cell G323   The service level =C318/B318

The Hammondsport ATM Simulation Model

We simulated the operation of the Hammondsport ATM waiting line system for 1000 customers. The spreadsheet used to carry out the simulation is shown again in Figure 16.20. Note that the simulation results for customers 6 through 995 have been hidden so that the results can be shown in a reasonably sized figure. If desired, the rows for these customers can be shown and the simulation results displayed for all 1000 customers. Let us describe the details of the Excel spreadsheet that provided the Hammondsport ATM simulation.

The data are presented in the first 9 rows of the spreadsheet. The interarrival times are described by a uniform distribution with a smallest time of 0 minutes (cell B4) and a largest time of 5 minutes (cell B5). A normal probability distribution with a mean of 2 minutes (cell B8) and a standard deviation of 0.5 minutes (cell B9) describes the service time distribution.

Simulation information for the first customer appears in row 16 of the spreadsheet. The cell formulas for row 16 are as follows:

Cell A16   Enter 1 for the first customer

Cell B16   Simulate the interarrival time for customer 1 (uniform
            distribution) =$B$4+RAND()*($B$5−$B$4)

Cell C16   Compute the arrival time for customer 1 =B16

Cell D16   Compute the start time for customer 1 =C16

Cell E16   Compute the wait time for customer 1 =D16−C16

Cell F16   Simulate the service time for customer 1 (normal distribution)
            =NORMINV(RAND(),$B$8,$B$9)

Cell G16   Compute the completion time for customer 1 =D16+F16

Cell H16   Compute the time in the system for customer 1 =G16−C16

Simulation information for the second customer appears in row 17 of the spreadsheet. The cell formulas for row 17 are as follows:

Cell A17   Enter 2 for the second customer

Cell B17   Simulate the interarrival time for customer 2 (uniform
            distribution) =$B$4+RAND()*($B$5−$B$4)

Cell C17   Compute the arrival time for customer 2 =C16+B17

Cell D17   Compute the start time for customer 2
            =IF(C17>G16,C17,G16)

Cell E17   Compute the wait time for customer 2 =D17−C17

FIGURE 16.20   SPREADSHEET SIMULATION OF THE HAMMONDSPORT SAVINGS BANK
WITH ONE ATM

	A	B	C	D	E	F	G	H
1	**Hammondsport Savings Bank with One ATM**							
2								
3	**Interarrival Times (Uniform Distribution)**							
4	Smallest Value	0						
5	Largest Value	5						
6								
7	**Service Times (Normal Distribution)**							
8	Mean	2						
9	Standard Dev	0.5						
10								
11								
12	**Simulation**							
13								
14		Interarrival	Arrival	Service	Wait	Service	Completion	Time
15	Customer	Time	Time	Start Time	Time	Time	Time	in System
16	1	1.4	1.4	1.4	0.0	2.3	3.7	2.3
17	2	1.3	2.7	3.7	1.0	1.5	5.2	2.5
18	3	4.9	7.6	7.6	0.0	2.2	9.8	2.2
19	4	3.5	11.1	11.1	0.0	2.5	13.6	2.5
20	5	0.7	11.8	13.6	1.8	1.8	15.4	3.6
1011	996	0.5	2496.8	2498.1	1.3	0.6	2498.7	1.9
1012	997	0.2	2497.0	2498.7	1.7	2.0	2500.7	3.7
1013	998	2.7	2499.7	2500.7	1.0	1.9	2502.5	2.8
1014	999	3.7	2503.4	2503.4	0.0	2.5	2505.8	2.5
1015	1000	4.1	2507.4	2507.4	0.0	1.9	2509.3	1.9
1016								
1017		**Summary Statistics**						
1018		Number Waiting			549			
1019		Probability of Waiting			0.6100			
1020		Average Wait Time			1.59			
1021		Maximum Wait Time			13.5			
1022		Utilization of ATM			0.7860			
1023		Number Waiting > 1 Min			393			
1024		Probability of Waiting > 1 Min			0.4367			

Cell F17   Simulate the service time for customer 2 (normal distribution)
=NORMINV(RAND(),$B$8,$B$9)

Cell G17   Compute the completion time for customer 2 =D17+F17

Cell H17   Compute the time in the system for customer 2 =G17−C17

Cells A17:H17 can be copied to cells A1015:H1015 in order to provide the 1000 customer
simulation.

Ultimately, summary statistics will be collected in order to describe the results of 1000 customers. Before collecting the summary statistics, let us point out that most simulation studies
of dynamic systems focus on the operation of the system during its long-run or steady-state

operation. To ensure that the effect of start-up conditions are not included in the steady-state calculations, a dynamic simulation model is usually run for a specified period without collecting any data about the operation of the system. The length of the startup period can vary depending on the application. For the Hammondsport Savings Bank ATM simulation, we treated the results for the first 100 customers as the start-up period. The simulation information for customer 100 appears in row 115 of the spreadsheet. Cell G115 shows that the completion time for the 100th customer is 247.8. Thus the length of the start-up period is 247.8 minutes.

Summary statistics are collected for the next 900 customers corresponding to rows 116 to 1015 of the spreadsheet. The following Excel formulas provided the summary statistics.

Cell E1018   Number of customers who had to wait (i.e., wait
    time > 0) =COUNTIF(E116:E1015,">0")

Cell E1019   Probability of waiting =E1018/900

Cell E1020   The average wait time =AVERAGE(E116:E1015)

Cell E1021   The maximum wait time =MAX(E116:E1015)

Cell E1022   The utilization of the ATM[4]
    =SUM(F116:F1015)/(G1015−G115)

Cell E1023   The number of customers who had to wait more than
    1 minute =COUNTIF(E116:E1015,">1")

Cell E1024   Probability of waiting more than 1 minute
    =E1023/900

Appendix 16.2   SIMULATION OF THE PORTACOM PROBLEM USING CRYSTAL BALL

In Section 16.1 we used simulation to perform risk analysis for the PortaCom problem, and in Appendix 16.1 we showed how to construct the Excel spreadsheet that provided the simulation results. Developing the spreadsheet simulation for the PortaCom problem using the basic Excel package was relatively easy. The use of add-ins enable larger and more complex simulation problems to be easily analyzed using spreadsheets. In this appendix, we show how Crystal Ball, an add-in package, can be used to perform the PortaCom simulation. Instructions for installing and starting Crystal Ball are included with the Crystal Ball software.

Formulating a Crystal Ball Model

We begin by entering the problem data into the top part of the spreadsheet. For the PortaCom problem, we must enter the following data: selling price, administrative cost, advertising cost, probability distribution for the direct labor cost per unit, minimum and maximum values for the parts cost per unit (uniform distribution), and the mean and standard deviation for first-year demand (normal distribution). These data with appropriate descriptive labels are shown in cells A1:F15 of Figure 16.21.

For the PortaCom problem, the Crystal Ball model contains the following two components: (1) cells for the probabilistic inputs (direct labor cost, parts cost, first-year demand), and (2) a cell containing a formula for computing the value of the simulation model output (profit). In Crystal Ball the cells that contain the values of the probabilistic inputs are called *assumption cells,* and the cells that contain the formulas for the model outputs are referred to as *forecast cells.* The PortaCom problem requires only one output (profit), and thus the

---

4. The proportion of time the ATM is in use is equal to the sum of the 900 customer service times in column F divided by the total elapsed time required for the 900 customers to complete service. This total elapsed time is the difference between the completion time of customer 1000 and the completion time of customer 100.

FIGURE 16.21   CRYSTAL BALL SPREADSHEET FOR THE PORTACOM PROBLEM

	A	B	C	D	E	F	G
1	**PortaCom Risk Analysis**						
2							
3		**Selling Price**	$249				
4							
5		**Administrative Cost**	$400,000				
6		**Advertising Cost**	$600,000				
7		**Total**	$1,000,000				
8							
9		**Direct Labor**			**Parts Cost per Unit**	**Uniform**	
10		**Cost per Unit**	**Probability**		**Minimum**	$80	
11		$43	0.1		**Maximum**	$100	
12		$44	0.2				
13		$45	0.4		**First-Year Demand**	**Normal**	
14		$46	0.2		**Mean**	15,000	
15		$47	0.1		**Standard Deviation**	4500	
16							
17	**Crystal Ball Model**						
18							
19			**Assumption**				
20			**Cells**				
21		**Direct Labor Cost**	$45				
22		**Parts Cost**	$90				
23		**First-Year Demand**	15,000				
24							
25			**Forecast**				
26			**Cell**				
27		**Profit**	$710,000				
28							

Crystal Ball model only contains one forecast cell. In more complex simulation problems more than one forecast cell may be necessary.

The assumption cells may only contain simple numeric values. In this model building stage, we entered PortaCom's best estimates of the direct labor cost ($45), the parts cost ($90), and the first year demand (15,000) into cells C21:C23, respectively. The forecast cells in a Crystal Ball model contain formulas that refer to one or more of the assumption cells. Because only one forecast cell in the PortaCom problem corresponds to profit, we entered the following formula into cell C27:

$$=(C3-C21-C22)*C23-C7$$

The resulting value of $710,000 is the profit corresponding to the base-case scenario discussed in Section 16.1.

Defining and Entering Assumptions

We are now ready to define the probability distributions corresponding to each of the assumption cells. We will begin by defining the probability distribution for the direct labor cost.

Step 1. Select cell C21
Step 2. Select the **Cell** pull-down menu
Step 3. Select the **Define Assumption** option
Step 4. When the **Cell 21: Distribution Gallery** dialog box appears:
Choose **Custom**
Select **OK**
Step 5. When the **Custom Distribution** dialog box appears:
Choose **Data**
Enter B11:C15 in the cell range box
Select **OK** to terminate the data entry process
Select **OK** to close the **Custom Distribution** dialog box

The procedure for defining the probability distribution for the parts cost is similar.

Step 1. Select cell C22
Step 2. Select the **Cell** pull-down menu
Step 3. Select the **Define Assumption** option
Step 4. When the **Cell 22: Distribution Gallery** dialog box appears:
Choose **Uniform**
Select **OK**
Step 5. When the **Cell C22: Uniform Distribution** dialog box appears:
Enter 80 in the **Min** box
Enter 100 in the **Max** box
Select **OK**

Finally, we perform the following steps to define the probability distribution for first-year demand.

Step 1. Select cell C23
Step 2. Select the **Cell** pull-down menu
Step 3. Select the **Define Assumption** option
Step 4. When the **Cell 23: Distribution Gallery** dialog box appears:
Choose **Normal**
Select **OK**
Step 5. When the **Cell C23: Normal Distribution** dialog box appears:
Enter 15000 in the **Mean** box
Enter 4500 in the **Std Dev** box
Select **OK**

Defining Forecasts

After defining the assumption cells, we are ready to define the forecast cells. The following steps show how to do it for C27, the forecast cell for the PortaCom problem.

Step 1. Select cell C27
Step 2. Select the **Cell** pull-down menu
Step 3. Select the **Define Forecast** option
Step 4. When the **Cell C27: Define Forecast** dialog box appears:
Enter Profit in the **Forecast Name** box
Select **OK**

The Define Forecast dialog box in step 4 allows you to change the forecast name and contains options for setting the forecast units, controlling the size of the forecast window, and determining when the forecast window is displayed.

Setting Run Preferences

We must now make the choices that determine how Crystal Ball runs the simulation. For the PortaCom simulation, we only need to specify the number of trials.

Step 1. Select the **Run** pull-down menu
Step 2. Select the **Run Preferences** option
Step 3. When the **Run Preferences** dialog box appears:
Select the **Trials** tab
Enter 500 in the **Maximum Number of Trials** box
Select **OK**

Running the Simulation

Crystal Ball repeats three steps on each of the 500 trials for the PortaCom simulation.

1. For each assumption cell, Crystal Ball generates a value at random according to the probability distribution defined.
2. Crystal Ball recalculates the value of the forecast cell (profit) corresponding to the values in the assumption cells.
3. The new profit value is added to the graph in the forecast window.

The following steps describe how to begin the simulation.

Step 1. Select the **Run** pull-down menu
Step 2. Select the **Run** option

When the run is complete, Crystal Ball displays the 500 simulated values of profit in the frequency chart shown in Figure 16.22. Other types of charts and output can be displayed in the forecast window. For instance, the following steps describe how to display the descriptive statistics corresponding to this simulation.

Step 1. Select the **View** pull-down menu in the forecast window (Figure 16.22)
Step 2. Select the **Statistics** option

FIGURE 16.22 CRYSTAL BALL FREQUENCY CHART FOR THE PORTACOM SIMULATION

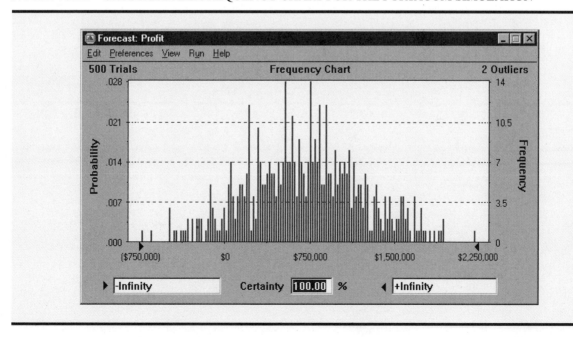

Figure 16.23 shows the forecast window with the descriptive statistics. Note that the worst result obtained in this simulation of 500 trials is a loss of $936,710, and the best result is a profit of $2,259,645. The mean profit is $709,305. These values are similar to the results obtained in Section 16.1. The differences result from the different random numbers used in the two simulations.

FIGURE 16.23   CRYSTAL BALL STATISTICS FOR THE PORTACOM SIMULATION

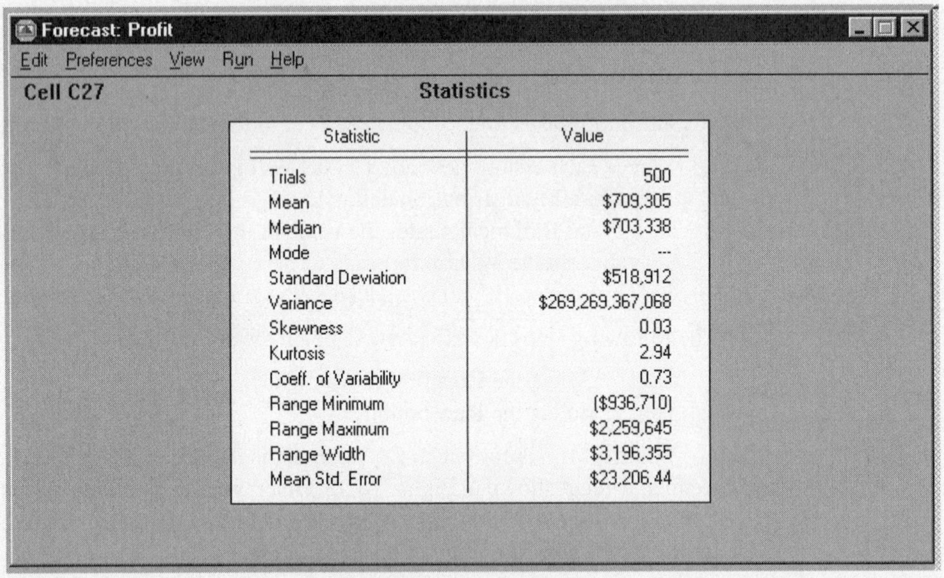

Forecast: Profit

Edit   Preferences   View   Run   Help

Cell C27   **Statistics**

Statistic	Value
Trials	500
Mean	$709,305
Median	$703,338
Mode	---
Standard Deviation	$518,912
Variance	$269,269,367,068
Skewness	0.03
Kurtosis	2.94
Coeff. of Variability	0.73
Range Minimum	($936,710)
Range Maximum	$2,259,645
Range Width	$3,196,355
Mean Std. Error	$23,206.44

PHARMACIA & UPJOHN, INC.*

BRIDGEWATER, NEW JERSEY

The companies that make up Pharmacia & Upjohn have been helping people live longer and healthier for more than 140 years. In all, more than 20 companies from Europe and the United States have merged to create one of the world's largest pharmaceutical groups. The merger between Pharmacia (1911) and Upjohn (1886) to form the Pharmacia & Upjohn Company occurred in 1995.

Quantitative Methods

The quantitative methods function is part of the Management Information and Office Services organization and offers a high-quality, professional problem-solving service to any part of the corporation. The mission of the group is to provide decision-making support for the company's customers, strategies, and priorities by using quantitative techniques to solve business problems and exploit business opportunities in a cost-effective manner. The primary areas of application are problem definition and analysis, modeling and simulation, capacity planning, resource allocation, scheduling, and project management.

A Computer Simulation Application

Demand for one long-standing product had remained stable for several years at a level easily satisfied by the company's manufacturing facility. However, changes in market conditions caused an increase in demand to a level beyond the capacity of the current facility. In the discussion that follows, we describe a simulation study successfully undertaken to determine the most cost-effective means of increasing production to meet the new level of demand.

*The authors are indebted to Dr. David B. Magerlein, Dr. James M. Magerlein, and Mr. Michael J. Goodrich of Pharmacia & Upjohn for providing this application.

The production process is shown in Figure 16.24. It consists of three independent subprocesses: raw material processing, bulk processing, and spent material reprocessing. Raw material processing takes purchased material as input and transforms it into material that can be used in bulk processing. Bulk processing (shown within the dashed line in Figure 16.24), which involves initial processing, assay, and final processing, converts the raw materials into a finished product. The key step occurs when an assay of the initial bulk processing output or intermediate is performed to determine whether the lot is ready for final processing. If the assay is acceptable, the lot proceeds to final processing and completion. If the assay is not acceptable, the intermediate is returned to initial bulk processing and several steps are repeated. The new intermediate material, which is input during the repeat processing, is obtained by reprocessing one of the spent materials generated during a prior initial bulk processing.

Each time the initial bulk process is run, a quantity of spent material is generated for possible reprocessing. Although the primary use of the reprocessed material is as input for repeat bulk processing, it also can be used as a replacement for the original raw material at the start of the bulk processing. Because the cost of the reprocessed material is significantly less than the cost of new raw material, using as much reprocessed material as possible is beneficial.

A simulation model of the production process was developed, and these questions were addressed:

1. What is the maximum throughput of the existing facility?
2. How can the production process be modified to increase the throughput of the existing facility?
3. How much equipment (tanks and centrifuges) must be added to the current facility to increase the capacity to meet the forecasted demand?

FIGURE 16.24   A PRODUCTION PROCESS

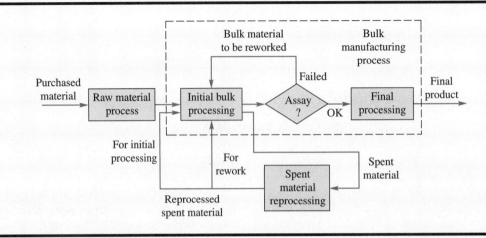

4. How should the reprocessed spent material be used to minimize the total production cost?
5. If a new facility is required, what is the optimal size and configuration?

The scope of the simulation model included the raw material and bulk and spent material processes already defined. The model was built in a modular flexible manner that allowed for the evaluation of resource levels within the facility, staffing levels and hours, changes in process times or equipment usage, changes in lot size, and/or yield changes. The logic of the process flow served as the core of the model and was developed in collaboration with the lead operators and supervisors of the production area. Because a good logical model is the key to good simulation results, a significant amount of time was spent defining the logic of the process flow. The model development process provided a secondary benefit in that production personnel got to review and evaluate the process as they explained it.

The computer simulation model has been used on several occasions over the past two years. Simulation results have assisted management in addressing capacity, resource allocation, and operating policy issues. Each time a request to evaluate an issue is made, a detailed experimental design is developed that defines the alternatives to be evaluated. The appropriate simulation runs are made, the results are evaluated and presented to production management and personnel, and follow-up actions are taken.

The computer simulation model was developed using the SLAMSYSTEM® Version 3.0 simulation language from the Pritsker Corporation. All simulation runs were made on a personal computer.

Benefits of the Simulation Model

The ongoing investigation of the production process using computer simulation has resulted in numerous benefits to the company, including the following:

1. Optimizing the use of reprocessed spent material to replace fresh raw material. Total material costs were reduced by approximately $3 million per year.
2. Demonstrating that the current facility, with some operating policy improvements, was large enough to satisfy the increased demand for the next several years. Expansion to a new facility was not necessary.
3. Determining the impact on facility throughput from alternative process changes. Numerous potential changes were investigated. The simulation model predicted how each change would affect total facility throughput. One change was identified that would increase throughput beyond what was needed for the 5-year forecasted demand.
4. Determining appropriate staffing levels within the facility. The model determined the number of operators required as production level increases in the future. This forecast ensures that the proper number of operators will be trained by the time they are needed.
5. Determining the required size and configuration for a new facility. Although the current facility was found adequate to meet demand, the model still allowed management to determine the cost required to build a new facility.

The final actions taken based on the simulation results included alterations in policies for using reprocessed spent material, priority implementation of the process change that most impacted increasing facility throughput, establishment of appropriate staffing levels, and cost minimization because the expense of building a new or expanded facility was avoided.

Questions

1. Briefly describe the production operation.
2. What was the primary reason for conducting a study of this operation?
3. Describe some of the factors that had to be included in the simulation model.
4. What were the advantages of simulation?

MARKOV PROCESSES

CONTENTS

Markov process models are useful in studying the evolution of systems over repeated trials. The repeated trials are often successive time periods where the state of the system in any particular period cannot be determined with certainty. Rather, transition probabilities are used to describe the manner in which the system makes transitions from one period to the next. Hence, we are interested in the probability of the system being in a particular state at a given time period.

Markov process models have been used to describe the probability that a machine that is functioning in one period will continue to function or will break down in the next period. They have also been used to describe the probability that a consumer purchasing brand A in one period will purchase brand B in the next period. In this chapter we present a marketing application that involves an analysis of the store-switching behavior of supermarket customers. As a second illustration, we consider an accounting application that involves transitioning accounts receivable dollars to different account-aging categories.

Because an in-depth treatment of Markov processes is beyond the scope of this text, the analysis in both illustrations is restricted to situations consisting of a finite number of states, the transition probabilities remain constant over time, and the probability of being in a particular state at any one time period depends only on the state in the immediately preceding time period. Such Markov processes are referred to as *Markov chains with stationary transition probabilities.*

17.1 MARKET SHARE ANALYSIS

Suppose we are interested in analyzing the market share and customer loyalty for Murphy's Foodliner and Ashley's Supermarket, the only two grocery stores in a small town. We focus on the sequence of shopping trips of one customer, and assume that the customer makes one shopping trip each week to either Murphy's Foodliner or Ashley's Supermarket, but not both.

Using the terminology of Markov processes, we refer to the weekly periods or shopping trips as the **trials of the process.** Thus, at each trial, the customer will shop at either Murphy's Foodliner or Ashley's Supermarket. The particular store selected in a given week is referred to as the **state of the system** in that period. Because the customer has two shopping alternatives at each trial, we say the system has two states, and because the number of states is finite, we can identify each state as follows:

State 1. The customer shops at Murphy's Foodliner

State 2. The customer shops at Ashley's Supermarket

If we say the system is in state 1 at trial 3, we are simply saying that the customer shops at Murphy's during the third weekly shopping period.

As we continue the shopping trip process into the future, we cannot say for certain where the customer will shop during a given week or trial. In fact, we realize that during any given week, the customer may be either a Murphy's customer or an Ashley's customer. However, using a Markov process model, we will be able to compute the probability that the customer shops at each store during any period. For example, we may find a 0.6 probability that the customer will shop at Murphy's during a particular week and a 0.4 probability that the customer will shop at Ashley's.

To determine the probabilities of the various states occurring at successive trials of the Markov process, we need information on the probability that a customer remains with the same store or switches to the competing store as the process continues from trial to trial or week to week.

Suppose that, as part of a market research study, we collect data from 100 shoppers over a 10-week period. Suppose further that these data show each customer's weekly shopping trip pattern in terms of the sequence of visits to Murphy's and Ashley's. To develop a Markov process model for the sequence of weekly shopping trips, we need to express the probability of selecting each store (state) in a given period solely in terms of the store (state) that was selected during the previous period. In reviewing the data, suppose that we find that of all customers who shopped at Murphy's in a given week, 90% shopped at Murphy's the following week while 10% switched to Ashley's. Suppose that similar data for the customers who shopped at Ashley's in a given week show that 80% shopped at Ashley's the following week while 20% switched to Murphy's. Probabilities based on these data are shown in Table 17.1. Because these probabilities indicate that a customer moves, or makes a transition, from a state in a given period to a particular state in the following period, these probabilities are called **transition probabilities.**

An important property of the table of transition probabilities is that the sum of the probabilities in each row is 1; each row of the table provides a probability distribution. For example, a customer who shops at Murphy's one week must shop at either Murphy's or Ashley's the next week. The entries in row 1 give the probabilities associated with each of these events. The 0.9 and 0.8 probabilities in Table 17.1 can be interpreted as measures of store loyalty in that they indicate the probability of a repeat visit to the same store. Similarly, the 0.1 and 0.2 probabilities are measures of the store-switching characteristics of the customers.

In developing a Markov process model for this problem, we are assuming that the transition probabilities will be the same for any customer and that the transition probabilities will not change over time.

TABLE 17.1   TRANSITION PROBABILITIES FOR MURPHY'S AND ASHLEY'S GROCERY SALES

Current Weekly Shopping Period	Next Weekly Shopping Period	
	Murphy's Foodliner	**Ashley's Supermarket**
Murphy's Foodliner	0.9	0.1
Ashley's Supermarket	0.2	0.8

The chapter appendix contains a review of matrix notation and operations.

Note that Table 17.1 has one row and one column for each state of the system. We will use the symbol p_{ij} to represent the transition probabilities and the symbol P to represent the matrix of transition probabilities; that is,

$$p_{ij} = \text{probability of making a transition from state } i \text{ in a given period to state } j \text{ in the next period}$$

For the supermarket problem, we have

A quick check for a valid matrix of transition probabilities is to make sure the sum of the probabilities in each row equals 1.

$$P = \begin{bmatrix} p_{11} & p_{12} \\ p_{21} & p_{22} \end{bmatrix} = \begin{bmatrix} 0.9 & 0.1 \\ 0.2 & 0.8 \end{bmatrix}$$

Using the matrix of transition probabilities, we can now determine the probability that a customer will be a Murphy's customer or an Ashley's customer at some period in the future. Let us begin by assuming that we have a customer whose last weekly shopping trip was to Murphy's. What is the probability that this customer will shop at Murphy's on the next weekly shopping trip, period 1? In other words, what is the probability that the system will be in state 1 after the first transition? The matrix of transition probabilities indicates that this probability is $p_{11} = 0.9$.

Now let us consider the state of the system in period 2. A useful way of depicting what can happen on the second weekly shopping trip is to draw a tree diagram of the possible outcomes (see Figure 17.1). Using this tree diagram, we see that the probability that the cus-

FIGURE 17.1   TREE DIAGRAM DEPICTING TWO WEEKLY SHOPPING TRIPS OF A CUSTOMER WHO SHOPPED LAST AT MURPHY'S

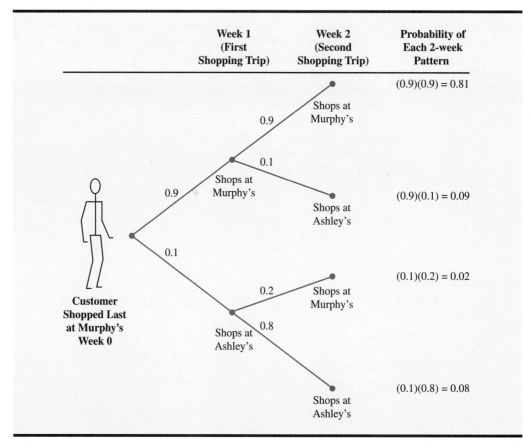

tomer shops at Murphy's during both the first and the second weeks is $(0.9)(0.9) = 0.81$. Also, note that the probability of the customer switching to Ashley's on the first trip and then switching back to Murphy's on the second trip is $(0.1)(0.2) = 0.02$. Because these options are the only two ways that the customer can be in state 1 (shopping at Murphy's) during the second period, the probability of the system being in state 1 during the second period is $0.81 + 0.02 = 0.83$. Similarly, the probability of the system being in state 2 during the second period is $0.09 + 0.08 = 0.17$.

As desirable as the tree diagram approach may be from an intuitive point of view, it becomes cumbersome when we want to extend the analysis to three or more periods. Fortunately, we have an easier way to calculate the probabilities of the system being in state 1 or state 2 for any subsequent period. First, we introduce a notation that will allow us to represent these probabilities for any given period. Let

$$\pi_i(n) = \text{probability that the system is in state } i \text{ in period } n$$

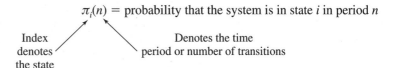

Index
denotes
the state

Denotes the time
period or number of transitions

For example, $\pi_1(1)$ denotes the probability of the system being in state 1 in period 1, while $\pi_2(1)$ denotes the probability of the system being in state 2 in period 1. Because $\pi_i(n)$ is the probability that the system is in state i in period n, this probability is referred to as a **state probability.**

The terms $\pi_1(0)$ and $\pi_2(0)$ will denote the probability of the system being in state 1 or state 2 at some initial or starting period. Week 0 represents the most recent period, when we are beginning the analysis of a Markov process. If we set $\pi_1(0) = 1$ and $\pi_2(0) = 0$, we are saying that as an initial condition the customer shopped last week at Murphy's; alternatively, if we set $\pi_1(0) = 0$ and $\pi_2(0) = 1$, we would be starting the system with a customer who shopped last week at Ashley's. In the tree diagram of Figure 17.1, we consider the situation where the customer shopped last at Murphy's. Thus,

$$[\pi_1(0) \quad \pi_2(0)] = [1 \quad 0]$$

is a vector that represents the initial state probabilities of the system. In general, we use the notation

$$\Pi(n) = [\pi_1(n) \quad \pi_2(n)]$$

to denote the vector of state probabilities for the system in period n. In the example, $\Pi(1)$ is a vector representing the state probabilities for the first week, $\Pi(2)$ is a vector representing the state probabilities for the second week, and so on.

Using this notation, we can find the state probabilities for period $n + 1$ by simply multiplying the known state probabilities for period n by the transition probability matrix. Using the vector of state probabilities and the matrix of transition probabilities, the multiplication[1] can be expressed as follows:

$$\Pi(\text{next period}) = \Pi(\text{current period})P$$

or

$$\Pi(n + 1) = \Pi(n)P \tag{17.1}$$

1. Appendix 17.1 provides the step-by-step procedure for vector and matrix multiplication.

Beginning with the system in state 1 at period 0, we have $\Pi(0) = [1 \quad 0]$. We can compute the state probabilities for period 1 as follows:

$$\Pi(1) = \Pi(0)P$$

or

$$[\pi_1(1) \quad \pi_2(1)] = [\pi_1(0) \quad \pi_2(0)]\begin{bmatrix} p_{11} & p_{12} \\ p_{21} & p_{22} \end{bmatrix}$$

$$= [1 \quad 0]\begin{bmatrix} 0.9 & 0.1 \\ 0.2 & 0.8 \end{bmatrix}$$

$$= [0.9 \quad 0.1]$$

The state probabilities $\pi_1(1) = 0.9$ and $\pi_2(1) = 0.1$ are the probabilities that a customer who shopped at Murphy's during week 0 will shop at Murphy's or at Ashley's during week 1.

Using equation (17.1), we can compute the state probabilities for the second week as follows:

$$\Pi(2) = \Pi(1)P$$

or

$$[\pi_1(2) \quad \pi_2(2)] = [\pi_1(1) \quad \pi_2(1)]\begin{bmatrix} p_{11} & p_{12} \\ p_{21} & p_{22} \end{bmatrix}$$

$$= [0.9 \quad 0.1]\begin{bmatrix} 0.9 & 0.1 \\ 0.2 & 0.8 \end{bmatrix}$$

$$= [0.83 \quad 0.17]$$

We see that the probability of shopping at Murphy's during the second week is 0.83, while the probability of shopping at Ashley's during the second week is 0.17. These same results were previously obtained using the tree diagram of Figure 17.1. By continuing to apply equation (17.1), we can compute the state probabilities for any future period; that is,

$$\Pi(3) = \Pi(2)P$$
$$\Pi(4) = \Pi(3)P$$
$$\vdots \qquad \vdots$$
$$\Pi(n + 1) = \Pi(n)P$$

Table 17.2 shows the result of carrying out these calculations for ten periods.

TABLE 17.2 STATE PROBABILITIES FOR FUTURE PERIODS BEGINNING INITIALLY WITH A MURPHY'S CUSTOMER

State Probability	Period (n)										
	0	1	2	3	4	5	6	7	8	9	10
$\pi_1(n)$	1	0.9	0.83	0.781	0.747	0.723	0.706	0.694	0.686	0.680	0.676
$\pi_2(n)$	0	0.1	0.17	0.219	0.253	0.277	0.294	0.306	0.314	0.320	0.324

The vectors $\Pi(1)$, $\Pi(2)$, $\Pi(3)$, . . . contain the probabilities that a customer who started out as a Murphy customer will be in state 1 or state 2 in the first period, the second period, the third period, and so on. In Table 17.2 we see that after a few periods these probabilities do not change much from one period to the next.

If we had started with 1000 Murphy customers—that is, 1000 consumers who last shopped at Murphy's—our analysis indicates that during the fifth weekly shopping period, 723 would be customers of Murphy's, and 277 would be customers of Ashley's. Moreover, during the tenth weekly shopping period, 676 would be customers of Murphy's, and 324 would be customers of Ashley's.

Now let us repeat the analysis, but this time we will begin the process with a customer who shopped last at Ashley's. Thus,

$$\Pi(0) = [\pi_1(0) \quad \pi_2(0)] = [0 \quad 1]$$

Using equation (17.1), the probability of the system being in state 1 or state 2 in period 1 is given by

$$\Pi(1) = \Pi(0)P$$

or

$$
\begin{aligned}
[\pi_1(1) \quad \pi_2(1)] &= [\pi_1(0) \quad \pi_2(0)]\begin{bmatrix} p_{11} & p_{12} \\ p_{21} & p_{22} \end{bmatrix} \\
&= [0 \quad 1]\begin{bmatrix} 0.9 & 0.1 \\ 0.2 & 0.8 \end{bmatrix} \\
&= [0.2 \quad 0.8]
\end{aligned}
$$

Proceeding as before, we can calculate subsequent state probabilities. Doing so, we obtain the results shown in Table 17.3.

In the fifth shopping period, the probability that the customer will be shopping at Murphy's is 0.555, and the probability that the customer will be shopping at Ashley's is 0.445. In the tenth period, the probability that a customer will be shopping at Murphy's is 0.648, and the probability that a customer will be shopping at Ashley's is 0.352.

As we continue the Markov process, we find that the probability of the system being in a particular state after a large number of periods is independent of the beginning state of the system. The probabilities that we approach after a large number of transitions are referred to as the **steady-state probabilities.** We shall denote the steady-state probability for state 1 with the symbol π_1 and the steady-state probability for state 2 with the symbol π_2. In other words, in the steady-state case, we simply omit the period designation from $\pi_i(n)$ because it is no longer necessary.

TABLE 17.3   STATE PROBABILITIES FOR FUTURE PERIODS BEGINNING INITIALLY WITH AN ASHLEY'S CUSTOMER

State Probability	Period (n)										
	0	1	2	3	4	5	6	7	8	9	10
$\pi_1(n)$	0	0.2	0.34	0.438	0.507	0.555	0.589	0.612	0.628	0.640	0.648
$\pi_2(n)$	1	0.8	0.66	0.562	0.493	0.445	0.411	0.388	0.372	0.360	0.352

Analyses of Tables 17.2 and 17.3 indicate that as n gets larger, the difference between the state probabilities for the nth period and the $(n + 1)$th period becomes increasingly smaller. This analysis leads us to the conclusion that as n gets large, the state probabilities at the $(n + 1)$th period are close to those at the nth period. This observation provides the basis of a simple method for computing the steady-state probabilities without having to actually carry out a large number of calculations.

In general, we know from equation (17.1) that

$$[\pi_1(n + 1) \quad \pi_2(n + 1)] = [\pi_1(n) \quad \pi_2(n)]\begin{bmatrix} p_{11} & p_{12} \\ p_{21} & p_{22} \end{bmatrix}$$

Because for sufficiently large n the difference between $\Pi(n + 1)$ and $\Pi(n)$ is negligible, we see that in the steady state $\pi_1(n + 1) = \pi_1(n) = \pi_1$, and $\pi_2(n + 1) = \pi_2(n) = \pi_2$. Thus, we have

$$[\pi_1 \quad \pi_2] = [\pi_1 \quad \pi_2]\begin{bmatrix} p_{11} & p_{12} \\ p_{21} & p_{22} \end{bmatrix}$$

$$= [\pi_1 \quad \pi_2]\begin{bmatrix} 0.9 & 0.1 \\ 0.2 & 0.8 \end{bmatrix}$$

After carrying out the multiplications, we obtain

$$\pi_1 = 0.9\pi_1 + 0.2\pi_2 \tag{17.2}$$

and

$$\pi_2 = 0.1\pi_1 + 0.8\pi_2 \tag{17.3}$$

However, we also know the steady-state probabilities must sum to 1 with

$$\pi_1 + \pi_2 = 1 \tag{17.4}$$

Using equation (17.4) to solve for π_2 and substituting the result in equation (17.2), we obtain

$$\pi_1 = 0.9\pi_1 + 0.2(1 - \pi_1)$$
$$\pi_1 = 0.9\pi_1 + 0.2 - 0.2\pi_1$$
$$\pi_1 - 0.7\pi_1 = 0.2$$
$$0.3\pi_1 = 0.2$$
$$\pi_1 = \tfrac{2}{3}$$

Then, using equation (17.4), we can conclude that $\pi_2 = 1 - \pi_1 = \frac{1}{3}$. Thus, using equations (17.2) and (17.4), we can solve for the steady-state probabilities directly. You can check for yourself that we could have obtained the same result using equations (17.3) and (17.4).[2]

---

2. Even though equations (17.2) and (17.3) provide two equations and two unknowns, we must include equation (17.4) when solving for π_1 and π_2 to ensure that the sum of steady-state probabilities will equal 1.

Thus, if we have 1000 customers in the system, the Markov process model tells us that in the long run, with steady-state probabilities $\pi_1 = \frac{2}{3}$ and $\pi_2 = \frac{1}{3}$, $\frac{2}{3}(1000) = 667$ customers will be Murphy's and $\frac{1}{3}(1000) = 333$ customers will be Ashley's. The steady-state probabilities can be interpreted as the market shares for the two stores.

Market share information is often quite valuable in decision making. For example, suppose Ashley's Supermarket is contemplating an advertising campaign to attract more of Murphy's customers to its store. Let us suppose further that Ashley's believes this promotional strategy will increase the probability of a Murphy's customer switching to Ashley's from 0.10 to 0.15. The revised transition probabilities are given in Table 17.4.

Given the new transition probabilities, we can modify equations (17.2) and (17.4) to solve for the new steady-state probabilities or market shares. Thus, we obtain

$$\pi_1 = 0.85\pi_1 + 0.20\pi_2$$

Substituting $\pi_2 = 1 - \pi_1$ from equation (17.4), we have

Can you now compute the steady-state probabilities for Markov processes with two states? Problem 3 provides an application.

$$\pi_1 = 0.85\pi_1 + 0.20(1 - \pi_1)$$
$$\pi_1 = 0.85\pi_1 + 0.20 - 0.20\pi_1$$
$$\pi_1 - 0.65\pi_1 = 0.20$$
$$0.35\pi_1 = 0.20$$
$$\pi_1 = 0.57$$

With three states, the steady-state probabilities are found by solving three equations for the three unknown steady-state probabilities. Try Problem 7 as a slightly more difficult problem involving three states.

and

$$\pi_2 = 1 - 0.57 = 0.43$$

Other examples of Markov processes include the promotion of managers to various positions within an organization, the migration of people into and out of various regions of the country, and the progression of students through the years of college, including eventually dropping out or graduating.

We see that the proposed promotional strategy will increase Ashley's market share from $\pi_2 = 0.33$ to $\pi_2 = 0.43$. Suppose that the total market consists of 6000 customers per week. The new promotional strategy will increase the number of customers doing their weekly shopping at Ashley's from 2000 to 2580. If the average weekly profit per customer is $10, the proposed promotional strategy can be expected to increase Ashley's profits by $5800 per week. If the cost of the promotional campaign is less than $5800 per week, Ashley should consider implementing the strategy.

This example demonstrates how a Markov analysis of a firm's market share can be useful in decision making. Suppose that instead of trying to attract customers from Murphy's Foodliner, Ashley's directed a promotional effort at increasing the loyalty of its own customers. In this case, p_{22} would increase, and p_{21} would decrease. Once we knew the amount of the change, we could calculate new steady-state probabilities and compute the impact on profits.

TABLE 17.4   REVISED TRANSITION PROBABILITIES FOR MURPHY'S AND ASHLEY'S GROCERY STORES

Current Weekly Shopping Period	Next Weekly Shopping Period	
	Murphy's Foodliner	**Ashley's Supermarket**
Murphy's Foodliner	0.85	0.15
Ashley's Supermarket	0.20	0.80

1. The Markov processes presented in this section have what is called the *memoryless property:* the current state of the system together with the transition probabilities contains all the information necessary to predict the future behavior of the system. The prior states of the system do not have to be considered. Such Markov processes are considered first-order Markov processes. Higher-order Markov processes are ones in which future states of the system depend on two or more previous states.

2. Analysis of a Markov process model is not intended to optimize any particular aspect of a system. Rather, the analysis predicts or describes the future and steady-state behavior of the system.

For instance, in the grocery store example, the analysis of the steady-state behavior provided a forecast or prediction of the market shares for the two competitors. In other applications, quantitative analysts have extended the study of Markov processes to what are called *Markov decision processes.* In these models, decisions can be made at each period that affect the transition probabilities and hence influence the future behavior of the system. Markov decision processes have been used in analyzing machine breakdown and maintenance operations, planning the movement of patients in hospitals, developing inspection strategies, determining newspaper subscription duration, and analyzing equipment replacement.

17.2 ACCOUNTS RECEIVABLE ANALYSIS

An accounting application in which Markov processes have produced useful results involves the estimation of the allowance for doubtful accounts receivable. This allowance is an estimate of the amount of accounts receivable that will ultimately prove to be uncollectible (i.e., bad debts).

Let us consider the accounts receivable situation for Heidman's Department Store. Heidman's has two aging categories for its accounts receivable: (1) accounts that are classified as 0–30 days old and (2) accounts that are classified as 31–90 days old. If any portion of an account balance exceeds 90 days, that portion is written off as a bad debt. Heidman's follows the procedure of aging the total balance in any customer's account according to the oldest unpaid bill. For example, suppose that one customer's account balance on September 30 is as follows:

Date of Purchase	Amount Charged
August 15	$25
September 18	10
September 28	50
	Total $85

An aging of accounts receivable on September 30 would assign the total balance of $85 to the 31–90-day category because the oldest unpaid bill of August 15 is 46 days old. Let us assume that one week later, October 7, the customer pays the August 15 bill of $25. The remaining total balance of $60 would now be placed in the 0–30-day category because the oldest unpaid amount, corresponding to the September 18 purchase, is less than 31 days old. This method of aging accounts receivable is called the *total balance method* because the total account balance is placed in the age category corresponding to the oldest unpaid amount.

Note that under the total balance method of aging accounts receivable, dollars appearing in a 31–90-day category at one point in time may appear in a 0–30-day category at a later point in time. In the preceding example, this movement between categories was true for $60 of September billings, which shifted from a 31–90-day to a 0–30-day category after the August bill had been paid.

Let us assume that on December 31 Heidman's shows a total of $3000 in its accounts receivable and that the firm's management would like an estimate of how much of the $3000 will eventually be collected and how much will eventually result in bad debts. The estimated amount of bad debts will appear as an allowance for doubtful accounts in the year-ending financial statements.

Let us see how we can view the accounts receivable operation as a Markov process. First, concentrate on what happens to *one* dollar currently in accounts receivable. As the firm continues to operate into the future, we can consider each week as a trial of a Markov process with a dollar existing in one of the following states of the system:

State 1. Paid category

State 2. Bad debt category

State 3. 0–30-day category

State 4. 31–90-day category

Thus, we can track the week-by-week status of one dollar by using a Markov analysis to identify the state of the system at a particular week or period.

Using a Markov process model with the preceding states, we define the transition probabilities as follows:

p_{ij} = probability of a dollar in state i in one week moving to state j in the next week

Based on historical transitions of accounts receivable dollars, the following matrix of transition probabilities, P, has been developed for Heidman's Department Store:

$$P = \begin{bmatrix} p_{11} & p_{12} & p_{13} & p_{14} \\ p_{21} & p_{22} & p_{23} & p_{24} \\ p_{31} & p_{32} & p_{33} & p_{34} \\ p_{41} & p_{42} & p_{43} & p_{44} \end{bmatrix} = \begin{bmatrix} 1.0 & 0.0 & 0.0 & 0.0 \\ 0.0 & 1.0 & 0.0 & 0.0 \\ 0.4 & 0.0 & 0.3 & 0.3 \\ 0.4 & 0.2 & 0.3 & 0.1 \end{bmatrix}$$

Note that the probability of a dollar in the 0–30-day category (state 3) moving to the paid category (state 1) in the next period is 0.4. Also, this dollar has a 0.3 probability it will remain in the 0–30-day category (state 3) one week later, and a 0.3 probability that it will be in the 31–90-day category (state 4) one week later. Note also that a dollar in a 0–30-day account cannot make the transition to a bad debt (state 2) in one week.

An important property of the Markov process model for Heidman's accounts receivable situation is the presence of *absorbing states*. For example, once a dollar makes a transition to state 1, the paid state, the probability of making a transition to any other state is zero. Similarly, once a dollar is in state 2, the bad debt state, the probability of a transition to any other state is zero. Thus, once a dollar reaches state 1 or state 2, the system will remain in this state indefinitely. We can conclude that all accounts receivable dollars will eventually be absorbed into either the paid or the bad debt state, and hence the name **absorbing state.**

When absorbing states are present, each row of the transition matrix corresponding to an absorbing state will have a single 1 and all other probabilities will be 0.

Fundamental Matrix and Associated Calculations

Whenever a Markov process has absorbing states, we do not compute steady-state probabilities because each unit ultimately ends up in one of the absorbing states. With absorbing states present, we are interested in knowing the probability that a unit will end up in each of the absorbing states. For the Heidman's Department Store problem, we want to know the probability that a dollar currently in the 0–30-day age category will end up paid (absorbing state 1) as well as the probability that a dollar in this age category will end up a bad debt (absorbing state 2). We also want to know these absorbing-state probabilities for a dollar currently in the 31–90-day age category.

The computation of the absorbing-state probabilities requires the determination and use of what is called a **fundamental matrix.** The mathematical logic underlying the fundamental matrix is beyond the scope of this text. However, as we show, the fundamental matrix is derived from the matrix of transition probabilities and is relatively easy to compute for Markov processes with a small number of states. In the following example, we show the computation of the fundamental matrix and the determination of the absorbing-state probabilities for Heidman's Department Store.

We begin the computations by partitioning the matrix of transition probabilities into the following four parts:

$$P = \begin{bmatrix} 1.0 & 0.0 & | & 0.0 & 0.0 \\ 0.0 & 1.0 & | & 0.0 & 0.0 \\ -&-&-&-&- \\ 0.4 & 0.0 & | & 0.3 & 0.3 \\ 0.4 & 0.2 & | & 0.3 & 0.1 \end{bmatrix} = \begin{bmatrix} 1.0 & 0.0 & | & 0.0 & 0.0 \\ 0.0 & 1.0 & | & 0.0 & 0.0 \\ -&-&-&-&- \\ & R & | & Q & \end{bmatrix}$$

where

$$R = \begin{bmatrix} 0.4 & 0.0 \\ 0.4 & 0.2 \end{bmatrix} \qquad Q = \begin{bmatrix} 0.3 & 0.3 \\ 0.3 & 0.1 \end{bmatrix}$$

A matrix N, called a *fundamental matrix,* can be calculated using the following formula:

$$N = (I - Q)^{-1} \tag{17.5}$$

where I is an identity matrix with 1s on the main diagonal and 0s elsewhere. The superscript -1 is used to indicate the inverse of the matrix $(I - Q)$. In Appendix 17.1 we present formulas for finding the inverse of a matrix with two rows and two columns.

Before proceeding, we note that to use equation (17.5), the identity matrix I must be chosen such that it has the *same size or dimensionality* as the matrix Q. In our example problem, Q has two rows and two columns, so we must choose

$$I = \begin{bmatrix} 1.0 & 0.0 \\ 0.0 & 1.0 \end{bmatrix}$$

Let us now continue with the example problem by computing the fundamental matrix.

$$I - Q = \begin{bmatrix} 1.0 & 0.0 \\ 0.0 & 1.0 \end{bmatrix} - \begin{bmatrix} 0.3 & 0.3 \\ 0.3 & 0.1 \end{bmatrix}$$
$$= \begin{bmatrix} 0.7 & -0.3 \\ -0.3 & 0.9 \end{bmatrix}$$

and (see Appendix 17.1)

$$N = (I - Q)^{-1} = \begin{bmatrix} 1.67 & 0.56 \\ 0.56 & 1.30 \end{bmatrix}$$

If we multiply the fundamental matrix N times the R portion of the P matrix, we obtain the probabilities that accounts receivable dollars initially in states 3 or 4 will eventually reach each of the absorbing states. The multiplication of N times R for the Heidman's Department Store problem provides the following results (again, see Appendix 17.1 for the steps of this matrix multiplication):

$$NR = \begin{bmatrix} 1.67 & 0.56 \\ 0.56 & 1.30 \end{bmatrix} \begin{bmatrix} 0.4 & 0.0 \\ 0.4 & 0.2 \end{bmatrix} = \begin{bmatrix} 0.89 & 0.11 \\ 0.74 & 0.26 \end{bmatrix}$$

The first row of the product NR is the probability that a dollar in the 0–30-day age category will end up in each absorbing state. Thus, we see a 0.89 probability that a dollar in the 0–30-day category will eventually be paid and a 0.11 probability that it will become a bad debt. Similarly, the second row shows the probabilities associated with a dollar in the 31–90-day category; that is, a dollar in the 31–90-day category has a 0.74 probability of eventually being paid and a 0.26 probability of proving to be uncollectible. Using this information, we can predict the amount of money that will be paid and the amount that will be lost as bad debts.

Establishing the Allowance for Doubtful Accounts

Let B represent a two-element vector that contains the current accounts receivable balances in the 0–30-day and the 31–90-day categories; that is,

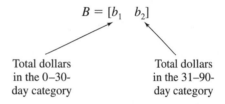

$$B = [b_1 \quad b_2]$$

Total dollars in the 0–30-day category

Total dollars in the 31–90-day category

Suppose that the December 31 balance of accounts receivable for Heidman's shows $1000 in the 0–30-day category (state 3) and $2000 in the 31–90-day category (state 4).

$$B = [1000 \quad 2000]$$

We can multiply B times NR to determine how much of the $3000 will be collected and how much will be lost. For example

$$BNR = [1000 \quad 2000] \begin{bmatrix} 0.89 & 0.11 \\ 0.74 & 0.26 \end{bmatrix}$$

$$= [2370 \quad 630]$$

Thus, we see that $2370 of the accounts receivable balances will be collected and $630 will be written off as a bad debt expense. Based on this analysis, the accounting department would set up an allowance for doubtful accounts of $630.

The matrix multiplication of BNR is simply a convenient way of computing the eventual collections and bad debts of the accounts receivable. Recall that the NR matrix showed a 0.89 probability of collecting dollars in the 0–30-day category and a 0.74 probability of collecting dollars in the 31–90-day category. Thus, as was shown by the BNR calculation, we expect to collect a total of $(1000)0.89 + (2000)0.74 = 890 + 1480 = \$2370$.

Suppose that on the basis of the previous analysis Heidman's would like to investigate the possibility of reducing the amount of bad debts. Recall that the analysis indicated that a 0.11 probability or 11% of the amount in the 0–30-day age category and 26% of the amount in the 31–90-day age category will prove to be uncollectible. Let us assume that Heidman's is considering instituting a new credit policy involving a discount for prompt payment.

Management believes that the policy under consideration will increase the probability of a transition from the 0–30-day age category to the paid category and decrease the probability of a transition from the 0–30-day to the 31–90-day age category. Let us assume that a careful study of the effects of this new policy leads management to conclude that the following transition matrix would be applicable:

$$
P = \begin{bmatrix} 1.0 & 0.0 & | & 0.0 & 0.0 \\ 0.0 & 1.0 & | & 0.0 & 0.0 \\ - & - & - & - & - & - \\ 0.6 & 0.0 & | & 0.3 & 0.1 \\ 0.4 & 0.2 & | & 0.3 & 0.1 \end{bmatrix}
$$

We see that the probability of a dollar in the 0–30-day age category making a transition to the paid category in the next period has increased to 0.6 and that the probability of a dollar in the 0–30-day age category making a transition to the 31–90-day category has decreased to 0.1. To determine the effect of these changes on bad debt expense, we must calculate N, NR, and BNR. We begin by using equation (17.5) to calculate the fundamental matrix N:

$$
N = (I - Q)^{-1} = \left\{ \begin{bmatrix} 1.0 & 0.0 \\ 0.0 & 1.0 \end{bmatrix} - \begin{bmatrix} 0.3 & 0.1 \\ 0.3 & 0.1 \end{bmatrix} \right\}^{-1}
$$

$$
= \begin{bmatrix} 0.7 & -0.1 \\ -0.3 & 0.9 \end{bmatrix}^{-1}
$$

$$
= \begin{bmatrix} 1.5 & 0.17 \\ 0.5 & 1.17 \end{bmatrix}
$$

By multiplying N times R, we obtain the new probabilities that the dollars in each age category will end up in the two absorbing states:

$$
NR = \begin{bmatrix} 1.5 & 0.17 \\ 0.5 & 1.17 \end{bmatrix} \begin{bmatrix} 0.6 & 0.0 \\ 0.4 & 0.2 \end{bmatrix}
$$

$$
= \begin{bmatrix} 0.97 & 0.03 \\ 0.77 & 0.23 \end{bmatrix}
$$

We see that with the new credit policy we would expect only 3% of the funds in the 0–30-day age category and 23% of the funds in the 31–90-day age category to prove to be uncollectible. If, as before, we assume a current balance of $1000 in the 0–30-day age category and $2000 in the 31–90-day age category, we can calculate the total amount of accounts receivable that will end up in the two absorbing states by multiplying B times NR. We obtain

$$
BNR = \begin{bmatrix} 1000 & 2000 \end{bmatrix} \begin{bmatrix} 0.97 & 0.03 \\ 0.77 & 0.23 \end{bmatrix}
$$

$$
= \begin{bmatrix} 2510 & 490 \end{bmatrix}
$$

Problem 11, which provides a variation of Heidman's Department Store problem, will give you practice in analyzing Markov processes with absorbing states.

Thus, the new credit policy shows a bad debt expense of $490. Under the previous credit policy, we found the bad debt expense to be $630. Thus, a savings of $630 − $490 = $140 could be expected as a result of the new credit policy. Given the total accounts receivable balance of $3000, this savings represents a 4.7% reduction in bad debt expense. After considering the costs involved, management can evaluate the economics of adopting the new credit policy. If the cost, including discounts, is less than 4.7% of the accounts receivable balance, we would expect the new policy to lead to increased profits for Heidman's Department Store.

SUMMARY

In this chapter we have presented Markov process models as well as examples of their application. We saw that a Markov analysis could provide helpful decision-making information about a situation that involves a sequence of repeated trials with a finite number of possible states on each trial. A primary objective is obtaining information about the probability of each state after a large number of transitions or time periods.

A market share application showed the computational procedure for determining the steady-state probabilities that could be interpreted as market shares for two competing supermarkets. In an accounts receivable application, we introduced the notion of absorbing states; for the two absorbing states, referred to as the paid and bad debt categories, we showed how to determine the percentage of an accounts receivable balance that would be absorbed in each of these states.

GLOSSARY

Trials of the process   The events that trigger transitions of the system from one state to another. In many applications, successive time periods represent the trials of the process.

State of the system   The condition of the system at any particular trial or time period.

Transition probability   Given the system is in state i during one period, the transition probability p_{ij} is the probability that the system will be in state j during the next period.

State probability   The probability that the system will be in any particular state. (That is, $\pi_i(n)$ is the probability of the system being in state i in period n.)

Steady-state probability   The probability that the system will be in any particular state after a large number of transitions. Once steady state has been reached, the state probabilities do not change from period to period.

Absorbing state   A state is said to be absorbing if the probability of making a transition out of that state is zero. Thus, once the system has made a transition into an absorbing state, it will remain there.

Fundamental matrix   A matrix necessary for the computation of probabilities associated with absorbing states of a Markov process.

PROBLEMS

1. In the market share analysis of Section 17.1, suppose that we are considering the Markov process associated with the shopping trips of one customer, but we do not know where the customer shopped during the last week. Thus, we might assume a 0.5 probability that the customer shopped at Murphy's and a 0.5 probability that the customer shopped at Ashley's at period 0; that is, $\pi_1(0) = 0.5$ and $\pi_2(0) = 0.5$. Given these initial state probabilities, develop a table similar to Table 17.2 showing the probability of each state in future periods. What do you observe about the long-run probabilities of each state?

2. Management of the New Fangled Softdrink Company believes that the probability of a customer purchasing Red Pop or the company's major competition, Super Cola, is based on the customer's most recent purchase. Suppose that the following transition probabilities are appropriate:

	To	
From	**Red Pop**	**Super Cola**
Red Pop	0.9	0.1
Super Cola	0.1	0.9

a. Show the two-period tree diagram for a customer who last purchased Red Pop. What is the probability that this customer purchases Red Pop on the second purchase?

b. What is the long-run market share for each of these two products?

c. A Red Pop advertising campaign is being planned to increase the probability of attracting Super Cola customers. Management believes that the new campaign will increase to 0.15 the probability of a customer switching from Super Cola to Red Pop. What is the projected effect of the advertising campaign on the market shares?

SELFtest

3. The computer center at Rockbottom University has been experiencing computer downtime. Let us assume that the trials of an associated Markov process are defined as one-hour periods and that the probability of the system being in a running state or a down state is based on the state of the system in the previous period. Historical data show the following transition probabilities:

	To	
From	**Running**	**Down**
Running	0.90	0.10
Down	0.30	0.70

a. If the system is initially running, what is the probability of the system being down in the next hour of operation?

b. What are the steady-state probabilities of the system being in the running state and in the down state?

4. One cause of the downtime in Problem 3 was traced to a specific piece of computer hardware. Management believes that switching to a different hardware component will result in the following transition probabilities:

	To	
From	**Running**	**Down**
Running	0.95	0.05
Down	0.60	0.40

a. What are the steady-state probabilities of the system being in the running and down states?

b. If the cost of the system being down for any period is estimated to be $500 (including lost profits for time down and maintenance), what is the breakeven cost for the new hardware component on a time-period basis?

5. A major traffic problem in the Greater Cincinnati area involves traffic attempting to cross the Ohio River from Cincinnati to Kentucky using Interstate 75. Let us assume that the probability of no traffic delay in one period, given no traffic delay in the preceding period, is 0.85 and that the probability of finding a traffic delay in one period, given a delay in the preceding period, is 0.75. Traffic is classified as having either a delay or a no-delay state, and the period considered is 30 minutes.

a. Assume that you are a motorist entering the traffic system and receive a radio report of a traffic delay. What is the probability that for the next 60 minutes (two time periods) the system will be in the delay state? Note that this result is the probability of being in the delay state for two consecutive periods.

b. What is the probability that in the long run the traffic will not be in the delay state?

c. An important assumption of the Markov process models presented in this chapter has been the constant or stationary transition probabilities as the system operates in the future. Do you believe this assumption should be questioned for this traffic problem? Explain.

6. Data collected from selected major metropolitan areas in the eastern United States show that 2% of individuals living within the city limits move to the suburbs during a 1-year period while 1% of individuals living in the suburbs move to the city during a 1-year period. Answer the following questions assuming that this process is modeled by a Markov process with two states: city and suburbs.

   a. Prepare the matrix of transition probabilities.

   b. Compute the steady-state probabilities.

   c. In a particular metropolitan area, 40% of the population live in the city, and 60% of the population live in the suburbs. What population changes do your steady-state probabilities project for this metropolitan area?

SELFtest

7. Assume that a third grocery store, Quick Stop Groceries, enters the market share and customer loyalty situation described in Section 17.1. Quick Stop Groceries is smaller than either Murphy's Foodliner or Ashley's Supermarket. However, Quick Stop's convenience with faster service and gasoline for automobiles can be expected to attract some customers who currently make weekly shopping visits to either Murphy's or Ashley's. Assume that the transition probabilities are as follows:

	To		
From	**Murphy's**	**Ashley's**	**Quick Stop**
Murphy's Foodliner	0.85	0.10	0.05
Ashley's Supermarket	0.20	0.75	0.05
Quick Stop Groceries	0.15	0.10	0.75

   a. Compute the steady-state probabilities for this three-state Markov process.

   b. What market share will Quick Stop obtain?

   c. With 1000 customers, the original two-state Markov process in Section 17.1 projected 667 weekly customer trips to Murphy's Foodliner and 333 weekly customer trips to Ashley's Supermarket. What impact will Quick Stop have on the customer visits at Murphy's and Ashley's? Explain.

8. The purchase patterns for two brands of toothpaste can be expressed as a Markov process with the following transition probabilities:

	To	
From	**Special B**	**MDA**
Special B	0.90	0.10
MDA	0.05	0.95

   a. Which brand appears to have the most loyal customers? Explain.

   b. What are the projected market shares for the two brands?

9. Suppose that in Problem 8 a new toothpaste brand enters the market such that the following transition probabilities exist:

	To		
From	**Special B**	**MDA**	**T-White**
Special B	0.80	0.10	0.10
MDA	0.05	0.75	0.20
T-White	0.40	0.30	0.30

What are the new long-run market shares? Which brand will suffer most from the introduction of the new brand of toothpaste?

10. Given the following transition matrix with states 1 and 2 as absorbing states, what is the probability that units in states 3 and 4 end up in each of the absorbing states?

$$P = \begin{bmatrix} 1.0 & 0.0 & 0.0 & 0.0 \\ 0.0 & 1.0 & 0.0 & 0.0 \\ 0.2 & 0.1 & 0.4 & 0.3 \\ 0.2 & 0.2 & 0.1 & 0.5 \end{bmatrix}$$

SELFtest

11. In the Heidman's Department Store problem of Section 17.2, suppose that the following transition matrix is appropriate:

$$P = \begin{bmatrix} 1.0 & 0.0 & 0.0 & 0.0 \\ 0.0 & 1.0 & 0.0 & 0.0 \\ 0.5 & 0.0 & 0.25 & 0.25 \\ 0.5 & 0.2 & 0.05 & 0.25 \end{bmatrix}$$

If Heidman's has $4000 in the 0–30-day category and $5000 in the 31–90-day category, what is your estimate of the amount of bad debts the company will experience?

12. The KLM Christmas Tree Farm owns a plot of land with 5000 evergreen trees. Each year KLM allows retailers of Christmas trees to select and cut trees for sale to individual customers. KLM protects small trees (usually less than 4 feet tall) so that they will be available for sale in future years. Currently 1500 trees are classified as protected trees, while the remaining 3500 are available for cutting. However, even though a tree is available for cutting in a given year, it may not be selected for cutting until future years. While most trees not cut in a given year live until the next year, some diseased trees are lost every year.

In viewing the KLM Christmas tree operation as a Markov process with yearly periods, we define the following four states:

State 1. Cut and sold
State 2. Lost to disease
State 3. Too small for cutting
State 4. Available for cutting but not cut and sold

The following transition matrix is appropriate:

$$P = \begin{bmatrix} 1.0 & 0.0 & 0.0 & 0.0 \\ 0.0 & 1.0 & 0.0 & 0.0 \\ 0.1 & 0.2 & 0.5 & 0.2 \\ 0.4 & 0.1 & 0.0 & 0.5 \end{bmatrix}$$

How many of the farm's 5000 trees will be sold eventually, and how many will be lost?

13. A large corporation has collected data on the reasons both middle managers and senior managers leave the company. Some managers eventually retire, but others leave the company prior to retirement for personal reasons including more attractive positions with other firms. Assume that the following matrix of one-year transition probabilities applies with the four states of the Markov process being retirement, leaves prior to retirement for personal reasons, stays as a middle manager, stays as a senior manager.

	Retirement	Leaves—Personal	Middle Manager	Senior Manager
Retirement	1.00	0.00	0.00	0.00
Leaves—Personal	0.00	1.00	0.00	0.00
Middle Manager	0.03	0.07	0.80	0.10
Senior Manager	0.08	0.01	0.03	0.88

    a. What states are considered absorbing states? Why?
    b. Interpret the transition probabilities for the middle managers.
    c. Interpret the transition probabilities for the senior managers.
    d. What percentage of the current middle managers will eventually retire from the company? What percentage will leave the company for personal reasons?
    e. The company currently has 920 managers: 640 middle managers and 280 senior managers. How many of these managers will eventually retire from the company? How many will leave the company for personal reasons?

14. Data for the progression of college students at a particular college are summarized in the following matrix of transition probabilities.

	Graduate	Dropout	Freshman	Sophomore	Junior	Senior
Graduate	1.00	0.00	0.00	0.00	0.00	0.00
Dropout	0.00	1.00	0.00	0.00	0.00	0.00
Freshman	0.00	0.20	0.15	0.65	0.00	0.00
Sophomore	0.00	0.15	0.00	0.10	0.75	0.00
Junior	0.00	0.10	0.00	0.00	0.05	0.85
Senior	0.90	0.05	0.00	0.00	0.00	0.05

    a. What states are absorbing states?
    b. Interpret the transition probabilities for a sophomore.
    c. Use The Management Scientist software package to compute the probabilities that a sophomore will graduate and that a sophomore will drop out.
    d. In an address to the incoming class of 600 freshmen, the dean asks the students to look around the auditorium and realize that about 50% of the freshmen present today will not make it to graduation day. Does your Markov process analysis support the dean's statement? Explain.
    e. Currently, the college has 600 freshmen, 520 sophomores, 460 juniors, and 420 seniors. What percentage of the 2000 students attending the college will eventually graduate?

Appendix 17.1   MATRIX NOTATION AND OPERATIONS

Matrix Notation

A *matrix* is a rectangular arrangement of numbers. For example, consider the following matrix that we have named D:

$$D = \begin{bmatrix} 1 & 3 & 2 \\ 0 & 4 & 5 \end{bmatrix}$$

The matrix D is said to consist of six elements, where each element of D is a number. To identify a particular element of a matrix, we have to specify its location. Therefore, we introduce the concepts of rows and columns.

All elements across some horizontal line in a matrix are said to be in a row of the matrix. For example, elements 1, 3, and 2 in D are in the first row, and elements 0, 4, and 5 are in the second row. By convention, we refer to the top row as row 1, the second row from the top as row 2, and so on.

All elements along some vertical line are said to be in a column of the matrix. Elements 1 and 0 in D are elements in the first column, elements 3 and 4 are elements of the second column, and elements 2 and 5 are elements of the third column. By convention, we refer to the leftmost column as column 1, the next column to the right as column 2, and so on.

We can identify a particular element in a matrix by specifying its row and column position. For example, the element in row 1 and column 2 of D is the number 3. This position is written as

$$d_{12} = 3$$

In general, we use the following notation to refer to the specific elements of D:

$$d_{ij} = \text{element located in the } i\text{th row and } j\text{th column of } D$$

We always use capital letters for the names of matrixes and the corresponding lowercase letters with two subscripts to denote the elements.

The *size* of a matrix is the number of rows and columns in the matrix and is written as the number of rows $\times$ the number of columns. Thus, the size of D is 2×3.

Frequently we will encounter matrixes that have only one row or one column. For example,

$$G = \begin{bmatrix} 6 \\ 4 \\ 2 \\ 3 \end{bmatrix}$$

is a matrix that has only one column. Whenever a matrix has only one column, we call the matrix a *column vector*. In a similar manner, any matrix that has only one row is called a *row vector*. Using our previous notation for the elements of a matrix, we would refer to specific elements in G by writing g_{ij}. However, because G has only one column, the column position is unimportant, and we need only specify the row the element of interest is in. That is, instead of referring to elements in a vector using g_{ij}, we specify only one subscript, which denotes the position of the element in the vector. For example,

$$g_1 = 6 \qquad g_2 = 4 \qquad g_3 = 2 \qquad g_4 = 3$$

Matrix Operations

Matrix Transpose.   The transpose of a matrix is formed by making the rows in the original matrix the columns in the transpose matrix, and by making the columns in the original matrix the rows in the transpose matrix. For example, the transpose of the matrix

$$D = \begin{bmatrix} 1 & 3 & 2 \\ 0 & 4 & 5 \end{bmatrix}$$

is

$$D^t = \begin{bmatrix} 1 & 0 \\ 3 & 4 \\ 2 & 5 \end{bmatrix}$$

Note that we use the superscript t to denote the transpose of a matrix.

Matrix Multiplication.   We demonstrate how to perform two types of matrix multiplication: (1) multiplying two vectors and (2) multiplying a matrix times a matrix.

The product of a row vector of size $1 \times n$ times a column vector of size $n \times 1$ is the number obtained by multiplying the first element in the row vector times the first element in the column vector, the second element in the row vector times the second element in the column vector, and continuing on through the last element in the row vector times the last element in the column vector, and then summing the products. Suppose, for example, that we wanted to multiply the row vector H times the column vector G, where

$$H = [2 \quad 1 \quad 5 \quad 0] \text{ and } G = \begin{bmatrix} 6 \\ 4 \\ 2 \\ 3 \end{bmatrix}$$

The product HG, referred to as a vector product, is given by

$$HG = 2(6) + 1(4) + 5(2) + 0(3) = 26$$

The product of a matrix of size $p \times n$ and a matrix of size $n \times m$ is a new matrix of size $p \times m$. The element in the ith row and jth column of the new matrix is given by the vector product of the ith row of the $p \times n$ matrix times the jth column of the $n \times m$ matrix. Suppose, for example, that we want to multiply D times A, where

$$D = \begin{bmatrix} 1 & 3 & 2 \\ 0 & 4 & 5 \end{bmatrix} \quad A = \begin{bmatrix} 1 & 3 & 5 \\ 2 & 0 & 4 \\ 1 & 5 & 2 \end{bmatrix}$$

Let $C = DA$ denote the product of D times A. The element in row 1 and column 1 of C is given by the vector product of the first row of D times the first column of A. Thus

$$c_{11} = [1 \quad 3 \quad 2] \begin{bmatrix} 1 \\ 2 \\ 1 \end{bmatrix} = 1(1) + 3(2) + 2(1) = 9$$

The element in row 2 and column 1 of C is given by the vector product of the second row of D times the first column of A. Thus,

$$c_{21} = [0 \quad 4 \quad 5] \begin{bmatrix} 1 \\ 2 \\ 1 \end{bmatrix} = 0(1) + 4(2) + 5(1) = 13$$

Calculating the remaining elements of C in a similar fashion, we obtain

$$C = \begin{bmatrix} 9 & 13 & 21 \\ 13 & 25 & 26 \end{bmatrix}$$

Clearly, the product of a matrix and a vector is just a special case of multiplying a matrix times a matrix. For example, the product of a matrix of size $m \times n$ and a vector of size $n \times 1$ is a new vector of size $m \times 1$. The element in the ith position of the new vector is given by the vector product of the ith row of the $m \times n$ matrix times the $n \times 1$ column vector. Suppose, for example, that we want to multiply D times K, where

$$D = \begin{bmatrix} 1 & 3 & 2 \\ 0 & 4 & 5 \end{bmatrix} \quad K = \begin{bmatrix} 1 \\ 4 \\ 2 \end{bmatrix}$$

The first element of DK is given by the vector product of the first row of D times K. Thus,

$$[1 \quad 3 \quad 2] \begin{bmatrix} 1 \\ 4 \\ 2 \end{bmatrix} = 1(1) + 3(4) + 2(2) = 17$$

The second element of DK is given by the vector product of the second row of D times K. Thus,

$$[0 \quad 4 \quad 5] \begin{bmatrix} 1 \\ 4 \\ 2 \end{bmatrix} = 0(1) + 4(4) + 5(2) = 26$$

Hence, we see that the product of the matrix D times the vector K is given by

$$DK = \begin{bmatrix} 1 & 3 & 2 \\ 0 & 4 & 5 \end{bmatrix} \begin{bmatrix} 1 \\ 4 \\ 2 \end{bmatrix} = \begin{bmatrix} 17 \\ 26 \end{bmatrix}$$

Can any two matrixes be multiplied? The answer is no. To multiply two matrixes, the number of the columns in the first matrix must equal the number of rows in the second. If this property is satisfied, the matrixes are said to *conform for multiplication.* Thus, in our example, D and K could be multiplied because D had three columns and K had three rows.

Matrix Inverse.   The inverse of a matrix A is another matrix, denoted A^{-1}, such that $A^{-1}A = I$ and $AA^{-1} = I$. The inverse of any square matrix A consisting of two rows and two columns is computed as follows:

$$A = \begin{bmatrix} a_{11} & a_{12} \\ a_{21} & a_{22} \end{bmatrix}$$

$$A^{-1} = \begin{bmatrix} a_{22}/d & -a_{12}/d \\ -a_{21}/d & a_{11}/d \end{bmatrix}$$

where $d = a_{11}a_{22} - a_{21}a_{12}$ is the determinant of the 2×2 matrix A. For example, if

$$A = \begin{bmatrix} 0.7 & -0.3 \\ -0.3 & 0.9 \end{bmatrix}$$

then

$$d = (0.7)(0.9) - (-0.3)(-0.3) = 0.54$$

and

$$A^{-1} = \begin{bmatrix} 0.9/0.54 & 0.3/0.54 \\ 0.3/0.54 & 0.7/0.54 \end{bmatrix} = \begin{bmatrix} 1.67 & 0.56 \\ 0.56 & 1.30 \end{bmatrix}$$

U.S. GENERAL ACCOUNTING OFFICE*
WASHINGTON, D.C.

The U.S. General Accounting Office (GAO) is an independent, nonpolitical audit organization in the legislative branch of the federal government. The GAO was created by the Budget and Accounting Act of 1921 and has three basic purposes:

1. To assist Congress, its committees, and its members in carrying out their legislative and oversight responsibilities, consistent with its role as an independent, nonpolitical agency.
2. To audit and evaluate the programs, activities, and financial operations of federal departments and agencies and to make recommendations toward more efficient and effective operations.
3. To carry out financial control and other functions with respect to federal government programs and operations including accounting, legal, and claims settlement work.

GAO evaluators, in fulfilling the main role in the GAO, determine the effectiveness of existing or proposed federal programs and the efficiency, economy, legality, and effectiveness with which federal agencies carry out their responsibilities. These evaluations culminate in reports to the Congress and to the heads of federal departments and agencies. Such reports typically include recommendations to Congress concerning the need for enabling or remedial legislation and suggestions to agencies concerning the need for changes in programs or operations to improve their economy, efficiency, and effectiveness.

GAO evaluators analyze policies and practices and the use of resources within and among federal programs, identify problem areas and deficiencies in meeting program goals, develop and analyze alternative solutions to problems of program execution, and develop and recommend changes to enable the programs to better conform to congressional goals and legislative intent. To effectively carry out their duties, evaluators must be proficient in interviewing, data processing, records review, legislative research, quantitative methods, and statistical analysis techniques.

Impact of Services on the Well-Being of Older People

GAO evaluators obtained data from a random sample of noninstitutionalized persons aged 65 and older living in Cleveland, Ohio. The health conditions of the sampled individuals in the 65- to 69-year-old groups were defined by the following three states:

- **Best.** Individual able to perform 13 identified activities of daily living without help.
- **Next best.** Individual able to perform the same 13 activities but required help for at least one activity.
- **Worst.** Individual unable to perform the same 13 activities even with help.

Using a 2-year period, GAO evaluators developed estimates of the year-to-year transition probabilities of individuals in the 65- to 69-year-old group. These estimates were then used to develop a transition probability matrix such as shown in the following table. Note that a death state has been added as an absorbing state.

Using the transition probabilities, a Markov process analysis can be used to determine the state probabilities for any number of periods (years) into the future. To verify the appropriateness of the Markov process model, GAO evaluators used the transition probabilities to determine the state probabilities for the 65- to 69-year-old age group 5 years into the future. The resulting state probabilities were compared with the health states of individuals in a known 70- to 74-year-old age group. No statistically significant difference occurred between the

*The authors are indebted to Bill Ammann of the U.S. General Accounting Office, Washington, D.C., for providing this application.

probabilities provided by the model and the actual state probabilities of the 70- to 74-year-old group.

Current Year Condition	Following Year Condition			
	Best	**Next Best**	**Worst**	**Death**
Best	p_{11}	p_{12}	p_{13}	p_{14}
Next Best	p_{21}	p_{22}	p_{23}	p_{24}
Worst	p_{31}	p_{32}	p_{33}	p_{34}
Death	0	0	0	1

Estimating the Likely Effects of Health Care Programs

The individuals in the original study were subdivided into two groups: those receiving appropriate health care and those not receiving appropriate health care. For the purpose of the study, a person was classified as receiving appropriate health care if the person was taking medication and/or treatment for each illness present and if the person was receiving help to perform each of the 13 activities of daily living as specifically needed. As a result, GAO evaluators developed two matrixes of transition probabilities: one for individuals receiving appropriate health care and one for individuals not receiving appropriate health care.

For any individuals not receiving appropriate help, the kind of additional help needed was determined, and the cost of that help was estimated. Then those persons were artificially aged using the transition probabilities to establish the likely benefits in terms of improved health states for the individuals. Over a 20-year period, a net savings occurred for the health care program provided all other factors remained equal. That is, the increased

cost to provide sufficient appropriate help to all persons was eventually offset by individuals either improving their health state or by not spending as much time in a worse state. Although benefits of health care are often proclaimed theoretically, the Markov process model provided evidence that indicated benefits would be achieved with the health care program.

This type of Markov analysis was also conducted for economic, social, and life view status as well as for the health status. In some instances, the Markov model showed that additional help and/or programs did not result in net savings over time.

Questions

1. Suppose the transition probabilities in the table were as follows:

$$\begin{bmatrix} 0.80 & 0.10 & 0.06 & 0.04 \\ 0.05 & 0.75 & 0.15 & 0.05 \\ 0.00 & 0.05 & 0.75 & 0.20 \\ 0.00 & 0.00 & 0.00 & 1.00 \end{bmatrix}$$

   Assume that a particular city has 1000 individuals in the best state, 2000 in the next best state, and 500 in the worst state. Estimate how many of each of these individuals will be in each state 2 years from now.

2. How might health care programs affect the matrix of transition probabilities in Question 1? What effect would you expect to see in the distribution of individuals across the four states 2 years from now?

Chapter 18

MULTICRITERIA DECISION PROBLEMS

CONTENTS

In previous chapters we have shown how a variety of quantitative methods can help managers make better decisions. Whenever we desired an optimal solution, we utilized a single criterion (e.g., maximize profit, minimize cost, minimize time). In this chapter we discuss techniques that are appropriate for situations in which the decision maker needs to consider multiple criteria in arriving at the overall best decision. For example, consider a company involved in selecting a location for a new manufacturing plant. The cost of land and construction may vary from location to location, so one criterion in selecting the best site could be the cost involved in building the plant; if cost were the sole criterion of interest, management would simply select the location that minimizes land cost plus construction cost. Before making any decision, however, management might also want to consider additional criteria such as the availability of transportation from the plant to the firm's distribution centers, the attractiveness of the proposed location in terms of hiring and retaining employees, energy costs at the proposed site, and state and local taxes. In such situations the complexity of the problem increases because one location may be more desirable in terms of one criterion and less desirable in terms of one or more of the other criteria.

To introduce the topic of multicriteria decision making, we consider a technique referred to as **goal programming.** This technique has been developed to handle multiple criteria situations within the general framework of linear programming. We next consider a *scoring model* as a relatively easy way to identify the best decision alternative for a multicriteria problem. Finally, we introduce a method known as the *analytical hierarchy process (AHP),* which allows the user to make pairwise comparisons among the criteria and a series of pairwise comparisons among the decision alternatives in order to arrive at a prioritized ranking of the decision alternatives.

18.1   GOAL PROGRAMMING: FORMULATION AND GRAPHICAL SOLUTION

To illustrate the goal programming approach to multicriteria decision problems, let us consider a problem facing Nicolo Investment Advisors. A client has $80,000 to invest and, as an initial strategy, would like the investment portfolio restricted to two stocks:

Stock	Price/Share	Estimated Annual Return/Share	Risk Index/Share
U.S. Oil	$25	$3	0.50
Hub Properties	$50	$5	0.25

U.S. Oil, which has a return of $3 on a $25 share price, provides an annual rate of return of 12%, whereas Hub Properties provides an annual rate of return of 10%. The risk index per share, 0.50 for U.S. Oil and 0.25 for Hub Properties, is a rating Nicolo has assigned to measure the relative risk of the two investments. Higher risk index values imply greater risk; hence, Nicolo has judged U.S. Oil to be the riskier investment. By specifying a maximum portfolio risk index, Nicolo will avoid placing too much of the portfolio in high-risk investments.

To illustrate how to use the risk index per share to measure the total portfolio risk, suppose that Nicolo chooses a portfolio that invests all $80,000 in U.S. Oil, the higher risk, but higher return, investment. Nicolo could purchase $80,000/$25 = 3200 shares of U.S. Oil, and the portfolio would have a risk index of 3200(0.50) = 1600. Conversely, if Nicolo purchases no shares of either stock, the portfolio will have no risk, but also no return. Thus, the portfolio risk index will vary from 0 (least risk) to 1600 (most risk).

Nicolo's client would like to avoid a high-risk portfolio; thus, investing all funds in U.S. Oil would not be desirable. However, the client agreed that an acceptable level of risk would correspond to portfolios with a maximum total risk index of 700. Thus, considering only risk, one *goal* is to find a portfolio with a risk index of 700 or less.

Another goal of the client is to obtain an annual return of at least $9000. This goal can be achieved with a portfolio consisting of 2000 shares of U.S. Oil (at a cost of 2000($25) = $50,000) and 600 shares of Hub Properties (at a cost of 600($50) = $30,000); the annual return in this case would be 2000($3) + 600($5) = $9000. Note, however, that the portfolio risk index for this investment strategy would be 2000(0.50) + 600(0.25) = 1150; thus, this portfolio achieves the annual return goal but does not satisfy the portfolio risk index goal.

Thus, the portfolio selection problem is a multicriteria decision problem involving two conflicting goals: one dealing with risk and one dealing with annual return. The goal programming approach was developed precisely for this kind of problem. Goal programming can be used to identify a portfolio that comes closest to achieving both goals. Before applying the methodology, the client must determine which, if either, goal is more important.

Suppose that the client's top-priority goal is to restrict the risk; that is, keeping the portfolio risk index at 700 or less is so important that the client is not willing to trade the achievement of this goal for any amount of an increase in annual return. But, as long as the portfolio risk index does not exceed 700, the client seeks the best possible return. Based on this statement of priorities, the goals for the problem are as follows:

Primary Goal (Priority Level 1)

Goal 1: Find a portfolio that has a risk index of 700 or less.

Secondary Goal (Priority Level 2)

Goal 2: Find a portfolio that will provide an annual return of at least $9000.

In goal programming with preemptive priorities, we never permit trade-offs between higher and lower level goals.

The primary goal is called a *priority level 1 goal,* and the secondary goal is called a *priority level 2 goal.* In goal programming terminology, these are called **preemptive priorities** because the decision maker is not willing to sacrifice any amount of achievement of the priority level 1 goal for the lower priority goal. The portfolio risk index of 700 is the **target value** for the priority level 1 (primary) goal, and the annual return of $9000 is the target value for the priority level 2 (secondary) goal. The difficulty in finding a solution that will achieve these goals is that only $80,000 is available for investment.

Developing the Constraints and the Goal Equations

We begin by defining the decision variables:

$$U = \text{number of shares of U.S. Oil purchased}$$
$$H = \text{number of shares of Hub Properties purchased}$$

Constraints for goal programming problems are handled in the same way as in an ordinary linear programming problem. In the Nicolo Investment Advisors problem, one constraint corresponds to the funds available. Because each share of U.S. Oil costs $25 and each share of Hub Properties costs $50, the constraint representing the funds available is

$$25U + 50H \leq 80,000$$

To complete the formulation of the model, we must develop a **goal equation** for each goal. Let us begin by writing the goal equation for the primary goal. Each share of U.S. Oil has a risk index of 0.50 and each share of Hub Properties has a risk index of 0.25, therefore the portfolio risk index is $0.50U + 0.25H$. Depending on the values of U and H, the portfolio risk index may be less than, equal to, or greater than the target value of 700. To represent these possibilities mathematically, we create the goal equation

$$0.50U + 0.25H = 700 + d_1^+ - d_1^-$$

where

$d_1^+ = $ the amount by which the portfolio risk index exceeds the target value of 700

$d_1^- = $ the amount by which the portfolio risk index is less than the target value of 700

To achieve a goal exactly, the two deviation variables must both equal zero.

In goal programming, d_1^+ and d_1^- are called **deviation variables.** The purpose of deviation variables is to allow for the possibility of not meeting the target value exactly. Consider, for example, a portfolio that consists of $U = 2000$ shares of U.S. Oil and $H = 0$ shares of Hub Properties. The portfolio risk index is $0.50(2000) + 0.25(0) = 1000$. In this case,

$d_1^+ = 300$ reflects the fact that the portfolio risk index exceeds the target value by 300 units; note also that since d_1^+ is greater than zero, the value of d_1^- must be zero. For a portfolio consisting of $U = 0$ shares of U.S. Oil and $H = 1000$ shares of Hub Properties, the portfolio risk index would be $0.50(0) + 0.25(1000) = 250$. In this case, $d_1^- = 450$ and $d_1^+ = 0$, indicating that the solution provides a portfolio risk index of 450 less than the target value of 700.

In general, the letter d is used for deviation variables in a goal programming model. A superscript of plus ($+$) or minus ($-$) is used to indicate whether the variable corresponds to a positive or negative deviation from the target value. If we bring the deviation variables to the left-hand side, we can rewrite the goal equation for the primary goal as

$$0.50U + 0.25H - d_1^+ + d_1^- = 700$$

Note that the value on the right-hand side of the goal equation is the target value for the goal. The left-hand side of the goal equation consists of two parts:

1. A function that defines the amount of goal achievement in terms of the decision variables (e.g., $0.50U + 0.25H$)
2. Deviation variables representing the difference between the target value for the goal and the level achieved

To develop a goal equation for the secondary goal, we begin by writing a function representing the annual return for the investment:

$$\text{Annual return} = 3U + 5H$$

Then we define two deviation variables that represent the amount of over- or underachievement of the goal. Doing so, we obtain

$d_2^+ = $ the amount by which the annual return for the portfolio is greater than the target value of \$9000

$d_2^- = $ the amount by which the annual return for the portfolio is less than the target value of \$9000

Using these two deviation variables, we write the goal equation for goal 2 as

$$3U + 5H = 9000 + d_2^+ - d_2^-$$

or

$$3U + 5H - d_2^+ + d_2^- = 9000$$

This step completes the development of the goal equations and the constraints for the Nicolo portfolio problem. We are now ready to develop an appropriate objective function for the problem.

Developing an Objective Function with Preemptive Priorities

The objective function in a goal programming model calls for minimizing a function of the deviation variables. In the portfolio selection problem, the most important goal, denoted P_1, is to find a portfolio with a risk index of 700 or less. This problem has only two goals, and the client is unwilling to accept a portfolio risk index greater than 700 to achieve the secondary annual return goal. Therefore, the secondary goal is denoted P_2. As we stated previously, these goal priorities are referred to as preemptive priorities because the satisfaction of a higher level goal cannot be traded for the satisfaction of a lower level goal.

Goal programming problems with preemptive priorities are solved by treating priority level 1 goals (P_1) first in an objective function. The idea is to start by finding a solution that comes closest to satisfying the priority level 1 goals. This solution is then modified by solving a problem with an objective function involving only priority level 2 goals (P_2); however, revisions in the solution are permitted only if they do not hinder achievement of the P_1 goals. In general, solving a goal programming problem with preemptive priorities involves solving a sequence of linear programs with different objective functions; P_1 goals are considered first, P_2 goals second, P_3 goals third, and so on. At each stage of the procedure, a revision in the solution is permitted only if it causes no reduction in the achievement of a higher priority goal.

We must solve one linear program for each priority level.

The number of linear programs that we must solve in sequence to develop the solution to a goal programming problem is determined by the number of priority levels. One linear program must be solved for each priority level. We will call the first linear program solved the priority level 1 problem, the second linear program solved the priority level 2 problem, and so on. Each linear program is obtained from the one at the next higher level by changing the objective function and adding a constraint.

We first formulate the objective function for the priority level 1 problem. The client has stated that the portfolio risk index should not exceed 700. Is underachieving the target value of 700 a concern? Clearly, the answer is no because portfolio risk index values of less than 700 correspond to less risk. Is overachieving the target value of 700 a concern? The answer is yes because portfolios with a risk index greater than 700 correspond to unacceptable levels of risk. Thus, the objective function corresponding to the priority level 1 linear program should minimize the value of d_1^+.

The goal equations and the funds available constraint have already been developed. Thus, the priority level 1 linear program can now be stated.

P_1 Problem

$$\text{Min} \quad d_1^+$$

s.t.

$$
\begin{array}{llll}
25U + & 50H & & \leq 80{,}000 & \text{Funds available} \\
0.50U + & 0.25H - d_1^+ + d_1^- & & = 700 & P_1 \text{ goal} \\
3U + & 5H & -d_2^+ + d_2^- & = 9000 & P_2 \text{ goal} \\
& U, H, d_1^+, d_1^-, d_2^+, d_2^- \geq 0
\end{array}
$$

Graphical Solution Procedure

One approach that can often be used to solve a difficult problem is to break the problem into two or more smaller or easier problems. The linear programming procedure we use to solve the goal programming problem is based on this approach.

The graphical solution procedure for goal programming is similar to that for linear programming presented in Chapter 7. The only difference is that the procedure for goal programming involves a separate solution for each priority level. Recall that the linear programming graphical solution procedure uses a graph to display the values for the decision variables. Because the decision variables are nonnegative, we consider only that portion of the graph where $U \geq 0$ and $H \geq 0$. Recall also that every point on the graph is called a *solution point*.

We begin the graphical solution procedure for the Nicolo Investment problem by identifying all solution points that satisfy the available funds constraint:

$$25U + 50H \leq 80{,}000$$

The shaded region in Figure 18.1, feasible portfolios, consists of all points that satisfy this constraint—that is, values of U and H for which $25U + 50H \leq 80{,}000$.

FIGURE 18.1   PORTFOLIOS THAT SATISFY THE AVAILABLE FUNDS CONSTRAINT

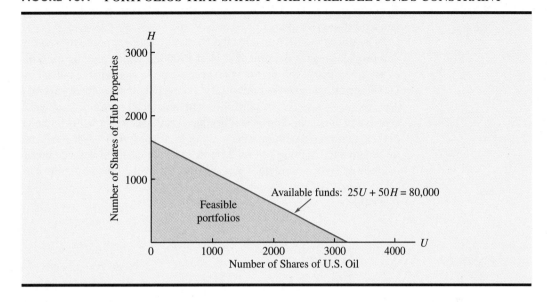

The objective for the priority level 1 linear program is to minimize d_1^+, the amount by which the portfolio index exceeds the target value of 700. Recall that the P_1 goal equation is

$$0.50U + 0.25H - d_1^+ + d_1^- = 700$$

When the P_1 goal is met exactly, $d_1^+ = 0$ and $d_1^- = 0$; the goal equation then reduces to $0.50U + 0.25H = 700$. Figure 18.2 shows the graph of this equation; the shaded region identifies all solution points that satisfy the available funds constraint and also result in the value of $d_1^+ = 0$. Thus, the shaded region contains all the feasible solution points that achieve the priority level 1 goal.

FIGURE 18.2   PORTFOLIOS THAT SATISFY THE P_1 GOAL

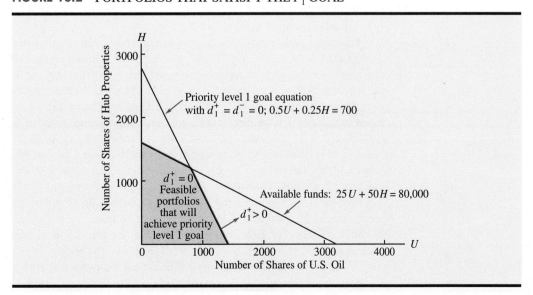

At this point, we have solved the priority level 1 problem. Note that alternative optimal solutions are possible; in fact, all solution points in the shaded region in Figure 18.2 maintain a portfolio risk index of 700 or less, and hence $d_1^+ = 0$.

The priority level 2 goal for the Nicolo Investment problem is to find a portfolio that will provide an annual return of at least $9000. Is overachieving the target value of $9000 a concern? Clearly, the answer is no because portfolios with an annual return of more than $9000 correspond to higher returns. Is underachieving the target value of $9000 a concern? The answer is yes because portfolios with an annual return of less than $9000 are not acceptable to the client. Thus, the objective function corresponding to the priority level 2 linear program should minimize the value of d_2^-. However, because goal 2 is a secondary goal, the solution to the priority level 2 linear program must not degrade the optimal solution to the priority level 1 problem. Thus, the priority level 2 linear program can now be stated.

P_2 Problem

Min d_2^-

s.t.

$$
\begin{array}{lrl}
25U + 50H & \leq 80{,}000 & \text{Funds available} \\
0.50U + 0.25H - d_1^+ + d_1^- & = 700 & P_1 \text{ goal} \\
3U + 5H \quad - d_2^+ + d_2^- & = 9000 & P_2 \text{ goal} \\
d_1^+ & = 0 & \text{Maintain achievement} \\
& & \text{of } P_1 \text{ goal}
\end{array}
$$

$$U, H, d_1^+, d_1^-, d_2^+, d_2^- \geq 0$$

Note that the priority level 2 linear program differs from the priority level 1 linear program in two ways. The objective function involves minimizing the amount by which the portfolio annual return underachieves the level 2 goal, and another constraint has been added to ensure that no amount of achievement of the priority level 1 goal is sacrificed.

Let us now continue the graphical solution procedure. The goal equation for the priority level 2 goal is

$$3U + 5H - d_2^+ + d_2^- = 9000$$

When both d_2^+ and d_2^- equal zero, this equation reduces to $3U + 5H = 9000$; we show the graph with this equation in Figure 18.3.

At this stage, we cannot consider any solution point that will degrade the achievement of the priority level 1 goal. Figure 18.3 shows that no solution points will achieve the priority level 2 goal and maintain the values we were able to achieve for the priority level 1 goal. In fact, the best solution that can be obtained when considering the priority level 2 goal is given by the point ($U = 800$, $H = 1200$); in other words, this point comes the closest to satisfying the priority level 2 goal from among those solutions satisfying the priority level 1 goal. Because the annual return corresponding to this solution point is $3(800) + $5(1200) = $8400, identifying a portfolio that will satisfy both the priority level 1 and the priority level 2 goals is impossible. In fact, the best solution underachieves goal 2 by $d_2^- = $9000 - $8400 = $600.

Thus, the goal programming solution for the Nicolo Investment problem recommends that the $80,000 available for investment be used to purchase 800 shares of U.S. Oil and 1200 shares of Hub Properties. Note that the priority level 1 goal of a portfolio risk index of 700 or less has been achieved. However, the priority level 2 goal of at least a $9000 annual return is not achievable. The annual return for the recommended portfolio is $8400.

FIGURE 18.3   BEST SOLUTION WITH RESPECT TO BOTH GOALS
(SOLUTION TO P_2 PROBLEM)

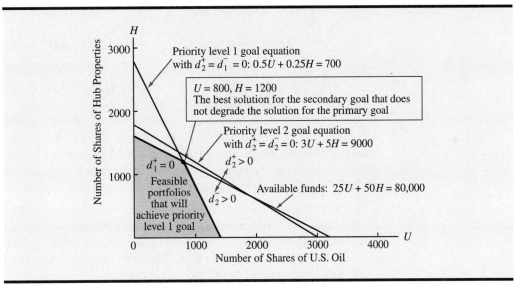

In summary, the graphical solution procedure for goal programming involves the following steps.

1. Identify the feasible solution points that satisfy the problem constraints.
2. Identify all feasible solutions that achieve the highest-priority goal; if no feasible solutions will achieve the highest priority goal, identify the solution(s) that comes closest to achieving it.
3. Move down one priority level, and determine the "best" solution possible without sacrificing any achievement of higher priority goals.
4. Repeat step 3 until all priority levels have been considered.

Problem 2 will test your ability to formulate a goal programming model and use the graphical solution procedure to obtain a solution.

Although the graphical solution procedure is a convenient method for solving goal programming problems involving two decision variables, the solution of larger problems requires a computer-aided approach. In Section 18.2 we illustrate how to use a computer software package to solve more complex goal programming problems.

Goal Programming Model

As we have stated, preemptive goal programming problems are solved as a sequence of linear programs: one linear program for each priority level. However, having a notation that permits writing a goal programming problem in one concise statement is helpful.

In writing the overall objective for the portfolio selection problem, we must write the objective function in a way that reminds us of the preemptive priorities. We can do so by writing the objective function as

$$\text{Min} \quad P_1(d_1^+) + P_2(d_2^-)$$

The priority levels P_1 and P_2 are not numerical weights on the deviation variables, but simply labels that remind us of the priority levels for the goals.

We now write the complete goal programming model as

Min $\quad P_1(d_1^+) + P_2(d_2^-)$

s.t.

$$
\begin{array}{rcll}
25U + 50H & & \leq 80{,}000 & \text{Funds available} \\
0.50U + 0.25H - d_1^+ + d_1^- & = & 700 & P_1 \text{ goal} \\
3U + 5H - d_2^+ + d_2^- & = & 9000 & P_2 \text{ goal} \\
U, H, d_1^+, d_1^-, d_2^+, d_2^- \geq 0 & & &
\end{array}
$$

With the exception of the P_1 and P_2 priority levels in the objective function, this model is a linear programming model. The solution of this linear program involves solving a sequence of linear programs involving goals at decreasing priority levels.

We now summarize the procedure used to develop a goal programming model.

1. Identify the goals and any constraints that reflect resource capacities or other restrictions that may prevent achievement of the goals.
2. Determine the priority level of each goal; goals with priority level P_1 are most important, those with priority level P_2 are next most important, and so on.
3. Define the decision variables.
4. Formulate the constraints in the usual linear programming fashion.
5. For each goal, develop a goal equation, with the right-hand side specifying the target value for the goal. Deviation variables d_i^+ and d_i^- are included in each goal equation to reflect the possible deviations above or below the target value.
6. Write the objective function in terms of minimizing a prioritized function of the deviation variables.

NOTES AND COMMENTS

1. The constraints in the general goal programming model are of two types: goal equations and ordinary linear programming constraints. Some analysts call the goal equations *goal constraints* and the ordinary linear programming constraints *system constraints*.
2. You might think of the general goal programming model as having "hard" and "soft" constraints. The hard constraints are the ordinary linear programming constraints that cannot be violated. The soft constraints are the ones resulting from the goal equations. Soft constraints can be violated but with a penalty for doing so. The penalty is reflected by the coefficient of the deviation variable in the objective function. In Section 18.2 we illustrate this point with a problem that has a coefficient of 2 for one of the deviation variables.
3. Note that the constraint added in moving from the linear programming problem at one priority level to the linear programming problem at the next lower priority level becomes a hard constraint. No amount of achievement of a higher priority goal may be sacrificed to achieve a lower priority goal.

18.2 GOAL PROGRAMMING: SOLVING MORE COMPLEX PROBLEMS

In Section 18.1 we formulated and solved a goal programming model that involved one priority level 1 goal and one priority level 2 goal. In this section we show how to formulate and solve goal programming models that involve multiple goals within the same priority level. Although computer programs have been specially developed to solve goal programming models, these programs are not as readily available as general purpose linear programming software packages. Thus, the computer solution procedure outlined in this section develops a solution to a goal programming model by solving a sequence of linear programming models with a general purpose linear programming software package.

Suncoast Office Supplies Problem

The management of Suncoast Office Supplies establishes monthly goals, or quotas, for the types of customers contacted. For the next 4 weeks, Suncoast's customer contact strategy calls for the sales force, which consists of four salespeople, to make 200 contacts with established customers who have previously purchased supplies from the firm. In addition, the strategy calls for 120 contacts of new customers. The purpose of this latter goal is to ensure that the sales force is continuing to investigate new sources of sales.

Making allowances for travel and waiting time, as well as for demonstration and direct sales time, Suncoast has allocated 2 hours of sales force effort to each contact of an established customer. New customer contacts tend to take longer and require 3 hours per contact. Normally, each salesperson works 40 hours per week, or 160 hours over the 4-week planning horizon; under a normal work schedule, the four salespeople will have $4(160) = 640$ hours of sales force time available for customer contacts.

Management is willing to use some overtime, if needed, but is also willing to accept a solution that uses less than the scheduled 640 hours available. However, management wants both overtime and underutilization of the workforce limited to no more than 40 hours over the 4-week period. Thus, in terms of overtime, management's goal is to use no more than $640 + 40 = 680$ hours of sales force time; and in terms of labor utilization, management's goal is to use at least $640 - 40 = 600$ hours of sales force time.

In addition to the customer contact goals, Suncoast has established a goal regarding sales volume. Based on its experience, Suncoast estimates that each established customer contacted will generate $250 of sales and that each new customer contacted will generate $125 of sales. Management wants to generate sales revenue of at least $70,000 for the next month.

Given Suncoast's small sales force and the short time frame involved, management has decided that the overtime goal and the labor utilization goal are both priority level 1 goals. Management also concluded that the $70,000 sales revenue goal should be a priority level 2 goal and that the two customer contact goals should be priority level 3 goals. Based on these priorities, we can now summarize the goals.

Priority Level 1 Goals

Goal 1:   Do not use any more than 680 hours of sales force time.

Goal 2:   Do not use any less than 600 hours of sales force time.

Priority Level 2 Goal

Goal 3:   Generate sales revenue of at least $70,000.

Priority Level 3 Goals

Goal 4:   Call on at least 200 established customers.

Goal 5:   Call on at least 120 new customers.

Formulating the Goal Equations

Next, we must define the decision variables whose values will be used to determine whether we are able to achieve the goals. Let

$$E = \text{the number of established customers contacted}$$
$$N = \text{the number of new customers contacted}$$

Using these decision variables and appropriate deviation variables, we can develop a goal equation for each goal. The procedure used parallels the approach introduced in the preceding section. A summary of the results obtained is shown for each goal.

Goal 1

$$2E + 3N - d_1^+ + d_1^- = 680$$

where

d_1^+ = the amount by which the number of hours used by the sales force is greater than the target value of 680 hours

d_1^- = the amount by which the number of hours used by the sales force is less than the target value of 680 hours

Goal 2

$$2E + 3N - d_2^+ + d_2^- = 600$$

where

d_2^+ = the amount by which the number of hours used by the sales force is greater than the target value of 600 hours

d_2^- = the amount by which the number of hours used by the sales force is less than the target value of 600 hours

Goal 3

$$250E + 125N - d_3^+ + d_3^- = 70,000$$

where

d_3^+ = the amount by which the sales revenue is greater than the target value of $70,000

d_3^- = the amount by which the sales revenue is less than the target value of $70,000

Goal 4

$$E - d_4^+ + d_4^- = 200$$

where

d_4^+ = the amount by which the number of established customer contacts is greater than the target value of 200 established customer contacts

d_4^- = the amount by which the number of established customer contacts is less than the target value of 200 established customer contacts

Goal 5

$$N - d_5^+ + d_5^- = 120$$

where

$d_5^+ =$ the amount by which the number of new customer contacts is greater than the target value of 120 new customer contacts

$d_5^- =$ the amount by which the number of new customer contacts is less than the target value of 120 new customer contacts

Formulating the Objective Function

To develop the objective function for the Suncoast Office Supplies problem, we begin by considering the priority level 1 goals. When considering goal 1, if $d_1^+ = 0$, we will have found a solution that uses no more than 680 hours of salesforce time. Because solutions for which d_1^+ is greater than zero represent overtime beyond the desired level, the objective function should minimize the value of d_1^+. When considering goal 2, if $d_2^- = 0$, we will have found a solution that uses *at least* 600 hours of salesforce time. If d_2^- is greater than zero, however, labor utilization will not have reached the acceptable level. Thus, the objective function for the priority level 1 goals should minimize the value of d_2^-. Because both priority level 1 goals are equally important, the objective function for the priority level 1 problem is

$$\text{Min} \quad d_1^+ + d_2^-$$

In considering the priority level 2 goal, we note that management wants to achieve sales revenues of at least $70,000. If $d_3^- = 0$, Suncoast will achieve revenues of *at least* $70,000, and if $d_3^- > 0$, revenues of less than $70,000 will be obtained. Thus, the objective function for the priority level 2 problem is

$$\text{Min} \quad d_3^-$$

Next, we consider what the objective function must be for the priority level 3 problem. When considering goal 4, if $d_4^- = 0$, we will have found a solution with *at least* 200 established customer contacts; however, if $d_4^- > 0$, we will have underachieved the goal of contacting at least 200 established customers. Thus, for goal 4 the objective is to minimize d_4^-. When considering goal 5, if $d_5^- = 0$, we will have found a solution with *at least* 120 new customer contacts; however, if $d_5^- > 0$, we will have underachieved the goal of contacting at least 120 new customers. Thus, for goal 5 the objective is to minimize d_5^-. If both goals 4 and 5 are equal in importance, the objective function for the priority level 3 problem would be

$$\text{Min} \quad d_4^- + d_5^-$$

However, suppose that management believes that generating new customers is vital to the long-run success of the firm and that goal 5 should be weighted more than goal 4. If management believes that goal 5 is twice as important as goal 4, the objective function for the priority level 3 problem would be

$$\text{Min} \quad d_4^- + 2d_5^-$$

Combining the objective functions for all three priority levels, we obtain the overall objective function for the Suncoast Office Supplies problem:

$$\text{Min} \quad P_1(d_1^+) + P_1(d_2^-) + P_2(d_3^-) + P_3(d_4^-) + P_3(2d_5^-)$$

As we indicated previously, P_1, P_2, and P_3 are simply labels that remind us that goals 1 and 2 are the priority level 1 goals, goal 3 is the priority level 2 goal, and goals 4 and 5 are the priority level 3 goals. We can now write the complete goal programming model for the Suncoast Office Supplies problem as follows:

$$\text{Min} \quad P_1(d_1^+) + P_1(d_2^-) + P_2(d_3^-) + P_3(d_4^-) + P_3(2d_5^-)$$

s.t.

$$
\begin{array}{rll}
2E + \quad 3N - d_1^+ + d_1^- & = & 680 \quad \text{Goal 1} \\
2E + \quad 3N \quad - d_2^+ + d_2^- & = & 600 \quad \text{Goal 2} \\
250E + 125N \quad - d_3^+ + d_3^- & = 70{,}000 \quad \text{Goal 3} \\
E \quad - d_4^+ + d_4^- & = & 200 \quad \text{Goal 4} \\
N \quad - d_5^+ + d_5^- & = & 120 \quad \text{Goal 5} \\
\end{array}
$$

$$E, N, d_1^+, d_1^-, d_2^+, d_2^-, d_3^+, d_3^-, d_4^+, d_4^-, d_5^+, d_5^- \geq 0$$

Computer Solution

The following computer procedure develops a solution to a goal programming model by solving a sequence of linear programming problems. The first problem comprises all the constraints and all the goal equations for the complete goal programming model; however, the objective function for this problem involves only the P_1 priority level goals. Again, we refer to this problem as the P_1 problem.

Whatever the solution to the P_1 problem, a P_2 problem is formed by adding a constraint to the P_1 model that ensures that subsequent problems will not degrade the solution obtained for the P_1 problem. The objective function for the priority level 2 problem takes into consideration only the P_2 goals. We continue the process until we have considered all priority levels. We illustrate the procedure for the Suncoast Office Supplies problem using the linear programming module of The Management Scientist software package.

To solve the Suncoast Office Supplies problem, we begin by solving the P_1 problem:

$$\text{Min} \quad d_1^+ + d_2^-$$

s.t.

$$
\begin{array}{rll}
2E + \quad 3N - d_1^+ + d_1^- & = & 680 \quad \text{Goal 1} \\
2E + \quad 3N \quad - d_2^+ + d_2^- & = & 600 \quad \text{Goal 2} \\
250E + 125N \quad - d_3^+ + d_3^- & = 70{,}000 \quad \text{Goal 3} \\
E \quad - d_4^+ + d_4^- & = & 200 \quad \text{Goal 4} \\
N \quad - d_5^+ + d_5^- & = & 120 \quad \text{Goal 5} \\
\end{array}
$$

$$E, N, d_1^+, d_1^-, d_2^+, d_2^-, d_3^+, d_3^-, d_4^+, d_4^-, d_5^+, d_5^- \geq 0$$

In Figure 18.4 we show The Management Scientist solution for this linear program. Note that D1PLUS refers to d_1^+, D2MINUS refers to d_2^-, D1MINUS refers to d_1^-, and so on. The solution shows $E = 250$ established customer contacts and $N = 60$ new customer contacts. Because D1PLUS = 0 and D2MINUS = 0, we see that the solution achieves both goals 1 and 2. Alternatively, the value of the objective function is 0, confirming that both priority level 1 goals have been achieved. Next, we consider goal 3, the priority level 2 goal, which is to minimize D3MINUS. The solution in Figure 18.4 shows that D3MINUS = 0. Thus, the solution of $E = 250$ established customer contacts and $N = 60$ new customer contacts also achieves goal 3, the priority level 2 goal, which is to generate a sales revenue of at least $70,000. The fact that D3PLUS = 0 indicates that the current solution satisfies goal 3 exactly at $70,000. Finally, the solution in Figure 18.4 shows D4PLUS = 50 and D5MINUS = 60. These values tell us that goal 4 of the pri-

FIGURE 18.4   THE MANAGEMENT SCIENTIST SOLUTION OF THE P_1 PROBLEM

```
Objective Function Value = 0.000

     Variable          Value          Reduced Costs
  --------------    -----------    --------------------

     D1PLUS           0.000             1.000
     D2MINUS          0.000             1.000
       E            250.000             0.000
       N             60.000             0.000
     D1MINUS          0.000             0.000
     D2PLUS          80.000             0.000
     D3PLUS           0.000             0.000
     D3MINUS          0.000             0.000
     D4PLUS          50.000             0.000
     D4MINUS          0.000             0.000
     D5PLUS           0.000             0.000
     D5MINUS         60.000             0.000
```

ority level 3 goals is overachieved by 50 established customers, but that goal 5 is underachieved by 60 new customers. As this point, both the priority level 1 and 2 goals have been achieved, but we need to solve another linear program to determine whether a solution can be identified that will satisfy both of the priority level 3 goals. Therefore, we go directly to the P_3 problem.

The linear programming model for the P_3 problem is a modification of the linear programming model for the P_1 problem. Specifically, the objective function for the P_3 problem is expressed in terms of the priority level 3 goals. Thus, the P_3 problem objective function becomes minimize D4MINUS + 2D5MINUS. The original five constraints of the P_1 problem appear in the P_3 problem. However, two additional constraints must be added to insure that the solution to the P_3 problem continues to satisfy the priority level 1 and priority level 2 goals. Thus, we add the priority level 1 constraint D1PLUS + D2MINUS = 0 and the priority level 2 constraint D3MINUS = 0. Making these modifications to the P_1 problem, we obtain the solution to the P_3 problem shown in Figure 18.5.

FIGURE 18.5   THE MANAGEMENT SCIENTIST SOLUTION OF THE P_3 PROBLEM

```
Objective Function Value = 120.000

     Variable          Value          Reduced Costs
  --------------    -----------    --------------------

     D1PLUS           0.000             0.000
     D2MINUS          0.000             1.000
       E            250.000             0.000
       N             60.000             0.000
     D1MINUS          0.000             1.000
     D2PLUS          80.000             0.000
     D3PLUS           0.000             0.008
     D3MINUS          0.000             0.000
     D4PLUS          50.000             0.000
     D4MINUS          0.000             1.000
     D5PLUS           0.000             2.000
     D5MINUS         60.000             0.000
```

Referring to Figure 18.5, we see the objective function value of 120 indicates that the priority level 3 goals cannot be achieved. Since D5MINUS = 60, the optimal solution of $E = 250$ and $N = 60$ results in 60 fewer new customer contacts than desired. However, the fact that we have solved the P_3 problem tells us the goal programming solution comes as close as possible to satisfying priority level 3 goals given the achievement of both the priority level 1 and 2 goals. Because all priority levels have been considered, the solution procedure is finished. The optimal solution for Suncoast is to contact 250 established customers and 60 new customers. Although this solution will not achieve management's goal of contacting at least 120 new customers, it does achieve each of the other goals specified. If management isn't happy with this solution, a different set of priorities could be considered. Management must keep in mind, however, that in any situation involving multiple goals at different priority levels, rarely will all the goals be achieved with existing resources.

NOTES AND COMMENTS

1. Not all goal programming problems involve multiple priority levels. For problems with one priority level, only one linear program needs to be solved to obtain the goal programming solution. The analyst simply minimizes the weighted deviations from the goals. Trade-offs are permitted among the goals because they are all at the same priority level.

2. The goal programming approach can be used when the analyst is confronted with an infeasible solution to an ordinary linear program. Reformulating some constraints as goal equations with deviation variables allows a solution that minimizes the weighted sum of the deviation variables. Often, this approach will suggest a reasonable solution.

3. The approach that we used to solve goal programming problems with multiple priority levels is to solve a sequence of linear programs. These linear programs are closely related so that complete reformulation and solution are not necessary. By changing the objective function and adding a constraint, we can go from one linear program to the next.

18.3   SCORING MODELS

A scoring model is a relatively quick and easy way to identify the best decision alternative for a multicriteria decision problem. We will demonstrate the use of a scoring model for a job selection application.

Assume that a graduating college student with a double major in finance and accounting has received job offers for the following three positions:

- A financial analyst for an investment firm located in Chicago
- An accountant for a manufacturing firm located in Denver
- An auditor for a CPA firm located in Houston

When asked about which job is preferred, the student made the following comments: "The financial analyst position in Chicago provides the best opportunity for my long-run career advancement. However, I would prefer living in Denver rather than in Chicago or Houston. On the other hand, I liked the management style and philosophy at the Houston CPA firm the best." The student's statement points out that this example is clearly a multicriteria decision problem. Considering only the *long-run career advancement* criterion, the financial analyst position in Chicago is the preferred decision alternative. Considering only the *location* criterion, the best decision alternative is the accountant position in Denver. Finally, considering only the *management style* criterion, the best alternative is the auditor position with the CPA firm in Houston. For most individuals, a multicriteria decision problem that requires a trade-off among the several criteria is difficult to solve. In this section, we describe how a **scoring model** can assist in analyzing a multicriteria decision problem and help identify the preferred decision alternative.

The steps required to develop a scoring model are as follows:

Step 1. Develop a list of the criteria to be considered. The criteria are the factors that the decision maker considers relevant for evaluating each decision alternative.

A scoring model enables a decision maker to identify the criteria and indicate the weight or importance of each criterion.

Step 2. Assign a weight to each criterion that describes the criterion's relative importance. Let

$$w_i = \text{the weight for criterion } i$$

Step 3. Assign a rating for each criterion that shows how well each decision alternative satisfies the criterion. Let

$$r_{ij} = \text{the rating for criterion } i \text{ and decision alternative } j$$

Step 4. Compute the score for each decision alternative. Let

$$S_j = \text{score for decision alternative } j$$

The equation used to compute S_j is as follows:

$$S_j = \sum_i w_i\, r_{ij} \tag{18.1}$$

Step 5. Order the decision alternatives from the highest score to the lowest score to provide the scoring model's ranking of the decision alternatives. The decision alternative with the highest score is the recommended decision alternative.

Let us return to the multicriteria job selection problem the graduating student was facing and illustrate the use of a scoring model to assist in the decision-making process. In carrying out Step 1 of the scoring model procedure, the student listed seven criteria as important factors in the decision-making process. These criteria are as follows:

- Career advancement
- Location
- Management style
- Salary
- Prestige
- Job security
- Enjoyment of the work

In Step 2, a weight is assigned to each criterion to indicate the criterion's relative importance in the decision-making process. For example, using a five-point scale, the question used to assign a weight to the career advancement criterion would be as follows:

Relative to the other criteria you are considering, how important is career advancement?

Importance	Weight
Very important	5
Somewhat important	4
Average importance	3
Somewhat unimportant	2
Very unimportant	1

By repeating this question for each of the seven criteria, the student provided the criterion weights shown in Table 18.1. Using this table, we see that career advancement and enjoyment of the work are the two most important criteria, each receiving a weight of 5. The management style and job security criteria are both considered somewhat important, and thus each received a weight of 4. Location and salary are considered average in importance, each receiving a weight of 3. Finally, because prestige is considered to be somewhat unimportant, it received a weight of 2.

The weights shown in Table 18.1 are subjective values provided by the student. A different student would most likely choose to weight the criteria differently. One of the key advantages of a scoring model is that it uses the subjective weights that most closely reflect the preferences of the individual decision maker.

In Step 3, each decision alternative is rated in terms of how well it satisfies each criterion. For example, using a nine-point scale, the question used to assign a rating for the "financial analyst in Chicago" alternative and the career advancement criterion would be as follows:

To what extent does the financial analyst position in Chicago satisfy your career advancement criterion?

Level of Satisfaction	Rating
Extremely high	9
Very high	8
High	7
Slightly high	6
Average	5
Slightly low	4
Low	3
Very low	2
Extremely low	1

A score of 8 on this question would indicate that the student believes the financial analyst position would be rated "very high" in terms of satisfying the career advancement criterion.

This scoring process must be completed for each combination of decision alternative and decision criterion. Because seven decision criteria and three decision alternatives need to be considered, $7 \times 3 = 21$ ratings must be provided. Table 18.2 summarizes the student's responses. Scanning this table provides some insights about how the student rates each decision criterion and decision alternative combination. For example, a rating of 9, corresponding to an extremely high level of satisfaction, only appears for the management style

TABLE 18.1   WEIGHTS FOR THE SEVEN JOB SELECTION CRITERIA

Criterion	Importance	Weight (w_i)
Career advancement	Very important	5
Location	Average importance	3
Management style	Somewhat important	4
Salary	Average importance	3
Prestige	Somewhat unimportant	2
Job security	Somewhat important	4
Enjoyment of the work	Very important	5

TABLE 18.2   RATINGS FOR EACH DECISION CRITERION AND EACH DECISION ALTERNATIVE COMBINATION

| | Decision Alternative | | |
	Financial Analyst Chicago	Accountant Denver	Auditor Houston
Criterion			
Career Advancement	8	6	4
Location	3	8	7
Management style	5	6	9
Salary	6	7	5
Prestige	7	5	4
Job security	4	7	6
Enjoyment of the work	8	6	5

criterion and the auditor position in Houston. Thus, considering all combinations, the student rates the auditor position in Houston as the very best in terms of satisfying the management criterion. The lowest rating in the table is a 3 that appears for the location criterion and the financial analyst position in Chicago. This rating indicates that Chicago is rated "low" in terms of satisfying the student's location criterion. Other insights and interpretations are possible, but the question at this point is how a scoring model uses the data in Tables 18.1 and 18.2 to identify the best overall decision alternative.

Step 4 of the procedure shows that equation (18.1) is used to compute the score for each decision alternative. The data in Table 18.1 provide the weight for each criterion (w_i) and the data in Table 18.2 provide the ratings of each decision alternative for each criterion (r_{ij}). Thus for decision alternative 1, the score for the financial analyst position in Chicago is

By comparing the scores for each criterion, a decision maker can learn why a particular decision alternative has the highest score.

$$S_1 = \sum_i w_i \, r_{i1} = 5(8) + 3(3) + 4(5) + 3(6) + 2(7) + 4(4) + 5(8) = 157$$

The scores for the other decision alternatives are computed in the same manner. The computations are summarized in Table 18.3.

TABLE 18.3   COMPUTATION OF SCORES FOR THE THREE DECISION ALTERNATIVES

		Decision Alternative					
		Financial Analyst Chicago		Accountant Denver		Auditor Houston	
	Weight	Rating	Score	Rating	Score	Rating	Score
Criterion	w_i	r_{i1}	$w_i r_{i1}$	r_{i2}	$w_i r_{i2}$	r_{i3}	$w_i r_{i3}$
Career advancement	5	8	40	6	30	4	20
Location	3	3	9	8	24	7	21
Management style	4	5	20	6	24	9	36
Salary	3	6	18	7	21	5	15
Prestige	2	7	14	5	10	4	8
Job security	4	4	16	7	28	6	24
Enjoyment of the work	5	8	40	6	30	5	25
Score			157		167		149

From Table 18.3, we see that the highest score of 167 corresponds to the accountant position in Denver. Thus, the accountant position in Denver is the recommended decision alternative. The financial analyst position in Chicago, with a score of 157, is ranked second, and the auditor position in Houston, with a score of 149, is ranked third.

The job selection example that we used to illustrate the use of a scoring model involved seven criteria, each of which was assigned a weight from 1 to 5. In other applications the weights assigned to the criteria may be percentages that reflect the importance of each of the criteria. In addition, multicriteria problems often involve additional subcriteria that enable the decision maker to incorporate additional detail into the decision process. For instance, consider the location criterion in the job selection example. This criterion might be further subdivided into the following three subcriteria:

- Affordability of housing
- Recreational opportunities
- Climate

In this case, the three subcriteria would have to be assigned weights, and a score for each decision alternative would have to be computed for each subcriterion. The Q. M. in Action Use of Scoring Models to Select Suppliers at Ford Motor Company illustrates how scoring models can be applied for a problem involving four criteria, each of which has several subcriteria. This example also demonstrates the use of percentage weights for the criteria and the wide applicability of scoring models in more complex problem situations.

Q. M. IN ACTION

USE OF SCORING MODELS TO SELECT SUPPLIERS AT FORD MOTOR COMPANY*

Ford Motor Company needed benchmark data in order to set performance targets for future and current model automobiles. A detailed proposal was developed and sent to five suppliers. Three suppliers were considered acceptable for the project.

Because the three suppliers had different capabilities in terms of teardown analysis and testing, Ford developed three project alternatives:

Alternative 1: Supplier C does the entire project alone.

Alternative 2: Supplier A does the testing portion of the project and works with Supplier B to complete the remaining parts of the project.

Alternative 3: Supplier A does the testing portion of the project and works with Supplier C to complete the remaining parts of the project.

For routine projects, selecting the lowest cost alternative might be appropriate. However, because this project involved many nonroutine tasks, Ford incorporated four criteria into the decision process.

The four criteria selected by Ford are as follows:

1. Skill level (effective project leader and a skilled team)

2. Cost containment (ability to stay within approved budget)
3. Timing containment (ability to meet program timing requirements)
4. Hardware display (location and functionality of teardown center and user friendliness)

Using team consensus, a weight of 25% was assigned to each of these criteria; note that these weights indicate that members of the Ford project team considered each criterion to be equally important in the decision process.

Each of the four criteria was further subdivided into subcriteria. For example, the skill-level criterion had four subcriteria: project manager—leadership; team structure—organization; team players—communication; and past Ford experience. In total, 17 subcriteria were considered. A team-consensus weighting process was used to develop percentage weights for the subcriteria. The weights assigned to the skill-level subcriteria were 40% for project manager—leadership; 20% for team structure—organization; 20% for team players—communication; and 20% for past Ford experience.

Team members visited all the suppliers and individually rated them for each subcriterion using a

1–10 scale (1-worst, 10-best). Then, in a team meeting, consensus ratings were developed. For Alternative 1, the consensus ratings developed for the skill-level subcriteria were 8 for project manager—leadership; 8 for team structure—organization; 7 for team players—communication; and 8 for past Ford experience. Because the weights assigned to the skill-level subcriteria are 40%, 20%, 20%, and 20%, the rating for Alternative 1 corresponding to the skill-level criterion is

$$\text{Rating} = .4(8) + .2(8) + .2(7) + .2(8) = 7.8$$

In a similar fashion, ratings for Alternative 1 corresponding to each of the other criteria were developed. The results obtained were a rating of 6.8 for cost containment, 6.65 for timing containment, and 8 for hardware display. Using the initial weights of 25% assigned to each criterion, the final rating for Alternative 1 = .25(7.8) + .25(6.8) + .25(6.65) + .25(8) = 7.3. In a similar fashion, a final rating of 7.4 was developed for Alternative 2, and a final rating of 7.5 was developed for Alternative 3. Thus, Alternative 3 was the recommended decision. Subsequent sensitivity analysis on the weights assigned to the criteria showed that Alternative 3 still received equal or higher ratings than Alternative 1 or Alternative 2. These results increased the team's confidence that Alternative 3 was the best choice.

*Based on Senthil A. Gurusami, "Ford's Wrenching Decision," *OR/MS Today* (December 1998): 36–39.

18.4   ANALYTIC HIERARCHY PROCESS

The **analytic hierarchy process (AHP),** developed by Thomas L. Saaty,[1] is designed to solve complex multicriteria decision problems. AHP requires the decision maker to provide judgments about the relative importance of each criterion and then specify a preference for each decision alternative using each criterion. The output of AHP is a prioritized ranking of the decision alternatives based on the overall preferences expressed by the decision maker.

To introduce AHP, we consider a car purchasing decision problem faced by Diane Payne. After a preliminary analysis of the makes and models of several used cars, Diane has narrowed her list of decision alternatives to three cars: a Honda Accord, a Saturn, and a Chevrolet Cavalier. Table 18.4 summarizes the information Diane has collected about these cars.

Diane decided that the following criteria were relevant for her car-selection decision process:

- Price
- Miles per gallon (MPG)
- Comfort
- Style

Data regarding the Price and MPG are provided in Table 18.4. However, measures of the Comfort and Style cannot be specified so directly. Diane will need to consider factors such as the car's interior, type of audio system, ease of entry, seat adjustments, and driver visibility in order to determine the comfort level of each car. The style criterion will have to be based on Diane's subjective evaluation of the color and the general appearance of each car.

AHP allows a decision maker to express personal preferences and subjective judgments about the various aspects of a multicriteria problem.

Even when a criterion such as price can be as easily measured, subjectivity becomes an issue whenever a decision maker indicates his or her personal preference for the decision alternatives based on price. For instance, the price of the Accord ($13,100) is $3600 more than the price of the Cavalier ($9500). The $3600 difference might represent a great deal of money to one person, but not much of a difference to another person. Thus, whether the Accord is considered "extremely more expensive" than the Cavalier or perhaps only "moderately more expensive" than the Cavalier depends upon the financial status and the

1. T. L. Saaty, *The Analytic Hierarchy Process* (New York: McGraw-Hill, 1988).

TABLE 18.4   INFORMATION FOR THE CAR SELECTION PROBLEM

Characteristics	Decision Alternative		
	Accord	**Saturn**	**Cavalier**
Price	$13,100	$11,200	$9500
Color	Black	Red	Blue
Miles per gallon	19	23	28
Interior	Deluxe	Above Average	Standard
Body type	4-door midsize	2-door sport	2-door compact
Sound system	AM/FM, tape, CD	AM/FM	AM/FM

subjective opinion of the person making the comparison. An advantage of AHP is that it can handle situations in which the unique subjective judgments of the individual decision maker constitute an important part of the decision-making process.

Developing the Hierarchy

The first step in AHP is to develop a graphical representation of the problem in terms of the overall goal, the criteria to be used, and the decision alternatives. Such a graph depicts the **hierarchy** for the problem. Figure 18.6 shows the hierarchy for the car selection problem. Note that the first level of the hierarchy shows that the overall goal is to select the best car. At the second level, the four criteria (Price, MPG, Comfort, and Style) each contribute to the achievement of the overall goal. Finally, at the third level, each decision alternative— Accord, Saturn, and Cavalier—contributes to each criterion in a unique way.

Using AHP, the decision maker specifies judgments about the relative importance of each of the four criteria in terms of its contribution to the achievement of the overall goal. At the next level, the decision maker indicates a preference for each decision alternative based on each criterion. A mathematical process is used to synthesize the information on the relative importance of the criteria and the preferences for the decision alternatives to provide an overall priority ranking of the decision alternatives. In the car selection problem, AHP will use Diane's personal preferences to provide a priority ranking of the three cars in terms of how well each car meets the overall goal of being the *best* car.

FIGURE 18.6   HIERARCHY FOR THE CAR SELECTION PROBLEM

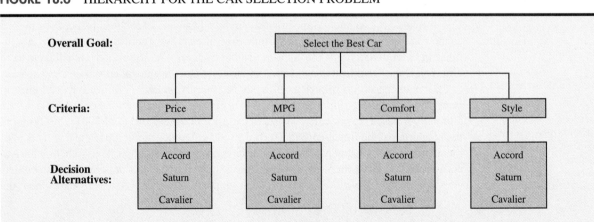

18.5   ESTABLISHING PRIORITIES USING AHP

In this section we show how AHP uses pairwise comparisons expressed by the decision maker to establish priorities for the criteria and priorities for the decision alternatives based on each criterion. Using the car selection example, we show how AHP determines priorities for each of the following:

1. How the four criteria contribute to the overall goal of selecting the best car
2. How the three cars compare using the Price criterion
3. How the three cars compare using the MPG criterion
4. How the three cars compare using the Comfort criterion
5. How the three cars compare using the Style criterion

In the following discussion, we demonstrate how to establish priorities for the four criteria in terms of how each contributes to the overall goal of selecting the best car. The priorities of the three cars using each criterion can be determined similarly.

Pairwise Comparisons

Pairwise comparisons form the fundamental building blocks of AHP. In establishing the priorities for the four criteria, AHP will require Diane to state how important each criterion is relative to each other criterion when the criteria are compared two at a time (pairwise). That is, with the four criteria (Price, MPG, Comfort, and Style) Diane must make the following pairwise comparisons:

Price compared to MPG

Price compared to Comfort

Price compared to Style

MPG compared to Comfort

MPG compared to Style

Comfort compared to Style

In each comparison, Diane must select the more important criterion and then express a judgment of how much more important the selected criterion is.

For example, in the Price-MPG pairwise comparison, assume that Diane indicates that Price is more important than MPG. To measure how much more important Price is compared to MPG, AHP uses scale with values from 1 to 9. Table 18.5 shows how the decision

TABLE 18.5   COMPARISON SCALE FOR THE IMPORTANCE OF CRITERIA USING AHP

Verbal Judgment	Numerical Rating
Extremely more important	9
	8
Very strongly more important	7
	6
Strongly more important	5
	4
Moderately more important	3
	2
Equally important	1

TABLE 18.6   SUMMARY OF DIANE PAYNE'S PAIRWISE COMPARISONS OF THE FOUR CRITERIA FOR THE CAR SELECTION PROBLEM

Pairwise Comparison	More Important Criterion	How Much More Important	Numerical Rating
Price-MPG	Price	Moderately	3
Price-Comfort	Price	Equally to moderately	2
Price-Style	Price	Equally to moderately	2
MPG-Comfort	Comfort	Moderately to strongly	4
MPG-Style	Style	Moderately to strongly	4
Comfort-Style	Style	Equally to moderately	2

maker's verbal description of the relative importance between the two criteria are converted into a numerical rating. In the car selection example, suppose that Diane states that Price is "moderately more important" than MPG. In this case, a numerical rating of 3 is assigned to the Price-MPG pairwise comparison. Using Table 18.5, we see "strongly more important" receives a numerical rating of 5 while "very strongly more important" receives a numerical rating of 7. Intermediate judgments such as "strongly to very strongly more important" are possible and would receive a numerical rating of 6.

Table 18.6 provides a summary of the six pairwise comparisons Diane provided for the car selection problem. Using the information in this table, Diane has specified that

Price is moderately more important than MPG

Price is equally to moderately more important than Comfort

Price is equally to moderately more important than Style

Comfort is moderately to strongly more important than MPG

Style is moderately to strongly more important than MPG

Style is equally to moderately more important than Comfort

AHP uses the numerical ratings from the pairwise comparisons to establish a priority or importance measure for each criterion.

As shown, the flexibility of AHP can accommodate the unique preferences of each individual decision maker. First, the choice of the criteria that are considered can vary depending upon the decision maker. Not everyone would agree that Price, MPG, Comfort, and Style are the only criteria to be considered in a car selection problem. Perhaps you would want to add safety, resale value, and/or other criteria if you were making the car selection decision. AHP can accommodate any set of criteria specified by the decision maker. Of course, if additional criteria are added, more pairwise comparisons will be necessary. In addition, if you agree with Diane that Price, MPG, Comfort, and Style are the four criteria to use, you would probably disagree with her as to the relative importance of the criteria. Using the format of Table 18.6, you could provide your own assessment of the importance of each pairwise comparison, and AHP would adjust the numerical ratings to reflect your personal preferences.

Pairwise Comparison Matrix

To determine the priorities for the four criteria, we need to construct a matrix of the pairwise comparison ratings provided in Table 18.6. Using the four criteria, the **pairwise comparison matrix** will consist of four rows and four columns as shown here:

	Price	MPG	Comfort	Style
Price				
MPG				
Comfort				
Style				

Each of the numerical ratings in Table 18.6 must be entered into the pairwise comparison matrix. To illustrate how this is done, consider the numerical rating of 3 for the Price-MPG pairwise comparison. Table 18.6 shows that for this pairwise comparison that Price is the most important criterion. Thus, we must enter a 3 into the row label Price and the column labeled MPG in the pairwise comparison matrix. In general, the entries in the column labeled Most Important Criterion in Table 18.6 indicate which row of the pairwise comparison matrix the numerical rating must be placed in. As another illustration, consider the MPG-Comfort pairwise comparison. Table 18.6 shows that Comfort is the most important criterion for this pairwise comparison and that the numerical rating is 4. Thus, we enter a 4 into the row labeled Comfort and into the column labeled MPG. Following this procedure for the other pairwise comparisons shown in Table 18.6, we obtain the following pairwise comparison matrix.

	Price	MPG	Comfort	Style
Price		3	2	2
MPG				
Comfort		4		
Style		4	2	

Because the diagonal elements are comparing each criterion to itself, the diagonal elements of the pairwise comparison matrix are always equal to 1. For example, if Price is compared to Price, the verbal judgment would be "equally important" with a rating of 1; thus, a 1 would be placed into the row labeled Price and into the column labeled Price in the pairwise comparison matrix. At this point, the pairwise comparison matrix appears as follows:

	Price	MPG	Comfort	Style
Price	1	3	2	2
MPG		1		
Comfort		4	1	
Style		4	2	1

All that remains is to complete the entries for the remaining cells of the matrix. To illustrate how these values are obtained, consider the numerical rating of 3 for the Price-MPG pairwise comparison. This rating implies that the MPG-Price pairwise comparison should have a rating of $\frac{1}{3}$. That is, since Diane has already indicated Price is moderately more important than MPG (a rating of 3), we can infer that a pairwise comparison of MPG relative to Price should be ⅓. Similarly, since the Comfort-MPG pairwise comparison has a rating of 4, the MPG-Comfort pairwise comparison would be ¼. Thus the complete pairwise comparison matrix for the car selection criteria is as follows:

	Price	MPG	Comfort	Style
Price	1	3	2	2
MPG	⅓	1	¼	¼
Comfort	½	4	1	½
Style	½	4	2	1

Synthesization

Using the pairwise comparison matrix, we can now calculate the priority of each criterion in terms of its contribution to the overall goal of selecting the best car. This aspect of AHP is referred to as **synthesization.** The exact mathematical procedure required to perform synthesization is beyond the scope of this text. However, the following three-step procedure provides a good approximation of the synthesization results.

1. Sum the values in each column of the pairwise comparison matrix.
2. Divide each element in the pairwise comparison matrix by its column total; the resulting matrix is referred to as the **normalized pairwise comparison matrix.**
3. Compute the average of the elements in each row of the normalized pairwise comparison matrix; these averages provide the priorities for the criteria.

To show how the synthesization process works, we carry out this three-step procedure for the criteria pairwise comparison matrix.

Step 1. Sum the values in each column.

	Price	MPG	Comfort	Style
Price	1	3	2	2
MPG	⅓	1	¼	¼
Comfort	½	4	1	½
Style	½	4	2	1
Sum	2.333	12.000	5.250	3.750

Step 2. Divide each element of the matrix by its column total.

	Price	MPG	Comfort	Style
Price	0.429	0.250	0.381	0.533
MPG	0.143	0.083	0.048	0.067
Comfort	0.214	0.333	0.190	0.133
Style	0.214	0.333	0.381	0.267

Step 3. Average the elements in each row to determine the priority of each criterion.

	Price	MPG	Comfort	Style	Priority
Price	0.429	0.250	0.381	0.533	0.398
MPG	0.143	0.083	0.048	0.067	0.085
Comfort	0.214	0.333	0.190	0.133	0.218
Style	0.214	0.333	0.381	0.267	0.299

The AHP synthesization procedure has provided the priority of each criterion in terms of its contribution to the overall goal of selecting the best car. Thus, using Diane's pairwise comparisons provided in Table 18.6, AHP has determined that Price with a priority of 0.398 is the most important criterion in the car selection process. Style with a priority of 0.299 ranks second in importance and is closely followed by Comfort with a priority of 0.218. MPG is the least important criterion with a priority of 0.085.

Consistency

A key step in AHP is the making of several pairwise comparisons as previously described. An important consideration in this process is the **consistency** of the pairwise judgments provided by the decision maker. For example, if criterion A compared to criterion B has a numerical rating of 3 and if criterion B compared to criterion C has a numerical rating of 2, perfect consistency of criterion A compared to criterion C would have a numerical rating of $3 \times 2 = 6$. If the A to C numerical rating assigned by the decision maker was 4 or 5, some inconsistency would exist among the pairwise comparison.

With numerous pairwise comparisons, perfect consistency is difficult to achieve. In fact, some degree of inconsistency can be expected to exist in almost any set of pairwise comparisons. To handle the consistency issue, AHP provides a method for measuring the degree of consistency among the pairwise comparisons provided by the decision maker. If the degree of consistency is unacceptable, the decision maker should review and revise the pairwise comparisons before proceeding with the AHP analysis.

A consistency ratio greater than 0.10 indicates inconsistency in the pairwise comparisons. In such cases, the decision maker should review the pairwise comparisons before proceeding.

AHP provides a measure of the consistency for the pairwise comparisons by computing a **consistency ratio.** This ratio is designed in such a way that a value *greater than* 0.10 indicates an inconsistency in the pairwise judgments. Thus, if the consistency ratio is 0.10 or less, the consistency of the pairwise comparisons is considered reasonable, and the AHP process can continue with the synthesization computations.

Although the exact mathematical computation of the consistency ratio is beyond the scope of this text, an approximation of the ratio can be obtained with little difficulty. The step-by-step procedure for estimating the consistency ratio for the criteria of the car selection problem follows.

Step 1. Multiply each value in the first column of the pairwise comparison matrix by the priority of the first item; multiply each value in the second column of the pairwise comparison matrix by the priority of the second item; continue this process for all columns of the pairwise comparison matrix. Sum the values across the rows to obtain a vector of values labeled "weighted sum." This computation for the car selection problem is as follows:

$$
0.398 \begin{bmatrix} 1 \\ \frac{1}{3} \\ \frac{1}{2} \\ \frac{1}{2} \end{bmatrix} + 0.085 \begin{bmatrix} 3 \\ 1 \\ 4 \\ 4 \end{bmatrix} + 0.218 \begin{bmatrix} 2 \\ \frac{1}{4} \\ 1 \\ 2 \end{bmatrix} + 0.299 \begin{bmatrix} 2 \\ \frac{1}{4} \\ \frac{1}{2} \\ 1 \end{bmatrix} =
$$

$$
\begin{bmatrix} 0.398 \\ 0.133 \\ 0.199 \\ 0.199 \end{bmatrix} + \begin{bmatrix} 0.255 \\ 0.085 \\ 0.340 \\ 0.340 \end{bmatrix} + \begin{bmatrix} 0.436 \\ 0.054 \\ 0.218 \\ 0.436 \end{bmatrix} + \begin{bmatrix} 0.598 \\ 0.075 \\ 0.149 \\ 0.299 \end{bmatrix} = \begin{bmatrix} 1.687 \\ 0.347 \\ 0.907 \\ 1.274 \end{bmatrix}
$$

Step 2. Divide the elements of the weighted sum vector obtained in Step 1 by the corresponding priority for each criterion.

$$
\text{Price} \qquad \frac{1.687}{0.398} = 4.236
$$

$$
\text{MPG} \qquad \frac{0.347}{0.085} = 4.077
$$

$$
\text{Comfort} \qquad \frac{0.907}{0.218} = 4.163
$$

$$
\text{Style} \qquad \frac{1.274}{0.299} = 4.264
$$

Step 3. Compute the average of the values found in step 2; this average is denoted λ_{max}.

$$
\lambda_{max} = \frac{(4.236 + 4.077 + 4.163 + 4.264)}{4} = 4.185
$$

Step 4. Compute the consistency index (CI) as follows:

$$
CI = \frac{\lambda_{max} - n}{n - 1}
$$

where n is the number of items being compared. Thus, we have

$$
CI = \frac{4.185 - 4}{4 - 1} = 0.0616
$$

Step 5. Compute the consistency ratio, which is defined as

$$
CR = \frac{CI}{RI}
$$

where RI is the consistency index of a *randomly* generated pairwise comparison matrix. The value of RI depends on the number of items being compared and is given as follows:

n	3	4	5	6	7	8
RI	0.58	0.90	1.12	1.24	1.32	1.41

Thus, for the car selection problem with $n = 4$ criteria, we have RI = 0.90 and a consistency ratio

$$CR = \frac{0.0616}{0.90} = 0.068$$

Problem 16 will give you practice with the synthesization calculations and determining the consistency ratio.

As mentioned previously, a consistency ratio of 0.10 or less is considered acceptable. Because the pairwise comparisons for the car selection criteria show CR = 0.068, we can conclude that the degree of consistency in the pairwise comparisons is acceptable.

Other Pairwise Comparisons for the Car Selection Problem

Continuing with the AHP analysis of the car selection problem, we need to use the pairwise comparison procedure to determine the priorities for the three cars using each of the criteria: Price, MPG, Comfort, and Style. Determining these priorities requires Diane to express pairwise comparison preferences for the cars using each criterion one at a time. For example, using the price criterion, Diane must make the following pairwise comparisons:

the Accord compared to the Saturn

the Accord compared to the Cavalier

the Saturn compared to the Cavalier

In each comparison, Diane must select the more preferred car and then express a judgment of how much more preferred the selected car is.

For example, using the Price as the basis for comparison, assume that Diane considers the Accord-Saturn pairwise comparison and indicates that the less expensive Saturn is preferred. Table 18.7 shows how AHP uses Diane's verbal description of the preference between the Accord and Saturn to determine a numerical rating of the preference. For example, suppose that Diane states that based on Price, the Saturn is "moderately more preferred" to the Accord. Thus, using the Price criterion, a numerical rating of 3 is assigned to the Saturn row and Accord column of the pairwise comparison matrix.

TABLE 18.7   PAIRWISE COMPARISON SCALE FOR THE PREFERENCE OF DECISION ALTERNATIVES USING AHP

Verbal Judgment	Numerical Rating
Extremely preferred	9
	8
Very strongly preferred	7
	6
Strongly preferred	5
	4
Moderately preferred	3
	2
Equally preferred	1

TABLE 18.8　PAIRWISE COMPARISON MATRIXES SHOWING PREFERENCES FOR THE CARS USING EACH CRITERION

Price

	Accord	Saturn	Cavalier
Accord	1	$\frac{1}{3}$	$\frac{1}{4}$
Saturn	3	1	$\frac{1}{2}$
Cavalier	4	2	1

MPG

	Accord	Saturn	Cavalier
Accord	1	$\frac{1}{4}$	$\frac{1}{6}$
Saturn	4	1	$\frac{1}{3}$
Cavalier	6	3	1

Comfort

	Accord	Saturn	Cavalier
Accord	1	2	8
Saturn	$\frac{1}{2}$	1	6
Cavalier	$\frac{1}{8}$	$\frac{1}{6}$	1

Style

	Accord	Saturn	Cavalier
Accord	1	$\frac{1}{3}$	4
Saturn	3	1	7
Cavalier	$\frac{1}{4}$	$\frac{1}{7}$	1

Table 18.8 shows the summary of the car pairwise comparisons that Diane provided for each criterion of the car selection problem. Using this table and referring to selected pairwise comparison entries, we see that Diane has stated the following preferences:

In terms of Price, the Cavalier is moderately to strongly more preferred than the Accord.

In terms of the MPG, the Cavalier is moderately more preferred than the Saturn.

In terms of Comfort, the Accord is very strongly to extremely more preferred than the Cavalier.

In terms of Style, the Saturn is moderately more preferred than the Accord.

Using the pairwise comparison matrixes in Table 18.8, many other insights may be gained about the preferences Diana has expressed for the cars. However, at this point, AHP continues by synthesizing each of the four pairwise comparison matrixes in Table 18.8 in order to determine the priority of each car using each criterion. A synthesization is conducted for each pairwise comparison matrix using the three-step procedure described previously for the criteria pairwise comparison matrix. Four synthesization computations provide the four sets of priorities shown in Table 18.9. Using this table, we see that the Cavalier is the preferred alternative based on Price (0.557), the Cavalier is the preferred

Practice setting up a pairwise comparison matrix and determine whether judgments are consistent by working Problem 20.

TABLE 18.9　PRIORITIES FOR EACH CAR USING EACH CRITERION

	Criterion			
	Price	MPG	Comfort	Style
Accord	0.123	0.087	0.593	0.265
Saturn	0.320	0.274	0.341	0.656
Cavalier	0.557	0.639	0.065	0.080

alternative based on MPG (0.639), the Accord is the preferred alternative based on Comfort (0.593), and the Saturn is the preferred alternative based on Style (0.656). At this point, no car is the clear, overall best. The next section shows how to combine the priorities for the criteria and the priorities in Table 18.9 to develop an overall priority ranking for the three cars.

18.6   USING AHP TO DEVELOP AN OVERALL PRIORITY RANKING

In Section 18.5, we used Diane's pairwise comparisons of the four criteria to develop the priorities of 0.398 for Price, 0.085 for MPG, 0.281 for Comfort, and 0.299 for Style. We now want to use these priorities and the priorities shown in Table 18.9 to develop an overall priority ranking for the three cars.

The procedure used to compute the overall priority is to weight each car's priority shown in Table 18.9 by the corresponding criterion priority. For example, the Price criterion has a priority of 0.398, and the Accord has a priority of 0.123 in terms of the Price criterion. Thus, $0.398 \times 0.123 = 0.049$ is the priority value of the Accord based on the Price criterion. To obtain the overall priority of the Accord, we need to make similar computations for the MPG, Comfort, and Style criteria and then add the values to obtain the overall priority. This calculation is as follows:

Overall Priority of the Accord:

$$0.398(0.123) + 0.085(0.087) + 0.218(0.593) + 0.299(0.265) = 0.265$$

Repeating this calculation for the Saturn and the Cavalier, we obtain the following results:

Overall Priority of the Saturn:

$$0.398(0.32) + 0.085(0.274) + 0.218(0.341) + 0.299(0.656) = 0.421$$

Overall Priority of the Cavalier:

$$0.398(0.557) + 0.085(0.639) + 0.218(0.065) + 0.299(0.080) = 0.314$$

Ranking these priorities, we have the AHP ranking of the decision alternatives:

Car	Priority
1. Saturn	0.421
2. Cavalier	0.314
3. Accord	0.265

Work Problem 24 and determine the AHP priorities for the two decision alternatives.

These results provide a basis for Diane to make a decision regarding the purchase of a car. As long as Diane believes that her judgments regarding the importance of the criteria and her preferences for the cars using each criterion are valid, the AHP priorities show that the Saturn is preferred. In addition to the recommendation of the Saturn as the best car, the AHP analysis has helped Diane gain a better understanding of the trade-offs in the decision-making process and a clearer understanding of why the Saturn is the AHP recommended alternative.

NOTES AND COMMENTS

1. The scoring model in Section 18.3 used the following equation to compute the overall score of a decision alternative.

$$S_j = \sum_i w_i \, r_{ij}$$

where

w_i = the weight for criterion i

r_{ij} = the rating for criterion i and decision alternative j

In Section 18.5 AHP used the same calculation to determine the overall priority of each decision alternative. The difference between the two approaches is that the scoring model required the decision maker to estimate the values of w_i and r_{ij} directly. AHP used synthesization to compute the criterion priorities w_i and the decision alternative priorities r_{ij} based on the pairwise comparison information provided by the decision maker.

2. The software package Expert Choice® marketed by Decision Support Software provides a user-friendly procedure for implementing AHP on a personal computer. Expert Choice will take the decision maker through the pairwise comparison process in a step-by-step manner. Once the decision maker has responded to the pairwise comparison prompts, Expert Choice will automatically construct the pairwise comparison matrix, conduct the synthesization calculations, and present the overall priorities. Expert Choice is a software package that should warrant consideration by a decision maker who anticipates solving a variety of multicriteria decision problems.

SUMMARY

In this chapter we used goal programming to solve problems with multiple goals within the linear programming framework. We showed that the goal programming model contains one or more goal equations and an objective function designed to minimize deviations from the goals. In situations where resource capacities or other restrictions affect the achievement of the goals, the model will contain constraints that are formulated and treated in the same manner as constraints in an ordinary linear programming model.

In goal programming problems with preemptive priorities, priority level 1 goals are treated first in an objective function to identify a solution that will best satisfy these goals. This solution is then revised by considering an objective function involving only the priority level 2 goals; solution modifications are considered only if they do not degrade the solution obtained for the priority level 1 goals. This process continues until all priority levels have been considered.

We showed how a variation of the linear programming graphical solution procedure can be used to solve goal programming problems with two decision variables. Specialized goal programming computer packages are available for solving the general goal programming problem, but such computer codes are not as readily available as are general purpose linear programming computer packages. As a result, we showed how the linear programming module of The Management Scientist software package can be used to solve a goal programming problem.

We then presented a scoring model as a quick and relatively easy way to identify the most desired decision alternative in a multicriteria problem. The decision maker provides a subjective weight indicating the importance of each criterion. Then the decision maker rates each decision alternative in terms of how well it satisfies each criterion. The end result is a score for each decision alternative that indicates the preference for the decision alternative considering all criteria.

We also presented an approach to multicriteria decision making called the analytic hierarchy process (AHP). We showed that a key part of AHP is the development of judgments concerning the relative importance of, or preference for, the elements being compared. A consistency ratio is computed to determine the degree of consistency exhibited by the decision maker in making the pairwise comparisons. Values of the consistency ratio less than or equal to 0.10 are considered acceptable.

Once the set of all pairwise comparisons has been developed, a process referred to as synthesization is used to determine the priorities for the elements being compared. The final step of the analytic hierarchy process involves multiplying the priority levels established for the decision alternatives relative to each criterion by the priority levels reflecting the importance of the criteria themselves; the sum of these products over all the criteria provides the overall priority level for each decision alternative.

GLOSSARY

Goal programming   A linear programming approach to multicriteria decision problems whereby the objective function is designed to minimize the deviations from goals.

Preemptive priorities   Priorities assigned to goals that ensure that the satisfaction of a higher level goal cannot be traded for the satisfaction of a lower level goal.

Target value   A value specified in the statement of the goal. Based on the context of the problem, management will want the solution to the goal programming problem to result in a value for the goal that is less than, equal to, or greater than the target value.

Goal equation   An equation whose right-hand side is the target value for the goal; the left-hand side of the goal equation consists of (1) a function representing the level of achievement and (2) deviation variables representing the difference between the target value for the goal and the level achieved.

Deviation variables   Variables that are added to the goal equation to allow the solution to deviate from the goal's target value.

Scoring model   An approach to multicriteria decision making that requires the user to assign weights to each criterion that describes the criterion's relative importance and to assign a rating that shows how well each decision alternative satisfies each criterion. The output is a score for each decision alternative.

Analytic hierarchy process (AHP)   An approach to multicriteria decision making based on pairwise comparisons for elements in a hierarchy.

Hierarchy   A diagram that shows the levels of a problem in terms of the overall goal, the criteria, and the decision alternatives.

Pairwise comparison matrix   A matrix that consists of the preference, or relative importance, ratings provided during a series of pairwise comparisons.

Synthesization   A mathematical process that uses the preference or relative importance values in the pairwise comparison matrix to develop priorities.

Normalized pairwise comparison matrix   The matrix obtained by dividing each element of the pairwise comparison matrix by its column total. This matrix is computed as an intermediate step in the synthesization of priorities.

Consistency   A concept developed to assess the quality of the judgments made during a series of pairwise comparisons. It is a measure of the internal consistency of these comparisons.

Consistency ratio   A numerical measure of the degree of consistency in a series of pairwise comparisons. Values less than or equal to 0.10 are considered reasonable.

PROBLEMS

1. The RMC Corporation blends three raw materials to produce two products: a fuel additive and a solvent base. Each ton of fuel additive is a mixture of 2/5 ton of material 1 and 3/5 ton of material 3. A ton of solvent base is a mixture of 1/2 ton of material 1, 1/5 ton of

material 2, and 3/10 ton of material 3. RMC's production is constrained by a limited avail-ability of the three raw materials. For the current production period, RMC has the follow-ing quantities of each raw material: material 1, 20 tons; material 2, 5 tons; material 3, 21 tons. Management wants to achieve the following P_1 priority level goals.

Goal 1: Produce at least 30 tons of fuel additive.

Goal 2: Produce at least 15 tons of solvent base.

Assume there are no other goals.

a. Is it possible for management to achieve both P_1 level goals given the constraints on the amounts of each material available? Explain.

b. Treating the amounts of each material available as constraints, formulate a goal pro-gramming model to determine the optimal product mix. Assume that both P_1 priority level goals are equally important to management.

c. Use the graphical goal programming procedure to solve the model formulated in part (b).

d. If goal 1 is twice as important as goal 2, what is the optimal product mix?

SELFtest

2. DJS Investment Services must develop an investment portfolio for a new client. As an ini-tial investment strategy, the new client would like to restrict the portfolio to a mix of two stocks:

Stock	Price/Share	Estimated Annual Return (%)
AGA Products	$ 50	6
Key Oil	100	10

The client has $50,000 to invest and has established the following two investment goals.

Priority Level 1 Goal

Goal 1: Obtain an annual return of at least 9%.

Priority Level 2 Goal

Goal 2: Limit the investment in Key Oil, the riskier investment, to no more than 60% of the total investment.

a. Formulate a goal programming model for the DJS Investment problem.

b. Use the graphical goal programming procedure to obtain a solution.

3. The L. Young & Sons Manufacturing Company produces two products, which have the following profit and resource requirement characteristics.

Characteristic	Product 1	Product 2
Profit/unit	$4	$2
Dept. A hours/unit	1	1
Dept. B hours/unit	2	5

Last month's production schedule used 350 hours of labor in department A and 1000 hours of labor in department B.

Young's management has been experiencing workforce morale and labor union prob-lems during the past 6 months because of monthly departmental workload fluctuations. New hiring, layoffs, and interdepartmental transfers have been common because the firm has not attempted to stabilize workload requirements.

Management would like to develop a production schedule for the coming month that will achieve the following goals.

Goal 1:   Use 350 hours of labor in department A.

Goal 2:   Use 1000 hours of labor in department B.

Goal 3:   Earn a profit of at least $1300.

a. Formulate a goal programming model for this problem, assuming that goals 1 and 2 are P_1 level goals and goal 3 is a P_2 level goal; assume that goals 1 and 2 are equally important.

b. Solve the model formulated in part (a) using the graphical goal programming procedure.

c. Suppose that the firm ignores the workload fluctuations and considers the 350 hours in department A and the 1000 hours in department B as the maximum available. Formulate and solve a linear programming problem to maximize profit subject to these constraints.

d. Compare the solutions obtained in parts (b) and (c). Discuss which approach you favor, and why.

e. Reconsider part (a) assuming that the priority level 1 goal is goal 3 and the priority level 2 goals are goals 1 and 2; as before, assume that goals 1 and 2 are equally important. Solve this revised problem using the graphical goal programming procedure and compare your solution to the one obtained for the original problem.

4. Industrial Chemicals produces two adhesives used in the manufacturing process for airplanes. The two adhesives, which have different bonding strengths, require different amounts of production time: the IC-100 adhesive requires 20 minutes of production time per gallon of finished product, and the IC-200 adhesive uses 30 minutes of production time per gallon. Both products use 1 pound of a highly perishable resin for each gallon of finished product. There are 300 pounds of the resin in inventory, and more can be obtained if necessary. However, because of the shelf life of the material, any amount not used in the next 2 weeks will be discarded.

The firm has existing orders for 100 gallons of IC-100 and 120 gallons of IC-200. Under normal conditions, the production process operates 8 hours per day, 5 days per week. Management wants to schedule production for the next 2 weeks to achieve the following goals.

Priority Level 1 Goals

Goal 1:   Avoid underutilization of the production process.

Goal 2:   Avoid overtime in excess of 20 hours for the 2 weeks.

Priority Level 2 Goals

Goal 3:   Satisfy existing orders for the IC-100 adhesive; that is, produce at least 100 gallons of IC-100.

Goal 4:   Satisfy existing orders for the IC-200 adhesive; that is, produce at least 120 gallons of IC-200.

Priority Level 3 Goal

Goal 5:   Use all the available resin.

a. Formulate a goal programming model for the Industrial Chemicals problem. Assume that both priority level 1 goals and that both priority level 2 goals are equally important.

b. Use the graphical goal programming procedure to develop a solution for the model formulated in part (a).

5. Reconsider the RMC data presented in Problem 1. Assume that the two P_1 priority level goals remain the same and that both goals are equally important to management. Suppose that management has learned that additional amounts of material 3 can be obtained from another RMC plant. Although management wants to obtain a solution that satisfies their

production goals using the 21 tons of material 3 currently available, it is willing to consider using additional amounts of material 3 from the other plant. With this new goal as a P_2 priority level goal, the problem goals can now be restated.

Priority Level 1 Goals

Goal 1:   Produce at least 30 tons of fuel additive.

Goal 2:   Produce at least 15 tons of solvent base.

Priority Level 2 Goal

Goal 3:   Use no more than 21 tons of material 3.

   a.   Treat the amounts of materials 1 and 2 available as problem constraints and formulate a goal programming model for this problem.
   b.   Use the goal programming computer procedure illustrated in Section 18.2 to solve the model formulated in part (a).
   c.   How many tons of material 3 need to be obtained from RMC's other plant?

6.   Michigan Motors Corporation (MMC) has just introduced a new luxury touring sedan. As part of its promotional campaign, the marketing department has decided to send personalized invitations to test drive the new sedan to two target groups: (1) current owners of an MMC luxury automobile and (2) owners of luxury cars manufactured by one of MMC's competitors. The cost of sending a personalized invitation to each customer is estimated to be $1 per letter. Based on previous experience with this type of advertising, MMC estimates that 25% of the customers contacted from group 1 and 10% of the customers contacted from group 2 will test drive the new sedan. As part of this campaign, MMC has set the following goals.

Goal 1:   Get at least 10,000 customers from group 1 to test drive the new sedan.

Goal 2:   Get at least 5000 customers from group 2 to test drive the new sedan.

Goal 3.   Limit the expense of sending out the invitations to $70,000.

Assume that goals 1 and 2 are P_1 priority level goals and that goal 3 is a P_2 priority level goal.
   a.   Suppose that goals 1 and 2 are equally important; formulate a goal programming model of the MMC problem.
   b.   Use the goal programming computer procedure illustrated in Section 18.2 to solve the model formulated in part (a).
   c.   If management believes that contacting customers from group 2 is twice as important as contacting customers from group 1, what should MMC do?

7.   A committee in charge of promoting a Ladies Professional Golf Association tournament is trying to determine how best to advertise the event during the 2 weeks prior to the tournament. The committee obtained the following information about the three advertising media they are considering using.

Category	Audience Reached per Advertisement	Cost per Advertisement	Maximum Number of Advertisements
TV	200,000	$2500	10
Radio	50,000	$ 400	15
Newspaper	100,000	$ 500	20

The last column in this table shows the maximum number of advertisements that can be run during the next 2 weeks; these values should be treated as constraints. The committee has established the following goals for the campaign.

Priority Level 1 Goal

Goal 1:   Reach at least 4 million people.

Priority Level 2 Goal

Goal 2:   The number of television advertisements should be at least 30% of the total number of advertisements.

Priority Level 3 Goal

Goal 3:   The number of radio advertisements should not exceed 20% of the total number of advertisements.

Priority Level 4 Goal

Goal 4:   Limit the total amount spent for advertising to $20,000.

a.   Formulate a goal programming model for this problem.
b.   Use the goal programming computer procedure illustrated in Section 18.2 to solve the model formulated in part (a).

8.   Morley Company is attempting to determine the best location for a new machine in an existing layout of three machines. The existing machines are located at the following x_1, x_2 coordinates on the shop floor.

$$\text{Machine 1:}\quad x_1 = 1, x_2 = 7$$
$$\text{Machine 2:}\quad x_1 = 5, x_2 = 9$$
$$\text{Machine 3:}\quad x_1 = 6, x_2 = 2$$

a.   Develop a goal programming model that can be solved to minimize the total distance of the new machine from the three existing machines. The distance is to be measured rectangularly. For example, if the location of the new machine is ($x_1 = 3$, $x_2 = 5$), it is considered to be a distance of $|3 - 1| + |5 - 7| = 2 + 2 = 4$ from machine 1. *Hint:* In the goal programming formulation, let

x_1 = first coordinate of the new machine location

x_2 = second coordinate of the new machine location

d_i^+ = amount by which the x_1 coordinate of the new machine
            exceeds the x_1 coordinate of machine i ($i = 1, 2, 3$)

d_i^- = amount by which the x_1 coordinate of machine i
            exceeds the x_1 coordinate of the new machine ($i = 1, 2, 3$)

e_i^+ = amount by which the x_2 coordinate of the new machine
            exceeds the x_2 coordinate of machine i ($i = 1, 2, 3$)

e_i^- = amount by which the x_2 coordinate of machine i
            exceeds the x_2 coordinate of the new machine ($i = 1, 2, 3$)

b.   What is the optimal location for the new machine?

SELFtest   9.   One advantage of using the multicriteria decision-making methods presented in this chapter is that the criteria weights and the decision alternative ratings may be modified to reflect the unique interests and preferences of each individual decision maker. For example, assume that another graduating college student had the same three job offers described in Section 18.3. This student provided the following scoring model information. Rank the overall preference for the three positions. Which position is recommended?

| | | Ratings | | |
Criteria	Weight	Analyst Chicago	Accountant Denver	Auditor Houston
Career advancement	5	7	4	4
Location	2	5	6	4
Management style	5	6	5	7
Salary	4	7	8	4
Prestige	4	8	5	6
Job security	2	4	5	8
Enjoyment of the work	4	7	5	5

10. The Kenyon Manufacturing Company is interested in selecting the best location for a new plant. After a detailed study of ten sites, the three location finalists are Georgetown, Kentucky; Marysville, Ohio; and Clarksville, Tennessee. The Kenyon management team provided the following data on location criteria, criteria importance, and location ratings. Use a scoring model to determine the best location for the new plant.

| | | Ratings | | |
Criteria	Weight	Georgetown, Kentucky	Marysville, Ohio	Clarksville, Tennessee
Land cost	4	7	4	5
Labor cost	3	6	5	8
Labor availability	5	7	8	6
Construction cost	4	6	7	5
Transportation	3	5	7	4
Access to customers	5	6	8	5
Long-range goals	4	7	6	5

11. The Davis family of Atlanta, Georgia, is planning its annual summer vacation. Three vacation locations along with criteria weights and location ratings follow. What is the recommended vacation location?

| | | Ratings | | |
Criteria	Weight	Myrtle Beach, South Carolina	Smoky Mountains	Branson, Missouri
Travel distance	2	5	7	3
Vacation cost	5	5	6	4
Entertainment available	3	7	4	8
Outdoor activities	2	9	6	5
Unique experience	4	6	7	8
Family fun	5	8	7	7

12. A high school senior is considering attending one of the following four colleges or universities. Eight criteria, criteria weights, and school ratings are also shown. What is the recommended choice?

Criteria	Weight	Ratings			
		Midwestern University	State College at Newport	Handover College	Tecumseh State
School prestige	3	8	6	7	5
Number of students	4	3	5	8	7
Average class size	5	4	5	8	7
Cost	5	5	8	3	6
Distance from home	2	7	8	7	6
Sports program	4	9	5	4	6
Housing desirability	4	6	5	7	6
Beauty of campus	3	5	3	8	5

13. Mr. and Mrs. Brinkley are interested in purchasing condominium property in Naples, Florida. The three most preferred condominiums are listed along with criteria weights and rating information. Which condominium is preferred?

Criteria	Weight	Ratings		
		Park Shore	The Terrace	Gulf View
Cost	5	5	6	5
Location	4	7	4	9
Appearance	5	7	4	7
Parking	2	5	8	5
Floor plan	4	8	7	5
Swimming pool	1	7	2	3
View	3	5	4	9
Kitchen	4	8	7	6
Closet space	3	6	8	4

14. Clark and Julie Anderson are interested in purchasing a new boat and have limited their choice to one of three boats manufactured by Sea Ray, Inc.: the 220 Bowrider, the 230 Overnighter, and the 240 Sundancer. The Bowrider weights 3100 pounds, has no overnight capability, and has a price of $28,500. The 230 Overnighter weights 4300 pounds, has a reasonable overnight capability, and has a price of $37,500. The 240 Sundancer weights 4500 pounds, has an excellent overnight capability (kitchen, bath, and bed), and has a price of $48,200. The Andersons provided the scoring model information separately as shown here.

Clark Anderson

Criteria	Weight	Ratings		
		220 Bowrider	230 Overnighter	240 Sundancer
Cost	5	8	5	3
Overnight capability	3	2	6	9
Kitchen/bath facilities	2	1	4	7
Appearance	5	7	7	6
Engine/speed	5	6	8	4
Towing/handling	4	8	5	2
Maintenance	4	7	5	3
Resale value	3	7	5	6

Julie Anderson

Criteria	Weight	Ratings		
		220 Bowrider	230 Overnighter	240 Sundancer
Cost	3	7	6	5
Overnight capability	5	1	6	8
Kitchen/bath facilities	5	1	3	7
Appearance	4	5	7	7
Engine/speed	2	4	5	3
Towing/handling	2	8	6	2
Maintenance	1	6	5	4
Resale value	2	5	6	6

    a. Which boat does Clark Anderson prefer?
    b. Which boat does Julie Anderson prefer?

15. Use the pairwise comparison matrix for the price criterion shown in Table 18.8 to verify that the priorities after synthesization are 0.123, 0.320, and 0.557. Compute the consistency ratio and comment on its acceptability.

SELFtest

16. Use the pairwise comparison matrix for the style criterion as shown in Table 18.8 to verify that the priorities after synthesization are 0.265, 0.656, and 0.080. Compute the consistency ratio and comment on its acceptability.

17. Dan Joseph was considering entering one of two graduate schools of business to pursue studies for an MBA degree. When asked how he compared the two schools with respect to reputation, he responded that he preferred school A strongly to very strongly to school B.
    a. Set up the pairwise comparison matrix for this problem.
    b. Determine the priorities for the two schools relative to this criterion.

18. An organization was investigating relocating its corporate headquarters to one of three possible cities. The following pairwise comparison matrix shows the president's judgments regarding the desirability for the three cities.

	City 1	City 2	City 3
City 1	1	5	7
City 2	⅕	1	3
City 3	⅐	⅓	1

    a.   Determine the priorities for the three cities.

    b.   Is the president consistent in terms of the judgments provided? Explain.

19. The following pairwise comparison matrix contains the judgments of an individual regarding the fairness of two proposed tax programs, A and B.

	A	B
A	1	3
B	⅓	1

    a.   Determine the priorities for the two programs.

    b.   Are the individual's judgments consistent? Explain.

SELFtest   **20.** Asked to compare three soft drinks with respect to flavor, an individual stated that

           A is moderately more preferable than B.

           A is equally to moderately more preferable than C.

           B is strongly more preferable than C.

    a.   Set up the pairwise comparison matrix for this problem.

    b.   Determine the priorities for the soft drinks with respect to the flavor criterion.

    c.   Compute the consistency ratio. Are the individual's judgments consistent? Explain.

21. Refer to Problem 20. Suppose that the individual had stated the following judgments instead of those given in Problem 20.

           A is strongly more preferable than C.

           B is equally to moderately more preferable than A.

           B is strongly more preferable than C.

Answer parts (a), (b), and (c) as stated in Problem 20.

22. The national sales director for Jones Office Supplies needs to determine the best location for the next national sales meeting. Three locations have been proposed: Dallas, San Francisco, and New York. One criterion considered important in the decision is the desirability of the location in terms of restaurants, entertainment, and so on. The national sales manager made the following judgments with regard to this criterion.

           New York is very strongly more preferred than Dallas.

           New York is moderately more preferred than San Francisco.

           San Francisco is moderately to strongly more preferred than Dallas.

    a.   Set up the pairwise comparison matrix for this problem.

    b.   Determine the priorities for the desirability criterion.

    c.   Compute the consistency ratio. Are the sales manager's judgments consistent? Explain.

23. A study comparing four personal computers resulted in the following pairwise comparison matrix for the performance criterion.

	1	2	3	4
1	1	3	7	$\frac{1}{3}$
2	$\frac{1}{3}$	1	4	$\frac{1}{4}$
3	$\frac{1}{7}$	$\frac{1}{4}$	1	$\frac{1}{6}$
4	3	4	6	1

a. Determine the priorities for the four computers relative to the performance criterion.
b. Compute the consistency ratio. Are the judgments regarding performance consistent? Explain.

SELFtest 24. An individual was interested in determining which of two stocks to invest in, Central Computing Company (CCC) or Software Research, Inc. (SRI). The criteria thought to be most relevant in making the decision are the potential yield of the stock and the risk associated with the investment. The pairwise comparison matrixes for this problem are

Criterion	Yield	Risk
Yield	1	2
Risk	$\frac{1}{2}$	1

Yield	CCC	SRI
CCC	1	3
SRI	$\frac{1}{3}$	1

Risk	CCC	SRI
CCC	1	$\frac{1}{2}$
SRI	2	1

a. Compute the priorities for each pairwise comparison matrix.
b. Determine the overall priority for the two investments, CCC and SRI. Which investment is preferred based on yield and risk?

25. The vice-president of Harling Equipment needs to select a new director of marketing. The two possible candidates are Bill Jacobs and Sue Martin, and the criteria thought to be most relevant in the selection are leadership ability (L), personal skills (P), and administrative skills (A). The following pairwise comparison matrixes were obtained.

Criterion	L	P	A
L	1	$\frac{1}{3}$	$\frac{1}{4}$
P	3	1	2
A	4	$\frac{1}{2}$	1

Leadership	Jacobs	Martin
Jacobs	1	4
Martin	$\frac{1}{4}$	1

Personal	Jacobs	Martin
Jacobs	1	$\frac{1}{3}$
Martin	3	1

Administrative	Jacobs	Martin
Jacobs	1	2
Martin	$\frac{1}{2}$	1

a. Compute the priorities for each pairwise comparison matrix.
b. Determine an overall priority for each candidate. Which candidate is preferred?

26. A woman considering the purchase of a custom sound stereo system for her car looked at three different systems (A, B, and C), which varied in terms of price, sound quality, and FM reception. The following pairwise comparison matrixes were developed.

	Criterion		
	Price	**Sound**	**Reception**
Price	1	3	4
Sound	⅓	1	3
Reception	¼	⅓	1

	Price		
	A	**B**	**C**
A	1	4	2
B	¼	1	⅓
C	½	3	1

	Sound		
	A	**B**	**C**
A	1	½	¼
B	2	1	⅓
C	4	3	1

	Reception		
	A	**B**	**C**
A	1	4	2
B	¼	1	1
C	½	1	1

a. Compute the priorities for each pairwise comparison matrix.
b. Determine an overall priority for each system. Which stereo system is preferred?

Case Problem   PRODUCTION SCHEDULING

EZ Trailers, Inc., manufactures a variety of general purpose trailers, including a complete line of boat trailers. Two of their best-selling boat trailers are the EZ-190 and the EZ-250. The EZ-190 is designed for boats up to 19 feet in length, and the EZ-250 can be used for boats up to 25 feet in length.

EZ Trailers would like to schedule production for the next two months for these two models. Each unit of the EZ-190 requires 4 hours of production time, and each unit of the EZ-250 uses 6 hours of production time. The following orders have been received for March and April.

Model	March	April
EZ-190	800	600
EZ-250	1100	1200

The ending inventory from February was 200 units of the EZ-190 and 300 units of the EZ-250. The total number of hours of production time used in February was 6300 hours.

The management of EZ Trailers is concerned about being able to satisfy existing orders for the EZ-250 for both March and April. In fact, it believes that this goal is the most important one that a production schedule should meet. Next in importance is satisfying existing orders for the EZ-190. In addition, management doesn't want to implement any production schedule that would involve significant labor fluctuations from month to month. In this regard, its goal is to develop a production schedule that would limit fluctuations in labor hours used to a maximum of 1000 hours from one month to the next.

Managerial Report

Perform an analysis of EZ Trailers's production scheduling problem, and prepare a report for EZ's president that summarizes your findings. Include a discussion and analysis of the following items in your report.

1. The production schedule that best achieves the goals as specified by management.
2. Suppose that EZ Trailers's storage facilities would accommodate only a maximum of 300 trailers in any one month. What effect would this have on the production schedule?
3. Suppose that EZ Trailers can store only a maximum of 300 trailers in any one month. In addition, suppose management would like to have an ending inventory in April of at least 100 units of each model. What effect would both changes have on the production schedule?
4. What changes would occur in the production schedule if the labor fluctuation goal was the highest priority goal?

Appendix 15.1   SCORING MODELS WITH SPREADSHEETS

A spreadsheet provides an efficient way to analyze a multicriteria decision problem that can be described by a scoring model. We will use the job selection application from Section 18.3 to demonstrate this procedure.

A spreadsheet for the job selection scoring model is shown in Figure 18.7. The criteria weights are placed into cells B6 to B12. The ratings for each criterion and decision alternative are entered into cells C6 to E12.

FIGURE 18.7   SPREADSHEET FOR THE JOB SELECTION SCORING MODEL

	A	B	C	D	E
1	**Job Selection Scoring Model**				
2					
3				**Ratings**	
4			**Analyst**	**Accountant**	**Auditor**
5	**Criteria**	**Weight**	**Chicago**	**Denver**	**Houston**
6	Career Advancement	5	8	6	4
7	Location	3	3	8	7
8	Management Style	4	5	6	9
9	Salary	3	6	7	5
10	Prestige	2	7	5	4
11	Job Security	4	4	7	6
12	Enjoy the Work	5	8	6	5
13					
14					
15	**Scoring Calculations**				
16			**Analyst**	**Accountant**	**Auditor**
17	**Criteria**		**Chicago**	**Denver**	**Houston**
18	Career Advancement		40	30	20
19	Location		9	24	21
20	Management Style		20	24	36
21	Salary		18	21	15
22	Prestige		14	10	8
23	Job Security		16	28	24
24	Enjoy the Work		40	30	25
25					
26	**Score**		157	167	149

The calculations used to compute the score for each decision alternative are shown in the bottom portion of the spreadsheet. The calculation for cell C18 is provided by the cell formula

$$=\$B6*C6$$

This cell formula can be copied from cell C18 to cells C18:E24 to provide the results shown in rows 18 to 24. The score for the financial analyst position in Chicago is found by placing the following formula in cell C26:

$$=SUM(C18:C24)$$

Copying cell C26 to cells D26:E26 provides the scores for the accountant in Denver and the auditor in Houston positions.

APPENDIXES

Appendix A: Binomial Probabilities

Entries in the following table give the probability of x successes in n trials of a binomial experiment, where p is the probability of a success on one trial. For example, with $n = 6$ trials and $p = 0.40$, the probability of $x = 2$ successes is 0.3110.

n	x	0.05	0.10	0.15	0.20	0.25	0.30	0.35	0.40	0.45	0.50
1	0	0.9500	0.9000	0.8500	0.8000	0.7500	0.7000	0.6500	0.6000	0.5500	0.5000
	1	0.0500	0.1000	0.1500	0.2000	0.2500	0.3000	0.3500	0.4000	0.4500	0.5000
2	0	0.9025	0.8100	0.7225	0.6400	0.5625	0.4900	0.4225	0.3600	0.3025	0.2500
	1	0.0950	0.1800	0.2550	0.3200	0.3750	0.4200	0.4550	0.4800	0.4950	0.5000
	2	0.0025	0.0100	0.0225	0.0400	0.0625	0.0900	0.1225	0.1600	0.2025	0.2500
3	0	0.8574	0.7290	0.6141	0.5120	0.4219	0.3430	0.2746	0.2160	0.1664	0.1250
	1	0.1354	0.2430	0.3251	0.3840	0.4219	0.4410	0.4436	0.4320	0.4084	0.3750
	2	0.0071	0.0270	0.0574	0.0960	0.1406	0.1890	0.2389	0.2880	0.3341	0.3750
	3	0.0001	0.0010	0.0034	0.0080	0.0156	0.0270	0.0429	0.0640	0.0911	0.1250
4	0	0.8145	0.6561	0.5220	0.4096	0.3164	0.2401	0.1785	0.1296	0.0915	0.0625
	1	0.1715	0.2916	0.3685	0.4096	0.4219	0.4116	0.3845	0.3456	0.2995	0.2500
	2	0.0135	0.0486	0.0975	0.1536	0.2109	0.2646	0.3105	0.3456	0.3675	0.3750
	3	0.0005	0.0036	0.0115	0.0256	0.0469	0.0756	0.1115	0.1536	0.2005	0.2500
	4	0.0000	0.0001	0.0005	0.0016	0.0039	0.0081	0.0150	0.0256	0.0410	0.0625
5	0	0.7738	0.5905	0.4437	0.3277	0.2373	0.1681	0.1160	0.0778	0.0503	0.0312
	1	0.2036	0.3280	0.3915	0.4096	0.3955	0.3602	0.3124	0.2592	0.2059	0.1562
	2	0.0214	0.0729	0.1382	0.2048	0.2637	0.3087	0.3364	0.3456	0.3369	0.3125
	3	0.0011	0.0081	0.0244	0.0512	0.0879	0.1323	0.1811	0.2304	0.2757	0.3125
	4	0.0000	0.0004	0.0022	0.0064	0.0146	0.0284	0.0488	0.0768	0.1128	0.1562
	5	0.0000	0.0000	0.0001	0.0003	0.0010	0.0024	0.0053	0.0102	0.0185	0.0312
6	0	0.7351	0.5314	0.3771	0.2621	0.1780	0.1176	0.0754	0.0467	0.0277	0.0156
	1	0.2321	0.3543	0.3993	0.3932	0.3560	0.3025	0.2437	0.1866	0.1359	0.0938
	2	0.0305	0.0984	0.1762	0.2458	0.2966	0.3241	0.3280	0.3110	0.2780	0.2344
	3	0.0021	0.0146	0.0415	0.0819	0.1318	0.1852	0.2355	0.2765	0.3032	0.3125
	4	0.0001	0.0012	0.0055	0.0154	0.0330	0.0595	0.0951	0.1382	0.1861	0.2344
	5	0.0000	0.0001	0.0004	0.0015	0.0044	0.0102	0.0205	0.0369	0.0609	0.0938
	6	0.0000	0.0000	0.0000	0.0001	0.0002	0.0007	0.0018	0.0041	0.0083	0.0156
7	0	0.6983	0.4783	0.3206	0.2097	0.1335	0.0824	0.0490	0.0280	0.0152	0.0078
	1	0.2573	0.3720	0.3960	0.3670	0.3115	0.2471	0.1848	0.1306	0.0872	0.0547
	2	0.0406	0.1240	0.2097	0.2753	0.3115	0.3177	0.2985	0.2613	0.2140	0.1641
	3	0.0036	0.0230	0.0617	0.1147	0.1730	0.2269	0.2679	0.2903	0.2918	0.2734
	4	0.0002	0.0026	0.0109	0.0287	0.0577	0.0972	0.1442	0.1935	0.2388	0.2734
	5	0.0000	0.0002	0.0012	0.0043	0.0115	0.0250	0.0466	0.0774	0.1172	0.1641
	6	0.0000	0.0000	0.0001	0.0004	0.0013	0.0036	0.0084	0.0172	0.0320	0.0547
	7	0.0000	0.0000	0.0000	0.0000	0.0001	0.0002	0.0006	0.0016	0.0037	0.0078

Binomial Probabilities (*Continued*)

						p					
n	x	0.05	0.10	0.15	0.20	0.25	0.30	0.35	0.40	0.45	0.50
8	0	0.6634	0.4305	0.2725	0.1678	0.1001	0.0576	0.0319	0.0168	0.0084	0.0039
	1	0.2793	0.3826	0.3847	0.3355	0.2670	0.1977	0.1373	0.0896	0.0548	0.0312
	2	0.0515	0.1488	0.2376	0.2936	0.3115	0.2965	0.2587	0.2090	0.1569	0.1094
	3	0.0054	0.0331	0.0839	0.1468	0.2076	0.2541	0.2786	0.2787	0.2568	0.2188
	4	0.0004	0.0046	0.0185	0.0459	0.0865	0.1361	0.1875	0.2322	0.2627	0.2734
	5	0.0000	0.0004	0.0026	0.0092	0.0231	0.0467	0.0808	0.1239	0.1719	0.2188
	6	0.0000	0.0000	0.0002	0.0011	0.0038	0.0100	0.0217	0.0413	0.0703	0.1094
	7	0.0000	0.0000	0.0000	0.0001	0.0004	0.0012	0.0033	0.0079	0.0164	0.0312
	8	0.0000	0.0000	0.0000	0.0000	0.0000	0.0001	0.0002	0.0007	0.0017	0.0039
9	0	0.6302	0.3874	0.2316	0.1342	0.0751	0.0404	0.0207	0.0101	0.0046	0.0020
	1	0.2985	0.3874	0.3679	0.3020	0.2253	0.1556	0.1004	0.0605	0.0339	0.0176
	2	0.0629	0.1722	0.2597	0.3020	0.3003	0.2668	0.2162	0.1612	0.1110	0.0703
	3	0.0077	0.0446	0.1069	0.1762	0.2336	0.2668	0.2716	0.2508	0.2119	0.1641
	4	0.0006	0.0074	0.0283	0.0661	0.1168	0.1715	0.2194	0.2508	0.2600	0.2461
	5	0.0000	0.0008	0.0050	0.0165	0.0389	0.0735	0.1181	0.1672	0.2128	0.2461
	6	0.0000	0.0001	0.0006	0.0028	0.0087	0.0210	0.0424	0.0743	0.1160	0.1641
	7	0.0000	0.0000	0.0000	0.0003	0.0012	0.0039	0.0098	0.0212	0.0407	0.0703
	8	0.0000	0.0000	0.0000	0.0000	0.0001	0.0004	0.0013	0.0035	0.0083	0.0176
	9	0.0000	0.0000	0.0000	0.0000	0.0000	0.0000	0.0001	0.0003	0.0008	0.0020
10	0	0.5987	0.3487	0.1969	0.1074	0.0563	0.0282	0.0135	0.0060	0.0025	0.0010
	1	0.3151	0.3874	0.3474	0.2684	0.1877	0.1211	0.0725	0.0403	0.0207	0.0098
	2	0.0746	0.1937	0.2759	0.3020	0.2816	0.2335	0.1757	0.1209	0.0763	0.0439
	3	0.0105	0.0574	0.1298	0.2013	0.2503	0.2668	0.2522	0.2150	0.1665	0.1172
	4	0.0010	0.0112	0.0401	0.0881	0.1460	0.2001	0.2377	0.2508	0.2384	0.2051
	5	0.0001	0.0015	0.0085	0.0264	0.0584	0.1029	0.1536	0.2007	0.2340	0.2461
	6	0.0000	0.0001	0.0012	0.0055	0.0162	0.0368	0.0689	0.1115	0.1596	0.2051
	7	0.0000	0.0000	0.0001	0.0008	0.0031	0.0090	0.0212	0.0425	0.0746	0.1172
	8	0.0000	0.0000	0.0000	0.0001	0.0004	0.0014	0.0043	0.0106	0.0229	0.0439
	9	0.0000	0.0000	0.0000	0.0000	0.0000	0.0001	0.0005	0.0016	0.0042	0.0098
	10	0.0000	0.0000	0.0000	0.0000	0.0000	0.0000	0.0000	0.0001	0.0003	0.0010
12	0	0.5404	0.2824	0.1422	0.0687	0.0317	0.0138	0.0057	0.0022	0.0008	0.0002
	1	0.3413	0.3766	0.3012	0.2062	0.1267	0.0712	0.0368	0.0174	0.0075	0.0029
	2	0.0988	0.2301	0.2924	0.2835	0.2323	0.1678	0.1088	0.0639	0.0339	0.0161
	3	0.0173	0.0853	0.1720	0.2362	0.2581	0.2397	0.1954	0.1419	0.0923	0.0537
	4	0.0021	0.0213	0.0683	0.1329	0.1936	0.2311	0.2367	0.2128	0.1700	0.1208
	5	0.0002	0.0038	0.0193	0.0532	0.1032	0.1585	0.2039	0.2270	0.2225	0.1934
	6	0.0000	0.0005	0.0040	0.0155	0.0401	0.0792	0.1281	0.1766	0.2124	0.2256
	7	0.0000	0.0000	0.0006	0.0033	0.0115	0.0291	0.0591	0.1009	0.1489	0.1934
	8	0.0000	0.0000	0.0001	0.0005	0.0024	0.0078	0.0199	0.0420	0.0762	0.1208
	9	0.0000	0.0000	0.0000	0.0001	0.0004	0.0015	0.0048	0.0125	0.0277	0.0537
	10	0.0000	0.0000	0.0000	0.0000	0.0000	0.0002	0.0008	0.0025	0.0068	0.0161
	11	0.0000	0.0000	0.0000	0.0000	0.0000	0.0000	0.0001	0.0003	0.0010	0.0029
	12	0.0000	0.0000	0.0000	0.0000	0.0000	0.0000	0.0000	0.0000	0.0001	0.0002
15	0	0.4633	0.2059	0.0874	0.0352	0.0134	0.0047	0.0016	0.0005	0.0001	0.0000
	1	0.3658	0.3432	0.2312	0.1319	0.0668	0.0305	0.0126	0.0047	0.0016	0.0005
	2	0.1348	0.2669	0.2856	0.2309	0.1559	0.0916	0.0476	0.0219	0.0090	0.0032

Binomial Probabilities (*Continued*)

							p				
n	*x*	0.05	0.10	0.15	0.20	0.25	0.30	0.35	0.40	0.45	0.50
	3	0.0307	0.1285	0.2184	0.2501	0.2252	0.1700	0.1110	0.0634	0.0318	0.0139
	4	0.0049	0.0428	0.1156	0.1876	0.2252	0.2186	0.1792	0.1268	0.0780	0.0417
	5	0.0006	0.0105	0.0449	0.1032	0.1651	0.2061	0.2123	0.1859	0.1404	0.0916
	6	0.0000	0.0019	0.0132	0.0430	0.0917	0.1472	0.1906	0.2066	0.1914	0.1527
	7	0.0000	0.0003	0.0030	0.0138	0.0393	0.0811	0.1319	0.1771	0.2013	0.1964
	8	0.0000	0.0000	0.0005	0.0035	0.0131	0.0348	0.0710	0.1181	0.1647	0.1964
	9	0.0000	0.0000	0.0001	0.0007	0.0034	0.0116	0.0298	0.0612	0.1048	0.1527
	10	0.0000	0.0000	0.0000	0.0001	0.0007	0.0030	0.0096	0.0245	0.0515	0.0916
	11	0.0000	0.0000	0.0000	0.0000	0.0001	0.0006	0.0024	0.0074	0.0191	0.0417
	12	0.0000	0.0000	0.0000	0.0000	0.0000	0.0001	0.0004	0.0016	0.0052	0.0139
	13	0.0000	0.0000	0.0000	0.0000	0.0000	0.0000	0.0001	0.0003	0.0010	0.0032
	14	0.0000	0.0000	0.0000	0.0000	0.0000	0.0000	0.0000	0.0000	0.0001	0.0005
	15	0.0000	0.0000	0.0000	0.0000	0.0000	0.0000	0.0000	0.0000	0.0000	0.0000
18	0	0.3972	0.1501	0.0536	0.0180	0.0056	0.0016	0.0004	0.0001	0.0000	0.0000
	1	0.3763	0.3002	0.1704	0.0811	0.0338	0.0126	0.0042	0.0012	0.0003	0.0001
	2	0.1683	0.2835	0.2556	0.1723	0.0958	0.0458	0.0190	0.0069	0.0022	0.0006
	3	0.0473	0.1680	0.2406	0.2297	0.1704	0.1046	0.0547	0.0246	0.0095	0.0031
	4	0.0093	0.0700	0.1592	0.2153	0.2130	0.1681	0.1104	0.0614	0.0291	0.0117
	5	0.0014	0.0218	0.0787	0.1507	0.1988	0.2017	0.1664	0.1146	0.0666	0.0327
	6	0.0002	0.0052	0.0301	0.0816	0.1436	0.1873	0.1941	0.1655	0.1181	0.0708
	7	0.0000	0.0010	0.0091	0.0350	0.0820	0.1376	0.1792	0.1892	0.1657	0.1214
	8	0.0000	0.0002	0.0022	0.0120	0.0376	0.0811	0.1327	0.1734	0.1864	0.1669
	9	0.0000	0.0000	0.0004	0.0033	0.0139	0.0386	0.0794	0.1284	0.1694	0.1855
	10	0.0000	0.0000	0.0001	0.0008	0.0042	0.0149	0.0385	0.0771	0.1248	0.1669
	11	0.0000	0.0000	0.0000	0.0001	0.0010	0.0046	0.0151	0.0374	0.0742	0.1214
	12	0.0000	0.0000	0.0000	0.0000	0.0002	0.0012	0.0047	0.0145	0.0354	0.0708
	13	0.0000	0.0000	0.0000	0.0000	0.0000	0.0002	0.0012	0.0045	0.0134	0.0327
	14	0.0000	0.0000	0.0000	0.0000	0.0000	0.0000	0.0002	0.0011	0.0039	0.0117
	15	0.0000	0.0000	0.0000	0.0000	0.0000	0.0000	0.0000	0.0002	0.0009	0.0031
	16	0.0000	0.0000	0.0000	0.0000	0.0000	0.0000	0.0000	0.0000	0.0001	0.0006
	17	0.0000	0.0000	0.0000	0.0000	0.0000	0.0000	0.0000	0.0000	0.0000	0.0001
	18	0.0000	0.0000	0.0000	0.0000	0.0000	0.0000	0.0000	0.0000	0.0000	0.0000
20	0	0.3585	0.1216	0.0388	0.0115	0.0032	0.0008	0.0002	0.0000	0.0000	0.0000
	1	0.3774	0.2702	0.1368	0.0576	0.0211	0.0068	0.0020	0.0005	0.0001	0.0000
	2	0.1887	0.2852	0.2293	0.1369	0.0669	0.0278	0.0100	0.0031	0.0008	0.0002
	3	0.0596	0.1901	0.2428	0.2054	0.1339	0.0716	0.0323	0.0123	0.0040	0.0011
	4	0.0133	0.0898	0.1821	0.2182	0.1897	0.1304	0.0738	0.0350	0.0139	0.0046
	5	0.0022	0.0319	0.1028	0.1746	0.2023	0.1789	0.1272	0.0746	0.0365	0.0148
	6	0.0003	0.0089	0.0454	0.1091	0.1686	0.1916	0.1712	0.1244	0.0746	0.0370
	7	0.0000	0.0020	0.0160	0.0545	0.1124	0.1643	0.1844	0.1659	0.1221	0.0739
	8	0.0000	0.0004	0.0046	0.0222	0.0609	0.1144	0.1614	0.1797	0.1623	0.1201
	9	0.0000	0.0001	0.0011	0.0074	0.0271	0.0654	0.1158	0.1597	0.1771	0.1602
	10	0.0000	0.0000	0.0002	0.0020	0.0099	0.0308	0.0686	0.1171	0.1593	0.1762
	11	0.0000	0.0000	0.0000	0.0005	0.0030	0.0120	0.0336	0.0710	0.1185	0.1602
	12	0.0000	0.0000	0.0000	0.0001	0.0008	0.0039	0.0136	0.0355	0.0727	0.1201
	13	0.0000	0.0000	0.0000	0.0000	0.0002	0.0010	0.0045	0.0146	0.0366	0.0739
	14	0.0000	0.0000	0.0000	0.0000	0.0000	0.0002	0.0012	0.0049	0.0150	0.0370

Binomial Probabilities (*Continued*)

		p									
n	*x*	0.05	0.10	0.15	0.20	0.25	0.30	0.35	0.40	0.45	0.50
	15	0.0000	0.0000	0.0000	0.0000	0.0000	0.0000	0.0003	0.0013	0.0049	0.0148
	16	0.0000	0.0000	0.0000	0.0000	0.0000	0.0000	0.0000	0.0003	0.0013	0.0046
	17	0.0000	0.0000	0.0000	0.0000	0.0000	0.0000	0.0000	0.0000	0.0002	0.0011
	18	0.0000	0.0000	0.0000	0.0000	0.0000	0.0000	0.0000	0.0000	0.0000	0.0002
	19	0.0000	0.0000	0.0000	0.0000	0.0000	0.0000	0.0000	0.0000	0.0000	0.0000
	20	0.0000	0.0000	0.0000	0.0000	0.0000	0.0000	0.0000	0.0000	0.0000	0.0000

Binomial Probabilities (*Continued*)

						p				
n	*x*	0.55	0.60	0.65	0.70	0.75	0.80	0.85	0.90	0.95
2	0	0.2025	0.1600	0.1225	0.0900	0.0625	0.0400	0.0225	0.0100	0.0025
	1	0.4950	0.4800	0.4550	0.4200	0.3750	0.3200	0.2550	0.1800	0.0950
	2	0.3025	0.3600	0.4225	0.4900	0.5625	0.6400	0.7225	0.8100	0.9025
3	0	0.0911	0.0640	0.0429	0.0270	0.0156	0.0080	0.0034	0.0010	0.0001
	1	0.3341	0.2880	0.2389	0.1890	0.1406	0.0960	0.0574	0.0270	0.0071
	2	0.4084	0.4320	0.4436	0.4410	0.4219	0.3840	0.3251	0.2430	0.1354
	3	0.1664	0.2160	0.2746	0.3430	0.4219	0.5120	0.6141	0.7290	0.8574
4	0	0.0410	0.0256	0.0150	0.0081	0.0039	0.0016	0.0005	0.0001	0.0000
	1	0.2005	0.1536	0.1115	0.0756	0.0469	0.0256	0.0115	0.0036	0.0005
	2	0.3675	0.3456	0.3105	0.2646	0.2109	0.1536	0.0975	0.0486	0.0135
	3	0.2995	0.3456	0.3845	0.4116	0.4219	0.4096	0.3685	0.2916	0.1715
	4	0.0915	0.1296	0.1785	0.2401	0.3164	0.4096	0.5220	0.6561	0.8145
5	0	0.0185	0.0102	0.0053	0.0024	0.0010	0.0003	0.0001	0.0000	0.0000
	1	0.1128	0.0768	0.0488	0.0284	0.0146	0.0064	0.0022	0.0005	0.0000
	2	0.2757	0.2304	0.1811	0.1323	0.0879	0.0512	0.0244	0.0081	0.0011
	3	0.3369	0.3456	0.3364	0.3087	0.2637	0.2048	0.1382	0.0729	0.0214
	4	0.2059	0.2592	0.3124	0.3601	0.3955	0.4096	0.3915	0.3281	0.2036
	5	0.0503	0.0778	0.1160	0.1681	0.2373	0.3277	0.4437	0.5905	0.7738
6	0	0.0083	0.0041	0.0018	0.0007	0.0002	0.0001	0.0000	0.0000	0.0000
	1	0.0609	0.0369	0.0205	0.0102	0.0044	0.0015	0.0004	0.0001	0.0000
	2	0.1861	0.1382	0.0951	0.0595	0.0330	0.0154	0.0055	0.0012	0.0001
	3	0.3032	0.2765	0.2355	0.1852	0.1318	0.0819	0.0415	0.0146	0.0021
	4	0.2780	0.3110	0.3280	0.3241	0.2966	0.2458	0.1762	0.0984	0.0305
	5	0.1359	0.1866	0.2437	0.3025	0.3560	0.3932	0.3993	0.3543	0.2321
	6	0.0277	0.0467	0.0754	0.1176	0.1780	0.2621	0.3771	0.5314	0.7351
7	0	0.0037	0.0016	0.0006	0.0002	0.0001	0.0000	0.0000	0.0000	0.0000
	1	0.0320	0.0172	0.0084	0.0036	0.0013	0.0004	0.0001	0.0000	0.0000
	2	0.1172	0.0774	0.0466	0.0250	0.0115	0.0043	0.0012	0.0002	0.0000
	3	0.2388	0.1935	0.1442	0.0972	0.0577	0.0287	0.0109	0.0026	0.0002
	4	0.2918	0.2903	0.2679	0.2269	0.1730	0.1147	0.0617	0.0230	0.0036
	5	0.2140	0.2613	0.2985	0.3177	0.3115	0.2753	0.2097	0.1240	0.0406
	6	0.0872	0.1306	0.1848	0.2471	0.3115	0.3670	0.3960	0.3720	0.2573
	7	0.0152	0.0280	0.0490	0.0824	0.1335	0.2097	0.3206	0.4783	0.6983
8	0	0.0017	0.0007	0.0002	0.0001	0.0000	0.0000	0.0000	0.0000	0.0000
	1	0.0164	0.0079	0.0033	0.0012	0.0004	0.0001	0.0000	0.0000	0.0000
	2	0.0703	0.0413	0.0217	0.0100	0.0038	0.0011	0.0002	0.0000	0.0000
	3	0.1719	0.1239	0.0808	0.0467	0.0231	0.0092	0.0026	0.0004	0.0000
	4	0.2627	0.2322	0.1875	0.1361	0.0865	0.0459	0.0185	0.0046	0.0004
	5	0.2568	0.2787	0.2786	0.2541	0.2076	0.1468	0.0839	0.0331	0.0054
	6	0.1569	0.2090	0.2587	0.2965	0.3115	0.2936	0.2376	0.1488	0.0515
	7	0.0548	0.0896	0.1373	0.1977	0.2670	0.3355	0.3847	0.3826	0.2793
	8	0.0084	0.0168	0.0319	0.0576	0.1001	0.1678	0.2725	0.4305	0.6634

Binomial Probabilities (*Continued*)

n	x	0.55	0.60	0.65	0.70	0.75	0.80	0.85	0.90	0.95
9	0	0.0008	0.0003	0.0001	0.0000	0.0000	0.0000	0.0000	0.0000	0.0000
	1	0.0083	0.0035	0.0013	0.0004	0.0001	0.0000	0.0000	0.0000	0.0000
	2	0.0407	0.0212	0.0098	0.0039	0.0012	0.0003	0.0000	0.0000	0.0000
	3	0.1160	0.0743	0.0424	0.0210	0.0087	0.0028	0.0006	0.0001	0.0000
	4	0.2128	0.1672	0.1181	0.0735	0.0389	0.0165	0.0050	0.0008	0.0000
	5	0.2600	0.2508	0.2194	0.1715	0.1168	0.0661	0.0283	0.0074	0.0006
	6	0.2119	0.2508	0.2716	0.2668	0.2336	0.1762	0.1069	0.0446	0.0077
	7	0.1110	0.1612	0.2162	0.2668	0.3003	0.3020	0.2597	0.1722	0.0629
	8	0.0339	0.0605	0.1004	0.1556	0.2253	0.3020	0.3679	0.3874	0.2985
	9	0.0046	0.0101	0.0207	0.0404	0.0751	0.1342	0.2316	0.3874	0.6302
10	0	0.0003	0.0001	0.0000	0.0000	0.0000	0.0000	0.0000	0.0000	0.0000
	1	0.0042	0.0016	0.0005	0.0001	0.0000	0.0000	0.0000	0.0000	0.0000
	2	0.0229	0.0106	0.0043	0.0014	0.0004	0.0001	0.0000	0.0000	0.0000
	3	0.0746	0.0425	0.0212	0.0090	0.0031	0.0008	0.0001	0.0000	0.0000
	4	0.1596	0.1115	0.0689	0.0368	0.0162	0.0055	0.0012	0.0001	0.0000
	5	0.2340	0.2007	0.1536	0.1029	0.0584	0.0264	0.0085	0.0015	0.0001
	6	0.2384	0.2508	0.2377	0.2001	0.1460	0.0881	0.0401	0.0112	0.0010
	7	0.1665	0.2150	0.2522	0.2668	0.2503	0.2013	0.1298	0.0574	0.0105
	8	0.0763	0.1209	0.1757	0.2335	0.2816	0.3020	0.2759	0.1937	0.0746
	9	0.0207	0.0403	0.0725	0.1211	0.1877	0.2684	0.3474	0.3874	0.3151
	10	0.0025	0.0060	0.0135	0.0282	0.0563	0.1074	0.1969	0.3487	0.5987
12	0	0.0001	0.0000	0.0000	0.0000	0.0000	0.0000	0.0000	0.0000	0.0000
	1	0.0010	0.0003	0.0001	0.0000	0.0000	0.0000	0.0000	0.0000	0.0000
	2	0.0068	0.0025	0.0008	0.0002	0.0000	0.0000	0.0000	0.0000	0.0000
	3	0.0277	0.0125	0.0048	0.0015	0.0004	0.0001	0.0000	0.0000	0.0000
	4	0.0762	0.0420	0.0199	0.0078	0.0024	0.0005	0.0001	0.0000	0.0000
	5	0.1489	0.1009	0.0591	0.0291	0.0115	0.0033	0.0006	0.0000	0.0000
	6	0.2124	0.1766	0.1281	0.0792	0.0401	0.0155	0.0040	0.0005	0.0000
	7	0.2225	0.2270	0.2039	0.1585	0.1032	0.0532	0.0193	0.0038	0.0002
	8	0.1700	0.2128	0.2367	0.2311	0.1936	0.1329	0.0683	0.0213	0.0021
	9	0.0923	0.1419	0.1954	0.2397	0.2581	0.2362	0.1720	0.0852	0.0173
	10	0.0339	0.0639	0.1088	0.1678	0.2323	0.2835	0.2924	0.2301	0.0988
	11	0.0075	0.0174	0.0368	0.0712	0.1267	0.2062	0.3012	0.3766	0.3413
	12	0.0008	0.0022	0.0057	0.0138	0.0317	0.0687	0.1422	0.2824	0.5404
15	0	0.0000	0.0000	0.0000	0.0000	0.0000	0.0000	0.0000	0.0000	0.0000
	1	0.0001	0.0000	0.0000	0.0000	0.0000	0.0000	0.0000	0.0000	0.0000
	2	0.0010	0.0003	0.0001	0.0000	0.0000	0.0000	0.0000	0.0000	0.0000
	3	0.0052	0.0016	0.0004	0.0001	0.0000	0.0000	0.0000	0.0000	0.0000
	4	0.0191	0.0074	0.0024	0.0006	0.0001	0.0000	0.0000	0.0000	0.0000
	5	0.0515	0.0245	0.0096	0.0030	0.0007	0.0001	0.0000	0.0000	0.0000
	6	0.1048	0.0612	0.0298	0.0116	0.0034	0.0007	0.0001	0.0000	0.0000
	7	0.1647	0.1181	0.0710	0.0348	0.0131	0.0035	0.0005	0.0000	0.0000
	8	0.2013	0.1771	0.1319	0.0811	0.0393	0.0138	0.0030	0.0003	0.0000
	9	0.1914	0.2066	0.1906	0.1472	0.0917	0.0430	0.0132	0.0019	0.0000
	10	0.1404	0.1859	0.2123	0.2061	0.1651	0.1032	0.0449	0.0105	0.0006
	11	0.0780	0.1268	0.1792	0.2186	0.2252	0.1876	0.1156	0.0428	0.0049

Binomial Probabilities (*Continued*)

						p				
n	x	0.55	0.60	0.65	0.70	0.75	0.80	0.85	0.90	0.95
	12	0.0318	0.0634	0.1110	0.1700	0.2252	0.2501	0.2184	0.1285	0.0307
	13	0.0090	0.0219	0.0476	0.0916	0.1559	0.2309	0.2856	0.2669	0.1348
	14	0.0016	0.0047	0.0126	0.0305	0.0668	0.1319	0.2312	0.3432	0.3658
	15	0.0001	0.0005	0.0016	0.0047	0.0134	0.0352	0.0874	0.2059	0.4633
18	0	0.0000	0.0000	0.0000	0.0000	0.0000	0.0000	0.0000	0.0000	0.0000
	1	0.0000	0.0000	0.0000	0.0000	0.0000	0.0000	0.0000	0.0000	0.0000
	2	0.0001	0.0000	0.0000	0.0000	0.0000	0.0000	0.0000	0.0000	0.0000
	3	0.0009	0.0002	0.0000	0.0000	0.0000	0.0000	0.0000	0.0000	0.0000
	4	0.0039	0.0011	0.0002	0.0000	0.0000	0.0000	0.0000	0.0000	0.0000
	5	0.0134	0.0045	0.0012	0.0002	0.0000	0.0000	0.0000	0.0000	0.0000
	6	0.0354	0.0145	0.0047	0.0012	0.0002	0.0000	0.0000	0.0000	0.0000
	7	0.0742	0.0374	0.0151	0.0046	0.0010	0.0001	0.0000	0.0000	0.0000
	8	0.1248	0.0771	0.0385	0.0149	0.0042	0.0008	0.0001	0.0000	0.0000
	9	0.1694	0.1284	0.0794	0.0386	0.0139	0.0033	0.0004	0.0000	0.0000
	10	0.1864	0.1734	0.1327	0.0811	0.0376	0.0120	0.0022	0.0002	0.0000
	11	0.1657	0.1892	0.1792	0.1376	0.0820	0.0350	0.0091	0.0010	0.0000
	12	0.1181	0.1655	0.1941	0.1873	0.1436	0.0816	0.0301	0.0052	0.0002
	13	0.0666	0.1146	0.1664	0.2017	0.1988	0.1507	0.0787	0.0218	0.0014
	14	0.0291	0.0614	0.1104	0.1681	0.2130	0.2153	0.1592	0.0700	0.0093
	15	0.0095	0.0246	0.0547	0.1046	0.1704	0.2297	0.2406	0.1680	0.0473
	16	0.0022	0.0069	0.0190	0.0458	0.0958	0.1723	0.2556	0.2835	0.1683
	17	0.0003	0.0012	0.0042	0.0126	0.0338	0.0811	0.1704	0.3002	0.3763
	18	0.0000	0.0001	0.0004	0.0016	0.0056	0.0180	0.0536	0.1501	0.3972
20	0	0.0000	0.0000	0.0000	0.0000	0.0000	0.0000	0.0000	0.0000	0.0000
	1	0.0000	0.0000	0.0000	0.0000	0.0000	0.0000	0.0000	0.0000	0.0000
	2	0.0000	0.0000	0.0000	0.0000	0.0000	0.0000	0.0000	0.0000	0.0000
	3	0.0002	0.0000	0.0000	0.0000	0.0000	0.0000	0.0000	0.0000	0.0000
	4	0.0013	0.0003	0.0000	0.0000	0.0000	0.0000	0.0000	0.0000	0.0000
	5	0.0049	0.0013	0.0003	0.0000	0.0000	0.0000	0.0000	0.0000	0.0000
	6	0.0150	0.0049	0.0012	0.0002	0.0000	0.0000	0.0000	0.0000	0.0000
	7	0.0366	0.0146	0.0045	0.0010	0.0002	0.0000	0.0000	0.0000	0.0000
	8	0.0727	0.0355	0.0136	0.0039	0.0008	0.0001	0.0000	0.0000	0.0000
	9	0.1185	0.0710	0.0336	0.0120	0.0030	0.0005	0.0000	0.0000	0.0000
	10	0.1593	0.1171	0.0686	0.0308	0.0099	0.0020	0.0002	0.0000	0.0000
	11	0.1771	0.1597	0.1158	0.0654	0.0271	0.0074	0.0011	0.0001	0.0000
	12	0.1623	0.1797	0.1614	0.1144	0.0609	0.0222	0.0046	0.0004	0.0000
	13	0.1221	0.1659	0.1844	0.1643	0.1124	0.0545	0.0160	0.0020	0.0000
	14	0.0746	0.1244	0.1712	0.1916	0.1686	0.1091	0.0454	0.0089	0.0003
	15	0.0365	0.0746	0.1272	0.1789	0.2023	0.1746	0.1028	0.0319	0.0022
	16	0.0139	0.0350	0.0738	0.1304	0.1897	0.2182	0.1821	0.0898	0.0133
	17	0.0040	0.0123	0.0323	0.0716	0.1339	0.2054	0.2428	0.1901	0.0596
	18	0.0008	0.0031	0.0100	0.0278	0.0669	0.1369	0.2293	0.2852	0.1887
	19	0.0001	0.0005	0.0020	0.0068	0.0211	0.0576	0.1368	0.2702	0.3774
	20	0.0000	0.0000	0.0002	0.0008	0.0032	0.0115	0.0388	0.1216	0.3585

Appendix B: Poisson Probabilities

Entries in the following table give the probability of x occurrences for a Poisson process with a mean λ. For example, when $\lambda = 2.5$, the probability of $x = 4$ occurrences is 0.1336.

x	λ									
---	0.1	0.2	0.3	0.4	0.5	0.6	0.7	0.8	0.9	1.0
0	0.9048	0.8187	0.7408	0.6703	0.6065	0.5488	0.4966	0.4493	0.4066	0.3679
1	0.0905	0.1637	0.2222	0.2681	0.3033	0.3293	0.3476	0.3595	0.3659	0.3679
2	0.0045	0.0164	0.0333	0.0536	0.0758	0.0988	0.1217	0.1438	0.1647	0.1839
3	0.0002	0.0011	0.0033	0.0072	0.0126	0.0198	0.0284	0.0383	0.0494	0.0613
4	0.0000	0.0001	0.0002	0.0007	0.0016	0.0030	0.0050	0.0077	0.0111	0.0153
5	0.0000	0.0000	0.0000	0.0001	0.0002	0.0004	0.0007	0.0012	0.0020	0.0031
6	0.0000	0.0000	0.0000	0.0000	0.0000	0.0000	0.0001	0.0002	0.0003	0.0005
7	0.0000	0.0000	0.0000	0.0000	0.0000	0.0000	0.0000	0.0000	0.0000	0.0001

x	λ									
---	1.1	1.2	1.3	1.4	1.5	1.6	1.7	1.8	1.9	2.0
0	0.3329	0.3012	0.2725	0.2466	0.2231	0.2019	0.1827	0.1653	0.1496	0.1353
1	0.3662	0.3614	0.3543	0.3452	0.3347	0.3230	0.3106	0.2975	0.2842	0.2707
2	0.2014	0.2169	0.2303	0.2417	0.2510	0.2584	0.2640	0.2678	0.2700	0.2707
3	0.0738	0.0867	0.0998	0.1128	0.1255	0.1378	0.1496	0.1607	0.1710	0.1804
4	0.0203	0.0260	0.0324	0.0395	0.0471	0.0551	0.0636	0.0723	0.0812	0.0902
5	0.0045	0.0062	0.0084	0.0111	0.0141	0.0176	0.0216	0.0260	0.0309	0.0361
6	0.0008	0.0012	0.0018	0.0026	0.0035	0.0047	0.0061	0.0078	0.0098	0.0120
7	0.0001	0.0002	0.0003	0.0005	0.0008	0.0011	0.0015	0.0020	0.0027	0.0034
8	0.0000	0.0000	0.0001	0.0001	0.0001	0.0002	0.0003	0.0005	0.0006	0.0009
9	0.0000	0.0000	0.0000	0.0000	0.0000	0.0000	0.0001	0.0001	0.0001	0.0002

x	λ									
---	2.1	2.2	2.3	2.4	2.5	2.6	2.7	2.8	2.9	3.0
0	0.1225	0.1108	0.1003	0.0907	0.0821	0.0743	0.0672	0.0608	0.0550	0.0498
1	0.2572	0.2438	0.2306	0.2177	0.2052	0.1931	0.1815	0.1703	0.1596	0.1494
2	0.2700	0.2681	0.2652	0.2613	0.2565	0.2510	0.2450	0.2384	0.2314	0.2240
3	0.1890	0.1966	0.2033	0.2090	0.2138	0.2176	0.2205	0.2225	0.2237	0.2240
4	0.0992	0.1082	0.1169	0.1254	0.1336	0.1414	0.1488	0.1557	0.1622	0.1680
5	0.0417	0.0476	0.0538	0.0602	0.0668	0.0735	0.0804	0.0872	0.0940	0.1008
6	0.0146	0.0174	0.0206	0.0241	0.0278	0.0319	0.0362	0.0407	0.0455	0.0540
7	0.0044	0.0055	0.0068	0.0083	0.0099	0.0118	0.0139	0.0163	0.0188	0.0216

Poisson Probabilities (*Continued*)

					λ					
x	2.1	2.2	2.3	2.4	2.5	2.6	2.7	2.8	2.9	3.0
8	0.0011	0.0015	0.0019	0.0025	0.0031	0.0038	0.0047	0.0057	0.0068	0.0081
9	0.0003	0.0004	0.0005	0.0007	0.0009	0.0011	0.0014	0.0018	0.0022	0.0027
10	0.0001	0.0001	0.0001	0.0002	0.0002	0.0003	0.0004	0.0005	0.0006	0.0008
11	0.0000	0.0000	0.0000	0.0000	0.0000	0.0001	0.0001	0.0001	0.0002	0.0002
12	0.0000	0.0000	0.0000	0.0000	0.0000	0.0000	0.0000	0.0000	0.0000	0.0001

					λ					
x	3.1	3.2	3.3	3.4	3.5	3.6	3.7	3.8	3.9	4.0
0	0.0450	0.0408	0.0369	0.0344	0.0302	0.0273	0.0247	0.0224	0.0202	0.0183
1	0.1397	0.1304	0.1217	0.1135	0.1057	0.0984	0.0915	0.0850	0.0789	0.0733
2	0.2165	0.2087	0.2008	0.1929	0.1850	0.1771	0.1692	0.1615	0.1539	0.1465
3	0.2237	0.2226	0.2209	0.2186	0.2158	0.2125	0.2087	0.2046	0.2001	0.1954
4	0.1734	0.1781	0.1823	0.1858	0.1888	0.1912	0.1931	0.1944	0.1951	0.1954
5	0.1075	0.1140	0.1203	0.1264	0.1322	0.1377	0.1429	0.1477	0.1522	0.1563
6	0.0555	0.0608	0.0662	0.0716	0.0771	0.0826	0.0881	0.0936	0.0989	0.1042
7	0.0246	0.0278	0.0312	0.0348	0.0385	0.0425	0.0466	0.0508	0.0551	0.0595
8	0.0095	0.0111	0.0129	0.0148	0.0169	0.0191	0.0215	0.0241	0.0269	0.0298
9	0.0033	0.0040	0.0047	0.0056	0.0066	0.0076	0.0089	0.0102	0.0116	0.0132
10	0.0010	0.0013	0.0016	0.0019	0.0023	0.0028	0.0033	0.0039	0.0045	0.0053
11	0.0003	0.0004	0.0005	0.0006	0.0007	0.0009	0.0011	0.0013	0.0016	0.0019
12	0.0001	0.0001	0.0001	0.0002	0.0002	0.0003	0.0003	0.0004	0.0005	0.0006
13	0.0000	0.0000	0.0000	0.0000	0.0001	0.0001	0.0001	0.0001	0.0002	0.0002
14	0.0000	0.0000	0.0000	0.0000	0.0000	0.0000	0.0000	0.0000	0.0000	0.0001

					λ					
x	4.1	4.2	4.3	4.4	4.5	4.6	4.7	4.8	4.9	5.0
0	0.0166	0.0150	0.0136	0.0123	0.0111	0.0101	0.0091	0.0082	0.0074	0.0067
1	0.0679	0.0630	0.0583	0.0540	0.0500	0.0462	0.0427	0.0395	0.0365	0.0337
2	0.1393	0.1323	0.1254	0.1188	0.1125	0.1063	0.1005	0.0948	0.0894	0.0842
3	0.1904	0.1852	0.1798	0.1743	0.1687	0.1631	0.1574	0.1517	0.1460	0.1404
4	0.1951	0.1944	0.1933	0.1917	0.1898	0.1875	0.1849	0.1820	0.1789	0.1755
5	0.1600	0.1633	0.1662	0.1687	0.1708	0.1725	0.1738	0.1747	0.1753	0.1755
6	0.1093	0.1143	0.1191	0.1237	0.1281	0.1323	0.1362	0.1398	0.1432	0.1462
7	0.0640	0.0686	0.0732	0.0778	0.0824	0.0869	0.0914	0.0959	0.1002	0.1044
8	0.0328	0.0360	0.0393	0.0428	0.0463	0.0500	0.0537	0.0575	0.0614	0.0653
9	0.0150	0.0168	0.0188	0.0209	0.0232	0.0255	0.0280	0.0307	0.0334	0.0363
10	0.0061	0.0071	0.0081	0.0092	0.0104	0.0118	0.0132	0.0147	0.0164	0.0181
11	0.0023	0.0027	0.0032	0.0037	0.0043	0.0049	0.0056	0.0064	0.0073	0.0082
12	0.0008	0.0009	0.0011	0.0014	0.0016	0.0019	0.0022	0.0026	0.0030	0.0034
13	0.0002	0.0003	0.0004	0.0005	0.0006	0.0007	0.0008	0.0009	0.0011	0.0013
14	0.0001	0.0001	0.0001	0.0001	0.0002	0.0002	0.0003	0.0003	0.0004	0.0005
15	0.0000	0.0000	0.0000	0.0000	0.0001	0.0001	0.0001	0.0001	0.0001	0.0002

Binomial Probabilities (*Continued*)

	λ									
x	5.1	5.2	5.3	5.4	5.5	5.6	5.7	5.8	5.9	6.0
0	0.0061	0.0055	0.0050	0.0045	0.0041	0.0037	0.0033	0.0030	0.0027	0.0025
1	0.0311	0.0287	0.0265	0.0244	0.0225	0.0207	0.0191	0.0176	0.0162	0.0149
2	0.0793	0.0746	0.0701	0.0659	0.0618	0.0580	0.0544	0.0509	0.0477	0.0446
3	0.1348	0.1293	0.1239	0.1185	0.1133	0.1082	0.1033	0.0985	0.0938	0.0892
4	0.1719	0.1681	0.1641	0.1600	0.1558	0.1515	0.1472	0.1428	0.1383	0.1339
5	0.1753	0.1748	0.1740	0.1728	0.1714	0.1697	0.1678	0.1656	0.1632	0.1606
6	0.1490	0.1515	0.1537	0.1555	0.1571	0.1587	0.1594	0.1601	0.1605	0.1606
7	0.1086	0.1125	0.1163	0.1200	0.1234	0.1267	0.1298	0.1326	0.1353	0.1377
8	0.0692	0.0731	0.0771	0.0810	0.0849	0.0887	0.0925	0.0962	0.0998	0.1033
9	0.0392	0.0423	0.0454	0.0486	0.0519	0.0552	0.0586	0.0620	0.0654	0.0688
10	0.0200	0.0220	0.0241	0.0262	0.0285	0.0309	0.0334	0.0359	0.0386	0.0413
11	0.0093	0.0104	0.0116	0.0129	0.0143	0.0157	0.0173	0.0190	0.0207	0.0225
12	0.0039	0.0045	0.0051	0.0058	0.0065	0.0073	0.0082	0.0092	0.0102	0.0113
13	0.0015	0.0018	0.0021	0.0024	0.0028	0.0032	0.0036	0.0041	0.0046	0.0052
14	0.0006	0.0007	0.0008	0.0009	0.0011	0.0013	0.0015	0.0017	0.0019	0.0022
15	0.0002	0.0002	0.0003	0.0003	0.0004	0.0005	0.0006	0.0007	0.0008	0.0009
16	0.0001	0.0001	0.0001	0.0001	0.0001	0.0002	0.0002	0.0002	0.0003	0.0003
17	0.0000	0.0000	0.0000	0.0000	0.0000	0.0001	0.0001	0.0001	0.0001	0.0001

	λ									
x	6.1	6.2	6.3	6.4	6.5	6.6	6.7	6.8	6.9	7.0
0	0.0022	0.0020	0.0018	0.0017	0.0015	0.0014	0.0012	0.0011	0.0010	0.0009
1	0.0137	0.0126	0.0116	0.0106	0.0098	0.0090	0.0082	0.0076	0.0070	0.0064
2	0.0417	0.0390	0.0364	0.0340	0.0318	0.0296	0.0276	0.0258	0.0240	0.0223
3	0.0848	0.0806	0.0765	0.0726	0.0688	0.0652	0.0617	0.0584	0.0552	0.0521
4	0.1294	0.1249	0.1205	0.1162	0.1118	0.1076	0.1034	0.0992	0.0952	0.0912
5	0.1579	0.1549	0.1519	0.1487	0.1454	0.1420	0.1385	0.1349	0.1314	0.1277
6	0.1605	0.1601	0.1595	0.1586	0.1575	0.1562	0.1546	0.1529	0.1511	0.1490
7	0.1399	0.1418	0.1435	0.1450	0.1462	0.1472	0.1480	0.1486	0.1489	0.1490
8	0.1066	0.1099	0.1130	0.1160	0.1188	0.1215	0.1240	0.1263	0.1284	0.1304
9	0.0723	0.0757	0.0791	0.0825	0.0858	0.0891	0.0923	0.0954	0.0985	0.1014
10	0.0441	0.0469	0.0498	0.0528	0.0558	0.0588	0.0618	0.0649	0.0679	0.0710
11	0.0245	0.0265	0.0285	0.0307	0.0330	0.0353	0.0377	0.0401	0.0426	0.0452
12	0.0124	0.0137	0.0150	0.0164	0.0179	0.0194	0.0210	0.0227	0.0245	0.0264
13	0.0058	0.0065	0.0073	0.0081	0.0089	0.0098	0.0108	0.0119	0.0130	0.0142
14	0.0025	0.0029	0.0033	0.0037	0.0041	0.0046	0.0052	0.0058	0.0064	0.0071
15	0.0010	0.0012	0.0014	0.0016	0.0018	0.0020	0.0023	0.0025	0.0029	0.0033
16	0.0004	0.0005	0.0005	0.0006	0.0007	0.0008	0.0010	0.0011	0.0013	0.0014
17	0.0001	0.0002	0.0002	0.0002	0.0003	0.0003	0.0004	0.0004	0.0005	0.0006
18	0.0000	0.0001	0.0001	0.0001	0.0001	0.0001	0.0001	0.0002	0.0002	0.0002
19	0.0000	0.0000	0.0000	0.0000	0.0000	0.0000	0.0000	0.0001	0.0001	0.0001

Poisson Probabilities (*Continued*)

					λ					
x	7.1	7.2	7.3	7.4	7.5	7.6	7.7	7.8	7.9	8.0
0	0.0008	0.0007	0.0007	0.0006	0.0006	0.0005	0.0005	0.0004	0.0004	0.0003
1	0.0059	0.0054	0.0049	0.0045	0.0041	0.0038	0.0035	0.0032	0.0029	0.0027
2	0.0208	0.0194	0.0180	0.0167	0.0156	0.0145	0.0134	0.0125	0.0116	0.0107
3	0.0492	0.0464	0.0438	0.0413	0.0389	0.0366	0.0345	0.0324	0.0305	0.0286
4	0.0874	0.0836	0.0799	0.0764	0.0729	0.0696	0.0663	0.0632	0.0602	0.0573
5	0.1241	0.1204	0.1167	0.1130	0.1094	0.1057	0.1021	0.0986	0.0951	0.0916
6	0.1468	0.1445	0.1420	0.1394	0.1367	0.1339	0.1311	0.1282	0.1252	0.1221
7	0.1489	0.1486	0.1481	0.1474	0.1465	0.1454	0.1442	0.1428	0.1413	0.1396
8	0.1321	0.1337	0.1351	0.1363	0.1373	0.1382	0.1388	0.1392	0.1395	0.1396
9	0.1042	0.1070	0.1096	0.1121	0.1144	0.1167	0.1187	0.1207	0.1224	0.1241
10	0.0740	0.0770	0.0800	0.0829	0.0858	0.0887	0.0914	0.0941	0.0967	0.0993
11	0.0478	0.0504	0.0531	0.0558	0.0585	0.0613	0.0640	0.0667	0.0695	0.0722
12	0.0283	0.0303	0.0323	0.0344	0.0366	0.0388	0.0411	0.0434	0.0457	0.0481
13	0.0154	0.0168	0.0181	0.0196	0.0211	0.0227	0.0243	0.0260	0.0278	0.0296
14	0.0078	0.0086	0.0095	0.0104	0.0113	0.0123	0.0134	0.0145	0.0157	0.0169
15	0.0037	0.0041	0.0046	0.0051	0.0057	0.0062	0.0069	0.0075	0.0083	0.0090
16	0.0016	0.0019	0.0021	0.0024	0.0026	0.0030	0.0033	0.0037	0.0041	0.0045
17	0.0007	0.0008	0.0009	0.0010	0.0012	0.0013	0.0015	0.0017	0.0019	0.0021
18	0.0003	0.0003	0.0004	0.0004	0.0005	0.0006	0.0006	0.0007	0.0008	0.0009
19	0.0001	0.0001	0.0001	0.0002	0.0002	0.0002	0.0003	0.0003	0.0003	0.0004
20	0.0000	0.0000	0.0001	0.0001	0.0001	0.0001	0.0001	0.0001	0.0001	0.0002
21	0.0000	0.0000	0.0000	0.0000	0.0000	0.0000	0.0000	0.0000	0.0001	0.0001

					λ					
x	8.1	8.2	8.3	8.4	8.5	8.6	8.7	8.8	8.9	9.0
0	0.0003	0.0003	0.0002	0.0002	0.0002	0.0002	0.0002	0.0002	0.0001	0.0001
1	0.0025	0.0023	0.0021	0.0019	0.0017	0.0016	0.0014	0.0013	0.0012	0.0011
2	0.0100	0.0092	0.0086	0.0079	0.0074	0.0068	0.0063	0.0058	0.0054	0.0050
3	0.0269	0.0252	0.0237	0.0222	0.0208	0.0195	0.0183	0.0171	0.0160	0.0150
4	0.0544	0.0517	0.0491	0.0466	0.0443	0.0420	0.0398	0.0377	0.0357	0.0337
5	0.0882	0.0849	0.0816	0.0784	0.0752	0.0722	0.0692	0.0663	0.0635	0.0607
6	0.1191	0.1160	0.1128	0.1097	0.1066	0.1034	0.1003	0.0972	0.0941	0.0911
7	0.1378	0.1358	0.1338	0.1317	0.1294	0.1271	0.1247	0.1222	0.1197	0.1171
8	0.1395	0.1392	0.1388	0.1382	0.1375	0.1366	0.1356	0.1344	0.1332	0.1318
9	0.1256	0.1269	0.1280	0.1290	0.1299	0.1306	0.1311	0.1315	0.1317	0.1318
10	0.1017	0.1040	0.1063	0.1084	0.1104	0.1123	0.1140	0.1157	0.1172	0.1186
11	0.0749	0.0776	0.0802	0.0828	0.0853	0.0878	0.0902	0.0925	0.0948	0.0970
12	0.0505	0.0530	0.0555	0.0579	0.0604	0.0629	0.0654	0.0679	0.0703	0.0728
13	0.0315	0.0334	0.0354	0.0374	0.0395	0.0416	0.0438	0.0459	0.0481	0.0504
14	0.0182	0.0196	0.0210	0.0225	0.0240	0.0256	0.0272	0.0289	0.0306	0.0324

Poisson Probabilities (*Continued*)

					λ					
x	8.1	8.2	8.3	8.4	8.5	8.6	8.7	8.8	8.9	9.0
15	0.0098	0.0107	0.0116	0.0126	0.0136	0.0147	0.0158	0.0169	0.0182	0.1094
16	0.0050	0.0055	0.0060	0.0066	0.0072	0.0079	0.0086	0.0093	0.0101	0.0109
17	0.0024	0.0026	0.0029	0.0033	0.0036	0.0040	0.0044	0.0048	0.0053	0.0058
18	0.0011	0.0012	0.0014	0.0015	0.0017	0.0019	0.0021	0.0024	0.0026	0.0029
19	0.0005	0.0005	0.0006	0.0007	0.0008	0.0009	0.0010	0.0011	0.0012	0.0014
20	0.0002	0.0002	0.0002	0.0003	0.0003	0.0004	0.0004	0.0005	0.0005	0.0006
21	0.0001	0.0001	0.0001	0.0001	0.0001	0.0002	0.0002	0.0002	0.0002	0.0003
22	0.0000	0.0000	0.0000	0.0000	0.0001	0.0001	0.0001	0.0001	0.0001	0.0001

					λ					
x	9.1	9.2	9.3	9.4	9.5	9.6	9.7	9.8	9.9	10
0	0.0001	0.0001	0.0001	0.0001	0.0001	0.0001	0.0001	0.0001	0.0001	0.0000
1	0.0010	0.0009	0.0009	0.0008	0.0007	0.0007	0.0006	0.0005	0.0005	0.0005
2	0.0046	0.0043	0.0040	0.0037	0.0034	0.0031	0.0029	0.0027	0.0025	0.0023
3	0.0140	0.0131	0.0123	0.0115	0.0107	0.0100	0.0093	0.0087	0.0081	0.0076
4	0.0319	0.0302	0.0285	0.0269	0.0254	0.0240	0.0226	0.0213	0.0201	0.0189
5	0.0581	0.0555	0.0530	0.0506	0.0483	0.0460	0.0439	0.0418	0.0398	0.0378
6	0.0881	0.0851	0.0822	0.0793	0.0764	0.0736	0.0709	0.0682	0.0656	0.0631
7	0.1145	0.1118	0.1091	0.1064	0.1037	0.1010	0.0982	0.0955	0.0928	0.0901
8	0.1302	0.1286	0.1269	0.1251	0.1232	0.1212	0.1191	0.1170	0.1148	0.1126
9	0.1317	0.1315	0.1311	0.1306	0.1300	0.1293	0.1284	0.1274	0.1263	0.1251
10	0.1198	0.1210	0.1219	0.1228	0.1235	0.1241	0.1245	0.1249	0.1250	0.1251
11	0.0991	0.1012	0.1031	0.1049	0.1067	0.1083	0.1098	0.1112	0.1125	0.1137
12	0.0752	0.0776	0.0799	0.0822	0.0844	0.0866	0.0888	0.0908	0.0928	0.0948
13	0.0526	0.0549	0.0572	0.0594	0.0617	0.0640	0.0662	0.0685	0.0707	0.0729
14	0.0342	0.0361	0.0380	0.0399	0.0419	0.0439	0.0459	0.0479	0.0500	0.0521
15	0.0208	0.0221	0.0235	0.0250	0.0265	0.0281	0.0297	0.0313	0.0330	0.0347
16	0.0118	0.0127	0.0137	0.0147	0.0157	0.0168	0.0180	0.0192	0.0204	0.0217
17	0.0063	0.0069	0.0075	0.0081	0.0088	0.0095	0.0103	0.0111	0.0119	0.0128
18	0.0032	0.0035	0.0039	0.0042	0.0046	0.0051	0.0055	0.0060	0.0065	0.0071
19	0.0015	0.0017	0.0019	0.0021	0.0023	0.0026	0.0028	0.0031	0.0034	0.0027
20	0.0007	0.0008	0.0009	0.0010	0.0011	0.0012	0.0014	0.0015	0.0017	0.0019
21	0.0003	0.0003	0.0004	0.0004	0.0005	0.0006	0.0006	0.0007	0.0008	0.0009
22	0.0001	0.0001	0.0002	0.0002	0.0002	0.0002	0.0003	0.0003	0.0004	0.0004
23	0.0000	0.0001	0.0001	0.0001	0.0001	0.0001	0.0001	0.0001	0.0002	0.0002
24	0.0000	0.0000	0.0000	0.0000	0.0000	0.0000	0.0000	0.0001	0.0001	0.0001

Poisson Probabilities (*Continued*)

					λ					
x	11	12	13	14	15	16	17	18	19	20
0	0.0000	0.0000	0.0000	0.0000	0.0000	0.0000	0.0000	0.0000	0.0000	0.0000
1	0.0002	0.0001	0.0000	0.0000	0.0000	0.0000	0.0000	0.0000	0.0000	0.0000
2	0.0010	0.0004	0.0002	0.0001	0.0000	0.0000	0.0000	0.0000	0.0000	0.0000
3	0.0037	0.0018	0.0008	0.0004	0.0002	0.0001	0.0000	0.0000	0.0000	0.0000
4	0.0102	0.0053	0.0027	0.0013	0.0006	0.0003	0.0001	0.0001	0.0000	0.0000
5	0.0224	0.0127	0.0070	0.0037	0.0019	0.0010	0.0005	0.0002	0.0001	0.0001
6	0.0411	0.0255	0.0152	0.0087	0.0048	0.0026	0.0014	0.0007	0.0004	0.0002
7	0.0646	0.0437	0.0281	0.0174	0.0104	0.0060	0.0034	0.0018	0.0010	0.0005
8	0.0888	0.0655	0.0457	0.0304	0.0194	0.0120	0.0072	0.0042	0.0024	0.0013
9	0.1085	0.0874	0.0661	0.0473	0.0324	0.0213	0.0135	0.0083	0.0050	0.0029
10	0.1194	0.1048	0.0859	0.0663	0.0486	0.0341	0.0230	0.0150	0.0095	0.0058
11	0.1194	0.1144	0.1015	0.0844	0.0663	0.0496	0.0355	0.0245	0.0164	0.0106
12	0.1094	0.1144	0.1099	0.0984	0.0829	0.0661	0.0504	0.0368	0.0259	0.0176
13	0.0926	0.1056	0.1099	0.1060	0.0956	0.0814	0.0658	0.0509	0.0378	0.0271
14	0.0728	0.0905	0.1021	0.1060	0.1024	0.0930	0.0800	0.0655	0.0514	0.0387
15	0.0534	0.0724	0.0885	0.0989	0.1024	0.0992	0.0906	0.0786	0.0650	0.0516
16	0.0367	0.0543	0.0719	0.0866	0.0960	0.0992	0.0963	0.0884	0.0772	0.0646
17	0.0237	0.0383	0.0550	0.0713	0.0847	0.0934	0.0963	0.0936	0.0863	0.0760
18	0.0145	0.0256	0.0397	0.0554	0.0706	0.0830	0.0909	0.0936	0.0911	0.0844
19	0.0084	0.0161	0.0272	0.0409	0.0557	0.0699	0.0814	0.0887	0.0911	0.0888
20	0.0046	0.0097	0.0177	0.0286	0.0418	0.0559	0.0692	0.0798	0.0866	0.0888
21	0.0024	0.0055	0.0109	0.0191	0.0299	0.0426	0.0560	0.0684	0.0783	0.0846
22	0.0012	0.0030	0.0065	0.0121	0.0204	0.0310	0.0433	0.0560	0.0676	0.0769
23	0.0006	0.0016	0.0037	0.0074	0.0133	0.0216	0.0320	0.0438	0.0559	0.0669
24	0.0003	0.0008	0.0020	0.0043	0.0083	0.0144	0.0226	0.0328	0.0442	0.0557
25	0.0001	0.0004	0.0010	0.0024	0.0050	0.0092	0.0154	0.0237	0.0336	0.0446
26	0.0000	0.0002	0.0005	0.0013	0.0029	0.0057	0.0101	0.0164	0.0246	0.0343
27	0.0000	0.0001	0.0002	0.0007	0.0016	0.0034	0.0063	0.0109	0.0173	0.0254
28	0.0000	0.0000	0.0001	0.0003	0.0009	0.0019	0.0038	0.0070	0.0117	0.0181
29	0.0000	0.0000	0.0001	0.0002	0.0004	0.0011	0.0023	0.0044	0.0077	0.0125
30	0.0000	0.0000	0.0000	0.0001	0.0002	0.0006	0.0013	0.0026	0.0049	0.0083
31	0.0000	0.0000	0.0000	0.0000	0.0001	0.0003	0.0007	0.0015	0.0030	0.0054
32	0.0000	0.0000	0.0000	0.0000	0.0001	0.0001	0.0004	0.0009	0.0018	0.0034
33	0.0000	0.0000	0.0000	0.0000	0.0000	0.0001	0.0002	0.0005	0.0010	0.0020
34	0.0000	0.0000	0.0000	0.0000	0.0000	0.0000	0.0001	0.0002	0.0006	0.0012
35	0.0000	0.0000	0.0000	0.0000	0.0000	0.0000	0.0000	0.0001	0.0003	0.0007
36	0.0000	0.0000	0.0000	0.0000	0.0000	0.0000	0.0000	0.0001	0.0002	0.0004
37	0.0000	0.0000	0.0000	0.0000	0.0000	0.0000	0.0000	0.0000	0.0001	0.0002
38	0.0000	0.0000	0.0000	0.0000	0.0000	0.0000	0.0000	0.0000	0.0000	0.0001
39	0.0000	0.0000	0.0000	0.0000	0.0000	0.0000	0.0000	0.0000	0.0000	0.0001

Appendix C: Areas for the Standard Normal Distribution

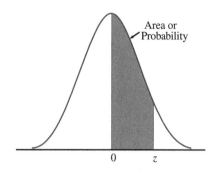

Area or Probability

Entries in the following table give the area under the curve between the mean and z standard deviations above the mean. For example, for $z = 1.25$ the area under the curve between the mean and z is 0.3944.

z	0.00	0.01	0.02	0.03	0.04	0.05	0.06	0.07	0.08	0.09
0.0	0.0000	0.0040	0.0080	0.0120	0.0160	0.0199	0.0239	0.0279	0.0319	0.0359
0.1	0.0398	0.0438	0.0478	0.0517	0.0557	0.0596	0.0636	0.0675	0.0714	0.0753
0.2	0.0793	0.0832	0.0871	0.0910	0.0948	0.0987	0.1026	0.1064	0.1103	0.1141
0.3	0.1179	0.1217	0.1255	0.1293	0.1331	0.1368	0.1406	0.1443	0.1480	0.1517
0.4	0.1554	0.1591	0.1628	0.1664	0.1700	0.1736	0.1772	0.1808	0.1844	0.1879
0.5	0.1915	0.1950	0.1985	0.2019	0.2054	0.2088	0.2123	0.2157	0.2190	0.2224
0.6	0.2257	0.2291	0.2324	0.2357	0.2389	0.2422	0.2454	0.2486	0.2518	0.2549
0.7	0.2580	0.2612	0.2642	0.2673	0.2704	0.2734	0.2764	0.2794	0.2823	0.2852
0.8	0.2881	0.2910	0.2939	0.2967	0.2995	0.3023	0.3051	0.3078	0.3106	0.3133
0.9	0.3159	0.3186	0.3212	0.3238	0.3264	0.3289	0.3315	0.3340	0.3365	0.3389
1.0	0.3413	0.3438	0.3461	0.3485	0.3508	0.3531	0.3554	0.3577	0.3599	0.3621
1.1	0.3643	0.3665	0.3686	0.3708	0.3729	0.3749	0.3770	0.3790	0.3810	0.3830
1.2	0.3849	0.3869	0.3888	0.3907	0.3925	0.3944	0.3962	0.3980	0.3997	0.4015
1.3	0.4032	0.4049	0.4066	0.4082	0.4099	0.4115	0.4131	0.4147	0.4162	0.4177
1.4	0.4192	0.4207	0.4222	0.4236	0.4251	0.4265	0.4279	0.4292	0.4306	0.4319
1.5	0.4332	0.4345	0.4357	0.4370	0.4382	0.4394	0.4406	0.4418	0.4429	0.4441
1.6	0.4452	0.4463	0.4474	0.4484	0.4495	0.4505	0.4515	0.4525	0.4535	0.4545
1.7	0.4554	0.4564	0.4573	0.4582	0.4591	0.4599	0.4608	0.4616	0.4625	0.4633
1.8	0.4641	0.4649	0.4656	0.4664	0.4671	0.4678	0.4686	0.4693	0.4699	0.4706
1.9	0.4713	0.4719	0.4726	0.4732	0.4738	0.4744	0.4750	0.4756	0.4761	0.4767
2.0	0.4772	0.4778	0.4783	0.4788	0.4793	0.4798	0.4803	0.4808	0.4812	0.4817
2.1	0.4821	0.4826	0.4830	0.4834	0.4838	0.4842	0.4846	0.4850	0.4854	0.4857
2.2	0.4861	0.4864	0.4868	0.4871	0.4875	0.4878	0.4881	0.4884	0.4887	0.4890
2.3	0.4893	0.4896	0.4898	0.4901	0.4904	0.4906	0.4909	0.4911	0.4913	0.4916
2.4	0.4918	0.4920	0.4922	0.4925	0.4927	0.4929	0.4931	0.4932	0.4934	0.4936
2.5	0.4938	0.4940	0.4941	0.4943	0.4945	0.4946	0.4948	0.4949	0.4951	0.4952
2.6	0.4953	0.4955	0.4956	0.4957	0.4959	0.4960	0.4961	0.4962	0.4963	0.4964
2.7	0.4965	0.4966	0.4967	0.4968	0.4969	0.4970	0.4971	0.4972	0.4973	0.4974
2.8	0.4974	0.4975	0.4976	0.4977	0.4977	0.4978	0.4979	0.4979	0.4980	0.4981
2.9	0.4981	0.4982	0.4982	0.4983	0.4984	0.4984	0.4985	0.4985	0.4986	0.4986
3.0	0.4986	0.4987	0.4987	0.4988	0.4988	0.4989	0.4989	0.4989	0.4990	0.4990

Appendix D: Values of $e^{-\lambda}$

λ	$e^{-\lambda}$	λ	$e^{-\lambda}$	λ	$e^{-\lambda}$
0.05	0.9512	2.05	0.1287	4.05	0.0174
0.10	0.9048	2.10	0.1225	4.10	0.0166
0.15	0.8607	2.15	0.1165	4.15	0.0158
0.20	0.8187	2.20	0.1108	4.20	0.0150
0.25	0.7788	2.25	0.1054	4.25	0.0143
0.30	0.7408	2.30	0.1003	4.30	0.0136
0.35	0.7047	2.35	0.0954	4.35	0.0129
0.40	0.6703	2.40	0.0907	4.40	0.0123
0.45	0.6376	2.45	0.0863	4.45	0.0117
0.50	0.6065	2.50	0.0821	4.50	0.0111
0.55	0.5769	2.55	0.0781	4.55	0.0106
0.60	0.5488	2.60	0.0743	4.60	0.0101
0.65	0.5220	2.65	0.0707	4.65	0.0096
0.70	0.4966	2.70	0.0672	4.70	0.0091
0.75	0.4724	2.75	0.0639	4.75	0.0087
0.80	0.4493	2.80	0.0608	4.80	0.0082
0.85	0.4274	2.85	0.0578	4.85	0.0078
0.90	0.4066	2.90	0.0550	4.90	0.0074
0.95	0.3867	2.95	0.0523	4.95	0.0071
1.00	0.3679	3.00	0.0498	5.00	0.0067
1.05	0.3499	3.05	0.0474	5.05	0.0064
1.10	0.3329	3.10	0.0450	5.10	0.0061
1.15	0.3166	3.15	0.0429	5.15	0.0058
1.20	0.3012	3.20	0.0408	5.20	0.0055
1.25	0.2865	3.25	0.0388	5.25	0.0052
1.30	0.2725	3.30	0.0369	5.30	0.0050
1.35	0.2592	3.35	0.0351	5.35	0.0047
1.40	0.2466	3.40	0.0334	5.40	0.0045
1.45	0.2346	3.45	0.0317	5.45	0.0043
1.50	0.2231	3.50	0.0302	5.50	0.0041
1.55	0.2122	3.55	0.0287	5.55	0.0039
1.60	0.2019	3.60	0.0273	5.60	0.0037
1.65	0.1920	3.65	0.0260	5.65	0.0035
1.70	0.1827	3.70	0.0247	5.70	0.0033
1.75	0.1738	3.75	0.0235	5.75	0.0032
1.80	0.1653	3.80	0.0224	5.80	0.0030
1.85	0.1572	3.85	0.0213	5.85	0.0029
1.90	0.1496	3.90	0.0202	5.90	0.0027
1.95	0.1423	3.95	0.0193	5.95	0.0026
2.00	0.1353	4.00	0.0183	6.00	0.0025
				7.00	0.0009
				8.00	0.000335
				9.00	0.000123
				10.00	0.000045

Appendix E   References and Bibliography

Chapter 1   The Role and Nature of Quantitative Methods

Churchman, C. W., R. L. Ackoff, and E. L. Arnoff. *Introduction to Operations Research.* Wiley, 1957.

Leon, Linda, Z. Przasnyski, and K. C. Seal. "Spreadsheets and OR/MS Models: An End-User Perspective," *Interfaces* (March–April 1996).

Powell, S. G. "Innovative Approaches to Management Science," *OR/MS Today* (October 1996).

Savage, S. "Weighing the Pros and Cons of Decision Technology and Spreadsheets," *OR/MS Today* (February 1997).

Winston, W. L. "The Teachers' Forum: Management Science with Spreadsheets for MBAs at Indiana University," *Interfaces* (March–April 1996).

Chapters 2 and 3   Probability

Anderson, D. R., D. J. Sweeney, and T. A. Williams. *Statistics for Business and Economics,* 7th ed. South-Western, 1999.

Barr, D. R. and P. W. Zehna. *Probability: Modeling Uncertainty.* Addison-Wesley, 1983.

Freund, J. E. and R. E. Walpole. *Mathematical Statistics,* 4th ed. Prentice-Hall, 1987.

Hogg, R. V. and Elliott A. Tanis. *Probability and Statistical Inference,* 4th ed. Macmillan, 1992.

Mendenhall, W., R. L. Scheaffer, and D. Wackerly. *Mathematical Statistics with Applications,* 4th ed. PWS-Kent, 1990.

Neter, J., W. Wasserman, and G. A. Whitmore. *Applied Statistics,* 4th ed. Allyn & Bacon, 1993.

Ross, S. M. *Introduction to Probability Models,* 5th ed. Academic Press, 1993.

Chapters 4 and 5   Decision Analysis

Berger, J. O. *Statistical Decision Theory and Bayesian Analysis,* 2d ed. Springer-Verlag, 1985.

Chernoff, H. and L. E. Moses. *Elementary Decision Theory.* Dover, 1987.

Clemen, R. T. *Making Hard Decisions,* 2d ed. Duxbury Press, 1996.

Goodwin, P. and G. Wright. *Decision Analysis for Management Judgment.* Wiley, 1997.

Gregory, G. *Decision Analysis.* Plenum, 1988.

Pratt, J. W., H. Raiffa, and R. Schlaiter. *Introduction to Statistical Decision Theory.* MIT Press, 1995.

Raiffa, H. *Decision Analysis.* McGraw-Hill, 1997.

Schlaiter, R. *Analysis of Decisions Under Uncertainty.* Krieger, 1978.

Chapter 6   Forecasting

Bowerman, B. L. and R. T. O'Connell. *Forecasting and Time Series: An Applied Approach,* 3d ed. Duxbury Press, 1993.

Box, G. E. P., G. M. Jenkins, and G. C. Reinsel. *Time Series Analysis: Forecasting and Control,* 3d ed. Prentice-Hall, 1994.

Hanke, J. E. and A. G. Reitsch. *Business Forecasting,* 6th ed. Prentice-Hall, 1998.

Makridakis, S. G., S. C. Wheelwright, and R. J. Hyndman. *Forecasting: Methods and Applications,* 3d ed. Wiley, 1997.

Wilson, J. H. and B. Keating. *Business Forecasting,* 3d ed. Irwin, 1998.

Chapters 7 to 11   Linear Programming, Transportation, Assignment, Transshipment Integer Programming Problems

Bazarra, M. S., J. J. Jarvis, and H. D. Sherali. *Linear Programming and Network Flows,* 2d ed. Wiley, 1990.

Carino, H. F. and C. H. Le Noir, Jr. "Optimizing Wood Procurement in Cabinet Manufacturing," *Interfaces* (March–April 1988): 10–19.

Dantzig, G. B. *Linear Programming and Extensions.* Princeton University Press, 1963.

Geoffrion, A. and G. Graves. "Better Distribution Planning with Computer Models," *Harvard Business Review* (July–August 1976).

Greenberg, H. J. "How to Analyze the Results of Linear Programs—Part 1: Preliminaries," *Interfaces* 23, no. 4 (July–August 1993): 56–67.

Greenberg, H. J. "How to Analyze the Results of Linear Programs—Part 2: Price Interpretation," *Interfaces* 23, no. 5 (September–October 1993): 97–114.

Greenberg, H. J. "How to Analyze the Results of Linear Programs—Part 3: Infeasibility Diagnosis," *Interfaces* 23, no. 6 (November–December 1993): 120–139.

Nemhauser, G. L. and L. A. Wolsey. *Integer and Combinatorial Optimization.* Wiley, 1988.

Sherman, H. D. "Hospital Efficiency Measurement and Evaluation," *Medical Care* 22, no. 10 (October 1984): 922–938.

Winston, W. L. *Operations Research: Applications and Algorithms,* 3d ed. Duxbury Press, 1994.

Chapter 12   Project Scheduling: PERT/CPM

Moder, J. J., C. R. Phillips, and E. W. Davis. *Project Management with CPM, PERT and Precedence Diagramming,* 3d ed. Blitz, 1995.

Wasil, E. A. and A. A. Assad. "Project Management on the PC: Software, Applications, and Trends," *Interfaces* 18, no. 2 (March–April 1988): 75–84.

Wiest, J. and F. Levy. *Management Guide to PERT-CPM,* 2d ed. Prentice-Hall, 1977.

Chapters 13 and 14   Inventory Management

Fogarty, D. W., J. H. Blackstone, and T. R. Hoffman. *Production and Inventory Management,* 2d ed. South-Western, 1990.

Hillier, F., and G. J. Lieberman. *Introduction to Operations Research,* 6th ed. McGraw-Hill, 1995.

Narasimhan, S. L., D. W. McLeavey, and P. B. Lington. *Production Planning and Inventory Control,* 2d ed. Prentice-Hall, 1995.

Orlicky, J. and G. W. Plossi. *Orlicky's Material Requirements Planning.* McGraw-Hill, 1994.

Vollmann, T. E., W. L. Berry, and D. C. Whybark. *Manufacturing Planning and Control Systems,* 4th ed. McGraw-Hill, 1997.

Chapter 15   Waiting Lines

Bunday, B. D. *An Introduction to Queuing Theory.* Wiley, 1996.

Gross, D. and C. M. Harris. *Fundamentals of Queueing Theory,* 3d ed. Wiley, 1997.

Hall, R. W. *Queueing Methods: For Service and Manufacturing.* Prentice-Hall, 1991.

Hillier, F. and G. J. Lieberman. *Introduction to Operations Research,* 6th ed. McGraw-Hill, 1995.

Kao, E. P. C. *An Introduction to Stochastic Processes.* Duxbury Press, 1996.

Saaty, T. *Elements of Queueing with Applications.* Dover, 1983.

Chapter 16   Simulation

Banks, J., J. S. Carson, and B. L. Nelson. *Discrete-Event System Simulation,* 2d ed. Prentice-Hall, 1995.

Fishwick, P. A. *Simulation Model Design and Execution: Building Digital Worlds.* Prentice-Hall, 1995.

Harrell, C. R. and K. Tumau. *Simulation Made Easy: A Manager's Guide.* Institute of Industrial Engineers, 1996.

Kelton, W. D., R. P. Sadowski, and D. A. Sadowski. *Simulation with Anema.* McGraw-Hill, 1998.

Law, A. M. and W. D. Kelton. *Simulation Modeling and Analysis,* 2d ed. McGraw-Hill, 1991.

Pidd, M. *Computer Simulation in Management Science,* 4th ed. Wiley, 1998.

Thesen, A. and L. E. Travis. *Simulation for Decision Making.* Wadsworth, 1992.

Chapter 17   Markov Processes

Bharucha-Reid, A. T. *Elements of the Theory of Markov Processes and Their Applications.* Dover, 1997.

Bhat, U. N. *Elements of Applied Stochastic Processes,* 2d ed. Wiley, 1984.

Filar, J. A. and K. Vrieze. *Competitive Markov Decision Processes.* Springer-Verlag, 1996.

Norris, J. *Markov Chains.* Cambridge, 1997.

Chapter 18   Multicriteria Decision Problems

Dyer, J. S. "A Clarification of Remarks on the Analytic Hierarchy Process," *Management Science* 36, no. 3 (March 1990): 274–275.

Dyer, J. S. "Remarks on the Analytic Hierarchy Process," *Management Science* 36, no. 3 (March 1990): 249–258.

Harker, P. T. and L. G. Vargas. "The Theory of Ratio Scale Estimation: Saaty's Analytic Hierarchy Process," *Management Science* 33, no. 11 (November 1987): 1383–1403.

Harker, P. T. and L. G. Vargas. "Reply to Remarks on the Analytic Hierarchy Process by J. S. Dyer," *Management Science* 36, no. 3 (March 1990): 269–273.

Ignizio, J. *Introduction to Linear Goal Programming.* Sage, 1986.

Keeney, R. L. and H. Raiffa. *Decisions with Multiple Objectives: Preferences and Value Tradeoffs.* Cambridge, 1993.

Saaty, T. *Decision Making for Leaders: The Analytic Hierarchy Process for Decisions in a Complex World,* 3d ed. RWS, 1995.

Saaty, T. and L. Vargas. *Fundamentals of Decision Making and Priority Theory with the Analytic Hierarchy Process.* RWS, 1994.

Saaty, T. *Multicriteria Decision Making,* 2d ed. RWS, 1996.

Saaty, T. L. "An Exposition of the AHP in Reply to the Paper Remarks on the Analytic Hierarchy Process," *Management Science* 36, no. 3 (March 1990): 259–268.

Saaty, T. L. "Rank Generation, Preservation, and Reversal in the Analytic Hierarchy Decision Process," *Decision Sciences* 18 (1987): 157–177.

Winkler, R. L. "Decision Modeling and Rational Choice: AHP and Utility Theory," *Management Science* 36, no. 3 (March 1990): 247–248.

Appendix F Answers to Even-Numbered Problems

Chapter 1

2. Methodological developments based on research advances in computer technology.

4. The problem is large, complex, important, new, and repetitive

6. Iconic—scale model of a new building
Analog—barometer
Mathematical—inventory cost equation

8. a. Max $10x + 5y$
s.t.
$$5x + 2y \leq 40$$
$$x \geq 0, y \geq 0$$

   b. Controllable inputs: x and y
Uncontrollable inputs: profit, labor-hours per unit, and total labor-hours available
   d. $x = 0, y = 20$, profit = \$100

10. If $a = 3, x = 13\frac{1}{3}$ and profit = \$133
If $a = 4, x = 10$ and profit = \$100
If $a = 5, x = 8$ and profit = \$80
If $a = 6, x = 6\frac{2}{3}$ and profit = \$67

12. A deterministic model with d = distance, m = miles per gallon, and c = cost per gallon, where total cost = $(2d/m)c$

14. Quicker to formulate, easier to solve, and/or more easily understood

16. a. 4706
   b. Loss of \$12,000
   c. \$23
   d. \$11,800

18. a. Max $6x + 4y$
   b. $50x + 30y \leq 80,000$
$\quad 50x \quad\quad \leq 50,000$
$\quad\quad\quad 30y \leq 45,000$

Chapter 2

2. $P(E_1) = 0.40, P(E_2) = 0.26, P(E_3) = 0.34$
The relative frequency method was used

4. a. 0.42
   b. 0.52
   c. 0.62
   d. 0.48

6. a. 0.31
   b. 0.69

8. a. 0.299, 0.222, 0.066
   b. Yes
   c. 0.521
   d. 0.288
   e. 0.413

10. P(part-time job or dean's list) = 0.50

12. a. 0.6667
   b. 0.80
   c. No; $P(A \mid B) \neq P(A)$

14. a. 0.44
   b. 0.15
   c. 0.0255
   d. 0.0025
   e. 0.136
   f. 0.106

16. a. 0.19
   b. 0.71
   c. 0.29

18. a. 0.25, 0.40, 0.10
   b. 0.25
   c. Independent; program does not help.

20. a. 0.10, 0.20, 0.09
   b. 0.51
   c. 0.26, 0.51, 0.23

22. a. 0.21
   b. Yes; Prob. of default > .20

24. a. 0.0625
   b. 0.0132
   c. Abandon after 3 consecutive dry wells.

26. a. $P(D_1 \mid S_1) = 0.2195, P(D_2 \mid S_1) = 0.7805$
   b. $P(D_1 \mid S_2) = 0.50, P(D_2 \mid S_2) = 0.50$
   c. $P(D_1 \mid S_3) = 0.8824, P(D_2 \mid S_3) = 0.1176$
   d. 0.1582 and 0.8418

Chapter 3

2. a. 0.05; probability of a \$200,000 profit.
   b. 0.70
   c. 0.40

4. a. 6
   b. 4.50
   c. 2.12

6. a. $f(x) \geq 0, \Sigma f(x) = 1$
   b. 3.64, 0.6704
   c. They do

8. a. Medium 145; large 140; prefer medium
   b. Medium 2725; large 12,400; prefer medium

10. a. $f(0) = 0.3487$
   b. $f(2) = 0.1937$
   c. 0.9298
   d. 0.6513
   e. 1
   f. $\sigma^2 = 0.9000$, $\sigma = 0.9487$

12. a. Probability of a defective part must be 0.03 for each trial; trials must be independent
   b. 2
   c.

Number of defects	0	1	2
Probability	0.9409	0.0582	0.0009

14. a. $f(x) = \dfrac{2^x e^{-2}}{x!}$

   b. $\mu = 6$ for 3 time periods

   c. $f(x) = \dfrac{6^x e^{-6}}{x!}$

   d. $f(2) = \dfrac{2^2 e^{-2}}{2!} = \dfrac{4(0.1353)}{2} = 0.2706$

   e. $f(6) = \dfrac{6^6 e^{-6}}{6!} = 0.1606$

   f. $f(5) = \dfrac{4^5 e^{-4}}{5!} = 0.1563$

16. a. 0.1465
   b. 1
   c. 0.8647

18. a. $f(x)$

   b. 0
   c. 0.50
   d. 0.60

20. a. $f(x)$

   b. 0.50
   c. 0.30
   d. 0.40

22. a. 1.96
   b. 0.61
   c. 1.12
   d. 0.44

24. a. 0.3830
   b. 0.1056
   c. 0.0062
   d. 0.1603

26. a. 0.7745
   b. 36.32
   c. 19%

28. $\mu = 19.23$

30. a. 0.94
   b. 0.52

32. a. 50 hours
   b. 0.3935
   c. 0.1353

34. a. 0.3333
   b. 0.2589
   c. 0.4078

Chapter 4

2. a. Optimistic: d_1
   Conservative: d_3
   Minimax regret: d_3
   c. Optimistic: d_1
   Conservative: d_2 or d_3
   Minimax regret: d_2

4. a. Decision: Which lease option to choose
   Chance event: Miles driven
   b.

	Annual Miles Driven		
	12,000	15,000	18,000
Forno	10,764	12,114	13,464
Midtown	11,160	11,160	12,960
Hopkins	11,700	11,700	11,700

   c. Optimistic: Forno Saab
   Conservative: Hopkins Automotive
   Minimax: Hopkins Automotive
   d. Midtown Motors
   e. Most likely: $11,160   Probability = 0.9
   f. Midtown Motors or Hopkins Automotive

6. a. d_1 **b.** d_4

8. a. d_2 is optimal for $p \leq 0.25$, d_1 is optimal for $p \geq 0.25$
   b. d_2
   c. As long as the payoff for $s_1 \geq 2$, then d_2 is optimal

10. a. If $p > 0.44$, location A; if $p < 0.44$, location C
   b. Location A because $0.65 > 0.44$

12. a. Decision: Whether or not to lengthen the runway
   Chance Event: The location decisions of Air Express and DRI
   Consequence: Annual Revenue
   b. $255,000
   c. $270,000

d. No

e. Lengthen the runway

14. a. If s_1, then d_1; if s_2, then d_1 or d_2; if s_3, then d_2

b. 192.5

c. d_1; 182.5

d. 10

16. b. If favorable, d_2

If unfavorable, d_1

EV = 292

18. b. d_2, 500

c. 195

d. If weak, then d_2; if average, then d_2; if strong, then d_3

e. 41.8

f. 21%

20. b. d_1, 1250

c. 1700

d. If N, d_1

If U, d_2; 1666

22. 0.1905, 0.2381, 0.5714

24. a. 0.695, 0.215, 0.090

0.98, 0.02

0.79, 0.21

0.00, 1.00

c. If C, Expressway

If O, Expressway

If R, Queen City

26.6 minutes

Chapter 5

2. a. d_2; EV(d_2) = \$5,000

b. p = probability of a \$0 cost

$1 - p$ = probability of a \$200,000 cost

c. d_1; EV(d_1) = 9.9

d. Expected utility approach; it avoids risk of large loss

4. a. Route B; EV = 58.5

b. p = probability of a 45-minute travel time

$1 - p$ = probability of a 90-minute travel time

c. Route A; EV = 7.6; risk-avoider

6. A: d_1; B: d_2; C: d_2

8. a.

	Win	Lose
Bet	350	−10
Do not bet	0	0

b. d_2

c. Risk takers

d. Between 0 and 0.26

10. a. Western; EV = 26%

b. p = probability of a 40% show

$1 - p$ = probability of a 15% show

c. Musical; risk taker

Chapter 6

2. a.

Week	4-Week	5-Week
10	19.00	18.80
11	20.00	19.20
12	18.75	19.00

b. 9.65, 7.41

c. 5-week

4. Weeks 10, 11, and 12: 18.48, 18.63, 18.27

MSE = 9.25; $\alpha = 0.2$ is better

6. b. The more recent data receive the greater weight or importance in determining the forecast

8. a. 33.1458

b. 32.9500

c. 33.2187

d. Exponential smoothing; it has the smallest MSE (1.24)

10. a. $\alpha = 0.2$

b. 46.1

12. 3117.01

14. $T_t = 20.7466 - 0.3514t$

Enrollment appears to be decreasing by an average of 351 students per year

16. a. Linear trend appears to be reasonable

b. $T_t = 19.993 + 1.774t$

Average cost increase of \$1.77 per unit per year

18. a. $T_t = -7.5 + 7.7714t$

b. 7.7714(\$M) per year

c. 46.9

20. a. A linear trend appears to exist

b. $T_t = -5 + 15t$

Average increase in sales is 15 units per year

22. a. A linear trend appears to be appropriate

b. $T_t = 12,899.98 + 2092.066t$

c. \$2,092,066

d. \$40,096,838 and \$42,188,904

24. a. Forecast for July is 236.97; forecast for August is 236.97

b. Forecast for July is 278.88; forecast for August is 297.33

c. Not fair; it does not account for upward trend in sales

26. 0.707, 0.777, 0.827, 0.966, 1.016, 1.305, 1.494, 1.225, 0.976, 0.986, 0.936, 0.787

28. a. Selected centered moving averages for $t = 5, 10, 15$, and 20 are 11.125, 18.125, 22.875, and 27.000

b. 0.899, 1.362, 1.118, 0.621

c. Quarter 2, prior to summer boating season

30. a. $T_t = 6.329 + 1.055t$

b. 36.92, 37.98, 39.03, 40.09

c. 33.23, 51.65, 43.71, 24.86

32. a. Yes, there is a seasonal effect; seasonal indexes are
1.696, 1.458, 0.711, 0.326, 0.448, 1.362
b. Forecast for 12–4 is 166,761.13; forecast for 4–8 is
146,052.99

34. a. $\hat{y} = 37.666 - 3.222x$
b. $3444

Chapter 7

10. $x_1 = {}^{12}\!/_7$, $x_2 = {}^{15}\!/_7$; Value of optimal solution = ${}^{69}\!/_7$

12. a. $x_1 = 3$, $x_2 = 1.5$; Value of optimal solution = 13.5
b. $x_1 = 0$, $x_2 = 3$; Value of optimal solution = 18
c. four: (0, 0), (4, 0), (3, 1.5), and (0.3)

14. a. Max $2400E + 1800L$
s.t.
$$6E + \quad 3L \le 2100$$
$$1L \le \ 280$$
$$2E + \ 2.5L \le 1000$$
$$E, L \ge 0$$

b. $E = 250$, $L = 200$, $960,000
c. Engine manufacturing time and assembly/testing time

16. a. $S = 300$, $D = 420$; Value of optimal solution = 10,560
b. $S = 708$, $D = 0$; Value of optimal solution = 14,160
c. Sewing constraint is redundant; optimal solution is still
$S = 540$, $D = 252$

18. Max $5x_1 + 2x_2 + \ 8x_3 + 0s_1 + 0s_2 + 0s_3$
s.t.
$$1x_1 - 2x_2 + 0.5x_3 + 1s_1 \qquad\qquad = 420$$
$$2x_1 + 3x_2 - \ 1x_3 \qquad + 1s_2 \qquad = 610$$
$$6x_1 - 1x_2 + \ 3x_3 \qquad\qquad + 1s_3 = 125$$
$$x_1, x_2, x_3, s_1, s_2, s_3 \ge 0$$

20. b. $x_1 = {}^{20}\!/_3$, $x_2 = {}^8\!/_3$; Value of optimal solution = $30\,{}^2\!/_3$
c. $s_1 = {}^{28}\!/_3$, $s_2 = 0$, $s_3 = 0$

22. a. Max $5R + 8C$
s.t.
$$1R + {}^3\!/_2C \le 900$$
$${}^1\!/_2R + {}^1\!/_3C \le 300$$
$${}^1\!/_8R + {}^1\!/_4C \le 100$$
$$R, C \ge 0$$

b. $R = 500$, $C = 150$
c. $3700
d. 725, 300, 100
e. 175, 0, 0

24. a. Max $50N + 80R$
s.t.
$$N + \quad R = 1000$$
$$N \qquad\quad \ge \ 250$$
$$R \ge \ 250$$
$$N - \ 2R \ge \quad 0$$
$$N, R \ge 0$$

b. $N = 666.67$, $R = 333.33$; Audience exposure = 60,000

26. a. Max $1W + 1.25M$
s.t.
$$5W + \quad 7M \le 4480$$
$$3W + \quad 1M \le 2080$$
$$2W + \quad 2M \le 1600$$
$$W, M \ge 0$$

d. $W = 560$, $M = 240$; Profit = 860

28. a. Max $15E + 18C$
s.t.
$$40E + 25C \le 50,000$$
$$40E \qquad\quad \ge 15,000$$
$$25C \ge 10,000$$
$$25C \le 25,000$$
$$E, C \ge 0$$

c. (375, 400); (1000, 400); (625, 1000); (375, 1000)
d. $E = 625$, $C = 1000$
Total return = $27,375

30.

Extreme Points	Objective Function Value	Surplus Demand	Surplus Total Production	Slack Processing Time
(250, 100)	800	125	—	—
(125, 225)	925	—	—	125
(125, 350)	1300	—	125	—

32. b. (4, 1), $({}^{21}\!/_4, {}^9\!/_4)$
c. $x_1 = 4$, $x_2 = 1$

34. a. Min $10,000T + 8,000P$
s.t.
$$T \qquad\qquad \ge \ 8$$
$$P \ge 10$$
$$T + \quad P \ge 25$$
$$3T + \ 2P \le 84$$

c. (15, 10); (21.33, 10); (8, 30); (8, 17)
d. $T = 8$, $P = 17$
Total cost = $216,000

36. a. Min $2.5A + \ 2B$
s.t.
$$2A + 1.5B \ge 1.7$$
$$2A + \ 3B \le 2.8$$
$$4A + \ 3B \le 3.6$$
$$A + \quad B = 1$$
$$A, B \ge 0$$

b. $A = 0.6$, $B = 0.4$; Cost = $0.022
c. 0.1, 0.4, 0, 0
d. $0.176

38. $P_1 = 30$, $P_2 = 25$, Cost = $55

40. Infeasibility

42. a. $x_1 = {}^{30}\!/_{16}$, $x_2 = {}^{30}\!/_{16}$; Value of optimal solution = ${}^{60}\!/_{16}$
b. $x_1 = 0$, $x_2 = 3$; Value of optimal solution = 6

44. a. 180, 20
b. Alternative optimal solutions
c. 120, 80

46. No feasible solution

48. $M = 65.45$, $R = 261.82$; Profit = \$45,818

50. $S = 384$, $O = 80$

52. a. Max $160M_1 + 345M_2$
s.t.
$$
\begin{aligned}
M_1 + \quad M_2 &\le 15 \\
M_2 &\le 10 \\
M_1 \qquad\quad &\ge 5 \\
M_2 &\ge 5 \\
40M_1 + \quad 50M_2 &\le 1000 \\
M_1, M_2 &\ge 0
\end{aligned}
$$

b. $M_1 = 12.5$, $M_2 = 10$

Chapter 8

2. a. $A = 6.5$, $B = 4.5$, 28.5
   b. 1.5
   c. 8 to 11.2
   d. 0.5 between 18 and 30

4. a. $X = 2.5$, $Y = 2.5$, 50
   b. -2
   c. 5 to 11
   d. -3 between 9 and 18

6. a. 4 to 12 and 3.33 to 10
   c. 725 to No Upper Limit; 133.33 to 400; 75 to 135
   d. \$560

8. a. More than \$7.00
   b. More than \$3.50
   c. None

10. a. $S = 4000$; $M = 10,000$; Total risk = 62,000
   b. 3.75 to No Upper Limit and No Lower Limit to 6.4
   c. \$60,000
   d. 5%
   e. 0.057 risk units
   f. 5.7%

12. a. 0, 25, 125, 0; Value = 525.0
   b. A and C
   c. B; 425 hours
   d. Yes

14. a. 7.30, 0, 1.89; Value = 139.73
   b. Two and three
   c. 0, -3.41, -4.43
   d. Decrease the right-hand side of constraint 3 from 20 to 19

16. a. All Pro: 1000; College: 200; High School: 0
   b. Sewing and minimum All Pro production requirement
   c. 4000 minutes of unused cutting and dyeing time; all the sewing time is being used; 5200 minutes of unused inspection and packaging time; only the minimum number of the All Pro model is being produced
   d. No Lower Limit to 5; 5 to No Upper Limit; No Lower Limit to 4

18. a. Max $0.07H + 0.12P + 0.09A$
s.t.
$$
\begin{aligned}
H + \quad P + \quad A &= 1{,}000{,}000 \\
0.6H - \ 0.4P - \ 0.4A &\ge 0 \\
P - \ 0.6A &\le 0 \\
H, P, A &\ge 0
\end{aligned}
$$

b. $H = \$400{,}000$, $P = \$225{,}000$, $A = \$375{,}000$
   Total annual return = \$88,750
   Annual percentage return = 8.875%
   c. No change
   d. Increase of \$890
   e. Increase of \$312.50 or 0.031%

20. a. Min $30L + \ 25D + \ 18S$
s.t.
$$
\begin{aligned}
L + \quad D + \quad S &= 100 \\
0.6L - \ 0.4D \qquad &\ge 0 \\
-0.15L - 0.15D + 0.85S &\ge 0 \\
-0.25L - 0.25D + \quad S &\le 0 \\
L \qquad\qquad &\le 50 \\
L, D, S &\ge 0
\end{aligned}
$$

b. $L = 48$, $D = 72$, $S = 30$
   Total cost = \$3780
   c. No change
   d. No change

22. a. 333.3, 0, 833.3; Risk = 14,666.7; Return = 18,000 or 9%
   b. 1000, 0, 0, 2500; Risk = 18,000; Return = 22,000 or 11%
   c. \$4000

24. a. Let M_1 = units of component 1 manufactured
   M_2 = units of component 2 manufactured
   M_3 = units of component 3 manufactured
   P_1 = units of component 1 purchased
   P_2 = units of component 2 purchased
   P_3 = units of component 3 purchased

Min $4.50M_1 + 5.00M_2 + 2.75M_3 + 6.50P_1 + 8.80P_2 + 7.00P_3$
s.t.
$$
\begin{aligned}
2M_1 + \quad 3M_2 + 4M_3 & & &\le 21{,}600 \quad \text{Production} \\
1M_1 + 1.5M_2 + 3M_3 & & &\le 15{,}000 \quad \text{Assembly} \\
1.5M_1 + \quad 2M_2 + 5M_3 & & &\le 18{,}000 \quad \text{Testing/Packaging} \\
1M_1 \qquad\qquad + 1P_1 & & &= 6{,}000 \quad \text{Component 1} \\
1M_2 \qquad + 1P_2 & & &= 4{,}000 \quad \text{Component 2} \\
1M_3 \qquad + 1P_3 & &= 3{,}500 \quad \text{Component 3} \\
M_1, M_2, M_3, P_1, P_2, P_3 &\ge 0
\end{aligned}
$$

b.

Source	Component 1	Component 2	Component 3
Manufacture	2000	4000	1400
Purchase	4000		2100

Total Cost \$73,550

c. Production: \$54.36 per hour
   Testing & Packaging: \$ 7.50 per hour
d. Dual prices = $-\$7.969$; it would cost Benson \$7.969 to add a unit of component 2

26. b. $G = 120,000$; $S = 30,000$; $M = 150,000$
   c. 0.15 to 0.60; No Lower Limit to 0.122; 0.02 to 0.20
   d. 4668
   e. $G = 48,000$; $S = 192,000$; $M = 60,000$
   f. The client's risk index and the amount of funds available

28. a. $L = 3$, $N = 7$, $W = 5$, $S = 5$
   b. Each additional minute of broadcast time increases cost by $100
   c. If local coverage is increased by 1 minute, total cost will increase by $100
   d. If the time devoted to local and national news is increased by 1 minute, total cost will increase by $100
   e. Increasing the sports by one minute will have no effect because the dual price is 0

Chapter 9

2. a. $x_1 = 77.89$, $x_2 = 63.16$, $3284.21
   b. Department A $15.79; Department B $47.37
   c. $x_1 = 87.21$, $x_2 = 65.12$, $3341.34
     Department A 10 hours; Department B 3.2 hours

4. a. $x_1 = 500$, $x_2 = 300$, $x_3 = 200$, $550
   b. $0.55
   c. Aroma, 75; Taste 84.4
   d. $0.60

6. 50 units of product 1; 0 units of product 2; 300 hours department A; 600 hours department B

8. Schedule 19 officers as follows:
3 begin at 8:00 A.M.; 3 begin at noon; 7 begin at 4:00 P.M.; 4 begin at midnight, 2 begin at 4:00 A.M.

10.

Product	Modern Line	Old Line
1	500	0
2	300	400

Cost = $3850

12. a. Purchase 5000 bases
   b. Same solution with objective function increased by $80
   c. Yes; Total cost = $24,293.33; $FCP = 1333$ and $FCM = 1667$

14. b.

Quarter	Production	Ending Inventory
1	4000	2100
2	3000	1100
3	2000	100
4	1900	500

16. x_i = number of 10-inch rolls processed by cutting alternative i
   a. $x_1 = 0$, $x_2 = 125$, $x_3 = 500$, $x_4 = 1500$, $x_5 = 0$, $x_6 = 0$, $x_7 = 0$; 2125 rolls with waste of 750 inches
   b. 2500 rolls with no waste; however, 1½-inch size is overproduced by 3000 units

18. a. 5 super, 2 regular, and 3 econo-tankers
   b. Total cost $583,000; monthly operating cost $4650

20. Produce 10,250 units in March, 10,250 units in April, and 12,000 units in May

22. 5, 515, 887 sq. in. of waste
   machine 3: 492 minutes

24. Investment strategy: 45.8% of A and 100% of B
   Objective function = $4340.40
   Savings/Loan Schedule

	Period			
	1	**2**	**3**	**4**
Savings	242.11	—	—	341.04
Funds from loan	—	200.00	127.58	—

26. b. Solution does not indicate that General Hospital is relatively inefficient
   c. General Hospital

28. c. No; E = 1 indicates that the amount of resources used by Hospital E are required to produce the outputs of Hospital E
   d. Hospital E

Chapter 10

2. a. Min $14x_{11} + 9x_{12} + 7x_{13} + 8x_{21} + 10x_{22} + 5x_{23}$
   s.t.

$$
\begin{array}{llll}
x_{11} + x_{12} + x_{13} & & & \leq 30 \\
& x_{21} + x_{22} + x_{23} & & \leq 20 \\
x_{11} & + x_{21} & & = 25 \\
x_{12} & + x_{22} & & = 15 \\
x_{13} & + x_{23} & = 10 \\
\end{array}
$$

$x_{11}, x_{12}, x_{13}, x_{21}, x_{22}, x_{23} \geq 0$
   b. $x_{11} = 5$, $x_{12} = 15$, $x_{13} = 10$, $x_{21} = 20$

4. b. $x_{12} = 300$, $x_{21} = 100$, $x_{22} = 100$, $x_{23} = 300$, $x_{31} = 100$
   Cost = 10,400

6. b.

Seattle–Denver	4000	Seattle–Los Angeles	5000
Columbus–Mobile	4000	New York–Pittsburgh	3000
New York–Mobile	1000	New York–Los Angeles	1000
New York–Washington	3000		

Cost = $150,000

   c.

Seattle–Denver	4000	Seattle–Los Angeles	5000
Columbus–Mobile	5000	New York–Pittsburgh	4000
New York–Los Angeles	1000	New York–Washington	3000

Cost actually decreases by $9000

8. Clifton Springs–D_2 4000   Clifton Springs–D_4 1000
   Danville–D_1 2000   Danville–D_4 1000
   Customer 2 has a shortfall of 1000; customer 3's demand is not satisfied

10. 1–A 300; 1–C 1200; 2–A 1200; 3–A 500; 3–B 500

12. b. Jackson–2, Ellis–1, Smith–3
    Total completion time = 64

14. b. Bostock–Southwest, Miller–Northwest

16. b. Toy to 2, Auto Parts to 4, Housewares to 3, Video to 1

18. a. Plano: Kansas City and Dallas
       Flagstaff: Los Angeles
       Springfield: Chicago, Columbus and Atlanta
       Boulder: Newark and Denver
       Cost = $216,000
    b. Nashville
    c. Columbus is switched from Springfield to Nashville
       Cost = $227,000

20. A to MS, B to Ph.D., C to MBA, D to undergrad
    Maximum total rating = 13.3

22. a.

Division	Supplier					
	1	2	3	4	5	6
1	614	660	534	680	590	630
2	603	639	702	693	693	630
3	865	830	775	850	900	930
4	532	553	511	581	595	553
5	720	648	684	693	657	747

b. Optimal solution:

Supplier 1–Division 2	$ 603
Supplier 2–Division 5	648
Supplier 3–Division 3	775
Supplier 5–Division 1	590
Supplier 6–Division 4	553
Total	$3169

24. c. $x_{14} = 320, x_{25} = 600, x_{47} = 300, x_{49} = 20, x_{56} = 300,$
    $x_{58} = 300, x_{39} = 380$
    Cost = $11,220

26. c. Note: Augusta: 1, Tupper Lake: 2, Albany: 3, Portsmouth: 4, Boston: 5, New York: 6, Philadelphia: 7

Variable	Value	Variable	Value
x_{13}	50	x_{36}	0
x_{14}	250	x_{37}	150
x_{23}	100	x_{45}	150
x_{24}	0	x_{46}	100
x_{35}	0	x_{47}	0

Objective function = 4300

28.

Optimal Solution	Units Shipped	Cost
Muncie–Cincinnati	1	6
Cincinnati–Concord	3	84
Brazil–Louisville	6	18
Louisville–Macon	2	88
Louisville–Greenwood	4	136
Xenia–Cincinnati	5	15
Cincinnati–Chatham	3	72
	Total	419

Two rail cars must be held at Muncie until a buyer is found

32. c. Regular-month 1: 275; overtime-month 1: 25; inventory at end of month 1: 150
    Regular-month 2: 200; overtime-month 2: 50; inventory at end of month 2: 150
    Regular-month 3: 100; overtime-month 3: 50; inventory at end of month 3: 0

Chapter 11

2. b. $x_1 = 1.43, x_2 = 4.29$; Value = 41.47
      Rounded: $x_1 = 1, x_2 = 4$; Value = 37
   c. $x_1 = 0, x_2 = 5$; Value = 40
      Not the same

4. a. $x_1 = 3.67, x_2 = 0$; Value = 36.7
      Rounded: $x_1 = 3, x_2 = 0$; Value = 30
      Lower bound = 30; Upper bound = 36.7
   b. $x_1 = 3, x_2 = 2$; Value = 36
   c. Alternative optimal solutions: $x_1 = 0, x_2 = 5$
      $x_1 = 2, x_2 = 4$

6. b. $x_1 = 1.96, x_2 = 5.48$; Value = 7.44
      Rounded: $x_1 = 1.96, x_2 = 5$; Value = 6.96
      Lower bound = 6.96; Upper bound = 7.44
   c. $x_1 = 1.29, x_2 = 6$; Value = 7.29

8. a. $x_3 = 1, x_4 = 1, x_6 = 1$; Value = 17,500
   b. Add $x_1 + x_2 \leq 1$
   c. Add $x_3 - x_4 = 0$

10. b. Choose locations B and E

12. a. $P \leq 15 + 15Y_P$
       $D \leq 15 + 15Y_D$
       $J \leq 15 + 15Y_J$
       $Y_P + Y_D + Y_J \leq 1$
    b. $P = 15, D = 15, J = 30$
       $Y_P = 0, Y_D = 0, Y_J = 1$; Value = 50

14. b. Modernize plants 1 and 3 or plants 4 and 5
    d. Modernize plants 1 and 3

16. b. Use all part-time employees

Bring on as follows: 9:00 A.M.–6, 11:00 A.M.–2, 12:00 noon–6, 1:00 P.M.–1, 3:00 P.M.–6
Cost = $672

c. Same as in part (b)

d. New solution is to bring on 1 full-time employee at 9:00 A.M., 4 more at 11:00 A.M. and part-time employees as follows:
9:00 A.M.–5, 12:00 noon–5, and 3:00 P.M.–2

18. a. New objective function: Min $25x_1 + 40x_2 + 40x_3 + 40x_4 + 25x_5$

   b. $x_4 = x_5 = 1$; modernize the Ohio and California plants

   c. Add the constraint $x_2 + x_3 = 1$

   d. $x_1 = x_3 = 1$

20. $x_1 + x_2 + x_3 = 3y_1 + 5y_2 + 7y_3$
    $y_1 + y_2 + y_3 = 1$

Chapter 12

2.

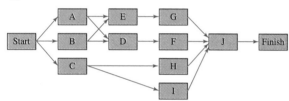

4. a. A–D–G

   b. No; Time = 15 months

6. a. A–D–F–H

   b. 22 weeks

   c. No, it is a critical activity

   d. Yes, 2 weeks

   e. ES = 3, LS = 4, EF = 10, LF = 11

8. b. B–C–E–F–H

   d. Yes, time = 49 weeks

10. a.

Activity	Time	Variance
A	5.00	0.11
B	9.00	0.11
C	8.00	0.44
D	8.83	0.25
E	7.17	0.25
F	6.00	0.11

   b. 23.83, 0.47

12. a. A–D–H–I

    b. 25.66 days

    c. 0.2578

14. a. A–D–F–G

    b. 1.5 days

    c. 29.5, 2.36

    d. 0.6293

16. a.

E(T)	Variance
16	3.92
13	2.03
10	1.27

   b. 0.9783, approximately 1.00, approximately 1.00

18. c. A–B–D–G–H–I, 14.17 weeks

    d. 0.0951, yes

20. b. Crash B(1 week), D(2 weeks), E(1 week), F(1 week), G(1 week)
       Total cost = $2427

    c. All activities are critical

22. b. Crash C(1 day) and E(1 day)

    c. $9300

24. c. A–B–C–F, 31 weeks

    d. Crash A(2 weeks), B(2 weeks), C(1 week), D(1 week), E(1 week)

    e. All activities are critical

    f. $112,500

Chapter 13

2. $164.32 for each; Total cost = $328.64

4. a. 1095.45

   b. 240

   c. 22.82 days

   d. $273.86 for each; Total cost = $547.72

6. a. 15.95

   b. $2106

   c. 15.04

   d. 16.62 days

8. $Q^* = 11.73$, use 12
   5 classes per year
   $225,200

10. $Q^* = 1414.21$
    $T = 28.28$ days
    Production runs of 7.07 days

12. $Q^* = 1000$; Total cost = $1200
    Yes, the change saves $300 per year

14. New $Q^* = 4509$

16. 135.55; $r = dm - S$; less than

18. 64, 24.44

20. $Q^* = 100$; Total cost = $3,601.50

22. $Q^* = 300$; Savings = $480

24. a. 500

    b. 580.4

26. a. 397

    b. 0.70

    c. 489, 0.35

28. a. 440
    b. 0.60
    c. 710
    d. c_u = $17

30. a. 13.68 (14)
    b. 17.83 (18)
    c. 2, $10; 6, $30

32. a. 31.62
    b. 19.86 (20); 0.2108
    c. 5, $15

34. a. 243
    b. 93, $54.87
    c. 613
    d. 163, $96.17
    e. Yes, added cost only $41.30 per year
    f. Yes, added cost would be $4130 per year

36. a. 40
    b. 62.25; 7.9
    c. 54
    d. 36

Chapter 14

2. a. Projected balance—week 6: 70
      Net requirement—week 4: 70
      Planned order release—week 3: 400
   b. Planned order release—week 1: 400
   c. None

4. a. Projected balance—week 3: 250
      Projected balance—week 6: 0
   b. Projected balance—week 3: 370
      Projected balance—week 6: 120
   c. Projected balance—week 3: 550
      Projected balance—week 6: 600
   d. Lot size of 800

6. a. Net requirements—week 3: 250
   b. Net requirements—week 3: 130
   d. Lot-for-lot rule

8. a. Projected balance—week 5: 100
      Net requirements—week 4: 150
   b. Projected balance—week 5: 0
      Net requirements—Week 4: 200
   c. Fixed lot size has higher holding costs

10. a. Net requirements—week 24: 400
       Planned order releases—week 21: 500
    b. Net requirements—week 21: 450
       Projected balance—week 23: 0

12. a. 800
    b. Week 15, 800 units
    c. Week 13, 800 units

14. 2000, 500, 200

Chapter 15

2. a. 0.4512
   b. 0.6988
   c. 0.3012

4. 0.3333, 0.2222, 0.1481, 0.0988, 0.1976

6. a. 0.3333
   b. 1.3333
   c. 0.1111 days (53.3 minutes)
   d. 0.6667

8. 0.20, 3.2, 4, 3.2, 4, 0.80
   Slightly poorer service

10. a. New: 0.3333, 1.3333, 2, 0.6667, 1, 0.6667
       Experienced: 0.50, 0.50, 1, 0.25, 0.50, 0.50
    b. New $74; experienced $50; hire experienced

12. a. 0.25, 2.25, 3, 0.15 hours, 0.20 hours, 0.75
    b. The service needs improvement

14. a. 8
    b. 0.3750
    c. 1.0417
    d. 12.5 minutes
    e. 0.6250
    f. Need to add a second consultant

16. a. 0.50
    b. 0.50
    c. 0.10 hours (6 minutes)
    d. 0.20 hours (12 minutes)
    e. Yes, W_q = 6 minutes is most likely acceptable for a marina

18. a. 0.5385
    b. 0.0593
    c. 0.0099 hours (0.59 minutes)
    d. 0.1099 hours (6.59 minutes)
    e. 0.1385

20. a. 0.2360, 0.1771, 1.5771, 0.0126 hours, 0.1126 hours
    b. P(wait) = 0.2024 for a 3-channel system

22.

Characteristic	A	B	C
a. P_0	0.2000	0.5000	0.4286
b. L_q	3.2000	0.5000	0.1524
c. L	4.0000	1.0000	0.9524
d. W_q	0.1333	0.0208	0.0063
e. W	0.1667	0.0417	0.0397
f. P_w	0.8000	0.5000	0.2286

The two-channel System C provides the best service

24. a. 0.0466, 0.05
    b. 1.4
    c. 11:00 A.M.

26. a. 0.2668, 10 minutes, 0.6667
    b. 0.0667, 7 minutes, 0.4669
    c. $25.33; $33.34; one-channel

28. a. 10, 9.6
    b. Design A with $\mu = 10$
    c. 0.05, 0.01
    d. A: 0.5, 0.3125, 0.8125, 0.0625, 0.1625, 0.5
       B: 0.4792, 0.2857, 0.8065, 0.0571, 0.1613, 0.5208
    e. Design B has slightly less waiting time

30. a. 0.1460, 0.3066, 0.3220, 0.2254
    b. 0.2254
    c. 1.6267
    d. 4; 0.1499

32. a. 31.03%
    b. 27.59%
    c. 0.2759, 0.1092, 0.0351
    d. 3, 10.92%

34. a. 0.4790
    b. 0.3110
    c. 0.8321
    d. 2.9854 minutes
    e. 7.9854 minutes
    f. 95.8 minutes; 35.8 minutes
    g. Yes, assistants spend too much time waiting at the copier

Chapter 16

2. a. Profit $= (50 - c)x - 30,000$
   b. 6000, $-22,200$, 41,400
   c. Helps estimate probability of loss

4. a. 0.00–0.08, 0.08–0.20, 0.20–0.48, 0.48–0.72, 0.72–0.86, 0.86–0.96, 0.96–1.00
   b. 2, 5, 2, 3, 2, 4, 2, 1, 1, 2
   c. 24 units

6. a. 0.00–0.83, 0.83–0.89, 0.89–0.94, 0.94–0.96, 0.96–0.98, 0.98–0.99, 0.99–1.00
   b. 4 claims paid; Total $= \$22,000$

8. a. Atlanta wins each game if random number is in interval 0.00–0.60, 0.00–0.55, 0.00–0.48, 0.00–0.45, 0.00–0.48, 0.00–0.55, 0.00–0.50.
   b. Atlanta wins games 1, 2, 4, and 6
      Atlanta wins series 4 to 2
   c. Repeat many times; record % of Atlanta wins

10. a. 0.00–0.40 for Yes; 0.40–1.00 for No
       If Yes, 0.00–0.30, 0.30–0.60, 0.60–1.00
       If No, 0.00–0.50, 0.50–0.90, 0.90–1.00
    b. Uncertain, definitely yes, definitely no
    c. Repeat many times; record % of definitely yes

12. a. $7, $3, $12
    b. Purchase: 0.00–0.25, 0.25–0.70, 0.70–1.00
       Labor: 0.00–0.10, 0.10–0.35, 0.35–0.70, 0.70–1.00
       Transportation: 0.00–0.75, 0.75–1.00
    c. $5
    d. $7
    e. Provide probability profit less than $5/unit

14. a. Most simulations between $5500 and $6500
    b. Most simulations between 0.24 and 0.30
    c. Project is too risky

16. Most simulations between 6 and 16 still working; 11 is the expected number

18. a. Most simulations between 0.60 and 0.65
    b. $775,000 roughly 0.82; $785,000 roughly 0.88
       Select $775,000

20. a. Results vary with each simulation run
       Approximate results: 50,000 provided $230,000
       60,000 provided $190,000
       70,000 less than $100,000
    b. Recommend 50,000 units
    c. Roughly 0.75

22. Very poor operation; some customers wait 30 minutes or more

Chapter 17

2. a. 0.82
   b. $\pi_1 = 0.5$; $\pi_2 = 0.5$
   c. $\pi_1 = 0.6$; $\pi_2 = 0.4$

4. a. $\pi_1 = 0.92$, $\pi_2 = 0.08$
   b. $85

6. a.

	City	Suburbs
City	0.98	0.02
Suburbs	0.01	0.99

   b. $\pi_1 = 0.333$; $\pi_2 = 0.667$
   c. City will decrease from 40% to 33%; suburbs will increase from 60% to 67%

8. a. MDA
   b. $\pi = 0.333$, $\pi_2 = 0.667$

10. .59 probability of $3 - 1$; .52 probability of $4 - 1$.

12. 3580 will be sold eventually; 1420 will be lost

14. a. Graduate and drop out
    b. P(Drop out) $= 0.15$, P(Sophomore) $= 0.10$, P(Junior) $= 0.75$
    c. 0.706, 0.294
    d. Yes; P(Graduate) $= 0.54$
       P(Drop out) $= 0.46$
    e. 1479 (74%) will graduate

Chapter 18

2. a. Min $P_1(d_1^-) + P_2(d_2^+)$
      s.t.
$$
\begin{aligned}
50x_1 + 100x_2 &\le 50,000 \\
3x_1 + 10x_2 - d_1^+ + d_1^- &= 4500 \\
x_2 - d_2^+ + d_2^- &= 300 \\
x_1, x_2, d_1^+, d_1^-, d_2^+, d_2^- &\ge 0
\end{aligned}
$$
   b. $x_1 = 250$, $x_2 = 375$

4. a. Min $P_1(d_1^-) + P_1(d_2^+) + P_2(d_3^-) + P_2(d_4^-) + P_3(d_5^-)$
s.t.

$$
\begin{aligned}
20x_1 + 30x_2 - d_1^+ + d_1^- &= 4800 \\
20x_1 + 30x_2 - d_2^+ + d_2^- &= 6000 \\
x_1 \qquad\quad - d_3^+ + d_3^- &= 100 \\
x_2 - d_4^+ + d_4^- &= 120 \\
x_1 + x_2 \quad - d_5^+ + d_5^- &= 300
\end{aligned}
$$

x_1, x_2, all deviation variables ≥ 0

b. $x_1 = 120, x_2 = 120$

6. a. Let $x_1 =$ number of letters mailed to group 1 customers
$x_2 =$ number of letters mailed to group 2 customers
Min $P_1(d_1^-) + P_1(d_2^-) + P_2(d_3^+)$
s.t.

$$
\begin{aligned}
x_1 \qquad - d_1^+ + d_1^- &= 40{,}000 \\
x_2 - d_2^+ + d_2^- &= 50{,}000 \\
x_1 + x_2 - d_3^+ + d_3^- &= 70{,}000
\end{aligned}
$$

x_1, x_2, all deviation variables ≥ 0

b. $x_1 = 40{,}000, x_2 = 50{,}000$

c. Optimal solution does not change

8. a. Min $d_1^- + d_1^+ + e_1^- + e_1^+ + d_2^- + d_2^+ + e_2^- + e_2^+ + d_3^- + d_3^+ + e_3^- + e_3^+$
s.t.

$$
\begin{aligned}
x_1 \qquad + d_1^- - d_1^+ &= 1 \\
x_2 + e_1^- - e_1^+ &= 7 \\
x_1 \qquad + d_2^- - d_2^+ &= 5 \\
x_2 + e_2^- - e_2^+ &= 9 \\
x_1 \qquad + d_3^- - d_3^+ &= 6 \\
x_2 + e_3^- - e_3^+ &= 2
\end{aligned}
$$

all variables ≥ 0

b. $x_1 = 5, x_2 = 7$

10. 178, 184, 151
Marysville

12. 170, 168, 190, 183
Handover College

14. a. 220 Bowrider (194)
b. 240 Sundancer (144)

16. CR = 0.028, acceptable

18. a. 0.724, 0.193, 0.083
b. CR = 0.057, yes

20. a.

	A	B	C
A	1	3	2
B	$\frac{1}{3}$	1	5
C	$\frac{1}{2}$	$\frac{1}{5}$	1

b. 0.503, 0.348, 0.148
c. CR = 0.415, no

22. a.

	D	S	N
D	1	$\frac{1}{4}$	$\frac{1}{7}$
S	4	1	$\frac{1}{3}$
N	7	3	1

b. 0.080, 0.265, 0.656
c. CR = 0.028, yes

24. a. Criterion: 0.667, 0.033
Yield: 0.750, 0.250
Risk: 0.333, 0.667
b. CCC, 0.611; SRI, 0.389
CCC is preferred

26. a. Criterion: 0.608, 0.272, 0.120
Price: 0.557, 0.123, 0.320
Sound: 0.137, 0.239, 0.623
Reception: 0.579, 0.187, 0.046
b. 0.446, 0.162, 0.392
System A is preferred

Chapter 1

4. A quantitative approach should be considered because the problem is large, complex, important, new, and repetitive

8. a. Max $10x + 5y$
    s.t. $5x + 2y \leq 40$
            $x \geq 0, y \geq 0$
   b. Controllable inputs: x and y
     Uncontrollable inputs: profit (10,5), labor-hours (5,2) and labor-hour availability (40)
   d. $x = 0$, $y = 20$; Profit = \$100
     (Solution by trial and error)

15. a. $TC = 1000 + 30x$
   b. $P = 40x - (1000 + 30x) = 10x - 1000$
   c. Break even when $P = 0$
     Thus $10x - 1000 = 0$
             $10x = 1000$
               $x = 100$

Chapter 2

1. The sample points are major defect, minor defect, no defect; in set notation S = {major defect, minor defect, no defect}; each is an experimental outcome

2. $P(E_1) = 0.40$, $P(E_2) = 0.26$, $P(E_3) = 0.34$
The relative frequency method was used

4. a. P(Internet access) = 21,733 / 51,745 = 0.42
   b. P(Internet access) = 7,286 / 14,012 = 0.52
   c. Total number of schools = 51,745 + 14,012 + 17,229
                             = 82,986
     P(Elementary) = 51,745/82,986 = 0.62
   d. Total number of schools with Internet access =
     21,733 + 7,286 + 10,682 = 39,701
     P(Internet access) = 39,701/82,986 = 0.48

6. a. $P(A) = P(150{-}199) + P(200 \text{ and over})$
     $= \dfrac{26}{100} + \dfrac{5}{100}$
     $= 0.31$
   b. $P(B) = P(\text{less than } 50) + P(50{-}99) + P(100{-}149)$
     $= 0.13 + 0.22 + 0.34$
     $= 0.69$

7. a. $P(A) = 0.40$, $P(B) = 0.40$, $P(C) = 0.60$
   b. $P(A \cup B) = P(E_1, E_2, E_3, E_4) = 0.80$; yes,
     $P(A \cup B) = P(A) + P(B)$
   c. $A^c = \{E_3, E_4, E_5\}$; $C^c = \{E_1, E_4\}$ $P(A^c) = 0.60$;
     $P(C^c) = 0.40$
   d. $A \cup B^c = \{E_1, E_2, E_5\}$; $P(A \cup B^c) = 0.60$
   e. $P(B \cup C) = P(E_2, E_3, E_4, E_5) = 0.80$

12. a. $P(A \mid B) = \dfrac{P(A \cap B)}{P(B)} = \dfrac{0.40}{0.60} = 0.6667$

   b. $P(B \mid A) = \dfrac{P(A \cap B)}{P(A)} = \dfrac{0.40}{0.50} = 0.80$

   c. No, because $P(A \mid B) \neq P(A)$

13. a.

	Reason for Applying			
	Quality	**Cost/ Convenience**	**Other**	**Total**
Full Time	0.218	0.204	0.039	0.461
Part Time	0.208	0.307	0.024	0.539
Total	0.426	0.511	0.063	1.000

   b. A student will most likely cite cost or convenience as the first reason: probability = 0.511; school quality is the first reason cited by the second largest number of students: probability = 0.426
   c. P(Quality | full time) = 0.218/0.461 = 0.473
   d. P(Quality | part time) = 0.208/0.539 = 0.386
   e. $P(B) = 0.426$ and $P(B \mid A) = 0.473$
     Since $P(B) \neq P(B \mid A)$, the events are dependent

20. a. $P(B \cap A_1) = P(A_1)P(B \mid A_1) = (0.20)(0.50) = 0.10$
     $P(B \cap A_2) = P(A_2)P(B \mid A_2) = (0.50)(0.40) = 0.20$
     $P(B \cap A_3) = P(A_3)P(B \mid A_3) = (0.30)(0.30) = 0.09$
   b. $P(A_2 \mid B) = \dfrac{0.20}{0.10 + 0.20 + 0.09} = 0.51$
   c.

Events	$P(A_i)$	$P(B \mid A_i)$	$P(A_i \cap B)$	$P(A_i \mid B)$
A_1	0.20	0.50	0.10	0.26
A_2	0.50	0.40	0.20	0.51
A_3	0.30	0.30	0.09	0.23
	1.00		0.39	1.00

25.

Events	$P(A_i)$	$P(D \mid A_i)$	$P(A_i \cap D)$	$P(A_i \mid D)$
Supplier A	0.60	0.0025	0.0015	0.23
Supplier B	0.30	0.0100	0.0030	0.46
Supplier C	0.10	0.0200	0.0020	0.31
	1.00		$P(S) = 0.0065$	1.00

a. $P(D) = 0.0065$
b. B is the most likely supplier if a defect is found

Chapter 3

1. a. Values: 0,1,2, . . . ,20
　　　discrete
b. Values: 0,1,2, . . .
　　　discrete
c. Values: 0,1,2, . . . ,50
　　　discrete
d. Values: $0 \leq x \leq 8$
　　　continuous
e. Values: $x \geq 0$
　　　continuous

3. a.

x	$f(x)$
1	3/20 = 0.15
2	5/20 = 0.25
3	8/20 = 0.40
4	4/20 = 0.20
	Total 1.00

b.

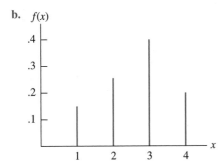

c. $f(x) \geq 0$ for $x = 1, 2, 3, 4$
　　$\Sigma f(x) = 1$

4. a.

x	$f(x)$	$xf(x)$
3	0.25	0.75
6	0.50	3.00
9	0.25	2.25
Totals	1.00	6.00

$E(x) = \mu = 6.00$

b.

x	$x - \mu$	$(x - \mu)^2$	$f(x)$	$(x - \mu)^2 f(x)$
3	−3	9	.25	2.25
6	0	0	.50	0.00
9	3	9	.25	2.25
				4.50

$\text{Var}(x) = \sigma^2 = 4.50$
c. $\sigma = \sqrt{4.50} = 2.12$

9. a. $f(1) = \binom{2}{1}(0.4)^1(0.6)^1 = \dfrac{2!}{1!1!}(0.4)(0.6) = 0.48$
b. $f(0) = \binom{2}{0}(0.4)^0(0.6)^2 = \dfrac{2!}{0!2!}(1)(0.36) = 0.36$
c. $f(2) = \binom{2}{2}(0.4)^2(0.6)^0 = \dfrac{2!}{2!0!}(0.16)(1) = 0.16$
d. $P(x \geq 1) = f(1) + f(2) = 0.48 + 0.16 = 0.64$
e. $E(x) = np = 2(0.4) = 0.8$
　　$\text{Var}(x) = np(1 - p) = 2(0.4)(0.6) = 0.48$
　　　$\sigma = \sqrt{0.48} = 0.6928$

12. a. Probability of a defective part being produced must be 0.03 for each trial; trials must be independent
b. Two outcomes result in exactly one defect
c. $P(\text{no defects}) = (0.97)(0.97) = 0.9409$
　　$P(\text{1 defect}) = 2(0.03)(0.97) = 0.0582$
　　$P(\text{2 defects}) = (0.03)(0.03) = 0.0009$

14. a. $f(x) = \dfrac{2^x e^{-2}}{x!}$
b. $\mu = 6$ for 3 time periods
c. $f(x) = \dfrac{6^x e^{-6}}{x!}$
d. $f(2) = \dfrac{2^2 e^{-2}}{2!} = \dfrac{4(0.1353)}{2} = 0.2706$
e. $f(6) = \dfrac{6^x e^{-6}}{6!} = 0.1606$
f. $f(5) = \dfrac{4^5 e^{-4}}{5!} = 0.1563$

18. a.

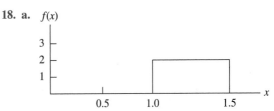

b. $P(x = 1.25) = 0$; the probability of any single point is zero because the area under the curve above any single point is zero
c. $P(1.0 \leq x \leq 1.25) = 2(0.25) = 0.50$
d. $P(1.20 < x < 1.5) = 2(0.30) = 0.60$

21. a. 0.2967
b. 0.4418
c. $0.5000 - 0.1700 = 0.3300$
d. $0.0910 + 0.5000 = 0.5910$
e. $0.3849 + 0.5000 = 0.8849$
f. $0.5000 - 0.2612 = 0.2388$

23. a. Look in the table for an area of $0.5000 - 0.2119 = 0.2881$; the value we are seeking is below the mean, so the z value must be negative; thus, for an area of 0.2881, $z = -0.80$
b. Look in the table for an area of $0.9030/2 = 0.4515$; $z = 1.66$

c. Look in the table for an area of 0.2025/2 = 0.1026; $z = 0.26$

d. Look in the table for an area of $0.9948 - 0.5000 = 0.4948$; $z = 2.56$

e. Look in the table for an area of $0.6915 - 0.5000 = 0.1915$; the value we are seeking is below the mean, so the z value must be negative; thus, $z = -0.50$

29. a. $P(x \leq x_0) = 1 - e^{-x_0/3}$

b. $P(x \leq 2) = 1 - e^{-2/3} = 1 - 0.5134 = 0.4866$

c. $P(x \geq 3) = 1 - P(x \leq 3) = 1 - (1 - e^{-3/3}) = e^{-1} = 0.3679$

d. $P(x \leq 5) = 1 - e^{-5/3} = 1 - 0.1889 = 0.8111$

e. $P(2 \leq x \leq 5) = P(x \leq 5) - P(x \leq 2) = 0.8111 - 0.4866 = 0.3245$

30. a. The mean time between fatalities is $\frac{1}{34}$ year, so for 1 month we have $\mu = \frac{12}{34}$ and
$P(x \leq 1) = 1 - e^{-1/(12/34)} = 1 - e^{-34/12} = 1 - e^{-2.833}$
$= 1 - 0.06 = 0.94$
$P(\text{no fatalities in one month}) = P(x > 1) = 1 - 0.94 = 0.06$

b. $P(x \leq 1 \text{ week}) = 1 - e^{-1/(52/34)} = 1 - e^{-34/52}$
$= 1 - 0.52 = 0.48$
Therefore, $P(x > 1 \text{ week}) = 0.52$

Chapter 4

1. a.

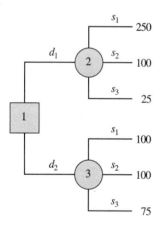

b.

Decision	Maximum Profit	Minimum Profit
d_1	250	25
d_2	100	75

Optimistic approach: Select d_1
Conservative approach: Select d_2

Regret or opportunity loss table:

Decision	s_1	s_2	s_3
d_1	0	0	50
d_2	150	0	0

Maximum regret: 50 for d_1 and 150 for d_2; select d_1

3. a. Decision: choose the best plant size from the two alternatives: a small plant and a large plant

Chance event: market demand for the new product line with three possible outcomes (states of nature): low, medium, and high

b. Influence Diagram:

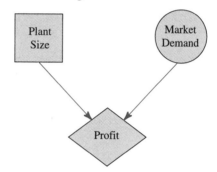

c.

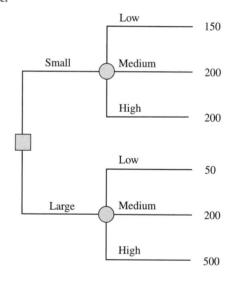

d.

Decision	Maximum Profit	Minimum Profit	Maximum Regret
Small	200	150	300
Large	500	50	100

Optimistic Approach: Large Plant
Conservative Approach: Small Plant
Minimax Regret: Large Plant

5. a. $EV(d_1) = 0.65(250) + 0.15(100) + 0.20(25) = 182.5$
$EV(d_2) = 0.65(100) + 0.15(100) + 0.20(75) = 95$
The optimal decision is d_1

7. a. $EV(\text{own staff}) = 0.2(650) + 0.5(650) + 0.3(600)$
$= 635$
$EV(\text{outside vendor}) = 0.2(900) + 0.5(600)$
$+ 0.3(300) = 570$
$EV(\text{combination}) = 0.2(800) + 0.5(650) + 0.3(500)$
$= 635$

Optimal decision: hire an outside vendor with an expected cost of $570,000

b.

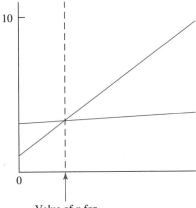

	Cost	Probability
Own staff	300	0.3
Outside vendor	600	0.5
Combination	900	0.2
		1.0

8. a. $EV(d_1) = p(10) + (1 - p)(1) = 9p + 1$
$EV(d_2) = p(4) + (1 - p)(3) = 1p + 3$

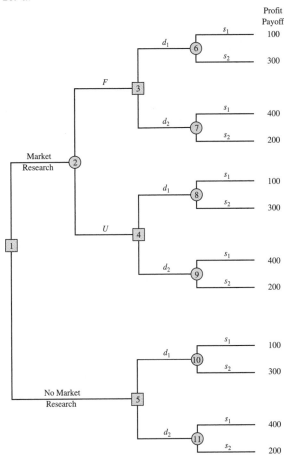

10

0

Value of p for
which EVs are equal

$9p + 1 = 1p + 3$ and hence $p = 0.25$
d_2 is optimal for $p \le 0.25$, d_1 is optimal for $p \ge 0.25$
b. d_2
c. As long as the payoff for $s_1 \ge 2$, then d_2 is optimal

14. a. If s_1, then d_1; if s_2, then d_1 or d_2; if s_3, then d_2
b. $EVwPI = 0.65(250) + 0.15(100) + 0.20(75) = 192.5$
c. From the solution to Problem 5, we know that $EV(d_1) = 182.5$ and $EV(d_2) = 95$; thus, recommended decision is d_1; hence, EVwoPI = 182.5
d. $EVPI = EVwPI - EVwoPI = 192.5 - 182.5 = 10$

16. a.

Profit
Payoff

b. $EV \text{ (node 6)} = 0.57(100) + 0.43(300) = 186$
$EV \text{ (node 7)} = 0.57(400) + 0.43(200) = 314$
$EV \text{ (node 8)} = 0.18(100) + 0.82(300) = 264$
$EV \text{ (node 9)} = 0.18(400) + 0.82(200) = 236$
$EV \text{ (node 10)} = 0.40(100) + 0.60(300) = 220$
$EV \text{ (node 11)} = 0.40(400) + 0.60(200) = 280$

$EV \text{ (node 3)} = \text{Max}(186,314) = 314 \, d_2$
$EV \text{ (node 4)} = \text{Max}(264,236) = 264 \, d_1$
$EV \text{ (node 5)} = \text{Max}(220,280) = 280 \, d_2$

$EV \text{ (node 2)} = 0.56(314) + 0.44(264) = 292$
$EV \text{ (node 1)} = \text{Max}(292,280) = 292$

$\therefore$ Market Research
If Favorable, decision d_2
If Unfavorable, decision d_1

Chapter 5

1. a. $EV(d_1) = 0.40(100) + 0.30(25) + 0.30(0) = 47.5$
$EV(d_2) = 0.40(75) + 0.30(50) + 0.30(25) = 52.5 \; \}d_2$
$EV(d_3) = 0.40(50) + 0.30(50) + 0.30(50) = 50.0$

b. Using utilities

Decision Maker A	Decision Maker B
$EU(d_1) = 4.9$	$EU(d_1) = 4.45$ Best
$EU(d_2) = 5.9$	$EU(d_2) = 3.75$
$EU(d_3) = 6.0$ Best	$EU(d_3) = 3.00$

c. Difference in attitude toward risk; decision maker A tends to avoid risk, whereas decision maker B tends to take a risk for the opportunity of a large payoff

5. a.

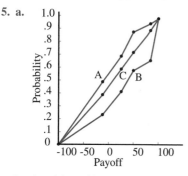

b. A—risk avoider
B—risk taker
C—risk neutral

c. Risk-avoider A, at $20 payoff $p = 0.70$
∴ EV(Lottery) = $0.70(100) + 0.30(-100) = \$40$
∴ Will Pay $40 - 20 = \$20$
Risk-taker B, at $20 payoff $p = 0.45$
∴ EV(Lottery) = $0.45(100) + 0.55(-100) = -\$10$
∴ Will Pay $20 - (-10) = \$30$

Chapter 6

1. a.

Month	Time Series Value	3-Month Moving Average Forecast	(Error)²	4-Month Moving Average Forecast	(Error)²
1	9.5				
2	9.3				
3	9.4				
4	9.6	9.40	0.04		
5	9.8	9.43	0.14	9.45	0.12
6	9.7	9.60	0.01	9.53	0.03
7	9.8	9.70	0.01	9.63	0.03
8	10.5	9.77	0.53	9.73	0.59
9	9.9	10.00	0.01	9.95	0.00
10	9.7	10.07	0.14	9.98	0.08
11	9.6	10.03	0.18	9.97	0.14
12	9.6	9.73	0.02	9.92	0.10
		Totals	1.08		1.09

MSE(3-month) = 1.08/9 = 0.12
MSE(4-month) = 1.09/8 = 0.14
Use a 3-month moving average.
b. Forecast = (9.7 + 9.6 + 9.6)/3 = 9.63

2. a.

Week	Time Series Value	4-Week Moving Average Forecast	(Error)²	5-Week Moving Average Forecast	(Error)²
1	17				
2	21				
3	19				
4	23				
5	18	20.00	4.00		
6	16	20.25	18.06	19.60	12.96
7	20	19.00	1.00	19.40	0.36
8	18	19.25	1.56	19.20	1.44
9	22	18.00	16.00	19.00	9.00
10	20	19.00	1.00	18.80	1.44
11	15	20.00	25.00	19.20	17.64
12	22	18.75	10.56	19.00	9.00
		Totals	77.18		51.84

b. MSE(4-week) = 77.18/8 = 9.65
MSE(5-week) = 51.84/7 = 7.41
c. For the limited data provided, the 5-week moving average provides the smallest MSE

4.

Week	Time Series Value	Forecast	Error	(Error)²
1	17			
2	21	17.00	4.00	16.00
3	19	17.40	1.60	2.56
4	23	17.56	5.44	29.59
5	18	18.10	-0.10	0.01
6	16	18.09	-2.09	4.37
7	20	17.88	2.12	4.49
8	18	18.10	-0.10	0.01
9	22	18.09	3.91	15.29
10	20	18.48	1.52	2.31
11	15	18.63	-3.63	13.18
12	22	18.27	3.73	13.91
			Total	101.72

MSE = 101.72/11 = 9.25
$\alpha = 0.2$ provided a lower MSE; therefore $\alpha = 0.2$ is better than $\alpha = 0.1$

5. a.

Month	Y_t	3-Month Moving Averages Forecast	$(Error)^2$	$\alpha = 2$ Forecast	$(Error)^2$
1	80				
2	82			80.00	4.00
3	84			80.40	12.96
4	83	82.00	1.00	81.12	3.53
5	83	83.00	0.00	81.50	2.25
6	84	83.33	0.45	81.80	4.84
7	85	83.33	2.79	82.24	7.62
8	84	84.00	0.00	82.79	1.46
9	82	84.33	5.43	83.03	1.06
10	83	83.67	0.45	82.83	0.03
11	84	83.00	1.00	82.86	1.30
12	83	83.00	0.00	83.09	0.01
		Totals	11.12		39.06

MSE(3-month) = 11.12/9 = 1.24
MSE($\alpha = 0.2$) = 39.06/11 = 3.55
Use a 3-month moving average
b. (83 + 84 + 83)/3 = 83.3

14. $\Sigma t = 21; \Sigma t^2 = 91; \Sigma Y_t = 117.1$;

$\Sigma tY_t = 403.7; n = 6$

$$b_1 = \frac{\Sigma tY_t - (\Sigma t \Sigma Y_t)/n}{\Sigma t^2 - (\Sigma t)^2/n}$$

$$= \frac{403.7 - (21)(117.1)/6}{91 - (21)^2/6}$$

$$= -0.3514$$

$b_0 = \bar{Y} - b_1\bar{t} = 19.5167 - (-.3514)(3.5) = 20.7466$

$T_t = 20.7466 - 0.3514t$

Conclusion: Enrollment appears to be decreasing by an average of approximately 351 students per year

25. a. Four-quarter moving averages beginning with
(1690 + 940 + 2625 + 2500)/4 = 1938.75
Other moving averages are

1966.25	2002.50
1956.25	2052.50
2025.00	2060.00
1990.00	2123.75

b.

Quarter	Seasonal-Irregular Component Values		Seasonal Index	Adjusted Seasonal Index
1	0.904	0.900	0.9020	0.900
2	0.448	0.526	0.4970	0.486
3	1.344	1.453	1.3985	1.396
4	1.275	1.164	1.2195	1.217
		Total	4.0070	

c. The largest seasonal effect is in the third quarter, which corresponds to the back-to-school demand during July, August, and September of each year

Note: Adjustment for seasonal index = 4.000/4.007 = 0.9983

33. a.

Restaurant (i)	x_i	y_i	x_iy_i	x_i^2
1	1	19	19	1
2	4	44	176	16
3	6	40	240	36
4	10	52	520	100
5	14	53	742	196
Totals	35	208	1697	349

$$\bar{x} = \frac{35}{5} = 7$$

$$\bar{y} = \frac{208}{5} = 41.6$$

$$b_1 = \frac{\Sigma x_iy_i - (\Sigma x_i \Sigma y_i)/n}{\Sigma x_i^2 - (\Sigma x_i)^2/n}$$

$$= \frac{1697 - (35)(208)/5}{349 - (35)^2/5}$$

$$= \frac{241}{104} = 2.317$$

$b_0 = \bar{y} - b_1\bar{x} = 41.6 - 2.317(7) = 25.381$

$\hat{y} = 25.381 + 2.317x$

b. $\hat{y} = 25.381 + 2.317(8) = 43.917$ or \$43,917

Chapter 7

1. Parts (a), (b), and (e) are acceptable linear programming relationships
Part (c) is not acceptable because of $-2x_2^2$
Part (d) is not acceptable because of $3\sqrt{x_1}$

Part (f) is not acceptable because of $1x_1x_2$
Parts (c), (d), and (f) could not be found in a linear programming model because they have the above non-linear terms

2. a.

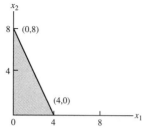

b.

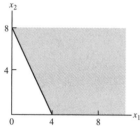

c.

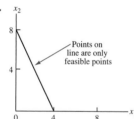

Points on line are only feasible points

6. $7x_1 + 10x_2 = 420$
$6x_1 + 4x_2 = 420$
$-4x_1 + 7x_2 = 420$

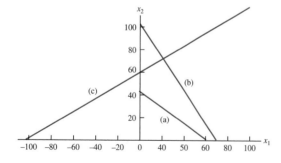

7.

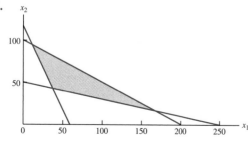

10.

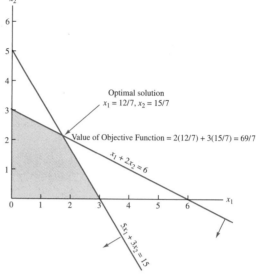

Optimal solution
$x_1 = 12/7, x_2 = 15/7$

Value of Objective Function $= 2(12/7) + 3(15/7) = 69/7$

$x_1 + 2x_2 = 6$

$5x_1 + 3x_2 = 15$

$$
\begin{array}{rll}
x_1 + 2x_2 = & 6 & (1) \\
5x_1 + 3x_2 = & 15 & (2) \\
5x_1 + 10x_2 = & 30 & (3)
\end{array}
$$

Equation (1) times 5:

Equation (2) minus equation (3): $-7x_2 = -15$

$x_2 = 15/7$

From equation (1): $x_1 = 6 - 2(15/7)$
$= 6 - 30/7 = 12/7$

13. a.

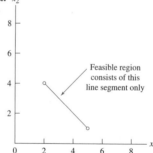

Feasible region consists of this line segment only

b. The extreme points are (5,1) and (2,4)

c.

Optimal solution
$x_1 = 2, x_2 = 4$

$x_1 + 2x_2 = 10$

18. Max $5x_1 + 2x_2 + 8x_3 + 0s_1 + 0s_2 + 0s_3$
s.t.

$$
\begin{array}{rl}
1x_1 - 2x_2 + 0.5x_3 + 1s_1 = 420 \\
2x_1 + 3x_2 - 1x_3 + 1s_2 = 610 \\
6x_1 - 1x_2 + 3x_3 + 1s_3 = 125
\end{array}
$$

$x_1, x_2, x_3, s_1, s_2, s_3 \geq 0$

22. a. Let R = number of units of regular model

C = number of units of catcher's model

Max $\quad 5R + 8C$

$\quad\quad 1R + \tfrac{3}{2}C \le 900 \quad$ Cutting and sewing

$\quad\quad \tfrac{1}{2}R + \tfrac{1}{3}C \le 300 \quad$ Finishing

$\quad\quad \tfrac{1}{8}R + \tfrac{1}{4}C \le 100 \quad$ Packaging and shipping

$\quad\quad\quad R, C \ge 0$

b.

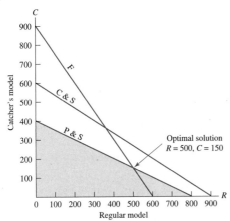

c. $5(500) + 8(150) = \$3,700$

d. C & S $\quad\quad 1(500) + \tfrac{3}{2}(150) = 725$

$\quad$ F $\quad\quad\quad\quad \tfrac{1}{2}(500) + \tfrac{1}{3}(150) = 300$

$\quad$ P & S $\quad\quad \tfrac{1}{8}(500) + \tfrac{1}{4}(150) = 100$

e.

Department	Capacity	Usage	Slack
Cutting and sewing	900	725	175 hours
Finishing	300	300	0 hours
Packaging and shipping	100	100	0 hours

29.

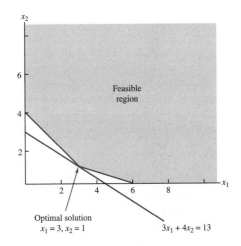

Objective function value = 13

32. a.

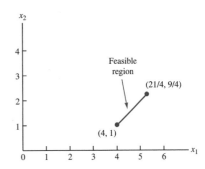

b. There are two extreme points

$$x_1 = 4 \quad\quad x_1 = 21/4$$
$$x_2 = 1 \quad\quad x_2 = 9/4$$

c. The optimal solution (see part (a)) is $x_1 = 4, x_2 = 1$

33. a. Min $\quad 6x_1 + 4x_2 + 0s_1 + 0s_2 + 0s_3$

$\quad$ s.t.

$$2x_1 + 1x_2 - s_1 \quad\quad\quad = 12$$
$$1x_1 + 1x_2 \quad\quad - s_2 \quad\quad = 10$$
$$1x_2 \quad\quad\quad\quad + s_3 = 4$$
$$x_1, x_2, s_1, s_2, s_3 \ge 0$$

b. The optimal solution is $x_1 = 6, x_2 = 4$

c. $s_1 = 4, s_2 = 0, s_3 = 0$

40.

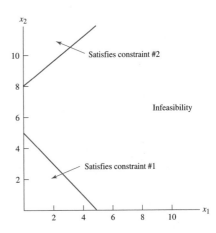

41.

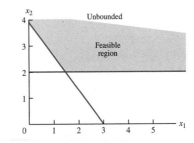

Chapter 8

1. a.

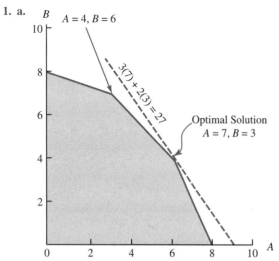

$A = 4, B = 6$

Optimal Solution
$A = 7, B = 3$

$3(7) + 2(3) = 27$

b. The same extreme point, $A = 7$ and $B = 3$, remains optimal; Value of the objective function becomes $5(7) + 2(3) = 41$

c. A new extreme point, $A = 4$ and $B = 6$, becomes optimal; Value of the objective function becomes $3(4) + 4(6) = 36$

d. The objective coefficient range for variable A is 2 to 6; the optimal solution, $A = 7$ and $B = 3$ does not change The objective coefficient range for variable B is 1 to 3; resolve the problem to find the new optimal solution

2. a. The feasible region becomes larger with the new optimal solution of $A = 6.5$ and $B = 4.5$

b. Value of the optimal solution to the revised problem is $3(6.5) + 2(4.5) = 28.5$; the one-unit increase in the right-hand side of constraint 1 improves the value of the optimal solution by $28.5 - 27 = 1.5$, therefore, the dual price for constraint 1 is 1.5

c. The right-hand-side range for constraint 1 is 8 to 11.2; as long as the right-hand side stays within this range, the dual price of 1.5 is applicable

d. The improvement in the value of the optimal solution will be 0.5 for every unit increase in the right-hand side of constraint 2 as long as the right-hand side is between 18 and 30

5. a. Regular glove = 500; Catcher's mitt = 150;
Value = 3700

b. The finishing, packaging, and shipping constraints are binding; there is no slack

c. Cutting and sewing = 0
Finishing = 3
Packaging and shipping = 28
Additional finishing time is worth $3 per unit, and additional packaging and shipping time is worth $28 per unit

d. In the packaging and shipping department, each additional hour is worth $28

6. a. 4 to 12
3.33 to 10

b. As long as the profit contribution for the regular glove is between $4.00 and $12.00, the current solution is optimal; as long as the profit contribution for the catcher's mitt stays between $3.33 and $10.00, the current solution is optimal; the optimal solution is not sensitive to small changes in the profit contributions for the gloves

c. The dual prices for the resources are applicable over the following ranges:

Constraint	Right-Hand-Side Range
Cutting and sewing	725 to No Upper Limit
Finishing	133.33 to 400
Packaging and shipping	75 to 135

d. Amount of increase = $(28)(20) = \$560$

10. a. $S = 4000$, $M = 10,000$, Total risk = 62,000

b.

Variable	Objective Coefficient Range
S	3.75 to No Upper Limit
M	No Lower Limit to 6.4

c. $5(4000) + 4(10,000) = \$60,000$

d. $60,000 / 1,200,000 = 0.05$ or 5%

e. 0.057 risk units

f. $0.057(100) = 5.7\%$

12. a. $x_1 = 0$; $x_2 = 25$; $x_3 = 125$; $x_4 = 0$
Value of solution = 525.0

b. The constraints on machine A and machine C hours are binding

c. Machine B has 425 hours of excess capacity

d. Yes, the allowable increase is only 0.05

13. a.

Variable	Objective Coefficient Range
x_1	No Lower Limit to 4.05
x_2	5.923 to 9
x_3	2 to 12
x_4	No Lower Limit to 4.5

b. There is no lower limit on the allowable decrease for the objective function coefficient of x_1; thus the percentage decrease is 0%

$$1.5/3 + 1/3.5 = 0.79$$

The accumulated percentage of allowable increases and decreases is 79%, which is less than 100%, so the optimal solution will not change.

c.

Constraint	Right-Hand-Side Range
Machine A hours	133.33 to 800
Machine B hours	275 to No Upper Limit
Machine C hours	137.5 to 825

d. Yes, because that is outside the range

Chapter 9

1. a. Let T = number of television advertisements
R = number of radio advertisements
N = number of newspaper advertisements

Max $100{,}000T + 18{,}000R + 40{,}000N$

s.t.

$2000T +$	$300R +$	$600N \leq 18{,}200$	Budget
T		$\leq$ 10	Max TV
	R	$\leq$ 20	Max radio
		$N \leq$ 10	Max news
$-0.5T +$	$0.5R -$	$0.5N \leq$ 0	Max 50% radio
$0.9T -$	$0.1R -$	$0.1N \geq$ 0	Min 10% TV
$T, R, N \geq 0$			

		Budget \$
Solution:	$T = 4$	\$ 8000
	$R = 14$	4200
	$N = 10$	6000
		\$18,200

Audience = 1,052,000

b. The dual price for the budget constraint is 51.30. Thus, a \$100 increase in the budget should provide an increase in audience coverage of approximately 5130. The right-hand-side range for the budget constraint will show that this interpretation is correct.

9. a. Decision variables A, P, M, H, and G represent the fraction or proportion of the total investment in each alternative

Max $0.073A + 0.103P + 0.064M + 0.075H + 0.045G$

s.t.

$A +$	$P +$	$M +$	$H +$	$G = 1$
$0.5A +$	$0.5P -$	$0.5M -$	$0.5H$	≤ 0
$-0.5A -$	$0.5P +$	$0.5M +$	$0.5H$	≤ 0
		$0.25M -$	$0.25H +$	$G \geq 0$
$-0.6A +$	$0.4P$			≤ 0
$A, P, M, H, G \geq 0$				

Objective function = 0.079; $A = 0.178$; $P = 0.267$; $M = 0.000$; $H = 0.444$; $G = 0.111$

b. Multiplying A, P, M, H, and G by the \$100,000 invested provides the following

Atlantic Oil	\$ 17,800
Pacific Oil	26,700
Huber Steel	44,400
Government Bonds	11,100
	\$100,000

c. 0.079(\$100,000) = \$7900

d. The marginal rate of return is 0.079

12. a. The only change is in the objective function with the price per unit for the number of bases purchased (BP) lowered from 0.60 to 0.55. The solution for the new model provides an objective function value of \$24,276.67, which is an overall savings of \$166.66

compared to the previous solution. Janders will now purchase all 5000 bases from the supplier. In addition, Janders will increase the manufacturing of financial cartridges from 667 to 2333 units to take advantage of the manufacturing capacity freed by the fact that the company no longer needs to manufacture bases.

b. By referring to the computer solution in Figure 9.5, we can answer the question without modifying and resolving the original problem. The objective coefficient range for TTP is No Lower Limit to \$0.875. Because the price increase to \$0.82 is within the range, the manufacturing and purchasing plan will not change. However, Janders purchases 2000 Technician tops. Thus, the price increase from \$0.78 to \$0.82 per unit will add \$0.04(2000) = \$80 to the total cost.

c. The only change in the original problem is to reduce the objective function coefficient for overtime (OT) premium from \$9 to \$2 per hour. This change enables Janders to use all 50 hours of overtime for manufacturing. The total cost is further reduced to \$24,293, but the company still needs purchases of 1333 financial cartridges (FCP), 3000 financial tops (FTP), and 2000 technician tops (TTP). The overtime is used to increase the manufacturing of financial cartridges (FCM) from 667 to 1667 units.

15. Let x_{11} = gallons of crude 1 used to produce regular
x_{12} = gallons of crude 1 used to produce high octane
x_{21} = gallons of crude 2 used to produce regular
x_{22} = gallons of crude 2 used to produce high octane

Min $0.10x_{11} + 0.10x_{12} + 0.15x_{21} + 0.15x_{22}$

s.t.

Each gallon of regular must have at least 40% A

$x_{11} + x_{21}$ = amount of regular produced
$0.4(x_{11} + x_{21})$ = amount of A required for regular
$0.2x_{11} + 0.50x_{21}$ = amount of A in $(x_{11} + x_{21})$ gallons of regular gas
$\therefore 0.2x_{11} + 0.50x_{21} \geq 0.4x_{11} + 0.40x_{21}$
$\therefore -0.2x_{11} + 0.10x_{21} \geq 0$

Each gallon of high octane can have at most 50% B

$x_{12} + x_{22}$ = amount high octane
$0.5(x_{12} + x_{22})$ = amount of B required for high octane
$0.60x_{12} + 0.30x_{22}$ = amount of B in $(x_{12} + x_{22})$ gallons of high octane
$\therefore 0.60x_{12} + 0.30x_{22} \leq 0.5x_{12} + 0.5x_{22}$
$\therefore 0.1x_{12} - 0.2x_{22} \leq 0$
$x_{11} + x_{21} \geq 800{,}000$
$x_{12} + x_{22} \geq 500{,}000$
$x_{11}, x_{12}, x_{21}, x_{22} \geq 0$

Optimal solution: $x_{11} = 266{,}667$, $x_{12} = 333{,}333$, $x_{21} = 533{,}333$, $x_{22} = 166{,}667$
Cost = \$165,000

19. a. Let x_{11} = amount of men's model in month 1
x_{21} = amount of women's model in month 1
x_{12} = amount of men's model in month 2
x_{22} = amount of women's model in month 2
s_{11} = inventory of men's model at end of month 1
s_{21} = inventory of women's model at end of month 1
s_{12} = inventory of men's model at end of month 2
s_{22} = inventory of women's model at end of month 2

Min $\quad 120x_{11} + 90x_{21} + 120x_{12} + 90x_{22} + 2.4s_{11} + 1.8s_{21} + 2.4s_{12} + 1.8s_{22}$

s.t.

$$
\left.
\begin{array}{l}
x_{11} - s_{11} = 130 \\
x_{21} - s_{21} = 95 \\
s_{11} + x_{12} - s_{12} = 200 \\
s_{21} + x_{22} - s_{22} = 150
\end{array}
\right\} \text{Satisfy demand}
$$

$$
\left.
\begin{array}{l}
s_{12} \geq 25 \\
\\
s_{22} \geq 25
\end{array}
\right\} \text{Ending inventory requirement}
$$

Labor-hours: Men's $2.0 + 1.5 = 3.5$
     Women's $1.6 + 1.0 = 2.6$

$$
\left.
\begin{array}{l}
3.5x_{11} + 2.6x_{21} \geq 900 \\
3.5x_{11} + 2.6x_{21} \leq 1100 \\
3.5x_{11} + 2.6x_{21} - 3.5x_{12} - 2.6x_{22} \leq 100 \\
-3.5x_{11} - 2.6x_{21} + 3.5x_{12} + 2.6x_{22} \leq 100
\end{array}
\right\} \text{Labor smoothing}
$$

$x_{11}, x_{12}, x_{21}, x_{22}, s_{11}, s_{12}, s_{21}, s_{22} \geq 0$

Solution: $x_{11} = 193$; $x_{21} = 95$; $x_{12} = 162$; $x_{22} = 175$
Total cost $= \$67,156$
Inventory levels: $s_{11} = 63$; $s_{12} = 25$; $s_{21} = 0$; $s_{22} = 25$
Labor levels: Previous   1000 hours
      Month 1 922.25 hours
      Month 2 1022.25 hours

b. To accommodate the new policy, the right-hand sides of the four labor-smoothing constraints must be changed to 950, 1050, 50, and 50, respectively; the new total cost is $67,175

Chapter 10

1.

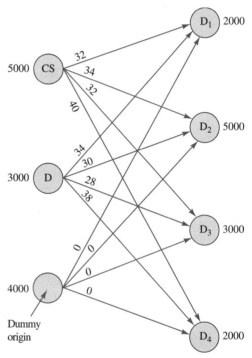

2. a. Let $\quad x_{11}$ = amount shipped from Jefferson City to Des Moines
    x_{12} = amount shipped from Jefferson City to Kansas City
      .
      .
      .
    x_{23} = amount shipped from Omaha to St. Louis

Min $\quad 14x_{11} + 9x_{12} + 7x_{13} + 8x_{21} + 10x_{22} + 5x_{23}$

s.t.

$$
\begin{array}{llll}
x_{11} + x_{12} + x_{13} & & & \leq 30 \\
& x_{21} + x_{22} + x_{23} & & \leq 20 \\
x_{11} & + x_{21} & & = 25 \\
x_{12} & + x_{22} & & = 15 \\
x_{13} & + x_{23} & & = 10
\end{array}
$$

$x_{11}, x_{12}, x_{13}, x_{21}, x_{22}, x_{23} \geq 0$

b.

Optimal Solution	Amount	Cost
Jefferson City–Des Moines	5	70
Jefferson City–Kansas City	15	135
Jefferson City–St. Louis	10	70
Omaha–Des Moines	20	160
	Total	435

8. The network model, in the linear programming formulation program and the optimal solution are shown. Note that the third constraint corresponds to the dummy origin; the variables x_{31}, x_{32}, x_{33}, and x_{34} are the amounts shipped out of the dummy origin and do not appear in the objective function since they are given a coefficient of zero.

Max $\quad 32x_{11} + 34x_{12} + 32x_{13} + 40x_{14} + 34x_{21} + 30x_{22} + 28x_{23} + 38x_{24}$

s.t.

$$
\begin{array}{llllll}
x_{11} + x_{12} + x_{13} + x_{14} & & & \leq 5000 \\
x_{21} + x_{22} + x_{23} + x_{24} & & & \leq 3000 \\
x_{31} + x_{32} + x_{33} + x_{34} & & \leq 4000 \\
x_{11} + x_{21} + x_{31} & & = 2000 \\
x_{12} + x_{22} + x_{32} & & = 5000 \\
x_{13} + x_{23} + x_{33} & = 3000 \\
x_{14} + x_{24} + x_{34} & = 2000
\end{array}
$$

$x_{ij} \geq 0 \quad$ for all i, j

Optimal Solution	Units	Cost
Clifton Springs–D2	4,000	$136,000
Clifton Springs–D4	1,000	40,000
Danville–D1	2,000	68,000
Danville–D4	1,000	38,000
	Total	$282,000

Customer 2 demand has a shortfall of 1000; customer 3 demand of 3000 is not satisfied

12. a.

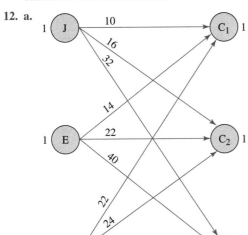

b.

Min $10x_{11} + 16x_{12} + 32x_{13} + 14x_{21} + 22x_{22} + 40x_{23} + 22x_{31} + 24x_{32} + 34x_{33}$

s.t.

$$
\begin{aligned}
x_{11} + x_{12} + x_{13} &\leq 1 \\
x_{21} + x_{22} + x_{23} &\leq 1 \\
x_{31} + x_{32} + x_{33} &\leq 1 \\
x_{11} \qquad\quad + x_{21} \qquad\qquad + x_{31} \qquad &= 1 \\
x_{12} \qquad\qquad + x_{22} \qquad\qquad + x_{32} \quad &= 1 \\
x_{13} \qquad\qquad + x_{23} \qquad\qquad + x_{33} &= 1 \\
x_{ij} \geq 0 \quad \text{for all } i, j
\end{aligned}
$$

Solution $x_{12} = 1$, $x_{21} = 1$, $x_{33} = 1$; total completion time = 64

23. a.

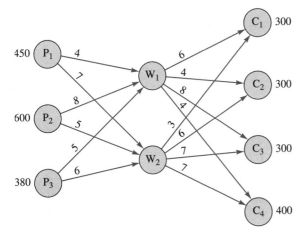

b.

Min $4x_{14} + 7x_{15} + 8x_{24} + 5x_{25} + 5x_{34} + 6x_{35} + 6x_{46} + 4x_{47} + 8x_{48} + 4x_{49} + 3x_{56} + 6x_{57} + 7x_{58} + 7x_{59}$

s.t.

$$
\begin{aligned}
x_{14} + x_{15} &\leq 450 \\
x_{24} + x_{25} &\leq 600 \\
x_{34} + x_{35} &\leq 380 \\
-x_{14} \quad - x_{24} \quad - x_{34} \quad + x_{46} + x_{47} + x_{48} + x_{49} &= 0 \\
- x_{15} \quad - x_{25} \quad - x_{35} \qquad\qquad + x_{56} + x_{57} + x_{58} + x_{59} &= 0 \\
x_{46} \qquad\qquad + x_{56} &= 300 \\
x_{47} \qquad\qquad + x_{57} &= 300 \\
x_{48} \qquad\qquad + x_{58} &= 300 \\
x_{49} \qquad\qquad + x_{59} &= 400
\end{aligned}
$$

c.

	Warehouse	
Plant	**1**	**2**
1	450	—
2	—	600
3	250	—

Total cost = $11,850

	Customer			
Warehouse	**1**	**2**	**3**	**4**
1	—	300	—	400
2	300	—	300	—

Chapter 11

2. a.

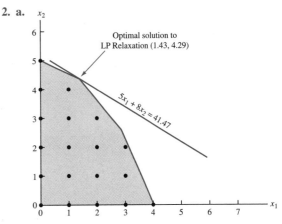

b. The optimal solution to the LP Relaxation is given by $x_1 = 1.43$, $x_2 = 4.29$ with an objective function value of 41.47. Rounding down gives the feasible integer solution $x_1 = 1$, $x_2 = 4$; its value is 37

c.

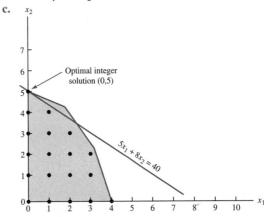

The optimal solution is given by $x_1 = 0$, $x_2 = 5$; its value is 40. It is not the same solution as found by rounding down; it provides a 3-unit increase in the value of the objective function

5. a. The feasible mixed-integer solutions are indicated by the boldface vertical lines in the graph

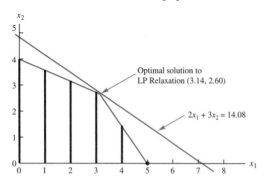

b. The optimal solution to the LP Relaxation is given by $x_1 = 3.14$, $x_2 = 2.60$; its value is 14.08
Rounding down the value of x_1 to find a feasible mixed-integer solution yields $x_1 = 3$, $x_2 = 2.60$ with a value of 13.8; this solution is clearly not optimal; with $x_1 = 3$, x_2 can be made larger without violating the constraints

c. The optimal solution to the MILP is given by $x_1 = 3, x_2 = 2.67$; its value is 14 as shown in the following figure

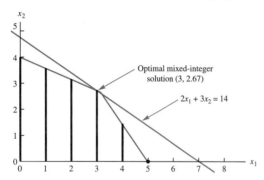

7. a. $x_1 + x_3 + x_5 + x_6 = 2$
b. $x_3 - x_5 = 0$
c. $x_1 + x_4 = 1$
d. $x_4 \leq x_1$
   $x_4 \leq x_3$
e. $x_4 \leq x_1$
   $x_4 \leq x_3$
   $x_4 \geq x_1 + x_3 - 1$

13. a. Add the following multiple-choice constraint to the problem
$y_2 + y_2 = 1$
New optimal solution: $y_1 = 1$, $y_3 = 1$, $x_{12} = 10$, $x_{31} = 30$, $x_{52} = 10$, $x_{53} = 20$
Value = 940
b. Because one plant is already located in St. Louis, it is only necessary to add the following constraint to the model
$y_3 + y_4 \leq 1$
New optimal solution: $y_4 = 1$, $x_{42} = 20$, $x_{43} = 20$, $x_{51} = 30$
Value = 860

Chapter 12

3.

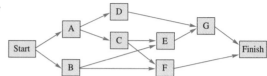

6. a. Critial path: A–D–F–H
b. 22 weeks
c. No, it is a critical activity
d. Yes, 2 weeks
e. Schedule for activity E:

Earliest start	3
Latest start	4
Earliest finish	10
Latest finish	11

10. a.

Activity	Optimistic	Most Probable	Pessimistic	Expected Times	Variance
A	4	5.0	6	5.00	0.11
B	8	9.0	10	9.00	0.11
C	7	7.5	11	8.00	0.44
D	7	9.0	10	8.83	0.25
E	6	7.0	9	7.17	0.25
F	5	6.0	7	6.00	0.11

b. Critical activities: B–D–F
Expected project completion time: $9.00 + 8.83 + 6.00 = 23.83$
Variance of projection completion time: $0.11 + 0.25 + 0.11 = 0.47$

13.

Activity	Expected Time	Variance
A	5	0.11
B	3	0.03
C	7	0.11
D	6	0.44
E	7	0.44
F	3	0.11
G	10	0.44
H	8	1.78

From Problem 6, A–D–F–H is the critical path, so
$E(T) = 5 + 6 + 3 + 8 = 22$
$\sigma^2 = 0.11 + 0.44 + 0.11 + 1.78 = 2.44$
$$z = \frac{\text{Time} - E(T)}{\sigma} = \frac{\text{Time} - 22}{\sqrt{2.44}}$$

                                                     Area

a. Time = 21: $z = -0.64$ 0.2389
      $P(21 \text{ weeks}) = 0.500 - 0.2389 = 0.2611$

b. Time = 22: $z = 0$ $\begin{array}{c}\text{Area}\\0.0000\end{array}$

$$P(22 \text{ weeks}) = 0.5000$$

c. Time = 25: $z = +1.92$ $\begin{array}{c}\text{Area}\\0.4726\end{array}$

$$P(25 \text{ weeks}) = 0.5000 + 0.4726 = 0.9726$$

21. a.

Activity	Earliest Start	Latest Start	Earliest Finish	Latest Finish	Slack	Critical Activity
A	0	0	3	3	0	Yes
B	0	1	2	3	1	
C	3	3	8	8	0	Yes
D	2	3	7	8	1	
E	8	8	14	14	0	Yes
F	8	10	10	12	2	
G	10	12	12	14	2	

Critical Path: A–C–E
Project completion time = $t_A + t_C + t_E = 3 + 5 + 6 =$ 14 days
b. Total cost = $8400

22. a.

Activity	Max Crash Days	Crash Cost/Day
A	1	600
B	1	700
C	2	400
D	2	400
E	2	500
F	1	400
G	1	500

Min $600Y_A + 700Y_B + 400Y_C + 400Y_D + 500Y_E + 400Y_F + 400Y_G$
s.t.
$$\begin{aligned}
X_A + Y_A &\geq 3\\
X_B + Y_B &\geq 2\\
-X_A + X_C + Y_C &\geq 5\\
-X_B + X_D + Y_D &\geq 5\\
-X_C + X_E + Y_E &\geq 6\\
-X_D + X_E + Y_E &\geq 6\\
-X_C + X_F + Y_F &\geq 2\\
-X_D + X_F + Y_F &\geq 2\\
-X_F + X_G + Y_G &\geq 2\\
-X_E + X_{FIN} &\geq 0\\
-X_G + X_{FIN} &\geq 0\\
X_{FIN} &\leq 12\\
Y_A &\leq 1\\
Y_B &\leq 1\\
Y_C &\leq 2\\
Y_D &\leq 2\\
Y_E &\leq 2\\
Y_F &\leq 1\\
Y_G &\leq 1\\
\text{All } X, Y &\geq 0
\end{aligned}$$

b. Solution of the linear programming model in part (a) shows

Activity	Crash	Crashing Cost
C	1 day	$400
E	1 day	500
	Total	$900

c. Total cost = Normal cost + Crashing cost
= $8400 + $900 = $9300

Chapter 13

1. a. $Q^* = \sqrt{\dfrac{2DC_0}{C_h}} = \sqrt{\dfrac{2(3600)(20)}{0.25(3)}} = 438.18$

b. $r = dm = \dfrac{3600}{250}(5) = 72$

c. $T = \dfrac{250Q^*}{D} = \dfrac{250(438.18)}{3600} = 30.43 \text{ days}$

d. $TC = \dfrac{1}{2}QC_h + \dfrac{D}{Q}C_0$

$= \dfrac{1}{2}(438.18)(0.25)(3) + \dfrac{3600}{438.18}(20) = \$328.63$

13. a. $Q^* = \sqrt{\dfrac{2DC_0}{(1 - D/P)C_h}}$

$= \sqrt{\dfrac{2(7200)(150)}{(1 - 7200/25{,}000)(0.18)(14.50)}} = 1078.12$

b. Number of production runs = $\dfrac{D}{Q^*} = \dfrac{7200}{1078.12} = 6.68$

c. $T = \dfrac{250Q}{D} = \dfrac{250(1078.12)}{7200} = 37.43 \text{ days}$

d. Production run length = $\dfrac{Q}{P/250}$

$= \dfrac{1078.12}{25{,}000/250} = 10.78 \text{ days}$

e. Maximum inventory = $\left(1 - \dfrac{D}{P}\right)Q$

$= \left(1 - \dfrac{7200}{25{,}000}\right)(1078.12)$

$= 767.62$

f. Holding cost = $\dfrac{1}{2}\left(1 - \dfrac{D}{P}\right)QC_h$

$= \dfrac{1}{2}\left(1 - \dfrac{7200}{25{,}000}\right)(1078.12)(0.18)(14.50)$

$= \$1001.74$

Ordering cost = $\dfrac{D}{Q}C_0 = \dfrac{7200}{1078.12}(150) = \$1001.74$

Total cost = $2003.48

g. $r = dm = \left(\dfrac{D}{250}\right)m = \dfrac{7200}{250}(15) = 432$

15. a. $Q^* = \sqrt{\dfrac{2DC_0}{C_h}\left(\dfrac{C_h + C_b}{C_b}\right)}$

$= \sqrt{\dfrac{2(12{,}000)(25)}{0.50}\left(\dfrac{0.50 + 5}{0.50}\right)} = 1148.91$

b. $S^* = Q^*\left(\dfrac{C_h}{C_h + C_b}\right) = 1148.91\left(\dfrac{0.50}{0.50 + 5}\right) = 104.45$

c. Max inventory $= Q^* - S^* = 1044.46$

d. $T = \dfrac{250Q^*}{D} = \dfrac{250(1148.91)}{12{,}000} = 23.94$ days

e. Holding $= \dfrac{(Q - S)^2}{2Q}C_h = \$237.38$

Ordering $= \dfrac{D}{Q}C_0 = \$261.12$

Backorder $= \dfrac{S^2}{2Q}C_b = \$23.74$

Total cost $= \$522.24$

The total cost for the EOQ model in Problem 4 was $547.72; allowing backorders reduces the total cost.

21. $Q = \sqrt{\dfrac{2DC_0}{C_h}}$

$Q_1 = \sqrt{\dfrac{2(500)(40)}{0.20(10)}} = 141.42$

$Q_2 = \sqrt{\dfrac{2(500)(40)}{0.20(9.7)}} = 143.59$

Because Q_1 is over its limit of 99 units, Q_1 cannot be optimal (see Problem 23); use $Q_2 = 143.59$ as the optimal order quantity.

Total cost $= \dfrac{1}{2}QC_h + \dfrac{D}{Q}C_0 + DC$

$= 139.28 + 139.28 + 4850.00 = \$5128.56$

25. a. $c_0 = 80 - 50 = 30$

$c_u = 125 - 80 = 45$

b. $P(D \leq Q^*) = \dfrac{c_u}{c_u + c_0} = \dfrac{45}{45 + 30} = 0.60$

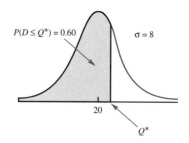

For an area of 0.60 below Q^*, $z = 0.25$

$Q^* = 20 + 0.25(8) = 22$

$P(\text{Sell all}) = P(D \geq Q^*) = 1 - 0.60 = 0.40$

29. a. $r = dm = (200/250)15 = 12$

b. $\dfrac{D}{Q} = \dfrac{200}{25} = 8$ orders/year

The limit of 1 stockout per year means that $P(\text{Stockout/cycle}) = 1/8 = 0.125$

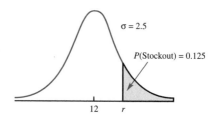

For area in tail $= 0.125$, $z = 1.15$

$z = \dfrac{r - 12}{2.5} = 1.15$

or

$r = 12 + 1.15(2.5) = 14.875 \approx 15$

c. Safety stock $= 3$ units

Added cost $= 3(\$5) = \$15$/year

33. a. $1/52 = 0.0192$

b. $M = \mu + z\sigma = 60 + 2.07(12) = 85$

c. $M = 35 + (0.9808)(85 - 35) = 84$

Chapter 14

1. a.

WHEEL SUBASSEMBLY Lot Size: 400	Lead Time: 2 Safety Stock: 0		Week				
			1	2	3	4	5	6
Gross requirements				250		300		260
Scheduled receipts				400				
Projected balance		80	80	230	230	330	330	70
Net requirements						70		
Planned order receipts						400		
Planned order releases				400				

b.

WHEEL SUBASSEMBLY Lot Size: 400	Lead Time: 2 Safety Stock: 0	Week					
		1	2	3	4	5	6
Gross requirements			250		300		260
Scheduled receipts			400				
Projected balance	180	180	330	330	30	30	170
Net requirements							230
Planned order receipts							400
Planned order releases						400	

c.

WHEEL SUBASSEMBLY Lot Size: 500	Lead Time: 2 Safety Stock: 0	Week					
		1	2	3	4	5	6
Gross requirements			250		300		260
Scheduled receipts			400				
Projected balance	80	80	230	230	430	430	170
Net requirements					70		
Planned order receipts					500		
Planned order releases			500				

3. a.

WHEEL SUBASSEMBLY Lot-for-Lot	Lead Time: 2 Safety Stock: 0	Week					
		1	2	3	4	5	6
Gross requirements			250		300		260
Scheduled receipts			400				
Projected balance	80	80	230	230	0	0	0
Net requirements					70		260
Planned order receipts					70		260
Planned order releases			70		260		

b.

WHEEL SUBASSEMBLY Lot-for-Lot	Lead Time: 2 Safety Stock: 0	Week					
		1	2	3	4	5	6
Gross requirements			250		300		260
Scheduled receipts			400				0
Projected balance	180	180	330	330	30	30	230
Net requirements							230
Planned order receipts							230
Planned order releases					230		

7. a.

DRAWER Lot size: 500	Lead Time: 1 Safety Stock: 30		Week					
			1	2	3	4	5	6
Gross requirements			450		300	250		500
Scheduled receipts			500					
Projected balance		0	50	50	250	500	500	500
Net requirements					280	30		30
Planned order receipts					500	500		500
Planned order releases				500	500		500	

The safety stock causes larger projected balances and therefore increases the inventory holding cost.

b.

DRAWER Lot size: 500	Lead Time: 1 Safety Stock: 100		Week					
			1	2	3	4	5	6
Gross requirements			450		300	250		500
Scheduled receipts			500					
Projected balance		120	170	170	370	120	120	120
Net requirements					230			480
Planned order receipts					500			500
Planned order releases				500			500	

The projected balances are the same as in part 4(b), so holding cost would not increase; however, over a longer planning period we could expect holding costs to be higher because the projected balance could not drop below 100.

10. a.

B Lot size: 500	Lead Time: 3 Safety Stock: 0		Week					
			21	22	23	24	25	26
Gross requirements				450		600		400
Scheduled receipts				500				
Projected balance		150	150	200	200	100	100	200
Net requirements						400		300
Planned order receipts						500		500
Planned order releases			500		500			

b.

D Lot-for-Lot	Lead Time: 1 Safety Stock: 0		Week			
			20	21	22	23
Gross requirements				500		500
Scheduled receipts						
Projected balance		50	50	0	0	0
Net requirements				450		500
Planned order receipts				450		500
Planned order releases			450		500	

Chapter 15

5. a. $P_0 = 1 - \dfrac{\lambda}{\mu} = 1 - \dfrac{10}{12} = 0.1667$

b. $L_q = \dfrac{\lambda^2}{\mu(\mu - \lambda)} = \dfrac{10^2}{12(12 - 10)} = 4.1667$

c. $W_q = \dfrac{L_q}{\lambda} = 0.4167$ hour (25 minutes)

d. $W = W_q + \dfrac{1}{\mu} = 0.5$ hour (30 minutes)

e. $P_w = \dfrac{\lambda}{\mu} = \dfrac{10}{12} = 0.8333$

11. a. $\lambda = 2.5$; $\mu = \dfrac{60}{10} = 6$ customers per hour

$L_q = \dfrac{\lambda^2}{\mu(\mu - \lambda)} = \dfrac{(2.5)^2}{6(6 - 2.5)} = 0.2976$

$L = L_q + \dfrac{\lambda}{\mu} = 0.7143$

$W_q = \dfrac{L_q}{\lambda} = 0.1190$ hours (7.14 minutes)

$W = W_q + \dfrac{1}{\mu} = 0.2857$ hours

$P_w = \dfrac{\lambda}{\mu} = \dfrac{2.5}{6} = 0.4167$

b. No; $W_q = 7.14$ minutes; firm should increase the mean service rate (μ) for the consultant or hire a second consultant

c. $\mu = \dfrac{60}{8} = 7.5$ customers per hour

$L_q = \dfrac{\lambda^2}{\mu(\mu - \lambda)} = \dfrac{(2.5)^2}{7.5(7.5 - 2.5)} = 0.1667$

$W_q = \dfrac{L_q}{\lambda} = 0.0667$ hour (4 minutes)

The service goal is being met

19. a. $k = 2$; $\lambda/\mu = 14/10 = 1.4$; $P_0 = 0.1765$

b. $L_q = \dfrac{(\lambda/\mu)^2 \lambda\mu}{1!(2\mu - \lambda)^2} P_0 = \dfrac{(1.4)^2(14)(10)}{(20 - 14)^2}(0.1765)$

$= 1.3451$

$L = L_q + \dfrac{\lambda}{\mu} = 1.3451 + \dfrac{14}{10} = 2.7451$

c. $W_q = \dfrac{L_q}{\lambda} = \dfrac{1.3453}{14} = 0.961$ hours (5.77 min.)

d. $W = W_q + \dfrac{1}{\mu} = 0.0961 + \dfrac{1}{10}$

$= 0.1961$ hours (11.77 min.)

e. $P_0 = 0.1765$

$P_1 = \dfrac{(\lambda/\mu)^1}{1!} P_0 = \dfrac{14}{10}(0.1765) = 0.2470$

$P(\text{wait}) = P(n \geq 2) = 1 - P(n \leq 1)$

$= 1 - 0.4235 = 0.5765$

21. From Problem 11, a service time of 8 minutes has $\mu = 60/8 = 7.5$

$L_q = \dfrac{\lambda^2}{\mu(\mu - \lambda)} = \dfrac{(2.5)^2}{7.5(7.5 - 2.5)} = 0.1667$

$L = L_q + \dfrac{\lambda}{\mu} = 0.50$

Total cost $= \$25L + \$16$
$= 25(0.50) + 16 = \$28.50$

Two channels: $\lambda = 2.5$; $\mu = 60/10 = 6$

Using equation (15.11) and $P_0 = 0.6552$, we get

$L_q = \dfrac{(\lambda/\mu)^2 \lambda\mu}{1!(2\mu - \lambda)^2} P_0 = 0.0189$

$L = L_q + \dfrac{\lambda}{\mu} = 0.4356$

Total cost $= 25(0.4356) + 2(16) = \$42.89$

Use one consultant with an 8-minute service time

25. $\lambda = 4$; $W = 10$ minutes

a. $\mu = \frac{1}{2} = 0.5$

b. $W_q = W - 1/\mu = 10 - 1/0.5 = 8$ minutes

c. $L = \lambda W = 4(10) = 40$

27. a. $\frac{2}{8}$ hours $= 0.25$ per hour

b. $1/3.2$ hours $= 0.3125$ per hour

c. $L_q = \dfrac{\lambda^2\sigma^2 + (\lambda/\mu)^2}{2(1 - \lambda/\mu)}$

$= \dfrac{(0.25)^2(2)^2 + (0.25/0.3125)^2}{2(1 - 0.25/0.3125)} = 2.225$

d. $W_q = \dfrac{L_q}{\lambda} = \dfrac{2.225}{0.25} = 8.9$ hours

e. $W = W_q + \dfrac{1}{\mu} = 8.9 + \dfrac{1}{0.3125} = 12.1$ hours

f. Same as $P_w = \dfrac{\lambda}{\mu} = \dfrac{0.25}{0.3125} = 0.80$

80% of the time the welder is busy

30. a. $\lambda = 42$; $\mu = 20$

i	$(\lambda/\mu)^i/i!$
0	1.0000
1	2.1000
2	2.2050
3	1.5435
Total	6.8485

j	P_j	
0	1/6.8485	$= 0.1460$
1	2.1/6.8485	$= 0.3066$
2	2.2050/6.8485	$= 0.3220$
3	1.5435/6.8485	$= 0.2254$
		1.0000

b. 0.2254

c. $L = \lambda/\mu(1 - P_k) = 42/20(1 - 0.2254) = 1.6267$

d. Four lines will be necessary; the probability of denied access is 0.1499

34. $N = 5$; $\lambda = 0.025$; $\mu = 0.20$; $\lambda/\mu = 0.125$

a.

n	$\dfrac{N!}{(N-n)!}\left(\dfrac{\lambda}{\mu}\right)^n$
0	1.0000
1	0.6250
2	0.3125
3	0.1172
4	0.0293
5	0.0037
Total	2.0877

$P_0 = 1/2.0877 = 0.4790$

b. $L_q = N - \left(\dfrac{\lambda + \mu}{\lambda}\right)(1 - P_0)$

$= 5 - \left(\dfrac{0.225}{0.025}\right)(1 - 0.4790) = 0.3110$

c. $L = L_q + (1 - P_0) = 0.3110 + (1 - 0.4790)$
$= 0.8321$

d. $W_q = \dfrac{L_q}{(N - L)\lambda} = \dfrac{0.3110}{(5 - 0.8321)(0.025)}$
$= 2.9854$ minutes

e. $W = W_q + \dfrac{1}{\mu} = 2.9854 + \dfrac{1}{0.20} = 7.9854$ minutes

f. Trips/day $=$ (8 hours)(60 minutes/hour)(λ)
$=$ (8)(60)(0.025) $= 12$ trips
Time at copier: $12 \times 7.9854 = 95.8$ minutes/day
Wait time at copier: $12 \times 2.9854 = 35.8$ minutes/day

g. Yes, five assistants $\times 35.8 = 179$ minutes (3 hours/day), so 3 hours per day are lost to waiting
$(35.8/480)(100) = 7.5\%$ of each assistant's day is spent waiting for the copier

Chapter 16

2. a. $c =$ variable cost per unit
$x =$ demand
Profit $= (50 - c)x - 30,000$

b. Base: Profit $= (50 - 20)1200 - 30,000 = 6,000$
Worst: Profit $= (50 - 24)300 - 30,000 = -22,200$
Best: Profit $= (50 - 16)2100 - 30,000 = 41,400$

c. Simulation will be helpful in estimating the probability of a loss

5. a.

Stock Price Change	Interval
-2	0.00 but less than 0.05
-1	0.05 but less than 0.15
0	0.15 but less than 0.40
$+1$	0.40 but less than 0.60
$+2$	0.60 but less than 0.80
$+3$	0.80 but less than 0.90
$+4$	0.90 but less than 1.00

b. Beginning price $39
0.1091 indicates -1 change; $38
0.9407 indicates $+4$ change; $42
0.1941 indicates 0 change; $42
0.8083 indicates $+3$ change; $45 (ending price)

9. a. Base-case based on most likely;
Time $= 6 + 5 + 14 + 8 = 33$ weeks
Worst: Time $= 8 + 7 + 18 + 10 = 43$ weeks
Best: Time $= 5 + 3 + 10 + 8 = 26$ weeks

b. 0.1778 for A: 5 weeks
0.9617 for B: 7 weeks
0.6849 for C: 14 weeks
0.4503 for D: 8 weeks; Total $= 34$ weeks

c. Simulation will provide an estimate of the probability of 35 weeks or less

14. Selected cell formulas for the spreadsheet shown in Figure S16.14 are as follows:

Cell	Formula
B13	=$C$7+RAND()*($C$8−$C$7)
C13	=NORMINV(RAND(),$G$7,$G$8)
D13	=($C$3−B13)*C13−$C$4

a. The mean profit should be approximately $6,000; simulation results will vary with most simulations having a mean profit between $5,500 and $6,500

b. 120 to 150 of the 500 simulation trials should show a loss; thus, the probability of a loss should be between 0.24 and 0.30

c. This project appears too risky.

18. Selected cell formulas for the spreadsheet shown in Figures S16.18 are as follows:

Cell	Formula
B11	=$C$4 + RAND()*($C$5−$C$4)
C11	=NORMINV(RAND(),$H$4,$H$5)
D11	=MAX(B11:C11)
G11	=COUNTIF(D11:D1010,"<750")
H11	=G11/COUNT(D11:D1010)

a. $750,000 should win roughly 600 to 650 of the 1000 times; the probability of winning the bid should be between 0.60 and 0.65

b. The probability of $775,000 winning should be roughly 0.82, and the probability of $785,000 winning should be roughly 0.88; a contractor's bid of $775,000 is recommended

FIGURE S16.14 SPREADSHEET FOR THE MADEIRA MANUFACTURING COMPANY

	A	B	C	D	E	F	G
1	**Madeira Manufacturing Company**						
2							
3	Selling Price per Unit		$50				
4	Fixed Cost		$30,000				
5							
6	**Variable Cost (Uniform Distribution)**				**Demand (Normal Distribution)**		
7	Smallest Value		$16		Mean		1200
8	Largest Value		$24		Standard Deviation		300
9							
10	**Simulation Trials**						
11		Variable					
12	Trial	Cost per Unit	Demand	Profit			
13	1	$17.81	788	($4,631)			
14	2	$18.86	1078	$3,580			

FIGURE S16.18 SPREADSHEET FOR THE CONTRACTOR BIDDING

	A	B	C	D	E	F	G	H
1	**Contractor Bidding**							
2								
3	**Contractor A (Uniform Distribution)**					**Contractor B (Normal Distribution)**		
4	Smallest Value		$600			Mean		$700
5	Largest Value		$800			Standard Deviation		$50
6								
7								
8	**Simulation**					**Results**		
9		Contractor	Contractor	Highest		Contractor's	Number	Probability
10	Trial	A's Bid	B's Bid	Bid		Bid	of Wins	of Winning
11	1	$673.4	$719.8	$719.8		750	629	0.629
12	2	$756.9	$654.8	$756.9		775	824	0.824
13	3	$705.5	$791.1	$791.1		785	887	0.887
14	4	$638.0	$677.1	$677.1				

Chapter 17

3. a. 0.10 as given by the transition probability

   b. $\pi_1 = 0.90\pi_1 + 0.30\pi_2$ (1)

   $\pi_2 = 0.10\pi_1 + 0.70\pi_2$ (2)

   $\pi_1 + \pi_2 = 1$ (3)

   Using (1) and (3),

   $$0.10\pi_1 - 0.30\pi_2 = 0$$
   $$0.10\pi_1 - 0.30(1 - \pi_1) = 0$$
   $$0.10\pi_1 - 0.30 + 0.30\pi_1 = 0$$
   $$0.40\pi_1 = 0.30$$
   $$\pi_1 = 0.75$$
   $$\pi_2 = (1 - \pi_1) = 0.25$$

7. a. $\pi_1 = 0.85\pi_1 + 0.20\pi_2 + 0.15\pi_3$ (1)

   $\pi_2 = 0.10\pi_1 + 0.75\pi_2 + 0.10\pi_3$ (2)

   $\pi_3 = 0.05\pi_1 + 0.05\pi_2 + 0.75\pi_3$ (3)

   $\pi_1 + \pi_2 + \pi_3 = 1$ (4)

   Using (1), (2), and (4) provides three equations with three unknowns; solving provides $\pi_1 = 0.548$, $\pi_2 = 0.286$, and $\pi_3 = 0.166$

   b. 16.6% as given by π_3

   c. Quick Stop should take

   $667 - 0.548(1000) = 119$ Murphy's customers

   and $333 - 0.286(1000) = \underline{\ 47\ }$ Ashley's customers

   Total   166 Quick Stop customers

   It will take customers from Murphy and Ashley

11. $I = \begin{bmatrix} 1 & 0 \\ 0 & 1 \end{bmatrix}$ $Q = \begin{bmatrix} 0.25 & 0.25 \\ 0.25 & 0.25 \end{bmatrix}$

   $(I - Q) = \begin{bmatrix} 0.75 & -0.25 \\ -0.05 & 0.75 \end{bmatrix}$

$$N = (I - Q)^{-1} = \begin{bmatrix} 1.3636 & 0.4545 \\ 0.0909 & 1.3636 \end{bmatrix}$$

$$NR = \begin{bmatrix} 1.3636 & 0.4545 \\ 0.0909 & 1.3636 \end{bmatrix} \begin{bmatrix} 0.5 & 0.0 \\ 0.5 & 0.2 \end{bmatrix} = \begin{bmatrix} 0.909 & 0.091 \\ 0.727 & 0.273 \end{bmatrix}$$

$$BNR = [4000 \quad 5000] \begin{bmatrix} 0.909 & 0.091 \\ 0.727 & 0.273 \end{bmatrix} = [7271 \quad 1729]$$

Estimate $1729 in bad debts

Chapter 18

2. a. Let x_1 = number of shares of AGA Products purchased
x_2 = number of shares of Key Oil purchased
To obtain an annual return of exactly 9%:

$$0.06(50)x_1 + 0.10(100)x_2 = 0.09(50{,}000)$$
$$3x_1 + 10x_2 = 4500$$

To have exactly 60% of the total investment in Key Oil:

$$100x_2 = 0.60(50{,}000)$$
$$x_2 = 300$$

Therefore, we can write the goal programming model as follows:

Min $P_1(d_1^-) + P_2(d_2^+)$
s.t.

$$\begin{aligned}
50x_1 + 100x_2 & & \leq 50{,}000 & \quad \text{Funds available} \\
3x_1 + 10x_2 - d_1^+ + d_1^- &= 4{,}500 & & \quad P_1 \text{ goal} \\
x_2 - d_2^+ + d_2^- &= 300 & & \quad P_2 \text{ goal}
\end{aligned}$$
$$x_1, x_2, d_1^+, d_1^-, d_2^+, d_2^- \geq 0$$

b. In the following graphical solution, $x_1 = 250$ and $x_2 = 375$

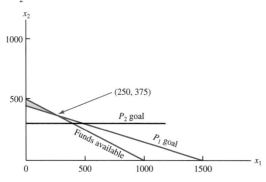

9. Scoring Calculations

Criteria	Analyst Chicago	Accountant Denver	Auditor Houston
Career advancement	35	20	20
Location	10	12	8
Management	30	25	35
Salary	28	32	16
Prestige	32	20	24
Job security	8	10	16
Enjoyment of the work	28	20	20
Totals	171	139	139

The analyst position in Chicago is recommended.

16. Step 1: Column totals are $^{17}/_4$, $^{31}/_{21}$, and 12
Step 2:

Style	Accord	Saturn	Cavalier
Accord	$^4/_{17}$	$^7/_{31}$	$^4/_{12}$
Saturn	$^{12}/_{17}$	$^{21}/_{31}$	$^7/_{12}$
Cavalier	$^1/_{17}$	$^3/_{31}$	$^1/_{12}$

Step 3:

Style	Accord	Saturn	Cavalier	Row Average
Accord	0.235	0.226	0.333	0.265
Saturn	0.706	0.677	0.583	0.656
Cavalier	0.059	0.097	0.083	0.080

Consistency Ratio
Step 1:

$$0.265 \begin{bmatrix} 1 \\ 3 \\ \frac{1}{4} \end{bmatrix} + 0.656 \begin{bmatrix} \frac{1}{3} \\ 1 \\ \frac{1}{7} \end{bmatrix} + 0.080 \begin{bmatrix} 4 \\ 7 \\ 1 \end{bmatrix}$$

$$\begin{bmatrix} 0.265 \\ 0.795 \\ 0.066 \end{bmatrix} + \begin{bmatrix} 0.219 \\ 0.656 \\ 0.094 \end{bmatrix} + \begin{bmatrix} 0.320 \\ 0.560 \\ 0.080 \end{bmatrix} = \begin{bmatrix} 0.802 \\ 2.007 \\ 0.239 \end{bmatrix}$$

Step 2: 0.802/0.265 = 3.028
2.007/0.656 = 3.062
0.239/0.080 = 3.007
Step 3: $\lambda_{max} = (3.028 + 3.062 + 3.007)/3 = 3.032$
Step 4: CI = (3.032 − 3)/2 = 0.016
Step 5: CR = 0.016/0.58 = 0.028
Because CR = 0.028 is less than 0.10, the degree of consistency exhibited in the pairwise comparison matrix for style is acceptable

20. a.

Flavor	A	B	C
A	1	3	2
B	$\frac{1}{3}$	1	5
C	$\frac{1}{2}$	$\frac{1}{5}$	1

b. Step 1: Column totals are $^{11}/_6$, $^{21}/_5$, and 8
Step 2:

Flavor	A	B	C
A	$^6/_{11}$	$^{15}/_{21}$	$^2/_8$
B	$^2/_{11}$	$^5/_{21}$	$^5/_8$
C	$^3/_{11}$	$^1/_{21}$	$^1/_8$

Step 3:

Flavor	A	B	C	Row Average
A	0.545	0.714	0.250	0.503
B	0.182	0.238	0.625	0.348
C	0.273	0.048	0.125	0.148

c. Step 1:

$$0.503 \begin{bmatrix} 1 \\ \frac{1}{3} \\ \frac{1}{2} \end{bmatrix} + 0.348 \begin{bmatrix} 3 \\ 1 \\ \frac{1}{5} \end{bmatrix} + 0.148 \begin{bmatrix} 2 \\ 5 \\ 1 \end{bmatrix}$$

$$\begin{bmatrix} 0.503 \\ 0.168 \\ 0.252 \end{bmatrix} + \begin{bmatrix} 1.044 \\ 0.348 \\ 0.070 \end{bmatrix} + \begin{bmatrix} 0.296 \\ 0.740 \\ 0.148 \end{bmatrix} = \begin{bmatrix} 1.845 \\ 1.258 \\ 0.470 \end{bmatrix}$$

Step 2: $1.845/0.503 = 3.668$
    $1.258/0.348 = 3.615$
    $0.470/0.148 = 3.123$
Step 3: $\lambda_{max} = (3.668 + 3.615 + 3.123)/3 = 3.469$
Step 4: $CI = (3.469 - 3)/2 = 0.235$
Step 5: $CR = 0.235/0.58 = 0.415$

Because $CR = 0.415$ is greater than 0.10, the individual's judgments are not consistent.

24. Criteria: Yield and Risk
Step 1: Column totals are 1.5 and 3
Step 2:

	Yield	Risk	Priority
Yield	0.667	0.667	0.667
Risk	0.333	0.333	0.333

With only 2 criteria, $CR = 0$; no need to compute CR
Preceding calculations for Yield and Risk provide

Stocks	Yield Priority	Risk Priority
CCC	0.750	0.333
SRI	0.250	0.667

Overall Priorities:
    CCC $0.667(0.750) + 0.333(0.333) = 0.611$
    SRI $0.667(0.250) + 0.333(0.667) = 0.389$
CCC is preferred

Index